# PLACING AESTHETICS

# PLACING AESTHETICS
## Reflections on the Philosophic Tradition

*Robert E. Wood*

*OHIO UNIVERSITY PRESS*
*Athens*

Ohio University Press, Athens, Ohio 45701
© 1999 by Robert E. Wood
Printed in the United States of America
All rights reserved

Ohio University Press books are printed on acid-free paper ∞ ™
03 02 01 00 99   5 4 3 2 1

Library of Congress Cataloging-in-Publication Data
Wood, Robert E., 1934–
    Placing aesthetics : reflections on the philosophic tradition /
Robert E. Wood.
        p.         cm. —(Series in Continental thought ; 26)
    Includes bibliograhical references and index.
    ISBN 0-8214-1280-9  (alk. paper).
    ISBN 0-8214-1281-7  (pbk. : alk. paper)
    1. Aesthetics—History        I. Title.  II. Series.
BH81.W66        1999
111'.85'09—dc21                                              99-27142
                                                                CIP

**Frontispiece.**   *Christus Africanus* by Robert E. Wood

*To Sue,*
*who, given but half a life, died at peace*

*and to Jim,*
*who, given two-thirds of a life, lived enough for three.*

# Contents

Contents

# Abbreviations

**Aquinas**
> *ST*      *Summa theologiae*

**Aristotle**
> *NE*      *Nicomachean Ethics*
> *OS*      *On the Soul*

**Dewey**
> *AE*      *Art as Experience*
> *ExN*      *Experience and Nature*
> FATE      "From Absolutism to Experimentalism"
> *RP*      *Reconstruction in Philosophy*

**Hegel**
> *ALFA*      *Aesthetics: Lectures on Fine Art* (Knox trans.)
> *EL*      *Encyclopaedia Logic*
> *HPM*      *[Hegel's] Philosophy of Mind*
> *PR*      *[Hegel's] Philosophy of Right*
> *PS*      *Phenomenology of Spirit*
> *SL*      *The Science of Logic*

**Heidegger**
> *BAT*      *Being and Time*
> BDT      "Building, Dwelling, Thinking," in *PLT*
> *EP*      *The End of Philosophy*
> *IM*      *An Introduction to Metaphysics*
> LH      "Letter on Humanism," in *Basic Writings*

| LP | "Language in the Poem," in *OWL* |
| MA | "Memorial Address" |
| NL | "The Nature of Language," in *OWL* |
| OWA | "The Origin of the Work of Art," in *PLT* |
| *OWL* | *On the Way to Language* |
| *PLT* | *Poetry, Language, and Thought* |
| *QCT* | *The Question Concerning Technology* |
| *WCT* | *What Is Called Thinking?* |
| *WP* | *What Is Philosophy?* |
| WPF | "What Are Poets For?" in *PLT* |

## Kant

| *CJ* | *Critique of Judgment* |
| *CPR* | *Critique of Pure Reason* |

## Nietzsche

| *BGE* | *Beyond Good and Evil* |
| *BT* | *The Birth of Tragedy* |
| *EH* | *Ecce Homo* |
| *GM* | *On the Genealogy of Morals* |
| *GS* | *Gay Science* |
| *TI* | *Twilight of the Idols* |
| *TSZ* | *Thus Spake Zarathustra* |
| *WTP* | *The Will To Power* |

## Plato

| *Rep* | *The Republic* |
| *Sym* | *Symposium* |

## Plotinus

| *Enn* | *The Enneads* |

## Schopenhauer

| *EA* | *Essays and Aphorisms* |
| *WWR* | *The World as Will and Representation* |

# *Preface*

The origins of this book are multiple: a love of solitude, of woods and mountains and clouds and fields, of the changing moods on the surface of the water, of the play of light and deepening shadow on brush and timber in late afternoon; a love of the shape and color of bleached bones, slightly porous, dull white; a love of smooth, shiny stones and shells gathered along the shores of Lake Michigan and the Pacific Ocean; the experience of being arrested from time to time by the realization of my own mortality; a few fleeting moments of the sense of eucharistic presence; the experience of the look of the human other—the absence-in-presence of the conscious person in the sensory gleam of that most fascinating of objects, the human eye, whose presence announces an absence that is more present than all objects; the sense of the endless and the encompassing in the open expanses of Lake Michigan, the Mediterranean Sea, and the Atlantic and Pacific Oceans as well as in the contemplation of the starry skies above; the sense of the virtual omnipresence of life by its absence atop high mountains; the sense of austerity in the desert surrounding the Dead Sea viewed from Masada; the sense of the sacred in the foothills of Parnassus at Delphi; the sense of the presence-in-absence of those long dead at those same sites.

Then there was the reappearance of mortality in Rachmaninoff's *Isle of the Dead*, together with Arnold Böcklin's painting of the same title: the rhythm of the waves washing against the island's shores mirroring the even deeper insistence of the rhythms of life moving toward death, the stern announcement of necessity and the lyrical, serene voice of acceptance; the reappearance of bones, trees, and mountains in the paintings of Georgia O'Keefe and the sculpture of Henry Moore, and of cypress trees, fields, rocks, and stars playing in relation to houses and people in van Gogh; the intertwining of people and landscape in Brueghel; the starkness of Grüne-wald's crucifixion; the piercing presence of Zeus-Poseidon in the bronze attributed to Phidias at the Athens museum; the power of Michelangelo's Moses at San Pietro in Vincoli in Rome and of his David in the Accademia in Florence; the elegance of the bronze busts of Benin and the expressive-ness of the Yoruba *akuaba* fertility doll; the sense of cradling in the Piazza Navona in Rome; the soaring heights and rhythmic coordinations of San Pietro in the Vatican, Cologne Cathedral, St. Vitus Church in Hradčany Castle in Prague, and Notre Dame in Paris. Earlier there was the music of Tchaikovsky, Rachmaninoff, and Beethoven; then of Sibelius, Shostakovich, and Stravinsky; and later of Mozart, Bach, and Vivaldi: music of longing and striving, of the brooding presence of nature, of discordance and reso-lution, of joy and energy; but also the simple, serene but soaring spiritual-ity of Gregorian chant; and the mix of presence and loss in the nature poetry of Blake, Keats, Wordsworth, and Hopkins.

One semester I spent all my free time making my way through western Europe. In addition to traveling along some of the great rivers, lakes and mountains—on one occasion climbing the face of the Gaisberg outside Salzburg—time spent lingeringly contemplating the churches and galleries of the great cities gave me a special taste for sculpture, particularly bronzes. Upon my return to America I decided to enroll in courses on clay sculp-ture. Subsequently I produced about four dozen pieces, the best of which—appearing on the cover of this book—I finally had cast in bronze. In addition to an enhanced sensitivity to form and texture, this gave me an appreciation of the process of artistic production. I include in an epilogue a description of that process, along with some general comments on the nature of sculpture that I learned from working, viewing, reading, and re-flecting on the art form.

All these special attractions drew me initially to the philosophy of Henri Bergson, the subject of my master's thesis, grounded in intuition and open to the mystical; drew me to the erotic in Plato, to the mysticism of Plotinus, John of the Cross, and Therese of Avila; to Buber's philosophy of presence and dialogue, the subject of my first book; to the comprehensive dialectic of Hegel that attempted to encompass the whole tradition, with his massive work on aesthetics introducing us to the character of the Final and Encompassing; to the thought of Heidegger, who covered much of the same historical-philosophical ground as Hegel, but who was more sensitive perhaps to the basis of speculative thought in the lifeworld *(Lebenswelt)* and to its articulation in poetry, architecture, and painting.

My first book, *Martin Buber's Ontology*, explored the possibility of an integral mode of relation to persons, things, and the encompassing whole in a dialogic philosophy carried by a sense of presence and a deep awareness of the ineradicable pluralism of thought.[1] My second book, *A Path into Metaphysics*, presented a phenomenological, hermeneutic, and dialogic approach, reading select highpoints in the history of thought about the ultimate and the encompassing in terms of the governing élan of each thinker.[2] The book was guided by the conviction introduced by Bergson that the center of every great speculative thinker was "aesthetic," a governing sense of the whole that furnished a basic generative gestalt.

The present book, employing the same methods, advances more explicitly into that aesthetic center by attending to select high points in the history of philosophic thought on matters aesthetic and attempting to locate these considerations within the view of the whole advanced by each of the thinkers treated. In this process I attempt to show that the aesthetic is no mere icing on the cake but is rather the dynamic center of the whole speculative enterprise. Following John Dewey, I would claim that the aesthetic is integral experience; but integral experience, pressed to its ultimate depth, involves a sense of the encompassing whole. Hence I begin the treatment of each thinker with a consideration of the interplay of the central concepts of his view of the whole within which his explicit reflection on aesthetics is placed. Thus the title, *Placing Aesthetics*. I could just as easily have used the title *Metaphysics and Aesthetics*, but the term *metaphysics* is currently in disrepute in most philosophical circles, even in those Heideggerian circles where "the question of Being" as the question of the whole is alive indeed. And in that same Heideggerian line, I anchor my consideration in an attempt at a phenomenological inventory of the fundamental structures of the field of experience as a whole, features that pose the question of the whole and allow of alternative construals as to its ultimate character. It is within that field that I will find a central place for what I mean by the aesthetic.[3]

That phenomenological grounding will provide us with a point of departure for reading the tradition, beginning, not with opinions of thinkers, but with "the things themselves" as they are displayed in and through the approach of each thinker. This work is an attempt to root philosophy in the lifeworld and in its intensification rather than in an abstract flight from it, whether conceptual or mystical. Attention to things themselves will also provide the basis for an ongoing response to the thinkers with a view toward building an aesthetic that will, I hope, be less exposed to the partiality that frequently afflicts both piecemeal argumentation and wholesale "system building." I will attempt to gather together the basic results of my inquiry in the concluding chapter.

—The University of Dallas

# PLACING AESTHETICS
*Reflections on the Philosophic Tradition*

# I

# INTRODUCTION
## *Fine Art and the Field of Experience*

THERE IS SURELY SENSE to the notion that one ought to approach every study in terms of empirical acquaintance with the objects of the study. In fact, how else could one begin? Thus in approaching matters aesthetic, one should have firsthand acquaintance with art objects as well as with the beauties of nature and, if possible, with artistic practice. We are surely not exempt from that requirement. However, every study except philosophy begins with certain presuppositions which it is not the task of that study to analyze. Thus Euclidean geometry takes its point of departure from the possibility of beginning with sensorily given examples as instances of theorems that it then proceeds to prove by deducing the theorems from fundamental axioms. It is the function of the philosophy of mathematics to carry out a meta-reflection upon the framework presupposed by the mathematician. Thus arise questions about the status of sensa, of theorems, of the relation between sensa and theorems, of the nature of deduction, of the peculiar angle of abstraction taken by geometry vis-à-vis sensorily given objects, about the nature of mind and its relation to consciousness on the one hand and to organic functioning on the other, about the value of mathematical inquiry in relation to other forms of inquiry, and about the value of inquiry in relation to the totality of interests sustained by humans.[1]

The philosophic mode of inquiry begins with a meta-reflection upon what is presupposed in other areas of human experience with a view toward developing a sense of the whole of that experience and what it entails. Philosophy involves an exposition of the fundamental framework of experience as presupposed in all that we think and do. Its distinction from other disciplines that deal only with the sensorily verifiable does not lie in its being given over to "airy speculation" or unverifiable supposition. Philosophy rather deals with the fundamentally and comprehensively verifiable, with what essentially we cannot do without, and on that basis it supplies a critical assessment of the limitations involved in the abstractions with which other disciplines operate.[2]

So in approaching aesthetics we will begin, not directly with aesthetic objects, but with the overarching, always present, and immediately verifiable framework of experience within which the work of art, the aesthetic object in general, artistic activity, and aesthetic experience can be located. My contention is that not only aesthetic understanding, but all fundamental understanding must move in that direction. Of course there is very much understanding to be had without attending to that framework, as one can very fruitfully work for one's whole life in mathematics without once asking the philosophic questions involved in the discipline. And just as pursuing such questions will not necessarily make one a better mathematician but might even distract one from mathematics, so also taking this approach to aesthetics may have the same irrelevant or even counterproductive relation to aesthetic matters. I say "may" because it is possible that, as a result of such inquiry, one could become more profoundly related to one's own discipline—art or mathematics or any other field—indeed to one's own *Lebenspraxis* as a whole. Here so much depends on the continual coming and going between philosophical reflection and live involvement with the area in question.

## The Threefold Structure of the Field of Experience

Anything we do or undergo takes place within the overarching field of experience to whose fundamental structures we rarely attend but upon which we necessarily rest. The fundamental character of that field is one of intentionality, of which volitional activity is only the most obvious form. Intentionality involves the manifestness of objects in their apparent independence of our awareness. And by *objects* here I do not mean only impersonal things; I mean anything other than the center of awareness that can be present to awareness, whether persons or things or principles. Intentionality involves the simultaneous focal manifestness of the appearing things and (prefocally) of our own selves as subjects of awareness to whom things appear. The self involved here is not only or even not basically the empirically objective organic body that appears as such an object both to others and to oneself. It is rather the conscious center, the essential nonobject, the fundamental condition for the possibility of the appearance of any appearing thing, the point of origin or pivot around which the appearing world arranges itself. My own sensory objectivity is obviously rooted in the reality of my bodily being, but its appearance depends on there being a subject of awareness whose object it is. Objects are appearances "thrown over against" *(ob-jecta)* subjects who are "thrown under" *(sub-jecta)* the field of manifestness. The apparent independence of objects has to be understood as an independence in being but not in appearing. As Edmund Husserl, founder of the discipline of phenomenology we are here practicing, put it: Things are given *for us* (in terms of our conditions) as existing *in themselves* (independently of those conditions).[3] What appear are objects costructured in their appearance by what they are and by the structural conditions of the subject of awareness. It is the task of phenomenology to carry out and maintain a descriptive inventory of the essential features *(logoi)* of this field of appearing *(phainomena)* as a co-constituting relation of conscious subject and appearing objects.[4] However, the conscious subject tends to disappear from attention because of its natural directedness to another for which it functions as the locus of manifestness. Further, because of the dominance of empirical objectiveness, it tends to understand itself as another empirical object. But it is this nonobjectifiable subject of awareness that initiates responses that are intentional in the ordinary sense of the term (i.e., are deliberate). There are subdivisions of such deliberate intentionality, like artistic activity and aesthetic appreciation. But deliberate intentionality is founded upon the spontaneously functioning intentionality of the field of awareness wherein, like it or not, things present themselves.[5] Awareness by nature intends objects. Choice as deliberate intentionality is solicited by the prior presentation of those objects in the mode of spontaneously functioning intentionality. Artistic intentionality in particular is peculiarly and sensitively rooted in that prior spontaneously functioning intentionality and makes it manifest to the artist's audience.

Now the field of intentionality, as it presents empirical objects, has a threefold structure, which we will designate as sensing, interpreting, and presence-to-being.[6] The first level seems clearest—at least it is the most obvious. There are the ever-present sensa: colors, sounds, tastes, smells, and the various features linked to tactility: hard and soft, rough and smooth, heavy and light, hot and cold, dry and moist. Color seems to dominate insofar as it is always present in the normal waking world, whereas the other features are either recessive or variable. However, we could also say that sound dominates insofar as encounter with the speaking other is the primary focus of most of our lives, for which the visual furnishes the background. The world of art, at least in its nonverbal forms, articulates the field of sensa, but with a peculiar focus upon the visual and audile features—a peculiarity to which we will return later.

First then the sensory field. The status of the sensa is problematic. For one thing, even though we tend to think of them as the most concrete evidences, as we speak of them in this way they are presented in a most abstract way vis-à-vis our ordinary experience. For we do not normally see colors, but trees and sky, buildings and people, paper and computers. We do not normally hear sounds, but voices, traffic, drills, bells sounding, the wind blowing through the trees—that is, the sensa are already configured in terms of modes of taking them up interpretatively.[7] As Bernard Lonergan once remarked, what is most obvious in knowing—namely, the sensa—is not what knowing most obviously is.[8] What, more exactly, is the field of sensation, considered apart from our specifically human way of taking it up?

Comprehensively considered and in abstraction from the other two levels, it is a synesthetic-kinesthetic whole displaying an appearance, a synthetic phantasma, a showing focused upon the surface of things other than the perceiving organism. It provides a realm of appearance filtered in terms of the functional needs of that organism and thus shot through and brought to focus by desire.[9] To ground those claims, first of all, we have to consider that each of the senses has its own way of selectively responding to the total set of causal impacts made by the environment on the organism by producing its own distinctive appearance. A sensory power is a selective filter in relation to those causal impacts. There is a sense in which, as Nietzsche noted, what the senses provide is a lie.[10] The apparently empty space between my eye and the text being read we know by instrumentally unaided reflection to be full of dust particles and sounds. But experimental work shows that it is also full of air molecules and of radio and TV waves. It is replete with photons and, in fact, with irradiation from across the whole electromagnetic spectrum. But of course, to be able to see all that would make recognition of approaching obstacles or dangers, and food or mate or offspring, virtually impossible. Seeing at all, it would seem, necessarily entails not being able to see all that is present. The visual field is a luminous bubble blown by the nervous system making a certain type of appearance possible so that an animal being can have a functional space available to meet its needs. Correlative to that appearance is the rising up of desire that moves the seer in the direction of the organically desirable or away from the undesirable. Thus the functionally manifest space is not only sensory but also sensuous, evoking desire or aversion or felt neutrality. Second, in view of organic functionality, the seen plays in relation to the heard and smelt, and eventually and most basically, the touched and tasted, for its mode of appearance aims at satisfying the desire for food or mate, which have to be tactually apprehended to fulfill such needs.[11] The field of the senses is thus, as I have said, a synesthetic-kinesthetic whole of selective appearance shot through with desire and constructed to fulfill the needs of the perceiving organism.

But though it is a perceiver-dependent appearance and not the inner reality of what appears, yet in order to fulfill its function, the sensuous field cannot be entirely a lie. It does not provide pseudofood and -mate but real food and mate, though the fullness of either is cloaked by the interest-laden selectivity of the appearance. Through the regularity of sensuous appearance manifest over time, the sensuously given displays patterns, both of functioning wholes and of coordination between functioning wholes. In particular, those functioning wholes we call living appear as setting themselves off from the causal networks within which they are embedded, providing both the model and in our case the matrix for a rational system as a coherently functioning whole.[12] Animal organisms organize the materials drawn from their environs so that the sensuous plenum comes to manifestness to the perceiving organism through the organs thus created. The objectively observable, shaped into an organ system, provides the conditions for the process of observation itself, which completes the organic process. Providing an instance of a more general principle enunciated by Hegel, here objectivity is completed in subjectivity as the condition for the manifestation of objectivity.[13]

As it appears in the field of animal awareness, each part of an organic being, whether viewed from without or lived through from within, is not simply sensorily there in a positivistic way; more basically, it expresses something of the character of the living whole within which it operates. And in the case of animal organisms, their behavior expresses the inwardness of desire that surges up teleologically out of an organic base. The recognition of such expressivity in organically functioning wholes is the central aspect in the recovery of natural form from the tendency to reduce it to its elements.[14] Now, expression and the interpretation of expression belong together. But at the animal level the sensory surface of another animal expresses support for, or antagonism or indifference to, satisfying the desires of the percipient animal who is locked into the circle of those desires. The sensory surface furnishes the basis for an organic dashboard knowledge, a mode of display sufficient to learn what to push, pull, and turn in order to get the required output.[15] Rooted in organic purpose, sensation reveals, not full being but filtered-off appearance co-constituted by the character of the perceiving organism and the way things in the environment interact physically with that organism.

Now what I have presented thus far is analogous to a geometrical analysis, like the isolation of a plane or a line or a point from the three-dimensional solidity of the world of ordinary objects. As noted previously, the things of ordinary experience are not simply colors or sounds, but things being revealed (and concealed) in various ways. And that revelation is a function of the way they are taken up into the field of awareness. We have been taking them up here, not in terms of their sensory particularity, but in terms of their immediately given universal features. But let us leave aside this mode of taking up for a moment (it will be crucial for the arts) and attend to the third level—even more crucial for our understanding of aesthetics: what I have called presence-to-being.

If sensa seem the most obvious features of the field of experience, presence-to-being is the least obvious, but it is deeply tied to the peculiar implicitness of the subject of awareness. To cite Augustine in a different but closely related context, presence-to-being is *interior interiori meo*, inside my inside, "more intimate to me than I to myself."[16] The sensa anchor awareness in the constantly flowing Now. If there is an indeterminate depth of space surrounding the luminous bubble of sensory appearance Here and uncovered in scientific investigation, there is no less the indeterminate depth of time surrounding the Now of such appearance. Space and time present themselves as indeterminately spread in such a way as to encompass the whole of all possible sensory presentation, including the Here and Now. Like a geometrical theorem, though in a more basic manner (more basic because it grounds geometry and all other human endeavors), the presentation of space and time as indeterminate wholes has itself an atemporal character.[17] Now, to say of space and time that each *is* given as all-encompassing in relation to the field of sensory presentation, to say that the sensory field *is* a luminous bubble blown by the nervous system *is* to bring into play the notion of being, the participial form of the verb *to be*, whose third person singular form *is* "is." It is a notion that encompasses space and time, the things appearing in the sensory field and the self to whom all this appears. The notion of being is given as absolutely unrestricted, including in itself even the forms of non-being we find present in experience, such as the no longer and the not yet, the absent, privation, and the like. It includes everything within it and everything about every thing.[18]

We can see the all-encompassing character of the notion of being if we think of the principle of noncontradiction co-given with it. This principle grounds the possibility of predication and inference, and thus also our ability to bring the whirl of experience into a consistent world. We know ahead of time that everything encounterable or even thinkable is such that it cannot both be and not be at the same time and in the same respect. Identity of things with themselves and their identity and nonidentity with each other in terms of certain predicates allow judgments to come to stand firm and hold over time and make possible inference as a linkage between judgments on the basis of the identity or nonidentity of the terms of the judgment with each other. For example, my being the identical person I am throughout the changes of my lifetime, the enduring possibility of my behaving rationally, and the enduring groundedness of responsibility in rationality, indicates my essential responsibility for my actions. Expressed syllogistically: Every rational being is responsible; I am a rational being; hence I am responsible. Each of the three linked propositions expresses an enduring identity of meaning in each term—*rational being, responsible, I*—and between the terms in each proposition, so that through my identity as a rational being I am linked to being responsible. These processes of identification and inference allow us to build up the world of immediate dwelling (the *Lebenswelt,* or lifeworld) and ground the extension through scientific inquiry of the field of sensa on which we base the constructions of the *Lebenswelt.* Beginning with immediately given sensa and the principles of inference, we come to construct the worlds of meaning that we inhabit.[19]

We might get another handle on what presence-to-being involves by considering the fact of religions. Religions are answers to the question central to human existence: How do we fit into the scheme of things? Answers to that question found different ways of life and hold them in place. Concern for the all, for the total scheme of things is central to being human. That question tends to surface explicitly when some of our deepest expectations are shattered, for then we ask seriously and not as a matter of mere curiosity: What's it all about? Though the typically offered answers are plural and not all mutually compatible, the fact of those attempts still shows the commonality of the question. To be human is to be referred by nature to the whole of what-is in the mode of a question.[20]

The human being exists wakefully in the ever-enduring Now of sensory surface, directed by nature to the whole, but initially only in the mode of questioning, since the whole is at first only emptily intended.

Taking the point of view of the whole encompasses the whole of space and time and thus exhibits a Now *sub specie aeternitatis,* a Now that eternally encompasses the flowing Now of sensory experience.[21] The initial emptiness of our reference to the whole makes it necessary to construct worlds of meaning that situate the ever-given sensory Now within the encompassing whole to which we are directed by our nature. The play between the needs of our biological ground and the need we have for seeing something of the character of our relation to the whole places human beings before certain fundamental decisions. These decisions are both possible and necessary because our relation to the whole sets us at an infinite distance from the givens of biology and thus "condemns us to choose."

In our case, sexuality drives male and female together but also poses a problem not solved by sheer natural drive, namely, How shall we care for the offspring that emerge from that togetherness? Nature addresses humankind in terms of problems not solved by nature; nature presses human freedom for decisions. The cluster of decisions provided by humankind in response to this question constitutes the history of the institutions of marriage and child rearing. Feelings of possessiveness and power, grounded in nature but focused by the sedimentation of decisions we call institutions, cluster about mates and offspring to furnish a second level, beyond natural organic feelings, of felt reverberations in the presence of sensa.

The togetherness of the family makes collective the first problems posed by nature, namely, How do I get enough to eat and drink? and How do I protect myself against the threats posed by the environment? Actually, because human beings are not born even relatively self-sufficient but require years of care, these questions an individual might ask regarding himself or herself actually originate from the questions, How do *we* get enough to eat? and How do *we* protect ourselves against the environment? The sedimentation of decisions in this realm gives rise to the history of economic institutions. The plurality of humans poses the problem of how we relate to others in and beyond those relations of mate and offspring grounded in sexuality and eventuates in determinate social practices. Of course, involved in all of this is the problem of authority: Who makes the decisions? and How do we pass on the results of these processes to those who follow us? This introduces not only the dialectic between individuals and groups who are coexistent, but, perhaps even more powerfully, that between the live community and the tradition of folkways, the sedimented set of decisions, now become second nature, that have allowed the community to survive against the more or less frequent hostility of the environment, natural and social. The answers we give to the questions posed by nature and by our sedimented responses to nature are not just ad hoc solutions but involve the establishment of anticipated possible regularity of response that could apply anywhere and any time we meet the same situations. By our decisions we help establish or disestablish both individual and collective principles for action.

But the questions posed to our freedom by our nature in relation to the natural and social environment are not the only questions. Our nature as oriented toward the whole of being poses to us the basic question of the meaning of the whole as object of our deepest human desire. It may not be the most immediately overpowering desire; but the latter ultimately pales into insignificance without some sense of its relation to the whole. After the height of orgasm one could readily ask if it "means" anything. And ultimate meaning, we suggest, is a matter of seeing and indwelling in the belonging together of humans and other entities within the whole. So we not only have to make fundamental decisions as to how we are to respond to the basic questions posed by nature in the realm of practice, we also stand under the requirement of certain interpretative decisions regarding the meaning of each entity within the whole. That they are, in a sense, decisions seems clear from the fact that there is a plurality of them. Yet neither type of decision—interpretive and practical—can be simply arbitrary and unconstrained, since they will not hold over time unless they are in some way compatible with the totality of what is given, both in terms of the encountered and in terms of our own needs, individual and collective. They are deeply tied to the sedimented history of decisions of those long dead that constitute the institutions within which a We exists. Fundamental decisions are responses to directions we are invited to walk, presented by the concrete situation in which we find ourselves, insofar as such decisions involve our place in the whole scheme of things.[22]

It is out of this question about the whole that the most powerful and sophisticated of all institutions emerges, namely the institution of language. In the first place, that structure makes possible for each individual that is given in the sensory field to function as an icon of the whole. Further, the factual reoccurrence, spatially and temporally, of types, of kinds of entities mediates the mode of manifestation in the individual's relation to the whole. It is language that allows us to retain our awareness of types. And in its mediation, language functions fundamentally in opening up the space from which decisions come, the space of meaning that emerges from the wedding between immersion in the problems posed by the sensory Now and our fundamental reference to the encompassing whole of being. Focus upon the rude artifacts from prehistorical times that archaeologists discover often makes us forget that "primitive peoples" for millennia were developing that most sophisticated of instruments to which we are still necessarily beholden: language.[23] Language, incarnated in the flow of sound generated by our lips, gathers about the immediately given sensa the whole as known and as imagined and endows the objects presented with emotional reverberations of extreme depth and subtlety. It is upon these reverberations that the arts play.

However, over and above, and indeed, I would argue, at the basis of all our conceptual articulations, there is the depth dimension of our fundamental presence to Being, whose subjective correlate is what a long tradition calls the heart.[24] Now there are several meanings that cluster around the term *heart* in a way that is remarkably constant across cultures, Eastern and Western. One thinks initially of the blood pump in the center of the chest, a mechanism in principle replicable by a man-made mechanical heart. But that is an abstraction from a more primordial, lived sense of the heart as burning with rage or skipping a beat in love: heart as the center of our lived experience known first before any knowledge of physiological mechanisms. The term is extended to an object in expressions like *sweetheart* or *heart of my heart*. Finally, it has a transcendental extension in expressions like *the heart of the matter* used to signify the essential, the core (Latin *cor*). Heart in the second sense is that to which, in biblical terms, God speaks.[25] As such it is the center, the source and receptacle for all the other distinctively human functions. And it is that, I would claim, which art articulates: the desires of the heart as our most fundamental lived presence to Being.

Being as the concrete wholeness of things within the wholeness of what-is cannot be simply object of intellectual operations directed at the abstract universal. Judgment linking the universal to the particular depends on a totalistic sense of things, out of which emerges *phronesis*, or practical wisdom in the moral-political order, and taste in the aesthetic order. Both operate at the level of "the heart" and depend on a totalistic attunement. In actual experience, things and persons are not equidistant items of information appearing within the field of a detached, judging intellect; some stand out as arresting presences, drawing near, gripping us at the level of the heart, setting up a field of magnetic attractions. And fundamental frameworks of evaluation are not present as neutral alternatives; we indwell in such frameworks, we in-habit them. The arts articulate those modes of indwelling, those senses of presence. That is why it can rightly be said that one of the most direct modes of access to a culture is through its art forms. Art gives expression to what counts most, to lived principles, to cherished persons and things in a mode appropriate to those matters. Like religion, art speaks to the heart. And both are as deep as they reach into the whole of what one is. As Mikel Dufrenne remarks, "The depth of the aesthetic object is measured by the depth of the existence to which it invites us."[26]

Reference to Being, linked to consideration of the organically dependent character of sensory manifestness, pushes us toward a distinction between the field of awareness constituted by complex relations of manifestness between subject and object and the underlying subjects of being anchoring both subject and object of awareness. The subject of awareness is "tuned," disposed, and oriented to interpret and act in certain ways from beneath the field of awareness by reason of its being in a determinate world. It comes to understand itself not simply by way of introspection of present states but more deeply by reflecting on the patterns of action it engages in over time. The object of awareness, co-constituted by the organically needy and intellectually finite subject of awareness and the underlying subject of encountered being, expresses itself in the field of awareness— that is, it rises up into that field to announce itself as indeterminately exceeding the mode of manifestness it displays in that field. It has consequently to be interpreted as well as observed. There is thus a clear distinction between appearance and reality, where the latter is understood as the full being of what is and the former as an awareness-dependent display that both reveals and conceals full being.

Reference to Being, reference to the whole, places us always at an infinite distance, not only from what we encounter, but from our very selves. A perpetual distinction between I and Me emerges. *Me* represents the objectifiable aspects of myself, what I am at any given moment outside the fact that I am always, as *I*, projected beyond it. *Me* is the resultant of (1) my genetic endowment and biological unfolding; (2) my being assimilated to, while assimilating, the institutions of my culture, beginning with language and passing through all the regularities of thought, feeling, and behavior I have received and continue to receive through the imprint of significant others—parents, siblings, friends, teachers, spouses, media, and so forth; and (3) the history of my past choices, based on the possibilities opened up by the genetic and cultural determinants and sedimented in the habit structures that both bear me up as skills and weigh me down as compulsions. All of this is Me, which—though a variation on general biological and cultural themes—is the artist's material, peculiar to me, which I as center of awareness cannot but choose to shape. The choices I make on the basis of genetic and cultural endowments sink back into the darkness from which the tuning of the field of my awareness is accomplished: they determine my heart, the desire I have to be and to act in a determinate way, to allow some persons and things to draw near and others to recede, the motivational source on the basis of which I am inclined to choose the way I do. The heart is the zone of the Me closest to the I, "the real Me." But as set at an infinite distance even from my heart, I am enabled to assess my heart, to transform my motivational basis or allow it to be transformed by a "conversion." Ultimately, I am the artist of my own life, empowered and constrained in each moment by the material I have to work with. And the specialized skills I may master as an artist in shaping sensory materials may allow me to give expression to the total way I am tuned toward being, the depths of my own heart, in artworks that come to embody my own peculiar style of inhabiting the common world, the lifeworld of my culture.

The threefold structure of the Weld of experience gives us a "vertical" cross-section verifiable at any given moment. And though the framework is concretely filled by the peculiar way in which a given culture enters into a given person's pattern of choices, individual meaning occurs by way of how that individual is in time or how the relation between past, present, and future is achieved. There are many possibilities of being in time. One could perhaps develop a logical table of the various possible ways we can be related experientially to those three dimensions. One can be fixed on acting intensely by focusing on one of the dimensions. For example, one can be so fixed on the future that one rushes past the present and repudiates the past. As Henry Ford had it, "History is bunk!" since he was opening the future for, as Aldous Huxley put it, "the year of our Ford." Or one can be so fixed on the past as to suffocate the future and reject the present. As one of my superconservative Americanist colleagues remarked: "Nothing worthwhile was written after 1781." So one engages in reactionary politics. One can also learn to be "with it," in the flowing Now, plunging excitedly into "the latest." Or one can be dreamily related to a Romanticized past or a Utopianized future. Again, one can simply drift in the present. One can also take it as one's project to appreciate the aesthetic deliverances of the past by attending carefully to what appears in the present. But when this happens in disregard of the obligations one has to others—familial, civic, contractual—one is engaged in an irresponsible aestheticism, of which Kierkegaard gives the most powerful description in philosophic literature.[27]

Heidegger has called attention to a distinction between "average everydayness," the basis for our ordinary mode of being in time and dealing with one another, and "appropriated" existence (*Eigenlichkeit*, usually translated as "authenticity"—which has the unfortunate consequence of suggesting that average everydayness is "phoniness," which it most certainly is not, for Heidegger and in fact). In average everydayness there is a flattened, stereotyped, routinized sliding along in the present, filling in time with rootless chatter, the future appearing as object of curiosity, the past appearing ambiguously as something over and done with but also as operative in the present. In appropriated existence the present has a tensed character and we learn to tarry appreciatively alongside what is present by virtue of a dedicated project whereby we take over an inheritance in the light of our sense of destiny. How we project our future determines how we take over our past. In a conversion experience, we tell our story quite differently than we did before because its meaning changes and different aspects are focused and highlighted and different events are retrieved through the new way we project our future. Ultimately, the properly tensed and deepened relation to the present depends on how we take over our Being-toward-death, for that provides us with the ultimate term of our projects in time. For one who learns to accept the irremovable conditions of existence, running ahead toward one's own term opens up the preciousness of the time we have.[28] As Buber put it, for one properly disposed toward death, "The script of life is so incomparably beautiful to read because we know that death looks over our shoulder."[29] And, as Schopenhauer noted, if we did not have to suffer and die, the great questions of life would not so grip our attention and life itself would become slack.[30] Both Buber and Heidegger went beyond that to a sense of what we might call vocational awareness. That is tied in with how we conceive of our relation to the whole, the preoccupation of both religion and traditional philosophy. In that context, things step out of indifference and become significant presences; they speak to the heart.[31] Art draws upon this level of experience: in Dufrenne's words, just as in the case of the look of the human other, the work of art magnetizes the environment.[32]

Art itself appears within the field of awareness in terms of how both artist and audience take over their existence in time. Futurism, for example, completely repudiated the past, referring to "Pheidian decadence" and "Michaelangelesque sins."[33] The various forms of revivalism that dominated academic architecture in the nineteenth century looked exclusively to the past and were instrumental in initially crushing the emergence of new forms in figures like Wright, Le Corbusier, and Gropius.[34] But much of the works that followed in the International Style were focused exclusively on the present and repudiated all relation to past forms. In reaction, so-called postmodern architecture allows the reentry of past quotations into present work—though often only ironically.[35]

In order to set the general framework within which aesthetic experience occurs, I have considered the structures of the field of experience both "vertically," or as a cross-section, and also "horizontally," in terms of how we are in time. Let us now move more explicitly into the consideration of art.

## The Manifold Forms of Art

Ordinary language usage is part of the inheritance into which we enter by being born into a culture. It delineates sets of distinctions based on the distinctions and relations that appear interlocked in a real functional world. If we attend to the use of the term *art* in ordinary language, we see that it encompasses a great variety of senses, from the most comprehensive to the most specific. Each meaning can be understood in terms of its contrast with other meanings.

1. The first and most comprehensive contrast is that between art and nature. Nature provides the fundamental framework of our existence, not only in the sense of the cosmos in general and the biological environment in particular, but also in the sense of the basic structure of our distinctively human being that makes possible the peculiarly human manifestness of the biological environment within the cosmos and, as a consequence, the ability to transform according to our choices aspects of what is manifest to us. As I have shown, the structure of human nature is bipolar. It consists, on the one hand, of physiological functions that provide us, in common with other animal beings, the sensa in relation to our basic biological needs and those appetites that lead us to seek to satisfy those needs. On the other

hand, our natural structure also consists of the founding reference to the whole that sets off our distinctively human nature. On the basis of this originary human nature, we have to choose to direct our lives in terms of principles (i.e., ways of situating the Now in reference to the whole). Beyond the founding minimum of distinctive humanness as reference to the whole and by reason of that founding minimum which sets the basic direction for human existence, everything else that is distinctively human does not come into being by reason of nature but by reason of art in the broad sense of the word—that is, in terms of the modification of the naturally given through concepts that provide understanding of the given and thus determinate ways to reach goals for our striving. The whole of culture is thus arti-ficial in the literal sense; that is, it is made by art.[36]

It is important here to attend to the old Latin adage *Cultura fit secunda natura,* culture becomes second nature. Culture produces a set of spontaneities, felt responses to things and situations whose very mode of action is just like nature. This is one of the senses in which art "imitates" nature. One should think here especially of language, of which one becomes much more acutely aware when one enters a foreign country. Think of the distinction between "natural" and artificial languages. Both are actually artificial as created by human art, but a so-called natural language comes into existence over generations in response to all the claims of the natural and social environment. It takes one up into it as into nature; and of both culture and nature it is true that one can never provide an encompassing inventory.[37] This is linked to the fact that they are tied to the comprehensive set of ends embedded in the complex interplay of nature and culture that is the human person. Artificial languages are precisely surveyable because they are made by individuals to suit specific ends. And even within a "natural" language, one still speaks of an artificial style, one that is not based on a comprehensive "sense" of the region of which one speaks, but which operates in terms of rules and tricks that betray a lack of full indwelling, full presence. Fine art, the central object of our attention in this work, has a special relation to the comprehensive sense of indwelling.

2. Within this most fundamental distinction between art and nature, one can go on to distinguish, on the art side, between art (more narrowly conceived) and science. Whereas the theoretical function of science is to act as a mirror of nature, the function of art is to transform nature. But one has to bear in mind that the mirroring function has itself to come into being by the choice on the part of human beings to pursue a science of nature in the first place, by their art of choosing hypotheses and shaping

more comprehensive theories better suited than competing theories for explaining what is observed and for suggesting fruitful lines of research, by their art of active observation and experimentation, creating instruments to open further the secrets of nature, and by their choice to assimilate the tradition of scientific inquiry upon which they will build. Science as the completed manifestness of nature is the sought-for term of the art of inquiry. Thus there is not only a scientific knowledge of nature or a scientifically based transformation of nature, there is also a dimension of art within the practice of science itself.

Even the comprehensive distinction between art and nature is transformed when one attempts to understand nature in terms of art as shaping the environment. Both the Hebrew and the Greek roots of our tradition proceed on the basis of the metaphor of art. For the biblical tradition, in the beginning God created heaven and earth; in Plato's *Timaeus* the *demiurgos* persuades the chaotic receptacle of space and time to take on intelligible form.[38] For Aristotle, even though there is no conception of a fashioner or creator of nature but only of a divine exemplar, art nonetheless furnishes the basic analogue for understanding nature as involving in their togetherness the causal factors that are separated by the imposition of form upon matter by the human artisan seeking his own ends.[39] A nature is a form energetically shaping matter for the sake of achieving its own immanently given ends. That fundamental metaphor of nature, understood most basically in terms of art, operates throughout the philosophical tradition even up to and including the atheists Schopenhauer and Nietzsche.[40]

3. We approach closer to the fine arts when we distinguish, within the distinction between art and science, the art of shaping human life from the art of shaping the things of the environment. In this respect Aristotle distinguished *phronesis*, or practical wisdom, from *techne*.[41] *Phronesis* is "the art of arts," the art of the comprehensive shaping of human behavior that operates in the interplay between the political and the personal.[42] Although for Aristotle and the premodern tradition, the highest aspect of human life is the comprehensive mirroring of the order of things, which he called *theoria*, nonetheless, it is in one sense subordinate to *phronesis* as the art of the prudential arrangement of one's life in which *theoria* is the highest aspect.[43] It was Karl Marx who pointed out that in shaping nature we are simultaneously shaping ourselves by the act of producing, but we are also being shaped by the products in the act of using or observing them.[44]

4. The art of shaping the environment has two forms: that directed to-

ward forming things that are essentially means to something else and that directed toward forming things that are in some sense ends in themselves. The latter is the province of what in modern times we have come to call the fine arts.[45] But there are overlapping forms: architecture is the classical example, for it is essentially meant to serve the ends for which a given building exists; but as a fine-art form it does this by an aesthetic shaping of its materials. And, indeed, in all shaping of the environment for practical purposes there is the matter of good design. The peculiar togetherness of the sensory features, the aesthetic form, may be said to be the common focus of all the arts insofar as they are fine arts.

The following diagram summarizes the four distinctions I have just made.

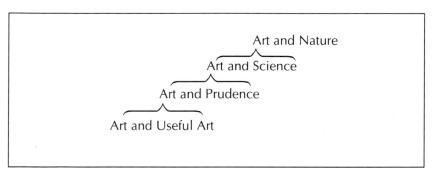

The term *art* is used in still another sense to describe the kind of institution in which a text such as this has been generated: a liberal arts school. In their origin, liberal arts were the arts of "the free man," of the leisure class not bound to the "servile" or "mechanical" arts. The former were divided into two sets: the quadrivium or "four ways" and the trivium or "three ways" which served respectively the theoretical and practical thrust of human existence. The trivium contained three arts: logic, or the art of valid thinking; grammar, or the art of correct expression; and rhetoric, or the art of persuasive expression, a fundamental art involved in the practice of political *phronesis*. *Art*, applied to the subjects of the trivium, has an instrumental sense: the arts of the trivium are useful for thinking, writing, and persuading.

The quadrivium (introduced in book 7 of Plato's *Republic*) comprised four mathematical "arts": arithmetic, geometry, astronomy, and music (understood as mathematical harmonics). *Art*, applied to the subjects of the quadrivium, seems a peculiar usage, for these subjects do not concern, like the trivium, how-to knowing. But they are understood as arts in the sense of being instrumental for the free operation of the mind, unconstrained by any other ends than purely theoretical observation. For Plato the quadrivium furnished ways to turn the soul from the realm of becoming to the realm of being, from the changeable to the eternal, freeing the mind from exterior demands to attend to what for him was its proper object.[46] As we shall see below, for Plato all arts are judged in terms of how they minister to that turn.

## A Preliminary Descriptive System of the Fine Arts

Understanding anything is a matter of seeing its relations to other things, showing how it is in some ways the same, in some ways different, as, for example, a human being shares properties with other material beings, with living things, with animals, especially the primates, but also has certain differentiating features.[47] "Basic" understanding of anything is a matter of seeing its most essential parameters in relation to the basic features of the encompassing field of experience. In this section I will focus in a preliminary way on the essential parameters of the various art forms in their togetherness. What I claim to do is to isolate some of the inescapable eidetic features of the world of art, features that are universal and necessary, that, like objects of geometrical proof, cannot be otherwise, but that, unlike geometrical proof, do not depend on postulates and abstract idealizations but on the immediate givenness of the regions of experience occupied by the fine arts. I will attempt to show some of the universal, essential, eidetic features involved in immediately given aesthetic particulars, just as redness and color and extension and quality, as universal forms, are found in red objects. The skeptic especially should note here the capacity to discern essential distinctions that are not matters of falsifiable empirical generalizations. One finds an immediate distinction between color as such and sound as such and is never tempted to mistake them. One finds too that color and sound are never presented to us nor are even imaginable except in a spatiotemporal context that indeterminately exceeds the immediate field of observation. There are eidetic constants in the interplay between awareness and its objects that transcend all opinions, personal and cultural, by making them possible.[48]

The field of the fine arts is the field of the senses—classically, not of all the senses, but only the fields of sight and sound. In common usage one does often speak of cooking or wine making or perfume making—although usually not of making love—as "fine arts" insofar as one develops forms that appeal to a palate capable of making fine discriminations in complex presentations of food or drink, or to a nose sensitive to subtle differences in aroma. One might well ask why these are not often listed under the fine arts in treatises on aesthetics, why the objects of seeing and hearing are the preferred locus of fine art.[49] From a purely aesthetic point of view, do the visual and audile arts not make the same appeal to a sensibility capable of refined discriminations in complex modes of presentation as do the culinary arts? What is there about seeing and hearing that sets off their field of operation from that of the other senses?

I would suggest, for one thing, that it has something to do with the fact that, in contrast with taste or smell or touch, which are "proximity" senses, seeing and hearing are "distance" senses. Taste and touch especially involve immediate contact with the object and thus a simultaneous somatic self-experience. Seeing and hearing operate over a significant distance and do not necessarily involve somatic self-experience. Under normal conditions of healthy functioning and of clear presentation of color or sound—where we do not have to strain to hear or see, are not pained by too much light or too loud a sound, or are not involved in some particular appetitive resonance—the appearing object fills the whole of our attention without a somatic self-experience. In this connection Thomas Aquinas speaks of sight as the most spiritual of the senses.[50] The distance involved, in sight especially, allows for the perception of unified wholes within the multiplicity of color presentation. And it is unified, sensorily manifest wholes or aesthetic forms that are the proximate and enduring objects of the fine arts. Functioning at a distance from individual somatic reverberations, sights and sounds are the focal points of a common world, a world we inhabit with others. As I noted earlier, sight dominates wakeful life as omnipresent, while sounds come and go. Nonetheless, because of the centrality of spoken language in our relation to the world and to one another, sound also has a centrality, but not so focally as sight. Hence we speak of all wakeful life through the metaphors associated with vision, as when we say, "See how this sounds or tastes or feels or smells, or how this geometric demonstration is carried out."

Sight displays aesthetic form in an immediately exemplary way. Colors, along with light and shadow, are set in tensive and harmonious relations of various sorts, playing within an overall spatial context of shapes that are spread out, discriminated, related, balanced, rendered rhythmic, and so on. Similarly, the temporality of sound admits of a unified togetherness through the diachrony of melodic lines and rhythmic repetitions and variations, and through the synchrony of harmonic relations. Furthermore, both the objects of vision and the objects of hearing admit of translation into mathematical ratios that virtually define what is meant by the harmonic, the proportionate, the rhythmic that constitute aesthetic experience. And in both cases, in the case of sights as well as of sounds, the capacity for unified togetherness allows for the expression of syntax and thus for reference to something other than sensuous surface. So the classical fine arts come to function as vehicles of expression of something other than sensuous surface through the peculiar shaping of sensuous surface. The harmonious play between the togetherness of sensory togetherness and referential togetherness constitutes the field of operation of aesthetic form.

One must note here, however, that the regular topographical transformability of a smooth surface admits of the tactual communication of language through Braille. But what would be the aesthetic shaping of a figure in Braille that would be the equivalent of painting or music? There is no publicly recognized Western art form dealing with the cultivation of tactility as there is for the gustatory and olfactory properties of things. Perhaps the *Kama Sutra* does this for the East; but the West has been too suspicious of sexuality to admit of a parallel cultivation for touch. And when we come to "high art," visual and audile arts take center stage insofar as they are tied to the communication, not simply of fine sensations, but of universally shareable meaning.

In religious liturgies—the Zen tea ceremony, for instance—an appeal is made to all the senses: seeing, smelling, hearing, tasting, the tactual cherishing of the utensils. Pre-Reformation Roman and Greek Christian liturgies used richly brocaded vestments, elaborately decorated liturgical vessels, music (vocal and instrumental, usually the organ), incense, bread and wine, set within elaborate architectural enclosures containing statuary and icons. Liturgical procession and drama alternated with sacred reading and oratory. The liturgies drew upon all the senses and artforms to convey a sense of the Holy recollected through the recounting of primordial religious history. But in either case, smelling and tasting are not highly cultivated, and tactility plays at best a very small role, purely subsidiary—perhaps in the handshake or embrace of peace. However, in the film *Babette's Feast* (*Babettes Gaestebud*, Danish-French, 1987), the heroine is presented as an artist who makes a sacrament of love out of a connoisseur's feast of food and wine, drawing together the assembled community whom she serves in such a way as to break down the barriers that separated them and to bring the event to culmination in celebratory dance. The movie recalls followers of the Reformation, whose bleak life involved only one aesthetic form, sacred music of the plainest sort, to the community-building power of the aesthetic sensuousness involved in pre-Reformation worship.

As I mentioned above, within the field of sensory operation there are two fundamental parameters necessarily involved: space and time. The fine arts settle into the various features of space and time by themselves and in relation, appealing to seeing and hearing either alone or together. Seeing color and shape has a special (but not exclusive) relation to the articulation of space, while hearing sound focuses and articulates time. But the situation is complicated by the fact of language. Though rooted in the here and now of sensory presence through sound patterns in speech or through visual patterns appearing in a text, language nonetheless has as its essential function to relate the here-and-now sensorily appearing individual things to the encompassing whole. The word as the sensory index of the universal concept is a kind of flight from the Now, grounded in the Now, a breaking out of the ever-flowing luminous bubble of sensory presence. The linguistic fine arts play in relation with the other fine art forms in a kind of complementary tension as primary carriers of the referential function of the mind.[51] But in addition, language contains the potential of music and dance in sonority and accent.[52] And so we can develop a preliminary descriptive system of the fine arts based on three parameters: space, time, and language, as they enter into the sensory field. Note that, as preliminary and descriptive, this systematic presentation does not broach the evaluative questions of good and bad art, high or low art, nor any possible expressive hierarchy within the arts. (See diagram on the following page of the basic relations between the art forms briefly discussed below.)

As a matter of fact, it is language that, allowing us to locate any encountered object and any experience within the space of a meaningful world, opens up the field for all the arts. So let us begin with the linguistic fine arts. Prose is the literary form closest to ordinary language. It occupies a range from a page of information, which operates in the visual field, to storytelling, which, like poetry, is meant to be heard. In between, arranged in an order of more naturally proximate to less naturally proximate to art, are forms like the novel, the biography, the historical essay, the philosophical dialogue, the treatise, and the scientific paper. All of these transcend the everyday use of language and become literary prose insofar as they take on aesthetic form, the latter genres lending themselves less to that form than

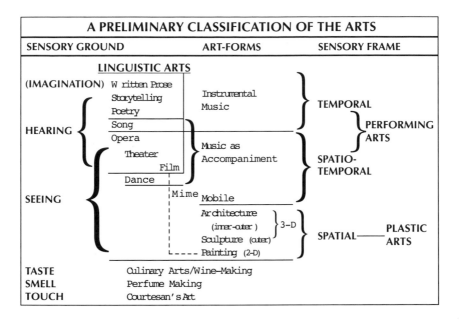

the former. An illuminated medieval manuscript or an illustrated page on one of Blake's poems or E. E. Cummings's arrangement of print in representational visual form seem calculated to work at the visual level the way melody works in relation to lyrics.

With the linguistic arts there is always a tension with the sensuous. At the level of written prose, immediate sensuousness has become wholly subordinated to the imaginative performance that the text leads us to undertake. A novel is not in the written text any more than the cake is in the recipe or the sonata in the musical staff. The written text is a series of directives for imaginative (or, in the case of music and theater, for physical) performance. The medium here is the imagination itself. Nonetheless, imaginative reconstruction or imaginative performance is a kind of second-order sensuousness that in principle can draw upon all the senses in literary description, only now transplanted from direct encounter into visual instructions for re-presentation in imagination.

Poetry is closer to sensuousness than storytelling and, a fortiori, than written prose, for poetry is meant to be heard, even though the invention of writing allows it to be read silently and thus only to be seen. But as read silently, its referential function takes over almost completely and its anchor in the sensuous is atrophied. Storytelling or dramatic reading entails the dynamics of speech: pacing, volume, expressiveness. But more than does storytelling, poetry accentuates the sonorousness of language. It sets up rhythms and rhyme schemes, it employs alliteration and attends to the interplay of various sound possibilities. Originally meters and rhyme schemes may have been mnemonic devices to help the minstrel, but over time the sonorousness takes on greater significance, perhaps initially by association with the accompanying lyre. On the side of reference, poetry creates metaphors that reconfigure the way things appear by recontextualizing the reference of the words, thus drawing upon novel associations to create a distinctive mode of presence. In its focus on sound relations, it functions to anchor language in the extended Now of living experience, from which we are prone to take flight into a world of imaginative or theoretical abstraction. As such it is related to song; and indeed, as in Homer, the function of the poet is to sing of heroes.

The art that isolates sound is instrumental music. It employs various features of the world of sound: tones and beats woven into a combination of melodies and rhythms, playing in relation to each other in harmonies and expressed in the timbre of various instruments. The first of musical instruments is the human voice, usually employing poetically shaped lyrics in song, in which the modulations of sound are even more emphasized than in poetry by itself. As employed in ordinary communication, language is an instrument wholly taken up in reference; it virtually disappears from focal awareness as does the baseball bat when we focus upon hitting the ball. But poetry sets up tension between sensuousness and reference. In song, musical accompaniment further accentuates the sensuousness. In opera, the lyrics often seem to furnish a mere occasion for the vocal elaboration of sound. In modern jazz, the development of "scat singing" plays with the various sound possibilities of the voice without employing them at all in the directly referential function they have in language.

Theater gathers together sights and sounds over time, with painting furnishing the backdrop and the enactment of the drama through words and deeds providing the focal point. The whole human body, together with its oral linguistic possibilities (from the latter of which dance abstracts), is the instrument of the art. Setting that to music leads to the idea of opera as the *Gesamtkunst*, the totalizing art, theoretically elaborated and actually practiced by Wagner. Set in the grandeur of the opera house, orchestral sound, lyrics, costuming, stage setting, and dramatic action (at times also involving dance) combine to present a single spatiotemporal, sound-and-color impression embracing a whole world of meaning. In a Wagnerian opera the natural tension between the sensuous form and the referentiality of language is resolved in the direction of the sensuous, where the "sea of harmony" is said to generate the text as well as the action. Wagner saw opera as performing the same liturgical function as ancient dramatic presentation, drawing upon all the artistic means to bring about a sense of participation, through the polis, in a cosmic whole.[53]

Film is *the* contemporary art form. It is wholly dependent on contemporary developments in technology. Film recording of motion and coordinated sound recording are very recent inventions. There is also the technology of special effects, which is increasingly more sophisticated. But film is the contemporary art form in another sense. It provides the most readily accessible presentation of all the art forms simultaneously. It functions, in a manner similar to opera, as a *Gesamtkunst*. It requires the cooperative artistry of script writers, actors, directors, camera operators, editors, costume makers, makeup artists, special effects experts, set-designers, musicians, and recording experts.[54] But in film the music is clearly accompaniment and thus strictly subordinate—unless the film is about musical performance. So much is that the case that I cannot recall movies that do not have musical accompaniment; even more, I am not usually aware at all of the musical soundtrack. However, the difference between action accompanied and not accompanied by music was demonstrated graphically in the PBS tribute to composer-director John Williams where a scene from *Jaws* was shown without and then with his accompanying musical score. The difference in emotional impact was amazing.

Of course, film, like painting and its allied arts, is two-dimensional. In terms of actual viewing, however, it creates a three-dimensional experiential world. In this it is closest to theater, except that in film the visual aspect takes on a much more powerful role, since the camera focuses for us by choosing the frame, the proximity or distance of the visual point of view, and, by fading the background, the focus itself. This focusing makes the viewer much more passive than in theater. Hence a greater immediacy and thus broader mass appeal is established. Furthermore, the camera can change settings immediately and range widely within a given setting, and can include flashbacks and superposition.[55] Film, in addition to popular music, with its relative lack of sophistication, is the art form most suitable to a mass democratic audience. Filmed opera expanded its possibilities when it moved from the visual-audial recording of stage performances (reaching a certain high point in Ingmar Bergman's work) to performances in real settings that gave the camera and the performance greater space in which to operate (e.g., *Carmen*, featuring Placido Domingo, 1984). In theater the word is the primary focus, standing in necessary tension with the visual enactment. Of course, both art forms can approach either end of the tension between the visual and the linguistic, between action and dialogue. Some films (e.g., *My Dinner with André*, 1981) give primacy to the dialogue, while some theater performances bring the action into greater prominence—though the dialogue still remains the center of the latter art form.

Considered in terms of their media, written prose, storytelling, poetry, song, and music in general are strictly temporal arts. Outside of written prose, the other art forms listed occupy the temporal field of sound. Written prose is a second-order art form, defocusing the immediately sensuous written page in order imaginatively to reconstruct the whole field of space-time sensuousness as displaying the context for the interaction of the characters. Opera, theater, and film are spatiotemporal arts since they appeal both to the space-and-time-occupying field of vision and to the time-occupying field of sound, the latter both in musical form and in linguistic form. There are also other forms of spatiotemporal art, such as dance or the mime that, like untitled instrumental music, are nonlinguistic. Beyond observable movement in space—a feature it shares with mime—dance introduces a further parameter insofar as it is usually linked with sound through music, thus bridging not only space and time, but also sight and sound. Mime and dance occupy two ends of a continuum of relation between reference and aesthetic form, while they stand over against acrobatics. Mime is wholly absorbed in reference ("imitation" as mirroring). Dance approaches mime when it is primarily referential (though always in the context of establishing a rhythmic whole), but dance can also operate in the free elaboration of form without reference. Dance is usually accompanied by music, or at least by the beat of a drum, the clapping of hands, or the stamping of feet, and thus appeals both to hearing and seeing, though the primary focus is seeing. Dance, whose material is the mobile possibilities of the body as a whole, has to be one of the primordial art forms. Perhaps it initially entailed communal coordination of movement through a simple common beat or rhythm associated with tasks that required cooperative effort, and then opened out into the possibility of complex movements of extraordinary grace achieved only with difficulty by individuals and groups, as in the development of ballet. Acrobatics stands over against both mime and dance in that it expresses nothing but exhibits the body reaching certain goals.[56] All the forms we have considered thus far are performing arts, in which temporality plays a central role. Each must be considered both from the point of view of the audience and from the point of view of the performer.

Let us consider next the plastic arts, which shape things in space. Chronologically, the first form is probably architecture, which is rooted in the biological need we have for protection from the elements. It shapes materials into a three-dimensional functional form.[57] As a fine art it attends to the articulation of space, and does that not only by providing certain boundaries and thus enclosing space. It also sets up an environmental space, alternating between focus on the vista and focus on more intimate places, gathering and opening for inhabitants and visitors the natural environment as well as the environment constituted by buildings already in place. It attends to the play of light and darkness at different times of the day and in different seasons. It attends to the appearance of different textures and colors under those conditions. It gathers all this together in such a way as to present a unified whole to one who walks around and through a building. Finally, it carries out this shaping process in such a way as to provide an environmental feel that suits the activities people will undertake in and around the building. It does all this as a functional form insofar as the formation of space inside and out fosters rather than inhibits what is to be done in and around the building. Allied to architecture would be the arts of interior decoration and landscape gardening, as well as the arts of design in furniture and utensils. Of all the art forms, these would seem to have the least overt referential function; they anchor us solidly in the Now of sensuous presence. And yet, especially in religious architecture, they are able to shape space in such a way as to communicate a sense of the sacred and the transcendent. Architecture is also linked to sculpture and painting by providing niches and walls for statues and paintings and to musical performance and drama by providing the space for performers and audience.

I will discuss sculpture more fully in the appendix. At this point I will anticipate only a few of its eidetic features. Traditionally it shapes only three-dimensional surface and thus, by disregarding the spatial interior, attends more one-sidedly to the three-dimensional whole than does architecture. It also tends to employ one material, like clay or wood or marble or bronze. But modern sculpture approaches architecture aesthetically—though not functionally—as it employs different materials in various combinations and opens up the interior of its materials through holes and hollows. It employs various textures and colors and sets up a play between light and shadow. The sculptural object occupies space and sets up a tension within the perceptual field between its own space and the surrounding space. One could indeed refer to architecture as a form of sculpture, as sculpture linked to utility. One could also speak of sculpture as a form of architecture, as architecture freed from utility.[58]

Grounded, like architecture, in functional need, but annexed in a sense to sculpture, clothing design comes to take on the form of a fine art. It both reveals and conceals the mobile three-dimensional human form and has its own decorative surface elaboration. Taking off from that is the art of jewelry making as a miniform of sculpture, usually "abstract," in which the quality of the materials is part of the central focus.

There is a form of plastic art (plastic in the extended sense of shaping visible materials) that works in a more abstract medium than architecture or sculpture, namely painting, together with those similar fine art forms like drawing, printmaking, and photography. They employ the abstractness of two-dimensional surface, establishing the play of color and shape, although in the case of black-and-white drawing or photography, they approach abstraction from all color. (Here I consider both black and white from a nontheoretical, wholly experiential point of view as the absence of color: black because our dominant experience of it is in the absence of light, where no colors show; white because it is usually that on which we begin to lay color on canvas or paper.) Representational forms of painting give the illusion of a third dimension; attention to surface texture gives a real three-dimensional character to a painting. The latter moves toward relief sculpture, which is a transitional form between two-dimensional and three-dimensional forms, from etchings to high relief. It is perhaps not without significance that the terms *art* and *artist* are used paradigmatically of painting and the painter, for it is in painting that the immediacy of integrated wholes is given all at once, whereas the architectural and sculptural wholes can be given only through moving in and around the three-dimensional forms. Painting (with its cognate forms) presents a standing Now as nothing else can do.

In terms of actual viewing, the arts of the two-dimensional surface approach a certain abstraction from time, since everything is present at once to the viewer. However, one must at least move one's eyes from point to point in order to enrich one's perception of the overall gestalt, and thus time necessarily enters in, not as simple endurance in the Now, but as continual change of focus. The arts that shape three-dimensional space add an indeterminate number of perspectives for viewing and require successive movements not only of our eyes but of our whole physical being as we move around and within the work. Architecture, insofar as it involves the changing play of light and dark through different seasons, may also be considered a temporal art: though the building does not change, its mode of presentation does. Perhaps one might say the same about sculpture. But painting and its allied art forms require optimal lighting conditions and thus are only accidentally temporal. The invention of mobile sculpture simultaneously occupies space and modifies that occupation through time; but it also allows stationary viewing, since it moves and thus does not require our whole body to move in order to grasp its overall gestalt. It is thus a spatiotemporal art.

In attending to any of the art forms, what is required is always what one might call imaginative performance, which is one reason I began my preliminary classification of the art forms with written prose, which most obviously demands such performance. The printed text provides the most idealized form of the act of attending operative in all art forms, even in the most immediate form of the two-dimensional plastic arts, as an act of imaginative performance. Reading a novel is the clearest case of taking the text as a set of recipes for imaginative construction. The author does not lay out a wholly complete world, no matter how detailed his descriptions, but indicates, through his linguistic constructions, a kind of core object around which we have to construct our own imaginative variations.[59] It requires a developed imagination to perform in response to the imaginative possibilities laid open on the printed page by a master novelist. When a novel is turned into a film, the imaginative possibilities are focused and rendered explicit in a single way. That is why a film version of a great novel is so disappointingly reduced compared to the richness of our imaginative performance in reading it. We might extend this observation to all the art forms, even to that which seems to be most explicit, namely painting. One must learn to "perform" the painting through gathering the details together, but also through indwelling in its immediate felt texture in order to reach the total gestalt. No art form lies open to immediate experience without some type of imaginative reenactment.[60]

At this point it would be fitting to follow a bit further the tension between linguistic reference and sensuousness in the arts. Consider the difference naming makes in how we attend to the sensuous. Arthur Danto tells the fictitious story of two artists, each of whom was commissioned to do a mural in a new science building. One mural was to be given the title *Newton's First Law*, the other *Newton's Third Law*. As it happened, each artist produced exactly the same painting: a single black line running straight across the white wall parallel to the floor and about a third of the way up from the bottom of the wall. But the titles make one attend to the same sensuous configuration differently. In the first case, following the inertial law that a body in motion will stay in motion in a straight line unless acted upon by an outside force, the line on the wall appears as a line segment tracing the path of motion of a projectile through space. In the second case, following the law that for every action there is an equal and opposite reaction, the line is a division between two white masses pressing against one another. Danto goes further: a physically identical painting might also be entitled *Sea and Sky at High Noon*. In another example, Danto suggests considering two possible titles for a painting that shows the sun shining from above on a landscape where a farmer is plowing his field while, in the lake below, two legs are shown of a figure splashing into the water. One would look at the painting differently if it were entitled *Work and Play*—or, as it actually is— *The Fall of Icarus*, by Brueghel.[61] Further, to take a musical example, would anyone think of the sea at sunrise or at high noon or in a storm if Debussy titled his work *Opus 34* instead of *La Mer* and gave no programmatic subtitles? Untitled paintings or instrumental music or purely abstract untitled sculpture represent attempts to attend to the pure aesthetic form without focusing on any direct reference. But then, as Henry Moore observed, there are always felt reverberations of forms and colors derived from past associations on which the abstract artist draws for at least an indirect kind of reference.[62] Pure aesthetic forms, scrubbed clean of all overt reference, nonetheless are peaceful or agitated, joyful or sad, strong or languid, and so on. As Aristotle observed of instrumental music, such forms produce states of mind similar to those obtained in the context of their real counterparts and are thus "the most imitative of artforms."[63] And because such forms appear in a field of awareness circumscribed by the lived disclosure of space and time as a whole, and, indeed, of *the* totality of meaningfulness, of "the world," works of art articulate a sense of indwelling in the whole; they establish a world. But, as Heidegger observed, it is language that opens up the space of such a world in the first place.[64]

One could draw up a scale of art forms, from those in which aesthetic form is purely subordinate to reference, to those in which overt reference disappears from purely aesthetic forms. At the level of dominant reference we would have, as a measure, the philosophic treatise in which no attention whatsoever is given to literary form. Then, as we enter the sphere of the aesthetic, we would have philosophy presented in dialogue form with judicious employment of drama, imagery, parable, and myth, as in a Platonic dialogue, or history written with great literary polish and descriptive power.

At a level next to that we would have the novel; then poetry in which the play with the possibilities of sound combinations takes a more dominant role; then song in which aural forms are still more dominant; then instrumental program music, then music with referential titles, and finally music with only genre and chronological series titles, as Sonata in G Minor, op. 4.

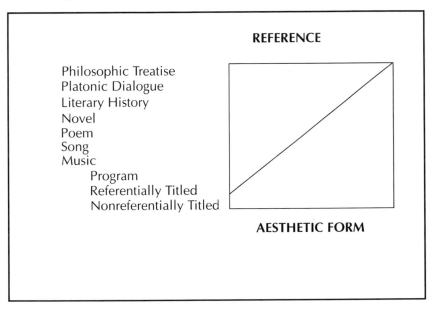

One could take art forms like painting and sculpture and show a similar scale exhibited by individual works within each of the forms, from the dominantly referential to the dominantly aesthetic-formal. Walter Pater once remarked that all art seeks the status of music.[65] Overtly referential or not, art forms bring about distinctive moods by reason of their organization of the sensuous. Like music, all art speaks to the heart and thus affects the emotional wellsprings of action, inclining us to act in the direction of the ways we are moved. That is why Plato and Aristotle spoke of the ethical character of music.

## Phenomenological, Hermeneutic, and Dialogic Approaches

The preliminary laying out of the field of experience for a discussion of the fine arts that I have just completed made use of a phenomenological method. Phenomenology is a permanent prolegomenon, acknowledged or not, to any philosophy. Phenomenology is, to begin with, descriptive explication of the essential structures *(logoi)* of the various modes of appearance *(phainomena)*, various relations of manifestness between conscious subjects and their differing types of objects. The sensorily given precisely as sensory, even though the most obvious aspect of manifestness, is only a starting point for knowledge, since to know something means to grasp it "as" something. To grasp something "as" something here is to bring to bear upon the sensa universal meanings expressible in words. What I have attempted is to lay out some of the fundamental eidetic features, the immanently present universal forms of the general structure of the field of experience and of the various aspects of the sensory domain within that field insofar as these aspects are the field of operation for the fine arts. I would claim that most of what was presented was not simply my opinion but inescapable eidetic features involved in the arts. In that sense I would claim to have presented features even more necessary than Euclidean geometry because they are immediately given features of the objects of experience presupposed in doing geometry or any thing else, whereas Euclidean geometry, resting on those features, operates in terms of abstract, idealized reconstruction of the quantitative aspects of the sensorily given.

But not all grasping of something "as" something is a matter of phenomenological description—that is, description of the immediately appearing, the immediately given. Very much of it is a matter of hermeneutics, a matter of interpreting the sensorily given, as the sciences furnish various interpretations (theories) of the nature of matter or of life, or as in everyday life we attempt to interpret the signs of someone's behavior in order to understand her basic character.[66]

The hermeneutical moment in this study is really twofold. On the one hand I am aiming at a philosophy of art and beauty, and thus must not only describe what occurs in the encounter with beauty and art and in the production of fine art; I must also furnish a comprehensive interpretation of the whole field of aesthetic phenomena. The development of that task is tied to the second hermeneutical aspect of my study, which lies in my major methodological decision, namely to approach the construction of an aesthetics through the study of a select portion of the great texts in the philosophy of art and beauty throughout the history of Western philosophy. The meaning of these texts does not lie on the surface. Philosophy is the attempt to think critically and comprehensively about the ultimate framework of all our dealings; and, since we are by nature referred to being, that involves thinking comprehensively about the whole of what is. That means that each concept cannot be understood until we see how it is related to all the basic concepts of a given philosophy. For example, even something so apparently self-evident as the meaning of the term *body* cannot be taken in identically the same way in the works of every philosopher, even though the starting point in the sensory givenness furnishes a point of reference for the more comprehensive meanings advanced by different philosophers.[67] Thus in my approach to each of the philosophers, I will not begin immediately with what they have to say about matters aesthetic, but with an interpretation of their comprehensive view of things within which we can begin to see the fuller significance of their aesthetic claims.

The second hermeneutical aspect leads to a third methodological factor, the dialogic. The structure of the field of experience gives us a common point of reference for all discussion provided both in the sensorily given and in the grounding reference to the whole of being. Every great philosopher has attempted to break through the sedimentation of meaning furnished by the cultural shaping he has received in order to get back to the basic phenomena and to construct his interpretation from there. But no constructive interpretation has ever been able to win over all intelligent, well-informed, diligent, and honest inquirers. Rather than allowing us to rest content with a selection of that which suits our own preferences and thus to fall into either a closed-minded dogmatism or an equally comfortable relativism, our founding reference to being pushes us out of the comfort of both dogmatism and relativism. It demands a dialogism, an entry into genuine conversation aimed at a more encompassing disclosure that will display the limits of our chosen views and thereby allow us a better grasp of the encompassing whole. It requires that we take a stand, that we judge as well as interpret the meanings of others, but also that we stand ready to be judged in terms of the possibly greater adequacy of those other views.[68] But we have the best chance of being less inadequate if we attend to the insights, both as phenomenological observations and as hermeneutic recommendations, offered by the great minds who have gone before us.

※ ※ ※

In concluding this introduction, let me lay out the path I will follow in this work. I will focus on certain central figures in the history of the philosophy of art and beauty. Among the Greeks I have selected Plato and Aristotle as by far the most outstanding, ground-breaking thinkers. Through his impact on Plotinus, Dionysius, and Augustine, Plato (whose works—except for the first third of the *Timaeus*—were unavailable before the Renaissance) indirectly influenced the thought of the Middle Ages and directly, through the translation of his works by Ficino in the fifteenth century, impacted upon the Renaissance. But it is surprising, especially in view of the unsurpassed beauty of the architectural achievements and the spiritually lofty Gregorian chant of the Middle Ages, that none of the major thinkers had much to say about art and beauty. And though the translation of Aristotle's works in the twelfth and thirteen centuries decisively shaped every phase of thought in the High Middle Ages, this was less so through his *Poetics,* his single sustained work on matters aesthetic (and that dealing with one artistic mode, namely tragedy). My approach to the Middle Ages will be more diffuse than the approach in the other chapters. Beginning with Plotinus, whose mode of thought decisively affected subsequent thinkers, I briefly consider Augustine, Dionysius, and Albertus Magnus, articulate the metaphysical frame that fused the Aristotelian and Platonist modes of thought in Aquinas, and conclude with Bonaventure.

The name *aesthetics* emerged as the term for the philosophy of art and beauty in the eighteenth century in the work of the German philosopher Alexander Baumgarten. At the same time the British tradition of taste developed. I will treat the latter in my discussion of David Hume's essay "Of the Standard of Taste," as an epilogue to an aspect of the German tradition which gained its first powerful expression in Immanuel Kant's *Critique of Judgment.* After Kant we have the rich development of the German philosophical tradition, which had a great deal to say about the arts. I will discuss the views of Hegel, Schopenhauer, Nietzsche, and Heidegger. I also include a chapter on John Dewey, one of America's greatest philosophers, who stands in the tradition of Hegel, but turned in a more empirical, pragmatic, and open-ended direction, for whom, nonetheless, the aesthetic is absolutely central, the aim and measure of all experience.

Throughout I will draw upon the structures I have explored in this introduction and work toward building a more comprehensive aesthetic by ending each chapter with an appreciative and critical response. In the conclusion I reflect somewhat systematically on the ground I have covered.

# II

# PLATO

IN MY TREATMENT OF Plato, the first of the great philosophers to address matters aesthetic, I begin to flesh out more fully the framework considerations I have offered in the previous chapter by an interpretation that builds a whole world of meaning, encompassing every aspect of human existence. There is a sense in which one might say that Plato's philosophy is essentially an aesthetic. Beauty plays a central role in his thought, though he has some harsh things to say about its appearance in art. However, in spite of the latter, his own works exhibit an artistry unmatched in the history of philosophy. The use of images and parables, the development of myths, the delineation of characters, the drama of their action and reaction in relation to the themes under discussion, and the overall structuring of the dialogues are neither pleasant accompaniments to philosophical argumentation nor irritating distraction therefrom. Though argumentation and rational construction are crucial to philosophy, they are essentially in a relation of mutual dependence upon a fuller sense of participation in life that affords the starting point, gives the basic insights about which we argue and from which we construct our theories, and finally, provides, in the holistic feel for things (the "lived aesthetic") that it involves, the basic test of all comprehensive claims.[1] Rational development stands in a dialectical relation with the heart as the felt residue of an interplay between a tradition and the individual thinker that provides our basic orientation toward things.

The key texts on beauty are in the *Phaedrus*, and especially in the *Symposium*. The key texts on art—and indeed on the pivotal ideas in Plato's thought—are in the *Republic*, which stands at the logical and chronological center of Plato's written work. The core idea of the latter dialogue is justice, but the key to understanding justice is understanding the relation between the city and philosophy. In that relation, beauty and art play an important role.

It may seem odd to begin a treatment of aesthetics with notions like justice, the city, and philosophy. Today we are used to a division of labor, with specialization even in "philosophy." We have fallen into that habit because of the astonishing success, both theoretically and technologically, of scientific method, which operates by specialized division of labor. Alexander Pope said, "Know then thyself, presume not God to scan; / the proper study of mankind is man."[2] Today thinkers have gone further: they would say that the proper study of humankind is bits and pieces of nature. In what many today call philosophy, we find a family resemblance to what the ancient tradition called philosophy. Then philosophy was "love of wisdom," where wisdom was understanding something of how we humans fit into the total scheme of things and how we might come into proper relation to the whole in our lives. It involved conceptual analysis and argumentation, but always within the overall matrix of the pursuit of the wider, more comprehensive vision—indeed, a vision governed in Plato by growth in a pervasive sense of awe before the strangeness of our situation.[3] In philosophy today conceptual analysis and argumentation conducted within regional specializations are the norm. In the more ancient view, represented in its first most powerful form by Plato, adequate understanding of any region involved understanding its place in the whole. Corollary to this is the view that each basic concept implies all the others. As Hegel later put it, "The truth is the whole."[4] I have begun this text by staking out the structure of the field of experience as it opens out to the whole of Being. I have gone on to locate art within that whole and to delineate the field of art by an analysis of the sensory fields and the spatiotemporal framework within which they operate. Following out that structure, I will approach each thinker by locating art and beauty within the whole of his thought. And that means seeing the place of the aesthetic within the whole of human life. Let us then take this approach to Plato's aesthetics.

## Art in the Purged City

In the *Republic*, Socrotes, Plato's spokesman, focuses on justice. After an introductory skirmish in which conventional ideas of justice (giving to each his due; giving benefits to allies and harm to enemies; and obeying the laws made in the self-interest of the stronger) are tested in a preliminary way by locating them in broader contexts to show their implications, and after the sources of those conventional ideas are explored, Socrates proposes to examine the justice of the individual in terms of the justice of the city.[5] He proceeds to do so by constructing several strata of a city, beginning with that involved in the provision of food, clothing, and shelter by a simple division of labor. Socrates calls this "the true, the healthy city." It is a city centered on health: it supplies basic biological needs. There is an additional aspect to this level: the citizens also sing hymns to the gods.[6] Here the aesthetic dimension, embodied in music, is subordinated to a sense of the sacred. Music emerges beyond biological need in conjunction with our metaphysical reference to the whole, since the gods are exhibitions of the community's sense of "the meaning of it all." Perhaps it is a "true and healthy city" because it satisfies not only biological need, but also metaphysical need, which is linked to the need for togetherness with others as simultaneously rooted in biology and in the metaphysical. Such a city would provide psychic health as well as health of body. It is a "true" (*alethes,* unconcealed) city in the sense that it is the most immediately manifest, though not the most developed. But it is unclear what Socrates' understanding of the status of the gods was at this level. At the third level of the city Socrates constructs (and which we will shortly consider), the gods are trimmed down to being projections of civic ideals. Are the gods here at this first level projections of the citizens' togetherness in their feasting and thus in their provision of biological necessities without further ideals? Whatever their putative status, the gods do exhibit a first articulation of our metaphysical need.

The citizens here are presented as moving out of this level by a desire for luxury: "sweetmeats and soft couches."[7] The promotion of luxury also introduces us to a surplus need, beyond biological necessity, that is distinctively human. It is the need for beauty, exhibited in the first city as subordinated to worship; but here it seems to be detached from any other consideration. Chefs, pastry cooks, cosmetologists, fashion designers, and musicians fill the city. No distinction is made between the cultivated satisfaction of biologically rooted appetites and the occurrence of a distinctive aesthetic experience. Culinary art and the art of the beauty parlor are placed on the same level as the art of music. What seems to stand at the center of the luxurious lifestyle is feeling good, having pleasurable sensations, being titillated, having goose bumps, feeling chills running up and down our spines. One remains locked within the immediacy of biologically based satisfaction, culturally stimulated and provided.[8]

Now, the first level of the city is described as the true and healthy city, but also as "a city for pigs," who have only biological needs to satisfy. Glaucon, who makes the observation, overlooks the hymns to the gods—although perhaps he understands them only too well at this level. This first level has a natural measure: what is required for biological well-being. But on the second level, where humans are driven by the desire for luxury, there is no natural measure. Because we are by nature not only rooted in biological appetites and sensations but also, at the other pole of our being, referred emptily to the whole, the play between these two poles in the field of awareness can lead to the indeterminacy of biological satisfaction, which we can endow with the character of the absolute and pursue measurelessly. At the cutting edge of our being we are indeterminate, forced by nature to choose our way and select our measure or go on and on endlessly and ultimately meaninglessly, now this way, now that. The city can consequently become measureless, bloated, feverish. People seek more and more as they are introduced, by those who would profit by them, to appetites they did not know they had. The city would seem to have undergone a fall from primitive simplicity, based on natural need, into measureless self-indulgence. But since human nature is not merely biological, and since the desire for beauty is distinctively human, the fall into the search for luxury is, so to speak, a fall upward. One cannot understand the peculiarly mixed character of this paradoxical upward fall until one grasps more fully the character of humanness which will also open up the possibility of another understanding of the divine. Plato introduces us to that bit by bit through a kind of dialectical inversion of the desire for luxury brought about by the logic of its own development.

Since the immediate environment cannot supply enough, the citizens of the bloated city begin a program of expansion. For this they need an army that also protects them, not only from the greedy eyes of outsiders but also from each other. It thus keeps order within the city. The introduction of an army involves the introduction of another lifestyle: a disciplined lifestyle that rises above the soft hedonism that drives the luxurious city. The discipline consists of gymnastics and music. Gymnastic exercise produces hardness and endurance, but, pursued one-sidedly, it also fosters brutality and insensitivity. It is offset by training in "music" which, without gymnastics, fosters softness, but which, together with gymnastic, tempers or tunes the dispositions.[9] Later, in Plato's *Laws*, the Athenian stranger discusses gymnastics as a form of dance and thus as an art form itself.[10] Dance is a fusion of gymnastic and music in which the whole body is the instrument. The perception thereof is visual for the observer but kinesthetic for the performer. The stranger focuses on the latter and stresses its effect in rendering the psyche graceful, rhythmic, orderly.

But returning to the discussion in the *Republic:* so that the "guard-dog" trainees do not prey upon the citizens, they must be trained to think in terms of dedication to the city as a whole.[11] The vehicle of such training is "music," understood basically as instrumentally accompanied poetry. That involves two components, beyond the relatively fixed character of the givenness of unconscious biological processes and corresponding to the two trainable aspects of human existence: psychic disposition and intellectual focus. Psychic disposition is trained here by the blend of gymnastic and music mentioned above. However, it is also affected by the aesthetic character of the visual and auditory ambiance. The cultural environment of visual and audile products that surround the citizenry from birth ought, says Socrates, to be characterized by grace, harmony, good rhythm. Socrates refers here to such visual products as paintings, clothing, utensils, furniture, and buildings.[12] It is important to notice that it is not the pictorial quality of paintings that is at stake here—how they mirror the outer world, as Socrates will ask us to think of them in book 10.[13] Linked with architecture, furniture, clothing, and utensil design, paintings are considered here in terms of their purely aesthetic properties. Design must consider not only function (although in book 10 Socrates does claim that form should follow function); design should also follow beauty.[14] The latter, however, should not simply be superadded to the former in an external way; rather beauty should support and flow from function. A culture that focuses exclusively on functional products without concern for the aesthetics of good design is a fractured culture: its world is either un- or anti-aesthetic (though maybe the former is impossible—"He who is not with me is against me")—or such a utilitarian culture, though having a place for beauty, separates art from the everyday.[15] The dispositional impact is what concerns Socrates here.

In the second book of his *Laws,* Plato has the Athenian stranger reject as senseless, along with the display of virtuosity for its own sake, tune and rhythm without words.[16] And in his *Republic* "melody *(harmonia)* and rhythm *(rhythmos)* will depend upon the word *(logos)*."[17] *Harmonia* referred to the relation between tones over time (hence "melody" in more modern terms), *rhythmos* to the beat found also in dance, and *logos* to the referent.[18] So it would seem that direct representation is what is important. Yet the stranger also says (and Aristotle will pick up on this) that all music is representative and imitative.[19] What does a tune on the lyre or the harp "represent" and "imitate"? Instrumental music, like the dance, can cover the ground between a rhythmic mime on the one hand and the elaboration of the synchronically and diachronically patterned togetherness of sensory elements on the other. Aristotle will suggest that the latter imitates character *(ethos)*. And that implies different moods and dispositions: happy or sad, vigorous or languid. But in the *Laws* the Athenian stranger insists on the association of the tunes and rhythms with the word. Association with the word will dominate until the eighteenth century, when musical forms will emerge whose only overt association with words will be a title indicating the genre (fugue or concerto, for example) and a chronological listing (opus 4).

In the *Republic*, Socrates advocates the same qualities in the audile modalities of music as he did in the plastic arts. Hence he calls for the repudiation of "Dionysian" music, which leads to high stimulation and wild abandon. He advocates "Apollonian" music, which fosters a sense of good order, grace, harmony, due proportion.[20] (In modern terms, one might think of acid rock versus Bach.) Notice that these are the same characteristics of good design in the plastic arts. Furthermore, the very timbre of different instruments tends to Dionysian or Apollonian effects. He thus advocates the lyre, the zither, and the shepherd's pipe, but not the "polyharmonic instruments," especially the flute,[21] the former set having a more calming effect, the latter one more exciting. (In contemporary terms, one might consider the effect of the electric versus the acoustic guitar.) Again in the second book of the *Laws*, the Athenian stranger returns to the discussion of Apollonian and Dionysian music, only here he says that the gift of Dionysus must no longer be condemned without qualification, for the music of Dionysus helps reduce the natural frenzy of youth through the imparting of rhythm.[22] Through music, Socrates says, good rhythm and harmony (or their opposites) sink deeply into the soul and affect our disposition to behave. And precisely because music affects the psychic disposition so profoundly, changes in the basic forms of music are linked to changes in political regimes.[23]

Socrates gives no further direct description of the properties he wishes to see promoted by art. They seem to be features which we have to learn to recognize by contrast with their opposites. He lists *eulogia,* or fine language; *euharmostia,* or easiness of temper; *euscheymosuney,* or gracefulness or good form; and *euruthmia,* or rhythmic order.[24] Fineness in language would seem to have to do both with conventional associations and with sound, though the two may not coincide. (Respondents who did not know English once selected "cellar door" as the most euphonious expression in a long list with which they were presented.) *Euharmostia* has affinities with harmony, and harmony implies the unity of parts such that all of them belong together, with all incongruities removed. Gracefulness involves the smooth transition between each aspect, primarily in temporal terms, but applicable also to spatial transitions. That which is graceful displays a kind of effortlessness, a lack of strain or tension. A grace is a gift, and gracefulness in performance is a matter of aligning oneself with one's gifts so that, as it were, "it" operates in me rather than "I" operate. Rhythm is the regular repetition of a pattern within a margin of variations, literally taken in the temporal order of sound, but transferable to spatial pattern as well. Order is the opposite of randomness; it obtains when there is a governing principle. In Greek all the terms are preceded by the prefix *eu-* which means "good." While each musical piece must have order, harmony, and rhythm so as to be something other than noise, only the graceful piece exhibits the dignity Socrates is intent on promoting at this point in the dialogue. Such grace seems to be the result of shaping by deliberate control based on thinking in terms of the unity of the whole polis. That is what *eu-* implies here. Art forms are to be promoted that open the psychic disposition to comprehensive rational shaping in terms of the needs of the polis.

There are three levels of human existence involved here. At the unconscious biological level, we have a natural model of a rational system: the harmonious synchronic and diachronic functioning of a complex multiplicity of parts—a fairly adequate description of health. Plato frequently uses the healthy organism as a symbol of psychic well-being—though it is much more than a symbol, being a lower-level phase of a complex psychosomatic unity.[25] At the basic level of psychic experience we have our emotions and their dispositions affected both by physiological state and the impact of past and present conscious life. Plato calls for measures to effect their harmonic tuning so as to produce a kind of prerational rationality. He says that such tuning will provide a fit matrix that will recognize and welcome fully reflective reason when it dawns.[26] The minimum presence of reflective reason awakens through the presence of the word. It is here that poetry plays a key role, for the poetic word not only opens up the world for reflective intelligence, it simultaneously provides it body and location in the lived world through the rhythmic and harmonic shaping of sound.

The referential function of the word is employed at this level of the exposition to furnish models of civic exemplarity for the military trainees.

Notice that it is not truth that is the issue here. One does not tell tales of the gods that speak of unseemly conduct (e.g., Zeus overthrowing his father, Cronus—"even if it were true.").[27] Furthermore, one does not present heroes trembling in fear at the imminent prospect of death, not to would-be soldiers.[28] Furthermore, one does not present the gods as changing forms, appearing in dreams and visions. Any kind of opening to what transcends the city is closed off. No revelation or special intervention is allowed. This referential level is the level of *musike* Plato has Socrates purge first, and he spends the most time with it. I have reversed the emphasis, stressing the consideration of aesthetic form apart from overt reference, because I believe that is, indeed, Plato's main intention here. The purgation of the referential function of literature is done with Adeimantus as interlocutor, an adamant, no-nonsense man—no laughter in *his* city—who wants to make rules to keep the citizenry in order. And the city Socrates builds for him allows no entry of revelation into or exit of human aspiration out of the city. It is not Adeimantus but Glaucon who is Socrates' interlocutor in moving from the healthy to the luxurious city, in discussing the aesthetic side of the purgation of the arts, and, later, in opening up Eros for Beauty Itself, which transcends the city. With Adeimantus, Socrates plays "moralist" of civic exemplarity, projected as protected cosmically by the gods; but with Glaucon, he works at tuning the dispositions that open out beyond the city to the whole and the Source.

Visual and audile art play an important role in the shaping of psychic disposition. Through connection with the word, the intellectual level of our being is given shape directly. Through music and visual art (and at this point "nonrepresentational" visual art in clothing, utensils, buildings, and furniture) one reaches what is announced as the (somewhat surprising) aim of education at this level: the appreciation of beautiful things.[29] The announcement of the aim is surprising because of the stolid emphasis on reference and moral exemplarity and the apparently—but only apparently—secondary character of aesthetic form. In a curious passage that indicates the several levels on which Plato moves here, he has Socrates speak of putting the guardhouse at the highest point of the city; but he goes on to say that that is the "fairest" sight, and further that they ought to put their guardhouse in music.[30] Everything turns on tuning the psychic disposition through harmonic visual and audile art in tandem with the formation of conscious human commitment to the city as a whole.

Having constructed a three-level city, Socrates parallels it with three levels of the soul: a desirous, a spirited, and a rational level, paralleling the majority of the population pursuing healthy and luxurious needs with the desirous level, the military with the spirited level, and its leadership with the rational.[31] He goes on to locate what came to be known as the cardinal virtues (meaning the hinges—from the Latin *cardo*—of fully functional human life), setting them in relation to each of the psychic levels, finding justice in the condition for the operation of each level: justice consists in each level performing its proper function, or doing its own thing.[32] That involves subordination of the desires to the rational level, which has concern for and knowledge of the whole of the city. A city so ordered is beautiful, a *kalipolis;* and that is rooted in the right ordering of the soul, paradigmatically in the rulers.

But it is crucial to understand what this implies, since the nobly disposed youths Glaucon and Adeimantus, who are Socrates' primary interlocutors, seem content with the city built up to the end of book 4 that harmonizes the soul in itself as a mirror of the harmony of the city. However, such a city is essentially faulty, since it recognizes no dimension of the soul that transcends the power of the polis. The text makes clear the insufficiency of the account, since Socrates says so several times.[33] But the interlocutors—and, I fear, too many readers, Karl Popper in particular—forget the caveats and consider the purged city to be Plato's realistic proposal.[34]

Something curious takes place in the dialogue at this point that is crucial to understanding Plato's thought. Socrates speaks as if he had finished with his argument, showing justice in a city and a soul that had been so structured that each part performed its proper function for the good of the whole and so that the harmony of each soul mirrored the harmony of the city as a whole. He is about to consider forms of order that deviate from the order he developed thus far—in effect skipping what turns out to be the very heart of the dialogue.[35] But his interlocutors are especially interested in one of his proposals. In order to foster the soldiers' identification with the city, Socrates had suggested two methods for breaking down preoccupation with narrower concerns: the elimination of private property for the higher classes, since such property tends to make them each preoccupied with themselves, and with the establishment of a community of wives and children, so that they would not be preoccupied with, or unduly favor their own families to the exclusion or diminishment of the interests of others within the city. All would be one family.[36] The interlocutors are interested in the community of wives—I suggest as a measure of sexual liberation. For Socrates proceeds to frame his response to their interest within two other claims whose connection with that interest is not immediately apparent. One is the claim (treated before he responds to their question) that women and men are equal, the other that philosophers should be kings.[37] I suggest that Socrates aims at a purging of their veiled erotic interest by suggesting the equality of women to men, in direct contrast to their subordination as mere sexual objects. But I also suggest, in view of the fact that all this is expressly constructed as an image of the soul, that what had been left out is the feminine dimension of the psyche: its receptivity to that which is above. Socrates says that thus far we have had the male drama; now begins the female drama, the drama of Eros.[38] However, he goes on to play to the erotic interest of his audience by proposing that the most valiant warriors will get the best mates and that those who are retired would be able to "frolic" with whom they pleased.[39] He introduces the notion of philosopher-king by describing him as a peculiar erotic type. In contrast to the lovers of beautiful things (and remember that the appreciation of the qualities of beautiful things, as distinguished from their titillating effect "in us," was the culmination of education for the warriors), philosophers are described as "lovers of the vision of Beauty Itself."[40] And what they do when they are "turned out to pasture" is "frolic" with the Ideas![41] What is going on here is an attempt at elevating the notion of beauty even further than it had been in the purged city. Socrates does so by considering it as the goal of Eros.

We are now at the heart of the dialogue, at the heart of Plato's understanding of beauty, and at the heart of Plato's philosophy as such. In the following, what may seem a distinctively nonaesthetic excursus will provide us with a further articulation of the ultimate framework constitutive of human experience, within which the nature and role of aesthetic experience and its objects—and indeed of any human experience and its objects—can be properly understood.

## The Center of Order

A line has been drawn between beautiful things and Beauty Itself. The duality this introduces is further articulated by the proclamation (without initial grounds) of the notion of the Good, which is placed on the side of Beauty Itself. The side of beautiful things is developed by an analysis of the three factors necessary for the visual perception of such things: visual object, eyeball with the power of seeing, and light source that makes seeing possible. That threefold structure furnishes an analogy of the Good that functions as metaphorical light source for the intellect, allowing it to ap-

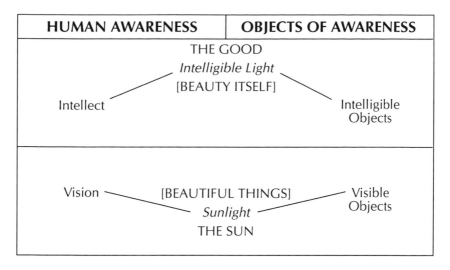

| HUMAN AWARENESS | OBJECTS OF AWARENESS |
|---|---|

THE GOOD
*Intelligible Light*
[BEAUTY ITSELF]

Intellect                                        Intelligible
                                                       Objects

Vision          [BEAUTIFUL THINGS]          Visible
                      *Sunlight*                    Objects
                      THE SUN

prehend "intelligible objects."[42] But once again, that is merely proclaimed, not grounded. The grounding occurs in the process of developing the Line of Knowledge in two directions. On the one hand, there is a horizontal division between the two regions named by the distinction between beautiful things and Beauty itself and initially articulated by the distinction between the two triplets paralleling physical vision and intellectual insight; on the other hand, there is a vertical division between human awareness and its objects.

Socrates asks us to take a line, dividing it by any proportion and dividing its segments, in turn, by the same proportion.[43] The upshot of such construction is found to produce a line divided into four portions such that the two central portions turn out always to be equal to one another. One could test this inductively by trying different proportions, such as 3:1, 2:1, or 10:1. But one could also "demonstrate" the more general theorem involved in such construction: *any* proportion used to divide a line and to subdivide its initial divisions yields a fourfold division such that its central portions are always and everywhere equal. When you are able to demonstrate that and reflect on what you have accomplished, you become aware of a basic distinction in experience between the particular visual object, drawn on paper and seen in the light by the eye, and the theorem, which is understood and demonstrated to apply to *all* lines constructed in the manner suggested: it is understood by the intellect "in the light of the Good." We have advanced in the articulation of the original line drawn between beautiful things and Beauty Itself. We are pointed, by the relations that obtain between the

| THE GOOD<br>(Beyond *"ousia"*) | |
|---|---|
| **STATES OF MIND** | **OBJECTS OF MIND** |
| *Noesis* $\left\{\begin{array}{l}\text{EPISTEME} \\[1em] \text{DIANOIA}\end{array}\right.$ | $\left.\begin{array}{l}\text{FORMS} \\[1em] \text{MATHEMATICS}\end{array}\right\}$ *Ousia* |
| *Doxa* $\left\{\begin{array}{l}\text{PISTIS} \\[1em] \text{EIKASIA}\end{array}\right.$ | $\left.\begin{array}{l}\text{THINGS} \\[1em] \text{"IMAGES"}\end{array}\right\}$ *Genesis* |

things we see, to a region of meaning that both appears in such objects and stands beyond them through its capacity of being present in *all* like objects. We arrive thus at a distinction in our own self-understanding between sensing and intellection.

The line drawn is a visual given. Reflection upon it leads us to the non-visually given (because universal) theorem that it exemplifies. Doubling reflection back upon that distinction leads us to understand the subject-object framework within which mathematical understanding occurs: the play of the fourfold of universal and particular, intellection *(noesis)* and sensation. Mathematical understanding leads us out of the cave of our sensibility and opinions, allows us to cross the Line to the region of intelligibility, which displays meaning in the sensory and measures our opinions about that meaning. Reflection upon the framework of mathematics is no longer mathematics but philosophy. Playing upon the double character of the Line, taken literally as exhibiting a theorem and taken figuratively as exemplifying the structural levels of the field of experience, and then reflecting the Line back upon itself, Plato locates mathematical understanding *(dianoia)* at the third level of the Line. Philosophic insight *(episteme)* is located at the fourth. The emptiness of the philosophic level is filled, at least partially, by the structures of the Line, the play of the fourfold, now understood, at least in a preliminary way.

One might ask where metaphoric reflection falls on the Line. I would suggest it falls at the third level, with mathematics as the object of *dianoia,* or insight *(noia)* through images *(dia)*. Plato names the lowest level of the Line—where we think in terms of, and are imprisoned within, sensory images—*eikasia* or knowing "icons." He also has a more extended notion of "image," which includes "images of justice in the lawcourts," where an "image" is an opinion *(doxa)* held without sufficient grounds. Plato himself constantly practices a *dianoetic eikasia,* a formation of sensory images—in the context within which we are working, the image of the divided Line correlated with the complex imagery of the Cave—which releases us from fixation on "images," whether in the realm of sensation proper or in the realm of opinions, by fixing our minds on the intelligible. Plato thus shows in practice the basis for the connection of the arts with wisdom.

But we have not yet arrived at an understanding of the Good and thus of Beauty Itself, the reason for offering the articulations thus far. By reflecting on the visible line and by reflecting on that reflection, we have arrived at a general articulation of the ultimate subject-object frame that makes mathematics, and indeed any level of understanding, possible: the play between sensible and intelligible and, correspondingly, between sensation and intellection. Socrates invites us to carry reflection one step further: to reflect on what makes the framework itself possible. The Good, he says, makes possible the mind, its intelligible objects, and both the ability to understand as well as the truth or unhiddenness *(aletheia)* of the objects.[44] At the very basis of what-is as a whole there is a mutual referredness of mind and things: things are intelligible and mind can understand. That must have a ground. Note that, because what is at stake in understanding is, initially, the instantiability of a theorem in an indefinite number of instances, wherever in time and whenever in space they might be found, the whole of the spatiotemporal universe is pregiven as a field for intellectual operation. The whole is somehow precontained in the reference of the mind which is thus sprung out of the Now of sensory presence. In the light of the openness of the whole we come to understand any particular. That is why the Good is called the principle of the whole.[45] As principle of the whole, it is not simply the principle of the intelligible but of the visible as well. Since this is the case, a reflection that follows the Line of Knowledge toward the Good will view the Line as the ascending curve of a circle that arises from the sensory toward the top, where we find the Good, which then, as principle of the whole, curves back to the beginning in the sensory to bind the whole together. This, we suggest, is why Plato employs imagery and story: they bring us back to where we always already are: this world here and now present in the sensory field, but illumined by the changeless field of the intelligible, at the summit of which is the Good, whose shining is Beauty Itself.[46]

There is this further consideration. When we come to understand (i.e., to demonstrate a geometric theorem), we proceed from a limited number of axioms, guided by a principle of unrestricted scope, the principle of non-contradiction, which allows us to deduce from that limited number of axioms, not only the theorem in question, but also the whole of the geometric region it inhabits. The relative fewness of the axioms generates the vast complexity of the theorems in a kind of cascading order of complexity. The employment of the principle of noncontradiction provides unity in that complexity by giving it coherence. What might have otherwise been scattered observations and isolated generalizations takes on the unity of a coherent scheme. If one reflects further upon the relative fewness of the axioms, one is led to ask whether that multiplicity might itself be located within a larger context and thus whether the different regions of experience might not be unified by appealing to a single principle, which we might then project as "the One." Plato calls this "the upward way," while deductive mathematics follows "the downward way."[47] Metaphorically speaking, it is "in the light of" our search for that One, drawn by the directedness of the mind toward the whole, that we are led to apprehend more and more of the coherence of the whole field of experience and its objects. The shining of that One, i.e. its functioning as ground and term of our search, generates the manifestation of the coherence of what is and draws us upward toward the fuller manifestness of that coherence.

We should note, however, that the "upward way" from mathematics toward the Good only covers part of the total field illumined by the Good. There is the whole dimension of psychic life, the locus of the display of the cosmic order which includes that life as its own inwardness. Once again, it is story and imagery that bring us to understand that life.

The Line presents us with a primal division within human experience between (1) what is first approached as the realm of the visible and (2) the realm of the intelligible to which Plato introduces us, first by mathematical reflection, then by reflection upon the subject-object framework presupposed by mathematics, and finally by reflection upon that reflection. Placing them in juxtaposition, we can discern some of the opposing predicates of the two realms: the visible is composed of sense-perceptible particular actualities presented in the here and now of bodily immediacy which have come into being, are subjected to change, and eventually pass out of being.

The mathematical theorem presents itself as both independent of and as extending to all its particular instances, actual or possible, throughout the whole of spatial and temporal relations. Though it came into awareness at a certain point in the history of culture, may have come to be known at a certain point in the reader's history, and may, through recursion to barbarism, pass out of awareness generally some time in the future, the theorem still presents itself as having always been true and thus as itself transcending change and thus also transcending spatio-temporal location and the conditions of its own knownness by a human. Nonetheless, its truth is resident in the particulars that are its instances. There is thus an identical core of meaning that can exist in a universal, atemporal mode or in a particular mode, immanent in a here and now. The understanding of bodily particulars would thus seem to involve two principles: (1) a principle of intelligibility in accordance with which the theorem is true of that particular, and (2) a principle that allows the multiplication of the principle in many times and in many places. Plato calls the former an idea, or *eidos* (Form); he calls the latter "the Receptacle" *(hypodoche)*, "the nurse of becoming," or what more recently Whitehead, following Plato, relates to the restless matrix of space-time.[48] It is as if the Receptacle were a flowing river on whose banks stood a tree. The wavelets make possible the multiple and transitory mirrorings of the tree as its image is held for a split second and in different ways by each of the wavelets. The flowing realm of space-time Plato refers to as the realm of *genesis* or Becoming; the intelligible realm he calls *to on* or *ousia* or Being, and the Good as source is considered to be "beyond *ousia*."[49] Becoming is made possible and thinkable by the ingredience of Being into the nonbeing of the Receptacle, of intelligibility into the flux. Time is the flowing of an ever-moving, unextended Now from the no longer to the not yet; space is the existent emptiness in which such flowing occurs. Space-time is existent negativity, a kind of nonbeing complex entering into the constitution and togetherness of the things that are—or perhaps better, within which spatio-temporal things are. Thus perceptible things are "mixtures of being and nonbeing."[50] By contrast, each changeless Form just "is" and does not come into being, change and pass out of being. This provides us with some of the essential eidetic features constituting the subject-object framework of our experience. In our Introduction we have attempted to fill in some of the eidetic features of the appearance of aesthetic objects.

The mathematical introduction to the region of intelligibility is relevant to the notion of Beauty since it leads us to understand Beauty Itself as related to the One radiating the light of intelligible coherence upon the whole. The mathematical approach is also relevant to the notion of Beauty in a way more directly tied to our sensory experience, for the mathematical is harmonic, proportionate, orderly, coherent. But Beauty at all levels is the harmonic: beauty of body, beauty of psychic disposition, beauty of mind, beauty of the belonging together of sensuous display and intelligible grounding.

## Mimesis

At this point we are able to consider one of the central notions of Plato's aesthetics: the notion of mimesis, or imitation. Following the lines we have considered thus far, not only mathematical objects but things in general as we encounter them (and we ourselves insofar as each of us is one of those things) are viewed as "images" or imitations of pure Forms in the flux of the Receptacle. Reflection upon the Line of Knowledge provides a mimetic vision of the entire universe of experience: a hierarchy of image-imaged relationships. At the very bottom are shadows, reflections, and dreams: all parasitic upon the things whose shadows, reflections, or images they are.[51] But all three of these types of images image the sensory surface, which has a subjective-objective structure (i.e., an image structure in relation to the underlying material things). Sensa are relations of things to our senses, relations of manifestness that, like the horizon and the perspectives of the object appearing within the horizon, are not there without the co-presence of things and a perceiver. The things so present exceed their manifestness within the circle of sensation.

Further, the reality of physical things whose external images appear in mirrors and dreams and are observed by us, is an "image" of the Forms. The mathematical level of the Forms is approached through images, beginning with figures drawn. The philosophical level transcends the pictured. And the whole region of Forms finally mirrors the One by exhibiting the unity of multiplicity that we call coherence. Even the region of Forms, though stable, involves nonbeing by participating in the Form of Otherness that accounts for the plurality of Forms. Just as Form mirrored in the negativity of the Receptacle (space-time) grounds physical things, so the One mirrored in the negativity of the Form of otherness grounds the region of Forms.[52] Thus the whole of reality has a mimetic structure as each lower level images the next higher level. That means that each level both exists in itself and has, as its ontological deep structure, its participation in the higher levels.

The process is complicated by the fact that human beings, who by their nature belong to the region of Being as well as to that of Becoming *(genesis)*, introduce a whole new set of images that we call culture, within which art appears. Culture is not only the set of artifacts that fill the sphere of sensa; it is also the "images of justice in the lawcourts,"[53] the interpretative structures that position us in the whole and link the ever-present Now of sensory immediacy to the whole in the mode of revealing and concealing. No way of understanding discloses the final character of reality as a whole and of ourselves within that whole. We become explicitly philosophic when we become aware of our directedness toward the whole. And yet for Plato *philo-sophia* can never become *sophia*. We can never look directly at the Sun (Good) else we would go blind. We are cautioned in Plato's *Laws*: "Let us not make darkness at noon by attempting to stare at the sun. Let us rather contemplate it in its images."[54] And those images are not simply the images provided by nature as sensa; they are, more deeply, the poetic images that provide us with our lived sense of the whole. Together with the sensa, such interpretive images help to weave the web of *doxa*, the field of immediate presentation of ourselves and the things with which we are engaged, constituting the collective mode of inhabitance that we call our world.

As a further delineation of the notion of imitation, Plato in his *Sophist*, in the context of a discussion of sculpture, distinguishes two forms of imitation, eikastic and phantastic.[55] The former presents an ikon, an exact and proportionate likeness of the original, the latter a phantasm, a distortion adjusted to the position of the perceiver to make the statue appear in the true proportions of the original. Such was the practice of Greek sculptors and architects. Huge statuary that would be seen only from the ground level was constructed with the upper parts proportionately larger so that they would appear proportionately normal from the ground. Socrates seems to be condemning the latter, but in fact he consistently practices phantastic imitation in adjusting his discussion to the character of his interlocutors, making the dialogues pedagogical studies of the blocks that stand in the way of the ascent of the soul. Hence his "poetry."

We should take note here of Socrates' distinction between "imitative" and "narrative" modes of poetic presentation in the *Republic*.[56] In the latter, author and narrator make clear, when they are describing something, that they stand at a distance psychically from what they narrate. What this means we can see by contrast with "imitative" presentation, where author and narrator pretend they are what they narrate. They imitate or mirror the object by giving the illusion of the object itself. An imitative narrator acts out what he describes by pretending to be Achilles or making sounds like a horse braying. An imitative author hides himself behind his writing.

Acting out, says Socrates, produces in the soul the disposition of what is imitated. Hence one may safely imitate the virtuous, but not inferior things like women in various emotional states or evil men or madmen or artisans or the sounds of animals or of other things of nature. He expressly includes in this prohibition imitating one overtaken by love. And given the high place assigned to Eros in the *Symposium* and the *Phaedrus,* one can again see the confining horizon within which this part of the dialogue occurs. Eros as the depth dimension of the soul is viewed as something lowly, belonging, from the perspective of the totalitarian city, to the lowest level of the soul, the desirous part.[57]

Reading the whole as an image of the soul, perhaps we are to understand the need to transcend the situation where we are mirrors of our social environment without attaining to that centeredness of existence that allows us to speak on our own. Further, it is at least curious that Plato's practice in the very section in question is to present his extremely controlled construction as if it were a direct transcription of Socrates' actual conversation. Plato clearly "imitates" rather than "narrates." Why? Because what he has to say here is confined within the perspective of the city, where one does not speak fully on one's own by basing himself on transcendence of the dominant opinions, reaching to the primordial evidences from which the opinions could be properly assessed.

Once we understand something of the depth dimension of the soul opened up by the center of the dialogue, we understand that the basic orientation of the soul to the whole cannot be contained within the city. Doing justice to the soul involves creating conditions for the possibility of its opening out to the whole, transcending not only the lower levels of bodily based desires, but also the limited tasks and basic opinions of the city.[58] A philosophy that understands that can also engage in the production of the seductive surface of art because it knows the antidote to that form of seduction that locks us into the sensory surface and the appetites correlative with it but also and simultaneously locks us into our socially conditioned presuppositions.[59]

## *The Treatment of Art in the* Republic

With that as a general background, we can now look to book 10 of the *Republic*. There, having completed the basic argument of the work on the superiority of justice—understood as ordering the soul in its directedness toward the whole—to injustice as the opposite, Socrates returns to a discussion of poetry, followed by a discussion of the rewards of justice in this life and the next, and capped off by the poetic creation of a myth of the afterlife. In the purged city, poetry is the chief element undergoing purgation. Here at the beginning of book 10 poetry is not purged but seemingly relegated to the lowest fringe of human experience. Yet it appears at the very end of the work in the myth of Er that Plato poetically concocts. It is this apparent contradiction that we have to understand.

Socrates considers poetry in book 10, not in terms of its support for the training of the military (the premise under which he operated in books 2–4), but for its truth-value. Remember, at the earlier stage truth was set aside in favor of civic exemplarity. "Don't tell tales of the gods engaged in unseemly conduct, *even if they are true!*" Approached now in terms of its truth, poetry, having passed through an analysis, in the middle of the work, of the truth of the soul as the soul's direct and evidential relation to truth transcending and thus ever in tension with the demands of the city, is compared to painting. And painting itself, as we noted earlier, is compared to a mirror held up to the sensory surface of things.[60]

The comparison with painting is seriously defective in terms of Socrates' own observation in the second and third books of the *Republic*, where what was important about painting was not its mirroring quality but its design properties. What makes a good painting is not that it is an exact likeness but that the frame is so selected that the space and the light and shadow are aesthetically distributed and the colors play in proper relation to one another so as to establish an overall organic presentation pervaded by a mood appropriate to the subject depicted. In the second book of the *Laws*, besides knowledge of the thing imitated and the correctness of the likeness, the excellence of the execution is an essential ingredient of any critical judgment.[61] Excellence of execution concerns the *how* of presentation, which is just what the passing reference to painting in the earlier part of the *Republic* entails. I suggest that in *Republic* 10, Socrates is deliberately downplaying art, focusing on its mirroring function in order to bring us, who have been exposed to a preliminary uncovering of the full dimensionally of psychic life as the locus of the manifestation of the truth of the whole, to bring us to reflect more deeply on the positive significance of art.

This is supported by the fact, already alluded to, that Socrates says that he would be willing to admit poets into the state if only a case could be made for them.[62] And he further points out that even though poets water our passions and aid their growth, thus diminishing our rational powers, we can attend to poetry without harm "if we know the antidote." I suggest that the antidote lies, not in the absence of passion in favor of a cold rationalism, but in the dialectical relation between Eros and Logos. Following the ladder of ascent to the beautiful described in the *Symposium* (something I will shortly treat), the space for the operation of reason is opened up and oriented beyond the cave of culturally mediated sensibility and beyond the limited constructions of reason toward the whole and its source. Thus the whole realm of poetic operation can be developed in such a way as to draw so-called reason on to greater and greater adequacy. One could then understand why Plato's own poetic work concludes the dialogue, which otherwise comes down so hard on poetry.

In the myth of Er Plato poetically concocts a story of the afterlife which becomes a paradigm for Virgil, Dante, and Milton. A fictitious world is created where *doxa* is removed and the soul is judged nakedly, not being clothed in the exteriority of appearance to others.

But to return to the linkage of the opening discussion of book 10 to the Line, in book 10 Socrates hearkens back to the Line and speaks of three levels: there is the thing made by man, say, a bed; there is, second, that to which the maker looks, the Idea of a bed ("made," Socrates says, "by god"); and there is the image of a bed made by the painter.[63] The middle level (the god's Idea) belongs on the upper part of the Line, on the side of Being; the types occupying the extremes in the verbal description belong below the Line, on the side of genesis, or Becoming, the painting occupying the lowest level. In the second book of the *Laws* Socrates calls attention to the possibility of a thousand representations of the same object available to sight, since spatially a given object affords an indeterminate number of perspectives.[64] A painting thus presents an extremely limited selection from the real multiplicity of aspects available.

We might note here that perspectivity, and thus an essential reference to the position of the viewer, is an essential feature of visible objects. Not the display of things in themselves, but of things in relation to the perceiver is what characterizes such evidences. A painting replicates one such subject-related perspective. Hence, in the *Republic,* the painting is located "three degrees removed from reality." This does not simply mean that it is an image of an object that imitates an Idea, since that gives us three levels and hence only two degrees. A painting is an image of an image (visual perspective) of a full object, which itself is more than the sum total of visible aspects, having also audile, tactile, and other sensory, as well as nonsensory, aspects that "imitate" the appropriate Idea. Plato gives no attention here to the peculiar focus a painter can give to an object that makes the Idea more clearly present than the thing's visible surface alone does. Plotinus, and later Schopenhauer and Hegel as well as Heidegger, will pick up on this and claim that the artist stands at the level of the Idea and thus a work of art can be higher than the natural sensorily given.[65] Martin Buber will observe that the artist is faithful not to appearance but to being, enhancing the expressivity of the appearance so that it more clearly displays the invisible interior.[66]

One wonders how serious Socrates is about the Idea of the bed as made by god. One would have thought the Idea was made up by the artisan. In the *Parmenides* Socrates agrees that his notion of Ideas is meant to cover things like justice or wisdom. He is not sure about natural species, and he is positive that there are no Forms of ugly things.[67] If no natural species are Forms, it would seem that the Ideas of human artifacts would also not be Forms. However, they are a function of the divine element in us, our intellect, that which we distinguish by reason of its being the locus of the manifestation of atemporal objects, objects that transcend the here and now of their instances.

Further in the discussion in book 10, Socrates makes a parallel distinction of three levels when he links the maker of a horse's bridle, the user of the bridle, and a painter of a picture of the bridle.[68] Here the user is the measure for the maker and occupies the same place as the god who "made" the Idea of the bed. This suggests that "the god" is the divine element in us that ought to govern the animal in us. He speaks in this connection of the world of the painter as not only three degrees removed from reality, but also three degrees removed from "the king" (i.e., the self-governing power in us).[69]

But all three images—the picture of the bed, the picture of the bridle, and the two-dimensional mirroring of the surrounding world—suggest a very peripheral role for imitation. Applied to poetry, we have the poet who learns to produce perspectival illusions, lacking the crucial depth dimension, of the solid activities in which humans engage—just what Plato has Socrates do in books 2 through 4!

A passage in Plato's *Sophist* delineates two forms of making, divine and human.[70] Each type divides into a form of reality and the corresponding form of an image of that reality. Thus a god makes physical things and their images in shiny surfaces, their shadows, and their appearance in dreams. As a craftsman, the human artisan makes artifacts and, as an artist, paintings of the artifacts. In the latter case, we have the same distinction as in book 10 of the *Republic*.

A passage in the *Gorgias* distinguishes among the human arts the arts of appearance or "sophistical arts" and the arts of reality.[71] As I noted in the introduction, human artifaction can be understood in a broad way to include arts like cooking, gymnastic training, and legislation. Socrates considers both arts of the body and arts of the soul. Regarding the body, the restaurant and the beauty parlor provide pleasure and cosmetic beauty, while medicine and gymnastic provide health and the natural bloom of a vigorously trained body. The "sophistical arts" give the appearance of beauty and the good; the arts of reality produce real physical beauty and real physical good. Regarding the soul, sophistry proper, along with poetry, are said to manipulate appearance, while, by contrast, wise legislation and philosophy foster real psychic development.

It might be possible to link up the consideration of "divinely made" dreams with the sources of inspiration tapped by the artist. In the *Phaedrus*, Socrates speaks of divine inspiration and of divinely inspired art, which seems to be distinguished from "imitative" art, the practitioners of which he places far down on a hierarchy of character types.[72] The divinely inspired artist not only has technical knowledge, but also *enthusiasmos*, that surplus spark of divine inspiration which, unlike *techne*, the artist cannot give himself.[73] But maybe we dismissed too readily the "divine" making of the Idea of the bed. Like artistic inspiration, the idea of an artifact "just comes," like a dream, to the first one to think of it. So a "god" (read: nonempirically present source of inspiration) creates in the artisan (at least in the first one who thought of it) the Idea of the bed.

Nonetheless, the difference between the two modes of inspiration—that of the creative artisan and that of the creative artist—is vast. The artisan qua artisan creates a form that is directed exclusively toward use, so that the artifact, so to speak, disappears from the focus of awareness in its functioning. In bed one might sleep or daydream or make love: in all three cases, the bed is not focal but purely peripheral to the field of awareness. (The selection of a bed for an example, followed by the example of the bridle, may not be incidental to the attempt at purging Eros that goes on in the *Republic* as well as in several other dialogues.) The artist, on the other hand, and even the artisan insofar as he is an artist as well, produces a work characterized by aesthetic form. Here the object does not disappear from or recede to the periphery of attention insofar as one is in the aesthetic mode. The well-formed object is precisely a significant presence, a focal object characterized by beauty.

## The Ladder of Ascent to Beauty Itself

The *Republic* can be understood as an attempt to purge the luxurious love of beauty that possesses Glaucon and those like him. The dialogue begins with Socrates and Glaucon headed "up to the city," when they are arrested by the threat of force on the part of several men whom Socrates has to persuade to let him and Glaucon continue their journey up to the city. The dialogue consists in persuading the actual city to let Socrates conduct, up to "the city laid out in heaven" and constructed in words, the Glaucons of this world,[74] those with a "musical and loving nature," as the *Phaedrus* puts it.[75] The actual conduct of the discussion is itself calculated to lead to that heavenly city. Glaucon moves the action out of the first city dedicated to physical well-being by his remark that it is "Pigsville," without "sweetmeats and soft couches" (i.e., distinctively human luxuries).[76] The purged city is introduced in a discussion with Adeimantus, who seems content with not telling the full truth about the gods because his vision is limited to the city; but Glaucon enters again when it is a question of the purely aesthetic (as distinct from the referential) features of *musike*.[77] Glaucon appears further as chief interlocutor when the study of the Good is introduced as rooted in the love of Beauty itself.[78] The discussion of the Line is meant to teach us how to move up the ladder of different levels of experience toward the vision of the Good itself, which is either identical with or closely related to Beauty Itself. The same ladder is discussed within the context of a much more explicit treatment of the notion of Eros in the *Symposium* as the teaching of Diotima on the ascent to Beauty. Diotima, a female, appears near the end of a male—indeed, male homosexual—discussion of Eros.[79] Again, first the male, then the female drama.[80] In both cases, the female drama far outstrips the male. Let us turn our attention then to Diotima's speech.

Diotima had proclaimed the fundamental character of Eros to be a desire of the mortal for the immortal aroused by a beautiful form and leading to productive activity.[81] This is clear enough at the level of sexual Eros, not indeed in the immediacy of the experience thereof, but in the inner directedness of its consummation to a term that outlasts both the momentariness of the experience and, in the normal course of things, the mortality of the couple. Sexual Eros produces offspring who produce offspring who produce offspring, and so on, as the establishment of the "immortality" of the species in time. This is true of animal organisms—indeed, of all organisms—in general.

Human Eros is cut into by the peculiar structure of the field of human awareness as open, beyond the Now of animal awareness, to the whole. Thus human beings are driven by a desire to become immortal through the recognition by others, present and to come, of their immortal deeds and works in battle, in sport, in art and literature, in the founding of institutions. These Diotima calls "the lesser works of love." There are also "the higher mysteries."[82] We enter into the latter by a definite progression that begins with the arousal of desire for one bodily being. The heightened state tends to produce "winged words" as the one in love bursts into poetic apostrophe. By a natural dynamic, the feeling of love tends to suffuse everything, so that the world itself seems beautiful. Again, in the course of development, such a state is gradually transformed into love for the beauty of the person that shines through the exterior. Here the sensory presence, especially of the eyes, "the windows of the soul,"[83] display the real presence of the consciousness of the other. And one may be led to see past, and thus reduce to the peripheral levels of our awareness, an otherwise uncomely exterior when the beauty of the person shines through.

Thus far everything seems to jibe with the ordinary course of experience. But Diotima seems to take an unanticipated leap when she claims that the next step is to learn to love the beauty of laws and institutions. However, the leap is reduced when we think of what tends to produce beauty of character. We realize that it is good upbringing, being shaped by the long accumulation of reinforced choices that constitute a tradition. One "falls in love with," becomes attached to, commits oneself to a tradition that has that power precisely because one is concerned with shaping and sustaining the beauty of souls. One becomes a "patriot."

This kind of natural dynamic of love still occurs "under the line," "inside the Cave," in history. If nature is a repetitive mirroring of the atemporal Forms, history is an ever-shifting approach to, and a falling away from an ideal arrangement in which reason governs prudentially, increasingly aware of the overarching order within which human life occurs and ever open to, and critically appreciative of, possibly higher forms of inspiration. In both cases, there is a measure, the discernment of which gives rise to the various sciences of nature (physics, biology), of the soul (psychology), of the virtues (ethics, politics), of being itself (metaphysics). Plato's *Statesman* delineates two types of measure: the quantitative and the qualitative. The quantitative concerns number (the abstract), length, breadth, and depth (the spatial) and the swift (the temporal), while the qualitative concerns the mean *(meson)* between excess and defect, the fit *(prepon)* in terms of preparedness to act, the opportune *(kairon)* in terms of the temporal rightness of action, and the due *(dikaios)* in terms of the obligations involved in action.[84] The quantitative appears initially as value-free measure, the qualitative as measure of value. However, the two types of measure overlap. In organisms, quantitative measures in spatial proportions and temporal rhythms are crucial to the qualitative well-being of the organism; and in works of art, spatial and temporal distribution according to ratios are constitutive of the aesthetic. Aristotle will remark that a well-formed drama is like an organism, in which everything is there that needs to be there to bring about the aesthetic effect and nothing that is there is such that its absence would not deter from the overall effect.[85] Here we have the idea of a mean between aesthetic excess and aesthetic defect. The differing modes of knowing are thus all concerned in some way with measure.

The pursuit of the sciences is an ever-developing process in which the underlying universal coherence is increasingly laid bare. The manifest togetherness of the Forms presents us with a deeper level of beauty, more stable than the ever-shifting, but law-governed realm of nature and the rise and fall of order in human history measured by the science of the human soul as the place of the cognitive display of cosmic order. The passion for such pursuit follows from the natural openness of the mind for the whole. It culminates in a vision of what Diotima calls Beauty Itself, which is presented in such a way that, far from being a mere analyzable concept that can be captured in a definition, it is the radiance of that which, as the One/Good, gathers the whole into unity and, being glimpsed as final object of human Eros, gathers the soul together into unity. Understanding human Eros in this way, we can see that, following the distinctions discussed in the *Symposium*, there is a pandemian or "common" and a uranian or "heavenly" Eros, and hence a higher and lower Dionysian function in Plato's thought.[86] In the fuller Platonic conception, the Apollonian level of *nous* rises out of the common Dionysian level, drawn on in its constructions by a heavenly Dionysian level of sublimated Eros. The purged city of the *Republic* is an Apollonian construction without the heavenly Dionysian and hence is a level of totalitarian closure and tyranny, subjecting the soul to complete subservience to the city and desublimating its fundamental human Eros. In a fuller view of Platonic thought, the last word belongs to a Dionysian height.

Now, just as we might have thought that we had left behind the world of the senses in passing outside the Cave, over the Line, from Becoming to Being, Socrates speaks, in the *Phaedrus*, of the privileged character of Beauty. Of all the Forms, it is the only one that is "perceptible by the eyes," a Real Presence, directly discernible and not merely inferentially available, in sensorily given things.[87] What has been going on is not at all a flight from the body and its senses, a disincarnation, but the hollowing out of an un-fathomable depth behind the sensory surface of things. Most especially, in the interpersonal context within which the *Phaedrus* is cast, the eyes of the other are the expressive media of the depth of the person and of the prepersonal depths of Eros for the Good that founds all personhood. In friendship, the deepest sense of the presence of Beauty Itself is found.[88] But this also raises the problem, treated in *Greater Hippias*, of the relation between "inward" beauty of character and outward display.[89] The beauti-ful ballerina who sadistically beats her grandmother comes to mind: beauty of external form set in motion through graceful action coexists with a character capable of doing ugly things. But that ugliness is also displayed in sensuous exteriority.

Amid all this talk of beauty, what has been said about that which is rec-ognized in all these stages of recognition? What is this feature called beauty? What are its properties? *Greater Hippias* proposes the notion of the appropriate *(to prepon)* as instanced in elements in relation to their context.[90] It raises the problem of the link of beauty with the useful. One must dis-tinguish the usefully appropriate from the aesthetically appropriate. But the *Republic* indicates that beauty in all things follows function.[91] Beauty thus has something to do with the way things appear functionally together in experience. In the *Republic*, as we saw, Socrates recommended being sur-rounded by works of visual and audile art that were characterized by grace, harmony, good order, good rhythm, good proportion. The "good" in all this is something directly perceived and is related as object to the right ordering of the soul, which subordinates the biologically grounded ap-petites to the ordering power of intellect and which aims intellect at an open search for the comprehensive order of things to which we are essen-tially directed by nature. Hence the togetherness of sensory surface sets up reverberations in all the other dimensions of our being, so that one can be led from the harmonious, graceful, well-proportioned, well-ordered togetherness of sensory surface to the perception of similar properties at progressively higher levels and vice versa. The mimetic structure of being, opened up in its multidimensional character by the pedagogy of the Line, is what makes possible this marvelous ascent. It is an ascent grounded in the look of the other, the encounter with which is developed in depth by sharing the pursuit of exploring and indwelling in the broader context of institutions, of nature and of cosmic ground, the direct relation to which constitutes the depth of being human.

Philosophy as introduced by Plato is love of the vision of the whole, aspiration toward which generates authentic human existence. Philosophy lives out reflectively the fundamental structure of the field of human experience. Unlike the poetic and religious modality of relation to the whole, philosophy is not simply inspired and proclamatory; it is also systematic, dialogic, and self-critical. It tests the adequacy of putative visions of the whole by their capacity to take into account all the features of the field of experience in their togetherness laid out in the reflective development of the Line. Yet by reason of its own essential incompleteness, it is open to poetic vision and, in philosophers like Plato, even generates its own poetic vision. It grows when it learns to respond to the admirable and the awesome. It is linked intimately to the arts and is anchored most especially in the beauty of the other person.

❧   ❧   ❧

## Response

How has this investigation of Plato aided our inquiry into aesthetics? First of all, it has developed, through his treatment of the Line of Knowledge, our understanding of the field of experience. What we can learn in a special way by beginning with Plato is how to approach any study within the context of the whole and thus to understand how regional specializations get carved out from the whole of experience. Plato is the unsurpassed philosopher of experience as he is also the dialectical explorer of alternate ways of configuring the whole of being to which experience always refers without possessing it in any final way. That totalistic concern looks to the effects of the aesthetic region on integral psychic functioning and thus lays the basis for the possibility of an ethical critique of art that is significantly more than a desire to stay within the mores of a community, since it involves the possibility of a critical assessment of those mores as well.

The Line of Knowledge presents, in its incipient analysis of sensation on the one hand and of the One/Good on the other, a developed version of the biological-ontological frame I have laid out in the introduction. Principle of the whole, the One/Good/Beautiful is the ultimate term of human Eros. I called the principle Being, though Plato had Socrates say that it is "beyond *ousia*," beyond beingness as involved in the intellect-Form correlation, and thus beyond the distinction between subject and object. I referred to our orientation toward it at first simply as "reference to Being," though I finally associated it with "the heart." Plato names our orientation Eros, the mortal's desire for the immortal that belongs to all the living. Eros concerns how we are related to time, which, together with space, is the enduring framework of all experience. As organisms we unfold, endure, and decline, exhibiting a definite temporal pattern from birth to death. As alert organisms, the effects of past experiences lead to routinized associations and responses. Also as alert organisms, our erotic desire leads, without our necessarily knowing it, to the transcendence of death in passing on our genes in our offspring. As humans our language gives expression to our capacity to isolate and relate recurrent types *(eide)* that we know to apply to all times and places where individuals of the type can be encountered. Space and time as a whole thus come into our purview; hence the "deathless" order of natural occurrence is capable of being made more explicit and refined in the sciences. On account of this apprehension of *eidos*, we are able to run ahead of our current and past organic situation and anticipate our term. Noting this distinctiveness, the Greeks referred to us as the mortals. Even though all living things die, we alone live out of an anticipation of our own term. Hence Eros and *Thanatos*, together with Logos as linguistic incarnation of the apprehension of the order of *eide*, belong inseparably together in human experience.

Current attacks on "Platonism" and "essences" in terms of "the theory-ladenness of perception" and "the deferral of presence" have to come to terms with Plato's observation that all arts depend on the recurrence of *eide.* Their recognition distinguishes the bungler from the expert. We might locate that in a more primordial region, that of life itself. The critics have to eat, and eating is a recognizably recurrent need for *all* organisms. It depends on the ability to distinguish the edible from the inedible, the noxious from the nonnoxious, the nourishing from the nonnourishing. The "theory" that accompanies and structures perception here is that of life itself. Here, in living form, there is the likewise currently odious "hierarchy" of functions, with the controlling center in the nervous system and lower and

higher centers of integration in the structures of the brain, from the reptil-
ian, through the mammalian, to the fully human cortical structures. These
are some of the *eide* differentiated by physiological research. They rest on
other *eide* ferreted out by physics, beginning with the periodic table. It is
knowledge of further recurrent structures that makes possible complex
building tasks and the "hi-tech" culture we live in today. As in Plato, recognition of recurrent *eide* makes possible all the arts. Nonetheless, it is important to observe that the *eide* we come to know are *eide* of appearance, of
modes of presentation and not of final ontological depth—a knowing Plato
sees as reserved "for the gods." Kant, Nietzsche, and Heidegger will underscore that with differing degrees of success.[92]

The reflective power of intellect as the capacity to apprehend universal Form directs Eros, oriented at the biological level toward a temporal
mirroring of the eternal, to the direct display of the unchanging and thus
"immortal" order governing the temporal. Or perhaps it is better to say
that intellect, drawn on by Eros, is able to clarify to itself what it is that all
life seeks. This places an aesthetic principle first: the totalistic desire of the
heart for the total-real. One should note here that the emphasis on Eros
moves beyond a "merely intellectual" relation to a more "totalistic" relation, a relation of "the whole person," of which Augustine will later make
much. It is the relation of what I have called "the heart," and of which the
biblical command, "Thou shalt love the Lord thy God with thy whole
heart," is the most revealing instance. In Plato there is thus a link between
"insight" into intelligible relations and "vision," which reverberates throughout the whole of experience. There is thus always a "visionary" aspect to
Platonic "intellectualism" that brings philosophy into close proximity to
the arts. This is a connection reinvoked more recently by Heidegger.

This relation, I suggest, is why the philosopher is presented by Socrates
first of all as the lover of the vision of Beauty Itself. That also recurs to the
opening line of the first work in Western metaphysics, Parmenides' *Peri
phuseos*, where "the steeds that bore me took me as far as my heart could desire," up from the realm of the mixture of darkness and light to the blazing
light of the identity of Being and thought.[93] Since such "vision" transcends
subject and object, it goes beyond the detachment of intellect into a participative identity with Being Itself.

The polar tension between our ontological reference, on the one hand,
expressed in the notion of the Good together with its subjective correlate,
human Eros, and, on the other hand, our biological ground, which gener-

ates the field of sensa together with the appetites correlative with it, sets up the tension between appearance and reality. Biology gives us our first access to things, a field of "images," of appearance relative to our biological needs. In my reading, the initial emptiness of our metaphysical Eros leads to the construction of cultures as ways of situating the here and now of bodily appearance within the Whole by means of the apprehension of universal Forms. But cultural constructions are plural, because, I would claim, culture rests on the *perspectival* apprehension of Forms or on different interpretive interweavings of nonperspectivally apprehended Forms. And precisely because of that perspectivity, culture in turn produces a second level of appearance, for example, "images of justice in the lawcourts," which open up certain possibilities of thinking, feeling, and acting, but which thereby close off deeper and, finally, normative possibilities for assessing the cultural images. Images articulate the very way things are present to us. The founding distance of humanness provided by reference to the totality via the notion of the Good as principle of the whole makes possible the re-formation of what is given by nature, not only to satisfy the demands of biological nature, but also to indicate, through aesthetic form, the way we are situated in the Whole. In this way, appeal is made to the whole of human experience, to our sense of participative identity with the Whole.

The Line of Knowledge, I claim, provides us with the irremovable and nonperspectival frame of human experience that, in turn, furnishes the fundamental orientation from which cultural images can be assessed. Each level of the Line exhibits a fundamental eidetic structure that, as apprehended, provides the initial filling for the fourth level of the Line, the metalevel of philosophic reflection on the other operative levels of experience. Hence the space between the always-present sensa and the One/Good is not entirely empty. The distinctions between sensing and the sensa and between the intellect and the intelligible are cut across by a distinction between subject and object on the one hand and between universal and particular on the other. Finally, the distinctions are surmounted by a principle of unity which grounds the play between all these distinctions and which is the ultimate term of inquiry.

Reflection on the status of sensa as images derived from biological interaction allows us to see that by themselves they are mute without our taking them up interpretively, without reading them as signs of expressive wholes that are not only expressive of their ontological ground in the togetherness of the Forms, but also, in the case of the other sensorily presented human being, expressive of the depths of psychic life. In the human case, a gap opens up between the beauty of the person and the character of its sensory display. And the beauty of the person, in turn, rests not only on subjective, purely idiosyncratic qualities, but on instantiating noble institutions in its behavior, displaying love of the beauty of cosmic order in its speech, manifesting Eros for the Good in its look.

The beauty recognized in sensory form in general instantiates laws of proportion, harmony, grace. And the creation of beautiful sensory form in the arts expresses the artist's apprehension of the universal harmonic. As the human psyche is displayed in its sensorily given behavior—in overt action, word, and look—so is it displayed in its own artifacts as sensorily available. If we can have disordered souls, we can have disordered and disordering artifacts. Expressive of a disordered psychic life, such artifacts tend to produce disorder in their observers. Our current culture furnishes a powerful demonstration of this claim.

Plato makes a clear distinction between what I have called aesthetic form and reference, between the harmonic shaping of sensory materials and the display of something other than the shaped object. He analyzes its operation in poetry, where he criticizes the civically undesirable things represented and the musical forms (rhythms and harmonies), modes of presentation (narrative or imitative), and instrumental timbres as well as musical styles (Dionysiac and Apollonian) through which the represented objects are presented. The fundamental Apollonian-Dionysian distinction is based, at one level, on the natural distinction between the biological pole and the possibilities for understanding and shaping that emerge from our ontological pole as initial empty reference to the whole. But at another level, the Dionysian rises from the lowest level of the soul toward the transintellectual One as object of complete Eros. At the highest level, Platonic thought is Dionysiac, erotically drawing us beyond Form to the Source, in continuity with the Eros that arises at the physiological level as a desire for eternity. In the *Republic,* Plato overtly places Eros at the lowest level of the soul, but covertly presents it as the vehicle of philosophic ascent to the Good. In the *Phaedrus* and the *Symposium* it overtly functions as the vehicle of ascent, but it is occasioned by the attractiveness of the human form. One might ask for the relation between the perception of art objects and the ascent made possible through Eros aroused by the perception of the human form. Plato advocates Apollonian style in all the arts by reason of its ability to bring harmony—and that means "rationality"—to the psychic field. How does that play in relation to the "madness" of Eros? In the *Republic* the philosophic type seems to furnish the *Aufhebung*, the sublimated synthesis of these two features, simultaneously Apollonian and Dionysian. Harmonic shaping is furnished by the Apollonian ambiance of the polis and thus has in principle a public character. Erotic attraction is in principle private, transcending the polis in its lower forms by recurring to the animal base and in its higher forms by philosophic ascent. In and through the aesthetic harmonization of Glaucon's soul, the sublimation of interpersonal Eros can lead out of the Cave and toward the heavenly city.

Plato further clarifies the distinction between aesthetic form and reference when he recommends being surrounded from birth to death by artifacts—and he lists buildings, furniture, utensils, and clothing, as well as paintings—that have the requisite rhythmic and harmonic properties without directly representing any object. Note here that painting is considered, not as in book 10 of the *Republic* in terms of its mirroring function in making perspectively manifest the exterior of a body, but in terms of its presentation of aesthetic form. It is in this that he lays the basis for the later focus on pure aesthetic form, originally in music, but also in painting and sculpture. But for Plato, music without words is meaningless, and so he cancels on the one hand what he opens on the other. Mikel Dufrenne speaks in this regard of the representational prejudice of classical aesthetics and carries on his discussion in terms of the expressivity of aesthetic form.[94] Plato's own treatment of Beauty Itself as a real presence in beautiful things points in the same direction, though in thus addressing the topic, he links such perception to erotic arousal in the presence of the beauty of a human body, not to the contemplation of artistic objects. Shorn of his heavy representational and interhuman erotic emphasis, Plato's observations about Apollonian aesthetic properties and the real presence of Beauty Itself in beautiful things could be considered the charter for abstract art.

Note also that rhythm and harmony are transferred from the musical arena, where they qualify sound, to the plastic, spatial arena, where they qualify visual objects. In both instances, through the plastic and the performing arts, music and harmony sink deeply into the soul. It is important to underscore this insight because it is so often overlooked in those who claim that Plato was basically hostile to the arts. In fact, Plato was more sensitive than most to the power of the arts. He thereby sought, not to oust them, but to employ them to bring what I have called prerational rationality to the soul, to shape the emotional wellsprings of action and attention in such a way as to foster the eventual emergence of an explicit rational pattern of experience, "with eyes fixed on the whole,"[95] aimed at that which exceeds it as principle of the Whole. By *rational pattern* I mean a whole style of attending that is capable of weighing and measuring both quantitatively and qualitatively, that is habituated to being intelligently alert to all the relevant parameters of a situation, that is aimed at the whole of reality within which human activity occurs, that is capable of attending to the long range as well as to the immediate, and that is capable of dispassionate assessment because it is moved by passionate (i.e., emotionally totalistic) commitment to the undisclosed Whole. Aware of the undisclosed Whole, philosophic Eros is capable of being sustained by an enduring awe that, far from being extinguished, is deepened as it understands more and more of the fuller context within which everyday awareness occurs.[96]

In fitting artistic activity and appreciation into that larger context, Plato treats various art forms in different ways. His major focus is on *musike* as instrumentally accompanied poetry. But he also treats sculpture, painting, dance, architecture, and manufacturing design in general. And whereas, regarding painting, his major focus in the *Republic* is on its mirroring function, he also treats it in passing, as we have noted, in terms of its purely aesthetic form. But he tends to subordinate aesthetic form to intellectually apprehensible meaning: he has one of his characters in the *Laws* claim that instrumental music without words is meaningless. He likewise has some significant things to say about the dance as a form of gymnastic for the soul. His focus here is not on the audience but on the performer. And here the object of the dance is not so much to train the body as it is to tune the soul, not only making it able to bear up under hardship, but also making it graceful, rhythmic, and harmonic. Indeed, all the art forms are considered in terms of their effect in tuning the soul so that it welcomes reason. For Plato beauty in everything turns on use, upon the proper functioning of the entity in question. So also, the beautification of the human being turns on health of body and soul, the latter being advanced by the perception of beautiful forms.

In Plato, beauty itself is extended from sensuous form to psychic disposition and from there to the objects of scientific treatment, not only the objects of mathematical harmonics that govern what is seen and heard, but also the objects of the philosophic sciences of psychic life, of ethics as its proper attunement, and of metaphysics as the unveiling of the harmony of the whole physical-psychic cosmos and perhaps of its Source. Beauty as a transcendent Form is privileged in that it appears in the sensory field it-

self as exceeding the locus of its manifestation, as being both in and beyond the beautifully seen (or heard) object. Plato thus points to a peculiar
experience of transcendence that gives a curious flavor to all he writes, but
which experience is implicit in, and the ground of, the fascination that sensuous beauty exercises on us all.

Beauty is that which binds the whole together: universal Form and
particular instance, intellectual apprehension and bodily resonance. The
abstract reflective movement out of the Cave of sensibility and culture into
the sunlight of intelligibility involves, as its necessary complement, a recu-
perative, concretizing reflection that binds the two realms of our experience together. Art, made reflectively aware by philosophic reflection of the
fundamental parameters and basic direction of psychic life, is able both to
set in motion the ultimate deepening of the lifeworld and to bring to significant, participative presence the intellectual depth carved out by philosophic reflection. But even further, in its intuitive flashes of insight into the
character of the whole, art gives rise not only to critical assessment on the
part of philosophy, but also to further possible rational development.

It is on the basis of these sets of connected insights that Plato is led to
the censorship of the arts and thus to infringe on artistic freedom, the one
unexamined absolute of the current artistic community. That community
seems to embody Plato's notion of democracy, where freedom to do what
you want is the central value and where every other value depends on the
choice of the individual, who is in principle free from all binding norms.
Art gives expression to such free individuality and creates whatever communities happen to gather around the idiosyncrasies of expression that
emerge. Tradition, order, rule, law—all represent limitations on artistic
freedom. We are in a similar cultural position as that encountered by Plato.
And his response to the situation is applicable to our own: the intrinsic nature of psychic life, oriented toward the whole and capable of rational ordering of its own life in attunement to the cosmic order, provides the
measure for the intrinsic value or disvalue of all cultural products. Do they
open out psychic life in such a way as to allow it both to exercise rational
judgment and to draw upon its total Eros for the whole, or do they in some
way inhibit both aspects of psychic development? Several things are rejected in principle: abandonment to biological appetites, total and uncriti-
cal immersion in culturally biased projects, and a rationalism that fails to
recognize its own need to transcend itself in our passion for the whole to
which our experience of the beautiful leads us.

Plato provides for us a rich harvest of aesthetic insights that move beyond the narrowness of art for art's sake into the breadth of art for the sake of the expanded, deepened, and harmonized human soul, attuned to the fineness of sensory surface expressive of the character of the whole and aware of unfathomed depths.

༄ ༄ ༄

## A Brief Excursus: Plato and Wright on Architecture

Locating beauty in the relation of form to function, Plato anticipates one of the fundamental principles of the mode of architecture represented in the twentieth century by Frank Lloyd Wright. Wright rejects the "pictorial view" of art that has dogged the tradition, just as Plato rejects "imitation" as holding a mirror to sensory surface.[97] The shape taken on by a work of art is that dictated by its function, just as in the case of any living form.[98] It is this that has been reborn in the industrial arts in the design of ships, airplanes, locomotives, and automobiles.[99] The more functionally adapted, the more streamlined and thus beautiful the objects appear. Architecture ought to translate this into the nonmobile forms of buildings: the form, stripped of all mere superadded decoration and rendered simple,[100] is determined by what is to be done in and around the building and thus by the essential human values involved.[101] Furthermore, as in things of nature, the form should also be adapted to the environment within which it essentially stands, expressing its belonging to the earth, and indeed, to this piece of earth, this peculiar environment.[102] To that extent, it is important for Wright to stress an intense appreciation for the qualities of the materials involved.[103] Furthermore, and as essential to his conception of *organic architecture*, there is a stress on the peculiarities of space, both inward and outward. A building is not walls and ceiling; it is the space these carve out.[104] In this stress on appreciation of materials, on the nature of space, and on belonging to a peculiar environment, it is not so clear that Wright would find an ally in Plato, for Plato most often seems more interested in the way out of the Cave. Where he is more like Plato is in his view of music as sublimated mathematics, furnishing him an image of architecture as similarly constituted.[105] Here both the mathematical and the sublimational are essential. And this is directly parallel to Wright's view that life itself is sublimated machinery, a mechanism that transcends itself. Mathematics and the machine are dead and spiritless, but they are the body in which the spirit realizes itself. Functionality is essentially linked to the character of the human spirit, whose inner experience is expressed in art and in religion, both of which exhibit a sense of the Whole.[106] The architect must therefore know something of the intrinsic order of the universe.[107] But where Wright would no doubt again stand strongly opposed to Plato is the low level at which Plato places democracy. Distinguishing with Plato liberty from license,[108] Wright nonetheless calls for and develops an architecture that is expressive of the democratic spirit in, among other things, his underscoring of the individual Usonian house on its own private acre.[109]

# III

# ARISTOTLE

## Meanings of the Term Art

THE APPROACH I TOOK in the introduction to locating fine art in the broader scheme of things human was basically Aristotelian. Let us review it at this point. I took an inventory of the uses of the term *art* in ordinary experience, ranging them in a hierarchy of broadest to narrowest usage and setting them in a system of contrasts. At the broadest level art is contrasted to nature. Aristotle expands on that by providing an insight into the nature of a nature: a nature *(phusis)* is a principle of motion and rest, of development and completion, that is intrinsic to a thing.[1] Natures head in their own directions or tend to endure in states toward which they have tended. A nature so conceived provides the frame within which art occurs.

Art is that which depends on choice.[2] Everything distinctively human has its origin in art in this broadest sense. Human nature is part of the frame of nature, since it involves a givenness that does not depend on human choice for its form, and that givenness involves structural features corresponding to tendencies to act along certain lines. Human nature involves a tension between two given factors: a biological-sensory factor and a factor of transcendence or of initially empty reference toward the whole of being. As Aristotle put it, "the human soul is, in a way, all things."[3]

The biological factor is comprised of basic vegetative processes, processes of anabolism and catabolism, of growth and sustenance, and of reproductive tendency.[4] Over and beyond that, it involves the level of sensory wakefulness and thus of the sensory manifestness of things. That manifestness takes place within the Now of the perspectives set up by our bodily position, by the limited thresholds of our perceptual organs, and by our organic needs. For Aristotle the sensa are the activations of the perceptibility of things in relation to the activation of the perceptual powers of the perceiver—indeed, in a relation of "intentional identity." ("The sensible in act is the sense [power] in act.")[5] As the horizon of vision and the perspective appearance of a material thing within that horizon are not absolute features of "the world outside," but conditions of manifestness relative to a biologically based percipient, so also with the sensa that appear within such perspectives. Such appearance is locked into the flowing Now but anchors all our wakefulness.

Our knowledge of the factor of transcendence has its root in the fact that we judge whatever we confront in that sensory field in terms of meanings that refer to all actual or possible instances of those meanings, whenever in time and wherever in space they might occur, even in such elementary sensorily focused experiences as seeing this page "as white." The whole of space and time is marginally pregiven as a term of reference for our judgments. But the judgments center on the employment of the notion of being whose reference is absolutely unrestricted. The judgment that something "is" such and such involves a reference to the wholeness of what is judged and to the encompassing whole that includes it, the one judging, and everything else as well. The way the human soul is all things is, initially, by way of empty reference. But it is precisely the emptiness of that reference that makes it necessary to choose how we are to work at uncovering that whole and how we are to arrange our lives so as to come to terms with the tasks imposed by our nature and the conditions of past choices, both our own and those of the tradition that bears us. Human nature is precisely that nature that has to choose to create culture. And since cultures are choices based on a necessary partiality in the manifestness of what-is and of all the parameters of our own being, they are necessarily plural and, alas, probably necessarily or at least contingently antagonistic.

There is then an art of producing culture in general. We might say that distinctively human nature is culture-producing nature, nature that operates by art, nature that produces forms. That includes the art of creating institutions—social, political, economic, educational, religious—that form a way of life. The art of producing culture also includes bringing theoretical knowledge *(theoria)* into being, the aim of which is the contemplation of the invariable, the frame of nature within which decisions are made.[6] Knowing how to introduce variations into nature presupposes knowing something of the invariants of what nature provides.

Under the narrower heading of art, as contrasted with *theoria*, Aristotle contrasts making *(poiesis)* with doing *(praxis)*.[7] The habit of the latter is prudence or practical wisdom *(phronesis)*, of the former it is art in a still narrower sense *(techne)*. *Techne* shapes something external; prudence shapes our own habits, individually and collectively. *Techne* thus falls under practical wisdom and is governed by it. Aristotle calls practical wisdom, in the broader usage of the term *art*, "the art of arts."[8] It is the habit of alert, intelligent focus on all the relevant parameters of our lives in the concrete situations in which we find ourselves. As a "habit" it is far from a dull routine, for it is concerned with building and breaking as well as sustaining routines, as the situation might require, in order to keep intelligently alert to the demands of changing contexts in the light of the naturally given human ends. It is a *hexis*, or habit (Latin *habitus*), or a "having," the fundamental way we possess ourselves, guided by the priority of concretely alert intelligence.[9] One way of looking at good or bad habits is in terms of whether we "have" ourselves (e.g., in skills) or whether we are "had" (e.g., in addictions)—although there is a fusion of the two, having and being had, in a passion for excellence, possessing ourselves in being possessed by what is worthy in itself.[10]

The "habit" of art in the narrower sense of *techne* is similar to the habit of practical wisdom. It is intelligent alertness to possible gestalten *(logoi)*, forms that can be brought into being externally. Aristotle defines *techne* as a habit (i.e., a mode of self-possession) concerned with making *meta logou alethou*.[11] We can see to what extent translation is interpretation by considering some possible renderings of this phrase. One is "involving a true course of reasoning";[12] another, "with true reason";[13] and again, "a rational quality . . . that reasons truly."[14] Antecedent to these we have Aquinas's *recta ratio factibilium*, "right reason regarding what can be made."[15] Interpreting what is involved in "a rational quality" or "right reason" and close to the phenomena of actual artistic production would be "according to the manifest togetherness of things." *Aletheia*, usually translated as "truth" and understood as correctness or rightness, actually involves a coming into presence of a form. Literally it means unconcealment.[16] *Logos*, rooted in *legein*, to gather, to read, involves a togetherness, a set of connections. The Latin *ratio* comes directly into English as *ratio*, or a set of relations, and indirectly as *reason*, which is actually a matter of seeing the peculiar relations that constitute things. Art is thus the habit of seeing connections for making. Reasoning is involved, but it is seeing that togetherness that is crucial. Elder Olson suggests that art involves a peculiar sort of hypothetical reasoning that works from whole to parts: granted a given whole, the idea of a possible form to be made, one proceeds to figure out how to bring it into actual materials.[17] So art involves two features: (1) a manifest togetherness, an idea as a possibility for shaping, and (2) a figuring out of the steps required to bring it into being. Aristotle will indicate something of the basic character of the manifest togetherness operative in one of the art forms in his *Poetics*, parts of which we will consider later.

Art as *techne* is often divided into useful and fine art, though the division overlaps in certain cases: for example, in the case of good design in architecture, utensils, furniture, clothing, and so forth, which Plato has Socrates advocate in the *Republic*. But the ancients had no significant distinction between useful and fine art. The fine is a desirable quality of whatever has been made, no matter how utilitarian. For Aristotle as well as for Plato, both aspects, the fine and the strictly utilitarian, are useful in effecting the tuning of psychic disposition. The good and the beautiful tended to coincide.

Almost all of Aristotle's aesthetic remarks turn on production and the character of the products. However, he makes observations in relation to temperance that have significant implications for aesthetic appreciation. Temperance *(sophrosune)*, he claims, is rooted in *sodzousa ten phronesin*, keeping your head, being able to direct yourself thoughtfully, preserving practical wisdom.[18] He notes that intemperance, as a matter of excess in sensuous indulgence, is not located in seeing or hearing, the typical "aesthetic" senses, nor, for that matter in smelling or even in tasting as such. One cannot be overindulgent in looking at paintings or sculptural pieces or the beauties of nature. Nor can one be overindulgent in hearing music or appreciating odors or developing a cultivated palate for food or wine. Intemperance, he notes, can be present in these matters only indirectly insofar as, in effect, the vegetatively based desires are involved (i.e., the desires linked to nourishment and reproduction). Here we can be intemperate by destroying our bodily base, clouding our ability to direct ourselves intelligently, and failing to attend to the fine qualities of things. Aristotle locates the problem of intemperance in tactility, though even here he refers to refined pleasures such as massages and warm baths, which, apart from other possible connections, pose no direct problem for temperance. He shows by contrast what an aesthetic experience is by noting that a dog loves the sight and smell of a rabbit, but only in connection with his desire to eat.

Kant will refer to a similar phenomenon in his often misunderstood notion of "disinterested satisfaction," which he connects to an "unconstrained favoring."[19] One is not forced by antecedent organic need to attend to the object. One attends freely to the fine qualities of the thing's presentation.

## Nature Illumined by Art: Plato and Aristotle

As I also noted in the introduction, the broad contrast between art and nature is not the last word. Both Plato and Aristotle, and later, Kant, Schelling, Schopenhauer, and Nietzsche, use the analysis of art to illuminate nature. For Plato, according to the mythos of the *Timaeus,* nature itself is the product of divine art: the cosmic demiurge looks to the eternal Ideas and persuades the Receptacle, the restless chaos of space-time, like the artist's clay, to take on intelligible form.[20]

Aristotle approaches nature differently, but takes his point of departure from an analysis of *techne.* He distinguishes four types of explanatory factor, four distinct strands, four "causes" or "(be)causes" *(aitiai)* that answer the question, Why did this occur? The artist is the one who brings about the work of art by his action: he is what comes to be called the efficient cause *(arche).* He works in terms of an idea that he intends to realize for a purpose that may or may not coincide with the work of art (e.g., he intends the work in order to pay his bills). The goal, posed initially as a creative idea, together with the purpose, are spoken of as the final cause, or *telos,* that for the sake of which something happens. The stuff the artist works with is the "material cause" *(hule,* lit., wood) which helps determine the quality of the finished product. Finally, the idea as realized in the material is the "formal cause" *(morphe,* lit., shape, and *eidos,* or intelligible look). The efficient and final causes are here "extrinsic causes" vis-à-vis the work of art. The material and formal causes are, by contrast, "intrinsic causes."[21]

Now artifaction *(techne)* occurs within the framework provided by nature *(phusis),* both the nature of the materials and of the artist himself as a product of a natural process. The artistic form, though ultimately immanent in the natural material, is imposed on it. The material itself has a natural form that is intrinsic to it and nonimposed. It developed as a process of nature. Its immanent natural form is a certain proportion of elements, describable in a formula *(logos).*[22] The elements—fire, air, earth, and water—are determinate forms that are subjectible to change. The basis of that subjectibility to change is what Aristotle calls *prote hule,* or prime matter, a pure potency, not empirically observable the way the elements are. It functions the way Plato's Receptacle functions, as a principle of both change and the multipliability of Form in a plurality of instances throughout the appropriate places and times.

The artist himself has a nature, the biological-transcendent, culture-creating nature described above. That nature is understood by Aristotle in terms of the immanentization of all four causal factors. The material cause involves the elements, but shaped through a developmental process by the psyche as entelechy, a self-formative principle that has its end within itself *(en telos echeia)*.[23] The biogenetic process involves the gathering of the elements into organs that are the instruments *(organoi)* for the activation of the psychic potentialities. The process heads toward the fully functional adulthood of the organism. Organs exhibit the same structural principles as the whole organism. The eye, for example, involves certain proportions of the elements "informed" by the unseeable power of seeing, both of which—observable organ and power of seeing—are fulfilled in actual (unseeable) seeing as the goal of the biogenetic process.[24] In the human case, the sensory furnishes the materials to be penetrated intelligently for the purpose of knowing and acting as a higher, ultimate goal, or telos (e.g., to understand the eyeball as an organ governed by the power of seeing). The psyche is the immanent formal, efficient, and final cause that gathers the material elements about itself; the psyche is the immanent artisan of its own developed nature as enmattered form.

Once again, then, as in Plato, art furnishes the starting point for the analysis of nature. However, in Aristotle's case, there is no external divine artisan, only immanent natures seeking their ends and shaping materials for realizing those ends. An Aristotelian god is a Pure Exemplar for those natures, a kind of telos rather than an agent. The world goes on because each nature seeks to be as like the divine as its nature allows: in the case of all material things, being in its proper place; in the case of all living things, being fully actualized and being immortal through reproduction; in the case of all animals, being aware and experiencing satisfaction; and in the case of all humans, being present to themselves as possessing cognitively the intelligible order of things.[25] Later, in Schelling, the underlying Artist is considered to work like the human artist, out of the inspiration of his unconscious and out of a need to discover himself in his creation. In Schopenhauer, as in Nietzsche, the underlying Cause, the One, is entirely blind, completely unconscious and brings forth the world by necessity; it should thus no longer be called God or a god.[26]

## Art as Imitation

As did Plato, Aristotle speaks of art as imitation. Art is related to nature not only for its materials but also for its forms. The form manifest for making "imitates" natural form. Here, however, *natural* has an extended meaning that includes every given, natural or man-made. Art has its origin in a native tendency to mimic that is found especially in children and is the chief means by which they learn. Children imitate their parents and thus learn to speak and behave in conventional ways. They imitate animals and even inanimate things and thus come to have an empathetic sense of the world. And humans learn not only by producing imitations, but also by attending to them. However, even when we do not recognize the object imitated, we naturally delight in the qualities of the presentation: the colors, the rhythms, the harmonies.[27]

Aristotle here distinguishes clearly the mirroring, referential function of art from the aesthetic form of the vehicle of reference. This form is found in the peculiar togetherness of the elements of the sensory presentation, its design properties. As in Plato, there is some question about how that last tendency might be annexed to imitation. Recall, Plato criticized the poets first of all in terms of verbal reference: they should not provide bad civic examples. He went on to consider types of melody and rhythm, the timbre of instruments, and the modes of presentation (narrative or dramatic). The consideration of melody, rhythm, and timbre turns more on the question of sensuous form. Plato, for one, called for a certain type of sensuous form, one exhibiting good (read: Apollonian) design properties in clothing, buildings, and utensils that are not themselves "imitations" but realities in their own right. If we consider instrumental music (untitled), we have *the* nonrepresentational form of art. But, Plato noted, through rhythm and harmony of sensuous form, the disposition of the soul is profoundly transformed.[28]

Aristotle picks up the same notion in his distinction here between imitation as a means of learning and delight in sensuous form as the twin origins of art. In the case of imitations that are to be considered artistic, fully aesthetic form must combine reference (imitation in the more obvious sense—i.e., as representation) and sensuous form, so that the latter is suitable to the former. But the notion of sensuous form as distinct from reference also has an imitative role for Aristotle. In what surprises modern readers, who would expect exactly the opposite, music, he says, is the most imitative of art forms. What it imitates is ethos, usually translated somewhat one-sidedly as "character."[29] Character involves that preconscious directedness of our dispositions out of which we spontaneously act: the sum total of our habits as they rise up to the level of felt tendency to act. Ethos as feeling and mood is what Aristotle has in mind with his remark on music's imitative character. Plato had spoken of the need for a blend of gymnastic and music in order to establish a kind of prereflective rationality of disposition. The organism itself was for him a model of a rational system: the coherence over time and space of a complex multiplicity of factors. It furnishes, according to Aristotle, an invariant ground for our action. Above it rises what he calls the ethos level, the level of emotions persuadable by reason that establishes character.[30] Plato refers to the same level as that of the desirous and the spirited parts of the soul. Harmonious sensuous form linked with reference into a full aesthetic form balances that dispositional ground and thus establishes another mode of rationality at this prereflective level of felt disposition. When fully reflective rationality begins to dawn, it will find a welcome matrix in such a disposition. For Aristotle, as for Plato, music, whether linked to the word and thus to overt reference or not, in its purely aesthetic modality produces harmony or disharmony in the psychic disposition to act.

We might note that music is not reduced to the causal factors involved in wave production. Like all sense qualities, for Aristotle, as for Plato, sound comes into being only in relation to perceivers, though that does not make it "merely subjective." It is a relation of manifestness of things to perceivers, establishing a novel "between" that overrides the modern subject-object dichotomy.[31] According to the latter, sound waves produce inner, subjective effects contained within the nervous system of the perceiver, leaving the problem of how we get to know the "objective" sound waves.[32] For Aristotle the imitative character of music lies in the effects it produces: feelings like those given by nature or culture (e.g., sorrow, joy, placidity, love, vigor, wrath). It is thus not the sound as such that is imitative but the emotional reverberations it sets up "in" us. Aesthetic form produces surrogate emotions. I should note, as Heidegger will later, that emotions, like observable sensory features of things, are not simply inner subjective experiences but ways in which we participate in the "life" of other entities, persons, or things—the way we are attuned to them. Emotions *(ethe)* are ways of opening onto the world, ways of disclosure.[33] What they disclose, I would claim, is the "inwardness" of the other, its wholeness, its surplus beyond what we cognitively apprehend, the mystery of its being, which is the way it belongs to the totality. But then, of course, we would have to consider emotions, not as raw animal feelings, but as distinctively human ways of feeling, rooted in an animal base but modified in terms of our founding reference to the totality as mediated by culture. Considering this dimension of aesthetic form, of the mode of presentation involved in all art, Walter Pater would later remark—as I noted in the introduction—that all art seeks the status of music as sheer play with the rhythmic and harmonic combinatory possibilities of its sensuous medium.[34] But both Plato and Aristotle note that such play produces states of mind like those produced by both natural and nonartistic cultural situations. It is these states of mind that art imitates.

Aristotle further remarks that art in general partially imitates and partially completes nature.[35] There are several ways in which this seems to occur. First, recalling that *techne* covers both useful art and what we today would call fine art, we could see art as an extension of the powers of human nature. The invention of tools in general enhances the powers nature already provided to humans. Aristotle notes the physiological inferiority of humans—animals have claws and wings for fight and flight. But humans have also by nature that peculiar relation of intelligence and hand—that "tool of tools"—that allows art to supplement what we lack by nature.[36] But specifically in fine art, there are at least four ways in which art goes beyond what is given by nature. First, in that it involves an exploration of the possible, art exhibits an understanding of the universal, that which would be the same under similar circumstances. Aristotle sees art as thereby more philosophic than history, which only presents the actual.[37] The materials of such exploration, however, are those provided by human experience, which is thus "imitated" by art but also surpassed in the direction of the possible. That gives a kind of generic sense of artistic imitation and completion that is realized in different ways. Even in the most fantastic fiction (e.g., in the Hobbit stories of Tolkien) the author works in a way analogous to the geometer. Once the characters and setting are laid down, the novel proceeds like a kind of deduction from these premises. It fails if it does not adhere to its premises. And what appears through such constructions are universal truths about human experience. In the Hobbit stories, you come into the presence of quest, honesty, the omnipresence of evil, and the like; and your understanding is thereby enriched in a concrete way. Indeed, the exploration of the fictively possible frees the universals immanent in human experience from the contingencies of their usual instantiations in order to allow them to stand forth more clearly.

In a second and more specific sense, art partly imitates and partly completes nature in that some forms of art present men, not as they are, but as they should be: art presents the obligatory. Aristotle reports here on Sophocles' claim.[38] Of course, one could say that art imitates (i.e., represents) nature as both the possible and the obligatory. Here *nature* is not in contrast to *history* but includes all actual occurrence. But in neither case does art merely reproduce surface, as Plato's mirror example might suggest. In Aristotle's sense, the representation of the possible and the obligatory would be a "completion" of nature, which is partially imitated in the construction of the work of art because the basis for the construction lies in knowledge of actual human life. The possibility art explores here is the moral ought.

In a third sense of imitation and completion, expressed in Schopenhauer and found originally in Polyclitus's Spearbearer (the *Doriphoros*) as a canon for treating the human body sculpturally (a sense Aristotle does not directly treat), art discerns certain ideal tendencies in actual physical forms and gives them embodiment in a work.[39] The actual human body could be considered the way a geometer considers actual triangles. Actual triangles can be compared as more or less adequate approximations to what is mentally projected as perfect triangularity. So Polyclitus, basing his work on the comparative study of actual human proportions running in tandem with a doctrine of certain harmonic proportional relations, projected an ideal human form for sculptors. The possibility art explores here is the physiological ideal, which Kant will explore in another way under the notion of "the ideal of beauty."[40]

The exploration of the moral ought and of ideal physiological proportions parallels the emergence of geometry as the projection of ideal figures and Plato's deliberately parallel projection of ideal humanness and of typical deviations from that ideal, both based on the hierarchy of human psychic structure. One might say that what is typically Greek is the power of this ideal-typical projection in geometry, in ethics, in sculpture, and in poetry.

In a fourth sense of imitation and completion, which gives the generic difference in the exploration of the possible that fine art explores, Aristotle calls attention to what we might call the *organicity* of the work of art, perhaps *the* defining criterion of art. An organism is a complex, integrated whole, a coherently functioning, harmonic system, each part of which requires all the others. So the organic character of a work of art means that each part ought to be such that its elimination would affect the fundamental character of the work. If the elimination of a part makes no essential difference to the character of the work, the part is aesthetically superfluous. If something essential to the character of the work is missing, there is aesthetic defect.[41] During the Renaissance, Alberti reformulated this principle for architecture.[42] By the criterion of organicity, most of what occurs in an actual event would be left out of its retelling in a story. In storytelling one picks out only the details that are relevant to the overall development of the story line. Actually mirroring the events dramatically would take as long as the events. Telling all the details of the events would be interminably longer. There are an amazingly complex set of factors existent and happening each second in an interpersonal exchange. Most are not relevant to the story. The attempt at full mirroring would be tedious rather than artistic. (Consider here the implausibility of the basic premise of the film *The Truman Show.*) The same could be said of a painting or a sculptural piece. The artistic sense of form is a peculiar capacity for abstraction from the actual even in strictly representational art. But then we are back to the consideration of aesthetic form playing in tandem with imitative reference. The peculiar togetherness of sensuous form in the case of untitled instrumental music and the peculiar togetherness of aesthetic form and reference in the representational arts is what is distinctively artistic. That togetherness has the character of organicity. The ability to grasp and bring into being gestalten having that character, making according to such a "manifest togetherness," is fine art. Such art thus imitates nature's productive organicity, rooted in and thus corresponding to the organic rhythmicity of human existence.

Aristotle gives piecemeal reference to the modes of imitation in different art forms. Music, as I have already noted, imitates character, which is the sum total of our dispositions to act. Music gives us dispositional states similar to their real counterparts. The difference, of course, lies in the nonreal character of the musical context. By that I mean that through performance a different world is added to the world of everyday experience. Music might induce longing or exultation or brooding depression or peacefulness, or any other mood whose real objects are not present. There is no beloved or victory or defeat or quiet achievement; but we are given to feel as if there were such in our lives. This is true whether the music in question is purely instrumental and without a title, is titled or, indeed, is fully "referenced" by accompanying a text. Drama, instrumentally accompanied or not, imitates character (again ethos), but character as interplaying with character through action and diction, in deeds and words.[43] I will return to that when I deal with Aristotle's analysis of tragedy, below.

By contrast with music, Aristotle claims that painting does not imitate ethos but only gives signs of it.[44] What it might imitate (i.e., mirror) would be sensuous surface, which might be adequate in the case of landscape, though here too, as in the case of photography, what makes it aesthetic is not exactitude of representation but frame and balance of shapes and colors, light and dark. The immediacy of musical experience reproduces the dispositional state underlying the surface portrait. The immediacy of a portrait reproduces surface but expresses the inwardness of disposition. What is peculiar here is the notion of sensuous surface because, in the case of the human being especially, its very character, particularly as found in the face, is to be expressive of inward, psychic disposition. It is modern Positivism that scrubs the surface clean of all expressivity and claims to find in sensuousness referred to sensuousness the whole meaning of things as far as our access to them is concerned.

## Division of the Performing Arts

In the beginning of his *Poetics*, Aristotle locates his chief subject matter, which was to be drama, both tragic and comic, within a division of the performing arts.[45] The basis for the division seems to lie in some of the basic characteristics of language, namely reference as carried by rhythmic and sonorous qualities. If we concentrate on rhythm alone and develop it, we have the basis for dance. If we isolate sonorousness and rhythm, we have the basis for instrumental music. Exclusive concentration on reference leads to ordinary prose, where sensuous form is lost in the reference. The process of learning to speak is parallel to learning to swing a golf club: one forgets about the club, indwells in it the way one indwells in his own body, and focuses attention on the ball. So in ordinary prose the words are defocused in terms of the what they make manifest. Finally, if we attend simultaneously to all the features—reference, rhythm, and melody—we have the basis for poetry. Here the reference is fully embodied in such a way that the rhythmic and sonorous qualities built into or accompanying the reference come into greater prominence and bring the referent into fuller presence. Think here of the difference musical background makes to a suspenseful or romantic movie. The fit between the visual presence and the musical background enhances the character of our participative presence. It is in such a context that drama, whether comic or tragic, fits.

Poetry for Aristotle's purposes in the *Poetics* is divided into serious and comic, and the former into epic and tragedy.[46] Epic and tragedy are differentiated in several ways. Epic presents a series of incidents covering a long time span, whereas tragedy focuses on one event, usually within a single day. Epic is narrated, while tragedy is enacted or "imitated." Epic is presented in a single meter, tragedy in several. Aristotle considers comedy a species of the inferior, indeed of the ugly, dealing with characters lower than the average type, whereas epic and tragedy deal with the higher character types.

In his *Politics* Aristotle discusses three roles for music: *paidia*, or amusement useful for relaxation (e.g., sleep, drink, and dancing); *paideia*, or education in virtue through pleasure in excellence; and *diagoge* and *phronesis*—a seemingly odd conjunction, since *diagoge* means a course of life or even pastime, though its linkage with practical wisdom places it significantly above *paidia*.[47] Amusement can be both relief from toil and a harmless end in itself. In its latter function, it is suited to the ends of human life. But beyond that, music contributes to ethical formation, for "virtue consists in rejoicing and loving and hating aright" and music produces those dispositions in us. It creates enthusiasm and sympathy and thus aids in developing the power of forming right judgments. It is in this context that Aristotle remarks that music is the most imitative of the arts as far as the fostering of ethos or felt disposition is concerned.[48] This is possible since the soul is, or at least possesses, harmony.

Now, his focus is on hearing the music, not playing. He regards the latter as fit only for slaves, and the higher class should only learn to play enough to be able to judge the performance of others. But whether as performer or member of an audience, one should be so cultivated as to be able to feel delight, not only in common music, which slaves, children, and even some animals can appreciate, but also and especially in "nobly beautiful *(kaloi)* melodies and rhythms."[49] Instruments that require great skill, such as the flute and the harp, should not be part of *paideia* because practice in these instruments takes too much time away from higher things. Besides, the flute is too exciting and one should only listen to it as furnishing relief from the passions—presumably part of the relief from toil referred to earlier. For Aristotle, the other problem with the flute is that one cannot use the voice with it, which seems related to what Plato had one of his characters advance in his *Laws*, namely that music without words is meaningless.

## The Definition of Tragedy

Aristotle defines tragedy as "the imitation of an action that is serious or heroic *[spoudaios]*, complete, having magnitude, in dramatic not narrative form, using language with pleasant accessories, to arouse pity and fear with a view toward their purgation."[50] I have already spoken of imitation. Let us focus first on action *(praxis)*. Analytical philosophy distinguishes and relates action and motion.[51] When my hand goes up, there is motion governed by mechanical laws. It may or may not be action, depending on whether it gives expression to the human life of meaning that animates the purely physical. Peter Sellers's Dr. Strangelove (in the film of the same name, 1964) deliberately restrains with his left hand his right hand's tendency to go up automatically in a *Sieg heil!* salute. The former is action, the latter mechanical motion—though, since Sellers is imitating the character, the depiction of pure motion is also action. Action is the level of meaning embodied in but surmounting the level of physical laws. Such action, however, is typically interaction between people, so that meaning here exists in the interplay and not in some purely private interiority.[52] One attends from one's own body to the other person(s) and the goals we share or about which we struggle. In either case, action takes place in a shared world of meaning. It is the realm of interaction with which tragedy deals.

The Greek adjective for "serious" or "heroic" *(spoudaios)* describes one of the characteristics that sets tragedy off from comedy. This may be linked to Aristotle's observation that tragedy deals with characters above the ordinary—hence "heroic." The nature of the seriousness is further specified by the emotions of pity and fear that are aroused by tragic performance. The interaction imitated constitutes a single action capable of being excised from the (fictional) whole life spans of the agents involved. As an action it itself has an organic wholeness: a definite beginning and a definite end tied to the beginning, not just chronologically but in terms of meaning.[53] The transition from one to the other constitutes a coherent singleness in spite of the multiplicity of its episodes.

*Teleios* (completeness) is from *telos* (goal), underscoring the direction of a process that furnishes its final explanation. The fully functional adult organism is the telos of the biogenetic process brought about by the psyche as *entelecheia* (having its end within itself). That is why a good "imitation" is "like an organism."

The reference to magnitude *(megethos)* is explained in terms of the ability of the ideal spectator to take in the object as a whole. Aristotle links that with beauty as relative to the perceiver, appealing to spatial size to illumi-nate the temporal. Too minute a creature cannot be appreciated, nor can that which is of vast size (he suggests something like 1,000 miles long).[54] So the beauty of a drama stands between too short and too long, relative to the ideal spectator. Here we have an anticipation of an aesthetic distinction Kant will make central to his analysis: the distinction between the beauti-ful and the sublime. The beautiful is rooted in forms we can take in, the sublime in those that exceed our capacity.[55]

The qualification "in dramatic not narrative form" underscores the si-multaneous appeal to the eyes and the ears in dramatic performance, as distinct from the purely auditory appeal of narration, though obviously one might listen to a reading of a drama or actually read the work silently to oneself—a more modern practice, especially fostered by "speed read-ing." Dramatic performance gives a more holistic imitation than does a reading—something that Plato has Socrates repudiate at one stage of the analysis in the *Republic*. In fact, Socrates repudiates even dramatic reading, insofar as the reader enters into the characters and becomes (at least a ver-bal) actor.

The discussion of language focuses on the particular embellishments of language proper to poetry. But it is located in a more elementary analy-sis of language. Aristotle presents a hierarchical list of the aspects of lan-guage taken up into discourse.[56] First of all, like an organism, spoken discourse has its elements *(stoikeia)*, based on the sonorous possibilities of the human oral cavity: vowels and consonants (which "sound together with" —*con-sonare*—the vowels by "clipping" them in various ways). Their ele-mentary combination yields syllables. Thus far the analysis is phonological. Next we reach the semantic level, the level of meanings. At the lowest level of meaning we have what the medievals will call the syncategorematic units which work together with *(syn)* the categories. Aristotle lists articles and "joints" (the latter have never been clearly identified). The categories or basic predicates are the lexical units of atemporal nouns set into tempo-ral contexts by verbs. Nouns and verbs together are subjected to inflection *(ptosis):* declensions (persons and cases) and conjugations (tenses, moods, and the like). The analytical hierarchy brings us to the sentence *(logos)* as the locus of realized meanings.

As Plato presented us with a preliminary eidetic analysis of poetic *musike* (reference, manner, rhythm, melody, style, and instrumental timber), so Aristotle presents us with a preliminary eidetic analysis of spoken lan-guage. In this treatment of the relation between the physical components of sound and the intentional components of meaning we find a direct expression of the body-mind relation—indeed it is one enactment of that relation. As in the organism visible material is gathered in such a way as to be expressive of the underlying psyche, so in language the physical vehicle, organized and inhabited by the soul, is subsidiary to the expression and reception of meaningful discourse as contact of mind to mind. But in poetry, mind and body, meaning and sound, are joined through the mediation of sound elaborated by musical harmony. Here soul in the full sense joins together intellect and body.

But all this is preliminary to the treatment of linguistic embellishment, Aristotle's primary focus here. He calls again for the mean, this time between the clarity of ordinary prose and the elevation of ornamental language: poetry needs the right mix of the two, both in order to contact ordinary meanings and to support the sense of elevation above the ordinary in the heroic characters presented.[57] Metaphor receives special attention here as the peculiar *alethes logos,* the special manifest togetherness that is the mark of genius *(euphuia).*[58] Hitting upon the novel expression that combines sameness and difference in such a way as to heighten the presence of the object, lifting it out of everyday manifestness, is one of the chief attributes of poetic *techne.* The pleasant accessories to language might also include musical accompaniment, used primarily in the choral odes that separate the various dramatic episodes.

The arousal of pity and fear with a view toward their purgation *(katharsis)* gives the main effect as well as the final purpose of tragedy in Aristotle's treatment. He explains this in his *Politics* by reference to certain religious rituals.[59] The sacred melodies induce frenzy, which releases the participants from the governing power of emotions like pity and fear. Their souls, he says, are lightened and delighted. Similarly, tragic performance provides an innocent cathartic pleasure. Here Aristotle seems to oppose the position advanced by Socrates in the *Republic* that the theatrical experience of emotions makes us all the more subject to them, and being subject to emotions makes it more difficult to discern the truth.[60] According to Aristotle's reading, the experience of a tragic performance does the opposite. And perhaps it does so by way of inoculating us against their absolute sway so that we might see clearly and judge rightly: we get a taste of pitiable and fearful situations, experiencing emotions that (as Aristotle said of music in general) "hardly fall short of the actual affections"—all the while knowing that the situations contemplated are fictional and thus not at all threatening either to the actors or to the audience. But there is further—though Aristotle does not mention it in the *Poetics*—the contemplation of the noble discussed in the *Nicomachean Ethics*.[61] Nobility is measured by how the character bears up under adversity. The release from pity and fear clears the ground for "the understanding of the universal" with regard to human action available through the poet's vision of the noble character and its dramatic enactment.

There is a second teleological element involved in Aristotle's treatment of tragedy. The art form has a historical genesis that has developed over time to reach what Aristotle calls "its natural form."[62] Tragedy begins in the Dionysiac religious festivals that consist in drinking and dancing to frenzy. The dancers form a circle, which constitutes a sacred space cut off from the secular everyday world. They represent satyrs—half-goat, half-human—brought to a state of high sexual excitement by the rituals. These goat songs *(tragoidiai)* gave the name to tragedy. At the beginning of the songs, and sometimes also between them, the leader recited stories of gods and heroes. The stories came to take on central importance. Aeschylus, the first of the great tragedians, diminished the role of the chorus, established the centrality of a single story, and brought two major actors onto the stage formed by the choral ring. Sophocles added the third character, along with scenery. For Aristotle, that brought tragedy to its fully mature natural form. Once brought to that level, it can fill its cathartic function most fully. What is curious about the claim to a natural form here is the apparent assimilation of culture to nature. Aristotle also speaks of different types of meter as naturally fitted to different forms of poetry.[63] In the interplay between various human faculties lie distinctive natural possibilities that require a fairly long cultural evolution, often spanning many generations, before they reach maturity. Such is the case likewise with the sciences. Given Aristotle's commitment to the eternity of species, for him humankind always existed and thus must have lost and found the sciences and the arts again and again.[64] That leads him to the position that mythology is decayed philosophy (or, alternatively, that philosophy is sublimated, purified mythology). Given evolution and given the development of science and technology as well as the emergence of different artistic genres and styles since Aristotle, one would have to extend considerably his notion of nature as applied to culture.

But to return to tragedy: Aristotle applies his form-matter analysis to it, distinguishing material parts, formal parts, and the overall form or 'soul' of tragedy as a third sense of telos.[65] The material parts are analogous to our own bodily components: they are the prologue followed by the first choral ode, called the parode, followed by the episodes of the play that are separated by various odes, culminating with the exode as the chorus leaves the stage.[66] The formal parts are—all but one—like our various functions, some more basically physical, some more basically psychological. They are mythos, character, thought, diction, melody, and spectacle.[67] *Charakter* is literally the stamp given to a person by antecedent conditions, internal and external. It involves the person's felt disposition to behave. Here it refers to the whole psychophysical agent whose deepest dimension is thought embodied particularly in diction, but also in visible action. Melody and spectacle provide support and setting for the action that occurs in the interplay between these components. But the animating principle, that which draws the whole together into unity, the "soul" of tragedy, is the mythos. Sometimes *mythos* is translated as "plot"; but plot is too skimpy a notion, a mere skeleton, as it were. Like psyche, whose work it is, mythos here is no disembodied abstraction, but the togetherness of the psychophysical whole, articulated down to its least member. The real dramatic art is the ability to see and display the organic togetherness of all the components, rhythmically paced, rising to the essential turning point, and unraveling to its organic conclusion in such a way as to arouse pity and fear in the audience and leave the spectators purged so that they might be able to contemplate the universal truths of the noble in action.

## Response

Aristotle's genius lay in his ability both to discern fine distinctions within the region of experience and to develop the inferences to what might stand beyond that field as its ground. He knew how, in Plato's terms, to carve along the joints of any region he explored and thus to distinguish regions for further exploration in the specialized sciences.[68]

Though, as basically a biological thinker, he was particularly intent on exploring the sensorily given, nonetheless, the sensorily given is always linked to the fact that the explorer, the human soul, "is, in a way, all things" (i.e., is always referred, beyond the sensory as such, to the totality within which the sensory is to be located). Aristotle exhibits the same basic structural analysis of the frame of human nature I presented in my introduction. Biologically based sensa he views fundamentally as relations of manifestness between a needy organism and a material being in the environment. But in the case of human awareness the sensory is found within a mind referred to the whole. That involves being able to take the sensory as the expressive indicator of the ontological depth of the sensorily given thing; and that, in turn, involves apprehending the intelligible, universal form as the proximate ground of the peculiar mode of sensory givenness in each case; that, finally, involves the apprehension of Pure Form as Self-Thinking Thought, as the self-presence of Form toward which all sensorily given being aspires as Primal Exemplar of actuality, eternality, and joy in the self-presence of the Whole. By reading the sensorily given in terms of its own expressivity based on the human reference to the Whole, Aristotle is able to locate wholeness, as with Plato, in the One/Good, which all things imitate. But, beyond Plato's own "idealism," Aristotle develops an idealism that reads the One/Good as the self-presence of Form. In the world we occupy, self-presence, in its various modalities, is not immediately given, but is the term of process. The sensorily given and we ourselves as correlate to it begin more as ordered bundles of active potentialities aimed at their integral actuation.

In that ultimate context, art is viewed, along with nature, as a source of coming into being. I have followed Aristotle's divisions in my introductory treatment of the various meanings of the term *art*. After being set over against *theoria* as the mirroring of the eternal order, art as *techne* is subdivided into the overarching political art of shaping human life (within which falls everything humans bring into being) and the art of shaping the environment. Aristotle enables us to extend the analysis of artifaction to an understanding of the nature it presupposes: the nature of the artist as a human being and the nature of the materials shaped. Based on a causal analysis of what is involved in artifaction, both the nature of the materials and the nature of the artist are viewed as form given to antecedent materials. In living things this takes place according to a teleological hierarchy of levels in which the lower levels are presupposed and subsumed by the higher, and in which the lowest is a level of pure passive potentiality to be shaped, at the antipode to the full actuality of Self-Thinking Thought.

Art in general is a possibility of human nature that supplements that which nature, both inside and outside us, provides. It involves the apprehension of a gestalt as a possibility for shaping and apprehension of the steps needed to bring it into being. More specific factors are involved in bringing particular art forms into being. In poetry, the focus of Aristotle's aesthetic analysis, he points to the sensitive, indeed even ecstatic character of genius (literally the ability to stand outside oneself) needed to indwell in the characters in order to give expression to the ethos or inward disposition expressed in their gestures, but also to see unusual sameness in differences that lies at the basis of the invention of one of the chief vehicles of poetic expression: the metaphor. And the general capacity involved in poetic creation is the capacity to grasp and form the plot as the concrete integral togetherness of all the factors involved in a piece, the vital soul of dramatic art, a concrete instance of the principle of organicity.

We might pursue here Aristotle's causal analysis of artifaction. Having distinguished the causal factors is one thing: material to be shaped, actual shaping, form to be brought into being, and reason for the shaping. The clarification of how they actually function is another. What is the relation between the extrinsic formal cause (the artist's idea) and the material cause (the stuff to be shaped)? That depends in part on the status of the idea. Perhaps at times it comes full-blown into mind, as Mozart is said to have conceived some of his pieces.[69] At other times it may come to clarity after a more or less lengthy process of playing with the idea in mind. Again, it may begin only as an impulsion, a sense of direction that grows and comes to fuller clarity as one works with the materials.[70] The measure of a mind here, as in any other region, is the quickness with which it comes to see the whole, to grasp significant unity in what otherwise would be a scattered multiplicity, to envisage form.

Furthermore, the relation of the idea to the materials is different in different art forms. In the plastic arts it is often the case that the materials talk back in the process of formation. In sculpture, shaping one way limits the possibilities for the next step; and especially with wood or marble, there is necessarily a process of discovering the limits as one uncovers the grain in the process of working the idea into the materials. In painting, laying on one color sets up tensions with other colors. Even in drawing, a line charges the space in which it is drawn and thus sets aesthetic limits to the next step. And in the creation of characters in the novel, their initial delineation leads them to object to any attempt to force them in a direction contrary to their constitution. Sensitivity to the play between the given and achieved factors on the one hand and the aura of possibilities in their significant relations on the other is crucial to every process of artistic shaping.

One might also inquire into the source of artistic ideas. How much is technical skill involved, how much a certain natural giftedness? To be a musical composer, one needs a developed sense of musical form and a fertile sense of novel possibilities similar to what is involved in a more restricted way in musical performance. A musician may learn to play according to a metronome; but unless one advances beyond that level, one never plays with the dynamics born of real human-felt inhabitance of a piece expressed in the right combination of louder and softer, faster and slower execution as they are relevant to the aesthetic unity of the whole piece. One arrives at that level only by being open in the moment of execution to the reception of whatever gifts one might have for musical performance. There is then the possibility of "inspired" playing that participates in the "vision" of the composer.

Aristotle, I said, exhibits a fine capacity to carve the field of experience and what it implies along the joints provided by nature. He is a master of analytic divisions. He locates poetry, the object of his one major treatise in aesthetics, within a division of the performing arts, which he seems to derive from, or at least relate to, aspects involved in linguistic expression: sonorousness, rhythm, and reference. Rhythm is the basis of dance; linked with sonorousness, it is the basis for instrumental music; both linked with reference, the basis for poetry. In discussing poetic diction, he analyzes language, as a specific instance of the body-mind relation, down to its physical units in the elements of sound and up to the various levels on which meaning enters into sound, culminating in the unity of discourse with felt inhabitance created in a poem. Aristotle thus not only situates poetry within the larger frameworks of the other arts and within a preliminary investigation of the nature of language, he also locates both within the still larger framework of human structure as referred to the cosmos that has been our primary focus from the very beginning.

He positions the tragic art within a division of poetry and analyzes it into its parts, both formal, pervasive parts, and material or sequential parts. As Plato provided us with the beginnings of an eidetic analysis of music, so Aristotle provides us with a parallel eidetic analysis of tragedy and, indeed, of language arts. He draws the whole together by an encompassing definition that finds its soul in the plot and its end in the catharsis of the audience. Unfortunately, Aristotle says very little about catharsis. And focus upon it leads to the absence of any reference to what many testify to in the experience of tragic drama: spiritual illumination. Perhaps purgation receives what seems to be a disproportionate emphasis because the passions stand in the way of facing, clearly and rationally, the tragic situation. But given Aristotle's powerful theoretical interests, one would have thought that the dimension of insight would have been central to his consideration here. One has to dredge them up by his introductory and undeveloped notion that poetry is more philosophical than history because it explores the possible and thus involves knowledge of the universal. However, perhaps the two aspects—spiritual illumination and purgation of pity and fear after their evocation—might be linked by the following observation. It is one thing to develop devices for arousing passions (one thinks of many of Stephen King's writings and the movies based on them); it is another to produce a work characterized by organicity. Following tragic art involves apprehending the organic gestalt of the emplotment. (One misunderstands the character of this apprehension in confusing it with being able to give the bare bones of a "plot summary." Paul Ricoeur understands better, I think, when he views emplotment, "the soul of tragedy" for Aristotle, as the whole organically functioning piece.)[71] Apprehension of the emplotment of a work encompasses and situates the experiences of pity and fear that follow from the artist's employment of the appropriate devices. Tragic depth follows from the depth of the apprehension expressed in the emplotment. One can be thus simultaneously purged and illumined by attention to the tragic performance. Consideration of the *Ethics* suggests that what emerges from tragic performance is the contemplation of the noble exhibited in the character's ability to bear up under extreme adverse conditions.

In focusing on tragedy, Aristotle shifts the focus of aesthetics from beauty and the Eros correlative to it to the horrible and the emotions of pity and fear aroused by it. Plato favors Apollo, but it is an Apollo as sublimated Dionysus, joyous and exultant in creating. Aristotle, one would have to say, favors a sober Apollo—all clarity, all order, but won by staring the Dionysus of destruction in the face. Distanced objectification of the horrible wins release from the disorienting emotions it evokes in order to allow us to contemplate the noble.

Aristotle's discussion of music is limited, even within the *Poetics*, where it seems to be confined to a consideration of meters. He does discuss its use in the *Politics*, but fails to attend to the way in which it aids in intellectual cultivation, which he only mentions. And he presents a challenge to the view that music is abstract as distinguished from imitative by claiming that music is the most imitative of the arts. In direct contrast to painting, which Plato presented in book 10 of his *Republic* as a clear example of mirroring, Aristotle considers music to imitate ethos or state of mind or mood by producing it in the audience, whereas painting can only give an exterior sign of such mood. I could, however, apply the same reasoning to painting and suggest, as Plato did in his passing treatment of it in the purged city, that the rhythm, harmony, play of colors, and distribution of forms likewise perform such "imitation" by evoking a mood appropriate to what is represented in "representational" painting or, just like purely instrumental music, evoking a mood without representation in "abstract" painting. I have cited Walter Pater's remark that all art seeks the status of music. It is remarkable how this runs like a refrain through modern artists. Kandinsky saw abstract art operating like music.[72] Gauguin claimed that color, like music, was able to express the inner force of nature by representing a mood rather than an object.[73] August Endell remarked that nonrepresentational art "can stimulate our souls as deeply as only the tones of music have been able to do."[74] Matisse claimed an analogy between the living harmony of colors in a painting and the relation of sounds in musical composition.[75] In Feininger, music suggested the rhythmic organization of his paintings.[76] It has also been suggested that in Art Nouveau generally, the symbolic power of the line corresponds to the melodious role of sound in Symbolist poetry.[77] Finally, Frank Lloyd Wright, as noted above, saw both music and architecture linked mathematically, while Schlegel saw architecture as "frozen music."[78]

In his treatment of tragedy, Aristotle introduces—though not by name—the central aesthetic notion of organicity by which we understand the mean between the extremes of aesthetic excess and aesthetic defect. Aristotle notes—and we should extend his observations to all art—that a tragedy should be so constructed that, as in an organism, nothing essential to its total operation is lacking and nothing is present that could be omitted without affecting that operation. Such organicity belongs both to the "soul" of the work's reference and the "body" of its sensory presentation in their integral togetherness as a unified meaning. In Kant this property will be located, along Aristotelian lines, in the *form* of the work of art.

Organicity relates human fabrication to the order of living things. In a sculptor like Henry Moore and an architect like Frank Lloyd Wright, living form is the archetype. In Kant, the origin of genius is spirit as animating principle of the creative faculties, producing vital works and evoking a sense of distinctively human life in the audience. (But we will see later that Kant has not the same relation to nonhuman life forms as Moore or Wright or Aristotle.) Kandinsky, the "inventor" of nonrepresentational painting, saw his very abstract work as preserving something of nature's organic growth.[79]

It is here that we might press a bit further into the basis for the two origins of poetry Aristotle suggests: the natural desire to imitate, through which we humans learn, and an innate appreciation for harmonies and rhythms. Through the first we are able to exist as political animals—that is, as sensate beings with biological survival needs whose empty reference to the whole is filled through our introduction into the sedimented words and

deeds, thoughts and actions, interpretations and choices of others that constitute the whole we call our culture. It is here that our imitative tendencies
help us to learn the culture. But that is set on a biological base; and the biological is a matter of inner rhythms and overall harmony of rhythms and
functions correspondent with an environment characterized by rhythms
and attunements—by the alternations of day and night, by the changes of
the seasons, by the phases of the moon, by the lapping of the waves and the
patter of the raindrops. For our own survival, our biorhythms must be attuned to the rhythms of the world surrounding us, a world of which we are
an integral part. And yet, because we are referred to the whole, we can
back off from biological need and let ourselves appreciate the rhythms and
harmonies that surround and comprise us at our basic level. We can also
learn to produce works that have rhythmic and harmonic properties and
bring them into organic unity. Such works are "fresh," "live," "vital," "organic," as distinguished from those that are "stale," "dead," "mechanical."

In general, Aristotle provides us with sober, workmanlike analyses.
There is no hint of something like Plato's passionate fascination with
beauty. In fact, Aristotle says very little of beauty beyond limiting it to what
a human can take in (between the petite and the monstrous), relativizing
it—in the case of human beauty—to different ages of human maturing,[80]
and listing (without explanation) the properties of order *(taxis)*, due proportion *(symmetria)*, and definedness *(horizmenon)*.[81] It would seem that for
Aristotle, the aesthetic is a subordinate region within the larger whole of
the human project, while for Plato it is the very center of that project.

Nonetheless, for both thinkers—as for all thinkers up to the nineteenth
and twentieth centuries—art is not a region that exists for its own sake.
Everything experienced, art included, is for the sake of enabling the
human being to become better attuned to the cosmic order, following out
the basic orientation of humanness toward the totality. But art's special
role is to locate that orientation in the here and now of bodily presence in
the world of the senses and thus to allow us to participate in that world
more fully.

# IV

## PLOTINUS AND
## THE LATIN MIDDLE AGES

THOUGH THE ARTISTIC PRACTICE of the Middle Ages was unparalleled, especially in the construction of the cathedrals that housed magnificent sculptural and pictorial works and were filled with the haunting sounds of Gregorian chant, it might not be too far off the mark to claim that, from the point of view of aesthetics (i.e., reflection on the nature of art and beauty), the thought of the Middle Ages was essentially derivative. Indeed, among the major thinkers, the great philosopher-theologians, besides citation and paraphrase of traditional sources, one finds very little sustained treatment of aesthetic matters, and almost nothing of any significance with regard to works of art. The one exception was the notion of divine beauty and the corresponding development of the transcendentality of beauty. Treatment of beauty was largely a matter of commenting on Dionysius, an early-sixth-century Syrian monk who leaned heavily upon pagan neo-Platonism. In the ninth century Scotus Eriugena developed a system of thought heavily dependent, in turn, on Dionysius. And in the High Middle Ages, commentary on the Dionysian corpus, begun in the ninth century with Scotus Erigena, attained new life with Albertus Magnus, who was followed in this by his pupils, Thomas Aquinas and Ulrich of Strasbourg.

The major texts dealing with aesthetic themes have been collected, like a series of pre-Socratic fragments, in Tatarkiewicz.[1] However, the difference between these and the earlier fragments is that they are found in whole

texts and operate out of a deliberate attempt to gather up and arrange positions handed down from previous ages.[2] The dominant philosophical
framework for the Middle Ages was Neoplatonic, developed especially by
Plotinus, and mediated by Augustine and Dionysius. And so we begin with
a treatment of Plotinus, the prince of Neoplatonists, who created a bridge
between Plato and medieval thought.

## Plotinus

Some six hundred years after Plato, Plotinus attempted to provide a
systematic account, in treatises arranged in groups of nine (hence called
*The Enneads* or *The Nines*) of the themes treated dialogically, dialectically,
and hence nonsystematically by Plato.[3] It is Plotinus's philosophy that provided the categories through which the Christian church interpreted the
biblical tradition, all too often in a dualistic, otherworldly direction. As
Thomas Aquinas pointed out, such a view posed great problems for understanding the central New Testament teachings of the Incarnation of
the Logos, the sacramentality of Christian worship, and the final Resurrection of the Body.[4]

In Plato's development of the Line of Knowledge, the question of the
status of the intellect was left open. Where do we stand when we each ascend beyond the privacy of our sensations, feelings, and preferences and
become the subject whose correlate is the eternality and necessity presented paradigmatically in mathematics? Later, the medieval Muslims,
Avicenna and Averroës, would speak of the one Agent Intellect in which
we all participate.[5] Thomas Aquinas, basing himself on the observation
that it is each of us individually who understands, labored strenuously
against this conception; but he retained a residue of it in his notion of the
agent intellect in each of us as "a certain participation in the divine light."[6]
Later still, Schopenhauer would speak of becoming "the one Eye of the
world" in contemplating the "Platonic Ideas."[7] And Hegel would speak of
God coming to His Self-awareness in human beings through the development of scientific, philosophic knowledge.[8] Earlier, Augustine held that we
are within the Logos when we grasp intelligible form.[9] In this they follow
Plotinus, who held that we are able to stand within the World Mind, the
Logos, which contains the intelligibility of the whole.[10]

Plotinus goes further in the direction indicated in Plato by what, in his
*Republic*, he calls the Good as the ground of intellect and intelligibility, beyond subject and object. As noted earlier, Plato also has Socrates refer to it

as "beyond *ousia*," usually translated as "beyond being." This becomes a staple in the Neoplatonic tradition and is made much of today by Emmanuel Levinas.[11] However, *ousia*, the term that, in Aristotle, was subsequently translated as substance, should, I suggest, be translated here as beingness. Plato refers to the Good as "the most manifest region of being" *(tou ontos to phanotaton).*[12] I would maintain that being *(to on)* is all-encompassing, for being is everything about everything, outside of which is absolutely nothing. It includes the realm of genesis, with its modes of relative nonbeing (pastness, futurity, potentiality, privation, absence), the realm of the *ousia* or beingness of beings (their intelligibility as correlate to intellect), and the Good as source of both *ousia* and *genesis*. What is important here is the testimony to a region beyond both what the senses can apprehend and what can be grasped by the abstract, conceptual, universalizing operations of the intellect. It is correlate to Eros as the desire of "the whole person."

In Plato the Good as the One, immediately irradiating the splendor of coherence upon the Forms, is, more profoundly, the principle of the whole. Its being "beyond," its utter transcendence, is at the same time its complete immanence. That is why the ascent from the Cave involves the return to the Cave: the One as *arche tou holou,*[13] as principle of the totality, circles back beneath the surface of the Cave images. If the Receptacle stands beneath things as the principle of their being spatiotemporal individuations of universal Forms, the One stands "beneath" the Receptacle just as it stands "above" the Forms. It is as Beauty that the One is a Real Presence in sensorily given things, healing the *chorismos*, the gap between the Forms and the sensory appearance.

The Good as the One is manifest in the peculiar experience of unity that we call the mystical, an experience described in similar terms in the East and in the West: "I and the All are one," "Atman is Brahman," "God and the soul are one."[14] Porphyry, Plotinus's biographer, reports on Plotinus's claim to have been drawn four times out of ordinary experience and into an ecstatic experience of unity with the One.[15] This gave him a peculiar appetite for being "alone with the Alone."[16] For Plotinus, following Diotima in Plato's *Symposium*, this One radiates itself in all things as Beauty, as the coherence, the harmony of each and all.[17] The initially experienced intoxication associated with sensory surface is suffused with a sense of the ultimate expressivity (i.e., the symbolic character of all things as mirrorings of the One in multiplicity). The sensory surface is therefore not simply color and pattern, but colored pattern illuminated by a underlying depth. For Plotinus there is nothing beautiful that does not express something more than beautiful.[18] Even Beauty Itself, irradiating all Forms and all things, which participate in and thereby express their Forms, is an expression of the One beyond.[19]

Focusing on beauty in all its forms and levels, Plotinus argues against a common ascription of symmetry to things as a necessary characteristic of beauty by pointing to symmetrical things like an ugly face that are not beautiful. Rather than symmetry, Plotinus argues for "dominance by form" as the essence of beauty in all its types; and by that he means unification, coherence, harmony of parts, the mirroring of the One in the manyness of matter, of functions, of concepts, but also simple instantiation of form. Full penetration by pattern, total unification, absolute coherence is, I suggest, precisely what Aristotle meant by the property I have described as organicity.[20] But there is also the simplicity of color with its luminosity (Plotinus uses the example of gold). Luminosity is the irradiation of the One, a surplus beyond pattern that makes pattern accessible. It bears witness to a "more" than what can be discriminated and united in intellectual operations, which stand at a distance from a given object. The beautiful object stands out from others as an arresting presence. It involves a participatory relation that overcomes the distance of subject detached from object in analytical and synthetic operations. Intuition of the Idea in relation to the sensory object that expresses it is participative presence.

For Plotinus, the Logos or World Mind flows out from the One as illumination from the source of light.[21] In so proceeding it can only go into multiplicity, first in the founding distinction of subject and object, and then in the progressive complexification of the realm of Idea-objects from unity to multiplicity.[22] From the realm of the Logos flows the World Soul as the last emanation within the eternal Trinity, turned, as creative power, toward the world of individual spirits. Eventually the One generates material multiplicity like light dispersing itself into darkness. Matter is the ultimate opposite of the One as the dark principle, the principle of dispersal, multiplying individuals under the same Form at different times and places, forcing the enmattered forms to struggle to develop themselves and maintain themselves and eventually to lose hold of themselves as they finally sink into the dispersal of the elements they employed in securing their peculiar and precarious hold on existence.[23] The material world came into being as a prison for the pure spirit, who falls from a higher realm so deeply that it forgets its own belonging to the supercelestial realm within the bosom of the divine Trinity.[24] Nonetheless, in order to be, things must mirror the

One and thus contain within themselves degrees of unification at various levels, answering to the level of the hierarchy of being they each occupy.

The hierarchy of beauties described by Diotima can then be meaningfully understood as more intensive and, at the same time, more comprehensive levels of unification. According to Plotinus, the perception of such intensive comprehensiveness, and thus also of sensuously formed objects as expressive thereof, depends on the achievement of a more intensive unification of our own individual lives, awakening from our fall into matter.[25] Even though at one level our intellect remains with the Logos, nonetheless we begin this life "sunk in matter," unconscious, floating in the darkness of the developmental processes of the embryo. As human form comes to dominate physiologically, awareness emerges as a stream of urges and impressions that are gradually shaped through the acquisition of language and patterned responses developing into motor habits. Such shaping is the aim of Plato's "primary education." The explicit intellectual pattern emerges later through the ability to con-centrate, literally to be at the center with something, to pull oneself together out of the flowing distractions of appetites and contingent impressions coming from the environment. Such concentration emerges more comprehensively in the philosopher. It is surmounted by an even more concentrated mode of existence when the higher Dionysian, mystical pattern emerges: that of participative knowing that co-implicates awareness and its object—only here subject and object are not only united as two in one; they are for Plotinus one and the same.[26]

But since not everyone can participate in such deep unity, then not everyone can attend to the deepest expressiveness of sensory surface. This is transparently clear in relation to the written and spoken word. But it is also the case with regard to the immediacy of sensuous form, whether visual or audile. In high art, the sensuous togetherness of form plays in relation to the depth of its capacity to express the profundity of things apprehended and given shape by the artist for the properly integrated receptivity of the perceiver.

Furthermore Plotinus, in keeping with Diotima's teaching in Plato's *Symposium*, also remarks that one cannot expect to reach the higher levels of contemplation unless one learns to contemplate the beauties given through sensation.[27] Ascending the Ladder of Beauty involves a turning around of the soul, wallowing in the pleasurable sensations occasioned by the sensorily given, to appreciate the beauty of individual sensuous forms themselves. The soul must be purged of its own self-indulgent proclivities, which

scatter its attention. Passing through the sensory surface to the person encountered and expressed in that surface requires an even deeper conversion; and moving beyond to the historic formative powers shaping personal
being, a conversion still deeper. As one moves more deeply within, one is
able—in a metaphoric inversion that always seems to accompany the
metaphor of depth[28]—to ascend to higher and higher levels of illumination. More inward power of concentration is required to grasp the eidetic
invariants that generate the observable particulars, and more power still to
bring the plurality of Ideas into the light of unity. But most of all, the deepest purgation is required to be drawn up into identity with the source of intelligible light: the One itself. This pattern, derived from Plato, becomes
the classic pattern for the "three ways" of the spiritual life in the Middle
Ages: the purgative way, the illuminative way, and the unitive way.[29]

The summit does not lie in becoming a spectator, but in having beauty
penetrate the whole soul so that contemplation turns into vision. Self-
knowledge becomes one with oneself.[30] Knowledge, even of oneself, loses
the external character of what we usually call knowledge and becomes
participatory, at one with the known, and thus self-knowledge and other-
knowledge at one. Ordinary separations—knowledge from participation,
knowledge of self from knowledge of the other—are here one.

Plato has Diotima claim that the highest level is the vision of Beauty
Itself, suggesting an ascent away from the sensuous starting point. However, Socrates in the *Phaedrus* claims that, of all the Forms, the privilege of
Beauty is that it is perceptible through the eyes as a "real presence" in
beautiful things. Plotinus similarly claims that, for one who has mounted
up to the higher levels, the sensuous surface is like the face of the beloved
which expresses, for one who loves, the depth of the beloved.[31] So there is
a kind of dialectic of an inward-upward move, beyond the Cave of culturally mediated sensibility, playing in tandem with a return to sensibility,
which is now participated in as expressive of the depth of Final Reality.
The move inward and upward carves out for the mature an infinite depth
beyond sensory surface in which the immature are fully enmeshed.[32]

Along these lines, even though Plotinus's remarks tend to devalue the
material world more deeply than some of the things Plato has his characters utter, Plotinus reverses the order of value in Plato's discussion of the
arts in *Republic* 10. Things, Socrates says, are images of Ideas and our sensations are perspectival images of things, whereas art, like a mirror, gives us
images of those images, "three degrees removed from reality." For Plotinus,
following Plato's remarks about inspired art as distinct from imitative art,

which mirrors sensory surface, the higher forms of art proceed from an apprehension of the generative Ideas.[33] Things are expressions of the World Soul working the potential chaos of matter into meaningful expressions of the unity of the Ideas. The high artist grasps the Ideas, not simply as static, atemporal unities, but, allied to the World Soul, as creative forces.

Schopenhauer will later distinguish the *unitas post rem,* a unity following the presentation of an entity, a reconstruction by analytical and synthetic intellectual operations of the *unitas ante rem,* the generative unity of the Idea that produces its instances in an atemporal vertical causality intersecting the horizontal temporal causality exhibited in observed antecedence and consequence.[34] So it seems that in Plotinus the Ideas themselves are not static forms, as they appear to be in Plato's dialogues when he takes his point of departure from mathematical form; they are generative forces. This is how artistic intuition apprehends them, since such intuition is essentially generative, essentially tied to the possibility of working the form into the externality of matter. For Plotinus, then, art imitates nature, not by reproducing sensuous surface, but by grasping her mode of production.[35]

Yet, because material embodiment is viewed as a fall of the soul, Plotinus considers art in the mind higher than its artistic expression in an actual work.[36] Boethius will mediate such a view to the Middle Ages in his remark that musical theory is more excellent than musical sound.[37] This is linked to the view that for an artist—Plotinus speaks specifically of the sculptor—the form is in the mind and not in the material.[38]

But even in the mind, the idea of the work is an idea expressed in images. This entails a link between imagination and intellect that parallels the link between sensation and imagination. For Plotinus imagination has two faces.[39] On the one hand, it stores and recombines the images received through sensation. Now sensation does not give us the thing in its ontological depth; it presents us with the surface of the thing appearing within the thresholds set up by our bodies and answering to our organic needs. However, art that proceeds out of the apprehension of nature's creative Ideas is no mere mirroring of that surface but an expression of the depth apprehension; hence the appearance of new images not simply derived from sensory surface.

Plotinus has astonishingly high praise for the power of images. He underscores the pictographic character of Egyptian hieroglyphs as transcending the discursiveness of propositions and expressing insight into the "wisdom of nature" that roots its creation of multiplicity in unity. Contemplation of the Forms is not consideration of propositions but experience of creative powers.[40] Grasp of Form is grasp of the expressive power of images, and is hence a creative intuition, an apprehension of the possibility of the transformation of sensory surface to express creative depth.

If the work of art, through the Idea it instantiates in its own creative way, brings us to the beauty of the One as the final object of human Eros, it is also linked with an intellectual "aesthetic" that is attuned to the togetherness of the Forms. All speculative thought is rooted in such an "aesthetic," a sense for wholeness that resists analytical dissolution and compartmentalization while recognizing the essential though subordinate role of analysis. Even speculative construction rests on the transconceptuality of the ultimate depth, correlate to the whole person. Every beauty stems from what is beyond and gives expression to a surplus that irradiates the conceptual work as it irradiates the work of the artist.[41]

## Aquinas among the Latin Medievals

Plotinus, as I have said, supplied the basic Neoplatonic philosophical framework for medieval interpretation of the scriptural tradition. Augustine remarks that very much of Christianity was in the Neoplatonists: Trinity as the One/Father producing the otherness of the Logos/Son, from which flows the World Soul/Spirit, followed by Creation, Fall, and Return of creatures to God. But Augustine further remarks that there is one central omission: that the Logos became flesh.[42] The claim that, minus this exception, much of Christianity is in Neoplatonism is an ambiguous claim, since the essence of Christianity is the incarnation and bodily resurrection of the Logos. Nonetheless, it was especially through Augustine in the West and Dionysius in the East that Neoplatonism entered into the Middle Ages.

Augustine's *Confessions* records the journey of a soul initially caught up in "fleshly beauty" and "worldly eloquence," converted first to Neoplatonism and then to Christianity. He laments: "O Beauty, ever ancient, ever new! Too late have I known thee!"[43] For he sought it in sensuous charms and warm embraces—he wallowed in the "seething caldron of unholy loves" in Carthage and had an illegitimate child (Adeodatus, "gift of God") by one of his mistresses—only to find that the Beauty he sought was not there. Following the Diotiman ladder of ascent in experience, turning within and upward, he came to a vision of Beauty Itself beyond all things. His personal experience thus gave him an ambivalent relation to physical beauty and also to art forms. Hans Urs von Balthasar speaks of an Augustinian "nervousness" regarding the senses.[44] In the *Confessions* Augustine acknowledges that he struggled with the issue of having music banned from the churches because it is so sensually enticing; but then, recalling that he had been moved to tears by music after his own conversion, he acknowledges that it might be an aid to "the weaker soul."[45]

Beauty in creatures he sees, in keeping with the Platonic and Aristotelian conceptions, as linked to objective properties rooted in form.[46] Following the *Book of Wisdom,* he identifies the properties as *modus, species, et ordo*—that is, measure or proportion, form (or type or even appearance) and order as ordination to an end.[47] These properties produce a concordance of parts to constitute a single unified whole.[48] This measured whole mirrors, in Platonic fashion, the realm of eternal numbers.[49] However, Augustine adds a new twist to aesthetic considerations: integral to the unification peculiar to beauty is an opposition of contraries that produces aesthetic tension.[50] Though Augustine stresses the objective properties, he also speaks of the beautiful as suiting our nature (i.e., as proportioned to or harmonious with our faculties)[51]—a position that Aquinas, following Aristotle, will stress as well. And anticipating a distinction Kant will later make, he also distinguishes beauty from *suavitas* (pleasantness or agreeableness) by distinguishing (differently than Kant) the perception of visual qualities from the perceptions of the other senses.[52]

Following Plotinus, Augustine claims that the artist must know the ideal form he wishes to embody and that his giving body to the form inevitably involves an inferior realization.[53] At best, when they are not the object of vain curiosity, the arts can assist in turning the soul inward and upward and thus away from the senses, for the goal of human existence is "spiritualization." Having to work through sensory imagery in order to communicate is a result of the Fall.[54] Such an attempt is justified ultimately under the aegis of charity,[55] but it amounts, in the words of Robert O'-Connell, to "an array of mud-huts, slapped together from the soul's own 'ruins.'"[56] In a comprehensive and critical—though not entirely unappreciative—study of Augustine's reflections on art, O'Connell summarizes Augustine's attitude toward artistic work, an attitude that will fatally stamp medieval thought: "Superbia, pride, the restless, 'curious' desire to be engaged in action, the arrogant will to construct a temporal imitation of the eternal world of beauty, the dissipation, literally, 'spilling forth' of its interior riches in a flight further and further from the divine to the outermost reaches of 'lesser and lesser' being—all the key elements of Plotinus' description in *Ennead* 3.7, of the fall from eternity into time are firmly in place."[57] Augustine seems to have had no sensitivity to painting, for he makes little mention of it. Indeed, he viewed both painting and the theater as species of lying.[58] And in his treatment of music, he is only concerned with rhythm (governed by number), the least sensuous of the features of music.[59] We have already taken note of his hesitation even to allow music in church. On the other hand, Augustine himself was a consummate rhetorician, as exhibited especially in the beauty of his *Confessions*. At times he displays an appreciation for the various marvels of human productivity, but then reminds himself and his readers that they are, after all, a result of the Fall into the body.[60] One of the results of the Fall is that we are immersed in the part and fail to see how it fits into the whole so as to constitute the poem of the universe.[61] This is one of the most fruitful aesthetic observations Augustine has made.

Dionysius—now called Pseudo-Dionysius because he passed himself off as Dionysius the Areopagite, disciple of St. Paul, even though he lived several centuries later—developed a *pankallism*, a vision of all things as manifestations of divine beauty.[62] Beauty is a transcendental property belonging to all things by reason of their participation in Beauty Itself, a real presence in beautiful things, as in Plato's *Phaedrus*. For Dionysius, beauty *(kallos)* is derived from calling *(kalloun)*, whereby the divine calls things to itself and to their place in the order of things. This call has two aspects: beauty functions as formal cause in giving things the being they have, but it also functions as final cause, which establishes in creatures an Eros for Beauty. Hence, as correlate to *pankallism* we have a *paneroticism*, the universality of desire that draws the creature to its source. In calling things to their place, Beauty thereby communicates the harmony of brightness of all things which flashes like light.[63] Two properties are linked together here: consonance and splendor, or harmonious relation between parts and a surplus "shining through" of what expresses itself from beyond the perceptible relations. Dionysius stressed the transcendence of the infinite divine in relation to everything positive we can say about the divinity. The last word about God is that we cannot say about God. He is essentially hidden, a mysterious Source: He is "beyond being."[64]

In a way reminiscent of Heidegger, Dionysius claims that Being itself, which Balthasar reads as equivalent to Aquinas's *esse commune*, is "the first of all the creatures," essentially other than all beings, which share in it.[65] Balthasar further suggests that this notion designates "the space of the spiritual life," a life that entails dwelling in the sense of totality and encompassment as the mysterious depth from which all things come and which ultimately mediates our lived relation to God.[66] The manifestation of harmonic properties in creatures is irradiated from within by the presence of the final mystery, giving to the perception of beauty a certain haunting character that takes us out of the everyday and suggests the presence of infinite depth. But as in Plotinus, the apprehension of the Beautiful and Good and One and the Same as such is made possible by the soul's entrance into itself from things without, being collected into unity.[67] Read in isolation from other counterbalancing tendencies, this carries out the Platonic-Neoplatonic tendency of shutting out the world of the senses in order to move "within" and "above." But read in a broader context, as I have already suggested, it carves out an experiential depth-dimension beyond our surface relation to all things, so that everything we encounter becomes sacramental, a theophany, a manifestation of the presence of divine Beauty.[68]

In the 1240s Albertus Magnus lectured on Dionysius's *Divine Names* to an audience that included Thomas Aquinas.[69] In *De pulchro et bono*—an opusculum formerly ascribed to Aquinas—Albert laid stress on terms that describe the surplus of beauty over goodness as a light, a shining, a radiance, a splendor, an incandescence, a resplendence, a lightning *(fulgor)*, a superfulgence, a *claritas* (linked to *clarus*, "famous," parallel to Greek *doxa* as "glory"), a supersplendence rooted in the substantial form.[70] In an otherwise austere scholastic presentation, this piling up and even manufacture of terms to describe a single property is indeed remarkable. Albert is clearly struggling to give expression to a surplus in the experience of beauty beyond the analyzable properties to which it might otherwise be reduced. In the expression *splendor formae* this luminescence is linked to proportion and consonance, which are understood as a relation of aspects within the object. But whatever the identifiable ratios involved, *splendor* is a surplus property. And in the Dionysian context, it is understood as the directly perceived expression of the depth of divine mystery irradiating all things.

Thomas Aquinas, according to Etienne Gilson one of the greatest arrangers of ideas in the history of thought, gathered up and synthesized what was available of Western intellectual tradition up to his time in the light of the newly available Aristotelian corpus, itself available until then only in fragments.[71] Aristotelian at the level of natural philosophy, assimilating the act-potency, substance-attribute, form-matter analysis of nature, and viewing the human being, not as a spirit externally related to matter, but as an essentially incarnate spirit, Aquinas was nonetheless Platonist at the deepest levels. Here the doctrines of participation, the divine Ideas, creation, and immortality were assimilated into the Aristotelian view.

The key concept of Aquinas's thought, his distinctive contribution, was the way he understood the distinction of essence and *esse*, originally introduced by Avicenna: as the most fundamental realization of the act-potency relationship, where *esse* is "the act of all acts," "form even with respect to substantial form," and essence is the receptive potentiality that limits the degree to which an entity is.[72] *Esse*, to be, is basic act, in every case individual; it is distinct from the limitation provided by a given essence. *Esse* is, however, by nature unlimited, so that its factual limitation in the beings of experience requires a Ground Whose Essence does not limit but is identical with His *Esse*, Who therefore cannot *not* be. Such a Ground is not in the deepest sense a once-upon-a-time Starter of the world-process, but— whether Starter as in Plato or Nonstarter as in Aristotle—a perpetual Source of being. Finite things are thus not simply initially but, more deeply, enduringly related to their infinite Source. As unlimited *Esse*, God is thus wholly other than all creation, utterly transcendent. However, as Source of being for creation, God is pervasively immanent in every creature, "more intimate to me than I to myself," as Augustine expressed it,[73] for without His constant creative sustenance and all-penetrating awareness, no finite thing can be at all.

In the Dionysian line, Aquinas developed a "negative theology," a theology of limits to conceptual comprehension. As infinite and one, God is beyond the limitations and distinctions with which our finite intelligence operates. For Aquinas we can infer the existence of Pure *Esse* and the presence of those attributes required for creation (power, wisdom, goodness, unity, infinity), but we cannot understand the infinity of the mode of existence and the identity of these attributes with one another in the infinite Ground. Hence inference has to be complemented by negation. For Aquinas our last word about God is that we do not comprehend God. But, by reason of the structure of creation, creatures express the presence of the ultimate unencompassable mystery of God to those sufficiently attuned to the depths.[74]

This provides the first division in the hierarchy of being: God as pure *Esse* unlimited by any essence, Whose essence is to be; creatures whose essence limits *esse*, participating in being in various degrees. The degrees are determined by the dominance of form over matter. Living beings are a step above the nonliving because of the unitary assimilation of the elements by the activity of their psychic form seeking its own ends. Beings that are aware are capable of "assimilating" the forms of other things "without the matter." Intellectual beings assimilate the same forms as purely sentient beings, without matter but also without the individuating conditions of matter, so that intellectual knowing is universal, laying the basis for language and for the sciences. Embodied intellectual beings, human beings, are hierarchized according to whether they live at the intellectual pole of their being, ultimately dwelling in the presence of God. And beyond humans are pure forms, angelic intelligences, each a distinct species rather than a variation on a species theme as individuated by matter.[75]

This view of hierarchy sets the framework for the doctrine of the transcendental properties of being, various aspects that display the richness of the *esse*, the to-be of things. Unity, thinghood, otherness, truth, and goodness are the properties laid out in the famous list in Aquinas's *De veritate* (1.1). Their historical origin lies in Plato's dialogues. They apply according to the formula: whatever is, insofar as it is, is one, good, and so on. The qualifying "insofar as it is" indicates the essentially hierarchical character of being. Enmattered beings are developmental, each beginning as a center of active potentialities and following a pattern of development until it reaches the fully adult actualization of those potentialities, so that the actual state is higher than its potentiality. And the potentialities are hierarchized according to the transcendence of matter involved: sensory operations are higher than unconscious physiological processes because they transcend their own material boundaries, while intellectual operations are higher than the sensory because, in the apprehension of the universal, they transcend the individuating conditions of matter and thus the immersion in the here and now present in both unconscious physiological processes and sensory apprehension. In this view, then, some things "are" more than others; and all "are" at some time more than they "are" at others. Accordingly, insofar as an entity actualizes its basic potentialities and occupies a rank on the hierarchy of types, it is unified, "thingly," other, intelligible, good.

Beauty does not make the list, but the elements are there for its inclusion. Aquinas, following Aristotle, sees beauty as involving a relation between knowing and desire. His description—*pulchrum est id quod visum placet:* beauty is that which, when seen, pleases—is not particularly helpful since truth also pleases; but that characterization does stress the appetitive response, the felt relation to the subject. For Aquinas, beauty brings the appetite to rest in the object.[76] There is thus a more holistic relation than in a purely intellectual act. In the definition, *visum* here might be taken, in the line of ordinary language, as analogously extended to all wakeful states: "*See* how this sounds, how this tastes, how that feels, how it smells; *see* the line of proof in this demonstration."[77]

Aquinas notes with Aristotle the peculiarity of human sense perception: only humans can come to delight in the beauty of sensible things in themselves and not simply in connection with their function in keeping us alive.[78] This could be understood in two opposed ways: on the one hand, the simple enjoyment of feelings produced by objects—which is characteristic of Plato's luxurious city; on the other, the appreciation of the sensory features of things themselves characteristic of Plato's purged city. There seems to be no clear discrimination of these two possibilities here.

We might note in this context Aquinas's view that sight is the most "spiritual" of the senses because it is filled with the object.[79] Contrary to touch, the lowest of the senses in Aquinas's estimation, in the sighting of the visual object qua visual (except in the case of the feeling of strain involved in an excess of brightness or darkness in the medium) there is no simultaneous experience of one's own body, which may distract attention from the characteristics of the object. However, the arousal of bodily feelings may accompany the sighting and thus deflect attention from the object to the feelings. Vision thus provides a kind of anticipation of the objectivity of intellect and points in the direction taken by Kant's emphasis on the "disinterested satisfaction" involved in aesthetic perception.[80]

This might be the place to note a shift from Cassiodorus, for whom all the senses perceived beauty,[81] to Aquinas, who restricted perception of beauty to sight and hearing,[82] and Thomas Gallus, who distinguished the higher senses of sight and hearing, which are annexed to the intellect, from the other and lower senses, which are annexed to affection.[83] Aquinas in the text cited claims that sight and hearing are maximally cognitive and that their objects are the only ones considered beautiful, in direct contrast to the objects of touch, taste, and smell. Even today, ordinary usage does not call the feel of velvet, the taste of wine, or the aroma of perfume beautiful—maybe exquisite, delicate, delightful, or fine, but not beautiful.

In considering what it is about the *visum* that pleases, Aquinas lists, without showing their interconnections, three properties of the beautiful.[84] The first is integrity or perfection, having all aspects together, being completely formed, a notion implicit in Albert's emphasis on form. The second property is Albert's feature of due proportion or consonance, which Aquinas considers in two different ways: the way Albert understood it, as a relation of one quantity to another,[85] to which Aquinas adds Augustine's observation of the relation to our cognitive power[86]—which itself parallels Aristotle's claim that beauty is relative to our capacity to perceive. Aquinas maintains that the senses are a kind of *ratio* or "reason," and that is the basis for our delight in the ratios of things: things beautiful by reason of the relations of their parts are suited to our own sensory faculties, which consist of corresponding ratios. The third property is Albert's *claritas*, which, as we have noted, carries more than the English *clarity*, including parallels to Greek *doxa*, which involves the notion of glory. Hence some translate it as "splendor" to maintain the connection with Albert's *splendor formae*. Jacques Maritain for one reads *claritas* as a kind of surplus of intelligible light available through the senses and lost when one turns from sense to abstraction and reasoning.[87] All three properties are associated with the notion of form,[88] picking up on Albert's notion of *splendor formae*.

Attempts have been made to correlate these three properties with the transcendental properties of unity, goodness, and truth respectively and then to import Bonaventure's notion of beauty as the fusion and seal of the transcendentals.[89] However, as I have noted, beauty did not make Aquinas's famous list of the transcendentals in *On Truth* (1.1). This may partly be explained by the close association the medievals saw between beauty and goodness viewed as perfection,[90] though, as I have noted, Aquinas claimed that beauty adds to goodness "a certain relation to the cognitive power." Qualifications such as *certain* are open invitations to interpretative ventures. In view of Aquinas's description of beauty as that which, when seen, pleases, the "certain relation" might be that of providing pleasure in the viewing. However, perfection or integrity is only one of the three features Aquinas offers and thus the identity of beauty and goodness as perfection cannot be sustained. Presumably there are completed entities—one thinks of some insects—that are not well proportioned, and presumably also some well-proportioned and completed entities through whom the splendor of the form does not shine. Beauty would require all three and to that extent would not be transcendental. Again, since proportion on Aquinas's reading involves, following Aristotle, a proportion to our powers, Umberto Eco suggests a further argument that beauty cannot be transcendental.[91] For Aquinas, since the mind is referred to being, both of its powers, intellect and will, entail the manifestness of the transcendental properties of truth and goodness respectively. One only has to distinguish sensory and ontological beauty to free the transcendentality of beauty. In his treatment of the Trinity, Aquinas correlates the three properties of beauty with the Word and thus locates beauty within the heart of the divinity.[92]

Eco notes that the weakest element in medieval aesthetics is its theory of art, which is essentially a theory of craftsmanship. For Aquinas art is, directly translating Aristotle, *recta ratio factibilium*, a phrase usually itself translated as something like "right reason regarding things to be made."[93] Eco goes on to say that the medievals had no notion of the creative power of art.[94] But Aquinas's borrowing of the revised notion of imitation from Plotinus contained that potential: art imitates nature, he says, in her manner of production.[95] This could be allied with the Aristotelian notion of the organicity of the work of art: as nature produces objects having the character of the integral togetherness of all its parts, so also art can come to produce artifacts not resembling any exterior form of entity, but possessing the crucial factor of organicity, thus providing distinctively human "growths."

Aquinas viewed the arts as inferior to intellectual communication. Artforms are superficial, standing on the empirical surface.[96] Poetry is *infima doctrina*, inferior teaching, having a defective mode of truth, but useful, as are all the arts, for communicating something of truth to the uneducated.[97] Furthermore, arts are considered inferior to the extent that their practice involves greater implication in the body[98]—an odd view for someone who fought for the Aristotelian notion of psychophysical holism against the dominant Neoplatonic dualism.

It is in the thought of Bonaventure, Aquinas's contemporary, that beauty not only takes on the character of a transcendental, but takes center stage as the final transcendental. Balthasar considers Bonaventure to be the high point and last glorious development of a sapiential theology, of monastic wisdom, rooted in *gustus experimentalis*, an experiential tasting of ultimate things.[99] The root of his theology is an experience of being overpowered by the fullness of reality,[100] an ecstatic *excessus*.[101] The key concept is *expression*:[102] creatures express God because God internally expresses Himself in His Son,[103] and each creature expresses itself to perceivers as an interior light shining in the exterior.[104] Again according to Balthasar, of all the medieval thinkers, Bonaventure had a most positive assessment of sensory knowledge and delight, wherein our grounding and enduring experience of expression is found.[105]

Bonaventure adopts Augustine's discussion of *modus, species,* and *ordo,* which he understands as expressing respectively the existence, the relation to other things, and the relation to its end of any creature.[106] It is the treatment of *species* that is particularly helpful, for it concerns especially the relation of manifestness, on account of which one of the terms used for beauty is *speciositas*. *Species,* before it becomes the word we define as "type," is appearance, relation to apprehending power, manifestness, display.

Beauty is the optimum mode of display. On the one hand we have the manifestation of the ordered character of the sensorily given, on the other the shining through of signification, ultimately of the presence of the divine. The one factor concerns the delight in apprehension, the other the delight in judgment. Because of the Fall we tend to be caught up in the first and are unable to read the language of creation. Anticipating Galileo, but with an entirely different sense of "reading," for Bonaventure nature is a book written by God and addressed to human beings; Scripture teaches us how to read it,[107] but only the mystics are proper readers.

Being drawn out of ourselves by beauty at all levels, we experience the integration of the transcendentals, for "beauty encompasses every cause"[108] and is the seal on the transcendentals. Bonaventure associates unity with the Father, truth with the Son, and goodness with the Holy Spirit, but beauty is their circumincession.[109] Insofar as all things mirror the Trinitarian ground—as traces in subhuman things, as images in humans, and as likenesses in perfected humans—beauty shines forth in them. The centrality of beauty in Bonaventure generated his fear that the "sapiential" center, the experiential "tasting" of ultimate things, was disappearing from theology in favor of the analytical and constructive rationalism of the Scholastic movement. "Splendor" began to disappear from view. Rationalism drives out aesthetics.

So the medieval thinkers were preoccupied with beauty primarily as an attribute of the divine and as a manifestation of the divine in the beings we encounter. But they did very little to advance the understanding of artistic production or appreciation. God, and nature as the manifestation of God, were more fundamental to the concern of the philosophers, who operated under the aegis of theology.

## Response

The culture of the Middle Ages stood in a constant tension between what it saw as the fact and implications of God's own Incarnation and the tendency toward disembodiment and otherworldliness coming out of pagan gnostic or Neoplatonic "saints." Following Plato's ascent out of the Cave of *doxa*, Neoplatonism developed severe ascetic practices linked to a real contempt for "bodiliness." So as not to be undone by these pagan "saints," Christians tried to outdo them in the severity of their asceticism and in their expressions of contempt for "the flesh." So, one finds in monastic literature reference to "filthy matter" close by reference to "filthy womanhood." This was assimilated into a tendency to establish first-class and second-class citizenship in the church: first-class belonged to those who have "renounced the world" with vows of poverty, chastity, and obedience, concessionary second-class to those who accumulated property, married, and made their own basic decisions. Not the family but the monastery was viewed as the cradle of Christian existence.[110] Even in Thomas Aquinas, who established an Aristotelian—and thus psychophysically holistic—hermeneutic of the biblical tradition, the practice of the nonverbal arts was a lower form of existence precisely because they involved greater implication in the body.

However, as in Plotinus, ascetic practice provided interior distance that allowed the surface of the sensory world to be reconfigured as the face of the Beloved One, so in the monastic tradition, for the soul purified of its bodily desires, the world was sacramental, a theophany, a manifestation of the presence of God precisely in and through its beauty, as we find in Francis of Assisi's *The Canticle of Brother Sun*.[111] As we will see, even in that most powerful anti-Platonic, anti-Christian thinker Friedrich Nietzsche, a measure of asceticism is an essential moment in the deepening and integration of any human life.[112] Here belongs Augustine's observation regarding our all-too-common tendency to immerse ourselves in the immediate and lose sight of the whole. For Augustine, this is part of the danger of the attractiveness of sensory beauty. It can too often stand in the way of our apprehension of the total "poem of the universe." However, deep art can have the opposite effect than that of which he warns us: it can draw us in and through the transformation of sensory surface to a sense of the encompassing whole.

I should underscore here the central image of light and the related terms *splendor, radiance, brilliance, shining*. With regard to the human face, it is when the face is most expressive of the depth of the person's joy that we speak of a radiance. Here we should assimilate Plotinus's way of speaking of the whole of the sensory surface as "the face of the beloved" (i.e., of the Origin Whose depth that surface expresses for one sufficiently attuned). This is in line with Plato's observation that Beauty Itself and not just the proportionate beauty of beautiful things is visible, shining through visible things. Here too belongs the Judeo-Christian notion of the *kabod*, the *doxa*, the glory of God as something seen.[113] One way in which this is represented artistically is by the halo surrounding the head of the saint or by the golden background commonplace in sacred icons. Vincent van Gogh thought that the radiance and vibration of colors paralleled the function of the halo in displaying eternity in the work.[114] The beautiful sensory surface is both harmonically proportionate in its parts and expressive of an ultimate depth. This state of affairs corresponds to the founding structure of distinctively human nature as biologically rooted, metaphysically referred field of awareness. There is, then, a sense of completion—or of glimpses of completion—in the epiphany of the brilliant.

Here also belongs the Plotinian, Dionysian reading of Plato's "beyond *ousia*" as a feature of the One that bears witness to a depth of experience transcending the analytic and synthetic work of what we have come to call intellect. There is an experience of wholeness aligned with the fullness of Being that cannot be adequately expressed conceptually nor met with sensorily. Yet, evoking the Eros of "the whole soul," it leads to comprehensive, constructive speculative vision and artistic fabrication. The constraints of conceptual construction are expressed in Dionysian and Aquinian apophatic or "negative" theology, which is a theology of limits. It lays the groundwork for a rereading of the role of the perception and creation of beauty that points beyond rational construction to being apprehended by the mystery of wholeness.

Here again belongs Dionysius's notion of Being which Balthasar links with Aquinas's *esse commune* and calls "the space of the spiritual life."[115] It is a complete encompassment and depth enclosing and surpassing every actual creature. It corresponds to Heidegger's notion of Being. According to Balthasar, it disappeared from theology after Bonaventure. It became the abstract, indifferent, empty notion of Being, Nietzsche's "last trailing cloud of evaporating reality."[116] The way back into the ground of spiritual life, the ground of all rational construction, thus the ground of metaphysics and theology, is the way of meditative dwelling with the whole of one's being in the encompassing mystery that grants what is given for human existence. It is the arts that can lead us to that way of thinking.

There is another aspect of Plotinus's thought that merits appropriative development in aesthetics. Reversing Socrates' judgment in the *Republic* that art mirrors surface, Plotinus, we noted, claims that profound art reaches to the generative Idea. Following our interpretation of Aristotle, we might inquire in this context whether there are not two distinguishable kinds of intuition here: the grasp of ideal form and the grasp of the steps needed to give the form material existence. The latter is tied to the development of motor habits correlated with knowledge of the properties of the media. The sensuous surface thus has to be seen, not simply in terms of the sensory togetherness of colors or sounds, but as *expressive* of underlying

Ideas operating as creative forces. The high artist is one who can grasp the universal forces and give them expression in his reformation of sensuous surface. This is in the line of Aristotle's observation that art partly imitates, partly completes nature. It is, indeed, reflected again and again in the work of modern painters, sculptors, and poets. Buber speaks of the artist as faithful, not to appearance, but to being.[117] Kandinsky, like Plato and Hegel, sees our routine relationship to things as losing touch with their inner nature.[118] The abstract artist awakens us to the real core of things hidden in the everyday. Henry Moore spoke of the inner forces evoked by the sculptor.[119]

I should comment here on Plotinus's notion that the form of the sculpture is not in the stone but in the mind of the artist. This may be true of clay (and also of paint and sounds), but it is not true of stone or wood. Plotinus's view is in direct contrast to Michelangelo, for whom the form is in the marble and the task of the artist is to find and release it. In his pessimism regarding the embodied condition, Michelangelo was deeply influenced by Neoplatonism, yet as a working sculptor, he appreciated the formal character of his material. Indeed, it seems that the notion of form imprisoned in marble was for him a symbol of the human condition.[120]

The monastic spirit that in Bernard of Clairvaux protested against the sumptuousness of the churches still fed the spirit that generated those same churches. The sense of harmony and proportionality throughout the sacred buildings, of gracefulness exhibited by the Gothic vaults, of the subtlety and splendor of color and light in the stained-glass windows, of playfulness and dignity in the transformed shapes of nature and humankind that decorated the facades and occupied their niches, the sense of the calm but dynamic, serene but soaring sonority of the Gregorian chant that filled the dizziness of the ascending spaces: here was, in its own way, a culmination of aesthetic sensitivity and mastery of media. Everything conspired to draw the heart in and through the transformation of materials to a sense of the splendor of the encompassing divine. A whole worldview gains presence and embodiment in such glorious works of art. A definite conception of our relation to the whole fills the empty space of our founding orientation to the whole, placed solidly on the earth of our biologically mediated encounters, but fills it in a way that transcends the detachment and abstraction of its intellectualized expression. Here the arts function at the center of a lifeworld that answers to the deepest desires of the human heart.

The High Gothic cathedral was all light and verticality. It spontaneously drew the heart upward to look to the source of light. It contrasts with the strong horizontality of the Greek temple and Wright's notion of the building belonging to the earth. Plutarch claimed that we learn speech from other humans and silence from the gods.[121] Silence, entering into building, opens us to what is above. Sacred architecture mediates the above and the below, setting our aspiration to the sacred onto the earth.

But one must ask what the medieval philosophizing theologians added intellectually to the understanding of this lifeworld beyond that presented by the pagan forebears. Practically everything said in these matters is a repetition of what the pagans have said. Only the ontological context is deepened, and that is significant gain indeed, though not directly for aesthetic theory.

# V

# KANT

ONCE ON IMMANUEL KANT's tombstone stood the words, "The starry skies above, the moral law within."[1] They are taken from the closing paragraphs of his *Critique of Practical Reason*, the second work in his critical project. The beginning of the quotation reads: "Two things fill the heart with ever new and increasing admiration and awe *[Bewunderung und Ehrfurcht]*. . . ."[2] The starry skies above are the object and model for mechanistic science. In Newtonian mechanics the laws that govern the stars govern all terrestrial motions as well. It was such knowing that furnished the exemplar of knowing analyzed in the first part of Kant's critical project: *The Critique of Pure Reason*.[3]

To determine the nature, limits, and interrelations of human powers, Kant attempted a systematic critical assessment, in turn, of the capacities of knowledge in the theoretical order—of willing-action in the moral order, and of feeling linked to judgment in the order of aesthetics and organics. "The moral law within" is the object of the second critique, which concludes with the sentiment of admiration and awe cited above. In the third critique, *The Critique of Judgment*, awe before the starry skies combines with awe before moral law to produce the feeling of the sublime.[4] In the presence of the overwhelming size of the starry skies we experience the dual emotion of sensing our own insignificance—hence the component of *Furcht*, or fear—and overcoming it with a sense of the sublimity of our own minds and their moral destiny—hence the component of *Ehre*, or honor, in *Ehrfurcht*, or awe. Checked initially by the sense of insignificance, powerful vital emotion bursts forth in the feeling of awe, which entails an emotional uplift. Among other things, the *Critique of Judgment* focuses attention on the sublime, the experience of which underlies the entire critical project. Awe before the starry skies and awe before the moral law combine in the aesthetic experience of the sublime. Like Plato's, Kant's philosophy is carried by the aesthetic.

## Critique of Pure Reason

In the first critique Kant introduced what has been called "the Copernican revolution in thought."[5] In astronomy Copernicus introduced the first revolution, contending that the spontaneous and ever-verifiable view of the motion of the sun around the earth is an appearance set up by the position of the observer and that the true view is the motion of the earth both around the sun and on its own axis. This accounts for the apparent view by situating it within the new context—an extremely important general methodological point.

Kant made a similar move with regard to the nature of human thought in general: he made the "transcendental turn," transcending or going beyond the traditional focus on objects to which humans have to adjust in knowing, and attending to the conditions in the knower to which appearing things have to adjust in order to appear and which thus limit our cognitive access to things.[6] He is guided here by the hypothetical distinction between an intellect that knows things exhaustively because its thinking makes them to be (an *intellectus archetypicus*, namely, God)—analogous to an artisan who in the practical order knows the form of the things he fabricates because such knowing is the origin of the form—and the human intellect, which, in the theoretical order, is receptively related to the impact of things upon our sensibility.[7] Because of the latter, we have to build up over time—over millennia—our knowledge of things. Hence Kant's fundamental distinction between *noumena* (correlate to Greek *nous*, intellect), which are things-in-themselves as completely transparent intuitive projects of a hypothetical divine, creative knowing and *phenomena* (from the Greek *phainomai*, I appear), which are things-for-us as ob-jects of finite, bodily situated, and thus discursively knowing sub-jects. Things that appear not only set conditions for our knowledge but have conditions set for their appearance by the structure of human receptive knowing.

We begin the knowing process in the mode of sensibility, passively being affected by things. Colors, sounds, smells, tastes, heat and cold, texture, and pressure are effects in us of what are in themselves physical transformations. Thus light, shining on a visible object, is partially absorbed, partially reflected; propagated through space, it enters the eye by passing through the pupil and the lens; it projects an inverted image of the object on the rods and cones of the retina, setting up electronic impulses that are carried by the optic nerve to the visual center in the back of the brain, where the color pattern is effected in the field of awareness. We thus begin our experience, not with things "out there," but with their effects "in" ourselves.[8] It was modern scientific experiments in physics and physiology that led to this view.

So the first conditions that have to be met for objects to appear are determined by the physiologically receptive apparatus that sets up certain thresholds within the field of sensory awareness governed by biological need. The apparatus, together with the incoming impulses, produce color as a subjective experience. There is no color apart from this process, though there are things and wave propagation—or so we think. But as Berkeley pointed out, if the only access we have to things and wave propagation is through subjectively experienced sensory qualities, these things are as subject related as are the sensory qualities.

Now there is also no immediate appearance of color apart from the experience of spatial location. And every spatial location is experienced in such a way as to be located in turn within an indeterminate spread of space beyond the horizon experienced in any given appearance of, for example, a color pattern. Space as a whole is co-given by an immediate intuition as the context for experienced spatial locations.[9] Similarly, nothing appears, whether outwardly or inwardly, except it appears in time, which is likewise co-given with any experienced temporal span as indeterminately exceeding what is experienced in time past, time present, and time to come.[10] The intuitions of space and time as invariant *forms of sensibility* are immediately co-given with—for Kant actually projected on—any experienced object. They are something like rose-colored glasses, which necessitate that everything we see appears rosy. The difference is that the forms of sensibility are inborn, like having rose-colored lenses in our eyeballs by nature. For Kant this accounts for the peculiarity of geometric demonstration that must have overwhelmed the Greeks when they discovered it. One can know a priori, without looking at all the instances, that certain theorems are necessarily true of *all* like objects in space, whenever and wherever we find them. One can further determine, without looking at *any* instances, that certain theorems follow, via the axioms of the geometric system, from other theorems with absolute necessity and can be subsequently observed to hold empirically. Plato thought that this introduced us to a noumenal realm of universal Forms according to which such objects have been made. Kant suggests that it introduces us to the inner optics of our own mental forms, within which every object has to appear.[11] Geometry is human and not at all divine knowing. It unpacks the implications of the forms of our mind. "Whenever" and "wherever" are a priori: we live out of relation to the whole of space and time.

There is a second level of a priori forms or lenses through which the world comes into explicit human focus for us. Space and time are empty as encompassing but individual wholes. But the second level of forms are empty as abstract universals: they are the categories of the understanding.[12] They furnish the principles for sorting and ordering the constant subjective flux of sensations into an objective and thus in-principle intersubjective world of coherent and enduring objects. The mind is not simply passive to sensations: it works them up into a world of meaningful objects through the employment of its innate principles.

In developing his system of categories Kant takes his cue from formal logic, which does not belong to the character of things but to the way the mind sets about thinking about things. It furnishes mechanisms for working out implications and inferences that, apart from the materials they are given to work with as starting points, yield only validity and not truth. Truth depends on the character of the starting points. And so we need a logic supplementary to formal logic, which is the logic of implication and inference; we need a transcendental logic of reference that yields the experiential starting points. Kant takes the table of types of judgment from formal logic and develops from them a table of categories of reference.[13] Basically they are arranged around the general headings *quantity, quality, relation,* and *mode,* which will appear throughout Kant's work, furnishing the basis for a systematic inventory of aspects of whatever objects he will treat. The most important aspects are found under the heading of *relation*: substance-accidents, cause-effect, and reciprocity. All objects appear, in and through the variations of their sensory accidents, as relatively independent and enduring functional wholes, as substances linked in causal chains of antecedence and consequence, and as involved in reciprocal relations with their contemporaries. Affording principles for sorting and organizing our sensory experience, such categories are always filled in our wakeful life.

In addition to these transcendental concepts there are empirical concepts like dog, tree, and cloud. In both cases there is the contrast of the sensory individuals and the universal concepts. For Kant the bridge between them is afforded by the imagination—"an art hidden in the depth of the soul"—which provides examples of empirical concepts and schemata of the categories. In the latter function such schematizing always involves some temporal feature: substance is endurance through time, causality antecedence and consequence in time, and so on.[14]

Through the operation of the categories via the imagination, experience comes to take on the character of a single whole of phenomena, of appearances. If all appearances are appearances *of* something—albeit for Kant an unknowable thing-in-itself—they are also always appearances *to* someone. In some way co-perceived or ap-perceived with whatever appears and yet ever transcending the sphere of objects and the formal and categorical conditions making objectivity possible, there is what Kant calls the transcendental unity of apperception, the "I think" that must accompany any representation.[15] It is always an "I" that takes up things through the functions described.

Beyond the categories employed by the "I think," there is a third level of a priori forms of the mind, corresponding to our reference to being as reference to the totality: the ideas of reason.[16] Kant uses the term *Vernunft* (reason), in contrast to *Verstand* (understanding employing the categories), to indicate the drive toward totality as the background or horizon against or within which all experience occurs. Based on three different ways in which we are related to the totality, reason operates with three totalizing ideas: the ideas of World, Soul, and God. The idea of World, or the cosmological idea, constitutes the horizon of all our attempts to build up and extend our understanding of what is given from without. It is a lure that draws us on in an ever-broadening but never-ending process toward completion of our knowledge of the cosmos. The idea of Soul functions in the same way regarding our attempts to understand our inward life, the life of consciousness. Finally, the idea of God functions as the Plotinian One, ground of the differentiation of experience into outward and inward, as that which, if known, would unify all our experience. It would make the universe to be a uni-verse, turning the plurality of experiences toward unity, displaying the ultimate coherence of all things. Contrary to the categories of understanding, which are always filled in ordinary experience, Ideas of Reason can never be filled by any experience or concept.

Kant's analysis begins with the streaming plurality of sensations as the lowest level; it terminates in the idea of the unity of the whole in the One.

In between, functioning in relation to the lowest level of enduring plurality in sensory givenness, we have the unfolding of more comprehensive levels of unification employed by the "I think" via the work of the imagination: the forms of space and time, the categories of understanding, and the ideas of reason under the One Being. This enables Kant to account for the various sciences that have emerged and developed since the time of the Greeks. Geometry, as the first science, has its origin in the a priori form of space; and mathematics in general unfolds different modes of possible spatial and temporal interrelation.[17] Formal logic emerges from analysis of the structures of implication and inference operative in geometry but extended to all experience. Physics operates out of a combination of mathematics with the categories, especially the notion of causality as necessary sequence of antecedents and consequents. Kant understands causality here in the manner of Newtonian science, where the whole state of the universe at a given time determines the whole state at a subsequent time to yield the Clockwork Universe. It is a world of universal determinism.[18] These stable and developing sciences clue us in to the responsible use of the mind in coming to know. Such use consists in unpacking and interrelating the forms of the mind with the sensory appearance of things. In this Kant insists that "thoughts without [sensory] intuition are empty; [sensory] intuitions without concepts are blind."[19] Only their interrelation yields responsible knowledge.

Then there is metaphysics, the putative queen of the sciences, which claims to know the fundamental principles of being, to be able to leap over the horizons established through patient work in other disciplines and to operate in the region of pure reason. Looking over the history of metaphysical thought and comparing it with formal logic, mathematics, and mathematical physics, we see that metaphysics, far from presenting itself like they do as a stable and developing science, appears as one great battlefield of contending factions.[20] Kant attempts to show that we are so related to the totality that there is no way of resolving the fundamental conflicting views that necessarily emerge from our position in relation to the whole. Thought that moves in this region necessarily generates irresolvable antinomies: for example, that the world had to have a beginning, as Bonaventure for one argued, since, among other things, there would have to be in any now an actual infinity of immortal souls that is being added to constantly;[21] or that the world cannot have a beginning, the opposite of which Aristotle called ridiculous, since the eternity of time follows from the nature of time as moving synthesis of the before and after in the now.[22] Aquinas recognized the antinomy and claimed that the issue was in principle undecidable by reason and can only be known by revelation.[23] Kant goes the round of such antinomies.[24]

Kant then attacks the alleged crown of metaphysics, the proofs for the existence of God. He discusses three possibilities: one is based on a particular experience—that of goal directedness; a second is based on experience in general; and a third is based on abstraction from all experience—which he calls the teleological, the cosmological, and the ontological proofs respectively.[25] The cosmological proof, if it proves, proves only a first cause without being able to determine its features. The teleological proof, again if it proves, proves that the causation involved entails intelligence, which—as Hume noted—could be plural, demonic, or value-indifferent, given what is given in experience. For the first two to work as proofs of an infinitely perfect God, Kant claims they need to invoke the ontological argument, an argument first advanced by Anselm and here given the name by Kant. It is based on the logic of the notion of being *(ontos)*. The notion of perfection, of fullness of being, is that than which no greater can be conceived; that which is outside merely being thought about is greater than what is merely thought about; hence the notion of perfection or the fullness of being contains the note of existing beyond merely being thought about.[26] But, Kant observes, as did Aquinas before him,[27] that this attempt supposes an unwarranted move from the necessity of thought to the necessity of existence. Hence all the proofs advanced ultimately do not prove in any necessary way but at best provide ways of making final sense of things. They are, in contemporary terms, hermeneutic rather than metaphysical.

The upshot of this analysis is that in this life our cognitive faculties are not made for insight into things-in-themselves. Responsible thinking resists the temptation to eschew patient, cooperative work in the established sciences and to leap beyond the horizon to the ultimate in the employment of "pure reason" (i.e., reason operating without the check of experience).[28] Our knowing is and will remain, in Nietzsche's terms, "human, all too human."

## Critique of Practical Reason

Cognitive experience is not our only experience. We also have the experience of being obligated, of having responsibility thrust upon us and of realizing that we are able either to assume the obligation or to abandon it.

This obviously raises the problem of how this is possible, given the absolute determinism of the Clockwork Universe. Kant refers to the experience of freedom involved in moral action as "the sole noumenal fact."[29] The entire analysis of the first critique yielded a world of phenomena, of appearance made possible by the character of our faculties. If the world *appears* as determined, that still leaves open the possibility that noumena, things-in-themselves, might not be so determined.[30] And our moral experience presents us with a demand for freedom as responsible self-determination.

Now this relation between freedom and obligation may seem unusual to most people, who see freedom as the ability to do what they like. But what we like is determined by antecedent conditions, beginning with native physiology and psychology and interplaying with cultural shaping. Liking is a welling up of feeling that can be explained deterministically. The experience of obligation awakens us to the possibility of not being determined by our spontaneous likes and dislikes but of determining ourselves over against them, of shaping and directing them through choices based on judgment.[31]

On the other hand, what is required for genuine moral behavior are criteria for assessing our own likes and dislikes as well as the obligations that a given society imposes on its members. Here Kant introduces what he calls the categorical imperative, which he contrasts with a hypothetical imperative.[32] The latter takes the form of an if-then proposition: *If* you wish to achieve X, *then* do Y,—basically, If you wish to be happy do X and avoid Y. By contrast, the categorical imperative poses no conditions but sets an absolute obligation. It takes several forms in Kant's articulation, three of which are particularly illuminating. The first, "So act that your principle for action can be made a norm for all humankind,"[33] is rooted in the universal orientation of the mind. The universalizability of our maxims is what is called for here. The second formulation, "Treat humanity, whether in yourselves or in others, always as an end and not simply as a means,"[34] looks to that same capacity to operate in terms of the universal (which he here calls our humanity) as significantly more than a mere means to the efficient gratification of our appetites. It is this which gives an inalienable dignity to every human being. The third formulation, "So act as if you were legislating for a kingdom of ends,"[35] looks to the togetherness of all humans as ends in themselves. Worked into the concrete, this involves the obligation both to the ongoing rational development of our faculties and to ongoing benevolence toward other persons in assisting their development.[36] Such principles allow us both to put our appetites in order and to judge the obligations laid upon individuals by a given social order, for the cannibal might feel obligated to eat the heart of his enemy and might experience extreme feelings of guilt if he chose not to, even though the practice involves the most extreme instance of treating a human being as a mere means and in no way as an end.

Morality involves not just acting *in accord with* such principles, it also involves acting *because of* such principles. One could, for example, act honestly and, like Ben Franklin, consider such action as the best policy; but one could also do so, not because of the moral obligation involved, but because people will trust you and therefore give you better business deals so you can make more money and thus gratify yourself more effectively. We might also follow moral rules, not because they are what we as humans ought to do, but because we wish to obtain some reward or to avoid some punishment.

But to operate in terms of such principles is to be involved in a struggle with our appetites and with those who refuse so to operate. Often those who strive to live up to such principles encounter great difficulty and are far from experiencing happy fulfillment, whereas those who fail or refuse often experience ease and contentment. For Kant this argues for postulating (not conclusively proving) the immortality of the soul so that there could be a coincidence between happiness and deservedness to be happy met with so infrequently in this life. Such coincidence Kant calls the *summum bonum*, in an anthropological transformation of the medieval concept, which applied to seeing God Himself.[37] Achievement of the human *summum bonum* also furnishes the basis for arguing to a Being Who can read the innermost movements of the human heart to see whether one has acted inwardly *because* of the moral order and not simply externally *in accord with* that order. It demands something approaching omniscience and omnipotence together with a sense of ultimate justice in One Who would be able to bring about the required coincidence. Beyond a first principle or a finite, plural, and morally indifferent cause or causes, the moral order implies all that we have come to recognize as God: omniscient, omnipotent, all-just creator and judge.[38] Freedom in relation to the deterministic World, the immortality of the Soul, and a moral God, inaccessible in a purely theoretical way, return as conditions for the moral order. Our shipwreck in the theoretical order points to the real purpose of our faculties: moral action in this world.[39]

The analysis of the first two critiques brings into focus a problem to which I called attention earlier, one of the deepest problems confronting reflection on the place of science in the modern world: the problem of the relation between determinism and freedom. Kant presents us here with two separated realms: determinism operates at the level of phenomena, of things appearing under conditions set by our faculties; freedom as rational self-determination implies transcendence of the phenomenal order. The question is how they are related. It is the third critique that attends to that interrelation.[40]

## Critique of Judgment

We reach the heart of the present exposition, the work in which the felt tonality, the aesthetic feeling of awe that governs the critical project is given its due. Its title does not immediately suggest its contents. The introduction presents judgment as the link between the universal concept and the experienced individual, a function previously assigned to the imagination. Kant goes on to distinguish two forms of judgment: determinate judgment and reflective judgment.[41] In the determinate judgment the universal is given and judgment subsumes the individual under it, as in the general operation of the categories as fundamental a priori; in the reflective judgment, the individual is given and the one judging seeks the universal under which that individual can be placed. It is reflective judgment that is Kant's focus here, and that in two specially chosen domains: the aesthetic and the teleological.

In the first critique Kant presented the principles for establishing objectivity in experience, for moving from a subjective "rhapsody of impressions"—presumably the situation of the infant—to an intersubjective world of coherence and consistency.[42] But those principles provide nothing of the *kinds* of objects that can so appear. For that we have to look to the regular collocations of sensations within the conditions of objectivity. When we pay attention to what is thus given, two orders jut into prominence: aesthetic objects (whether works of art or things of nature, whether evoking the experience of beauty or of sublimity) and living forms in their logically hierarchical relations of genera and species.[43]

The key experience is our awareness of our ability to transform nature through concepts, which is Kant's definition for art in general, whether that of the plow maker or of the sculptor.[44] It seems not accidental but fitting that the discussion of art appears in the center of the work, with the notion of genius occupying the exact center because this provides the analogue for a series of reflective judgments that attempt to make comprehensive sense out of what is given in experience.[45] For Kant they amount to projecting onto nature itself our experience of operating according to preconceived goals. Thus when we attend to living things, we see that, though they cannot violate the laws of mechanics, they operate in a way that we can only understand on an analogy with our own transformative activity. Thus we introduce, in addition to mechanism, the notion of teleology, or operation in terms of a prior conception *(logos)* of a goal *(telos)* we seek. Living forms display themselves *as if* they were operating on some such grounds when they form themselves through the articulation of their organs as instruments for the realization of vital purposes and when they search outside themselves for food, drink, and mate.[46]

In the second book of his *Physics* Aristotle makes the same move.[47] From an analysis of artefaction as externally imposed form caused by an artisan operating on some material in terms of a preconceived goal, Aristotle internalizes formal, final, and efficient causes in the psyche, the basic formal and self-forming principle of living beings orchestrating material elements to suit its natural purposes.[48] Kant's contention is that, though this is our only way to make sense out of living forms, it is a projection, not an insight into the metaphysical constitution of things. Organisms act *as if* unconsciously they were operating like we do consciously. (Since *logos* suggests conscious conception, instead of teleo-*logy*, theoretical biologists today have introduced the term *teleonomy*, where *nomos* refers, not to a concept, but to a law of goal seeking.)[49] Kant thereby moves us both backward, behind modern mechanistic physics, to an earlier view of nature, and forward to the biological views of the twentieth century. Thereby he also points out a large region in which mechanisms are naturally taken up into purposes, smoothing the way for thinking of human self-determining freedom as able to operate in the universe described in physics by subsuming its mechanisms under human purposes.

The second region where Kant projects human purposiveness is the aesthetic region. In beautiful forms and in situations evoking the feeling of the sublime, it is as if nature were so arranged as to bring about the peculiar feelings that indicate the presence of such forms and situations.[50] Of course, in the case of artistic forms, nature *is* rearranged for that purpose, only in that case the artist does not operate entirely in the same way as the plow maker. The production of artistic forms requires genius, the gift through which, as Kant has it, "nature gives the rule to art."[51] It is his or her inborn nature even more than it is mastery of certain knowable techniques that makes the artist. In really inspired art, the artist has no awareness of the wellsprings of his or her novel ideas. Here again, as in the case of natural beauty, it is as if nature, working through the artist as the source of inspiration, had the purpose of bringing about the peculiar aesthetic feelings. Indeed, for Kant it is inspired art that sensitizes us to the beauties of nature.[52] It is as if through the artist nature is teaching us to appreciate her own beauties. We retain something of this insight when we refer to a scene or a person as being "pretty as a picture." Kant thus speaks of the whole aesthetic region as exhibiting "purposiveness without a purpose"—that is, appearing as if it had a purpose without our being able definitively to assign a real purpose, as we can in ordinary human activity. So the general concept arrived at by reflective judgment for thinking both the organic and the aesthetic regions is "purposiveness."[53] Pleasure itself—aesthetic or otherwise—Kant understands as the sign that a purpose has been fulfilled.[54] That is what gives unity to what otherwise seem to be two unrelated regions.

Besides the regions of natural organic form and aesthetic form, there is a third region where Kant deals with purposiveness. Considering the whole of nature as a purposive system, Kant finally projects the notion of God as a divine artist operating through ideas of species and ultimately through the overarching moral idea, creating an arena for the development of human faculties through the work of culture under the moral law. The notion of an ultimate "technic of nature" in a divine moral Artisan will thus draw the whole critical work of reason into unity with itself.[55] But, note well, it is only in the mode of "as if." This is the way to make sense out of the whole of our experience, but it does not guarantee that this is the way things as a whole finally are. We are still in the realm of phenomena. Our awareness is always "human, all too human."[56]

In the aesthetic region Kant focuses on two distinguishable objects: the beautiful and the sublime. I will deal with each in turn.

## The Beautiful

Kant's analysis of the beautiful exhibits two basic movements that are clarified by his distinction between free and dependent beauty.[57] Free beauty is pure (i.e., abstracted from all admixture of concepts); dependent beauty involves a relation to concepts. Kant begins with an analysis of free or pure beauty, separating beauty from features with which it is for the most part mixed and therefore often confused. There is the empiricist confusion of beauty with what simply produces agreeable sensations; there is the rationalist confusion of beauty with perfection, whether physical or moral, measured by some conceptual and therefore intellectual standard.[58] While, more often than not, agreeable sensations and concepts of what a given object ought to be accompany beautiful objects, for Kant these features do not constitute their beauty. We have then first to separate out beauty from its usual accompaniments and view it by itself; then we have to fold it back into its relation to its usual accompaniments. Pure beauty is trivial beauty, yielding only aesthetic surface; it is literally super-ficial. Kant uses as examples of pure beauty flowers, bird plumage, and seashells in the natural order and arabesque drawings (wallpaper design) as well as musical fantasias (without words) in the artistic order.[59] Nontrivial beauty is dependent beauty, requiring the unity of aesthetic surface with concepts expressing something more significant, especially in what Kant will term the Ideal of Beauty (of which more later).[60]

Kant begins his aesthetic with an analysis of free beauty. He arranges his analysis around the four basic genera of logical judgments I have mentioned earlier: quality, quantity, relation, and mode. Schopenhauer considers this exercise a procrustean bed, where the given has to be either stretched or chopped off to get it to fit into the forms of the first critique.[61] Jean-François Lyotard suggests that the exercise is intended to show the uselessness of the direct application of the categories: the aesthetic given escapes the logic of the categories and produces "logical monsters."[62]

Beginning with *quality*, he notes that the judgment of taste involved in the perception of the beautiful is based on a feeling of pleasure and is thus subjective. But aesthetic pleasure is a peculiar sort. Our bodily pleasures are what he calls "interested": feeling has to do here with how the object can be used.[63] As Aristotle noted, the hound loves the look of the hare, but only because it is potential food.[64] And whatever pleasure we might find in the good is likewise "interested," though in a different way. Aesthetic pleasure is, by contrast, "disinterested," a feature of a state of mind in which we attend, Kant says, not to "existence," but only to the sheer appearance of the object.[65] By the term *existence* Kant presumably here refers to such features as the process of the coming to be of the object or the causal consequences that follow from the reality of what appears as well as the real substructure of the object. In the case of food, one of the features of existence is that it will be consumed to nourish the body; in the case of an art work—for example, a painting—there is the chemical composition of the gesso and paint as well as the nature of the canvas and the support of the stretcher. None of this is a matter of direct aesthetic concern. Aesthetically we contemplate the beauty of an object's display without concern for any such "existential" features and therefore "what we can get out of it." We thus obtain "disinterested pleasure." One could profitably consider here the difference between an aesthetic and an erotic satisfaction in attending to nude statuary. Detached from the compulsion of our own bodily appetites and from all desire to subsume the object under our projects, we are able to give the object what Kant calls free favoring, treating it for its own sake. Here one needs to distinguish a focus on one's own feelings from a focus on certain features of the object. Hence, even though distinctively aesthetic feeling is the first criterion of the presence of the beautiful,[66] Kant will swing attention from the peculiar pleasure involved in aesthetic perception to the object of such perception. He will attend to what he calls the "form" of the object.[67]

The feeling involved is variously described as one of harmony, of enlivening, and of free play—all attributed to the peculiar relation between imagination and understanding.[68] *Harmony* by itself suggests something static—and this seems to be the way Schopenhauer was to understand it. But *enlivening* and *free play* suggest something more dynamic. Unfortunately, Kant does very little to elaborate on these features. In his discussion of art, he notes that a symbol creates an indeterminate set of associations governed by their harmonizing with the disposition proper to a given form, so that the mind is set in motion to move freely among these associated images and—presumably—among the concepts that might be associated with them. There would then be a certain creative moment even in the reception of the beautiful object, so that, as one commentator suggests, the meaning of free play is creativity.[69]

The judgments listed under quality in logic are affirmative, negative, and infinite, where *infinite* combines the affirmative and the negative, negating the negation to arrive at a new affirmation.[70] Perhaps that is what disinterested satisfaction involves: the positivity of interested satisfaction from the point of view of the perceiver involves the negation of the object's independence; but the aesthetic stance of "unconstrained favoring" negates that negation, allows the object to present itself "for its own sake" and thus provides a higher level of positive subjective satisfaction, not limited by the object's subordination to need.

Under the heading of *quantity*, Kant speaks of the judgment of taste as providing a "subjectively universal" satisfaction.[71] A satisfaction focused on the beautiful appearance for its own sake and not generated by any individual interest on the part of the viewing subject raises one above the peculiarities of one's private subjectivity, but not in the way a concept does. The universality involved is not objective but subjective: it lays a claim upon all human beings to respond to the beautiful object, which is itself not a universal but a distinctively individual object.[72]

The formal logical categories under the heading of quantity are: universal, particular, and individual, where, once more, the third synthesizes the first two.[73] A particular merely instantiates the type that is a universal over against the particulars that fall under it. An individual is such that in it the type is not only instantiated but fully realized. In the aesthetic object, the universality of the claim of beauty has a peculiar fulfillment, making the beautiful object a distinctive individuality. Furthermore, Kant focuses on the universality of the claim that the distinctive individuality of the aesthetic object makes: that all should respond to it appreciatively. Here we must distinguish between "I like it" and "It is beautiful." The former might refer to the merely agreeable, and regarding that one might say: "Different strokes for different folks." But the latter appeals to all observers.[74]

In connection with this Kant distinguishes the charm of particular sensory features and the form exhibited by the beautiful object. Compare a melody played on a violin with the same played on a tuba. The differing instrumental timbres might appeal differently to different people, depending on what pleases them. More, or even most, people might prefer the violin. But it is not the sensory mode as such that, according to Kant, constitutes the beautiful; it is the *form* of the melody. To prefer the sound of the tuba to that of the violin is not a defect in the perceiver; but to fail to appreciate the beauty of the form *is* considered a defect. The beautiful is such that all *ought* to appreciate it. The sensory charms, which strike different persons differently, merely serve to bring into focus the form, which all should learn to appreciate as the sameness in the difference.

It is in this context that Kant also disallows the entry of an explicit concept into the aesthetic judgment qua aesthetic. As we noted in the first moment, the judgment of taste with regard to the beautiful is based on a peculiar feeling, not on a concept, not even the concept of perfection, otherwise we would have an intellectual and not an aesthetic judgment.[75] But for Kant there is ultimately an *implicit* concept involved, since the judgment is an interplay of the universal and the particular.[76] In fact, for Kant it is the judgment that generates the aesthetic feeling.[77] As I indicated previously, that feeling he identifies as one of harmony in the free play of the relation between imagination and understanding.[78] That relation is the form of judgment, the form of the togetherness of the faculties required for any judgment: imagination to synthesize the manifold of sensations, under-standing to provide the concept for that manifold.[79]

There is not a little ambiguity in Kant's formulations. On the one hand, in the initial moment, the judgment of the beautiful is based on a feeling; on the other hand, the feeling is based on a judgment. Judgment involves a certain detachment, a holding one's own in the face of the given, and yet the experience of the beautiful involves being taken by the form of the object, which demands unconstrained favoring. On the one hand, the experience involved is that of the form of the judgment; on the other, the form of the object. The whole region involves a certain tension of oppo-sites. What is involved in each of the features indicated is the reciprocal emergence of judgment and feeling, of detachment and attachment, of the form of the judgment and the form of the beautiful thing. But Kant gives the priority to the judgment because it alone releases us from "con-strained favoring" and allows us to let the object be itself.

Free play suggests not being bound by the ordinary operation of judg-ment. Kant claims that an aesthetic idea gives rise to much thought with-out being fully determined to one thought.[80] A beautiful work is overdetermined: it sets the cognitive faculties in peculiar motion to play within certain limits. This relation of free play is the ground of the claim to universality, for it is that which makes any knowing and any distinctively human communication possible: that imagination as the faculty of gather-ing up sensations harmonizes with our faculty of providing universals fit for understanding such a gathering. According to Kant, the feeling of the a priori form of the judgment as the harmonic relation between imagina-tion and understanding is what is evoked by and reciprocally tied to the coming into focus of the form of the beautiful sensible thing, produced in works of art through aesthetic ideas.[81] And just as Kant speaks of the form as the play of figures in space or of sounds in time,[82] so the form of the judgment to which it corresponds involves the free play of the cognitive faculties. Play, whether of figures or of cognitive faculties, indicates a free-dom from domination by purposes, appetitive or moral. The aesthetic is a space of fully free activity, though finally it is tied in several ways to our ul-timately moral destiny. But it is the reflective distance afforded by this rela-tion between the universal and the particular that pulls us out of the merely private subjectivity of the life of the senses and allows for the uni-versal communicability of aesthetic feelings.[83]

Eventually Kant identifies the implicit concept involved in the judg-ment of the beautiful as that of the supersensuous ground of experience (presumably the same as the notion of the noumenon, or thing-in-itself), an indeterminate concept of reason that can never be filled.[84] Indeed, it is that concept that gets differentiated, by reason of the relation of exterior and interior involved in all experience, into the ideas of World and Soul on the one hand and the idea of God as ground of their relationship on the other. There is then a reference to the noumenal that provides the peculiar attraction of the beautiful, though for Kant, and contrary to Plato, this noumenal cannot itself appear. And since our fundamental relation to the noumenal is moral, Kant ultimately aligns the beautiful with the moral, not as a means thereto but as a symbol thereof.[85] The beautiful has its own constitution, and it is only when we attend to it as such that it can function as a symbol. Thus even colors come to take on the qualities of human action: bold, soft, stately, and so on.

The presence of the indeterminate concept of the supersensible as the horizon of all human wakefulness allows Kant to solve what he calls the antinomy of taste, which arises when we reflect on the aesthetic[86] One side of that antinomy is expressed in the often-quoted proverb *De gustibus non disputandum* (regarding taste there ought not to be dispute).[87] The other side of the antinomy is the factual dispute that goes on throughout the ages. Insofar as the dispute claims to rest on determinate concepts from which one could rationally argue, for Kant dispute is beside the point, for the judgment of taste rests on a feeling and not a determinate concept. Nonetheless, by reason of its alignment with the indeterminate concept of the supersensible, taste generates dispute because there is a universal claim made in the attribution of beauty. The *de gustibus* proverb applies to the agreeable, to our attention to sensuous charm rather than to beautiful form. Beautiful form evokes the harmony of the cognitive faculties and refers, beyond this, to the indeterminate concept of the supersensuous, which receives determination through the moral order.

Dependent beauty ties the beautiful thing to determinate concepts of what a thing ought to be and thus to the notion of perfection. In this connection Kant introduces the so-called Ideal of Beauty, which he locates in the depiction of the idealized form of the human being as morally expressive.[88] In this case the beauty of the form is tied to its expression of something not directly perceptible by the senses, a state of mind. When the moral state of mind finds a bodily display in a form that itself constitutes a norm for the species, we have the Ideal of Beauty. State of mind and state of sensory display have to be proportionate to one another for ideal beauty to be realized. However, for Kant, as distinct from Plato, the moral state of mind is not itself beautiful but is only said to be so by metaphoric analogy. The Ideal of Beauty is the result of a conceptual amalgam of two distinct but related regions: sensory exteriority and moral inwardness.[89]

In discussing the expressive fusion of a moral state of mind with a species norm, Kant suggests that one arrives at such a norm—remember it is a norm of display—by a kind of superimposition of experienced forms of the same kind until an average form is delineated. It suggests a type, an aesthetic idea with which nature itself can be thought to operate in producing the inexperienceable substructure in the thing that will display itself in approximation to that norm.[90] Given Kant's description here, the art that carries the ideal most fully would be sculpture and, to a lesser extent because limited to two-dimensional presentation, painting. The other art forms would seem to be excluded.

In his analysis of the judgment of the beautiful, under the genus of *relation*, Kant refers to the feature of what he calls "purposiveness without a purpose," something we have already considered: beautiful objects appear when the perception of their form brings about the free play between imagination and understanding, *as if* nature had produced beautiful forms for that purpose.[91] It is helpful to recall the categories Kant located in the first critique under relation: substance-accidents, cause-effect, reciprocity.[92] The notion of purpose gathers them up in the notion of an organism, governed by purpose, reciprocally cause and effect of itself, whose accidents, caused by the substance, cause the substance itself to become actual.[93] That notion, as we have already noted, locates the beautiful, together with the organic, in the larger view of purposiveness.

Under the genus of *mode* Kant calls attention to the peculiar necessity attending the judgment of taste. Under the logical genus of mode are the categories of actuality, possibility, and necessity, together with their opposites.[94] For Kant it is possible for any representation to be bound up with pleasure. A pleasant representation actually produces pleasure. But an aesthetic representation has a necessary reference to pleasure.[95] There is an appeal to a kind of necessity in the form of an obligation laid upon all humankind to attend appreciatively to what can be designated as beautiful. Being able to do this involves the development of a *sensus communis*, a common sense.[96] This common sense is to be distinguished, on the one hand, from the kind of understanding common to a given community regarding proper operation in that community (better called common understanding). On the other hand, it is different than the Scholastic *sensus communis*, the single root of the sense powers that allows us to integrate their differing objects into a single phantasm, making possible the appearance of a given individual or type in and through the multiple perspectives afforded by the operations of each of the sense powers—a notion derived from Aristotle.[97] As contrasted with common understanding and Scholastic common sense, an aesthetic common sense is a kind of ideal to be striven for: a capacity to judge beautiful objects built up through attention to the classical models that have emerged and stood the test of time by their continued ability to draw the attention of sensitive and reflective individuals throughout the ages.[98]

This does not mean that the past furnishes the unalterable set of rules for judgment and operation in the present, as certain neoclassical critics would have it. Proper attention to the classics involves the ability to contact the same sources of judgment and activity that the original geniuses contacted in the production of their works. They teach us how to see and, if we also are gifted with genius, to create works that are both original and exemplary.[99] For Kant there is no substitute for direct encounter with the beautiful, for direct experience of form without having to appeal to explicit criteria. There is here a kind of aesthetic autonomy parallel to moral autonomy. One has to learn to see for oneself. Rules derived from past experience or from what others—especially the experts—tell us can get in the way of being open to the emergence of novelty in the work of genius.

Kant attempted to analyze the necessity he saw in judgments of the beautiful which is indicated in the difference between the two claims "It is beautiful," which testifies to a peculiar subjective feeling of any properly disposed spectator in its presence, and "I like it," which testifies to a subjective but also merely private state in relation to what I find agreeable. The former requires cultivation of attention and is based on a judgment; the latter has the character of undisciplined immediacy. That cultivation is made possible by attention to the classics. Particular claims we might make could be mistaken and we are given pause by appeal to the community, living and dead, of the cultivated judges. However, the ultimate appeal has to be, not to that community and its judgments, but to one's own direct perception. What they say has to be validated directly by each, so that the community's judgment might be shifted by a single perceiver getting that community to see what it otherwise missed in the object. There is thus a pivotal relation between judgment and perception here. According to Kant, the feeling the cultivated observer has in the presence of the object is precisely a feeling of that harmonious relation between understanding and imagination involved in all judgment. This might be why those who are so cultivated tend to be those who are involved in professions and who are regularly called upon to use their judgment in often novel ways in their professional work.[100]

## The Sublime

In terms of the historical genesis of the third critique, the notion of the sublime was added to the project.[101] Kant himself refers to it as an appendage *(Anhang)*.[102] In Lyotard's reading, through the notion of the sublime, "the teleological machine [the attempted gathering together of reason in the notion of cosmic purpose] explodes." Rather than bringing reason into harmony, the sublime exposes the "spasmodic state" critical thought experiences when it reaches its limit, the "principle of fury" as the demand for the unconditioned, which the critique restrains.[103] This, however, seems extreme. Reference to the totality coupled with the notion of the *summum bonum* and of immortality introduces a principle of hope to which, in my reading, the experience of the sublime bears witness.[104]

However, Kant's own later insertion into the plan of the third critique and his designation of it as an appendage seems to challenge our interpretation of the sublime as the dispositional ground of the critical project as a whole. This seems strange, since he had already written *Observations on the Feeling of the Beautiful and the Sublime* during his precritical period (1764).[105] What is crucial is that, in the text from the second critique cited in the introduction to this chapter, he highlighted the disposition of awe accompanying the contemplation of "the starry skies above and the moral law within" without designating it explicitly as the sublime. In the third critique, the *Bewunderung und Ehrfurcht* provoked by the starry skies above and the moral law within, supreme instances of the objects of the first and second critiques respectively, are focused on both regions together, as the overwhelming magnitude of the distance between us and the stars schematizes the superiority of our ultimately moral relation to the totality. The cool feeling of *Achtung* or respect in relation to the moral law is turned in the direction of an emotional, stirring experience on the occasion of encountering something overwhelming in the outer world. In Kant's analysis, what overwhelms us in nature threatens our empirical insignificance: the stars make us appear tiny indeed. As the Psalmist says, "When I look at the heavens, the work of your fingers, . . . what are human beings that you are mindful of them?" But what follows is significant for Kant's analysis: "You have made them a little lower than God. . . . "[106] An instrumentally aided empirical inspection linked to calculation and scientific theory shows us as flyspecks on the surface of this flyspeck we call the earth. But our founding mental reference to the totality places us infinitely beyond even the largest conceivable finite extension and power. The initial emotional putdown brought about by the empirical consideration checks and dams up our spontaneous feeling of life. An awakening to the incomparable character of our own mind releases the dammed up feeling to produce a feeling of exaltation. This analysis lies at the background of Rudolph Otto's notion of the Holy as the *mysterium tremendum et fascinans*—the mystery that simultaneously repels and attracts us, that causes us to tremble in fear and to be bound to it in fascination.[107] Such an experience requires a certain level of mental cultivation to resist the purely negative feeling produced in us by nature's magnitude. The savage cowers in fear; one who has been awakened to the transcendent character of the human mind is in a position to experience the sublime.

The sublime exhibits the same four moments as the beautiful (disinterested satisfaction, subjective universality, purposiveness without a purpose, and necessary satisfaction), but it has another basis.[108] However, whereas the beautiful involves the feeling of harmonious interplay between understanding *(Verstand)* and imagination, the sublime involves a tension between imagination and reason *(Vernunft)*. Through the emergence of beautiful form within the space created by distancing oneself from the pressure of need-based perception, imagination and understanding experience their harmonious relation; we find ourselves at home in the world. But if beauty involves loving something without interest, sublimity involves esteeming something *against* sensory interest.[109] The deep background of psychic harmony in tune with the appearing environment lies in being pried loose from any being-at-home by reason's horizonal reference to the totality. Mind is directed to an unreachable beyond. As Lyotard would have it: "The absolute is never there, never given in a presentation, but it is always 'present' as a call to think beyond the 'there.' Ungraspable, but unforgettable. Never restored, never abandoned."[110] This creates a fundamental tension within the human being, an irremovable *Widerstreit*. Paralleling Derrida, Lyotard speaks of it as the *differend*, that which is different than anything that falls within the field of our experience and must be permanently deferred in coming to presence. Lyotard makes this differend the center of his thought.[111] This both wounds imagination as the faculty of presentation by the essential nonpresentability of the encompassing Beyond and gives imagination an extension it would not otherwise have by luring it into the construction of symbols. The sublime *(das Erhaben)* performs an *Aufhebung* of imagination, both canceling it and taking it up.[112] It generates alternative traditions in the history of art such as Mannerism or the Baroque or Surrealism, which embody an aesthetics of excess, and Suprematism or Abstract Art in general, which embody a minimalist aesthetic, both standing over against classical representationalist realism of the beautiful. This embodies the basic controversy between the Moderns and the Ancients, between "an aesthetic of 'presence' and the pagan poetics of good form," between the presence-in-absence of an unreachable (because infinite) encompassment and the full-bodied observation of familiar objects idealized.[113] In the Chinese tradition, we have the alternation between the Confucian focus on being together with others in familiar society and the Taoist belonging to the mysterious cosmic whole.[114]

Kant actually refers to three types of sublime experience. The two that are focal in his exposition appear on the basis of nature in relation to cognition and desire respectively; the third appears in relation to persons. Regarding the cognitive side of reason there is what Kant calls the mathematical sublime, an instance of which is the starry skies above. The experience of our own insignificance in this instance is linked to our ability to think beyond any given magnitude of the encompassing totality. From the point of view of understanding, this introduces us to a *progressus ad infinitum*, which Hegel will later designate as "the spurious [or bad] infinite."[115] However, what is at stake in relation to reason is the ability to think *the absolute totality* as the substrate underlying all experience. Reason runs ahead of the *progressus* of understanding to encompass it absolutely—though only in thought.[116] The empirically based experience of being *abgestossen* (repelled) joins with the reflectively based experience of our relation to the totality, to which we are simultaneously *angezogen* (attracted). This is the fundamental experience of the antinomic character—not simply of the *thinking* of the totality, but of the *existence* of human reality manifest to itself experientially as held in the tension between the at-home and the Beyond.

But the experience of the "mathematical" sublime, the sublime in relation to quantity, has a higher finality in relation to the desire of reason, which is the will. For Kant human reality does not culminate in the contemplative or theoretical but in the practical. The antinomies of theoretical reason block the way of theoretical completion but point to "the sole noumenal fact" of freedom under law, which leads into the immortality of the soul and the divine as omniscient, omnipotent, and just judge. The mathematical sublime is surmounted by the dynamically sublime, manifest in the encounter with the overpowering aspects of nature, nature under the aspect of causality.[117] In relation to the storm at sea or the tornado, what is threatened is not only the sense of one's significance in the massive order of space, but one's very existence. One is reminded of Pascal's reflection on the human being as a "thinking reed" that a mere vapor can destroy, but whose whole dignity consists in thought.[118] But for Kant thought itself points to an awareness of the ultimate superiority of our moral vocation.[119] For Kant, then, nature in these displays is not sublime; sublime in the proper sense of the term is our vocation as possessors of reason. Nature's display only serves as a symbol of this distinctively human superiority.[120] It would seem to be another way, beyond the beauties of nature and art, in which we gain some indication that "we are meant" by the world process, that we are in some sense the purpose of what appears in the world. Only in this case, the tendency of the beautiful to make us feel at home in the world is unsettled by our ever-unfulfilled reference to the undisclosed totality.

However, in addition to his major focus on objects occasioning the feeling of the sublime, Kant's discussion of the sublime in his General Comment on aesthetic judgments also focuses on persons and thus slides over into sublime dispositions. He includes enthusiasm as an affective straining of our forces by ideas that establishes a powerful and permanent disposition. Among the Jews, in their prohibition of graven images, that very negation in relation to the infinity of God produces a most exalted feeling of the sublime. But because enthusiasm deprives the mind of its ability to engage in free deliberation about principles, it falls prey to fanaticism, which substitutes ferment for insight and easily slides into superstition. For Kant, every vigorous affect is sublime. He mentions here anger and indignation, which lead us to overcome powerful resistance. But more sublime is the noble character pursuing its principles with vigor and without affect. Among the sublime dispositions Kant also includes isolation from society, provided it rests, not on misanthropy or anthropophobia, but on ideas that resist our sensible interest—indeed, any case of setting aside our own needs for the sake of principle Kant regards as sublime.[121] It would seem that in art the presentation of such a disposition in an ideal human form is what the Ideal of Beauty is all about.

## *Art and Genius*

As I have already indicated, art plays a pivotal role in the third critique. If we conceive of nature as divine art, ultimately as the work of a divine moral Artist working in the way in which a human artist operates with aesthetic ideas, we can bring the initially segregated realms of mechanistic nature and moral freedom into relation. We can thus bring the three regions of reason—cognitive, moral, and aesthetic—into harmony.

As I have said, for Kant genius is the inborn character through which nature gives the rule to art. His point is that genius does not operate according to explicitly known rules—or rather, though certain rules (e.g., those of technique or genre) might be implicitly operative, the distinctive character of genius is the emergence of something original, which then may be shown to exhibit rules. Like Aristotelian *phronesis*, genius in its exemplary originality is primordially rule generating rather than explicitly rule following.[122] Similarly, Giordano Bruno had maintained, in his "Discourse of Poets," that poetry is not born in rules, but rules in poetry;[123] in the 1750s in England, Joseph Warton and Edmund Young advocated a total rejection of rules in art, whether technical or aesthetic rules;[124] and what was at stake in the *Sturm und Drang*, which had swept Germany during the time just before Kant was writing his third critique, was the proclamation of the absolute radicality of genius, breaking with the past and establishing the new.[125]

In the creation of beautiful art—and it is the rendering rather than the theme that makes it beautiful—the same harmonious interplay of imagination and understanding that takes place in appreciation also takes place. But whereas appreciation is animated by the work, creation is animated by the emergence of inspiration, the fruit of "spirit" *(Geist)* as origin of aesthetic ideas.[126] Spirit for Kant does not seem to be another faculty but refers to the unknown source "in nature" that inspires as the animation of all the faculties. The ancients referred to muses or angels; Kant refers to spirit as nature giving the rule without specifying what that nature is. It is another case of a situation in which it seems "as if" there were a purposive agency operating from behind the phenomenal screen inspiring the genius to original creation.

But originality is not sufficient, for one can produce original nonsense. Rather, originality has finally to be subjected to the judgment of taste cultivated, as in Hume, by a study of the diversity of classical pieces in diverse genres and styles, a taste that has learned to discern aesthetic form and to be ready for the emergence of yet-to-be classical pieces. Genius also involves mastery of a medium in order to give body to the spirit.[127] In this way genius produces works of exemplary originality. Genius thus consists in the animation of the harmonious interplay of imagination and understanding by spirit as the source of aesthetic ideas that, linked to the judgment of taste, result in the emergence of novel works, styles, and genres that become exemplary for others.

Kant's analysis involves certain inversions of the notion of the matter-form relation as it obtains in art. On the one hand, mastery of a medium provides the material that is informed, animated by genius. But, on the other hand, genius also provides the material that is formed by taste. There is involved here a reciprocity between tradition and innovation in the relation between craft and genius on the one hand and in the relation between taste and genius on the other.

Kant goes into some detail in describing what he means by an aesthetic idea. It is the inverse of a rational Idea which, as I have previously indicated, is a concept for which no intuition is adequate, an open, horizonal concept that functions as a lure for further exploration. World, Soul, and God are the basic ideas of reason. As I suggested earlier, they articulate the founding notion of being in terms of the bifurcation of experience into empirical object and conscious subject governed by the drive for their common ground. An aesthetic idea, by contrast, is an intuition of the imagination for which no concept is adequate. An aesthetic idea gives rise to much thought without any thought being able to encompass it. Both types of ideas are similar in their calling for some kind of elaboration, the rational calling for experientially grounded conceptual filling, the aesthetic for further interpretive articulation.[128]

Kant deals with such ideas as they cluster around objects of pure beauty and of dependent beauty. Music, untitled and unaccompanied by program or text, is a prime example of pure beauty. Paralleling Aristotle, Kant sees it as a kind of language of the affections; but, beyond Aristotle, he sees it as giving expression to an indeterminate whole of an incredible wealth of thought.[129] One can see it in this way by linking it to the indeterminate concept of the supersensuous Beyond, which lures understanding toward comprehensive rationality. In this he prefigures and probably gives rise to Schopenhauer and, following him, Nietzsche, both of whom consider music as the expression of final ontological depth.[130] In the Pythagoreanizing line of Plato, Kant goes on to link music with the mathematical study of harmonics.[131] Nonetheless, he seems to backtrack on these suggestive notions by claiming that music is the lowest of the art forms, easily sliding into the merely agreeable and doing least for informing the mind. In this it is the polar opposite of poetry, the most informative of all the arts.[132]

When we come to dependent beauty, Kant sees the role of aesthetic ideas as that of providing symbolic schematization for rational ideas.[133] Thus, for example, Plato's Myth of Er, Dante's *Divina Commedia*, and Milton's *Paradise Lost* give symbolic expression to the ideas of the afterlife, of final judgment, of heaven, hell, and purgatory, all of which are morally important but cognitively empty. We can know nothing definitive about the afterlife, but we can make meaningful practical postulates that can be brought closer to us by means of imaginative symbolization. But even in relation to actual experience, art can give such things as love, death, and envy such expression as to bring them significantly closer to us than any theoretical consideration can. Artistic presentation thus sets the mind in motion, thinking more deeply about actual experience and pondering the larger implications of experience, all the while deepening our sense of presence.[134]

Kant discusses both the beautiful and the sublime in terms of the relation between imagination and the higher faculties of understanding and reason: the beautiful produces harmony in the relation between imagination and understanding; the sublime produces tension between imagination and reason. In the case of understanding within the cognitive field, imagination is, first of all, a retentive and synthesizing faculty, gathering about a single object present in the sensory field other experiences of the same sense at different times and of different senses at the same and at different times, furnishing thereby the sensory manifold that the concept is meant to comprehend.[135] In relation to the concepts generated therefrom, imagination likewise furnishes schematic examples as bridges between a given manifold and the concept. More deeply, imagination furnishes the temporal schemata that build the bridge from the pure concepts of the understanding (the categories) to the individual given in the field of sensation. Thus the category of substance is schematized as endurance through time of an entity in and through the variation of its accidents, while the category of cause and effect is schematized in terms of the temporal antecedence and consequence of linked substances in a regular way.[136] But in the aesthetic field, imagination provides the symbols that give fuller presence to the things we already know and that also bring us into a meaningful but noncognitive relation with rational ideas of the afterlife like eternity, heaven, hell, purgatory.[137] Imagination thus plays a key role in the life of the mind.

Kant presents a possible division of the arts based on the notion of art as expressive of aesthetic ideas.[138] Expression involves articulation, gesticulation, and tone. Under articulation he locates poetry and rhetoric, the basic linguistic arts. Under gesticulation we find arts of sensible truth and of sensible illusion. The first includes architecture and sculpture, providing us with three-dimensional real things; the second involves representational painting, which provides an illusion of three-dimensionality, but also (somewhat surprisingly) landscape gardening. Included in the arts of tone are music, which provides sound-tones, and nonrepresentational painting, which furnishes visual tones. Then there are mixed forms: drama is rhetoric combined with pictorial exhibition; song is poetry combined with music; the play of sound and of figures is dance; all these forms are combined in opera.

Kant goes on to provide a judgment of the relative worth of the individual arts, assigning poetry the highest value since it is the most communicative. Instrumental music is assigned the lowest level, shading off into the merely agreeable and furnishing a mere mood, for example as background for a dinner party. He does not assess the other art forms in between these two extremes.

## Nature's Ultimate and Final Purpose

The aesthetic, I said, is set within the larger context of an attempt to bring nature and freedom together via the projection of the notion of purposiveness onto nature in various ways. From an aesthetic point of view Kant looks at nature as if it were oriented in a threefold manner: (1) toward bringing about the harmony of the faculties in the presentation of the beautiful, whether directly in natural phenomena or indirectly through the natural inspiration of genius; (2) toward awakening us to the sublimity of our own calling in the presentations of overwhelming magnitude and power; and (3) toward easing the transition between our biological responses to the sensorily given and our moral obligation by teaching us a disinterested relation to the sensa.[139] In the latter way, beauty becomes a symbol of the morally good.

From the point of view of organic phenomena, Kant projects purposiveness into things, not in relation to us, but in relation to the ends they seem to seek. Thus we can only make sense out of living processes if we consider them as seeking their own growth, sustenance, and reproduction —though we have to subtract from such seeking the state of awareness involved in our own deliberate seeking.[140] In sexual reproduction we have to think of the function of each of the sexes as aimed at the other by nature. And when we consider the variety of species, we see them linked in what appears to be a systematic way, where minerals function as nutrient for vegetative life, and plants in turn as food for herbivores, which, in their turn, are food for carnivores.[141] But all of them are material for humans, who have the distinct capacity to set goals and impose them on the rest of nature. The conditions for the possibility of setting and carrying out goals involve two components of culture: a culture of discipline that clears the space for those functions by learning the control of appetites, and a culture of skills that enable us to reach the goals most efficiently. The basis for this process is civil society as a condition of freedom under law, where each person's pursuit of goals is checked by denying infringement on all others' similar pursuit.[142] It is as if nature had in mind this capacity to project and reach goals in orienting all other presentations of both natural and cultural development to this as its ultimate end. But even beyond this, for Kant there is a final end, an end that does not need anything else as condition, and that is the moral end: acting in accordance with the categorical imperative.[143] That points us ultimately beyond the phenomenal world in which we live to the noumenal realm as our final destiny. And it is here that we reach consideration of the Cause of all as a moral Artist-Artisan, arranging nature as an arena for human moral activity.

Kant links the aesthetic to our moral destiny in several ways. First, there is the distancing from appetite involved both in aesthetic and moral experience. Second, there is, linked to this, the aesthetic symbolization of the moral, first by that very appetitive distancing, but also by natural forms spontaneously taking on moral qualities like the stateliness of trees or the purity of snow. Third, there is the Ideal of Beauty as the presentation of the human form displaying moral action. Fourth, there is the awakening to our moral destiny through the experience of the sublime. Finally, there is the formation of aesthetic community based on the imperative of favoring the beautiful, the respect for aesthetic autonomy in allowing direct encounter with the form of the object as the final criterion for judgment, and the study of the classics as the vehicle for developing aesthetic perception.

Understanding, which was the core of the first critique, points to a supersensible substratum of appearance that is wholly indeterminate; judgment provides the possibility of determination by intellectual power; and reason provides the determination through moral law. Judgment thus occupies the point of transition from the concept of nature (as appearance) to the concept of freedom (as "sole noumenal fact").[144] The whole region of reflective judgment—the beautiful, the sublime, and the organic—points to the possibility of the insertion of causality through concepts into the mechanical world of nature and thus serves to bring together the fractured halves of the field of thought brought about in the first and second critiques.

## Response

Kant's approach to aesthetics is set within the context of his own critical project. Within that project it is aimed at unifying the antithetical regions of mechanically necessitated knowing and moral responsibility grounded in human freedom. And it carries on that operation by an analysis of the power of judgment linked, at first in a seemingly implausible way, to the experience of pleasure. The complication of the context makes difficult a critical assimilation to our own aesthetic project. The difficulty is eased a bit by reason of the common phenomenological ground of our introductory approach and Kant's attention to the modes of givenness of aesthetic objects.

One of the most serious difficulties is the apparent arbitrariness in the first critique's limitation of "theoretical knowledge" of causality to mechanical causation. In the second critique Kant is driven to acknowledge the "causality of freedom," and in the third, the reciprocal relation of cause and effect in the self-causation of organic process.[145] It seems more reasonable to begin with the full phenomenology of causation and view mechanical causation as the lowest level, clearly subsumed under organic causation (e.g., in our own eating), with both mechanical and organic causation in turn subsumed under causation-through-concepts in human choice (e.g., to eat in a elegant manner or to fast).

Kant's phenomenology of feeling focuses on four distinctively different kinds of feeling: of the agreeable (sensation), of the beautiful (taste), of the sublime (awe), and of the moral (respect).[146] The two feelings occupying the center in our list are the center of Kant's analysis in the third critique, while the two modes flanking the center are means of contrast.

We thought we detected a parallel distinction between the agreeable and the beautiful in Plato's distinction between the objects of attention in the luxurious and the purged city. Luxury moves beyond the biologically necessary, the healthful (which governed the first city), in the direction of measureless self-indulgence. What would satisfy such desire is the re-formation through human ingenuity of what is given by nature. Here the criterion seems to be what will produce positive somatic reverberations. The emergence of artistic form here is not for the sake of the appreciation of the form itself, but for the sake of the gratification it produces. Reading this situation in terms of the Cave allegory: in the luxurious phase we are chained to the cave of our own sensory appetites, for whose gratifications new industries are created. But the aim of the purged city is the turning around of the soul, and its education at this level is said to culminate in the appreciation of beautiful things. Appreciation here is a state of soul attuned to the things themselves in their display, while luxurious gratification seeks merely a pleasing state of the organism.

Kant's distinction between the beautiful and the sublime parallels the distinction implicit in Aristotle between the aesthetic of the beautiful in music and painting and that of the horrible as represented in tragedy. The sublime is occasioned by that which threatens our existence. For Kant, the horrible or the ugly as represented in art contains beauty in its mode of treatment. The artist does a "beautiful" (read: excellent) job of representing the horrors of the crucifixion.

Kant focuses his insights within the broader context of his analysis of the general conditions for objectivity functioning in a biologically receptive knower who begins with being-affected sensorily and learns, through a priori principles, to separate out the merely subjective from the intersubjective elements in the stream of bodily impressions and to stitch them together into a coherent world of appearance. Aesthetic objects appear within such conditions for objectivity and are especially able to affect pleasurable responses. For Kant it is the character of the sensory as such that produces agreeable or disagreeable sensations, since we are not photo- or audio-receptors but needy organisms shot through with desires. And though there are general tendencies for certain sensa to produce similar pleasurable reactions in large numbers of individuals, there is no universal necessity in such reactions. Strawberries taste good to most people, but are not similarly pleasing to all. (Note, however, that pleasure in taking in nourishment and in sexual activity is a necessary accompaniment of these activities, given their linkage to natural organic ends.) However, the very capacity we have to objectify—to set out sensations over-against *(ob-iectum)* the subjectivity of the self in judgment—makes possible our attending, through the given sensa, to the form of the togetherness of the sensa, the configuration of sensory features. A certain reflective distance is established as one focuses attention on the character of the thing's presentation. Reflective distance is distance from one's own organic need, so that one is free to attend, not to the satisfaction the object produces, but to the form of the object. Kant calls such satisfaction "disinterested," "unconstrained" by need, able to give "free favoring."[147] Nietzsche scoffs at the notion of "disinterest" in the presence of the artistic nude.[148] But if a nonhomosexual male might appreciate Michelangelo's *David* in a nonsexual manner, so also might a heterosexual female, as a heterosexual male might learn aesthetic appreciation of Bernini's *Madame Canova*. And, indeed, one's appreciative response to one of Cezanne's paintings of fruit might not be one of drooling in hungry anticipation.

"Disinterested" attention does involve a satisfaction, though one that is fixated on the qualities of the object rather than on the satisfaction itself. In general, our reflective distance and our capacity to understand rather than simply undergo sensations make it possible both that we deliberately eat for nourishment and have sexual relations for procreating as well as that we are able to separate the pleasures found in both from their natural ends and cultivate them explicitly. Puritanism would find the latter morally reprehensible. But deliberate cultivation is not submission to appetite; it is another expression of rising above animal proclivity by shaping it. Kant locates aesthetic satisfaction in what he calls the harmonious free play of the cognitive faculties, namely, imagination and understanding. It quickens our sense of distinctively human life—not our animal life sunk in itself, wallowing in its own gratifications, but our cognitive life, rooted in our ability to make good judgments beyond merely felt preference. Thus there are two directions pleasurable experiences can take: the direction of our own organic reverberations and the direction of objects. Attention to the latter in the form of display they take in the sensory field awakens us to our distinctive humanness.

But a genuine aesthetic favoring likewise does not essentially involve the employment of concepts, such as "rules of taste" or concepts of physical or moral perfection, that would supposedly determine what the object ought to be. Furthermore, aesthetic judgment abstracts from what Kant calls the "existence" of the objects, which I understand to be their substantial underpinning and causal context, both in terms of their origin and their consequences as physical things. Aesthetic judgment attends only to their sheer display in the sensory field—that is, their relation to a bodily situated perceiver.

The object of aesthetic experience is the form or the mode of presentation, the how of an object's presence to our perception. It is reciprocally tied to the experience of the form of the judgment, the harmony of the imagination and the understanding. Mikel Dufrenne suggests that aesthetic form is actually composed of several factors in a progression: contour, the unity of the sensuous qualities, the unity of meaning, the unity of style, the unity of spectator and work.[149] "The form is less the shape of an object than the shape of the system which the subject forms with the object" founded on "the logos of feeling."[150]

Kant's connection of the aesthetic with the teleological in the third critique as a whole invites comparison between notions of form in both cases. In living form we have the presentation of a functional whole whose sensory display is expressive of its own striving to reach its ends. In the aesthetic realm, form might be isolated apart from what it expresses—though in art it always in some way expresses the aesthetic idea of the artist, even in the most abstract forms, like untitled instrumental music. But form most often accompanies and thus expresses its referent.

In the visual realm, Kant sees form primarily in the pictorial line, with color a mere pleasant accompaniment that, unless it operates to make the line more focal, is an aesthetic distraction. Here he is opposed by turn-of-the-century notions like those of Cezanne, who saw painting as an essential synthesis of line and color.[151] Cezanne remarked, "Form is at its fullest when color is at its richest."[152] Matisse likewise considered color harmonies as the primary form of painting.[153]

Having separated aesthetic judgment from both "interest" and "concept," Kant goes on to fold in both. Thus his first step is to separate out the genuinely aesthetic from other factors that might be confused with it. Then he can more safely relate it to those separated factors. He does this by a distinction between free and dependent beauty. As examples of the former he focuses on things like bird plumage on the one hand and arabesque drawings on the other. However, what we experience here is only trivial beauty. This first move seems to place Kant against the tradition rooted in Plato's Ladder of Beauty and having the greatest impact on the Middle Ages. In

Kant's view, the beauty of the person, of the laws that form persons, the beauty of the sciences, which study the principles of cosmic harmony as well as the principles for judging the adequacy of human laws, and "the vision of Beauty Itself" do not involve literal instances of beauty but metaphoric extensions. As far as the "beauty of the sciences" is concerned, even the conceptual study of harmonics is not the study of beauty but of extractable relations considered apart from the aesthetic experience. Kant suggests we should call mathematical demonstrations (as we often do) elegant rather than beautiful. For him, beauty strictly speaking lies in the form present in sensory display. However, Kant's notion of dependent beauty allows for some extension in the expressivity of the presentation in relation to the inwardness of character realized in his Ideal of Beauty.

"The vision of Beauty Itself" in Plato and the carryover of that into Plotinian mysticism and medieval notions of divine Beauty—making allowance for the differences in these assimilations—does claim to have an experiential basis. Augustine picks up on the Platonic-Plotinian line in his exclamation in the *Confessions* where, referring to God, he exclaims, "O Beauty ever ancient, ever new! Too late have I known Thee!"[154] Here we have an essential transformation of the pagan experience, which spoke in terms of encounter with an encompassing region or a type or principle. The Augustinian and subsequent medieval assimilation involves the experience of the presence of a Person. Why would Plato call the vision he speaks of one of Beauty Itself and why would the Christian tradition speak of divine Beauty? Kant speaks here of the danger of illuminism, fanaticism, and superstition, short-circuiting the hard labor of the intellect in favor of supposedly privileged intuitions.[155] But the real question is what we make of the experiences to which these various traditions bear witness.

However, there is a Kantian parallel to the experience of Beauty Itself or Himself in the experience of the sublime. Sensorily appearing objects of great magnitude of size and power provoke a feeling of awe. Such feeling expresses the antinomic sense of both insignificance and exaltation, since, though our bodies are tiny and impotent in the face of such magnitudes, our intellects can think beyond any magnitude and our wills are called to a realm transcending the whole domain of the sensory. For Kant, strictly speaking, nature is not sublime; it is only our reason, practical and theoretic, that is so. The experience of the sublime, which, I have claimed, grounds the whole critical project, is a mode of *self*-discovery. Kant's interpretation parallels the anthropological reduction he performs in the notion of the *summum bonum*. As I noted previously, whereas for the tradition in general and for the medievals especially God is the *summum bonum*, for Kant the *summum bonum* is the coming together of happiness with deservedness to be happy (by reason of consistently acting from moral principle) for which God functions as means. (No matter that this seems to violate in the highest instance the categorical imperative to treat the person as an end and never simply as a means.) However, Kant does claim that the experience of the sublime can schematize for us such notions of the wrath of God.[156] He further claims that there is no more sublime poetry than the Hebrew, which bases itself on the essential unrepresentability of Yahweh and that it is that very unrepresentability that can evoke the most profound feelings, which, unchanneled by rational considerations, can erupt into the wildest fanaticism. Here Kant is clearly working with what I have initially described as the emptiness of the notion of Being and is recommending how to understand its all-encompassing character. He clearly seems to recognize the functioning of Platonic Eros, born of poverty and plenty and thus always empty, always longing, having designs upon absolute plenitude. Only he keeps turning it back upon itself rather than bringing it into relation with that nonobjective Object, transcendent of the Enlightenment's Supreme Being, which no concept can encompass. Contrary to Kant, the sublime typically does not involve a focus on ourselves but on our sense of the Beyond, which is expressed in encounters with overwhelming magnitude and might, a Beyond that draws us and gives us a sense of belonging to it. I suggest that Kant turns the experience back to humanness because of the way he understands autonomy.

Kant's ethics involves the rational individual being absolutely self-determining, completely autonomous. This, in turn, involves a certain distancing from any mode of being drawn by inclination, and thus the appearance of being antithetical to any notion of grace. However, in the notion of genius we see an area in which the notion of grace appears: genius is that power through which nature gives the rule to art. Certain individuals are gifted in being able to act beyond rules in such a way as to be both original and exemplary, not so much following rules as generating rules. In Kant such grace functions in establishing aesthetic community, binding humans together synchronically and diachronically through the communication of that which would otherwise seem purely private, namely, the inwardness of feeling.

Art likewise teaches us to view the beauties of nature. The Alps appeared merely tedious to the pragmatic Romans, who saw in them obstacles to their imperial and engineering ambitions until Petrarch's poetry began to teach people to see them otherwise.[157] Even Winckelmann, the originator of a renewed appreciation for the originality of the Greeks in art over against what were subsequently viewed as the merely derivative Romans, found the Alps a bore.[158] The same was true of Rousseau's *Reveries of the Solitary Walker* in relation to the pragmatic tendencies of the age of Enlightenment: Rousseau reintroduced an aesthetic appreciation for mountains.[159] Thus through the work of genius both art and nature serve to bring our cognitive faculties into harmony and thereby to bring us more in harmony with each other. By drawing upon the study of the products of genius throughout the centuries, Kant assimilates Hume's standard of taste: the dialogic community of critics whose taste is honed on the study of classical forms.

The genius works through aesthetic ideas, the intuition of forms for shaping materials. Such ideas thereby give rise to much thought in their viewers without any particular thought being adequate to encompass the works. In this way aesthetic ideas obversely parallel rational ideas, which can never attain to intuitive filling. But in this way also they "schematize rational ideas" by giving them body, presenting them in such a way that they "draw near" and are more present. Consider here Plato's Myth of Er, Dante's *Divina Commedia*, Milton's *Paradise Lost*. But aesthetic ideas can also bring human traits closer to us: love, death, virtue—perhaps not closer than an actual experience of them in our own lives and in the lives of others, especially those close to us—but closer than the mere thought of them, no matter how carefully worked out conceptually. It is in effecting this "sense of presence" that art is most effective. And it is in this that we come to *realize* what we might already *know*.

Dufrenne suggests that such "realization" is the work of imagination, which "gives full weight to the real by assuring us of the presence of the hidden and distant."[160] In Kant the link with the noumenal is the link with what is in principle hidden and ultimately distant from all our determinations. Looking forward to Heidegger, I contend that the notion of Being opens up the notion of the encompassing and unencompassable to which we are essentially referred, the mystery that surrounds the dashboard of both our everyday and our scientific dealings. The depth of our lives pivot about the extent to which we live out of a sense of the hidden and distant.

### Epilogue: Hume's Notion of Aesthetic Community

Central to Kant's aesthetics is the notion of aesthetic community, built out of the study of classical models. Kant does little to develop this notion. But in the epoch immediately preceding Kant's, David Hume, in his short essay "Of the Standard of Taste," offered a penetrating analysis of the way aesthetic community comes to be formed. Since the reflections are independent of the foundations in his general philosophic approach, being based rather on more commonsensical discussions, I append a brief discussion of this work.

Hume's "Of the Standard of Taste," which Peter Kivy, with justification, regards as "the most mature aesthetic document to come out of the British Enlightenment, and one of the few real masterpieces of which the philosophy of art can boast."[161] In this essay Hume comes to terms with the key problem involved in the adage: *De gustibus non disputandum.*[162] One should not dispute about taste—because, apparently, different people have different tastes. How then even speak about a standard in this realm?

Hume begins by noting the often observed—because readily observable—differences in taste, and even goes on to deepen the case by noting the less obvious differences that underlie apparent verbal agreements. In this he is much like Alasdair MacIntyre today (an editor of Hume's moral writings very likely clued to the notion by Hume), who argues a similar thesis in *Whose Justice? Which Rationality?*[163] This plurality of taste is so, Hume claims, because beauty is not a property of things but a relation to the mind.[164] (Of course, strictly speaking, in Hume's general philosophy, everything experienceable is a relation to—literally, in—the mind.) In spite of that, he goes on to suggest that some standard could be developed. It turns out that the "standard" is a dialogic community of cultivated observers.

One way of reducing the plurality is to point to differences in native capacities: on one end of the scale some have sensory deficiencies, and, on the other, some possess an uncommon delicacy of taste or imagination. Hume calls attention here to two characters in Cervantes's *Don Quixote* who were able to detect the most subtle iron and leather flavors, unnoticed by most others, in a cask of wine. Though taste is a subjective being-affected, it yet has a kind of objectivity because it is related to certain constancies detectable by more common means—in this case a key with a leather thong attached to it found at the bottom of the cask when the cask was emptied. The two characters' taste provided a standard for others less sensitive to the properties in question.[165]

In the case of works of art, granted a certain basic sensitivity, nonetheless a certain cultivation is also required. Hume wants to find the equivalent of the leather-thonged key and thus another medium to defend the immediacy of cultivated sensibility. One has, first of all, to learn the purpose of a given art work; then one has to attend to the coherence (consistency) of the whole in view of its purpose; and, finally, one has to observe how its design properties serve that purpose. In order to be able to achieve such perception in any given situation, one has to attain to a serenity of mind, free from all agitation, along with an ability to recollect past experiences that clue one in on how to attend to a given piece and provide one with the means for assessment. These conditions make possible the final condition: a careful, undistracted attention to the object given.[166] In this process one moves from simple immediacy of response through reflective distance to a mediated immediacy.

Granted such attention, Hume goes on to note how cultivation could then expand on native sensitivities. One who practices an art is in a better position to appreciate its qualities than one who does not. Presumably the practitioner has a better understanding of both the materials and ways of construction so as to be better attuned to the way these appear in the finished work. But Hume's notion of practice here seems to refer more to the practice of reflective attention rather than the production of art works. One who, in addition, contemplates the plurality of works and styles, past and present, in a given species of art is in a better position than one who merely practices his own style or attends to only one style. Further, one who compares species of art and degrees of excellence in each species is more likely to have better judgment than one who does not. Such a one operates within a more expanded field of awareness and can appreciate diversity. Again, one who returns to a work again and again is able to judge and thus appreciate better than one who attends to only a single superficial viewing. A work of art is a complex unity-in-multiplicity such that every aspect cannot be taken in during a single limited period of attention. And a classic is, by definition, that which merits continually renewed attention by reason of providing renewed satisfaction by many people in different epochs and by the same person at different times. But in order to attend properly to a work, in any given context one must have serenity of mind, a recollective state, and a proper focus on the object.

Note here that the study of art forms takes its point of departure from the preexistence of models of excellence in each form. A traditional canon guides the development of taste.[167] What one learns by this study is, negatively speaking, freedom from confining prejudgments in order to let a given work work upon him. Through the cultivated contemplation of a plurality of arts, genres, styles, and degrees of excellence, such a critic, far from being locked into the past, learns openness to the different, to the new. All this puts the critic in the position to make personal judgments, to articulate them verbally, and to test them against the judgments of similarly cultivated critics. Relation to other critics involves the analysis of components and the synthesis of those components into a whole, the translation of cultivated perception into language, and the explicitation, defense, and transformation of criteria. It is the joint verdict of critics so operating that constitutes for Hume the standard of taste.[168] The standard of taste then involves a peculiarly qualified dialogic community.

Hume is quite aware of the fragility of such a standard, though he claims that, when one looks over the history of thought, one finds that it is more stable than theology or even than science. Plato, Aristotle, Epicurus, and Descartes successively yield to each other, but Terence and Virgil still hold sway. There will, however, always be differences in preference owing to differences in individual constitution, in age, and in moral and religious commitments.[169] Nonetheless, the cultivation of taste along the lines suggested will mitigate the differences in judgment. Indeed, one might learn to recognize degrees of excellence in a genre or a style without any great personal love of that genre or style. Granted also those differences that are irremovable, the dialogic community of critics should also have a measure of tolerance for diversity within limits.

Hume claims that such a process would lead to a knowledge of the rules that define the limits of diversity.[170] Unfortunately, "Of the Standard of Taste" provides little specific guidance in this regard beyond a few comments on what is good and what is bad in Ariosto's work: good are force and clearness of expression, readiness and variety of inventions, natural depiction of the passions; bad are improbable fictions, mixture of comic and tragic styles, lack of narrative coherence, and continual interruption in narration. Hume says no more about these features than simply listing them.[171]

## Response

Taste is a peculiarly modern phenomenon. It seems to go back to Renaissance *gusto*, a notion promoted by Balthasar Gratian. In contrast to simple liking or disliking, taste is a capacity that requires cultivation. It involves rising above one's own proclivities and those of one's contemporaries, selecting and rejecting in a way that produces overall harmony.

It seems to me undeniable that, in addition to aesthetic preferences based on uncultivated proclivities, the cultivated study, along the lines suggested by Hume, of the full range of art works and types judged excellent throughout the ages opens one to qualities to which one would otherwise have no access. An aesthetic canon is capable of freeing one from one's own idiosyncrasies and from the prejudices of one's epoch or group. But one has to learn to move beyond mere acquaintance with and thus ability to talk about past works, to a sensitivity to the qualities of their real presence.

The canon is an indispensable aid in the cultivation of such taste, and gender ought have nothing to do with it. If it were possible, it would almost be better not to know the first names of a given artist, for it is not simply a question of the work of white males—or of males of any color—but excellence of aesthetic form playing in tandem with depth of reference that are worthy of consideration here. The works that exhibit such excellence and depth are those that have continued to appeal, throughout the ages, to sensitive, informed, reflective, and critical observers.[172]

Hume's skeptical empiricism lessens the scope of his own appreciation. Above all, his reductionist assumptions about human mentality (thought as the little agitation of the brain)[173] disallow his following out what is involved in his observation about the encompassing darkness surrounding the island of light provided by sensations. We are aware of the Beyond—indeed, as I have attempted to show throughout, everything distinctively human is based on the fact that we are directed, though by nature only emptily, to the totality via the notion of Being. Not being by nature directed beyond the empirical circle, the animal evidently experiences no lure of what lies beyond its current functioning. Hume's own claims about the essential character of sensations and the acute discrimination of types he makes throughout presuppose an ability to be beyond the Now of sensory impression by eidetic insight which situates the given in the whole of space and time as the field of possibility for the individual instantiation of the types. This presupposes the prior givenness of that field as the condition for the possibility of the apprehension of types. Cultivating the reference to Being as the ultimate condition for this possibility involves a sensitivity to the mystery of wholeness in each appearing thing, and especially in the self as the locus of the revealing/concealing of the Whole. The attempt to articulate that sensitivity has been the role of the arts from time immemorial. Lack of such sensitivity involves an essential closure to the deepest work of the works of art that come to us from the past. Hume has lost that sensitivity, and in this he is paradigmatic of much of modern taste.

Hume thought that the community he described could develop "rules of taste." It was just such rules that governed late-nineteenth-century academic art, against which all twentieth-century movements in art were directed. The rules became a procrustean bed rather than a framework within which possibilities could be explored. Kant will release the first great protest against such a conception. The study of the classics is essential but not so that we might practice servile imitation. Rather, we should learn to contact the same creative source—*die ewige Anfang*, the eternal beginning, as Schelling would have it[174]—in order to bring forth or recognize works that are both original and exemplary.

One of the problems one has to encounter in dealing with the nature of taste is the variability it has shown throughout the ages, not only in the obvious area of clothing styles, where the present style is king, but also in the shifts in appreciation that occur in aesthetic communities. The Renaissance and the Enlightenment viewed the Gothic cathedrals as irrational monstrosities,[175] expressions of the irrationalism of the Dark Middle Ages, while poets like Goethe set in motion a Gothic revival[176] and historian-architects like Viollet-le-Duc even went so far as to claim and demonstrate that the Gothic cathedral showed an immense rational mastery.[177] Frank Lloyd Wright condemned the architecture of the Renaissance as inauthentically derivative from Roman and Greek forms, which he also viewed negatively, along with the eclecticism of later nineteenth-century building practice; but he had high praise for Mayan, Egyptian, and Japanese architecture.[178] Futurist Umberto Boccione spoke of "Phidian decadence" and "Michaelangelesque [*sic*] sins,"[179] while Henry Moore favorably annexed both Phidias and Michelangelo to their more overtly powerful antecedents, going back to Assyrian, Babylonian, Egyptian, and Mayan sculptural forms.[180] Gaugin and Picasso introduced an appreciation for what was previously considered primitive barbarism.[181] The 1913 Armory Show in New York, which displayed paintings from Europe since the turn of the century, produced strong negative reaction from the critics, only for the works to become standard museum pieces.[182] In its premiere performance, Stravinsky's *Rite of Spring* almost caused a riot and the composer had to leave through a window, even though the piece has now become part of the standard repertoire of the symphony orchestra. Shakespeare himself had been in eclipse during the Enlightenment as a kind of undisciplined barbarian until Addison began to rescue him and Dr. Johnson sprang to his defense. Futurist Carlo Carra, in a complete reversal of traditional aesthetics, went so far as to advocate a need for inner disharmony brought about by new forms.[183] Taste clearly swings in all the arts.

What is positive about the current situation is that, through the invention of what André Malraux calls "the museum without walls," namely the art book, people have access to the art of all the world.[184] Hitherto one had continuing access only to what was in one's own collection or in the local museum and had to remember what one had seen elsewhere. In the case of the visual arts, one can follow Hume's admonition significantly further than he and those prior to recent times were able to do and learn to appreciate the beauties of the widest possible variety of genres and styles. In the case of literature, we are in a position to extend the canon to the founding texts of East Asia in India, China, and Japan. One is not then tied in, as tends to be the case with clothing styles, to the current, but can range over all of human history.

Hans-Georg Gadamer noted a distinction between taste and fashion. Fashion is simply what is currently in, and will soon be out: for example, the best-seller in literature, the latest rage in clothing styles, the most recent school of philosophy. Taste involves, negatively, a certain distancing from one's own uncultivated proclivities and from what surrounds one in the present, a distancing brought about by attention to a wide range of artifacts available from the past. Positively, taste involves a holistic sensibility, also made possible by that distance, which allows one to select or forego what the present offers as that can or cannot be assimilated into a sense of wholeness.[185] In a era when the decontextualization of choice has rendered individual "freedom" an absolute and all standards are rejected, it is crucial to learn to expose oneself sensitively and reflectively, along the lines suggested by Hume, to the wide variety of exemplars made available by modern methods or reproduction in order to learn what harmonious sensibility has meant in differing contexts. For what is at stake is not simply individual preference but integrated or disintegrated living. Goethe remarked that the greatness of a nature is shown by the capacity to absorb the greatest multiplicity without suffering disharmony. In today's situation of pluralism, the need to cultivate such integrated personality is greater than ever before in history.

# VI

# HEGEL

## Hegel, Enlightenment, and Christianity

A FIRST APPROACH TO G. W. F. Hegel may be taken in terms of a comparison between two ideal-typical positions: what I will call the Enlightenment heritage and Orthodox Christian Theology. The approach is ideal-typical in that it develops in terms of a projection of certain tendencies in different thinkers that are viewed as heading toward an ideal term that may be held *in toto* by none of them, but that illuminates tendencies in them all. And I want to approach the three positions—Enlightenment, orthodox Christian, and Hegelian—in three areas: theology, anthropology, and Christology. I take this approach partly because it allows us to fill in something of the thought movements to which we have paid insufficient attention, but which are required by an overview of the salient points in the whole of Western thought; but mainly because it is particularly illuminating with regard to Hegel. Some of the typical contemporary rejections of Hegel have the same basis in the Enlightenment as some of the typical rejections of orthodox Christianity (which is not to say that Hegel was entirely orthodox).

In the Enlightenment theological heritage, there is the tendency to consider God as a separate entity, absolutely one and apart from things, in a manner one might envision the separation of one atom from another in Greek atomic theory. Creation is the fashioning of preexistent material by this God as a Divine Architect or Watchmaker.[1] In the area of anthropology, there is a tendency to view the human Spirit as spatially locatable, inside the head. Locke's view comes to mind: awareness as a dark, empty chamber into which light enters through the slits of the senses.[2] Spirit is considered as either separated from the brain, as in Locke's "inner chamber," or identical with it, as in Hobbes's or La Mettrie's materialism or Hume's phenomenalism.[3] In either case, experience is something subjective that occurs inside the head as an effect of exterior causal processes, which tend to be viewed as so all-encompassing that even so-called free acts are explained in terms of antecedent causal processes. On the social level, there is social atomism. Paralleling methodical procedure in classical physics, society is considered in terms of its ultimate constituents, isolated individuals, starting from which we attempt to construct a comprehensive view of society through the positing of a founding contract between those isolated individuals.[4] Original innocence belongs to human nature, which becomes corrupted through social structures.[5] The Good Life is viewed as satisfaction of appetite and thus as freedom from pain. Medical research aims especially at the latter, technological advancement in general at the former.[6] Humankind progresses in enlightenment as we learn the mechanisms of nature and use them for our benefit (i.e., the procurement of pleasure and the avoidance of pain).[7] If we wish to retain Christianity in such a view, Christ is viewed as the good man, the moral exemplar.[8] Grace, if considered at all, is conceived of as an outside aid in reaching the Good Life.[9]

If we compare this set of related views with an ideal-typical analysis of orthodox Christian theology (at least pre-sixteenth-century orthodoxy), we find a significant contrast on all scores. Many of the things for which people blame Hegel are actually closely related to the claims of this traditional Christian theology. Among other things, Hegel is trying to give a conceptual transcription of that theology. He claims that Christianity has revealed the basic truth; but he also claims, following Lessing, that revelation was not rational when it occurred (it was received from without and not at all understood in its basic grounds), yet it is directed toward our rational comprehension.[10] Thomas Aquinas says something similar in his *Summa theologiae* where he talks about things that are available through philosophic inference as well as through revelation. Aquinas includes in the latter such things as the existence of God, those of His attributes inferable as the causal grounds of the objects of experience, and the natural moral order, specifically the Ten Commandments. They were revealed, according to Aquinas, because they are necessary for proper human behavior, but they can only be discovered through reason by thinkers of significant capacity, with great effort, over long stretches of time, and with significant admixture of error. But once given, such truths can be underpinned and fully integrated into our lives by reaching them through the extensions of our experience by means of the work of reason. However, there is a limit: for Aquinas some truths—those that are not inferable as causally implicated in what we can experience—can only be known through revelation.[11] That includes the central Christian dogmas of the Trinity, the Incarnation, and the nature of the Sacraments. Hegel, on the contrary, acknowledges no limits: we can give a conceptual transcription of revelation that makes sense out of it (i.e., integrates it into our experience as a whole) and that likewise makes sense out of the entire history of Western philosophy.[12]

In the orthodox Christian theology I am considering, the first truth is that God is Trinity.[13] This is one of the things that Aquinas places beyond the scope of reason's power of inference. Not so for Hegel: God as sheer identity, the One as First Principle, is dead; God as Trinity, as identity-in-difference, is alive, a moving Ground, the very paradigm of Reason.[14] In the traditional teaching, common to both Plotinus and Augustine, God "others" Himself in the Logos, which is the basis for the outpouring of the otherness of creation.[15] The Logos precontains all the ways the Father/One can be mirrored outside the Godhead in creation. The Holy Spirit is the union of the otherness of the Father and the Logos-Son. Being is trinitarian in its ground. These were some of the basic truths, essential to Christianity, that Augustine claimed to find in the Platonists.[16] In traditional orthodox Christology, the Logos was made flesh in Christ, who was not only the good man, the holy rabbi, the great teacher, but God in his otherness.[17] Only the Logos, as the internal otherness of the Father, could enter into the otherness of creation.[18]

In creating, God does not simply remain separate, but, by reason of the fact of perpetually giving complete being to creation, He is, in the words of Augustine, nearer to creatures than they are to themselves.[19] God, being absolutely infinite as the ground of the total being of the finite, is more transcendent than the Watchmaker God of the Enlightenment, who fashions matter separate from Him, or, for that matter, more transcendent than the finite, noncreating, exemplar divinity of Aristotle. At the same time, He is more immanent than in either view as the Ground of being of all that is, having to sustain knowingly and freely all that is. God is not simply Fashioner but Creator, not simply giving form and furnishing exemplarity, but also giving full being to all outside Himself.[20]

And only humanness, as sole locus of openness to the Infinite in material creation, constitutes the external condition for the possibility of being assumed by the Logos in the God-Man.[21] Humanness is understood as the image of God and is thus not wholly locked up in the finite, but is finite-infinite, finite having designs on the infinite. The human being as the image of God consequently involves a view of Spirit that is not simply identical with the body, nor simply contained within the head or even totally within finite conditions. The human being as aware and responsible, having intellect and will, is openness to the totality of Being.[22] However, historically human beings are in a darkened condition brought about by an Original Fall that is passed on to the whole race.[23] This transmission is linked to the fact that a human being is not an atomic individual, but is intrinsically social, and, indeed, as believer, a member of the Mystical Body of Christ, the Incarnate Logos. That is not intended merely as a metaphor but as an ontological reality.[24] There is an internal connection between all believers, who share in a common life, the life of grace, which is not only an outside aid but, more deeply, a participation in the divine life, the indwelling of the Trinity in our own togetherness as a community of love. Love as the bond of the Spirit in the community is an identity-in-difference: not simply an external connection or an interior merging, but the fostering of difference by identifying with it and discovering one's own identity in the process. This becomes the formula for Being itself. God is an identity-in-difference as divine Love; so also with God and creation, Spirit and body, individual and community—they are intelligible as identities-in-difference, each dyad in its own way. God is love. Trinity expresses that: the Spirit is the bond of love between the Father and the Son, Who are other than one another and yet are united in the deepest and most complete manner possible.[25] That has implications for thinking about interpersonal relationships.

The trinitarian structure of identity-in-difference is the logical "genetic code" for all reality. Creation is God's own othering for Hegel—though this is far from being orthodox. In orthodoxy the Trinity is complete before creation, needing nothing outside Itself. God creates out of love and out of choice to share divine goodness.[26] In Hegel, by contrast, God is empty possibility developing out of the empty notion of Being and requiring, needing instantiation in the concrete realms of Nature and History.[27] For Hegel, God *needs* creation and *must* create. Creation for orthodoxy is *other than*, not the *othering of* God. The latter is, in orthodoxy, the Incarnation. Further, the point of creation is that God be manifest in knowledge and love, and in orthodoxy the Incarnation is the in-principle final manifestation of God that is completed in fact through the completion of history.[28] Finally, in Christianity one does not flee from pain but, when it is inevitable, embraces it, not masochistically but by identifying with Christ on the Cross, Who asked precisely not to have to undergo it—though one finds it difficult to resist seeing masochism in much of the spiritual tradition. It is through His suffering and death that His Resurrection and consequently our redemption occurs.[29]

There is clearly a vast difference between the Enlightenment heritage, which we all share rather spontaneously and are inclined to defend "rationally," and the Christian tradition, which Hegel attempted to interpret rationally in the modern era. He claimed to be an orthodox Lutheran to the end of his life, but the claim has been challenged (in different ways, based on differing interpretations of what he actually did).[30]

## The Starting Point of the Hegelian System

Hegel is the great synthesizer, who sought to contain the entire philosophic tradition, with its Greco-Roman and Judeo-Christian sources, in a single system of astonishing power and insight. There is a very real sense in which he establishes a persuasive synthesis of Parmenides, Plato, and Aristotle, mediated by the dominant symbols of Christianity and grounded in the turn to the subject focused in a special way in Descartes.

Parmenides opened Western metaphysics with the proclamation of the identity of thought and being and presented a claim to knowledge of the essential features of being. He described a goddess revealing to him that "'It is' and 'It is not' is not." He proceeded to a conceptual analysis that removes all elements of nonbeing ("It is not") from the notion of being ("It is"). If we perform that analysis, being shows itself as changeless and absolutely one: changeless because change involves the nonbeing of the no-longer and the not-yet in the never-finally-there of the moving Now; absolutely one, and not a one of many that is itself composed of a multiplicity, because any one among many is *not* the others, and any one composed of multiplicity is such that one aspect is likewise *not* the others.[31] However, for Hegel, as for Nietzsche, such being is not the fullness of reality but "the last trailing cloud of evaporating reality."[32]

If we think how we might arrive at such a notion starting from the things of experience, we might set in motion a sorting process that, by leaving aside concrete differences, arrives at progressively higher order (i.e., more universal, more encompassing) logical classes. Beginning with the multiplicity of actual people, we leave aside the many interesting things that distinguish each of them to arrive at the notion of humanness, which is their common identity. Thinking in terms of the next wider class, we arrive at the identical notion of animal, which leaves aside the concrete differences between the various species of animals, humans included. Moving further upward and leaving progressively more aside, we arrive at the identical notion of organism, and further still at the notion of body. Finally, in the Aristotelian line, we reach the category of so-called substance (*ousia,* beingness), which includes the bodily and the mental.[33] Going back to the concrete things from which analysis began, we are able to sort out common features in all substances: quantitative features such as weight or extension, qualities such as sensory features or powers or habits, relations of various sorts, including the spatial and temporal, actions and passivities and the like. The features fall into the general notion of attributes (*symbebekota,* things that are "yoked together" with the basic beingness of things). Substance and attributes are described as being-in-itself and being-in-another respectively: a substance, such as a person or a tree, exists as self-grounded ("in itself"), in opposition to the features of things, such as their color or height, which exist only in and on the basis of the things that ground them. Hegel takes us one step further: leaving aside the "in itself" and the "in another," we arrive at the pure notion of being. Since (as we followed in the line of substance) every logically higher order, i.e. more inclusive category, can be inclusive of broader ranges of things only insofar as it leaves aside more and more differentiating aspects of those things in order to concentrate upon commonalities, the last move, isolating the notion of being from the two modes of being-in-itself and being-in-another, leaves us with a notion that is completely empty. Hence it turns out to be identical with its opposite, nothingness or nonbeing. But then, far from being changeless, as Parmenides claimed, such a notion is identical with becoming or process, for, as Plato indicated, process is the mixture or synthesis of being and nonbeing: being no longer what it was and not yet being what it is to be.[34]

Here we find Aristotle's notion of *phusis.* The notion of being is not only the empty notion of process; it is also all-encompassing, for outside being there is nothing. Hence the empty notion of being strains toward its own unfolding in the totality of the concrete universe. Being has an erotic structure in the Platonic sense of the term *erotic:* it is emptiness that has designs on plenitude. But in contrast to Plato, it is the Eternal having designs on the temporal for Its fulfillment. At the same time, Parmenides' claim that "thought and being are one" gives the telos to the process: being in its inner nature is directed to manifestness, is intrinsically related to Spirit and is completed in being understood.[35] So, it would make no final sense to have a world in which Spirit did not appear. Hence the embarrassment that surfaces today in the all too common epiphenomenalist notion of spirit that is left over once we turn over all explanation in the sciences to observation and mechanism. In such a view, spirit as awareness is a residual by-product of the nervous system that is able to do absolutely nothing, not even practice science.[36] Its functional place is taken by brain mechanisms; its appearance is undeniable, but also inexplicable because—by hypothesis—totally inactive. It is the locus of a wholly passive display of part of the workings of the nervous system. But if nature can be understood, so, contrary to the epiphenomenalist, can the locus of its manifestness, namely human understanding. And nature comes to fuller manifestness when we understand that it strains to produce, in increasingly more complex and centralized animal organisms, the conditions for its own progressive manifestation. It is this link between being and manifestness that sets the immediate context for Hegel's view of art. Far from being irrational, such a view leaves no dangling irrationals such as appear in that scientific view that leaves out conscious Spirit, except as functionless epiphenomenon.

Being-Nonbeing-Becoming constitutes the first triad of Hegel's System and exhibits the kind of formulaic structure that Fichte had described as thesis-antithesis-synthesis.[37] The synthesis is called *Aufhebung*, an ordinary German term that can mean three apparently quite different and even opposing things: cancellation, preservation, and elevation. The notion of Becoming cancels out the one-sidedness contained in the notions of Being and Nonbeing, preserves what is seen in each of them in isolated fashion, and elevates the insights contained in them to a new and higher level of mutual compatability.[38] In a sense this is the strategy for approaching any great thinker in the history of thought. What we have to realize is that each classic has a hold on something of crucial significance, else it would not have continually drawn the attention of those who think seriously in these matters. But thinkers hold opposite views. What is seen by a given thinker? Preserve that. What is one-sided about the understanding of what is seen? Cancel that. How can we put these two insights together and do justice to what is seen in them singly? The Spirit drives in this way over time through all partialities to a more comprehensive understanding of things: generating positions, evoking counterpositions and finding higher syntheses.

When we arrive at the empty notion of Being we find something that is there for Spirit as something manifest to us. So going back to Parmenides, the first great metaphysician, there is a sense in which thought and being are one. The question is, in what sense are they one? At least in this sense, that being is there for manifestation to Spirit and that manifestness is an identity-in-difference. We stand over against what is being revealed to us; it is being manifest precisely as it is and where it is, other than us; but it is also "in" us as our knowledge. Thus there is also a kind of identity: what is called in the Scholastic tradition an intentional or cognitive identity. Knowing is, in Scholastic terminology, being the other as other.[39] Being other is change; knowing is being *the* other, precisely as it is other than the consciousness to which it is manifest. Thought is not just present to itself in blank self-identity. The whole of being is there for manifestness; the point of being is to be there for manifestness.

So what we get in the Parmenidean formula on the identity of thought and Being is a statement of the fundamental teleology of the process of reality. The reality process is not simply that of empty Being trying to become fully what it can be—though that is the case; it is, more fundamentally, Being as aimed at creating the conditions for its being fully manifest by producing the conditions for the locus of manifestness: human existence.

## The Development of the System

Nature strives to produce from itself complex and centralized organic structures that culminate, on one level, in the animal senses, which manifest aspects of the environment relative to the needs of the organism; but on another level, there is a leap to another genus when fully reflective Spirit appears. The human Spirit is the goal of nature's own hierarchical process that strives for its own manifestations.[40] Spirit working at the manifestations of nature is the history of thought. The history of the uncovering of nature is the history of the uncovering of that which aims at producing Spirit. And that uncovering is only possible through the production of culture in the broader sense: language, family, economy, political organization. The aim of political organization is ultimately to make possible the display of the whole.[41] In this sense Hegel is continuous with the line from Plato and Aristotle to Aquinas. The highest activity in this universe of physical reality is contemplative thought, speculative thought (from *speculum*, the mirror, the "spectacle"). The ultimate aim of thought is to mirror the whole: the Spirit is, in this way, all things. At the base of things, thought and Being are one in intention; thought and being strain toward becoming one in actuality as the telos of things.

Nature elaborates for itself *in concreto* what that Logos system is in itself and *in abstracto*.[42] Here Hegel is in the line of Plato, Plotinus, Augustine, and Aquinas: the Logos precontains the ways in which the infinite divine can be imitated in the finitude of nature. The One, for Hegel an empty primordial process, spills over into the multiplicity of intelligible principles that constitute the Logos system, the system of possibilities for the One to be realized in multiplicity. The Christian thinkers had put together Platonism and the prologue to St. John's Gospel: In the beginning was the Logos, *with* God and *as* God, through Whom all things were made and Who was the Light illuminating all men. Within the Trinity, the Logos is the othering of the Father that makes possible the otherness of creation and the entry of God Himself into that otherness in Christ the God-Man. The task of the sciences is to uncover the Logos-system mirrored in things. But in Hegel, the Logos-system consists of mere possibilities for existence. He calls it "God in Himself."[43] Reversing Plato, the Ideas are not real being from which things instantiating the Ideas in space and time are derivative and secondary;[44] rather, following Aristotle, things are real being *(prote ousia)* and the universal Ideas are being in a secondary sense as the fulfillment of concrete things in their intelligible manifestness to Spirit.[45] Abstract universals are intelligibilities actualized by the Spirit in its relations of manifestness to things. In the Aristotelian view, "the intelligible in act is the intellect in act."[46] So for Hegel the Logos-system needs Nature and the emergence of Spirit out of Nature in order that the Logos become actual. Hence the Trinity *requires* spilling over into creation because in Itself It is only an intelligible system of possibilities.[47]

For Hegel, the first triad, Being-Nonbeing-Becoming, spills over into a second, Essence, and is related to it as inner to outer insofar as intelligibility involves a move from surface to depth.[48] The two are joined synthetically by the Notion *(Begriff)*, in which the show of the process occurs, although at this stage it is the notion of the show, the concept of manifestness, not the manifestness itself. Real manifestness requires concrete Nature worked up to the point of humanness. The inner is transformed from intelligible interiority to conscious interiority. And the latter is not a withdrawal from the publicity of things, but the locus of their manifestness. The actual Spirit is the place where the manifestness of the whole occurs. Here is a retrieval of Parmenides' "Thought and being are one" and Aristotle's "The soul is, in a way, all things."

Within the context of the Logic we find the grounds for correcting what is perhaps the most frequent misunderstanding of Hegel's System. Those grounds lie in Hegel's demonstration of—paradoxically expressed—the necessity of contingency. When the System—the necessarily coimplicated structures of Logic, Nature, and Spirit—spills over into spatiotemporal existents, it enters into the realm of vast contingency. For Hegel there is no way one could deduce—Laplace-like—the position and velocity of any particle in the universe or the coming into being of any particular entity or the vast plurality of species. These all belong to the empirical realm, replete with contingency, that is the domain of continuing empirical scientific exploration. The System claims to present the necessity of the coming into being of just those general levels of actuality—physical, living, animal—requisite to the emergence of the human Spirit.

Spirit in its actuality is a product of Nature, indeed the goal of nature. Spirit has its other, namely body, as a moment of outwardness required for the emergence of Spirit.[49] Spirit needs the sensorily given other to come to apprehend the intelligible inwardness revealed and concealed in the sensory surface. But such surface can only be manifest through the bodily organs. (Here we begin to see the location and glimpse something of the role of art.)

The manifestness of the whole is the Notion of notion or the Idea fully returned to itself in comprehensive thought.[50] Hegel uses the image of a tree to give a graphic conception of the main lines of his System. The first triad of the Logos gives what we might today call the basic "genetic code" and the Logos system constitutes the seed. Nature is the tree ramifying into its various branches according to the logical genetic code. The Logos-system is being-in-itself, or potentiality; Nature is being-outside-itself, or spatiotemporal existence; and Spirit in its history is being-in-and-for-itself, or actualization, being returned in manifestness to the Logos-system. Spirit divides into three forms: Subjective, Objective, and Absolute Spirit. Subjective Spirit is the bud on the tree of life; Objective Spirit the flower; Absolute Spirit the fruit, the telos of the tree. Subjective spirit divides into three again: anthropology, as the physical articulation of the organism, grounds phenomenology, or the realm of the appearance of things and persons to awareness and thus of an inwardness that makes manifestness possible; both are surmounted by psychology, which comprehends the subjective conditions for intelligent fashioning and intelligible manifestness.[51] The ultimate distance from the Now (which Hegel calls "negative," or "formal freedom") afforded by our reference to the whole makes possible both freedom of choice in the practical order and intelligible manifestness in the theoretical order.[52] Freedom of choice introduces a vast level of contingency, in and beyond the contingencies of Nature, of arbitrariness, irrationality, and also of creativity characteristic of humanness. The structures displayed at this level are the conditions for the possibility of the next two levels: Objective and Absolute Spirit.

The essentially embodied Spirit is, to begin with, merely Subjective Spirit, merely the basic set of human potentialities in concrete individuals. It requires Objective Spirit—that is, the development of the objectifications of thought in institutions, habits, customs, ways of life, traditions, in order that, through time, Spirit might come more fully to itself through the growing manifestness of the whole. (Here we begin to see the role of tradition in the development of the conditions for art.) Subjective Spirit does not develop its potentialities without a social matrix, which is the objectification brought about by past and present human subjects. One does not arrive at even a rudimentary self-consciousness without the presence of the human other, threatening or confirming.[53] But that does not occur without a developed institutional matrix, beginning with the institution of language. Objective Spirit is the other in relation to the Subjective Spirit, the instantiations of which—human individuals—stand in dialectical relation to one another. The development of Subjective Spirit is thus not only dependent on society, but also on history.

History itself has a goal. Not all people are on the same level except as Subjective Spirit, which, from the point of view of the telos, can participate in history further as it unfolds. Social, political, and economic institutions become, in a sense, more rational over time, not only in the sense of becoming more subjectable to calculation, but also in the sense of becoming more articulated and more understood, providing more amplitude for the exercise of individual choice, and, above all, coordinate with and supportive of the growing manifestness of the intelligibility of the whole of Being. Intelligibility and freedom develop because intelligence objectifies itself more and more through history.[54]

One has to understand here another of Hegel's oft-quoted and mostly misunderstood claims: "The rational is the real and the real is the rational."[55] That has to be related to his claim to the necessity of contingency in nature and to both contingency and irrationality brought into being by human choice in history. It has also to be related to his teleological view of nature and history. "Real" translates *wirklich,* which indicates the reaching of a goal, the actualization of a directed potentiality. The rational is what has reached its fulfillment. What has not reached it, though factual, is not real or actual and thus irrational. In this context, also note Hegel's seemingly arrogant claim that if the facts do not measure up to the Concept, so much the worse for the facts. All that means is that if a fertilized ovum develops into a functionless cripple, so much the worse for the factual cripple; if a functional adult fails to become mature, reflective, and responsible, so much the worse for the factual adult; if the factual arrangements in a society fail to evoke or tend to block the emergence of mature, reflective, and responsible citizens, so much the worse for the society. The cripple, the immature adult, and the repressive society are all factual but "unreal." The task of thought is to penetrate through the contingencies and irrationalities to detect the underlying rationality operative in nature and in history.

Objective Spirit is, again, divided into three: the abstract sphere of right,[56] the inner sphere of "morality" *(Moralität)* or conscience,[57] and that which puts the two together, the concrete ethical community (*Sittlichkeit,* from *Sitte,* customs, the concrete ways of life for a people).[58] Ethical life, in turn, exists along three levels: family, civil or contractual society, and the state. They are related in the following way: Family is immediate and concrete, growing up spontaneously through time out of natural sexual and consequent parent-child relations.[59] Civil society is the abstract and mediated level of contract based on the modern notion of abstract rational individuals taking initiative and entering into contractual relations.[60] Ethical life is the encompassing concreteness of a given society bonded together by customs and group feeling. Modern civil society drives a wedge into traditional society, opposing it as the explicitly rational over against the spontaneous and traditional, but grounding the possibility of an enriched ethical community realized in the modern state. Led by patriotic feeling, we are willing to sacrifice our private interests and our very lives for the good of the more encompassing whole.[61]

Now we should underscore, contrary to an army of critics beginning with Kierkegaard, that Hegel's view does not involve the swallowing up of the individuals but rather their location within a vision of the whole. Furthermore, the development Hegel envisions is rational precisely insofar as it advances in maximizing opportunities for individual choice—of occupation, marriage partner, religious affiliation, speech, assembly, and the like—though within the structures that make possible "substantial freedom" (i.e., identification with family, state, and God), and ultimately making possible "absolute knowledge" as the comprehensive view of the whole.[62] Even then, what speculative knowing comprehends is the moral necessity of a community, rooted in the inwardness of the presence of the divine Spirit of love revealed historically through Christ. Such community is characterized by its awareness of the necessity of each—whether at the level of taking responsibility for oneself or at various hierarchical levels for the community—to choose a course of action existent within contingent contexts and generative of consequences that cannot be fully envisioned—hence the necessity of the fallibility of choice. But by reason of being bound to the community, there is also the necessity of offering grounds for the course chosen and being open to correction by others. By reason also of the bond of the community, there is the correlative need for forgiveness for mistaken choices. Absolute knowing is the manifestation of the necessary interrelatedness of categories, which culminates in the coming into being of such a fallible, dialogical community bound together by the spirit of sharing in the divine.[63]

For Hegel the coming into being of such a community and its development through time according to the lines of the System follows Christ's pronouncement that "it is expedient for you that I go [from you into heaven]. If I do not go the Spirit of the Father will not come. When he comes he will teach you to worship in spirit and truth."[64] Spirit reaches its deepest inwardness by appearing in bodily presence and withdrawing therefrom into inwardness and encompassment of all bodily presence. We will see this theme developed especially in the coming into being of the Gothic cathedral.

Objective Spirit is not the goal but merely the flower that precedes the goal. The final fruit of the tree of Being is the realm of Absolute Spirit or Spirit absolved from the mere abstract possibility characterizing the Logos-system considered by itself, the concrete but non-self-present realm of Nature, and the conscious but finitely bounded realm of human awareness constituting history prior to the emergence of the Hegelian System. Through history Spirit returns to itself. This occurs first in the realm of *art*, where the Absolute is displayed in sensory form; then in the realm of *religion*, where the turn within, to the heart, is accomplished. The process is completed by the comprehension made possible over time through the development of *philosophy*.[65] We will return to art shortly.

The mode of interiority that rises above art is religion, which gives expression to the human heart's rising up from the everyday to the encompassing eternal.[66] But religion thinks about the absolute in pictorial terms: God is a father, the Logos a son, the Spirit a dove.[67] In the development of theology, it thinks conceptually, but only with the static, regional abstractions *(Vorstellungen)* of the understanding *(Verstand)*, not in the developmental and comprehensively related categories *(Begriffen)* of all-encompassing Reason *(Vernunft)*. One has to give the conceptual cash value of the pictures and life to the abstractions through philosophic comprehension, which thus rises above religion, moving even more inward because it reaches the very inwardness of Spirit.[68]

Philosophy begins in Parmenides with the notion of Being and the proclamation that thought and Being are one.[69] But this occurs at the beginning only abstractly and apart from the world of our everyday experience. It has to descend into the world to comprehend it totally. Its in-principle comprehension is displayed in the System we have sketched. Such a system not only comprehends the main lines of Nature, it also, and especially, includes the main lines of History. For Hegel, the divine Spirit operates even more in History than it does in Nature.[70] Providence governs what occurs, driving toward the full disclosure of the meaning of the whole. But History, like Nature, is no serene unfolding of a harmonious whole: it involves the pain of struggle and destruction, even at the level of the history of philosophy. However, in and through the cross of contradiction, suffering, and destruction, the meaning of the whole is progressively displayed.[71] For Hegel, art is a critical dimension of that display.

## The Nature of Art

Rather than focusing on the transcendentality of beauty in which natural beauty has a central place, as in the Platonic and medieval traditions, Hegel focuses on art. The beauty of nature for Hegel is a mirror of human moods and is in itself too indeterminate for a science of beauty.[72] Subhuman nature cannot exhibit the kind of unity capable of expression in a single form such as we find in human beings precisely because in humans Spirit as such is active.[73] And even the human being, enmeshed in "the hunger of Nature" and "the prose of everyday life," is not capable of exhibiting the full ideality of Spirit.[74] Art, on the other hand, has already passed through the medium of Spirit, which allows for a more determinate conceptual treatment and thus stands on a higher level than the beauty of nature.[75] In fact, art allows for the possibility of the presentation, not only of surface beauty, but of ideality, and that because it is the expression of Spirit.[76] What appears in art is like the human eye, in which the unity of the whole behind the surface is expressed. The whole is concentrated in the external show.[77] In art we are detached from the limited manifestness characteristic of animal desire and human need and have returned to ourselves as free spirits in our proper infinity. Art shows the inner repose of the human spirit, even in the midst of outward tensions; it exhibits the ideality behind the surface show. In a lyrical line anticipating Nietzsche, Hegel remarks: "Even in the expression of suffering the sweet tones of the plaint must penetrate and clarify the sorrows, so that it continually may seem to us worth all the suffering to arrive at such sweetness of plaint in its expression. And this is the sweetness of melody, the singing of every kind of art."[78]

Hegel begins his introduction to the study of art by confronting various views. One view considers art something frivolous, mere phenomenal froth covering the deeper things of life. By contrast, Hegel notes that in art people have given expression to some of their deepest insights.[79] He thus pushes beyond Kant's initial concentration on taste in relation to sensory surface (arabesques, bird plumage, and the like) as "free beauty" and follows the direction indicated by Kant's "ideal of beauty" in that form of "dependent beauty," which is the human being acting under moral laws. Taste, says Hegel, only deals with the surface.[80] We must press beyond to that which is expressed in the highest forms of art: the noblest ideals and the deepest insights of humankind.

Another view, encountered in the tenth book of Plato's *Republic*, claims that art by its nature deals with a medium of mere exteriority, surface, even deception and is thus unworthy of serious study. Hegel counters with the claim, backed up by and central to his System, that *appearance is essential to being* and that the appearance of things in art is more revelatory of the heart of things than the surface nature presents in ordinary experience.[81] Art is born of Spirit, and that alone places it higher than all of prehuman nature.[82] Indeed, one might say that the manifestation of Spirit is itself the meaning of nature: when Spirit manifests itself, nature gains something of its own telos. But art in its higher forms doubly manifests Spirit: it displays

Spirit's insight into that which stands beyond the sensory surface and thus beyond subjective Spirit. Indeed, even and perhaps especially as mediated by common interpretation, objects in the lifeworld close off more of their underlying meaning than they disclose. That spontaneously appearing surface, product of the interplay between animal senses and cultural interpretation, is more deceptive than the higher forms of art, for it presents itself as final "reality," though it is merely mediated surface. It is a hard rind through which thought must penetrate to reach toward the depths it conceals.

While accepting the view that art gives expression to deep insights, others think that the aesthetic is still a dispensable coating on the ideas, like sugarcoating on a pill.[83] But for Hegel art effects a mediation between abstract ideas and presence in the sensory environment. In art the spiritual is sensualized and the sensuous spiritualized.[84] Art "consists precisely in the reciprocal relation, affinity, and substantive fusion of significance and form."[85] However, having its origin in insight that is one with the emotions of its creator, it attains to an alien existence in its expression in the work of art that calls for a return to the Spirit through the work of appreciative, and eventually of comprehending, thought.[86]

The ground of the work of art is the insight of genius who needs technical ability to translate his insight into external form.[87] Those who place nature higher than art on the grounds that nature is God's creation, which we cannot rival, fail to see that God operates in human beings as well—and even more deeply. It is He who inspires the genius with ideas which rise above mere nature to manifest its significance as the matrix for spirit.[88] Through such manifestness nature itself comes to fulfillment. The work expresses both its subject matter and who the artist himself is. If the work that emerges from such inspiration is great art, it is purged of all that is merely idiosyncratic both in the object and in the vision of the artist.[89]

Hegel confronts various views of the purpose of art. One is that art imitates nature. If that is understood to mean copying the sensuous surface, Hegel considers it superfluous when successful, since nature does a far better and more consistent job of creating that surface—and here Hegel agrees with the critics who hold to art's essential superficiality. Even in the case of Zeuxis, who painted grapes so realistic that doves pecked at them, creating illusions is not a very exalted business. For Hegel the invention of hammer and nails was far more important. If the imitation is to rank as fine art, the object and the mode of presentation must be beautiful. And in visual presentation, the frame must be so selected as to present a well-proportioned use of space. Further, the object also must undergo transformation from a mere natural fact to something expressive of spiritual life. So art must elevate its object from the everyday to the ideal.[90] And even further, some arts are not given over to such imitation as their essence: consider especially architecture and music. However, natural shapes constitute an indispensable foundation for art, from time to time rescuing it from the stiffness and staleness of convention into which it often falls. Yet such imitation is not the end of art, only a sort of beginning.[91]

A second view of the aim of art is that it is to arouse the heart to sympathize with the whole range of human feelings. But these feelings are both good and bad, noble and ignoble, based on insight and based on illusion. Art would thus only serve to magnify the inner contradictions from which we all suffer. Thus the question emerges of the unity to be attained in this vast welter of conflicting feelings aroused by art. One suggestion, related to Aristotle's notion of catharsis, is that art's end is to mitigate the fierceness of desires. It does this by giving us the distance afforded by objectification. We do not simply live in our passions: we observe them in the objects of art. The talk about "oneness with nature" in feeling is mere barbarism: art dissolves that oneness and makes us more human—in other words, more in possession of ourselves as rational agents by granting us distance from nature, which is itself a lower phase of being.[92]

And we have to go further since the view in question still does not separate the pure from the impure in passion itself. Art is thus said to aim at moral instruction as its essential end. Art has been in fact the first instructor of a people, not only for moral purposes but also in terms of general worldview.[93] But considered this way, art seems superfluous coating on what is available prosaically in its full truth. Form and content are separated into the delightful, which is inessential, and the didactic, which makes the work of art a dispensable means. The sensuously individual and the spiritually general become external to one another.[94] In the context of the time in which Hegel wrote, which is still in many ways our time, the conflict between the polarities of existence was especially stark. In the dominant Kantianism, the moral realm, which in one view it is art's sole task to teach, is based on a separation of will from impulse, whether noble or ignoble, and denies their reconcilability. But the conflict extends further to the more general conflict between essential reality and actual existence, between abstract law and individual phenomenon, between reason and sensory experience, spirit and matter.[95] Kant both heightened the antitheses, especially in his view of morality, and provided, in his third critique,

*(margin note)* historical and objectification

the basic direction for their overcoming. Hegel sees in the Kantian notion of purposiveness the notion that reconciles the universal and the particular since the encompassing end subsumes the particular parts and phases of a biological process and since, in the work of art, the concept is wholly united with the aesthetic form. Correspondingly, in our aesthetic perception understanding and sensibility are fused.

In Hegel's view, art's fundamental mission is to reconcile these antitheses. Thought, by reason of its empty orientation to the whole via the notion of Being, sets up an abstract realm in opposition to the sensuously given immediate. It is art's mission to heal the rift thus generated. Art ought to be "generality made absolutely individual and sensuously particularized."[96] It is not fundamentally subservient to moral instruction or, indeed, to education in basic worldview. It has its end in itself: to reveal the Absolute in sensuous form, to display Spirit as the encompassing ground and telos operative here and now in the sensuous display of the natural materials reshaped by genius in such a way that the Ideal wholly penetrates all the details of the presentation. Here Hegel expressly puts forth the school of Phidias as an exemplar of ideal presentation.[97] One should note that the fundamental character of the re-formation of the sensuous material is historically correlated with the character of Spirit's awareness of the Absolute. This yields several different stages in the development of art.

### The Basic Stages and Forms of Art

As Hegel sees it, there are three stages in the history of art: symbolic, classical, and romantic. They are based on three relations of art forms to the idea of art as the display of the Absolute, the meaning of the whole, in sensuous form.[98] To begin with, Spirit is present to the sensuously given Now against the background of the whole of being that is initially present as empty intention. Spirit strains to give sensuous expression to the empty whole that appears as the mysterious Beyond. Spirit does not grasp the character of the whole but only stands before it in awe. This gains expression first of all in the monstrous, the huge, the distorted and strained—but also in the simple reproduction of the everyday (a cat, a lion, a beetle, an ibis) as containing some feature symbolic of the Beyond. All this is characteristic of what Hegel calls the *symbolic* stage of art, as it appears, for example, in the ancient Egyptians, Hindus, and Chinese. Its basic vehicle of expression is found in architecture, which deals with massive forms, many of which are not directly imitative of nature but symbolize (i.e., suggest) the strangeness of the mysterious Beyond: the overpowering massiveness of the temples appearing in all ancient empires, the geometric perfection of the Egyptian pyramids, the distortions of sculptural forms on Chinese and Indian temples.[99] Yearning, fermentation, mystery, and sublimity are characteristic of this stage.

The second relation of Spirit to the sensuous as the display of the Absolute occurs in *classical art* when Spirit begins to grasp the inner intelligible nature of reality and the adequate natural expression of that inwardness in the human body as Spirit's own natural otherness. Classical art reaches its high point in Greek classical sculpture, where the ideal proportions of the body—freed from the blemishes of factual contingency—give expression to the repose of Spirit in its inwardness as perfectly united to its exteriority. At the end of the development of Greek thought in Aristotle, the divine Spirit is viewed as finite unitary ground and center of all. Leading up to that we have the notion of the divine split into various divinities that are, in fact, projections of human powers.[100] Greek sculpture presents that finitely understood divine in human form as the statues of the gods. The human body is that sensuously appearing form naturally suited to the expression of finite Spirit. Consequently, this is the stage in which art is wholly adequate to the conception of the divine reached up to that point. Viewed in terms of its highest mission, this is the high point of art, which is identical with a religion of art: it is the classical phase of art. At this stage of human penetration into the encompassing Beyond, art is the vehicle for relating us adequately to the Absolute conceived as finite Mind.[101]

In Christianity both the encompassing infinity of God and human identity with that infinity are manifest. The sensuous as finite presentation is consequently inadequate in principle to give sufficient expression to it. As a result, the classical stage is left behind and we reach thereby what Hegel calls the *romantic* stage of art. The term *romantic* here does not refer simply to the period from the end of the eighteenth to the middle of the nineteenth centuries in the West. It refers to the art that emerged after primitive Christianity—the art that appeared beginning in the Christian Roman Empire. Perhaps one should read the term as *Roman*-tic. In this phase there is a return to the symbolic insofar as the infinity of the divine Beyond cannot be adequately expressed in the sensuous the way finite divine Spirit can in the gestures of the human body. But there is an advance insofar as the Beyond is no longer empty nor full in its finite viewing; it is manifest as Infinite Spirit.[102] Art in this phase is art transcending itself into inwardness and a sense of grounding encompassment.

In one—of many—of his most disputed phrases, one that especially drives art lovers to paroxysms, Hegel speaks here of "the end of art." One fails to note the qualification: "in its highest mission."[103] Once Christianity announced the infinity of God, art was no longer the adequate instrument for that communication. By contrast, at the level of comprehension of the Beyond as finite Spirit reached by the Greeks in the classical age, art became fully adequate to giving expression to such a view, since the human body's external show *is* the natural expression of Spirit. That is what made it classical in the sense of unsurpassable in its type. Religion and art were then capable of identification. But with revealed religion, art could no longer carry on the highest mission because the finite sensuous and the infinite Beyond are not commensurable. Hence the end of art in its highest mission. But Christianity opened up art to a greater range of thematic explorations because of its announcement of the identity of the divine and the human, so that anything in which humans took an interest became expressions of the divine in some way. Hence when modernity opened up the centrality of subjectivity implicit in Christianity from its inception, artistic activity, especially in painting and music, burst into full flower.[104] Hegel went on to claim that, even though its highest mission is a thing of the past, achieved in the classical age of the Greeks, in the future one could expect art to develop different modes of technical elaboration.[105] But the great modern flowering of art has occurred simultaneous with the development of modern philosophy, which culminated in the ultimate inwardness of final intelligible manifestation in the Hegelian System.

The romantic phase is especially characterized by its emphasis on the heart, as in Pascal's expression, "The heart has its reasons, of which 'reason' knows nothing."[106] In Hegel such "reason" is *Verstand*, while *Vernunft* as the faculty of totality deeply involves the heart. One of the fundamental imperatives of human existence is the unity of heart and head. Hegel speaks of "the possibility of a culture of the intellect which leaves the heart untouched . . . and of the *heart without the intellect*—of hearts which in a one-sided way want intellect, and *heartless intellects*—[which] only proves at most that bad and radically untrue existences occur."[107] Religion has its locus in the heart as articulated in terms of our founding openness to the totality. The properly attuned heart is rendered intuitive to all the nuances of any region of thought or practice, and indeed to everyday existence as a whole.[108] Heart is "concentrated individuality" whose special form is genius.[109] It is on this that the arts are based, and it is to this that the romantic phase of art is particularly attentive.

The romantic phase is expressed especially in painting and music. Here physical dimensionality begins to disappear. In painting it is reduced to a two-dimensional surface, to which the viewer has to add the third dimension through his imaginative vision, supplying for the intrinsic deficiency of the medium but adding inwardness thereby.[110] In music we have a complete abstraction from three-dimensional palpability in the concrete presence of sound, which Spirit has to continue to gather since sound rapidly disappears as it moves through time.[111] But music is not mere registration of sound impressions; it is, as Aristotle noted, productive of ethos, the inward dispositions of the heart. These art forms become progressively central vehicles of expression as the basic Christian view pervades institutions, especially flowering in modernity, when subjectivity, inwardness, freedom take center stage. Music is the art of inwardness; and as it develops in modern times into "absolute music," detached from any attempt to portray or imitate, it corresponds to the formal freedom of the abstract ego, which simultaneously surfaced in modern politics. "For musical expression therefore it is only the inner life of soul that is wholly devoid of an object that is appropriate, in other words, the abstract personal experience simply. This is our entirely empty ego, the self without further content."[112]

On the other hand, with Christianity there is a peculiar emphasis on the work of the Spirit as establishing community. Hegel lays great emphasis on community. Absolute knowing, I suggested above, develops the categories that show the teleological completion of the world process in the fallibilistic, dialogic community of confession and forgiveness within the larger structures that expand the arena for individual choice and responsibility while anchoring the individual solidly in family, in state, and in the divine. The enlarged arena for artistic creativity is addressed precisely to that community. And yet Hegel claims that the most suitable subject matter for artistic treatment is taken from the heroic ages—either the early phases of civilization or those transitional phases when an old order has crumbled. It is in these times that order rests on individual virtue and not on an articulated set of laws and practices, as in the modern state. Here it was that the meaning of the whole could be concentrated better in a single figure.[113]

Poetry is a peculiar art form that appears centrally in all three historical phases—symbolic, classical, and romantic—through which art passes.[114] Poetry is able to abstract completely from all direct sensuous mediation in order to appeal directly to the imagination, the central organ of art in all its forms and phases. Thus it uses either sound or written language, being, in a sense, indifferent to either.[115] Nonetheless, Hegel does note the peculiar relation to sound that constitutes poetry—meter, rhyme, alliteration, and the general harmony of sounds—that effects a reconciliation between meaning and sensuousness that Hegel considers to be the mission of all art.[116] In Hegel's treatment of the beauty of art, he actually spends the most time describing the content most suitable for epic and dramatic poetry: the heroic individual in a definite situation, full of conflict. And in dealing with particular art forms, he devotes by far the most space to poetry.[117] By contrast, sculpture and painting are extremely limited in their ability to depict situation and character.[118]

Poetry takes three forms: the universal art of epic, which presents the encompassing community; the individual art of the lyric, which gives expression to individual inward sentiment; and the reconciliation of universal and individual in drama. But the latter goes beyond the other two forms insofar as it gathers together all the other art forms. Aimed at performance, it is both visual and audile; developed as language, it is the bearer of articulate meaning; accompanied by music, dance, and set, and contained within an architectural setting, it is, indeed—to employ a term soon to be made popular by Wagner—the *Gesamtkunst*, the totalizing art form.[119]

Though certain art forms take center stage in each historical phase of development in art history, nonetheless, the advancement of spirit in penetrating the character of the Encompassing leads to the further development of the specific art forms. This is especially the case for Hegel in architecture. Although it carries the highest mission of the spirit at the symbolic phase in expressing the apprehension of the divine as empty and mysterious Beyond, architecture reaches its own perfection only at the romantic phase, in the Gothic cathedral. Romantic architecture, found in the Gothic, is especially well suited to express the turn within and the upward soaring of the spirit to the Infinite through the sensuous and beyond the sensuous.[120] And so in the romantic we have a return to the symbolic, not because the Beyond is dark, but because its infinity is revealed as Infinite Spirit, as I have noted previously. In Gothic architecture the community is set apart from the outside world and through plastic, musical, and poetic forms, in tandem with the upward movement of the architectural interior, the community together is drawn beyond the sensuous.

Poetry is peculiar, since it has a certain independence from the three chronological phases through which the other art forms develop.[121] This is perhaps linked to its basic operation in the medium of imagination, where it becomes the basic vehicle of religious expression.[122] All art in its earlier forms is linked to religion. Thus epic is the linguistic art, which reaches perfection in an early phase of a culture. And lyric and drama reach a certain high point as well in the classical age, though the modern age seems to have surpassed that period in these forms (e.g., in Shakespeare and in the Romantic lyric poets).[123] And though poetry is surpassed in philosophy and Romantic poetry in Hegelian thought, nonetheless it remains the province of poetry—and indeed of the arts in general—"to translate speculative thought into terms of the imagination, giving a body to the same in the sphere of intelligence itself."[124]

Considering the highest function of the arts as the revelation of the divine, Hegel sees architecture as providing the setting for the god who appears in sculpture. He further sees the arts of painting, music, and poetry, which call for completion in the observer-hearers, as informing the community within which the Spirit dwells.[125] Formed by the community, the individual is most its own self in liturgical communion with others—except when raised to the level of totalistic philosophic comprehension on the basis of that communion. But maybe even philosophy is completed in oral communication with the community.

The different aspects in the development of the Spirit are coordinate with one another. The great forms of symbolic art emerge on the basis of a society settled in some way by law and written records in the Oriental empires of China, India, Assyria, Persia, Babylonia, and Egypt.[126] The arts develop as religious expressions on the basis of awareness of the existence of the encompassing All and our special relation to it, but also on the basis of ignorance of Its nature. Thus politics, art, religion, and reflective thought emerge as coordinate forms of the Spirit.

At the next level, Greek institutions in the classical age, though based on a slave substratum, recognize the freedom of the citizens.[127] That makes possible free inquiry and thus the rise of philosophy as self-critical and systematic thought. As a consequence, the Encompassing is no longer seen as empty mystery but as that which is coordinate with reflective thought—ultimately, in Aristotle's God, as Self-thinking Thought. The "other side" of sensory immediacy and everyday functional attention is thought. Classical art gives expression to that in the statues of the gods, finding that sensuous form fit by nature to express finite Spirit, namely the form of humanness.

Christianity, in proclaiming the identity of God and Man in Christ, set in motion a political process that culminates in modern institutions that recognize the freedom and dignity of all humans.[128] In proclaiming the Infinity of God, Christianity also reduced art to a secondary role because its media are no longer adequate to the message.[129] Christianity also, through its Logos doctrine, opened the way to absolute Idealism in philosophy. But, in initiating the romantic phase in art, Christianity indirectly opened art to all that is of interest to human beings.

## Response

I have devoted what some might regard as an inordinate amount of space to my sketch of the Hegelian System. But it was necessary in view of Hegel's claim that the truth is the whole, and that only by seeing the whole can we grasp the fuller significance of the parts. It also provides us with a way of looking back on the historical ground we have covered in its fullest context. Art, as a part, must be seen in its relation to the whole. I am partial to that view and partial to very much Hegel has to say. Such partiality dictates the general form of my work, which covers select highlights in the history of aesthetics, but does so by locating the aesthetic within the overall context of each philosopher's thought. Further, however, I attempt to carry on thereby not merely a series of reports on particular thinkers, but a series of developing reflections on the nature of art and beauty. The play between the thinkers furnishes the means by which, in and through and beyond the "opinions of the philosophers," certain features of the aesthetic realm itself come to be displayed.

Perhaps the central feature of Hegel's thought is his focus on appearance and on its mode of completion in art. Plato tends to treat the realm of appearance *(doxa)* as an obscuring of the Idea; Kant, as an occlusion of the noumenal; and some common interpreters of modern science, as an inexplicable, functionless epiphenomenon that percolates out of the workings of the nervous system uncovered in natural science. For Hegel, being reaches its telos in appearance and one of the highest modes of that telos in art. We are not inexplicably caught in appearance; it is rather appearance that explains the point of the mechanisms of nature. Everything preconscious in nature is simply the condition for the possibility of consciousness and therefore of its own manifestness through the inquiry initiated by consciousness.[130] As in Plato, so for Hegel there *is* an obscuring of the Idea in everyday awareness—the appearance of "the hard rind of nature" tied to the functional adjustment of the organism to its environment and of the individual member to its own limited projects and to society; but it is in art that such obscuring is overcome by clarity. Art is the appearance of spirit and, in its highest forms, not simply, as in everyday behavior, the display of limited intentions, but, as in religion and in philosophy, the mediated display of an apprehension of the meaning of the Whole.

The appearance of the meaning of the Whole in limited forms is one of the most important insights developed in this work. Plato initiated this with his notion of the epiphany of Beauty Itself as the display of cosmically encompassing plenitude in beautiful things. Beauty is spoken of as the only Form perceptible with the eyes; all the other Forms require a turn within and above, away from the sensorily given which reminds us of this Other. On the contrary, we are talking here of a Real Presence in things and not of a reminder in things that leads us away from the reminder to the Presence. In this regard, Hegel claims that it is art that "heals the rift" created by reflection between the encompassing Beyond and the here-and-now present sensorily given. Plato's focus in this regard is not on art but on natural beauty, and, most particularly, the beauty of the human form as object of Eros.

For Hegel the beauties of nature are insufficiently determinate to serve as objects of a science of beauty. Nature mirrors back to us our own moods, which are themselves indeterminate in relation to the clarity of the Concept. Because art has passed through Spirit, it is placed on a higher level than all nature. But passing through Spirit means ultimately being in proximity to the Concept. Nature by itself is more distant from the Concept, but has Concept as its own teleological ground. Nature points to humanness as its completion and humanness, in turn, points to the Concept as *its* own completion.

But there is a sense in which the works of Spirit can themselves constitute a screen between Spirit and its reference to the whole. There is the vanity of "culture" (better pronounced here as "culchah"); there is the "world," which the New Testament says we are not to love. In the Stoics, in Francis of Assisi, in Chinese Taoism, and in Rousseau there is a movement "back to nature" that has its roots in this observation. Nature itself is the whole or the expression of its Origin and civilization is a movement *contra naturam*. Martin Buber distinguished between form and object in relation to works of culture, a distinction that is a subspecies of his distinction between I-Thou and I-It relations. Object appears within networks of identification and use constituting the everyday appearance of things; form appears when the object is haunted by a sense of encompassing mystery and transforms our relation to everything.[131] A work of art may be object of art-historical analysis, exhibition of the psychology of its author or the sociology of the author's general situation; but its fundamental work is addressing the viewer as a significant presence beyond all objectification. Hegel is not unaware of something like this: as we have noted, he speaks of the "hard rind" of the everyday appearance of things; he also speaks of a rising up of the heart, the center of feeling, out of the quotidian to a sense of the eternal and encompassing; and he claims that in art we find a healing of the rift between the sensory surface and our enduring, founding reference to the whole. But it is art and not the immediate appearance of nature that seems so to function for him. Yet in common with those movements and thinkers I have mentioned, in Hegel the return to nature breaks through the staleness of culture to stimulate the development of new artistic forms.

As the preface to this work indicated, my own sense of things is deeply saturated with the sense of prehuman nature in its glorious, haunting, mysterious encompassment. I see the recurrent movement against civilization and back to nature as a healthy corrective, but also as an equally one-sided view of our relation to nature. With Hegel, I see human nature as a part of nature, above "nature" in the limited sense that dualisms have assigned to the term *nature,* and the telos of subhuman nature. Human nature is creative in relation to prehuman nature outside and inside itself, but in such a way as to be able to bring that nature to its own unfolding. Art is a wedding between Spirit and nature in which Spirit finds itself and its own history at one with nature. Back to Nature movements tend to leave no place for history and the works of Spirit; certain humanisms view nature only as adversary. In the line of Hegel, I see the relation as dialectical. As in Kant, art sensitizes us to the beauties of nature while aligning us with our moral task; but it also opens us up to what I would regard as the ultimate point of morality: the appreciation of Being, relishing the role of each type of entity and each individual within the Whole as the basis for appropriate action. Such appreciation avoids what would violate the integrity of each thing and promotes its fullest unfolding within the order of the whole.

There are several meanings of the term *nature.* One is sensory surface —that in which Impressionism often seemed to take exclusive delight. Another is that which is the depth generating that surface. Great portrait artists are interested in such a nature in individuals. A subset of that meaning of nature is that of an archetype expressed in an individual of a species. Classical and neoclassical art was interested in that meaning of nature. Leonardo calls for drawing to attend to the forms displayed immediately in the surface.[132] It is this that Hegel recommends as a rejuvenating sense for even the most abstract forms of art. Henry Moore advocated the same attention. But Moore looked for formative powers beneath the surface.[133] Frank Lloyd Wright suggested a similar move for architecture. But architecture is peculiar in that it must attend to the structural principles of natural forms under penalty of collapsed structures. It is linked to nature more directly than any other art form. Architecture requires engineering knowledge of physical principles. But beyond this, for Wright, it requires the study of living nature in order to learn how to establish, through building in and with the environment, an organic whole.[134]

Hegel's work in aesthetics displays a keen awareness of the eidetic features of each artistic genre, but he is especially focused on the way in which each feature is related to the communication of meaning, which can eventually be sublimated into the conceptual system. However, contrary to Kierkegaard, the individual—person, work of art, or natural thing—is not "swallowed up" in the System. It is rather located than swallowed, directed than coerced. The universal *requires* its instantiations. And in the case of things human—persons and works—freely choosing individuality is central. Works of art, individual lifestyles, cultural worlds are not mere expressions of subjective idiosyncrasies nor simply means for grasping abstractions but the rich ways in which the power of the universal is displayed. The System sets the frame for the appearance of human creativity. One measure of the rationality of the political system is the development of opportunities for choice and thus for creativity.

In response to the further Kierkegaardian critique that philosophers construct huge thought castles and dwell in miserable shacks nearby, a central tenet of Hegel's thought is the notion of dwelling and its locus, the heart. In the heart is the possibility of healing the rift set up by the abstractive work of mind between its own work and the Now of our encounters. Indeed, that the work of reason penetrate to the heart is a central Hegelian imperative. But the work of reason is not restricted to its deliberate phase in philosophy: before it rises to explicit conceptual manifestation, it is already operative in nature and history generally, and specifically in the life experience of a community and of those on the leading edge of development. In my introduction, I emphasized the heart in connection with reference to the totality via the notion of Being. The heart is the center of the Me from which the I as reference to totality stands initially at an infinite distance. The central human task is to bring the heart into coincidence with that founding reference. In that task the arts play an essential role by establishing significant presences. Hegel has the distinction of bringing both the arts and the notion of the heart to the center of the human-cosmic drama.

Kant noted that we can only understand what we make, displaying the essentially manipulative character of Newtonian science;[135] but his complementary view of the appearance of the purposive in life forms and in art forms was linked to a sense of the unencompassable noumenal. Giambattista Vico noted the same basic constructive-noetic principle and then claimed that, since we have made history, that alone is what we can understand.[136] Hegel, in effect, linked the three principles—the constructive-noetic, the teleological, and the historical—by viewing nature and history as constructed by Spirit for the purpose of manifesting to itself its own nature as rising out of nature and history as its own preconditions. Both Kant and Vico displayed a sense of awe before the encompassing as final mystery. For Hegel, it would seem that, although the "rising up of the heart from the quotidian to a sense of the eternal encompassing" is the enduring ground of philosophic comprehension and that the healing of the rift between the eternally encompassing Beyond and the flowing sensuous Now is the perennial task of art, the sense of mystery seems to evaporate in conceptual comprehension.[137] And for us that is a great loss.

# VII

# SCHOPENHAUER

*A Synthesis of Kant, Plato, and the Indian Tradition*

ONE WAY OF LOOKING at Arthur Schopenhauer's thought is to view it as a synthesis between Kant and Plato (together with Plotinus) on the one hand and the Indian tradition on the other. Schopenhauer's early work *On the Fourfold Root of the Principle of Sufficient Reason* was straight Kantian analysis.[1] Recall in Kant the three levels of form, which function as filters or glasses through which the world of appearance is constituted. The first level is that of the forms of sensibility—space and time—which furnish the encompassing frame of all appearance; the second, the level of the categories of the understanding, which sort the flow of experiences and form them into a world of consistent objects; and the third, the level of the ideas of reason, which set the goal of unifying experience as a whole through time. All these are functions of the "I think," the transcendental unity of apperception whereby all experience is unified by the coperceived I as conscious self-employing of the categories of the understanding and striving toward the systematic unity of the whole.

Now in *On the Fourfold Root of the Principle of Sufficient Reason,* Schopenhauer develops the foundations for the various sciences along Kantian lines, resting on the distinctions just recalled. Mathematics is rooted in the forms of sensibility. Natural science is based on the operation of the categories of the understanding, specifically causality. Reason is the ground of logic through which we attempt to establish consistency throughout the whole of our experience. And if we consider the human subject, not only as a center of knowing but also as a source of feeling and of action or willing, we have the basis for the humanities. Everything has a sufficient reason, an explanatory ground; but the explanations are different because of the different regions of experience. In each case, providing a reason consists in establishing relations. However, Schopenhauer does more than merely repeat and amplify Kant.

I said that Schopenhauer's thought could be understood in terms of a kind of fusion between Kant and Plato together with Plotinus. In Plato there is, on the part of the knower, the realm of *doxa,* of opining-appearing, which is, ontologically, the realm of genesis, or Becoming. This is intersected and surmounted by the realm of Being, of *ousia,* locus of the Ideas or noumena (objects of *nous*), which are eternal and universal. They, in turn, are surmounted by the Good, which is also the One, irradiating the Beauty of coherent manifestness on all below it. When we analyze particulars as intelligible particulars—things that can be understood (and being able to be understood means being able to be exhibited as instances of universal meanings)—we require two basic principles: a principle of intelligibility, which comes to be called form, and a principle of both mutability and the multipliability of the same form at different places and times and for different durations. Plato names the latter principle the Receptacle *(hypodoche),* which Whitehead calls "the restlessness of space-time." Aristotle terms it *prote hyle,* or prime matter. Matter so understood grounds both space and time. Spatiality involves having parts outside of parts and thus mutability, the capacity to come apart, and consequently also temporality. Reality as we see it in individual things is a mirroring of changeless and universal principles in a changing and manifold matrix. Matter is thus also spoken of in medieval times as the *principium individuationis,* or the principle of individuation. Schopenhauer uses this expression to refer, not to matter, but to matter's derivatives, space and time together.[2] The principle operates to reflect and multiply what he calls Platonic Ideas. For Schopenhauer, Platonic Ideas specifically include the Ideas of animal species.[3] It is these and other natural forms that are filtered through the *principium individuationis,* so that sensorily given things are expressions of their corresponding Platonic Ideas, jutting into the net of phenomenal relations explored by the sciences with their sufficient reasons. But for Schopenhauer, as for Plato, the Ideas in turn are expressions of something more primordial.

## *The World as Will and Representation*

Schopenhauer's main work is *The World as Will and Representation [Vorstellung]*. Following Kant, his claim here is that the world as we experience it is not noumenal reality, but our representation of that reality. In its actuality it is, first of all, the direct expression of Platonic Ideas that present themselves in and through the phenomenal realm analyzed by Kant. We have to think here of Kant's third critique, *The Critique of Judgment*, in relation to the first critique. *The Critique of Pure Reason* analyzed the conditions for the possibility of objectivity, of intersubjective verifiability, of thing-hood, as distinguished from merely subjective, private, personal experiences. The analysis does not determine what *kinds* of things appear objectively. Kant notes that the appearances of things are capable of being arranged in hierarchies of genera and species, as if Nature met the mind's need for logical order halfway by providing such appearances. Nature can be viewed as if a Divine Artist arranged matter into organic forms, giving expression to His intuition of the specific aesthetic ideas. For Schopenhauer, fortified by the development of German Idealism from Fichte and Schelling to Hegel, the "as if" is lifted: the kinds of things that appear *are* expressions of Platonic Ideas. Each individual is an expression of an ideal form of the species whose perfection it strives to reach, hampered by the complexity of the material conditions of the instantiation of the form. Here Schopenhauer sets himself in opposition to Positivism, according to which the knowable is the sensory in the regularity of its sequences. Hume was the great early modern proponent of this position: we exist, he said, within the great sea of surrounding darkness, inhabiting a small island of light, which is the realm of sensory impressions. He admonishes us to forget about the surrounding whole and to pay attention to surveying and extending the island of light so that we may learn to harness it to our purposes. Auguste Comte gave the name Positivism to this position.[4] The optometrist practices it when he measures the eyeball. But when he does so he abstracts from the fundamental expressivity of the eye. Driven by the will, he views only those aspects of the phenomena that serve our purposes.[5] Schopenhauer, following Kant's third critique, reintroduces the notion of the expressivity of all phenomena that allow for contemplation detached from the interest of the will.

As I have said, what are expressed in experience are Platonic Ideas passed through the *principium individuationis*, which is the realm of the Kantian forms of sensibility (space and time). But the Ideas, in turn, are expressions of what stands behind or above them. In Plato/Plotinus, Ideas are expressions of the One. In Schopenhauer it is not clear whether both the immediately experienced individuals and the Platonic Ideas are the realm of phenomena or whether the individuals are phenomenal and the Ideas noumenal. However, it is clear that both are the world as representation. Whether, like the immediately sensed individuals, they are relative to our modes of understanding and perception, Platonic Ideas give expression to what underlies them. In Plotinus it is the One, in Schopenhauer it is the Will.[6]

Schopenhauer goes back to Kant here and the idea expressed at the end of the third critique that freedom is the sole noumenal fact, where freedom for Kant means our capacity to direct ourselves by our own will over against our being directed by our inclinations, by our passions, by the law-governed movements of our nature. Schopenhauer accepts the will as the escape hatch from the phenomenal, governed by the *principium individuationis,* to the noumenal. However, will is now understood as desire, not as transcendence of desire. Everything phenomenal is expression of underlying desire. Thus the bodily organs express their corresponding desires: the mouth is hunger and thirst incarnate, the sexual organs incarnate Eros.[7] Conscious desire emerges out of a more primordial process of natural desire that Schopenhauer terms Will. Escape from desire transcends the principle of individuation and leads to the notion of a universal subject, as in Plotinus's World-Mind. Basing himself on the mystical experience of identity with the One, Plotinus in effect raised the question implicit in Plato and taken up by the medieval Arabian thinkers and by the German Idealists: where are we and who are we when we rise above the privacy and individuality of our feelings and opinions and are able to uncover the universal, public necessities of science? How can a private interiority uncover a public exteriority, an individual come to know a universal, a temporal being contain an atemporal truth? The answer given in Plotinus and followed in the traditions cited is, in Schopenhauer's terms: when we reach the level of Platonic Ideas we become the World-Mind, "the single eye of the world" as subjects of will-less contemplation, since we have to suspend the peculiarities of our own desires to let what-is appear "for its own sake."[8] In aesthetic contemplation what we apprehend is the Platonic Idea expressed in the individual contemplated.

Plotinus saw his view of things as similar to that of the Hindus. So did Schopenhauer. In the Hindu view the surface of things, the everyday world of experience, is Maya, the veil of illusion, cloaking the basic truth that underlying everything is Brahman, the One, identical with Atman, the Self. Our immersion in the everyday world causes us to lose sight of that and to believe that plurality, difference is fundamental.[9]

But now comes the most decisive thing for Schopenhauer. The ultimate character of the single underlying Will has to be read in terms of what gives expression to it in the sensory surface. If we follow the ancient tradition, the world is a harmonious totality that expresses the One, which is the Good. But if we look carefully, we see conflict, tragedy in the world: "nature, red in tooth and claw," as Tennyson put it.[10] Species are so constituted as to prey upon species. Beneath the tranquil meadow happily reflecting the light and warmth of the noonday sun in early spring, insect preys on insect while the hawk circles above seeking her prey and we sit tranquilly by nibbling on a lamb-chop sandwich. The eternal slaughter goes on. Human history itself is the history of fragile periods of peace strung over continually potential and, all too often, actual war and devastation. Disease, decline, and dissolution follow the bloom of youth. Pain, physical and psychological, dogs conscious existence at every step. As one drooling inmate of Peter Weiss's *Marat/Sade* has it, "Man is a mad animal. . . . I've helped commit a million murders. . . . We few survivors walk over a quaking bog of corpses always under our feet. . . ."[11] In Tennessee Williams's *Suddenly Last Summer*, the poet around whom the play centers wandered one summer day onto a beach in which sea turtles had laid their eggs. At a given time each year, the female turtles slowly crawl up out of the sea. Each laboriously digs a hole in the sand and deposits up to two hundred eggs in its nest. After covering the eggs, she drags herself, exhausted, back to the sea. The sun incubates the eggs, and over time the sand begins to move and then to boil as the tiny turtles hatch, emerge from the sand nests, and instinctively start to make their way to the sea. But beforehand, birds of prey have begun gathering on the cliffs nearby, watching for the first signs of the hatch. When the newborn turtles commence their dash to the sea, the birds swoop down, turn them over, and make a feast of their entrails. The devastation is mighty, and only a small number of the hatchlings make it safely to the water—only to be confronted by the predators of the sea. Of the original two hundred little turtles, one or two from each nest survive to carry on the perennial process. And the poet said, "Suddenly last summer I saw the face of God."[12] Down on that beach, he saw that God was intrinsically vicious. This is at the heart of the Schopenhauerian vision: the underlying ground that all things express is not ultimately the Good/One/Beautiful or the loving Father, but a single, vicious, self-contradictory Will. This is a complete reversal of the traditional view. Schopenhauer would say that it is rooted in a willingness to view reality on its own terms without the possibility of mythological consolation. "God" is actually blind, indifferent, intrinsically conflicting underlying Will spewing up a world that expresses His reality.[13]

The conflict and tragedy that afflicts the external world, both in the relations of natural species and in the relations between people as individuals and as communities at various levels of comprehensiveness, is also found within each of us as the conflict between our animal natures and our higher aspirations. If we escape serious disease and natural disaster, we are constant prey to inward tensions, rarely achieving inward peace.[14] If we could see psyches rather than bodies, we would see something that would resemble Napoleon's army retreating from Moscow: beaten, bruised, battered—an eye missing in one, an arm or a leg blown off in another, crawling, hobbling, painfully attempting to make our way home. And in the end we are food for worms.

Here we can see a kind of sea change in the whole tradition. A completely different sense of the underlying realm emerges. In Hegel, the underlying Spirit was good, but it developed through contradiction and suffering, rising out of its initial emptiness and blindness. In Schopenhauer, the underlying Will is full but blind, causing suffering in what it produces. It is itself not fulfilled but canceled in those who learn to rise above it.[15] Here Schopenhauer turns to the Indian tradition again. He moves close to the thought of the Buddha, who proclaimed the Four Noble Truths. The first is that reality is suffering. The second is that suffering occurs because of desire. The third is that one can gain release from suffering by "the blowing out of desire," the achievement of Nirvana. The fourth is that Nirvana is achieved through the Eightfold Path, beginning with right speech and right occupation and culminating in right meditation. The idea is to attain release from the anguish that afflicts us because of the structure of desire: only the saint attains salvation. And it is along these lines that Schopenhauer understands the Christian asceticism of Meister Eckhart, Angelus Silesius, Bonaventura, Madame Guyon, Johann Tauler, and the New Testament itself.[16]

Schopenhauer picks that up and weaves it into his peculiar combination of Kantian and Platonic/Plotinian themes. His claim is that the underlying reality expressed in the phenomenal order is intrinsically self-canceling, not only in terms of species biting into species because of their basic constitution, but also and especially because of our own basic internal organization that produces psychological tensions, particularly that between the higher aspirations and bodily desires. And the bodily desires themselves are so constituted as to produce the deceptive satisfaction we call pleasure. We are often and foolishly tempted to identify such pleasure with the good. However, it is intrinsically related to pain, not only by producing phenomena like the proverbial hangover after a night of revelry, but also by way of opening up the pain of longing after its temporary satiation. Pleasure itself is simply momentary release from such pain and has no status apart from it. Once satisfied, it only rests for a while and then the pain begins all over again. One way of obtaining release from the will is in aesthetic contemplation, freed of desire.[17] Another is in sympathetic identification with the sufferings of others—not simply human beings, but also other living things as well. Attention is defocused from our own desire and attached to the sufferings Will produces in others.[18] Here we have a seeming recurrence to a basic Hindu notion involved in the ritual formula *Tat tvam asi,* "That art thou," giving expression to the experience of the basic identity of all creatures.[19] But, by reason of the intrinsically conflicting character of Schopenhauer's Will, sympathetic identification is not because of the substantial identity of all things with Brahman, but because of the sage's nonidentity with the One/Will through detachment. Here we have a parallel to the Compassionate Buddha, who, in the Hindu line, learns identification with the suffering of others.[20] Such a one stands above being immersed in the natural struggle of species and of individuals within species expressed in our appetites: he learns to feel for and with others. But the Buddha teaches only release from suffering, not identity with final reality, about which he offers no doctrine.[21] For Schopenhauer identification would seem to have no metaphysical grounds. Rather, he argues for a self-imposed nonidentification with the Will, about which he has a definite doctrine: it is the origin of suffering and destruction as well as of delight and creation. The highest way of escape for Schopenhauer is the achievement of Nirvana, the final aim of the Buddhist way of life.[22]

I underscore that this is not (as in Plotinian and Hindu, as well as in Christian, mysticism) becoming identified with the Will that underlies everything, but precisely becoming detached from it, since It creates suffering in and among Its individuated expressions. Mystical union with the One is definitely not the aim of Schopenhauer's teaching because the underlying One is not good. The task is to get away from It, to blow out the desire that immerses us in It.

## Aesthetic Experience and the Work of Art

Aesthetic experience, like sympathetic identification with others and the achievement of Nirvana, is a means for release from the Will. In aesthetic contemplation the bodily desires are stilled for a moment.[23] Here Schopenhauer follows Kant again: the basic characteristic of aesthetic experience is disinterested satisfaction, a release from bodily based desire in order to let the sensory surface appear in its own integrity. But for Schopenhauer it is not simply the sensory surface in its formal properties that is the object of contemplation. More fundamentally, it is the Platonic Ideas expressed in that surface. For Schopenhauer as for Plotinus, though atemporal, the Idea is not simply the finished form of a developmental process, but includes as well the stages of the process, for the Idea is not simply archetype but generative form.[24] For Schopenhauer, all things are beautiful in their own way, but the things that stand out and arrest us in their beauty are the things in whom their Idea is most visible. In the aesthetic experience of such objects, one becomes the will-less subject of contemplation. Though in this way one attains release from the intrinsic contradictoriness of Will as it appears in us, aesthetic contemplation only releases us for a time. Sympathetic identification as a basic disposition endures over time, but still involves care. Radical release only occurs in the achievement of Nirvana. But aesthetic experience, owing to its more frequent occurrence, helps us to understand the ultimate possibility: final release from the Will.

As did Kant, Schopenhauer considers genius to be the source of art.[25] But he also extends the notion so that it is required for any aesthetic experience, though to a lesser degree in appreciating than in originating the work of art. Genius is the capacity for objectivity, for letting the thing stand out in its own right and not simply as subsumed under our needs.[26] Ordinary experience likewise presents the surface of things through the filters of the *principium individuationis* and the categories of the understanding. In ordinary experience the Platonic Idea is distorted. Creative genius runs ahead of such experience and grasps what nature is stammeringly trying to say.[27] Bringing it forth in a work of art, genius in effect exclaims to nature, "This is what you were aiming at!" That is one way of understanding Aristotle's claim that art partly completes, partly imitates nature. Similarly, perceptive genius, present in various degrees in all of us, discerns through aesthetic experience the presence of the Platonic Idea in such works and in those things of nature where it is most evident. However, the depth of the work is not only what is given to the senses; that must be "born in the imagination of the beholder, though begotten by the work of art."[28] Schopenhauer here anticipates Dewey and Heidegger, who claim that the work of art is what it does to the beholder. I will return to this shortly when I talk about the various art forms.

Ordinary knowledge, subservient as it is to our will, to our striving to live and to satisfy ourselves, and scientific knowledge, an extension of ordinary knowledge indirectly related to that same striving, are governed by the principle of sufficient reason and yield up to us only knowledge of relations, not of things-in-themselves.[29] Such knowing is linked to the ongoing "horizontal" series of causes and effects in space and time. We are driven to such knowledge by our own needs, revealing that about things which allows us to transform them for our purposes. But such knowing is also shot through by the Platonic Idea as a "vertical" component, an eternal ingredient entering into the ongoing flux of events.

It is crucial here to follow Schopenhauer's distinction between concept and Idea.[30] The former we have readily available in ordinary and scientific language in our terms for species and universal forces. But this only gives us the *unitas post rem*, the unity after the thing, affording concepts that yield no more than we put into them. They are our constructs. An Idea, on the other hand, is a *unitas ante rem*, a unity eternally antecedent to things, a Plotinian creative force of which things are the expression. Following Kant's notion of aesthetic ideas, they are intuitions to which no concept is adequate. They are apprehended by the artist, but not in an abstractly universal way, the jejune way of concepts. They are apprehended in individual objects of perception as creative forces expressing themselves in those objects.[31]

Again, as did Kant, Schopenhauer distinguishes the experience of the beautiful from that of the sublime. He does so by way of the latter's naturally hostile relation to the human will: the objects that occasion the experience of the sublime are those natural things that threaten to crush us by their overwhelming power or remind us, by their immensity, of our own bodily insignificance. In the perception of the beautiful, the will is spontaneously removed and pure knowledge gains the upper hand without struggle. In the perception of the sublime, such knowledge is gained only by a forcible breaking with the will. Schopenhauer goes further, presenting us with levels of the sublime from those close to the beautiful to those most far removed, based on the threat to our existence posed by the object. The beauty of light shining on a cold wintry day presents "the faintest trace of the sublime in the beautiful," since we are aware of the threat to life that the bitter cold presents. The silence of boundless uninhabited prairies under clear skies furnishes a second example, forcing us out of our usual relations and needs. The desert, removed from those organic forms that sustain our life, is more sublime still. Then there is nature in turbulent motion against which we are forced to struggle—especially when the turbulence is large-scale. Here we have the full impression of the dynamically sublime. In a different way, the mathematically sublime appears in the spatial and temporal immensity of the known universe as well as in the towering character of architectural monuments, where the insignificance of our own size is brought home to us in a powerful way. Finally, the sublime also appears in a character who has learned to view things, even those inimical to himself, in an objective manner. Here one who can contemplate the sublime becomes himself sublime.[32]

In addition to the two aesthetic modes Kant distinguished—namely, the beautiful and the sublime—Schopenhauer further distinguished the graceful and the characteristic. Beauty has a spatial, grace a temporal character. Grace has to do with movement: with smooth transitions among coordinated parts. But grace presupposes beauty: a well-formed body is a prerequisite for graceful activity. The characteristic has to do with human beings, the one case where the individual stands out from the species and has its own "Idea." A portrait artist in particular tries to capture what is peculiarly characteristic of that individual—whether it be beautiful or graceful or not.[33] So with Schopenhauer we get four distinct aesthetic categories, and not simply the classical two, traceable back to Longinus's discussion of the sublime.[34]

## The Forms of Art

Like Hegel, Schopenhauer refers to the various art media, all of which are such that they require completion in the imagination, for exact depiction of individuals, as in a waxworks reproduction, reveals only individuals and not the Platonic Idea.[35] Recall the two-dimensional depiction of three-dimensional objects in painting (Schopenhauer adds the linear sketch thereof in drawing); recall also the restriction of space to the point of abstract motion through time that constitutes the medium of music; recall finally the relative indifference to visual or audile medium in poetry (and, indeed, in all verbal expression). Schopenhauer adds sculpture to the list with the observation that painted statuary is far inferior to the bare marble of a Grecian statue precisely because the former leaves less to the imagination. He praises the infallible Greek aesthetic sensibility that observed this rule, not knowing that the statues were originally painted. (Of course, that does not alter his principle.)

Attend next to the specific functions of each of the art forms. Among them, pure instrumental music has a privileged place. All other art forms give expression to Platonic Ideas: at the lowest end, architecture expresses the struggle between gravity and rigidity and between light and shadow;[36] at the highest level, the struggle between persons and between Fate and humanity finds expression in tragedy. Drama is the most perfect expression of human existence.[37] Schopenhauer sees the individual human being as presenting the highest Platonic Idea, suggesting an ideal of each human expressed (e.g., in portraiture), but also a hierarchy of humanness embodied in individuals. The novel at its best is most revelatory of the inwardness of the individual. The height of that artistic genus is found in *Tristram Shandy, La nouvelle Héloïse, Wilhelm Meister,* and *Don Quixote.*[38] Music, however, reaches beyond the Ideas to that which they themselves express: the Will. Music is the language of desire. It reaches into the heart of things and expresses the continuing alternations between conflict and resolution. Here we have the basis for the Wagnerian conception of music. The word itself is a secondary expression of the emotions expressed in music.[39] But Schopenhauer also opposes in advance the Wagnerian conception of opera as totalizing art *(Gesamtkunst)*. He goes so far as to say that "pictorial," or what comes to be called program, music is in principle objectionable and that opera, by piling up the means to aesthetic enjoyment, confuses and barbarizes music. It is "an unmusical invention for the benefit of unmusical minds," making them less receptive to "the sacred, mysterious, intimate language of music."[40] Music reaches to the heart of things. Parallel to that, the deepest dimension of the self is the heart, of which the intellect and its prose is the expression.

Seemingly along Hegelian lines, Schopenhauer says that philosophy is related to the arts as wine to grapes.[41] However, philosophy itself has to be understood as ultimately intuition into the heart of things and not simply conceptual understanding. The latter only presents the *unitas post rem*, the unity we are able to construct after the fact, so to speak, semiartificially building up out of scattered pieces that which is essentially unitary. Intuitive philosophy reaches the Platonic Idea as the *unitas ante rem*, the unity that generates the thing and that can only be grasped by artistic, that is to say, generative insight. There is a sense of the generative and unitary ground of the object contemplated. Here Schopenhauer again draws upon Plotinus, who claimed that the artist reaches to the Idea, which the thing expresses and the mirror only superficially represents. Indeed, as I already remarked, for Schopenhauer the artist grasps that which Nature is only stammeringly trying to say and proceeds to say it better. One thinks here of Aristotle's notion that art partly imitates, partly completes nature. Presumably philosophy rests on the same intuitional capacity, but brings the multiplicity of such intuitions to some final intuitive synthesis.

## Response

One of the chief claims of Schopenhauer is the distinctiveness of music vis-à-vis the other art forms. He picks up on Kant's observation that music is the language of affections, which gives rise to the aesthetic idea of an indeterminate whole of an immense wealth of thought. But he reverses Kant's assessment of its value, which was based on the dimming of the priority of verbal-intellectual manifestness evident in poetry. For Schopenhauer, music gives direct expression to the encompassing Will while other art forms point to it indirectly by expressing the Platonic Ideas, which, in turn, are expressions of the Will. The metaphysical claim parallels the Neoplatonic notion of the relation between the One and the *Nous*, locus of the cosmic Logos. The One is beyond the Logos, transcending every distinction, including the distinction between subject and object that frames the region of the Logos. There is a distinctive relation to the One: a non-dualistic experience of identity beyond concepts and words. In orthodox Christian theology the Logos, though one with the Father in a unity closer than any other mode of unity, is other than the Father, being His mirroring in otherness. In a direct parallel, for Schopenhauer the Will lies beyond the Platonic Ideas which are its expression. At the level of art, music provides the mood, which generates the word and thus mirrors the world process. Interestingly, this reverses the understanding, common in the Christian tradition, of the priority of the word, both in terms of the creation story in *Genesis*, where God's speech is the origin of things, and in the prologue to John's gospel, where it is announced that in the beginning was the Word. This also goes back to Plato, for whom—at least in the *Laws*—music without words is nonsensical, suggesting a merely supportive role for music. It is found also in neoclassical aesthetic. Surprisingly, on this point Schopenhauer's view seems more in keeping with the trinitarian doctrine of the Origin beyond the Word. Obviously different, however, is Schopenhauer's reversal of traditional value, finding in the ultimate Ground—because of suffering, struggle, and death in its expressions—a repelling rather than an attracting source. Contemplation through music, rather than uniting us to the grounding Will, frees us from it.

As we have previously noted, the position on the priority of music over the word is opposed by Gregorian chant, in which, following the prologue to St. John's gospel ("In the beginning was the Word"), music is essentially subordinated to the word. Schopenhauer would probably say that even such a view betrays itself when it musically elaborates the Alleluia at great length after the sufferings of Lent, an emotional breakthrough revealing something of the real underlying character of things. Hegel likewise sees music as an intermediary form of art, leaving exterior form behind and straining toward the interiority of poetry. Poetry itself approaches philosophic prose as the highest manifestation of the ultimate depth of interiority, which music only expresses inadequately. Schopenhauer reverses that: the word is derivative and essentially inadequate expression of that which music alone most fully expresses.

In poets like Schiller and Poe, a "musical mood" gives rise to the poetry. Poe, for example, discusses the origin of "The Raven" in the attempt to express the feeling of sadness. He searched for a word that would best express that and arrived at *nevermore*. Lenore, night, the black raven, and so on followed therefrom.[42] Dufrenne speaks of "an atmosphere" that crystallizes into a represented world. He insists that "it is on the basis of music that one must understand the realism of the representational arts, not vice versa."[43]

One serious ambiguity in Schopenhauer's general view is the conflation under the term Will of the appetites we share in common with the animals and our possibility of acting over against those appetites, and then his projecting into the Ground of being the blindness of those appetites over against the principles we consciously select as the bases for our choices. There does not seem in general to be an explanation for how we are able to put ourselves in a position to transcend "the will" (as appetite) except through the active cooperation of our "will" (in traditional terms, as ability to choose over against our appetites), which is aligned with our capacity for insight. Nor does there seem to be an explanation of how the arts emerge, which allow us to transcend our ground in the Will through contemplative distance. In Kant it is as if the ground of things through the genius aimed at bringing us above our appetites in aesthetic contemplation and thus bringing us halfway to the moral state of the organization of our appetitive life to support our respect for Humanity in ourselves and in others. In Schopenhauer, by contrast, the emergence of the arts seems groundless. It just happens that the Will produces an open field that transcends its own unconscious aims through conscious contemplation.

There is also a tension in his account of our relation to others. It is the same capacity of rising above the self-centeredness of appetites that makes possible both aesthetic contemplation and identification with other beings who are suffering. But in aesthetic contemplation we are detached from the objects of contemplation, whereas in sympathetic identification we are united. Again, no ground for the possibility of such identification seems forthcoming.

To switch to a positive note, Schopenhauer's focus on the negative factors in the world and in our self-experience is a realistic corrective to an all too idyllic notion of the harmony of nature. But unlike Hegel, who takes account of the power of the negative as a conceptual translation of the Christian focus on the Cross, Schopenhauer provides no resolution outside of escape, while Hegel, following the Christian tradition, links the negative factors with an invitation to move to a more encompassing view of things and thus to a richer and deeper life. Schopenhauer in a sense returns to elements of the Greek approach to tragedy—a return that forms the point of departure for Friedrich Nietzsche.

In his view of pure beauty, Kant set in motion a view of art that focuses on aesthetic surface to the exclusion of all other reference: art for art's sake was the result. However, Kant himself considered pure beauty only for the sake of isolating the strictly aesthetic moment as object of conceptless disinterest before he folded back in both concepts and interests. In this way he was able to move from a trivial surface aesthetic to what one might call a depth aesthetic. It is the depth aesthetic that interests Schopenhauer, especially in assimilating Kant's notion of aesthetic ideas to Platonic Ideas as the archetypes of natural species and as the special objects of art. Here he brings to the fore the key notion of the *expressivity* of sensory surface that was implicit in Plotinus especially. Indeed, in the Neoplatonic line, sensory surface is expressive of ontological depth in the individual, which is expressive of the even deeper realm of the Forms, which, in turn, are expressive of the ultimate One. One must distinguish here the surface copier, who exhibits fine hand-eye coordination and who was, for the most part, rendered superfluous by the camera, from the visionary artist, who, grasping the underlying generative Form expressed in individuals, transforms surface to express depth. But as we distinguish different Forms, we must realize that the human is a peculiar Form. An individual human is not simply an instance of a general archetype. Oriented toward the level of the universal, humans must choose what they are to be, individually and collectively. Hence every human is unique in a way that no other instance of a species is unique. And the more profound the level at which the individual operates, the more unique his or her existence. Hence for Schopenhauer there is opened up for the artist the possibility of apprehending and giving expression to the peculiar idea of an individual human, especially of the great individual. Such an individual would more adequately express the One that is expressed in everything—only for Schopenhauer the One is contradictory, whereas the fully achieved individual human would be harmonious. Schopenhauer even confesses the inadequacy of his view when he suggests at the very end of his magnum opus that there might be something positive corresponding to his negative notion of nirvana as the essence of sainthood.[44]

Schopenhauer followed the example of Kant in developing a view of hierarchy among the arts. For Schopenhauer the hierarchy is rooted in his metaphysics and thus is based, not primarily on aesthetic form, but on reference: there are corresponding levels of depth within the arts. First of all there is the hierarchy of types of referents, from the depiction of landscape through animal forms to human forms. Since humans are the highest types and tragedy reveals the essence of things, tragedy is the highest art form depicting types. Then there is the transcendence of music beyond those types to give expression to the Will, which all types express, each in their own ways. Apart from the hierarchy of reference, in its aesthetic form architecture displays an aspect of universal struggle at the level of the lowest forms: the struggle of gravity and rigidity on the one hand and of light and darkness on the other. Architecture and music bear witness to the fact that even aesthetic form is, in its own way, referential. And in this we return to Aristotle. But one must ask why it is that, though struggle often is an explicit theme, whether directly referential in tragic drama, or indirectly in musical tension, nonetheless, the aesthetic experience is one of resolution and harmony, producing disinterested calm. And beyond this, not every referent treated aesthetically exhibits struggle—perhaps the majority of thematic works do not—so that Schopenhauer seems to skew his theory by selectively attending to works and aesthetic forms that fit his theory.

We should note here Schopenhauer's departure from Kant on the notion of the sublime. Where Kant maintained that what we call sublime objects are really only occasions which remind us of our own sublimity,

Schopenhauer does not depart from ordinary usage: what is sublime is what is hostile to our desire. But then how does one distinguish between the threatening and the sublime unless it be in our regarding of it?

Schopenhauer will be aligned with Nietzsche in pushing for a priority of music over the other art forms. In this he is in opposition to a line that begins in Plato and goes through Kant and Hegel. Plato had said that music alone without lyrics is meaningless; Kant had placed music at the bottom of the hierarchy of the art forms because it is basically an art of the agreeable, not of the beautiful or sublime, giving us least information about what is; Hegel is said to have had little sympathy for orchestral music.[45] In all three cases, it seems that a view of the superiority of reason is the reason. On the other hand, in Plato I have attempted to show that there is a priority of Eros that leads reason, constantly incomplete, to transcend itself; and in Kant it is clear that reason points beyond that which we can conquer cognitively in the phenomenal order.

# VIII

# NIETZSCHE

## *Nietzsche's Horizon*

ONE MIGHT SAY THAT the founding experience of Friedrich Nietzsche's philosophy is the experience of the death of God. It is announced, like Plato's thought, in poetic form through the Parable of the Madman in *The Gay Science*. Nietzsche describes a madman who lit a lantern in the morning hours and went in search of God, like Diogenes, who claimed that the light of day was not sufficient to reveal an honest man. The madman's audience of unbelievers mocked him, asking whether God had gotten lost or emigrated. The madman proclaimed that God was dead and that he and they together had killed Him. He wondered at the power that made this possible, for the act was equivalent to drinking up the sea of meaning within which we swim, wiping away the horizon that locates us, unchaining the earth from the sun, which, holding us in place, illuminates us. And with that act there is no longer any absolute direction, no up or down. We stray as through an infinite nothing, feeling the breath of empty space, the chill that sets in without the sun, the darkness. God is dead and is in the process of decomposition. Yet people are still oblivious to it. It takes time for the stench to reach their nostrils. They have not yet attained the ears to hear the proclamation of the event. The madman, realizing he had come too soon, threw down his lantern, and its flame was extinguished. But he went about the churches, tombs of the dead God, singing: *Requiem aeternam deo.* Eternal rest unto God![1]

Nietzsche here hearkens back to Plato's *Republic* and the notion of the Good symbolized by the sun.[2] That dialogue attempted to determine, by its argument, its structure, and its action, an absolute "up" and "down" for human existence. It begins "down in the Piraeus" and goes down further in reflection to Hades, from which it rises through the construction of several levels of a city until it reaches the highest level that is drawn "out of the Cave" upward to the sunlight of the Good. Inside the Cave is the realm of matter and change, of nature and history; outside the Cave is the realm of Forms, eternal measures, universal and changeless, illuminated by the unifying power of the One/Good. This constitutes one of the two roots of the Western tradition. The Judeo-Christian tradition is the other root, gathering all explanation and all aspiration into Yahweh/God. The two roots, Platonic and Hebrew-Christian, came together in Patristic theology and governed together the entire Western tradition until relatively recently.

Today, in the era of deconstruction, there is no longer any sun, any single center of reference. There is a pluralism in principle, with not even the dream of a totality or of any kind of a fundamental principle or foundation, any kind of ultimate point of reference. There is no longer a measure, no up or down. And what follows from it is an experience of emptiness.[3]

If we look back over some of the thinkers from the modern era I have covered in this text, we see a transformation of the Platonic-Christian center. In Kant we see the beginning of an inversion of the tradition in this sense, that the *summum bonum*, the highest good, is not God as it was for the medievals or, in a sense, for Plato (insofar as the Agathon functioned as the highest end). Rather, for Kant the *summum bonum* is the coming together in a human afterlife of happiness and deservedness to be happy for which God is the guarantor. It is not God that we seek, but our own final happiness.[4] Correlative to this, the aesthetic experience of the sublime is transformed from that which pulls us out of ourselves and might become symbolic of the divine, to that which reminds us of our own sublimity.[5] In the ancient-medieval tradition seeing God is our final happiness.[6] In Hegel the notion of the divine is the notion of an eternally antecedent realm that by itself is mere possibility. For Hegel what we call God in the Christian tradition is, before creation, possibility of realization. God is unconscious or not fully self-conscious and comes to consciousness in Nature and in History, which are His own self-unfolding. When we say that God realizes Himself in the realization of full humanness, we are saying in effect that God is nothing but humanness fully realized, as Feuerbach and the other

Left Hegelians realized. Feuerbach saw in the statement that God is all-knowing, all-powerful, all-wise, all-just, and all-loving a projection of the immanent ideals of human existence, the approach to which is the meaning of Nature. Nature's meaning is to produce human beings whose own significance lies in reaching asymptotically toward complete knowledge, complete control, full wisdom, justice, and love. These are all human characteristics drawing us into the deep future of fuller humanness. In the notion of God we have an alienated projection of such ideals. We are driven toward such projection because of the ignorance, impotence, foolishness, injustice, and lack of love that afflicts human history and that alienates us from our true essence as humans. The ideals are given with human nature as the kind of being that is open to the Whole, aiming at the Whole in the modalities of knowing, acting, and feeling.[7] In Schopenhauer the underlying is also unconscious, but the character of the underlying is no longer good. The ground of things, the Will, is intrinsically contradictory. And if that is God, He is not to be loved but avoided. One should flee from such a God. Here we have a complete reversal of the tradition on that point. And coming off of Schopenhauer we have Nietzsche.

Nietzsche expressed mixed feelings at the discovery of the death of God. There is a kind of sadness, a feeling of emptiness, a sense of what he calls nihilism that follows from the realization of the death of God. In high culture, the very function of God has been transmuted, then negated, then reversed. There is nothing that takes the place of God: there is no measure, no final up or down anymore. The place defined by the Platonic Good that was taken over by and melded with the Hebrew-Christian God is now no longer occupied—indeed the very existence of the place is in question. There is no ground for values; there is a nothingness of values, a value nihilism.[8] This first vision of nihilism brings about a kind of emptiness and despair. What gave meaning to the earth, the holy, the sacred, is no longer seen as a viable option.

One who stands outside the prevalent sense of rationality seems, by comparison, to be mad. Nietzsche himself is the madman, yet one who comes too early. It takes a long time for corpses to decay and for their stench to reach the nostrils of the many. Nietzsche claims, in effect, to have a better nose than most: he can smell the decay of the flesh of the divine. In another place he says that great deeds take a long time before they are heard; the deed of the killing of God may take a hundred years before it will be heard.[9] Almost a hundred years later, on the cover of *Time* magazine, the organ of proclamation to the many, there appeared the question, "Is God Dead?"[10] It brought to light the discovery that Nietzsche had sniffed out in the third quarter of the nineteenth century.

But though on the one hand there is a feeling of emptiness, on the other hand there is the notion that we have to become gods ourselves to be worthy of the deed. And there Nietzsche finds the basis for a certain kind of exultation: the sea is open, the horizons free;[11] we can ourselves become the sun.[12] The very context within which this appears, *The Gay Science*, is a book about learning how to laugh and dance—and that not in oblivion of the negative factors of existence.[13] Quite the contrary. There are many such factors, as Schopenhauer never tired of pointing out and as Nietzsche was not afraid to face. But in spite of that, for Nietzsche life is indescribably fertile, creative, rising up again and again in new forms, in spite of the conflict and destructiveness that stands internal to its very character. Rejoicing in the creative upsurge of life is the exultant side in the discovery of the death of God.[14]

This turns upon realizing that the place of the Good as the origin of the realm of Being in Plato's view and in the Christian tradition is itself nihilistic. There is thus a second and deeper kind of nihilism. In the first type, there is sadness at the disappearance of that which defines ultimate meaning for most people and has defined it throughout Western history: the Good/Yahweh/God. But for Nietzsche this is itself a deeper form of nihilism: the very place of value is nihilistic. The reason is that Plato has to posit another realm in order to find worthy the realm in which we live, the realm of becoming, of embodiment—or better, *because* he finds life unworthy, Plato posits another life. In fact, according to Nietzsche, the Platonic-Christian view is a derogation of, a blasphemy against this life, a slur upon existence, for it claims that the only thing that gives meaning to this life is something beyond it and that this life is consequently a shadow life, life in a cave, a valley of tears.[15] For some of the early Christian Platonists, like Origen, the realm of matter existed because Adam and Eve, who were pure spirits, fell; and their fall generated this world as the land of their exile.[16] For Gregory of Nyssa, the sexual origin of life is the result of the Fall.[17] Nietzsche reports Pope Innocent III's repetition of Augustine's judgments on the "filth" of human origins.[18] This life, this world is a dark place, a bad place. We do not belong here. We should keep ourselves safe from its allurements and pray that we get out of it as soon as possible. But woe to those who are happy, rich, talented, successful, famous. Blessed are the downtrodden, the poor, those at the bottom, the worst.[19] Christianity becomes Platonism for the people,[20] a way of reconciling oneself to the negative factors of existence—as well as a convenient prop for political establishments, a civil religion that keeps control over the many.

Nietzsche takes the Platonic-Christian teaching on the afterlife as a slur on this life, a saying No! to life: "I had always sensed strongly the furious, vindictive hatred of life implicit in that system of ideas and values. . . . Christianity spelled life loathing itself. . . . A hatred of the 'world,' a curse on the affective urges, a fear of beauty and sensuality, a transcendence rigged up to slander mortal existence, a yearning for extinction. . . ."[21] Nietzsche wants to affirm against that the exultation of existence, joy in the rising of life in spite of destruction and pain. Life is inexhaustibly good. Say Yes! to it![22] Life is constant process, constant metabolism and catabolism. It is like a flame that is constantly being fueled. Platonism proclaims the superiority of fixity—in effect, of deadness—and thus is the extreme opponent of life. Platonism really consists in a set of abstractions made from the flux of life. Thus there is nihilism in the very way the value question is posed in the tradition.

Whatever the grounds offered, Nietzsche notes an intrinsic order to life itself. Rank and hierarchy are intrinsic to being. There is a higher and lower: higher men and lower men. There is a kind of natural morality, which Nietzsche calls master morality, in which the operative terms are *good* and *bad*. They basically mean competent and incompetent respectively. Name any kind of functional capacity, including sainthood, and you have rank: there are those farthest removed from it, those who most deeply epitomize it, and many grades scattered in between. Artist, athlete, chemist, entrepreneur, financier, philosopher, saint—any individual who aspires to instantiate any one of these types can be shown to occupy a rung on an empirically discernible hierarchy relative to others who perform the same function, a hierarchy intrinsic to the very nature of things. Master morality is an order in which the omni-competent are on top because they ought to be there, and those on the bottom belong there because they are incompetent.[23]

But historically there came a slave revolt in morality and a reversal. Good and bad are inverted into a corresponding evil and good.[24] Nietzsche has in mind the Sermon on the Mount with its woes to the rich, the happy, the laughing, and its blessings on the poor, the sad, the mourning.[25] Evil are those who are proudly exultant in their success and superiority. Good are those on the bottom. In proportion as one has less one is to be rewarded hereafter; in proportion as one has more, one is to be deprived. The last shall be first and the first last. Many of these things in the Christian bloodstream are rooted in ressentiment: those on the bottom resent the fact that they are on the bottom and desire the fall of those on top.[26] Nietzsche presents an amalgam between the slave revolt and Platonism in his view of Christianity as Platonism for the masses. Down here, in this life, we have the rich and the poor; there, in the afterlife above, the rank is inverted. Those who proclaim this view attempt to uproot their ties with this life through vows of poverty, chastity, and obedience, to become disembodied, otherworldly spirits who hate the body and this "land of exile," this "vale of tears." But those who proclaim this also hold the greatest power over those whom they persuade.[27]

The upshot of the slave revolt is, in secularized terms, democratic socialism—socialism where everybody works for everybody else, and democracy in which every man is equal. That leads to a flattening out of all hierarchy, in particular the financial hierarchy, and is rooted in resentment of any kind of natural superiority. Democratic socialism is secularized Christianity, which continues the inversion of the natural, master morality.[28] Nietzsche calls for a transvaluation of values, an inversion of the slave inversion, getting back to the natural order of intrinsic rank and hierarchy.[29]

Natural order is governed by what Nietzsche called Will-to-Power, a variation on the Schopenhauerian theme of Will as fundamental ground, as comprehensive basis expressed in each entity. Will-to-Power is the world "viewed from the inside."[30] Nietzsche was stimulated by Schopenhauer, but went beyond Schopenhauer. Nietzsche's development led him to stress creativity, the origin of form and the self-surpassing involved in creativity. It becomes difficult to see in Schopenhauer any ground for creativity if art, like religion, is essentially life denying. In the notion of the Will-to-Power, Nietzsche preserves the continuity of the realm of art, and indeed of culture as a whole, with the realm of nature. And, contrary to Schopenhauer, he celebrates both.

Will-to-Power is *Wille zur Macht*, where *Macht* is rooted in *machen*, to make, so that Will-to-Power should be understood as will to create.[31] Such a will-to-create produces ever higher forms—that is, forms with ever more developed capacity to create unity in ever more complex multiplicities. Life is a matter in each instance of gathering power to itself, of appropriating the nonliving and the living, but also of creating beyond itself on the basis of that gathering of power. We kill plant and animal life to permit the expansion and sustenance of our own power. Life in each case destroys in order to build and, through reproduction as well as in the formation of culture, to create beyond itself, exulting in such creation.

Going back to Heraclitus (but also to the Old Testament *Book of Wisdom*),[32] Nietzsche views the operation of the Will-to-Power as play—according to Eugen Fink, the central concept of Nietzsche's philosophy.[33] The notion stresses unpredictability and transsubjectivity, the latter in the sense that in play the individual subject is not in full control but is rather dependent on the direction the total play complex takes.[34] Will-to-Power has consequently to be understood in an individual case as knowing how to let oneself be taken, to go along, as well as to take whatever control is possible in order to achieve form. This links with Nietzsche's later emphasis on *amor fati*, the love of one's fate, the lot one is given, the hand one is dealt—in Heidegger's terms, one's *Geschick*, one's destiny following one's *Geworfenheit*, one's thrownness.[35] As Fink puts it, world-play involves the "cosmic agreement *[Einklang]* of man and world in the play of necessity."[36]

The human being stands at the top of the hierarchy of forms that emerge from the world-play. The tradition stemming from Platonism seized upon the work of intellect and will as the directive center of consciousness and claimed the alien descent of the intellectual-volitional subject from another realm, a fall into the body with its passions. Nietzsche deconstructs the notion of subject so conceived, displaying the complexity of the "simple" act of willing[37] and calling attention to the operation of instinct in the life of "intellect."[38] He constantly refers to the whole human being as "physiological" and as a play of forces.[39] But on the other side of such relocation of the subject of awareness within the transformed physiological context there is the exaltation of the creative type, that is one who requires discipline, bringing the chaos of passions into order, "chaining the dogs in the basement," gaining simplicity by keeping the most extreme opposites in tension, ideally without effort, extending the temporal horizon of one's awareness through holding himself to long-term projects, gaining power over himself, and becoming—like Goethe, Nietzsche's lifelong model[40]—a whole person. Such wholeness is measured by the extent to which one can contain multiplicity in unity,[41] learning to "'live resolutely' in wholeness and fullness of being."[42] Far from dissolving the human being into the play of forces that are factually operative in him, far from exalting self-indulgence in one's passions as the exhibition of the "free spirit," Nietzsche saw his free spirit as just the opposite.[43] It is the lower types—and this includes too many who claim descent from Nietzsche—that wallow in the "liberation" of passions. Nietzsche's aim is "to make asceticism natural again."[44] This is an indispensable condition for "the higher men."

One of the higher levels on which the will-to-power operates is that of a political state as the fusing together of multiplicities of different individuals and groups over long periods of time.[45] The most powerful way in which that is achieved is not by means of weaponry, which conquers only the body, but by means of the conquest of the soul through the bestowal of comprehensive meaning. This is the work of "the higher men" who embody more fully the most fundamental metaphysical ground, which is the Will-to-Power. They operate in Hegel's realm of Absolute Spirit: artists, philosophers, and saints.[46] Who are some of the higher men? Lao-tzu, Confucius, Buddha, Socrates, Jesus, Muhammad, Shakespeare, Goethe—all of them poets of a sort who create a comprehensive form of life that governs billions of people for thousands of years. They create the horizon of meaning within which the many come to find meaning, whatever their hierarchical rank otherwise. All life—and thus all human life—needs a horizon within which to live.[47] One cannot live with unlimited horizons. Human beings need a "ring of myths" that give the stamp of eternity to the quotidian, providing a creative womb for those who operate within the ring.[48] We human beings, however, are peculiar in that we are always pushed to create limited horizons and to strain at their edges, so to speak. We have to create culture whose fundamental structures lie in the definition of the horizons of meaning, within which everything else occurs. The great religions do precisely that through their founders, the great creative types, those who embody the Will-to-Power most deeply.

One problem with modern democratic socialism is that it does not promote the higher men but, as noted above, flattens out natural rank and hierarchy.[49] Democratic socialism produces what Nietzsche calls "the last man," who "invents happiness" (i.e., a universally available, easy gratification that the technological system produces for the many).[50] It is supposed to give meaning to the earth, but ends in recurrent boredom and the need for constant novel stimulation. The last man loses the meaning horizon provided by the higher men and falls into meaningless distraction. The higher type is the meaning of the earth through his ability to create a horizon of meaning that is existentially compelling, that grips his followers, who freely adhere to his message.

The higher men are not hedonists but disciplined types, often ascetics of the most rigorous sort. This seems to be out of step with Nietzsche's notion that life itself is the ground of meaning, for asceticism seems to express a denial of life. Nietzsche distinguishes the ascetic *ideal*, which is life denying, from asceticism as a natural condition for all higher creativity. In any case, we would have to get beneath the various meaning structures in order to understand what it is that produces them (i.e., life in its creative upsurge). Discipline, especially self-discipline, is the indispensable condition for an enduring form of life.[51] But even further, the life-denying forms of life are also expressions of a way of giving meaning to life creatively. This leads the great creative one to form illusions.

Illusions, however, are not necessarily bad; they are often life sustaining. "Truth" (i.e., the claim to ultimate meaning) is the lie we need in order to live.[52] Truth is the creation of a horizon of meaning that defines the ultimate meaning structure for those who come to exist under it. An analogue to this—and more than an analogue, another expression of the character of life—is animal perception. Perception is a "lie" that is needed in order to adjust to the environment. In ordinary experience, it looks like the space between my eyeball and this book is empty; it feels like the desk is smooth and stable. As a matter of fact, the space is full of unobserved entities and the desk is rough and in constant agitation at the subatomic level. Perception simplifies and gives the illusion of fixity and stability in order that the organism be able to adjust to its environment and thus survive. Perception is a "lie" invented by life to promote life.[53]

Project that into the distinctively human realm. Not only is there the initial lie that perception itself creates for us, but also the "lie" that characterizes each of the meaning systems. Each poses itself as absolute and encompassing; and yet by the very nature of the case, each is only a perspective.[54] Whatever it discloses, it simultaneously closes other ways of ultimate conception. But that again is a lie needed in order to allow people to grow up and adjust—a kind of second womb created by culture. The horizon of meaning is a "lie" created by life through the higher types. Nietzsche is here paralleling Plato, who in his *Republic* has Socrates observe that, in teaching children, the rule is, "The false before the true."[55] To begin with, we tell children fables, fairy tales; later we go on to the true picture—Nietzsche would say, the adult tissue of lies that has us in its grip as our way of coping with life. Indeed, for Nietzsche, "in art the lie becomes consecrated, the will to deception has good conscience at its back."[56]

There are several further remarks on truth we should consider here. One is Nietzsche's claim that we have art lest we perish from truth.[57] The truth here is that of the true horrors, the suffering and destruction endemic to life at every level. I elaborated on that a bit in the previous chapter on Schopenhauer. Life is truly like that—no "lie" involved. Nietzsche even claims that the measure of character is how much of such truth one can bear.[58] The second is that dedication to truth leads to the canceling of

Christianity—and indeed of theism, unmasking what the genealogy and history of Christianity reveal: resentment of the gifted and successful, contempt for the earth, self-contempt, and the operation of power.[59] But, third, Nietzsche sees—and this is one of the most difficult things to construe credibly—belief in truth itself as something to be overcome.[60] One aspect of this is his frequent equation of truth with Platonism—that is, with acceptance of "another world" of fixed and eternal forms and the corresponding dualism of soul and body.[61] It is that which he calls metaphysics and which falls to perspectivism and "physiology." Even science involves such Platonistic faith. As a counter to this Nietzsche suggests that truth is a woman;[62] and woman he sees as surface, lightness, delighting in appearances,[63] also as given to seduction,[64] but as the very image of mother earth, of life itself.[65] Here is where, facing the truth of the horrors of existence, one sees in art, with its preoccupation with surfaces and the beauty of appearance, an overcoming of "truth"—both in the sense of creatively coming to terms with life and in the sense of repudiating the Platonism of another and better world. The ultimate conclusion to the faith in truth is that appearance, "the lie," is divine.[66] Ultimately, Nietzsche claims, art is worth more than truth.[67] It is in this connection, he says that life requires truth and deception,[68] and by that I would understand the recognition of perspectivity, afforded by the artistry of life, which reveals and conceals. Finally, he claims that the will to truth is a mask for the will to power.[69] This should at least lead the inquirer to ask, In what is *my* will to truth rooted? Is it a desire to be able to tell others what to do? Is it a way of calling attention to my superiority, attracting the attention of others like the little boy in knee pants reciting his repertoire of nursery rimes to the oohs and ahs of the adulating adults? But Nietzsche evidently has something further also in mind: truth in the service of life.[70] In his early work he praised truth only as connected with justice and thus repudiated the search for trivial truths, which afflicts the scholar.[71] What enhances one's capacity to do, to create, to produce something beyond the perishing moment of pleasure or pain? Is it the fact that he who does "the truth" enters into the light?

The higher types are all, in a sense, artists: they create out of inspiration. And the definition of horizon they create is great insofar as it comprehensively unifies the multiplicity of things actual in a culture. This requires attunement to the materials available at the time, a sense of all the parameters of existence that are operative in the culture, and creation of comprehensive form, which takes account of and fuses that multiplicity. There are more powerful and less powerful definitions of horizon. But the greater visions create forms of such power that the "lie" lasts for thousands of years in binding a people together. Perspectival disclosure holds people under its sway for millennia as the putative absolute disclosure of final meaning (the very definition of ultimate horizon). But the meaning systems eventually come apart as time moves forward and we await the bringer of new meaning, the creator of a new horizon that can bring together and put the stamp of eternity on the plurality of directions functioning in a culture.[72]

Socrates created what we recognize as the philosophic type that came to play a central role in Western culture to this day.[73] But that type so conceived is rooted in a contempt for the earth. It is a high type because of the power it has exhibited: it touched a nerve in human existence and led to a form that lasted for millennia. People recognized it and responded by saying, "Yes, that makes sense; let's live that way"—and they continued to do so throughout the centuries. But there are plural ways of horizon definition. The latter is both arbitrary and not: arbitrary in that there is a decision involved, but not arbitrary in that, if it is profound it will last, if superficial it will fade.

The very way the definition of the horizon has occurred historically through the great higher types is such as to be by and large one that is still nihilistic. One needs to get beneath that to see that life itself is the ground for the creation of these forms. Life itself is the fundamental value. What Nietzsche calls us to do is to say Yes! to life.[74] We have to realize that we do not cognitively possess the whole, and the manifestness of the whole is rooted in the myth of a knower before whom the whole is manifest. There is no uncovering of the whole, but there is the uncovering of horizons that are more or less adequate. Thus we have different perspectives. But it is life, the will to create, that surges up in the higher types and leads them to form the horizon within which the many come to exist. There is no need for metaphysical justification that appeals to another life, to Being apart from Becoming; life in its creative upsurge is justification enough.

Consider a football stadium and see the definition of existence it represents: "Sunday observance," which gives meaning to the drabness of the workweek, identifying with the "saints," seeing the battle of "good and evil," and finding a center of meaning without needing any further metaphysical ground. (As I look out my office window at Texas Stadium, home of the Dallas Cowboys, I see Revival Tent Architecture.) People find significance through activity governed by the creation of an arbitrary set of rules that are rigidly enforced. If someone does not follow the rules, they spoil the game for others. There is nothing in the nature of things that says we have to play this game or play it with these rules, since rules are made up and continually modified. Generalizing that: the game of human life is operative at the level of problems posed by nature, such as the need to eat and the need to take care of the relation of the sexes because of the offspring that emerge from that relation and the need to find a way to make these decisions collectively. The problems posed by these needs can be solved in terms of different games: different economic games, different social games, different political games. But all this also can be, has been and *must be* encompassed and given ultimate horizon by some system of ultimate meaning. It is important to have rigid rules and adhesion to those rules, but not such that they cancel out powerful urges. Urges ought rather to be channeled. So we get the powerful instincts of athletes channeled and honed along certain lines determined by rules. The rules allow them to concentrate their powers and to find significance in that concentration, celebrating the upsurge of life. But there is no one, encompassing, *natural* societal form, no one defining horizon: they are all artistic fabrications on the part of great creative geniuses. One of those geniuses was Socrates, another was Jesus, but there are others. We do not need metaphysical justification appealing to another life, to Being apart from Becoming, for this exhibits contempt for life. Life in its own creative upsurge is justification enough. Nietzsche calls upon us to celebrate life: not to say No! like the otherworldly ascetics, but to say Yes! to being as it is.

The top of Nietzsche's natural hierarchy is what he calls the Overman *(Übermensch)*. Nietzsche says that man is a rope stretched from ape to Overman.[75] Man is a transitional species, suggesting something in the future. The Overman, he says, is the meaning of the earth.[76] The Overman and what he calls *the higher men* are related to one another.[77] The higher men—like Homer, Socrates, Moses, and Jesus—have been the most powerful definers of the ultimate horizon in our tradition. But they were all under the illusion that they were taking heavenly dictation, that some divine entity or its emissary—a muse or an angel—was whispering in their ear.[78] With the experience of the death of God, the essential ingredient in the prevailing definition of the horizon can no longer hold. Enter the "free spirit," the spirit of the higher men become fully self-conscious, aware of its historical self-alienation in Absolute Spirit.

Nietzsche has Zarathustra, the inventor of dualism, repent his error through the "discovery of solitude," thus freeing the human spirit.[79] On the mountaintop he encountered, not a higher entity or its emissary, but rather absolute solitude. There was no one besides himself. That discovery makes possible the emergence of the Overman. Like the higher men, he will appear unpredictably and will create the horizon of meaning for the many; but, unlike the higher men, he will be free of the illusion of divine inspiration. That does not mean he will be free of inspiration—quite the contrary: he remains, like all great artists, a medium, a mouthpiece for overpowering forces.[80] Ideally for Nietzsche he will be—in another variation on a Platonic theme—a saint-emperor, "the Roman Caesar with Christ's soul."[81] He will not proclaim another life tied in with contempt for this life. He will teach us how to celebrate this life, how to laugh and dance. He will teach the Gay Science.

Three fundamental concepts interplay in Nietzsche's understanding: the Overman, Will-to-Power, and Eternal Recurrence of the Same. The Overman expresses the Will-to-Power as the will to create form, which occurs in terms of the Eternal Recurrence of the Same. The latter is Nietzsche's way of coming to terms with the two worlds of Platonism and thus of the tradition where Being lies beyond Becoming. For Nietzsche, Eternal Recurrence installs Being within Becoming.[82] Eternity lies inside Becoming and not outside it. There is something in the very character of life, expressed in joy, that seeks eternity. In one of the middle chapters of Nietzsche's major work, *Thus Spake Zarathustra,* there is a song for whose stanzas the concluding verse is: "All joy seeks eternity, seeks deep, deep eternity."[83] That is in a sense a retrieval of Diotima's claim in the *Symposium* as to the nature of Eros: the mortal seeking the immortal, the temporal seeking the eternal.[84] Procreation is the establishment of eternity in time. The eternal repetition of the same is, for one thing, the eternal proliferation of individuals under a given species. This is in Aristotle as well as in Plato, except that for both there is a claim to something superior beyond time: Self-thinking Thought, Pure Form as the Unmoved Mover in Aristotle[85] and the realm of Forms surmounted by the One/Good in Plato.[86] Within time Eros constitutes that in the perishable which surpasses perishing. But for Plato as for Aristotle, that is because the perishing seeks to emulate that which stands eternally beyond time. Nietzsche, however, seeks to install the eternal within time in the self-surpassing creativity of life's Eros.

There are various ways in which Nietzsche talks about eternal recurrence. In *The Will to Power,* posthumously published, he speaks of eternal recurrence as a kind of scientific hypothesis.[87] The basis for it is the supposition of a finite number of entities in the universe and an infinity of time. Given that, the combinatory possibilities will have to repeat themselves again and again. We have to think about eternity seriously in this context. There is an example in the Hindu tradition about the duration of the fundamental unit of time, the kalpa: if a bird drags a piece of the finest silk over the highest mountain peak once every hundred years, a kalpa is the time it would take to flatten that mountain. That constitutes but one unit, like a single second, in the eternity of time itself.[88] If the thought of infinite empty space brought Pascal up short,[89] the thought of infinite time should do so as well. Given that, all combinations would seem to have to repeat themselves eventually.

The doctrine of Eternal Recurrence is also the basis for a kind of categorical imperative to prevent the Overman from complete arbitrariness in his creation of form. In the first announcement of Eternal Recurrence in 1882, Nietzsche says something like: So create that you can will what is created to reoccur forever and ever.[90] In a sense that is equivalent to thinking in Christian terms about heaven or hell. Whatever path we choose in life will be with us forever. Nietzsche proposes the equivalent within time. One wonders how literally the teaching is to be taken, and whether it is itself not a kind of myth directed at the problem of the temptation to absolute arbitrariness in the Overman's creative activity. It gives an infinite weight to each decision.

However we understand Eternal Recurrence, for Nietzsche nature strains to gather power that unifies otherwise independent centers of power. In human form, it strains to produce political states that unify human beings. But states have as their own telos, and thus as the ultimate goal of nature, the production of the artistic genius, who gives meaning to the togetherness of humans in a state. And for Nietzsche, the highest artistic creator is the tragic artist who reveals to us something of the real character of existence.[91]

## Nietzsche's Aesthetics

In his posthumously published notes titled *The Will to Power,* Nietzsche remarks that hitherto reflection on art has been largely restricted to "woman's aesthetics," which he identifies as emphasis on the recipient, the perceiver of the art work.[92] His own focus is on the creative aspect, the origin of the work of art, the creation of form. One of the features of form creation lies in bringing to some kind of interpenetration two facets of human existence. The first is the upsurge of instinct that Nietzsche names Dionysus and the other is the urge toward form that he calls Apollo, given prominence in his first work, *The Birth of Tragedy out of the Spirit of Music*, a work in which all the major themes of his thought are prefigured.[93] The Dionysian represents the forces of the unconscious that find expression in orgiastic religious experience: drinking, singing, and dancing to intoxication, being caught up in a kind of mass emotional infection in which the participants experience an immersion in the Great All, of which each individual is an expression. The principle of individuation is lost sight of, not simply for the sake of an escape from routine but by way of a religious sensibility that seeks a lived relation to the Whole. The Apollonian impulse runs counter to this: it is characterized by clarity, order, restraint, harmony. If the Dionysian principle is analogous to intoxication, losing oneself in a whirl of religious enthusiasm, Nietzsche likens the Apollonian principle to a dream where the individual figures stand out. The Apollonian provides the eternal in the realm of appearance while the Dionysian speaks out of the inexhaustible depth of the noumenal.[94] The roots are clearly Schopenhauerian: the underlying Will expresses itself in Platonic Ideas, which, in turn, are expressed in the phenomenal order by passing through the *principium individuationis*. But there is also a more sober Greek parallel in the notions of *peras* and *apeiron*, limit and the unlimited.[95] The turn Nietzsche gives it is the focus on the human instantiation of the notions.

Though in the beginning of *The Birth of Tragedy* Nietzsche speaks of two origins operative in the arts—the Apollonian "dream" state as the origin of the plastic arts and epic, the Dionysian state of "intoxication" as the origin of music, song, dance—nonetheless, ultimately the two are fused and the whole Apollonian realm is understood as a projection of the underlying Dionysian.[96] As regions of art forms, both have their origin in psychic states that break with the everyday world and in which something other than the controlling ego is operative in us. But beyond nature's production of these states in the ordinary individual, there is nature's production in the artist, which leads to reconfigurations within the everyday world that put us in contact, not simply with private psychic states, but, more important, with what we might call encompassing powers of being. The Dionysiac is a single, underlying creative totality, a sea of energy that expresses and limits itself in clearly definable Apollonian forms. In Dionysian experience, "the spell of individuation is broken, and the way lies open to . . . the innermost heart of things."[97] In the experience of tragic art we become "one with the primordial joy in existence," in spite of fear and pity aroused by struggle, pain, and destruction.[98]

The Apollonian is expressed among the Greeks in the Homeric gods, clearly individuated types that stand over against the Dionysiac nature forces. Mythically, the rule of Zeus, king of the Olympians, comes about through the overthrow of his father, Cronus, who governed the age of the Titans. The Titans as savage, monstrous nature forces are overcome by the more humanized Olympians.[99] Nietzsche goes back to the story of King Midas, who confronted the satyr Silenus and asked what the greatest thing in life might be. Silenus responded: The greatest thing is not to have been born; the next greatest is to die as soon as possible.[100] Life is terrible under the governance of the nature forces, under all those aspects on which Schopenhauer focused our attention. But after the age of the wisdom of Silenus, the Greeks created the Olympians. This allowed them to live in spite of the terror of existence, in such a way that, with Homer's Achilles, one would rather be a serf in this world than a king in the underworld.[101] The artist Homer created the illusion of the Olympians, which allowed the post-Homeric Greeks to celebrate this life rather than, following the wisdom of Silenus, to flee from it. Nietzsche's claim is that the fusion of the Dionysian and Apollonian forms was achieved in Greek tragedy, where "Dionysus speaks the language of Apollo; and Apollo finally the language of Dionysus."[102] This echoes Schiller's unity of the sensuous impulse and the form impulse in the play impulse.[103] Its major message is that, in spite of the destruction of the tragic hero, life is superabundantly fertile.[104] Here Nietzsche opposes the Aristotelian view, "half-medicinal, half-moral," of the aim of tragedy as purgation from the sway of the emotions of fear and pity and yet aligns himself in his own way with the Aristotelian view that poetry is more philosophic than history, allowing us to grasp the universal—even though the character of the universal and the nature of the grasp differs substantially from Aristotle's view.[105]

As in Schopenhauer, great plastic art presents to us representatives of regional forms precisely as representative (i.e., as types); music presents to us representatives of the creative source itself. In poetry the two are fused insofar as "the musical mood" generates the word (Nietzsche cites with approval Schiller's observation on his own poetic practice).[106] But it is in Greek drama and in Wagnerian opera that we arrive at a *Gesamtkunst* where the body of the actors and dancers become the primary instrument.

It is important to stress that the fusion works a transformation of both Apollonian and Dionysian forms. The individual is not a dreamlike flight from reality, nor is he or she swallowed up in the Dionysian. Rather, the individual stands out as an expression of the underlying Dionysian and becomes sublime rather than horrible,[107] appearing "surrounded with a higher glory."[108] The individual becomes a symbol of the underlying Dionysian and does not stand simply in a truth relation to what it expresses, but rather exists sui generis.[109] At the same time, the art form transfigures everyday life. As Richard Schacht has it, "Dionysian reality is sublimated and Apollinian ideality is brought down to earth. Both meet on the plane of individual human existence and yield a transfigured representation of it in which the conditions of human existence are at once preserved and transformed."[110]

Emphasis on the Dionysian sea of energy and the shattering of the principle of individuation appear again later in Nietzsche's work in his deconstruction of the ego, the subject, into a play of forces held together by a grammatical fiction.[111] The creative one becomes a channel through which the Dionysian announces itself in the emergence of form from the potential chaos of forces. As we have noted, such creativity presupposes a prior organization of one's life, a certain asceticism of instincts, and thus— paradoxically—control by the "grammatical fiction." And creativity is both grounded in and produces a system of control, a tradition of shaping. For Nietzsche, "every mature art has a host of conventions as its basis. . . . Convention is the condition of great art, *not* an obstacle."[112] The controlling ego is resituated, not only in relation to its own instinctual life, but also in relation to its historical context—the two dominant aspects evoking *amor fati*.

Contrary to modern dogma, for Nietzsche the true artist is not one who expresses his peculiar subjectivity. One might think such of the lyric poet in particular. But for Nietzsche, subjective art is just bad art.[113] For one thing, art is not merely subjective, idiosyncratic "expression."[114] As Nietzsche said, great art, like language, rests on "a host of conventions." Furthermore, the true artist is "the medium through which the one truly existent subject celebrates his release in appearance."[115] The true artist speaks universally because he is a channel for the underlying encompassing ground, which Nietzsche, in common with the Idealist tradition, here identifies as *subject*. However ambiguous that might be in this context, it will be clearly superseded in *The Gay Science* by the announcement of the death of God and his repudiation of all "metaphysical consolation" in his 1886 "Attempt at a Self-Criticism" directed at *The Birth of Tragedy*.[116] That does not involve repudiation of inspiration. In *Ecce Homo* Nietzsche says: "one accepts, one does not ask who gives," for there is no Who, only the enigma of visions and inspiration.[117]

The origin of Greek drama in the Dionysiac rituals actually locates "the spirit of music" first in the dance, because it is the dance circle that was the prototype of the stage, setting off the sacred from the profane. The rhythmic movement of the body is the basic instrument in the expression of personal participation in the primordial power of being, recognized as primordial and all-encompassing—hence something more than mere privatized—or even socialized—intoxication, whether in the individual or in the mass emotional affection of a group. The original Dionysian dance circle survives as the chorus. The chorus creates a sacred space within its circling dance. Through the revelry and frenzy of the dance, the image of the god appears in their midst and is embodied in the leader of the chorus, who eventually dons a mask of Dionysus. The characters of tragedy come out of that original form. They are rooted back in a kind of Dionysian sea and yet emerge as clear characters occupying the region of Apollo.[118]

For Nietzsche, the high point of the Apollonian-Dionysian fusion occurred in the tragedies of Aeschylus and Sophocles. But then came Socrates and with him Euripides, his putative disciple. Socrates introduced the philosophic type, who corroded the tragic synthesis. "Aesthetic Socratism" arose: to be beautiful (and good and true) is to be a matter of clear knowledge.[119] Dionysian rapture is smothered by the cold blanket of Socratic reason. According to Nietzsche, Euripides never understood the Dionysian depths of his predecessors: in place of the large mythic figures of earlier tragedy, Euripides presents us with the ordinary man. Life is flattened to the everyday. The Dionysiac becomes "fiery emotions," and the Apollonian "clear ideas." Here we have a psychologistic reduction of the larger cosmic-religious function of the notions in Aeschylus and Sophocles.

According to Nietzsche, aesthetic Socratism moves in that direction: the theoretical type that Socrates introduces is interested in the unveiling of nature and in the cast off garments; he loses the great artist's interest in the hidden depths.[120] When that attains to one of its consequences, we then hear talk of "Greek cheerfulness" (*Heiterkeit:* cheerfulness, serenity, clearness), which is actually a species of superficiality without any awareness of the metaphysical depths plumbed in pre-Euripidean tragedy.[121] Art eventually becomes froth, the bubbly exterior of life, with nothing of its relation to the cosmic depths. One has to think that observation in relation to Nietzsche's other claims regarding art's celebration of surface. Is it that Platonism is surface, seduction, appearance, and that tragic art creates an appearance that tells the real truth?

"Greek serenity" seems the equivalent of Schopenhauerian aesthetic contemplation as the stilling of the will. Heidegger for one thinks that Schopenhauer's interpretation of Kant's "disinterested satisfaction" was based on a misunderstanding that became the standard interpretation of Kant. Heidegger sees Kant as actually closer to Nietzsche: "disinterested satisfaction" is "unconstrained favoring."[122] Schopenhauer's view of art as pointing toward the blowing out of desire was the main thing that set Nietzsche in opposition. For Nietzsche art is not a narcotic or a flight from life but the stirring and rapturous celebration of life.[123] Where Schopenhauer advocates saying No! to life because of the immense suffering it inflicts, Nietzsche advocates saying Yes! to it in spite of suffering and because of the rapture of creativity in the will to power. But then Nietzsche notes that the function of art depends on the character of the perceiver: one who is overwrought because of desire seeks the stilling of Will; one who is languid requires stimulus.[124]

Nietzsche was particularly concerned with the "Alexandrianism" that stemmed from the introduction of the theoretical type. In the transition to the Hellenistic age, whose center was Alexandria in Egypt, the scholar replaced the creator. An essentially shrunken creature in Nietzsche's view, the scholar confines himself to a small circle of soluble problems.[125] Nietzsche was particularly sensitive to the difficulties this entailed since he studied classical philology in an era when the aim of classical study was shifting— and precisely along Alexandrian lines. Up to that point it had been *Bildung*, the shaping of human life through the study of the classics. Now it was becoming *Altertumswissenschaft*, the science of antiquity, the objective determination of facts with no concern for the comprehensive shaping, through such study, of the ones who read the classics.[126] Granted, *Bildung* still operated within the general horizon of Platonism and Christianity; but it also operated within a horizon that informed life with comprehensive meaning. As in Alexandria, the modern scholar becomes a specialist. Nietzsche's project was to consider the scholar in terms of the artist and the artist in terms of life.[127]

For the Nietzsche of *The Birth of Tragedy* at least, the German tradition provided the basis for a Greek Renaissance that went back to the Dionysiac origins. This moves beyond the Apollonian classicism admired by Winckelmann, who had reawakened appreciation for the Greeks where the Renaissance doted on the Romans. One line of this further recovery moves musically from Luther through Bach and Beethoven to Wagner.[128] The other moves philosophically from Kant to Schopenhauer. Both limited the operation of logic to phenomenality and opened the way to a wisdom beyond logic.[129]

The whole, nature and society together, is a kind of aesthetic phenomenon. The great artist is life itself. As its darling, life produces those higher types that, as in Kant, are the geniuses through which nature gives the rules. And these higher types come to define the fundamental forms of life, the fundamental games that constitute cultures. For Nietzsche some of the greatest works of art are the Jesuit Order and the Prussian Officers Corps—scarcely something his contemporary Dionysian followers would approve.[130] For such works to succeed there has to be "the will to tradition, to authority, to centuries-long responsibility, to *solidarity* between succeeding generations backwards and forwards *in infinitum*."[131] This is what is involved in the instinct for institutions eroded by the rise of democracy and liberalism. Today, "that which *makes* institutions is despised, hated, rejected. . . ."[132] However, this stands in tension with Nietzsche's praise of "the will to be oneself, to stand out—that which I call *pathos of distance* [which] characterizes every *strong* age."[133] As I have indicated previously, for Nietzsche this entails, in each individual, a will to "compel the chaos that is within to take on form,"[134] to have the hounds in the basement quietly chained, to enjoy the clear air at the top storey as a condition for all great productivity.[135] The aim is ultimately "the grand style," to become simple, logical, even mathematical, to become law, holding together opposites without tension, and thereby taking up becoming into being.[136] The tension entails distinguishing the herd from the masters. But even the master's will to stand out entails respect, even reverence for their real equals and thus a real ability to discern quality.[137] The ideal of mastership in the Overman involves, as we noted before, "the Roman Caesar with Christ's soul."[138]

Nietzsche returns to the more comprehensive Greek meaning of art expressed in Aristotle's description of politics as the art of arts. Art in the narrower sense is not the locus of aesthetic detachment; rather it gives the umbrella of meaning within which such enduring lifestyles can succeed by receiving ultimate legitimation. But art in the narrower sense also sets such meaning systems upon the earth of bodily encounters. Of course, cultures are in conflict; but that produces conditions for the creation of new forms, keeping us from falling back into a general slackness as Hegel also maintained. Life goes on, continually spewing out new forms in nature and in history. To identify with it is not only to accept the inevitability of conflict and destruction, but, even more so, to exult in life's boundless creativity.

## Response

Nietzsche's work might be viewed as parallel with Kant's sublime: threat to life producing exultation. The tame aesthetics of Schopenhauerian-Kantian "coming to rest" in the detached contemplation of beautiful form is set aside. Schopenhauer's understanding of the sublime is itself based on detached contemplation, the sublimity of detachment measured by the degree of potential threat to one's own life exhibited by the sublime occasion. In contrast to the beautiful, which brings us to rest (though in the quickening of the feeling of distinctive human life in the free play of the relation between understanding and the imagination in the capacity to make a judgment), Kant's understanding of the sublime links it to an upsurge of emotion, of the feeling of life—and here Kant sees life not in its distinctively human form, but in the general form of living existence—in the face of occasions that would threaten it. For Nietzsche tragic performance brings us face to face with the destructive power of the Dionysian, but evokes exultation in the Apollonian creativity of that same power instantiated by the tragic artwork itself, and not simply by what it represents. Nietzsche's scorn for "disinterested satisfaction" understands it the way Schopenhauer understood it, as on the way toward the "blowing out" of desire. Nietzsche fails to attend to the context of Kant's understanding of that expression. For Kant art has its origin in genius, in the work of spirit, which animates all the faculties; it has its immediate terminus in a work characterized as fresh, vital, organic, in contrast to the dead and mechanical; and it effects a quickening of the sense of distinctively human life. The difference between Kant and Nietzsche lies more in how they view that stimulation of the sense of life. For Kant life here lies in the capacity to make good judgments; for Nietzsche it is closer to the religious "enthusiasm" and "illuminism" Kant repudiated: a kind of cosmic intoxication. This brings us back to Nietzsche's proximity to Plotinus in the transcendence of Eros over nous.

In assigning priority to the Dionysian dance circle, Nietzsche retrieves and develops a suggestion present in Plato, the only other thinker I have treated—and the only other major philosopher of which I am aware— who gives a major role to dance among the art forms. And, as in Nietzsche, dance for Plato is linked to a certain priority of music among the art forms. Remember that in the *Republic*, Socrates joins together music and gymnastics as the instruments of the first stage of *paideia*—initially as ways of tuning the soul and the body respectively, but eventually as cooperative in tuning the psyche in the balanced tension between softness and hardness of disposition. In the *Laws* the gymnastic required is dance, which imparts order to the chaotic flux of emotion in the life of the young. Note that dance here is a kind of psychotherapy, a moral tool for tuning the dispositions, not, as in Nietzsche, a way of participating in the depths of the cosmos.

Socrates said that through music order and harmony sink most deeply into the soul. What are we to make of those "depths"? Are they to be taken as real and not just metaphorical opposites to "the heights" gained by going out of the Cave of temporality and sensibility and ascending to the region of pure intelligible light, the light of Beauty Itself? Are "the depths" the region of the emotions tied to the organism? In the *Republic* bodily based feelings occupy the lowest (deepest?) level of the psyche and include hunger, thirst, and Eros. However, we know from the *Symposium* and the *Phaedrus* that Eros is exalted into relation with the region of the eternal as the intermediary, tying the temporal and the eternal, the very realm in which philosophy operates, so that the depth of Eros is the vehicle of aspiration toward the heights. Without Eros reason becomes calculation in the service of one's own egoistic ends or, at best, in service to the city. It is that Eros which reappears in Nietzsche.

Plato extends the harmonic tuning of the psyche achievable by music into the region of the spatial arts, surrounding the psyche from birth to death with artifacts—buildings, furniture, utensils, clothing, paintings—having the properties of order, grace, harmony, proportion. We have several times noted Walter Pater's remark that all art seeks the status of music —that is, an ordered aesthetic totality, representative or not. As such, other arts have the same effect as music in effecting an emotional tonality. Here we see an antecedent to Nietzsche's "grand style." Nonetheless, such rhythmic tuning through seeing and hearing is all in the receptive mode. Plato adds another dimension in dance, an active mode, a performance mode in which the body as a whole is the instrument. Kinesthetic feelings, feelings of the balance of our own bodily movements, join the feelings that come through the eye and the ear. Nietzsche reinstates and recommends such aesthetic priority.

In Plato, the upward ascent of the soul involves the prior harmonizing of the emotional life so that, with the emergence of the rational pattern of experience, which seeks to unveil the cosmic harmony, it will find a welcome matrix in the already rationally ordered psychic life. Yet, as I have said, the dance and the music that bring about that order do not seem to involve the display of the primordial and all-encompassing as they do in Nietzsche.

In Plato the ultimate aim is to harmonize the whole human psyche, whose basic nature is philosophic—that is, occupying the region between the eternal and the temporal as the mortal having designs on the immortal, in the mode of rational exploration and rational ordering of life as a whole within the never fully revealed cosmic Whole. Rationality is led by Eros, which might be understood participatively as the complement to noetic detachment. It is in this direction that Plotinus takes us: the One/Good/Beautiful as correlate to Eros is that with which we are finally to be identified in the field of awareness in its mystical completion. (Doesn't Plotinus also speak of the Dionysiac here?) But that mystical moment is the anchor of a fully rational life that orders the life of the body and the world around us and that alternates between the discernment of rational order and participation in the Source.

This is both near and far in relation to Nietzsche. For him the desideratum is "the grand style": compelling the chaos that is in us to become form, giving the stamp of the eternal on the quotidian linked to an exultant sense of participating in the creative-destructive cosmos. And achieving that involves a certain asceticism of the instinctive life so as to achieve a clear sense of things. But whereas in Plotinus this is tied up with a certain contempt for things and a desire to be with that which lies beyond it all, in Nietzsche it is linked with the affirmation of this life and a repudiation of claims to an absolute transcendent. Nietzsche sees a close relation between the two: affirmation of a transcendent is linked to contempt for this life.

A professor of ethics at a secular university found it astonishing that his avowedly Christian students regularly announced that they would have no reason to be moral if there were no God who would punish and reward them for their deeds. Should it not be the other way around: finding something about the intrinsic value of life leads us to the affirmation of God? (I take this to be what is at stake in Dostoyevsky's *Brothers Karamazov*.) In fact, if we look at what Plato does in the *Republic*, we see that he develops the argument about the nature and superiority of justice over injustice explicitly, *without* any appeal to the gods or an afterlife. The Ring of Gyges has the function of making one hypothetically disappear from men *and gods*, so that thoughts of external rewards and punishment do not enter into the heart of the argument.[139] In considering what the nature of justice is and whether it is better than injustice, all we would have to deal with would be the intrinsic order or disorder of our own experience. Plato pulls us away from that which too many people today consider the indispensible ground of ethics: a divine Legislator, Judge, Rewarder, and Punisher in a life hereafter. Plato temporarily puts that in brackets. When the argument is completed, he restores the appearance to others: over the long haul, even in this life, the truly just man is found out, as is the truly unjust; and in the afterlife, it is likely that rewards and punishments will be justly administered.[140] But this restoration of the external appearance *(doxa)* of the soul is precisely superadded, not constitutive of the intrinsic grounds of moral action. For Plato, contrary to many of his followers, especially many of his Christian followers, the right way is immanent in life itself. But even so, the way Plato establishes the right order is by appealing to the realm of Being and the Good, which stand outside the realm of time and life. In virtue of this we tend to view ourselves dualistically as souls separate from bodies, imprisoned in our bodies and thus in our passions. And our aim is thus disembodiment.[141] Hence Nietzsche's critique of Platonism in favor of life. However, there are countervailing texts in Plato. *Phaedo* appeals to the psychological blocks that feelings arising from the body set in the way of the emergence of a concentrated rational pattern of experience; but the *Timaeus* presents the basis for an ontology (as distinct from a descriptive psychology) of the body as the house of the soul (i.e., the place where the rational soul is at home in the cosmos).[142]

Contemporary enthusiasts for Nietzsche heed his emphasis on standing above the herd and his praise of the creative individual without attending equally to his attack on private subjectivity and his reading of great art as expressive of the concrete universality of encompassing life. Along with this goes his emphasis on the need for discipline—for a measure of asceticism, for a chaining of the dogs in the basement of one's life, for a measure of chastity, humility, and poverty—as a condition of creativity. There is as well his stress on tradition as a general condition and of artistic convention as a specific condition of artistic creativity. These are measures that "Dionysiac artists" in the twentieth century have ignored, often invoking the authority of Nietzsche.

One major criterion of form creation is efficacy, the pragmatic test, something like a scientific theory. The theory is regarded as true insofar as it is not only able to take account of known regularities of nature, but is also fruitful in suggesting lines of experimentation that uncover more and more of the context of nature. However, the theory is discarded insofar as

226

a more comprehensive theory arises that unifies the lines of research achieved and going forward at a given time, suggests further lines of exploration, and is able to do justice to the anomalies that resist penetration under the older theory.[143] Something analogous to this takes place at a more encompassing level in the comprehensive horizons of meaning, which deal, not simply with one aspect of experience, but with whole ways of life that have, ingredient in and grounding them, definitions of the umbrella of meaning, of what finally counts, what is finally "up" or "down" for human existence. The creation of meaning systems has to be fruitful in bringing about the possibility that various subforms of human life, different types of functions and personalities come to live under these umbrellas. There is something about them that is true the way a scientific theory is true: it is not finally but hypothetically true, contextually true, perspectively true. It discloses certain facets of the surrounding world and allows for certain connections to emerge in our experience without being the final disclosure. As you get one scientific theory substituting for another, so you get various religious and philosophic systems contending with and often driving out others. Only in that case we have a tendency to settle down in one or another without the drive beyond emerging in so central a fashion as we have in the scientific tradition. (Perhaps the inherently ongoing, self-corrective character of science ought to be present also in the philosophic tradition. Dewey, as we shall see in the next chapter, calls for an application of the scientific method so conceived especially to ethics.[144] But this is largely not the case, because philosophy has tended to model itself on the absoluteness of religious claims. One might wonder whether that absoluteness is tied to the fear both of chaos that ontological openness sets on an animal base and of the ultimate emptiness correlated with that very openness.) The more comprehensive character of the horizons of meaning lies in their opening out perspectives not only theoretically but also practically and aesthetically: paths for thinking, doing, and feeling. But none of them are anything but perspectives, and to that extent they are all "lies," but are also disclosures as well. Heidegger will pick up on that: Being reveals and conceals itself in all the philosophies that have emerged in such a way that none has been able to drive the others out.[145]

The will-to-power is the will to create beyond the level at which one exists. The criteria for creation lie in the fusion of complexity. The more comprehensive and powerful the unification, the higher the type of horizon creation.[146] Ultimately and ideally it would seem that the highest form would be one in which every individual would find a way of tapping his or her potentialities consonant with the unity of the whole. This would seem to be the final projection of form, which comes to terms with all the life forms present. Whether or not that is possible is a question. To create a perspective is to load the dice in one or the other direction. Creating conditions for the emergence of certain lifestyles inhibits the emergence of other forms. The predominance of a disciplined lifestyle inhibits the emergence of a loose, self-indulgent form and vice-versa. In individual lives, the nature of decision is not only to cut off deliberation about possibilities, but also to cut off all those possibilities except the lines opened up by that on which we actually decide. Choosing one way allows one to tap potentialities unavailable without commitment to that way; but that means that other possibilities have to lie fallow. The pursuit of one is the exclusion of the others. A society likewise cannot choose to foster equally all styles of life but only a limited set of forms compatible with one another. If we try to let all forms go forward simultaneously, chaos results. The context within which all forms, and especially all higher forms (i.e., more complex forms, having more prerequisites for their achievement), would be inhibited.

The choices that have been made historically involve an elite class that depends on a slave class. Whether they are called slaves in some direct way or are slaves indirectly—Marx's "wage slaves"—there are people who have to be at the bottom, an essentially servile class.[147] Whether they are given greater latitude one way or another, there has to be some class at the bottom that makes possible an elite from which the Overmen can come—except in democratic socialism, in which meaning dies because of antipathy against any elite. The highest elite are the creators of comprehensive meaning, the supreme artists. What I want to stress first of all is the parallel between such meaning creation and scientific procedure. Traditionally, meaning systems have been viewed statically. Scientific procedure suggests that we consider them dynamically. But I also want to stress, along with Nietzsche, a certain priority of the aesthetic. It is exemplary unification of mind and feeling, of sensibility and intellect, of individual and group, of the Now and the Whole. It binds together what the priority of abstractive intellect takes apart. It teaches us "how to dance," a celebratory fidelity to the earth, a paean to creation.

For Nietzsche art is produced by nature and functions both as supplement to and overcoming of nature.[148] This is linked to Nietzsche's various statements about truth. Platonistic eternal, nonperspectival Truth is out: it is a lie concocted to help us deal with suffering. A true life is one of "fidelity to the earth." There is also truth in the service of life as distinct from the collection of trivial truths. Wisdom is higher than such truth seeking. Further, the truth is that life is full of horrors, but also that it is indescribably fertile, creative. To be creative is thus to be true to life. For Nietzsche, finally, art is worth more than truth—either Platonistically conceived or, more truthfully, in terms of the horrors and the trivialities we find in life. But art is most fully true to itself when it stems from and exhibits a unified life, a life in which reason, will, and sensibility are one, in which the theoretical is united with the practical.

One of the deep problems with Nietzsche is the status of his own claims. If all is perspectivism, how can we know that? And does he really want to say that the deepest truths, both in the theoretical and the practical order, are merely perspectives? I have tried to maintain throughout this work the proximate and enduring priority of the structures of the field of experience that give us the conditions for possibility of our perspectival construals of the character of the Whole to which the deepest structure of the field of experience emptily points. The skeletal framework of the field of experience and what is implicit in that recognition can be animated by different worldviews. But that very fact, linked to our directedness by nature to the whole, entails a heuristic and dialogic imperative to remain open to what is other than what presents itself within the perspective we currently occupy. Finally, all that we deal with appears within the perspective of human, all too human awareness and is linked to the fostering of that distinctive form of life.

# IX

# DEWEY

OUTSIDE OF HEGEL AND Schelling, there is no major philosopher who has devoted as much attention to the aesthetic or given it as central a role as John Dewey. This may come as a surprise to some. In their standard two-volume survey of American philosophy, Elizabeth Flower and Murray Murphey do not even mention Dewey's *Art as Experience,* in spite of their relatively extensive period-by-period, work-by-work survey of his publications.[1] And yet for Dewey the aesthetic furnishes the basic measure of everything human.

The centrality of the aesthetic is linked to the centrality of experience, for in Dewey's view, the aesthetic is "experience in its integrity."[2] Attention to the features given in experience returns us from the region of ultimate ontological construals, which is a battlefield of contending views, to that which is always already there when we set about to think. To the extent that he makes this turn, Dewey exhibits many parallels with the phenomenological orientation of this book.

Though he falls, with C. S. Peirce and William James before him, in the general line of American Pragmatism, Dewey's basic position is more accurately described by what he calls *Instrumentalism,* which indicates the fundamental character of an idea.[3] Generally speaking, the common view of the nature of an idea in the tradition has been to conceive of it as either an intrinsic and higher reality (e.g., Plato and Hegel) or a mirror of such, whether relatively clear (Aristotle) or initially distorted by the medium (Locke). In any case, according to Dewey, for the tradition generally an idea is essentially retrospective, related to the past, to what has been; the idea is to that extent essentially a priori.[4] In contrast, Dewey himself, reflecting on the function of modern scientific ideas, sees an idea as essentially prospective, future oriented, tied in with our action on things in experimentation and modified or rejected in terms of testable consequences. This view is related to his general strategy of trying to overcome the dualisms that occur within experience and that tend to be canonized by philosophers, especially those that are introduced in the Platonic tradition, which turns on the status of the Idea. The tendency toward dualisms is exacerbated in modern times by Descartes, who in some sense falls within the Platonic line. For Dewey it is the aesthetic which finally heals all such splits, for the aesthetic, as I have said, is experience in its integrity.[5]

## Overcoming the Platonic Splits

The basic split in the Platonic tradition is that between Being and Becoming, the stable and the changing, the eternal and the temporal, to which we have access through the distinction between Ideas and the things that mirror them.[6] To recur to things noted in my first historical chapter, for Plato the Idea is superior since it does not come into being and pass out of being, though it may come into awareness and pass out of awareness. *Idea* is a technical term that does not cover any "bright idea" I might happen to have, but rather indicates something essentially objective that the mind sees or mirrors when it is properly attentive. Take, for example, the geometric demonstration that the internal angles of a triangle are equal to 180 degrees. When seen, it shows itself to have a kind of atemporal validity, to have been true even before it was seen. Thus an Idea in the technical Platonic sense is not a subjective state of mind, although some of the things *we* call ideas are subjective states of mind. A Platonic Idea is an eternal truth over against the plurality of instances that mirror it in the changing context of the world of nature as well as in the changing character of human culture and human individual minds. Culture and the minds that carry it may be such that a given Idea never enters into their field of awareness or, having entered, has passed out of it; but the Idea remains an eternal measure of the things that instantiate it and the minds that mirror it. This sets up a basic split between the eternality of Ideas on the one hand, and the temporality of things and empirical states of awareness on the other.

Parallel to this is a split between mind and body. Mind as intellect discovers itself only when it pulls itself away from its bodily involvement and is able to concentrate, to "become a center together with" the object on which it centers its attention. In order to achieve this it has to pull itself out of the flowing distractions of its bodily existence.[7] A split between mind and body thus follows the split between Idea and thing. On the Platonic reading, both of them are expressions of the split between Being and Becoming. The Idea always "is," as compared with the things of our ordinary focus, which at one time were not, at one time will not be, and, when they are, are always such that they are no longer what they were and not yet what they will be. Their mode of being is one of becoming, and their degree of being is the degree to which they realize the fullness of their type.

Linked to the mind-body split is the split between reason and emotion. In the *Republic*, Plato has Socrates present Eros, together with hunger and thirst, at the lowest level of the soul (*epithumia*, desire) and criticize art for watering the desires rather than drying them up, as is required for the emergence of the rational from the biological pattern of experience. Along Pythagorean lines, the *Phaedo* has Socrates present the bodily desires as virtually the tomb of the rational soul.[8] These positions are the ancestors of Stoic *apatheia*, or lack of passion, and parallel Buddhist nirvana, which gained Western expression in Schopenhauer's philosophy.

The split between mind and body, linked to the separation and superiority of the Idea over the thing, leads to the priority of *theoria*, or the contemplative life over the realm of praxis, which puts us in contact with the grubby things of material reality.[9] The latter is the sort of thing with which the slave class, along with their immediate overseers, is preoccupied, but from which the lords are removed. Theory and practice are split off from one another and each is located in a different stratum of society. An elite class is ideally given over to the higher pursuit of *theoria;* those less gifted intellectually and dispositionally engage in the workaday world for the sake of the elite's leisure to pursue contemplation.[10] This view is maintained even in the synthesis of Christianity and Greek thought in Thomas Aquinas.[11]

We can see then that these various splits are systematically connected with one another and follow from a certain quite natural conception of the status of an Idea. Dewey offers a counterposition to this conception. As I indicated earlier, rather than being a mirror of an eternally existent order, for Dewey an idea is essentially an instrument fashioned for a purpose. It arises when we face problems posed by the relations we find in our overall social and biological environment while carrying on the tasks involved in living our lives. By reason of the continually shifting character of the environment and our relationship to it, our ideas are always capable of change —indeed, must change or suffer the penalty of diminished effectiveness in carrying out our life tasks.[12]

Natural science presents us with such a conception of an idea: it operates by hypothesis, which is retained insofar as it is fruitful in bringing about an expansion of our awareness and control through continued experiment; it is modified or discarded when it does not. Contrary to the basically retrospective, backward-looking character of the Platonic Idea, Dewey's conception of an idea is, as I already remarked, essentially prospective, future oriented. Contrary to the eternality of the Platonic Ideas, in Dewey's view ideas are necessarily capable of transformation over time. Dewey's conception does not place us in the state of contemplative inaction, but calls for bodily action on the environment in the form of experimentation. It does not fortify us in our complacency but establishes a methodically self-corrective process. Stimulated by the environment and calling for action, such an idea integrates thought and action, mind and body, organism and environment, thus overcoming many of the splits that have afflicted the history of thought, especially since Plato.[13]

## Overcoming the Cartesian Splits

But there were several distinctively modern splits that emerged in the sixteenth and seventeenth centuries and which both added to and reenforced the Platonic splits that lay in the deep structure of Western history. The Reformation that arose within Western Christendom in the sixteenth century led not only to the breakup of Christendom as a social-political system, but also to a lengthy period of bloody religious wars. Out of that experience emerged the search for a new ground of human togetherness independent of religious belief: a separation of church and state, the tolerance of competing belief systems and the pursuit of value-free natural science tied to the transformation of the environment to serve the more obvious aspects of human well-being. It was the way this new science was conceived that produced a new set of splits within experience.

That science had its first philosophical grounding in René Descartes, who reduced the world to two sets of differing substances: extensive material substance, exhaustively treatable by quantitative methodology, and thought, the whole field of awareness, considered as spiritual substance.[14]

234

Natures other than human were reduced to mechanisms without awareness, and human nature became what Gilbert Ryle later called "the ghost in the machine."[15] Entailed in all this was Galileo's way of conceiving a distinction between primary and secondary qualities. Based on discoveries in physics and physiology, the measurable properties were considered to belong to material things as primary qualities, while the sensory features, considered secondary and derivative, were located within—in the literal sense of the term *within*—the human perceiver as subjective effects of the primary qualities belonging to the object. Color, for example, was an effect inside the head—and, following casually thereupon, inside awareness—of the agitation of the retina by light waves.[16]

Descartes arrived at this view by beginning with a methodic doubt in order to sort out levels of certitude within experience. The upshot of his employment of that doubt was the indubitable self-presence of awareness to itself expressed in the famous *Cogito ergo sum*.[17] The problem that generated was the problem of how to get out of the initial confinement of the *cogito*. That problem was directly connected with the way, following Galileo, Descartes conceived of the distinction and relation of primary and secondary qualities. If we have initial access only to our own being-affected in the form of colors, sounds, and the like, how do we come to know the primary qualities and things external to us?

Methodic doubt is an intellectual invention aimed at sorting out levels of certitude in experience. The everyday world is subjected to such theoretical doubt by noting the occurrence of illusions in waking experience and of dreams while sleeping. In the latter case we have as vivid a sense of reality as in wakefulness. The Chinese Taoist sage Chuang Tzu once dreamt he was a butterfly, but then awoke to find he was still Chuang Tzu. He then reflected that he might really be a butterfly dreaming he is Chuang Tzu.[18] Finding no absolute certitude in that direction, Descartes turns next to mathematics, only to undermine the absolute character of the certitude available therein by appealing to the admittedly wild hypothesis of a hypothetical evil genius tinkering with awareness to make it *think* it has certitude. Then Descartes presents his basic discovery, the Archi-medean point of his thought: even if such a wildly hypothetical being were constantly deceiving me, he could not deceive me about one thing: my self-presence in the act of being deceived. *Cogito ergo sum* I think, therefore I am.[19] No matter what I am thinking about, no matter how deceived I might be with respect to that object, I am indubitably present to myself while I think. So indubitably is this true that any attempt to doubt it exhibits it, for to doubt is a mode of thinking, which necessarily involves self-presence. And so there is an intellectual Archimedean point around which everything can be made to pivot—or better, from which one can move the world intellectually, reconstructing our understanding of things through the employment of rigorous method.

But notice that this *cogito* is, to begin with, disengaged from its embodiment. Descartes eventually canonized such disengagement by claiming that a human being is really two substances: a thinking substance—the mind—and an extended substance—the body—with nothing in between.[20] There are thus two regions and two kinds of entities with only external—though "intimate"—connection between one another, a ghost in a machine. The machine notion prefigures the way modern science has gone on thinking about the body, in principle explicable in terms of mechanical laws. Then there is the ghostly thing haunting the machine, an angel or a devil, or a merely epiphenomenal ethereal thing that does not appear in the observable mechanical context, namely thinking (Descartes's generic term for the whole field of awareness).

From this position, Descartes attempted to work his way out to God as truthful Creator of the mind and thus as guarantor of truth when the mind seeks it in responsible, i.e. methodologically certified, ways.[21] Then Descartes returned attention to the external world. The latter is shorn of the colors, sounds, tastes, smells, and tactile features that it has in everyday experience: they are merely subjective qualities as effects of physical processes. The external world delivers its secrets through mathematical physics, which separates the quantitative causes from the sensory effects.[22] The self-enclosed mind is a subject initially separated from its deceptive everyday objects as well as from its body, which is the source of the original deceptions. The outer world and the body within it return in methodically purified form as objects of mathematical physics and the criteria for distinguishing wakefulness from dream or illusion in ordinary experience are found in implicitly employed principles of coherence and consistency (prefiguring Kant's position, which I have briefly discussed earlier).[23] The initial state of being locked up inside our own minds, dealing only with the subjective contents of our personal experience, is a peculiar modern legacy picked up by Empiricism and by Kant. In Descartes, the ontology of matter has to develop in correlation with observation and experimentation in the sensory field to discover which of the possibilities of mechanical sequence compatible with first principles has been realized in fact.[24]

The initial disregard of the senses is linked with the enduring downplay of the life of feeling, which is tied in with our intimate association with the body. This sounds like the Socrates of the *Republic*, but not like the Socrates of the *Symposium* and the *Phaedrus*, for whom there are deeper, more metaphysical dimensions to the passionate life. And so we have again the emphasis on a fundamental split between reason and emotion and an implicit rendering of the whole aesthetic region as peripheral and merely decorative.

At the same time, this self-involuted intellect, shorn of all passion, seeking certitude through careful methodological procedure, methodically cut itself off from the context of the tradition in which it exists, viewed as a source of confused and conflicting interpretations. Hence we have a psychological foundation and reinforcement for a social atomism: the individual, the self-initiating, self-sustaining, self-made person who is the arbiter over the whole tradition, reconstructing the world of knowledge and action from his own internal resources.

Another distinctively modern split occurs, based predominantly on Cartesian foundations: the fact-value split. The world turns out to be a set of mechanically governed facts shorn of intrinsic value. This is tied to the elimination of substantial forms and consequently of teleology in nature, a position that can be traced back to ancient atomism.[25] Things are the result of the accidental shuffling of particles; they are not "headed in the direction" of actualizing the potentialities of their natural forms. In the dominant tradition from Plato and Aristotle through the Middle Ages, there are grades of excellence in nature based on a hierarchy of substantial forms and on the degree to which individuals of a species fulfill the nature given by their substantial forms. Value is coterminous with the fulfillment of a thing's natural goals and with the place a thing occupies in the hierarchy of being. All this disappears with the emergence of modern physics: in place of a hierarchy of natures seeking their ends, we find colorless, odorless, valueless matter in motion according to fixed mechanical laws, with phenomenal organisms appearing like froth spewed forth by the ocean waves. Absent from this view were Aristotelian natures, formative principles organizing material for the sake of realizing their own natural ends. Nature eventually became "the clockwork universe," a single whole composed of atomic particles combining and separating according to invariant laws. Learning those laws enabled us to transform materials for our purposes, making us "masters and possessors of nature."[26]

Reinforcing the Platonic dualisms, there are thus several peculiarly modern dualisms: of mind and body, of subject and object, of fact and value, of individual and community, of past and present. Descartes's methodic doubt pried him loose from bodily sensations and passions and from traditional modes of understanding and behavior—precisely Plato's cave of *doxa*. The method placed him at one remove from things and persons, having immediate access only to his own consciousness, the famous *cogito* from which we have to reason our way to the world outside. The physical world is stripped of the colors, sounds, tactile, gustatory, and olfactory features that are now located in the mind as effects of the measurable features that inhere in the single property of *extension*. Extension, in turn, operates according to invariant mechanical laws to yield a clockwork universe. Primary qualities take center stage, secondary qualities are reduced to subjectivity, and all Aristotelian forms as final causes, and thus as values—or what Dewey will call tertiary qualities—have been banished.

Dewey attempts to overcome the splits that have their origins in the Platonic and Cartesian traditions, on the one hand by his instrumentalist theory of idea (which I have already briefly discussed) and, on the other hand, by his biological theory of mind. The biological theory of mind, derived from Darwinian impulses and mediated through the work of William James, erodes the Cartesian model in that awareness is displayed as a function of the broad context of physical-physiological interaction on which awareness itself rests.[27] Awareness is possible only within a biological matrix that involves the habitual storage of routes of response to the impact of the environment on the organism. This region of response constitutes a kind of iceberg from which consciousness emerges as its tip. Consciousness itself, though essentially future oriented at the level of intelligence, is intelligible both in terms of its grounding in past interaction routes, and also in present interplay with the environment, only part of which is ever manifest in the present—indeed, only a part is *ever* manifest, even in science.[28] In this process the conscious mind does not display itself as an entity but as a function that, though pivotal in our lives, is linked to the massive set of habit structures that are continuous with the motor routes that our "body" has inscribed within it. For Dewey, awareness itself is a flickering process over against the more enduring aspect of mind that is empatterned in the "meat." Mind is enduring in the sense that my knowledge and my skills remain "in my mind" even though they are for the moment out of my awareness. Awareness itself flickers in the sense that its "light" goes on in the morning and goes out at night, occasionally dimming and brightening in between.[29] Awareness is thus not identical with mind but is its cutting edge, the relatively self-directive aspect of mind. In this way, Dewey thinks, much along the lines of Aristotle, of a psychophysical whole that is itself a node of partially manifest interaction with the environment.

But, as in Aristotle, all this is not viewed as a purely internal matter, not simply a private, inward, enclosed state—which is the tendency in modern accounts of experience, beginning with Galileo and Descartes and going through Locke and Berkeley to Hume and Kant. Experience in that tradition is a self-enclosed effect of physical causation, giving us the problem of how we get outside to know other persons and things—indeed, to know the physical causation that produces sensation in our subjective privacy. It is the Cartesian problem in empiricist terms. For Dewey, interaction-based awareness brings us outside our privacy into the manifestness of the world, as we will see in Heidegger as well.[30] Experience in general is not an internal occurrence but the transformation of physical interaction into participation in what lies without.[31] Interaction is what occurs in photoelectric cells, computers, and robot mechanisms. But experience is heightened vitality that involves being taken, beyond both the spatial internality of the impact of the environment on our organism and the privacy of our internal sensations, into active and alert commerce with the world. At its height experience signifies complete interpenetration of self and the world of objects and events. Though based on physical interaction, experience is much more. It attains a certain height in those all-encompassing emotions that bring us outside ourselves and into deepest communion with things, the emotions upon which great art develops.[32]

To say that the Cartesian mind-body split is overcome by a biological theory of mind does not mean that for Dewey we are "meat" and nothing but meat (even though, in many prevailing accounts, perhaps coexistent with an epiphenomenal awareness). Dewey is in some sense close to Nietzsche's "physiology" here, which, as Heidegger explains, has to be understood in a manner quite different than in modern biological thought. The latter is fundamentally "meat" analysis and presupposes the Cartesian split that allows us to prescind from awareness in the living being and treat the body as a meaty mechanism. But the body is not simply something externally observable; it is, more fundamentally, something I as a conscious-unconscious entity *live through*. This position is basically Aristotelian in that we are not composed of mind *and* body but are each a psychophysical whole comprised, in Aristotle's terms, of soul and body as a form-matter or act-potency relationship. For Aristotle, the very structure of the body *is* the soul in one of its moments of activation. The soul builds up its own body as an instrumental complex in order to allow the higher powers of the soul, the powers of sensory and eventually rational awareness, to emerge. In this view there is no inner spiritual substance somehow linked to an outer physical substance. There is but a single entity that is multilayered and in which the very character of the "physiological" (in the modern sense) is the condition for the possibility for the development of the higher levels. Something like this Dewey, along with Nietzsche, is also after.

Taking it further, mind is functionally embedded in a material matrix that is not fully nonmind. By reason of evolution, "matter" itself is that which, through complexification and centralization, becomes actually what it is potentially: enminded and aware. The typical way of understanding evolution misses this feature of matter because it operates under the Cartesian split. It continues to think comprehensively in terms of mechanical explanation based on visual observation for which awareness—visual or otherwise—is an embarrassing epiphenomenon. Explanation proceeds from the lower, earlier, less complex to the higher, later, more complex. For Dewey, resisting the Cartesian split, there is a co-modification of the ideas of "mind" and "matter" such that deeper explanation proceeds from the later forms to grasp what is merely potential in the earlier. Emergent evolutionism encompasses and situates mechanistic evolutionism. "Matter" is a relatively unintegrated state of what in integration is the ground for the emergence of the manifestness of things.[33] As Schelling put it, working along similar lines, mind-body duality is the ground for the manifestation of mind-body unity.[34] In this (as in several other matters) Dewey is not so far from Hegel. "Mind" is the meaning of "matter."

Here Dewey also attempts to overcome the fact-value dichotomy that runs through modern thought from its inception. Mind possessing ends is no stranger to nature, and nature as manifest to mind exhibits culminating phases, aesthetically displayed in the appearance of form. There is value as soon as there is life, which involves not mere mechanical sequence but patterns of development, processes leading toward an end.[35] Dewey thus in effect reintroduces Aristotelian substantial form as entelechy, the actualization of ends immanent in its initial stages. Only, beyond Aristotle, such forms are not eternal; they are temporary solutions to problems posed by the environment for the realization of the comprehensive goals of life.[36]

At the same time that Dewey overcomes the split between mind and body, he also overcomes the split between individual and society-tradition.[37] Tradition is the deep past and the society the residue of the past in the present. Mind is conditioned by that matrix. We are not brought up as rational animals. Rational animality is a goal, not only for individuals in their upbringing to adulthood, but also for society. We are assimilated to a society in such a way that the societal structures enter into the rhythms of our being, into our feelings about things, our spontaneous responses, our patterns of thought. We are conditioned and relatively determined by the whole fabric of interaction with the biological environment as well as with our parents, siblings and the people with whom we associate as we continue our lives.[38] Philosophies themselves are emergents out of this kind of matrix and tend to be justifications for it as a prior sense of the Whole that guides our philosophizing.[39] One constructs arguments for his prior sense of the Whole and against its opponents. If the arguments fail, the vision is not abandoned; one makes up other arguments. Prior to reflectively rational articulation is societal articulation. Not that awareness is simply a pure reflex of the society—a typical Marxist view.[40] The situation is rather dialectical or interactional, in which the individual is the cutting edge of the modification of the tradition on the basis of the tradition, just as awareness is the cutting edge of the modification of previous habit structures in the individual.[41]

If we attend to the fully concrete context within which we operate, we find that a global rejection of tradition is impossible because tradition has entered into the concrete fabric of our being. We might reject some dominant strands of a tradition, as Dewey himself rejected his own religious upbringing; but we are still necessarily enmeshed in countless other strands, beginning with the language we employ. There is no comprehensive handling of all the concrete factors of our existence. We as conscious agents always remain carried more or less—"thrown," as Heidegger for one will strongly emphasize. But part of our task is to become more extensively aware and thus more intelligently self-directive, individually and societally. Education for Dewey is thus not simply initiation of students into the societal way of doing things, into the tradition. More fundamentally, it provides the conditions to make intelligence emerge more clearly in the operative life of the society as the responsible cutting edge of the tradition.[42]

## Further Modifications of Traditional Notions

Linked to the Platonic view of things is the notion of the One/Good as the final cause of everything. All things aim at a single end. Against such a view, Dewey first observes that, by reason of evolution, there are not simply fixed ends for species. Complex interactional situations pose new problems solved often by the coming into being of new species. Ends are thus ends-in-situation or ends-in-view.[43] Secondly, Dewey proposes an ultimate and irreducible plurality of ends among human beings: different people in society seeking different ends, with intelligence operating in order to bring about those ends, formulating ideas, checking their experienced consequences, and modifying them in the light of those consequences. The plurality of ends is worthwhile promoting: business, art, farming, sports, engineering, and so forth.[44] Dewey finds criteria for distinguishing such examples from the ends most people would call criminal by following out the conditions for the possibility of intelligently creative cooperative existence. But for Dewey it is not the case that we can set up a hierarchy among these pursuits: they are simply different. Intellect functions as an instrument to bring about and modify the character of the many ends to which people find it worth their while to dedicate their lives.

But if we think solely of a plurality of ends, we have the grounds for chaos. One of the necessary conceptions is that of the creation of a social whole out of that plurality. That is where the development of social ethics comes into the picture.[45] One way to work this out is to conceive of society as oriented around a single end and enforced by a single body of power and opinion. But for Dewey a better way—better because it is closer to the actual character of life—is to draw upon the operative intelligence of the various interests, formulating organizational ideas and testing them out in the arena of social action in a kind of democratic process operating through rational debate tied to actual practice.[46] As in natural science, so also in society: we ought to have an experimental method in ethics and politics. The social whole has to be continually reconfigured to take account of emergent and divergent interests and of more extensive knowledge of the actual context of our operations.[47]

When Dewey eschews fixity of ends, he seems to be thinking more of strategies or rules. But even evolution has certain "fixed ends": growth and sustenance of the individual organism and reproduction of the type. What is not absolutely fixed are the strategies and transformations that have to be changed to realize those ends. We might call this more generalized level of ends "meta-ends." Dewey himself maintains several such ends. He sometimes says that "the only fixed end is growth."[48] However, in organisms one has to distinguish healthy and cancerous growth. Healthy growth involves harmony among various components heading toward and sustaining the fully functional adult form of a given species. Human growth heads toward some kind of psychic balance, but also one that is rich in proportion to its ability to contain within itself variety-in-unity.[49] For Dewey, association of people is the condition for the possibility of the emergence of distinct individuals with rich experience. The state is the widest coordinating agency measured by how it elicits intelligently responsible, creative, and cooperative individuals, and individuals are measured correspondingly by how they act intelligently, responsibly, creatively, and cooperatively.[50]

Full integration at the human level is aesthetic integration, the integral togetherness of all the parameters of experience. Thus, as we have indicated before, the aesthetic is the real meta-end. How it is achieved in multiple circumstances always involves some kind of transformation. Crucial to achieving aesthetic integration is the emergence of the pattern of intelligence, one of the fundamental ends of education. Intelligence is the capacity to make explicit what is implicit in ordinary experience, to analyze and synthesize, to grasp the possibility of achieving significant integrations, to apprehend consequences, and thus to move from spontaneous emotional prizing to thoughtful appraising. Intelligence is the cutting edge of conscious mind.[51]

Growth under patterns of intelligent aesthetic integration has conditions for its possibility. Health is one; self-restraint sufficient to apprehend clearly and shape significantly is another; courage and persistence in carrying through what intelligence projects is a third; initiative, learning, sensitivity, balance of interests are also entailed. However, a human being is no isolated monad but is dialectically tied to a definite community shaped by a specific set of traditions. Relatedness to others and thus obligation is ingredient in humanness; hence wide sympathy, justice, and friendship are essential to integral humanness; democratic society follows from respect for individuals and their ends.[52] By the time we ferret out these conditions, we see that we are to a large extent back on the territory mapped out long ago by Plato and Aristotle. We also see that one essential difference is the Christian addition of the dignity of individuals developed along distinctively modern lines in terms of enlarging the scope for freedom of choice, as Hegel pointed out.

Thus we see that there are several related meta-ends in Dewey's thought, expressed in several fixed criteria: the criterion of growth, the intellectual criterion, the moral criteria—individual and social—all integrated into the aesthetic criterion. Integral experience intelligently achieved in the relation of individuals in society working toward richer and deeper integrations: this is the comprehensive meta-end that guides Dewey's thought. He installs us in life more sensitively and more intelligently. And in this process he is especially concerned with appreciation of the everyday world, the cave of *doxa,* and the concrete complex of problems people of all sorts have to face in that world. He is concerned to focus on the kind of knowledge required to come to terms with that world and the way that occurs individually and socially.

There is a consequence for educational theory that follows from the Platonic notion of idea but that is not necessarily Platonic. There is a tendency to think that, by reason of knowledge already being there in some eternally valid and unshakable way, all that teachers have to do is pass it on through lectures and writing. Learning is a process in which the teachers who have such knowledge hand it over to the students, who receive it passively. By contrast, Dewey conceives of education as an interactive process in which the ideas of the teacher, which are largely residues of the past, are challenged and modified in terms of the interaction that goes on with colleagues and the students. In this way, school is not simply a preparation for life, but is itself a slice of life wherein interaction dominates and ought to dominate.[53]

Dewey's notion of education is often misunderstood as overly tolerant and permissive, aimed at a pragmatism understood as a kind of grubby materialism seeking "success." But for Dewey education is first of all a societal affair; society has a stake in how it educates its children. Education ought to draw upon the initiative of the students, but it should also constantly shape them through the teachers, whose end is both to mediate the tradition and to bring about the increasing emergence of intelligence, creativity, and cooperation in what tend to be animal or socially reflexive centers of action. Society is measured by its capacity to produce from within itself individuals who are creative and take intelligent initiative in such a way as not simply to foster their own ends, but to pursue the common good of the society. But the common good of society always has a stake in promoting creative individuals. The individual and social poles interpenetrate in the work of intelligent construction.[54]

Another split that tends to arise in the context Dewey is dealing with is that between the sacred and the profane. The sacred is contained spatially within churches and is pursued temporally on the Sabbath; the profane is temporally the workaday week and spatially the world outside the churches. Outside our minimal sacral activity lies the worldly activity with which we are predominantly preoccupied, alternating between work and leisure. On Dewey's reading the sacred has been separated off from its origin in the character of civic togetherness. Athena was a projection of the experience of the Athenians as to the sacredness, the inviolability of their common bond. She expressed and celebrated the sacred character of that bond by embodying the common ideals of the citizenry, but was no real entity that stood beyond that togetherness. Here Dewey parallels Feuerbach in his notion of God as a projection of the ideals of humanness—only the Greek gods were not perceived as alien but as immanent. The sacred is initially discovered in the promises people make to one another and in their togetherness as generations bound by group piety. The sacred is not simply end, but both end and means.[55]

Parallel with this is the split between the world of art and the workaday world. Art is set in museums; the workaday world is one in which—if one conceives of the sacred and the beautiful as in some sense ends—we develop as pure means in order to arrive at the leisure to pursue the things that are considered ends in themselves: aesthetic, intellectual, or religious goals. If the world of everyday work is mere means, then aesthetic and religious values tend to disappear from it and we get the antiaesthetic, all-too-secular environment of the modern factory. But for Dewey, art, like the sacred, ought to penetrate the workaday world, bringing the experience of those who operate within it to a greater integration.[56]

Here Dewey resists the notion, deeply embedded in the tradition, that some things are mere means and other things simply ends. Education is thought of as securing the means for the work world, while the work world is means for aesthetic, intellectual, or religious ends. For Dewey means and ends interpenetrate, so what is from one point of view an end is also a means and vice-versa.[57] As education is both preparation for life and a slice of life, so the aesthetic, the intellectual, and the religious are both ends within life and, when bound together with the workaday world, means toward fuller life.

Dewey is dispositionally opposed to any splits, which he sees as rooted in departing from the wholeness of experience. They have institutional expressions and epistemological and metaphysical defenses. We have to lead all these things back to their origins in experience to discover where the splits occur in order to bring about their overcoming. In this he follows an Hegelian model of overcoming antitheses through the detection of identity in difference. Throughout, the antithetical relations are transformed into dialectical relations of mutual interpenetration: ends and means, mind and body, body and environment, society and individual, the current state of society and tradition, theory and practice, sacred and profane, education and life, and finally, the aesthetic and the workaday. We will now turn to a fuller consideration of that final and central relation.

## Dewey's Aesthetics

Current practice, reinforced by a long tradition, places art on a pedestal, locating it high above ordinary life and viewing it as one of the exalted ends for which the workaday is mere means. For Dewey, it is precisely this exaltation and separation that stands in the way of understanding art.[58] Its causes lie in modern developments: consider the rise of nationalism and imperialism—for example, Napoleon's filling the Louvre with the spoils of war and thereby removing art works from their original location in the life of a people; consider capitalism, which promoted the private collector; consider the development of industry, which pushed the artist aside into a ghetto of individualistic "self-expression" apart from community functions; finally, following from all this, consider art theories, which emphasize the purely contemplative aspects of an art so separated from the rest of life, especially those theories that focus on form apart from matter.[59] Dewey's aim, as we said, is to reverse this separatist tendency and to reconnect art with its origins in human life as a whole.[60]

As we have pointed out, in spite of his overt rejection of a single end, for Dewey the aesthetic is, in a sense, the goal of the development of individuals and societies. The aesthetic measures everything else. Indeed, Dewey goes so far as to say that art is "the complete culmination of nature."[61] The aesthetic is experience in its integrity, as distinct from what happens in science or philosophy. The latter always involve second-order developments in relation to even ordinary experience because they are *features* of experience, *aspects* of experience. A scientific statement *points to* an experience, but an aesthetic statement *constitutes* an experience, a special experience that brings together all the facets into an integral whole.[62] Individual lives and institutional arrangements are measured by Dewey in terms of their ability to support that kind of experience.

The end character of the aesthetic follows the notion of natural form as the integral functioning of all the rhythmic processes that constitute the life of an organism.[63] But the aesthetic end is not apart from the other things we do, including the *pursuit* of aesthetic ends. Nor are other things mere means to this more exalted end. As we have said, for Dewey nothing should be treated as mere means, since that leads to an un- and antiaesthetic treatment of the development of means. If one thinks interactively or dialectically, the ends-means relation ought not to be conceived of in this one-way manner. In some sense the means ought to be ends, and the ends means. For Dewey, corollary to this is the imperative, which we have seen first enunciated by Plato, that art ought to pervade the instrumental world of everyday life. One of the problems of modern society is the way in which ugliness suffuses the workaday world, especially in the factories, where, during Dewey's time, most people worked. The unaesthetic and antiaesthetic character of the working situation results from viewing that context as one of pure means for some other, perhaps more exalted, ends. The individual workers are seen as means for the profit of the owners and vice versa. The work itself is considered a means for each of them being able to purchase certain goods in the context of their leisure—whatever the character of those goods may be. In the case of most people, the purchasable goods involve some kind of sensory gratification as escape from the ugliness of the everyday world. As Marx observed, in the modern factory system, men tend to feel at home in their more animal functions: eating, drinking, having sex; whereas in their distinctively human function of transforming the world by praxis, they are alienated by the work situation.[64] If ends and means ought to influence one another reciprocally, the aesthetic as well as the intellectual and the sacred ought to pervade the workplace. In Dewey's view, aesthetic resolution of the conflicts that emerge in the intersecting rhythms of life at certain moments, though a kind of overarching meta-end, is itself a means, providing us with an exemplar to help us work at such resolution with different materials when dispersal necessarily sets in. Learning aesthetic perception teaches us how to go about any other facet of life that we would otherwise tend to treat as mere means. Dewey thus finds the distinction between fine arts and useful arts wrongheaded. "It is this degree of completeness of living in the experience of making and of perceiving that makes the difference between what is fine or esthetic in art and what is not. Whether the thing made is put to use, as are bowls, rugs, garment, weapons, is, *intrinsically* speaking, a matter of indifference." In fact, art is "useful in the ultimate degree" when it contributes to "an expanded and enriched life."[65]

Originally, the aesthetic served a fundamental function in the life of a people. It was not a separate region of museums or concert halls where one goes to look at or listen to something called art that is largely the concern of an elite class that cultivates a special attention on special days, just as originally religion itself was not simply something participated in on the Sabbath, but something that pervaded the life of the people. All the higher-order "ethereal things" were grounded in the life of the people. Those who built the Parthenon built it, not as a "work of art," but as a civic commemoration to serve a civic function.[66] And the people who build and are served are not some kind of aliens fallen from a higher realm into the context of natural processes but are continuous with the rhythmic processes of nature itself. The aim of Dewey's aesthetic is to recover contact with experience in its integrity.

Dewey's integrating move focuses first on reconnecting the aesthetic to its origins in natural rhythms, those involved in the activity of the human organism—inhaling and exhaling, the systolic and diastolic rhythms of the heart, the cadences of walking and of repetitive action upon the environment, the rhythms of waking and sleeping, hunger and satiety, work and rest, birth and death—as well as the rhythms observed and adjusted to in nature outside the organism—the action of the waves, the ebb and flow of tides, the alternation of day and night, the phases of the moon, the changes of the seasons, the rhythmic patterns of color in animal markings and bird plumage. The organism itself is a balance of rhythmic functions interplaying with the rhythms of the environment, standing in tension with it, falling out of phase and coming into balance through adjustment. Emotional tension develops and is satisfied in this coming into rhythmic balance. Here is the natural germ of aesthetic experience.[67] Rhythm in general is "ordered variation of manifestation of energy."[68] It is "rationality among qualities."[69] Central to these observations is the notion of organic form, the unification of rhythms centralized in the organically based field of awareness.[70] "Underneath the rhythm of every art and of every work of art there lies, as a substratum in the depths of the subconsciousness, the basic pattern of the relations of the live creature to his environment."[71]

And as I noted earlier, experience in general is the transformation of physical-physiological interaction with the environment into conscious participation in it. We are brought out of privacy into the publicity of the outer world. The founding vehicle of this process is the operation of the sense organs.[72] They are the means of being outside oneself, and any derogation of the senses puts us out of contact with real things. As Dewey has it: "Oppositions of mind and body, soul and matter, spirit and flesh all have their origin fundamentally in fear of what life may bring. They are marks of contraction and withdrawal. . . . The unity of sense and impulse, of brain and eye and ear exemplified in animal life [can be] saturated with conscious meanings derived from communication and deliberate expression."[73] That unity of sense and impulse saturated with conscious meanings derived from human communication is the goal of art, in which meaning penetrates into the sensory. Consciousness adds regulation, selection, and redisposition to sensory elements.[74] The process culminates in full interpenetration of animal and human in the joy of aesthetic experience, which is to be distinguished from pleasure found in our animal functions. Though the latter is by no means to be despised, joy is distinguished from pleasure by the wholeness ingredient in it.[75]

Besides the integration of sensation and impulse with distinctively human meaning, there is the further integrative feature found in the fact that, although in art works one or the other senses is primarily operative, the experience itself is synesthetic. The visually perceived surface, for example, is suffused with tactual qualities, and what we hear calls forth visual and tactual experience. This is so because what we perceive are not isolated "inner sensations" but qualities of things that function as magnetic poles, drawing together our various experiences upon the things, making perception not an instantaneous snapshot, but a process developing in time.[76] Because of this synesthetic character of perception, Dewey resists divisions of the arts in terms of distinct sensory fields and spatial or temporal modes, such as I have offered in the introduction—at least insofar as they lead us to think of isolated sensory fields rather than of synesthesia.[77] But it is obvious that in the various art forms, different senses take the lead. What Dewey underscores is that the other senses are still implicitly operative in the field of awareness, in which one element is focal.

Reflection on the process of deliberate artistic transformation of sensory materials eventually leads to the idea of art as "the greatest intellectual achievement of humanity," the idea of being able to shape the whole of human existence in terms of ideas.[78] Among the Greeks, the notion of art extended beyond what we have come to call both fine and mechanical arts and applied even more deeply to the art of shaping human life as a whole. As we have noted, Aristotle called *phronesis* the art of all arts. Dewey expressly appeals to the Greek *kalos-kagathos*, the beautiful and good (which Britishers sometimes translate, characteristically, as "the gentleman"), a fusion of ethics and aesthetics, establishing proportion, grace, and harmony in human conduct.[79] Rooted in such a holistic form of life, poetry, art, and religious feeling spontaneously flower.[80] Dewey extends the notion of art as aesthetic process so far as to say that the intelligent mechanic who takes pride in his work and takes care of his tools is engaged in an artistic activity.[81]

Experience, I said, was pivotal for Dewey's aesthetics. Art is that which celebrates those moments in the stream of experience of which we can say that it was "an experience": *that* party, *that* trip, *that* day. Dewey elaborates on the characteristics of those special moments: "Every successive part flows freely without seam and without unfilled blanks in what ensues. At the same time there is no sacrifice of the self-identity of the parts. . . . [There is] a unity constituted by a single quality that pervades the entire experience in spite of the variation of its constituent parts. This unity is neither emotional, practical nor intellectual, for these terms name distinctions that reflection can make within it."[82] The pervasive quality lies at the center of what makes experience aesthetic.[83] Here Dewey notes several times the aesthetic quality of real intellectual activity. It is guided by a sense of the region within which it operates, the "aura" in which facts and theories swim. There is an emotional attraction for certain ideas.[84] Hence the term *beauty* has been applied both to sensuous charm—within whose region Kant restricts the use of the term—and to the harmonious proportion of parts, the latter of which encompasses both the sensuous and whatever else we may focus attention on.[85] (The exclamation "Beautiful!" spontaneously arises in the excellent execution of a play in football or the successful liftoff of a rocket.) But the difference between intellectual and aesthetic or artistic experience is that in the latter the pervasive quality is found in the very medium of expression, so that art mediates this quality from which intellectual expression—even though rooted in such quality— abstracts.[86] It is this quality that leads in the construction of the art object to the selection of some items and the rejection of others. It binds together the various elements into a living whole rather than a mechanical and artificial construction. In spite of the emotional character of this pervasive character, Dewey considers it a mistake to hold that the content of art is emotion. Emotions, like sensations, are "intentional," are *of* or *about* something; and it is our relation to the "something" that art is all about.[87]

Dewey further adds that in the special experiences within which art is rooted, time is brought to a kind of unity: the past reinforces the present and the future quickens what now exists to give a sense of fulfillment.[88] The moment of which we can say that it was *an* experience can be excised from the flow of life because it has a certain unity in itself. These observations directly parallel features of Aristotle's description of the exemplary work of art having the property of aesthetic organicity. Aristotle spoke of tragedy as having a beginning, middle, and end, not simply in terms of chronological succession but in terms of meaning, so that it begins in order to reach an end, and the middle is the meaningful transition between the beginning and the end. The whole constitutes a unity that is like a living organism, such that each part requires all the others, none is intelligible without the whole, and none may be eliminated without damaging the character of the whole. According to Dewey, that organic property is derived from those moments of each of which we can say that it was *an* experience.

Consider the hunt. The narrative art begins in recounting experiences such as this, creating overall qualitative unity, leaving aside irrelevancies, which, though required for human experience to be such, are not necessary to the story—otherwise the storytelling would take infinitely longer than it took to live through the event. The aesthetic enters into the character of experience, but it is concentrated, focused, and refashioned in story to make it the subject of an art form.[89] "[T]he work of art . . . , just because it is a full and intense experience, keeps alive the power to experience the common world in its fullness. It does so by reducing the raw materials of that experience to matter ordered through form."[90] In this way all art is "abstract," distilling the aesthetically relevant from the aesthetically irrelevant in nonartistic experience. But even abstract art has a limit as art: unless it is to lapse into the purely private, it must still present common qualities found in experience.[91] Abstract art is not the antithesis to nature but a mode of its fulfillment. What stands in antithesis to nature is "arbitrary conceit, fantasy, and stereotyped convention."[92] Many forms of "realistic" art are not truly naturalistic because they reproduce details while missing their moving and organizing rhythms, which may indeed be picked up in "abstract" forms of art. Naturalism, in Dewey's sense, is the escape from convention to perception insofar as convention hampers genuine attending. As in Plato's Cave and Hegel's hard rind of everyday surface, for Dewey art involves the breaking of stereotypes to arrive at more careful attention to what is there.[93] Ordinary experience typically involves mere recognition and set responses; it does not linger over its objects long enough to let experience of them develop to some sense of completeness. Art teaches us how to let our experience develop to its integral fullness.[94]

Aesthetic form is realized through achieving "the completeness of relations within a chosen medium." However, contrary to intellectual modes of interrelation, relations within an artistic medium are dynamically interactive. Indeed, in keeping with the grounding of the artistic in the natural, form is found in *"the operation of forces that carry the experience of an event, object, scene, and situation to its own integral fulfillment."*[95] Precisely because aesthetic experience is developmental, the formal conditions of aesthetic form are continuity, cumulation, conservation, tension, anticipation, and fulfillment.[96] It would seem that such an analysis is derived from the performing arts; but Dewey applies it to all the arts. In the plastic arts, as I noted in the introduction, the eye has not only to take in the total gestalt, it has to traverse the piece from aspect to aspect and from these aspects to the overall gestalt as a deepening and enriching process. Here Dewey seems to follow the same lines as Plato, transferring the rhythmic, harmonic qualities found in music to the plastic arts.

The abstraction of the aesthetically relevant from the aesthetic clutter of everyday or even extraordinary experience and its concentration into form is ingredient in the expression of an artist. In this regard Dewey devotes special attention to the notion of expression.[97] The mere giving way to an impulse, like sneezing for example, does not constitute expression in the aesthetic sense. Such an act is expressive, not in itself, but in the interpretation of an observer. Expression, like impulse, does involve an urge from within; but, Dewey says, "it must be clarified and ordered by taking up within itself the values of prior experience before it can become aesthetic expression. And these values are not called into play save by objects in the environment that offer resistance to the direct discharge of emotion and impulse."[98] Three things are thus involved in artistic expression: an impulse, a conscious drawing upon prior experience, and interaction with materials to be shaped in terms of a knowledge of the techniques of shaping. Expression is rich in proportion to the depth of the impulse, the breadth of prior experience, and the mastery of the medium. The impulse is that which generates the "pervasive quality" that guides all artistic production. Prior experience "thickens" the character of present involvement, beyond what is immediately given; it mediates our relation to the fuller context, which makes the immediately given—say a static thing visually appearing from a single fixed perspective—not only sensorily present but meaningful.[99] Indeed, it is past experience that creates "the aura and penumbra in which a work of art swims"—a favorite metaphor of Dewey's which he applies also to the peculiar emotional tonality of ideas for one who really can advance them.[100] The mastery of a medium involves a real love of the qualities of materials and an experimental spirit intent on exploring the expressive capacities of a given medium.[101] It also involves a measure of resistance to our designs by the materials, without which we would not be challenged to develop—a specialized application of a general feature found in the relation of the live creature to its environment. Indeed, the evolution of technique is linked to the emergence of new kinds of experience.[102] Without the mastery of materials, expression is clearly hampered: it becomes discharge or exhibition rather than expression. Without reflective drawing upon rich experience, there is no significant compression that grounds significant expression. In the interplay between the emotion that initiates and guides the process, a kind of Aristotelian mean is required: too much emotion disturbs recollection and technical mastery, too little emotion leads at best to a formally correct but sterile product.[103] With the unity of profound impulse, broad experience, and mastery of materials—through a Wordsworthian "emotion recollected in tranquillity"[104]—both the material environment and our own experience come to take on significant lived form.[105] But even here, in the process of expression, the originating emotional impulse itself undergoes transformation. This marks the difference between immediacy and refinement. In that process things in the environment come to function as "metaphors" for the generating emotion, as in a poem skylarks, stars, the moon, still ponds, and rushing torrents come to stand in relation to love, and love itself is refined in a relation beyond animal immediacy.[106] In that process, though "realistic" objects might enter into an art piece, they enter purged of their aesthetic irrelevancies and transformed.[107] Here we see the basis for the possibility of a difference between the artistic treatment of a nude and a pornographic treatment: brought into relation to the totality of elements that compose a picture animated by an impulse other than lust, "realistic" associations are downplayed in the art piece and another mode of appreciation emerges.[108]

Regarding the "work" of art, Dewey holds a similar position to that which we have met in Schopenhauer and will meet again in Heidegger. The work of art is not the art product, the objective thing, but the experience it effects.[109] So understood, the work of art, to begin with, is perception. The objective thing is the agent of the perception. For Dewey the inadequacy of many theories of art lies in their confining attention to the art product, which is separated from the conditions of production, often taken out of the context in which it was originally meant to operate, and considered apart from experience. But experience is the origin and end of the art product. There is, however, no univocal experience of a given work. It provokes different experiences in different people, different epochs and in different encounters by the same person, including the artist. Though, in the case of the plastic arts, the product retains its identity (except for the natural wear of time), it generates indeterminately many different experiences of itself.[110] In the case of the performing arts, each performance is different, a variation on the identity of the score or script. (However, modern duplicating techniques in audio and video recordings have enabled us to replay past performances, to hear or see identical versions of the same performance at different times and in different places. The performance becomes a kind of "universal" instantiated in different spatiotemporal instances.)

Aesthetic viewing is not a matter of mere passivity. The work of the art product also involves the working of the perceiver. In reading a novel the reader uses what is written as a recipe to perform an imaginative construction. The result is as rich as the constructive imagination of the reader. The same might not seem to be the case with regard to a painting. There the object is present to direct frontal viewing. Nonetheless, as we observed several times, the perceiver has to learn to move from an initially apprehended gestalt in order to focus on particular aspects and back again to the whole so that the richness of the piece has a chance to do its work in a continuously spiraling process.[111]

Crucial to Dewey's view of aesthetic perception is an initial being-seized by a pervasive quality intuitively apprehended. Its parallel on the side of artistic creation is the impulsion of "the musical mood" that Schiller indicated as generative of the words of the poem (and, as we noted, he was followed in this by Nietzsche). Indeed, like Walter Pater, Dewey considers "an harmonious ensemble in any art" to be "the musical quality of that art." Discrimination of parts comes after the intuitive seizure, but the parts must be distinguished as belonging to the pervasive quality that animates them. Aesthetic perception is a matter of learning to be apprehended by an integral whole, an exemplary togetherness of aspects that evokes the togetherness of all the aspects of experience, within which intellectual discrimination plays a subordinate role. But it is reflective discrimination that learns to distinguish between being the victim of cheap theatrical tricks that might arrest attention by shocking or horrifying and being in the presence of genuine aesthetic quality.[112] Furthermore, one learns to discriminate the mechanically repetitive rhythms in certain forms of popular art, especially music, from the more complex vitality produced by higher art forms. Dewey singles out gospel hymns, as governed by an external and imposed rhythm, that are correlated with the relatively impoverished sentiment they invoke. Richly aesthetic rhythms sum up and carry forward rather than simply repeat. Variation within an integral whole producing tensions and leading to culminations of experience is central to works that become classic. One is able to grasp a symmetry in which the whole is seen to "hold together within itself the greatest variety and scope of opposed elements."[113] On the other hand, Dewey views such culmination as simultaneously "leading to a new longing," so that "the completeness of the integration of these two offices [of accumulation and anticipation] . . . by the *same* means . . . measures artistry of production and perception."[114]

That brings us back to the discussion of form and reference and the relation of sensory surface to the theme treated in that surface. In the case of purely decorative art, we would seem to have a case of superficiality in the literal sense: setting upon the surface. But as Plato noted, even without explicit reference, art forms having properties of grace, harmony, and proportion sink into the depths of our souls and produce like properties in us. The "superficial" in this region is the vehicle for the profound insofar as it reaches into the emotional depth of the soul. This is especially the case with music, which, in its nonprogrammatic, nonverbally tied form, affects us most deeply. But more fully referenced art pieces can do their work as we come to understand more fully the context of their reference. This does not mean that the work furnishes an occasion for reverie or free association. In order for the work of art to do its specific work, whatever connected meanings we discern have to find their place in the sensuousness of the mode of presentation so that there is a complete fusion of reference and form as we are brought out of our privacy into the world of aesthetic objects.[115]

But the work of art is, beyond the immediate experience, its impact on how we conduct our lives. This brings us to Dewey's observation, following Shelley, that poetry affects that which produces morality, namely our whole sensibility. Art civilizes, not in the sense of domesticating, but in the sense of deepening our sensitivity. Poets for Shelley are the founders of civil society, "the unacknowledged legislators of mankind."[116] Imagination is the chief instrument of the good. It develops our ability to put ourselves in the place of others and it makes us more alert to the actual context in which we are called on to operate. As Dewey has it, "Art is more moral than moralities, for the latter either are or tend to become consecrations of the status quo, reflections of custom, reinforcements of the established order. The moral prophets of humanity always have been poets, even though they spoke in free verse or by parables."[117]

Dewey presupposes that, in human life as in life in general, fixity is only and ought to be only relative—especially in institutions, customs, and laws.[118] In his view, one ought to learn to grow constantly, expanding and unifying experience, coming to terms with all the relevant parameters functioning in experience—which involves constantly moving beyond where one has been to broader, deeper, and more integrated experience.

Transformation is always called for, at some times more than at others. And that involves the imaginative capacity expanded by art.

The common enjoyment of works of art is the sign of a unified collective life, but the work of the art product is also the bringing about of such a life. Art both forms and gives expression to something beyond the quirks of a "sensitive and creative individual"; it forms and gives expression to the togetherness of a community, bringing together people who would otherwise be apart.[119] The work of art thus overcomes the opposition of individual and universal, subjective and objective, freedom and order, which has captivated the philosophic tradition, by binding them together.[120] Dewey pushes the expansiveness and unifying power of art into the appreciation of cultures foreign to ours, the main access to which we have through their art. Art is a kind of universal language because it arises from the universal fact of encounter with the rhythms and energies in the active interchange of the live creature with its environment. It thus builds communicative bridges within a given community and allows access to what is foreign.[121]

Finally, one must distinguish significant levels of aesthetic depth, culminating in a sense of the universe itself made available through art. As Dewey says, "The sense of an extensive and underlying whole is the context of every experience and it is the essence of sanity."[122] Meaninglessness lies in isolation from that encompassing Whole. The work of art brings into focus not only the quality of being an integral whole but also of belonging to a larger, all-inclusive Whole, which is the universe in which we live. Religious experience accompanies intensive aesthetic perception precisely as this feeling of the universal Whole. For Dewey this is "the mystical" in the positive sense of the term. In a profound work of art, "we are, as it were, introduced to a world beyond this world, which is nevertheless the deeper reality of the world in which we live in our ordinary experiences. We are carried out beyond ourselves to find ourselves."[123]

This goes back to Aristotle: the human soul is, *in a way*, all things; and to Parmenides' claim that thought and being are one. A powerful work of art brings us into a concrete sense of the enveloping whole, present, and manifest in the particular—which is quite close in many ways to Plato's notion of Beauty as the radiance of the One really present and perceptible through the eyes—and Hegel's notion of beauty as the Absolute manifest in sensuous form. If the aesthetic is the basic measure and meta-end in relation to everything else in human life, the range of the aesthetic reaches from the superficial to the profound. The final measure would be how we grow in the sense of the depth of the Whole behind the surface of the present, with alert sensitivity to the features of the here and now.

Dewey contrasts two views of how this sense of the depth dimension arises: one, presumably Platonic, is that is descends from above; the other—his own—that it arises from below by assimilation and transformation of the rhythms involved in the interaction of the live creature with its environment. For him there is no ultimate adjudication between these two views: one is left with a choice. But the choice he makes is tied deeply to the sense of alienation and the fracturing of integral experience that has dogged the Platonic view and led to a mysticism of flight from the here and now.[124] As in Hegel, it is art that mediates between our bodily-sensory insertion into the here and now and our founding reference to the Whole.

## *Response*

There are several parallels between Nietzsche and Dewey that lead into the aesthetic. Both Dewey and Nietzsche are attempting to overcome the Cartesian splits but also the Platonic tradition that lies at the larger cultural background. Both of them are in some respects close to an Aristotelian conception that involves a "biological" theory of mind. (Note that Aristotle's treatment of the soul appears in his general treatise in biology, *On the Soul,* which is the theoretical part for which such works as *The Parts of Animals* and *The History of Animals* supply the empirical part.) The priority of Becoming or process over Being is also common to both Dewey and Nietzsche. That is also an Hegelian thesis: Being is Becoming (which is likewise true for Aristotle at the level of *phusis*). A third parallel is their common rejection of anything that transcends nature. Both of them view the notion of a transcendent God as rooted in a condition of contempt for life on this earth. A fourth parallel is the priority of aesthetics in human life. For Nietzsche life is redeemed aesthetically. It is aesthetic creation that allows us to live with the terrors of existence by carrying the Dionysian upsurge of nature into the creation of dynamic form. Art is the full meaning of nature. There is a fifth parallel: contrary to Schopenhauer, both Nietzsche and Dewey view art as emotionally moving. However, for Dewey art at the same time produces an ordering of the emotional response through our being drawn out to appreciate the character of the art object. This is not that far from Kant insofar as "disinterested satisfaction" allows for "unconstrained favoring" of the object and the resultant pleasure is an experience of the quickening of life. But for Kant that means the quickening of the distinctive human capacity to judge in the free play of the relation between imagination and understanding. This is not a matter of emotion, of a being drawn out of the whole person in relation to the object, for Kant restricts that to the effect of the sublime brought about by a tension between the finitude of the imagination and the infinite orientation of reason. For Kant the experience of the beautiful is rather one of harmony, thus giving rise to Schopenhauer's view of the aesthetic as akin to the more advanced "blowing out of desire" in Buddhist nirvana.

Thus although, like Nietzsche's, Dewey's thought appears as a challenge to the tradition of philosophic thought, it is in many ways continuous with that tradition, especially in its Aristotelian and its Hegelian forms. But that is only in keeping with his overall strategy of overcoming splits. In this case, the old and the new interpenetrate. As I have indicated, Dewey's thought is Aristotelian not only in its "biological" holism but also in the priority of *phronesis* as directedness through intelligent alertness to all relevant parameters of the concrete environment. But Dewey's thought is Aristotelian without the fixity of species, the priority of *theoria* and its correlates, Self-thinking Thought on the one hand and elitist society on the other. Dewey's thought is Hegelian in his dialectical style of resolving antitheses, in its capacity to come to terms with an evolving universe, but also in his emphasis on the sense of the Whole functioning as the background of all experience and as the explicit focus of certain moments of aesthetic experience. But his thought is Hegelian without the notion of the Absolute and thus without an absolutist reading of art, religion, and philosophy. Ideas are not ends but instruments. It is the idea of art that gives us the model for all human operation.

I am dispositionally favorable to Dewey's overall philosophic strategy of tracing dualities back to their origin in the field of experience and turning them, as in Hegel, from dualities into dialectical relations within an overarching whole. Art in particular has tended in modern, especially post-Kantian, times to occupy a separate region, unconnected with other regions of human experience. Kant himself performed a theoretical kind of surgical separation in his first two critiques, severing the region of knowing from the region of moral responsibility. And, in his attempt in the third critique at healing the rift he had created, Kant compounded the splits initially by separating aesthetic form from its relation to biological appetite on the one hand and rational conception on the other. Though he went on to reconnect the aesthetic with both poles of our being and to use it as a hermeneutic model for understanding the character of the Whole as the product of divine art, in the course of the nineteenth century aesthetic thought often tended to follow his initial move of separating the aesthetic and hence produced the movement of "art for art's sake."

Dewey himself attempted to link the aesthetic to the other facets of human existence, so that the aesthetic would pervade the whole of human life. This is actually an old Platonic theme: from birth to death the citizenry should be surrounded by objects—clothing, buildings, utensils, furniture, paintings—that have the properties of order, grace, harmony, proportion. Ideally such an environment tends to produce the same qualities in the emotional lives of the citizenry. And such prereflective emotional rationality creates a fit matrix for the development of reflective rationality that extends such sensibility to the cosmic Whole.

Kant also viewed the aesthetic as an integrating center in the field of human experience; but his mode of integration is significantly different than Dewey's. For Kant the aesthetic lifts us off of our animal relations and ultimately sets us in relation to the moral order. For Dewey and for us, esthetics has its origin in the live creature's relation to its environment. Embued by nature with rhythmic sensitivity, human beings, by reason of their primordial distance from the immediacy of the sensorily given and the appetites linked thereto, are capable of choosing to transform themselves and their environment rhythmically: dance and song as well as poetic storytelling modify the natural temporal rhythms, and the design of utensils, clothing, housing, and furniture, which use decorative elaboration of utilitarian artifacts, as well as self-decoration through tattooing or other cosmetic devices, modify natural spatial rhythms and harmonies.

Drawing upon the rhythmic relation of the live creature to its environment, art provides a level of access, a kind of language, that cuts across the Babel of tongues found throughout the earth. One can come to a kind of direct access to the generative sensitivity of foreign culture. While we could grant that, nonetheless, it is the fusion of form and substance, of sensuous shaping with reference that leaves such access largely at the level of suggestion, for it is the mother tongue that gives expression to the deeper meanings that contextualize what is directly accessible. If we recur to Danto's discussion of Brueghel's *Fall of Icarus* cited in the introduction, we see that one ignorant of the language and mythological tradition would only have access to "work and play on a summer's day." And that would be far from what is actually "in" the painting.

By reason of their founding reference to the whole, human beings must take up the sensorily given interpretively and thus deepen the natural reference to biologically functional surface by divining the ontological depth. The primary vehicle of this interpretive movement is language that prearticulates the character of the whole, linking given particulars to their kinds and fitting their kinds into a world of meaning. In functioning through language as carrier of the referential feature of human artefaction, ideally the rhythmic modification of materials fuses with reference to constitute a single whole. Dewey contrasts this fusion of the referential function and the aesthetic function, which we have seen distinguished from Plato onward, with the purely referential function of ordinary language and of the specialized languages of science and philosophy. The latter *refer* to experiences, while the art object *constitutes* experiences; the prosaic functions *re-present* things, while the aesthetic functions *present* things; the former operate in absence, the latter in presence. However, presence here is not a matter of sheer immediacy. The art object passes through the mediation of the artist's own past experience and evokes the mediated response of aesthetic perception. Like Schopenhauer before him and Heidegger after, Dewey properly distinguishes the art object from the *work* of art, the physical reality from the experience it evokes. However, Dewey does not understand by this that the art object functions as an occasion for reverie; rather, he maintains that the experience evoked brings us out of ourselves and into an enriched contact with the environment. He emphasizes what phenomenologists call the *intentionality* of emotions, their referredness to that which lies outside the inwardness of the experience, their capacity to disclose something beyond the privacy of the individual perceiver.

Perhaps most significantly, Dewey testifies to the extent of that disclosive capacity when he calls attention to the sense of an enveloping whole, the wholeness of the universe itself, that is often evoked by the work of art. Here we meet with a theme I laid down in the beginning and have followed throughout the course of this study: that the field of human experience is ultimately referred to the whole of being as one of its poles, while anchored in sensory presence as another. In the work of art there is an intensified sensory presence of a unique individual that, at the same time, functions as a vehicle through which we gain an intensified sense of the Whole, within which it and we as perceivers exist.

The meeting and indeed fusion of these two poles of the field of human reference deepens our sense of presence and transforms our relation to everything. As Dewey puts it, art affects that which produces the moral order: our sensitivity to things. This is a different route within the aesthetic arena to Kant's moral end. The work of art not only can bring about a peculiar experience in relation to an individual object, it can also transform most deeply the substratum of all experience as referred to the whole. Thinking about art can thus lead to comprehensive thinking about the whole of human experience and the whole of its field of reference. More than that, however, as in Hegel, art is capable of healing the rift that thought produces between itself and the sensuous givenness of our life-world. Indeed, for Dewey and in fact, the way it treats aesthetic experience is a peculiar measure for the adequacy of a philosophy, provided one understands the aesthetic as stretched along a continuum from sensory surface to encompassing depth.[125] But once we do that, we are in essential continuity with the tradition we have been examining from Plato onward.

Dewey contrasts two incompatible views of the origin of art, with no means for adjudication between them other than choice (viz., the notion that beauty "descends from above" or that it "arises from below"). But one wonders how far apart they really are, at least at one level. The crucial factors are: (1) that there is an encompassing depth beyond sensory surface, (2) that, correspondingly, human reality is a reference to that encompassing depth, and (3) that there is a mode of access to it that takes place in sensory presence rather than in mere re-presentation. "Descent from above" and "arising from below" may be two metaphoric ways of speaking about the same kind of experience. If we talk about the real presence of Beauty Itself in beautiful things discernible through the eyes as in Plato or the presentation of the Absolute in sensuous form as in Hegel, how different is that from the sense of a world beyond this world as the depth of this very world to which Dewey calls attention? But where the crucial difference finally lies is in the experience of being addressed by a personal encompassing Ground, as in the biblical tradition and in contemporary thinkers like Martin Buber or Emmanuel Levinas. It is in terms of such an "aesthetic" that medieval thinkers assimilated the Platonic tradition into the biblical tradition of personal address. And it is in such aesthetic that we are essentially interested. A Deweyan approach anchors the aesthetic most firmly in this world, in the world of biological existence, and, with Nietzsche, admonishes those who would despise this world, to remain faithful to the earth which, having created, Yahweh saw as good.

One could go quite far in paralleling the ancient tradition with Dewey's sense of the nonfixity of particular ends and his implicit notion of a series of meta-ends encompassed by the aesthetic. We find a kind of Deweyan meta-end in Plato's notion of the Good, which involves the notion of oneness to be mirrored creatively in our individual and collective lives in different contexts as one comes to terms intelligently with the concrete. Aristotelian *phronesis* as the capacity to achieve the good situationally is precisely the habit of forming and breaking habits intelligently, with full alertness to the requirements of situations and the general (meta-)ends of humanness. It is a habit of not falling into habits in the sense of unintelligent fixed routines incapable of being modified without great difficulty. The achievement of *phronesis* is possible only if we have some control over our passions, and that is why temperance and fortitude are required. The structure of the virtues in their togetherness are not rule governed but rule generating. And though the aesthetic accent is not so pronounced and central in Aristotle as in Dewey, flexibility and intellectual alertness in relation to the given environment put us quite close to Dewey's peculiar aesthetic. The general Greek ideal of the *kalos kagathos*, the beautiful and good person, is something to which Dewey makes explicit appeal.

The fixity of meta-ends in spite of Dewey's preference for change and relativity has its parallel in Dewey's notion of ideas. It cannot account for itself (i.e., for the fixity of the notions of idea and intelligence). We might note here, with Lonergan, that everything is subject to revision except the conditions for the possibility of revision.[126] In prehuman life the meta-ends of growth, sustenance, repair, and reproduction are realized in changing contexts to produce the evolution of species. In human life, growth tied to the emergence of intelligence taking the lead in establishing integral experience for creative and cooperative individuals are the fixed meta-ends operative in changing contexts. So also, reflection on these processes presupposes fundamental conditions for reflection aiming at the display of the general and concrete character of the Whole within which we are operative.

# X

# HEIDEGGER

## Situating Heidegger

FROM MARTIN HEIDEGGER'S FIRST major work, *Being and Time,* his thought has focused on the notion of Being, but the method of his approach was phenomenology, the method characterizing my own introduction. Heidegger's approach falls in the line of his teacher, Edmund Husserl, the founder of Phenomenology. Husserl understood Phenomenology to be comprehensive philosophy; it is at least permanent prolegomenon, acknowledged or not, to any philosophy. Phenomenology comes from two Greek terms, *phainomenon,* appearance, and *logos,* essence. Phenomenology is a comprehensive descriptive inventory of all the essential ways in which appearance—that is, presence to consciousness—occurs: direct evidence in sensation, imaginative presentation, recollection in memory, judging, inference, willing, desiring, feeling, presence to oneself as conscious, "apperception" of other persons, and so on.[1] Phenomena are appearances, modes of manifestation, always involving particular modalities of awareness at their base, always involving a conscious subject related to a manifest object. Consciousness itself is the intending of those modes of manifestness: such intentionality is the basic feature of awareness. All consciousness—deliberate or not—intends, that is, points toward and thus manifests some object. Further, human awareness always involves an eidetic component, an element of universality. The sensorily given "this" is always seen *as* something: as a tree or a dog or a book, which notions apply, beyond "this," to all actual or possible instances of the type given in this instance. The universal feature is usually emptily intended and only partially filled. A tree is a whole, only aspects of which I concretely know. Microbiology and physics press at a more complete filling of what a tree is, but not necessarily all that any given tree is. The whole of treeness is revealed and concealed in what we actually know of trees. Introduction of other conscious entities complicates the analysis by *appresenting* the other's awareness as a kind of absence in the fullness of sensory presence.[2] The consciousness of another is co-given expressively with the givenness of positively identifiable sensory features, but not at all in the way colors and sounds are given. Each science operates in terms of a certain angle of abstraction from the ever-pregiven, all-encompassing *Lebenswelt* or lifeworld of meaning and inhabitance built up out of the interrelation of human beings over countless generations. Phenomenology aims at sustaining a systematic inventory of the lifeworld. But all science and the lifeworld itself are subjected to a process of historical sedimentation whereby the basic phenomena are covered over by the mediations of a tradition. Tradition works with words and, through words, with ready-made concepts whose origins in direct experience and whose limitations are no longer thought. One can repeat the words; further, one can learn something of their meaning; further still, as in every science, one can even carry on deductions from ready-made concepts which, by reason of their founding—though abstract—relation to their origins in lifeworld experience, have functional consequences. But none of these abstract processes gets us back to the originary phenomena to which phenomenology leads us.[3]

Historically Husserl goes back to Kant and to Descartes. The latter made the fundamental discovery of the *cogito* and the multiple realm of "seeming" that is its enduring correlate. But he did not pursue the fruitfulness of the "seeming" theme, preferring to follow the direction of theoretical reconstructions.[4] Kant distinguished phenomena and noumena and thus, according to Ricoeur, founded phenomenology.[5] Contrary to Descartes, he resolutely confined his attention to phenomena, but nonetheless remained under the influence of the theoretical abstractions of Newtonian cosmology.

Heidegger has significant relations to all three thinkers. Husserl gave him his point of departure: phenomenological inventory. Heidegger's first and most famous book, *Being and Time,* was dedicated to Husserl. Heidegger devoted several books to the study of Kant: *Kant and the Problem of Metaphysics, What Is a Thing?,* and *Phenomenological Interpretation of Kant's Critique of*

*Pure Reason.*[6] The first highlighted the significance of time and imagination; the second opened up considerations that would lead, in other writings, to the priority of the work of art; the third, an earlier lecture course, lays the background for the ontic-ontological distinction. However, for Heidegger phenomena are not thereby cut off from noumena, but provide us with various revealings—and concealings—of the being of things.[7] Such revealing and concealing follows out Husserl's distinction between empty intentions and their partial filling on the one hand, and his *Lebenswelt* analysis on the other.[8] Radicalizing Descartes and Husserl, Heidegger attempted to find—in the words of one of his essays—"The Way Back into the Ground of Metaphysics."[9] In this connection he introduces a basically Kierkegaardian distinction between abstract thought, with which philosophy has always been engaged, and concrete dwelling. Abstract thought sets things at a distance, splitting subject from object. Especially in Descartes and the modern tradition stemming from him, the subject-object split becomes a separation: we begin, according to these thinkers, inside the private chamber of our awareness and are confronted with the problem of winning our way out. For Heidegger, on the contrary, we begin as being-in-the-world—that is, as indwelling, inhabiting a world, built up through a tradition, where we are "outside" our privacy and close to persons and things.[10] We have to pry ourselves loose deliberately from such involvement to arrive at the artificial problem of a separate *cogito*. Furthermore, the world we inhabit is not simply a physical cosmos, but, more deeply, a world of functional meaning prearticulated for us by the work of prior generations. Such a world is made possible by the fundamental character of humanness, which Heidegger calls *Dasein*, often hyphenated as *Da-Sein* to indicate Heidegger's particular emphasis. *Dasein* is the "there" *(da)* of Being *(Sein)*, the place where the whole of what is is disclosed as a matter of question, for which the various worlds of meaning provided by different cultures and different epochs are the putative answers.[11] A cultural epoch entails, beyond implicit phenomenological description, *interpretation* of what underlies the directly available and how that fits into the Whole. Hence phenomenology turns in a hermeneutic direction.[12] Here Heidegger supplies underpinning for Nietzsche's observations on the essentially interpretive, perspectival disclosures of the meaning of the Whole provided by the "higher men," that is, the artists, philosophers, and saints.

Descartes had reversed the medieval notions of subjectivity and objectivity. For example, in Aquinas objectivity is an aspect of things related to the abstracting attention of cognitive subjectivity: objectivity is the face things present to finite cognition—their "over-againstness" *(ob-iectivitas);* and both cognitive subjectivity and objectivity rest on the more basic "subjectivity of being" in both knower and known. At the basis of there being subjects of awareness and their objects, there are subjects of being, namely human beings and things, only aspects of which we humans know. Heidegger underscores the indeterminate receding of the subject of being in whatever we encounter as it rises up to present to us an object, an aspect, relative to our awareness. But, especially in his early classic, *Being and Time,* he emphatically underscores the noncoincidence of human reality with awareness and indicates, with the notion of *Dasein,* the full being of humanness, which tunes the field of awareness. Such full being is biologically grounded, culturally fashioned being-in-a-world with others determined in its essential features by those long dead. The Greek notion of *charakter* or "stamp" indicates the preconscious determination that "tunes" the subject of awareness, inclining it to see and act along certain predetermined lines. In-habiting a world is being so spontaneously tuned. The reflective *cogito,* the methodically controlling "I," emerges out of such a matrix. It was this especially that attracted Heidegger to Aristotle's ethics and its requirement of the prior shaping of one's ethos through the right upbringing.[13]

Attend at this point to our original view of human nature. Human nature involves a biological ground that gives us the ever-present sensory surface yielding aspects of things in the environment related to our biological needs. The sensory circle reveals something about things, but it conceals much more. And, as Nietzsche remarked, the way it reveals is "a lie," fundamentally misleading if we take it alone as revealing of the way things finally and fully are. On the other hand, human nature involves a transcendent direction: it operates in terms of the notion of being; it involves openness to the totality of each being within the totality of what is. This is the old Aristotelian notion that the human soul is, in a way, all things, and the even older Parmenidean notion that thought and being are one—something to which we have constantly recurred in this book and to which Heidegger gave renewed attention. Being is not simply minimal being outside nothing, but everything about everything, because outside being there is nothing at all. Being as a whole, however, is not known but is referred to by the character of what we are: openness to the totality. Openness to the totality and, for us, the initial emptiness of the totality outside of the positive presence of sensa, requires that the immediate presence of these sensa be brought into interpretative relation to the Whole. Such a bringing of the sensory surface into relation with the Whole necessitates the development of culture. Culture is the establishment of a world of meaning that is not simply a theoretical way of looking (this, after all, came very late in human history), but is a way of being for a people, a lived-in, dwelt-in sense of the Whole involving modes of thought linked immediately to modes of operation. Thought, feeling, and action are interpenetrating elements involved in the inhabitance of a world. Inhabitance, or dwelling, is crucial here. To in-habit, as Dewey also observed, is to become habituated in a certain way, to have a way of standing toward things as a quasi-permanent orientation. This involves an opening up of the totality from a certain perspective. It involves the Whole coming out of its initial concealment into a disclosure of meaning within which we can come to formulate propositions and check their correspondence with experience. Correctness of representation or correspondence to what is opened up depends on a prior opening up of a sense of meaning of the Whole within which propositions can be formulated. Any given opened-up totality is, however, only one way of disclosure: it is essentially perspectival manifestation of the Whole. For everything revealed there is the underside of concealment. What we are dealing with finally is orientation toward the absolute mystery of Being, which always lies beyond any rational mastery.[14]

In this respect, consider science as a kind of progressive, ongoing, self-corrective way of thinking about the world, no state of which is definitive, but each state of which shows something of the character of what is, though never in such a way as to include the Whole exhaustively. But science is a limited theoretical project, resting on the more encompassing project, which is that of being-in-the-world, inhabiting the world. The scientist, before, during, and after his acting as a scientist, belongs to a culture, shares its lifeworld. *World* here does not mean physical totality but world of meaning, as in the classical Greek world, the primitive Christian world, the twentieth-century Western world, the ancient Egyptian world, the Chinese world. These are ways of disclosure, primarily practical, governing in a global fashion how we conduct our lives. Heidegger underscores the dominance of world disclosure in the expression "the world worlds": rather than being at our disposal, world does something to us; it holds us in its grips and discloses/closes our fundamental possibilities.[15]

At its deepest level, such a world of meaning is governed by the fundamental meaning of the term *Being* operative within it.[16] Thus for Heidegger, the history of Western thought is essentially the history of the notion of Being. Heidegger calls attention to "the ontological difference" between Being *(Sein)* and beings *(Seienden)*, which includes entities and their beingness *(Seiendheit)* or the principles that constitute them as beings—the latter subdistinction found, for example, in Plato's distinction between things in the realm of genesis and being, which lies in their Forms. Being for Heidegger is that which grants access to entities and their principles. It is correlated with the fundamental structure of humanness as *Da-Sein*, as openness to the Whole. However, the Western tradition focused attention on entities and principles and failed to attend to that which granted them. For all its focus on the beingness of beings, it is characterized by the forgottenness of what Heidegger names Being. Furthermore, it is governed throughout all its variations by the Greek experience of Being as standing presence. What is is Now, exemplified particularly by Plato's notion of Form, but opened initially by Parmenides. This sets Being in opposition to becoming, to appearing, to thought, and to the ought, which are, in different ways, other than Being so conceived. The Being of the things we encounter and of our own selves lies in unchanging principles.[17] But what governs *that* distinction is the experience of Being as standing presence.[18] For Heidegger, Being as what makes possible the distinction between forms/principles and things needs to be rethought in terms of how time enters into that conception, how the Now dominates, but also how the Now is itself constituted by retention of the past and protention of the future, two notions to which Husserl gave close attention.[19]

The interplay of the three temporal dimensions focuses on "presencing" as the way in which things draw near to us and thus engage us. The essential dimension in this presencing process is the future. How I draw up my past and thus stand in the present depends on how I am related to my future. If my fundamental project is amassing a fortune, the study of metaphysics, though perhaps required by a particular curriculum, is not something to which I would be inclined to be deeply present, for it is hard to see how such could contribute to my fundamental project. If, however, I undergo a conversion and project my future differently, I will look at my past differently and tell a new story about my life, for different things will jut into significance and others sink into indifference. I might even come to find the study of metaphysics worthy of my sustained attention. The depth and quality of my relation to the Whole might take center stage and my plutocratic project might then sink into indifference or become transformed into a means for philanthropy. Modern science emerged when a different "ground plan of nature" was projected, a non-Aristotelian view of what was henceforth to count as nature: there are no longer natures seeking immanent goals, but a single Nature, a world machine built from elementary particles combining and separating according to fixed mechanical laws. Under that projection very much of the mechanisms of nature have been uncovered, but, among other things, at the price of the separation of fact from value and the concealing of the process of revealing itself.[20] And at the most fundamental level, the way each of us relates to the ultimate future of the end of our being-in-the-world, our own death, determines how we are present to all our projects. Among the ancients, humans are characterized by being "the mortals"—not simply because we will die (that is true of all living forms), but because we live out of an *anticipation* of our not-being-in-the-world. How we face that ultimate term—embracing it or fleeing from it—determines how we are present in any given Now.[21]

For the most part we live in an "inauthentic"—or better, "unappropriated" *(uneigenlich)*—mode, determined by what "they" say, what "they" are doing, what is "in." Our past enters into how we are present, but in a way that is ambiguous with regard to what is really disclosed and ambiguous with regard to what *I* determine and what is determined in me by my tradition. Our future is an object of curiosity: we are attracted by this and that prospect, but we run from the thought of our ultimate term. We huddle together in the present, filling the time with endless and meaningless chatter as we wait to die—a thought from which we flee into chatter and busyness.[22] What awakens us to "authenticity" and allows us to appropriate for ourselves what is available is letting our own death enter into our lives as a "real presence." It can then happen that, in a "moment of vision," our mortality lays hold of us. Pried loose from our unappropriated belonging to the "they," we are enabled resolutely to engage in projects lived within their ultimate temporal perspective. The unsettled character of our being-toward-death opens up a pervasive and irremovable anxiety as our own being-toward-death has to be understood in terms of our being toward the Whole expressed in the notion of Being itself as the revealing-concealing of the Whole.

This is most basic for Heidegger. Any disclosure of the Whole is simultaneously a concealing of what does not show itself within the way of revealing characteristic of a given world of meaning. Hence the finitude of any given world, and hence the notion of the historicity of Being itself.[23] Hans-Georg Gadamer suggests that Heidegger's basic contribution was to shift phenomenology from concern for the given to concern for the hidden.[24] In this regard, the historicity of Being is linked to Heidegger's notion of essence. Contrary to the Platonic tradition, essence is no atemporal endurance, definable once and for all. It is rather endurance through time, displaying itself now this way now that. The display is essentially connected with the perspectival character of the disclosure of the whole. This means that thought has to be essentially historical.

In working through the historical character of the manifestation of Being, Heidegger follows Kierkegaard's distinction between thinking and dwelling by distinguishing two modes of thinking: one is "representative-calculative"; the other is "meditative," thinking as dwelling.[25] The former constructs and is ultimately governed by the will-to-power, to cognitive or practical mastery. The latter "lets things be" in appreciatively dwelling on them. Representative-calculative thinking devises methods and makes progress.[26] Meditative thinking follows a way and returns recollectively to where we always already are. The former operates in absence; the latter in presence. The former speaks to what we have come to call *the intellect,* the con-centrated point detached from our whole mode of indwelling; the latter speaks to *the heart,* the core, the center of our being and ground of thinking, acting and feeling, which articulates our mode of indwelling.[27] Parallel to the distinction between these two modes of thinking is Heidegger's distinction between two modes of truth, linked to two Greek terms, *orthotes* and *aletheia.* The former, coming into English in such terms as *ortho-doxy,* or correct opinion, is truth as correspondence between mind and things that attains to correctness of representation. For Heidegger truth as correctness is essentially derivative from the more primordial notion of truth as *a-letheia,* or un-concealment. The formulation of propositions and their being checked against the availability of evidence both presuppose the prior opening up of a space of meaning. The term *un-concealment* calls attention to the link between revealing and concealing and embodies the notion of direct presencing. Correct propositions which correspond to what is are derived from the coming to presence, out of concealment, of what is, in such a way that what is manifest remains rooted in the mystery of what is and will remain concealed. *A-letheia* is linked to *lethe,* unconcealment to the essentially concealed. *Dasein* has an essential stake in how its relation to the *lethe,* the hidden mystery of Being, is preserved.[28] This is intimately linked to the role of the arts.

There is a further Heideggerian thesis connected with this: the priority of language. Before our employment of language in addressing others, language addresses us: "Language speaks."[29] Language is not a mere instrument by which we give expression to fully formed thoughts. Rather, language, which we first learned functionally as children, has us in its grips, prearticulates our world of meaning in the mode of indwelling, and makes possible our discovery of what we think. Language primordially gives rise to thought. Functioning in our lifeworld, language is like our own body: we presuppose it in thinking how and what we think. As the ground of our being-in-the-world, language is the ground of our essential historicity. Language, history, *Da-Sein*, along with the founding structure of our own embodiment as an expression of our belonging to nature: together they constitute the framework that supports the field of explicit awareness.[30] All that we do within that field can never overtake and encompass the framework that makes it possible. *Orthotes* can never overtake *aletheia*, for the latter is the condition for the possibility of the former, not vice-versa.

The history of Western thought is in part the history of the notion of truth. For Heidegger, it begins among the Greeks as *aletheia*, but focus shifts permanently to *orthotes*. As a variation on that theme, with Descartes truth becomes certitude: the presence of things is transformed in accordance with our methodologically purified representations. In more recent times, certitude gives way to what Heidegger calls *enframing (Gestell)*: the approach to things as "standing reserve" *(Bestand)* for our projects.[31] This describes the nature of modern science as in essence technological. Given the dominance of this mode of revealing (experimental science as the exclusive way of revealing), we tend to view ourselves as photoelectric cells, computer brains, robot mechanisms. Much is revealed in this approach, but what is essentially concealed is the very character of revealing.[32] Awareness is ignored or explained away or admitted as an embarrassingly functionless epiphenomenon.[33] The world that emerges in this way is increasingly planned for efficiency, but it is no longer a world in which we can fully dwell. As a consequence, though it becomes increasingly "rational," it also becomes increasingly meaningless in the holistic sense: the world is no longer our dwelling place. But the technological view was already prefigured in the way in which Plato conceived Being as Form, object of an intelligible look, functioning as plan for the demiurge to fashion material for his purposes.[34] And that view set itself up in direct opposition to the arts. Plato considered the arts as the primordial articulation of the Cave, the sheltering, confining semidarkness, semilight of the lifeworld. The origin of philosophy is the battle with poetry.

At this point, then, we turn to the arts. Heidegger reinstates the battle between philosophy and poetry; but rather than subordinating poetry to philosophy, he almost tends to the opposite. "Poetry" articulates being-in-the-world, which guides the way of philosophy. For Heidegger, the arts provide "the saving power" in the epoch of enframing. The arts operate in the meditative mode of "letting things be," rather than dominating them conceptually and practically. It is within the modality of the sensitive dwelling afforded by the arts that we can learn to await the new advent of meaning in the era of the darkening of the world expressed in "the flight of the gods, the destruction of the earth, the transformation of man into a mass, the hatred and suspicion of everything free and creative, the pre-eminence of the mediocre."[35]

## *"The Origin of the Work of Art"*

One of the chief statements of Heidegger's aesthetic views is his "Origin of the Work of Art," written in 1935 and 1936.[36] It would be helpful to begin at the end of this rather convoluted essay, wherein the notion of origin tends to be lost sight of, and work backward. There, at the very end, Heidegger remarks: "The origin of the work of art,—that is, the origin of both the creators and the preservers, which is to say of a people's historical existence, is art. This is so because art is by nature an origin, a distinctive way in which truth comes into being, that is, becomes historical."[37]

There are several things here that require expansion. First of all, the work of art is not fundamentally and properly the thing that stands there, but rather is the work it does. Heidegger's thought parallels Dewey's and Schopenhauer's in that respect. What stands in a museum and is dusted by the cleaning personnel is something at hand, like a table or a mop board or a shelf. It is labeled as a work of art, but that is a kind of extrinsic denomination. For Heidegger, it is largely a work that was; now it is a labeled, locatable, viewable, dustable object.[38]

Second, the work of art does not simply involve an isolated genius creator and a small coterie of preservers; it involves a way for a people, the world of a people. Art is a way in which the world is exposed. This remark is tied to a view of personhood as necessarily embedded in a tradition or a complex web of traditions. If we regard ourselves as self-made individuals, it is only possible on the basis of having been shaped and sustained in a certain way by a peculiar tradition. Preservers are those who are brought through the work, in an uncommon way, into a world of common inhabitance.[39]

Third, art is the setting-into-work of truth.[40] What is truth? For Heidegger, as I have said, there are two senses: the ordinary view and a more profound view. Truth as correctness of representation is derived from *aletheia*, unconcealment, which has, as its other side, concealment. We indwell in the Whole in the modality of a world that furnishes the meaning field within which things are accessible and within which we come to formulate and test our propositions for their (orthotic) truth. In Heidegger's view, world is more in being than any of the things that are. It is not merely the collection of things present-at-hand nor a merely imaginative framework added to such things. It is neither "objective facts" nor "subjective construals" nor theories about the facts. World is something more than the tangible and perceptible in which we think we are at home.[41] Here we must recall again that in our ordinary wakeful life we are not dealing with sensations but with things, in the disclosure of which sensations are subsidiary. Sensations by themselves are abstractions from the concrete reality of things: they are the vehicles of our access to things, not the typical focus of our attention. And we have access to things through the mode of disclosure of the Whole that has us in its grips antecedent to reflective thought. Art is one of the origins of the disclosure of a world. It is the setting into a work of the truth (i.e., the disclosure of a world). The art work is a peculiar kind of thing that opens up the space of a world and does so for its preservers. Through this disclosure, truth becomes historical—that means it becomes effective, operative. It is that which, before people come to think about it, has them in its grips.

The historicity of truth also means perspectival disclosure of the whole and thus involves struggle among various modes of putative final disclosure. Those raised Christian will be Christian before they even come to think about it. Those raised in the modern world spontaneously come to think about the world scientifically: they are held in the grip of a mode of revealing that is characterized as technical, calculative. Within contemporary people these two modes of revealing, Christian and scientific, are involved in some sort of tensive relation to one another. They inaugurate a struggle for dominance as the primordial mode of revealing. But as perspectival, the modes of revealing are always tied to concealing, to the Not *(das Nichts)*, the Nothing in relation to the world of disclosure.[42] Because we are gripped by the scientific mode of revealing—a relatively recent phenomenon in the history of mankind—we can come to do science without necessarily reflecting on the peculiar angle of abstraction afforded by that particular way of coming at things. We take it to be simply definitive, *the* way of revealing—until we think about it. What grounds the scientific mode of revealing? Once we press that we see that we need something more than science as observation and theory: we need, to begin with, a phenomenological reflection on the mode of revealing that characterizes the scientist himself and that rests on the broader context of the scientist's inhabitation of a common world. He talks to other people in ordinary language; he lives with his family; makes political and moral decisions, decides to devote himself to science, and maybe even prays—not on the basis of his science, but on the basis of the disclosure of the lifeworld out of which science comes as a peculiar kind of abstract angle. The notion of a world becomes crucial as a way in which the historical existence of a people is established. The work of art is a way in which that world is set up.

But art is only one of the ways. Others include the action that grounds a political state, the experience of the nearness of the divine, essential sacrifice, the thinker's questioning of being.[43] The latter is Heidegger's own direction: making us see the hidden in what we think is clear and definitive, the mystery that is involved in the everyday, and the antecedent decisions, most of which each of us has not made, which are involved in the way in which we come to think, act, and feel. Science is not an original opening out of truth, but the extension of a domain already opened up, the discovery of the right, the correct within the more primordial establishment of a horizon of meaning.[44]

One would have to ask here how these various ways of opening out of the whole for dwelling are related to one another. Heidegger does not explicitly deal with the question when he presents this list. However, if we return to his consideration of art near the end of the essay in question, we will see aspects of a possible answer. Art is essentially poetry, of which poesy (or poetry in the usual sense) is only one expression. However, poesy is a privileged mode because it is *the* language art and language is the primary articulation of our mode of being in the world. All the other arts take shape in the space opened up by language.[45] So also political founding, essential sacrifice, experiencing the presence of the divine, and the thinker's questioning of being are all rooted in the poetic art. In seeming agreement with Dewey, who follows Shelley: the poet is the unacknowledged legislator of mankind.

## What Is a Thing?

Moving on from the end of "The Origin of the Work of Art," let us consider its overall structure. It has three parts whose topics overlap:

*Thing and Work*

*Work and Truth*

*Truth and Art*

We have looked at the relation of truth and art. Let us consider the relation between thing and work. Heidegger spends a great deal of time discussing the notion of "the thing" here and elsewhere. As we have already noted, he has an entire book dedicated to the question *What Is a Thing?* as well as a shorter essay titled "The Thing."[46] The essay under consideration here focuses once more on that notion. Nothing would seem more obvious and less problematic. But it is the obvious that is the aspect of experience we least think about. Our ordinary modes of thought are actually past decisions—the decisions of those long dead—over against other possible decisions: they conceal as well as reveal. And Heidegger tries to get us to question our ordinary conceptions in order to understand their modes of concealment. Heidegger tries to approach the work of art from the beginning of the essay in terms of the notion of the thing, since the work of art is one of the things that we meet.

As noted above, the cleaning personnel in the museum dust the statue, the frame of the painting, the door, the mop board: these are all equally things from the point of view of the duster. Heidegger focuses on three traditional conceptions of the thing that are all correct (orthotic), but none of which is fundamental.[47] There is the Aristotelian notion of the thing as the bearer of properties, the Berkeleyan notion of the thing as the unity of the sensory manifold (i.e., the togetherness of the multiplicity of sensory features); and there is, again, the Aristotelian notion of formed matter. For Heidegger, all the notions are too general to come to terms with the peculiar thinghood involved in the work of art. The first involves the notion of at-hand *(vorhanden)* objectness, which places the thing too far away from the immediate involvement required by the work of art.[48] Furthermore, it parallels the subject-predicate structure of sentences and leads us to question whether linguistic structure mirrors the structure of the thing or whether we read linguistic structure into the thing. The second notion actually brings the thing too close to our bodily being in the sense that it is reduced to its effect relative to our senses. The sensory surface is entirely subsidiary in our ordinary dealings with things where we hear, not auditory phenomena, but fan motors, planes overhead, voices, doors slamming, and the like. Third, the notion of formed matter does not apply primarily to things but to equipment. In the second book of Aristotle's *Physics,* where the form-matter relation is discussed, Aristotle begins his analysis by talking about equipment as the occasion for reaching the notions of form and matter.[49] Aristotle makes no distinction here between the making of a piece of equipment and the making of a work of art. So the form-matter distinction is itself too wide to deal with the thinghood of the work of art—and also too narrow for the notion of thing itself.

In developing his own approach, Heidegger views the thingly character of a thing as turning upon its belonging to the Earth.[50] Here *Earth* does not mean a chemical mass located in the solar system. Earth is rather the self-closing, purposeless bearer of things in our world, a bearer that is set in opposition to the openness of the world of a people. The conflict of World and Earth appears in the figure of the work of art and reveals the nature of equipment and things as such. Heidegger uses van Gogh's painting of a peasant's shoes as an example. The shoes are equipment used by a peasant woman. In their daily use they disappear from attention. This is what Heidegger means by the ready-to-hand character of equipment. When they are not in use, they are set aside in their ordinariness, perhaps to become simply present-at-hand, describable scientifically. But in the painting the belonging of the shoes to the world of the peasant woman and to the earth of her dwelling are manifest.[51] Van Gogh's mode of treatment brings that world to presence in a way that the objectivity of observation, whether through a casual glance at the shoes in the corner or through careful inspection, could never do. The latter modes yield facts, data; the former brings to presence, restores "being" to things.

Heidegger distinguishes in this respect the ready-to-hand, the present-at-hand, and the work of art. In *Being and Time* Heidegger talks about a hammer as that which fits into a context of operations in the world of the carpenter.[52] It is not simply its being at-hand as a thing that can be sensorily described which manifests it as hammer; it is its having a function, the context of which has to be already disclosed, which allows us to identify it specifically as a hammer—that is, a tool used primarily for pounding and extracting nails. One who has no knowledge of the world of the carpenter will only be able to describe the thing at hand without having access to what it is—like many primitive artifacts that are found in museums of fine art today. This parallels the scientific approach to organic bodies, which are alive with sensuous and rational life but which are treated in biology solely in terms of their sensorily descriptive properties. When we understand things we bring to them something more than their immediately verifiable properties. When we live with things, the functional context is disclosed.

It is the work of art that sets that functional context more deeply into the character of Earth and the character of World. In the work of art,

World is manifest as a world of inhabitance and Earth as native soil. Native soil is not something a chemist could ever analyze. Native soil is revealed by the peculiar sense of being at home that opens up when we inhabit it for some time. There is a kind of nostalgia experienced by remembering the smell of burning leaves in autumn up north back in the 1950s, linked to long walks, the chill in the air after early frost, raking leaves after school, and awaiting a supper of hot homemade soup with your family before getting down to homework and anticipating a well-deserved rest. Inhabitance of a world, a way of being, effects the sense of native soil. It is in the work of art that World and Earth are brought together focally.

Earth is "the unpurposed self-closer." Earth resists disclosure as a mystery of darkness for what we have come to call intellect. We describe its properties and break it apart to carry on the description. But that is always treating it in terms of its "for-us" (i.e., in terms of its relation to our senses). That makes possible what Owen Barfield describes as "dashboard knowledge," which allows us to manipulate the surface in order to get our desired responses, but which leaves hidden and forgotten the final depth of things.[53] In itself, Earth withdraws even as it juts up into the field of sensation. The claim that Earth is "unpurposed" suggests the elements that enter into the form of living things. Living things can be understood up to a point in terms of their telos. By contrast, Earth is simply there, in itself without a purpose, but capable of being taken up into the purposes of the living, prehuman as well as human. Earth is simply there in its supportive opacity. And even the things that are alive cannot be fully understood in terms of purpose. Heidegger likes to quote Angelus Silesius, who said: "The rose is without a why."[54] Why are there roses? Who knows? Furthermore, there is something unexplainable about the way in which earth displays itself in terms of sensory properties. Why should it be the case that having the kind of "meat" we do involves the disclosure of colors or sounds? Why should disclosure be tied up with "meat"? Earth itself, which enters into the rose and into the meat of our own bodies, is ultimately purposeless in itself.

In the work-being of the work not only is equipment manifest in its belonging to world and earth, but other things too are so manifest. The ordinary comes to take on an extraordinary character as we recognize it, so to speak, for the first time. The depth of meaning involved in belonging to a world of dwelling and the rich sensuousness involved in belonging to native soil meet in the coming to presence of a work of art. In the work of art, contrary to the character of equipment, the sensuous is not subsidiary, disappearing in its function; it enters into the focal character of significant presence.[55]

Heidegger highlights the feature of *polemos*, or struggle, brought about by the work of art, the aesthetic tension to which Augustine called attention. The work appears as a gestalt, a form that bears the tension between Earth and World. But here the tension between Earth and World involves the tension between a tendency to concealment and a tendency to unconcealment respectively, only Earth is the essentially concealed that rises up to partial manifestness in sensuousness, and World is the opening up of paths for thinking, acting, and feeling that contains the partial concealment of its own possibilities. World disclosure opens up a future whose actual texture and concrete disclosure of new possibilities is not revealed. The work of art as a form establishes that tension and thereby provides an aura of meaning, a measure of "world space" in which the everyday appears as extraordinary.[56]

In Heidegger's later work, Earth is absorbed into World as one of the regions that constitute the Fourfold of the World.[57] *Earth* again has to be understood here, not as a location in the solar system and not as a chemical mass, for these are abstractions from native soil, from the sensuousness of rhythm and melody that sound in our words, from the radiance of color, from our own lived embodiment. It is part and parcel of our speaking that it rises up from the sensuousness, the "earthiness" of language, not as that which we control with full deliberateness (we know how artificial "studied" style is), but as that which grows up in us. It is in the latter that Earth appears primordially as Earth. Language that rises up poetically from this Earth is foundational natural language, of which ordinary language is a sedimented resultant, and scientific and philosophic languages, flattened out abstractions. World that includes Earth so considered is a world for dwelling. That is why a scientific world is uninhabitable. That is why contemporary literature is filled with the experience of alienation. Insofar as the world we live in is increasingly and totalistically a technologically reconstructed world, it is not a world that brings us to ourselves. It is a world in which presences have become increasingly absent. Inhabitance shrivels through the priority of the work of the reflective *cogito*, that has forgotten the soil in which it is rooted.

Earth always interplays with the second region, Sky, as the open expanse that allows Earth to appear and that sets the measures for our time on earth, generating the days and the seasons. It encircles our lives and by its vastness gives us a sense of our smallness and our simultaneously be-longing to that vastness, which animals could not notice. It is the region of Kantian awe: "the starry skies above."

Mortals are the third world region. We humans belong to the earth: we come from the earth and are made of the earth. The human (Latin *hu-manus*) is humus, earth as soil. Biblically, human beings are made from the slime of the earth, or from its clay. Earth in turn flowers forth in our speech and in our art. But we also return inevitably to earth. We are mortal. That, however, does not mean simply that each of us will one day fall apart, de-caying into the earthly elements of which we are composed—though that is also correct. Much more basically, we humans are "the mortals"—those who live out of an awareness of having to die and are likewise distin-guished as the ones who speak. Death and language belong together. One for whom the Whole is opened up through language is one who lives out of an awareness of the whole of its temporal span and thus out of an antici-pation of the temporal termination of its being. Mortals are speakers, for whom therefore there is language, for whom the wholeness of their own being as stretched from birth to death is opened up by a rebound from both terms and becomes the echo chamber of the Whole.

Called out from Earth and living under the Sky, Mortals take the mea-sure of their being from the Gods, the fourth world region. Gods here are to be taken as messengers of what is highest, sources of inspiration regard-ing those things that set the measure, the Sacred, the inviolable. As Mortals are linked to the Earth, so are Gods linked to the Sky, to that above us which measures us, which reveals what is most high, which encompasses us with its vastness. For Heidegger, the Gods are linked to the dimension of concealment manifest as such—as essentially concealed, by the Sky, which presents an essential unreachability. It is the domain of the hidden God.

World is, for Heidegger, the interplay of these four regions: Earth and Sky, Mortals and Immortals. The peculiar character of the interplay differs in different cultures, and indeed in different epochs within a culture. That is why manifestness is essentially historical. *Seinsgeschichte*, history of Being, is the essentially perspectival, essentially mutable, essentially temporal open-ing up of the Whole.[58] When the four regions play together in our silent lis-tening, when we are not intent on mastery, but are open, meditatively, thankfully letting things be manifest, the poetic word arises. With this word things become significant presences, and with this play of things and word, world comes to hold sway.

What then is a thing? Thing is that which assembles the Fourfold and which is assembled by the Fourfold. The German for "thing," *Ding*, originally meant "assembly." Heidegger parallels that with the Greek term *logos*, especially as it appears in the fragments of the pre-Socratic philospher Heraclitus. *Logos* as the gathering performed by the word is the origin of our term *logic* as the kind of gathering we call reasoning, but it is ever so much richer. Logic cultivates the sphere of what is opened up and is thus derivative of that which opens up a region. *Logos* is related to *legein*, which means to read but also to gather; it also applies to that which is read, namely the word. (*Logos* in the prologue to John's Gospel is translated as "Word.") According to Heidegger, for Heraclitus *logos* is primarily the gathering together of the Whole in things that occurs when the appropriate word arises.[59] That gathering together of the Whole, for which humanness *(Da-Sein)* furnishes the locus, is the opening out of a world for a people. In one of Heidegger's most difficult yet more compressed and revealing statements: "If we let the thing be present in its thinging from out of the worlding world, then we are thinking of the thing as thing."[60] The disclosure of thing and world is reciprocal. It is not something we do but something done to us: things "thing" us by "thinging" (i.e., gathering a world); world "worlds" by holding us and things together, presenting things in a way that has us in its grip. The play of thing and world in the clearing granted to *Da-Sein* comes to pass in and through the poetic word. And such a word stands at the origin of every work of art.

Art, in revealing the fundamental character of the thing as an assembling of the whole for dwelling, leads us back from the abstract one-sidedness of science, the all-sided abstractness of philosophy, and the partiality of all our particular interests to the wholeness of meaning. Art brings us from our various modes of absence and imposition to the presencing of the Whole in the sensuously present. It teaches us to "let things be"; it speaks directly to the heart, the center of thought, action, and feeling; it teaches us meditative rather than simply calculative and representative thinking. It brings us back to the ground of metaphysics: it articulates our sense of Being as the whole within which we come to find our own wholeness.

## Philosophy, Science, Art, and the Lifeworld

I will draw together many of the themes I have articulated, expand some of them, and bring them closer to us by considering six ways of life focused throughout Heidegger's work.[61] This will highlight what being-in-the-world involves as the ground of metaphysics and will bring to light the central role of the artist-poet, reinvoking Plato's battle between philosophy and poetry for primacy in articulating the lifeworld. For Heidegger philosophy does not stand above poetry, as it does for Plato; rather philosopher and poet "occupy twin peaks equidistant from the valley" of everyday life.[62] I will call these ways of life that of the peasant, the artist-poet, the philosopher, the scientist, the man on the street, and the thinker. The peasant and the contemporary man on the street exhibit ways of life that have to be constructed out of Heidegger's concerns, but they throw light on the other ways of life. They help illuminate what being-in-the-world entails. The first two ways, that of the peasant and that of the artist-poet, the latter furnishing the framework of meaning for the former, antedate the emergence of philosophy as a design on the Whole and continue as possible ways thereafter. The way of the scientist as specialist follows the emergence of philosophy and that of the contemporary man on the street follows from the technological impact of science on society as a whole. The way of the thinker is poised somewhat ambiguously between philosophy and poetry. The peasant, the artist-poet, and the thinker operate in the medium of the lifeworld and thus fall on the side of poetry in the historic battle between philosophy and poetry. The philosopher, the scientist, and even the man on the street suffer from a certain abstraction from the full medium of experience. I will treat them in what is, for the most part, a kind of chronological order and conclude with some comparisons between them.

*The Peasant.* I use the term *peasant* to refer to those like Heidegger's Schwarzwald neighbors, for whom he exhibits the greatest respect. The peasant world is the world of Heidegger's own origins and the chosen milieu within which he primarily thought. So respectful was he of those who dwelt in this world that he asked and followed the advice of one old farm neighbor when he received a call to come to teach in Berlin in the early days of the Nazi regime.[63] The peasant represents a mode of being-in-the-world largely untouched by philosophy, science, and modern technology, but not by poetry in the large sense of the term.

The peasant (German *Bauer*) lives in an order of building *(bauen)*—that is, both cultivating and constructing—for the sake dwelling or inhabiting (becoming habituated to and familiar with) his world. At his best, he treasures things through thinking meditatively (i.e., recollectively, appreciatively). He learns to let things be present, making their claim upon him.[64] He is engaged in his daily tasks, where things appear in equipmental contexts.[65]

Undertaking those tasks, he dwells on the earth as his native soil, under the sky. He allows the alternation of night and day and the cycles of the seasons to govern his life. He entrusts his crops and cattle to the earth and cultivates them.[66] He has a place in his home for a reminder of death: the *Totenbaum,* the niche awaiting the corpse of the next family member to die.[67] There is also a place near the common table: the *Herrgottswinkel,* the Lord God's corner, surmounted by a crucifix.[68] The peasant heeds the announcements of the Most High, the inspirations that give him fundamental orientation in life, mediated by his own religious tradition.[69] He walks over the bridge that blends into the banks and is surmounted by a statue of a saint, a bridge that becomes a living image of his own transition from mortal to immortal shores.[70] He respects the ways passed down to him from ancestral times into which he initiates his own children.

Solitude is an essential part of this life. It affords the power of "projecting our whole existence into the vast uncommonness of the presence of all things."[71] The *Bauer* lives out a sense of the environing Mystery, from which everything arises into his field of awareness.[72] One who dwells thoughtfully in this element knows how "to receive the blessing of the earth and to become at home in the law of this reception in order to shepherd the mystery of Being and watch over the inviolability of the possible."[73] He comes to know the ancient *phusis* as "the arising and receding of all that is present in its presencing and absencing."[74] He gathers things into his heart in respectful repose.

The key notion here is the heart, the old Anglo-Saxon word for the thinking of which is *thanc.*[75] It is not a merely emotional but an essentially dispositional notion. It is the region of our basic stance toward what is, inclining us habitually to attend and act in certain directions. It is tied essentially to gratitude, to appreciation, to thankfulness. It treasures past blessings and hence is essentially linked to memory. Memory, in turn, is originally tied to the holy and the gracious, the inviolable which grants the poetic inspiration.

Heidegger refers to the characteristic activity of the heart so conceived as *das andenkendes Denken,* thinking that recalls, or meditative thinking.[76] Such recollective thinking is the supreme thanks. It evokes devotion.[77] Recollection and devotion, turned in gratitude toward what has been granted and devoted to acting in accordance with it, gathers time together and in so doing deepens present being by providing it with the ultimate lived context of the Mystery. Since it rests on the structure of *Dasein* as relation to the Whole, such thinking reaches out most fully to the outermost limits as well as to the most inward—that is, it develops a sense of the encompassing whole of what is, while simultaneously reaching inward to what is deepest in *Dasein*.[78]

Meditative thinking is not given to abstraction and logical arrangement. It thinks in the medium of the lifeworld, in the mode of dwelling, of inhabitance. Such meditative dwelling is a mode of thinking that belongs to humankind as such and is distinguished from the modes of thinking characteristic of specially talented types: mathematicians, scientists, philosophers, theologians.[79] Heidegger attests that his own philosophic work "belongs right in the midst of the peasants' work," rooted in the Alemannian-Swabian soil.[80] So much is that the case that he reported in a letter to Gadamer that the *Kehre*, the turn in his thought from *Dasein* to Being, "came to me in a rush"—*Ereignis* like, event like—as he returned home to Freiburg and the Black Forest and began "to feel the energy of his old stomping ground."[81] We should take that claim with the utmost seriousness.

Among contemporary intellectuals, it is precisely this that has been the object of resistance, even ridicule. Heidegger's background and chosen milieu incline him toward what is regarded as the closed society of the peasant, an anti-intellectual society, suspicious of strangers, resistant to the other, the outsider, opposed to the city, to democracy, debate, compromise, to technological and scientific advance, the components of the chosen milieu of modern intellectuals. What surfaces here is an essential tension between freedom and *pietas*, reflected respectively in modern society and its intellectual apologists on the one hand and, on the other, in Heidegger's peasant society and the apologetic ingredient in his own thought. *Denken als Danken* (thinking as thanking) is the reinvocation of ancient *pietas*, given expression in Aristotle, in Cicero, and in Aquinas,[82] as an attitude of gratitude for gifts that is rooted in a sense of an indebtedness that cannot be repaid, for the gift provided is the whole context of one's life. *Pietas*, exercised toward one's family, toward the tradition, and toward God, involves the recognition of the origin of all of one's real possibilities: the family brings one into being and provides (expressed in Greek) one's *charakter*, one's fundamental stamp, mediating the ways of one's community, which afford the concrete possibilities for any effective action, suffused with a sense that the whole context—one's own being included—is provided by the divine. Modern freedom had to fight an uphill battle against such *pietas*, which tended quite naturally to hold one in thrall to the given economic-social-political order.

Hegel's work may be viewed as an attempt to establish ancient *pietas* within modern civil society based on individual freedom of inquiry and operation.[83] Heidegger's work—at least at a fundamental level—reinvokes such *pietas* against the civil society of his contemporary critics. And it is in the element of *pietas* that poetry especially operates.[84]

*The Artist-Poet.* Even living in the way described, the peasant, like everyone, falls into a mode of everydayness, into the "they," the anonymous "one."[85] Mystery tends to disappear. Routine and surface come to dominate as things become flattened out. It is the artist, and especially the poet, who provides what Heidegger refers to as a "world space" in which the mysterious depth of the thing announces itself as emerging from and as sheltered within that which encompasses everything.[86] Indeed, the peasant moves in a world opened up by the creative ones, basically the poets and the founders.[87] One should think here of the role the biblical authors play in providing for the West the ultimate framework and feeling for the world. In the light of the poetically achieved world space everything is taken out of the commonplace; in Heidegger's terms, it receives its "being."[88]

The artist-poet struggles with everyday appearance, fights the battle between World and Earth, establishes figure in the rift between the two, and thus opens up the "inwardness of things."[89] In the 1930s especially, the *polemos* of Heraclitus tends to take center stage: struggle, battle, the praise of the strong.[90] But it is not the physical strength exhibited in overpowering others that is involved here; it is the spiritual strength to win back a sense of the depth that surrounds us from the tendency toward superficiality in everyday appearance. The struggle is essentially with such a fallen appearance for the sake of "being" as depth and as encompassing in relation to the everyday surface.[91]

Humans learn to dwell when they stand in the play of the fourfold of Earth and Sky, Mortals and Immortals. It is the poets who initiate that dwelling. Through them we learn to liberate the Earth from domination; welcome the Sky, which guides the seasons; hold ourselves ready for the announcements of the Immortals; and lead other Mortals toward their authentic death.[92] Things *are* in Heidegger's sense, they have their being, they appear charged with significance, as they gather a world of inhabitance. In so doing they "thing" us—they lay hold of us and gather us together insofar as we are available to "let them be." Things are not simply passive to our projects; they can also take hold of us, absorb us, magnetize our attention. And they can so "thing" us insofar as world "worlds" (i.e., insofar as an encompassing way of thinking, acting, and feeling has us in its grip), for things appear meaningfully present as they stand in webs of meaning relations that ultimately stretch to the Whole. It is paradigmatically in art that things come to "thing" us and world comes to "world" us.[93]

The artist as shaper of materials—of sound, of paint, and of glass, of stone and wood, clay and bronze—depends on the most primordial of artists, the poet, who gives shape to language, which opens up the Whole. Language gives expression to the *Logos* which gathers a community over time as it gathers together the coming to presence of the Whole for the community.[94] Poetry creates the primary music that sets linguistic meaning upon the earth of sonority. Within the space of its meanings all other art forms come into being.[95]

Art in general operates in the same medium of meditative dwelling charactertistic of the peasant, who takes things to heart, who is thoughtful. *Mnemosune*, memory as devotion, is the mother of the Muses, but also the daughter of Sky and Earth.[96] Thinking that recalls is the origin of poetry.[97] It proclaims the Holy, which, for Heidegger, is ancillary to consideration of the divine. The Holy, announced by the poet, is a dimension of encompassment and demand that calls for devotion. Only in letting things be— devotedly, thoughtfully—can the true sense of the divine dawn.[98] Great art occasions such thinking for a community. Great art is grateful letting be.

The dialogue that Heidegger conducts between thinking and poetry focuses on the nature of language. Language is the element in which we live, the relation of all relations, the openness in which everything appears.[99] As Heidegger sees it, in a reversal of what one might have thought, everyday language itself is flattened-out poetry.[100] We tend to see things differently because we live off an inheritance of the view of language that goes back at least to Aristotle, according to which language is an instrument we use to express previously complete thoughts.[101] Poetry would then be a kind of ornamentally embellished ordinary language. But for Heidegger, following a line of thought that appeared earlier in Heraclitus's notion of the logos, it is language that first addresses us.[102] And the vehicle of that primordial address is the poet who hears that logos. The poet gains entrance into the relation of word and thing.[103] The Aristotelian view is correlated with the view of truth as *orthotes*, whereas the poet opens up truth as *aletheia*. In the "needy time" wherein we live, a time of the flight of the gods, several poets—in particular Friedrich Hölderlin and Stefan George—turned to the nature of language.[104]

Heidegger spends a good bit of time in two different pieces meditating on the final line of George's poem "The Word": "Where word breaks off, no thing can be."[105] Poetry allows the thing to *be*—that is, to emerge into appearance *(bhu-)*, to come alive *(es)*, to enter into a world of dwelling *(wesan)*.[106] Reflecting these Sanskrit roots of the Indo-European conjugations of the forms of the verb *to be* (German *bin, ist, wesen;* English *been, is, were*), Heidegger's apparently idiosyncratic usage squares with those sedimented meanings long since forgotten in the common notion of being as being-outside-nothing—for Nietzsche, "the last trailing cloud of evaporating reality." It also parallels George's peculiar usage in the passage cited. The poetic word permits the thing to enter into a world of human dwelling. And dwelling is entering into the play of the Fourfold.[107]

The thinker, Heidegger says, thinks Being, whereas the poet names the holy. But the George passage seems to suggest that it is the poet who names Being. In the *Letter on Humanism,* Heidegger sets up a kind of order: thinking of Being is a prelude to thinking the holy, which, in turn, opens up the divine; this then allows us to think what God might be.[108] So we have what Heidegger would call "a calculative ordering": Being, the holy, the divine, God. To the thinker he assigns the task of bringing about a relation to the first, beyond the region of things and their principles dominating Western philosophy and science. To the poet he assigns the proclaiming of the holy. He plays on terms for wholeness, the healthy, the hale, healing, linked to *das Heilige,* especially in Rilke. The divine is the region of the immortals, the messengers of the Most High. In George, word breaks off when it returns us to the soundlessness of the pealing of silence, wherein healing occurs.[109]

As the art of language, poetry creates the context for all the arts. For Sophocles' *Antigone* chorus, the human being is the strangest *(deinotaton)* of all the creatures on earth, who creates cities and ways, but is essentially without city or way.[110] For Georg Trakl, the poet is called apart so that the stranger finds a home on the earth.[111] Every poet speaks out of a single center that remains unsaid.[112] Trakl's center, according to Heidegger, is the notion of *Abgeschiedenheit,* that apartness of the poet from the everyday that makes possible the creation of a home on earth.[113] Such being-at-home involves a sense of nearness (neighborliness). At its most authentic, neighborliness happens through the poet preserving farness in a creative tension between opposites that gives a depth to our experience.[114] We must distinguish modes of nearness and farness: (1) at the personal level, certain persons and projects are "near and dear to my heart"; (2) as an abstraction out of that comes the measurable nearness and distance of the sciences; and (3) at the root of both is the way the whole appears as measure of the near and dear. At the latter level we have the coincidence of nearness and distance in the mystery of encompassment involved in being, awareness, language, history, nature. Poetry gives expression to our relation to the mystery.

Though poetry is rooted in *mnemosune*, it is yet attentive to destiny, which comes from the future.[115] As we already noted, in ancient mythology, *mnemosune*, in turn, is the daughter of earth and sky. For Hölderlin, as a student of classical Greece, earth and sky form the site of the wedding feast of gods and men to establish the fourfold.[116] The play of the Fourfold, which brings things to presence, is set in the relation between past and future. As we noted before, for Heidegger the past comes to us from the future.[117] In "authentic" existence, the relation between the three temporal dimensions is tensed: the present takes on depth when the emergence of a project allows us to take over the past as the history that leads to the project. The fully tensed relation to time provides a sense of destiny, a kind of vocational awareness, a sense of a life project to be achieved. But this occurs in such a way that one is not simply looking past the present and thus is unable to tarry with things. On the contrary, the deepest tarrying with the present occurs through the activation of the other two temporal dimensions, with the priority of the future as vocation.[118] This frees us from an irresponsible aestheticism. The poet who becomes the vehicle for this sense of destiny is thus no dandy tarrying at the fringes of a culture but is rather one who establishes its basic sense of being.[119]

In a needy time, to be a poet is to attend, singing, to the traces of the fugitive gods.[120] The poet attends to the holy, which forms the basis or provides the element for the epiphany of the divine or the Immortals as messengers of the Most High, or of God Himself. Is the holy then the togetherness of the Fourfold? But in relation to humanness, Being precedes the Holy. Thinking of Being does not operate as song. It is song that would establish relation to the Earth. The medium of poetry and of the arts in general is sensuousness, belonging to the Earth. Earth flowers from the mouth of the poet (Hölderlin). Song is that flowering as the celebration of existence.[121] Singing and thinking are twin stems in the neighborhood of poetry.[122]

Rilke adds another dimension that runs along the lines of Heidegger's central preoccupation. Rilke's central image of the "globe of being" as the integral totality of things is parallel to Parmenides' thinking of Being. Rilke distinguished the center of this globe as encompassing, other than all objectification, and corresponding to the heart, the inner dimension of human dwelling. In such dwelling pain, love, and death belong together. Loss of the center involves a fracturing and a loss of that belonging together. Afflicted by care because of death and pain, we create security for ourselves through objectification; yet we are thereby removed from the center, the boundless and open, which is beyond all security. An eye on the integral Whole may allow for a transcendence of technology through formative power.[123] Heidegger's observations on technology have one of their roots in his dialogue with Rilke. Generally, in the later Heidegger the poets become his chief interlocutors, for he attempted to find the way back to the ground of the metaphysical tradition, which opened modern science and thus contemporary technology. That ground lies in the sense of Being corresponding to our mode of dwelling, whose center lies in the heart. It is the formation of the heart that is the task of the arts in general, but of poetry in particular.

*The Philosopher.* Philosophy is a distinctively Greek phenomenon. For Heidegger, as for Hegel, there is no non-Western philosophy but only a certain family resemblance to philosophy *stricto sensu*.[124] Philosophy emerges in the West in the train of Anaximander, Parmenides, and Heraclitus, who were primordial thinkers and not yet philosophers—indeed, at least for the Heidegger of 1951, they were too great to be philosophers.[125]

Philosophy has what we might call its proto-origin in a poetic-intellectual experience of Being in Heraclitus and Parmenides as emerging into presence, which they termed *phusis*, whose stems stress emergence *(phuo)* and manifestness *(phainomai)*.[126] Plato and Aristotle focus on the "what" in what emerges into presence, but the coming to presence is itself unfocused.[127] The "what" is idea or *eidos*, the intelligible look, the face things present to intellectual looking, the ever-Now, always already there, perpetually standing intelligible.[128] Here we see what Dominique Janicaud has described as "the transition in metaphysics from Being-present to Being-essential."[129] The distinction between Being so conceived and beings who appear as its instances still occupies, in Heidegger's view, the level of beings *(Seienden,* as things and principles) and does not rise to the level of Being *(Sein)* as that which grants the distinction.

However, in his reading of Plato and Aristotle, Heidegger claims that for them, as the first philosophers, philosophy still plants its roots in awe; it feeds on astonishment before the mystery of the Whole and grows in such astonishment as it carries on its essential questioning.[130] It is led to ask about the most fundamental things, to unsettle all the settled so as to get to the roots of things. Like art, philosophy too creates so much world space that in its light even the ordinary appears extraordinary.

But just as in art what comes to be is subjectible to the everydayness that flattens out all appearance, so also with philosophy. The astonishment allied with the peculiar coming to presence of that which is given for thought disappears and one falls into argumentation and construction far removed from fundamental awe. The passing on of problems within a given horizon fails to think the unconcealed horizon in relation to the concealed encompassing out of which it comes. Philosophic problems are subject to what Heidegger—perhaps thinking originally of the Sophists, but not only of them—calls "the cheap acid of a merely logical intelligence."[131]

The history of philosophy, precisely as metaphysics, becomes the history of the forgottenness of Being as mysterious encompassment coming to presence in what it grants for thought. But though there is a reigning forgetfulness from the very inception of philosophy as metaphysics, nonetheless, metaphysics is not false or wrong.[132] But unless it is led back to its own ground, what is essential to *Dasein* is lost. And that entails a relation of philosophy, through thinking its ground, to the arts.

*The Scientist.* For Heidegger science operates in the conceptual space opened up by philosophy.[133] Scientific thinking is derived from philosophy.[134] But the development of the sciences is their separation from and completion of philosophy.[135] Science always and necessarily operates on the basis of what is manifest in the lifeworld, but only insofar as that has been transformed by conceptual transcription. After distinctions have been conceptually inventoried, specializations can be cultivated that are no longer concerned with their origins or their relations with one another. Just as one can operate within the functional circle of the everyday world, unaware that, as Kierkegaard put it, "we float on waters 70,000 fathoms deep," so in science we can master cybernetic functions without ontological meaning, without questioning the framework of manifestness within which science itself occurs.[136]

Scientific specializations emerge in the wake of Plato and Aristotle.[137] But distinctively modern science emerges through a distinctive projection of the ground plan of nature that sets it in decisive contrast to the Aristotelian view, which it supplanted. For Heidegger, this is not necessarily a progression *tout court*—although there is clearly a progressive manifestation of features of nature under the modern paradigm. What holds sway in modern science is the essence of technology, a view made thematic in Nietzsche, for whom being itself is will-to-power.[138] Nature is made over into what it has to be in order to be progressively controlled, assimilated into our projects. In the Galilean-Newtonian view, there are no longer natures seeking to actualize their forms; there is only Nature, a single system of colorless, odorless, tasteless, soundless, valueless, irreducible elements located in an empty container space and, simultaneously, in a flowing, riverlike time, combining and separating according to invariant laws.[139] As a consequence, from the point of view of science, natures can thus no longer be violated. Aristotelian natures, substantial forms each seeking their respective *teloi* are considered mere phenomenal appearances of what has been called the dance of the atoms. And learning how they dance without us enables us to becomes conductors of the dance. In this way, for Heidegger, things lose their "being" and become data.[140] But for Heidegger also, this was already prepared for when Plato thought the Being of beings as intelligible looks that were archetypes for divine production.[141]

In the first emergence of modern science, we have the age of the world picture: Nature is the in-principle viewable. But then, with twentieth-century physics, nature disappears into the objectlessness of standing reserve: *Gegenstand* becomes *Bestand*, standing-over-against becomes standing-at-hand.[142] In contrast with Nature for the peasant, modern Nature is placed under demand, no longer entrusted with sustaining us and our works. Standing within Nature, attuned to its essential rhythms and fitting human projects within it, the peasant is disposed by a basic *pietas* for the Nature God or the gods have provided. In contrast, in the modern disposition, humanness stands over against Nature, which it summons to appear in such a way as to provide maximum yield for humanity's projects: Nature is a field for the operation of unbounded human freedom. Rather than the shepherd of Being, modern man seeks to become the lord and master of Nature.[143] Held in the grips of the scientific-technological way of viewing, we allow no other view of Nature to stand. People look to science to decide on the place of human being in the Whole and to set the standards for human decision.[144] Much is revealed, but what is concealed is revealing itself, and thus *Dasein*, as the locus of manifestness.[145]

Though a scientist may, as a reflective person, shift into the philosophic mode, science does not, as science—indeed, cannot as science—think its own presuppositions, its own rootedness in the structure of *Dasein;* hence science is in the dark regarding its own nature.[146] In Heidegger's not too rhetorically wise way of putting it: "Science does not think."[147] Its thoughtlessness regarding its own encompassment is rooted in its essential one-sidedness.[148] And the great danger that attends this movement is that *Dasein* itself will disappear into the standing reserve: human beings will themselves become simply on hand for the projects of some Overman.[149]

*The Man on the Street.* Human reality as *Dasein* is thrown being-in-the-world, on account of which we are always inauthentic in the sense of not being fully self-possessed, being in the grip of a world articulated long before we entered on the scene.[150] But there is a massive difference between the world of the peasant and the world of the contemporary man on the street. The inauthenticity of the peasant was still the expression of a world that had a place for the essential things he could thinkingly take to heart. An essential part of his world was the heeding of the poets—again, consider here the biblical authors.

The contemporary man on the street is held in the grip of the same mode of revealing characteristic of modern science as its technological essence has come to clearer focus. Scientific technology holds sway; and for it there is no longer any room for that which falls outside the scope of its methods, for action not guided by its attitude of dominance, hence for the Holy, which places its demands on us.

In lines reminiscent of Nietzsche's about the last man,[151] Heidegger speaks of the devastation of the earth as the condition for a guaranteed high standard of living and happiness for all, leading to the "high-velocity expulsion of Mnemosyne,"[152] of meditative thinking, of thoughtful recollection attuned to the Holy. For Heidegger we live in a time of "the darkening of the world, the flight of the gods, the destruction of the earth, the transformation of men into a mass, the hatred and suspicion of everything free and creative."[153] The sense of history vanishes (one recalls Henry Ford's famous remark: "History is bunk!") and the boxer (or today the multimillion-dollar athlete) is hero. Devotees of speed and of time-saving devices, we seem to have no time.[154] If we think of the Whole at all, we think of it in scientific-technological terms. The arts are pleasant diversion, entertainment, prettification—not manifestations of the fundamental. The Holy, which great art proclaims, has disappeared from our purview. For Heidegger "perhaps what is distinctive about this world-epoch consists in the closure of the dimension of the hale [*das Heiligen*]."[155]

Modern humanity is essentially homeless.[156] It has lost the element in which *Dasein* by nature lives. Even the contemporary farmer no longer lives in Nature as the ever-environing, nurturing Whole, unencompassable by science. Technology in the form of radio and television invades his silence and prevents his meditative thought.[157] Language as simultaneously the home of Being and the dwelling place of humankind degenerates into an instrument for communicative purposes[158] and further into "a mere container for their sundry preoccupations."[159] Without the sense of Being, humankind is like a fish out of water.[160]

*The Thinker.* Given what Heidegger understands by thinking, logic is not, as logicians claim, the requisite thinking on thinking.[161] In fact, if we cannot think beyond logic, we are left with the previously designated "cheap acid of a merely logical intelligence." And science does not "think." Both science and logic cultivate a domain already open. Thinking is concerned with coming back reflectively upon that opening.

Heidegger regularly refers to philosophers as thinkers, in contrast to scientists, who are said not to think insofar as philosophy deals with the frameworks presupposed by science. Socrates, for example, is the purest thinker of the West,[162] and Nietzsche is a great thinker.[163] Aristotle, Plato, and Kant are thinkers.[164] Presumably philosophy has to do with conceptual elaboration, construction, and argumentation as a means of working out that thought. But Heidegger also distinguishes philosophy, which is in essence metaphysics, from thinking, which concerns the ground of metaphysics and thus enters into proximity with the element in which the arts live.[165] As we have noted earlier, for Heidegger, Heraclitus and Parmenides were thinkers but were of too great stature to be philosophers. Here, from Socrates to Nietzsche, something essential loses focus. Metaphysics is the ultimate conceptual framework presupposed in all our dealings, scientific and otherwise; but its practitioners do not think that which it itself presupposes, the way Being itself comes to presence. Metaphysics thus contributes to the forgottenness of Being—indeed, because it is considered the most fundamental form of thought, it is the major culprit in the occlusion of Being that holds sway in Western philosophy and science.[166]

Because philosophy, observing and inferring, operates from out of the perspectives granted in each case but does not think the granting, the history of philosophy calls for a "destruction,"[167] a dismantling *(Abbau)* of "representations that have become banal and vacuous,"[168] a desedimentation that leads back to the ground of original givenness, originary coming to presence. This allows one to stake out the positive possibilities of the tradition. Such a process involves an overcoming *(Überwindung)* of metaphysics. Heidegger insists that the destruction or overcoming of the history of metaphysics is not its elimination because metaphysics is not false or wrong.[169] He later admitted that the term *destruction* had lent itself to a misunderstanding "of insuperable grotesqueness."[170] He rejects as superficial an interpretation that would, as Janicaud puts it, "consist in setting oneself against metaphysics, in rejecting it as an opinion, or else in dismissing it as a discipline now obsolete. Metaphysics is less overcome than assigned to limits."[171] In fact, for Heidegger metaphysics belongs to the nature of humanness—presumably, like science, available in principle to any fully capable human.[172] "Even overcome, metaphysics does not disappear. It returns in another form and maintains its supremacy."[173] As Joan Stambaugh observes, "overcoming" metaphysics signifies not elimination but incorporation.[174] Heidegger says that what is involved is "neither a destruction nor even a denial of metaphysics. To intend anything else would be childish presumption and a demeaning of history."[175] In this sense, overcoming is related to authenticity, in which, instead of taking for granted and going along, we each appropriate and thus take radical responsibility for the "inauthentic," which is our irremovable ground as the prior genetic and cultural shaping we have and must have received. According to Jean-François Mattéi, deconstruction is "the *return* toward the original site of metaphysics in order to appropriate it within its own limits and to prepare a new beginning."[176] Thought climbs back down from metaphysical abstraction into the nearness of the near.[177]

Furthermore, in Heidegger's view, each philosophy, which is at base metaphysics, is inexhaustible. "Overcoming" metaphysics is transforming it by replanting it in the soil in which it originated, the soil of fundamental awe.[178] But this requires a loosening up of the soil. In what does this loosening up consist? Heidegger uses another metaphor here: it involves attempting to "get into the draft," which draws the thinker, guiding him in his conceptual articulations.[179] Concepts have to be brought back to their origins in the lifeworld. Rootless elaboration of problems that follow from previous formulations, argumentation of positions pro and con, construction of explanations, elaboration of systematic connections: all this philosophic work has to be led back to its origins, not simply in specialized experiences, but in the encompassing field of the lifeworld, which, above all, includes our orientation toward the Whole.[180]

We accomplish this leading back by thinking the unthought, presumably the lifeworld payoff, the deepening of the sense of real presences, for thinking takes place in the medium of the lifeworld,[181] as Heidegger identifies the locus of his own thinking in the lifeworld of the Swabian peasant. In leading the conceptual apparatus back to the lifeworld, we see that, primordially considered, philosophy is lived correspondence with the Being of beings.[182] But then, without some form of such correspondence, we would not be able to speak: the Whole has to be opened up in a certain way through language. However, for Heidegger, philosophy—adequately understood—is *fulfilled* correspondence.[183] Presumably, in maintaining some distinction between philosophy and primordial thinking, the fulfilled correspondence is not simply the demonstrable circle of concepts, but the experiential filling of that circle, the rising up and return of conceptualization to the sense of holistic attunement to the Whole, revealed and concealed in and through the peculiarity of a given philosophic circle of concepts.[184]

The thinker's task is to make clear the perspectives we occupy in relation to the encompassing mystery. In so doing he operates within the element thematized by the artist-poet but also implicitly constituting the lifeworld of the peasant. Thinking, Heidegger says, is "memory, devotion and thanks," features that characterized the meditative taking to heart of his peasant friends.[185] "Thinking" operates prethematically in the peasant, the artist-poet, and even in the philosopher. But it is not attended to explicitly in any of them. That is the task for what Heidegger comes to call, paradigmatically, the thinker. He is ultimately "the shepherd of being,"[186] one who cares for the presencing in what is present. Heidegger uses another metaphor: he is the one who "works at building the house of Being," the house that is language.[187] He builds linguistically by setting language into the element in which it lives.[188]

In this regard, Heidegger's understanding of Parmenides is central. He focuses particularly on two Parmenidean dicta: *to gar auto estin noein te kai einai,* usually translated as, "Thought and being are one";[189] and *chre to legein te noein to eon emmenai,* often rendered as, "One should both say and think that being is."[190] Thought in its primordial sense is the place where the sense of the Whole opens up. It *is* this opening up. Early Heidegger calls this place *Dasein,* human reality as the "there" of the dawning of the meaning of Being *(Sein).* The thought of Being is the being-taken by that meaning, being attuned to it, living in it. *Noein,* thinking, is taking to heart, which is letting be; nous is the *thanc.*[191] Taking-to-heart allows the presence of what is present to make its claim.[192] "Apprehension [*noein*] is the happening which has man."[193] Taking to heart presupposes the gathering *(legein)* performed by language that lets things be present in the way they are present. Linguistically mediated manifestness precedes taking to heart as letting lie before. But it also follows as safeguarding in the gathering of what is taken to heart.[194] The two together, *legein* and *noein,* rooted in language and the heart, show what thinking is.[195] Letting-lie-before corresponds to the theoretical moment, but taking-to-heart fulfills our belonging to Being. Philosophy and its development in the special sciences is aimed at conquest, possession. Philosophy as fulfilled attunement to Being sets the conceptually elaborated within the framework of fundamental awe attuned to the encompassing mystery, out of which all that comes to presence comes to presence. It is finally a mode of letting be, which is a mode of being possessed.[196]

Contrary to what it might seem from very much that Heidegger says and from much that his readers draw from him, he is not calling for a repudiation of technology, of science, or of metaphysics.[197] They are part of the history of what has been granted to us. What is needed is a "friend of the house of Being" who, as he says, "in equal manner and with equal force is inclined toward both the technologically constructed world-edifice *and* the world as a house for a more original dwelling," one who is able "to re-entrust the calculability and technicity of nature to the open mystery of a newly experienced naturalness of nature."[198]

*Conclusion.* The thinker, the artist-poet, and the peasant operate out of meditative thinking. Each has a peculiar sense of the environing mystery to which we essentially belong—belong, that is, as called upon to be aware of it and to listen for the essential claims it makes on us. But each operates with a different vehicle: the thinker operates negatively in the sphere of concepts, loosening them to get a sense of the unsaid draft that draws on the philosopher; the artist-poet operates in the medium of what is most immediately insistent in the lifeworld, sensory manifestness, within the context of a lived sense of the Whole. The artist-poet, by bringing sensuousness, earthiness to focal presence, works to win back the sense of the whole and thus the depth of each least thing from the flattening out that tends to constitute everyday appearance. The paradigmatic peasant occupies the sphere of everyday experience pervaded by tasks but knows the nearness of the environing mystery, which he takes to heart. Peasant, artist-poet, and thinker—they are all friends of the simple who have experienced its quiet force.

In a sense counterpoised to these are the philosopher, the scientist, and the contemporary man on the street. The former operates constructively in the sphere of the concept, feeding off fundamental generative intuitions that produce encompassing frameworks. The modern scientist operates as a specialist out of a peculiar, more encompassing framework that transforms Nature into what it has to be in order for us to manipulate it. The contemporary man on the street is the recipient of the scientific-technological framework, which tends to drive out of consideration other modes of revealing. The latter two types—scientist and man on the street—are in principle, insofar as they think exclusively in the dominant framework, alienated from the element proper to humankind, the element of meditative thinking. The philosopher seems to be a transitional figure. He thinks in terms of the presuppositions of science and the lifeworld, but he fails to think the mystery in the element proper to it because he is dominated by the thought of Being as standing Now. Insofar as he is an essential thinker, he is sustained by fundamental awe and lives in a deepened presence of the Whole appearing in all things; but apparently, qua philosopher, he does not *think* that off which he lives. In attending questioningly to the ground of metaphysics, Heidegger has performed an essential service: in the words of Janicaud, he "has altered the light in which the landscape was bathed."[199]

Getting back behind what holds sway in Western thought from its inception leads to the possibility of a second beginning. It leads into the element in which the arts operate. It could provide, in the darkened era in which we now live, the "saving grace," for the reinvoking of a lifeworld, like the lifeworld of the peasant, which has a place for the Holy. However, such a reinvocation can occur only in relation to the context of scientific-technological orientation, which is the dominant mode of revealing granted to us today. In the element of the lifeworld we can relearn how to correspond to the mystery that surrounds us. In this element we can learn a mode of thinking other than the representative-calculative mode that currently dominates us. We can learn again meditatively taking to heart. And in this task the arts and thinking on the arts take the lead.

## Response

Heidegger has provided much of the orientation that guides this text. In particular, the distinction between two modes of thinking, representative-calculative and meditative—and, correspondingly, the distinction between the intellect and the heart—has been pivotal. These parallel sets of distinctions are crucial in approaching the different roles in human life of the sciences (taken in a broad sense that includes philosophy) and the arts.

Representation *(Vorstellung)* abstracts from our coimplication with things and persons, from our participative presence, where we find ourselves involved with what is other than ourselves; it places them before our minds *(vor-stellen)*, at a distance; it re-presents them. Even in the presence of things, it abstracts from their presencing, the way they lay hold of us. Such representation makes calculation possible. In the broad sense Heidegger uses the term, calculation involves the ordering of things, placing them in frameworks, outlines, schemata. Mathematical calculation is only one form of calculative thinking in this sense. What is crucial is the underlying stance involved in these two aspects of what we have come to call the work of intellect. Based on abstraction from the claim beings have on us in our total life situation, in the *Lebenswelt*, we are enabled to arrange things to suit our projects, theoretical or practical. In its extreme form, representative-calculative thinking creates the *Gestell*, the enframing that turns all beings, not only into objects *(Gegen-stände)* set over against us in function of our abstract representations, which allow them to appear in a certain manner, but (more radically, though along the same lines) such thinking turns things and persons into a reservoir of resources *(Bestand)* for our technological transformation along whatever lines we will. This is the situation in which we now find ourselves, the world we inhabit or the world that is uninhabitable, the mode of manifestation that has us thoughtlessly in its grip.

Meditative thinking *(das andenkendes Denken)* is thinking which returns us to where we already are, to the lifeworld, to our co-implication with things and persons, to participative presencing. Meditative thinking learns, not to master calculatively, but to let persons and things be present. It learns to let them draw near, lay hold of us ever more deeply. Meditative thinking "treasures things in the heart"; it is essentially appreciative thinking, thinking as thanking. It is attuned to our essential giftedness, our having been granted what and who we are and thus our place among things. Meditative thinking belongs, not simply to intellectually gifted types (as representative-calculative thinking belongs to mathematicians, scientists, philosophers); it belongs to human beings as such. It naturally expands to the essential space of *Dasein:* attending to the announcements of what is highest through what the Greeks called Muses and the Hebrews, Angels, the sources of inspiration speaking through the poets and prophets; recalling our essential mortality, the necessary closing off of all our possibilities for being in the world, thus bringing our life as a whole into focus and allowing at the same time for the deep and essential to come into focus over against the superficial and accidental; attending, finally, to the enduring presence of the sensuously given, our root contact with beings, framed by earth and sky. And precisely because it is called upon to heed whatever might emerge as an indication of the Most High, meditative thinking is aware of the finiteness of its apprehension and is thus attuned to the vastness of what is hidden behind all that is manifest. It learns to let whatever appears be ever more deeply present as the announcement of the ultimate encompassing Mystery to which we belong essentially as humans.

Now that space of meditative thinking is, for Heidegger, the space in which the arts operate. It is the space belonging to the heart, the core, the unifying center of humanness, whose correlate is significant presences drawing us into and beyond the whole of beings as the Mystery at the heart of Being. If intellectual thinking re-presents in absence, meditative thinking operates in presence; it presents. The medium of intellectual thinking is the language of prose in which the medium itself disappears in its function of revealing abstract meaning. The medium of meditative thinking is the language of poetry, in which the medium, coming into focus qua sensuous, places us upon the earth. It corresponds to and deepens our dwelling, our inhabitance of the lifeworld. Poetry opens the lifeworld to appreciative thinking as it opens the space within which the other art forms operate.

In the line of Heidegger, Dufrenne insists that the "objective world" is founded upon the world of inhabitance, which is, first and foremost, a world of feeling. Even science is possible only by reason of a certain sympathy for the subject matter.[200] Feeling is thus not merely something private, merely subjective; it manifests something of the Being of things. Above all, it is capable of showing "the mysterious splendor of being which precedes men and objects," a splendor on which primitive religions rest and which the arts at their highest evoke.[201]

Like Dewey, Heidegger distinguishes the empirically present art product from the *work* of art. The latter involves for Heidegger the opening up of a world for dwelling. The form of the work appears only insofar as we are taken up in the struggle between World and Earth, or, as Heidegger later puts it, in the play of the Fourfold. However, the works we find in museums are typically works that *were,* for the character of the world that produced them is long gone. This raises the problem of what he calls the preservers. And by this he does not mean those who practice the technique of art restoration, for these only preserve the art product. How do we relate to works that have been?

Consider a work of art intended to give expression to the depth of religious experience; consider a loving treatment of the Madonna and Child. An animal looking at the painting presumably sees only visual patterns without connection to biological needs and thus the picture appears in a mode of indifference. The aesthetically and religiously uncultivated viewer sees a picture of a woman holding her baby. The aesthetically sensitive see an organized framing of a richly textured surface of color relations and of the play of light and shadow appropriate to the display of the relation of mother and child. If not believers, they might still gain a sense of the fulfilling character of the way of life associated with what is depicted; but they might not be moved to accept it as true. As Hegel remarked, though we can appreciate the beauty of a Medieval or Renaissance work depicting the Madonna and Christ child, we no longer bend our knee because we stand at another level in the development of the human Spirit.[202] George Santayana spent his last years in a convent in Spain, not because he believed in Catholicism, but because he found the whole ambiance most beautiful.[203] Along the same lines, Walter Kaufmann bemoaned the fact that religion, which had produced some of the greatest works of art known to humankind, was essentially a thing of the past. For Kaufmann the regret was not that the moribund religions furnished a right relation to things as that they generated such incomparably beautiful art, the likes of which we will probably never see again in a world from which the sacred has virtually disappeared.[204] In contrast, religiously sensitive viewers see a holy picture that might not only touch them deeply but also reinforce their commitment to a whole way of life associated with that Mother and her Child. They stand, not in the mode of "as if" in the presence of an aspect of a charming story; the work of art helps them to realize what they already accept.

But insofar as epochal transformations of the horizon of meaning entail translation of a faith tradition into a different mode, believers too stand in relation to past art works as works that were. There is a sense in which, just as the teachings of the faith require a reinterpretation as we gain distance from the epochs within which beliefs have been formulated, so also the expression of the lifeworld of faith requires new artistic mediation in different epochs. But both a faith hermeneutic and novel art work are deepened insofar as they are related in a mode of critical retrieval to the works that were.

With Nietzsche and Dewey, Heidegger senses the endangering of the lifeworld that emerged with the emergence of philosophy in Plato. The lifeworld for Plato is the Cave of sensibility and of tradition; its architects are the poets, its decorators the other artists. From the time of Plato onward, philosophy and its saintly followers have been all too inclined to contemn the world of the senses and thus the arts. Christianity, breathing deeply the vapors of disembodied spirituality and otherworldliness generated by the pagan gnostic and Neoplatonic saints, became, in its institutionalized form, "Platonism for the people," as Nietzsche remarked. It inclined toward a view of first-class and second-class citizenship in the church based on the degree of remotion one achieved from one's bodily experience. Sexuality above all was strongly suspect and almost condemned, allowed as an instrument of procreation but begrudgingly accepted as a result of the Fall. But the central doctrines of the Incarnation and Final Resurrection of the Body exerted a countervailing power and the arts were assimilated to the liturgy of the pre-Reformation church. The church of the Reformers paradoxically reinstated sexuality by eliminating celibacy as an ideal and contemned the arts, while simultaneously purging churches of all art except music, which operates with the least material medium.

With Nietzsche and Dewey, Heidegger sees the arts as articulating our belonging to the earth, though in no case is it a matter of collapsing humanness into bodily encapsulation, where aesthetics is simply a matter of fine, physiologically internal feelings. For all three art takes us out of such an enclosed self; and in the great work of art something of the character of both sensorily present things and the whole in which they are installed is displayed. For Nietzsche eternity is installed in time; for Dewey the encompassing Whole is revealed as the depth behind the sensory announcement; for Heidegger the Whole is opened up as a world for human dwelling under the measure of the Most High. Art sets us on the earth as it brings near the meaningful character of the Whole. And yet, whereas Nietzsche and Dewey eliminate anything beyond the world as it now is, for Heidegger a Transcendent is still an open question philosophically and an essential space is created for theophany. That is his historical mission and his essential grandeur as a thinker.

Aside from the fact that the restoration of the thing rather than encounter with the human other is the center of his focus, one thing for which Heidegger could be faulted in his meditations on art is the absence of any discussion of the temporal arts—and that despite the centrality of the notion of time for his thought about Being. Perhaps, however, there is a connection between his neglect of reflection on the human other and his ignoring of dramatic art, in which the person is the center. But what about music, the pure articulation of time in and through sound? About that he says, to my knowledge, absolutely nothing significant. I find that astonishing. Van Gogh's painting of a pair of peasant's shoes, the Greek temple, and nature poetry or poetry about poetry are his primary focus when discussing the arts. Why this fixation on things? Why this neglect of the person? Why this ignoring of music?

Recall especially the close connection discerned by Plato and Aristotle between music and morality, with music sinking most deeply into the soul and affecting our disposition to behave. If language gives focus to our felt dwelling in the world, music presents the tonality of that very indwelling. Aside from architecture, which is the pervasive art form in every civilization, and film, which is the distinctive art form of our culture, music pervades our culture as it did no other. But one has only to scan the radio channels surrounding any of our large cities to find one or perhaps two classical channels. The dominant music forms today both express and give shape to the felt tonality of dwelling in the world of the twentieth-century West. And those musical forms, along with the culture they articulate, are rapidly spreading throughout the world. When I was in Germany during the fall of the Berlin wall one of my expatriate American colleagues remarked: "You can't stop rock and roll!" That is worlds removed from the culture articulated by Bach, Mozart, Vivaldi, and Beethoven. The world of enframing is a world expressed by a music of a self-indulgent wallowing in uncultivated feelings. But music itself expresses most deeply our mode of being in time.

# XI

# CONCLUSION

In conclusion, let me summarize, clarify, and extend my leading contentions, focusing discussion on the interrelation of form and what I am calling *the aesthetic center*.[1] In so doing, I will rehearse the primary evidences on which I have rested throughout. I have been developing a series of related theses: first, that human nature is culture creating, condemned by its nature to giving form, to shaping by choice, in itself and its offspring, the potential chaos that ontological openness sets on an animal base; second, that the region aesthetics addresses is the heart as the developed center between intellect, will, and sensibility, whose correlate is significant presences; and third, that aesthetic form plays a significant role in shaping that center.

As my most fundamental point of departure, I have maintained that the field of experience is by nature bipolar: on the one hand there is the ever present and fully actual field of sensa, which rises up out of our desirous organism in interaction with its environment; on the other hand there is the empty reference to the whole of what is via the all-inclusive notion of being, which sets us at an infinite distance from that environment. That is the founding structure of what Hegel called Subjective Spirit. The distance established by reference to the Whole poses for us by nature a twofold task: linking the biologically given plenum with the emptily given Whole through eidetic description and interpretation, and choosing to act among the possibilities provided by the given and our understanding of it. As interpretations and choices play in relation to the biologically given over time and the empty space between the sensuously manifest Now and the Whole gets filled with what we call culture in the widest sense of the term, felt proclivities develop so that some features in that total field of awareness draw near and become significant presences while others recede into relative indifference. We have come to call the capacity for interpretation *intellect,* and the capacity for choosing, *will,* while the region of felt proclivities and significant presences has been named the *heart.* It is in this latter region that we find the aesthetic.

The dominant tradition underscores moral and intellectual development. Most people have emphasized the moral and downplayed the intellectual, while academics have emphasized the intellectual. In theological circles there has been a stress on the primacy of orthodoxy; in the last half of the twentieth century, there has been a counterstress on the primacy of orthopraxy.[2] However, theologian Hans Urs von Balthasar has called attention to the priority, going back into the Old Covenant and still present centrally in theology until the end of the thirteenth century, of what we might call—following the orthodoxy and orthopraxy emphases—ortho-aesthetic, a right sense of things, a right modality of felt presence.[3] Ortho-aesthetic plays in relationship to both intellectual and practical operations; and, in fact, the intellectual and the practical are, for the most part, rooted in and sustained by the aesthetic. Interestingly enough, in this emphasis theologian Balthasar parallels many of the observations advanced by secularist John Dewey. As we have seen, for Dewey the aesthetic is integral experience. It provides the sensibility that generates moral rules and practices and suggests comprehensive interpretations. It opens out into a sense of the depth of the world surrounding the pragmatic surface of experience.[4] This region of integral experience is, again, what I am calling the heart. I have attempted to show throughout how the aesthetic operates at the center of the thinkers we have considered.

In this conclusion I want to treat the aesthetic at three levels: the sensory field as the primary field for the operation of the arts, the field of culture, which provides the world of meaning brought to expression in the arts, and the all-encompassing field opened up by our reference to the whole. These correspond to Heidegger's notions of Earth, of World, and of Mystery as they come to presence in the work of art and address the heart.[5] In my reflections I am following Heidegger's *Schritt zurück,* a reflective step back, from philosophy as generally practiced, into "the ground of metaphysics" in our mode of being present to things. And, in the Heideggerian manner, the focus on "the things themselves" has allowed us to mine the tradition of thought in such a way that certain conventional ways of understanding are loosened up by being brought back to their founding modes of givenness, thereby uncovering alternative lines of thought. Hence the approach I have taken—appearances to the contrary notwithstanding—involves not simply reporting the opinions of philosophers nor an eclectic sampling of various positions, but the extraction of the phenomenological yield from the ore of each system, attempting to show how things are manifest within the perspective of each thinker.

In the process of concluding exposition, since the levels we have considered interpenetrate to form the total field of experience, it has been difficult to separate them completely. Consequently—and appropriately in a work dealing with aesthetic—this final exposition will be musical in structure. It will have three movements. And its development is not so much linear as spiral, returning again and again to the same themes, but each time at a higher level and consequently with varying emphases. In my execution I will bring in at different times different voices we have heard throughout this work: Heidegger, Plato, and Kant will take the main parts; but Aristotle, Nietzsche, Hegel, Dewey, and Albertus Magnus will join the chorus. And, indeed, at the deepest level we will from time to time hear from Martin Buber. At each level I will first review the fundamental features of that level and then link it to aesthetic considerations.

## The Sensory Field

Consider first the sensory field. It involves a bodily based presentation of the appearance of other bodily individuals in the surrounds of our own bodies within thresholds set up by our biological apparatus, mediated by the needs of our organisms and thus shot through with biological desire. Our body carves out a field of limited manifestness from the totality of influences impacting it from the environment for the purpose of fostering its own natural ends of growth, sustenance, and reproduction. Plato called such a field of appearance a Cave in which the intellectual soul was buried; Nietzsche called it a lie; Hegel considered it a hard rind that had to be penetrated with effort; Heidegger considered it, parallel to the work of intellect, both a revealing and concealing. What is shown is sufficient for our biological adjustment; what is concealed can, at one level, be progressively dug out by the tandem work of intellectual inference and active experimentation.

Vision displays an apparently empty space separating stable objects from the eye of the viewer, whereas reflection and experimentation show that the space is full and the objects significantly more dynamic at levels beyond immediate experience. The visual field appears as it does, first of all, in order to meet the organic needs of the perceiver, so that what appears visually is no epistemically neutral datum but is powerfully affect laden, immediately evoking organically based appetites. The visual field is, as it were, a luminous bubble blown by the nervous system, making a certain type of appearance possible so that an animal being can have a functional space available to meet its needs. Though vision is the lead sense, it plays in relation to the audile and olfactory fields and, most basically, the gustatory and tactual, for its mode of appearance aims at satisfying the desire for food or mate, which have to be tactually apprehended to fulfill such needs.[6] The field of the senses is thus, as I said, a synesthetic-kinesthetic whole of selective appearance shot through with desire and constructed to fulfill the needs of the perceiving organism. Its mode of revelation conceals the wholeness of what is encountered within that field, with the appearing things subserving organic need.

But in spite of the truth involved in Nietzsche's claim, the sensuous field cannot be entirely a lie, since it provides what the organism needs for its survival and prospering. And the organism itself is a functioning whole that constructs, from the materials available in its environment, a system of instruments for self-formation, self-sustenance, self-repair, and reproduction. Thus its mode of appearance *expresses* the inwardness of desire that surges up out of the organic base. For the perceiving animal, the sensory surface furnishes the basis for an organic dashboard knowledge, a mode of display sufficient to learn what to push, pull, and turn in order to get the required output.

Such a field of limited manifestness is the enduring biological pole of the field of awareness. Meditation on these considerations should lead to a sense of the strangeness of the taken-for-granted sensory givenness. Focused on this appetitively mediated surface, we live our lives within this cave, this internally luminous, externally opaque bubble. The sense of strangeness in the everyday opens up the field both for philosophic penetration and for artistic creation, the former seeking to comprehend, the latter to evoke the sense of strangeness in order to haunt the everyday with the awareness of that More which everydayness conceals.

This sensuous field is the field of operation of the arts and the basis of aesthetic experience in general. In discussing the aesthetic, Kant underscored the distinctive human capacity for disengaging the perceptual object within that field from organismic desire so as to provide a condition of what he called "unconstrained favoring." It culminates in a feeling of "disinterested satisfaction" in the epiphany of the beautiful beyond what is merely agreeable to our animal nature. Not coerced by biological desire, without interest in anything other than sheer sensory appearance, one is able to bring into focus the *form* of the display, the peculiar togetherness of sensory elements, where, in the first sense of the term, we have learned to find beauty.

Plato isolated certain features in the form of presentation in his *Republic* when he distinguished, in Socrates' purgation of the arts, between the referents of poetry—namely, gods and heroes—and its aesthetic features—namely, musical modes and instrumental timbres. In shifting attention to purely aesthetic considerations, Socrates pointed to two basic kinds of music, Apollonian and Dionysian. The Dionysian evokes the organismic desires. The Apollonian reveals harmony, order, proportion, and grace and produces those same properties in the emotions of the perceiver. The differentiation between those two modes turns, in the perceiver, upon the distinction between luxurious wallowing in good somatic feelings brought about by pleasing objects and a turning around of the soul so that its education at this level culminates in an appreciation of beautiful things themselves. Plato goes further in this direction, transferring the Apollonian aesthetic from the temporal arts of poetry and music to the spatial arts of architecture, painting, and design in the areas of clothing, furniture, and utensils. I must underscore painting here, since what is at stake is not the mirroring of surface alluded to in book 10 of the *Republic*, but the aesthetic features of composition. Surrounded visually and audiely from birth to death with an aesthetic ambiance characterized by order, proportion, harmony, and grace, the citizenry will have its dispositions so tuned as to supply a fit matrix for the emergence of nous opened to the harmonics of the larger cosmic order within which our sensory environment is located and to which we are by nature directed. What is crucial here is, as Nietzsche observed, "compelling the chaos within to take on form," becoming simple, holding opposites in tension without effort, achieving "the grand style."

Regarding the object of aesthetic focus, Kant spoke of form and Plato gave us a list of formal properties. Aristotle, in the restricted region of tragic art, presented us with what I regard as the most fundamental feature of aesthetic form, its organicity. Aristotle said that, just as an organism has in itself all that it needs for its functioning as a whole and nothing irrelevant to that functioning, so also a tragedy should be such that everything that needs to be there to produce the total effect is there and nothing that is there is irrelevant to that end. So the aesthetic character of a tragedy lies in a mean between aesthetic defect and aesthetic excess. This is one way in which art partly imitates and partly completes nature, conceived of here as what occurs outside art. The artist abstracts from all the details of what might actually occur in order to select and organize only what fits within the aesthetic whole. Of course, in focusing on tragic art, Aristotle has gone beyond the sensuous form of our immediate concern to the expression of the inwardness of character in the sensory forms of language and gesture. However, that observation of the organicity of a good tragic work can be generalized to cover every work of art. Organicity is *the* defining property of the work of art: the work functions as a whole and is thus fresh and live and not dead or mechanical. That links it back to the naturally organic. Indeed, the link between the organic and art is so close in Aristotle that, before Kant called attention to it, Aristotle used the causal factors in human artefaction to read the four causes back into nature. And as Plotinus noted—in this he was copied by Aquinas—art imitates nature in her mode of production. Two factors are linked in that observation: art operates like organic nature by shaping materials to reach a preconceived goal; but also, and more significant for our immediate purpose, the art product at its best has the character of organicity. We could consider "abstract" music here— non-text-accompanying, nonprogrammatic, nonreferentially titled music— a fugue, for example. Such music is an autonomous growth from the nature of the human being as culture-producing animal—an organism that freely creates organic objects. It refers immediately to nothing beyond itself. It is sheer sensuous display of an organic whole, resembling nothing externally presented in nature. And I should extend that along the lines of Walter Pater's by now oft cited claim that all art seeks the status of music (i.e., seeks the production of aesthetic form). Matisse observed similarly that photography freed painting to be painting, so that the latter would not simply be a mirroring of the pregiven but the production of visual form, the organized togetherness of visual elements that may or may not draw directly from previously observed natural form.[7] But whether painting does so draw or not, it is the organicity of the form that makes it good art.

However, Aristotle made another remark that puts even abstract art back into the orbit of mimesis and links up with Plato's focus on aesthetic form: it is the startling claim that music is the most imitative of art forms. What it imitates, Aristotle says, is *ethos,* usually translated as "character," but actually focused on what is most intimate to character, the wellsprings of action in felt proclivities to act. Shaping that is the chief task of ethics. Music produces states of mind, feelings akin to those aroused in encounter with nonartistic situations. (I hasten to add that the likeness also includes immense difference: sorrowful music like Ravel's *Pavane for a Dead Princess* is akin to, but also a world's remove from, sorrow at the death of one's own daughter.) The imitative character does not lie in the audile medium as such—or better, the character of the musically audile is not simply heard sound but the emotional tuning accompanying it, since sensation occurs in function of organic desire. Though we must note that such desire is transformed by rising into the full human field of culturally mediated, personally appropriated reference to the Whole that allows the unconstrained favoring of the form of sensuous display detached from physiological need.

Kant noted that the disinterested satisfaction brought about by concentration on the form of sensory presentation produces a certain quickening of the sense of distinctively human life, a life of the interplay between imagination rooted in the sensory and understanding that provides the basis for aesthetic distancing from biological desire. On the part of the artist, Kant noted that the aesthetic idea emerges from the animation of all the faculties and culminates in a work characterized by liveliness, freshness, organicity. For him the whole region of the aesthetic exhibits— in artist, work, and audience—an awakening, an animation, a quickening of the sense of the distinctive life of the rational animal. The region of beauty, located in the distinterested appreciation of the form of the sensuous, is, for Kant, *the* peculiarly human region, for animals have sensations and hypothetical pure intelligences would have thoughts; only humans can attend to the form of the sensuous display.

Thinking along these lines, Dewey worked the link between art and the organic further and more holistically. The organicity involved in the work of art is not simply derived from observing living things; it is also derived from the fact that artist and audience are themselves organic. That is, human beings, who both make and appreciate works of art, are organically functioning wholes. As such, our minds are not simply apart from the physiological—though there is obviously a sense in which they are apart, and thus our propensity to nonholistic, abstract forms of living; our minds are a significant aspect of our psychophysical totality. What we have come to call *reason* is *ratio*, or ratio, a matter of recognizing or becoming attuned to proportionate, harmonic relations, rooted in the biologically given environment, as they fit within the context of the harmonic totality, the ordered cosmos, to which mind is an aspiration. Organically functioning wholes— living forms which are organically formative processes—are such only because of their capacity to adjust to the totality of the environments within which alone they can live. So also, at the highest level of the organism, with reason as the capacity to apprehend and adjust to the total context of human existence.

It is in this direction that we could assimilate Feuerbach's criticism of Christian thinkers whose dream of being elsewhere distracts them from being here and makes them ashamed of being embodied.[8] We could also appreciate Nietzsche's observations about contempt for the earth exhibited by what became the mainline of Platonism and by Christianity insofar as it became Platonism for the masses. Being a psychophysical whole, an organism alive with a sense of the encompassing Whole or, in biblical terms, made from the clay or the slime of the earth and animated with a divine breath, the human being belongs to the earth. Art underscores the goodness of that belonging.

As Heidegger observed, in art earth rises up in sensuousness to bring the sensuous features to a mode of appearance they do not enjoy in our usual more pragmatic modes of disclosure. Color is most fully manifest as color in the painting. In our other modes of relation, the sensuous is strictly subsidiary. In ordinary language use, sound recedes from attention to bring the communicated into focus. This is the case in an audience's following what a speaker has to say, unless there are those who have lost interest and all that registers is the ongoing droning of the speaker's voice. But in poetic speech, sonority is part of the message and no mere vehicle. It is sonority that brings what is communicated into a more intensive mode of presence by entering into the communicated. And, indeed, it is a certain style of delivery that turns ordinary speech into a kind of art form that enhances the presence of what is communicated.

## The Cultural World

What I have attended to thus far is the sensuous field within which art works appear, and the functioning of art works within that field. But I had to move beyond that in several of my observations, and my last considerations introduced the larger whole of human awareness through the observation of language. Language bears witness to our essentially belonging to a tradition. It involves a peculiar capacity to attend differently than in an animal mode to the Now of sensory actuality and plenitude, relating that plenum to the nonsensory—ultimately and always horizontally to the emptily intended Whole. Language also allows one to absent oneself from the presently given in order to roam over the past in reverie, over the future in hope, over the purely fanciful in imagination, or over the abstract in thought. This enables the work of art to refer through the sensuous form to something beyond the sensuous.

Heidegger spoke of the work of art as a gestalt, a form appearing in the rift brought into being by what he referred to as "fighting the battle of Earth and World." We have considered Earth in the rising up of sensuousness to a new focus in the work of art; but as Earth interplays with World, it becomes native soil, suffused with a sense of belonging to a given, sensorily present place where people together inhabit the world of meaning brought into being by their tradition. World appears over time as the world of a people set on the earth. It comes into being as a requirement of the bipolar structure of the field of experience.

By nature the distinctively human pole, reference to Being, is vacuous, infinite in the sense of indeterminate, but also in the sense of emptily intending all determinations. The ontological reference hollows out a depth behind the animal surface but simultaneously opens up an indeterminate set of possibilities for interpretation and action. The guided circle of animal presentation, the security of instinctively following out natural purpose, is opened up in human beings to the precariousness of the possibilities for human choice. Ontological reference blows the lid off of human instinctual life. The ontological animal becomes the chaotic animal. So Nietzsche's admonition: "Compel the chaos that is within to take on form!" is the challenge to individuals and communities posed by the structure of human nature. The distinctively human task is to develop a coherent mode of understanding in relation to the totality of what is given, to provide a set of related choices for action, and to develop a sense of felt significance that can integrate an individual over a lifetime and a community over generations. Through those felt modes we learn to dwell in a world, to in-habit it. The choices that created those spontaneities are passed on to others as those who pass them on pass on. They become what Hegel called Objective Spirit, Spirit arising in subjectivity but enduring in objectivity beyond the lifetime of its originators. However, the choices of those long dead appear to those who are born into them, not as matters of choice at all, but as the way things are. Hence the tendency to resist any change in traditional forms. But the plurality of such worlds is the clearest proof that they are, in the broad sense in which Heidegger uses the expression, decisions, matters of choice.

Belonging to a world involves in-habitation, having patterns of interpretation and response developed that have become customary, habitual, and that allow things to draw near or to be set at a distance. Indwelling in a world articulates the heart of our personal being. Individual beings appear as endowed with a significance that corresponds to their meaningful place in that world. And such appearance can be located either in natural objects, in works of art, or, arguably, also in transcendent "objects."

One should stress creativity and adaptability in world construction, especially since the philosophic tradition has been dominated theoretically from early times by the notion of nonevolving species, more recently by the notion of sheer mechanism, and in the order of behavior by the idea of a fixed pattern.[9] If the organism furnishes the model of a rational system, exhibiting what existential coherence means, changes in its environment establish a disequilibrium that calls for flexible adaptability and leads to higher integrations. Human creativity introduces another level of disequilibrium, potentially and at times actually chaotic, but also potentially and at times actually fruitful in generating alternate forms of order in keeping with the spiral rather than circular repetitiveness of the ever-creative cosmos within which we are inserted.

By reason of the mediations of being formed within a world, our typical knowledge is, as in the animal mode, still "dashboard knowledge," but now extended beyond the functional circle of animal awareness by a tradition of interpretation and practice. Growing up is a matter of learning input and output correlations within the functional circle of our animal based, culturally mediated awareness. "Growing up" is largely a matter of learning to glance, stereotype, and respond in routinized ways that allow both for coordination of groups and for adjustment to the physical environment. Routinized attention defocuses sensory surface until it becomes subsidiary to our modes of adjustment. Furthermore, such attention also stands in tension between the disclosed and the merely passed on, so that it is replete with mere hearsay knowledge or claims to knowledge. This is precisely Plato's Cave of *doxa*, in which we are chained by nature to sensa and by culture to modes of interpretation. It is Heidegger's world of average everydayness, of *das Man*, the anonymous "one" or "they." It is Hegel's hard rind of everyday surface appearance, extended from the sensa to cultural interpretation, which covers up much more than it reveals and calls forth art to establish a more fully revelatory appearance of what underlies it. It is also related to Buber's "world of It," of experience and use, the relation to which he called *orientation*, knowing our way around in a region, be it pragmatic or intellectual.[10] Now it is absolutely crucial to see, as these various thinkers have seen, that this "real world" is precisely an appearance, constructed by our animal nature, our cultural upbringing, and our past modes of attention, functionally revealing, but more deeply concealing what is fully there. It is in this orientational world of It that one's awareness of the Thou as the hidden fullness that rises up to address us in nature and in art, as well as in other persons can disappear. In the It-world, as Buber noted, "morality" can come to hide the face of our fellowman and religion the face of God;[11] in it, from age to age religion takes the lead in perfecting the armor of invulnerability against the revelation that the Bible claims can speak to us in the everyday. But in the name of the Book, we look away from where we really are. We fail to read "the signs of the times." We fall in love with "the world," even and perhaps especially the world of Christendom.[12]

Born into a cultural world, every human individual is stamped in a peculiar way by genetic endowment and cultural upbringing, which together furnish the concrete possibilities for individual choices. Choices are made possible and necessary because, by reason of the founding reference to the Whole, each human being is an I, set at a distance from all determinations, from every objectifiable feature of its own total selfhood.[13] Hence emerges the distinction between the I and the Me. Genetic and cultural stamping furnishes the nonchosen Me. The history of choice based on this stamping furnishes a variation, the Me I have chosen to be from the possibilities afforded by my situation. The past sediments in the space provided by my nature between the sensuous plenum and empty reference to the Whole to form the historically constituted Me. At any given moment that peculiar Me is the artist's material given to the I to shape within the limits of its concrete possibilities.

The center of the Me is the heart, that which is closest to the I. And the I tends to move in the direction of the heart's desires. The heart is fixed on what is personally closest—though perhaps spatially far away—around which whatever else that appears falls into circles of decreasing relevance, shading off into indifference. Heart develops over time: anticipation and recall are governed automatically by that on which my heart is set. There are regions within me of anonymous functionings, beginning with my physiology; there are registrations of past experiences, development of motor skills—like being able to play a musical instrument—that may not lie close to my heart. Yet what is close is that which spontaneously solicits my attention.

To repeat, cultural formation opens up the concrete possibilities each I has for further determination of the stamp given it, without its asking, by genetics and culture. In the past, realization of this fact evoked *pietas*, a sense of gratitude for unpayable debts to parents, to country, and to God for allowing to come into being what would otherwise lay fallow within general human possibilities.[14] How many potentially great classical pianists roamed the jungles thousands of years ago, none of whom could actualize that potentiality prior to the development of the instrument, the technique, and the repertoire afforded by the tradition of classical piano? *Pietas* expresses what Hegel called *substantial freedom*, a certain fulfillment brought about by identification with what would otherwise seem to be simply other, alien to subjectivity. But the freedom provided by the primordial distance of the I—what Hegel called *formal* or *abstract freedom*—makes possible the deliberate abandonment of *pietas* and the deliberate attempt to repudiate as much as possible of the formation given to us by culture. Absolutized, it can dissolve most of the obvious external institutions. Today we see it expressed in the formlessness filling the contemporary sections of our museums of fine art. I choose to do with Me whatever I choose, for whatever reasons. The last two considerations have already moved us ahead to the aesthetic considerations of this part of my recapitulation.

Brought up in a cultural world, humans have regions of distinctive concerns: pragmatic, cognitive, and moral regions carved out by the tradition. And as these, along with biological need, absorb most of our attention, sensory surface is usually subsidiary to them, parallel to the way in which that surface functions in animal life. In opening up access to the aesthetic, Kant not only separated it from animal need, he also disengaged it from these other concerns that emerge in the course of cultural development. In the aesthetic mode one does not view an object in terms of the use to which it can be put or in terms of its providing occasion for some form of inference or explanation, or its giving us some form of moral instruction. Kant pushes very hard to achieve what Gadamer has called *aesthetic differentiation,* a complete lifting off of the form of sensory display from any other consideration, physiological or cultural.[15]

But for Kant, the defocusing of attention from any form of interest is only an initial, though quite important move. He himself viewed the appreciation of beauty more holistically. Disinterested focus on the form of sensory togetherness gives us the entrance ticket to the region of the beautiful. To this end, Kant isolated what he called *free beauty*, as found in bird plumage, seashells, arabesque drawings, or in purely instrumental music—in the appreciation of which, as he said, there is no antecedent notion of what the object ought to be, no concept governing our judgment, no other end than appreciation. Beauty is found in sheer sensory display. But such focus by itself gives us only what is for Kant ultimately trivial beauty.

Having established the entrance ticket to the realm of the beautiful in the form of sensuous display, Kant goes beyond that to the notion of *dependent beauty* and ultimately to the notion of *the ideal of beauty*. Most of what we consider beautiful is accompanied by some concept that refers us to a nonsensory content, articulated in the field of meaning of a given culture, of which the sensory display is an expression. In this case, the peculiar togetherness of the sensory features is governed by its suitability to what is being displayed. So, for example, Lawrence Welk's "champagne music" would be inappropriate accompaniment for the text of St. Matthew's Passion. The beauty of the music would here be dependent on what it brings to sensuous presence. The function of the sensuous form is to give to the referent a closeness it would not otherwise have in merely prosaic presentation.

For Kant the highest form of dependent beauty is what he calls "the ideal of beauty." It is found in an empirically derived archetype of the sensory presentation of the human form expressing moral qualities. In Kant's view of things, it is the moral that is the highest level of human experience, linking the phenomenal—the appearance of things relative to us—to the noumenal—being-in-itself beyond all appearance. But again, what makes the display of moral qualities in the human form beautiful is not the moral qualities; it is the *form* of the display. Now in this case, such display is expressive of something of what a noble human is as rising to presence in sensation, but simultaneously sinking back into unencompassable depth.

For Kant, in nature it is the organism that is a primary locus of such expressiveness. He calls this feature expressed in the sensory appearance of the organism "purposiveness" *(Zweckmäßigkeit)*, which he also claims to be basic to the aesthetic object. Even free beauty in nature expresses something of the belonging together of the display and the human capacity for perception of that display, as if the display were arranged for our aesthetic perception, intended by what underlies sensory surface. The deepest aspect of that belonging together lies in the founding human reference to the totality Kant terms *Vernunft*, a drive toward the totality of what-is, a drive realized most deeply in the moral disposition to act according to principle by arranging the empirically given to conform to our moral disposition.

Kant's initial disinterested focus on the form of sensory presentation, even as it operates in dependence on what it expresses, is the background to the nineteenth-century movement of art for art's sake, which appeared (for example) in France in Théophile Gautier and in England in Walter Pater. Pater's observation, often cited, that all art seeks the status of music is aligned with such aestheticism, the aim of which is to fill one's life as full as possible with a multiplicity of aesthetic experiences.[16] Artistically displayed form, whether in the free or dependent mode, becomes one's ultimate commitment. All life can be considered "aesthetically" in the sense of detached appreciation.

For Heidegger, on the contrary, art perishes in purely aesthetic experience.[17] And Kierkegaard leveled a powerful and persuasive attack on such an "aesthetic life."[18] Kant too recognized the problem of immoral artistic dilettantes.[19] We must distinguish between aestheticism and a more holistic mode of being moved. Art, seen in a larger perspective, requires participation, a holistic sharing both in what is communicated and in the mode of presentation as well. And as Hegel noted, it was in art that a people presented their deepest wisdom, their sense of what it means for humans to belong to the Whole.

The mode of presentation is originally meant to communicate not simply the content but also the proper mode of participative response. The work of art fuses sensory form and reference into a single gestalt wherein the sensory form brings about the disposition proper to the referent. The referent becomes a real presence instead of a merely intellectually intended or sensorily noted object. More than merely content, the artistic mode of presentation establishes a peculiar "feel" for the content, the way one is present to it. One does not only affirm the content; it becomes a living presence; it touches us; it moves our heart; we share in it. We can come to have not only what Newman would call a *notional assent,* but also something like a *real assent* (i.e., an assent that entails a realization).[20] A purely aesthetic approach will yield something like a real assent without a real assent. The aesthetic shows us something of what it is to live a belief, not in conduct alone but in the sense of realization, of attaining to significant presence, that lies at the basis of modes of conduct and belief—only art itself does this, not in the mode of belief, but in the mode of "as if." The problem is both in appreciatively distinguishing the aesthetic and in vitally relating it to the other aspects of human experience.

For Heidegger, the art work, within which Earth rises up in sensuousness as native soil, opens up simultaneously a World of inhabitance; it solicits the larger sense of indwelling in a world with its peculiar "feel" and is not simply a matter of isolated feelings aroused by isolated objects. The struggle between Earth and World, parallel to the struggle between closure and disclosure, creates the rift in the everyday surface, the lightning flash that creates the peculiar space for the form of the work. Art's isolation (e.g., through framing techniques) places the work outside ordinary experience—Plato's Cave, Hegel's hard rind of everyday appearance, Buber's world of It—but in order to bring us back to the whole of that experience in a different way. The work of art can bring about a transformation of one's general attunement, one's deep-seated way of holding oneself toward things, and thereby affect one's disposition to act. As Heidegger remarked, great art creates such world space that through it even the ordinary appears extraordinary. In Dewey's surprising way of putting it, art brings us from the focus of ordinary life to the fringe that always surrounds it. In so doing, it awakens what he calls "the mystical" as a sense of belonging to the universe, introducing us to a world beyond this world that is nonetheless the depth of this very world.

An artist may be interested in giving expression in his or her work to aesthetic surface or to the quotidian or the pornographic or the patriotic or the mystical or the idiosyncratic or whatever. What I want to emphasize is the founding structures that make that possible, whether or not they come to focal awareness in the artist or in the art produced. Indeed, those same structures make possible the observer's approach to the work of art, so that one could bring a superficial or a more or less reflective and encompassing awareness to bear on any given work. Nonetheless, from the point of view of art, the quality of treatment, the handling of aesthetic surface is what is crucial, even for an artisan wholly absorbed in that surface. And that can evoke appreciation from the most reflectively developed awareness, which has, so to speak, caught up with its own grounding in habitual lived direction toward the encompassing.

Aesthetic deepening depends on initiation into aesthetic community. As both Hume and Kant noted, the presentation of exemplars helps shape our ability to make meaningful discriminations among different types of aesthetic presentations. However, it may also tend to lock us into what has been unless we learn the lesson of essential plurality and novelty. As many dispositional conservatives never seem to learn, classics had to come into being; and when they did so, they were novelties. A study of the plurality of classics teaches us the perception of meaningful form in different arts, different genres, different styles. It frees us from our confining preconceptions and permits us the inner space to let the new work work upon us to show what it can do in comparison with previous forms. But as it does this, it also builds aesthetic community based on a distancing from our private selves and an adhesion to values sharable in principle by all properly attuned participants. For Kant this is the chief value of art. As civilization advances, people are given over more and more to communication rooted in the aesthetic, both in creating aesthetic forms and in verbally articulating and intellectually evaluating such experiences.

As I indicated in the beginning of this book, art works enter into a culture over the millennia following the articulation of the field of the senses. I laid out a preliminary system of the arts in terms of three parameters: the senses appealed to, the frameworks of space and time (separate and in their interrelations), and language, which situates the sensorily given within the culturally prearticulated Whole. I tried, within that preliminary division, to lay out some of the eidetic features of the different art forms. Plato and Aristotle advanced that endeavor, tying it to their own advancement in the understanding of the Whole that deepened and situated interpretively our preliminary descriptive presentation. Hegel extended that. But Dewey in particular warns against such divisions, calling attention to the concrete interplay of all the parameters of experience in each of the art forms. Heeding his warning, we nevertheless must note—as Dewey did—the focal priority of some parameters in certain art forms and in different styles. Thus, for example, the sculptural object is a spatial form appealing focally to vision, though it surely draws on associative values derived from the other senses, especially touch, and the other parameters in our division.

But our preliminary division paid no attention either to what is communicated or to a possible value hierarchy between the arts. Hegel in particular argued for a hierarchy based on the relative limitations in communicative possibilities among the art forms. Poetry ranked the highest because its linguistic medium had the greatest possible range. Music was second because it spans the whole range of emotional life—as Plato said, music sinks most deeply into the soul; and Aristotle claimed it the most imitative because most able to produce inner ethos. But in both cases this concerns the emotional life, or the "depths," of the soul. The "heights" are occupied by *nous*—or at least so it seems. But in Plato, Eros rises above *nous*, so that there is an emotional range in Plato that extends from the depths to the heights. Schopenhauer and Nietzsche argued for the priority of music over the apprehension of "Platonic Forms" or over the Apollonian. They both fall on this issue in the Platonic-Neoplatonic line of attending to that which exists *epekeina tes ousias,* beyond the correlate to nous in the Forms. In all cases, the visual arts stand lower in the hierarchy. Kant is an exception regarding the place of music: for him it is the least communicative, poised on the borderline between the agreeable and the beautiful.

Appearing within a world of communally constituted meaning, a work of art takes on form by drawing one from surface to depth and encompassment. But then, the world of meaning changes as time goes by or as the piece is approached by one who does not occupy the world from which it stems and to which it speaks. In the latter case it becomes a mere at-hand product and, as Heidegger said, a work that has been. In Buber's terms, it passes from form to object.[21] Apart from the purely aesthetic modality of a Walter Pater, the work of art can be studied in terms of the scientific aspects of the composition of its materials, in terms of the exhibition of techniques of construction, of its fitting within the history of the development of the artist's style, which can itself be located within a comparative schema of different artistic styles, in different epochs and cultures; it can further be considered in terms of autobiographical and sociological factors. It becomes an object of art history. In Dewey's way of putting it, it passes from work that effects the integration of the properly disposed viewer through disclosing a depth behind the surface, to become an art product, a sensorily present object in space and time, another mere thing accumulating dust for the cleaning personnel, which begins Heidegger's exposition of the thinghood of the work of art. But for those who learn to preserve the working of the work of art by standing in the space of its manifestness, it can bring about a sense of the ontological mystery.

## Transcendence

Mention of the ontological mystery leads into my final section. It is at this point that I want to focus more closely on the third feature of the context within which the aesthetic operates: that of our natural, empty reference to the Whole via the notion of being and its relation to the heart —though I could not help invoking it at other points in my exposition. The opposite pole to the sensory is that fundamental reference to the totality of what-is, expressed in the "is" of the judgment that articulates the notion of Being, outside of which there is nothing. By nature this reference is initially empty; but it provides, as an aspect of its anticipation of the totality, an anticipation of the whole of space and time that makes possible abstraction of universal forms and thus linguistic expression that refers an encountered form to all its instances wherever in space and whenever in time they might be found. It likewise furnishes the unrestricted generality of the principle of noncontradiction, which makes possible the development of inference and the building up of a progressively extended and consistent view of the Whole. Further, it raises the question of that which might exist beyond the finitude of our grasp. The grounding presence of this reference to the totality makes necessary our interpretatively locating whatever we encounter within that totality: what kinds of things appear in the sensory field and out of what depths do they appear? Pried loose from the Now by that reference, just as we are forced to interpret, so we are "condemned to choose" from the possibilities afforded by the givens of our biology and our reflective capacity. The congealing of interpretive and practical decisions settles into the initially empty space between the Now of sensation and the Whole of what is to constitute a cultural world that opens up pathways for acting, thinking, and feeling for those who have been assimilated to it as a second nature manifest most clearly in one's native language.

The notion of being is contracted in every judgment to the being on which we are focusing attention and to the peculiar manifest features in virtue of which we are attending. Nonetheless, it refers us beyond the limitation of the mode of manifestness—sensory and intellectual—to the underlying wholeness of the thing encountered. In the case of encounter with the expressivity of an organism or a person or a work of art where the way the sensory appears gives access to the nonsensory, which rises to manifestness, at the same time the unobserved powers and the underlying nature of a given organism recede into an ultimately unretrievable depth of which humans, distanced by nature from the dashboard surface of animal sensation and cultural mediation, can become aware. As Aquinas put it, "We do not know the essence of anything, not even of a simple fly."[22] But, beyond and essentially connected with that, the notion of being refers us to the encompassing whole surrounding the thing and ourselves as experiencing and passing judgment on it. This dual reference—to the wholeness of the encountered being within the encompassing wholeness of being itself—is the reason why we come to understand anything by fitting it into a world of meaning, the Whole as articulated by language. But language only emptily intends the ontological fullness of what in each case it partially delineates.[23]

Further, it is precisely because of our natural reference to the wholeness of each thing within the wholeness of all that we are each an I, a center referred beyond all objectification, even of the most intimate aspects of our own Me, beyond one's own heart. Each I is thus able to function as the center before which everything makes its distinctive mode of appearance and able—no, forced to take responsibility, to choose what I am to do with

Me. What I want to underscore at this point is that the reference to the Whole that founds the I is not simply neutral reference but fundamental Eros in the Platonic sense of poverty having passionate designs on plenty. If sensuous appearance occurs in function of organismic desire, the presence of the nonappearance of the plenitude of being is correlated with the peculiarity of ontological desire as passion for the absent totality. This gives the final depth dimension to the heart explored in a significant way by Augustine.[24]

Now one can make these observations, which I take to be true judgments. One might go on—bypassing contemporary dogmas about the impossibility of "onto-theo-logy"—and make responsible inferences as to the existence of an ever-present, ever-operative, and even personal Source Who is the Infinite Fullness of Being, *Ipsum esse subsistens,* imitated in finite ways by the works of His generosity, yet infinitely beyond any adequate comprehension on our part. But the modality of those judgments is impersonal. For the real life of the human being they sketch out the possibility of an all-encompassing Presence that may Itself flash through the cracks of our dashboard knowledge like lightning and transform our whole sense of things in the most radical way. If and when that happens, from then on it tends to hover in the background of all our wakefulness and may rise again from time to time in explicit presentness.

Buber reserves the term *presence* for the experience of the full gathering of the self in relation to the fullness of any encountered other, met but not comprehended, revealed as inexhaustible mystery and opening experientially to being heard as a word addressed by the Eternal Thou.[25] For Buber this is the core of biblical revelation: the world as spoken by God, the Presence Who will be present in whatever way He chooses, but whose Presence is announced in the speech that is creation.[26] If the world of It gives us orientation, the Thou is a matter of *realization.* But what is realized in meeting with the Thou is simultaneously threefold: first, the unencompassable fullness of what is encountered and second, the fullness of oneself—both standing beyond the partiality of what is available for our orientation, whether intellectually or practically, beyond the human dashboard; but the third aspect of ontological plenitude is the epiphany of the encompassing Mystery as personal address, which Buber calls the Eternal Thou. In this threefold display there is manifest a deep otherness rising to presence and receding into mystery to which we may refer intellectually—as I am now doing—but which is only available as a presence to the heart. Ontological reference gives the ultimate depth to the human heart—it reveals our heart of hearts, which is restless until its relation to the fullness of what manifests its deep otherness culminates in the coming to presence of the Eternal Thou.

We now move to our final aesthetic consideration, linked to the consideration of the deepest native concern of our hearts. Kant noted, as I have before, that in art we can give a new mode of presence to things already lying within our field of experience, like love, hate, and anger. But he also noted that it is in art that we are able to develop an imaginative-symbolic exploration of ideas deeply connected with the most fundamental interest of our reference to the Whole, ideas like the afterlife and the Four Last Things (judgment, heaven, hell, purgatory), such as we find instanced in the myths of Plato and in the works of Dante and Milton. Strictly speaking, we know virtually nothing about these things, even if we accept revelation. But the symbolic-imaginative extensions created by such poetic thinkers bring these matters close to us and bind them tightly to our mode of living as haunting presences.

However, the extended field of such exploration opens out to another kind of aesthetic experience. Kant put the aesthetic of the beautiful in contrast with the aesthetic of the sublime by setting the limited character of conceptuality exhibited in dependent beauty against the unlimited striving for totality characteristic of *Vernunft*. The contrast between the beautiful and the sublime deals with form and the transcendence of form respectively. In the latter, Kant hearkens back to the medievals and ultimately to Plotinus and Plato. Kant's own mode of philosophizing was underpinned by awe provoked by the moral law within, analyzed in the second critique. and by the starry skies above, whose exhibition of the principles of mechanical motion furnished the exemplary object of knowledge analyzed in the first critique. In the third critique, awe is presented as a peculiar aesthetic state: the simultaneous feeling of insignificance and exultation, rooted respectively in the animal and rational poles of our existence. Outside, "the starry skies above", the overwhelming character of whose vast spaces filled the pious Pascal with fear, play in relation to "the moral law within" which indicates the sublimity of our vocation as human beings. The combination of these two contrary dispositions yields awe as the sense of the sublime that transcends and locates the limited character of the appearance of the beautiful form. It is this awe that suffuses the otherwise seemingly dry and austere character of Kantian analysis and helps sustain his distinction between phenomenal surface and noumenal depth.

This hearkens back to Plato, for whom, as Heidegger noted,[27] philosophy has its pervasive and enduring principle in *thaumazein*, a state of astonishment attributed mythically to Iris, the messenger of the god Thaumas.[28] The mythic reference takes it out of the region of mere curiosity and links the philosophic enterprise to the divine. Precisely as the kind of philosopher he was, a philosopher of fully comprehensive reflectiveness, Plato wrote in such a way that the severity of conceptual elaboration always drew upon our peculiar Eros for the whole and returned his attentive readers to the world of our inhabitance through myths, imagery, and the concrete interchange between characters in dialogue. Philosophy for Plato is not simply curiosity about conceptual puzzles nor satisfaction in understanding the samenesses and differences exhibited in how things present themselves: it is rooted in ever-growing awe as the fuller context of our existence comes to light through inquiry aimed, as Socrates said, at the wholeness of each thing within the all-encompassing Whole of being.[29] Astonishment is deeply linked to the realization that we live in the cave of *doxa*, of animally grounded, culturally mediated appearance, complacently taking such appearance for reality. But it is also and simultaneously linked to the development of distinctively human Eros.[30]

Now Nietzsche saw Socrates, in his alleged influence on Euripides, to have defocused the erotic Dionysian in favor of the Apollonian and thus to have been the originator of that "aesthetic Socratism" which dominated Western existence and, in the form of science and technology, still dominates it. This focuses something important in understanding Western culture and things aesthetic, but it is one-sided. As Plato set the central focus of aesthetic consideration on beauty, Aristotle set it on the horrible presented in tragedy. Nonetheless, Platonic Eros was also Dionysiac, evoking the Dionysus of exultant creation, generating Apollonian forms. Aristotle, soberly nonerotic, won, from the objectification of the destructive Dionysus, purgation from the disorienting emotions of fear and pity, which the confrontation with destruction involves. A similar contrast between the Apollonian and the Dionysian appears in Kant's distinction between the beautiful and the sublime. What is central to a Platonic aesthetic is precisely the Dionysian, evoked by the beauty of form, but drawn beyond, ultimately toward the Whole and the Source of the Whole through the sublimation of erotic desire. For Plato art plays in the space between animal-like feelings and a sense of encompassing Beauty associated in his *Republic* with the Good, shaping such feelings into form, which ultimately gives expression to the epiphany of that encompassment. It is this that is announced in

Diotima's description of Beauty Itself as an overwhelming presence that suddenly bursts like lightning into the life of the aspirant. And in the *Phaedrus*, Socrates further claims that the privilege of this Beauty is that its presence is available through the eyes, expressed, that is, in the field of the sensuous as exceeding it. The character of that excess is indicated in the *Republic*, where the Source and End, the One/Good, is referred to as an incomparable Beauty beyond *ousia*. Here we see a move through form beyond form, whether "aesthetic" in the sensory sense or eidetic as correlate to intellect, toward that which we seek from the bottom or at the height or from the center of our psychophysical totality—all three metaphors appear in the tradition to focus on this feature. The move is in a direction laid out in Kant's notion of *Vernunft* as a drive toward totality and which I ground in the notion of Being. All form—sensory or intellectual, natural or artistic—points to a Beyond that it ultimately expresses to a psyche that is not fulfilled either in sensory or intellectual achievement, but only in dwelling with the fullness of one's being in relation to that ultimately mysterious Source of the all.

Kant and Plato clash over the limitation and extension of the notion of beauty. Plato follows out the structures of the field of experience in the *Symposium*, where Socrates presents Diotima's Ladder of Beauty. In the human case, the beauty of sensuous display stands in tension with the beauty of character. Kant places the ideal of beauty in their relationship, though *beauty* said of character is, for Kant, a metaphoric extension of the term, which applies properly to the form of sensuous display alone. Plato goes on to extend the term to the beauty of institutions and laws, since these are what shape the beauty of character. And both the beauty of sensuous display and the beauty of character, along with what shapes it, are measured by universal principles, whether in the mathematical sciences of material ordering or in the philosophic sciences of psychic structure grounding ethico-political shaping. Hence Plato goes on to speak of the beauty of the sciences. Kant employs the term *elegance* here and again repudiates the metaphoric extension of the term *beauty*. And yet what is displayed in the natural and human sciences provokes his awe, the subjective correlate to what he calls the sublime: the starry skies above, the moral law within. Kant reduces the being-drawn-out in this experience to an exalted mode of self-experience. What is sublime is, in relation to the vastness of nature's display, human thought's ability to exceed it, or, in relation to the power of nature's display, human moral destiny. This is linked to Kant's reduction of the *summum bonum* from its traditional location in the loving vision of God to the coincidence of happiness with deservedness to be happy in the just person. For Kant, God as omniscient, omnipotent, and just judge is the condition of the possibility of this coincidence. Platonic intoxication with the vision of Beauty Itself as the object of philosophic aspiration and the linkage of that Beauty to encounter with a divine Person in religious experience are repudiated by Kant as "enthusiasm," which generates the pretension of special insight and superstitious practices. Though one must admit the serious danger of self-deception in these matters, the tandem development of the rational and the mystical in the Platonic tradition furnishes the possibility of a corrective. And Augustine's "Beauty ever ancient, ever new" simply reverses the direction of Kant's sense of the sublime from its deflection back to the human.

As a long philosophical tradition maintains in common with primitive animism, everything gives expression to an underlying force, the depth beyond all depths, the center and ground of the whole, correlate to the human mind's reference to the Whole via the notion of Being. Plato sees it as the One/Good/Beautiful; Aristotle personifies it as Self-Thinking Thought; the Judeo-Christian tradition views it as the Creator-Redeemer-Judge, Whose glory is displayed in nature and in history. Indeed, as it attains philosophic expression in Hegel, the Christian view grounds the expressivity of things in the expressivity within God Himself: the Father expresses Himself in His Son, with Whom He unites in the Spirit of Love. Bonaventure locates beauty finally in the togetherness of the Trinity, wherein the Father is the One, the Son the True as mirror of the Father, the Spirit the Good as the Spirit of Love, and Beauty the seal on the transcendentals, the splendor of the Holy Trinity. Correlatively, the human relationship to the divine is being drawn out by ecstasy toward the divine Beauty expressed in all things. All things are traces of God; the human person is made in His image; the mature human, "returned to the Source" through contemplation and giving to others the fruits of contemplation, is the likeness of the divine.

Now it is this that was the special object of medieval aesthetic and which generated its theologies, culminating in the work of Bonaventure. But it was not something that became, in most thinkers, an object of extended attention, especially as it appears in works of art. As Umberto Eco noted and anyone can verify by searching around the writings of the scholastics, the medieval philosopher-theologians were severely deficient in reflection on the nature of art, for all the magnificence their artists and musicians produced and for all the efforts made by neo-Scholastic "fans" to make them appear otherwise.[31]

In Plotinus, the pagan source of the fundamental philosophic underpinning of much of patristic and medieval theology, that move beyond form appears in both the sensory and the intellectual mode through the distinction between harmonic properties on the one hand and in the shining of the One that makes those properties visible. And here he follows the direction laid out in Plato's notion of the Good. In modern times Schopenhauer reinvoked that distinction within the context of the arts by distinguishing between the art forms that exhibit Platonic Forms, or idealized types, and music, which gives expression to the ultimate Source of all (which he termed the Will). The attunement that music expresses is the underpinning of all aesthetic creation. Musical attunement generates form. Here Schopenhauer was also echoing Schiller, for whom the musical mood produced the poetic word, and anticipating Dewey, for whom all creativity is rooted in a felt aura in which ideas swim. It was this which Nietzsche picked up immediately from Schopenhauer in his analysis of the birth of tragedy from the spirit of music. For Schopenhauer and Nietzsche, such aesthetic creation became the fundamental cipher for world generation.

In medieval thought that distinction between form and a surplus giving a peculiar access to form reappears united in Albertus Magnus's expression *splendor formae*, a radiance beyond the objective recognizability of the form. In an otherwise severe scholastic presentation, he manufactures and piles up adjectives, laying stress on terms that describe the surplus of beauty over goodness as a light, a shining, a radiance, a splendor, a supersplendence, an incandescence, a resplendence, a lightning *(fulgor)*, a superfulgence, a *claritas* (understood, not as clarity but as glory, linked to the adjective *clarus*, famous). The property indicated is, nonetheless, rooted in the substantial form. In a typical scholastic presentation, this piling up and even manufacture of terms to describe a single property is indeed remarkable. Albertus was clearly struggling to give expression to a surplus in the experience of beauty beyond the intellectually analyzable properties to which it might otherwise be reduced. In the expression *splendor formae* this luminescence is linked to proportion and consonance, which are understood as a relation of aspects within the object. But whatever the identifiable ratios involved, *splendor* is a surplus property. And in the Dionysian context within which Albertus thought, that property is understood as the expression of the depth of divine mystery irradiating all things.

It was that sense of the divine light shining through proportionate form that created the splendor of the Gothic cathedral and that was suggested by the golden halo or the gilded background on the sacred icons. The silence of the cathedral's soaring spaces called forth the haunting sounds of the Gregorian chant, a music that arose out of the depths of its makers' silence and set its hearers back into the silence of our ultimate distance. For all the otherworldliness that currents of one-sided Neoplatonism tended to generate, the artists brought the other world here, into the field of sensuousness, where we as full human beings belong. That only spells out more fully the fundamentally incarnate character of Christian religion, rooted in the belief in God's own incarnation and culminating in the resurrection of the body.

❧ ❧ ❧

This brings us to the end of my presentation. I have set about to explore the major parameters of the field of experience. I have tried to show that at its center lies the heart. The heart is relation to being in the mode of significant presence. It is the core, the center of the self, the single root of the soul's powers, that from which everything in us arises and to which everything should return. The heart may be superficial or profound, it may be scattered or integrated. It is the center of the "Me," the sedimented resultant of the whole of my past—genetic, cultural, personal-psychological—which moves me spontaneously in certain directions. Yet, rooted in the ultimate distance from any determination afforded by my primordial reference to the whole, "I" am judging and choosing self in relation to the spontaneities of the heart, which I can follow or resist. The task of life is to align the spontaneous heart with the growing display of the whole context of existence. In this the arts work in tandem with intellectual development as they each in their own way disclose the Whole in more encompassing ways. The heart operates by an intuitive affinity with beings, situations, and regions based on the whole of our past dealings, bringing new directions to conceptual work; the intellect, based on a history of development in its own region, brings the intuitive to judgment by providing it with systematic context through explicit conceptualization. The arts explore the region of human dwelling, giving body and presence to intellectual apprehensions, but also providing direction for intellectual development as linked to the most comprehensive region of human dwelling. It is to the heart that the work of art appeals by establishing form as a charged presence appearing in the sensory field. By reason of the bipolar structure of humanness, the heart can be brought to its own fullness by being taken up into a mystical sense of the encompassing and even into a personal address by the Creative Source or it can slide down into the dissipation of sensory indulgence. Just so, art can make its appeal to the mystical in genuine religious art or to the prurient by creating the pornographic. But whether in nature or in art, the overall form of presence exhibits its arising into sensuousness out of the depth of mystery, into which it recedes. Correlated with the thrust of human awareness toward Being or toward the totality, or toward everything about everything, the depth of mystery in what is encountered is the mystery of the totality, within which everything is rooted and out of which all appearance—sensory and intellectual—occurs. Intellectual reference draws upon a significant aspect of ourselves in relation to whatever we apprehend of the objects that appear within our field of experience. Reference to being, which grounds both the thrust to understand and the requirement to choose in a manner consonant with understanding, calls us to holistic presence, to a recognition of the Not and the More than what is immediately revealed. The whole that encompasses everything can itself become a presence haunting the dashboard manifest in our usual modes of attention. The fullness calls to our hearts through the forms that arise in the between of appearance. But as reference to the Whole stemming from an organic base, our fully human response to it ought not to be simply a flight into the Beyond; it ought to be a renewed attentiveness set on the earth of sensuous presence that creates a world of inhabitance.

Throughout the ages, the call of the Mystery continually gives rise to new forms and leads to new formative institutions. In an epoch of the widespread dissolution of form, there opens up the possibility of a new epoch of form arising through attention to that which stands beyond and announces itself through all form as the object of our restless hearts' search.

# Appendix

## ON SCULPTURAL PRODUCTION

> *Our aesthetics hitherto has been a woman's aesthetics to the extent that only the receivers of art have formulated their experience of "what is beautiful?" In all philosophy hitherto the artist is lacking.*
>
> —Friedrich Nietzsche, *The Will to Power*

THE ATTEMPT TO UNDERSTAND art and beauty philosophically is usually developed on the experiential basis of the spectator as the philosopher watches or listens to aesthetic products. But one might be helped further by the actual practice of an art form. In what follows I will give an account of the process of following out particular lines of forms as they came to me while trying to develop as an amateur sculptor, as well as the process of assigning names and thus meanings to what I produced. This will furnish the basis for some more general remarks on the nature of sculpture.

### Descriptions

As a spatially oriented thinker who feels lost until conceptual relations can be given diagrammatic and thus spatial form, and as one who has scored very high in three-dimensional visualization tests, I decided to take up sculpture—or at least I think that is why I decided to take up sculpture. Actually, during a semester teaching in Rome I spent a good deal of time in museums throughout Europe and was attracted by sculptural pieces, especially by bronzes, and in particular by Phidias's Zeus-Poseidon in the Athens museum. As I wandered and wondered through the museum, I was drawn again and again to the power of presence in that work. It was as if it said to me, "I want you!" as a kind of command approaching irresistibility. I could understand a bit how one might consider such works the real presence of the divinity. Upon my return to the states, I decided to take up sculpture as a sideline while I continued my teaching and writing in aesthetics. It was my "aesthetics lab experience."

The old sculpture teacher, Heribert Bartscht, trained at the Academy of Art in Munich, started us out on eye-hand coordination exercises. The first assignment: a mask—like a death mask—of a human being. What astonished me was how little I knew of how the various parts of the human head related to one another. I found myself staring at other people during committee meetings. I had to learn not simply to glance and stereotype but really to *see* how heads actually appeared. I remember being especially astonished at how deeply the eyes were set into the head. There followed several other exercises: copying my left hand, copying live models. Old Heri once remarked, when looking at the works of the various students, how differently people see the same object. I remarked that it was not so much a matter of differently seeing at this point in Sculpture I; it was a matter of a different level of achievement of eye-hand coordination. "Seeing" would come later, if at all.

Then Heri asked us to do something "abstract." While I appreciated abstract painting and sculpture and played with elaboration of patterns in doodling, it took me a while before I had an abstract idea for sculpting. Why, I did not know, but I thought of drawing the letter C, then drawing its reverse and interrelating the two forms. I then determined that I would build up this simple drawing three-dimensionally by ascending to a high point and that I would work only with curved, not straight lines. Again, why, I do not know for sure. Perhaps it was a sense that staying consistently within certain parameters would give a kind of unity to the piece, much like holding oneself to certain rules, which will, as Nietzsche remarked, "compel the chaos that is within us to take on form."[1]

The clay we worked with fired pinkish and one of the ways we finished it was with brown shoe polish, which we then washed with turpentine to even the distribution and allow the color to settle into the grooves so as to bring out the texture of the surface. We completed the process with clear paste wax brought through buffing to a satin glow. But in the case of this abstract piece, I soon noticed that the shape it took, were it to be finished off with a brown patina, would strongly resemble feces. I therefore sprayed it white! (Knowing the reason why I did this, one of my students named it *Albino Feces.*) Because some of the subforms that appeared in this piece suggested other forms (which I shall shortly describe), I subsequently called this piece *The Matrix* (fig. a).

I found that, for the most part, as I followed out the lines of connected forms that emerged, I had to sit with the piece for quite a while after it was completed, sometimes waiting for months before I was able to assign a name that fit what I had produced. I became interested only in exploring related lines of shapes, not in "saying" something. Hence when a ceramics student once asked me what I was trying to say with a particular piece (she always had an "intellectual" message behind her pieces), I was a bit irritated and said, "What I want to say is: 'Look, this is an interesting form!' My own professional craft is with words, and if I want to say something, I *say* it!"

One part of the original piece resembled a leg in a squatting position, so I decided to follow with a human figure in such a position. For no apparent reason I thought to build the piece as if it were made out of potatoes of various sizes—though now it occurs to me that perhaps it was because the brownish patina of the first pieces I produced resembled the

Figure a.  *The Matrix*  Figure b.  *Melancholy*

surface of potatoes. As I worked with building such forms into a human figure, I saw that the one side of the chest area that was exposed required another round form to interrelate the parts in a way that satisfied my sense of spatial distribution, so I inserted a small, rounded "potato" and the figure became female! Because of the general mood of the piece, especially the way the head was tilted, I subsequently named it *Melancholy* (fig. b).

Another aspect of *The Matrix* resembled a peach. *The Matrix* was generating a fruit and vegetable period. I made three interlocking stylized pieces of fruit: a peach joined to an orange, which was joined to a pear, which, in turn, joined the peach again in a circular dance. The dividing line that I ran through the side of the peach facing the viewer tilted upward in such a way as to suggest prolongation into a spiral that culminated in the top of the pear. But here the choice of these particular fruits suggested a female peach and a male pear, with the orange their offspring. I called it *Fruit Family* (fig. c). It is this piece that has haunted me with a call to turn it into a large outside installation. There's even a peculiar opening in a wooded area outside the art department that beckons for this purpose. It would be a concrete piece, eight feet tall, with the same earth tones as the small original, only set on a square base, at least one and a half feet high. I see it again and again. Maybe I'll get the time and the cooperation to bring it into being.

Figure c. **Fruit Family**    Figure d. **Fruitfulness**

Figure e.  *Dance of Life*                    Figure f.  *Empty Womb*

After the original *Fruit Family* I played with the possibility of developing a half-peeled orange and gave it up in favor of opening out the peach and the orange forms, peeling and emptying them. But the empty spaces called for some positive form and so I inserted an egg form in each. The result I called *Fruitfulness* (fig. d).

The next step along this line was to work with onion forms using a variation on the same triple motif. A small onion is linked, via a common base, to a larger onion that has developed a slit in its surface; and this is followed by a still larger onion that had opened up and out of which spilled several small onions, which joined the small one with which I had started. I called this piece *Dance of Life* (fig. e).

This led to a stylized peapod, opened and showing three peas. This picked up and orchestrated four formal elements that had been developing: the vegetable motif, the round, the opening motif, and the triad. Unfortunately it was dropped and smashed to pieces in a move into a new office.

Following out the peeling of the fruit forms in *Fruitfulness* and the onion forms in *Dance of Life*, I pulled a single onion form out of the *Dance of Life*, elongated it, opened it up, and hollowed it out. I attempted two variations on the same theme. Sometime later I entitled each of them *Empty Womb* (fig. f).

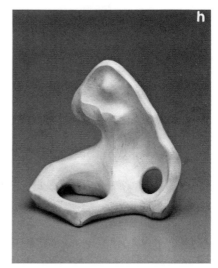

Figure g.  *Couple*            Figure h.  ***Madonna without Child***

The same elongation of the onion I kept solid and joined two forms of differing sizes together. Both tops were finished off with a slightly concave oval top that opened upward. The figures faced one another, with the tops curved in such a way that extending the lines of their curves into the surrounding space created above the negative space of two intersecting parabolas opened upward, and created below another negative space between them that resembled a heart. I called the piece *Couple* (fig. f). I attempted a triple with the same motifs and called it *Family*, but I am not pleased with the resulting form, which looks like a three-legged person diving into a lake.

Going back to the *Empty Womb:* tipped over, this form resembled a bird's skull, so I tried to make a form that looked like such a skull. My first attempt I destroyed because of bad execution. But it was transitional to an interest in skulls and bones. I did a human skull and two cow skulls. I began at this time to collect several skull and bone specimens. Studying a pelvic bone, I saw the possibility of developing a female form out of one half of such a bone. This led to two versions of *Madonna without Child*, in which the form provides an empty cradle (fig. h).

I was next led to join the pelvic bone motif with a kind of stylized tree. Four trunks ascended from a single base, joined at the top and the middle to a central form. From the top the joinings create a cross. Viewed frontally the two opposing trunks are connected by an arching, cradling, bonelike structure with two symmetrical oval hollows on top and two symmetrical archways on the bottom. Viewed from the side, the two opposing trunks, which lean backward, are joined to the middle by a sloping connector, slightly suggesting a Cycladic figure connected with its lyre I had recently seen at an exhibition. After a while I named it, with Heideggerian connections in mind, *The Play of the Fourfold* (fig. i).

The next piece was my most complicated. It consisted of two intertwined forms, intended as male and female, though their stylization made it impossible to determine which was which. The curves and holes of *Madonna without Child* as well as the interior negative space of *Empty Womb* played throughout this work. The two forms are both joined in one continuous form and separated by complicated negative spaces. The curves are arranged so that following out their directions visually leads into the surrounding space in such a way that the space of the whole so prolonged curls back upon itself. I called it *Family* (fig. j).

Meanwhile, the skulls suggested a more stylized version of a symmetrical, hollowed form with the use of negative spaces suggested by the quasi-ovals of *Fruitfulness* and the bilateral symmetry of the skulls. I pushed these forms in the direction of geometrical exactitude. I was not satisfied with

Figure i. ***The Play of the Fourfold***        Figure j. ***Family***

the first such form and never gave it a name. What followed it was more interesting. I began with a round form from which I carved two symmetrical ovals, within which I carved two smaller ovals, within which, in turn, I located a third set of ovals. I further pierced the resultant divider between the two great oval hollows with another oval space at right angles with the other ovals. Behind the triple-carved sets I entered the round form from behind in order to let the light shine through. The head of the art department saw the piece at this time and suggested that I set the form on a column—which I proceeded to do, making the column three times the original form in height and slightly smaller in circumference. I mediated the column and the hollowed out figure with a double collar a bit larger than the width of the divider between the two sets of ovals and I continued the line of that divider, after the gap created by the collar, down the length of the column to the bottom. The top form had an owlish look, with austere, un-

Figure k.
*The Categorical Imperative*

blinking eyes, and the column made it appear lofty. I began to see it as the owl of Minerva, symbol of wisdom, applied to the moral order. I subsequently called it, following Kant, *The Categorical Imperative.* It says, in effect, "I don't care how you feel; you *must* do it!" (fig. k).

Bilaterally symmetrical shapes alternating negative and positive round shapes and playing out sets of ovals led to a mother goddess form with a frontal oval for a head and an oval base at right angles with the stylized head, two hollows for eyes, two cupped hollows for hands and corresponding full round forms for breasts and derriere, with a large bulging oval form for the stomach. I called it *Mother Goddess.* Unfortunately, someone stole it from my office before I had time to have it photographed!

The mother goddess form put me in mind of African Yoruba *akuaba*s, fertility dolls that expectant mothers carried. I made one from memory of those I had seen in the local museum (fig. l).

This, in turn, brought me to a kind of culmination of my attempts, reaching the form that would be worthy of being cast in bronze. As I developed the akuaba, I noted its cruciform shape and thought that I could flatten it and turn it into a male crucified figure. The eyes were the hollows I had introduced into the Mother Goddess. I bypassed the mouth and produced a set of male genitalia that corresponded to the eye-nose relationship

Figure l. *African Yoruba (made by author from memory of examples in local museum)*

Figure m. *Imago Dei*

on the head, only with the positive spaces below matching the negative spaces above. I slightly hollowed and divided the chest area and also hollowed the stomach area. In this move I was guided not only by the shapes, but also by what I sought to express: the marital relation between the Crucified and His Church, for the negative mold of this figure matched in its slightly protruding breasts and slightly distended abdomen, as well as in its recessed genitalia, the female forms corresponding to the male figure. The whole was perfectly symmetrical. The arms and legs, though half-rounds, were stiff and flattened on the ends, paralleling the stiff and flattened horizontal and vertical beams of the cross. The round head was located in the center of the lower half of a surrounding oval halo, while the stomach and breasts corresponded below to the oval halo above. While the arms were perfectly horizontal, the straight lines of the legs each deviated from verticality, imaginatively extending to embrace the bottom edge of the halo. It was a study in alternating straight lines and oval shapes, flats and rounds, concave, flat, and convex surfaces. I called the piece *Christus Africanus* because of its akuaban origin. (See the frontispiece of this book.) But I also saw that formally it paralleled the Egyptian ankh, an androgynous symbol of eternal life. Three symbolic traditions representing life came together, two by design, one by accident: the Yoruba fertility doll; the Christian Cross, source of eternal life; and the Egyptian ankh. I subsequently made the negative mold into a corresponding female figure and have exhibited the two of them together. I called the pair *Imago Dei*, the image of God, after the statement in Genesis: "In His image and likeness He made them; male and female He made them" (fig. m). This was for me a culmination: it was that toward which, unbeknown to me, I had been pressing from the beginning.

One more effort virtually closed the lines I had been pursuing. Inspired by the African antelope headdresses I had often admired in the local museum and following the skull motif, I began with a stylized antelope skull, which I prolonged from the top of the head to curl back upon itself. Along the curve I developed a rhythmically decorated mane using alternating negative ovals on the surface, creating a regularly undulating edge outside and set of alternating positive and negative flat toothlike spaces inside. The decorated curve was linked to a base continuous with both sides of the form, skull and curve. The whole somewhat resembled an ear. One art student said I had made a gear. Linking that to the antelope I eventually called it, playfully, *The Ear Gear Deer* (fig. n). Subsequently I thought of an appropriate quasi-poem.

Figure n. *The Ear Gear Deer*

*List' to the sound of the Ear Gear Deer*
*Ground in the wheels of the earth.*
*Hark to the round of the near-fear tear*
*Bound in the seals of its birth.*

There were a few other works after this. There were circular plaques showing variations on the theme of trinity, with dominant focus on the Spirit in the form of a dove. The outer circle represents the Father, the origin; the smaller inner circle is the Son, like the Father but in some sense subordinate, derivative. The Spirit is larger because the focus is on the relation to us of the trinitarian Godhead. Specially interesting to me is what a colleague noted: that I had produced, unbeknown to me, a "tongue of flame" in the dove form. Later I noticed that the dove was also an exact replica of the "angel fish" doodles I frequently make. Dove and fire, symbols of the Spirit; fish, symbol of Christianity—and angel fish at that! Subsequently I made a medal of the form and cast it in silver.

There followed an undistinguished recollection of an African mask, two statues of Saint Francis of Assisi, and several portrait busts, which I regard as secondary to my main interest in sculpting. The busts I had done now and then from the beginning of my productive period. On commission from Cedric Messina, producer of the BBC Shakespeare series, who directed our university's production of *The Merchant of Venice*, I did a terra cotta bust of Portia's father, made to look like the sire of the woman who played Portia, but as a joke made it bald as counterpoint to the leonine mane of tight red curls that adorned the leading lady. It was wheeled in and out of the set as the centerpiece that dominated the action.

But administrative duties, the editing of a journal, and the authoring of a couple of books, including the present one, turned my energies away from sculptural production and on toward further reflection. Maybe I will be moved again to take up the sculptural task anew, maybe not. I sometimes feel the itch to get back to the clay. But I think I learned something important about the productive process and I did arrive at a form that satisfied me.

## Reflections

What has struck me most about this process is that it began with a random relation of shapes I found particularly attractive and went on to generate lines of shapes to which meanings later accumulated and suggested names. One shape would call forth others, moving in a certain direction; then the lines would crisscross and run in still other directions. It was the shapes rather than the meanings that occupied my deliberate attention, until I arrived at the idea for *Christus Africanus*, where meaning and shape emerged together. Fruitful forms, family forms, symbols of life and death, of fundamental human relations, sexual and familial, and basic religious forms, trinitarian and cruciform, all rooted firmly in earthiness, in vital embodiment: these were the symbolic meanings playing around in my pursuit of lines of shapes. Perhaps the interlocking Cs, one facing forward, one reversed, that was the basis of *The Matrix*, was an unconscious symbol of coupling, since the fertility-dominated shapes sprang forth from it. I came to see more clearly that the choice of shapes was tied deeply to the things that mattered most to me, the things that gripped my heart, even though my focal interest was initially in the shapes. Henry Moore remarked that certain natural shapes are spontaneously symbolic[2]—an observation Herbert Read exploited in his Jungian interpretation of Moore's work.[3] Though Moore found the human figure the object of deepest interest, nonetheless he found principles of form and rhythm in the study of pebbles, rocks, bones, trees, shells, and plants, thus linking the human to the natural order from which it has arisen.[4] I found natural affinities with Moore in my spontaneous attraction to the same natural forms. Unusually shaped pebbles with smooth surfaces and transitions, sprinkled with small pods of various sorts stand in front of me on my desk, while a collection of seashells peers at me from a display case. Vertebrae and half a pelvic bone from a horse stand on or below my bookshelves along with the skull of a racoon. Several plants surround me in my home and office, while five large oaks shade the front of the house. The combined formal properties of these natural objects give a sense of form and texture deeply relevant to what guides the eye and hand in sculptural production. As Herbert Read noted, "the eye of the artist feeds unconsciously on whatever formal motes come its way."[5]

The smooth transitions and the overall unity of the bones as well as the comprehensive structure and patterns of the seashells are linked to their being functional parts of organic wholes and teach us to produce organic wholes. Trees and plants, of course, *are* organic wholes. The stones, on the other hand, are not organic wholes. They have to be collected by an eye already sensitized to organic form from the overwhelming numbers of randomly generated forms produced by the grinding and washing process of the ocean and lake waves rubbing them against other stones. Having a visual understanding of the formal properties of such objects allows for the production of visual objects that do not necessarily represent or replicate the appearance of naturally produced objects appearing in the world of everyday attention.

Hence for Moore, Greco-Roman idealistic representation is but one conception. There is a broader conception, capable of doing justice to the whole range of differing styles of sculpture that have emerged historically, from the more primitive to the most modern. To see it, he said, one must remove the Greek spectacles.[6] Here he is less dogmatic than the Futurists, like Boccione, who speak of "the Phidian period and its decadence" and "Michaelangelesque [sic] sins."[7] Moore sees the great sculpture of the world in Sumerian, early Greek, Etruscan, Ancient Mexican, Fourth- and Twelfth-Dynasty Egyptian, Romanesque, and early Gothic styles.[8] What redeems Phidias for Moore is that he still maintained the fundamental sculptural principles of the archaic Greeks, which express an intense vitality, as certain figures of the Renaissance still remained close to primitive grandeur and simplicity. So-called "classical" periods arise on the basis of "primitive" art and then slowly fade into technical tricks and intellectual conceits.[9] Indeed, the realistic ideal of physical beauty in art was "only a digression from the main world tradition of sculpture, while . . . Romanesque and Early Gothic are in the main line."[10] Here Moore shares common ground with Brancusi, who said, "What is real is not the external form, but the essence of things. Starting with this truth it is impossible for anyone to express anything essentially real by imitating its exterior surface."[11] Along the same lines, Rodin makes a distinction between imitation of "form" and imitation of "life."[12] In this view, what is important is not beauty but vitality and power of expression.[13] The inclusivist conception Moore advances is sensitive to the intrinsic emotional significance of shapes and the importance of the materials employed.[14] Here Moore articulates a view identical with the architectural view of Frank Lloyd Wright[15] and parallel to the one advanced by Plotinus against Plato's (perhaps ironic) presentation of art as surface imitation. Unfortunately, it is Plato's overt view that has determined most people's expectation of the work of art. Moore sees the historical mission of Brancusi's work lying in a process of simplification that eliminated all surface distraction that has cluttered shape since the end of the Gothic. Brancusi's work thereby makes us more shape conscious.[16] In moving toward that consciousness, Wright, Brancusi, and Moore paid special attention to the nature of materials in their work.[17]

In my own work, at first asymmetrical organicity was the dominant formal motif, the belonging together of spatial configurations that ultimately harmonized, one with all the others, to compose a single whole. In sculpture the problem is much more complex than in painting, for in painting one has to satisfy "organistic" conditions only in two dimensions. The addition of the third dimension adds an indeterminate number of perspectives, each of which has to be respected to produce an integral piece. As Moore remarked, this makes sculpture the most difficult of all arts.[18] One has to learn how to perceive in three dimensions, so that today people are often more attracted to sculpture at first through photographic reproduction.[19] But to capture and express the vitality of the work, the sculptor has to occupy the center of gravity of the piece, which holds all the perspectives together.[20]

Producing works that are closer to relief is more like painting: the problem of organicity here is basically two-dimensional. But in the fully three-dimensional pieces, working the material from one perspective immediately modifies the other perspectives. This makes portrait busts particularly difficult. One has to capture the subject from all angles simultaneously. More freely creative work is easier because one does not have to attend to exactitude of resemblance with a given subject and is freer to pursue the aesthetic possibilities. Nonetheless, it is virtually impossible to conceive of a work from all angles simultaneously, so that one inevitably has to create as one goes along. And each decision one makes limits the possibilities for the next decision. Clay is easier in this respect, since one can always reverse a whole set of decisions—something that marble or wood does not allow. Furthermore, marble or wood does a lot more independent talking back by revealing the limits of the grain's ability to cooperate with the emerging form, for one ought not simply impose the form on the marble or the wood, but develop it in relation to the grain of the material. Michelangelo immortalized this relation between the material and the artist in the famous lines, "Non ha l'ottimo artista alcun concetto / Ch' un marmo solo in se non circonscriva." (The best artist has no concept that a piece of marble alone does not circumscribe within itself.) This is a notion that has passed into the fundamental character of twentieth-century sculpture.[21]

In my work, the process of production typically began with a rather vague idea that took on more determinate shape as I worked with the materials. Moore claims the creative process can begin from either of two ends of human experience, which he calls order and surprise, intellect and imagination, conscious and unconscious. One can have an expressed idea, after which one must figure out how to render it in the appropriate medium, or one can simply begin vaguely and let the idea come to fruition in the process of production.[22] The latter has been my typical mode of procedure.

In my own work, following the move from groups of vegetative forms to single animal and human forms via the interest in skulls, the dominant formal motif shifted for the most part from the belonging together of asymmetrical forms to bilateral symmetry, a subspecies of which is the vertebrate organic, involving a balance of two sides of a piece such that each side replicates the other. After the shift from vegetable and fruit to animal and human forms, the three-dimensional forms all display this. However, the plaques and medal maintain an asymmetrical internally organic preoccupation. What is tempting about bilateral symmetry is that it is an easy way to bring about a kind of harmony. It is the way followed by paper cutouts, kaleidoscopes, and Rorschach inkblots and also by Georgian architecture. The real aesthetic challenge, however, is the same in both forms, symmetrical or not: to create harmony or organic unity among the elements of either side so that a side could exist as a unity all its own. A human profile is an example of this challenge. Symmetry makes the elements correspond point by point with their symmetrical opposite and so adds balance to the piece. Either form displays wholeness.

The medium too has its own symbolic value. Bronze and stone, and to a lesser extent wood or ceramic clay fired at extreme temperatures, have a fixity, a solidity less subject to the decay of time than paint on canvas or plaster. A sculpted piece suggests an endurance, a hardness, a resistance and is particularly fit for memorializing. It renders its subject "immortal." The medium also determines treatment: modeling (e.g., with clay or wax, often linked with casting as a second step), carving (e.g., wood, stone, ivory), and, in more recent times, construction. Some dogmatic purists—and there are as many of them in the world of art as there are in religion— insist that carving is the only true form. R. H. Wilenski, for example, down-plays modeling as more suited to Romanticism, which focuses on individu-alism and loses the more universal expressiveness involved in carving.[23] Others who claim "truth to materials" in too one-sided a way miss the sense of pleasant surprise involved in shifting from one medium to another in casting what is originally conceived in clay or wax or even in a hard (and thus carved) medium. Nonetheless, there is something important in Wilen-ski's observation that there is a formal meaning in each substance with which the true sculptor has to reckon.[24]

The sense of space is integral to sculpture, and not only the filling of space by mass. As Boccione notes, the different aspects of shapes interplay in such a way as to set up a dynamic relation between the parts and a kind of charge in the surrounding space.[25] The lines that determine a given form and the negative spaces within it suggest prolongation into that envi-roning space. They make visible a translation into the sculptural medium of "those atmospheric planes that link and intersect things," giving "plas-tic form to the mysterious sympathies and affinities that the reciprocal for-mal influences of the planes of objects create."[26] Opening the forms provides a whole new dimension to a sculptural piece: a sense of inward-ness and a sense of containment. The hole opens a third dimension, as, for example, in the work of Henry Moore and Barbara Hepworth (paralleled by the painting of her husband, Ben Nicholson, and the pelvic bone paint-ings of Georgia O'Keefe).[27] For Moore, the hole immediately creates the sense of the third dimension, while simultaneously evoking the mystery of the cave.[28] Together, external and internal space add, as it were, another dimension to traditional focus on mass.[29] Hollows and full forms of similar shape call out to one another; dissimilar shapes establish a counterpoint; and both play in relation to occupied space. In interplay with such shapes, the parts take on a kind of rhythm and harmony suggesting, as in every art form, a certain mood.[30] One might note here that the focus on space as a kind of material all its own is a peculiarity of modern art forms. The International Style in architecture for example, was dedicated to the shaping of space.[31]

My focus has been on free-standing sculpture. Mention of architecture calls attention to one of the dominant traditions, where sculpture is subservient to architecture. It was this tradition that almost wholly occupied the attention of John Ruskin, who claimed that "perfect sculpture must be a part of the severest architecture. . . . The first office of that sculpture is not to represent the things it imitates but to gather out of them those arrangements of form which shall be pleasing to the eye in their intended places."[32] Ruskin was particularly attentive to the medieval cathedrals, where the statuary was designed to fit into the niches provided by the architecture of the building, but where also sculpted decoration, often employing vegetative motifs, developed its own stylized rhythm. This entailed a play between representation and stylization that characterizes all good art, even the most "imitative."

In sculpture as well as in architecture, texture is particularly important. It sets up a play between light and shadow on the surface of the piece to help create the dominant mood of the work. An overly smooth piece might take on a boring character compared with the surface of one of Rodin's nudes which ripples and flashes as one moves around the work.

Though the ancient Greeks painted the surface of many of their statues, time has worn it off, presenting us today with naked marble or bronze. Schopenhauer, who should have known this fact, praised the Greeks for their "infallible good taste," as over against painted wax sculpture, since they are said to have left work for the imagination of the viewer.[33] Taste has largely moved in the direction dictated by the ravages of time: color, beyond that provided by the medium itself, with some addition of a patina, has usually not been associated with high-level sculpture. Of course, in contemporary times, no canons of taste are followed. Three-dimensional painted pieces, fusing painting and sculptural construction, are commonplace. And waxworks realism is found in many contemporary exhibitions. (In the Stuttgart museum I almost said "Pardon me" to the cleaning lady, until I noticed she did not move!)

In this regard, I am reminded of Hegel's remark regarding the legendary competition between Zeuxis and Parrhasios in which Zeuxis remarked that he had painted grapes so realistically that he deceived the birds, who tried to peck at them. Parrhasios then directed the braggart to pull back the drapes to see a real painting, only to have the grape painter discover that the drapes were painted! One who could fool humans is a greater painter than one who can fool birds![34] But, as Hegel remarked: So someone has such hand-eye coordination as to be able to fool perceivers into thinking the work of art is its real counterpart—so what? Where is the value of being able so to deceive? The invention of hammer and nails was much more significant to the development of humankind![35] Kant noted that the creation of illusion pleases for only a short time and we are soon bored with it.[36] Such illusionary art turns us back to the artist to admire his or her dexterity. It is an art of conspicuous display, much like the rich throwing money about to show their own ability to accumulate.

Of course, artists can do what they want. But art functions at a more profound level when it so transforms our ordinary "dashboard" relationship to things as to give us a sense of meaningful presence and of the underlying depths and encompassing wholeness, which are nonetheless anchored in the individual, sensorily present work. Art haunts us and has the ability to bring us both to an enhanced appreciation of sensory surface and, simultaneously, to a sense of lived meaning. And it can do this because it arises within and appeals to the field of human experience, which is anchored in the sensuous here and now and referred to the encompassing Whole through the mediations of cultural tradition. We have examined that structure throughout this work.

# Notes

## Preface

1. Robert E. Wood, *Martin Buber's Ontology: An Analysis of* I and Thou (Evanston, Ill.: Northwestern University Press, 1969).

2. Robert E. Wood, *A Path into Metaphysics: Phenomenological, Hermeneutical, and Dialogical Studies* (Albany: State University of New York Press, 1991).

3. I have presented a lengthy exposition of a seven-volume work (the first part of a trilogy on beauty, goodness, and truth) that advances that thesis against the background of the whole history of Western literature, philosophy, and theology in "Philosophy, Aesthetics, and Theology," *American Catholic Philosophical Quarterly* 67.3 (Summer 1993): 355–82.

## I. Introduction

1. I contend that this is exactly what is involved in Plato's Line of Knowledge. Cf. Robert E. Wood, "Plato's Line Revisited: The Pedagogy of Complete Reflection," *Review of Metaphysics* 44 (March 1991): 525–47.

2. Alfred North Whitehead, *Process and Reality: An Essay in Cosmology* (New York: Harper, 1960).

3. Edmund Husserl, *General Introduction to a Pure Phenomenology*, trans. F. Kersten, vol. 1 of *Ideas Pertaining to a Pure Phenomenology and to a Phenomenological Philosophy* (The Hague: Martinus Nijhoff, 1982), 21.

4. For an exposition of the major phenomenologists—Husserl, Scheler, Heidegger, Sartre, Merleau-Ponty—in relation to Plato's Line of Knowledge, see Robert E. Wood, "The Phenomenologists" in *Reading Philosophy for the Twenty-First Century*, ed. G. McLean (Lanham, Md.: University Press of America, 1989), 131–60.

5. On functioning intentionality, cf. Edmund Husserl, *The Crisis of European Sciences and Transcendental Phenomenology: An Introduction to Phenomenological Philosophy*, trans. D. Carr (Evanston, Ill.: Northwestern University Press, 1970), 109.

6. This is analogous to the threefold structure that governs Mikel Dufrenne's treatment in *The Phenomenology of Aesthetic Experience,* trans. E. Casey et al. (Evanston, Ill.: Northwestern University Press, 1973). Dufrenne distinguishes the sensous, the represented object, and the expressed world as aesthetic developments of presence, representation, and reflection (333ff.). It is in the relation between reflection and feeling that he locates what I am calling presence-to-being, as both distinguished from and found in the presence he locates as the sensuous component. I have explored these matters a bit more fully in *Path into Metaphysics,* especially in chapters 2 and 3.

7. Cf. Martin Heidegger, "The Origin of the Work of Art" (henceforth OWA), in *Poetry, Language, and Thought,* trans. A. Hofstadter (New York: Harper and Row, 1971), 26 (henceforth *PLT*).

8. Bernard Lonergan, *Insight: A Study of Human Understanding* (London: Longmans, Green, 1958), 416.

9. In what follows, I would claim fidelity to the acute observations of Aristotle throughout his *On the Soul* in close correlation with Hegel's work in *Philosophy of Mind,* where he claims direct descent from Aristotle's work. G. W. F. Hegel, *Hegel's Philosophy of Mind,* trans. W. Wallace (Oxford: Clarendon Press, 1971), 3 (henceforth *HPM*). For more recent accounts drawing upon contemporary research, see also Maurice Merleau-Ponty, *The Structure of Behavior,* trans. A. Fisher (Boston: Beacon Press, 1963), 59–114 and Errol Harris, in *Hypothesis and Perception: The Roots of Scientific Method* (London: George Allen and Unwin, 1970), 249–92 as well as *The Foundation of Metaphysics in Science* (Lanham, Md.: University Press of America, 1983), 388–419.

10. Cf. Friedrich Nietzsche, "On Truth and Lie in an Extra-moral Sense," in *The Portable Nietzsche,* ed. and trans. W. Kaufmann (New York: Viking, 1954), 42–47.

11. Cf. Aristotle, *On the Soul,* trans. W. Hett (Cambridge, Mass.: Harvard University Press, 1975), 3.12.434a23ff. (henceforth *OS*). Descartes understood this: see *Meditations on First Philosophy,* trans. D. Cress (Indianapolis: Hackett, 1979), 6.50ff.

12. Cf. Harris, *Foundation,* 163ff.

13. Cf. Robert E. Wood, "Being and Manifestness: Philosophy, Science, and Poetry in an Evolutionary Worldview," *International Philosophical Quarterly* 35.4 (December 1995): 437–47.

14. The recovery of natural form and teleology by Kant in the mode of "as if"—*Critique of Judgment,* trans. W. Pluhar (Indianapolis: Hackett, 1987), §§64–65.248–55 (henceforth *CJ*)—was made central to nonhypothetical expressivity in Schopenhauer, *The World as Will and Representation,* trans. E. Payne, 2 vols. (New York: Dover, 1966), vol. 1, bk. 2, §18, 99ff. (henceforth *WWR*). Cf. also Hans Urs von Balthasar, *Seeing the Form,* trans. E. Leiva-Merikakis, vol. 1 of *The Glory of the Lord* (San Francisco: Ignatius Press, 1982), 118, 151, 442, 444.

15. The felicitous metaphor of "dashboard knowledge" is Owen Barfield's in *Saving the Appearances: A Study in Idolatry* (New York: Harcourt, Brace and World, 1957), 28–35.

16. Aurelius Augustine, *Confessions,* trans. W. Watts, 2 vols. (Cambridge, Mass.: Harvard University Press, 1977), 3.6.

17. On the givenness of space and time as the framework of all experience, see Immanuel Kant, *Critique of Pure Reason,* trans. N. K. Smith (New York: St. Martin's Press, 1929), B 38/A 24f., 68–69 (henceforth *CPR*). There is the obvious question, made current in contemporary physics, of the real separability of space and time. Plato's notion

of the *receptacle (hupodoche)* interrelates the two; Plato, *Timaeus,* trans. R. Bury (Cambridge, Mass.: Harvard University Press, 1977), 49. For a correlation of time and space with subject and object, see Dufrenne, *Phenomenology,* 346ff.

18. Cf. Lonergan, *Insight,* 348ff.

19. For a treatment of the principle of noncontradiction, see Aristotle, *Metaphysics,* trans. H. Tredennick, 2 vols. (Cambridge, Mass.: Harvard University Press, 1967), bk. 4, 1005b ff. See Aristotle's *Organon* for the foundations of logic. Hegel's challenge to the principle in his *Logic* does not eliminate but only locates it: in fact, people do contradict one another and themselves, though they each remain what they are in spite of that. Existential contradiction in organisms becomes the motor for establishing an identity that strives to remove the contradiction. On contradiction, see *Hegel's Science of Logic,* trans. A.V. Miller (London: George Allen and Unwin, 1969), 431ff.; on the organism, 770 (henceforth *SL*).

20. Cf. Martin Heidegger, *Being and Time,* trans. J. Macquarrie and E. Robinson (New York: Harper, 1962), 32–35 (henceforth *BAT*).

21. Cf. Baruch Spinoza, *Ethics,* trans. R. Elwes (New York: Dover, 1955), pt. 2, prop. 44, cor. 2, 117.

22. On the notion of "decision" in this context, cf. Heidegger, OWA, 67. For a wider discussion of the nature of freedom see Robert E. Wood, "Aspects of Freedom," *Philosophy Today* 15.1 (Spring 1991): 106–15.

23. Cf. Lewis Mumford, *The Myth of the Machine: Technics and Human Development* (New York: Harcourt Brace Jovanovich, 1966), 51.

24. On the notion of the heart, see Stephen Strasser, *Phenomenology of Feeling: An Essay on the Phenomena of the Heart,* trans. and intro. R. Wood (Pittsburgh: Duquesne University Press, 1977).

25. For a systematic sketch of these meanings, see my introduction to Strasser, *Phenomenology,* 11–14.

26. Dufrenne, *Phenomenology,* 398, 402–7.

27. Søren Kierkegaard, *Either/Or,* vol. 1, trans. D. Swenson and L. M. Swenson (Garden City, N.Y.: Anchor Books, 1959).

28. Cf. Heidegger, *BAT,* 278–311.

29. Martin Buber, *Daniel: Dialogues on Realization,* trans. M. Friedman (New York: McGraw-Hill, 1965), 91.

30. Schopenhauer, *WWR,* vol. 2, chap. 17, 161.

31. Cf. Dufrenne, *Phenomenology,* 137.

32. Ibid., 154.

33. Cf. Umberto Boccione, "The Futurist Manifesto" in *Theories of Modern Art,* ed. H. Chipp (Berkeley: University of California Press, 1968), 298–304.

34. Cf. Sigfried Giedion, *Space, Time, and Architecture: The Growth of a New Tradition* (Cambridge, Mass.: Harvard University Press, 1980), 385ff.; also Peter Collins, *Changing Ideals in Modern Architecture, 1750–1950* (Kingston, Ont.: McGill-Queen's University Press, 1984), 128ff.

35. Cf. Mark Taylor, *Disfiguring: Art, Architecture, Religion* (Chicago: University of Chicago Press, 1992), 242ff. Cf. Friedrich Nietzsche's suggestive comments on historical existence in *On the Uses and Disadvantages of History for Life,* in *Untimely Meditations,* trans. R. Hollingdale (London: Cambridge University Press, 1983).

36. Cf. Plato, *Politicus,* 259b, where *techne* and *episteme* are used interchangeably; *Politicus, Philebus, Ion,* trans. H. Fowler and W. Lamb (Cambridge, Mass.: Harvard University Press, 1975). See also Kant, *CJ,* §43.170; cf. also Aristotle, *Nichomachean Ethics,* trans. H. Rackham (Cambridge, Mass.: Harvard University Press, 1975), 4.3 (henceforth *NE*); and Paul Kristeller, "The Modern System of Fine Arts," in *Renaissance Thought and the Arts: Collected Essays* (Princeton, N.J.: Princeton University Press, 1990), 166.

37. Cf. Martin Heidegger, *The Question Concerning Technology, and Other Essays,* trans. W. Lovitt (New York: Harper and Row, 1977), 175 (henceforth *QCT*).

38. Plato, *Timaeus,* 28. As we will see below (chap. 10), Heidegger considers the West to have been dominated in its view of Being by the notion of production. Being is considered to lie in the enduring form, which is the goal of the production process. Cf. Martin Heidegger, *The Basic Problems of Phenomenology,* trans. A. Hofstadter (Bloomington: Indiana University Press, 1988), 99ff.

39. Cf. chap. 3.

40. As we will see below (chaps. 8, 9).

41. Aristotle, *NE,* 6.1140a.

42. *NE,* 1.2.1094a28.

43. *NE,* 10.1177a12ff.

44. Karl Marx, "From Excerpt—Notes of 1844," in *Writings of the Young Marx on Philosophy and Society,* ed. and trans. L. Easton and K. Guddat (Garden City, N.Y.: Doubleday, 1967), 281.

45. Cf. Kristeller, "Modern System," 163–227.

46. Plato, *The Republic,* trans. P. Shorey, 2 vols. (Cambridge, Mass.: Harvard University Press, 1969), 7.521b ff. (henceforth *Rep*).

47. See Plato's *Sophist* and *Politicus* for early illustrations of this insight into understanding as the display of samenesses and differences.

48. For a report on a more in-depth systematic treatment of the arts, see Robert E. Wood, "Metaphysics and Aesthetics," in *The Philosophy of Paul Weiss,* ed. L. Hahn, Library of Living Philosophers (Carbondale: Southern Illinois University Press, 1995), 615–35. Weiss's work appeared in *The World of Art* and *Nine Basic Arts* (Carbondale: Southern Illinois University Press, 1961).

49. Cf. Dufrenne, *Phenomenology,* 358; Umberto Eco, *Art and Beauty in the Middle Ages,* trans. H. Bredin (New Haven: Yale University Press, 1986), 66.

50. Thomas Aquinas, *Summa theologiae* (New York: Benziger Brothers, 1947), 1.78.3 (henceforth *ST*).

51. Cf. Robert E. Wood, "Heidegger on the Way to Language," in *Semiotics 1984,* ed. J. Deely (Lanham, Md.: University Press of America, 1985), 661–20 and "Martin Buber's Philosophy of the Word," *Philosophy Today* 30 (Winter 1986): 317–24.

52. Cf. Dufrenne, *Phenomenology,* 102.

53. Richard Wagner, *The Art-work of the Future,* trans. W. Ellis (London, 1892).

54. For a discussion of each of the art forms entailed, see Paul Weiss, *Cinematics* (Carbondale: Southern Illinois University Press, 1975).

55. For a penetrating treatment of film, see Stanley Cavell, *The World Viewed: Reflections on the Ontology of Film* (New York: Viking, 1971).

56. Cf. Dufrenne, *Phenomenology,* 77.

57. For a fuller discussion of architecture, see Robert E. Wood, "Architecture: Confluence of Art, Technology, Politics, and Nature" in *The Nature of Technology*, Proceedings of the American Catholic Philosophical Association (Washington, D.C.: The Catholic University of America, 1996), 79–93. One of the best books on the philosophy of architecture is Karsten Harries, *The Ethical Function of Architecture* (Cambridge, Mass.: MIT Press, 1997).

58. Cf. Constantin Brancusi, *Brancusi*, ed. Ionel Jianou (London: Adam, 1963), 69.

59. For the development of this concept, cf. Roman Ingarden, *The Cognition of the Literary Work of Art*, trans. R. Crowley and K. Olson (Evanston, Ill.: Northwestern University Press, 1973).

60. Schopenhauer makes much of this insight in *WWR*, 2, suppl. to bk. 3, chap. 34, 408.

61. Arthur Danto, *The Transfiguration of the Commonplace: A Philosophy of Art* (Cambridge, Mass.: Harvard University Press, 1983), 115ff.

62. Henry Moore, "A View of Sculpture," in *Henry Moore* (New York: George Wittenborn, 1968), 1:xxx.

63. Aristotle, *The Politics of Aristotle*, trans. E. Barker (Cambridge: Oxford University Press, 1970), 8.5.1340a1ff.

64. Heidegger, OWA, 73.

65. Walter Pater, *The Renaissance*, in *Selected Writings of Walter Pater*, ed. Harold Bloom (New York: Columbia University Press, 1974), 55–57.

66. For one of the major sources of modern hermeneutic thinking, see Hans Georg Gadamer, *Truth and Method*, trans. G. Barden and J. Comming (New York: Crossroad, 1982).

67. Thus there is a difference between a Platonic, an Aristotelian, a Cartesian, a Hobbesian, and a Whiteheadian body—even though all of them take their point of departure in some way from sensory presentation. See Wood, "Being and Manifestness."

68. Cf. Martin Buber, "Dialogue," in *Between Man and Man* (Boston: Beacon Press, 1961).

## II. Plato

1. For an illustration of how this works in Plato's central dialogue and for a general orientation in the *Republic*, see Robert E. Wood, "Image, Structure and Content: On a Passage in Plato's *Republic*," *Review of Metaphysics* 40 (March 1987): 495–514.

2. Alexander Pope, *An Essay on Man*, ed. F. Brady (Indianapolis: Bobbs-Merrill, 1965), 2.1.17.

3. Cf. *Theaetetus* (155c), in which Socrates says that the principle of philosophy is awe. Plato, *Theaetetus* and *Sophist*, trans. H. Fowler (Cambridge, Mass.: Harvard University Press, 1977). Heidegger picks that up again more recently in *What Is Philosophy?* trans. W. Kluback and J. Wilde (New York: Twayne, 1958), 78–85 (henceforth *WP*).

4. G. W. F. Hegel, *Phenomenology of Spirit*, trans. A. Miller (Oxford: Clarendon Press, 1977), preface, §20.11 (henceforth *PS*).

5. *Rep*, 2.268d.

6. *Rep*, 2.272b.

7. *Rep*, 2.272d.

8. Dufrenne, *Phenomenology*, 62–63: there are works that "flatter our subjectivity," but "authentic art turns us away from ourselves and toward itself."

9. *Rep*, 3.410d.

10. Plato, *The Laws of Plato*, trans. T. Pangle (New York: Basic Books, 1980), 2.672e (henceforth *Laws*).

11. *Rep*, 3.412d–e, 420e.

12. *Rep*, 3.401a.

13. *Rep*, 10.596d.

14. *Rep*, 10.601d.

15. We will see this discussed in some detail in chapter 9, on the aesthetics of John Dewey.

16. *Laws*, 2.698b f.

17. *Rep*, 3.399d.

18. See Carl Dahlhaus, *The Idea of Absolute Music*, trans. R. Lustig (Chicago: University of Chicago Press, 1989), 8. It is precisely this priority of the word that will be challenged in the emergence of "absolute music" and its metaphysical grounding in Schopenhauer.

19. *Laws*, 2.668a; cf. Aristotle, *Politics*, 1340a.

20. *Rep*, 3.400e.

21. *Rep*, 2.399c–d. It is not clear what *polyharmonic* means here, especially with regard to the flute.

22. *Laws*, 2.672a.

23. *Rep*, 4.424c.

24. *Rep*, 3.400e.

25. For the body as a harmonic whole, see, for example, *Rep*, 1.350a, where it is implicit, and *Rep*, 3.401a.

26. *Rep*, 3.402a.

27. *Rep*, 2.378a.

28. *Rep*, 3.386a ff.

29. *Rep*, 3.403c.

30. *Rep*, 3.415d; 4.124d.

31. *Rep*, 4.427e ff.

32. *Rep*, 4.433a ff.

33. *Rep*, 4.434d–37a.

34. Karl Popper, *The Open Society and Its Enemies* (Princeton, N.J.: Princeton University Press, 1950), 11ff. Cf. Thomas Thorson, ed., *Plato: Totalitarian or Democrat?* (Englewood Cliffs, N.J.: Prentice-Hall, 1963).

35. *Rep*, 5.449a.

36. On community of wives and children, see *Rep*, 4.423e; on property, see 416d.

37. On the equality of women and men, see *Rep*, 4.451c ff.; on the philosopher-king, see 473d ff.

38. *Rep*, 5.451c.

39. *Rep*, 5.459d, 461c; 6.490b, 499b; 7.540b.

40. *Rep*, 5.476a.

41. *Rep*, 7.540a.

42. *Rep,* 6.507d ff.

43. *Rep,* 6.509d. For a further elaboration of what follows, see Robert E. Wood, "Plato's Line Revisited: The Pedagogy of Complete Reflection," *Review of Metaphysics* 44 (March 1991): 525–47.

44. *Rep,* 6.508e.

45. *Rep,* 6.511b.

46. For a development of this theme see my "Self-reflexivity in The *Theaetetus:* On the Lifeworld of a Platonic Dialogue," *The Review of Metaphysics* [forthcoming].

47. *Rep,* 6.510b.

48. *Timaeus,* 49b–53c; cf. A. N. Whitehead, *Adventures of Ideas* (New York: Free Press, 1967), 150; for an exposition of Whitehead's Platonism, see Wood, *Path into Metaphysics,* chap. 15.

49. *Rep,* 6.509b.

50. *Rep,* 5.478e.

51. *Sophist,* 266c; cf. also *Rep,* 6.509e.

52. *Sophist,* 257a–59d.

53. *Rep,* 7.520c.

54. *Laws,* 10.897d.

55. *Sophist,* 264d f.

56. *Rep,* 3.392d.

57. *Rep,* 4.439d.

58. I tried to demonstrate that in "Image, Structure, and Content."

59. *Rep,* 10.607c.

60. *Rep,* 10.596d.

61. *Laws,* 2.669a.

62. *Rep,* 10.607c.

63. *Rep,* 10.597b f.

64. *Laws,* 2.668d.

65. Plotinus, *The Enneads,* trans. A. H. Armstrong, Loeb Classical bilingual edition (Cambridge, Mass.: Harvard University Press, 1989), 5.8.5 (henceforth *Enn*); Hegel, *Philosophy of Fine Art,* trans. F. Osmaston (London: G. Bell, 1920), 1:9–10; Schopenhauer, *WWR,* 2, suppl. to bk. 3, chap. 34, 408; Heidegger, OWA, 50.

66. Martin Buber, "Man and His Image Work," in *The Knowledge of Man: A Philosophy of the Interhuman,* trans. M. Friedman and R. G. Smith (New York: Harper and Row, 1965), 159.

67. Plato, *Parmenides,* trans. H. Fowler (Cambridge, Mass.: Harvard University Press, 1963), 130d.

68. *Rep,* 10.601c.

69. *Rep,* 10.597e.

70. *Sophist,* 465b.

71. Plato, *Gorgias,* in *Lysis, Symposium, Gorgias,* trans. W. Lamb (Cambridge, Mass.: Harvard University Press, 1975), 464b f.

72. Plato, *Phaedrus,* in *Euthyphro; Apology; Crito; Phaedo; Phaedrus,* trans. H. Fowler (Cambridge, Mass.: Harvard University Press, 1957), 248d.

73. Cf. also *Ion,* 533e ff.

74. *Rep,* 1.327a.

75. *Phaedrus,* 248d.

76. *Rep,* 2.372d.

77. *Rep,* 3.398c.

78. *Rep,* 6.506d.

79. *Symposium,* 201e (henceforth *Sym*).

80. *Rep,* 5.451c.

81. *Sym,* 206b.

82. *Sym,* 210a.

83. *Phaedrus,* 255c.

84. *Politicus,* 283b ff.

85. Aristotle, *Poetics,* trans. W. Fyfe (Cambridge, Mass.: Harvard University Press, 1973), 8.1451a30ff.; 23.1459a20.

86. *Sym,* 180c.

87. *Phaedrus,* 250d.

88. *Phaedrus,* 255c.

89. Plato, *Greater Hippias,* in *Cratylus; Parmenides; Greater Hippias; Lesser Hippias,* trans. H. Fowler (Cambridge, Mass.: Harvard University Press, 1963), 294c.

90. Ibid., 290c, 293e.

91. *Rep,* 10.601d.

92. I have attempted to lay out what I regard as the inescapable eidetic structures involved in all experience in "Taking the Universal Viewpoint: A Descriptive Approach," *Review of Metaphysics* 50 (June 1997): 69–78.

93. See Wood, *Path into Metaphysics,* chap. 6, for a treatment of this opening.

94. Dufrenne, *Phenomenology,* 117ff.

95. *Theaetetus,* 175a.

96. *Theaetetus,* 155c.

97. Frank Lloyd Wright, *The Future of Architecture* (New York: Mentor, 1953), 115. For a fuller treatment, see Wood, "Architecture."

98. Wright, *Future of Architecture,* 160, 206–8.

99. Ibid., 141.

100. Ibid., 156ff. On surface decoration, see 93.

101. Ibid., 33. Cf. the whole chapter "The Cardboard House," 143–62.

102. Ibid., 144, 152, 155.

103. Ibid., 94ff.

104. Ibid., 66.

105. Ibid., 60, 234.

106. Ibid., 70, 123.

107. Ibid., 221.

108. Ibid., 104. On 195, Wright calls for "ordered freedom" and an essential distinction between creative joy and mere pleasure seeking.

109. Ibid., 101.

## III. Aristotle

1. Aristotle, *The Physics,* trans. P. Wicksteed and F. Cornford (Cambridge, Mass.:

Harvard University Press, 1980), 2.1.192b8–19 and 4.195b31ff.; 9.199b34ff.; *Metaphysics,* 7.7.1032a13.

2. *NE,* 3.2.111b4ff.

3. *OS,* 3.425b27.

4. *OS,* 3.4.415b1.

5. *OS,* 3.425b27.

6. *NE,* 6.1.1139a7.

7. *NE,* 6.1141a.

8. *NE,* 1.2.1094a28.

9. *NE,* 2.1103a14.

10. See Wood, "Aspects of Freedom."

11. *NE,* 6.4.1140a1ff.

12. *Nicomachean Ethics,* W. D. Ross translation in R. McKeon (ed.), *The Basic Works of Aristotle* (New York: Random House, c. 1941), 1025

13. Aristotle, *Aristotle's Nicomachean Ethics,* trans. Hippocrates G. Apostle (Grinell, Iowa: Peripatetic Press, 1984), 104.

14. *NE* (Rackham trans.), 335.

15. Aquinas, *ST,* 1–2.57.3.

16. This is one of Heidegger's basic distinctions. See below, chap. 10, 5.

17. Elder Olson, "The Poetic Method in Aristotle," in *Aristotle's* Poetics *and English Literature,* ed. E. Olson (Toronto: University of Toronto Press, 1965), 181.

18. *NE,* 3.1118a21–3.

19. Cf. chap. 5.

20. Plato, *Timaeus,* 49.

21. *Physics,* 2.2-3.194a, 22–195b, 30. Cf. also my treatment of Aristotle in *Path into Metaphysics,* chap. 8.

22. *Physics,* 2.193a10 ff.

23. *OS,* 3.425b27.

24. *OS,* 2.1.412b.

25. *Metaphysics,* 12.1072b.

26. Cf. chaps. 7 and 8, below.

27. *Poetics,* 4.1448b.

28. Cf. chap. 2, above.

29. *Politics,* 8.5.1340a1ff.

30. *NE,* 2.1102a26.

31. *OS,* 3.2.425b26. For a similar position advanced by Socrates, see *Theaetetus,* 153d.

32. This seems to be a constant from Galileo and Kepler through Descartes, Locke, Hume, Kant, on up to Russell.

33. Heidegger, *BAT,* §29.172ff. Cf. also "What Is Metaphysics?" in *Martin Heidegger: Basic Writings,* ed. and trans. D. Krell (New York: Harper and Row, 1977), 101ff.

34. Walter Pater, *The Renaissance,* in *Selected Writings of Walter Pater,* ed. Harold Bloom (New York: Columbia University Press, 1974), 55–57.

35. *Physics,* 2.8.199a15.

36. *OS,* 3.432a1.

37. *Poetics,* 9.1451b.

38. *Poetics*, 25.1460b34.

39. For Polyclitus see Galen, *De placitis Hippocratis et Platonis*, 5, ed. Mueller, 425, and Quintilian, *Institutio oratoria*, 5.12.21, cited in J. J. Pollitt, *The Art of Ancient Greece: Sources and Documents* (Cambridge: Cambridge University Press, 1990), 76–77; for Schopenhauer see *WWR*, vol. 1, bk. 3, sec. 2, §45.222. Johann Winckelmann saw the Greek genius in the ability to depict nature in its visual ideality, "as it should be," in *Reflections on the Imitation of Greek Works in Painting and Sculpture*, trans. E. Heyer and R. Norton (LaSalle, Ill.: Open Court, 1987), 21–25.

40. Neither Polyclitus's treatise nor his *Doryphorus* are extant. See R. H. Wilenski, *The Meaning of Modern Sculpture* (Boston: Beacon Press, 1961), 37. For Kant, see below, chap. 7, n.88.

41. *Poetics*, 8.1451a30ff.; 23.1459a20.

42. Leon Battista Alberti, *The Ten Books of Architecture: The 1755 Leoni Edition* (New York: Dover, 1986), bk. 6, chap. 2.

43. *Poetics*, 6.1449b.25ff.

44. *Politics*, 8.5.1340a30.

45. *Poetics*, 1.1447a20.

46. *Poetics*, 4, 1448b, 24.

47. *Politics*, 8.5.1339a ff.

48. *Politics*, 8.5.1340a20.

49. *Politics*, 8.5.1341a15.

50. *Poetics*, 6.1449b24.

51. Cf. Jerome Schaefer, *The Philosophy of Mind* (Englewood Cliffs, N.J.: Prentice-Hall, 1968), 77ff.

52. Cf. Hegel, *PS*, §399ff., on action as communitarian.

53. *Poetics*, 7.1450b25.

54. Ibid.

55. Cf. chap. 5.

56. *Poetics*, 20.1457a ff.

57. *Poetics*, 22.1458a32.

58. *Poetics*, 22.1459a5.

59. *Politics*, 8.7.1342a5.

60. Plato, *Rep*, 10.606d.

61. *NE*, 1.1100b20.

62. *Poetics*, 4.1229a10ff.

63. *Poetics*, 24.1459b30.

64. *Politics*, 8.10.1329b24.

65. *Poetics*, 6.1450b1.

66. *Poetics*, 12.1452b16.

67. *Poetics*, 6.1450a37.

68. *Politicus*, 287b.

69. Erich Hertzmann, "Mozart's Creative Process," in *The Creative World of Mozart*, ed. Paul Henry Lang (New York: Norton, 1963), 17–30.

70. Cf. Dufrenne, *Phenomenology*, 34–35.

71. Paul Ricoeur, *The Rule of Metaphor*, trans. R. Czerny, K. McLaughlin, J. Costello (Toronto: University of Toronto Press, 1977), 35–41.

72. Sam Hunter and John Jacobus, *Modern Art: Painting, Sculpture, Architecture* (Englewood Cliffs, N.J.: Prentice-Hall, 1985), 112b.

73. Ibid., 112b, 118a.

74. Ibid., 55a.

75. Ibid., 110a.

76. Ibid., 110a.

77. Ibid., 56b.

78. This is attributed to Friedrich von Schlegel by G. W. F. Hegel, *Aesthetics: Lectures on Fine Art*, trans. T. Knox (Oxford: Clarendon Press, 1975), 2:662 (henceforth *ALFA*). In future citations, I will also refer to Hegel, *The Philosophy of Fine Art*, trans. F. Osmaston (London: G. Bell, 1920), following the Knox translation in parentheses with volume and page number, and thus here: (3:65). Schopenhauer traces it back to Goethe in Schopenhauer, *WWR*, 2, suppl. to bk. 3, chap. 35, 453–54.

79. Hunter and Jacobus, *Modern Art*, 28b; cf. Collins, *Changing Ideals*, 272.

80. *Rhetoric*, 1.1361b8.

81. *Metaphysics*, 13.1078b1.

## *IV. Plotinus*

1. Wladyslaw Tatarkiewicz, *History of Aesthetics*, vol. 2, *Medieval Aesthetics* (The Hague: Mouton, 1972).

2. In particular, Edgar le Bruyne in *The Aesthetics of the Middle Ages*, trans. E. Hennessey (New York: Ungar, 1969), and Umberto Eco in *Art and Beauty*, as well as in *The Aesthetics of Thomas Aquinas*, trans. H. Bredin (Cambridge, Mass.: Harvard University Press, 1988), have attempted to provide a continuous thematic and dialectical context for these scraps.

3. See chap. 2, n. 65.

4. Thomas Aquinas, *On the Truth of the Catholic Faith: Summa contra gentiles*, trans. A. Pegis et al. (Garden City, N.Y.: Doubleday, 1955), 4.29, 4.56, 4.79 ff.

5. On Avicenna, see Etienne Gilson, *History of Christian Philosophy in the Middle Ages* (New York: Random House, 1955), 204; on Averroës, 224–25.

6. *ST*, 1.84.5.

7. Schopenhauer, *WWR*, 1.3.§38.198.

8. Hegel, *HPM*, §564.298.

9. Cf. Gilson, *Christian Philosophy*, 76.

10. *Enn*, 5.3.

11. Emmanuel Levinas, *Totality and Infinity: An Essay on Exteriority*, trans. A. Lingis (Pittsburgh: Duquesne University Press, 1969), 102–5.

12. *Rep*, 6.518c–d.

13. *Rep*, 6.511b.

14. Cf. for example *Bṛhadāraṇyaka Upaniṣad*, 3.4.1 in S. Radhakrishnan and C. Moore, eds., *A Sourcebook in Indian Philosophy* (Princeton, N.J.: Princeton University Press, 1957), 83.

15. Porphyry, *The Life of Plotinus*, 23, in *Enn*, 71.

16. This is a constant theme: cf. *Enn*, 5.1.6; 6.7.34; 6.9.11.

17. The chief texts on beauty are *Enn*, 1.6; 5.8.

18. Cf. Hans Urs von Balthasar, *The Realm of Metaphysics in Antiquity*, trans. B. McNeil et al., vol. 4 of *The Glory of the Lord* (San Francisco: Ignatius Press, 1989), 307.

19. Actually Plotinus is ambivalent on this: the place of Beauty is the place of the Forms, with the Good beyond; *or* the Good and Beauty are on the same level, though Beauty is still also at the level of the Forms (cf. *Enn*, 1.6, 6 and 9).

20. *Enn*, 6.1.

21. *Enn*, 5.2.

22. *Enn*, 5.1.4.

23. *Enn*, 1.4.12–16. There is a line of texts that claims that all is form, including matter itself as the lowest level of form. (Cf. *Enn*, 5.8.7).

24. *Enn*, 4.8.4.

25. *Enn*, 1.6.9.

26. *Enn*, 5.8.11.

27. *Enn*, 2.9.16.

28. Cf. Huston Smith, *Forgotten Truth* (New York: Harper and Row, 1976), 19–33

29. Cf. Adolphe Tanquerey, *The Spiritual Life: A Treatise on Ascetical and Mystical Theology* (Belgium: Desclée, 1930), 297ff.

30. *Enn*, 5.8.10–11.

31. *Enn*, 2.9.16.

32. Cf. Paul Ricoeur, *Fallible Man*, trans. C. Kelbley (Chicago: Regnery, 1965), 103–5.

33. *Enn*, 5.8.1–5.

34. Cf. below, chap. 8.

35. *Enn*, 5.8.5.

36. *Enn*, 5.8.1.

37. *De institutione musica*, 1.34; *Medieval Aesthetics*, 2.86.

38. *Enn*, 5.8.1.

39. *Enn*, 4.3.30.

40. *Enn*, 5.8.5, 6.

41. Cf. Robert O'Connell, *Art and the Christian Intelligence in St. Augustine* (New York: Fordham University Press, 1978), 68, on the shift of accent in Plotinus from the earlier "On Beauty" (*Enn*, 1.6) to the later "On the Intelligible Beauty" (5.8).

42. Augustine, *Confessions*, 7.9.

43. *Confessions*, 9.10.

44. Hans Urs von Balthasar, *Studies in Theological Style: Clerical Styles*, trans. A. Louth, F. McDonagh, and B. McNeil, vol. 2 of *The Glory of the Lord* (San Francisco: Ignatius Press, 1984), 121.

45. *Confessions*, 10.33.

46. *De immortalitate animae*, 13; *On the Immortality of the Soul*, trans. G. Leckie in *Basic Writings of St. Augustine*, ed. Whitney Oates (New York: Random House, 1948), 313.

47. *De natura boni*, 3; *Medieval Aesthetics*, 2.60. Cf. Eco, *Aesthetics of Thomas Aquinas*, 66–67.

48. *De vera religione*, 30.55, 32.59, 40.76, MA, 2.59; *Confessions*, 4.13.

49. *De ordine*, 2.15.42, MA, 2.60.

50. *De civitate dei*, 11.18, MA, 2.61.

51. *De musica*, 6.12.38, MA, 2.61.

52. From *De ordine*, cited in Eco, *Aesthetics of Thomas Aquinas*, 50.

53. *De immortalitate*, 4, Basic Writings, 304.

54. *The Greatness of the Soul*, trans. J. Colleran (New York: Newman Press, 1950), 28.54.81.

55. *Greatness*, 33.76.104–6

56. O'Connell, *Art*, 88, commenting on *De musica*, 6.44.

57. O'Connell, *Art*, 78.

58. *Soliloquia*, 2.10.18, MA 2.65.

59. *De musica*, 1.12.

60. *Greatness of the Soul*, 33.72.100–101; 34.78.107–8.

61. Balthasar, *Clerical Styles*, 127, citing *De musica*, 6.20.

62. Cf. Eco, *Art and Beauty*, 18.

63. Dionysius, *On Divine Names*, in Pseudo-Dionysius, *Complete Works*, trans. C. Luibhead (New York: Paulist Press, 1987), 4.7.46.

64. Dionysius, *Mystical Theology*, *Works*, 4.141.

65. Dionysius, *Divine Names*, *Works*, 5.5.99 and 11.6.124.

66. Hans Urs von Balthasar, *The Realm of Metaphysics in the Modern Age*, trans. O. Davies, A. Louth, B. McNeil, J. Saward, and R. Williams, vol. 5 of *The Glory of the Lord* (San Francisco: Ignatius Press, 1991), 12–27.

67. Dionysius, *Divine Names*, *Works*, 4.9.78.

68. Cf. Balthasar, *Clerical Styles*, 164ff.

69. Cf. Eco, *Art and Beauty*, 84.

70. The expressions are scattered throughout the opusculum *De pulchro et bono*, a work originally attributed to Thomas Aquinas, but later discovered to be from the hand of Albert. Cf. Thomas Aquinas, *S. Thomae Aquinatis opera omnia: Aliorum medii aevi auctorum scripta* 61, ed. R. Busa (Stuttgart-Bad Cannstatt: Friedrich Frommann Verlag, 1980), 43–47.

71. Cf. Gilson, *Christian Philosophy*, 361ff. For a fuller presentation and the citation of texts pertinent to this exposition, see Wood, *Path into Metaphysics*, 177–203.

72. Aquinas, *ST*, 1.3.4; *Summa contra gentiles*, 2.52.

73. Augustine, *Confessions*, 3.6.

74. Thomas Aquinas, *On the Power of God* (Westminster: Newman Press, 1952), 7, 5, ad 14.

75. Thomas Aquinas, *On Being and Essence*, trans. A. Maurer (Toronto: Pontifical Institute of Medieval Studies, 1949), 4:43ff.

76. *ST*, 1-2.27.1, ad 3.

77. Cf. Augustine, *Confessions*, 10.27.

78. *ST*, 1.91.3, ad 3; 2-2.141.4, ad 3.

79. *ST*, 1.78.3.

80. Cf. below, chap. 6.

81. Le Bruyne, *Aesthetics*, 27.

82. *ST*, 1-2.27.1, ad 3.

83. Cf. Eco, *Art and Beauty*, 115.

84. *ST*, 1.39 ad 8. For an interpretation of these properties against the background of their development in Western thought before Aquinas, see Eco, *Aesthetics*, 64–121.

85. *ST*, 1.12.1, ad 4.

86. *ST*, 1.5.4, ad 1.

87. Jacques Maritain, *Art and Scholasticism* and *the Frontiers of Poetry* (New York: Scribners, 1962), 164.

88. *ST,* 1.5.4.

89. Maritain, *Art,* 132, 173. Eco does not find this notion of fusion in Aquinas: *Aesthetics of Thomas Aquinas,* 39.

90. *Disputed Questions On Truth,* vol. 3, trans. R. Schmitt (Chicago: Regenery, 1954), 22.1, ad 12.

91. Eco, *Aesthetics,* 37. Eco contradicts his own position here in the conclusion to the book, where the relation to the subject is what allows the transcendentality of beauty to show itself (*Aesthetics,* 191).

92. *ST,* 1.39.8.

93. *ST,* 1–2.57.4. Cf. my own translation of Aristotle's original phrase in chapter 3.

94. Eco, *Art and Beauty,* 92–95

95. *Commentary on the Physics of Aristotle,* trans. R. Blackwell, R. Spath, W. Thirlkel (New Haven: Yale University Press, 1963), 2.4.

96. *ST,* 1.77.1, ad. 7.

97. *ST,* 1–2.101.2, ad 2.

98. *ST,* 1–2.57.3, ad 3.

99. *De septem donis Spiritus Sancti,* 2.7.1, *Opera Omnia,* ed. A. Peltier (Paris: Vivès, 1866), 7.635b; for Balthasar, see *Clerical Styles,* 276-77.

100. Cf. Balthasar, *Clerical Styles,* 263.

101. *De sc. Chr.* q. 7 (Quaracchi edition, 5.43a–b), cited in Balthasar, *Clerical Styles,* 268.

102. Balthasar, *Clerical Styles,* 335.

103. Ibid., 283.

104. Bonaventure, *Itinerarium mentis in deum,* 1, *Opera,* 12.1.5–6; Balthasar, *Clerical Styles,* 346.

105. Balthasar, *Clerical Styles,* 318–19, 335.

106. Bonaventure, *In sententias,* 3.1, dubium 3, *Opera,* 4.7.

107. Bonaventure, *Breviloquium,* prologue, *Opera* 7.244.

108. Balthasar, *Clerical Styles,* 335.

109. Ibid.

110. See Hans Urs von Balthasar, *Studies in Theological Styles: Lay Styles,* A. Louth, J. Saward, M. Simon and R. Williams, vol. 3 of *The Glory of the Lord* (San Francisco: Ignatius Press, 1986), 406ff.

111. Francis of Assisi, "Canticle of Brother Son," in *The Little Flowers of St. Francis,* trans. R. Brown (Garden City, N.Y.: Image Books, 1958), 317–18.

112. Friedrich Nietzsche, *On the Genealogy of Morals,* trans. W. Kaufmann (New York: Vintage, c. 1967), 2.17.86 (henceforth *GM*).

113. Cf. Hans Urs von Balthasar, *Theology: The Old Covenant,* trans. B. McNeil and E. Leiva-Merikakis, vol. 6 of *The Glory of the Lord* (San Francisco: Ignatius Press, 1991), 62; *Theology: The New Covenant,* trans. B. McNeil, vol. 7 of *The Glory of the Lord* (San Francisco: Ignatius Press, 1989), 239.

114. Hunter and Jacobus, *Modern Art,* 47a.

115. Balthasar, *Seeing the Form,* trans. E. Leiva-Merikakis, vol. 1 of *The Glory of the Lord* (San Francisco: Ignatius Press, 1982), 158.

116. Friedrich Nietzsche, *Twilight of the Idols*, trans. R. Hollingdale (Baltimore: Penguin, 1968), 37 (henceforth *TI*).

117. Martin Buber, "Man and His Image Work," in *Knowledge of Man*, 159.

118. Wassily Kandinsky, *Concerning the Spiritual in Art*, trans. M. Sadler (New York: Dover, 1977), 1ff.

119. Henry Moore, "The Sculptor's Aims," in *Henry Moore*, xxxi, b.

120. Cf. the discussion of Michelangelo in Wilenski, *Modern Sculpture*, 95. Michelangelo expresses the reverse in Plotinus's view here in a sonnet that begins, "Non ha l'ottimo artista alcun concetto / Ch' un marmo solo in se non circonscriva."

121. Plutarch, cited in Max Picard, *The World of Silence* (Chicago: Regnery, 1952), 154–55.

## V. Kant

1. Friedrich Paulsen, *Immanuel Kant: His Life and Doctrine*, trans. J. Creighton and A. Lefevre (New York: Ungar, 1972), 53.

2. Immanuel Kant, *Critique of Practical Reason*, trans. L. W. Beck (Indianapolis: Bobbs-Merrill, 1956).

3. For references to *CPR*, I will cite the Akademie edition references to the first and second editions of *CPR* as A or B, each followed by their respective page numbers in Akademie where the treatment begins. The reference will be completed by inclusive page numbers from the Smith translation: e.g., *CPR*, B 25/A 12, (59).

4. *CJ*, §§23–29.98ff. (244ff.). All references to *CJ* give the section number, followed by the page numbers of the Pluhar translation and, in parentheses, the Akademie edition.

5. *CPR*, preface to the 2d ed., B xv (22).

6. *CPR*, A 12/B 25, (59).

7. *CPR*, B 145 (161); A 671/B 699 (550). Cf. *CJ*, §77.408–9 (292–93).

8. *CPR*, B 45/A 30 (73). For three basic views of the nature of the sensa see Wood, *Path into Metaphysics*, 165.

9. *CPR*, A 22/B 37 (67ff.).

10. *CPR*, B 46/A 31 (74ff.).

11. *CPR*, A 24/B 39 (68ff.).

12. *CPR*, B 102/A 76 (111ff.).

13. *CPR*, A 70/B 95 (106ff.).

14. *CPR*, A 145/B (183ff.).

15. *CPR*, B 133ff.; A 341/B 399.

16. *CPR*, A 3212/B 377 (315–22).

17. Cf. Immanuel Kant, *Prolegomena to Any Future Metaphysics*, trans. P. Carus, rev. J. Ellington (Indianapolis: Hackett, 1977), 28off. (25ff.).

18. *CPR*, A 532/B 560 (464ff.).

19. *CPR*, A 57/B 75 (93).

20. *Prolegomena*, 1–2 (256).

21. Bonaventure, *II Sent*, 1.1.1.2.

22. Aristotle, *Metaphysics*, 2.1071b1; *Physics*, 251b12.

23. Aquinas, *ST*, 1.46, 2.

24. *CPR*, A 405/B 432 (384ff.).

25. *CPR*, A 590/B 618 ff. (499ff.).

26. *CPR*, A 592/B 620 ff. (500ff.); cf. Anselm, *Proslogion*, chap. 2–4, in *Opera omnia*, ed. F. Schmitt (Stuttgart: Friedrich Frommann, 1968), 1:101–4.

27. Aquinas, *ST*, 1.2.1, ad 2.

28. *CPR*, A 671/B 699 (550).

29. *CJ*, §91.468 (362), 474 (368).

30. *CPR*, A 542/B 570 (469).

31. Immanuel Kant, *Foundations of the Metaphysics of Morals*, trans. L. W. Beck (Indianapolis: Bobbs-Merrill, 1959), 64–67.

32. Ibid., 31ff.

33. Ibid., 39.

34. Ibid., 47.

35. Ibid., 49, 55.

36. Immanuel Kant, *The Metaphysical Principles of Virtue*, trans. J. Ellington (Indianapolis: Bobbs-Merrill, 1964), 50ff. (391ff.).

37. *Critique of Practical Reason*, 114, 126ff.

38. Ibid.; *CJ*, §86.444 (333).

39. *Critique of Practical Reason*, 37ff. (133ff.).

40. *CJ*, introduction, 2.174ff. (12ff.).

41. *CJ*, introduction, 4.179 (18–19).

42. *CJ*, introduction, 4.179ff. (18ff.).

43. *CJ*, introduction, 5.185 (24).

44. *CJ*, §43.303 (170).

45. *CJ*, §46.307 (174); cf. "First Introduction," 2.204 (393), 5.215 (403), 9.232 (421). This holds even though it seems that the consideration of art was a later addition to the Critique of Taste, projected in 1787. Zammito complains of the infelicity of its placement. John Zammito, *The Genesis of Kant's* Critique of Judgment (Chicago: University of Chicago Press, 1992), 4, 129.

46. *CJ*, §64.369-70 (248–49).

47. Aristotle, *Physics*, 2.3.194b16ff.

48. Cf. Aristotle, *OS*, 2.1.112a1ff.

49. David Hull, *Philosophy of Biological Science* (Englewood Cliffs, N.J.: Prentice-Hall, 1974), 103ff.

50. *CJ*, §10.220ff. (64ff.).

51. *CJ*, §46.307 (174).

52. *CJ*, §45.306 (174). Winckelmann, who seems to be in the background of Kant's discussion, suggests that Bernini, for example, was sensitized to the beauty of nature through the study of Greek statuary. Winckelmann, *Imitation of Greek Works*, 19.

53. Cf. *CJ*, introduction, 5-9.181ff. (20ff.); first introduction, 5.211ff. (399ff.). For a laying out of the underlying scheme of purposiveness in the third critique, see Robert E. Wood, "Aesthetics within the Kantian Project," in *Philosophy and Art*, ed. D. Dahlstrom (Washington, D.C.: Catholic University of America Press, 1991), esp. 176–80.

54. *CJ*, introduction, 6.187 (27); cf. also the comment following §29.266 (126). In the famous letter to Reinhold projecting a Critique of Taste, Kant paralleled the faculties of cognition, of feeling pleasure and pain, and of desire with theoretical philosophy,

*teleology,* and practical philosophy (cited in Zammito, *Genesis,* 46–47). Feeling and teleology are here thought together.

55. *CJ,* §86.442ff. (331ff.).

56. Friedrich Nietzsche, *Human, All Too Human: A Book for Free Spirits,* trans. M. Faber and S. Lehmann (Lincoln: University of Nebraska Press, 1984).

57. *CJ,* §16.229 (76).

58. *CJ,* §13.223 (68); §15.226 (73).

59. *CJ,* §4.207 (49); §16.229–30 (76–77).

60. *CJ,* §17.231ff. (79ff.).

61. Schopenhauer, *WWR,* 1, app., 528.

62. Jean-François Lyotard, *Lessons on the Analytic of the Sublime,* trans. E. Rottenberg (Stanford: Stanford University Press, 1994), 44–49.

63. *CJ,* §2.204 (45).

64. Aristotle, *NE,* 3.1118a21–23.

65. *CJ,* §5.209 (51).

66. *CJ,* §1.203 (44).

67. *CJ,* §13.223 (68–69).

68. *CJ,* §9.217–18 (62–63).

69. Cf. Zammito, *Genesis,* 131.

70. Cf. *CPR,* A72/B97 (108).

71. *CJ,* §6.212 (54).

72. Cf. Dufrenne, *Phenomenology,* 191.

73. *CPR,* A 70/B 95 (107). The corresponding pure concepts are unity, plurality, and totality (A 80/B 106, [113]), of which Kant does not seem to make even implicit use here.

74. *CJ,* §7.212 (55).

75. *CJ,* §8.213ff. (57ff.); §15.226ff. (73ff.).

76. *CJ,* introduction, 4.179 (18). He later identifies the indeterminate concept as that of the supersensible ground; *CJ,* §57.339ff. (211ff.).

77. *CJ,* §9.216ff. (61ff.); first introduction, 8, comment. 230 (419).

78. *CJ,* §20–21.238ff. (87ff.).

79. *CJ,* §35.287 (151): §38.289–90 (155–56); first introduction, 8.224 (413).

80. *CJ,* §49.314 (182).

81. *CJ,* §40.294 (160).

82. *CJ,* §14.225 (72).

83. *CJ,* §39–40.291ff. (157ff.).

84. *CJ,* §57.339ff. (211ff.).

85. *CJ,* §59.351ff. (225ff.).

86. *CJ,* n§57.339ff. (211ff.).

87. *CJ,* §56.338 (210).

88. *CJ,* §17.231ff. (79ff.).

89. Cf. *CJ,* general comment following §29.270 (130).

90. *CJ,* §17.234 (82–83). The Polyclitian canon seems to involve another element, namely a doctrine of harmonic proportions that need not necessarily be the kind of statistical average Kant suggests. Here we have a case of a kind of empirical-rational tension in arriving at a norm. Kant seem to have had in mind the descriptions of

Winckelmann in *Imitation of Greek Works* and *History of Ancient Art*, trans. G. Lodge, 4 vols. (Boston: Little, Brown, 1856–73). Cf. the discussion of Winckelmann in Alex Potts, *Flesh and the Ideal: Winckelmann and the Origins of Art History* (New Haven: Yale University Press, 1994), esp. 155ff.

91. *CJ*, §10.219ff. (64ff.).

92. *CPR*, A 80/B 106 (113).

93. *CJ*, §65.372ff. (251ff.).

94. *CPR*, A 80/B 106 (113).

95. *CJ*, §18.236ff. (85ff.).

96. *CJ*, §20–22.238ff. (87ff.); §40.293ff. (159ff.).

97. Aristotle, *OS*, 3.2.426b4ff.

98. *CJ*, §32.282ff. (145ff.).

99. Ibid.; *CJ*, §46.308 (175).

100. Cf. Dufrenne, *Phenomenology*, 416–18.

101. Zammito, *Genesis*, 269ff. Kant's notion of the sublime has received a great deal of attention recently. Significant essays have been gathered in Jean-François Courtine, *Of the Sublime: Presence in Question*, ed. and trans. J. Librett (Albany: State University of New York Press, 1993). I have already referred to Jean-François Lyotard's *Lessons on the Analytic of the Sublime*, which is a careful reading of pertinent sections of the third critique, leaning heavily on the concepts of reflection in the first critique.

102. *CJ*, §23.246 (100).

103. Lyotard, *Lessons*, 54–56.

104. Kant still has room for a transcendence beyond this world. It would seem that for Lyotard the door to such considerations has been definitively closed.

105. Immanuel Kant, *Observations on the Feeling of the Beautiful and Sublime*, trans. J. Goldthwait (Berkeley: University of California Press, 1960).

106. Psalms 8:3–5, New Revised Standard Edition.

107. Rudoph Otto, *The Idea of the Holy*, trans. J. Harvey (New York: Oxford University Press, 1964), 12–40.

108. *CJ*, §23.244ff. (97ff.).

109. *CJ*, general comment to §29.267–68 (127–28).

110. Lyotard, *Lessons*, 150.

111. Ibid., 123ff., 159, 214, 234; cf. also Lyotard, *The Differend: Phrases in Dispute* (Minneapolis: University of Minnesota Press, 1983) and *The Inhuman: Reflections on Time* (Stanford: Stanford University Press, 1988). For Derrida, see "Differance" in *Margins of Philosophy*, trans. A. Bass (Chicago: University of Chicago Press, 1982), 1–27.

112. Lyotard, *Lessons*, 129.

113. Ibid., 74, 76, 153–57.

114. Wing-tsit Chan, trans. and comp., *A Sourcebook in Chinese Philosophy* (Princeton, N.J.: Princeton University Press, 1963), 136–210.

115. G. W. F. Hegel, *The Encyclopaedia Logic*, trans. T. Geraets, W. Suchting, and H. Harris (Indianapolis: Hackett, 1991), §94.149 (henceforth *EL*).

116. Cf. Lyotard, *Lessons*, 111ff.

117. *CJ*, §24.247 (101).

118. Blaise Pascal, *Pensées* (New York: Modern Library, 1941), 6.§347.

119. *CJ*, general comment to §29.269 (129).

120. *CJ*, §26.256 (113).

121. *CJ*, general comment to §29.272ff. (132ff.).

122. *CJ*, §46.308 (175).

123. Cited in Katharine Gilbert and Helmut Kuhn, *A History of Aesthetics* (New York: Dover, 1972), 199.

124. Zammito, *Genesis*, 26–28.

125. Ibid., 34ff.

126. *CJ*, §49.313ff. (181ff.).

127. *CJ*, §43.304 (304).

128. *CJ*, §49.314 (182).

129. *CJ*, §53.328 (199).

130. See chaps. 8 and 9. Cf. Dahlhaus's detailed discussion of the full cultural context of this in *Absolute Music*.

131. *CJ*, §53.329 (199).

132. *CJ*, §53.326 (196ff.).

133. *CJ*, §49.314 (182–83).

134. See Lyotard, *Lessons*, 214.

135. *CPR*, A120 (144).

136. *CPR*, A137/B176ff. (180ff.); *CJ*, §59.351 (227).

137. *CJ*, §49.314 (182–83).

138. *CJ*, §51–52.320ff. (189ff.).

139. *CJ*, §59.354 (230).

140. *CJ*, §64.370ff. (248ff.).

141. *CJ*, §82.426 (313–14).

142. *CJ*, §83.429ff. (317ff.).

143. *CJ*, §84.434ff. (321ff.).

144. *CJ*, introduction, 9 (196), 37.

145. Ibid., 36–37.

146. *CJ*, general comment to §29.266ff. (126ff.).

147. Cf. the essays developing and criticizing this notion in George Dickie and Richard Sclafani, eds., *Aesthetics: A Critical Anthology* (New York: St. Martin's Press, 1977): Edward Bullough, "Psychical Distance as a Factor in Art and an Aesthetic Principle," 758–82; Allan Casebier, "The Concept of Aesthetic Distance," 783–99; and George Dickie, "All Aesthetic Attitude Theories Fail: The Myth of the Aesthetic Attitude," 800–15.

148. Cf. Nietzsche, *GM*, 3.6.104.

149. Dufrenne, *Phenomenology*, 55, 138–46.

150. Ibid., 231.

151. Hunter and Jacobus, *Modern Art*, 29a.

152. Ibid., 32a.

153. Ibid., 110a. Also see Dufrenne, *Phenomenology*, 284–85.

154. Augustine, *Confessions*, 10.27.

155. *CJ*, general comment to §29.272ff. (132ff.).

156. *CJ*, §28.263 (122).

157. Francesco Petrarca [Petrarch], " The Ascent of Mont Ventoux," in *The Renaissance Philosophy of Man*, ed. E. Cassirer, P. Kristeller, and J. Randall (Chicago: University of Chicago Press, 1971), 36–46.

158. Cf. Giedion, *Space*, 432.

159. Jean-Jacques Rousseau, *The Reveries of the Solitary Walker*, trans. C. Butterworth (New York: Harper and Row, 1979).

160. Dufrenne, *Phenomenology*, 357.

161. Peter Kivy, "Recent Scholarship and the British Tradition: A Logic of Taste—The First Fifty Years," in *Aesthetics*, ed. Dickie and Sclafani, 636.

162. David Hume, "Of the Standard of Taste," in *Aesthetics*, ed. Dickie and Sclafani, 592–606.

163. Alasdair MacIntyre, *Whose Justice? Which Rationality?* (Notre Dame, Ind.: University of Notre Dame Press, 1988).

164. Hume, "Taste," 592.

165. Ibid., 597.

166. Ibid., 597–600.

167. Ibid., 598.

168. Ibid., 601.

169. Ibid., 603.

170. Ibid., 597.

171. Ibid., 595.

172. Commenting on Hume's "ideal observer," Peter Kivy asks, "Should the ideal aesthetic observer be passionate or cold-blooded, emotional, or cerebral? Poet or peasant, of the elite or the masses? In the ivory tower, or in the ash can? Political or apolitical, moral or immoral? Sensitive to craftsmanship or aesthetic surface, technique or impression? Quick to judge or slow in judgment? All these questions have been part and parcel of the evolution of artistic and aesthetic movements and schools, just as much as have questions about the recommended aesthetic properties of works of art." "Logic of Taste," 639. Our reading of Plato and Hume would lead us to collapse some of the dichotomies, requiring passion and detachment, poet and peasant, inhabitance of the polis and its transcendence, an *Aufhebung* of conventional morality through critique rooted in the structures of experience, a holism that would appreciate surface and technique, but which would surely not advocate quick judgment over deliberation (who but a fool would?).

173. David Hume, *Dialogues Concerning Natural Religion*, ed. N. K. Smith (Indianapolis: Bobbs-Merrill, 1947), 2:148.

174. Cf. Joseph Lawrence, *Die ewige Anfang: Zum Verhältnis von Natur und Geschichte bei Schelling* (Tübingen: Köhler, 1984).

175. Cf. Le Corbusier, *Towards a New Architecture*, trans. F. Etchells (New York: Praeger, 1960), 32; Le Corbusier reports the judgment without sharing it.

176. Hegel, *ALFA*, 2:684 (3:89).

177. Eugène-Emmanuel Viollet-le-Duc, *The Foundations of Architecture: Selections from the Dictionnaire Raisonné*, trans. K. Whitehead (New York: George Braziller, 1990), 70ff., 163, 182ff., 259ff.

178. Wright, *Future of Architecture*, 51ff.

179. Umberto Boccione, "Technical Manifesto of Futurist Sculpture," in *Art and Its Significance: An Anthology of Aesthetic Theory*, ed. S. Ross (Albany: State University of New York Press, 1984), 537–38.

180. Henry Moore, "Mesopotamian Art," in *Henry Moore*, xxxii, a; "Primitive Art" (1941), in *Henry Moore*, xxxvi, a; xxxvii, b.

181. Cf. Hunter and Jacobus, *Modern Art*, 38b ff., 136a ff.

182. Meyer Shapiro, *Modern Art: Nineteenth and Twentieth Centuries* (New York: George Braziller, 1982), 135ff.

183. Carlo Carra, *La pittura dei suoni* (Rome: Archivi del Futurismo, 1958), 1:74, cited in Michael Benedikt, *Deconstructing the Kimbell* (New York: SITES/Lumen Books, 1991), 115, n. 44.

184. André Malraux, *Voices of Silence*, trans. S. Gilbert (Princeton, N.J.: Princeton University Press, 1978), 13ff.

185. Gadamer, *Truth and Method*, 33–39.

## VI. Hegel

1. Cf. *EL*, §128, ad, 198. For a general account see Preserved Smith, *A History of Modern Culture*, vol. 2, *The Enlightenment, 1687–1776* (New York: Collier, 1962), 410ff.

2. John Locke, *An Essay Concerning Human Understanding*, ed. P. Nidditch (Oxford: Clarendon Press, 1975), bk. 2, chap. 11, 17.

3. See, for example, Hume, *Dialogues*, 2:148.

4. John Locke, *The Second Treatise of Government* (Indianapolis: Bobbs-Merrill, 1952), bk. 2, chap. 2, 4; Thomas Hobbes, *Leviathan*, ed. M. Oakschott (New York: Collier, 1973), First Part, chap. 13.

5. Cf. the treatment of the issue in the Enlightenment by Ernst Cassirer, *The Philosophy of the Enlightenment*, trans. F. Koelln and J. Pettegrove (Boston: Beacon Press, 1951), 137–60.

6. Smith, *Enlightenment*, 202–11.

7. Ibid.

8. Cf. Hegel, *Lectures on the Philosophy of Religion*, ed. P. Hodgson, trans. R. Brown et al. (Berkeley: University of California Press, 1988), 458 (henceforth *LPR*).

9. *LPR*, 422.

10. *LPR*, 144ff.; cf. Gotthold Ephraim Lessing, *Die Erziehung des Menschengeschlechts und andere Schriften* (Stuttgart: Reclam, 1965), §72.

11. Aquinas, *ST*, 1.1.1.

12. Cf. *LPR*, 418.

13. Cf. Aquinas, *ST*, 1.27ff.

14. Cf. *HPM*, §566–70.299–301; also *LPR*, 418.

15. Plotinus, *Enn*, 6.1; Augustine, *On the Trinity*, bk. 15, 23ff.

16. Augustine, *Confessions*, 7.9.

17. Aquinas, *ST*, 3.2.

18. Cf. Karl Rahner, *Foundations of Christian Faith: An Introduction to the Idea of Christianity*, trans. W. Dych (New York: Seabury, 1978), 223ff.; cf. also Karl Rahner, ed., *Encyclopedia of Theology: The Concise Sacramentum mundi* (New York: Seabury, 1975), 1755ff.

19. Augustine, *Confessions*, 3.6.

20. For fuller exposition and references, see Wood, *Path into Metaphysics*, 9:187ff.

21. Cf. Rahner, *Encyclopedia of Theology*, 690ff.

22. Cf. Wood, *Path into Metaphysics*, chap. 2, 3.

23. Cf. Rahner, *Encyclopedia of Theology*, 1148ff.

24. Pius XII, *The Mystical Body of Christ*, trans. J. Bluett (New York: The America Press, 1943).

25. Aquinas, *ST,* 1.37.1 and 2.

26. *ST,* 1.46.1, ad 6.

27. *EL,* §212, ad. There is the enigmatic and undeveloped declaration in the *Encyclopedia of Logic* that "God is eternally complete and eternally completing Himself" that seems to give the lie to understanding the Trinity as "in itself" the realm of possibility and thus empty and requiring creation of nature as its own fulfillment. In the *Science of Logic* (50) logic is said to consider God in his eternal essence before creation. There is also the declaration in *The Philosophy of History* that "spirit is immortal; with it there is no past, no future, but an essential *now*. . . . What Spirit is it has always been essentially." Trans. J. Sibree (New York: Dover, 1956), 79 (henceforth *PH*).

28. *Letter to the Ephesians* 3:6.

29. Aquinas, *ST,* 3.49.

30. G. W. F. Hegel, *Lectures on the History of Philosophy,* trans. E. Haldane (Lincoln: University of Nebraska Press, 1995), 1.73 (henceforth *LHP*).

31. Cf. Wood, *Path into Metaphysics,* 6:125–32.

32. *SL,* 82ff.; Nietzsche, *TI,* 37.

33. Cf. Aristotle, *Categories,* 5.2a11.

34. *SL,* 105ff.

35. *SL,* 479ff.

36. Cf. Dean Wooldridge, *Mechanical Man: The Physical Basis of Intelligent Life* (New York: McGraw-Hill, 1968).

37. Cf. Walter Kaufmann, "The Hegel Myth and Its Overcoming," in *From Shakespeare to Existentialism* (Garden City, N.Y.: Doubleday, 1960), 95ff.

38. *EL,* §96, ad.

39. Jacques Maritain, *The Degrees of Knowledge,* trans. G. Phelan (New York: Scribners, 1959), 112.

40. Cf. *Hegel's Philosophy of Nature,* ed. and trans. M. Petry, 3 vols. (London: George Allen and Unwin, 1970), 3:22. In spite of the rejection of evolution, Hegel's thought is so close to evolutionary thinking that it could readily pass over into such thinking when sufficient evidence had been gathered. That is precisely one of the major contentions of the lifework of Errol Harris. Cf. Harris, *Nature, Mind, and Modern Science* (London: George Allen and Unwin, 1958), 246.

41. *HPM* gives a short version Objective Spirit in §§483–552; it is elaborated in *Hegel's Philosophy of Right,* trans. T. Knox (London: Oxford University Press, 1952) (henceforth *PR*).

42. *SL,* 843–44.

43. *SL,* 50.

44. Cf. Plato, *Sophist,* 248b.

45. Aristotle, *Categories,* 5.2a11.

46. Aristotle, *OS,* 3.7.430a1–25; *Metaphysics,* 12.1072b22.

47. See note 28.

48. *SL,* 389ff.

49. *HPM,* §389.29–34.

50. *SL,* 576ff. See my "Being and Manifestness" for an attempt to articulate that notion in the contemporary context.

51. This is the basic outline of the level of subjective spirit in *HPM,* §387–482.25–240.

52. *HPM*, §465.224; §469.228; §481–82.238–40.
53. *PS*, §175ff. on self-consciousness.
54. See *PH*, 54ff., 69ff.
55. Preface to *PR*, 10; also 283; cf. also *EL*, §6.29; and *PH*, 36.
56. *PR*, §§34–104.37–74.
57. *PR*, §§105–41.75–104.
58. *PR*, §§142–360.106–223.
59. *PR*, §§158–81.110–22.
60. *PR*, §§182–256.122–55.
61. *PR*, §§257–360.155–223.
62. On freedom of property, cf. *PR*, §62.51; on freedom of the press, of speech, and of thought, §319.205–6; on freedom of conscience, §124.84, on freedom to choose a marriage partner, §162.111.
63. *PS*, §§641–71.
64. John 16:7–8; *PH*, 325; *ALFA*, 1:80 (1:108).
65. *IIPM*, §§553–77.292–315.
66. G. W. F. Hegel, *Lectures on the Philosophy of Religion*, trans. E. Speirs and J. B. Sanderson (London: Kegan Paul, Trench, Trübner, 1895), 1:4. This is an alternative to the Hodgson version of Hegel's lectures, which was based on the 1827 series.
67. *LPR*, 146.
68. *LPR*, 144ff.; cf. *ALFA*, 1:108 (1:149): *Vorstellung* includes images but also abstract concepts like "man" and "the quality of blueness," while *Begriff* contains opposite factors in unity.
69. *LHP*, 1:249ff.
70. *PH*, 15; *ALFA*, 1:30 (1:40).
71. *LPR*. Cf. *ALFA*, 1:97 (1:133).
72. *ALFA*, 1:132 (1:182–83).
73. *ALFA*, 1:152 (1:208).
74. *ALFA*, 1:148–52 (1:203–8).
75. *ALFA*, 1:1 (1:2).
76. *ALFA*, 1:114 (1:157).
77. *ALFA*, 1:153 (1:209), 156 (1:213), 163 (1:222).
78. *ALFA*, 1:159 (1:217); cf. also 176–79 (1:238–41).
79. *ALFA*, 1:3–4 (1:8–9), 279 (1:377).
80. *ALFA*, 1:33–34 (1:45–46).
81. *ALFA*, 1:8–9 (1:10–11).
82. *ALFA*, 1:44 (1:60).
83. *ALFA*, 1:51 (1:70).
84. *ALFA*, 1:39 (1:53).
85. *ALFA*, 1:304 (2:9).
86. *ALFA*, 1:89 (1:120).
87. *ALFA*, 1:26ff. (1:35ff.), 283ff. (1:384ff.).
88. *ALFA*, 1:29–30 (1:39–40).
89. *ALFA*, 1:291–92 (1:395–96), 294–98 (1:400–405).
90. *ALFA*, 1:290 (1:394).
91. *ALFA*, 1:45 (1:62); cf. also 1:254–55 (1:342–43).

92. *ALFA*, 1:49 (1:68).

93. *ALFA*, 1:7 (1:9).

94. *ALFA*, 1:51 (1:70).

95. *ALFA*, 1:52–55 (1:72–77).

96. *ALFA*, 1:51 (1:70).

97. *ALFA*, 1:55 (1:77), 111 (1:154), 173 (1:235).

98. *ALFA*, 1:76ff. (1:103ff.), 81 (1:110).

99. *ALFA*, 1:76 (1:103–4), developed in 1:303–426 (2:8–168); on architecture, see 2:630–700 (3:25–108).

100. *ALFA*, 1:226–28 (1:300–303).

101. *ALFA*, 1:77–79 (1:104–6), developed in 1:427–516 (2:175–281); on sculpture, see 2:701–91 (3:109–216).

102. *ALFA*, 1:79–81 (1:106–10), developed in 1:517–611 (2:282–401).

103. *ALFA*, 1:9–11 (1:11–13); cf. 1:102–4 (1:141–42).

104. *ALFA*, 1:86 (1:116).

105. *ALFA*, 1:104 (1:142).

106. Pascal, *Pensées*, 4.§277.

107. *HPM*, §445.188.

108. *HPM*, §447.194.

109. *HPM*, §405.96.

110. *ALFA*, 1:87 (1:117–18); for further development see 2:797–958 (3:223–337).

111. *ALFA*, 1:87–88 (1:118–19); for further development see 2:888–958 (3:338–430).

112. *ALFA*, 1:254–55 (1:342). For a penetrating treatment of the development of the idea of absolute music in the time immediately preceding and following Hegel, see Dahlhaus, *Absolute Music*.

113. *ALFA*, 1:185ff. (1:249ff.), 263 (351ff.). Hegel sees such individuals as world-historical figures. In his own time, he reported his impressions on seeing Napoleon, "the world-spirit on horseback," riding triumphantly through the streets of Jena, as just such a figure in which the meaning of the whole is concentrated. Cited in Franz Wiedmann, *Hegel: An Illustrated Biography*, trans. J. Neugroschel (New York: Pegasus, 1968), 38.

114. *ALFA*, 2:966–7 (4:12–13), 977 (4:26).

115. *ALFA*, 2:964 (4:10), 968 (4:16).

116. Cf. *ALFA*, 1002 (4:58), 1011 (4:70), esp. 1036–37 (4:101–2), for the priority of sonorousness in poetry, which is like color to a mere outline.

117. On the general content of art, see *ALFA*, 1:177–298 (1:240–320), esp. 217–20 (289–91); on poetry, see the whole of *ALFA* 2:959–1238 (4:3–350).

118. *ALFA*, 1:204 (1:273).

119. *ALFA*, 2:1037–9 (4:102–4). For a development of the epic, see 2:1040–110 (4:106–192); of lyric, 2:111–57 (4:193–247); of drama, 2:1159–239 (4:248–347).

120. *ALFA*, 2:684–700 (3:89–108).

121. *ALFA*, 2:977 (4:27).

122. *ALFA*, 1:89 (1:120).

123. On epic see *ALFA*, 2:1114 (4:196); on lyric, 2:1152 (4:242.); on Shakespeare, 2:1227 (4:337) and 2:1235–36 (4:348).

124. *ALFA*, 2:976–7 (4:26).

125. *ALFA*, 1:83–86 (1:112–16).

126. *PH*, 61.

127. *PH*, 18.

128. *PH*, 340ff.; *HPM*, §482.239–40.

129. *ALFA*, 1:102–3 (1:141–42).

130. Cf. Wood, "Being and Manifestness."

131. Cf. Wood, *Martin Buber's Ontology*, 34ff.

132. Leonardo da Vinci, *Leonardo on Painting: An Anthology of Writings*, ed. Martin Kemp (New Haven: Yale University Press, 1989), 193.

133. Cf. Henry Moore, "The Sculptor's Aims," in *Henry Moore*, xxxi, b.

134. Cf. Wright, *Future of Architecture*, 221.

135. Kant, *CPR*, B xiii.

136. Cf. Giambattista Vico, *The New Science of Giambattista Vico*, trans. T. Bergin and M. Fisch (Ithaca, N.Y.: Cornell University Press, 1991), bk. 1, sect. 3, 1.331.96.

137. Cf. *ALFA*, 1:314–15 (2:23–24).

## VII. Schopenhauer

1. Arthur Schopenhauer, *On the Fourfold Root of the Principle of Sufficient Reason*, trans. E. Payne (LaSalle, Ill.: Open Court, 1974).

2. *WWR*, 1.2.§25.127.

3. *WWR*, 1.3.§30.169ff.

4. Auguste Comte, *Introduction to Positive Philosophy*, ed. and trans. Frederick Ferré (Indianapolis: Bobbs–Merrill, 1970).

5. Arthur Schopenhauer, *Essays and Aphorisms*, trans. R. Hollingdale (Harmondsworth: Penguin, 1986), 157 (henceforth *EA*).

6. *WWR*, 1.4.§28.153ff.; cf. also 2.3.§34.408.

7. *WWR*, 1.2.§18.99ff.

8. *WWR*, 1.3.§38.198.

9. *WWR*, 1.3.§53.274.

10. Alfred, Lord Tennyson, *In memoriam*, 56.15.

11. Peter Weiss, *Marat/Sade*, trans. G. Skelton (New York: Simon and Schuster, 1965), 53.

12. Tennessee Williams, *Suddenly Last Summer*, in *The Theatre of Tennessee Williams*, vol. 3 (New York: New Directions, 1971).

13. *WWR*, 2.4.50.645.

14. *WWR*, 2.4.46.373–88.

15. *WWR*, 1.4.§68.397.

16. *WWR*, 1.4.§68.381ff.

17. *WWR*, 1.3.§53.267.

18. *WWR*, 1.4.§67.375.

19. *WWR*, 1.4.§64.355.

20. *WWR*, 1.§66.372ff.

21. *WWR*, 2.47.623.

22. *WWR*, 1.§63.356; 2.608–9. See Radhakrishnan and Moore, *Sourcebook:* "The

Synopsis of Truth" (from *Majjhima-nikaāya*, in *Further Dialogues of the Buddha*, trans. Lord Chalmers), 275–78; and "Examination of Nirvana," (from the *Mādhyamika-sāstra* of Nāgārjuna, trans. Th. Stcherbatsky), 342–45.

23. *WWR*, 1.4.§68.378ff.

24. *EA*, 158.

25. Ibid.

26. *WWR*, 1.3.§36.185.

27. *WWR*, 1.3.§45.222

28. *WWR*, 2.3.34.408.

29. *WWR*, 1.2.§17.97.

30. *EA*, 158–59.

31. *WWR*, 1.2.§27.145ff.

32. *WWR*, 1.3.§39.200–207.

33. *WWR*, 1.3.§45.223ff.

34. Longinus, *On the Sublime*, trans. W. Hamilton Fyfe, in *Aristotle:* The Poetics, *"Longinus,"* On the Sublime, and *Demetrius:* On Style (Cambridge, Mass.: Harvard University Press, 1973), 119–254.

35. *EA*, 160.

36. *WWR*, 1.3.§43.214–18.

37. *EA*, 164.

38. *EA*, 165.

39. *WWR*, 1.3.§52.257.

40. *EA*, 162–63.

41. *WWR*, 2.3.34.407.

42. Edgar Allan Poe, "The Philosophy of Composition," in *Selected Poetry and Prose of Edgar Allan Poe*, ed. T. Mabbott (New York: Modern Library, 1951). On Schiller, see chap. 8, n. 111.

43. Dufrenne, *Phenomenology*, 187, 516.

44. *WWR*, 2.4.50.644.

45. Cf. Osmaston's remark in his translation of Hegel's *Philosophy of Fine Art*, 1:386, n. 1.

## VIII. Nietzsche

1. Friedrich Nietzsche, *The Gay Science*, 3.§125, trans. W. Kaufmann (New York: Vintage, 1974), 181–82 (henceforth *GS*).

2. Plato, *Rep*, 7.508C.

3. *GS*, 3.§151.196. Cf. Taylor, *Disfiguring*, for the playing out of this process in the interplay of the plastic arts, philosophy, and religion.

4. Kant, *Critique of Practical Reason*, 114, 126ff.

5. Kant, *CJ*, §28.120–21 (261–62).

6. Cf. Aquinas, *ST*, 1–2.3.8.

7. Ludwig Feuerbach, *The Essence of Christianity*, trans. G. Eliot (New York: Harper, 1957), 13ff., 155ff.

8. Friedrich Nietzsche, *The Will to Power*, trans. W. Kaufmann and R. Hollingdale (New York: Vintage, 1967), 1:9ff. (henceforth *WTP*).

9. *GS*, 3.§125.182.

10. "Toward a Hidden God: Is God Dead?" *Time* 87 (April 1966): 82–87.

11. *GS*, 5.§343–44.279–80.

12. *GS*, 4.§293–94.236; §320.254.

13. *GS*, §107.164.

14. *GS*, §§382–83.346–48.

15. Cf. the whole of Friedrich Nietzsche, *The Anti-Christ*, trans. R. Hollingdale (Baltimore: Penguin, 1968); on Plato, see *GM*, 3.25.153–54.

16. Friedrich Nietzsche, *Ecce Homo*, trans. W. Kaufmann (New York: Vintage, c. 1967), 334 (henceforth *EH*).

17. Gregory of Nyssa, *Hexaëmeron*, *Patrologia Graeca*, 44, 189 b–192 a. Cf. Nietzsche, *TI*, 110.

18. *GM*, 2.7.67.

19. *GM*, 1.8.34.

20. Friedrich Nietzsche, *Beyond Good and Evil: Prelude to a Philosophy of the Future*, trans. W. Kaufmann (New York: Vintage, 1966), 3 (henceforth *BGE*). Cf. *TI*, 106, where Nietzsche calls Plato an "antecedent Christian."

21. Friedrich Nietzsche, *The Birth of Tragedy*, W. Kaufmann (New York: Vintage, 1967) (henceforth *BT*), §5, 21; cf. also *GM*, 3.25.154.

22. *EH*, 273; *TI*, 109; *WTP*, 4.1.§1041.536.

23. *GM*, 1.3–5.27–31.

24. *GM*, 1.11.40.

25. Matthew 5.

26. *GM*, 1.10.36.

27. *GM*, 3.15.126.

28. *BGE*, §202–3.116–18; *WTP*, 4.§860.458; *WTP*, 1.2.§125.77.

29. Cf. the subtitle of *The Will to Power: Towards a Transvaluation of Values*.

30. *BGE*, §36.48.

31. *GM*, 2.12.78.

32. Friedrich Nietzsche, *Thus Spake Zarathustra*, in *The Portable Nietzsche*, ed. and trans. W. Kaufmann (New York: Viking, 1954), 3.278 (henceforth *TSZ*); *WTP*, 3.4.§797.419.

33. Eugen Fink, *Nietzsches Philosophie* (Stuttgart: Kohlhammer, c. 1960), 31, 108, 188.

34. Cf. Gadamer, *Truth and Method*, 9ff.

35. *GS*, 4.§276.223; *WTP*, §1041.536.

36. Fink, *Philosophie*, 189.

37. *BGE*, §19.25.

38. *BGE*, §3.11.

39. For an interpretation of Nietzsche's "physiology" see Martin Heidegger, *Nietzsche*, trans. D. Krell (San Francisco: Harper and Row, 1979–87), 3:39ff.

40. From 1872 in *The Birth of Tragedy*, where Nietzsche features Goethe's adage: "to live resolutely in wholeness and fullness," to 1886, where he repeats it in his "Attempt at Self-Criticism" (*BT*, 26), through *The Gay Science*, in which Goethe is presented as a supreme representative of authentic culture (§103.159), on to *Twilight of the Idols* (1889), where he refers to Goethe as the last German before whom he feels reverence (104) and as one who aspires to totality against the separation of reason, sensuality, feeling, and will (102), and on, finally, to *Will to Power*, where Goethe again is representative of one

who forms a totality of himself (§95.60), the spiritualizer of the senses (§118.70), an exemplar of "the grand style," of giving form to one's chaos (§842.444).

41. *BGE*, §211.137.

42. *BT,* §18.113; ASC (1886), §7.26. This is a quote from Goethe's *Generalbeichte* (cf. Kaufmann's note in *BT,* 113, n. 4).

43. *WTP,* 4.§957.503.

44. *WTP,* 4.§915.483.

45. *GM*, 2.17.86; *TI*, 93.

46. Cf. Friedrich Nietzsche, *Schopenhauer as Educator,* in *Untimely Meditations,* trans. R. Hollingdale (London: Cambridge University Press, 1983), 159ff.

47. *Uses and Disadvantages of History,* 63; cf. also *BGE,* 3.

48. *BT,* §23.135–37.

49. *TSZ,* 398.

50. *TSZ,* prologue, §5.129.

51. *GM,* 3.9.247; cf. *WTP,* 4.§912ff.482ff.

52. Cf. *BGE,* §5.12; *TSZ,* 2.198.225.

53. Friedrich Nietzsche, "Truth and Lie," 42–47; cf. also *Daybreak: Thoughts on the Prejudices of Morality,* trans. R. Hollingdale (Cambridge: Cambridge University Press, 1982), §117.73.

54. *GM,* 3.12.119; *BGE,* 3.

55. Plato, *Rep,* 2.377a.

56. *GM,* 3.25.153.

57. *WTP,* 3.4.§822.435.

58. *EH,* 218.

59. *GM,* 3.27.160; *GS,* 5.§357.507.

60. *GM,* 3.24.150.

61. *EH,* 334; *GM,* 3.24.150–53. Cf. *GS,* 4.§344.280–83.

62. *BGE,* preface, 2.

63. *GS,* preface, §4.38; *BGE,* §232.163; *WTP,* 3.4.§943.497.

64. *GS,* 4.§339.271–72.

65. *TSZ,* 3.336–43.

66. *WTP,* 4.§1011.523.

67. *WTP,* 3.4.§853.453.

68. *BGE,* §2.10; *WTP,* 5.§344.281.

69. *GS,* 1.§13.87; *BGE,* §211.136.

70. *BGE,* 9.

71. *Uses and Disadvantages of History,* §6.89.

72. *BT,* §23.137.

73. *BT,* §15.94.

74. *GS,* 4.§276.223.

75. *TSZ,* 1.126.

76. *TSZ,* 1.125.

77. *BGE,* §62.74–75.

78. *GM,* 3.§5.103.

79. *EH,* 334.

80. *EH,* 300–301.

81. *WTP,* 4.§983.513.

82. *TSZ,* 3.339ff.; *WTP,* 4.3.§1057–67.544ff.

83. *TSZ,* 3.329–30; 4.435–36.

84. Plato, *Sym,* 207a.

85. Aristotle, *Metaphysics,* 12.9.1074b.34.

86. Plato, *Rep,* 6.508e; 7.524d.

87. *WTP,* 4.3.1066.

88. Nancy Ross Wilson, *Three Ways of Asian Wisdom: Hinduism, Buddhism, Zen, and Their Significance for the West* (New York: Simon and Schuster, 1966), 65–66.

89. Pascal, *Pensées,* §206.

90. *GS,* §341.273–74.

91. Friedrich Nietzsche, "Aus dem Gedankenkreis der Geburt der Tragödie," in *Der griechische Staat* (1871; Stuttgart: Alfred Kroener, 1955), 206, 216–18.

92. *WTP,* 3.4.811.

93. Cf. Fink, *Philosophie,* 32. Fink makes the plausible case that his subsequent attraction to the Enlightenment, expressed in *The Gay Science* and *Daybreak,* merely cut him loose from his dependence on Schopenhauer and Wagner that dominates the first work. In *Thus Spake Zarathustra* and in the posthumously published *Will to Power* Nietzsche returns to elaborate the major insights of his *Birth of Tragedy.* The last parts of *Will to Power* (3.4, "Will to Power as Art," and 4.2, "Dionysus") fortify that case powerfully.

94. *BT,* §1.33ff.

95. Cf. Fink, *Philosophie,* 18.

96. *BT,* §25.143; 4.44ff.

97. *BT,* §16.99–100.

98. *BT,* §17.104–5.

99. *BT,* §3.41ff.

100. *BT,* §3.42.

101. *BT,* §3.43.

102. *BT,* §21.130.

103. Friedrich Schiller, *On the Aesthetic Education of Man in a Series of Letters,* trans. R. Snell (New York: Ungar, 1965), twelfth–sixteenth letter, 64–81.

104. *BT,* §18.109–10.

105. *WTP,* 3.4.§852.450.

106. *BT,* §5.49.

107. This is the burden of Richard Schacht's argument in "Nietzsche on Art in *The Birth of Tragedy,*" in *Aesthetics,* ed. Dickie and Sclafani, 269–312. Cf. esp. 301, 309.

108. *BT,* §3.43.

109. Schacht, "Nietzsche on Art," 289.

110. Ibid., 305.

111. *BGE,* §12.20.

112. *WTP,* 3.4.§809.428.

113. *BT,* §5.48.

114. *WTP,* 3.4.809.

115. *BT,* §5.48ff.

116. *BT,* 26.

117. *EH,* 300.

118. *BT*, §8.61ff.

119. *BT*, §§10–12.75ff.

120. *BT*, §15.94.

121. *BT*, §11.78.

122. Martin Heidegger, "The Will to Power as Art," in *Nietzsche*, part 4, 107ff.

123. *TI*, 24.81; *WTP*, 3.4.§802.422; §851.449; §853.453.

124. *GM*, 3.§5.105.

125. *BT*, §17.109.

126. Cf. M. S. Silk and J. P. Stern, *Nietzsche on Tragedy* (Cambridge: Cambridge University Press, 1981), 12ff. This work gives a comprehensive treatment of the general context and basic character of the *Birth of Tragedy*.

127. *BT*, §2.19.

128. *BT*, §19.119.

129. *BT*, §18.112.

130. *WTP*, 3.4.§796.419.

131. *TI*, 93.

132. *TI*, 39, 94.

133. *TI*, 37, 91.

134. *WTP*, 3.4.§842.444.

135. *GM*, 3.8.243.

136. *WTP*, 3.4.§803.422; §842.444.

137. *BGE*, §265.215.

138. *WTP*, 4.§983.513.

139. Plato, *Rep*, 2.367e.

140. For a consideration of rewards and punishments as a consequence but not as a motive for a just life, see Plato, *Rep*, 10.608c ff.

141. Plato, *Phaedo*, 82e

142. Plato, *Timaeus*, 41.

143. This is, of course, the familiar thesis advanced by Thomas Kuhn in *The Structure of Scientific Revolutions* (Chicago: University of Chicago Press, 1962).

144. John Dewey, *Reconstruction in Philosophy* (Boston: Beacon Press, 1957), ix (henceforth *RP*).

145. Martin Heidegger, *The End of Philosophy*, trans. J. Stambaugh (New York: Harper and Row, 1973), 4ff., 79 (henceforth *EP*).

146. Cf. *WTP*, 4.§883.471.

147. *Daybreak*, §296.126.

148. *BT*, §24.140.

## IX. Dewey

1. Elizabeth Flower and Murray Murphey, *A History of Philosophy in America*, 2 vols. (New York: Capricorn, 1977), 2:809–87.

2. John Dewey, *Art as Experience* (New York: Capricorn, c. 1934), 46 (henceforth *AE*).

3. John Dewey, "From Absolutism to Experimentalism" in *On Experience, Nature, and Freedom*, ed. R. Bernstein (Indianapolis: Bobbs-Merrill, 1960), 15 (henceforth FATE); *RP*.

4. *RP*, 159.

5. FATE, 10

6. *RP,* 107ff.

7. Cf. Plato, *Phaedo,* 67d.

8. Ibid., 86a. In this matter one should also recall the countervailing positions presented in other dialogues on the status of eros: the *Phaedrus* presents it as the wings of the soul, as a form of divine madness that allows the soul to ascend to the highest things (245b). Moreover, in that same dialogue the latter are discerned as really present in visible things under the aspect of the Beautiful Itself (250d); and the *Symposium* presents eros as occupying the same place as philosophy, in the mediating realm between being and becoming and thus implicitly between rational soul and body (202d).

9. *RP,* 109ff., 115.

10. *AE,* 20–21; *RP.*

11. Aquinas, *ST,* 2–2.182.1.

12. *RP,* 112ff., 145. This entails a view of reality as process, "the most revolutionary discovery yet made" (*RP,* xiii).

13. We should note that, in spite of these observations, Dewey remarked (in 1930) that Plato "still provides my favorite philosophic reading," but Plato as "dramatic, restless, co-operatively inquiring," "whose highest flight of metaphysics always terminated with a social and practical turn" (FATE, 12–13).

14. René Descartes, *Discourse on Method,* D. Cress (Indianapolis: Hackett, 1980), 4 (AT), 32–33; 5 (AT), 56.

15. Gilbert Ryle, *The Concept of Mind* (New York: Barnes and Noble, 1949), 15–16.

16. Galileo Galilei, *The Assayer,* in *Discoveries and Opinions of Galileo,* trans. S. Drake (New York: Doubleday, 1957), 274.

17. Descartes, *Discourse on Method,* 4 (AT), 32. For a general approach to Descartes, see Wood, *Path into Metaphysics,* chap. 10.

18. The *Chuang Tzu,* in Chan, *Sourcebook in Chinese Philosophy,* 190.

19. Cf. Descartes, *Discourse on Method,* 4 (AT), 32.

20. Gueroult claims that Descartes actually has a third notion of substance: the human composite of thinking and extended substance. Cf. Martial Gueroult, *Descartes' Philosophy Interpreted According to the Order of Reasons,* vol. 2, *The Soul and the Body,* trans. R. Ariew (Minneapolis: University of Minnesota Press, 1985), 116–17.

21. Descartes, *Meditations,* 3 (AT, Latin, 45ff.; French, 35ff.); 5 (AT, Latin, 65ff.; French, 52ff.).

22. Ibid., 6 (AT, Latin, 74ff.; French, 59ff.).

23. Ibid. (AT, Latin, 89; French, 71).

24. Descartes, *Discourse on Method,* 6 (AT), 65.

25. Reported in Diogenes Laertius 9.31, Kirk and Raven, 409–10.

26. Descartes, *Discourse on Method,* 6 (AT), 62.

27. FATE, 15–17; *RP,* 84, 91.

28. *RP,* 87.

29. John Dewey, *Experience and Nature* (New York: Dover, 1958), 303 (henceforth *ExN*).

30. *AE,* 19.

31. *AE,* 22, 58.

32. *AE,* 67–69.

33. Cf. *ExN,* 73–75, 110ff.

34. Friedrich Schelling, "System of Transcendental Idealism," in *Philosophies of Art and Beauty,* ed. A. Hofstadter and R. Kuhns (Chicago: University of Chicago Press, 1964), 5.1.359. Cf. my "Being and Manifestness" for a parallel approach.

35. *AE,* 14–15.

36. *ExN,* 48ff., 92ff.

37. *RP,* 187ff.

38. *AE,* 270.

39. *AE,* 32, 37, 73, 120.

40. Cf. Joseph Stalin, *Dialectical and Historical Materialism* (New York: International Publishers, 1940), 20–21.

41. Even Descartes did not escape from this process. Etienne Gilson, the prominent historian of medieval thought, began his life project by demonstrating the medieval bases of Descartes's thought (e.g. in *Index scolastico-cartésien,* Paris: Alcan, 1912–13). Though Descartes thought he was constructing things anew, the very way he went about his construction was a function of the distinctions and directions provided by his upbringing

42. Cf. *RP,* 183–86. Cf. also *The Child and the Curriculum* (c. 1900; rev. ed. 1915) and *The School and Society* (c. 1902; Chicago: University of Chicago Press, 1971).

43. *ExN,* 102ff.

44. *RP,* 176.

45. *RP,* 203.

46. *RP,* 209.

47. Cf. *RP,* ix.

48. *RP,* 177.

49. *RP,* 177, 186.

50. *RP,* 194, 203.

51. *ExN,* 401; *AE,* 144–46.

52. *RP,* 164–69.

53. The passive view of education is not Platonic, since interaction is the way learning goes on in a Socratic context, as indicated in a Platonic dialogue. Socrates calls upon his interlocutors to take their own position and then helps them work out the consequences. The dialogues are protreptic and proleptic, leading the reader on and suggesting, without following out convergent directions for the reader's thought. Even the *Republic,* which, after its first book, seems to present a teaching, does not simply hand out answers. The character of the imagery, the nature of the interlocutors, the dramatic movement, the general form, and all the apparent fallacies and strange turns and qualifications of claims are calculated to set up in the reader the attentiveness that allows him to follow the direction indicated proleptically, by way of hint, in the various features of the dialogue. There is no way to get what Plato is after in a direct way. (See Wood, "Image, Structure, and Content" for an illustration of these features in Plato's *Republic.*) Dewey himself calls for a return to the Platonic dialogues as instantiating a more active form of education than has all too often been the case in the modern curriculum: he calls for an interactional model of learning (FATE, 13).

54. *RP,* 183–86, 209.

55. *RP,* 105. Cf. also John Dewey, *A Common Faith* (New Haven: Yale University Press, 1934), 59–60, 87.

56. *AE*, 4–9.

57. *RP,* 170ff.

58. *AE*, 3, 337.

59. *AE*, 6–11, 131, 252ff.

60. *AE*, 3–4, 10, 150.

61. *ExN,* 358.

62. *AE*, 85.

63. *AE*, 14ff.

64. *AE*, 4–10.

65. *AE*, 26–7.

66. *AE*, 4.

67. *AE*, 14ff., 147ff., 162ff.

68. *AE*, 154, 164.

69. *AE*, 169.

70. *AE*, 13, 137ff.

71. *AE*, 150.

72. *AE*, 19.

73. *AE*, 22.

74. *AE*, 25.

75. *AE*, 17, 121.

76. *AE*, 125–26, 175. This is a notion that goes back to Plato's *Theaetetus* (184c) and Aristotle's *OS* (3.1.425).

77. *AE*, 29, 50, 53, 100, 121–22, 218.

78. *AE*, 25.

79. *AE*, 39.

80. *RP,* 212–13.

81. *AE*, 5.

82. *AE*, 36ff., 67, 192.

83. Cf. the parallel discussion in Dufrenne, *Phenomenology,* 327.

84. *AE*, 33, 37–38, 73, 120, 123.

85. *AE*, 129–30.

86. *AE*, 38, 119–20.

87. *AE*, 67–69, 192.

88. *AE*, 19.

89. *AE*, 84.

90. *AE*, 133.

91. *AE*, 93–94, 100ff., 151–52, 208, 313.

92. *AE*, 152.

93. *AE*, 173.

94. *AE*, 177.

95. *AE*, 137, 117. Emphasis Dewey's.

96. *AE*, 138, 145.

97. *AE*, 6off.

98. Ibid.

99. *AE*, 71, 89, 98, 155.

100. *AE*, 123. This is a notion underscored by Hegel in *HPM,* §447, 194 and, more

recently, by physicist-philosopher Michael Polanyi in *Personal Knowledge: Towards a Post-Critical Philosophy* (New York: Harper and Row, 1964), 134ff.

101. *AE*, 140ff.

102. *AE*, 143.

103. *AE*, 70. Dufrenne speaks in this connection of academic art in which the artist is "only a hand without a heart" (*Phenomenology*, 104).

104. *AE*, 70.

105. *AE*, 65.

106. *AE*, 74ff.

107. *AE*, 92.

108. *AE*, 95, 178.

109. *AE*, 162ff., 106–9, 139. This is a central theme in Dufrenne, *Phenomenology*, 15, 24ff.

110. *AE*, 108.

111. *AE*, 144ff., 182.

112. *AE*, 145.

113. *AE*, 180.

114. *AE*, 169. Dewey's emphasis.

115. *AE*, 109.

116. Percy Bysshe Shelley, *A Defence of Poetry*, in *The Complete Works of Percy Bysshe Shelley*, ed. R. Ingpen and W. Peck (New York: Gordian Press, 1965), 7:140.

117. *AE*, 348.

118. *ExN*, 41.

119. *AE*, 81.

120. *AE*, 92.

121. *AE*, 105, 270, 335.

122. *AE*, 194; cf. *Common Faith*, 18–19, 85.

123. *AE*, 195.

124. *AE*, 107, 184–85.

125. *AE*, 274.

126. Lonergan, *Insight*, 335–36.

## X. Heidegger

1. Cf. Edmund Husserl, *General Introduction* and *Studies in the Phenomenology of Constitution*, trans. R. Rojcewicz and A. Schuwer, *Ideas Pertaining to a Pure Phenomenology and to a Phenomenological Philosophy*, bk. 2 (Dordrecht: Kluwer, 1989). For a general approach from within the movement, see Heidegger's *History of the Concept of Time: Prolegomena*, trans. T. Kisiel (Bloomington: Indiana University Press, 1985), 13–134. For an approach that links phenomenology with Plato's Line, see Wood, "Phenomenologists," 130–60.

2. Cf. Husserl, *Cartesian Meditations: An Introduction to Phenomenology*, trans. D. Cairns (The Hague: Martinus Nijhoff, 1960), §50.109.

3. Cf. Husserl, *Crisis*, 26–27; Heidegger, *BAT*, 60–61.

4. Husserl, *Cartesian Meditations*, 7, 18–24; *Crisis*, 73ff. Cf. Descartes, *Meditations*.

5. Paul Ricoeur, *Husserl: An Analysis of His Phenomenology*, trans. E. Ballard and L. Embree (Evanston, Ill.: Northwestern University Press, 1967), 201; cf. Husserl, *General Introduction*, 183.

6. Martin Heidegger, *Kant and the Problem of Metaphysics*, trans. J. Churchill (Bloomington: Indiana University Press, 1965); *What Is a Thing?* trans. W. Barton and V. Deutsch (Chicago: Regnery, 1967); *Phenomenological Interpretation of Kant's Critique of Pure Reason*, trans. P. Emad and K. Maly (Bloomington: Indiana University Press, 1997).

7. *BAT,* 247ff.

8. Edmund Husserl, *Logical Investigations*, trans. J. Findlay, 2 vols. (New York: Humanities Press, 1970), 2:741–42.

9. Martin Heidegger, "The Way Back into the Ground of Metaphysics," trans. W. Kaufmann, in *Existentialism from Dostoevsky to Sartre*, ed. W. Kaufmann (Cleveland: World Publishing, 1956), 206–21.

10. *BAT,* 78ff.

11. *BAT,* 27, 67ff.

12. Cf. *BAT,* 61–62.

13. *NE* 1.4.1095b7. See Martin Heidegger, *Plato's Sophist*, trans. R. Rojcewicz and André Schuwer (Bloomington: Indiana University Press, 1997), 33–40, 91–123.

14. Martin Heidegger, "Memorial Address," in *Discourse on Thinking*, trans. J. Anderson and E. Freund (New York: Harper and Row, 1966), 54–56 (henceforth MA).

15. "Language," in *PLT,* 203.

16. *An Introduction to Metaphysics*, trans. R. Manheim (New Haven: Yale University Press, 1959), 37 (henceforth *IM*).

17. *IM,* 180ff.

18. *IM,* 194, 202; Martin Heidegger, *What Is Called Thinking?* trans. J. Glenn Gray (New York: Harper and Row, 1968), 102 (henceforth *WCT*).

19. *BAT,* 370ff. and 456ff.; Edmund Husserl, *Phenomenology of Internal Time-Consciousness*, trans. J. Churchill (Bloomington: Indiana University Press, 1964), 50ff., 76ff.

20. Martin Heidegger, *What Is a Thing?* trans. W. Barton and V. Deutsch (Chicago: Henry Regnery, 1967), 66ff. Cf. also *QCT,* 37.

21. *BAT,* 278–311.

22. *BAT,* 149ff.

23. Martin Heidegger, "On the Essence of Truth," in *Basic Writings from* Being and Time *(1927) to* The Task of Thinking *(1964)*, ed. and trans. D. Krell (New York: Harper and Row, 1977), 132.

24. Hans-Georg Gadamer, *Heidegger's Ways*, trans. J. Stanley (Albany: State University of New York Press, 1994), 123.

25. MA, 46; cf. *WCT,* 139ff.; and "What Are Poets For?" (henceforth WPF), in *PLT,* 127ff.

26. Martin Heidegger, *On the Way to Language*, trans. P. Hertz (San Francisco: Harper and Row, 1971), 93 (henceforth *OWL*).

27. Cf. note 25.

28. "Essence of Truth," 132ff.

29. *OWL,* 95.

30. *QCT,* 175.

31. *QCT,* 17–20.

32. *QCT,* 27.

33. Cf. Wooldridge, *Mechanical Man*, 84–86, 158–62.

34. *IM,* 62–63.

35. *IM,* 38.
36. OWA, 17–87.
37. OWA, 78.
38. OWA, 19.
39. OWA, 74 ff.
40. OWA, 50.
41. OWA, 44.
42. Martin Heidegger, "What Is Metaphysics?" in *Basic Writings,* 99ff.
43. OWA, 62.
44. *IM,* 26; *WCT,* 131.
45. OWA, 73.
46. *PLT,* 165–82.
47. OWA, 22ff., 68.
48. Cf. *BAT,* 96ff.
49. Aristotle, *Physics,* 2.3.194b ff.
50. OWA, 42ff.

51. Meyer Shapiro challenged Heidegger's identification and claimed they were the painter's own shoes; Derrida undercuts the narrowness of Shapiro's observations in terms of Heidegger's basic concern in the essay. Cf. Jacques Derrida, *The Truth in Painting,* trans. G. Bennington and I. McLeod (Chicago: University of Chicago Press, 1987), 257ff.

52. *BAT,* 98.

53. Cf. Barfield, *Saving the Appearances,* 28–35.

54. Martin Heidegger, *The Principle of Reason,* trans. R. Lilly (Bloomington: Indiana University Press, 1991), 35ff. Cf. John Caputo, *The Mystical Element in Heidegger's Thought* (New York: Fordham University Press, 1986).

55. OWA, 46–47.

56. *IM,* 26

57. Martin Heidegger, "Building, Dwelling and Thinking" (henceforth *BDT*), in *PLT,* 49–51; cf. also "The Thing," in *PLT,* 172–82.

58. Cf. *EP.*

59. *IM,* 128.

60. Cf. "The Thing," in *PLT,* 181. "Wenn wir das Ding in seinem Dingen aus der weltenden Welt Wesen lassen, denken wir an das Ding als Ding:" *Das Ding* in *Vorträge und Aufsätze,* p. 173.

61. This section is an adaptation of Robert E. Wood, "Six Heideggerian Figures," in *Martin Heidegger,* ed. John D. Caputo, special issue of *American Catholic Philosophical Quarterly,* Spring 1995, 311–31. For an approach that links Heidegger to two cognate twentieth-century thinkers, see Robert E. Wood, "Silence, Being, and the Between: Picard, Heidegger, and Buber," *Man and World* 27 (1994): 121–34.

62. Martin Heidegger, postscript to "What Is Metaphysics?" in *Existence and Being,* ed. and trans. W. Brock (South Bend, Ind.: Regnery, 1949), 360.

63. Martin Heidegger, "Why Do I Stay in the Provinces?" trans. T. Sheehan, *Listening* 12 (1977): 124. Unless otherwise indicated, all works referred to henceforth are those of Heidegger.

64. BDT, 146ff.

65. *BAT,* 95ff.

66. *QCT,* 15.

67. Martin Heidegger, "Hebel—Friend of the House," trans. B. Foltz and M. Heim, *Contemporary German Philosophy* 3 (1983): 93. Cf. also BDT, 160.

68. "Why Do I Stay?" 123.

69. BDT, 149 .

70. *QCT,* 153.

71. "Why Do I Stay?" 123.

72. MA, 55.

73. *EP,* 109.

74. "Hebel," 97.

75. Cf. *WCT,* 139–48 for what follows. Cf. also WPF, 127ff. and my introduction to Strasser's *Phenomenology of Feeling.*

76. "The Thing," in *PLT,* 181.

77. Hans-Georg Gadamer suggests the relation between *Andenken,* or remembrance, and *Andacht,* or devotion, though etymologically dubious, may have been intended to convey the proximity of such thinking to religious experience. See *Heidegger's Ways,* 27.

78. OWA, 36.

79. MA, 47.

80. "Why Do I Stay?" 123.

81. Gadamer, *Heidegger's Ways,* 117.

82. Cf. Aquinas, *ST,* 2-2.101.1. As antecedents he cites Aristotle, *NE,* 9.12.1162a4ff. and Cicero, *De Inv. Rhet, ii.*

83. Cf. Hegel's *Philosophy of Right.* The section on Ethical Life is divided into sections on Family, Civil Society, and State (§§142–340.105–216), in which the flanking notions—the loci of "substantial freedom"—set the limiting frame for the central section, which deals with modern freedoms—market, marriage, press, occupation, assembly, and the like.

84. Cf. Plato's *Phaedrus,* 245a5.

85. *BAT,* 149ff.

86. *IM,* 26.

87. Cf. OWA, 62, 74. Jacques Taminiaux points to a fundamental shift from the first version of the OWA lecture in November 1935 to the third, one year later. In the first two Heidegger was still in continuity with the contempt for everydayness evidenced in *Being and Time* and in *Introduction to Metaphysics;* in the third he shows a renewed appreciation for the strangeness of the familiar. See "The Origin of 'The Origin of the Work of Art,'" in *Reading Heidegger: Commemorations,* ed. J. Sallis (Bloomington: Indiana University Press, 1993), 392–404. This may dovetail with Gadamer's report (see note 20, above) on the transformation Heidegger experienced on his return to the Black Forest.

88. *IM,* 11, 63.

89. OWA, 63. On innerness, see WPF, 126–30. Cf. Michael Zimmerman, *Heidegger's Confrontation with Modernity: Technology, Politics, and Art* (Bloomington: Indiana University Press, 1990), 123; cf. 117 on the connection of Heidegger with *Innerlichkeit* as the center of Hölderlin's thought.

90. For a treatment of the notion of *Kampf* (struggle) in Heidegger, cf. John Caputo, *Demythologizing Heidegger* (Bloomington: Indiana University Press, 1993), 39–59.

91. *IM*, 61ff. Caputo claims that Heidegger moved from an early concern with the thematics of New Testament *kardia*, or the heart, to the *Kampf* of faith and thus to *polemos* as central orientation (*Demythologizing Heidegger*, 6, 39ff.). Need the two be incompatible? It seems to me that for Heidegger it is only through struggle with the tendency to settle down in surface appearances that beings draw near. In such drawing near, they speak to the heart. At any rate, it is clear that, for later Heidegger, the heart again becomes a focal notion (cf. above, n. 25).

92. Cf. Jean-François Mattéi, "The Heideggerian Chiasmus [*sic*]," in Dominique Janicaud and Jean-François Mattéi, *Heidegger: From Metaphysics to Thought*, trans. M. Gendre (Albany: State University of New York Press, 1995), 112. Leading humans in this way seems to be the sole locus, scarcely focused and developed, of *Mitdasein* in later Heidegger. Essentially following Levinas, Caputo notes Heidegger's predominant concern for things and not-so-predominant concern for people, and especially not for those other than fully functional adults (*Demythologizing Heidegger*, 65). But he notes further that what is required is more than an extension of "letting things be" from things to people, but a more radical openness to what is other (146).

93. "Language" in *PLT*, 199, 203.

94. Cf. Wood, "Heidegger on the Way to Language," 611–20.

95. OWA, 73–74.

96. Cf. Mattéi, "Heideggerian Chiasmos," 133.

97. *WCT*, 11.

98. Martin Heidegger, "Letter on Humanism" (henceforth LH), in *Basic Writings*, 230.

99. Martin Heidegger, "Way to Language," in *OWL*, 112–13.

100. Martin Heidegger, "Language," in *PLT*, 208.

101. Martin Heidegger, "The Nature of Language" (henceforth NL), in *OWL*, 97; "Way to Language," 115.

102. "Words," in *OWL*, 155.

103. NL, 66.

104. WPF, 91.

105. NL, 60ff.; "Words," in *OWL*, 140ff.

106. *IM*, 70–73.

107. Cf. "Poetically Man Dwells . . . ," in *PLT*, 218; NL, 62.

108. LH, 230.

109. NL, 78.

110. *IM*, 152.

111. Martin Heidegger, "Language in the Poem," (henceforth LP), in *OWL*, 172.

112. LP, 160.

113. LP, 172.

114. BDT, 147; "The Thing," in *PLT*, 177–78; "A Dialogue on Language," in *OWL*, 12.

115. "A Dialogue on Language," in *OWL*, 10.

116. WPF, 93.

117. Nietzsche, *BAT*, 373.

118. *BAT*, 169ff.

119. LP, 196–97.

120. WPF, 94.

121. NL, 99.

122. Martin Heidegger, "The Thinker as Poet," in *PLT*, 13.

123. WPF, 97–128.

124. *WCT*, 224; *WP*, 31.

125. *WP*, 53.

126. *IM*, 14, 101. I find little ground for Zimmerman's contention that Heidegger did not adequately emphasize the first stem (*Confrontation*, 225). The text cited seems to me to make that transparent.

127. *WP*, 53.

128. *IM*, 180ff.; *WCT*, 233, 238.

129. Dominique Janicaud, "Heideggeriana," in Janicaud and Mattéi, *Heidegger*, 16.

130. *WP*, 79. There is much in the Platonic dialogues that supports this way of reading *thaumazein*. However, when Aristotle explicitly treats it in his *Metaphysics* (1.1.982b12), it is not awe but curiosity as that which disappears when one can offer an explanation. I suspect Heidegger reads this into Aristotle because he had even greater respect for him than for Plato, whom, Gadamer suggests, Heidegger never really understood (*Heidegger's Ways*, 144). In general, Heidegger read Plato in the light of Aristotle, as is clearly indicated by his spending the first 237 pages of his 668-page *Platon: Sophistes (Gesamtausgabe*, vol. 2, Frankfurt am Main: Vittorio Klostermann, 1992) on Aristotle.

131. *IM*, 26; cf. also 120–21. We should underscore the "merely" since Heidegger is not repudiating but rather situating logic. When logic claims priority, it tends to dissolve the deeper sensitivity Heidegger is cultivating.

132. *WCT*, 103, 211.

133. *WCT*, 131; *WP*, 31–33.

134. *IM*, 26.

135. *On Time and Being*, trans. J. Stambaugh (New York: Harper and Row, 1972), 57.

136. *Time and Being*, 58.

137. LH, 232-33.

138. *QCT*, 75ff.

139. *What Is a Thing?* 8off.

140. *IM*, 62–63.

141. *Basic Problems*, 282-83. Cf. Reiner Schürrmann, *Heidegger on Being and Acting: From Principles to Anarchy* (Bloomington: Indiana University Press, 1990), 75: philosophy had its roots in Greek astonishment before things produced by man. This accounts for the dominance of "teleocracy" in all Western thinking (83). Metaphysics then becomes "the generalization of modes of thought appropriate to only *one* region of phenomena—artifacts" (105, Schürrmann's emphasis). For a critique of the Platonic origins of this notion, see Stanley Rosen, *The Question of Being: A Reversal of Heidegger* (New Haven: Yale University Press, 1993), 10–21, 43. Rosen thinks that, among other things, Heidegger fails to deal adequately with Platonic Eros, which operates in the crucial relation between mythos and logos (29). We noted above Gadamer's claim regarding Heidegger that the Platonic dialogues "remained inaccessible to this impatient questioner" (*Heidegger's Ways*, 144).

142. *QCT*, 17.

143. LH, 210; cf. Descartes, *Discourse on Method*, 33 (AT, 62).

144. *WCT*, 43.

145. *QCT*, 27.

146. *WCT*, 43.

147. *WCT,* 8. Schürmann suggests that this parallels Kant's distinction between thinking and knowing (*Being and Acting,* 291). This would seem to imply that science does not think because it knows—though it does not know what exceeds, situates and makes itself possible.

148. *WCT,* 32ff.

149. Cf. Zimmerman (*Confrontation,* 58–59) on Heidegger's relation to Jünger: human beings are viewed as standing reserve to be stamped with the gestalt of the worker. Meditation on Hölderlin led to the opposite view of drawing out of forms that are already there (76).

150. *BAT,* 219.

151. Cf. *WCT,* 57ff.

152. *WCT,* 30.

153. *IM,* 38.

154. *WCT,* 101.

155. LH, 230.

156. LH, 218.

157. MA, 48.

158. *OWL,* 58.

159. LH, 239.

160. LH, 195.

161. *WCT,* 21.

162. *WCT,* 17.

163. *WCT,* 50.

164. *WCT,* 77.

165. Cf. "Ground of Metaphysics."

166. Ibid., 276.

167. *BAT,* 44.

168. Martin Heidegger, *The Question of Being,* trans. W. Kluback and J. Wilde (New Haven: College and University Press, 1958), 92 (henceforth *QB*).

169. *WCT,* 103, 211.

170. *QB,* 92.

171. Dominique Janicaud, "Overcoming Metaphysics," in Janicaud and Mattéi, *Heidegger,* 5, 7. I agree completely with Mattéi's judgment that Heidegger is concerned with "displacing the metaphysical *point* of view on Being—not in order to cancel it, but to show its essential insufficiency in the absence of a premetaphysical *counterpoint*" ("Heideggerian Chiasmus" in *Heidegger,* 74). Janicaud correctly remarks: "At stake is the question of taking metaphysics upon oneself, and not leaving it aside" (Janicaud, "Heidegger in New York" in *Heidegger,* 197). I think then that Derrida is off the mark in claiming that Heidegger dealt with metaphysics in order to "send it packing" (*On Spirit,* trans. G. Bennington and R. Bowlby [Chicago: University of Chicago Press, 1989], 75).

172. *EP,* 87; cf. "Ground of Metaphysics," 267.

173. *Vorträge und Aufsätze,* 72.

174. *EP,* 84ff. Cf. Stambaugh's note 1. It seems to me that Gadamer is on firm ground when he claims that Heidegger's work gave metaphysics new strength and was calculated to do so (*Heidegger's Ways,* 82, 184–85).

175. *OWL*, 20.

176. Mattéi, "Heideggerian Chiasmus," *Heidegger*, 54.

177. LH, 231.

178. *EP*, 85.

179. Cf. WPF, 105ff.

180. On the notion of "sedimentation of concepts," cf. Husserl, *Crisis*. Gadamer notes the astonishment of himself and his fellow students as Heidegger demonstrated that, instead of charting out relations and formally linking judgments, thinking is showing and getting things to show themselves in and through the thinkers he examined, with whose horizons he fused his own (*Heidegger's Ways*, 61–62, 70, 141). He thus showed that the break with the tradition was "just as much an incomparable renewal of the tradition" (70).

181. WCT, 31.

182. In view of everything I have pointed out, I find it mind-boggling for Rosen to claim that Heidegger has detached philosophy from everyday life (*Reversal*, 272), only insofar as Rosen might understand that as not providing any guidance for living our lives except for "listening to the voice of Being," which Rosen regards as vacuous (217, 263).

183. *WP*, 75, 79.

184. If this interpretation is correct, Heidegger already circumvents Janicaud's objection that Heidegger creates a solidified dichotomy between metaphysics and the thought of being that disallows a "rational dwelling" in terms of a "non-techno-logical-scientific rational thinking . . . [which] reigned freely in the Medievals' theory of *analogia*" ("Heideggerian Chiasmus," *Heidegger*, 35, 29).

185. *WCT*, 163.

186. LH, 221.

187. LH, 192, 236.

188. *OWL*, 98ff.

189. *WCT*, 241.

190. *WCT*, 174. Heidegger spends the rest of the book (to 244) explicating this and the sentences that follow.

191. *WCT*, 202, 207; also WPF, 127ff.

192. *WCT*, 241.

193. *IM*, 141.

194. *WCT*, 208.

195. *WCT*, 209.

196. Cf. Dufrenne, *Phenomenology*, 427–30.

197. There's always been a problem with Heidegger's rhetoric, which may go deeper than rhetoric. For example, in the use of terms like *authentic* and *inauthentic*, surrounded in his own usage with high moral tone, Heidegger still denies any moral features to the notions involved. He seems to attack metaphysics and then to reinstate it; he does the same with technology.

198. "Hebel," 98.

199. Janicaud, "Heideggeriana," *Heidegger*, 22. I have tried to approach select high points in the history of metaphysics by leaning especially on Heidegger's notion of *aletheia* and developing a set of "secular meditations" that follow that lead in *Path into*

*Metaphysics.* Cf. especially chapter 1, on meditation, and chapter 16, on Heidegger. I have also linked Heidegger with the poet-essayist Max Picard and with Martin Buber in "Silence, Being, and the Between: Picard, Heidegger, and Buber," *Man and World* 27 (1994).

200. Wood, *Path into Metaphysics*, 190–98.

201. Ibid., 225. This is indeed the basic thesis of Balthasar's seven-volume *Glory of the Lord*, which he sees as an effort to appropriate Heidegger's project (vol. 5, *The Realm of Metaphysics in the Modern Age*, 449–50).

202. Hegel, *Philosophy of Fine Art*, 2.390; cf. also *PS*, §753.456.

203. Cf. Irving Singer, introduction to *The Last Puritan* by George Santayana (Cambridge, Mass.: MIT Press, 1994), xxii.

204. Walter Kaufmann, *Religions in Four Dimensions: Existential and Aesthetic, Historical and Comparative* (New York: Reader's Digest Press, 1976).

## XI. Conclusion

1. A variation on this concluding chapter has been presented as "Recovery of the Aesthetic Center," the 1994–95 presidential address to the American Catholic Philosophical Association. It appeared in *Recovery of Form*, Proceedings of the American Catholic Philosophical Association, Washington, D.C.: Catholic University of America, 1995, 1–25.

2. Cf. Gustavo Gutiérrez, *A Theology of Liberation: History, Politics, and Salvation*, trans. and ed. C. Inda and J. Eagleson (Maryknoll, N.Y.: Orbis, 1973).

3. For a development of this theme, drawing upon literature, philosophy, and theology from the early Greeks and Hebrews to the present, see his massive seven-volume *The Glory of the Lord: A Theological Aesthetics* to which I have several times referred. I have tried to indicate this direction earlier in "Art and the Sacred," *Listening* 18.1 (Winter 1983): 30–40.

4. Dewey, *AE;* on integral experience, see 46; on morality, 346–49; on depth, 193–95.

5. On the notions of earth and world, cf. Heidegger, *OWA*, 42ff.; on mystery, cf. "Essence of Truth," 132 ff. and MA, 55.; on the notion of the heart, *WCT*, 139–48 and WPF, 127ff.

6. Cf. Aristotle, *OS*, 3.12.434a23ff.

7. Henri Matisse, *Henri Matisse*, ed. Jack D. Flam (Berkeley: University of California Press, 1994), 48, 66, 92, 140.

8. Feuerbach, *The Essence of Christianity*, 12–32.

9. Cf. Peter Berger and Thomas Luckmann, *The Social Construction of Reality: A Treatise in the Sociology of Knowledge* (Garden City, N.Y.: Doubleday, 1966).

10. Martin Buber, *I and Thou*, trans. W. Kaufmann (New York: Scribners, 1970), 63–64, 73–74, 80–82, 87–88.

11. Buber, "Dialogue," *Between Man and Man*, 18.

12. This is, of course, a basic complaint of Kierkegaard, who strongly influenced Buber's thought. Cf. *Kierkegaard's Concluding Unscientific Postscript*, trans. D. Swenson (completed by W. Lowrie) (Princeton, N.J.: Princeton University Press, 1941), esp. 248–52. On Buber's relation to Kierkegaard, see Buber, *Between Man and Man*, 40ff., 161–63.

13. Cf. Hegel, *PM*, §381, *Zusatz* 11. Cf. also his *PR*, §7.21–24.

14. Cf. Aquinas, *ST,* 2.2.101, ad 1. As antecedents he cites Aristotle, *NE,* 9.12.1162a4ff. and Cicero, *De Inv. Rhet., ii.*

15. Gadamer, *Truth and Method,* 76.

16. Pater, *Renaissance,* 159.

17. OWA, 68, 79.

18. Cf. esp. Kierkegaard, *Either/Or.*

19. Kant, *CJ,* 42.165.

20. John Henry Newman, *An Essay in Aid of a Grammar of Assent* (Garden City, N.Y.: Doubleday, 1955), 49–92.

21. Buber, *I and Thou,* 117–19.

22. Thomas Aquinas, *Commentary on Aristotle's* De anima, 1.1, n. 15; *Disputed Questions on Spiritual Creatures,* 11, ad 3; *On Truth,* 4.1, ad 8. I have used this reference to mystery as a way of relating Aquinas and Heidegger in "Aquinas and Heidegger: Personal *Esse,* Truth, and Imagination," in *Postmodernism and Christian Philosophy,* ed. R. Ciapalo (Washington, D.C.: Catholic University of America Press, 1997), 268–80.

23. I have tried to delineate the fundamental phenomena here by triangulating through the work of three thinkers in "Silence, Being, and the Between."

24. Cf. Augustine's *Confessions,* beginning with the famous I I on the "restless heart," through the equally famous "tolle, lege" passage in 8.12, where his heart was suffused with light, to the "confessions of the heart" in book 10, culminating in the vision of "Beauty ever ancient ever new" of 10.27.

25. Buber, *I and Thou,* 44, 110;, cf. Wood, *Martin Buber's Ontology,* 54ff., 104–5.

26. Martin Buber, *Moses, The Revelation, and the Covenant* (New York: Harper, 1959), 52; cf. also *The Eclipse of God* (New York: Harper, 1952), 62.

27. Heidegger, *WP,* 78–85.

28. Plato, *Theaetetus,* 155c.

29. Ibid., 174a–175a.

30. For a different way of developing the link between metaphysics, the aesthetic, and the emotional, see Wood, "Metaphysics and Aesthetics," 615–35. For the way in which an enlarged sense of the aesthetic functions at the center of Weiss's thought, see Robert E. Wood, "Weiss on Adumbration," *Philosophy Today* 22 (Winter 1985): 339–48.

31. Eco, *Art and Beauty,* 92ff.

## *Appendix*

1. Nietzsche, *WTP,* 3.4.842.444.

2. Moore, "View of Sculpture," xxx.

3. Herbert Read, *A Concise History of Modern Sculpture* (New York: Praeger, 1964), 176ff. Read has a more extended work devoted entirely to this interpretation of Moore: *Henry Moore* (London: Zwemmer, 1934).

4. Moore, "View of Sculpture," xxxi, a. Cf. Naum Gabo on the emotional value of materials deriving from our own belonging to the material order. Naum Gabo, "Sculpture: Carving and Construction in Space," in *Theories of Modern Art: A Sourcebook by Artists and Critics,* ed. H. Chipp (Berkeley: University of California Press, 1968), 331.

5. Read, *Modern Sculpture,* 167.

6. Moore, "View of Sculpture," xxx, a.

7. Boccione, "Technical Manifesto," 537–38.

8. Moore, "Mesopotamian Art," in *Henry Moore,* xxxii, a.

9. Moore, "Primitive Art" (1941), in *Henry Moore,* xxxvi, a. In this observation Moore roughly follows a tradition represented by Winckelmann, for whom sculpture passes through several more primitive phases until it enters a classical culmination followed by decline, although Moore completely changes the evaluative perspective represented by Winckelmann, who had little sympathy for anything less than perfect idealized representation. Cf. Winckelmann's *History of Ancient Art,* 4 vols., trans. G. Lodge (Boston: Little, Brown, 1856–73).

10. Moore, "Primitive Art," xxxvii, b.

11. Cited in Hunter and Jacobus, *Modern Art,* 77a–78b.

12. Cited in ibid., 67a.

13. Moore, "The Sculptor's Aims," in *Henry Moore,* xxxi, b. Cf. Read, *Modern Sculpture,* 163. Cf. also R. H. Wilenski, *Modern Sculpture,* 162.

14. Moore, "View of Sculpture," in *Henry Moore,* xxx.

15. Wright, *Future of Architecture,* 104.

16. Moore, "Notes on Sculpture," in *Henry Moore,* xxxiv, a.

17. See Nicholas Penny, *The Materials of Sculpture* (New Haven: Yale University Press, 1993), for a detailed discussion of the significance of the use of various materials for sculpturing employed throughout history.

18. Ibid., xxxiii, b. Plato made the same observation about the indeterminate number of perspectives involved in sculpture in his *Laws* 2.

19. Moore, "Mesopotamian Art," xxxiii, a.

20. "Notes on Sculpture," xxxiv, a.

21. Cf. Wilenski, *Modern Sculpture,* 95, 101.

22. Moore, "Notes on Sculpture," xxxv, b.

23. Wilenski, *Modern Sculpture,* 25, 92–106.

24. Ibid., 100.

25. Boccione, "Technical Manifesto," 537.

26. Ibid.

27. Hunter and Jacobus, *Modern Art,* 240.

28. Moore, "Notes on Sculpture," xxxiv, b.

29. Cf. Gabo, "Sculpture," 332.

30. Cf. ibid., 336; Moore, "Notes on Sculpture," xxxv, b.

31. Cf. Giedion, *Space,* xlvii–lvi.

32. John Ruskin, *The Seven Lamps of Architecture* (New York: Dover, 1989).

33. Schopenhauer, *WWR,* 2, suppl. to book 3, chap. 34, 408.

34. Pliny, *Natural History,* 35.61–66, reported in Pollitt, *Art of Ancient Greece,* 150.

35. Hegel, *ALFA,* 1:42 (1:59).

36. Kant, *CJ,* 42.166 (299).

# Bibliography

Alberti, Leon Battista. *The Ten Books of Architecture: The 1755 Leoni Edition*. New York: Dover, 1986.

Albertus Magnus. *De pulchro et bono*. In *Aquinatis opera omnia: Aliorum medii aevi auctorum scripta* 61, ed. R. Busa, 43–47. Stuttgart: Friedrich Frommann, 1980.

Anselm. *Proslogion*. In *Opera omnia*, vol. 1, ed. F. Schmitt. Stuttgart: Friedrich Frommann, 1968.

Aquinas, Thomas. *Commentary on the Physics of Aristotle*. Trans. R. Bladewell, R. Spath, W. Thirlkel. New Haven: Yale University Press, 1963.

———. *Disputed Questions on Truth*. 3 vols. Trans. R. Mulligan, R. Schmitt, J. McGlynn. Chicago: Regnery, 1952–54.

———. *On Being and Essence*. Trans. A. Maurer. Toronto: Pontifical Institute of Medieval Studies, 1949.

———. *On the Power of God*. Westminster: Newman Press, 1952.

———. *On the Truth of the Catholic Faith: Summa contra gentiles*. 4 vols. Trans. V. Bourke, C. O'Neil, A. Pegis. Garden City, N.Y.: Doubleday, 1955.

———. *Summa theologiae*. 3 vols. New York: Benziger Brothers, 1947.

Aristotle. *Aristotle: The Art of Rhetoric*. Trans. J. Freese. Cambridge, Mass.: Harvard University Press, 1965.

———. *Aristotle's Nicomachean Ethics*, trans. Hippocrates G. Apostle (Grinell, Iowa: Peripatetic Press, 1984).

———. *The Basic Works of Aristotle*. Ed. R. McKeon; trans. W. D. Ross. New York: Random House, c. 1941.

———. *The Categories; On Interpretation*. Trans. H. Cooke. *Prior Analytics*. Trans. H. Tredennick. Cambridge, Mass.: Harvard University Press, 1962.

———. *Metaphysics*. 2 vols. Trans. H. Tredennick. Cambridge, Mass.: Harvard University Press, 1967.

———. *The Nicomachean Ethics*. Trans. H. Rackham. Cambridge, Mass.: Harvard University Press, 1975.

———. *On the Soul; Parva natura; On Breath*. Trans. W. Hett. Cambridge, Mass.: Harvard University Press, 1975.

———. *The Physics*. Trans. P. Wicksteed and F. Cornford. Cambridge, Mass.: Harvard University Press, 1980.

———. *The Poetics*. Trans. W. Fyfe. Cambridge, Mass.: Harvard University Press, 1973.

———. *The Politics of Aristotle*. Trans. E. Barker. Cambridge: Oxford University Press, 1970.

Augustine, Aurelius. *The City of God*. Trans. M. Dods. New York: Modern Library, 1950.

———. *The Greatness of the Soul*. Trans. J. Colleran. New York: Newman Press, 1950.

———. *On the Immortality of the Soul*. Trans. G. Leckie in *Basic Writings of St. Augustine*. Ed. Whitney Oates. New York: Random House, 1948.

———. *Saint Augustine's Confessions*. Trans. W. Watts. 2 vols. Cambridge, Mass.: Harvard University Press, 1977.

———. *The Trinity*. Trans. J. Rotelle. Brooklyn: New City Press, 1990.

Balthasar, Hans Urs von. *The Glory of the Lord: A Theological Aesthetics*. Vol. 1, *Seeing the Form*. Trans. E. Leiva-Merikakis. San Francisco: Ignatius Press, 1982.

———. *The Glory of the Lord*. Vol. 2, *Studies in Theological Style: Clerical Styles*. Trans. A. Louth, F. McDonagh, and B. McNeil. San Francisco: Ignatius Press, 1984.

———. *The Glory of the Lord*. Vol. 3, *Studies in Theological Style: Lay Styles*. Trans. A. Louth, J. Saward, M. Simon, and R. Williams. San Francisco: Ignatius Press, 1986.

———. *The Glory of the Lord*. Vol. 4, *The Realm of Metaphysics in Antiquity*. Trans. B. McNeil, A. Louth, J. Saward, R. Williams, and O. Davies. San Francisco: Ignatius Press, 1989.

———. *The Glory of the Lord*. Vol. 5, *The Realm of Metaphysics in the Modern Age*. Trans. O. Davies, A. Louth, B. McNeil, J. Saward, and R. Williams. San Francisco: Ignatius Press, 1991.

———. *The Glory of the Lord*. Vol. 6, *Theology: The Old Covenant*. Trans. B. McNeil and E. Leiva-Merikakis. San Francisco: Ignatius Press, 1991.

———. *The Glory of the Lord*. Vol. 7, *Theology: The New Covenant*. Trans. B. McNeil. San Francisco: Ignatius Press, 1989.

Barfield, Owen. *Saving the Appearances: A Study in Idolatry*. New York: Harcourt, Brace and World, 1957.

Benedikt, Michael. *Deconstructing the Kimbell: An Essay on Meaning and Architecture*. New York: SITES/Lumen Books, 1991.

Berger, Peter, and Thomas Luckmann. *The Social Construction of Reality: A Treatise in the Sociology of Knowledge*. Garden City, N.Y.: Doubleday, 1966.

Boccione, Umberto. "The Futurist Manifesto." In *Theories of Modern Art: A Sourcebook by Artists and Critics*, ed. H. Chipp, 298–304. Berkeley: University of California Press, 1968.

———. "Technical Manifesto of Futurist Sculpture." *Art and Its Significance: An Anthology of Aesthetic Theory*, ed. S. Ross. Albany: State University of New York Press, 1984.

Bonaventura. *Opera Omnia.* 15 vols. Paris: Vivès, 1876–.

Brancusi, Constantin. *Brancusi*. Ed. Ionel Jianou, ed. London: Adam, 1963.

Buber, Martin. *Between Man and Man*. Boston: Beacon Press, 1961.

———. *Daniel: Dialogues on Realization*. Trans. M. Friedman. New York: McGraw-Hill, 1965.

———. *Eclipse of God: Studies in the Relationship between Religion and Philosophy*. New York: Harper, 1952.

———. *I and Thou*. Trans. W. Kaufmann. New York: Scribners, 1970.

———. *The Knowledge of Man: A Philosophy of the Interhuman*. Trans. M. Friedman and R. G. Smith. New York: Harper and Row, 1965.

———. *Moses, The Revelation, and the Covenant*. New York: Harper, 1959.

Bullough, Edward. "Psychical Distance as a Factor in Art and an Aesthetic Principle." In *Aesthetics: A Critical Anthology*, ed. G. Dickie and R. Sclafani, 758–82. New York: St. Martin's Press, 1977.

Caputo, John. *Demythologizing Heidegger*. Bloomington: Indiana University Press, 1993.

———. *The Mystical Element in Heidegger's Thought*. New York: Fordham University Press, 1986.

Casebier, Allan. "The Concept of Aesthetic Distance." In *Aesthetics: A Critical Anthology*, ed. G. Dickie and R. Sclafani, 783–99. New York: St. Martin's Press, 1977.

Cassirer, Ernst. *The Philosophy of the Enlightenment*. Trans. F. Koelln and J. Pettegrove. Boston: Beacon Press, 1951.

Cavell, Stanley. *The World Viewed: Reflections on the Ontology of Film*. New York: Viking, 1971.

Chan, Wing-tsit, trans. and comp. *A Sourcebook in Chinese Philosophy*. Princeton, N.J.: Princeton University Press, 1963.

Collins, Peter. *Changing Ideals in Modern Architecture, 1750–1950*. Kingston, Ontario: McGill-Queen's University Press, 1984.

Comte, Auguste. *Introduction to Positive Philosophy*. Ed. and trans. Frederick Ferré. Indianapolis: Bobbs-Merrill, 1970.

Corbusier, Le. *Towards a New Architecture*. Trans. F. Etchells. New York: Praeger, 1960.

Courtine, Jean-François. *Of the Sublime: Presence in Question*. Ed. and trans. J. Librett. Albany: State University of New York Press, 1993.

Dahlhaus, Carl. *The Idea of Absolute Music*. Trans. R. Lustig. Chicago: University of Chicago Press, 1989.

Danto, Arthur. *The Transfiguration of the Commonplace: A Philosophy of Art*. Cambridge, Mass.: Harvard University Press, 1983.

Derrida, Jacques. "Differance." In *Margins of Philosophy*, trans. A. Bass. Chicago: University of Chicago Press, 1982.

———. *On Spirit*. Trans. G. Bennington and R. Bowlby. Chicago: University of Chicago Press, 1989.

———. *The Truth in Painting*. Trans. G. Bennington and I. McLeod. Chicago: University of Chicago Press, 1987.

Descartes, René. *Discourse on the Method of Rightly Conducting One's Reason and of Seeking Truth in the Sciences*. Trans. D. Cress. Indianapolis: Hackett, 1980.

———. *Meditations on First Philosophy*. Trans. D. Cress. Indianapolis: Hackett, 1979.

Dewey, John. *Art as Experience*. New York: Capricorn, c.1934.

———. *The Child and the Curriculum* and *The School and Society*. Chicago: University of Chicago Press, 1971.

———. *A Common Faith*. New Haven: Yale University Press, 1934.

———. *Experience and Nature*. New York: Dover, 1958.

———. "From Absolutism to Experimentalism." In *On Experience, Nature, and Freedom: Representative Selections*, ed. R. Bernstein. Indianapolis: Bobbs-Merrill, 1960.

———. *Reconstruction in Philosophy*. Boston: Beacon Press, 1957.

Dickie, George. "All Aesthetic Attitude Theories Fail: The Myth of the Aesthetic Attitude." In *Aesthetics: A Critical Anthology*, ed. G. Dickie and R. Sclafani, 800–815. New York: St. Martin's Press, 1977.

Dickie, George, and Richard Sclafani, eds. *Aesthetics: A Critical Anthology*. New York: St. Martin's Press, 1977.

Dufrenne, Mikel. *The Phenomenology of Aesthetic Experience*. Trans. E. Casey with A. Anderson, W. Domingo, L. Jacobson. Evanston, Ill.: Northwestern University Press, 1973.

Eco, Umberto. *The Aesthetics of Thomas Aquinas*. Trans. H. Bredin. Cambridge, Mass.: Harvard University Press, 1988.

———. *Art and Beauty in the Middle Ages*. Trans. H. Bredin. New Haven: Yale University Press, 1986.

Feuerbach, Ludwig. *The Essence of Christianity*. Trans. G. Eliot. New York: Harper, 1957.

Fink, Eugen. *Nietzsches Philosophie*. Stuttgart: Kohlhammer, c.1960.

Flower, Elizabeth, and Murray Murphey. *A History of Philosophy in America*. 2 vols. New York: Capricorn, 1977.

Gadamer, Hans Georg. *Heidegger's Ways*. Trans. J. Stanley. Albany: State University of New York Press, 1994.

———. *Truth and Method*. Trans. G. Barden and J. Comming. New York: Crossroad, 1982.

Galilei, Galileo. "Excerpts from *The Assayer*." In *Discoveries and Opinions of Galileo*, trans. S. Drake. New York: Doubleday, 1957.

Giedion, Sigfried. *Space, Time, and Architecture: The Growth of a New Tradition*. 5th ed. Cambridge, Mass.: Harvard University Press, 1980.

Gilbert, Katharine, and Helmut Kuhn. *A History of Aesthetics*. Rev. ed. New York: Dover, 1972.

Gilson, Etienne. *History of Christian Philosophy in the Middle Ages*. New York: Random House, 1955.

———. *Index scolastico-cartésien*. Paris: Alcan, 1912–3.

Gueroult, Martial. *The Soul and the Body*. Vol. 2 of *Descartes' Philosophy Interpreted According to the Order of Reasons*. Trans. R. Ariew. 2 vols. Minneapolis: University of Minnesota Press, 1985.

Gutiérrez, Gustavo. *A Theology of Liberation: History, Politics, and Salvation*. Trans. and ed. C. Inda and J. Eagleson. Maryknoll, N.Y.: Orbis, 1973.

Harries, Karsten. *The Ethical Function of Architecture*. Cambridge, Mass.: MIT Press, 1997.

Harris, Errol. *The Foundation of Metaphysics in Science*. Lanham, Md.: University Press of America, 1983.

———. *Hypothesis and Perception: The Roots of Scientific Method*. London: George Allen and Unwin, 1970.

———. *Nature, Mind, and Modern Science*. London: Allen and Unwin, 1968.

Hegel, Georg Wilhelm Friedrich. *Aesthetics: Lectures on Fine Art*. Trans. T. Knox. Oxford: Clarendon Press, 1975.

———. *The Encyclopaedia of Logic*. Trans. T. Geraets, W. Suchting, and H. Harris. Indianapolis: Hackett, 1991.

————. *Hegel's Philosophy of Mind.* Trans. W. Wallace. Oxford: Clarendon Press, 1971.

————. *Hegel's Philosophy of Nature.* 3 vols. Ed. and trans. M. Petry. London: George Allen and Unwin, 1970.

————. *Hegel's Philosophy of Right.* Trans. T. Knox. London: Oxford University Press, 1952.

————. *Hegel's Science of Logic.* Trans. A. V. Miller. London: George Allen and Unwin, 1969.

————. *Lectures on the History of Philosophy.* Trans. E. Haldane. Lincoln: University of Nebraska Press, 1995.

————. *Lectures on the Philosophy of Religion.* Trans. E. Speirs and J. B. Sanderson. London: Kegan Paul, Trench, Trübner, 1895.

————. *Lectures on the Philosophy of Religion.* Ed. P. Hodgson. Trans. R. Brown, P. Hodgson, and J. Stewart. Berkeley: University of California Press, 1988.

————. *Phenomenology of Spirit.* Trans. A. Miller. Oxford: Clarendon Press, 1977.

————. *Philosophy of Fine Art.* 4 vols. Trans. F. Osmaston. London: G. Bell, 1920.

————. *The Philosophy of History.* Trans. J. Sibree. New York: Dover, 1956.

Heidegger, Martin. *The Basic Problems of Phenomenology.* Trans. A. Hofstadter. Bloomington: Indiana University Press, 1988.

————. *Being and Time.* Trans. J. Macquarrie and E. Robinson. New York: Harper, 1962.

————. *The End of Philosophy.* Trans. J. Stambaugh. New York: Harper and Row, 1973.

————. *Existence and Being.* Ed. and trans. W. Brock. South Bend, Ind.: Regnery, 1949.

————. "Hebel—Friend of the House." Trans. B. Foltz and M. Heim. *Contemporary German Philosophy* 3 (1983).

————. *History of the Concept of Time: Prolegomena.* Trans. T. Kisiel. Bloomington: Indiana University Press, 1985.

————. *An Introduction to Metaphysics.* Trans. R. Manheim. New Haven: Yale University Press, 1959.

————. *Kant and the Problem of Metaphysics.* Trans. J. Churchill. Bloomington: Indiana University Press, 1965.

————. "Memorial Address." In *Discourse on Thinking.* Trans. J. Anderson and E. Freund. New York: Harper and Row, 1966.

————. *Nietzsche.* Trans. D. Krell. 4 vols. San Francisco: Harper and Row, 1979–87.

————. "On the Essence of Truth." In *Basic Writings from* Being and Time *(1927) to*

The Task of Thinking *(1964)*. Ed. and trans. D. Krell. New York: Harper and Row, 1977.

———. *On the Way to Language*. Trans. P. Hertz. San Francisco: Harper and Row, 1971.

———. *On Time and Being*. Trans. J. Stambaugh. New York: Harper and Row, 1972.

———. "The Origin of the Work of Art." In *Poetry, Language, Thought*, trans. A. Hofstadter. New York: Harper and Row, 1971.

———. *Phenomenological Interpretation of Kant's Critique of Pure Reason*. Trans. P. Emad and K. Maly. Bloomington: Indiana University Press, 1997.

———. *Plato's Sophist*. Trans. R. Rojcewicz and André Schuwer. Bloomington: Indiana University Press, 1997.

———. *Poetry, Language, Thought*. Trans. A Hofstadter. New York: Harper and Row, 1971.

———. *The Principle of Reason*. Trans. R. Lilly. Bloomington: Indiana University Press, 1991.

———. *The Question Concerning Technology, and Other Essays*. Trans. W. Lovitt. New York: Harper and Row, 1977.

———. *The Question of Being*. Trans. W. Kluback and J. Wilde. New Haven: College and University Press, 1958.

———. "The Way Back into the Ground of Metaphysics." Trans. W. Kaufmann. In *Existentialism from Dostoevsky to Sartre*, ed. W. Kaufmann. Cleveland: World Publishing, 1956.

———. *What Is a Thing?* Trans. W. Barton and V. Deutsch. Chicago: Regnery, 1967.

———. *What Is Called Thinking?* Trans. J. Glenn Gray. New York: Harper and Row, 1968.

———. *What Is Philosophy?* Trans. W. Kluback and J. Wilde. New York: Twayne, 1958.

———. "Why Do I Stay in the Provinces?" Trans. T. Sheehan. *Listening* 12 (1977).

Hertzmann, Erich. "Mozart's Creative Process." In *The Creative World of Mozart*, ed. Paul Henry Lang, 17–30. New York: Norton, 1963.

Hobbes, Thomas. *Leviathan*. Ed. M. Oakschott. New York: Collier, 1973.

Hull, David. *Philosophy of Biological Science*. Englewood Cliffs, N.J.: Prentice-Hall, 1974.

Hume, David. *Dialogues Concerning Natural Religion*. Ed. N. K. Smith. Indianapolis: Bobbs-Merrill, 1947.

———. "Of the Standard of Taste." In *Aesthetics: A Critical Anthology*, ed. G. Dickie and R. Sclafani, 592–606. New York: St. Martin's Press, 1977.

Hunter, Sam, and John Jacobus, eds. *Modern Art: Painting, Sculpture, Architecture*. Englewood Cliffs, N.J.: Prentice-Hall, 1985.

Husserl, Edmund. *Cartesian Meditations: An Introduction to Phenomenology.* Trans. D. Cairns. The Hague: Martinus Nijhoff, 1960.

———. *The Crisis of European Sciences and Transcendental Phenomenology: An Introduction to Phenomenological Philosophy.* Trans. D. Carr. Evanston, Ill.: Northwestern University Press, 1970.

———. *General Introduction to a Pure Phenomenology.* Trans. F. Kersten. *Ideas Pertaining to a Pure Phenomenology and to a Phenomenological Philosophy,* book 1. The Hague: Nijhoff, 1982.

———. *Logical Investigations,* 2 vols. Trans. J. Findlay. New York: Humanities Press, 1970.

———. *The Phenomenology of Internal Time-Consciousness.* Trans. J. Churchill. Bloomington: Indiana University Press, 1964.

———. *Studies in the Phenomenology of Constitution.* Trans. R. Rojcewicz and A. Schuwer. *Ideas Pertaining to a Pure Phenomenology and to a Phenomenological Philosophy,* book 2. Dordrecht: Kluwer, 1989.

Ingarden, Roman. *The Cognition of the Literary Work of Art.* Trans. R. Crowley and K. Olson. Evanston, Ill.: Northwestern University Press, 1973.

Janicaud, Dominique, and Jean-François Mattéi. *Heidegger: From Metaphysics to Thought.* Trans. M. Gendre. Albany: State University of New York Press, 1995.

Kandinsky, Wassily. *Concerning the Spiritual in Art.* Trans. M. Sadler. New York: Dover, 1977.

Kant, Immanuel. *Critique of Judgment.* Trans. W. Pluhar. Indianapolis: Hackett, 1987.

———. *Critique of Practical Reason.* Trans. L. W. Beck. Indianapolis: Bobbs-Merrill, 1956.

———. *Critique of Pure Reason.* Trans. N. K. Smith. New York: St. Martin's Press, 1929.

———. *Foundations of the Metaphysics of Morals* and *What Is Enlightenment?* Trans. L. W. Beck. Indianapolis: Bobbs-Merrill, 1959.

———. *Kants Werke,* photocopied from the Preußishen Academie der Wissenschaften edition of *Kants Gesammelten Werken* of 1902. Berlin: Walter de Gruyter, 1968.

———. *The Metaphysical Principles of Virtue.* Trans. J. Ellington. Indianapolis: Bobbs-Merrill, 1964.

———. *Observations on the Feeling of the Beautiful and Sublime.* Trans. J. Goldthwait. Berkeley: University of California Press, 1960.

———. *Prolegomena to Any Future Metaphysics That Will Be Able to Come Forward as Science.* Trans. P. Carus; rev. J. Ellington. Indianapolis: Hackett, 1977.

Kaufmann, Walter. *From Shakespeare to Existentialism.* Garden City, N.Y.: Doubleday, 1960.

————. *Religions in Four Dimensions: Existential and Aesthetic, Historical and Comparative.* New York: Reader's Digest Press, 1976.

Kierkegaard, Søren. *Either/Or.* 2 vols. Vol. 1 trans. D. Swenson and L. M. Swenson; vol. 2 trans. W. Lowrie. Garden City, N.Y.: Anchor Books, 1959.

————. *Kierkegaard's Concluding Unscientific Postscript.* Trans. D. Swenson; completed by W. Lowrie. Princeton, N.J.: Princeton University Press, 1941.

Kivy, Peter. "Recent Scholarship and the British Tradition: A Logic of Taste—The First Fifty Years." In *Aesthetics: A Critical Anthology,* ed. G. Dickie and R. Sclafani, 626–42. New York: St. Martin's Press, 1977.

Kristeller, Paul. "The Modern System of Fine Arts." In *Renaissance Thought and the Arts: Collected Essays.* Princeton, N.J.: Princeton University Press, 1990.

Kuhn, Thomas. *The Structure of Scientific Revolutions.* Chicago: University of Chicago Press, 1962.

Lawrence, Joseph. *Die ewige Anfang: Zum Verhältnis von Natur und Geschichte bei Schelling.* Tübingen: Köhler, 1984.

Le Bruyne, Edgar. *The Aesthetics of the Middle Ages.* Trans. E. Hennessey. New York: Ungar, 1969.

Leonardo da Vinci. *Leonardo on Painting: An Anthology of Writings.* Ed. Martin Kemp. New Haven: Yale University Press, 1989.

Lessing, Gotthold Ephraim. *Die Erziehung des Menschengeschlechts und andere Schriften.* Stuttgart: Reclam, 1965.

Levinas, Emmanuel. *Totality and Infinity: An Essay on Exteriority.* Trans. A. Lingis. Pittsburgh: Duquesne University Press, 1969.

Locke, John. *An Essay Concerning Human Understanding.* Ed. P. Nidditch. Oxford: Clarendon Press, 1975.

————. *The Second Treatise of Government.* Indianapolis: Bobbs-Merrill, 1952.

Lonergan, Bernard. *Insight: A Study of Human Understanding.* London: Longmans, Green, 1958.

Longinus. *On the Sublime.* Trans. W. Hamilton Fyfe. In *Aristotle:* The Poetics, *"Longinus":* On the Sublime, and *Demetrius:* On Style. Cambridge, Mass.: Harvard University Press, 1973.

Lyotard, Jean-François. *The Differend: Phrases in Dispute.* Minneapolis: University of Minnesota Press, 1983.

————. *The Inhuman: Reflections on Time.* Stanford: Stanford University Press, 1988.

————. *Lessons on the Analytic of the Sublime: Kant's Critique of Judgment.* Trans. E. Rottenberg. Stanford: Stanford University Press, 1994.

MacIntyre, Alasdair. *Whose Justice? Which Rationality?* Notre Dame, Ind.: University of Notre Dame Press, 1988.

Malraux, André. *Voices of Silence.* Trans. S. Gilbert. Princeton, N.J.: Princeton University Press, 1978.

Maritain, Jacques. *Art and Scholasticism* and *The Frontiers of Poetry.* New York: Scribners, 1962.

———. *The Degrees of Knowledge.* Trans. G. Phelan. New York: Scribners, 1959.

Marx, Karl. *Writings of the Young Marx on Philosophy and Society.* Ed. and trans. L. Easton and K. Guddat. Garden City, N.Y.: Doubleday, 1967.

Matisse, Henri. *Henri Matisse.* Ed. J. Flam. Berkeley: University of California Press, 1994.

Merleau-Ponty, Maurice. *The Structure of Behavior.* Trans. A. Fisher. Boston: Beacon Press, 1963.

Moore, Henry. "A View of Sculpture." In *Henry Moore.* Vol. 1. New York: George Wittenborn, 1968.

Mumford, Lewis. *The Myth of the Machine: Technics and Human Development.* New York: Harcourt Brace Jovanovich, 1966.

Newman, John Henry. *An Essay in Aid of a Grammar of Assent.* Garden City, N.Y.: Doubleday, 1955.

Nietzsche, Friedrich. *The Anti-Christ.* Trans. R. Hollingdale. Baltimore: Penguin, 1968.

———. "Aus dem Gedankenkreis der Geburt der Tragödie." In *Der griechische Staat.* Stuttgart: Alfred Kröner, 1955.

———. *Beyond Good and Evil: Prelude to a Philosophy of the Future.* Trans. W. Kaufmann. New York: Vintage, 1966.

———. *The Birth of Tragedy.* Trans. and ed. W. Kaufmann. New York: Vintage, 1967.

———. *Daybreak: Thoughts on the Prejudices of Morality.* Trans. R. Hollingdale. Cambridge: Cambridge University Press, 1982.

———. *Ecce Homo.* Trans. W. Kaufmann. New York: Vintage, c. 1967.

———. *The Gay Science.* Trans. W. Kaufmann. New York: Vintage, 1974.

———. *Human, All Too Human: A Book for Free Spirits.* Trans. M. Faber and S. Lehmann. Lincoln: University of Nebraska Press, 1984.

———. *On the Genealogy of Morals.* Trans. W. Kaufmann. New York: Vintage, c. 1969.

———. *On the Uses and Disadvantages of History for Life.* In *Untimely Meditations.* Trans. R. Hollingdale. London: Cambridge University Press, 1983.

———. "On Truth and Lie in an Extra-Moral Sense." In *The Portable Nietzsche,* ed. and trans. W. Kaufmann. New York: Viking, 1954.

————. *Schopenhauer as Educator*. In *Untimely Meditations*. Trans. R. Hollingdale. London: Cambridge University Press, 1983.

————. *Thus Spake Zarathustra*. In *The Portable Nietzsche*, ed. and trans. W. Kaufmann. New York: Viking, 1954.

————. *Twilight of the Idols*. Trans. R. Hollingdale. Baltimore: Penguin, 1968.

————. *The Will to Power*. Trans. W. Kaufmann and R. Hollingdale. New York: Vintage, 1967.

O'Connell, Robert. *Art and the Christian Intelligence in St. Augustine*. New York: Fordham University Press, 1978.

Olson, Elder. "The Poetic Method in Aristotle," In *Aristotle's Poetics and English Literature: A Collection of Critical Essays*, ed. E. Olson. Toronto: University of Toronto Press, 1965.

Otto, Rudoph. *The Idea of the Holy*. Trans. J. Harvey. New York: Oxford University Press, 1964.

Pascal, Blaise. *Pensées*. New York: Modern Library, 1941.

Pater, Walter. *The Renaissance*. In *Selected Writings of Walter Pater*, ed. Harold Bloom. New York: Columbia University Press, 1974.

Paulsen, Friedrich. *Immanuel Kant: His Life and Doctrine*. Trans. J. Creighton and A. Lefevre. New York: Ungar, 1972.

Petrarca, Francesco [Petrarch]. "The Ascent of Mont Ventoux." In *The Renaissance Philosophy of Man*, ed. E. Cassirer, P. Kristeller, and J. Randall. Chicago: University of Chicago Press, 1971.

Picard, Max. *The World of Silence*. Chicago: Regnery, 1952.

Pius XII. *The Mystical Body of Christ*. Trans. J. Bluett. New York: The America Press, 1943.

Plato. *Cratylus; Parmenides; Greater Hippias; Lesser Hippias*. Trans. H. Fowler. Cambridge, Mass.: Harvard University Press, 1963.

————. *Euthyphro; Apology; Crito; Phaedo; Phaedrus*. Trans. H. Fowler. Cambridge, Mass.: Harvard University Press, 1957.

————. *The Laws of Plato*. Trans. T. Pangle. New York: Basic Books, 1980.

————. *Lysis, Symposium, Gorgias*. Trans. W. Lamb. Cambridge, Mass.: Harvard University Press, 1975.

————. *Politicus, Philebus, Ion*. Trans. H. Fowler and W. Lamb. Cambridge, Mass.: Harvard University Press, 1975.

————. *The Republic*. 2 vols. Trans. P. Shorey. Cambridge, Mass.: Harvard University Press, 1969.

————. *Theaetetus; Sophist.* Trans. H. Fowler. Cambridge, Mass.: Harvard University Press, 1977.

————. *Timaeus; Critias; Cleitophon; Menexenus; Epistles.* Trans. R. Bury. Cambridge, Mass.: Harvard University Press, 1977.

Plotinus. *The Enneads.* Trans. A. H. Armstrong. Loeb Classical bilingual edition. Cambridge, Mass.: Harvard University Press, 1989.

Poe, Edgar Allan. "The Philosophy of Composition." In *Selected Poetry and Prose of Edgar Allan Poe,* ed. T. Mabbott. New York: Modern Library, 1951.

Polanyi, Michael. *Personal Knowledge: Towards a Post-Critical Philosophy.* New York: Harper and Row, 1964.

Pollitt, J. J. *The Art of Ancient Greece: Sources and Documents.* Cambridge: Cambridge University Press, 1990.

Pope, Alexander. *An Essay on Man.* Ed. F. Brady. Indianapolis: Bobbs-Merrill, 1965.

Popper, Karl. *The Open Society and Its Enemies.* Princeton, N.J.: Princeton University Press, 1950.

Potts, Alex. *Flesh and the Ideal: Winckelmann and the Origins of Art History.* New Haven: Yale University Press, 1994.

Pseudo-Dionysius. *The Complete Works.* Trans. C. Luibhead. New York: Paulist Press, 1987.

Radhakrishnan, Sarvepalli, and Charles Moore, eds. *A Sourcebook in Indian Philosophy.* Princeton, N.J.: Princeton University Press, 1957.

Rahner, Karl. *The Foundations of Christian Faith: An Introduction to the Idea of Christianity.* Trans. W. Dych. New York: Seabury, 1978.

————, ed. *Encyclopedia of Theology: The Concise* Sacramentum mundi. New York: Seabury, 1975.

Ricoeur, Paul. *Fallible Man.* Trans. C. Kelbley. Chicago: Regnery, 1965.

————. *Husserl: An Analysis of His Phenomenology.* Trans. E. Ballard and L. Embree. Evanston, Ill.: Northwestern University Press, 1967.

————. *The Rule of Metaphor.* Trans. R. Czerny, K. McLaughlin, and J. Costello. Toronto: University of Toronto Press, 1977.

Rosen, Stanley. *The Question of Being: A Reversal of Heidegger.* New Haven: Yale University Press, 1993.

Rousseau, Jean-Jacques. *The Reveries of the Solitary Walker.* Trans. C. Butterworth. New York: Harper and Row, 1979.

Ryle, Gilbert. *The Concept of Mind.* New York: Barnes and Noble, 1949.

Schacht, Richard. "Nietzsche on Art in *The Birth of Tragedy.*" In *Aesthetics: A Critical An-*

*thology*, ed. G. Dickie and R. Sclafani, 269–312. New York: St. Martin's Press, 1977.

Schaefer, Jerome. *The Philosophy of Mind*. Englewood Cliffs, N.J.: Prentice-Hall, 1968.

Schelling, Friedrich. "A System of Transcendental Idealism." In *Philosophies of Art and Beauty*, ed. A. Hofstadter and R. Kuhns. Chicago: University of Chicago Press, 1964.

Schiller, Friedrich. *On the Aesthetic Education of Man in a Series of Letters*. Trans. R. Snell. New York: Ungar, 1965.

Schopenhauer, Arthur. *Essays and Aphorisms*. Trans. R. Hollingdale. Harmondsworth: Penguin, 1986.

———. *On the Fourfold Root of the Principle of Sufficient Reason*. Trans. E. Payne. LaSalle, Ill.: Open Court, 1974.

———. *The World as Will and Representation*. 2 vols. Trans. E. Payne. New York: Dover, 1966.

Schürrmann, Reiner. *Heidegger on Being and Acting: From Principles to Anarchy*. Bloomington: Indian University Press, 1990.

Shapiro, Meyer. *Modern Art: Nineteenth and Twentieth Centuries*. New York: George Braziller, 1982.

Shelley, Percy Bysshe. *A Defence of Poetry*. In *The Complete Works of Percy Bysshe Shelley*, ed. R. Ingpen and W. Peck, vol. 7. New York: Gordian Press, 1965.

Silk, M. S., and J. P. Stern. *Nietzsche on Tragedy*. Cambridge: Cambridge University Press, 1981.

Singer, Irving. Introduction to *The Last Puritan* by George Santayana. Cambridge, Mass.: MIT Press, 1994.

Smith, Huston. *Forgotten Truth: The Primordial Tradition*. New York: Harper and Row, 1976.

Smith, Preserved. *A History of Modern Culture*. Vol. 2, *The Enlightenment, 1687–1776*. New York: Collier, 1962.

Spinoza, Baruch. *Correspondence on the Improvement of the Understanding, The Ethics*. Trans. R. Elwes. New York: Dover, 1955.

Stalin, Joseph. *Dialectical and Historical Materialism*. New York: International Publishers, 1940.

Strasser, Stephen. *Phenomenology of Feeling: An Essay on the Phenomena of the Heart*. Trans. and intro. R. Wood. Pittsburgh: Duquesne University Press, 1977.

Taminiaux, Jacques. "The Origin of 'The Origin of the Work of Art.'" In *Reading Heidegger: Commemorations*, ed. J. Sallis. Bloomington: Indiana University Press, 1993.

Tanquerey, Adolphe. *The Spiritual Life: A Treatise on Ascetical and Mystical Theology.* Belgium: Desclée, 1930.

Tatarkiewicz, Wladyslaw. *History of Aesthetics.* Vol. 2, *Medieval Aesthetics.* The Hague: Mouton, 1972.

Taylor, Mark. *Disfiguring: Art, Architecture, Religion.* Chicago: University of Chicago Press, 1992.

Thorson, Thomas, ed. *Plato: Totalitarian or Democrat?* Englewood Cliffs, N.J.: Prentice-Hall, 1963.

Vico, Giambattista. *The New Science of Giambattista Vico.* Trans. T. Bergin and M. Fisch. Rev. ed. Ithaca, N.Y. : Cornell University Press, 1991.

Viollet-le-Duc, Eugène-Emmanuel. *The Foundations of Architecture: Selections from the* Dictionnaire raisonné. Trans. K. Whitehead. New York: George Braziller, 1990.

Wagner, Richard. *The Art-work of the Future.* Trans. W. Ellis. London, 1892.

Weiss, Paul. *Cinematics.* Carbondale: Southern Illinois University Press, 1975.

———. *Nine Basic Arts.* Carbondale: Southern Illinois University Press, 1961.

———. *The World of Art.* Carbondale: Southern Illinois University Press, 1961.

Weiss, Peter. *Marat/Sade.* Trans. G. Skelton. New York: Simon and Schuster, 1965.

Whitehead, Alfred North. *Adventures of Ideas.* New York: Free Press, 1967.

———. *Process and Reality: An Essay in Cosmology.* New York: Harper, 1960.

Wiedmann, Franz. *Hegel: An Illustrated Biography.* Trans. J. Neugroschel. New York: Pegasus, 1968.

Wilenski, R. H. *The Meaning of Modern Sculpture.* Boston: Beacon Press, 1961.

Williams, Tennessee. *Suddenly Last Summer.* In *The Theatre of Tennessee Williams*, vol. 3. New York: New Directions, 1971.

Wilson, Nancy Ross. *Three Ways of Asian Wisdom: Hinduism, Buddhism, Zen, and Their Significance for the West.* New York: Simon and Schuster, 1966.

Winckelmann, Johann Joachim. *The History of Ancient Art.* 4 vols. Trans. G. Lodge. Boston: Little, Brown, 1856–73.

———. *Reflections on the Imitation of Greek Works in Painting and Sculpture / Gedanken über die Nachahmung der griechischen Werke in der Malerei und Bildhauerkunst.* English and German texts. Trans. from the German by E. Heyer and R. Norton. LaSalle, Ill.: Open Court, 1987.

Wood, Robert E. "Aesthetics within the Kantian Project." In *Philosophy and Art*, ed. D. Dahlstrom. Washington, D.C.: Catholic University of America Press, 1991.

———. "Aquinas and Heidegger: Personal *Esse*, Truth, and Imagination." In *Postmod-*

*ernism and Christian Philosophy*, ed. R. Ciapalo, 268–80. Washington, D.C.: Catholic University of America Press, 1997.

———. "Architecture: The Confluence of Art, Technology, Politics, and Nature." In *The Nature of Technology*, Proceedings of the American Catholic Philosophical Association, 79–93. Washington, D.C.: Catholic University of America, 1996.

———. "Art and the Sacred." *Listening* 18.1 (Winter 1983): 30–40.

———. "Aspects of Freedom." *Philosophy Today* 15.1 (Spring 1991): 106–15.

———. "Being and Manifestness: Philosophy, Science, and Poetry in an Evolutionary Worldview." *International Philosophical Quarterly* 35.4 (December 1995): 437–47.

———. "Heidegger on the Way to Language." In *Semiotics 1984*, ed. J. Deely. Proceedings of the Ninth Annual Semiotic Society of America, 11–14 October, Bloomington, Ind. Lanham, Md.: University Press of America, 1985.

———. "Image, Structure and Content: On a Passage in Plato's *Republic*." *Review of Metaphysics* 40 (March 1987): 495–514.

———. Introduction to *Phenomenology of Feeling: An Essay on the Phenomena of the Heart* by Stephen Strasser, 3–39. Pittsburgh: Duquesne University Press, 1977.

———. *Martin Buber's Ontology: An Analysis of* I and Thou. Evanston, Ill.: Northwestern University Press, 1969.

———. "Martin Buber's Philosophy of the Word." *Philosophy Today* 30 (Winter 1986).

———. "Metaphysics and Aesthetics." In *The Philosophy of Paul Weiss*, ed. L. Hahn. Library of Living Philosophers. Carbondale: Southern Illinois University Press, 1995.

———. *A Path into Metaphysics: Phenomenological, Hermeneutical and Dialogical Studies.* Albany, N.Y.: State University of New York Press, 1990.

———. "The Phenomenologists." *Reading Philosophy for the Twenty-First Century*, ed. G. McLean, 131–60. Lanham, Md.: University Press of America, 1989.

———. "Philosophy, Aesthetics, and Theology: A Review of Hans Urs von Balthasar's *The Glory of the Lord*." *American Catholic Philosophical Quarterly* 67.3 (Summer 1993): 355–82.

———. "Plato's Line Revisited: The Pedagogy of Complete Reflection," *Review of Metaphysics* 44 (March 1991): 525–47.

———. "Recovery of the Aesthetic Center." *The Recovery of Form*, 1–25. Proceedings of the American Catholic Philosophical Association. Washington, D.C.: Catholic University of America, 1995.

———. "Silence, Being, and the Between: Picard, Heidegger and Buber." *Man and World* 27 (1994).

————. "Six Heideggerian Figures." *Martin Heidegger*, ed. John D. Caputo. Special issue of the *American Catholic Philosophical Quarterly*, Spring 1995.

————. "Taking the Universal Viewpoint: A Descriptive Approach." *Review of Metaphysics* 50 (June 1997): 69–78.

————. "Weiss on Adumbration." *Philosophy Today* 22 (Winter 1985): 339–48.

Wooldridge, Dean. *Mechanical Man: The Physical Basis of Intelligent Life*. New York: McGraw-Hill, 1968.

Wright, Frank Lloyd. *The Future of Architecture*. New York: Mentor, 1953.

Zammito, John. *The Genesis of Kant's* Critique of Judgment. Chicago: University of Chicago Press, 1992.

Zimmerman, Michael. *Heidegger's Confrontation with Modernity: Technology, Politics, and Art*. Bloomington: Indiana University Press, 1990.

# Index of Names

# Subject Index

# E C O N O M I C S

## PRINCIPLES / PROBLEMS / DECISIONS

### S E V E N T H    E D I T I O N

# ECONOMICS
## PRINCIPLES/PROBLEMS/DECISIONS

# EDWIN MANSFIELD

*DIRECTOR / CENTER FOR ECONOMICS AND TECHNOLOGY / UNIVERSITY OF PENNSYLVANIA*

## SEVENTH EDITION

**W•W•NORTON & COMPANY**

*NEW YORK • LONDON*

To Edward Deering Mansfield (1801–1880)
and his brother-in-law Charles Davies (1798–1876)
neither of whom should be held responsible
for the views expressed here.

Printed in the United States of America.

The text of this book is composed in Garamond Light, with the display set in Futura Book Bold. Composition by TSI Graphics. Manufacturing by Arcata Hawkins.

Library of Congress Cataloging-in-Publication Data

Mansfield, Edwin.
    Economics: principles, problems, decisions / Edwin Mansfield.—7th ed.
        p. cm.
    Includes index.
    1. Economics. I. Title.
    HB171.5.M266  1992
    330—dc20                                         91-12312

ISBN 0-393-96138-9

W. W. Norton & Company, Inc., 500 Fifth Avenue, New York, N.Y. 10110
W. W. Norton & Company Ltd., 10 Coptic Street, London WCIA 1PU

1 2 3 4 5 6 7 8 9 0

# CONTENTS

## PART THREE    MONEY, BANKING, AND STABILIZATION POLICY

# PART SIX  MARKET STRUCTURE AND ANTITRUST POLICY

# PREFACE

Textbooks, like firms and economies, do not change at a constant rate; instead, some revisions are minor, while others are extensive and fundamental. This seventh edition, while it shares the same objectives as its predecessor, is a very substantial departure from it. The macroeconomics chapters have been almost completely rewritten to reflect the many developments and controversies in recent years. Some of the microeconomics chapters have also been revised almost completely for the same reason. A dozen of the major changes are briefly described below.

1. *Additional material on the new classical macroeconomics (including real business cycle models) and New Keynesianism.* There is now a new chapter (Chapter 14) devoted almost entirely to these topics, which were given much less attention in the previous edition.

2. *New chapter on the federal budget deficit.* There is now an entire chapter (Chapter 15) dealing with the size and effects of the federal deficit, including treatments of Ricardian equivalence and a variety of other topics relating to theoretical and policy differences in this area.

3. *Expanded treatment of the role of expectations.* A much more complete discussion of the theory of rational expectations is provided in Chapter 13, together with a thorough treatment of the role of expectations in models of inflation and unemployment.

4. *Much more emphasis on aggregate demand and supply curves.* Beginning now in Chapter 5, aggregate demand and supply curves are used and emphasized; the simple Keynesian model is confined largely to Chapter 6, where it is used mainly to derive the aggregate demand curve.

5. *Earlier and more continual discussion of the controversies between policy activists and their critics.* From Chapter 5 on, there are now continual references to the differences of opinion between activists and their critics; this new emphasis both enhances the liveliness of the text and makes the discussion more balanced and complete.

6. *Open economy assumed from the start.* Beginning in Chapter 4, the models presented in the text include exports and imports; and early in our discussion of fiscal policy (Chapter 9) and monetary policy (Chapter 12) we take up the workings of each type of policy, recognizing that the United States is an open economy.

7. *Added emphasis on relationship between business fluctuations and economic growth.* In keeping with the recent tendency of economists to view business fluctuations and growth as part of essentially the same dynamic process, the material on economic growth has been moved forward to Chapter 16 and has been integrated more clearly with the discussion of business fluctuations.

8. *New oligopoly chapter with emphasis on game theory.* The coverage of game theory has been expanded greatly, with sections on the Prisoners'

Dilemma, tit-for-tat, non-credible threats, entry deterrence, and other topics; the coverage is unusually full, but nonetheless is readily accessible to the average student.

9. *New treatments of principal-agent problems, asymmetric information, education as a signaling device, diversification, and the capital asset pricing model.* In Chapters 21, 28, and 29, there are discussions of these important new microeconomic concepts and techniques; these discussions are integrated with other relevant and related materials, not walled off in a separate chapter.

10. *Much more coverage of the major changes that have occurred in Eastern Europe (and the Soviet Union and China).* Beginning in Chapter 3, there is a prominent discussion of the historic economic changes in Poland and elsewhere in Eastern Europe. In Chapter 35, the treatments of the Soviet Union and China have been thoroughly revised.

11. *Improved organization.* Many chapters have been moved to improve the organization of the book. The introductory discussion of the business firm has been moved to Chapter 21, the material on economic growth has been moved to Chapter 16, and the chapters on government spending and taxation have been moved to Chapters 31, 32, and 33. Isoquants are now taken up in the Appendix to Chapter 22. As noted above, the macroeconomic chapters have been entirely reorganized.

12. Based on the positive reaction of both students and instructors to the sections on central economic problems in the previous edition, each two or more pages long, this feature has been maintained and refined. Four out of seven of the new multipage inserts on *Central Economic Issues* are new: (1) How to Make the Transition from Communism to Capitalism: The Case of Poland, (2) Will the Banks Go the Way of the Savings and Loan Industry? (3) Medical Care: Can Benefit-Cost Analysis Be Used? and, (4) What Should Be Done about Global Warming? These new features should be of great use in whetting the interests of students and in helping them to thread their way through complex contemporary issues.

As in previous editions, the boxed inserts and examples are designed to make economics more relevant and interesting to students. Well over half of the boxed inserts are new: (1) Toting up the Costs of the War against Saddam Hussein, (2) How Asymmetric Information Affects the Market for Used Cars, (3) The First Estimates of GNP in the United States, (4) Why So Much Unemployment in Europe? (5) How a Shift in the Consumption Function Can Upset a Forecast, (6) President Eisenhower and Automatic Stabilizers, (7) The Failure of the Knickerbocker Trust in 1907, (8) *P*-Star: A Useful Guide to Long-Run Inflation? (9) Expectations and Interest Rates, (10) The Design of Macroeconomic Policy: The CEA Criticizes Its Predecessors, (11) How Inflation Distorts the Deficit, (12) Should Eisenhower Have Tried to Balance the Budget? (13) Restrictions on U.S. Imports of Japanese Autos, (14) International Policy Coordination, (15) Are Foreigners Buying up the United States at Bargain Prices? (16) Using Diversification to Reduce Risk, (17) The Principal-Agent Problem, (18) The Coca-Cola Company and the Price of Inputs, (19) Diversifiable Risk, Nondiversifiable Risk, and the Capital Asset Pricing Model, (20) Why the Tennessee Valley Authority? and (21) The Clash over the Protection of Intellectual Property. These inserts take up a wide variety of topics of current interest, as well as a number of new theoretical topics. They are very important in showing how economics can be used to help solve a host of major problems. Also, four of the boxed examples are new: (1) Can Profit-Sharing Be Used to Reduce Unemployment?, (2) The Costs of a Small

Machine Shop, (3) Economies of Scale in Cable Television, and (4) What Will Be on the Covers of *Newsweek* and *Time?*

Most textbooks do not encourage the student to get involved in the subject. They simply lay out the material, leaving the student to absorb it passively. In previous editions, I have invited students to *do* economics in order to understand it better. Scores of examples were provided, each describing a real (or realistic) situation and then calling on the student to work through the solution. Also, in each chapter there were two problem sets, both designated "Test Yourself" that enabled students to check their comprehension of what they had just read. The reaction of instructors and students was very favorable, and the emphasis on doing economics is maintained in this Seventh Edition.

All of the empirical and policy-oriented chapters have been updated. Since a text should reflect current conditions and concerns, the government policies in all the major economic areas—fiscal, monetary, incomes, farm, energy, environmental, antitrust, and international—are reviewed in depth. The latest data available have been incorporated in the tables, diagrams, and discussions, while revisions in sections on economic forecasting, reserve requirements, Social Security, and a variety of other topics have brought them into line with current developments.

Since instructors differ considerably in their choice and ordering of topics, the Seventh Edition, like its predecessors, is organized for maximum flexibility. Many instructors take up microeconomics before macroeconomics. This book will work just as well for these instructors as for those who prefer to present macroeconomics first. (A suggested ordering of chapters is presented for them on p. XX.) As an alternative to reversing the chapter sequence in the one-volume edition, some instructors may want to consider the two-volume paperbound version, *Principles of Microeconomics* and *Principles of Macroeconomics*, Seventh Editions.

This book can also be adapted for use in one-semester courses. Pages XX–XXI present outlines for a one-semester course stressing microeconomics, a one-semester course stressing macroeconomics, and a one semester course covering both.

As supplements to this text, I have prepared both a book of readings and a study guide containing problems and exercises. The book of readings is in two parts, *Principles of Macroeconomics: Readings, Issues, and Cases,* Fourth Edition, and *Principles of Microeconomics: Readings, Issues, and Cases,* Fourth Edition. It provides a substantial set of supplementary articles, carefully correlated with the text for instructors who want to introduce their students to the writings of major contemporary economists. It is designed to acquaint the student with a wide range of economic analysis, spanning the spectrum from the classics to the present-day radicals. The emphasis, as in the text, is on integrating theory, measurement, and applications.

The *Study Guide*, Seventh Edition, contains, in addition to problems, review questions, and tests, a large number of cases that require the student to work with quantitative material in applying concepts to practical situations. Both students and instructors have reported that such cases are important in motivating students and illuminating economic theory.

An *Instructor's Manual* has been prepared by Michael Claudon of Middlebury College to accompany the text. A *Test Item File*, prepared by Herbert Gishlick of Rider College, is available both in printed form and on computer disk. *Transparency Masters* are also available to instructors who adopt the text.

Finally, it is a pleasure to acknowledge the debts that I owe to the many teachers at various colleges and universities who have commented in detail on various parts of the manuscript. The first, second, and third editions benefited greatly from the advice I received from the following distinguished economists, none of whom is responsible, of course, for the outcome: Wallace Atherton, California State University at Long Beach; Bela Balassa, Johns Hopkins; Robert Baldwin, University of Wisconsin (Madison); Arthur Benavie, North Carolina; Lee Biggs, Montgomery College; Donald Billings, Boise State; William Branson, Princeton; Martin Bronfenbrenner, Duke; Edward Budd, Penn State; Phillip Burstein, Purdue; Wade Chio, U.S. Air Force Academy; Michael Claudon, Middlebury; Warren Coates, Federal Reserve; Richard Cooper, Yale; Alan Deardorff, Michigan; William Desvousges, Missouri (Rolla); F. Trenery Dolbear, Brandeis; Robert Dorfman, Harvard; James Duesenberry, Harvard; William Dugger, North Texas State University; Richard Easterlin, University of Southern California; Jonathan Eaton, Princeton; David Fand, Wayne State; Judith Fernandez, University of California (Berkeley); David Gay, University of Arkansas; Howard A. Gilbert, South Dakota State University; Gerald Goldstein, Northwestern; Robert Gordon, Northwestern; Edward Gramlich, Michigan; Herschel Grossman, Brown; William Gunther, Alabama; Jerry Gustafson, Beloit; Judith Herman, Queens College; Alan Heston, University of Pennsylvania; Albert Hirschman, Harvard; Ronald Jones, Rochester; John Kareken, Minnesota; Ann Krueger, Duke; Robert Kuenne, Princeton; Simon Kuznets, Harvard; William Leonard, St. Joseph's; Richard Levin, Yale; Raymond Lubitz, Columbia and the Federal Reserve; John F. MacDonald, Illinois (Chicago Circle); Sherman Maisel, University of California (Berkeley); Leonard Martin, Cleveland State University; Thomas Mayer, University of California (Davis); William McEachern, University of Connecticut; Joseph McKinney, Baylor; Edward McNertney, Texas Christian University; Steven Morrison, University of California (Berkeley); John Murphy, Canisius; Arthur Okun, Brookings Institution; Lloyd Orr, Indiana; R. D. Peterson, Markenomics Associates (Fort Collins); E. Dwight Phaup, Union College; Roger Ransom, University of California (Berkeley); Charles Ratliff, Davidson College; Albert Rees, Sloan Foundation; Edward Renshaw, State University of New York (Albany); Anthony Romeo, Unilever; Vernon Ruttan, Minnesota; Warren St. James, Nassau County Community College; Steven Sacks, University of Connecticut; Allen Sanderson, William and Mary; David Schulze, Florida, Edward Shapiro, University of Toledo; William Shugart, Arizona; Paul Sommers, Middlebury; Nicolas Spulber, Indiana; Charles Tone, Swarthmore; Richard Sutch, University of California (Berkeley); Frank Tansey, City University of New York; Michael Taussig, Rutgers; Thomas Tidrick, Clayton Junior College; Fred Westfield, Vanderbilt; Simon Whitney, Iona College; William Whitney, University of Pennsylvania; and Harold Williams, Kent State University.

Among the teachers who contributed comments and suggestions for the changes in subsequent editions are: Werner Baer, University of Illinois; Willie Belton, Georgia Institute of Technology; Don Billings, Linfield College; Steven Cunningham, University of Connecticut; Eric Engen, UCLA; Carl Enomoto, New Mexico State University; Edwin Fujii, University of Hawaii; Otis Gilley, University of Texas at Austin; Herbert Gishlick, Rider College; Marvin E. Goodstein, University of the South; Clyde A. Haulman, College of William and Mary; Marc Hayford, Loyola University; Bruce Herrick, Washington and Lee University; William Keeton, Yale; Michael Knetter, Dartmouth College; Stuart Lynn, Assumption College;

Thomas Maloy, Muskegon Community College; Walter Misiolek, University of Alabama; Edward Montgomery, Michigan State University; Jennifer Roback, Yale; Newton Robinson, Alfred University; Leonard Schifrin, William and Mary; Thomas Shea, Springfield College; Calvin D. Siebert, University of Iowa; and Robert Withington, Jr., State University of New York at Plattsburgh.

I would like to thank Elisabeth Allison of Harvard University and Nariman Behravesh of Oxford Economics USA for contributing the inserts that appear (over their initials) in various chapters, and Catherine Wick and W. Drake McFeely of W. W. Norton for their efficient handling of the publishing end of the work. As always, my wife, Lucile, has contributed an enormous amount to the completion of this book.

*Philadelphia, 1991*                                                                        E.M.

## Outline of a One-Year Course with Macroeconomics Following Microeconomics.

1 Economic Problems and Analysis
2 Economic Models and Capitalism, American-Style
3 The Price System
19 Market Demand and Price Elasticity
20 Getting behind the Demand Curve: Consumer Behavior
21 A Guided Tour of the Business Firm
22 Optimal Input Decisions by Business Firms
23 Cost Analysis
24 Perfect Competition
25 Monopoly and Its Regulation
26 Oligopoly, Game Theory, and Monopolistic Competition
27 Industrial Organization and Antitrust Policy
28 Determinants of Wages
29 Interest, Rent, and Profits
30 Income Inequality and Poverty
4 National Income and Product
5 Unemployment and Inflation: A First Look

6 Aggregate Demand: The Foundations
7 Aggregate Demand and Supply Curves
8 Business Fluctuations
9 Introduction to Fiscal Policy
10 Money and the Economy
11 The Banking System and the Quantity of Money
12 Monetary Policy
13 Inflation, Unemployment, and the Role of Expectations
14 Controversies over Stabilization Policy: The New Classical Macroeconomics and the New Keynesians
15 The Budget Deficit and the National Debt
16 Economic Growth
17 International Trade
18 Exchange Rates and the Balance of Payments
31 The Economic Role of the Government
32 Government Expenditures and Taxation
33 Government and the Environment
34 The Less Developed Countries
35 The Communist Countries and Marxism

## Outline of a One-Semester Course Emphasizing Microeconomics.

1 Economic Problems and Analysis
2 Economic Models and Capitalism, American-Style
3 The Price System
4 National Income and Product
5 Unemployment and Inflation: A First Look
6 Aggregate Demand: The Foundation
7 Aggregate Demand and Supply Curves
8 Business Fluctuations
9 Introduction to Fiscal Policy
10 Money and the Economy
11 The Banking System and the Quantity of Money
12 Monetary Policy
19 Market Demand and Price Elasticity

20 Getting Behind the Demand Curve: Consumer Behavior
21 A Guided Tour of the Business Firm
22 Optimal Input Decisions by Business Firms
23 Cost Analysis
24 Perfect Competition
25 Monopoly and Its Regulation
26 Oligopoly, Game Theory, and Monopolistic Competition
27 Industrial Organization and Antitrust Policy
31 The Economic Role of the Government
30 Income Inequality and Poverty [Optional]

## Outline of a One-Semester Course Emphasizing Macroeconomics.

## Outline of a One-Semester Course Emphasizing Macroeconomics and Microeconomics.

# PART ONE

## INTRODUCTION TO ECONOMICS

# ECONOMIC PROBLEMS AND ANALYSIS

GEORGE BERNARD SHAW, the great playwright, once said, "The only time my education was interrupted was when I was in school." Fortunately, economics, if properly presented, can contribute mightily to your education—and you can learn it without leaving school. Let's look at a sample of the major problems economists deal with; you'll find that each of them could have a big effect on your own life.

## ECONOMIC PROBLEMS: A SAMPLER

### Unemployment and Inflation

The history of the American economy is for the most part a story of growth. Our output—the amount of goods and services we produce annually—has grown rapidly over the years, giving us a standard of living that could not have been imagined a century ago. For example, output per person in the United States was about $22,000 in 1990; in 1900, it was much, much smaller. Nonetheless, the growth of output has not been #9 steady or uninterrupted; instead, our output has tended to fluctuate and so has unemployment. In periods when output has fallen, thousands, even millions, of people have been thrown out of work. In the Great Depression of the 1930s over 20 percent of the labor force was unemployed (see Figure 1.1).

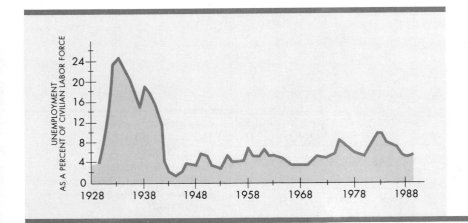

Figure 1.1
Unemployment Rates, United States, 1929–90
The unemployment rate has varied substantially from year to year. In the Great Depression, it reached a high of over 24 percent. In late 1990, it was about 6 percent.

The first of our sample of economic problems is: *What determines the extent of unemployment in the American economy, and what can be done to reduce it?* This problem is complicated by a related phenomenon: The level of prices may rise when we reduce the level of unemployment. In other words, inflation may occur. Thus the problem is not only to curb unemployment, but to do this without producing an inflation so ruinous to the nation's economic health that the cure proves more dangerous than the ailment. Consequently, another major accompanying question is: *What determines the rate of inflation, and how can it be reduced?* As Figure 1.2 shows, we have experienced considerable inflation since 1929; the dollar has lost over four-fifths of its purchasing power during the past forty years alone. Moreover, in the 1970s and early 1980s, our economy often was bedeviled by "stagflation": a combination of high unemployment and high inflation.

During the past 50 years, economists have learned a great deal about the factors that determine the extent of unemployment and inflation.

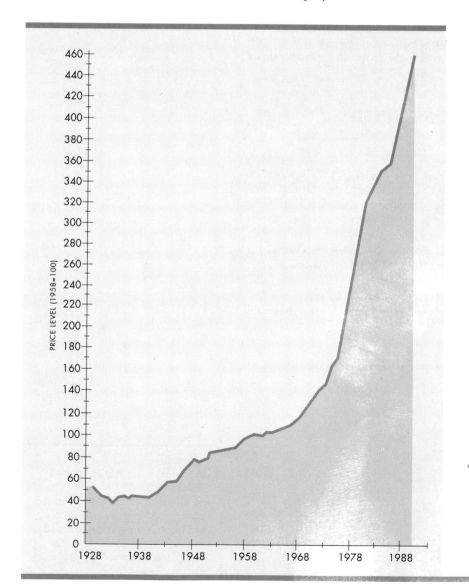

**Figure 1.2**
**Changes in Price Level, United States, 1929–90**
The price level has increased steadily since the 1930s, and is now over five times as high as it was in 1950.

Nonetheless, this topic remains the center of a great deal of controversy. Any responsible citizen needs to know what economists have learned—and to be aware of the differences of opinion among leading economists on this score. To understand many of the central political issues of the day, and to vote intelligently, this knowledge is essential. Also, to understand the fallacies in many apparently simple remedies for the complex economic problems in this area, you need to know some economics.

## U.S. Competitiveness in World Markets and the Productivity Slowdown

During recent decades, American manufacturers have been experiencing increased difficulty in competing with their rivals in Japan, Germany, and elsewhere. In industries like steel, machine tools, consumer electronics, and autos, American firms, once world leaders, are confronted with foreign producers that can produce at lower cost than they can. Our second example of an economic problem is: *Why are American firms finding it so difficult to compete, and how can their competitiveness be enhanced?*

One factor that is relevant in this regard is the recent history of labor productivity in the United States. **Labor productivity** is defined as the amount of output that can be obtained per hour of labor. All nations are interested in increasing labor productivity, since it is intimately related to a nation's standard of living. Many factors, including new technologies like microelectronics and biotechnology, influence the rate of increase of labor productivity.

Historically, labor productivity has increased relatively rapidly in the United States; but beginning in the late 1960s, U.S. labor productivity rose at a slower pace. At first, it was unclear whether this slowdown was only temporary, but during the 1970s the situation got worse, not better. Between 1977 and 1980, labor productivity in the United States actually declined. (In other words, less was produced per hour of labor in 1980 than in 1977!) During the 1980s, productivity growth picked up, but was still below what it was in the 1960s. (And again in 1989 and 1990, labor productivity fell.)

Many observers regard this productivity slowdown as being partly responsible for the decline of American competitiveness. If so, this leads us to a further set of questions: *What determines the rate of increase of labor productivity? Why has this productivity slowdown occurred in the United States? What measures can and should be adopted to cope with it?* Economics provides a considerable amount of information on this score. Not only does economics tell us a good deal about the broad factors influencing national productivity levels; in addition, it provides rules and principles that are useful in increasing the productivity and efficiency of individual firms (and government agencies).

## The Economic Ferment in Eastern Europe

While the United States has its share of economic troubles, it is regarded with envy by most of the world. One of the most startling developments of the 1990s has been the movement of the East European countries like Poland and Czechoslovakia away from central planning and toward capitalism. Under capitalism, individual firms make their own decisions concerning what to produce and how to produce it. This is in marked contrast to centrally planned economies where these decisions are made by planners in government agencies.

To make the transition from central planning to a more capitalistic system, factories owned by the state have been sold to private organizations and individuals, and governments have loosened their control over the prices of goods and services. In 1990, price controls were reported to have been removed in Poland and East Germany virtually overnight. In Czechoslovakia, the administration of Vaclav Havel asked the nation's Parliament to approve a strategy of rapid price decontrol. These are enormous and fundamental changes that have surprised even the most knowledgeable observers.

Our third example of an economic problem is: *What are the advantages of a capitalistic system? What do these countries hope to achieve by adopting such a system?* In 1990, it was obvious to practically any Soviet citizen that the Soviet economy was in trouble. Food was scarce, output was declining, and the price level was rising. According to the available estimates, Soviet workers had to labor a great deal longer than Americans to obtain television sets or beef. But what made some Soviet leaders believe that the Soviet Union would be better off if it embraced capitalism, which for decades had been its arch foe?

The Berlin Wall comes down, November 11, 1989

It is important to recognize that the American brand of capitalism is built on the idea that firms should compete with one another. Thus the producers of steel, automobiles, oil, toothpicks, and other goods are expected to set their prices independently and not to collude. Certain acts of Congress, often referred to as the antitrust laws, make it illegal for firms to get together and set the price of a product. This leads to another question: *Why is competition of this sort socially desirable?* Of course, one reason why Americans have traditionally favored competition over collusion, and relatively small firms over giant ones, is that they have mistrusted the concentration of economic power, and obviously, this mistrust was based on both political and economic considerations. But beyond this, you should know when competition generally benefits society, and when it does not. Economists have devoted a huge amount of time and effort to help answer this question.

## The Elimination of Poverty

As pointed out by Philip Wicksteed, a prominent twentieth-century British economist, "A man can be neither a saint, nor a lover, nor a poet, unless he has comparatively recently had something to eat." Although relatively few people in the United States lack food desperately, about 32 million American people, approximately 13 percent of the population of the United States, live in what is officially designated as **poverty.** These people have frequently been called invisible in a nation where the average yearly income per family is about $35,000; but the poor are invisible only to those who shut their eyes, since they exist in ghettos in the wealthiest American cities like New York, Chicago, and Los Angeles, as well as near Main Street in thousands of small towns. They can also be found in areas where industry has come and gone, as in the former coal-mining towns of Pennsylvania and West Virginia, and in areas where decades of farming have depleted the soil.

Table 1.1 shows the distribution of income in the United States in 1989. Clearly, there are very substantial differences among families in income level. You as a citizen and a human being need to understand the social mechanisms underlying the distribution of income, both in the United States and in other countries, and how reasonable and just they are. Our fourth economic problem is: *Why does poverty exist in the world today, and what can be done to abolish it?* To help the poor effectively, we must understand the causes of poverty.

Since poverty is intimately bound up with our racial problems and the decay of our cities, the success or failure of measures designed to eradicate poverty may also help us determine whether we can achieve a society where equality of opportunity is more than a slogan and where people do not have to escape to the suburbs to enjoy green space and fresh air. Nor does the economist's concern with poverty stop at our shoreline. One of the biggest problems of the world today is the plight of the poor countries of Asia, Africa, and Latin America—the so-called less developed countries. The industrialized countries of the world, like the United States, Western Europe, Japan, and the Soviet Union, are really just rich little islands surrounded by seas of poverty. Over half of the world's population lives in countries where per capita income is less than $5,000 per year. These countries lack equipment, technology, and education; sometimes (but by no means always) they also suffer from overpopulation. Economists have devoted considerable attention to the problems of the less developed countries, and to developing techniques to assist them.

**Table 1.1**
**Percentage Distribution of Households, by Annual Money Income, United States, 1989**

| MONEY INCOME (DOLLARS) | PERCENT OF ALL HOUSEHOLDS |
|---|---|
| Under 5,000 | 5 |
| 5,000 – 9,999 | 10 |
| 10,000 – 14,999 | 10 |
| 15,000 – 24,999 | 18 |
| 25,000 – 34,999 | 16 |
| 35,000 – 49,999 | 17 |
| 50,000 – 74,999 | 15 |
| 75,000 – 99,999 | 5 |
| 100,000 and over | 4 |
| Total | 100 |

*Source:* U.S. Bureau of the Census.

# WHAT IS ECONOMICS?

## Human Wants and Resources

According to one standard definition, *economics is concerned with the way resources are allocated among alternative uses to satisfy human wants*. This definition is fine, but it does not mean much unless we define what is meant by *human wants* and by *resources*. What do these terms mean?

**Human wants** are things, services, goods, and circumstances that people desire. Wants vary greatly among individuals and over time for the same individual. Some people like sports, others like books; some want to travel, others want to putter in the yard. An individual's desire for a particular good during a particular period of time is not infinite, but, in the aggregate, human wants seem to be insatiable. Besides the basic desires for food, shelter, and clothing, which must be fulfilled to some extent if the human organism is to maintain its existence, wants stem from cultural factors. For example, society, often helped along by advertising and other devices to modify tastes, promotes certain images of "the good life," which frequently entails owning an expensive car and living in a $200,000 house in the suburbs.

**Resources** are the things or services used to produce goods which then can be used to satisfy wants. **Economic resources** are scarce, while **free resources,** such as air, are so abundant that they can be obtained without charge. The test of whether a resource is an economic resource or a free resource is price: economic resources command a nonzero price, but free resources do not. The number of free resources is actually quite limited. For instance, although the earth contains a huge amount of water, it is not a free resource to the typical urban or suburban home owner, who must pay a local water authority for providing and maintaining his or her water supply. In a world where all resources were free, there would be no economic problem, since all wants could be satisfied.

Economic resources can be classified into three categories, each of which is described below:

**1. LAND.** A shorthand expression for natural resources, land includes minerals as well as plots of ground. Clearly, land is an important and valuable resource in both agriculture and industry. Think of the fertile soil of Iowa or Kansas, from which are obtained such abundant crops. Or consider Manhattan island, which supports the skyscrapers, shops, and theaters in the heart of New York. In addition, land is an important part of our environment, and it provides enjoyment above and beyond its contribution to agricultural and industrial output.

**2. LABOR.** Human efforts, both physical and mental, are included in the category of labor. Thus, when you study for a final examination or make out an income tax return, this is as much labor as if you were to dig a ditch. In 1992, over 100 million people were employed (or looking for work) in the United States. This vast labor supply is, of course, an extremely important resource, without which our nation could not maintain its current output level.

**3. CAPITAL.** Buildings, equipment, inventories, and other nonhuman producible resources that contribute to the production, marketing, and distribution of goods and services all fall within the economist's definition of capital. Examples are machine tools and warehouses; but not all types of capital are big or bulky: for example, a hand calculator, or a pencil for that matter, is a type of capital. American workers have an enormous amount of capital to work with. Think of the oil refineries in New Jersey and Philadelphia, the electronics plants in Silicon Valley and Texas, the aircraft plants in Washington and Georgia, and the host of additional types of capital we have and use in this country. Without this capital, the nation's output level would be a great deal less than it is.

Land

## Technology and Choice

As pointed out above, economics is concerned with the way resources are allocated among alternative uses to satisfy human wants. An important determinant of the extent to which human wants can be satisfied from the amount of resources at hand is technology. **_Technology_** is society's pool of knowledge concerning the industrial arts. It includes the knowledge of engineers, scientists, artisans, managers, and others concerning how goods and services can be produced. For example, it includes the best existing knowledge regarding the ways in which an automobile plant or a synthetic rubber plant should be designed and operated. The level of technology sets limits on the amount and types of goods and services that can be derived from a given amount of resources.

To see this, suppose that engineers and artisans do not know how an automobile can be produced with less than 500 hours of labor being used in its manufacture. Clearly, this sets limits on the number of automobiles that can be produced with the available labor force. Or suppose that scientists and engineers do not know how to produce a ton of synthetic rubber with less than a certain amount of capital being used in its manufacture. This sets limits on the amount of synthetic rubber that can be produced with the available quantity of capital.

Labor

Given the existing technology, the fact that resources are scarce means that only a limited amount of goods and services can be produced from them. In other words, the capacity to produce goods and services is limited—*far more limited than human wants*. Thus there arises the necessity for **choice.** Somehow or other, a choice must be made as to how the available resources will be used (or if they will be used at all). And somehow a choice must be made as to how the output produced from these resources will be distributed among the population.

Economics is concerned with how such choices are made. Economists have spent a great deal of time, energy, and talent trying to determine how such choices *are* made in various circumstances, and how they *should* be made. Indeed, as we shall see in the next section, the basic questions that economics deals with are problems of choice of this sort. Note that these problems of choice go beyond the problems of particular individuals in choosing how to allocate their resources; they are problems of social choice.

## Central Questions in Economics

Economists are particularly concerned with four basic questions regarding the working of any economic system—ours or any other. These questions are: (1) What determines what (and how much) is produced? (2) What determines how it is produced? (3) What determines how the society's output is distributed among the members? (4) What determines the rate at which the society's per capita income will grow? These questions lie at the core of economics, because they are directed at the most fundamental characteristics of economic systems. And as stressed in the previous section, they are problems of choice.

To illustrate the nature and basic importance of these questions, suppose that, because of war or natural catastrophe, your town is isolated from the adjoining territory. No longer is it possible for the town's inhabitants to leave, or for people or goods to enter. (Lest you regard this as fanciful, it is perhaps worthwhile to note that Leningrad was under siege in World War II for over two years.) In this situation, you and your fellow townspeople must somehow resolve each of these questions. You must decide what goods and services will be produced, how each will be produced, who will receive what, and how much provision there will be for increased output in the future.

In a situation of this sort, your very survival will depend on how effectively you answer these questions. If a decision is made to produce too much clothing and too little food, some of the townspeople may starve. If a decision is made to produce wheat from soil that is inappropriate for wheat, but excellent for potatoes, much the same result may occur. If a decision is made to allot practically all of the town's output to friends and political cronies of the mayor, those who oppose him or her may have a very rough time. And if a decision is made to eat, drink, and be merry today, and not to worry about tomorrow, life may be very meager in the days ahead.

Because we are considering a relatively small and isolated population, the importance of these questions may seem more obvious than in a huge country like the United States, which is constantly communicating, trading, and interacting with the rest of the world. But the truth is that these questions are every bit as important to the United States as to the isolated town. And, for this reason, it is important that we understand

Capital

how these decisions are made, and whether they are being made effectively. Just as in the hypothetical case of the isolated town, your survival depends on these decisions—but in the United States the situation isn't hypothetical!

---

## TEST YOURSELF

1. Explain why each of the following resources is or is not capital: (a) iron ore in Minnesota that is still in the ground; (b) a Boeing 747 airplane operated by American Airlines; (c) a Chrysler dealer's inventory of unsold cars; (d) a telephone used by the University of Oklahoma.

2. Alfred Marshall, the great British economist, defined economics as follows: "Economics is a study of [people] as they live and move and think in the ordinary business of life. But it concerns itself chiefly with those motives which affect, most powerfully and most steadily, [people's] conduct *in the business part of life*. . . . [The] steadiest motive to ordinary business work is the desire for the pay which is the material reward of work." Does this definition encompass all of the examples of economic analysis and problems contained so far in this chapter?

3. C. J. Blank and E. Rosinski of Mobil Research and Development Corporation invented a new type of catalyst which enables all refiners to save an estimated 200 million barrels of crude oil per year. Has this invention altered the technology of the oil refining industry? Has it changed the amount of goods and services that can be derived from a given amount of resources? Were resources used to obtain this invention? If so, what types of resources were used?

4. We described four basic questions that any economic system must answer. Which of these questions is involved in each of the following specific problems: (a) Should the United States use natural gas to produce ammonia? (b) Should taxes on the poor be lower? (c) Should American consumers save more? (d) Should more of our nation's industry be used to produce food?

---

## OPPORTUNITY COST: A FUNDAMENTAL CONCEPT

In previous sections, we have emphasized that economics is concerned with the way resources are allocated among alternative uses to satisfy human wants. To help determine how resources should be allocated, economists often use the concept of **opportunity cost.** We turn now to an introductory discussion of this concept, which should help to acquaint you with how it is used.

Since a specific case is more interesting than abstract discussion, let's return to the case of the town that is isolated from the adjoining territory because of a war or natural catastrophe. Suppose that you are a member of the town council that is organized to determine how the town's resources should be utilized. To keep things simple, suppose that only two goods—food and clothing—can be produced. (This is an innocuous assumption that allows us to strip the problem to its essentials.) You must somehow figure out how much of each good should be produced. How can you go about solving the problem?

Clearly, the first step toward a solution is to list the various resources contained within the town. Using the technology available to the townspeople, each of these resources can be used to produce either food or clothing. Some of these resources are much more effective at producing one good than the other. For example, a tailor probably is better able to produce clothing than to produce food. But nonetheless most resources can be adapted to produce either good. For example, a tailor can be put to work on a farm, even though he or she may not be very good at farming.

After listing the various available resources and having determined how effective each is at producing food or clothing, the next step is to see how much food the town could produce per year, if it produced nothing but food, and how much clothing it could produce per year, if it produced nothing but clothing. Also, you should determine, if various amounts of food are produced per year, the maximum amount of clothing that the town can produce per year. For example, if the town produces 100 tons of food per year, what is the maximum amount of clothing it can produce per year? If the town produces 200 tons of food per year, what is the maximum amount of clothing it can produce per year? And so on.

Having carried out this step, suppose that the results are as shown in Table 1.2. According to this table, the town can produce (at most) 200 tons of clothing per year if it produces nothing but clothing (possibility A). Or it can produce (at most) 400 tons of food per year if it produces nothing but food (possibility E). Other possible combinations (labeled B, C, and D) of food and clothing output are specified in Table 1.2.

The data in Table 1.2 put in bold relief the basic problem of choice facing you and the other members of the town council. Because the town's resources are limited, the town can only produce limited amounts of each good. There is no way, for example, that the town can produce 200 tons of clothing per year and 200 tons of food per year. This is beyond the capacity of the town's resources. If the town wants to produce 200 tons of clothing, it can produce no food—which is hardly a pleasant prospect. And if the town wants to produce 200 tons of food, it can produce 150 (not 200) tons of clothing per year.

**Table 1.2**
**Combinations of Output of Food and Clothing That the Town Can Produce per Year**

| POSSIBILITY | AMOUNT OF FOOD PRODUCED PER YEAR (TONS) | AMOUNT OF CLOTHING PRODUCED PER YEAR (TONS) |
|---|---|---|
| A | 0 | 200 |
| B | 100 | 180 |
| C | 200 | 150 |
| D | 300 | 100 |
| E | 400 | 0 |

## More Food Means Less Clothing

A very important fact illustrated by Table 1.2 is that, whenever the town increases its production of one good, it must cut back its production of the other good. For example, if the town increases its production of food from 100 to 200 tons per year, it must cut back its production of clothing from 180 to 150 tons per year. Thus *the cost to the town of increasing its food output from 100 to 200 tons per year is that it must reduce its clothing output from 180 to 150 tons per year.*

Economists refer to this cost as **opportunity cost** (or **alternative cost**): it is one of the most fundamental concepts in economics. *The opportunity cost of using resources in a certain way is the value of what these resources could have produced if they had been used in the best alternative way.* In this case, the opportunity cost of the extra 100 tons of food per year is the 30 tons of clothing per year that must be forgone. This is what the town must give up in order to get the extra 100 tons of food. Why is opportunity cost so important? Because for you and the other members of the town council to determine which combination of food and clothing is best, you should compare the value of increases in food output with the opportunity costs of such increases.

# TOTING UP THE COSTS OF THE WAR AGAINST SADDAM HUSSEIN

In late 1990 and early 1991, the United States and its allies were engaged in a full-scale war against Iraq. A half million soldiers and their equipment were transported to the Persian Gulf and maintained there. Thousands of missiles were used in the hostilities. According to the Bush administration, the cost of the war to the Pentagon was about $50 billion, but was this the cost to the United States? Absolutely not.

Because the allies pledged to contribute $53.9 billion to the United States to help pay for the war, the United States may more than recoup the Pentagon's expenses. Moreover, this is particularly likely since the Bush administration's cost estimate of $50 billion may have been too high. For example, the Pentagon seems to have overestimated the effects of the war on the price of oil—and hence on its fuel bills.

Further, many of the weapons lost in the war may really have been redundant. At the beginning of hostilities, the United States had 267,000 TOW anti-tank missiles, 428,000 multi-launch rocket systems, 5,000 Patriot missiles, and over 2,000 Tomahawk cruise missiles. This huge inventory of weapons was built up during the days when the Soviet Union was regarded as a much more dangerous threat than in the early 1990s. Many observers have questioned whether Congress would ever be willing to replace many of the weapons lost in the war.

On the other hand, many of the costs of the war are much more subtle than indicated by a simple listing of the expenses of the Pentagon. According to many economists, including Alan Greenspan, the chairman of the Federal Reserve, the war helped to bring about the reduction in national output and the increase in unemployment that occurred in the United States in late 1990 and early 1991. (Why? Be-

cause it raised oil prices and reduced consumer and business confidence in the future. The reasons why higher oil prices and reduced confidence may have had these effects are given in subsequent chapters.) If Greenspan is right, it is obvious that, even if the United States is paid in full by its allies for the expenses incurred by the Pentagon, the war may nonetheless have been costly.

Here, as in so many other areas, the concept of opportunity cost is of fundamental importance. To determine the actual cost of the war to the United States, you must try to determine what the United States really gave up by engaging in this war. Clearly, the actual cost was quite different from the amount the Pentagon spent.

For example, suppose that the town council is considering whether or not to increase food output from 100 to 200 tons per year. To decide this question, the council should compare the value of the extra 100 tons of food with the opportunity cost of the extra food (which is the 30 tons of clothing that must be given up). If the town council feels that the extra 100 tons of food are worth more to the town's welfare than the 30 tons of clothing that are given up, the extra food should be produced. Otherwise it should not be produced.

**PARKS AND OPPORTUNITY COSTS.** As we have just seen, the concept of opportunity cost can be used to help solve the hypothetical problem of the town council described above. Used in a similar way, the concept of opportunity cost can throw significant light on many important real problems as well. For example, suppose that a bill is presented to Congress to set aside certain wilderness areas as national parks. At first glance, it may appear that such a step entails no cost to society, since the land is not being utilized and the resources required to designate the areas as national parks are trivial. But using the concept of opportunity cost, it is clear that this step may have very substantial costs to society. For instance, if these lands are made part of the national parks system, the minerals, timber, and other natural resources contained within the areas cannot be extracted nor can the lands be used as sites for factories or processing plants. As pointed out above, the opportunity cost of using resources in one way is the value of what these resources could have produced had they been used in the best alternative way. Suppose that if these lands are not turned into national parks, their most valuable alternative use is for development of copper mines which would produce benefits amounting to $25 million per year to society. Then the actual cost to society of using these lands as parks is $25 million per year, since this is the amount that society is giving up when it uses them in this way (rather than selecting the most valuable alternative). Thus, whether these lands should be used as parks depends on whether the society believes that it is worth $25 million or more to do so.

The concept of opportunity cost is very important in analyzing personal, managerial, and judicial issues, as well as questions involving government policy. Example 1.1 shows how this concept can be applied to determine the true costs to a student of going to college. Example 1.2 indicates how this concept was used in a legal case to assess damages. Like the examples in subsequent chapters, they should be studied carefully.

# THE IMPACT OF ECONOMICS ON SOCIETY

Economics has influenced generations of statesmen, philosophers, and ordinary citizens, and has played a significant role in shaping our society today.

## Adam Smith, Father of Modern Economics

To illustrate the importance of economic ideas, let's consider some of the precepts of Adam Smith (1723–90), the man who is often called the father of modern economics. Much of his masterpiece *The Wealth of Nations*[1]

[1] Adam Smith, *The Wealth of Nations*, New York: Modern Library, 1937. Originally published in 1776.

seems trite today, because it has been absorbed so thoroughly into modern thought, but it was not trite when it was written. On the contrary, Smith's ideas were revolutionary. *He was among the first to describe how a free, competitive economy can function—without central planning or government interference—to allocate resources efficiently. He recognized the virtues of the "invisible hand" that leads the private interest of firms and individuals toward socially desirable ends, and he was properly suspicious of firms that are sheltered from competition, since he recognized the potentially undesirable effects on resource allocation.*

In addition, Smith—with the dire poverty of his times staring him in the face—was interested in the forces that determined the evolution of the economy—that is, the forces determining the rate of growth of average income per person. Although Smith did not approve of avarice, he felt that saving was good because it enabled society to invest in machinery and other forms of capital. Accumulating more and more capital would, according to Smith, allow output to grow. In addition, he emphasized the importance of increased specialization and division of labor in bringing about economic progress. By specializing, people can concentrate on the tasks they do best, with the result that society's total output is raised.

All in all, Smith's views were relatively optimistic, in keeping with the intellectual climate of his time—the era of Voltaire, Diderot, Franklin, and Jefferson, the age of the Enlightenment, when men believed so strongly in rationality. Leave markets alone, said Smith, and beware of firms with too much economic power and government meddling. If this is done, there is no reason why considerable economic progress cannot be achieved. Smith's work has been modified and extended in a variety of ways in the past 200 years. Some of his ideas have been challenged and, in some cases, discarded. But his influence on modern society has been enormous.

## The Influence of Economics Today

Turning from Adam Smith's day to the present, economics continues to have an enormous influence over the shape of our society. Economics, and economists, play an extremely important part in the formulation of public policy. Skim through the articles in a daily newspaper. Chances are that you will find a report of an economist testifying before Congress, perhaps on the costs and benefits of a program to reduce unemployment among black teenagers in the Bedford-Stuyvesant area of New York City, or on the steps to be taken to make American goods more competitive with those of Japan or Germany. Still another economist may crop up on the editorial page, discussing the pros and cons of various proposed ways to reduce the federal deficit.

Economics and economists play a key role at the highest levels of our government. The president, whether a Democrat or a Republican, relies heavily on his economic advisers in making the decisions that help to shape the future of the country. In Congress, too, economics plays a major role. Economists are frequent witnesses before congressional committees, staff members for the committees, and advisers to individual representatives and senators. Many congressional committees focus largely on economic matters. For example, in 1991, many members of Congress spent large chunks of their time wrestling with budgetary and tax questions.

Paul Volcker, former chairman of the Federal Reserve, before a congressional committee

## EXAMPLE 1.1 HOW MUCH DOES IT COST TO GO TO COLLEGE?

According to the College Board, the average college student incurred the following annual costs in 1990–91:

| | PRIVATE COLLEGE | PUBLIC COLLEGE |
|---|---|---|
| | (DOLLARS) | |
| Tuition and fees | 9,400 | 1,800 |
| Meals, room, books, travel, and other expenses | 5,900 | 5,200 |
| Total | 15,300 | 7,000 |

(a) Is $15,300 the total cost to the student of a year at a private college? (*Hint:* Are there opportunity costs?) (b) John Martin is a 40-year-old executive; James Miller is an 18-year-old with no job experience. They are both full-time students. Although both must pay the same costs (given above), the true cost to Martin is more than the true cost to Miller. Why? (c) Is $1,800 the total cost to the typical public college of a student's going there for a year? (d) Is $15,300 the total cost to society of a student's going to a private college for a year?

### Solution

(a) No, the true cost of going to college is considerably in excess of the out-of-pocket expenses because one can obtain wages by working rather than attending classes and studying. In other words, the time spent in school has opportunity costs, since it could be devoted to a job rather than to education. For example, if the student could earn $8,000 during a school year if he or she worked rather than going to college, the true total annual cost of a college education is $15,300 + $8,000 = $23,300. (b) Martin can earn much more than Miller if, rather than going to school, he were to work. Thus the opportunity cost of his time spent in school is greater than for Miller. (c) No. Tuition and fees cover only part of the public college's costs; the rest are covered by government support, alumni contributions, and other payments. (d) No. The cost to society equals the value to society of the resources used to teach, house, feed, and maintain the student, as well as the opportunity cost to society of his or her time. Although it is not easy to pin down all of the social costs, they clearly do not equal $15,300.

Perhaps the most dramatic evidence of the importance of economics in the formulation of public policy is provided during presidential elections, like that in 1992 (or the 1988 election that pitted George Bush against Michael Dukakis). Each candidate—with his or her own cadre of economic advisers supplying ideas and reports—stakes out a position on the major economic issues of the day. This position can be of crucial importance in determining victory or defeat, and you, the citizen, must know some economics to understand whether a candidate is talking sense or nonsense (or merely evading an issue). For example, if a candidate promises to increase government expenditures, lower taxes, and reduce the federal deficit, you can be pretty certain that he is talking through his hat. This may not be obvious to you now, but it should be later on.

Also, economics and economists play an extremely important role in private decision making. Their role in the decision-making process in business firms is particularly great, since many of the nation's larger corporations hire professional economists to forecast their sales, reduce their

# ADAM SMITH ON THE "INVISIBLE HAND"

Adam Smith (1723–90) lived during the Industrial Revolution and was one of the first scholars to understand many of the central mechanisms of a free, or unplanned, economy. Much of his life was spent as professor of moral philosophy at the University of Glasgow in Scotland. In 1759, he published *The Theory of Moral Sentiments,* which established him as one of Britain's foremost philosophers; but this was not the book for which he is famous today. His masterpiece, published in 1776 (while the American colonists were brewing rebellion), was *The Wealth of Nations,* a long encyclopedic book twelve years in the writing. It was not an instant success, but the laurels it eventually won undoubtedly compensated for its early neglect.

One of Smith's central contentions was that firms and individuals, by pursuing their own objectives, often will promote the general welfare. In a famous passage, he stated that:

``It is only for the sake of profit that any man employs [his] capital in the support of industry, and he will always, therefore, endeavor to employ it in the support of that industry of which the produce is likely to be of greatest value, or to exchange the greatest quantity either of money or of other goods. But the annual revenue of every society is always precisely equal to the exchangeable value of the whole annual produce of its industry, or rather is precisely the same thing with that exchangeable value. As every individual, therefore, endeavors as much as he can both to employ his capital in the support of domestic industry, and so to direct that industry that its produce may be of the greatest value, every individual necessarily labors to render the annual revenue of the society as great as he can: He generally, indeed, neither intends to promote the public interest, nor knows how much he is promoting it. . . . He intends only his own security; and by directing that industry in such a manner as its produce may be of the greatest value, he intends only

his own gain, and *he is in this, as in many other cases, led by an invisible hand to promote an end which was no part of his intention.* Nor is it always the worse for the society that it was no part of it. *By pursuing his own interest he frequently promotes that of the society more effectually than when he really intends to promote it.* I have never known much good done by those who affected to trade for the public good. It is an affectation, indeed, not very common among merchants, and very few words need be employed in dissuading them from it. . . ."[1]

[1] Adam Smith, *The Wealth of Nations,* London: George Routledge, 1900, p. 345. Originally published in 1776. (Italics added.)

costs, increase their efficiency, negotiate with labor and government, and carry out a host of other tasks. Judging from the fancy salaries business economists are paid, the firms seem to think they can deliver the goods, and in fact, the available evidence seems to indicate that they do provide important guidance to firms in many areas of their operations.

## Positive Economics versus Normative Economics

Before concluding this chapter, it is essential that we recognize the distinction between positive economics and normative economics. ***Positive economics*** *contains descriptive statements, propositions, and predictions about the world*. For instance, an economic theory may predict that the price of copper will increase by $.01 a pound if income per person in the United States rises by 10 percent; this is positive economics. Positive economics tells us only what will happen under certain circumstances. It says nothing about whether the results are good or bad—or about what we should do. ***Normative economics,*** *on the other hand, makes statements about what ought to be, or about what a person, organization, or nation ought to do*. For instance, a theory might say that Chile should introduce new technology more quickly in many of its copper mines; this is normative economics.

Clearly, positive economics and normative economics must be treated differently. Positive economics is science in the ordinary sense of the word: Propositions in positive economics can be tested by an appeal to the facts. In a nonexperimental science like economics, however, it is sometimes difficult to get the facts you need to test particular propositions. For example, if income per person in the United States does not rise by 10 percent, it may be difficult to tell what the effect of such an increase would be on the price of copper. Moreover, even if per capita income does increase by this amount, it may be difficult to separate the effect of the increase in income per person on the price of copper from the effect of other factors. But nonetheless, we can, in principle, test propositions in positive economics by an appeal to the facts.

In normative economics, this is not the case. *In normative economics, the results you get depend on your values or preferences*. For example, if you believe that reducing unemployment is more important than maintaining the purchasing power of the dollar, you will get one answer to certain questions; whereas if you believe that maintaining the purchasing power of the dollar is more important than reducing unemployment, you are likely to get a different answer to the same questions. This is not at all strange. After all, if people desire different things (which is another way of saying that they have different values), they may well make different decisions and advocate different policies. It would be strange if they did not.

This book will spend a lot of time on the principles of positive economics—the principles and propositions concerning the workings of the economic system about which practically all economists tend to agree. Normative economics will also be treated, since we must discuss questions of policy—and all policy discussions involve individual preferences, not solely hard facts. In these discussions, we shall try to indicate how the conclusions depend on one's values. Then you can let your own values be your guide. The purpose of this book is not to convert you to a particular set of values. It is to teach you how to obtain better solutions to economic problems, whatever set of values you may have.

# EXAMPLE 1.2   THE ASSESSMENT OF DAMAGES

In a well-known legal case, the United States was sued by O'Brien Bros., Inc., the owner of a Brooklyn-bound barge that was sunk by a U.S. Navy tug that collided with the barge. O'Brien Bros. received damages stemming from the collision. The calculation of the damages was turned over to a commissioner, who found them to be as follows:

| | DOLLARS |
|---|---|
| Costs of raising the wreck | 7,732.21 |
| Repairs | 43,245.22 |
| Compensation for loss of earnings from the barge during the time it was unavailable for work | 6,620.25 |
| Miscellaneous costs | 3,423.91 |
| Total | 61,021.59 |

(a) Why should O'Brien Bros. be compensated for the loss of earnings? It did not pay out $6,620.25 to anyone. Why should it receive this amount in damages? (b) The United States appealed the decision. Government attorneys introduced evidence that a similar barge could have been built new for $33,000. Does this mean that the damages should have been $33,000? (c) Suppose that O'Brien Bros. could have bought a similar barge for $25,000 and that its forgone earnings during the time elapsing from the sinking of the old barge to the availability of the new barge was $5,000. If the sunk barge would cause no problems either to O'Brien Bros. or anyone else, should it have been raised and repaired? (d) Suppose that O'Brien Bros. could have obtained $8,500 for the wreck (for scrap metal, salvageable parts, and so forth), if it was raised? Should it have been raised?

## Solution

(a) If the barge had not been sunk, O'Brien Bros. would have earned this amount. It is the opportunity cost of the barge's being sunk. (b) No. The barge that was sunk may have been worth less than $33,000, since it was not new. On the other hand, the figure of $33,000 takes no account of lost earnings in the time interval until the barge was replaced. (c) No. The cost of raising and repairing it exceeded the cost of buying a similar barge. (d) Yes, because the amount that could be obtained for the wreck would exceed the cost of raising it.*

* For further description of this case, see "O'Brien Bros., Inc. v. The Helen B. Moran et al." in R. Byrns and G. Stone, Jr., *An Economics Casebook: Applications from the Law*, Santa Monica: Goodyear, 1980.

# TEST YOURSELF

1. In a famous passage from The Wealth of Nations, Adam Smith said that: "It is the maxim of every prudent master of a family, never to make at home what it will cost him more to make than to buy." Suppose that Mrs. Harris spends an hour preparing a meal. She is a psychologist in private practice and can obtain $50 per hour for her services. What is the cost to the Harris family of her preparing this meal? Explain.

2. "Resources are scarce and once a decision is made to use them for one purpose, they are no longer available for another. One opportunity cost of reading [an] . . . article, for example, is not simultaneously being able to read [another article]." Explain, and relate to the question of how a student should allocate his or her time among various course assignments.

3. Suppose that it costs a college student $1,000 per year more for room and board than if he or she works (and lives at home). If this assumption is correct, why is this amount, rather than the full cost of room and board, the proper amount to use in Example 1.1?

4. On the basis of positive economics alone, which of the following statements can be determined to be true or false? (a) The tax cut of 1981 reduced unemployment in the United States by 3 percentage points. (b) The tax cut was timed improperly. (c) The tax cut was a less equitable way of reducing unemployment than a program whereby the unemployed were hired by the government to perform important social functions.

# SUMMARY

1. According to one standard definition, economics is concerned with the way resources are allocated among alternative uses to satisfy human wants. A resource is a thing or service used to produce goods (or services) which can satisfy wants. Not all resources are scarce. Free resources, such as air, are so abundant that they can be obtained without charge.

2. Those resources that are scarce are called economic resources. The test of whether a resource is an economic resource or a free resource is price: economic resources command a nonzero price but free resources do not. Economists often classify economic resources into three categories: land, labor, and capital.

3. Since economic resources are scarce, only a limited amount of goods and services can be produced from them, and there arises the necessity for choice. For example, if an isolated town has a certain amount of resources, it must choose how much of each good it will produce from these resources. If it increases the amount produced of one good, it must reduce the amount produced of another good.

4. The opportunity cost (or alternative cost) of using a resource to increase the production of one good is the value of what the resource could have produced had it been used in the best alternative way. To illustrate the use of the concept of opportunity cost, which is one of the most important in economics, we discussed the cases of public parks and a college education.

5. Economists are particularly concerned with four basic questions regarding the working of any economic system, ours or any other. These questions are (1) What determines what (and how much) is produced? (2) What determines how it is produced? (3) What determines how the society's output is distributed among the members? (4) What determines the rate at which the society's per capita income will grow?

6. Economists often distinguish between positive economics and normative economics. Positive economics contains descriptive statements, propositions, and predictions about the world; whereas normative economics contains statements about what ought to be, or about what a person, organization, or nation ought to do.

7. In normative economics, the results you get depend on your basic values and preferences; in positive economics, the results are testable, at least in principle, by an appeal to the facts.

# CONCEPTS FOR REVIEW

| | | |
|---|---|---|
| Unemployment | Resources | Technology |
| Inflation | Economic resources | Choice |
| Labor productivity | Free resources | Opportunity cost |
| Poverty | Land | Alternative cost |
| Economics | Labor | Positive economics |
| Human wants | Capital | Normative economics |

# ECONOMIC MODELS AND CAPITALISM, AMERICAN-STYLE

THE UNITED STATES, LIKE all other nations, is beset by many economic problems. As pointed out in Chapter 1, the early 1990s were a period when the competitiveness and efficiency of many American industries were questioned, and in late 1990 the unemployment rate rose. Also, there were problems in controlling the federal deficit and in bringing our exports and imports into balance. Yet, despite these problems, the American economy is among the most prosperous in the world. The average American family has plenty of food, clothing, housing, appliances, and luxuries of many kinds. The tremendous strength and vitality of the American economy should be recognized, as well as its shortcomings. Nothing is gained by overlooking either the successes or the faults of our system.

As a first step toward understanding why we are so well off in some respects and so lacking in others, we need to understand how our economy works. Of course, this is a big task. Indeed, you could say that this whole book is devoted to discussing this subject. So we will not try to present a detailed picture of the operation of the American economy at this point. All we will do now is give a preliminary sketch, a basic blueprint of what an economic system must do and how our mixed capitalistic system works.

First, however, we must provide a brief description of the role of model building in economics, since this will introduce you to the methods used by economists. Without such an introduction to economic methodology, it would be difficult, if not impossible, for you to understand fully much of the material that follows in this and succeeding chapters. Only after these preliminary matters are covered will we be able to turn to a discussion of the tasks of an economic system and the way our economy functions.

## THE METHODOLOGY OF ECONOMICS

### Model Building in Economics

Like other types of scientific analysis, economics is based on the formulation of ***models***. *A model is a theory. It is composed of a number of assumptions from which conclusions—or predictions—are deduced.* An astronomer who wants to formulate a model of the solar system might represent each planet by a point in space and assume that each would change position in accord with certain mathematical equations. Based on this model, the astronomer might predict when an eclipse would occur, or estimate the probability of a planetary collision. The economist proceeds along similar lines when setting forth a model of economic behavior.

There are several important points to be noted concerning models:

**1. TO BE USEFUL, A MODEL MUST SIMPLIFY THE REAL SITUATION.** The assumptions made by a model need not be exact replicas of reality. If they were, the model would be too complicated to use. The basic reasons for using a model is that the real world is so complex that masses of detail often obscure underlying patterns. The economist faces the familiar problem of seeing the forest as distinct from just the trees. Other scientists must do the same; physicists work with simplified models of atoms, just as economists work with simplified models of markets. However, this does not mean that *all* models are good or useful. A model may be so oversimplified and distorted that it is utterly useless. The trick is to construct a model so that irrelevant and unimportant considerations and variables are neglected, but the major factors—those that seriously affect the phenomena the model is designed to predict—are included.

**2. THE PURPOSE OF A MODEL IS TO MAKE PREDICTIONS ABOUT THE REAL WORLD; AND IN MANY RESPECTS THE MOST IMPORTANT TEST OF A MODEL IS HOW WELL IT PREDICTS.** In this sense, a model that predicts the price of copper within plus or minus $.01 a pound is better than a model that predicts it within plus or minus $.02 a pound. Of course, this does not mean that a model is useless if it cannot predict very accurately. We do not always need a very accurate prediction. For example, a road map is a model that can be used to make predictions about the route a driver should take to get to a particular destination. Sometimes, a very crude map is good enough to get you where you want to go, but such a map would not, for instance, serve the hiker who needs to know the characteristics of the terrain through which he plans to walk. How detailed a map you need depends on where you are going and how you want to get there.

**3. A PERSON WHO WANTS TO PREDICT THE OUTCOME OF A PARTICULAR EVENT WILL BE FORCED TO USE THE MODEL THAT PREDICTS BEST, EVEN IF THIS MODEL DOES NOT PREDICT VERY WELL.** The choice is not between a model and no model; it is between one model and another. After all, a person who must make a forecast will use the most accurate device available—and any such device is a model of some sort. Consequently, when economists make simplifying assumptions and derive conclusions that are only approximately true, it is somewhat beside the point to complain that the assumptions are simpler than reality or that the predictions are not always accurate. This may be true, but if the predictions based on the economists' model are better than those obtained on the basis of other models, their model must, and will, be used until something better comes along. Thus, if a model can predict the price of copper to within plus or minus $.01 per pound, and no other model can do better, this model will be used even if those interested in the predictions bewail the model's limitations and wish it could be improved.

1.2

## Economic Measurement

To utilize and test their models, economists need facts of many sorts. For example, suppose that an economist constructs a model which predicts

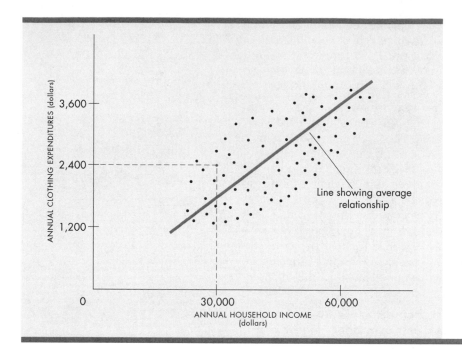

**Figure 2.1**
**Relationship between Annual Clothing Expenditures and Annual Household Income**
Each family is represented by a dot. The line shows the average relationship. The line does not fit all families exactly, since all the points do not fall on it. The line does, however, show average clothing expenditure for each income level.

that a household's annual clothing expenditure tends to increase by $60 when its income increases by $1,000. To see whether this model is correct, he or she must gather data concerning the incomes and clothing expenditures of a large number of households and study the relationship between them. Suppose that Figure 2.1 shows the relationship the economist finds. The line represents an average relationship between household income and household clothing expenditure. Judging by Figure 2.1, his or her model is reasonably accurate, at least for households with incomes between $30,000 and $60,000 per year.[1]

Measurements like those in Figure 2.1 enable economists to *quantify* their models; in other words, they enable them to construct models that predict *how much* effect one variable has on another. The economist above has shown that a $1,000 increase in a household's income results, on the average, in a $60 increase in clothing expenditures. Notice how much more useful this specific relationship is than simply saying that with more income, a person will tend to buy more clothes. You do not need an economist to tell you that.

## GRAPHS AND RELATIONSHIPS

To conclude our brief discussion of economic methodology, we must describe the construction and interpretation of graphs, such as Figure 2.1, which economists use to present data and relationships. Such graphs are used repeatedly throughout this book, and it is essential that the following three points be understood:

[1] It is worth noting that, although it is useful to see how well a model would have fit the historical facts, this is no substitute for seeing how well it will predict the future. As a distinguished mentor of mine once observed. "It's a darned poor person who can't predict the past."

1. A graph has a horizontal axis and a vertical axis, each of which has a scale of numerical values. For example, in Figure 2.1, the horizontal axis shows a household's annual income, and the vertical axis shows the annual amount spent by the household on clothing. The intersection of the two axes is called the origin and is the point where both the variable measured along the horizontal axis and the variable measured along the vertical axis are zero. In Figure 2.1, the origin is at the lower lefthand corner of the figure, labeled "0."

2. To show the relationship between two variables, one can plot the value of one variable against the value of the other variable. Thus, in Figure 2.1, each family is represented by a dot. For example, the colored dot is in the position shown in Figure 2.1 because it represents a family whose income was $30,000 and whose clothing expenditure was $2,400. Clearly, the line showing the average relationship does not fit all the families exactly, since all the points do not fall on the line. This line does, however, give the average clothing expenditure for each level of income: it is an average relationship.

3. The relationship between two variables is *direct* if, as in Figure 2.1, the line of average relationship is upward sloping. In other words, if the variable measured along the vertical axis tends to increase (decrease) in response to increases (decreases) in the variable measured along the horizontal axis, the relationship is direct. On the other hand, if the line of average relationship is downward sloping, as in Figure 2.2, the relationship is *inverse*. In other words, if the variable measured along the vertical axis tends to decrease (increase) in response to increases (decreases) in the variable measured along the horizontal axis, the relationship is inverse.

To illustrate how one can graph a relationship between two variables, consider Table 2.1, which shows the amount of tennis balls demanded in a particular market at various prices. Putting price on the vertical axis and quantity demanded on the horizontal axis, one can plot each combination of price and quantity in this table as a point on a graph; and that is precisely what has been done in Figure 2.2 (points *A* to *E*).

**Table 2.1
Quantity of Tennis Balls Demanded in a Particular Market at Various Prices**

| PRICE OF A TENNIS BALL (DOLLARS) | QUANTITY OF TENNIS BALLS DEMANDED (MILLIONS) |
| --- | --- |
| 1.50 | 1 |
| 1.20 | 2 |
| 0.90 | 3 |
| 0.60 | 4 |
| 0.30 | 6 |

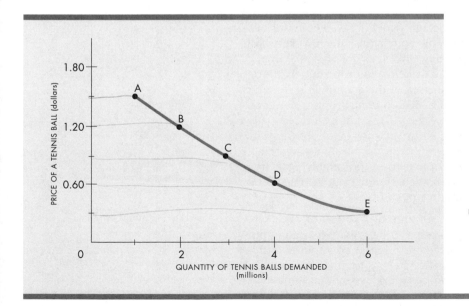

**Figure 2.2
Relationship between Quantity Demanded and Price of Tennis Balls (as shown in Table 2.1)**

# THE TASKS OF AN ECONOMIC SYSTEM

Having discussed the nature and quantification of economic models, we now can turn to the primary purpose of this chapter, which is to provide a preliminary sketch of what an economic system must do and how our mixed capitalistic system works. In this section, we describe what an economic system—*ours or any other*—must do. Basically, as we saw in Chapter 1, there are four tasks that any economic system must perform:

**1. AN ECONOMIC SYSTEM MUST DETERMINE THE LEVEL AND COMPOSITION OF SOCIETY'S OUTPUT.** That is, it must answer questions like: To what extent should society's resources be used to produce new aircraft carriers and missiles? To what extent should they be used to produce sewage plants to reduce water pollution? To what extent should they be used to produce low-cost housing for the poor? Pause for a moment to think about how important—and how vast—this function is. Most people simply take for granted that somehow it is decided what we as a society are going to produce, and far too few people really think about the social mechanisms that determine the answers to such questions.

**2. AN ECONOMIC SYSTEM MUST DETERMINE HOW EACH GOOD AND SERVICE IS TO BE PRODUCED.** Given existing technology, a society's resources can be used in various ways. Should the skilled labor in Birmingham, Alabama, be used to produce cotton or steel? Should a particular machine tool be used to produce aircraft or automobiles? The way questions of this sort are answered will determine the way each good and service is produced. In other words, it will determine which resources are used to produce which goods and services. If this function is performed badly, society's resources are put to the wrong uses, resulting in less output than if this function is performed well.

**3. AN ECONOMIC SYSTEM MUST DETERMINE HOW THE GOODS AND SERVICES THAT ARE PRODUCED ARE TO BE DISTRIBUTED AMONG THE MEMBERS OF SOCIETY.** In other words, how much of each type of good and service should each person receive? Should there be a considerable amount of income inequality, the rich receiving much more than the poor? Or should incomes be relatively equal? Take your own case. Somehow or other, the economic system determines how much income you will receive. In our economic system, your income depends on your skills, the property you own, how hard you work, and prevailing prices, as we shall see in succeeding chapters. But in other economic systems, your income might depend on quite different factors. This function of the economic system has generated, and will continue to generate, heated controversy. Some people favor a relatively egalitarian society where the amount received by one family varies little from that received by another family of the same size. Other people favor a society where the amount a family or person receives can vary a great deal. Few people favor a thoroughly egalitarian society, if for no other reason than that some differences in income are required to stimulate workers to do certain types of work.

**4. AN ECONOMIC SYSTEM MUST DETERMINE THE RATE OF GROWTH OF PER CAPITA INCOME.** An adequate growth rate has come to be regarded as an important economic goal, particularly in the less developed countries of Africa, Asia, and Latin America. There is very strong pressure in these countries for changes in technology, the adoption of superior techniques, increases in the stock of capital resources, and better and more extensive education and training of the labor force. These are viewed as some of the major ways to promote the growth of per capita income.

## TEST YOURSELF

1. Suppose that the quantity of corn demanded annually by American consumers at each price of corn is as follows:

| PRICE (DOLLARS PER BUSHEL) | QUANTITY OF CORN (MILLIONS OF BUSHELS) |
|---|---|
| 1 | 2.0 |
| 2 | 1.0 |
| 3 | 0.5 |
| 4 | 0.4 |

How much will farmers receive for their corn crop if it is 2 million bushels? If it is 1 million bushels? If you owned all of the farms producing corn, would you produce 2 million bushels? Why, or why not?

2. Plot the relationship between price and quantity demanded in Question 1 on a graph. Is the relationship direct or inverse? Based on your graph, estimate how much corn is likely to be demanded if the price is (a) $1.50, (b) $2.50, and (c) $3.50.

3. Suppose that Americans begin to take up tennis in much larger numbers. Will the curve in Figure 2.2 shift? If so, will it shift to the right or to the left? Explain.

4. Suppose that you wanted to construct a model to explain and predict the breakfast food that your neighbor will choose tomorrow. What factors would you include? How well do you think you could predict?

# THE ECONOMIC SYSTEM: A SIMPLE INTRODUCTORY MODEL ⁴

## The Production Possibilities Curve and the Determination of What Is Produced

We've seen that economists use models to throw light on economic problems. At this point, let's try our hand at constructing a simple model to illuminate the basic functions any economic system, ours included, must perform. To keep things simple, suppose that society produces only two goods, food and tractors. This, of course, is unrealistic, but, as we've seen, a model does not have to be realistic to be useful. Here, by assuming that there are only two goods, we eliminate a lot of unnecessary complexity and lay bare the essentials. In addition, we suppose that society has at its disposal a certain amount of resources, and that this amount is fixed for the duration of the period in question. This assumption is quite realistic. So long as the period is relatively short, the amount of a society's resources is relatively fixed (except, of course, under unusual circumstances, such as if a country annexes additional land). Finally, we suppose as well that society's technology is fixed. So long as the period is relatively short, this assumption too is realistic.

Under these circumstances, it is possible to figure out the various amounts of food and tractors that society can produce. Specifically, we can proceed as in Chapter 1, where we determined the amounts of food and clothing that an isolated town could produce. Let's begin with how many tractors society can produce if all resources are devoted to tractor production. According to Table 2.2, the answer is 15 million tractors.

Next, let's consider the opposite extreme, where society devotes all its resources to food production. According to Table 2.2, it can produce 12 million tons of food in this case. Next, let's consider cases where both products are being produced. Such cases are represented by possibilities *B* to *F* in the table. As emphasized in Chapter 1, the more of one good that is produced, the less of the other good that can be produced. Why? Because to produce more of one good, resources must be taken away from the production of the other good, lessening the amount of the other good produced.

Figure 2.3 shows how we can use a graph to show the various production possibilities society can attain. It is merely a different way of presenting the data in Table 2.2; the output of food is plotted on the horizontal axis and the output of tractors on the vertical axis. The curve in Figure 2.3, which shows the various combinations of output of food and tractors that society can produce, is called a ***production possibilities curve.***

The production possibilities curve sheds considerable light on the economic tasks facing any society. It shows the various production possibilities open to society. According to Figure 2.3, society can choose to produce 4 million tons of food and 12 million tractors (point *C*), or 6 million tons of food and 10 million tractors (point *D*), but it cannot choose to produce 6 million tons of food and 12 million tractors (point *H*). Point *H* is inaccessible with this society's resources and technology. Perhaps it will become accessible if the society's resources increase or if its technology improves, but for the present, point *H* is out of reach.

If resources are fully and efficiently utilized, *the first function of any economic system—to determine the level and composition of society's output—is really a problem of determining at what point along the production possibilities curve society should be.* Should society choose point *A, B, C, D, E, F,* or *G*? In making this choice, one thing is obvious from the production possibilities curve: *you cannot get more of one good without giving up some of the other good.* In other words, you cannot escape the problem of choice. So long as resources are limited and technology is less

**Table 2.2**
**Alternative Combinations of Outputs of Food and Tractors That Can Be Produced**

| POSSIBILITY | FOOD (MILLIONS OF TONS) | TRACTORS (MILLIONS) |
|---|---|---|
| *A* | 0 | 15 |
| *B* | 2 | 14 |
| *C* | 4 | 12 |
| *D* | 6 | 10 |
| *E* | 8 | 7 |
| *F* | 10 | 4 |
| *G* | 12 | 0 |

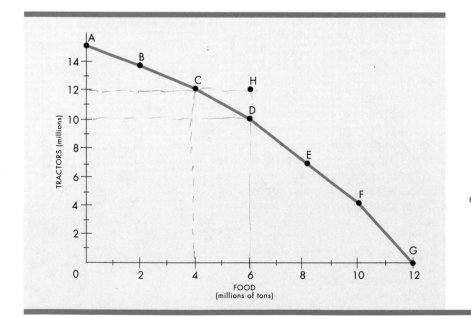

**Figure 2.3**
**Production Possibilities Curve**
This curve shows the various combinations of tractors and food that can be produced efficiently with given resources and technology. Point *H* is unattainable.

# EXAMPLE 2.1    HAY AND GRAIN IN IOWA

According to studies carried out at Iowa State University, the following combinations of grain and hay could be produced from 100 acres of land in a particular part of Iowa:

| NUMBER OF ACRES DEVOTED TO EACH USE | | TOTAL PRODUCTION (POUNDS) | |
|---|---|---|---|
| HAY | GRAIN | GRAIN | HAY |
| 0 | 100 | 224,000 | 0 |
| 25 | 75 | 212,920 | 89,600 |
| 33 | 67 | 166,194 | 96,400 |

That is, if all 100 acres were devoted to grain, 224,000 pounds of grain could be produced; if 75 of the 100 acres were devoted to grain, 212,920 pounds of grain and 89,600 pounds of hay could be produced; and so on.

(a) If a 100-acre farm in this part of Iowa was producing 212,920 pounds of grain and 89,600 pounds of hay, what was the approximate cost of increasing its production of grain by 1 pound? (b) Suppose that the profit to be made from a pound of grain was five times the profit to be made from a pound of hay, and that the owner of this farm claimed that, because this was the case, he should produce no hay. Would he be correct? (c) Suppose that, if hay production was increased from zero to about 100,000 pounds, the production of grain *increased,* not *decreased* (because hay contributed elements to the soil needed in the production of grain). Under these circumstances, would the slope of the production possibilities curve be negative at all points? Would it be rational for a farmer to produce no hay? (d) Would the production possibilities curve for a farm of this sort be the same now as in the 1940s?

**Solution**

(a) If it increased its grain output by 11,080 pounds (from 212,920 to 224,000 pounds), it had to reduce its hay output by 89,600 pounds. Thus an extra pound of grain output cost the farm about 89,600÷11,080, or 8.09 pounds of hay. (b) No. If he produced 212,920 pounds of grain, and 89,600 pounds of hay, his profits would be larger than if he produced no hay, because the profit from the extra 89,600 pounds of hay was greater than the profit from the 11,080 pounds of grain forgone. (c) No. No, because by producing up to 100,000 pounds of hay, the farmer increased the output of grain too. (d) No, because of changes in technology.

---

than magic, you must reckon with the fact (emphasized in Chapter 1) that more of one thing means less of another. The old saw that you don't "get something for nothing" is hackneyed but true, so long as resources are fully and efficiently utilized.

## The Law of Increasing Cost
*opportuny*

In the previous section, we stressed that an increased output of one good (say, food) means a decreased output of the other good (say, tractors). This amounts to saying (in the language of Chapter 1) that the opportunity cost of producing more food is the output of tractors that must be forgone. In this section, we go a step further; we point out that, *as more and more of a good is produced, the production of yet another unit of this good is likely to entail a larger and larger opportunity cost* and we explain why this is true.

This so-called law of increasing cost can be demonstrated in Figure 2.3. As more and more food is produced, the cost of increasing food output by 2 million tons increases. To see this, note that the *first* 2 million tons of food cost 1 million tractors (because this is the amount that tractor output must be reduced if food output increases from 0 to 2 million tons). The *second* 2 million tons of food cost 2 million tractors (because this is the amount that tractor output must be reduced if food output increases from 2 to 4 million tons). Skipping to the *sixth* 2 million tons of food, the cost of this additional food output is 4 million tractors (because this is the amount that tractor output must be reduced if food output increases from 10 to 12 million tons). Clearly, the more food that is already being produced, the greater the cost of producing an additional 2 million tons.

Why is this the case? Basically, it is because resources are not as effective in producing one good as in producing the other. When society only produces a small amount of food, it can use in food production those resources that are well suited to producing food and not so well suited to producing tractors. But as society produces more and more food, it tends to run out of such resources, and must absorb into food production those resources that are less suited to producing food and better suited to producing tractors. To increase food output by 2 million tons with the latter type of resources, a greater reduction must occur in tractor output than when the 2-million-ton increase in food output occurred with the resources that were well suited to food production (and not so well suited to producing tractors). Thus the cost of producing an additional 2 million tons of food tends to increase as more food is already being produced.

This law of increasing cost explains why a production possibilities curve has the shape shown in Figure 2.3. That is, it explains why the production possibilities curve has the "bowed out" shape (rather than the "bowed in" shape) indicated in Figure 2.4. Because the cost of increasing food output by a certain amount increases as more of it is already produced, the production possibilities curve tends to fall more steeply as one moves from left to right along the horizontal axis—which explains why the production possibilities curve has the "bowed out" shape.

## 4.3 The Production Possibilities Curve and the Determination of How Goods Are Produced

Let's turn now to the second basic function of any economic system: to determine how each good and service should be produced. In Table 2.2, we assumed implicitly that society's resources would be fully utilized and that the available technology would be applied in a way that would get the most out of the available resources. In other words, we assumed that the firms making food and tractors were as efficient as possible and that there was no unemployment of resources. But if there is widespread unemployment of people and machines, will society still be able to choose a point on the production possibilities curve? Clearly, the answer is no. Since society is not using all of its resources, it will not be able to produce as much as if it used them all. Thus, *if there is less than full employment of resources, society will have to settle for points inside the production possibilities curve*. For example, the best society may be able to do under these circumstances is to attain point *K* in Figure 2.5. *K* is a less desirable point than *C* or *D*—but that is the price of unemployment.

Suppose, on the other hand, that there is full employment of resources but that firms are inefficient. Perhaps they promote relatives of the boss, regardless of their ability; perhaps the managers are lazy or not much interested in efficiency; or perhaps the workers like to take long coffee breaks and are unwilling to work hard. Whatever the reason, will society still be able to choose a point on the production possibilities curve? Again, the answer is no. Since society is not getting as much as it could out of its resources, it will not be able to produce as much as it would if its resources were used efficiently. Thus, *if resources are used inefficiently, so-*

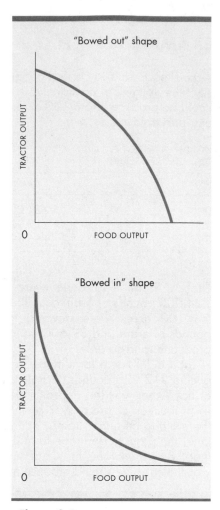

**Figure 2.4**
**Shape of the Production Possibilities Curve**
So long as the law of increasing cost holds true, the production possibilities curve will have the shape at the top ("bowed out"), *not* the shape at the bottom ("bowed in").

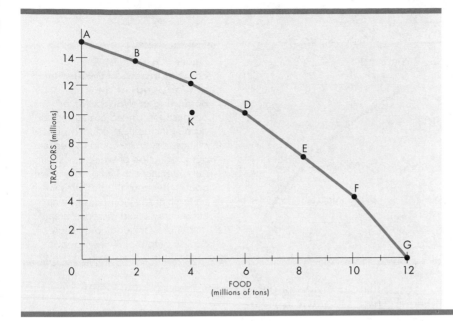

**Figure 2.5**
**Production Possibilities Curve**
This curve, like Figure 2.3, shows
the various combinations of tractors and food that can be produced efficiently with given
resources and technology. Point *K*
is less desirable than points *C* or
*D*, because less output is produced
at this point. But because of unemployment or inefficiency, society
may wind up at point *K*.

ciety will have to settle for *points inside* the production possibilities curve.
Perhaps in these circumstances, too, the best society can do may be point
*K* in Figure 2.5. The difference between this less desirable position and
positions on the production possibilities curve is the price of inefficiency.

At this point, it should be obvious that our model at least partially answers the question of how each good and service should be produced.
The answer is to *produce each good and service in such a way that you
wind up on the production possibilities curve, not on a point inside it.* Of
course, this is easier said than done, but at least our model indicates a
couple of villains to watch out for: unemployment of resources and inefficiency. When these villains are present, we can be sure that society is not
on the production possibilities curve.

If there is unemployment or inefficiency, society may be able to increase its output of one good without producing less of another good.
Otherwise this cannot be done, as long as technology and the quantity of
resources are fixed. Thus the old saw is wrong, and it is possible to "get
something for nothing" when society is inside the production possibilities
curve. Society need not give up anything—in the way of production of
other goods—to increase the production of this good under these circumstances.

For example, consider the sequence of events in two different countries at the beginning of World War II. In the Soviet Union, the war effort
meant a substantial decrease in the standard of living on the home front.
Resources had to be diverted from the production of civilian goods to the
production of military goods, and the war struck a severe blow at the living standards of the civilian population. In the United States, however, it
was possible to increase the production of military goods without making
such a dent in the living standards of the civilian population. How was
this possible? The United States at the beginning of World War II was still
struggling to emerge from the Great Depression, and several million people were still unemployed. The Soviet Union, however, was suffering no
such unemployment. Thus we could increase the production of both guns
and butter, whereas they could not.

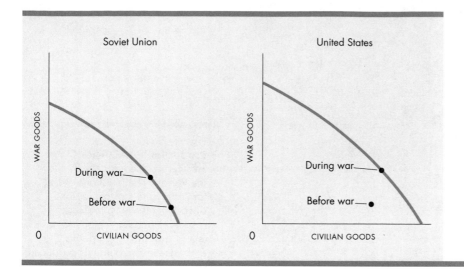

**Figure 2.6**
**Effect of Increased Production of War Goods at the Beginning of World War II**
Because the United States was at a point inside its production possibilities curve, we could increase our production of war goods without reducing production of civilian goods. Because the Russians were on their production possibilities curve, they could increase their output of war goods only by reducing output of civilian goods.

To put this comparison in a diagram, suppose that we divide all goods into two classes: war goods and civilian goods. Then, as shown in Figure 2.6, *we were inside our production possibilities curve at the beginning of the war, while the Soviets were not.*

## The Production Possibilities Curve, Income Distribution, and Growth

Let's return now to the case where our economy produces food and tractors. The third basic function of any economic system is to distribute the goods and services that are produced among the members of society. Each point on the production possibilities curve in Figure 2.5 represents society's total pie, but to deal with the third function, we must know how the pie is divided up among society's members. Since the production possibilities curve does not tell us this, it cannot shed light on this third function.

Fortunately, the production possibilities curve is of more use in analyzing the fourth basic function of any economic system: to determine the society's rate of growth of per capita income. Suppose that the society in Figure 2.5 invests a considerable amount of its resources in developing improved processes and products. It might establish agricultural experiment stations to improve farming techniques and industrial research laboratories to improve tractor designs. As shown in Figure 2.7, the production possibilities curve will be pushed outward. This will be the result of improved technology, enabling more food and/or more tractors to be produced from the same amount of resources. Thus one way for an economy to increase its output—and its per capita income—may be to invest in research and development.

Another way is by devoting more of its resources to the production of capital goods rather than consumers' goods. **Capital goods** consist of plant and equipment that are used to make other goods; **consumers' goods** are items that consumers purchase like clothing, food, and drink. Since capital goods are themselves resources, a society that chooses to produce lots of capital goods and few consumers' goods will push out its production possibilities curve much farther than a society that chooses to produce lots of consumers' goods and few capital goods.

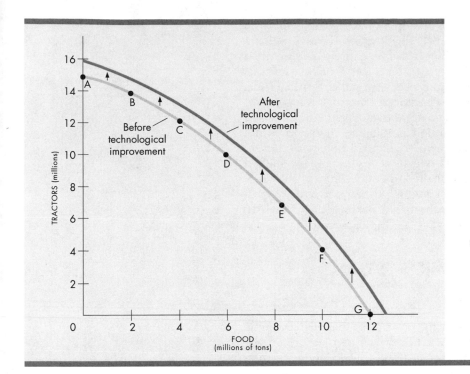

**Figure 2.7**
**Effect of Improvement in Technology on Production Possibilities Curve**
An improvement in technology results in an outward shift of the production possibilities curve.

To illustrate this point, consider our simple society that produces food and tractors. The more tractors (and the less food) this society produces, the more tractors it will have in the next period; and the more tractors it has in the next period, the more of both goods—food and tractors—it will be able to produce then. Thus the more tractors (and the less food) this society produces, the farther out it will push its production possibili-

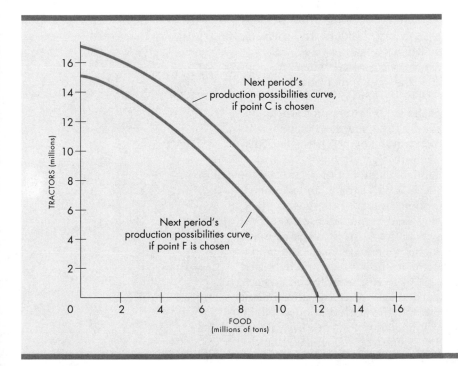

**Figure 2.8**
**Effect of Increase in Capital Goods on Production Possibilities Curve**
An increase in the amount of capital goods results in an outward shift of the production possibilities curve. The choice of point *C* means the production of more capital goods than the choice of point *F*.

ties curve—and the greater the increase in output (and per capita income) that it will achieve in the next period. If this society chooses point $F$ (shown in Figures 2.7, 2.5, or 2.3), the effect will be entirely different than if it chooses point $C$. If it chooses point $F$, it produces 4 million tractors, which we assume to be the number of tractors worn out each year. Thus, if it chooses point $F$, it adds nothing to its stock of tractors; it merely replaces those that wear out. Since it has no more tractors in the next period than in the current period, the production possibilities curve does not shift out at all if point $F$ is chosen. On the other hand, if point $C$ is chosen, the society produces 12 million tractors, which means that it has 8 million additional tractors at the beginning of the next period. Thus, as shown in Figure 2.8, the production possibilities curve is pushed outward. By producing more capital goods (and less consumers' goods) our society has increased its production possibilities and its per capita income.

## CAPITALISM: AN ECONOMIC SYSTEM

### What Is Capitalism?

In previous sections we have discussed the basic tasks that any economic system must perform. Now we must look at how our own economic system performs these tasks. The particular kind of economic system adopted by the United States is **capitalism.** Capitalism is one of those terms that is frequently used but seldom defined, and even less frequently understood. Its operation is complex, but its principal characteristics can be lumped into four major categories.

**1. PRIVATE OWNERSHIP OF CAPITAL.**   Under capitalism you or I can buy the tools of production. We can own factories, equipment, inventories, and other forms of capital. In a capitalistic system, somebody owns each piece of capital—and receives the income from it. Each piece of equipment has some sort of legal instrument indicating to whom it belongs. (If it belongs to a corporation, its owners basically are the stockholders who own the corporation). Moreover, each piece of capital has a market value. This system is in marked contrast to a communist or socialist state where the government owns the capital. In these states, the government decides how much and what kinds of capital goods will be produced; it owns the capital goods; and it receives and distributes the income they produce. In the Soviet Union or China, no one can buy or put up a new steel plant; it simply isn't allowed. (However, as noted above, in the early 1990s some Russian leaders favored moving toward capitalism.)

The United States is basically a capitalistic system, but there are certain areas where the government, not individuals, owns capital, and where individual property rights are limited in various ways by the government. The government owns much of the tooling used in the defense industries; it owns dams and the Tennessee Valley Authority; and it owns research laboratories in such diverse fields as atomic energy, space exploration, and health. Further, the government determines how much of a deceased person's assets can go to his or her heirs. (The rest goes to the government in the form of estate and inheritance taxes.) Also, the government can make a person sell his or her property to allow a road or other public project to be built. There are many such limitations on property rights. Ours is basically a capitalistic system, but it must be recognized that the government's role is important.

# THE ROLE OF SAVING IN THE INDUSTRIAL REVOLUTION AND JAPANESE ECONOMIC GROWTH

One of the most remarkable developments in human history was the Industrial Revolution. Until the middle of the eighteenth century, industry (as distinct from agriculture or commerce) played a small role in the economies of Europe or America. But during the late eighteenth and early nineteenth centuries a host of important technological innovations, such as James Watt's steam engine and Richard Arkwright's spinning jenny, made possible a very rapid growth in the output of industrial goods (like textiles and pig iron). And accompanying this growth of industrial output was the advent of the factory—a social and economic institution that is taken for granted today, but which was largely unknown prior to the Industrial Revolution.

The Industrial Revolution was characterized by major improvements in technology and by large increases in the amount of capital resources available to society. Both the improvements in technology and the additional capital resulted in an outward shift in the production possibilities curve in England, where the Industrial Revolution first took hold. (See Figure 2.7 and 2.8). Due to this shift, the standard of living in England, as measured by per capita income (total income divided by population), grew at an unprecedented rate. As the Industrial Revolution spread, this rise in living standards occurred too on the European continent and in the United States; it remained one of the lasting effects of industrialization.

As stressed above, the Industrial Revolution was characterized by considerable increases in capital. How did England (and other countries) bring about this increase in capital? By saving and investing. In other words, the English people had to set aside some of their resources and say in effect, "These resources will *not* be used to satisfy the current needs of our population for food, clothing, and other forms of consumption. Instead, they will be used to produce capital—factories, machines, equipment, railroads, and canals—which will increase our future productive capacity." Much more will be said about this saving process in subsequent chapters. For now, the essential point is that this saving process was one of the necessary conditions that made possible the Industrial Revolution.

Turning from the Industrial Revolution to the present, one of the reasons for Japan's remarkable increase in output during the period since World War II has been the very high Japanese savings rate. In the period during the 1960s and early 1970s when output in Japan was growing at about 10 percent per year, the Japanese were saving about 25 percent of their income. Like the English during the Industrial Revolution, the Japanese said in effect: "These resources will be used for factories, equipment, and other forms of investment, not for consumption." The result was an outward shift of the production possibilities curve, as in Figure 2.8.

**2. FREEDOM OF CHOICE AND ENTERPRISE.** Another important characteristic of capitalism is freedom of choice and freedom of enterprise. ***Freedom of choice*** means that consumers are free to buy what they please and reject what they please; that laborers are free to work where, when, and if they please; and that investors are free to invest in whatever property they please. By ***freedom of enterprise***, we mean that firms are free to enter whatever markets they please, obtain resources in whatever ways they can, and organize their affairs as best they can. Needless to say, this does not mean that firms can run roughshod over consumers and workers. Even the strongest champions of capitalism are quick to admit that the government must set "rules of the game" to prevent firms from engaging in sharp or unfair practices. But granting such limitations, the name of the game under capitalism is economic freedom.

Freedom to do what? Under capitalism, individuals and firms are free to pursue their own self-interest. Put in today's idiom, each individual or firm can do his, her, or its own thing. However, it is important to note that this freedom is circumscribed by one's financial resources. Consumers in a capitalistic system can buy practically anything they like—if they have the money to pay for it. Similarly, workers can work wherever or whenever they please—if they don't mind the wages. And a firm can run its business as it likes—if it remains solvent. Thus an important regulator of economic activity under capitalism is the pattern of income and prices that emerges in the marketplace.

**3. COMPETITION.** Still another important characteristic of capitalism is ***competition***. Firms compete with one another for sales. Under perfect competition, there are a large number of firms producing each product; indeed, there are so many that no firm controls the product's price. Because of this competition, firms are forced to jump to the tune of the consumer. If a firm doesn't produce what consumers want—at a price at least as low as other firms are charging—it will lose sales to other firms. Eventually, unless it mends its ways, such a firm will go out of business. Of course, in real-life American markets, the number of producers is not always so large that no firm has any control over price. (Much more will be said about this below.) But in the purest form of capitalism, such imperfections do not exist. Also, lest you think that competition under capitalism is confined to producers, it must be remembered that owners of resources also compete. They are expected to offer their resources—including labor—to the buyer who gives them the best deal, and buyers of resources and products are supposed to compete openly and freely.

**4. RELIANCE UPON MARKETS.** Finally, another very important characteristic of capitalism is its reliance upon markets. *Under pure capitalism, the market—the free market—plays a central role.* Firms and individuals buy and sell products and resources in competitive markets. Some firms and individuals make money and prosper; others lose money and fail. Each firm or individual is allowed freedom to pursue its or his or her interests in the marketplace, while the government guards against shady and dishonest dealings. Such is the nature of the economic system under pure capitalism.

## How Does Capitalism Perform the Four Basic Economic Tasks?

The ***price system*** lies at the heart of any capitalist economy. In a purely capitalist economy, it is used to carry out the four basic economic functions discussed above. The price system is a way to organize an economy. Under such a system, every commodity and every service, including labor, has a price. We all receive money for what we sell, including labor, and we use this money to buy the goods and services we want. If more is wanted of a certain good, the price of this good tends to rise; if less is wanted, the price of the good tends to fall. Producers base their production decisions on the prices of commodities and inputs. Thus increases in a commodity's price generally tend to increase the amount of it produced, and decreases generally tend to decrease the amount produced. In this way, firms' output decisions are brought into balance with consumers' desires.

The very important question of how the price system performs the basic economic functions we discussed above will be answered in some detail in the next chapter. All we can do here is provide a preliminary sketch.

**1. HOW DOES THE PRICE SYSTEM DETERMINE WHAT SOCIETY WILL PRODUCE?** In a substantially capitalistic economy, such as ours, consumers choose the amount of each good that they want, and producers act in accord with these decisions. The importance consumers attach to a good is indicated by the price they are willing to pay for it. Of course, the principle of **consumer sovereignty**—producers dancing to the tune of consumers' tastes—should not be viewed as always and completely true, since producers do attempt to manipulate the tastes of consumers through advertising and other devices, but it is certainly a reasonable first approximation.

**2. HOW DOES THE PRICE SYSTEM DETERMINE HOW EACH GOOD AND SERVICE WILL BE PRODUCED?** Prices indicate the desires of workers and the relative value of various types of materials and equipment as well as the desires of consumers. For examples, if plumbers are scarce relative to the demand for them, their price in the labor market—their wage—will be bid up, and they will tend to be used only in the places where they are productive enough so that their employers can afford to pay them the higher wages. The forces that push firms toward actually carrying out the proper decisions are profits and losses. Profits are the carrot and losses are the stick used to eliminate the less efficient and less alert firms and to increase the more efficient and the more alert.

**3. HOW DOES THE PRICE SYSTEM DETERMINE HOW MUCH IN THE WAY OF GOODS AND SERVICES EACH MEMBER OF THE SOCIETY IS TO RECEIVE?** In general, an individual's income depends largely on the quantities of resources of various kinds that he or she owns and the prices he or she gets for them. For example, if a man both works and rents out farm land he owns, his income is the number of hours he works per year times his hourly wage rate plus the number of acres of land he owns times the annual rental per acre. Thus the distribution of income depends on the way resource ownership—including talent, intelligence, training, work habits, and, yes, even character—is distributed among the population. Also, to be candid, it depends on just plain luck.

**4. HOW DOES THE PRICE SYSTEM DETERMINE THE NATION'S RATE OF GROWTH OF PER CAPITA INCOME?** A nation's rate of growth of per capita income depends on the rate of growth of its resources and the rate of increase of the efficiency with which they are used. In our economy, the rate at which labor and capital resources are increased is motivated, at least in part, through

# TRADE, SPECIALIZATION, AND COMPARATIVE ADVANTAGE

Trade plays an important role in capitalism, as we have seen. Why do individuals trade with one another? Consider the hypothetical case of Jane Barrister, a lawyer, divorced with two children. The Barrister family, like practically all families, trades continually with other families and with business firms. Since Ms. Barrister is a lawyer, she trades her legal services for money which she uses to buy the food, clothing, housing, and other goods and services her family wants. Why does the Barrister family do this? What advantages does it receive through trade? Why doesn't it attempt to be self-sufficient?

To see why the Barrister family prefers to opt for trade rather than self-sufficiency, let's compare the current situation—where Ms. Barrister specializes in the production of legal services and trades the money she receives for other goods and services— with the situation of self-sufficiency. In the latter case, the Barristers would have to provide their own transportation, telephone service, foodstuffs, clothing, and a host of other things. Ms. Barrister is a lawyer—a well-trained, valuable, productive member of the community. But if she were to try her hand at making automobiles—or even bicycles— she might be a total loss. Thus, if the Barrister family attempted to be self-sufficient, it might be unable to provide many of the goods it now enjoys.

*Trade permits specialization, and specialization increases output.* In our hypothetical case, it is obvious that, because she can trade with other families and with firms, Ms. Barrister can specialize in doing what she is good at—practicing law. Consequently, she can be more productive than if she were forced to be a Jane-of-all-trades, as she would have to be if she could not trade with others.

Let's turn now from individuals to nations. Basically, the same reasons exist for trade among nations as for trade among individuals. Because the United States can trade with other nations, it can specialize in the goods and services it produces particularly well. Then it can trade them for goods that other countries are especially good at producing. Thus both we and our trading partners benefit.

Some countries have more and better resources of

An immigration lawyer conferring with her client before a court hearing

certain types than others. Saudi Arabia has oil, Canada has timber, Japan has a skilled labor force, and so on. *International differences in resource endowments, and in the relative quantity of various types of human and nonhuman resources, are important bases for specialization.* Consider countries with lots of fertile soil, little capital, and much unskilled labor. They are likely to find it advantageous to produce agricultural goods, while countries with poor soil, much capital, and highly skilled labor will probably do better to produce capital-intensive, high-technology goods. We must recognize, however, that the bases for specialization do not remain fixed over time. Instead, as technology and the resource endowments of various countries change, the pattern of international specialization changes as well. For instance, the United States specialized more in raw materials and foodstuffs a century ago than it does now.

Surprising as it may seem, even if one country is able to produce everything more cheaply than another country, it still is likely that they both can benefit from specialization and trade. This proposition, known as *the law of comparative advantage,* will be discussed at length in Chapter 17. To illustrate why this law is valid, consider Jane Barrister and her friend, Ann Jones. Suppose that Jane is ten times as good at legal work and twice as good at typing as Ann. Should Jane do both legal work and typing? By no means. She should hire Ann to do the typing. Why? Because she earns so much more by specializing in law that it pays her to turn the typing over to Ann.

While Ann is half as good a typist as Jane, she is only a tenth as good a lawyer. Thus, by doing the typing, she is engaged in the type of work where she is best *comparatively.* Similarly, by doing the legal work, Jane is engaged in the type of work where she is best *comparatively.* (Recall that she is ten times as good a lawyer as Ann but only twice as good a typist.) If each does the type of work where she has a comparative advantage, both can benefit. This is true for countries as well as for individuals. Even if one country is more efficient than another in the production of everything, both countries can improve their lot by specializing in the production of the things where they have a comparative advantage.

the price system. Higher wages for more skilled work are an incentive for an individual to undergo further education and training. Capital accumulation occurs in response to the expectation of profit. Increases in efficiency, due in considerable measure to the advance of technology, are also stimulated by the price system.

## OUR MIXED CAPITALIST SYSTEM

Since the days of Adam Smith, economists have been fascinated by the features of a purely capitalistic economic system—an economy that relies entirely on the price system. Smith, and many generations of economists since, have gone to great pains to explain that in such an economic system, *the price system, although it is not controlled by any person or small group, results in economic order, not chaos.* The basic economic tasks any economy must perform can, as we have said, be carried out in such an economic system by the price system. It is an effective means of coordinating economic activity through decentralized decision making based on information disseminated through prices and related data.

But does this mean that the American economy is purely capitalistic? As we have noted repeatedly, the answer is no. A purely capitalistic system is a useful model of reality, not a description of our economy as it exists now or existed in the past. It is useful because a purely capitalistic economy is, for some purposes, a reasonably close fit to our own. However, this does not mean that such a model is useful for all purposes. Many American markets are not perfectly competitive and never will be; they are dominated by a few producers or buyers who can influence price and thus distort the workings of the price system. Moreover, *the American economy is a mixed capitalistic economy, an economy where both government and private decisions are important.* The role of the government in American economic activity is very large indeed. Although it is essential to understand the workings of a purely capitalistic system, any model that omits the government entirely cannot purport to be adequate for the analysis of many major present-day economic issues.

To create a more balanced picture of the workings of the American economy, we must recognize that, although the price system plays an extremely important role, it is not permitted to solve all of the basic economic problems of our society. Consumer sovereignty does not extend — and cannot realistically be extended — to all areas of society. For example, certain public services cannot be left to private enterprise. The provision of fire protection, the operation of schools, and the development of weapons systems are examples of areas where we rely on political decision making, not the price system alone. Moreover, with regard to the consumption of commodities like drugs, society imposes limits on the decisions of individuals.

In addition, certain consequences of the price system are, by general agreement, unacceptable. Reliance on the price system alone does not ensure a just or equitable or optimal distribution of income. It is possible, for example, that one person will have money to burn while another person will live in degrading poverty. Consequently, society empowers the government to modify the distribution of income by imposing taxes that take more from the rich than the poor, and by welfare programs that try to keep the poor from reaching the point where they lack decent food, adequate clothing, or shelter. Besides providing public services and maintaining certain minimum income standards, the government also carries out a variety of regulatory functions. Industries do not police the actions of their constituent firms, so it falls to the government to establish laws that impose limits on the economic behavior of firms. For example, these laws say that firms must not misrepresent their products, that child labor must not be employed, and that firms must not collude and form monopolies to interfere with the proper functioning of the price system. In this way, the government tries, with varying degrees of effectiveness, to establish the "rules of the game" — the limits within which the economic behavior of firms (and consumers) should lie.

## TEST YOURSELF

1. Suppose that a society's production possibilities curve is as follows:

OUTPUT(PER YEAR)

| POSSIBILITY | FOOD (MILLIONS OF TONS) | TRACTORS (MILLIONS) |
|---|---|---|
| A | 0 | 30 |
| B | 4 | 28 |
| C | 8 | 24 |
| D | 12 | 20 |
| E | 16 | 14 |
| F | 20 | 8 |
| G | 24 | 0 |

(a) Is it possible for the society to produce 30 million tons of food per year? (b) Can it produce 30 million tractors per year? (c) Suppose this society produces 20 million tons of food and 6 million tractors per year. Is it operating on the production possibilities curve? If not, what factors might account for this?

2. Plot the production possibilities curve in Question 1 on a graph. At what point along the horizontal axis does the curve cut the axis? At what point along the vertical axis does the curve cut the axis?

3. Suppose that, because of important technological improvements, the society in Question 1 can double its production of tractors at each level of food production. If so, is this society on its new production possibilities curve if it produces 20 million tons of food and 16 million tractors? Plot the new production possibilities curve. At what point along the horizontal axis does the new curve cut the axis? At what point along the vertical axis does it cut the axis?

4. "[Some people] . . . fail to realize that the price system is, and ought to be, a method of coercion. . . . The very term 'rationing by the purse' illustrates the point. Economists defend such forms of rationing, but they have to do so primarily in terms of its efficiency and its fairness." Comment.

5. "The great advantage of the [price system] . . . is that it permits wide diversity. It is, in political terms, a system of proportional representation. Each man can vote, as it were, for the color of tie he wants and get it; he does not have to see what color the majority wants and then, if he is in the minority, submit." Comment.

## SUMMARY

1. The methodology used by economists is much the same as that used in any other kind of scientific analysis. The basic procedure is the formulation and testing of models.

2. A model must in general simplify and abstract from the real world. Its purpose is to make predictions, and in many respects the most important test of a model is how well it predicts. To test and quantify their models, economists gather data and utilize various statistical techniques.

3. The production possibilities curve, which shows the various production possibilities a society can attain, is useful in indicating the nature of the economic tasks any society faces.

4. Society has to recognize that it cannot get more of one good without giving up some of another good, if resources are fully and efficiently used. However, if they are not fully and efficiently used, society will have to settle for points inside the production possibilities curve—and it will be possible to obtain more of one good without giving up some of another good.

5. The task of determining how each good and service should be produced is, to a considerable extent, a problem of keeping society on its production possibilities curve, rather than at points inside the curve. The production possibilities curve does not tell us anything about the distribution of income, but it does indicate various ways that a society can promote growth in per capita income.

6. The American economy is a capitalistic economy, an economic system in which there is private ownership of capital, freedom of choice, freedom of enterprise, competition, and reliance upon markets.

7. Under pure capitalism, the price system is used to perform the four basic economic tasks. Although it is not controlled by any person or small group, the price system results in order, not chaos.

8. A purely capitalistic system is a useful model of reality, not a description of our economy as it exists now or in the past. The American economy is a mixed capitalistic economy, in which both government and private decisions are important.

## CONCEPTS FOR REVIEW

**Model**
**Production possibilities curve**
**Capital goods**
**Consumers' goods**

**Capitalism**
**Freedom of choice**
**Freedom of enterprise**

**Competition**
**Price system**
**Consumer sovereignty**

# THE PRICE SYSTEM

IN THE EARLY 1990s, POLAND adopted an ambitious plan to make the transition from communism to capitalism, a step that would have seemed utterly impossible only a few years before. This plan called for the transfer of industry from government to private hands, and for reliance on market prices. As we shall see in this chapter, economists played a major role in the formulation of this plan, which in effect called for Poland to adopt the price system.

This chapter takes up the nature and functions of the price system, as well as some applications of our theoretical results to real-life problems. For example, we show how the price system determines the quantity produced of a commodity like wheat, and how the pricing policies of the Broadway theater have hurt show business in a variety of ways. These applications, like the fascinating case of Poland, help to illustrate the basic theory and indicate its usefulness.

The Polish parliament building in Warsaw

## CONSUMERS, FIRMS, AND MARKETS

We begin by describing and discussing consumers and firms, the basic building blocks that make up the private, or nongovernmental, sector of the economy.

**CONSUMERS.** Sometimes—for example, when a person buys a beer on a warm day—the consumer is an individual. In other cases—for example, when a family buys a new car—the consumer may be an entire household. *Consumers* purchase the goods and services that are the ultimate products of the economic system. When a man buys tickets to a ball game, he is a consumer; when he buys himself a Coke at the game, he is a consumer; and when he buys his wife a book on baseball for their twentieth wedding anniversary, he is a consumer.

**FIRMS.** There are over 10 million firms in the United States. About nine-tenths of the goods and services produced in this country are produced by firms. (The rest are provided by government and not-for-profit institutions like universities and hospitals.) A *firm* is an organization that produces a good or service for sale. In contrast to not-for-profit organizations, firms attempt to make a profit. It is obvious that our economy is centered around the activities of firms.

**MARKETS.** Consumers and firms come together in a market. The concept of a market is not quite as straightforward as it may seem, since most markets are not well defined geographically or physically. For example, the New York Stock Exchange is an atypical market because it is located principally in a particular building. For present purposes, a **market** can be defined as a group of firms and individuals that are in touch with each other in order to buy or sell some good. Of course, not every person in a market has to be in contact with every other person in the market. A person or firm is part of a market even if it is in contact with only a subset of the other persons or firms in the market.

Markets vary enormously in their size and procedures. For some goods like toothpaste, most people who have their own teeth (and are interested in keeping them) are members of the same market; while for other goods like Picasso paintings, only a few dealers, collectors, and museums in certain parts of the world may be members of the market. And for still other goods, like lemonade sold by neighborhood children for a nickel a glass at a sidewalk stand, only people who walk by the stand—and are brave enough to drink the stuff—are members of the market. Basically, however, all markets consist primarily of buyers and sellers, although third parties like brokers and agents may be present as well.

Markets also vary in the extent to which they are dominated by a few large buyers or sellers. For example, in the United States, there was for many years only one producer of aluminum. This firm, the Aluminum Company of America, had great power in the market for aluminum. In contrast, the number of buyers and sellers in some other markets is so large that no single buyer or seller has any power over the price of the product. This is true in various agricultural markets, for example. When a market for a product contains so many buyers and sellers that none of them can influence the price, economists call the market **perfectly competitive.** In these introductory chapters, we make the simplifying assumption that markets are perfectly competitive. We will relax that assumption later.

## THE DEMAND SIDE OF A MARKET

Every market has a demand side and a supply side. *The **demand** side can be represented by a **market demand curve**, which shows the amount of the commodity buyers would like to purchase at various prices.* Consider Figure 3.1, which shows the demand curve for wheat in the American market during the early 1990s.[1] The figure shows that about 2.4 billion bushels of wheat will be demanded annually if the farm price is $2.80 per bushel, about 2.5 billion bushels will be demanded annually if the farm price is $2.40 per bushel, and about 2.6 billion bushels will be demanded annually if the farm price is $2.00 per bushel. The total demand for wheat is of several types: to produce bread and other food products for domestic use, as well as for feed use, for export purposes, and for industrial uses. The demand curve in Figure 3.1 shows the total demand—including all these components—at each price. Any demand curve pertains to a particular period of time, and the shape and position of the demand curve depend on the length of this period.

Take a good look at the demand curve for wheat in Figure 3.1. This simple, innocent-looking curve influences a great many people's lives.

[1] I am indebted to officials of the U.S. Department of Agriculture for providing me with this information. Of course, these estimates are only rough approximations, but they are good enough for present purposes.

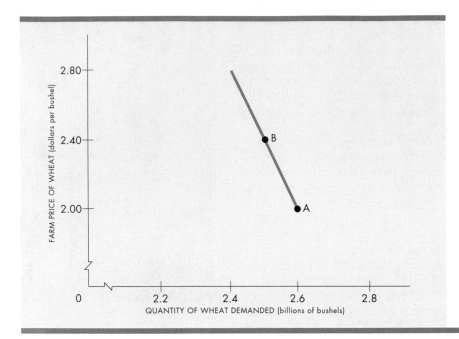

**Figure 3.1**
**Market Demand Curve for Wheat, Early 1990s**
The curve shows the amount of wheat buyers would demand at various prices. At $2.00 per bushel, about 8 percent more wheat can be sold than at $2.80 per bushel.

After all, wheat is the principal grain used for direct human consumption in the United States. To states like Kansas, North Dakota, Oklahoma, Montana, Washington, Nebraska, Texas, Illinois, Indiana, and Ohio, wheat is a mighty important cash crop. Note that the demand curve for wheat slopes downward to the right. In other words, the quantity of wheat demanded increases as the price falls. This is true of the demand curve for most commodities: they almost always slope downward to the right. This makes sense; one would expect increases in a good's price to result in a smaller quantity demanded.

Any demand curve is based on the assumption that the tastes, incomes, and number of consumers, as well as the prices of other commodities, are held constant. Changes in any of these factors are likely to shift the position of a commodity's demand curve, as indicated below.

**CONSUMER TASTES.** If consumers show an increasing preference for a product, the demand curve will shift to the right; that is, at each price, consumers will desire to buy more than previously. On the other hand, if consumers show a decreasing preference for a product, the demand curve will shift to the left, since, at each price, consumers will desire to buy less than previously. Take wheat. If consumers become convinced that foods containing wheat prolong life and promote happiness, the demand curve may shift, as shown in Figure 3.2; and the greater the shift in preferences, the larger the shift in the demand curve.

**INCOME LEVEL OF CONSUMERS.** For some types of products, the demand curve shifts to the right if per capita income increases; whereas for other types of commodities, the demand curve shifts to the left if per capita income rises. Economists can explain why some goods fall into one category and other goods fall into the other, but, at present, this need not concern us. All that is important here is that changes in per capita income affect the demand curve, the size and direction of this effect varying from product to product. In the case of wheat, a 10 percent increase in per

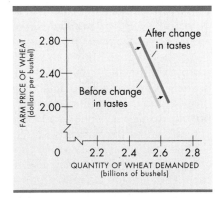

**Figure 3.2**
**Effect of Increased Preference for Wheat on Market Demand Curve**
An increased preference for wheat would shift the demand curve to the right.

capita income would probably have a relatively small effect on the demand curve, as shown in Figure 3.3.

**NUMBER OF CONSUMERS IN THE MARKET.** Compare Austria's demand for wheat with the United States'. Austria is a small country with a population of less than 8 million; the United States is a huge country with a population of over 200 million. Clearly, at a given price of wheat, the quantity demanded by American consumers will greatly exceed the quantity demanded by Austrian consumers, as shown in Figure 3.4. Even if consumer tastes, income, and other factors were held constant, this would still be true simply because the United States has so many more consumers in the relevant market.[2]

**LEVEL OF OTHER PRICES.** A commodity's demand curve can be shifted by a change in the price of other commodities. Whether an increase in the price of good B will shift the demand curve for good A to the right or the left depends on the relationship between the two goods. If they are substitutes, such an increase will shift the demand curve for good A to the right. Consider the case of corn and wheat. If the price of corn goes up, more wheat will be demanded since it will be profitable to substitute wheat for corn. If the price of corn drops, less wheat will be demanded since it will be profitable to substitute corn for wheat. Thus, as shown in Figure 3.5, increases in the price of corn will shift the demand curve for wheat to the right, and decreases in the price of corn will shift it to the left.[3]

## The Distinction between Changes in Demand and Changes in the Quantity Demanded

It is essential to distinguish between a *shift in a commodity's demand curve* and a change in the *quantity demanded of the commodity*. A shift in a commodity's demand curve is a change in the *relationship* between price and quantity demanded. Figures 3.2, 3.3, and 3.5 show cases where such a change occurs. A change in the quantity demanded of a commodity may occur even if *no* shift occurs in the commodity's demand curve. For example, in Figure 3.1, if the price of wheat increases from $2.00 to $2.40 per bushel, the quantity demanded falls from 2.6 to 2.5 billion bushels. This change in the quantity demanded is due to a *movement along* the demand curve (from point *A* to point *B* in Figure 3.1), not to a *shift* in the demand curve.

When economists refer to an *increase in demand,* they mean a *rightward shift* in the demand curve. Thus Figures 3.2, 3.3, and 3.5 show increases in demand for wheat. When economists refer to a *decrease in demand,* they mean a *leftward shift* in the demand curve. An increase in demand for a commodity is not the same as an increase in the quantity demanded of the commodity. In Figure 3.1, the quantity demanded of wheat increases if the price falls from $2.40 to $2.00 per bushel, but this is

[2] Note that no figures are given along the horizontal axis in Figure 3.4. This is because we do not have reasonably precise estimates of the demand curve in Austria. Nonetheless, the hypothetical demand curves in Figure 3.4 are close enough to the mark for present purposes.

[3] If goods A and B are complements, an increase in the price of good B will shift the demand curve for good A to the left. Thus an increase in the price of gin is likely to shift the demand curve for tonic to the left. Why? Because gin and tonic tend to be used together. The increase in gin's price will reduce the quantity of gin demanded, which in turn will reduce the amount of tonic that will be demanded at each price of tonic.

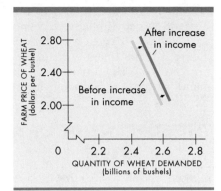

**Figure 3.3**
**Effect of Increase in Income on Market Demand Curve for Wheat**
An increase in income would shift the demand curve for wheat to the right, but only slightly.

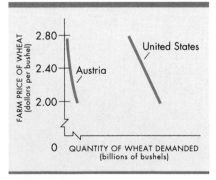

**Figure 3.4**
**Market Demand Curve for Wheat, Austria and the United States**
Since the United States has far more consumers than Austria, the demand curve in the United States is far to the right of Austria's.

not due to an increase in demand, since there is no rightward shift of the demand curve. Similarly, a decrease in demand for a commodity is not the same as a decrease in the quantity demanded of the commodity. In Figure 3.1, the quantity demanded of wheat *decreases* if the price rises from $2.00 to $2.40 per bushel, but this is not due to a decrease in demand, since there is no leftward shift of the demand curve.

## THE SUPPLY SIDE OF A MARKET

So much for our first look at demand. What about the other side of the market: supply? *The* **supply** *side of a market can be represented by a* **market supply curve** *that shows the amount of the commodity sellers would offer at various prices.* Let's continue with the case of wheat. Figure 3.6 shows the supply curve for wheat in the United States in the early 1990s, based on estimates made informally by government experts.[4] According to the figure, about 2.3 billion bushels of wheat would be supplied if the farm price were $2.00 per bushel, about 2.5 billion bushels if the farm price were $2.40 per bushel, and about 2.7 billion bushels if the farm price were $2.80 per bushel.

Look carefully at the supply curve shown in Figure 3.6. Although it looks innocuous enough, it summarizes the potential behavior of thousands of American wheat farmers—and their behavior plays an important role in determining the prosperity of many states and communities. Note that the supply curve for wheat slopes upward to the right. In other words, the quantity of wheat supplied increases as the price increases. This seems plausible, since increases in price give a greater incentive for farms to produce wheat and offer it for sale. Empirical studies indicate that the supply curves for a great many commodities share this characteristic of sloping upward to the right.

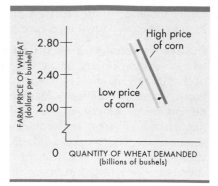

**Figure 3.5**
**Effect of Price of Corn on Market Demand Curve for Wheat**
Price increases for corn will shift the demand curve for wheat to the right.

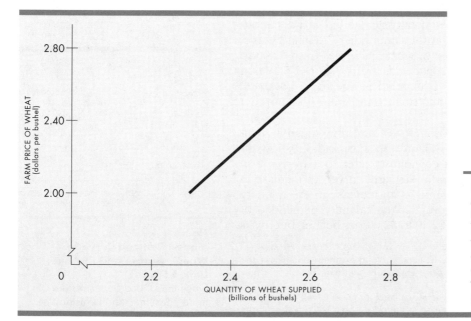

**Figure 3.6**
**Market Supply Curve for Wheat, Early 1990s**
The curve shows the amount of wheat sellers would supply at various prices. At $2.80 per bushel, about 17 percent more wheat would be supplied than at $2.00 per bushel.

[4] Officials of the U.S. Department of Agriculture provided me with these estimates. Although rough approximations, they are good enough for present purposes.

Any supply curve is based on the assumption that technology and input prices are held constant. Changes in these factors are likely to shift the position of a commodity's supply curve, as indicated below.

**TECHNOLOGY.** Recall that technology was defined in Chapter 1 as society's pool of knowledge concerning the industrial arts. As technology progresses, it becomes possible to produce commodities more cheaply, so that firms often are willing to supply a given amount at a lower price than formerly. Thus technological change often causes the supply curve to shift to the right. This certainly has occurred in the case of wheat, as shown in Figure 3.7. There have been many important technological changes in wheat production, ranging from advances in tractors to the development of improved varieties, like semi-dwarf wheats.

**INPUT PRICES.** The supply curve for a commodity is affected by the prices of the resources (labor, capital, and land) used to produce it. Decreases in the price of these inputs make it possible to produce commodities more cheaply, so that firms may be willing to supply a given amount at a lower price than they formerly would. Thus decreases in the price of inputs may cause the supply curve to shift to the right. On the other hand, increases in the price of inputs may cause it to shift to the left. For example, if the wage rates of farm labor increase, the supply curve for wheat may shift to the left, as shown in Figure 3.8.

An *increase in supply* is defined to be a *rightward shift* in the supply curve; a *decrease in supply* is defined to be a *leftward shift* in the supply curve. A change in supply should be distinguished from a change in the quantity supplied. In Figure 3.6, the quantity supplied of wheat will increase from 2.3 to 2.5 billion bushels if the price increases from $2.00 to $2.40 per bushel, but this is not due to an increase in supply, since there is no rightward shift of the supply curve in Figure 3.6.

## EQUILIBRIUM PRICE

The two sides of a market, demand and supply, interact to determine the price of a commodity. Recall from the previous chapter that prices in a capitalistic system are important determinants of what is produced, how it is produced, who receives it, and how rapidly per capita income grows. It behooves us, therefore, to look carefully at how prices themselves are determined in a capitalist system. As a first step toward describing this process, we must define the equilibrium price of a product.

An **equilibrium** is a situation where there is no tendency for change: in other words, it is a situation that can persist. Thus an **equilibrium price** is a price that can be maintained. Any price that is not an equilibrium price cannot be maintained for long, since there are basic forces at work to stimulate a change in price.

For example, consider the wheat market. Let's put both the demand curve for wheat (in Figure 3.1) and the supply curve for wheat (in Figure 3.6) together in the same diagram. The result, shown in Figure 3.9, will help us determine the equilibrium price of wheat.

We begin by seeing what would happen if various prices were established in the market. For example, if the price were $2.80 per bushel, the demand curve indicates that 2.4 billion bushels of wheat would be demanded, while the supply curve indicates that 2.7 billion bushels would be supplied. Thus, if the price were $2.80 a bushel, there would be a mis-

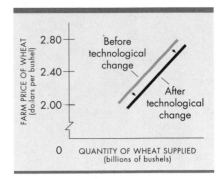

**Figure 3.7**
**Effect of Technological Change on Market Supply Curve for Wheat**
Improvements in technology often shift the supply curve to the right.

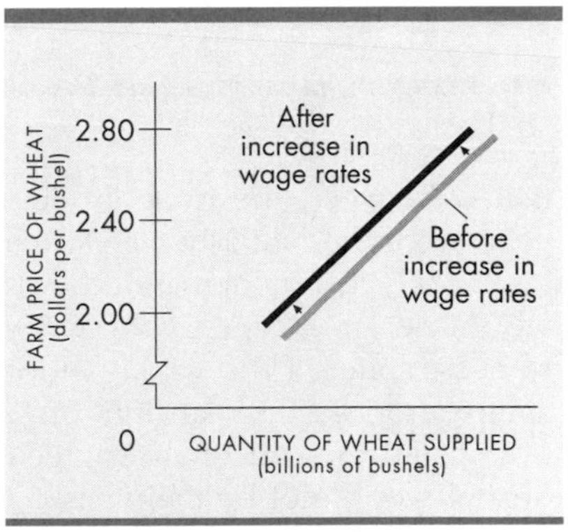

**Figure 3.8**
**Effect of Increase in Farm Wage Rates on Market Supply Curve for Wheat**
An increase in the wage rate might shift the supply curve to the left.

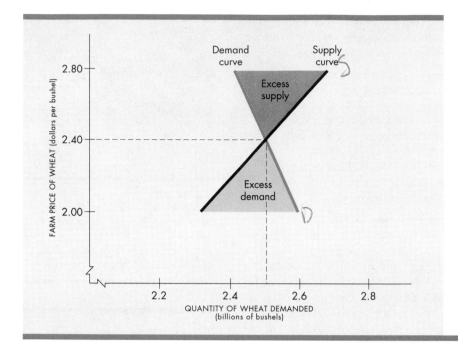

**Figure 3.9**
**Determination of the Equilibrium Price of Wheat, Early 1990s**
The equilibrium price is $2.40 per bushel, and the equilibrium quantity is 2.5 billion bushels. At a price of $2.80 per bushel, there would be an excess supply of 300 million bushels. At a price of $2.00 per bushel, there would be an excess demand of 300 million bushels.

match between the quantity supplied and the quantity demanded per year, since the rate at which wheat is supplied would be greater than the rate at which it is demanded. Specifically, as shown in Figure 3.9, there would be an *excess supply* of 300 million bushels. Under these circumstances, some of the wheat supplied by farmers could not be sold, and, as inventories of wheat built up, suppliers would tend to cut their prices in order to get rid of unwanted inventories. Thus a price of $2.80 per bushel would not be maintained for long—and for this reason $2.80 per bushel is not an equilibrium price.

If the price were $2.00 per bushel, on the other hand, the demand curve indicates that 2.6 billion bushels would be demanded, while the supply curve indicates that 2.3 billion bushels would be supplied. Again we find a mismatch between the quantity supplied and the quantity demanded per year, since the rate at which wheat is supplied would be less than the rate at which it is demanded. Specifically, as shown in Figure 3.9, there would be an *excess demand* of 300 million bushels. Under these circumstances, some of the consumers who want wheat at this price would have to be turned away empty-handed. There would be a shortage. And given this shortage, suppliers would find it profitable to increase the price, and competition among buyers would bid the price up. Thus a price of $2.00 per bushel could not be maintained for long—so $2.00 per bushel is not an equilibrium price.

*Under these circumstances, the equilibrium price must be the price where the quantity demanded equals the quantity supplied. Obviously, this is the only price at which there is no mismatch between the quantity demanded and the quantity supplied; and consequently the only price that can be maintained for long.* In Figure 3.9, the price at which the quantity supplied equals the quantity demanded is $2.40 per bushel, the price where the demand curve intersects the supply curve. Thus $2.40 per bushel is the equilibrium price of wheat under the circumstances visualized in Figure 3.9, and 2.5 billion bushels is the equilibrium quantity.

## ACTUAL PRICE

The price that counts in the real world, however, is the ***actual price,*** not the equilibrium price, and it is the actual price that we set out to explain. In general, economists simply assume that the actual price will approximate the equilibrium price, which seems reasonable enough, since the basic forces at work tend to push the actual price toward the equilibrium price. Thus, if conditions remain fairly stable for a time, the actual price should move toward the equilibrium price.

To see that this is the case, consider the market for wheat, as described in Figure 3.9. What if the price somehow is set at $2.80 per bushel? As we

## EXAMPLE 3.1  HOW THE ORANGE MARKET WORKS

In recent years, many oranges grown in California and Arizona have been provided to cattle for feed or given away to juicing plants. An 11-member committee of farmers and shippers establishes the number and size of oranges that can be sold. Anyone selling oranges without the committee's permission can face civil and criminal prosecution by the Department of Justice. Although some industry representatives claim that the oranges held off the market are too small to be sold, it is reported that the industry's figures show that some of these oranges are as large as those sent to market.

(a) In the absence of government intervention, suppose that the demand and supply curves for oranges would be as shown below:

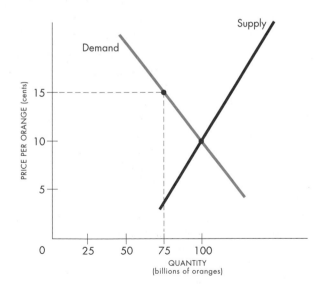

What would be the equilibrium price under these circumstances? (b) If the committee says that the quantity of oranges that can be sold must be 25 percent less than what would be sold in a free market, what will be the equilibrium price? (c) Under the committee's edict, will the growers receive more or less for their crop than under the free market? How much more or less? (d) How are consumers affected by the committee's edict?

### Solution

(a) 10 cents per orange. (b) In a free market, 100 billion oranges would be sold. If this quantity is reduced by 25 percent, only 75 billion oranges can be sold. Based on the demand curve, this amount can be sold for 15 cents per orange. Thus this will be the price. (c) Under the committee's edict, growers will sell 75 billion oranges at 15 cents each, so they will receive $11.25 billion. Under the free market, they will sell 100 billion oranges at 10 cents each, so they will receive $10 billion. Thus they will receive $1.25 billion more under the committee's edict than under the free market. (d) They consume fewer oranges and pay more for those they do consume.

saw in the previous section, there is downward pressure on the price of wheat under these conditions. Suppose the price, responding to this pressure, falls to $2.70. Comparing the quantity demanded with the quantity supplied at $2.70, we find that there is still downward pressure on price, since the quantity supplied exceeds the quantity demanded at $2.70. The price, responding to this pressure, may fall to $2.60, but comparing the quantity demanded with the quantity supplied at this price, we find that there is still a downward pressure on price, since the quantity supplied exceeds the quantity demanded at $2.60.

So long as the actual price exceeds the equilibrium price, there will be a downward pressure on price. Similarly, so long as the actual price is less than the equilibrium price, there will be an upward pressure on price. Thus there is always a tendency for the actual price to move toward the equilibrium price. But it should not be assumed that this movement is always rapid. Sometimes it takes a long time for the actual price to get close to the equilibrium price. Sometimes the actual price never gets to the equilibrium price because by the time it gets close, the equilibrium price changes (because of shifts in either the demand curve or the supply curve or both). All that safely can be said is that the actual price will move toward the equilibrium price. But of course this information is of great value, both theoretically and practically. For many purposes, all that is needed is a correct prediction of the direction in which the price will move.

## TEST YOURSELF

1. Assume that the market for electric toasters is competitive and that the quantity supplied per year depends as follows on the price of a toaster:

| PRICE OF A TOASTER (DOLLARS) | NUMBER OF TOASTERS SUPPLIED (MILLIONS) |
|---|---|
| 12 | 4.0 |
| 14 | 5.0 |
| 16 | 5.5 |
| 18 | 6.0 |
| 20 | 6.3 |

Plot the supply curve for toasters. Is this a direct or inverse relationship? Are supply curves generally direct or inverse relationships?

2. Suppose that the quantity of toasters demanded per year depends as follows on the price of a toaster:

| PRICE OF A TOASTER (DOLLARS) | NUMBERS OF TOASTERS DEMANDED (MILLIONS) |
|---|---|
| 12 | 7.0 |
| 14 | 6.5 |
| 16 | 6.2 |
| 18 | 6.0 |
| 20 | 5.8 |

Plot the demand curve for toasters. If the price is $14, will there be an excess demand of toasters? If the price is $20, will there be an excess demand? What is the equilibrium price of a toaster? What is the equilibrium quantity? (Use the data in Question 1.)

3. Suppose that the government imposes a price ceiling on toasters. In particular, suppose that it decrees that a toaster cannot sell for more than $14. Will the quantity supplied equal the quantity demanded? What sorts of devices may come into being to allocate the available supply of toasters to consumers? What problems will the government encounter in keeping the price at $14? What social purposes, if any, might such a price ceiling serve? (Use the data in Questions 1 and 2.)

4. Suppose that the government imposes a price floor on toasters. In particular, suppose that it decrees that a toaster cannot sell for less than $20. Will the quantity supplied equal the quantity demanded? How will the resulting supply of toasters be taken off the market? What problems will the government encounter in keeping the price at $20? What social purposes, if any, might such a price floor serve? (Use the data above.)

5. If the demand curve for butter is $Q_D = 20 - 4P$

(where $Q_D$ is the quantity demanded and $P$ is the price of butter) and the supply curve for butter is $Q_S = 2P$ (where $Q_S$ is the quantity supplied), what is the equilibrium price? What is the equilibrium quantity? (Both $Q_D$ and $Q_S$ are measured in millions of pounds, and price is measured in dollars per pound.)

## THE EFFECTS OF SHIFTS IN THE DEMAND CURVE

Heraclitus, the ancient Greek philosopher, said you cannot step in the same stream twice: everything changes, sooner or later. One need not be a disciple of Heraclitus to recognize that demand curves shift. Indeed, we have already seen that demand curves shift in response to changes in tastes, income, population, and prices of other products, and that supply curves shift in response to changes in technology and input prices. Any supply-and-demand diagram like Figure 3.9 is essentially a snapshot of the situation during a particular period of time. The results in Figure 3.9 are limited to a particular period because the demand and supply curves in the figure, like any demand and supply curves, pertain only to a certain period.

What happens to the equilibrium price of a product when its demand curve changes? This is an important question because it sheds a good deal of light on how the price system works. Suppose that consumer tastes shift in favor of foods containing wheat, causing the demand curve for wheat to shift *to the right,* as shown in Figure 3.10. It is not hard to see the effect on the equilibrium price of wheat. Before the shift, the equilib-

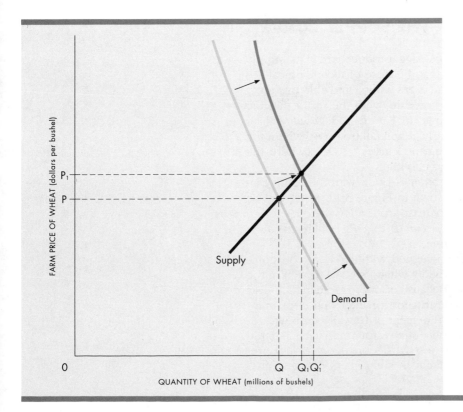

**Figure 3.10**
**Effect on the Equilibrium Price of a Shift to the Right of the Market Demand Curve**
This shift of the demand curve to the right results in an increase in the equilibrium price from $OP$ to $OP_1$ and an increase in the equilibrium quantity from $OQ$ to $OQ_1$.

rium price is *OP*. But when the demand curve shifts to the right, a shortage develops at this price.[5] Consequently, suppliers raise their prices. After some testing of market reactions and trial-and-error adjustments, the price will tend to settle at $OP_1$, the new equilibrium price, and quantity will tend to settle at $OQ_1$.

On the other hand, suppose that consumer demand for wheat products falls off, perhaps because of a great drop in the price of corn products. The demand for wheat now shifts *to the left*, as shown in Figure 3.11. What will be the effect on the equilibrium price of wheat? Clearly, the equilibrium price falls to $OP_2$, where the new demand curve intersects the supply curve.

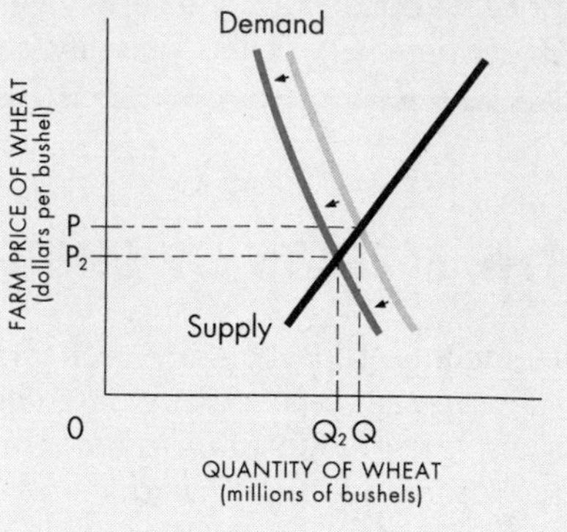

In general, *a shift to the right in the demand curve results in an increase in the equilibrium price, and a shift to the left in the demand curve results in a decrease in the equilibrium price*. This is the lesson of Figures 3.10 and 3.11. Of course, this conclusion depends on the assumption that the supply curve slopes upward to the right, but, as we noted in a previous section, this assumption is generally true.

At this point, since all of this is theory, you may be wondering how well this theory works in practice. In 1972 and 1973, there was a vivid demonstration of the accuracy of this model in various agricultural markets, including wheat. Because of poor harvests abroad and greatly increased foreign demand for American wheat, the demand curve for wheat shifted markedly to the right. What happened to the price of wheat? In accord with our model, the price increased spectacularly, from about $1.35 a bushel in the early summer of 1972 to over $4.00 a year later. Anyone who witnessed this phenomenon could not help but be impressed by the usefulness of this model.

## THE EFFECTS OF SHIFTS IN THE SUPPLY CURVE

What happens to the equilibrium price of a product when its supply curve changes? For example, suppose that, because of technological advances in wheat production, wheat farmers are willing and able to supply more wheat at a given price than they used to, with the result that the supply curve shifts *to the right*, as shown in Figure 3.12. What will be the effect on the equilibrium price? Clearly, it will fall from *OP* (where the original supply curve intersects the demand curve) to $OP_3$ (where the new supply curve intersects the demand curve).

On the other hand, suppose the weather is poor, with the result that the supply curve shifts *to the left*, as shown in Figure 3.12. What will be the effect? The equilibrium price will increase from *OP* (where the original supply curve intersects the demand curve) to $OP_4$ (where the new supply curve intersects the demand curve).

In 1990, law enforcement officers concerned with narcotics consumption in the United States were shown vividly what a shift to the left in the supply curve of a commodity will do. Because of poor marijuana harvests in the United States, as well as the destruction or interception of marijuana by federal agents (for example, 90 percent of Hawaii's crop was reported to be destroyed), the supply curve for marijuana shifted dramatically to the left. The result was just what our theory would predict: a big jump in the price of marijuana. In some parts of the United

**Figure 3.11**
**Effect on the Equilibrium Price of a Shift to the Left of the Market Demand Curve**
This shift of the demand curve to the left results in a decrease in the equilibrium price from *OP* to $OP_2$ and a decrease in the equilibrium quantity from *OQ* to $OQ_2$.

[5] This shortage is equal to $OQ'_1 - OQ$ in Figure 3.10.

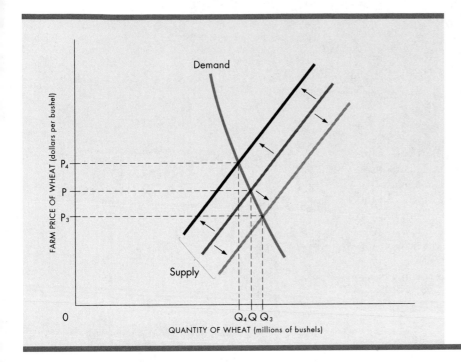

Figure 3.12
Effects on the Equilibrium
Price of Shifts in the Market
Supply Curve
The shift of the supply curve to the
right results in a decrease in the
equilibrium price from *OP* to *OP₃*.
The shift of the supply curve to the
left increases the equilibrium price
from *OP* to *OP₄*.

States, marijuana sold in 1990 for $2,000 per pound, up from about
$1,200 a year before.

In general, *a shift to the right in the supply curve results in a decrease
in the equilibrium price, and a shift to the left in the supply curve results
in an increase in the equilibrium price.* Of course, this conclusion depends on the assumption that the demand curve slopes downward to the
right, but, as we noted in a previous section, this assumption is generally
true.

## HOW THE PRICE SYSTEM DETERMINES WHAT IS PRODUCED

Having described how prices are determined in free markets, we can
now describe somewhat more fully how the price system goes about performing the four basic tasks that face any economic system. Let's begin
by considering the determination of what society will produce: How does
the price system carry out this task? Consumers indicate what goods and
services they want in the marketplace, and producers try to meet these
wants. More specifically, the demand curve for a product shows how
much of that product consumers want at various prices. If consumers
don't want much of it at a certain price, its demand curve will indicate
that fact by being positioned close to the vertical axis at that price. In
other words, the demand curve will show that, at this price for the product, the amount consumers will buy is small. On the other hand, if consumers want lots of the product at this price, its demand curve will be far
from the vertical axis.

A product's demand curve is an important determinant of how much
firms will produce of the product, since it indicates the amount of the
product that will be demanded at each price. From the point of view of

# HOW ASYMMETRIC INFORMATION AFFECTS THE MARKET FOR USED CARS

In some markets, like the market for used cars, buyers and sellers do not have the same information. Suppose that you are selling a used car. Given that you have operated the car for a while (and paid the bills for repairs and other expenses), you have a pretty good idea of the car's virtues and defects. If it is a lemon (that is, a defective car), you know it. On the other hand, if you are thinking of buying such a used car, you are likely to know little about how it will perform. Unless you have a considerable amount of detailed knowledge concerning automobiles, you can easily be fooled.

Thus there is an asymmetry of information, in the sense that sellers have more information than buyers about the quality of the product. This asymmetry of information influences how the market for used cars works. To see that this is the case, suppose for simplicity that all new cars are good or defective, that after a person buys a new car, he or she finds out whether it is good or defective, and that, if this car is offered for sale (as a used car), a potential buyer will not be able to determine (before buying it) whether it is good or defective.

Because the buyer of a used car cannot tell the difference between a good car and a defective car, both good and defective used cars must sell for the same price. Obviously, this price must be below the price of a new car. Otherwise, it would pay to purchase a new car, find out whether it is defective, and (if it turns out to be defective) sell it and purchase another new car. Unless the price of a used car is below the price of a new one, there would be no demand for used cars.

Defective cars—that is, lemons—are likely to constitute a large proportion of the used cars offered for sale. If a person owns a good used car, he or she will be unlikely to offer it for sale because the equilibrium price of a used car is relatively low. And since defective used cars may constitute a large number of the used cars offered for sale, potential buyers—

wary of buying a lemon—are even more inclined to offer relatively low prices for used cars.

Perhaps the most important point to note is the following: *The buyer of a used car would be willing to pay more than the equilibrium price if he or she were sure of getting a good one, and the seller of a good used car would be happy to agree to such a transaction. But the asymmetry of information—the fact that the seller knows whether the used car is defective or good, but the buyer does not—makes it hard for such trades to occur.* How do sellers of used cars try to deal with this situation? They attempt in various ways to *signal* potential purchasers that their car is good. They provide information about the car, they encourage the potential purchaser to have his or her experts inspect it before purchase, and they offer free service contracts or money-back guarantees.[1]

---

[1] For a famous article on this topic, see G. Akerlof, "The Market for Lemons," *Quarterly Journal of Economics,* August 1970.

the producers, the demand curve indicates the amount they can sell at each price. In a capitalist economy, firms are in business to make money. Thus the manufacturers of any product will turn it out only if the amount of money they receive from consumers exceeds the cost of putting the product on the market. Acting in accord with the profit motive, firms are led to produce what the consumers desire. As we have seen, if consumers' tastes shift in favor of foods containing wheat, the demand curve for wheat will shift to the right, which will result in an increase in the price of wheat. This increase will stimulate farmers to produce more wheat. For example, when the demand curve shifts to the right in Figure 3.10, the equilibrium quantity produced increases from $OQ$ to $OQ_1$. Given the shift in the demand curve, it is profitable for firms to step up their production. Acting in their own self-interest, they are led to make production decisions geared to the wants of the consumers.

Thus the price system uses the self-interest of the producers to get them to produce what consumers want. Consumers register what they want in the marketplace by their purchasing decisions—shown by their demand curves. Producers can make more money by responding to consumer wants than by ignoring them. Consequently, they are led to produce goods and services consumers want—and for which they are willing to pay enough to cover the producers' costs. Note that costs as well as demand determine what will be produced, and that producers are not forced by anyone to do anything. They can produce air conditioners for Eskimos if they like—and if they are prepared to absorb the losses. The price system uses prices to communicate the relevant signals to producers, and metes out the penalties and rewards in the form of losses or profits.

## HOW THE PRICE SYSTEM DETERMINES HOW GOODS ARE PRODUCED

Next, consider how society determines how each good and service is produced. How does the price system carry out this task? The price of each resource gives producers an indication of how scarce this resource is, and how valuable it is in other uses. Clearly, firms should produce goods and services at minimum cost. Suppose that there are two ways of producing tables: Technique A and Technique B. Technique A requires 4 hours of labor and $10 worth of wood per table, whereas Technique B requires 5 hours of labor and $8 worth of wood. If the price of an hour of labor is $5, Technique A should be used since a table costs $30 with this technique, as opposed to $33 with Technique B.[6] In other words, Technique A uses fewer resources per table.

The price system nudges producers to opt for Technique A rather than Technique B through profits and losses. If each table commands a price of $45, then by using Technique A, producers make a profit of $45 – $30 = $15 per table. If they use Technique B, they make a profit of $45 – $33 = $12 per table. Thus producers, if they maximize profit, will be led to adopt Technique A. Their desire for profit leads them to adopt the techniques that will enable society to get the most out of its resources. No one commands firms to use particular techniques. Washington officials do not order steel plants to substitute the basic oxygen process for open

[6] To obtain these figures, note that the cost with Technique A is 4 hours times $5 plus $10, or $30, while the cost with Technique B is 5 hours times $5 plus $8, or $33.

hearths, or petroleum refineries to substitute catalytic cracking for thermal cracking. It is all done through the impersonal marketplace.

You should not, however, get the idea that the price system operates with kid gloves. Suppose all firms producing tables used Technique B until this past year, when Technique A was developed: in other words, Technique A is based on a new technology. Given this technological change, the supply curve for tables will shift to the right, as we have seen, and the price of a table will fall. Suppose it drops to $32. If some firm insists on sticking with Technique B, it will lose money at the rate of $1 a table; and as these losses mount, the firm's owners will become increasingly uncomfortable. The firm will either switch to Technique A or go bankrupt. The price system leans awfully hard on producers who try to ignore its signals.

## HOW THE PRICE SYSTEM DETERMINES WHO GETS WHAT

Let's turn now to how society's output will be distributed among the people: How does the price system carry out this task? How much people receive in goods and services depends on their money income, which in turn is determined under the price system by the amount of various resources that they own and by the price of each resource. Thus, under the price system, each person's income is determined in the marketplace: the person comes to the marketplace with certain resources to sell, and his or her income depends on how much he or she can get for them.

The question of who gets what is solved at two levels by the price system. Consider an individual product—for example, the tables discussed in the previous section. For the individual product, the question of who gets what is solved by the equality of quantity demanded and quantity supplied. If the price of these tables is at its equilibrium level, the quantity demanded will equal the quantity supplied. Consumers who are willing and able to pay the equilibrium price (or more) get the tables, while those who are unwilling or unable to pay it do not get them. It is just as simple—and as impersonal—as that. It doesn't matter whether you are a nice guy or a scoundrel, or whether you are a connoisseur of tables or someone who doesn't know good workmanship from poor workmanship: all that matters is whether you are able and willing to pay the equilibrium price.

Next, consider the question of who gets what at a somewhat more fundamental level. After all, whether a consumer is able and willing to pay the equilibrium price for a good depends on his or her money income. Thus the super-rich can pay the equilibrium price for an astonishing variety of things, whereas those in abject poverty can scrape up the equilibrium price for very little. As we have already seen, a consumer's money income depends on the amount of resources of various kinds that he or she owns and the price that he or she can get for them. Some people have lots of resources: they are endowed with skill and intelligence and industry, or they have lots of capital or land. Other people have little in the way of resources. Moreover, some people have resources that command a high price, while others have resources that are of little monetary value. The result is that, under the price system, some consumers get a lot more of society's output than do other consumers.

# HOW THE PRICE SYSTEM DETERMINES THE RATE OF ECONOMIC GROWTH

Let's turn now to the task of determining a society's rate of growth of per capita income. How does the price system do this? As pointed out in the previous chapter, a nation's rate of increase of per capita income depends on the rate of growth of its resources and the rate of increase of the efficiency with which they are used. First, consider the rate of growth of society's resources. The price system influences the amount society invests in educating, training, and upgrading its labor resources. To a considerable extent, the amount invested in such resource-augmenting activities is determined by the profitability of such investments, which is determined in turn by the pattern of prices.

Next, consider the rate of increase of the efficiency with which a society's resources are used. Clearly, this factor depends heavily on the rate of technological change. If technology is advancing at a rapid rate, it should be possible to get more and more out of a society's resources. But if technology is advancing rather slowly, it is likely to be difficult to get much more out of them. The price system affects the rate of technological change in a variety of ways: it influences the profitability of investing in research and development, the profitability of introducing new processes and products into commercial practice, and the profitability of accepting technological change—as well as the losses involved in spurning it.

The price system establishes strong incentives for firms to introduce new technology. Any firm that can find a cheaper way to produce an existing product, or a way to produce a better product, will have a profitable jump on its competitors. Until its competitors can do the same thing, this firm can reap higher profits than it otherwise could. Of course, these higher profits will eventually be competed away, as other firms begin to imitate this firm's innovation. But lots of money can be made in the period during which this firm has a lead over its competitors. These profits are an important incentive for the introduction of new technology.

# TWO CASE STUDIES

## The Price System in Action behind Enemy Lines

The real story of a World War II prisoner-of-war camp affords an excellent view of the price system in action. Just as certain elementary forms of life illustrate important biological principles in a simple way, so the economic organization of a prisoner-of-war camp is an elementary form of economic system that illustrates certain important economic principles simply and well. What made the camp's economic system so elementary was the fact that no goods were produced there. All commodities were provided by the country running the camp, by the Red Cross, and by other outside donors. Each prisoner received an equal amount of food and supplies—canned milk, jam, butter, cookies, cigarettes, and so on. In addition, private parcels of clothing, cigarettes, and other supplies were received, with different prisoners, of course, receiving different quantities. Because no goods were produced in the prisoner-of-war camp, the first two tasks of an economic system (What will be produced? How will it be produced?) were not relevant; neither was the fourth task (What provision is to be made for growth?)

# HOW TO MAKE THE TRANSITION FROM COMMUNISM TO CAPITALISM: THE CASE OF POLAND

The price system seems to be gaining adherents throughout the world. After decades of criticizing capitalism, the governments of many communist countries, particularly in Eastern Europe, have begun to talk seriously about abandoning central planning and turning to the price system. Unquestionably, this is one of the most dramatic and significant economic developments of the 1990s. Practically everyone—including the most sophisticated observers—has been struck by how quickly the movement toward economic reform has progressed in some of these countries.

Poland is at the vanguard of this movement. At the beginning of 1990, Poland adopted a bold and controversial plan to make the transition from communism to capitalism. Specifically, this plan called for the transfer of industry from government to private hands, for an end to government subsidies, and for reliance on market prices. Also, in contrast to earlier days, bankruptcy and unemployment would now be tolerated. Unlike other East European countries, Poland jumped into capitalism like a child enters a swimming pool—feet first. Critics said this economic plan was "cold turkey" or "shock treatment."

Why are Poland and its East European neighbors abandoning central planning? As the Council of Economic Advisers has pointed out,

Jeffrey Sachs

A fundamental distinguishing feature of centrally planned economies is that state authorities, not private citizens, own and control most of the means of production. Instead of allocating resources through markets that establish prices based on supplies and demands, the state authorities generally formulate detailed plans for inputs and outputs. Coordinating this process properly requires an immense amount of information, making it exceedingly difficult for a centralized system of managers to allocate scarce resources according to what people want, or to respond to changes in demands, supplies and technologies. The lack of private ownership implies that individuals have little stake in improving resource allocation. Of course, the population as a whole would gain if resources were used to produce goods and services they valued more highly.

Although the operation of centrally planned systems is very complex, a simple polar example illustrates key issues. Consider an enterprise producing shirts. In a centrally planned economy, planners would typically determine the amounts of cloth, dye, thread, and other inputs the enterprise would receive and the source and price of each input. Workers would be assigned to the enterprise, and often allocated to particular tasks. The plan would also set targets for output of each type of shirt and determine the final prices to households.

The contrast with a market economy is striking. In a centrally planned economy, prices of labor, goods, and services do not adjust to reflect supplies and demands, and production decisions are not motivated by profitability. Unlike a market system, producers typically have no leeway to reduce prices or production when inventories accumulate or to raise prices or production as inventories decline—even if consumers form long queues. The enterprise does not base hiring decisions on its assessment of needs and worker quality, nor does it choose where to purchase inputs so as to minimize production costs. Furthermore, state-owned enterprises are allocated the credit needed to finance operations through a centralized banking system. Most centrally planned economies have never developed laws to deal with bankruptcies, because enterprises are typically bailed out if costs exceed revenues. Consider the implications for U.S. firm behavior if the Federal Government promised to mail a check to cover the losses of every business that lost money. Such a system severely weakens the incentives for producers to use resources efficiently.

Because individuals in centrally planned economies own few of the factories or other productive assets, individuals have little incentive to respond to market signals about resource scarcity, even if such signals exist. Instead, the central planning system puts a premium on meeting output targets. The lack of private ownership also provides little incentive for innovation or quality control. New firms cannot simply enter the market to take advantage of better management or new ideas.[1]

Given these problems, Poland has decided to abandon central planning and to adopt the price system. In many respects, this is an unprecedented experiment. Although the world has plenty of experience with the functioning of a price system, very little is known about how to get a price system started. In the case of Poland, the government's "cold turkey" program, devised in considerable part by Harvard's Jeffrey Sachs, has undoubtedly caused pain. Critics point to the fact that substantial unemployment has occurred, that inflation has been very serious, and that living standards have fallen. Because of the huge increase in food prices, working families in early 1990 spent over half of their income on food. (See Table 1.) Some assert that the treatment may be as bad as the ailment.

But Sachs and others argue that a gradual transition from central planning will not work. In his view, "A step-by-step approach can't work for very good and deep and solid economic, financial, and political reasons. You get trapped in a mass of contradictions. You have to go far beyond simply decentralizing the economy. You have to go all the way to embracing a full market economy with private ownership, free international trade, and prices set according to supply and demand."[2]

Not all economists and politicians agree. For example, Mikhail Gorbachev, president of the Soviet Union, decided in 1990 not to emulate the Polish model. Instead, he proposed a gradual transition to a "regulated market economy." Criticizing the propo-

Lech Walesa, president of Poland

nents of a quick transition, he said, "They want to take a gamble. [They say that] everything should be thrown open tomorrow. Let market conditions be put in place everywhere. Let's have free enterprise and give the green light to all forms of ownership, private ownership. Let everything be private. Let us sell the land, everything. I cannot support such ideas, no matter how decisive and revolutionary they might appear. These are irresponsible ideas, irresponsible."[3]

Will Poland's bold new program work? It is a safe

### Table 1 Percentage of Workers' Incomes Spent on Various Items, 1989 and 1990

| ITEM | 1989 | 1990 |
|---|---|---|
| Food | 38 | 52 |
| Clothing | 21 | 12 |
| Rent | 11 | 11 |
| Energy | 3 | 3 |
| Entertainment | 10 | 7 |
| Transportation | 6 | 6 |
| Health Care | 4 | 3 |
| Other | 7 | 6 |
| Total | 100 | 100 |

*Source: New York Times, July 29, 1990.*

[1] *Economic Report of the President,* Washington, D.C.: Government Printing Office, 1990, pp. 227–28.
[2] "The Debt Offensive," *Philadelphia Inquirer,* May 6, 1990.
[3] "How Gorbachev Rejected Plan to "Shock Treat" the Economy," *New York Times,* May 14, 1990.

bet that the price system by itself will not be a cure for all of Poland's economic ills. Poland's output per capita is only about one-fourth of that in the United States. It lacks modern equipment and sophisticated managers, among other things. According to the Joint Economic Committee of Congress, economic performance and living standards in Poland may decline in the near term as a result of this program.[4] But in the longer term, there is reason to believe that the price system will enable Poland to raise its standard of living.

### Probing Deeper

1. Why does the coordination of the process of allocating resources in a centrally planned economy

require "an immense amount of information"?

2. Why does the lack of private ownership of capital in a centrally planned economy imply "that individuals have little stake in improving resource allocation"?

3. Why does the lack of private ownership provide "little incentive for innovation or quality control"?

4. In 1990, Poland tried to sell a dozen large state enterprises to private groups, but failed. What are some of the problems in auctioning off enterprises of this sort?

5. Why do economists feel that it is a good idea to end government subsidies of enterprises?

6. Why has Poland decided that bankruptcy and unemployment should be tolerated? Aren't they to be avoided?

[4] "Jobless to Soar in a Free-Market East," New York Times, May 17, 1990.

All that did matter in this elementary economic system was the third task: to determine who would consume the various available goods. At first blush, the answer may seem obvious: each prisoner would consume the goods he received from the detaining country, the Red Cross, and private packages. But this assumes that prisoners would not trade goods back and forth ("I'll swap you a cigarette for some milk"), which is clearly unrealistic. After all, some prisoners smoked cigarettes, others did not; some liked jam and didn't like canned beef, others liked canned beef and didn't like jam. Thus there was bound to be exchange of this sort, and the real question is in what way and on what terms such exchange took place.

How did the prisoners go about exchanging goods? According to one observer, the process developed as follows:

> Starting with simple direct barter, such as a nonsmoker giving a smoker friend his cigarette issue in exchange for a chocolate ration, more complex exchanges soon became an accepted custom. . . . Within a week or two, as the volume of trade grew, rough scales of exchange values came into existence. [Some prisoners], who had at first exchanged tinned beef for practically any other foodstuff, began to insist on jam and margarine. It was realized that a tin of jam was worth one-half pound of margarine plus something else, that a cigarette issue was worth several chocolate issues, and a tin of diced carrots was worth practically nothing. . . . By the end of the month, there was a lively trade in all commodities and their relative values were well known, and expressed not in terms of one another—one didn't quote [jam] in terms of sugar—but in terms of cigarettes. The cigarette became the standard of value.[7]

Thus the prisoners used the price system to solve the problem of allocating the available supply of goods among consumers. A market developed for each good. This market had, of course, both a demand and a supply side. Each good had its price but this price was quoted in

[7] R. A. Radford, "The Economic Organization of a P.O.W. Camp," reprinted in E. Mansfield, *Principle of Microeconomics: Readings, Issues, and Cases,* 4th ed., New York: Norton, 1983.

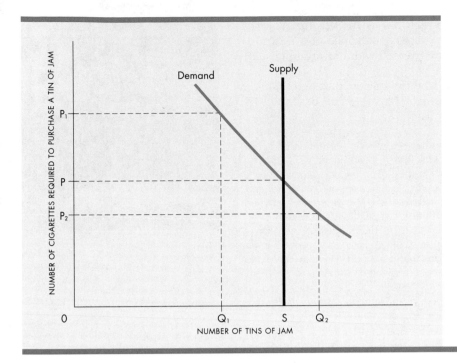

**Figure 3.13**
**Determinants of Equilibrium Price of a Tin of Jam (in terms of cigarettes) in a P.O.W. Camp**
The market supply for jam is fixed at $OS$ tins. Thus the equilibrium price of a tin of jam is $OP$ cigarettes. If the price were $OP_1$, $OQ_1$ tins would be demanded; if the price were $OP_2$, $OQ_2$ tins would be demanded.

cigarettes, not dollars and cents. These markets were not started in a self-conscious, deliberate way. No one said, "Let's adopt the price system to allocate available supplies," or "Let's vote on whether or not to adopt the price system." Instead, the system just evolved . . . and it worked.

To see how the supply of a particular good—jam, say—was allocated, look at Figure 3.13, which shows the market supply curve for jam. In the short run, this supply was fixed, so this supply curve is a vertical line. Figure 3.13 also provides the market demand curve for jam, which shows the amount of jam the prisoners wanted to consume at various prices of jam—expressed in terms of cigarettes. For example, the prisoners wanted $OQ_1$ tins of jam when a tin of jam cost $OP_1$ cigarettes, and $OQ_2$ tins of jam when a tin of jam cost $OP_2$ cigarettes. For the quantity demanded to equal the available supply, the price of a tin of jam had to be $OP$ cigarettes; one tin of jam had to exchange for $OP$ cigarettes. At this price, the available supply of jam was rationed, without resort to fights among prisoners or intervention by the prison authorities. Those prisoners who could and would pay the price had the jam and there were just enough such consumers to exhaust the available supply. Moreover, this held true for each of the other goods (including cigarettes) as well.

## The Price System in Action on the Great White Way

It is a long way from a prisoner-of-war camp to the Broadway theater, but economics, like any good tool of analysis, applies to a very wide variety of problems. In this section, we discuss the theater's pricing problems and the role of the price system in helping to solve these problems. Prices for tickets to Broadway shows are established at levels that are much the same whether the show is a success or a flop. An orchestra ticket to *Kelly* (which managed to hold out for one performance before closing) cost about as much as an orchestra ticket to such hits as *Les Misérables* or *The Phantom of the Opera*. And once a play opens, the price of a ticket remains much the same whether the play is greeted with universal praise or with discontented critics and customers.

Because of these pricing methods, the Broadway theater has been beset for many years by serious problems. Here they are described by two veteran observers of the Broadway stage:

> For centuries the sale of theater tickets has brought on corruption and confusion. When there are more buyers than sellers, a black market results. The so-called "retail" price, the price printed on the ticket, becomes meaningless. Speculation doubles, triples, or quadruples the "real" as opposed to the "legal" asking price. A smash hit on Broadway means "ice"—the difference between the real and legal prices—a well-hidden but substantial cash flow that is divided among shadowy middlemen. Ticket scandals break out in New York as regularly as the flu. The scenario is familiar. A play opens and becomes a superhit. Tickets become difficult, then impossible, to obtain. There are letters to the newspapers. . . . Shocking corruption is discovered. Someone . . . is convicted of overcharging and accepting illegal gratuities. Someone may even go to jail. The black market, valiantly scotched, *never stops for a single moment*.[8]

Besides enriching crooked box-office workers and managers, as well as other shadowy elements of society, the black market for theater tickets has the additional undesirable effect of excluding the authors, composers, directors, and stars of the play from participation in the premium revenue. Almost all of these people receive a percentage of the play's revenues; and if the revenues at the box office are less than what customers pay for their seats (because of "ice"), these people receive less than they would if no black market existed. The amount of "ice" can be substantial. For example, Rodgers and Hammerstein estimated that, at one performance of their play, *South Pacific,* the public probably paid about $25,000 for tickets with a face value of $7,000, the amount turned in at the box office.

To focus on the problem here, let's look at the market for tickets to a particular performance of *A Chorus Line* (Broadway's longest-running show) when it was at the height of its popularity. Since the supply of tickets to a given performance of this play is fixed, the market supply curve, shown in Figure 3.14, is a vertical line at the quantity of tickets corresponding to the capacity of the theater. The price set officially on a ticket was about $30. But because the show was enormously popular, the market demand curve was $D$ in Figure 3.14, and the equilibrium price for a ticket was $60.[9]

Figure 3.14 makes the nature of the problem apparent: at the official price of $30, the quantity of tickets demanded is much greater than the quantity supplied. Supply and demand don't match. Obviously, there is an incentive for people to buy the tickets from the box office at $30 and sell them at the higher prices customers are willing to pay. There is also an incentive for box-office workers to sell them surreptitiously at higher prices and turn in only $30. The price system cannot play the role it did in the prisoner-of-war camp for jam and other goods. It cannot act as an effective rationing device because, to do so, the price of tickets would have to increase to its equilibrium level, $60.

[8] S. Little and A. Cantor, *The Playmakers,* New York: Norton, 1970, p. 220.
[9] This figure is only a rough estimate, but it is good enough for present purposes.

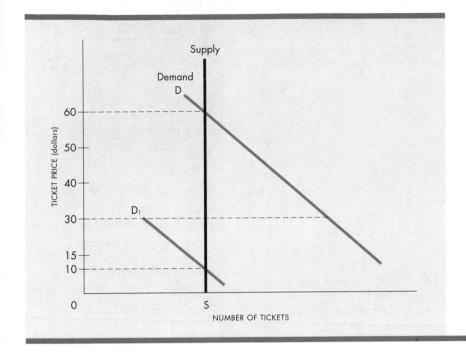

**Figure 3.14**
**Equilibrium Price for Tickets to**
**A Chorus Line**
The market supply for tickets is fixed at OS per performance. If the demand curve is D, the equilibrium price of a ticket is $60. (If the demand curve is $D_1$, the equilibrium price is $10.) If the demand curve is D and the price of a ticket is $30, the quantity of tickets demanded will far exceed the quantity supplied.

Many theater experts believe that the solution to Broadway's pricing problems lies in allowing the price system to work more effectively by permitting ticket prices to vary depending on a show's popularity. For example, the official ticket price would have been allowed to rise to $60 for *A Chorus Line*. On the other hand, if *A Chorus Line* had been much less popular and its market demand curve had been $D_1$ in Figure 3.14, its official ticket price would have been allowed to fall to $10. In this way, the black market for tickets would be eliminated, since the equilibrium price—which equates supply and demand—would be the official price. "Ice" would also be eliminated, since there would be no difference between the official and the actual price paid, and the people responsible for the show would receive its full receipts, not share them with crooked box-office workers and illegal operators.[10]

## PRICE CEILINGS AND PRICE SUPPORTS

During national emergencies, the government sometimes puts a lid on prices, not allowing them to reach their equilibrium levels. For example, during World War II, the government did not allow the prices of various foodstuffs to rise to their equilibrium levels, because it felt that this would have been inequitable (and highly unpopular). Under such circumstances, the quantity demanded of a product exceeds the quantity supplied. In other words, the situation is like that in Figure 3.14, where the quantity of tickets demanded for *A Chorus Line* exceeded the quantity supplied at a price of $30. There is a shortage.

[10] Steps have been taken toward somewhat greater price flexibility for Broadway shows. For example, in the mid-1970s, a booth was established in Times Square where tickets to some shows were on sale at (approximately) half of the official ticket price. In this way, a show was enabled to cut its price, if it was unable to fill the theater at the official ticket price. Apparently, this has worked quite well, both for the producers of the shows and the theatergoing public.

Since the price system is not allowed to perform its rationing function, some formal system of rationing or allocating the available supply of the product may be required. Thus, in World War II, families were issued ration coupons which determined how much they could buy of various commodities. And in the 1970s, when the Organization of Petroleum Exporting Countries cut back oil production and reduced exports of oil to the United States, there was serious talk that gasoline and oil might be rationed in a similar way. Such rationing schemes may be justified in emergencies (of reasonably short duration), but they can result eventually in serious distortions, since prices are not allowed to do the job normally expected of them.

To illustrate the sorts of problems that can arise when price ceilings are imposed, consider the rent ceilings that exist on some apartments in New York City. Originally imposed to prevent dwelling costs from soaring during World War II, these ceilings have been defended on the ground that they help the poor, at least in the short run. Although this may be so, they have also resulted in a shortage of housing in New York City. Because they have pushed the price of housing below the equilibrium price, less housing has been supplied than has been demanded. The depressed price of housing has discouraged investors from building new housing, and has made it unprofitable for some owners of existing housing to maintain their buildings. Thus, although it would be socially desirable to channel more resources into New York housing, the rent ceilings have prevented this from occurring.

Government authorities may also impose price floors—or price supports, as they often are called. These floors are generally defended on the ground that they enable the producers of the good in question to make a better living. For example, the federal government has imposed price supports on a wide range of agricultural commodities, the purpose being to increase farm incomes. Just as in the case in Figure 3.14 where the demand curve is $D_1$ and where a price floor of \$30 exists, the result is that the quantity supplied exceeds the quantity demanded at the support price. Thus there is a surplus of the commodity—and, in the case of agricultural commodities, the government has had to buy up and store these surpluses. As in the case of a price ceiling, the result is that the price system is not allowed to do the job expected of it.

Whether price ceilings or floors are socially desirable depends on whether the loss in social efficiency resulting from them is exceeded by the gain in equity they achieve. As indicated above, their purpose is to help or protect particular parts of the population which would be treated inequitably by the unfettered price system. Since one person's view of what is equitable differs from another person's, this is an area of considerable controversy. More will be said about both price ceilings and floors in subsequent chapters, particularly Chapters 19 and 31.

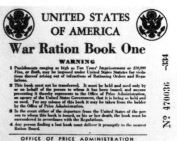

Ration coupons from World War II

## THE CIRCULAR FLOWS OF MONEY AND PRODUCTS

So far we have been concerned largely with the workings of a single market—the market for wheat or tables or jam or tickets to *A Chorus Line*. But how do all of the various markets fit together? This is a very important question. Perhaps the best way to begin answering it is to distinguish

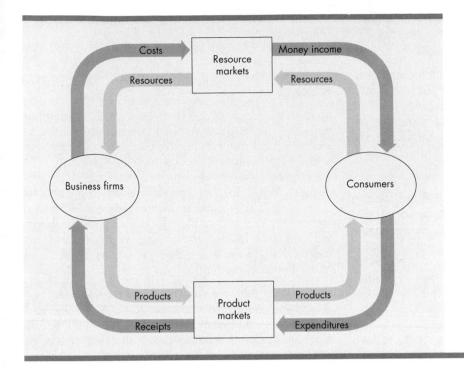

**Figure 3.15**
**The Circular Flows of Money and Products**
In product markets, consumers exchange money for products and firms exchange products for money. In resource markets, consumers exchange resources for money and firms exchange money for resources.

between product markets and resource markets. As their names indicate, **product markets** *are markets where products are bought and sold; and* **resource markets** *are markets where resources are bought and sold.* Let's first consider product markets. As shown in Figure 3.15, firms provide products to consumers in product markets, and receive money in return. The money the firms receive is their receipts; to consumers, on the other hand, it represents their expenditures.

Next, let's consider resource markets. Figure 3.15 shows that consumers provide resources—including labor—to firms in resource markets, and they receive money in return. The money the consumers receive is their income; to firms, on the other hand, it represents their costs. Note that the flow of resources and products in Figure 3.15 is counterclockwise: that is, *consumers provide resources to firms which in turn provide goods and services to consumers.* On the other hand, the flow of money in Figure 3.15 is clockwise: that is, *firms pay money for resources to consumers who in turn use the money to buy goods and services from the firms.* Both flows—that of resources and products, and that of money—go on simultaneously and repeatedly.

So long as consumers spend all their income, the flow of money income from firms to consumers is exactly equal to the flow of expenditure from consumers to firms. Thus these circular flows, like Ole' Man River, just keep rolling along. As a first approximation, this is a perfectly good model. But as we pointed out in Chapter 1, capitalist economies have experienced periods of widespread unemployment and severe inflation that this model cannot explain. Also, note that our simple economy in Figure 3.15 has no government sector. Under pure capitalism, the government would play a limited role in the economic system, but in the mixed capitalistic system we have in the United States, the government plays an important role indeed.

# TEST YOURSELF

1. Will each of the following tend to shift the demand curve for toasters to the right, to the left, or not at all? (a) Consumer incomes rise by 20 percent. (b) The price of bread falls by 10 percent. (c) The price of electricity increases by 5 percent. (d) Medical reports indicate that toast prevents heart attacks. (e) The cost of producing a toaster increases by 10 percent.

2. Will each of the following tend to shift the supply curve for toasters to the right, to the left, or not at all? (a) The wage of workers producing toasters increases by 5 percent. (b) The price of the metal used to make toasters falls by 10 percent. (c) The price of bread falls by 10 percent. (d) Consumer incomes rise by 20 percent. (e) New technology makes toaster production much more efficient.

3. If both the demand and supply curve for a product shift to the right, can one predict whether the product's equilibrium price will increase or decrease? Can one predict whether its equilibrium quantity will increase or decrease?

4. In 1987, apple growers in the state of Washington expected their crop to exceed the previous record by more than 25 percent. (a) Washington apple growers spent $1.5 million to market their fruit overseas. Did this influence the demand curve or the supply curve for apples? Why? (b) Growers said their best hope for preventing a severe price decline was a new storage technology that allows them to keep apples fresh tasting and fresh looking for up to a year after they are picked. Using supply and demand curves, show the effects of this new technology on price.

5. Suppose that the American public becomes convinced that beets are more desirable than they have been, and string beans are less so. Describe the shifts that will occur in the demand and supply curves in the relevant markets, and the mechanisms that will signal and trigger a redeployment of resources.

# SUMMARY

1. There are two sides of every market: the demand side and the supply side. The demand side can be represented by the market demand curve, which almost always slopes downward to the right and whose location depends on consumer tastes, the number and income of consumers, and the prices of other commodities.

2. The supply side of the market can be represented by the market supply curve, which generally slopes upward to the right and whose location depends on technology and resource prices.

3. The equilibrium price and equilibrium quantity of the commodity are given by the intersection of the market demand and supply curves. If conditions remain reasonably stable for a time, the actual price and quantity should move close to the equilibrium price and quantity.

4. Changes in the position and shape of the demand curve—in response to changes in consumer tastes, income, population, and prices of other commodities—result in changes in the equilibrium price and equilibrium output of a product. Similarly, changes in the position and shape of the supply curve—in response to changes in technology and resource prices, among other things—also result in changes in the equilibrium price and equilibrium output of a product.

5. To determine what goods and services society will produce, the price system sets up incentives for firms to produce what consumers want. To the extent that they produce what consumers want and are willing to pay for, firms reap profits; to the extent that they don't, they experience losses.

6. The price system sets up strong incentives for firms to produce goods at minimum cost. These incentives take the form of profits for firms that minimize costs and losses for firms that operate with relatively high costs.

7. To determine who gets what, the price system results in each person's receiving an income that depends on the quantity of resources he or she owns and the prices that they command.

8. The price system establishes incentives for activities that result in increases in a society's per capita income. For example, it influences the amount of new capital goods produced, as well as the amount society spends on educating its labor force and improving its technology.

9. There are circular flows of money and products in a capitalist economy. In product markets, firms provide products to consumers and receive money in return. In resource markets, consumers provide resources to firms, and receive money in return.

# CONCEPTS FOR REVIEW

Consumers

Firms

Markets

Perfect competition

Demand

Market demand curve

Supply

Market supply curve

Equilibrium

Equilibrium price

Actual Price

Product market

Resource market

# PART TWO

## NATIONAL OUTPUT, INCOME, AND EMPLOYMENT

# NATIONAL INCOME AND PRODUCT

ABOUT 70 YEARS AGO, a Russian-born immigrant came to the United States and, after teaching himself English in a summer, became an economist. His name was Simon Kuznets, and, as we shall see in this chapter, he constructed some of the first crude estimates of ***gross national product***. Put in the simplest terms, gross national product—or GNP, as it is often called—is the value of the total amount of final goods and services produced by our economy during a particular period of time. This measure is important for its own sake, and because it helps us to understand both inflation and unemployment.

The federal government and the business community watch GNP figures avidly. Government officials, from the president down, are interested because these figures indicate how prosperous we are, and because they are useful in forecasting the future health of the economy. Business executives are also extremely interested in GNP figures because the sales of their firms are related to the level of GNP, and so the figures are useful in forecasting the future health of their businesses. All in all, it is no exaggeration to say that the gross national product is one of the most closely watched numbers in existence. In this chapter, we discuss the measurement, uses, and limitations of the gross national product, as well as a variety of other commonly used measures of national income and output.

## GROSS NATIONAL PRODUCT

As noted above, gross national product is a measure of how much the economy produces in a particular period of time. But the American economy produces millions of types of goods and services. How can we add up the output of everything from lemon meringue pies to helicopters, from books to houses? The only feasible answer is to use money as a common denominator and to make the price of a good or service—the amount the buyer is willing to pay—the measure of value. In other words, we add up the value in money terms of the total output of goods and services in the economy during a certain period, normally a year, and the result is the gross national product during that period.

Although the measurement of gross national product may seem straightforward ("just add up the value in money terms of the total output of the economy"), this is by no means the case. Some of the more important pitfalls that must be avoided and problems that must be confronted are the following:

**AVOIDANCE OF DOUBLE COUNTING.** Gross national product does not include the value of *all* goods and services. It includes only the value of *final* goods and services produced. ***Final goods and services*** are those destined for the ultimate user. For example, flour purchased for family consumption is a final good, but flour to be used in manufacturing bread is an ***intermediate good,*** not a final good. We would be double counting if we counted both the bread and the flour used to make the bread as output. Thus the output of intermediate goods—goods that are not destined for the ultimate user, but are used as inputs in producing final goods and services—must not be included in gross national product.

Steel used in the production of automobiles and cotton used in the production of blue jeans must not be included. They will be counted when we count the automobiles and jeans, which are final goods. The value of the steel will be included in the price of the automobiles, and the value of the cotton will be included in the price of the jeans.

**VALUATION AT COST.** Some final goods and services that must be included in gross national product are not bought and sold in the marketplace, so they are valued at what they cost. Consider the services performed by government—police protection, fire protection, the use of the courts, defense, and so forth. Such services are not bought and sold in any market (despite the old saw about the New Jersey judge who was "the best that money could buy"). Yet they are an important part of our economy's final output. Economists and statisticians have decided to value them at what they cost the taxpayers. This is by no means ideal, but it is the best practical solution advanced to date.

**NONMARKET TRANSACTIONS.** It is necessary for practical reasons to omit certain types of final output from gross national product. In particular, some nonmarketed goods and services, such as the services performed by homemakers, are excluded from the gross national product. This is not because economists fail to appreciate these services, but because it would be extremely difficult to get reasonably reliable estimates of the money value of a homemaker's services. At first glance, this may seem to be a very important weakness in our measure of total output, but so long as the value of these services does not change much (in relation to total output), the variation in gross national product will provide a reasonably accurate picture of the variation in total output—and, for many purposes, this is all that is required.

**NONPRODUCTIVE TRANSACTIONS.** Purely financial transactions are excluded from gross national product because they do not reflect current production. Such financial transactions include government transfer payments, private transfer payments, and the sale and purchase of securities. ***Government transfer payments*** are payments made by the government to individuals who do not contribute to production in exchange for them. Payments to welfare recipients are a good example of government transfer payments. Since these payments are not for production, it would be incorrect to include them in GNP. ***Private transfer payments*** are gifts or other transfers of wealth from one person or private organization to another. Again, these are not payments for production, so there is no reason to include them in GNP. The sale and purchase of securities are not payments for production, so they too are excluded from GNP.

# THE FIRST ESTIMATES OF GNP IN THE UNITED STATES

It is hard to find a copy today of the small report to the United States Senate titled simply "National Income, 1929–32," but when it was first printed in 1934, it was something of a bestseller; 4500 copies sold in eight months—at 20 cents each. It was not yet called the "gross national product"; that title would come later with refinements, but as one expert noted, in terms of looking at the entire American economy, this is when time began.

Senator Robert La Follette of Wisconsin was a key figure in getting the U.S. Department of Commerce to make estimates of GNP for the three previous years, starting with the peak of the nation's growth spurt, 1929. The late Simon Kuznets spearheaded this effort. Born in Russia, Kuznets came to America in 1921, taught himself English in one summer, and five years later had completed his Ph.D. in economics at Columbia University. He joined the National Bureau of Economic Research where he began looking for ways to refine the statistical measurements of national income and output. Kuznets's work was the foundation of the Commerce Department's estimates.

It took a year to calculate the industry-by-industry income once the definitions had been clarified. On January 4, 1934, the completed report was sent to the Senate and the nation had its first overall measure, one that brought home the bad news. National output had fallen from $89 billion in 1929 to $49 bil-

Simon Kuznets

lion at the end of 1931. Simon Kuznets, who was awarded the Nobel Prize in economics in 1971, was the first to warn that GNP did not measure how well off we are as a people. He emphasized that an attempt "to make GNP a gauge of scientifically determined, real welfare of the population involves an unwarranted optimism as to the validity of sciences concerning human nature."

N.B.

**SECONDHAND GOODS.** Sales of secondhand goods are also excluded from gross national product. The reason for this is clear. When a good is produced, its value is included in GNP. If its value is also included when it is sold on the secondhand market, it will be counted twice, thus leading to an overstatement of the true GNP. Suppose that you buy a new bicycle and resell it a year later. The value of the new bicycle is included in GNP when the bicycle is produced. But the resale value of the bicycle is not included in GNP; to do so would be double counting.

# ADJUSTING GNP FOR PRICE CHANGES

## Current Dollars versus Constant Dollars

In Chapter 1, we stressed that the general price level has changed over time. (Recall the rapid inflation of the 1970s and early 1980s.) Since gross national product values all goods and services at their current prices, it is bound to be affected by changes in the price level as well as by changes in total output. If all prices doubled tomorrow, this would produce a doubling of gross national product. Clearly, if gross national product is to be a reliable measure of changes in total output, we must correct it somehow to eliminate the effects of such changes in the price level.

To correct for price changes, economists choose some base year and express the value of all goods and services in terms of their prices during the **base year.** For example, suppose we want to compare beef output in 1989 with that in subsequent years. If 1989 is taken as the base year and if the price of beef was $3 per pound in 1989, beef is valued at $3 per pound in all other years. Thus, if 100 million pounds of beef were produced in 1992, this total output is valued at $300 million even though the price of beef in 1992 was actually higher than $3 per pound. In this way, distortions caused by changes in the price level are eliminated.

Gross national product is expressed either in current dollars or in constant dollars. Figures expressed in **current dollars** are actual dollar amounts, whereas those expressed in **constant dollars** are corrected for changes in the price level. Expressed in current dollars, gross national product is affected by changes in the price level. Expressed in constant dollars, gross national product is not affected by the price level because the prices of all goods are maintained at their base-year level. GNP, after being corrected for changes in the price level, is called **real gross national product.**

Figure 4.1 shows the behavior of both real GNP and GNP expressed in current dollars. GNP expressed in current dollars has increased more rapidly (due to inflation) than GNP in constant dollars.

## Price Indexes

It is often useful to have some measure of how much prices have changed over a certain period of time. One way to obtain such a measure is to divide the value of a set of goods and services expressed in current dollars by the value of the same set of goods and services expressed in constant (or base-year) dollars. Suppose that a set of goods and services costs $100 when valued at 1992 prices, but $70 when valued at 1989 prices. Apparently, prices have risen an average of 43 percent for this set of goods between 1989 and 1992. How do we get 43 percent? The ratio of the cost in 1992 prices to the cost in 1989 prices is $100 \div 70 = 1.43$; thus prices must have risen on the average by 43 percent for this set of goods.

The ratio of the value of a set of goods and services in current dollars to the value of the same set of goods and services in constant (base-year) dollars is a **price index.** Thus 1.43 is a price index in the example above. An important function of a price index is to convert values expressed in current dollars into values expressed in constant dollars. This conversion, known as **deflating,** can be achieved simply by dividing values expressed in current dollars by the price index. In the illustration above,

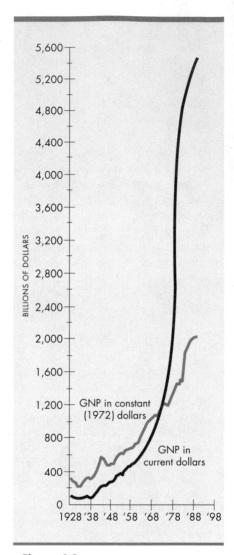

**Figure 4.1**
**Gross National Product, Expressed in Current Dollars and 1972 Dollars, United States, 1929–90**
Because of inflation, GNP expressed in current dollars has increased more rapidly in recent years than GNP in constant (1972) dollars. This was particularly true in the 1970s and early 1980s, reflecting the price surge then.

values expressed in 1992 dollars can be converted into constant (i.e., 1989) dollars by dividing by 1.43. This procedure is an important one, with applications in many fields other than the measurement of gross national product. For example, firms use it to compare their output in various years. To correct for price changes, they deflate their sales by a price index for their products.

In many cases, price indexes are multiplied by 100; that is, they are expressed as percentage changes. Thus, in the case described in the previous paragraph, the price index might be expressed as $1.43 \times 100$, or 143, which would indicate that 1992 prices on the average were 143 percent of their 1989 level. In the next chapter, we shall say more about price indexes that are expressed in this way. For now, we assume that the price index is not multiplied by 100.

## Using Price Indexes

To illustrate how a price index can be used to deflate some figures, suppose that we want to measure how much the output of bread rose *in real terms*—that is, in constant dollars—between 1989 and 1993. Let us suppose that the value of output of bread in current dollars during each year was as shown in the first column of Table 4.1, and that the price of bread during each year was as shown in the second column. To determine the value of output of bread in 1989 dollars, we form a price index with 1989 as the base year, as shown in the third column. Then dividing the figures in the first column by this price index, we get the value of output of bread during each year in 1989 dollars, shown in the fourth column. Thus the fourth column shows how much the output of bread has grown in real terms. The real output of bread has risen by 19 percent—$(1,900 - 1,600) \div 1,600$—between 1989 and 1993.

Next, let's take up an actual case. The first column of Table 4.2 shows the gross national product in selected years. The second column shows the relevant price index for GNP for each of these years. (The base year is 1972). Using this price index, we can determine real GNP in each year. For example, what was real GNP in 1989? To answer this question, we must divide GNP in current dollars in 1989 by the price index for 1989. Thus the answer is $4,118 billion divided by 2.5300, or $1,628 billion. In other words, when expressed in constant 1972 dollars, GNP in 1989 was $1,628 billion. What was real GNP in 1978? Applying the same principles, the answer is $2,156 billion divided by 1.5005, or $1,437 billion. In other

**Table 4.1**
**Use of Price Index to Convert from Current to Constant Dollars**

| YEAR | (1) OUTPUT OF BREAD IN CURRENT DOLLARS | (2) PRICE OF BREAD (DOLLARS) | (3) PRICE INDEX (PRICE ÷ 1989 PRICE) | (4) OUTPUT OF BREAD IN 1989 DOLLARS[a] |
|------|------|------|------|------|
| 1989 | 1,600 million | 0.50 | 1.00 | 1,600 million |
| 1990 | 1,768 million | 0.52 | 1.04 | 1,700 million |
| 1991 | 1,980 million | 0.55 | 1.10 | 1,800 million |
| 1992 | 2,090 million | 0.55 | 1.10 | 1,900 million |
| 1993 | 2,204 million | 0.58 | 1.16 | 1,900 million |

[a] This column was derived by dividing column 1 by column 3.

**Table 4.2**
**Calculation of Real Gross National Product**

| YEAR | GNP IN BILLIONS OF CURRENT DOLLARS | PRICE INDEX (1972 = 1.0000) | REAL GNP (BILLIONS OF 1972 DOLLARS) |
|------|------|------|------|
| 1972 | 1,171 | 1.0000 | 1,171 (=1,171 ÷ 1.0000) |
| 1975 | 1,529 | 1.2718 | |
| 1978 | 2,156 | 1.5005 | 1,437 (=2,156 ÷ 1.5005) |
| 1989 | 4,118 | 2.5300 | 1,628 (=4,118 ÷ 2.5300) |

words, when expressed in constant 1972 dollars, GNP in 1978 was $1,437 billion. To test your understanding, see if you can figure out the value of real GNP in 1975. (To check your answer, consult footnote 1.)[1]

## USING VALUE-ADDED TO CALCULATE GNP

We have pointed out that gross national product includes the value of only the final goods and services produced. Obviously, however, the output of final goods and services is not due solely to the efforts of the producers of the final goods and services. The total value of an automobile when it leaves the plant, for example, represents the work of many industries besides the automobile manufacturers. The steel, tires, glass, and many other components of the automobile were not produced by the automobile manufacturers. In reality, the automobile manufacturers only added a certain amount of value to the value of the intermediate goods— steel, tires, glass, and so forth—they purchased. This point is basic to an understanding of how the gross national product is calculated.

To measure the contribution of a firm or industry to final output, we use the concept of value-added. ***Value-added*** means just what it says: *the amount of value added by a firm or industry to the total worth of the product.* It is a measure in money terms of the extent of production taking place in a particular firm or industry. Suppose that $160 million of bread was produced in the United States in 1992. To produce it, farmers harvested $50 million of wheat, which was used as an intermediate product by flour mills, which turned out $80 million of flour. This flour was used as an intermediate product by the bakers who produced the $160 million of bread. What is the value-added at each stage of the process? For simplicity, assume that the farmers did not have to purchase any materials from other firms in order to produce the wheat. Then the value-added by the wheat farmers is $50 million; the value-added by the flour mills is $30 million ($80 million – $50 million); and the value-added by the bakers is $80 million ($160 million – $80 million). The total of the value-added at all stages of the process ($50 million + $30 million + $80 million) must equal the value of the output of final product ($160 million), because each stage's value-added is its contribution to this value.

Table 4.3 shows the value-added by various industrial groups in the United States in 1990. Since the total of the value-added by all industries must equal the value of all final goods and services, which, of course, is gross national product, it follows that $5,465 billion—the total of the fig-

[1] The real GNP in 1975 equaled $1,529 billion divided by 1.2718, or 1,202 billion of 1972 dollars.

ures in Table 4.3—must have been equal to gross national product in 1990. It is interesting to note that most of the value-added in the American economy in 1990 was not contributed by manufacturing, mining, construction, transportation, communication, or electricity or gas. Instead, most of it came from services—wholesale and retail trade, finance, insurance, real estate, government services, and other services. This is a sign of a basic change taking place in the American economy, which is turning more and more toward producing services, rather than goods.

## NET NATIONAL PRODUCT

One major drawback of GNP as a measure of national output must now be faced: it does not take into account the fact that plant and equipment wear out with use, and that a certain amount of each year's national output must be devoted to replacing the capital goods worn out in producing the year's output. Economists have therefore developed another important measure, **net national product** *(NNP), which equals gross national product minus depreciation.* To obtain net national product, government statisticians estimate the amount of depreciation—the amount of the nation's plant, equipment, and structures that are worn out during the period—and deduct it from gross national product. Net national product is a more accurate measure of the economy's output than gross national product because it takes depreciation into account, but estimates of net national product contain whatever errors are made in estimating depreciation (which is not easy to measure).

As we shall see in succeeding chapters, data on gross national product are more often used, even if net national product may be a somewhat better measure. Actually, since GNP and NNP move together quite closely, which one you use doesn't matter much for most practical purposes. (See Figure 4.2.)

## THE LIMITATIONS OF GNP AND NNP

It is essential that the limitations of both gross national product and net national product be understood. Although they are very useful, these figures are by no means ideal measures of economic well-being. At least five limitations of these measures must always be borne in mind.

**POPULATION.** GNP and NNP are not very meaningful unless one knows the size of the population of the country in question. For example, the fact that a particular nation's GNP equals $50 billion means one thing if the nation has 10 million inhabitants, and quite another thing if it has 500 million inhabitants. To correct for the size of the population, GNP per capita—GNP divided by the population—is often used as a rough measure of output per person in a particular country.

**LEISURE.** GNP and NNP do not take into account one of mankind's most prized activities, leisure. During the past century, the average work week in the United States has decreased substantially. It has gone from almost 70 hours in 1850 to about 40 hours today. As people have become more affluent, they have chosen to substitute leisure for increased production. Yet this increase in leisure time, which surely contributes to our well-being, does not show up in GNP or NNP. Neither does the personal satisfaction (or displeasure and alienation) people get from their jobs.

**Table 4.3**
**Value-Added by Various Industries, United States, 1990**

| INDUSTRY | VALUE-ADDED (BILLIONS OF DOLLARS) |
|---|---|
| Agriculture, forestry, and fisheries | 117 |
| Mining | 83 |
| Construction | 259 |
| Manufacturing | 1,013 |
| Transportation and public utilities | 483 |
| Wholesale and retail trade | 865 |
| Finance, insurance, and real estate | 941 |
| Other services | 1,019 |
| Government[a] | 649 |
| Rest of the world | 38 |
| Gross national product | 5,465[b] |

[a] Equals wages and salaries of government workers.
[b] Because of rounding errors and a statistical discrepancy, figures do not sum to total.
*Source:* Preliminary estimates.

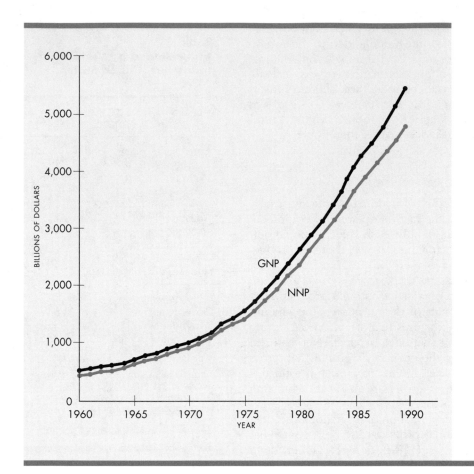

**Figure 4.2**
**Gross National Product and Net National Product, United States, 1960–90**
It is evident that GNP and NNP move together quite closely. Thus, for many practical purposes, which one you use doesn't matter much.

**QUALITY CHANGES.** GNP and NNP do not take adequate account of changes in the quality of goods. An improvement in a product is not reflected accurately in GNP and NNP unless its price reflects the improvement. For example, if a new type of drug is put on the market at the same price as an old drug, and if the output and cost of the new drug are the same as the old drug, GNP will not increase, even though the new drug is twice as effective as the old one. Because GNP and NNP do not reflect such increases in product quality, it is sometimes argued that the commonly used price indices overestimate the amount of inflation, since although prices may have gone up, quality may have gone up too.

**VALUE AND DISTRIBUTION.** GNP and NNP say nothing about the social desirability of the composition and distribution of the nation's output. Each good and service produced is valued at its price. If the price of a Bible is $10 and the price of a pornographic novel is $10, both are valued at $10, whatever you or I may think about their respective worth. Moreover, GNP and NNP measure only the total quantity of goods and services produced. They tell us nothing about how this output is distributed among the people. If a nation's GNP is $500 billion, this is its GNP whether 90 percent of the output is consumed by a relatively few rich families or whether the output is distributed relatively equally among the citizens.

**SOCIAL COSTS.** GNP and NNP do not reflect some of the social costs arising from the production of goods and services. In particular, they do not reflect the environmental damage resulting from the operation of our nation's factories, offices, and farms. It is common knowledge that the atmosphere and water supplies are being polluted in various ways by firms, consumers, and governments. Yet these costs are not deducted from GNP or NNP, even though the failure to do so results in an overestimate of our true economic welfare.

Economists are beginning to correct the GNP figures to eliminate some of these problems. For example, William Nordhaus and James Tobin, both of Yale University, have tried to correct the GNP figures to take proper account of the value of leisure, the value of homemakers' services, and the environmental costs of production, among other things. Unquestionably, more work along this line is needed, and will be done. However, it is also worth noting that many of these adjustments and corrections are necessarily quite rough, since there is no accurate way to measure the relevant values and costs.

## TEST YOURSELF

1. The following table shows the value of GNP in the nation of Puritania. The figures shown are in millions of 1970 dollars and current dollars. Fill in the blanks.

| YEAR | GNP IN MILLIONS OF 1970 DOLLARS | GNP IN MILLIONS OF CURRENT DOLLARS | PRICE INDEX $\left(\dfrac{\text{CURRENT PRICE LEVEL}}{\text{1970 PRICE LEVEL}}\right)$ |
|------|------|------|------|
| 1974 | 1,000 | ____ | 1.00 |
| 1976 | ____ | 1,440 | 1.20 |
| 1978 | 1,300 | ____ | 1.40 |
| 1980 | 1,500 | ____ | 1.60 |
| 1992 | ____ | 2,720 | 1.70 |

2. If George Bush wins $100,000 from Mario Cuomo in a poker game, will this increase, decrease, or have no effect on GNP? Explain.

3. If a paper mill produces $1 million worth of paper this year, but adds considerably to the pollutants in a nearby river, are the social costs arising from this pollution reflected in the gross national product? If so, how? Should these costs be reflected in the GNP? If so, why?

4. A (small) country contains only ten firms. William Moran, the country's top statistician, calculates the country's GNP by totaling the sales of these ten firms. Do you agree with this procedure? Why, or why not?

## TWO APPROACHES TO GNP

Suppose that we want to measure the market value of an automobile. One way to do this is to look at how much the consumer pays for the automobile. Although this is the most straightforward way to measure the automobile's market value, it is not the only way it can be done. Another, equally valid way is to add up all of the wage, interest, rental, and profit incomes generated in the production of the automobile. As pointed out in the circular flow model in Chapter 3 (Figure 3.15), the amount that the automobile producer receives for this car is equal to its profit (or loss) on the car plus the amount it pays the workers and other resource owners who contributed their resources to its production. Thus, if we add up all of the wage, interest, rental, and profit incomes resulting from the production of the automobile, the result is the same as if we determine how much the consumer pays for the automobile.

By the same token, there are two ways to measure the market value of the output of the economy as a whole. Or, put differently, there are two ways of looking at GNP. One is the *expenditures approach,* which regards GNP as the sum of all the expenditures on the final goods and services produced this year. The other is the *income approach,* which regards GNP as the sum of incomes derived from the production of this year's total output.

Since both of these approaches are valid, it follows that GNP can be viewed as either the total expenditure on this year's total output or as the total income stemming from the production of this year's total output. In other words,

$$\begin{array}{c}\text{The total}\\\text{expenditure on}\\\text{this year's total}\\\text{output}\end{array} = \text{GNP} = \begin{array}{c}\text{The total}\\\text{income}\\\text{stemming from}\\\text{the production}\\\text{of this year's}\\\text{total output.}\end{array}$$

This is an identity; the left-hand side of this equation must equal the right-hand side. (More precisely, the right-hand side should also include depreciation and indirect business taxes, as we shall see later. But this refinement can be ignored at this point.)

It is important to understand both the income and the expenditures approaches to GNP. In the following sections, we describe both approaches in more detail, and provide a more formal proof that they do in fact provide the same result.

## THE EXPENDITURES APPROACH TO GNP

To use the **expenditures approach** to determine GNP, one must add up all the spending on final goods and services. Economists distinguish among four broad categories of spending, each of which is taken up below.

### Personal Consumption Expenditures

**Personal consumption expenditures** include the spending by households on durable goods, nondurable goods, and services. This category of spending includes your expenditures on items like food and drink, which are **nondurable goods.** It also includes your family's expenditures on a car or on an electric washer or dryer, which are **durable goods.** Further, it includes your payments to a dentist, who is providing a **service** (painful though it sometimes may be). Table 4.4 shows that in 1990 personal consumption accounted for about two-thirds of the total amount spent on final goods and services in the United States. Expenditures on consumer durable goods are clearly much less than on consumer nondurable goods, whereas expenditures on services are now larger than expenditures on either durable or nondurable goods.

### Gross Private Domestic Investment

**Gross private domestic investment** consists of all investment spending by U.S. firms. As shown in Table 4.4, three broad types of expenditures are included in this category. First, all *final purchases of tools, equipment,*

**Table 4.4
Expenditures on Final Goods and Services, United States, 1990**

| TYPE OF EXPENDITURE | | AMOUNT (BILLIONS OF DOLLARS) |
|---|---|---|
| Personal consumption | | 3,657 |
| Durable goods | 480 | |
| Nondurable goods | 1,194 | |
| Services | 1,983 | |
| Gross private domestic investment | | 741 |
| Expenditures on plant and equipment | 524 | |
| Residential structures | 222 | |
| Increase in inventories | –5 | |
| Net exports | | –31 |
| Exports | 673 | |
| Imports | 704 | |
| Government purchases of goods and services | | 1,098 |
| Federal | 424 | |
| State and local | 674 | |
| Gross national product | | 5,465 |

*Source:* U.S. Department of Commerce.

and machinery are included. Second, all *construction expenditures,* including expenditures on residential housing, are included. (One reason why houses are treated as investment goods is that they can be rented out.) Third, the *change in total inventories* is included. An increase in inventories is a positive investment; a decrease in inventories is a negative investment. The change in inventories must be included, because GNP measures the value of all final goods and services produced, *even if they are not sold this year.* Thus GNP must include the value of any increases in inventories that occur during the year. On the other hand, if a decrease occurs during the year in the value of inventories, the value of this decrease in inventories must be subtracted in calculating GNP because these goods and services were produced prior to the beginning of this year. In other words, a decline in inventories means that society has purchased more than it has produced during the year.

Gross private domestic investment is "gross" in the sense that it includes all additions to the nation's stock of investment goods, whether or not they are replacements for equipment or plant that are used up in producing the current year's output. *Net private domestic investment* includes only the addition to the nation's stock of investment goods after allowing for the replacement of used-up plant and equipment. To illustrate the distinction between gross and net private domestic investment, consider the situation in 1990. In that year, the nation produced $741 billion worth of investment goods; thus gross private domestic investment equaled $741 billion. But in producing the 1990 GNP, $576 billion worth of investment goods were used up. Thus net private domestic investment equaled $741 billion minus $576 billion, or $165 billion. This was the net addition to the nation's stock of investment goods.

Net private domestic investment indicates the change in the nation's stock of capital goods. If it is positive, the nation's productive capacity, as gauged by its capital stock, is growing. If it is negative, the nation's productive capacity, as gauged by its capital stock, is declining. As pointed out in Chapter 1, the amount of goods and services that the nation can produce is influenced by the size of its stock of capital goods. (Why? Because these capital goods are one important type of resource.) Thus this year's net private domestic investment is a determinant of how much the nation can produce in the future.

## Government Purchases of Goods and Services

This category of spending includes the expenditures of the federal, state, and local governments for the multitude of functions they perform: defense, education, police protection, and so forth. It does not include transfer payments, since they are not payments for current production. Table 4.4 shows that government spending in 1990 accounted for about one-fifth of the total amount spent on final goods and services in the United States. State and local expenditures are bigger than federal expenditures. Many of the expenditures of the federal government are on items like national defense, health, and education, while at the state and local levels the biggest expenditure is for items like education and highways.

## Net Exports

***Net exports*** equal the amount spent by other nations on our goods and services less the amount we spent on other nations' goods and services.

This factor must be included since some of our national output is destined for foreign markets, and since we import some of the goods and services we consume. There is no reason why this component of spending cannot be negative—indeed in 1990 it was negative, since imports exceeded exports. The quantity of net exports tends to be quite small. Table 4.4 shows that net exports in 1990 were equal (in absolute terms) to about 1 percent of the total amount spent on final goods and services in the United States.

### Putting Together the Spending Components

Finally, because the four categories of expenditure described above include all possible types of spending on final goods and services, their sum equals the gross national product. In other words,

$$GNP = \text{personal consumption expenditures} +$$
$$\text{gross private domestic investment} +$$
$$\text{government purchases of goods and}$$
$$\text{services} +$$
$$\text{net exports.}$$

As shown in Table 4.4, the gross national product in 1990 equaled 3,657 + 741 + 1,098 − 31, or $5,465 billion.

# THE INCOME APPROACH TO GNP

To use the *income approach* to determine GNP, one must add up all of the income stemming from the production of this year's output. This income is of various types: compensation of employees, rents, interest, proprietors' income, and corporate profits. In addition, for reasons described in detail in a later section, we must also include a capital consumption allowance and indirect business taxes. Each of these items is defined and discussed below.

### Compensation of Employees

This is the largest of the income categories. It includes the wages and salaries that are paid by firms and government agencies to suppliers of labor. In addition, it contains a variety of supplementary payments by employers for the benefit of their employees, such as payments into public and private pension and welfare funds. These supplementary payments are part of the employers' costs and are included in the total compensation of employees.

### Rent

In the present context, **rent** is defined as a payment to households for the supply of property resources. For example, it includes house rents received by landlords. Quite different definitions of rent are used by economists in other contexts.

## Interest

*Interest* includes payments of money by private businesses to suppliers of money capital. If you buy a bond issued by General Motors, the interest payments you receive are included. Interest payments made by the government on Treasury bills, savings bonds, and other securities are excluded on the grounds that they are not payments for current goods and services. They are regarded as transfer payments.

## Proprietors' Income

What we have referred to as profits are split into two parts in the national income accounts: proprietors' income and corporate profits. ***Proprietors' income*** consists of the net income of unincorporated businesses—businesses that are not corporations.

## Corporate Profits

***Corporate profits*** consist of the net income of corporations. (A corporation is a fictitious legal person separate and distinct from the stockholders who own it. Much more will be said about corporations in Chapter 21.) This item is equal to corporate profits before the payment of corporate income taxes.

## Depreciation

All of the items discussed above—compensation of employees, rents, interest, proprietors' income, and corporate profits—are forms of income. In addition, there are two nonincome items, depreciation and indirect business taxes, that must be added to the sum of the income items to obtain GNP. As we know from an earlier section, ***depreciation*** is the value of the nation's plant, equipment, and structures that are worn out this year. In the national income accounts, depreciation is often called a *capital consumption allowance,* because it measures the value of the capital consumed during the year. The reason why depreciation must be added to the sum of the income items to obtain GNP is given in a subsequent section.

## Indirect Business Taxes

The government imposes certain taxes, such as general sales taxes, excise taxes, and customs duties, which firms treat as costs of production. These taxes are called ***indirect business taxes*** because they are not imposed directly on the business itself, but on its products or services instead. A good example of an indirect business tax is the tax on cigarettes; another is the general sales tax. Before a firm can pay out incomes to its workers, suppliers, or owners, it must pay these indirect business taxes to the government. As shown in the next section, these indirect business taxes, like depreciation, must be added to the total of the income items to get GNP.

## Putting Together the Income Components

The sum of the five types of income described above (plus depreciation and indirect business taxes) equals gross national product. In other words,

GNP = compensation of employees + rent + interest + proprietors' income + corporate profits + depreciation + indirect business taxes.

A proof that this is true is contained in the next section.

# GNP EQUALS THE TOTAL CLAIMS ON OUTPUT: A PROOF

We can prove that GNP exactly equals the total claims on output—the sum total of the wages of the workers who participated in the productive efforts, the interest paid to the investors who lent money to the firms that produced the output, the profits of the owners of the firms that produced the output, and the rents paid to the owners of land or buildings used to produce the output, as well as indirect business taxes and depreciation.

To do so, let's start with a single firm, the Miller Company. For this (or any other) firm, profit is defined as sales minus costs. In other words,

$$\text{profit} = \text{sales} - \text{costs}. \qquad (4.1)$$

Thus it follows that

$$\text{sales} = \text{costs} + \text{profit}. \qquad (4.2)$$

Suppose we put the value of Miller's output (i.e., its sales) on the left-hand side of Table 4.5 and its costs and profits on the right-hand side. Clearly, by Equation (4.2), the total of the right-hand side must equal the total of the left-hand side.

Now, suppose that we deduct one element of costs, "Intermediate products bought from other firms," from both sides of Table 4.5, and

---

**Table 4.5**
**Sales, Costs, and Profit, Miller Company, 1992**

| SALES (MILLIONS OF DOLLARS) | | COSTS AND PROFIT (MILLIONS OF DOLLARS) | |
|---|---|---|---|
| Sales | 160 | Employee compensation | 81 |
| | | Interest and rent | 22 |
| | | Depreciation | 14 |
| | | Indirect business taxes | 12 |
| | | Intermediate products bought from other firms | 10 |
| | | Total costs | 139 |
| | | Profits | 21 |
| Total | 160 | Total | 160 |

**Table 4.6**
**Value-Added and Claims against Output, Miller Company, 1992**

| VALUE ADDED (MILLIONS OF DOLLARS) | | CLAIMS AGAINST OUTPUT | |
|---|---|---|---|
| Sales | 160 | Employee compensation | 81 |
| | | Interest and rent | 22 |
| *Subtract* : Intermediate products bought from other firms: | 10 | Profits | 21 |
| | | Depreciation | 14 |
| | | Indirect business taxes | 12 |
| Value-added | 150 | Total | 150 |

present the results in Table 4.6. Since the left-hand total equals the right-hand total in Table 4.5, the same must hold in Table 4.6. The total of the left-hand side of Table 4.6 equals value-added, since Miller's value-added equals its sales minus its expenditures on intermediate goods bought from other firms. The total of the right-hand side of Table 4.6 equals the total claims against Miller's output, which is the total income paid out (or owed) by the firm—wages, interest, rent, profits—plus indirect business taxes and depreciation. And, as pointed out above, the total of the left-hand side must equal the total of the right-hand side of Table 4.6.

Next, imagine constructing a table like Table 4.6 for each employer in the economy, putting sales less intermediate products bought from other firms on the left and costs plus profits less intermediate products bought from other firms on the right. For every employer, the total of the left side must equal the total of the right side. Thus, if we add up the total of the left-hand sides for all employers in the economy, the result must equal the total of the right-hand sides for all employers in the economy. But what is the total of the left-hand sides for all employers in the economy? It is the sum of value-added for all employers, which, as we saw earlier, equals gross national product. And the total of the right-hand sides for all employers in the economy is the total of all income paid out (or owed) in the economy—wages, interest, rent, profits—plus indirect business taxes and depreciation. Consequently, gross national product must equal the total of all income paid out (or owed) in the economy plus indirect business taxes and depreciation.

Table 4.7 shows the total amounts of various types of income paid out (or owed) in the American economy during 1990. It also shows depreciation and indirect business taxes. You can see for yourself that the total of these items equals gross national product. Besides helping to prove the point stated at the beginning of this section, this table is an interesting description of the relative importance of various types of income. For example, it shows the great importance of wages and salaries in the total income stream in the United States. In 1990, roughly 60 percent of gross national product was paid out in employee compensation.

Finally, to see how these income flows are related to the flows of output and expenditure, look carefully at Figure 4.3, which shows diagrammatically the relationships among them. Beginning at the top left-hand side of the figure, we see that the total claims on output equal GNP. Then moving to the right, we see that part of the income goes to firms, part goes to the government, and the rest goes to households. These receipts are then used by households, firms, and the government to buy the gross

**Table 4.7**
**Claims on Output, United States, 1990**

| TYPE OF CLAIM ON OUTPUT | AMOUNT OF CLAIM (BILLIONS OF DOLLARS) |
|---|---|
| Employee compensation | 3,244 |
| Rental income | 7 |
| Interest | 467 |
| Income of proprietors and professionals | 403 |
| Corporate profits | 298 |
| Indirect business taxes | 440 |
| Depreciation | 576 |
| Statistical discrepancy[a] | 30 |
| Gross national product | 5,465 |

[a] This also includes some minor items that need not be of concern here. See the source.
*Source:* U.S. Department of Commerce.

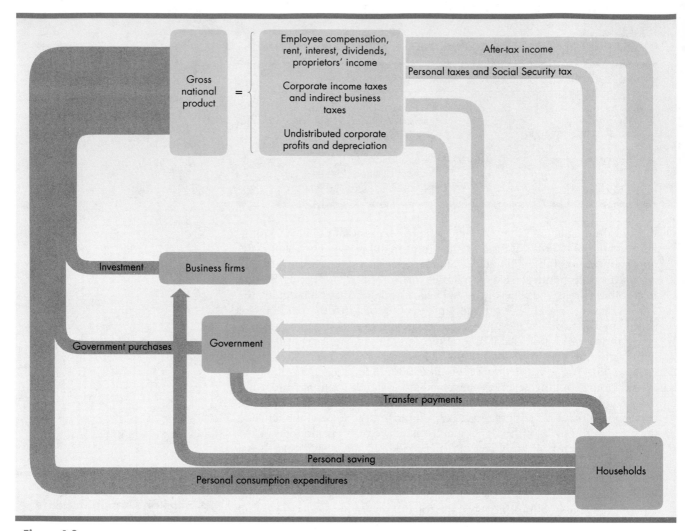

**Figure 4.3**
**Flows of Output, Income, and Expenditures in the National Economy**
This diagram shows that (1) gross national product equals total income plus depreciation plus indirect business taxes; (2) part of these claims goes to households, part goes to firms, and part goes to government; and (3) households, firms, and government spend these receipts on GNP.

national product, as shown on the left-hand side of the figure. (For simplicity, this figure assumes that net exports are zero and that the government has a balanced budget. While neither has been true in the 1990s, this figure is still a good first approximation.)

## NATIONAL INCOME, PERSONAL INCOME, AND DISPOSABLE INCOME

Besides gross national product and net national product, there are several other national accounting concepts that are of importance—namely, national income, personal income, and disposable income. In this section, we describe each of these concepts.

**NATIONAL INCOME.**   We are sometimes interested only in the total amount of wages, interest, rents, and profits paid out (or owed) by employers, an amount called **national income.** It is easy to derive national income if you know gross national product. All you have to do is subtract indirect business taxes and depreciation from gross national product. Or putting it another way, all you have to do is subtract indirect business taxes from net national product, since gross national product minus depreciation equals net national product.[2] Table 4.8 shows the result for 1990.

**PERSONAL INCOME.**   For some purposes, we may need to know how much the people of a nation receive in income. This is **personal income,** and it differs from national income in two ways. First, some people who have a claim on income do not actually receive it. For example, although all a firm's profits belong to the owners, not all of its profits are paid out to them. Part of the profits are plowed back into the business, and part go to the government for corporate income taxes; only dividends are received by owners of corporations. Also, wage earners do not actually receive the amounts they and their employers pay currently for Social Security. Second, some people receive income that is not obtained in exchange for services rendered. You will recall from an earlier section that government transfer payments are made to welfare recipients, people receiving unemployment compensation or Social Security, and so forth. Also, there are business transfer payments—pensions and other payments made by firms that are not in exchange for current productive services.

Knowing national income, it is easy to derive personal income. You begin by subtracting corporate profits from national income and adding dividends to the result. This will correct for the fact that profits not distributed as dividends do not actually enter people's hands. Then you must deduct contributions for social insurance, and add government and business transfer payments. (Note once again that interest paid by governments on their debt is regarded as a transfer payment, on the grounds that it is not a payment for current goods and services.) These calculations are shown in detail in Table 4.8.

**DISPOSABLE INCOME.**   It is also useful for many purposes to know how much of their personal income people get to keep after personal taxes. This is **disposable income.** Having calculated personal income, you can obtain disposable income by deducting personal taxes from personal income, as shown in Table 4.8. Disposable income plays a very important role in subsequent chapters because it has a major influence on how much consumers spend. According to Table 4.8, disposable income equaled about 70 percent of gross national product in 1990.

**Table 4.8**
**Gross National Product, Net National Product, National Income, Personal Income, and Disposable Income, United States, 1990**

| MEASURE | AMOUNT[a] (BILLIONS OF DOLLARS) |
|---|---|
| Gross national product | 5,465 |
| Subtract: Depreciation | 576 |
| Net national product | 4,889 |
| Subtract: Indirect business taxes | 440 |
| Business transfers | 35 |
| Statistical discrepancy | –2 |
| Add: Subsidies less surpluses of government enterprises | 3 |
| National income | 4,418 |
| Subtract: Corporate profits | 298 |
| Contributions for social insurance | 507 |
| Add: Government transfers to persons | 660 |
| Dividends | 124 |
| Business transfers | 35 |
| Other items | 214 |
| Personal income | 4,646 |
| Subtract: Personal taxes | 699 |
| Disposable income | 3,946 |

[a] Because of rounding errors, figures do not always sum to totals.
*Source:* U.S. Department of Commerce.

[2] Two other small items must also be taken into account. As shown in Table 4.8, we must subtract *business transfer payments*—pensions and other payments made by firms that are transfer payments—and add *subsidies less surpluses of government enterprises,* which corrects for the fact that some government agencies pay out more to income recipients than they produce in value-added. In addition, of course, there is a statistical discrepancy that must be recognized. It is purely a statistical matter.

1. Given the following data (in millions of dollars) concerning the Puritanian economy in 1992, compute its gross national product and net national product.

| | |
|---|---|
| Gross private domestic investment | 400 |
| Personal consumption expenditure | 1,000 |
| Exports | 300 |
| Imports | 100 |
| Government purchases | 300 |
| Increase in inventories | 50 |
| Depreciation | 100 |

2. An economic historian, after careful research, makes the following estimates (in millions of dollars) concerning the Puritanian economy in 1910.

| | |
|---|---|
| Disposable income | 400 |
| Business transfer payments | 0 |
| Statistical discrepancy | 0 |
| Subsidies less surpluses of government enterprises | 0 |
| Net national product | 600 |
| National income | 550 |
| Personal income | 460 |

How much were personal taxes and indirect business taxes in Puritania in 1910?

3. Based on the following data (in millions of dollars), use the income approach to determine GNP.

| | |
|---|---|
| Compensation of employees | 50 |
| Interest | 10 |
| Rents | 5 |
| Indirect business taxes | 8 |
| Corporate profits | 10 |
| Transfer payments | 22 |
| Proprietors' income | 6 |
| Depreciation | 4 |

4. What is the difference between gross private domestic investment and net private domestic investment? Can the former be less than the latter? If the latter is negative, does this mean that the nation's capital stock is increasing or decreasing? Explain.

5. In 1989, there was a $28.3-billion increase in business inventories. Why should this be regarded as a form of investment? Explain why GNP would be calculated incorrectly if this increase in inventories were ignored?

6. Which of the following are included in calculating GNP this year? (a) Interest on a government bond; (b) Payment by the government to a naval officer; (c) Wages paid by the University of Michigan to a professor; (d) Payment for a secondhand car by a Florida student; (e) The amount a husband would be willing to pay for his wife's housekeeping services; (f) The amount John Jones pays for 30 shares of IBM stock; (g) The allowance a father gives his 12-year-old child.

## SUMMARY

1. One of the key indicators of the health of any nation's economy is the gross national product, which measures the total value of the final goods and services the nation produces in a particular period.[3] Since gross national product is affected by the price level, it must be deflated by a price index to correct for price-level changes. When deflated in this way, GNP is called real GNP, or GNP in constant dollars.

2. There are many pitfalls in calculating the gross national product. One must avoid counting the same output more than once. Purely financial transactions that do not reflect current production must be excluded. Also, some final goods and services that must be included in GNP are not bought and sold in the marketplace, so they are valued at what they cost.

3. GNP is not an ideal measure of total economic output, let alone a satisfactory measure of economic well-being. It takes no account of a nation's population, the amount of leisure time, or the distribution of income. It does not reflect many changes in the quality of goods and many social costs like pollution.

4. One approach to GNP is the expenditures approach, which regards GNP as the sum of all the expenditures that are involved in taking the total output of final goods and services off the market.

5. Another approach to GNP is the income approach, which regards GNP as the sum of incomes derived from the

[3] Note that investment goods are one form of final goods produced, and that inventory changes are part of investment. Recall our discussion of Table 4.4.

production of this year's output (plus depreciation and indirect business taxes).

6. Economists distinguish among four broad categories of spending: personal consumption expenditures, gross private domestic investment, government purchases, and net exports.

7. Net national product is gross national product minus depreciation. It indicates the value of net output when account is taken of capital used up. National income is the total amount of income paid out (or owed) by employers; personal income is the total amount people actually receive in income; and disposable income is the total amount they get to keep after taxes.

## CONCEPTS FOR REVIEW

**Gross national product**
**National income accounts**
**Final goods and services**
**Intermediate goods**
**Transfer payments**
**Base year**
**Current dollars**
**Constant dollars**
**Real gross national product**
**Price index**
**Deflating**

**Value-added**
**Net national product**
**Expenditures approach to GNP**
**Personal consumption expenditures**
**Gross private domestic investment**
**Government purchases**
**Net exports**
**Income approach to GNP**

**Compensation of employees**
**Rent**
**Interest**
**Proprietors' income**
**Corporate profits**
**Depreciation**
**Indirect business taxes**
**National income**
**Personal income**
**Disposable income**

# UNEMPLOYMENT AND INFLATION: A FIRST LOOK

THE AMERICAN ECONOMY ADDED about 17 million new jobs between 1980 and 1988. As we shall see in this chapter, the "great American job machine" was the envy of Western Europe where the unemployment rate remained close to 10 percent from 1984 to 1988. Unemployment is widely feared, both here and abroad. So is inflation, as we saw in Chapter 1. In this chapter, we take an introductory look at both of these economic problems.

## UNEMPLOYMENT

Almost a century ago, Pope Leo XIII said, "Among the purposes of a society should be to arrange for a continuous supply of work at all times and seasons."[1] Why should we be concerned about the unemployed? Because some of them become demoralized, suffer loss of prestige and status, and their families tend to break apart. Sometimes they are pushed toward crime and drugs; often they feel despair. Their children may be innocent victims, too. Indeed, perhaps the most devastating effects of unemployment are on children, whose education, health, and security may be ruined.

Of course, this does not mean that all unemployment, whatever its cause or nature, should be eliminated. (For example, some unemployment may be voluntary.) According to the U.S. government, any person 16 years of age or older who does not have a job and is looking for one is unemployed. Since this definition is necessarily quite broad, it is important that we distinguish among several different kinds of unemployment.

### Frictional Unemployment

Some people quit their jobs and look for something better. They may get angry at their bosses, or they may feel that they can get more money elsewhere. Others, particularly ex-students, are looking for their first job. Still others are temporarily laid off because their work is seasonal, as in the construction industry. Unemployment of this sort is called **frictional un-**

---

[1] Pope Leo XIII, "Encyclical Letter on the Conditions of Labor," May 15, 1891.

**employment.** Frictional unemployment is inevitable, since people find it desirable to change jobs, and such job changes often involve a period of temporary unemployment.

John Caruso may quit his job after the boss calls him a fathead. It may take him a month to find another job, perhaps because he is unaware of job opportunities or perhaps because the boss was right. During this month, he is numbered among the unemployed. We don't necessarily think that unemployment of this sort is a good thing, but it would not make much sense to try to eliminate it entirely. On the contrary, a free labor market could not function without a certain amount of frictional unemployment.

## Structural Unemployment

Changes continually occur in the nature of consumer demand and in technology. For example, consumers grow tired of one good and become infatuated with another. And new technologies supplant old ones. Thus some workers are thrown out of work, and because the new goods and the new technologies call for different skills than the old ones did, they cannot use their skills elsewhere. Unemployment of this sort is called **structural unemployment.** It exists when jobs are available for qualified workers, but the unemployed do not have the necessary qualifications. This sort of unemployment results from a mismatch between job requirements and the skills of the unemployed. Consider the case of Mary Jones, a 58-year old bookkeeper who was thrown out of work by the introduction of a new technology and who lacks the skills needed to get a job in another field. Ms. Jones is one of the structurally unemployed.

## Cyclical Unemployment

**Cyclical unemployment** occurs when, because of an insufficiency of aggregate demand, there are more workers looking for work than there are jobs. Cyclical unemployment is associated with business fluctuations, or the so-called business cycle. Industrialized capitalistic economies have been subject to fluctuations, with booms often succeeding busts and vice versa. (More will be said about the nature and recent history of business fluctuations in Chapter 8.) One feature of these fluctuations has been that the American economy has periodically gone through depressions, during which unemployment has been high. The Great Depression of the 1930s was particularly long and severe, and when World War II ended, many Americans worried that the gigantic social costs of the enormous unemployment of the 1930s might be repeated in the postwar period. In response, Congress passed the Employment Act of 1946, which says,

> It is the continuing policy and responsibility of the Federal Government to use all practicable means . . . [to create and maintain] conditions under which there will be afforded useful employment opportunities, including self-employment, for those able, willing, and seeking to work and to promote maximum employment, production, and purchasing power.

In subsequent chapters, we shall see how, and with what success, the federal government has tried to meet this commitment to combat cyclical unemployment.

# THE MEASUREMENT AND INCIDENCE OF UN-EMPLOYMENT

Having discussed various types of unemployment, we must look next at the way in which the unemployment rate is measured in the United States and at the characteristics of the unemployed.

## The Unemployment Rate

Each month, the federal government conducts a scientific survey of the American people, asking a carefully selected sample of the population whether they have a job, and, if not, whether they are looking for one. According to most expert opinion, the resulting figures are quite reliable but subject to a number of qualifications. One of these is that the figures do not indicate the extent to which people are underemployed. Some people work only part-time, or at jobs well below their level of education or skill, but the government figures count them as fully employed. Also, some people have given up looking for a job and are no longer listed among the unemployed, even though they would be glad to get work if any was offered. To be counted as unemployed in the government figures, one must be actively seeking employment.

To obtain the unemployment rate, the Bureau of Labor Statistics (the government agency responsible for producing the unemployment data) divides the estimated number of people who are unemployed by the estimated number of people in the *labor force*. To be in the labor force, a person must either be employed or unemployed. Note that the unemployment rate can rise either because people who formerly were employed are thrown out of work or because people who formerly were not in the labor force decide to look for jobs. For example, an increasing number of married women who decide to enter the labor force may tend to raise the unemployment rate.

Some critics of the official unemployment statistics would use a definition of unemployment that focuses attention on "serious" cases of joblessness. They would exclude unemployed people with a working spouse, unemployed teenagers living with a parent with a job, and unemployed people who have been out of work less than a month. Also, they would have the government try harder to find out whether those who say they are unemployed are making a serious effort to find work. Officials of the Bureau of Labor Statistics reply that such a change in definition would convert the statistics into a measure of hardship rather than of unemployment.

In interpreting the unemployment statistics, do not jump to the conclusion that unemployment means starvation. For one thing, unemployed workers may receive unemployment insurance. In most states, the average worker, if fired or laid off, can collect about one-half of his or her wages for up to 26 weeks. (However, in 1989, only a minority of the unemployed were eligible.) According to many economists, unemployment insurance increases unemployment, since it encourages (or at least enables) some of the jobless to remain unemployed longer than they otherwise would. Estimates of the size of the increase in the unemployment rate due to unemployment insurance range from about 0.2 to 1.2 percentage points.

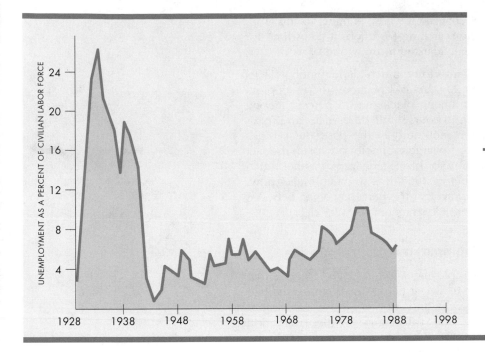

**Figure 5.1**
**Unemployment Rates, United States, 1929-90**
The unemployment rate has varied substantially. Fortunately, since World War II it has not approached the very high levels of the Great Depression of the 1930s. But the recession of 1981 showed that the nation is not immune to severe bouts of unemployment.

## How Much Unemployment Is There?

To get some idea of the extent of unemployment, we can consult Figure 5.1, which shows the percent of the labor force unemployed during each year from 1929 to 1990. Note the wide fluctuations in the unemployment rate, and the very high unemployment rates during the 1930s. Fortunately, unemployment since World War II has never approached the tragically high levels of the Great Depression of the 1930s. Between 1958 and 1964, it averaged about 6 percent, and then declined steadily until it fell below 4 percent in 1966–69. In 1970–74, it bounced back up to 5 or 6 percent, and then rose to 8.5 percent in 1975, after which it receded to 5.8 percent in 1979. In 1981 and 1982, it rose to about 9.5 percent, after which it fell to about 5.2 percent in 1989, after which it began to rise in 1990 and 1991. Although many of these variations in the unemployment rate may seem small, they are important. With a labor force of over 100 million in the United States, a 1 percentage point increase in the unemployment rate means that over 1 million more people are unemployed.

## Who Are the Unemployed?

The overall unemployment rate indicates what percentage of the labor force is out of work, but it doesn't tell us whether the unemployed are young or old, white or black. A closer look at the unemployed is in order.

TEENAGERS.    The unemployment rate tends to be higher among younger than older segments of tha labor force. As shown in Table 5.1, the unemployment rate among teenagers is extremely high. In 1990, it was 14 percent for white males, 13 percent for white females, 32 percent for black males, and 30 percent for black females. To a considerable extent, this is

**Table 5.1**
**Unemployment Rate, Selected Segments of the Population, United States, 1990**

| POPULATION SEGMENT | UNEMPLOYMENT RATE |
|---|---|
| Whites | |
| Males | |
| 16–19 years | 14.2 |
| 20 years and over | 4.3 |
| Females | |
| 16–19 years | 12.6 |
| 20 years and over | 4.1 |
| Blacks | |
| Males | |
| 16–19 years | 32.1 |
| 20 years and over | 10.4 |
| Females | |
| 16–19 years | 30.0 |
| 20 years and over | 9.6 |

*Source:* Economic Report of the President, 1991. ·

frictional unemployment. Many teenagers are new entrants to the labor force. They must spend some time searching for a job. It takes time for them to find a suitable job and to get adjusted to the world of work.

**BLACKS.** The unemployment rate tends to be much higher among blacks than among whites. Among males 20 years old or more, the unemployment rate in 1990 was 10 percent among blacks and 4 percent among whites (Table 5.1). To some extent, of course, this difference can probably be explained by discrimination, now and in the past. But puzzles exist. For example, experts seem to be largely unable to explain the fact that, whereas the unemployment rate for black teenagers was not much different than for white teenagers before 1955, it is so much higher now. Moreover, this occurred despite the fact that the percentage gap between black and white adult unemployment rates has not risen for decades.

## Duration and Reasons for Unemployment

A noteworthy characteristic of unemployment in the United States is that most of it is quite temporary. In 1990, almost half of the unemployed had been without jobs for less than 5 weeks, and another third had been jobless for 5 to 14 weeks. However, as shown in Figure 5.2, the proportion of the unemployed out of work for 27 weeks or longer goes up during years like 1982, when the unemployment rate is high.

Also, as pointed out above, unemployment is not always due to a per-

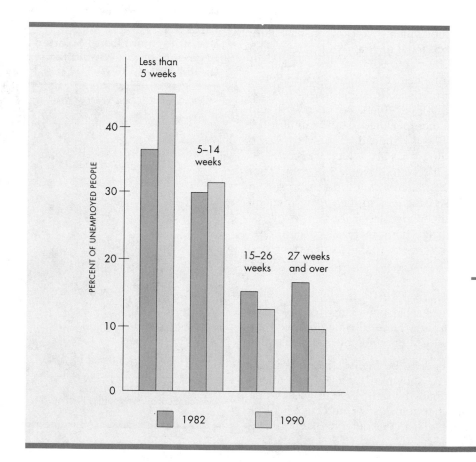

**Figure 5.2**
**Duration of Unemployment, 1982 and 1990**
The bulk of the unemployed have been without jobs for a relatively short period of time. However, the percentage that are jobless for substantial periods of time is greater in years of relatively high unemployment, such as 1982, than in years of prosperity.

son's losing his or her job. In 1990, only about half of the unemployed had lost their jobs; the rest had left their jobs or were re-entering the labor force or entering it for the first time.

## The Costs of Unemployment

Most economists believe that very high levels of unemployment impose great costs on society. In this section, we describe these costs, which are both economic and noneconomic, in more detail.

### Economic Costs

According to most economists, *unemployment can result in substantial economic costs, since it reduces the amount of goods and services produced by society.* To determine how much society loses in this way by tolerating an unemployment rate above the minimum level resulting from frictional (and some structural) unemployment, economists estimate the **potential GNP**, which is the level of gross national product that could be achieved if there had been full employment. Thus, if full employment is defined as a 5 percent unemployment rate, potential GNP can be estimated by multiplying 95 percent of the labor force times the normal hours of work per year times the average output per hour of work at the relevant time.

If actual GNP is less than potential GNP, the estimated gap between actual and potential GNP is a measure of what society loses by tolerating less than full employment. Figure 5.3 shows the estimated size of this gap from 1952 to 1990. (Note than both actual and potential GNP are expressed in 1972 prices.) Clearly, the economic costs of unemployment have been substantial. Consider 1975, a recession year when unemployment was about 8.5 percent. As shown in Figure 5.3, society lost about $100 billion in that year alone. Although this estimate is very rough, it is

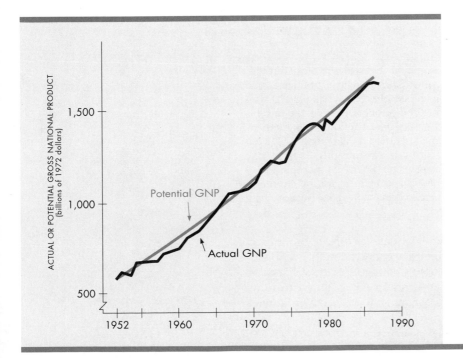

**Figure 5.3**
**Actual and Potential GNP, United States, 1952–90**
When potential GNP exceeds actual GNP, the gap is a measure of what society loses because there is less than full employment. In Figure 8.1, we show this gap in earlier years.

accurate enought to suggest the social waste that accompanies large-scale unemployment.

One important problem in estimating this gap stems from the difficulty of defining "full employment." For many years, a common definition of *full employment* was a 4 percent unemployment rate, since it was felt that frictional and structural unemployment could not be reduced below this level. During the seventies, there was criticism of this definition on the grounds that an unemployment rate of about 5 percent was a more realistic measure because there were more young people, women, and minority workers in the labor force. All of these groups find it relatively difficult to find jobs. In the 1980s, many economists felt that 6 percent (or higher) was a more appropriate figure. More will be said on this score in the section after next.

## Noneconomic Costs

Unemployment can strike at the social fabric of families and societies; it is not merely an economic phenomenon. Since general descriptions of the plight of the unemployed often have relatively little impact, a real-life case study may give you a better feel for what unemployment is like. Consider Joseph Torrio, a New Haven factory worker who was laid off after 18 years on the job. He describes in his own words how he spent several mornings:

> Up at seven, cup of coffee, and off to Sargent's. Like to be there when the gang comes to work, the lucky devils. Employment manager not in. Waited in his outer office. . . . Three others waiting, two reporting for compensation. Other one laid off two weeks ago and said he called at office every day. He inquired what I was doing and when I said "looking for work" he laughed. "You never work here? No? What chance you think you got when 400 like me who belong here out?" Employment manager showed up at 9:30. I had waited two hours. My time has no value. A pleasant fellow; told me in a kind but snappy way business was very bad. What about the future, would he take my name? Said he referred only to the present. Nothing more for me to say, so left. Two more had drifted into office. Suppose they got the same story. Must be a lot of men in New Haven that have heard it by now.
>
> [On May 21], interview with sales manager of the Real Silk Hosiery Mills. Had seen their ads for salesmen in the paper. Sales manager approached me with his hand sticking out, the first one who had offered to shake hands with me. I told him my name and inquired about the position. He took me into his private office, well furnished, and asked me if I had had any selling experience. I told him that I hadn't any but I thought I could do the work. . . . Asked me to report at 9 A.M. the next morning for further instructions. . . . [On May 22], I kept my appointment with the sales manager. Spent the morning learning different kinds of stockings. Made another appointment for the afternoon which I did not keep because he wanted me to bring along $6 as security on a bag and some stock. I did not have the $6.[2]

No single case study can give you an adequate picture of the impact on people of being without a job. There are a wide variety of responses to involuntary unemployment. Some people weather it pretty well, others sink into despair; some people have substantial savings they can draw on, others are hard pressed; some people manage to shield their families

[2] E.W. Bakke, *The Unemployed Worker*, Hamden, Conn.: Archon, 1969, pp. 168, 169, 174, 175.

from the blow, others allow their misfortunes to spread to the rest of the family. But despite these variations, being without work can deal a heavy blow to a person's feeling of worth. It can hit hard at a person's self-image, indicating that he or she is not needed, cannot support a family, is not really a full and valuable member of society. The impact of widespread and persistent unemployment is most clearly visible at present among the blacks and other racial minorities, where unemployment rates are much higher than among the white population. Unquestionably, the prevalence of unemployment among blacks greatly influences how they view themselves, as well as the way they interact with others in the community.

## The Natural Rate of Unemployment

The **natural rate of unemployment** is the unemployment rate when the economy is at full employment. As pointed out in the section before last, full employment is hard to define, and controversies swirl over the level of the natural rate of unemployment. Nonetheless, many economists regard the natural rate of unemployment as a useful concept. Basically, economists try to measure it by finding the unemployment rate that does not result in an increase (or decrease) in the rate of inflation. The idea is that, if the unemployment rate were pushed below the natural rate, the rate of inflation would rise unacceptably.[3]

In the early 1990s, many economists believed that the natural rate of unemployment in the United States was between 5 and 6 percent. As pointed out in the section before last, there is a widespread belief that the natural rate of unemployment tended to increase during the 1960s, 1970s, and early 1980s. In part, this was because teenagers and minorities increased as a percentage of the labor force. Since these groups have high unemployment rates, this would be expected to raise the overall unemployment rate. Also, unemployment insurance became more generous in the late 1960s and 1970s than in the 1950s and early 1960s. Consequently, unemployed workers probably searched less intensively for a new job and were more reluctant to take low-paying employment. Further, because of an increase in the amount of resource reallocation among industries and areas (the decline of the auto and steel industries, the problems of the midwestern Rust Belt, and so on), structural unemployment rose.

During the middle and late 1980s, there was evidence that the natural rate of unemployment reversed direction and fell, due in considerable measure to the aging of people who formerly were teenagers. In other words, the baby-boom generation moved into age groups with lower frictional and structural unemployment rates. According to the Council of Economic Advisers, this contributed about 0.5 percentage point to the decline in the natural unemployment rate in the 1980s.

While many economists use the concept of the natural rate of unemployment, this does not mean that questions do not exist concerning its interpretation. For example, according to studies by MIT's Olivier Blanchard and Harvard's Lawrence Summers, the natural rate of unemployment depends on the actual rate of unemployment. This phenomenon is known as **hysteresis**. If this is the case, the natural rate of unemployment is not determined only by factors like the age distribution of the

Olivier Blanchard

Lawrence Summers

[3] Another name for the natural rate of unemployment is the "non-accelerating-inflation rate of unemployment," or NAIRU.

population, the size of unemployment insurance benefits, and the amount of resource reallocation among industries and areas. Instead, it will tend to rise if the actual unemployment rate rises, and it will tend to fall if the actual unemployment rate falls. However, this is not a settled matter: many questions have been raised concerning the extent to which hysteresis really is present in the American economy.

In addition, there is controversy over what can and should be done about high levels of unemployment. Many economists argue that the natural rate of unemployment is between 5 and 6 percent, and that unemployment above the natural rate should not be tolerated. But not all economists agree. As we shall see, some think that the natural rate of unemployment is variable and that the fluctuations in the actual unemployment rate are due in considerable measure to the variation in the natural rate. This controversy will be discussed at length in subsequent chapters.

## THEORIES OF UNEMPLOYMENT

### The Classical View of Unemployment

Until the 1930s, most economists were convinced that the price system, left to its own devices, would hold unemployment to a reasonable minimum. Thus most of the great names of economics in the nineteenth and early twentieth centuries—including John Stuart Mill, Alfred Marshall, and A.C. Pigou—felt that there was no need for government intervention to promote a high level of employment. To be sure, they recognized that unemployment was sometimes large, but they regarded these lapses from high employment as temporary aberrations that the price system would cure automatically. We begin by taking an initial, brief look at why the classical economists felt this was true. (More will be said below and in later chapters about their theories.)

The classical economists recognized the fact that the level of total spending determines the unemployment rate. They believed that total spending was unlikely to be too small to purchase the full-employment level of output, because of **Say's Law** (named after the nineteenth-century French economist, J.B. Say). According to this law, the production of a certain amount of goods and services results in the generation of an amount of income which, if spent, is precisely sufficient to buy that output. (Recall the circular flow discussed in Chapters 3 and 4.) In other words, *supply creates its own demand, since the total amount paid out by the producers of the goods and services to resource owners must equal the value of the goods and services. Thus, if this amount is spent, it must be sufficient to purchase all of the goods and services that are produced.*

But what if resource owners do not spend all of their income, but save some of it instead? How, then, will the necessary spending arise to take all of the output off the market? The answer the classical economists offered is that each dollar saved will be invested. Therefore, investment (made largely by business firms) will restore to the spending stream what resource owners take out through the saving process. Recall that the economist's definition of investment is different from the one often used in common parlance. To the economist, investment means expenditure on plant, equipment, and other productive assets. The classical economists believed that the amount invested would automatically equal the amount saved because the interest rate—the price paid for borrowing

The ideas of **John Stuart Mill** (1806–73) and his arguments in support of individual freedom are particularly famous. He was one of the great philosophers of the nineteenth century. He was also a great economist; his *Principles of Political Economy* (1848) is his best-known work. He advocated many social reforms, including shorter working hours and tax reform.

money—would fluctuate in such a way as to maintain equality between them. In other words, there is a market for loanable funds, and the interest rate will vary so that the quantity of funds supplied equals the quantity demanded. Thus, since funds are demanded to be used—that is, invested—the amount saved will be invested.

Further, the classical economists said that the amount of goods and services firms can sell depends upon the prices they charge, as well as on total spending. For example, $1 million in spending will take 100 cars off the market if the price is $10,000 per car, and 200 cars off the market if the price is $5,000 per car. Recognizing this, the classical economists argued that firms would cut prices to sell their output. Competition among

---

# EXAMPLE 5.1 SHOULD WE LOOK AT EMPLOYMENT, NOT UNEMPLOYMENT?

Some economists believe that the rate of employment is a better measure of job availability than the rate of unemployment. The civilian rate of employment is the number of persons employed (over 16 years of age) in the civilian labor force divided by the number of persons (over 16) in the noninstitutional population (which excludes people in penal, mental, and nursing institutions). Changes over time in the rate of employment and the rate of unemployment are shown in the graph below.

(a) What advantages are there in using the rate of employment? (b) Does it make any real difference as to which of these measures we use? (c) According to some economists, the gradual increase in the labor force participation of women has increased the rate of employment. Do you think that it has also influenced the unemployment rate? (d) Should we forget about the unemployment rate and focus attention only on the employment rate?

## Solution

(a) One advantage is that it does not depend on a judgment as to whether a person really is "available for work" or "actively seeking employment." Some economists feel that some people say they are looking for work, but really aren't. Other people who want work may be discouraged and give up looking for it. (b) Yes. For example, in the late 1970s, the rate of employment was high and growing, indicating that the economy was providing lots of job opportunities. At the same time, however, the unemployment rate also was high. (c) Yes. Female workers tend to move in and out of the labor force more than men. Also, men with working wives are under less pressure to stay at their present jobs or to minimize the length of time they are unemployed. (d) No. A high unemployment rate indicates that the labor market is not functioning efficiently. Both the employment rate and the unemployment rate should be considered.

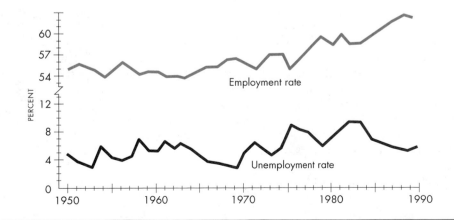

firms would prod them to reduce their prices in this way, with the result that the high-employment level of output would be taken off the market.

Looking at this process more closely, it is obvious that the prices of resources must also be reduced under such circumstances. Otherwise firms would incur losses because they would be getting less for their product, but paying no less for resources. The classical economists believed that it was realistic to expect the prices of resources to decline in such a situation. Indeed they were quite willing to assume that the wage rate—the price of labor—would be flexible in this way. Through the processes of competition for jobs, they felt that wage rates would be bid down to the level where everyone who really wanted to work could get a job.

## The Keynesian View of Unemployment

Son of a British economist who was famous in his own right, John Maynard Keynes (1883-1946) was enormously successful in a variety of fields. He published a brillant book on the theory of probability while still a relatively young man. Working for a half-hour in bed each morning, he made a fortune as a stock market speculator. He was a distinguished patron of the arts and a member of the Bloomsbury set, a group of London intellectuals who were the intellectual pacesetters for British society. He was a faculty member at Cambridge University and a key figure at the British Treasury. In short, he was an extraordinarily gifted and accomplished man.

In 1936, while the world was still in the throes of the Great Depression, Keynes published his *General Theory of Employment, Interest, and Money*.[4] His purpose in this book was to explain how the capitalist economic system could get stalled in the sort of depressed state of equilibrium that existed in the 1930s. He also tried to indicate how governments might help to solve the problem. Contrary to the classical economists, Keynes concluded that no automatic mechanism in a capitalistic society would generate a high level of employment—or, at least, would generate it quickly enough to be relied on in practice. Instead, the equilibrium level of national output might for a long time be below the level required to achieve high employment. His reasons for believing that this could be the case are discussed in detail in this and subsequent chapters.

There were at least two basic flaws in the classical model, as Keynes and his followers saw it. First, in their view, *there is no assurance that intended saving will equal intended investment at a level ensuring high employment*. The people and firms who save are often not the same as the people and firms who invest, and they often have quite different motivations. In particular, a considerable amount of saving is done by families who want to put something aside for a rainy day or for a car or appliance. On the other hand, a considerable amount of investment is done by firms that are interested in increasing their profits by expanding their plants or by installing new equipment. According to Keynes, one cannot be sure that changes in the interest rate will bring about the equality of saving and investment visualized by the classical economists. In his view, intended saving may not equal intended investment at a level ensuring high employment. Instead, they may be equal at a level corresponding to considerable unemployment (or to considerable inflation). Thus a purely

Crowd outside employment office, 1931

[4] John Maynard Keynes, *The General Theory of Employment, Interest, and Money*, New York: Harcourt, Brace, 1936.

# WHY SO MUCH UNEMPLOYMENT IN EUROPE?

During 1980-82, the unemployment rate rose from about 5 percent to 10.percent in Europe, as shown in the graph below. In the United States, too, the unemployment rate rose substantially during this period. This was the time of the 1981-82 recession, when national output dropped in many countries, so an increase in unemployment was to be expected. But subsequently, whereas the unemployment rate fell substantially in the United States, it did not change at all in Europe. From 1984 to 1988, the unemployment rate remained close to 10 percent in Europe. Moreover, in many European countries, most of the unemployed were without a job for over a year.

Further, they claim that high European tax rates have discouraged the formation of small firms, which have played an important role in the growth of employment in the United States. In their view, all of these factors have increased the natural rate of unemployment in Europe.

*Other economists attribute the increase in the natural rate to hysteresis.* They argue that the natural rate goes up or down in response to increases or decreases in the actual unemployment rate. Thus, because of the substantial and more-or-less continuous increase in the actual unemployment rate in Europe from about 1960 to about 1985, the natural rate rose.

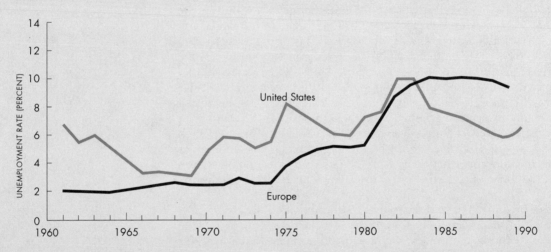

According to many economists, the natural rate of unemployment in Europe during 1987-89 was about 9 to 9.5 percent. This was much higher than in the United States where, as we have seen, it was estimated to be about 5 or 6 percent. Also, it was much higher than it had been in Europe about a quarter of a century before; in the early 1960s, it seemed to be only about 2 percent.

*Some economists believe that European unemployment is high because of a disease they call Eurosclerosis, which manifests itself in excessive government regulation, overly generous unemployment insurance, and high tax rates.* For example, they cite layoff regulations, restrictions on shop-opening hours, and plant-closing laws as factors that increase unemployment. Also, they hold that unemployment benefits have been great enough to shield the jobless from the necessity of searching seriously for a job.

Why? Because long-term unemployment resulted in a decrease in the skills of the jobless, because the productive capacity of the economy fell during the period of substantial unemployment, and for other reasons.

Without further research, it is impossible to tell whether the first hypothesis (Eurosclerosis) or the second hypothesis (hysteresis) or some mixture of both is closest to the mark. But no further research is needed to confirm the fact that the American economy added about 17 million new jobs between 1980 and 1988. Clearly, we did a great deal better than Europe in this regard. Indeed, the Europeans often refer with unconcealed envy to the "great American job machine."[1]

[1] This discussion is based in considerable part on R. Gordon, *Macroeconomics*, fifth edition, Glenview, Ill.: Scott Foresman, 1990.

capitalist economic system, in the absence of appropriate government policies, has no dependable rudder to keep it clear of the shoals of serious unemployment or of serious inflation.

Second, *Keynes and his followers objected to the classical economists' assumption that prices and wages are flexible.* They contended that, contrary to the classical economists' view, the modern economy contains many departures from perfect competition that are barriers to downward flexibility of prices and wages. In particular, many important industries are dominated by a few producers who try hard to avoid cutting prices. Even in the face of a considerable drop in demand, such industries have sometimes maintained extraordinarily stable prices. Moreover, the labor unions fight hard to avoid wage cuts. In view of these facts of life, Keynes believed that the classical assumption of wage and price flexibility was unrealistic, and he questioned whether price and wage reductions can be depended on to maintain full employment.

## The New Classical Macroeconomists and the New Keynesians

Over forty years have elapsed since Keynes's death, and theories of unemployment have continued to develop and change. Even during the 1950s and 1960s, Keynes's views were challenged by an influential minority of economists known as the *monetarists*. This group, discussed in Chapter 10, stresses the influence of changes in the money supply on the economy. During the 1970s and 1980s, other groups—such as the supply-side economists, discussed in Chapter 9, and the *new classical macroeconomists* discussed in Chapter 14—mounted an attack on Keynesian views. In many respects, the new classical macroeconomists harked back to the classical view of unemployment; in particular, they rejected Keynes's argument that prices and wages are inflexible. (Macroeconomics is the part of economics that deals with the behavior of economic aggregates like national output, the price level, and the level of unemployment.)

Keynes's own ideas have been extended and modified. Just as there is a new classical macroeconomics, so there is a new Keynesianism. Like the original Keynesians, the new Keynesians do not believe that markets clear continuously; that is, they do not believe that the quantity demanded of a product or input always equals the quantity supplied. In their view, the economy can stay in a state of disequilibrium for years if prices adjust slowly enough. But whereas old Keynesians merely assumed that wages tend to be rigid and that prices are sticky, new Keynesians have developed theories (described in Chapter 14) to help explain why such wage and price stability can be expected, given the rational behavior of individuals and firms.

It is essential to understand at the outset that the new classical macroeconomists view unemployment in an entirely different way than do the new Keynesians. *The new classical macroeconomists believe that the wage rate (which is the price of labor) is flexible.* To see what this means, suppose that the demand curve for labor is as shown in panel A of Figure 5.4. Thus, if the price of labor (that is, the wage rate) is $12 per hour, employers will demand 84 million workers, whereas if it is $8 per hour, employers will demand 90 million workers. Suppose too that the supply curve for labor is as shown in panel A of Figure 5.4. Thus, if the wage rate is $12 per hour, 98 million workers will be willing to work, whereas if it is $8 per hour, 90 million workers will be willing to work.

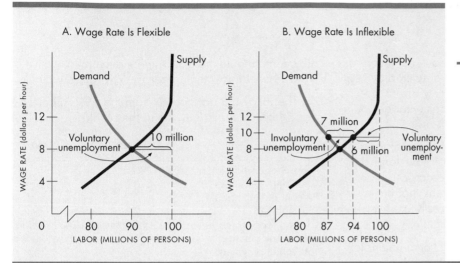

**Figure 5.4**
**Involuntary and Voluntary Unemployment, Where the Wage Rate Is Flexible or Inflexible**
If the wage rate is completely flexible, as in panel A, no involuntary unemployment exists, whereas if the wage rate is inflexible, as in panel B, there is involuntary employment (7 million in panel B). In panel A, voluntary unemployment equals 10 million; in panel B, it equals 6 million.

In this situation, the new classical macroeconomists argue that the wage rate will move to the level where the quantity of labor demanded equals the quantity supplied. In other words, the wage rate will move from whatever it was in the past to $8, the new equilibrium level. At this level, there is no involuntary unemployment. All of the people who are willing to work at this wage rate can find jobs. In particular, 90 million workers seek work when the wage rate is $8 per hour; all find jobs.

Of course, this does not mean that there is no unemployment. If the total number of people who can work is 100 million, there must be 10 million who are unemployed (since 90 million will find jobs, according to panel A of Figure 5.4). But the point is that they are *voluntarily unemployed*. According to the new classical macroeconomists, there is no involuntary unemployment.

On the other hand, *the new Keynesians, like the original Keynesians, believe that the wage rate is inflexible.* Suppose that the demand and supply curves for labor are the same as in panel A of Figure 5.4, but that the wage rate in the past has been about $10 per hour. If the wage rate falls only to $9.50 per hour, panel B of Figure 5.4 shows that the quantity of labor supplied will exceed the quantity of labor demanded. Specifically, 94 million workers will seek work at this wage rate, but only 87 million will find jobs. Thus 7 million workers will be involuntarily unemployed. In addition, 6 million workers will be voluntarily unemployed.

Why do the new Keynesians insist that wages are inflexible? Basically, because wage rates are set for a considerable period of time, and are not adjusted frequently. According to the new Keynesians, there are many costs involved in changing the wage rates that a firm pays, so changes are made only at intervals of perhaps a year or more. Union contracts typically extend for three years. In addition, a variety of other arguments are given by the new Keynesians, as we shall see in Chapter 14.

In subsequent chapters, much more will be said about the controversies among various groups of economists—classical, Keynesian, monetarist, supply-side, new classical, and new Keynesian—over the determinants and interpretation of unemployment. But at the outset, it should be recognized that whereas most economists regard unemployment as a social waste, not all economists do. In particular, the new classical macroeconomists view unemployment typically as being voluntary.

## TEST YOURSELF

1. "Unemployed workers make about as much as when they were employed because of unemployment insurance, so the nation need not worry about the unemployed." Specify at least two fundamental errors in this statement.

2. The unemployment rate shows the percentage of the labor force out of work, but not how long they have been out of work. Does the average duration of unemployment matter too? Do you think that the average duration of unemployment is directly or inversely related to the unemployment rate? Explain.

3. Explain the differences among frictional unemployment, structural unemployment, and cyclical unemployment. Should the government attempt to reduce all types of unemployment to zero? Why, or why not?

4. The following data came from the 1991 *Economic Report of the President*. Fill in the blanks.

|  | 1989 | 1990 |
|---|---|---|
| Percent of civilian labor force unemployed | 5.3 | 5.5 |
| Percent of civilian labor force employed | ____ | ____ |
| Civilian labor force | 123.9 million | 124.8 million |
| Total employment | ____ | ____ |
| Total unemployment | ____ | ____ |

## INFLATION

Economic problems as well as economic theories have changed in the forty-five years since Keynes's death. The Great Depression of the 1930s is a distant memory, while double-digit inflation is fresh in the minds of everyone over 30 years of age. The unemployment problem is still of concern to the American people, but the electorate has learned to fear inflation as well as unemployment.

It is hard to find anyone these days who does not know the meaning of inflation firsthand. Try to think of commodities you regularly purchase that cost less now than they did several years ago. Chances are that you can come up with precious few. *Inflation* is a general upward movement of prices. In other words, inflation means that goods and services that currently cost $10 may soon be priced at $11 or even $12, and wages and other input prices increase as well. It is essential to distinguish between the movements of individual prices and the movement of the entire price level. As we saw in Chapter 3, the price of an individual commodity can move up or down with the shifts in the commodity's demand or supply curve. If the price of a particular good—corn, say—goes up, this need not be inflation, since the prices of other goods may be going down at the same time, so that the overall price level—the general average level of prices—remains much the same. Inflation occurs only if most prices for goods and services in the society move upward—that is, if the average level of prices increases.

In periods of inflation, the value of money is reduced. A dollar is worth what it will buy, and what it will buy is determined by the price level. Thus a dollar was more valuable in 1940, when a Hershey chocolate bar was 5 cents, than in 1991, when it was about 50 cents. But it is important to recognize that inflations may vary in severity. ***Runaway inflations*** wipe out the value of money quickly and thoroughly, while ***creeping inflations*** erode its value gradually and slowly. There is a lot of difference between runaway inflation and creeping inflation, as the following examples indicate.

UPHILL RACER

*Uphill Racer.* A 1980 cartoon shows the peril of soaring prices

## Runaway Inflation

The case of Germany after World War I is a good example of runaway inflation. Germany was required to pay large reparations to the victorious Allies after the war. Rather than attempting to tax its people to pay these amounts, the German government merely printed additional quantities of paper money. This new money increased total spending in Germany, and the increased spending resulted in higher prices because the war-devastated economy could not increase output substantially. As more and more money was printed, prices rose higher and higher, reaching utterly fantastic levels. By 1923, it took a *trillion* marks (the unit of German currency) to buy what one mark would buy before the war.

The effect of this runaway inflation was to disrupt the economy. Prices had to be adjusted from day to day. People rushed to the stores to spend the money they received as soon as possible, since very soon it would buy much less. Speculation was rampant. This inflation was a terrible blow to Germany. The middle class was wiped out; its savings became completely worthless. It is no wonder that Germany has in recent years been more sensitive than many other countries to the evils of inflation.

## Creeping Inflation

For the past 50 years, the price level in the United States has tended to go one way only—up. In practically all years during this period, prices have risen. Since 1955, there hasn't been a single year when the price level has fallen. Certainly, this has not been a runaway inflation, but it has resulted in a very substantial erosion in the value of the dollar. Like a beach slowly worn away by the ocean, the dollar has gradually lost a considerable portion of its value. Specifically, prices now tend to be about 5 times what they were 40 years ago. Thus the dollar now is worth about a fifth of what it was worth then. Although a creeping inflation of this sort is much less harmful than a runaway inflation, it has a number of unfortunate social consequences, which we describe in detail after indicating how inflation is measured.

# THE MEASUREMENT OF INFLATION

The most widely quoted measure of inflation in the United States is the Consumer Price Index, published monthly by the Bureau of Labor Statistics. Until 1978, the purpose of this index was to measure changes in prices of goods and services purchased by urban wage earners and clerical workers and their families. In 1978, the index was expanded to include all urban consumers (although the narrower index was not discontinued). The first step in calculating the index is to find out how much it costs in a particular month to buy a market basket of goods and services that is representative of the buying patterns of these consumers. Then this amount is expressed as a ratio of what it would have cost to buy the same market basket of goods and services in the base period (1982–84),[5] and this ratio is multiplied by 100. In contrast to the price indices in the previous chapter, this (like most commonly used indices) shows the *percentage,* not the proportional, change in the price level. For example, the Consumer Price Index equaled 133.8 in December 1990, which meant that it cost 33.8 percent more to buy this market basket in December 1990, than in 1982–84.

[5] Other base periods, such as 1967, have been used in the past.

To obtain results based on the previous chapter's definition of a price index, all we have to do is divide this index by 100.

The market basket of goods and services that is included in the Consumer Price Index is chosen with great care and is the result of an extensive survey of people's buying patterns. Among the items that are included are food, automobiles, clothing, homes, furniture, home supplies, drugs, fuel, doctors' fees, legal fees, rent, repairs, transportation fares, recreational goods, and so forth. Prices, as defined in the index, include sales and excise taxes. Also, real estate taxes, but not income or personal property taxes, are included in the index. Besides the overall index, a separate price index is computed for various types of goods or services, such as food, rent, new cars, medical services, and a variety of other items. Also, a separate index is computed for each of 28 metropolitan areas, as well as for the entire urban population.

The Consumer Price Index is widely used by industry and government. Labor agreements often stipulate that, to offset inflation, wages must increase in accord with changes in the index. Similarly, pensions, welfare payments, royalties, and even alimony payments are sometimes related to the index. However, this does not mean that it is an ideal, all-purpose measure of inflation. For one thing, it does not include the prices of industrial machinery or raw materials. For another thing, it is not confined to currently produced goods and services. For some purposes, it is less appropriate than other indices, such as the GNP deflator or the Producer Price Index.

Figure 5.5 shows the behavior of the Consumer Price Index since 1946. As pointed out in the previous section, the price level has increased considerably in the United States in the past 40 years. Substantial inflation followed World War II; the price level increased by about 24 percent be-

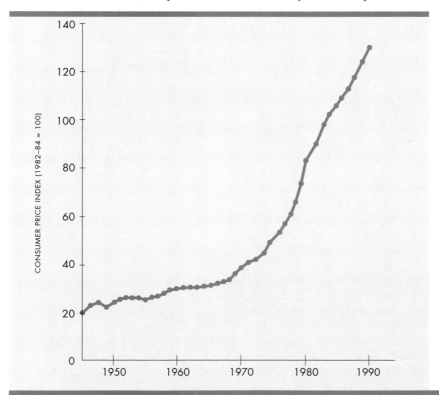

**Figure 5.5**
**Consumer Price Index, 1946–90**
Inflation has been a continual problem in the United States, particularly in the late 1970s and early 1980s.

tween 1946 and 1948. Bursts of inflation recurred during the Korean War and then during the Vietnam War. The 1970s were a period of particularly high inflation; between 1969 and 1979 the price level doubled. The 1980s began with more double-digit inflation, but there was a reduction in the inflation rate in 1982–91. How long this respite will continue is by no means certain.

## IMPACT OF INFLATION

Citizens and policy makers generally agree that inflation, like unemployment, should be minimized. Indeed, in 1981, the Council of Economic Advisers identified inflation as the chief economic problem confronting the United States. Even during 1991, when inflation had subsided substantially, there was widespread fear that it would increase again. Why is inflation so widely feared? What are its impacts? Inflation affects the distribution of income and wealth, as well as the level of output, as indicated below.

### Redistributive Effects

Because all money incomes do not go up at the same rate as prices, inflation results in an arbitrary redistribution of income. People with relatively fixed incomes, lenders, and savers tend to be hurt by it, and major inflations tend to cripple total output as well. To understand the redistributive effects of inflation, it is necessary to distinguish between **money income** and **real income.** A family's money income is its income measured in current dollars, whereas its real income is adjusted for changes in the price level. During periods of inflation, a family with a relatively fixed money income will experience a declining real income.

Suppose that the Murphy family earns $41,000 this year and $40,000 last year, and that the price level is 10 percent higher this year than last year. Under these circumstances, the Murphy family's money income has increased by $1,000, but its real income has fallen (because its money income has risen by a smaller percentage than the price level). This is the sort of effect that inflation has on people with relatively fixed incomes, lenders, and savers—three groups that tend to be hit hard by inflation.

FIXED MONEY INCOMES.    Inflation may seem no more than a petty annoyance; after all, most people care about relative, not absolute, prices. For example, if the Howe family's money income increases at the same rate as the price level, the Howe family may be no better or worse off under inflation than if its money income remained constant and no inflation occurred. But not all people are as fortunate as the Howes. Some people cannot increase their wages to compensate for price increases because they work under long-term contracts, among other reasons. These people take a considerable beating from inflation. One group that sometimes is particularly hard hit by inflation is the elderly, since old people often must live on pensions and other relatively fixed forms of income. Thus inflation sometimes has a substantial, inequitable, and unwelcome impact on our older citizens.

LENDERS.    Inflation hurts lenders and benefits borrowers, since it results in the depreciation of money. A dollar is worth what it will buy, and what it will buy is determined by the price level. If the price level increases, a dollar is worth less than it was before. Consequently, if you lend Bill

Dvorak $100 in 1991 and he pays you $100 in 1999—when a dollar will buy much less than in 1991—you are losing on the deal. In terms of what the money will buy, he is paying you less than what he borrowed. Of course, if you anticipate considerable inflation, you may be able to recoup by charging him a high enough interest rate to offset the depreciation of the dollar, but it is not so easy to forecast the rate of inflation and protect yourself.

**SAVERS.** Inflation can have a devastating and inequitable effect on savers. The family that works hard and saves for retirement (and a rainy day) finds that its savings are worth far less, when it finally spends them, than the amount it saved. Consider the well-meaning souls who invested $1,000 of their savings in United States savings bonds in 1939. By 1949, these bonds were worth only about 800 1939 dollars, including the interest received in the 10-year period. Thus these people had $200 taken away from them, in just as real a sense as if someone had picked their pockets.[6]

---

# EXAMPLE 5.2 MONEY WAGES AND REAL WAGES IN MANUFACTURING

In many situations, ranging from discussions of government economic policy to a particular labor negotiation between management and a union, it is important to distinguish between *money* and *real* wages. Money wages are wages expressed in current dollars, whereas real wages are adjusted for changes in the price level. The average weekly earnings in U.S. manufacturing are shown below for 1947–90, together with the Consumer Price Index for the same years.

| YEAR | AVERAGE WEEKLY EARNINGS (CURRENT DOLLARS) | CONSUMER PRICE INDEX (1982–84 = 100) |
|---|---|---|
| 1947 | 49.13 | 22.3 |
| 1957 | 81.59 | 28.1 |
| 1967 | 114.49 | 33.4 |
| 1977 | 228.50 | 60.6 |
| 1990 | 442.27 | 130.7 |

(a) Convert the above money wages into real wages expressed in 1982–84 dollars. (b) In percentage terms, did real money wages in U.S. manufacturing increase as much during 1967–77 as during 1947–57? (c) John Murphy, a vegetarian who spends the bulk of his income on spinach, cauliflower, and books, received the above wages during 1947–90. Are you confident that the changes in real wages you calculated in (a) are a good indication of the changes in Mr. Murphy's standard of living during this period?

(d) If the Consumer Price Index had been calculated so that 1977 = 100, would the value of this index for 1967 have been higher or lower than that shown above?

**Solution**

(a) 1947: $49.13 ÷ .223 = $220.31
1957: $81.59 ÷ .281 = $290.36
1967: $114.49 ÷ .334 = $342.78
1977: $228.50 ÷ .606 = $377.06
1990: $442.27 ÷ 1.307 = $338.39

(b) During 1967–77, real wages increased by 10.0 percent (from $342.78 to $377.06). During 1947–57, they increased by 31.8 percent (from $220.31 to $290.36). Thus, percentagewise, they rose less during 1967–77 than during 1947–57. (c) No, because the prices of the goods on which he spends most of his income may have behaved quite differently from the Consumer Price Index (since the goods he buys are quite different from the market basket of goods and services bought by all urban consumers). Also, his standard of living may depend on the extent of his assets as well as the size of his earnings. (d) It would have been higher. If the 1977 price level were set equal to 100, the 1967 price level would have to be more than 33.4.

---

[6] However, it is important to recognize that the form of the savings matters. If one can put his or her savings in a form where its monetary value increases as rapidly as the price level, the saver is not harmed by inflation. But this isn't always easy to do.

## Effects of Anticipated and Unanticipated Inflation

Economists are fond of pointing out that the effects of anticipated inflation tend to be less severe than those of unanticipated inflation. To see why this is the case, suppose that everyone anticipates (correctly) that the price level will be 6 percent higher next year than this year. In such a situation, everyone will build this amount of inflation into his or her decisions. Workers will realize that their money wage rates must be 6 percent higher next year just to avoid a cut in their real wage rates. The Murphy family, which earns $41,000 this year, will realize that it must earn $1.06 \times$ $41,000$, or $43,460$, next year if it is to avoid a reduction in its real earnings. And people who are thinking of lending money for a year will recognize that they must charge 6 percent interest just to break even. Why? Because when the money is repaid next year, $1.06 will be worth no more in real terms than $1.00 is now.

Because people build the anticipated rate of inflation into their calculations, the effects of anticipated inflation are likely to be less pronounced than those of unanticipated inflation. However, in the real world in which we all live, this frequently is of small comfort, since it is very difficult to anticipate the rate of inflation correctly. Even the most sophisticated econometric models have not had a very distinguished record in forecasting the rate of inflation. Thus it seems foolish to believe that the typical citizen (like those who invested in United States savings bonds in 1939) can anticipate inflation well enough to protect himself or herself against its consequences.

## An Arbitrary "Tax"

While inflation hurts some people, it benefits others. Those who are lucky enough to invest in goods, land, equipment, and other items that experience particularly rapid increases in price may make a killing. For this reason, speculation tends to be rampant during severe inflations. However, it is important to recognize that the rewards and penalties resulting from inflation are meted out with little or no regard for society's values or goals. As the late Arthur Okun, a former chairman of the Council of Economic Advisers, put it, " 'sharpies' . . . make sophisticated choices and often reap gains on inflation which do not seem to reflect any real contribution to economic growth. On the other hand, the unsophisticated saver who is merely preparing for the proverbial rainy day becomes a sucker." This is one of the most undesirable features of inflation, and it helps to account for inflation's sometimes being called an arbitrary "tax."

## Effects on Output

Creeping inflation, unlike unemployment, does not seem to reduce national output; in the short run, output may increase, for reasons taken up in subsequent chapters. But, although a mild upward creep of prices at the rate of a few percent per year is not likely to reduce output, a major inflation can have adverse effects on production. For one thing, it encourages speculation rather than productive use of savings. People find it more profitable to invest in gold, diamonds, real estate, and art (all of which tend to rise in monetary value during inflations) than in many kinds of productive activity. Also, managers of firms tend to be discouraged from carrying out long-range projects because of the difficulty of

Economic problems, like smugglers, have no respect for international boundaries. In the late 1980s and early 1990s, unemployment and inflation afflicted most of the industrialized world, as shown in the accompanying table. Compared with previous experience since World War II, recent unemployment rates have been high. For example, in 1969, West Germany's unemployment rate was only 0.9 percent, as compared with 5.7 percent in 1989.

A comparison of the U.S. unemployment rate with that in other countries shows that our 1990 unemployment rate was lower than that in all major noncommunist countries other than Japan and Germany. To some extent, these international differences in unemployment rates are due to the fact that unemployment is defined differently in one country than in another. In some countries, to be counted as unemployed, you must register with government unemployment exchanges. Another reason for the international differences in unemployment rates is that institutional and cultural arrangements differ from country to country. In Japan many large firms commit themselves to a policy of lifetime employment for workers. This is one reason for Japan's relatively low unemployment rates.

As for the rate of inflation, the accompanying table shows that U.S. performance seemed better than in some of the other countries, although it was not as good in this regard as in Canada, France, Germany, or Japan. A 5 percent annual rate of inflation is high, relative to 30 years ago. Many economists, and citizens as well, would be glad to return to the days when the price level seldom rose at more than a couple of percentage points per year—and unemployment rarely exceeded 4 or 5 percent.

## Unemployment and Inflation Rates in the United States and Six Other Countries

| | UNEMPLOYMENT RATE | | INFLATION RATE[a] | |
| | 1989 | 1990 | 1989 | 1990 |
|---|---|---|---|---|
| United States | 5.3 | 5.5 | 4.8 | 5.4 |
| Canada | 7.5 | 8.1 | 5.0 | 4.8 |
| France | 10.1 | 9.4 | 3.6 | 3.6 |
| Germany | 5.7 | 5.2 | 2.7 | 2.7 |
| Italy | 7.8 | 7.0 | 6.6 | 6.1 |
| Japan | 2.3 | 2.1 | 2.3 | 2.3 |
| Great Britain | 6.4 | 6.4 | 7.8 | 9.5 |

[a] Estimates in *Economic Report of the President,* 1990 and 1991. The figures are rough estimates but sufficiently reliable for present purposes. The data are not comparable with those given in other tables. For 1989, they pertain to 1988–89. For 1990, they pertain to 1989–90 (or in some cases, 1988–89).

forecasting what future prices will be. If the rate of inflation reaches the catastrophic heights that prevailed in Germany after World War I, the monetary system may break down. People may be unwilling to accept money. They may insist on trading goods or services directly for other goods and services. The result is likely to be considerable inefficiency and substantially reduced output.

## AGGREGATE DEMAND AND AGGREGATE SUPPLY

At this point, you should have a pretty clear idea of what unemployment and inflation are—and why they are regarded as economic evils. But how do economists explain and analyze unemployment and inflation? What sorts of models do they use? Although it would be premature to try to answer these questions fully, it is worthwhile to provide an early peek at the sorts of models that we will study.

Fundamentally, the level of national output and the price level are determined by the **aggregate demand curve** and the **aggregate supply curve,** as shown in Figure 5.6. Specifically, the level of total real output in the economy and the price level tend to equal $OQ$ and $OP$, the values corresponding to the point where the aggregate demand and supply curves cross. Even a glance at Figure 5.6 is likely to remind you of the supply-and-demand analyses in Chapter 3, where we analyzed the determinants of price and output of individual commodities like wheat. But although the similarities are obvious, there are basic differences between the aggregate demand and supply curves and the demand and supply curves of an individual commodity—the most fundamental difference

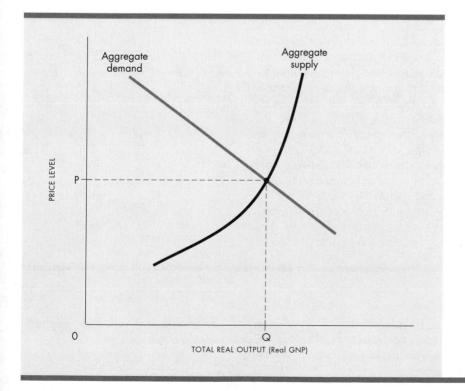

**Figure 5.6**
**Aggregate Demand and Aggregate Supply Curves**
The aggregate demand curve shows the level of total real output demanded at each price level. The aggregate supply curve shows the level of total real output supplied at each price level. The equilibrium level of the price level is $OP$, and the equilibrium level of total real output is $OQ$.

being that the aggregate demand and supply curves pertain to the entire economy, not an individual commodity.

*The aggregate demand curve shows the level of total real output in the economy that will be demanded at each price level.* As we know, the price level is the average price of all goods and services. Increases in the price level tend to reduce the quantity of total real output that will be demanded. Figure 5.6 indicates that this is the case, since the aggregate demand curve slopes downward to the right. In the next two chapters, we will devote a great deal of attention to the factors determining the shape and position of the aggregate demand curve, and to the reasons why it slopes downward to the right. For now, it is sufficient to take on faith that this is the case.

*The aggregate supply curve shows the level of real output in the economy that will be supplied at each price level.* Increases in the price level tend to increase the quantity of total real output that will be supplied. Figure 5.6 indicates that this is the case, since the aggregate supply curve slopes upward to the right. In Chapter 7, we will study the factors determining the shape and position of the aggregate supply curve, and the reasons why it slopes upward to the right. For now, it is sufficient to know that it does slope upward to the right. (As you will see in Chapter 7, the aggregate supply curve shown in Figure 5.6 is a particular kind of aggregate supply curve—a short-run aggregate supply curve—but that too need not concern us at present.)

*The point is that, if we understand the factors determining the shape and position of the aggregate demand and supply curves, we will understand why total real output and the price level are what they are.* After all, as shown in Figure 5.6, both total real output and the price level are determined by these curves. Why? Because the equilibrium level of total real output and the equilibrium level of the price level are given by the intersection of these curves. (In Figure 5.6, they are *OQ* and *OP.*)

Further, *if we know why total real output and the price level are what they are, we will have gone a long way toward understanding why the unemployment rate and the inflation rate are what they are.* As we have seen, decreases in total real output tend to cause the unemployment rate to rise, and increases in total real output tend to cause the unemployment rate to fall. And if we know how the price level varies, it is only a matter of simple arithmetic to calculate the inflation rate.

Thus, to understand the determinants of the unemployment rate and the inflation rate, we must study the determinants of the shape and position of the aggregate demand and supply curves. In the following chapter, we begin this study by looking in detail at the relationships between national income, national expenditure, and national output. As we shall see in Chapter 7, these relationships are the foundations of the aggregate demand curve.

## TEST YOURSELF

1. "The Employment Act of 1946 should be amended to include the goal of stabilizing the purchasing power of the dollar as well as the goal of maintaining high-level employment." Comment and evaluate.

2. "Inflation is a necessary cost of economic progress." Comment and evaluate.

3. Suppose that a family's money income remains constant at $40,000, and that the price level increases

10 percent per year. How many years will it take for the family's real income to be cut in half?

4. If you believe that the United States is about to suffer severe inflation, would you be better off to invest money in land or in governmental bonds? Explain your answer.

5. According to a 1976 statement by the Research and Policy Committee of the Committee for Economic Development, "The inflation rate has receded substantially from its double-digit levels of 1974, but it still remains unacceptably high, particularly for a period in which the economy is operating far below its potential." Why do they say this is particularly true for a period when output is far less than its potential? Explain.

## SUMMARY

1. Unemployment is of various types: frictional, structural, and cyclical. The overall unemployment rate conceals considerable differences among types of people. The unemployment rate tends to be higher for teenagers than for older people, and for blacks than for whites.

2. According to most economists, high levels of unemployment impose costs on society. The economic costs of unemployment include the goods and services that could have been produced (but weren't) by the unemployed. The gap between actual and potential GNP is a measure of the economic costs of high unemployment. The natural rate of unemployment is the unemployment rate when the economy is at full employment.

3. John Maynard Keynes, in the 1930s, developed a theory to explain how the capitalist economic system remained mired in the Great Depression, with its tragically high levels of unemployment. Contrary to the classical economists, he concluded that there was no automatic mechanism in a capitalistic system to generate and maintain full employment—or, at least, to generate it quickly enough to be relied on in practice.

4. Keynes's ideas were challenged by the monetarists, and in more recent years by the new classical macroeconomists. In many respects, the new classical macroeconomists hark back to the classical view of unemployment; in particular,

they do not accept Keynes's argument that prices and wages are inflexible. On the other hand, the new Keynesians have developed theories to help explain why such inflexibility might be expected.

5. Inflation is a general upward movement of prices. Runaway inflation occurs when the price level increases very rapidly, as in Germany after World War I. Creeping inflation occurs when the price level rises a few percent per year, as in the United States during the late 1980s and early 1990s. The Consumer Price Index, published monthly by the Bureau of Labor Statistics, is a key measure of the rate of inflation.

6. High rates of inflation produce considerable redistribution of income and wealth. People with relatively fixed incomes, such as many of the elderly, tend to take a beating from inflation. Inflation hurts lenders and benefits borrowers. The penalties (and rewards) resulting from inflation are meted out arbitrarily, with no regard for society's values or goals. Substantial rates of inflation may also reduce efficiency and total output.

7. The level of national output and the price level are determined by the aggregate demand curve and the aggregate supply curve. The aggregate demand curve shows the level of total real output that will be demanded at each price level. The aggregate supply curve shows the level of total real output that will be supplied at each price level.

## CONCEPTS FOR REVIEW

**Unemployment**
**Frictional unemployment**
**Structural unemployment**
**Cyclical unemployment**
**Potential GNP**
**Full Employment**

**Natural Rate of Employment**
**Hysteresis**
**Say's Law**
**Inflation**
**Runaway inflation**

**Creeping inflation**
**Money income**
**Real income**
**Aggregate demand**
**Aggregate supply**

# AGGREGATE DEMAND: THE FOUNDATIONS

REDUCTIONS IN NATIONAL output tend to trigger increases in the unemployment rate. Thus, to understand why unemployment sometimes rises substantially, we must study the forces determining national output. As we saw at the end of the previous chapter, the level of national output is determined by the aggregate demand curve and the aggregate supply curve. To understand the derivation of the aggregate demand curve, it is useful to study the determinants of national output when the price level is held constant. Our purpose in this chapter is to take up this topic.

Basically, the simple model we present in this chapter is the one put forth in the 1930s by John Maynard Keynes, who was discussed at length in the previous chapter. Given that recent decades have seen persistent inflation, not a constant price level, this model is obviously incomplete, although it throws useful light on the factors influencing aggregate demand. We begin our discussion by describing the consumption function, after which we take up the determinants of investment expenditure. Then we discuss the determinants of the equilibrium level of national output in a closed economy (no exports, no imports) with no government. Finally, we relax the assumptions that the economy is closed and that there is no government. All of this is based on the assumption that the price level is held constant.

John Maynard Keynes

## THE CONSUMPTION FUNCTION

An important part of our theory is the **consumption function,** *which is the relationship between consumption spending and disposable income.* It seems clear that *consumption expenditures—whether those of a single household or the total consumption expenditures in the entire economy— are influenced heavily by income.* Families with higher incomes spend more on consumption than families with lower incomes. Of course, individual families vary a good deal in their behavior; some spend more than others even if their incomes are the same. But, on the average, a family's consumption expenditure is tied very closely to its income.

What is true for individual families also holds for the entire economy: total personal consumption expenditures are closely related to disposable income. This fact is shown in Figure 6.1, where personal consumption expenditure in each year (from 1929 to 1990) is plotted against disposable income in the same year (from 1929 to 1990). The points fall very near the straight line drawn in Figure 6.1, but not right on it. For most practical purposes, however, we can regard the line drawn in Figure 6.1 as representing the relationship between personal consumption expenditures and disposable income. In other words, we can regard this line as the consumption function.

## The Marginal Propensity to Consume

Suppose that we know what the consumption function for a given society looks like at a particular period in time. For example, suppose that it is given by the figures for disposable income and personal consumption expenditure in the first two columns of Table 6.1. Based on our knowledge of the consumption function, we can determine the *extra* amount families will spend on consumption if they receive an *extra* dollar of disposable income. *This amount—the fraction of an extra dollar of income that is spent on consumption—is called the* **marginal propensity to consume.** For reasons discussed later in this chapter, the marginal propensity to consume, shown in column 3 of Table 6.1, plays a major role in our theory.

To make sure that you understand exactly what the marginal propensity to consume is, consult Table 6.1. What is the marginal propensity to consume when disposable income is between $1,000 billion and $1,050 billion? The second column shows that, when income rises from $1,000 billion to $1,050 billion, consumption expenditure rises from $950 billion to $980 billion. Consequently, the fraction of the extra $50 billion of income that is consumed is $30 billion ÷ $50 billion, or 0.60. Thus the marginal propensity to consume is 0.60.[1] Based on similar calculations, the marginal propensity to consume when disposable income is between $1,050 billion and $1,100 billion is 0.60; the marginal propensity to consume when disposable income is between $1,100 billion and $1,150 billion is 0.60; and so forth.

The marginal propensity to consume can be interpreted geometrically as the slope of the consumption function. The slope of any line is the ratio of the vertical change to the horizontal change when a small movement occurs along the line. As shown in Figure 6.2, the vertical change is the change in personal consumption expenditure, and the horizontal change is the change in disposable income. Thus the ratio of the vertical change to the horizontal change must equal the marginal propensity to consume.

In general, the marginal propensity to consume can differ, depending on the level of disposable income. For example, the marginal propensity to consume may be higher at lower levels than at higher levels of disposable income. Only if the consumption function is a straight line, as in Figure 6.1 and Table 6.1, will the marginal propensity to consume be the same at all levels of income. For simplicity, we assume in much of the subsequent analysis that the consumption function is a straight line, but this assumption can easily be relaxed without affecting the essential aspects of our conclusions.

---

[1] Students with some knowledge of mathematics will recognize that this is an approximation since $50 billion is a substantial change in income, whereas the marginal propensity to consume pertains to a small change in income. But this is an innocuous simplification. Similar simplifications are made below.

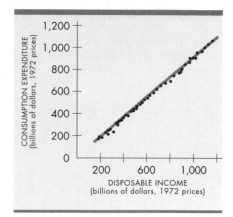

**Figure 6.1**
**Relationship between Personal Consumption Expenditure and Disposable Income, United States, 1929–90 (excluding World War II)**
There is a very close relationship between personal consumption expenditure and disposable income in the United States. In this figure a dot is given for each year. The dot's horizontal distance from the origin measures the disposable income that year, and its vertical distance from the origin measures the consumption expenditure that year. As you can see, the dots generally are very close to the line.

## The Average Propensity to Consume

It is important to distinguish between the marginal propensity to consume and the ***average propensity to consume.*** The average propensity to consume equals the proportion of disposable income that is consumed. In other words, it equals

$$\frac{\text{personal consumption expenditure}}{\text{disposable income}}.$$

Clearly, this will not in general equal the marginal propensity to consume, which is

$$\frac{\text{change in personal consumption expenditure}}{\text{change in disposable income}}.$$

The point is that the marginal propensity to consume is the proportion of *extra* income consumed, and this proportion generally is quite different from the proportion of *total* income consumed. For example, in Table 6.1, the average propensity to consume when disposable income is $1,100 billion is 0.92; but the marginal propensity to consume when disposable income is between $1,050 billion and $1,100 billion is 0.60.

## THE SAVING FUNCTION

If people don't devote their disposable income to personal consumption expenditure, what else can they do with it? Of course, they can save it. When families refrain from spending their income on consumption goods and services—that is, when they forgo present consumption to provide for larger consumption in the future—they save. Thus we can derive from the consumption function the total amount people will save at each level of disposable income. All we have to do is subtract the total personal con-

**Table 6.1**
**The Consumption Function**

| DISPOS-ABLE INCOME (BILLIONS OF DOLLARS) | PERSONAL CONSUMP-TION EXPEN-DITURE (BILLIONS OF DOLLARS) | MARGINAL PROPENSITY TO CONSUME | AVERAGE PROPENSITY TO CONSUME |
|---|---|---|---|
| 1,000 | 950 | | .95 |
| | | $\frac{30}{50} = .60$ | |
| 1,050 | 980 | | .93 |
| | | $\frac{30}{50} = .60$ | |
| 1,100 | 1,010 | | .92 |
| | | $\frac{30}{50} = .60$ | |
| 1,150 | 1,040 | | .90 |
| | | $\frac{30}{50} = .60$ | |
| 1,200 | 1,070 | | .89 |
| | | $\frac{30}{50} = .60$ | |
| 1,250 | 1,100 | | .88 |
| | | $\frac{30}{50} = .60$ | |
| 1,300 | 1,130 | | .87 |

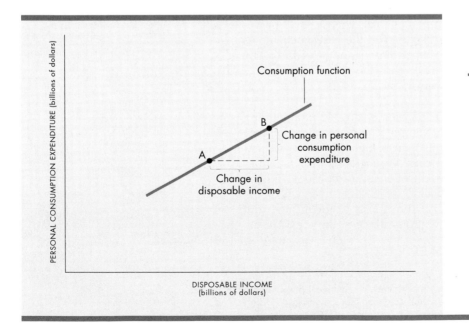

**Figure 6.2**
**The Marginal Propensity to Consume Equals the Slope of the Consumption Function**
The slope of the consumption function between points *A* and *B* equals the vertical change (which is the change in personal consumption expenditure) divided by the horizontal change (which is the change in disposable income). Since the marginal propensity to consume equals the change in personal consumption expenditure divided by the change in disposable income, it follows that the slope equals the marginal propensity to consume.

**Table 6.2**
**The Saving Function**

| DISPOSABLE INCOME (BILLIONS OF DOLLARS) | PERSONAL CONSUMPTION EXPENDITURE (BILLIONS OF DOLLARS) | SAVING (BILLIONS OF DOLLARS) | MARGINAL PROPENSITY TO SAVE |
|---|---|---|---|
| 1,000 | 950 | 50 | |
| | | | $\frac{20}{50} = .40$ |
| 1,050 | 980 | 70 | |
| | | | $\frac{20}{50} = .40$ |
| 1,100 | 1,010 | 90 | |
| | | | $\frac{20}{50} = .40$ |
| 1,150 | 1,040 | 110 | |
| | | | $\frac{20}{50} = .40$ |
| 1,200 | 1,070 | 130 | |
| | | | $\frac{20}{50} = .40$ |
| 1,250 | 1,100 | 150 | |
| | | | $\frac{20}{50} = .40$ |
| 1,300 | 1,130 | 170 | |

sumption expenditure at each level of disposable income from disposable income. The difference is the total amount of saving at each level of disposable income. This difference is shown in the next to last column of Table 6.2. We can plot the total amount of saving against disposable income, as in Figure 6.3. The resulting relationship between total saving and disposable income is the **saving function.** Like the consumption function, it plays a major role in our theory.

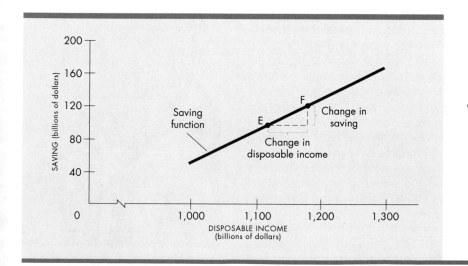

**Figure 6.3**
**The Saving Function**
The saving function describes the total amount of saving at each level of disposable income. The slope of the saving function equals the change in saving divided by the change in disposable income. Thus the slope of the saving function equals the marginal propensity to save.

## The Marginal Propensity to Save

If we know the saving function, we can calculate the marginal propensity to save at any level of disposable income. The ***marginal propensity to save*** *is the proportion of an extra dollar of disposable income that is saved*. To see how to calculate it, consult Table 6.2 again. The third column shows that, when income rises from $1,000 billion to $1,050 billion, saving rises from $50 billion to $70 billion. Consequently, the fraction of the extra $50 billion of income that is saved is $20 billion ÷ $50 billion, or 0.40. Thus the marginal propensity to save is 0.40. Similar calculations show that the marginal propensity to save when disposable income is between $1,050 billion and $1,100 billion is 0.40; the marginal propensity to save when disposable income is between $1,100 billion and $1,150 billion is 0.40; and so forth.

Note that, *at any particular level of disposable income, the marginal propensity to save plus the marginal propensity to consume must equal one*. By definition, the marginal propensity to save equals the proportion of an extra dollar of disposable income that is saved, and the marginal propensity to consume equals the proportion of an extra dollar of disposable income that is consumed. The sum of these two proportions must equal one, for, as stated above, the only things that people can do with an extra dollar of disposable income are consume it or save it. Table 6.2 shows this fact quite clearly.

Finally, it is worth noting that the marginal propensity to save equals the slope of the saving function—just as the marginal propensity to consume equals the slope of the consumption function. As pointed out above, the slope of a line equals the vertical distance between any two points on the line divided by the horizontal distance between them. Since (as shown in Figure 6.3) the vertical distance is the change in saving and the horizontal distance is the change in disposable income, the slope of the saving function must equal the marginal propensity to save.

# THE PERMANENT-INCOME AND LIFE-CYCLE HYPOTHESES

The consumption function, as described in previous sections, is a relationship between *current* consumption expenditure and *current* disposable income. In Figure 6.1, for example, it is presumed that current consumption expenditure in a given period depends upon disposable income in that same period. Some economists, led by Milton Friedman of Stanford University, Franco Modigliani of the Massachusetts Institute of Technology, and Albert Ando of the University of Pennsylvania, have challenged this presumption. In their view, a household's current personal consumption expenditure does not depend on current disposable income; instead, it depends on the household's expected stream of disposable income over a long period of time (as well as the household's wealth). Thus two households that have the same current disposable income may spend quite different amounts on consumption goods, if their expected income streams over the long term are quite different.

To illustrate what these economists mean, consider two hypothetical families: the Rosenbergs and the Goulds. Although both Mr. Rosenberg and Ms. Gould will earn $12,000 this year, their long-run income

Franco Modigliani

prospects are quite different. Mr. Rosenberg is a businessman who ordinarily makes $100,000 per year, but whose income is much lower this year because of a foolish decision by one of his employees that caused a sizable one-time loss to Rosenberg's firm. Based on all available evidence, Rosenberg's annual income will return to about $100,000 in the future. Ms. Gould, on the other hand, has been unemployed for many years, and there is no prospect that she will return to work. Her $12,000 income this year was due to her having won a lottery. What Friedman, Modigliani, and Ando are saying is that one would expect each family to spend an amount on consumption goods this year that is commensurate with its long-term income, not just its income this year. Thus one would expect the Rosenbergs to spend a lot more on consumption goods than the Goulds, even though their current incomes are the same.

Although Friedman's theory (often called the **permanent-income hypothesis**) differs in many respect from the Modigliani-Ando theory (often called the **life-cycle hypothesis**), the differences need not concern us here. What is important for present purposes is that both of these theories predict that a transitory change in income may not have much impact on a household's consumption expenditure, if the household's long-run income prospects remain relatively unaffected. In contrast, the basic consumption function discussed earlier in this chapter assumes that consumption expenditure is dependent on current disposable income. To keep the analysis as simple as possible, we generally shall use the basic consumption function in subsequent chapters; but the fact that it is a simplification should be recognized. (In discussing the effect of temporary tax changes in Chapter 9, we shall put the Friedman and Modigliani-Ando theories to good use.)

# DETERMINANTS OF INVESTMENT

In Chapter 4, we stressed that investment consists largely of the amount firms spend on new buildings and factories, new equipment, and increases in inventory. Investment plays a central role in the theory of output and employment. To understand this theory, it is essential that you understand the factors determining the level of gross private domestic investment. Basically, there are two broad determinants of the level of gross private domestic investment—the expected rate of return from capital, and the interest rate.

## Rate of Return

The **expected rate of return from capital** is the perceived rate of return that managers of firms believe they can obtain if they put up new buildings or factories, add new equipment, or increase their inventories. Each of these forms of investment requires the expenditure of money. The rate of return measures the profitability of such an expenditure; it shows the annual profits to be obtained per dollar invested. Thus a rate of return of 10 percent means that, for every dollar invested, an annual profit of 10 cents is obtained. Clearly, the higher the expected rate of return from a particular investment, the more profitable the investment is expected to be.

## Interest Rate

The **_interest rate_** is the cost of borrowing money. More specifically, it is the annual amount that a borrower must pay for the use of a dollar for a year. Thus, if the interest rate is 8 percent, a borrower must pay 8 cents per year for the use of a dollar. And if the interest rate is 12 percent, a borrower must pay 12 cents per year for the use of a dollar. Anyone with a savings account knows what it is to earn interest; anyone who has borrowed money from a bank knows what it is to pay interest.

# THE INVESTMENT DECISION

_To determine whether to invest in a particular project (a new building, piece of equipment, or other form of investment), a firm must compare the expected rate of return from the project with the interest rate._ If the expected rate of return is less than the interest rate, the firm will lose money if it borrows money to carry out the project. For example, if the firm invests in a project with a 10 percent rate of return and borrows the money to finance the project at 12 percent interest, it will receive profits of 10 cents per dollar invested and pay out interest of 12 cents per dollar invested. So it will lose 2 cents (12 cents minus 10 cents) per dollar invested.

Even if the firm does not borrow money to finance the project, it will be unlikely to invest in a project where the expected rate of return is less than the interest rate. Why? Because, if the firm can lend money to others at the prevailing interest rate, it can obtain a greater return from its money by doing this than by investing in the project. Thus, if the interest rate is 12 percent and an investment project has an expected rate of return of 10 percent, a firm will do better, if it has a certain amount of money, to lend it out at 12 percent than to earn 10 percent from the investment project.

Since firms are likely to invest only in projects where the expected rate of return exceeds the interest rate, it is clear that _the level of gross private domestic investment depends on the total volume of investment projects where the expected rate of return exceeds the interest rate._ For example, if the interest rate is 10 percent, the level of investment depends on the total volume of investment projects where the expected rate of return exceeds 10 percent. The more such projects there are, the higher will be the level of investment. The fewer such projects there are, the lower will be the level of investment. In the following sections, we discuss a number of factors that influence how many such projects there are.

## Technological Change

The rate of technological change can have an important influence on the volume of investment projects where the rate of return exceeds the interest rate. New technology frequently opens up profitable investment opportunities. For example, in the late 1980s, Nucor Corporation, the nation's largest mini-mill company, built a new steel mill in central Indiana to exploit a technological breakthrough—an advanced caster to pour molten steel into very thin slabs, thus saving energy, labor, and materials. The new mill was a substantial investment, costing about $225 million. In 1990, Nucor announced that it would build a second such plant for $300 million in Arkansas.

Advanced caster technology at Nucor Corporation

In general, *a more rapid rate of technological change is likely to result in a greater dollar amount of investment projects where the rate of return exceeds the interest rate. Thus a more rapid rate of technological change is likely to increase the level of investment.*

## Existing Stock of Capital

Another factor that influences the volume of investment projects where the rate of return exceeds the interest rate is the size of the existing stock of capital (relative to the level of sales). As a firm's sales go up, its need for plant, equipment, and inventories clearly goes up as well. Beyond some point, increases in sales result in pressure on the capacity of existing plant and equipment, so that the firm finds it profitable to invest in additional plant and equipment. The crucial relationship is between a firm's sales and its stock of capital goods—that is, its stock of plant, equipment, and inventories. If its sales are well below the amount it can produce with its stock of capital goods, there is little pressure on the firm to invest in additional capital goods. But if its sales are at the upper limit of what can be produced with its capital goods, the firm is likely to view the purchase of additional capital goods as yielding a high rate of return.

In general, *the smaller the existing stock of capital goods—relative to present and prospective sales levels—the greater the dollar amount of investment projects where the expected rate of return exceeds the interest rate.* Conversely, *the bigger the existing stock of capital goods—relative to present and prospective sales levels—the smaller the dollar amount of investment projects where the expected rate of return exceeds the interest rate.*

## Business Expectations

Still another factor that influences the volume of investment projects where the expected rate of return exceeds the interest rate is the state of business expectations. Sometimes business executives are optimistic; sometimes they are pessimistic. If they believe that their sales are about to drop dramatically, they will be unlikely to invest much in additional capital goods. On the other hand, if they believe that their sales are about to increase greatly, they may be led to invest heavily in capital goods. Firms must make investment decisions on the basis of forecasts. There is no way any firm can tell exactly what the future will bring, and the investment decisions it makes will be influenced by how optimistic or pessimistic its forecasts are. This, in turn, will depend on existing business conditions, as well as on many other factors. Sometimes government actions and political developments have an important impact on business expectations. Sometimes unexpected changes in the profits of one industry have a major effect on expectations in other industries.

In general, *the more optimistic business expectations are, the larger the dollar amount of investment projects where the expected rate of return exceeds the interest rate. Conversely, the more pessimistic business expectations are, the smaller the dollar amount of investment projects where the expected rate of return exceeds the interest rate.*

## Level of the Interest Rate

Finally, the volume of investment projects where the expected rate of return exceeds the interest rate clearly depends on the level of the interest rate. The higher the interest rate, the smaller the volume of projects that have expected rates of return exceeding the interest rate. Suppose that a firm is considering the six investment projects shown in Table 6.3. If the interest rate is 6 percent, all of them have expected rates of return exceeding the interest rate. If the interest rate is 10 percent, only three of them (projects A, B, and D) have expected rates of return exceeding the interest rate. And if the interest rate is 15 percent, none of them has an expected rate of return exceeding the interest rate.

In general, *increases in the interest rate tend to reduce investment, while decreases in the interest rate tend to increase investment.* In late 1990 and 1991, the federal government reduced interest rates to promote additional investment; at other times it has raised interest rates to discourage investment.

**Table 6.3**
**Expected Rates of Return from Investment Projects Considered by a Firm**

| PROJECT | EXPECTED RATE OF RETURN (PERCENT) |
|---------|-----------------------------------|
| A | 12 |
| B | 14 |
| C | 8 |
| D | 11 |
| E | 7 |

## TEST YOURSELF

1. Suppose that only three families inhabit a nation and that (regardless of the level of its income) each family spends 90 percent of its income on consumption goods. For the nation as a whole, what is the marginal propensity to save? How much difference is there between the marginal propensity to consume and the average propensity to consume? To what extent does the nation's marginal propensity to consume depend on the distribution of income? Is this realistic?

2. Assume that the consumption function is as follows:

| DISPOSABLE INCOME (BILLIONS OF DOLLARS) | PERSONAL CONSUMPTION EXPENDITURE (BILLIONS OF DOLLARS) |
|------------------------------------------|--------------------------------------------------------|
| 900 | 750 |
| 1,000 | 800 |
| 1,100 | 850 |
| 1,200 | 900 |
| 1,300 | 950 |
| 1,400 | 1,000 |

(a) How much will be saved if disposable income is $1,000 billion? (b) What is the average propensity to consume if disposable income is $1,000 billion? (c) What is the marginal propensity to consume if disposable income is between $1,000 billion and $1,100 billion? (d) What is the marginal propensity to save if disposable income is between $1,000 billion and $1,100 billion?

3. Suppose that the relationship between personal consumption expenditure and disposable income in the United States were as follows:

| CONSUMPTION (BILLIONS OF DOLLARS) | DISPOSABLE INCOME (BILLIONS OF DOLLARS) |
|------------------------------------|------------------------------------------|
| 750 | 700 |
| 830 | 800 |
| 910 | 900 |
| 970 | 1,000 |
| 1,030 | 1,100 |
| 1,100 | 1,200 |

Draw the consumption function on a graph. On another graph, draw the saving function. Is the marginal propensity to consume constant, or does it vary with the level of disposable income? Does the average propensity to consume rise or fall as disposable income rises?

4. "Unless firms make profits, they cannot invest in plant and equipment. Profits set an upper limit on how much they can invest." Comment and evaluate.

5. What effect would each of the following have on the amount of investment? That is, would each increase it, decrease it, or have no effect on it? (a) Expectations of greater likelihood of impending recession by firms; (b) a decrease in interest rates; (c) increased rate of invention of important new synthetic materials; (d) a marked reduction in the percent of existing plant that is utilized; (e) an increase in the perceived profitability of building up inventories.

# THE EQUILIBRIUM LEVEL OF GROSS NATIONAL PRODUCT: A CLOSED ECONOMY WITH NO GOVERNMENT

At this point, we can show how the equilibrium level of GNP is determined if the price level is held constant. Three simplifying assumptions, all of which are relaxed subsequently in this or later chapters, are made:

1. We assume that there are no government expenditures and that the economy is closed (no exports or imports). Thus *total spending on final output—that is, on gross national product—in this simple case equals consumption expenditure plus gross investment.*[2] (Why? Because the other two components of total spending—government expenditures and net exports—are zero.) These assumptions will be relaxed in the latter part of this chapter.

2. We assume that there are no taxes, no transfer payments, and no undistributed corporate profits. Indeed, we assume that GNP *equals disposable income in this simple case,* because the items in Table 4.8 that are taken from, or added to, GNP to get disposable income total zero. Later chapters relax this assumption.

3. We shall assume that the total amount of intended investment is *independent* of the level of gross national product. This, of course, is only a rough simplification, since, as we noted in a previous section, the amount firms invest will be affected by the level of national output. But this simplification is very convenient and in Chapter 8 it will be relaxed.

As stressed in Chapter 3, an equilibrium is a situation where there is no tendency for change; in other words, it is a situation that can persist. There we studied the equilibrium value of a product's price. Here we are interested in the equilibrium value of gross national product. In Chapter 3, we saw that price is at its equilibrium value when the quantity demanded equals the quantity supplied. Here we shall see that GNP is at its equilibrium value when the flow of income (generated by this value of GNP) results in a level of spending that is just sufficient (not too high, not too low) to take this level of output off the market. To understand this equilibrium condition, it is essential to keep the circular flow of the macroeconomy in mind:

1. *Output determines income:* The production of goods and services results in a flow of income to the workers, resource owners, and managers who help to produce them. Each level of GNP results in a certain flow of income. More specifically, under the assumptions made here, GNP equals disposable income. Thus, whatever the level of GNP may be, we can be sure that the level of disposable income will be equivalent to it.

2. *Income determines spending:* The level of spending on final goods and services is dependent on the level of disposable income. As we saw earlier in this chapter, consumption expenditure depends on the level of disposable income. (For the moment, we assume that investment is independent of the level of output in the economy.) Thus, if we know the level of disposable income, we can predict what level of spending will be forthcoming.

---

[2] Since personal consumption expenditure and gross private domestic investment are cumbersome terms, we shall generally use consumption expenditure and gross investment (or simply investment) instead in this and subsequent chapters.

*3. Spending affects output:* If producers find that they are selling goods faster than they are producing them, their inventories will decline. If they find that they are selling goods slower than they are producing them, their inventories will rise. *If GNP is at its equilibrium value, the intended level of spending must be just equal to GNP.* Why? Because otherwise there will be an unintended increase or decrease in producers' inventories—a situation which cannot persist. Much more will be said on this score in the sections that follow.

## AGGREGATE FLOWS OF INCOME AND EXPENDITURE

Let's look in more detail at the process whereby national output (that is, GNP) determines the level of income, which in turn determines the level of spending. Suppose that the first column of Table 6.4 shows the various possible output levels—that is, the various possible values of GNP—that the economy might produce this year. This column shows the various output levels that might be produced, *if producers expect that there will be enough spending to take this much output off the market at the existing price level.* And, as stressed above, disposable income equals GNP.

Since disposable income equals GNP (under our current assumptions), the first column of Table 6.4 also shows the level of disposable income corresponding to each possible level of GNP. From this, it should be possible to determine the level of spending corresponding to each level of GNP. Specifically, suppose that the consumption function is as shown in Table 6.1 (page 110). In this case, intended consumption expenditure at each level of GNP will be shown in column 2 of Table 6.4. For example, if GNP equals $1,000 billion, intended consumption expenditure equals $950 billion.

But consumption expenditure is not the only type of spending. What about investment? Suppose that firms want to invest $90 billion regardless of the level of GNP. Under these circumstances, total spending at each level of GNP will be as shown in column 5 of Table 6.4. (Since total intended spending equals intended consumption expenditure plus intended investment, column 5 equals column 2 plus column 4.)

**Table 6.4**
**Determination of Equilibrium Level of Gross National Product**
**(Billions of Dollars)**

| (1) GROSS NATIONAL PRODUCT (=DISPOSABLE INCOME) | (2) INTENDED CONSUMPTION EXPENDITURE | (3) INTENDED SAVING | (4) INTENDED INVESTMENT | (5) TOTAL INTENDED SPENDING (2) + (4) | (6) TENDENCY OF NATIONAL OUTPUT |
|---|---|---|---|---|---|
| 1,000 | 950 | 50 | 90 | 1,040 | Upward |
| 1,050 | 980 | 70 | 90 | 1,070 | Upward |
| 1,100 | 1,010 | 90 | 90 | 1,100 | No change |
| 1,150 | 1,040 | 110 | 90 | 1,130 | Downward |
| 1,200 | 1,070 | 130 | 90 | 1,160 | Downward |
| 1,250 | 1,100 | 150 | 90 | 1,190 | Downward |

*For GNP to be at its equilibrium value, total **intended spending** on final goods and services must equal GNP.* Consider Table 6.4. Column 5 of this table shows the level of total intended spending at each level of national output (and income). The equilibrium value of GNP is $1,100 billion, where total intended spending equals GNP. In this and the following section, we prove this is the case.

The easiest way to prove this is to show that, if intended spending is not equal to GNP, GNP is *not* at its equilibrium value. The following discussion provides such a proof. First we show that, if intended spending is greater than GNP, GNP is not at its equilibrium level. Then we show that, if intended spending is less than GNP, GNP is not at its equilibrium level.

If intended spending is *greater* than GNP, what will happen? Since the total amount that will be spent on final goods and services exceeds the total amount of final goods and services produced (the latter being, by definition, GNP), firms' inventories will be reduced. Consequently, firms will increase their output rate to avoid continued depletion of their inventories and to bring their output into balance with the rate of aggregate demand. Since an increase in the output rate means an increase in GNP, it follows that GNP will tend to increase if intended spending is greater than GNP. GNP therefore is not at its equilibrium level.

On the other hand, what will happen if intended spending is *less* than GNP? Since the total amount that will be spent on final goods and services falls short of the total amount of final goods and services produced (the latter being, by definition, GNP), firms' inventories will increase. As inventories pile up unexpectedly, firms will cut back their output to bring it into better balance with aggregate demand. Since a reduction in output means a reduction in GNP, it follows that GNP will tend to fall if intended spending is less than GNP. Once again, GNP is not at its equilibrium level.

Since GNP is not at its equilibrium value when it exceeds or falls short of intended spending, it must be at its equilibrium value only when it equals intended spending.

## WHY GNP MUST EQUAL INTENDED SPENDING: THREE CASES

To get a better idea of why GNP will be at its equilibrium value only if it equals intended spending, consider three possible values of GNP—$1,050 billion, $1,100 billion, and $1,150 billion—and see what would happen in our simple economy (in Table 6.4) if these values of GNP prevailed.

### Case 1: GNP = $1,050 Billion

What would happen if firms were to produce $1,050 billion of final goods and services? Given our assumptions, disposable income would also equal $1,050 billion (since disposable income equals GNP), so that consumers would spend $980 billion on consumption goods and services. (This follows from the nature of the consumption function: see column 2 of Table 6.4.) Since firms want to invest $90 billion, total intended spending would be $1,070 billion ($980 billion + $90 billion, as shown in column 5). But the amount spent on final goods and services under these circumstances would exceed the total value of final goods and services produced by $20 billion ($1,070 billion – $1,050 billion), so that firms' inventories would be drawn down by $20 billion. Clearly, this situation could not persist very long. As firms become aware that their inventories are becoming depleted, they would step up their production rates, so that the value of output of final goods and services—GNP—would increase.

### Case 2: GNP = $1,150 Billion

What would happen if firms were to produce $1,150 billion of final goods and services? Given our assumptions, disposable income would also equal $1,150 billion (since disposable income equals GNP), with the result that consumers would spend $1,040 billion on consumption goods and services. (Again, this follows from the consumption function: see column 2 of Table 6.4.) Since firms want to invest $90 billion, total spending would be $1,130 ($1,040 billion + $90 billion, as shown in column 5). But the total amount spent on final goods and services under these circumstances would fall short of the total value of final goods and services produced by $20 billion ($1,150 billion – $1,130 billion), so that firms' inventories would increase by $20 billion. Clearly, this situation, like the previous one, could not continue very long. When firms see that their inventories are increasing, they reduce their production rates, causing the value of output of final goods and services—GNP—to decrease.

### Case 3: GNP = $1,100 Billion

What would happen if firms were to produce $1,100 billion of final goods and services? Disposable income would also equal $1,100 billion (since disposable income equals GNP), so that consumers would spend $1,010 billion on consumption goods and services. (Once again, this follows from the consumption function: see column 2 of Table 6.4.) Since firms want to invest $90 billion, total spending would be $1,100 billion ($1,010 billion + $90 billion, as shown in column 5). Thus the total amount spent on final goods and services under these circumstances would exactly equal the total value of final goods and services produced. There would be no reason for firms to alter their production rates, making this an equilibrium situation—a set of circumstances where there is no tendency for GNP to change.

These three cases illustrate the process that pushes GNP toward its equilibrium value (and maintains it there). Whether GNP is below or above its equilibrium value, there is a tendency for production rates to be altered so that GNP moves toward its equilibrium value. Eventually, GNP will reach its equilibrium value, and the situation will be like that described in our third case. The important aspect of the third case—the equilibrium situation—is that for it to occur, intended spending must equal GNP.

## USING A GRAPH TO DETERMINE EQUILIBRIUM GNP

For the sake of absolute clarity, we can represent the same argument in a diagrammatic, rather than tabular, analysis. Let's show again that the equilibrium level of GNP is at the point where intended spending equals GNP, but now using a graph. Since disposable income equals gross national

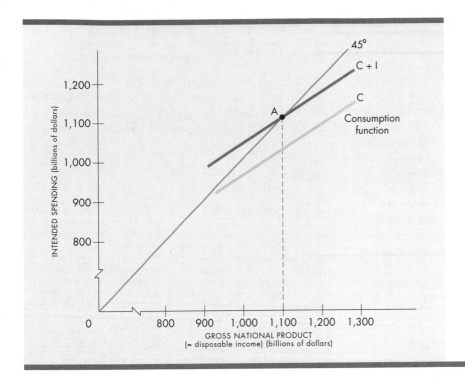

Figure 6.4
**Determination of Equilibrium
Value of Gross National Product**
The consumption function is *C*, and the
sum of consumption and the investment
expenditure is *C* + *I*. The equilibrium
value of GNP is at the point where the
*C* + *I* line intersects the 45-degree line,
here $1,100 billion.

product in this simple case, we can plot consumption expenditure (on
the vertical axis) versus gross national product (on the horizontal axis), as
shown in Figure 6.4. This is the consumption function. Also, we can plot
the sum of consumption expenditure *(C)* and investment expenditure *(I)*
against GNP, as shown in Figure 6.4. This relationship, shown by the *C* +
*I* line, indicates the level of total intended spending on final goods and
services for various amounts of GNP. Finally, we can plot a **45-degree
line,** as shown in Figure 6.4. This line contains all points where total intended spending equals gross national product.

We are concerned with one of these points in particular, the one that
also lies on the *C* + *I* line. The *equilibrium level of GNP will be at the point
on the horizontal axis where the C + I line intersects the 45-degree line*. In
Figure 6.4, this occurs at $1,100 billion. Under the conditions assumed
here, no other level of GNP can be maintained for any considerable period of time.

Why can we be sure that the point where the *C* + *I* line intersects the
45-degree line is the point where intended spending equals GNP? Because a 45-degree line is, by construction, a line that includes all points
where the amount on the horizontal axis equals the amount on the vertical axis. In this case, as noted above, intended spending is on the vertical
axis and GNP is on the horizontal axis. Thus at point *A,* the point where
the *C* + *I* line intersects the 45-degree line, intended spending must equal
GNP, because point *A* is on the 45-degree line.

# EFFECTS OF CHANGES IN INTENDED
# INVESTMENT

Looking at the highly simplified model we constructed in previous sections to explain the level of national output, what is the effect of a change

# EXAMPLE 6.1    ASKING "WHAT IF" QUESTIONS

Economists find it useful to ask "what if" questions. For example, what if GNP in a particular country assumed various alternative values? What would be the results? Suppose that you know four things about the country in question. First, in this country, personal consumption expenditure = $100 million + 0.75 $D$, where $D$ is disposable income. Second, intended investment in this country equals $150 million. Third, this country has a primitive economy with neither a government nor foreign trade. Fourth, the price level in this country is fixed.

(a) Suppose that GNP in this country assumes the alternative values shown below. What are the corresponding values of intended consumption expenditure, intended investment, and total intended spending? Fill in the blanks below.

| GROSS NATIONAL PRODUCT | INTENDED CONSUMPTION EXPENDITURE | INTENDED INVESTMENT | TOTAL INTENDED SPENDING |
|---|---|---|---|
| | (MILLIONS OF DOLLARS) | | |
| 800 | _____ | _____ | _____ |
| 900 | _____ | _____ | _____ |
| 1,000 | _____ | _____ | _____ |
| 1,100 | _____ | _____ | _____ |

(b) What is the equilibrium level of gross national product? (c) If GNP equals $900 million, what is the intended value of saving? (d) At what value of GNP does intended saving equal intended investment?

## Solution

(a) The complete table is:

| GROSS NATIONAL PRODUCT | INTENDED CONSUMPTION EXPENDITURE | INTENDED INVESTMENT | TOTAL INTENDED SPENDING |
|---|---|---|---|
| | (MILLIONS OF DOLLARS) | | |
| 800 | 700 | 150 | 850 |
| 900 | 775 | 150 | 925 |
| 1,000 | 850 | 150 | 1,000 |
| 1,100 | 925 | 150 | 1,075 |

(b) $1,000 million, since at this level of GNP total intended spending equals GNP. (c) $900 million minus $775 million, or $125 million. (d) When GNP equals $1,000 million, both intended saving and intended investment equal $150 million.

in the amount of intended investment? Specifically, if firms increase their intended investment by $1 billion, what effect will this increase have on the equilibrium value of gross national product, according to this model?

This is an interesting question, the answer to which sheds light on the reasons for changes in national output. The following sections are devoted to answering it. For simplicity, we assume that the change in investment is autonomous, not induced. An *autonomous* change in spending is one that *is not* due to a change in income or GNP. An *induced* change in spending is one that *is* due to a change in income or GNP.

## The Spending Chain: One Stage after Another

If there is a $1 billion increase in intended investment, the effects can be divided into a number of stages. In the first stage, firms spend an additional $1 billion on plant, equipment, or inventories. This extra $1 billion is received by workers and suppliers as extra income, which results in a second stage of extra spending on final goods and services. How much of their extra $1 billion in income will the workers and suppliers spend? If the marginal propensity to consume is 0.6, they will spend 0.6 times $1 billion, or $.6 billion. This extra expenditure of $.6 billion is received by firms and disbursed to workers, suppliers, and owners as extra income, bringing about a third stage of extra spending on final goods and services. How much of this extra income of $.6 billion will be spent? Since the marginal propensity to consume is 0.6, they will spend 60 percent of this $.6 billion, or $.36 billion. This extra expenditure of $.36 billion is received by firms and disbursed to workers, suppliers, and owners as extra income, which results in a fourth stage of spending, then a fifth stage, a sixth stage, and so on.

## Totaling Up the Stages

Table 6.5 shows the total increase in expenditure on final goods and services arising from the original $1 billion increase in intended investment. The total increase in expenditures is the increase in the first stage, plus the increase in the second stage, plus the increase in the third stage, and so on. Since there is an endless chain of stages, we cannot list all the increases. But because the successive increases in spending get smaller and smaller, we can determine their sum, which in this case is $2.5 billion. Thus the $1 billion increase in intended investment results—after all stages of the spending and responding process have worked themselves out—in a $2.5 billion increase in total expenditures on final goods and services. In other words, it results in a $2.5 billion increase in GNP.

**WHY $2.5 BILLION?**   Why does the $1 billion increase in intended investment result in a $2.5 billion increase in GNP? Because 0.6 is the marginal propensity to consume, a $1 billion increase in intended investment will result in increased total spending of $(1 + .6 + .6^2 + .6^3 + \ldots)$ billions of dollars. This is evident from Table 6.5, which shows that the increased spending in the first stage is $1 billion, the increased spending in the second stage is $.6 billion, the increased spending in the third stage is $.6^2$ billion, and so on. But it can be shown that $(1 + .6 + .6^2 + .6^3 + \ldots)$

$= \dfrac{1}{1 - .6}$ (See footnote 3.) Consequently, since $1/(1 - .6) = 2.5$, the total increase in GNP must be $2.5 billion.

Since the marginal propensity to save equals $(1 - .6)$, another way to state the finding of the previous paragraph is: *a $1 billion increase in intended investment results in an increase in equilibrium GNP of (1/MPS) billions of dollars, where MPS is the marginal propensity to save.*

### Table 6.5
### The Multiplier Process

| STAGE | AMOUNT OF EXTRA SPENDING (BILLIONS OF DOLLARS) |
|---|---|
| 1 | 1.00 |
| 2 | .60 |
| 3 | .36 |
| 4 | .22 |
| 5 | .13 |
| 6 | .08 |
| 7 | .05 |
| 8 | .03 |
| 9 and beyond | .03 |
| Total | 2.50 |

[3] To see this, let's divide 1 by $(1 - m)$, where $m$ is less than 1. Using the time-honored rules of long division, we find that

$$
1 - m \overline{\smash{\big)}\,\begin{array}{l} 1 + m + m^2 + m^3 + \ldots \\ \hline 1 \end{array}}
$$
$$
\begin{array}{r}
\underline{1 - m} \\
m \\
\underline{m - m^2} \\
m^2 \\
\underline{m^2 - m^3} \\
m^3 \\
\underline{m^3 - m^4} \\
m^4
\end{array}
$$

Thus letting $m = 0.6$, it follows that 1 divided by $(1 - .6)$ equals $1 + .6 + .6^2 + .6^3 + \ldots$

# THE MULTIPLIER

Since the marginal propensity to save is less than one, it follows from the previous paragraph that a $1 billion increase in intended investment results in a more than $1 billion increase in GNP. In the simple model considered here, it results in an increase in equilibrium GNP of (1/MPS) billions of dollars. The term (1/MPS) is called the **multiplier** for its role in translating the spending change into the corresponding change in the level of output. If you want to estimate the effect of a given increase in intended investment on GNP, multiply the increase in intended investment by (1/MPS). The result will be the increase in GNP. This means that GNP is relatively sensitive to changes in intended investment.

Suppose that the marginal propensity to save is 1/3. If so, a $1 billion increase in intended investment will increase equilibrium GNP by $1 \div 1/3$ billion dollars; that is, by $3 billion. Or take a case where the marginal propensity to consume equals 3/4. What is the effect of a $1 billion increase in intended investment? Since the marginal propensity to save must equal $1 - 3/4$, or 1/4, the answer must be $1 \div 1/4$ billion dollars. That is, equilibrium GNP will increase by $4 billion.

The same multiplier holds for decreases in intended investment as well as for increases. That is, a dollar less of intended investment results in (1/MPS) dollars less of GNP. Consequently, if you want to estimate the effect of a given change in intended investment (positive or negative) on GNP, multiply the change in intended investment by (1/MPS).

Since MPS is less than one, *the multiplier must be greater than one.* In other words, an increase in intended investment of $1 will result in an increase in GNP of more than $1. As noted above, this means that GNP is relatively sensitive to changes in intended investment. Moreover, since the multiplier is the reciprocal of the marginal propensity to save, the smaller the marginal propensity to save, the higher the multiplier—and the more sensitive is GNP to changes in intended investment.

# DETERMINANTS OF CONSUMPTION: NONINCOME FACTORS

The multiplier applies to consumption spending as well as to investment. In previous sections, we were concerned with the effects on GNP of changes in investment spending. Now we must consider the effects of changes in consumption expenditure. It is important to recognize that many other factors besides disposable income have an effect on personal consumption expenditure. Holding disposable income constant, personal consumption expenditure is likely to vary with the amount of wealth in the hands of the public, the ease and cheapness with which consumers can borrow money, the expectations of the public, the amount of durable goods on hand, the income distribution, and the size of the population. In this section, we discuss the effects of these nonincome factors on consumption expenditure.

**AMOUNT OF WEALTH.** Holding disposable income constant, it is clear that personal consumption expenditure will be higher if the public has a large amount of wealth—stocks, bonds, savings accounts, and so on—than if it has a small amount. Why? Because people are more willing to spend out of current income when they have large assets to tide them over if their incomes fall. Thus, if the Merriwether family has $100,000 in stocks and bonds, it is more likely to spend a large percentage of its income than if it has little or nothing in wealth.

**EASE AND CHEAPNESS OF BORROWING.** Holding disposable income constant, it is clear that personal consumption expenditure will be higher if the public can borrow money easily and cheaply. This is particularly important for expenditures on consumer durables like automobiles and appliances. If required down payments are increased, and interest rates go up, some potential buyers will be persuaded (or forced) to postpone purchases of such items. For example, the Merriwethers may want a new car, and they may be quite willing to borrow the money to pay for it at 10 percent per year. But if the interest rate is raised to 15 percent per year, they may decide to stick with their old car until it is run into the ground.

**EXPECTATIONS.** Holding disposable income constant, personal consumption expenditure may be higher if the public feels that price increases are in the wind or that goods will become harder to get. Why? Because the public may want to stock up on goods before their prices rise and while they are still available. (In the late 1970s, the expectation of price rises with regard to such items as autos and sugar seems to have had such an effect.) But this may not always occur. The expectation of price increases may have the opposite effect if the public is alarmed by inflation, and wants to build up its savings to cushion it against hard times ahead.

**AMOUNT OF DURABLE GOODS ON HAND.** Holding disposable income constant, personal consumption expenditure may be higher if the public has few durable goods on hand. For example, during World War II, very few automobiles were produced for ordinary civilian purposes. When such goods became available once again immediately after the war, there was an increase in the proportion of disposable income spent on durable goods, particularly since the public came out of the war with considerable savings and liquid assets.

**DISTRIBUTION OF INCOME.** Holding disposable income constant, personal consumption expenditure would be expected to increase as a nation's income becomes more nearly equally distributed. Why? Because one would expect that the marginal propensity to consume would be higher (and the marginal propensity to save would be lower) among poor families than among rich ones. Thus, if a dollar of income is transferred from a rich family to a poor one, the poor family would be expected to save a smaller proportion of this extra dollar than the rich family from whom it was taken. Consequently, total consumption expenditure would be expected to increase as a result of transfers of income of this sort.

**SIZE OF POPULATION.** Holding disposable income constant, personal consumption expenditure would be expected to increase as a nation's population increases. As there are more and more mouths to feed, bodies to clothe, and families to house, one would expect that more would be spent on consumption goods, and less saved.

## SHIFTS IN THE CONSUMPTION FUNCTION

Suppose that a change occurs in one of the factors discussed in the previous section. For example, suppose that there is a marked increase in the amount of wealth in the hands of the public. What effect will this have on the consumption function? Obviously, it will shift the consumption function upward, as from position 1 to position 2 in Figure 6.5. Or suppose that it becomes more difficult and expensive for consumers to borrow money. What effect will this have on the consumption function? Obviously, it will shift the consumption function downward, as from position 1 to position 3 in Figure 6.5.

### Shifts in Functions versus Movements Along Them

It is important to distinguish between a *shift* in the consumption function and a *movement along* a given consumption function. A **shift in the consumption function** means that the public wants to spend a different amount on consumption goods out of a given amount of disposable income than in the past. Thus, if the consumption function shifts to position 2 in Figure 6.5, this means that the public wants to spend more on consumption goods out of a given amount of disposable income than when the consumption function was at position 1. And if the consumption function shifts to position 3 in Figure 6.5, this means that the public wants to spend less on consumption goods out of a given amount of disposable income than when the consumption function was at position 1. When the consumption function shifts upward, this is called an *autonomous increase in consumption*; when it shifts downward, this is called an *autonomous decrease in consumption*.

In contrast, a movement along a given consumption function is a change in personal consumption expenditure induced by a change in disposable income, with no change in the relationship between personal consumption expenditure and disposable income. For example, the movement from point *A* to point *B* is a movement along a consumption function (in position 1). Similarly, the movement from point *C* to point *D* is a movement along a consumption function (in position 2). Such movements are called *induced changes in consumption*.

## EFFECTS OF SHIFTS IN THE CONSUMPTION FUNCTION

Earlier in this chapter, we showed that changes in intended investment have an amplified effect on GNP, with the extent of the amplification measured by the multiplier. It is important to recognize that a shift in the consumption function will also have such an amplified effect on GNP. For example, in Figure 6.6, if the consumption function shifts from $C_1$ to $C_2$, this means that at each level of disposable income, consumers intend to spend $1 billion more on consumption goods and services than they did before. *This $1 billion upward shift in the consumption function will have precisely the same effect on equilibrium GNP as a $1 billion increase in intended investment.*[4]

Moreover, a *$1 billion downward shift in the consumption function will have precisely the same effect on equilibrium GNP as a $1 billion decrease in intended investment*. Thus both upward and downward shifts in the consumption function—due to changes in tastes, assets, prices, population, and other things—will have a magnified effect on GNP. In other words, GNP is sensitive to shifts in the consumption function in the same way that it is sensitive to changes in intended investment. This is an im-

[4] For an algebraic demonstration that this is true, see the Appendix to this chapter.

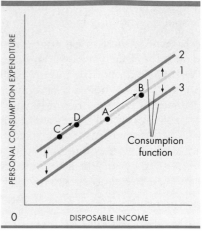

**Figure 6.5**
**A Shift versus a Movement in the Consumption Function**
If the consumption function moves from position 1 to position 2 (or position 3), this is a *shift* in the consumption function. A movement from A to B (or from C to D) is a *movement along* a given consumption function.

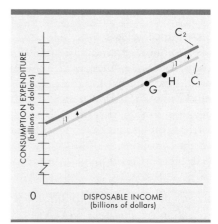

**Figure 6.6**
**Shift in Consumption Function**
If the consumption function shifts from $C_1$ to $C_2$, then at each level of disposable income consumers intend to spend $1 billion more on consumption goods and services. Such a shift results in an increase of $(1/MPS)$ billions of dollars in equilibrium GNP.

# HOW A SHIFT IN THE CONSUMPTION FUNCTION CAN UPSET A FORECAST

During World War II, economists, using the best models then available, were able to forecast the pace of the economy reasonably well. When the war was coming to an end, they were charged with forecasting the level of national product in 1946, the year immediately after the war. This was an important task, since the government was worried that the economy might suffer severe postwar unemployment. The Great Depression of the 1930s was a recent—and still bitter—memory.

To forecast gross national product in 1946, these Washington economists began by using prewar data to estimate the consumption function. Then they estimated the amount of investment that would take place in 1946. To obtain their forecast of the change in GNP, they computed the multiplier (1/MPS) and multiplied it by their estimate of the prospective change in intended investment. Then since their model (unlike ours up to this point) included government spending and taxes, other calculations had to be made as well. The result was a forecast of a gross national product in 1946 of about $170 billion.

This forecast caused a severe chill in many parts of the government, as well as among business executives and consumers. A GNP of only about $170 billion would have meant a great deal of unemployment in 1946. Indeed, according to some predictions, about 8 million people would have been unemployed in the first quarter of 1946. Unfortunately for the forecasters—but fortunately for the nation—the GNP in 1946 turned out to be not $170 billion, but about $190 billion. And unemployment was only about a third of the forecasted amount.

What went wrong in the Washington economists' forecast? For one thing, they failed to recognize that the consumption function would shift upward. When World War II ended, households had a great deal of liquid assets on hand. They had saved money during the war. There had been rationing of many kinds of goods, and other goods—like automobiles or refrigerators—could not be obtained at all. When the war

Here's your style leader and star performer... 1947's thrill car...the postwar Studebaker!

ended and these goods flowed back on the market, consumers spent more of their income on consumption goods than in the previous years. In other words, there was a pronounced upward shift of the consumption function.

To see why this shift in the consumption function caused the forecasters to underestimate GNP in 1946, recall from the previous sections that an upward shift of $1 billion in the consumption function will result in an increase of (1/MPS) billions of dollars of national product. Bearing this in mind, suppose the forecasters assumed that the consumption function remained fixed, when in fact there was an $8 billion shift upward. Then if the multiplier— (1/MPS)—was 2½, national product would turn out to be $20 billion higher than the forecasters expected. (Since (1/MPS) is assumed to be 2½, national product will increase $2.5 billion for every $1 billion shift in the consumption function, so an $8 billion shift in the consumption function will result in a $20 billion increase in national product.)

portant point. Finally, to prevent misunderstanding, recall from the previous sections that a *shift* in the consumption function is quite different from a *movement along* a given consumption function. (An example of the latter would be the movement from point *G* to point *H* in Figure 6.6.) We are concerned here with shifts in the consumption function, not movements along a given consumption function.

## THE EQUILIBRIUM LEVEL OF GROSS NATIONAL PRODUCT: AN OPEN ECONOMY WITH GOVERNMENT SPENDING

Having taken up the determinants of GNP in the highly simplified case where the economy is closed (no exports, no imports) and where no government exists, we now extend our analysis to include exports and imports as well as government spending. As pointed out in Chapter 4, gross national product equals consumption expenditure plus gross investment plus government expenditure plus net exports. Thus, if government expenditures and net exports are no longer assumed to be zero, total intended spending on final goods and services equals

$$C + I + G + (X - M_I),$$

where $C$ is intended consumption expenditure, $I$ is intended gross investment expenditure, $G$ is intended government expenditure on final goods and services, $X$ is intended exports, and $M_I$ is intended imports.

For simplicity, we take the values of $G$ and $(X - M_I)$ as given. In Chapter 9, a detailed discussion of the determinants and effects of government expenditure (and taxes) is provided. In Chapters 8 and 17, there is a detailed treatment of the determinants and effects of net exports. For now, it is convenient to assume that both intended government expenditure and intended net exports are given (and the same, regardless of GNP). In other words, we treat $G$ and $(X - M_I)$ in the same way that we have treated $I$ throughout this chapter.

For GNP to be at its equilibrium value, total intended spending on final goods and services must equal GNP. This is one of the central points stressed in this chapter. Thus, if the consumption function and intended investment are as shown in Table 6.4, and if intended government spending equals \$30 billion, and intended net exports equal \$10 billion, the equilibrium value of GNP equals \$1,200 billion. To see why, look carefully at Table 6.6, which shows all of the relevant information. As you can see, if GNP is *less* than \$1,200 billion, total intended spending is *more* than GNP, which means that there is a tendency for GNP to *rise*, since firms' inventories are going down. On the other hand, if GNP is *greater* than \$1,200 billion, total intended spending is *less* than GNP, which means that there is a tendency for GNP to *fall*, since firms' inventories are going up. Thus, as shown in Table 6.6, total intended spending equals GNP only when GNP equals \$1,200 billion—which means that this is the equilibrium value of GNP.

Figure 6.7 shows the same thing graphically. The $C + I + G + (X - M_I)$ line shows the level of total intended spending—that is, $C + I + G + (X - M_I)$ at each level of GNP. *The equilibrium level of GNP will be at the point on the horizontal axis where the* $C + I + G + (X - M_I)$ *line intersects the 45-degree line.* As shown in Figure 6.7, we get the same result as in

## Table 6.6
## Determination of Equilibrium Level of Gross National Product
## (Billions of Dollars)

| (1) GROSS NATIONAL PRODUCT (= DISPOSABLE INCOME)[a] | (2) INTENDED CONSUMPTION EXPENDITURE | (3) INTENDED INVESTMENT | (4) INTENDED NET EXPORTS | (5) INTENDED GOVERNMENT EXPENDITURE | (6) TOTAL INTENDED SPENDING (2)+(3) +(4)+(5) | (7) TENDENCY OF NATIONAL OUTPUT |
|---|---|---|---|---|---|---|
| 1,000 | 950 | 90 | 10 | 30 | 1,080 | Upward |
| 1,050 | 980 | 90 | 10 | 30 | 1,110 | Upward |
| 1,100 | 1,010 | 90 | 10 | 30 | 1,140 | Upward |
| 1,150 | 1,040 | 90 | 10 | 30 | 1,170 | Upward |
| 1,200 | 1,070 | 90 | 10 | 30 | 1,200 | No change |
| 1,250 | 1,100 | 90 | 10 | 30 | 1,230 | Downward |

[a] For simplicity, we assume here, as in Table 6.4, that GNP equals disposable income. In Chapter 9, we will relax this assumption.

Table 6.6: the equilibrium level of GNP is $1,200 billion. Of course, it will always be true that a tabular analysis and a graph of this sort will produce the same answer. (The $C + I$ line in Figure 6.4 is a special case of the $C + I + G + (X - M_I)$ line in Figure 6.7; it is valid when $G$ and $(X - M_I)$ are zero, as assumed in Figure 6.4.)

Increases in net exports tend to push up GNP. Suppose, for example, that net exports increase from $10 billion to $30 billion. If the situation is as shown in Figure 6.8, the equilibrium value of GNP will rise from $1,200 billion to $1,250 billion. Increases in spending on net exports have a multiplier effect, which is like the multiplier effect for investment or

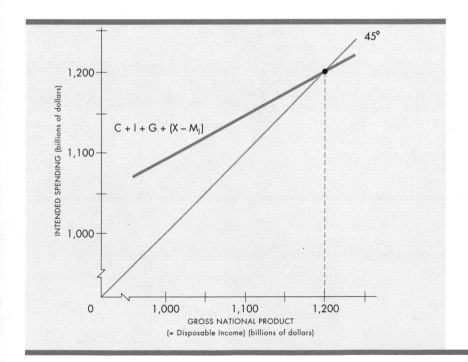

**Figure 6.7**
**Determination of Equilibrium Value of Gross National Product, Open Economy with Government Spending**
The $C + I + G + (X - M_I)$ line shows total intended spending—the sum of consumption, investment, and government expenditure plus net exports—at each level of GNP. The equilibrium value of GNP is at the point where the $C + I + G + (X - M_I)$ line intersects the 45-degree line, here $1,200 billion.

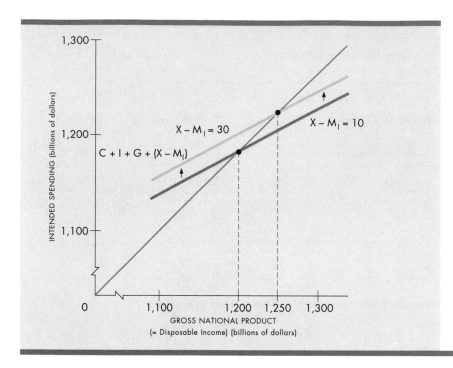

**Figure 6.8**
**Effect on Equilibrium GNP of Increase in Net Exports**
If net exports $(X - M_I)$ increase from $10 billion to $30 billion, the $C + I + G + (X - M_I)$ line moves upward, as shown above, the result being that equilibrium GNP increases from $1,200 billion to $1,250 billion.

shifts in the consumption function. Thus a $1 increase in intended spending on net exports results in more than a $1 increase in GNP. Since governments during the 1930s wanted desperately to increase their GNP to reduce unemployment, it is clear why they tried hard to increase their net exports at that time.

Increases in government spending also tend to push up GNP, and there is a multiplier effect, as in the case of investment, shifts in the consumption function, and net exports. Chapter 9 is devoted entirely to government expenditure, as well as to taxation, which has not been included in our present model. For an algebraic proof that government spending— as well as investment, shifts in the consumption function, and net exports—have this multiplier effect, see the Appendix to this chapter.

In conclusion, it is important to note once again that we have assumed in this chapter that the price level is constant. The model that we have presented—the simple Keynesian model—sheds light on the determinants of aggregate demand. In the following chapter, we show how our results can be used to derive the aggregate demand curve.

## TEST YOURSELF

1. Suppose that the consumption function in a particular economy is given by the following table:

| DISPOSABLE INCOME (BILLIONS OF DOLLARS) | CONSUMPTION EXPENDITURE (BILLIONS OF DOLLARS) |
| --- | --- |
| 400 | 300 |
| 500 | 360 |
| 600 | 410 |
| 700 | 440 |
| 800 | 470 |

Suppose that the sum of intended investment, government spending, and net exports increases from $140 billion to $141 billion. Using a graph showing the old and new $C + I + G + (X - M_I)$ line, indicate what effect this will have on the equilibrium value of GNP. (Assume the price level is fixed.)

2. In Question 1, suppose that consumers want to spend $50 billion more at each level of disposable income than is shown in the table. Using the $C + I + G + (X - M_I)$ line, show what effect this will have on the equilibrium value of GNP. (Assume that $I + G + (X - M_I)$ equals $140 billion.)

3. Suppose that the consumption function in a particular economy is $C = 100 + 0.8D$, where $C$ is consumption expenditure and $D$ is disposable income. What is the value of the multiplier?

4. Intended investment increases by $1000 in an economy where the marginal propensity to save is .2. What is the amount of extra spending in the *first* stage of the spending and respending process?

5. If the marginal propensity to consume is three times the marginal propensity to save, what is the multiplier? Why?

## SUMMARY

1. To understand the nature and derivation of the aggregate demand curve, it is useful to study the determinants of national output when the price level is held constant. The resulting model focuses on the forces influencing consumption expenditure, investment, government spending, and net exports.

2. The consumption function is the relationship between consumption expenditure and disposable income. From the consumption function, one can determine the marginal propensity to consume, which is the proportion of an extra dollar of income that is spent on consumption, as well as the saving function (the relationship between total saving and disposable income) and the marginal propensity to save (the proportion of an extra dollar of income that is saved).

3. The level of gross private domestic investment is determined by the expected rate of return from capital and the interest rate. The expected rate of return from capital is the perceived rate of return that businesses expect to obtain if new buildings are put up, new equipment is added, or inventories are increased. The interest rate is the cost of borrowing money. The level of investment is directly related to the expected rate of return from capital, and inversely related to the interest rate.

4. The equilibrium level of gross national product will be at the point where intended spending on final goods and services equals GNP. If intended spending exceeds GNP, GNP will tend to increase. If intended spending falls short of GNP, GNP will tend to fall.

5. A $1 billion change in intended investment will result in a change in equilibrium GNP of $\left(\frac{1}{\text{MPS}}\right)$ billions of dollars where MPS is the marginal propensity to save. In other words, the multiplier is $\left(\frac{1}{\text{MPS}}\right)$. The multiplier can be interpreted in terms of—and derived from—the successive stages of the spending process.

6. Holding disposable income constant, personal consumption expenditure is likely to depend on the amount of wealth in the hands of the public, the ease and cheapness with which consumers can borrow money, the expectations of the public, the amount of durable goods on hand, the income distribution, and the size of the population. Changes in these factors are likely to cause shifts in the consumption function.

7. A shift in the consumption function will also have an amplified effect on GNP, a $1 billion shift in the consumption function resulting in a change of $\left(\frac{1}{\text{MPS}}\right)$ billions of dollars in GNP.

8. Increases in net exports also have an amplified effect on GNP, as do increases in government spending on final goods and services. Much more will be said about the effects of government spending and net exports on GNP in subsequent chapters.

## CONCEPTS FOR REVIEW

**Consumption function**

**Marginal propensity to consume**

**Average propensity to consume**

**Saving function**

**Marginal propensity to save**

**Permanent-income hypothesis**

**Life-cycle hypothesis**

**Expected rate of return**

**Interest rate**

**Intended spending**

**45-degree line**

**Multiplier**

**Shifts in the consumption function**

# APPENDIX 6.1: USING BASIC ALGEBRA TO DERIVE THE MULTIPLIER

Equations speak more clearly to some than words, and so for those with a taste for (elementary) algebra, we will show how some of the principal results of this chapter can be derived algebraically. We begin by recalling that the equilibrium value of GNP is attained at the point where GNP equals total intended spending on output. This condition can be expressed in the following equation:

$$GNP = C + I + G + (X - M_I), \qquad (6.1)$$

which says that GNP must equal intended expenditure on consumption goods ($C$), plus intended investment ($I$), plus government expenditure ($G$), plus net exports ($X - M_I$). Since intended consumption expenditures plus intended investment plus government expenditure plus net exports equals total intended spending, it follows that this equation states that GNP must equal total intended spending.

Next, let's introduce a friend from this chapter, the consumption function. The consumption function in the first two columns of Table 6.4 can be represented by the following equation:

$$C = 350 + 0.6D, \qquad (6.2)$$

which says that desired consumption equals $350 billion plus 0.6 times disposable income ($D$). Figure 6.9 shows the consumption function. As you can see, $350 billion is the intercept on the vertical axis, while 0.6 is the slope of the consumption function. Since—as we noted in this chapter—the slope of the consumption function equals the marginal propensity to consume, 0.6 equals the marginal propensity to consume.

The next step is to substitute the right-hand side of Equation (6.2) for $C$ in Equation (6.1). The result is:

$$GNP = 350 + 0.6D + I + G + (X - M_I). \qquad (6.3)$$

But recall that disposable income is equal to GNP in our simplified economy since taxes are omitted here. (Taxes are discussed at length in Chapter 9.) Consequently, we can substitute GNP for $D$ in this equation to get

$$GNP = 350 + 0.6GNP + I + G + (X - M_I). \qquad (6.4)$$

And going a step further, we can subtract 0.6 times GNP from both sides of Equation (6.4), which gives

$$GNP - 0.6GNP = 350 + I + G + (X - M_I), \qquad (6.5)$$

or collecting terms,

$$0.4GNP = 350 + I + G + (X - M_I). \qquad (6.6)$$

Finally, dividing both sides by 0.4, we have

$$GNP = \frac{350}{0.4} + \frac{I}{0.4} + \frac{G}{0.4} + \frac{(X - M_I)}{0.4}. \qquad (6.7)$$

Now we can see what happens to GNP if there is a $1 billion increase in $I$. In other words, suppose that $I$ is increased from some amount, $R billion, to $(R + 1)$ billion. How much will this increase GNP? From Equa-

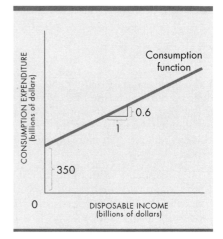

**Figure 6.9**
**Consumption Function**
The consumption function is derived from the data in Table 6.4. The marginal propensity to consume is 0.6, so the slope is 0.6.

tion (6.7), it is clear that GNP will equal

$$\frac{350}{0.4} + \frac{R}{0.4} + \frac{G}{0.4} + \frac{(X - M_\text{I})}{0.4}$$

if intended investment equals $R$ billion. It is also clear from Equation (6.7) that GNP will equal

$$\frac{350}{0.4} + \frac{(R + 1)}{0.4} + \frac{G}{0.4} + \frac{(X - M_\text{I})}{0.4}$$

if intended investment is equal to $(R + 1)$ billion. Consequently, the increase in GNP due to the $1 billion increase in intended investment is equal to

$$\frac{R + 1}{0.4} - \frac{R}{0.4}$$

$$= \frac{R}{0.4} + \frac{1}{0.4} - \frac{R}{0.4} = \frac{1}{0.4}$$

That is, a $1 billion increase in intended investment will result in an increase of $\frac{1}{0.4}$ billion dollars in GNP. Recalling that 0.6 is the marginal propensity to consume and that the sum of the marginal propensity to consume and the marginal propensity to save equals one—it follows that *a $1 billion increase in intended investment will result in an increase of* $\left(\frac{1}{MPS}\right)$ *billions of dollars in GNP, where MPS is the marginal propensity to save—0.4 in this case.*

This is precisely the same conclusion we arrived at in the text of the chapter. Thus we have derived the value of the multiplier by an algebraic route rather than the other routes used before.

In addition, Equation (6.7) can be used to determine the effects of a shift in the consumption function. A $1 billion·shift upward in the consumption function causes the intercept to increase from its former amount, $350 billion, to $351 billion. What is the effect of this increase in the intercept on the equilibrium value of GNP? If the intercept is $350 billion, the equilibrium value of GNP will equal

$$\frac{350}{0.4} + \frac{I}{0.4} + \frac{G}{0.4} + \frac{(X - M_\text{I})}{0.4}.$$

If the intercept is $351 billion, the equilibrium value of GNP will equal

$$\frac{351}{0.4} + \frac{I}{0.4} + \frac{G}{0.4} + \frac{(X - M_\text{I})}{0.4}.$$

Consequently, the increase in GNP from the $1 billion upward shift in the consumption function is

$$\frac{351}{0.4} - \frac{350}{0.4} = \frac{1}{0.4}.$$

That is, a $1 billion upward shift in the consumption function results in an increase of $\frac{1}{0.4}$ billions of dollars in GNP. Recalling that 0.4 = MPS, it follows that *a $1 billion upward shift in the consumption function will result in an increase of $\left(\frac{1}{MPS}\right)$ billions of dollars in GNP*. This is precisely what we said on this score in this chapter.

Finally, let's consider the effects on the equilibrium value of GNP of a $1 billion dollar increase in either $G$ or $(X - M_I)$. From Equation (6.7) it is clear that, if either $G$ or $(X - M_I)$ goes up by $1 billion, GNP will go up by $\frac{1}{0.4}$ billions of dollars. (To prove this to yourself, let either $G$ or $(X - M_I)$ increase by $1 billion, and use Equation (6.7) to see what the effect is on GNP.) In other words, a $1 billion increase in intended government spending or net exports will result in an increase of $\frac{1}{0.4}$ billion dollars of GNP. Since 0.4 is the marginal propensity to save, it follows that *a $1 billion increase in intended government expenditure or net exports will result in an increase of $\left(\frac{1}{MPS}\right)$ billions of dollars in GNP*. This agrees exactly with what was said on this score in the chapter.

## APPENDIX 6.2: EFFECTS OF THE MARGINAL PROPENSITY TO IMPORT ON THE MULTIPLIER

In this chapter (as well as Appendix 6.1), we assumed that net exports are given. In other words, net exports were assumed to be the same, regardless of GNP. In fact, however, *a country's net exports tend to decline as its GNP rises*. Why? Because its imports rise as its GNP goes up. Increases in GNP mean increases in consumers' incomes; and as their incomes rise, consumers tend to spend more on imported goods and services. Also, increases in GNP mean increases in firms' outputs, and as their outputs go up, firms tend to spend more on imported components and materials. On the other hand, a country's exports are not much affected by its own GNP. (What influences a country's exports is the GNP of other countries.) Thus, since exports are unaffected by GNP and imports are directly related to GNP, net exports—that is, exports minus imports—must be inversely related to GNP. (More will be said on this score in Chapter 8.)

Once we recognize that this is the case, we must change the simple formula for the multiplier that we presented in this chapter (and that we derived in Appendix 6.1). No longer is it true that the multiplier equals $\left(\frac{1}{MPS}\right)$; instead, it equals

$$\frac{1}{MPS + MPI}$$

where MPI is the marginal propensity to import, which is defined as the proportion of an extra dollar of income that is spent on imports.

To see how this formula can be applied, suppose that intended investment spending goes up by $1 billion. If the marginal propensity to save equals .2 and if the marginal propensity to import equals .1, the multiplier equals ⅓, or 3⅓. Thus the $1 billion in extra investment will result in a $3⅓ billion increase in GNP.

It is important to note that *the value of the multiplier is inversely related to the marginal propensity to import*. That is, the larger the marginal propensity to import, the smaller the multiplier. Consequently, in our previous discussion in this chapter, we overestimated the multiplier because we assumed implicitly that the marginal propensity to import was zero. To see that this is true, recall that we said that the multiplier equals $\frac{1}{\text{MPS}}$, whereas it really equals $\frac{1}{\text{MPS} + \text{MPI}}$. Clearly, our former estimate was too high—since $\frac{1}{\text{MPS}}$ must be bigger than $\frac{1}{\text{MPS} + \text{MPI}}$.

This is not the only reason why the simple multiplier formula presented in this chapter is likely to be too high. As stressed repeatedly, this chapter assumes that the price level is fixed; when the price level is allowed to vary, the size of the multiplier will be reduced. Also, this chapter ignores the fact that any autonomous increase in spending is likely to raise interest rates, which may also lower the multiplier. Further, we have ignored the income tax, which also reduces the multiplier. Each of these topics will be taken up in subsequent chapters.

# AGGREGATE DEMAND AND SUPPLY CURVES

IN 1991, IT WAS HARD TO FIND A newspaper, magazine, or television program dealing with business issues that did not mention changes, actual or forecasted, in GNP or the price level. Practically everyone is interested in these topics because they are intimately bound up with the economic health of our country—and with our own economic well-being. In this chapter, we show how national output and the price level are determined. (In contrast to the previous chapter, we no longer make the simplifying assumption that the price level is held constant.) As pointed out at the end of Chapter 5, our theory is built around aggregate demand and supply curves.

After reviewing what is meant by an aggregate demand curve, we use the results of the previous chapter to show how such a curve can be derived. Then we take up the aggregate supply curve in the short run, after which we discuss the determinants of total real output and the price level. Finally, we describe the shape and significance of the aggregate supply curve in the long run.

**GNP WILL POST A GAIN THIS QUARTER** The current swing in inventories will have its greatest impact on real gross national product in the third quarter, but that lift will not carry into the fourth quarter without more help from consumers. The government's latest revision to GNP shows a 0.1% drop in the second quarter, compared with the 0.4% gain originally reported. Consumer spending was not as strong as first reported, and inventory liquidation was much larger.

The revision makes three consecutive quarterly declines in real GNP, but the economy will undoubtedly post a gain in the third quarter. Inventories have now been cut deeply for three consecutive quarters (chart).

*Source: Business Week, September 9, 1991, p. 23.*

## AGGREGATE DEMAND AND SUPPLY

Before we become immersed in the details, it is worthwhile sketching out what this chapter is trying to do. In Chapter 3, we described the demand and supply curves for an individual commodity like wheat. Using these demand and supply curves, we analyzed the forces determining the price and output of a commodity in a competitive market. For example, we saw that a shift to the right in the demand curve for wheat tends to increase both the price and output of wheat.

In this chapter, we will analyze the changes in the price level and output of the entire economy. That is, we are going to determine why the price level increases in some periods, but not in others, and why real GNP soars in some periods and plummets in others. To understand the factors underlying inflation and unemployment, we must know why changes occur in the price level and in national output. (Why do we need to know the reasons for changes in national output in order to understand why changes occur in unemployment? Because more output tends to mean more employment.)

Can we use demand and supply curves for the entire economy in much the same way as we did in individual markets? Are there demand and supply curves for the whole economy that are analogous to the demand and supply curves for individual products like wheat? In Chapter 5, we said that the answer to both questions is *yes,* and we briefly described these aggregate demand and supply curves. In this chapter, we provide a much more complete treatment of each of these curves.

# THE AGGREGATE DEMAND CURVE

To begin with, consider the **aggregate demand curve.** As we know from Chapter 5, *the aggregate demand curve shows the level of real national output that will be demanded at each price level.* (Recall from Chapter 4 that real national output is measured by real gross national product. Thus real national output is composed of the output of food, automobiles, machine tools, ships, and the host of other final goods and services that are produced.) As can be seen in Figure 7.1, the aggregate demand curve slopes downward to the right. In other words, when other things are held equal, the higher the price level, the smaller the total output demanded will be; and the lower the price level, the higher the total output demanded will be. This might be expected, since the demand curve for an individual product also slopes downward to the right, as we saw in Chapter 3.

It is important to recognize the differences between the aggregate demand curve and the demand curve for an individual commodity. The aggregate demand curve, unlike the demand curve for any particular commodity, relates the economy's total real output to the price level. When the price level falls, the average price of *all* goods and services falls.[1] Unlike the demand curve for an individual commodity, there is not just a single price that falls, with the result that consumers find the relevant commodity relatively cheap and buy more of it.

In the following sections, we will show how the aggregate demand curve can be derived, using the $C + I + G + (X - M_I)$ line discussed in the

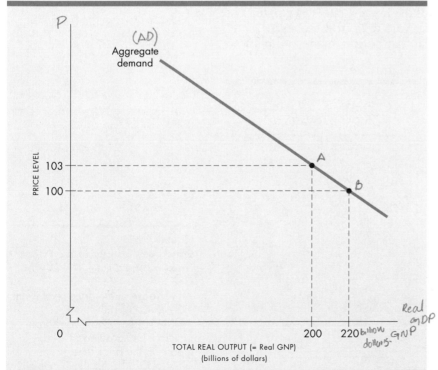

**Figure 7.1**
**Aggregate Demand Curve**
The aggregate demand curve shows the level of total real output that will be demanded at each price level. If the price level is 100, a total real output of $220 billion will be demanded. If the price level is 103, a total real output of $200 billion will be demanded.

[1] Of course, this does not mean that the price of each good and service falls when the price level falls. Only the *average* falls.

previous chapter. Then we will explain why the aggregate demand curve slopes downward to the right.

## Effects of Changes in the Price Level on the $C + I + G + (X - M_I)$ Line

The aggregate demand curve is intimately related to the $C + I + G + (X - M_I)$ line we encountered in Chapter 6. Recall that the $C + I + G + (X - M_I)$ line shows total intended spending at each level of GNP. To understand the relationship between the $C + I + G + (X - M_I)$ line and the aggregate demand curve, you must know one simple fact: *An increase in the price level lowers the* C + I + G + (X − M_I) *line; a decrease in the price level raises the* C + I + G + (X − M_I) *line.* The purpose of this section is to prove that this is true; in the next section we show how this fact can be used to derive the aggregate demand curve.

Suppose that the $C + I + G + (X - M_I)$ line is in position 1 in Figure 7.2. As we know from Chapter 6, this line is based on the assumption that the price level is constant. But suppose that the price level rises. Why will this lower the $C + I + G + (X - M_I)$ line (say from position 1 to position 2)? *One reason is that the increase in the price level will tend to push up interest rates.* In constructing the aggregate demand curve, it is assumed that the supply of money in the economy is fixed. An increase in the price level increases the average money cost of each transaction because the price of each good tends to be higher. Thus, if the price level increases considerably, people will have to hold more money in their wallets and checking accounts to pay for the items they want to buy. Since the supply of money is fixed, and the demand for money increases, there will be an increase in the price of money, which is the interest rate. (As pointed out in Chapter 6, the interest rate is the price paid to borrow money.)

When the interest rate goes up, firms that borrow money to invest in

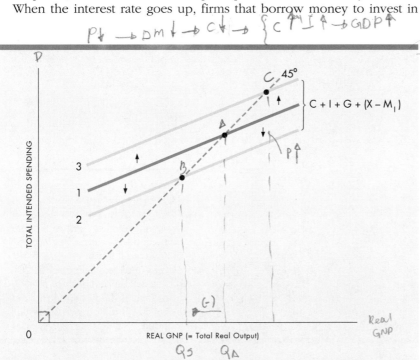

Figure 7.2
Effects of Changes in the Price Level on the $C + I + G + (X - M_I)$ Line
An increase in the price level (from $OP_1$ to $OP_2$) shifts the $C + I + G + (X - M_I)$ line downward (from position 1 to position 2). A decrease in the price level (from $OP_1$ to $OP_3$) shifts the $C + I + G + (X - M_I)$ line upward (from position 1 to position 3).

plant and equipment tend to cut down on their spending on these items. Due to the higher interest rates, the cost of borrowing money is greater, and hence some of these investment projects no longer seem profitable. (Recall our discussion in Chapter 6.) Since $I$ is reduced, $C + I + G + (X - M_I)$ must fall, which means that the $C + I + G + (X - M_I)$ line will shift downward. At each level of GNP, $C + I + G + (X - M_I)$ will be less than it was prior to the increase in the price level.

But the fact that an increase in the price level will tend to push up interest rates is not the only reason why it will lower the $C + I + G + (X - M_I)$ line. In addition, *the increase in the price level reduces the real value of the currency and government bonds held by the public.* Clearly, a \$1,000 bank account represents less purchasing power if a hamburger costs \$5 than if it costs 50 cents. Thus an increase in the price level reduces the real value of people's wealth, much of which is held in the form of assets (like currency, bank accounts, and government bonds) with a fixed dollar value. As pointed out in Chapter 6, such a reduction in people's wealth is likely to cause a downward shift in the consumption function. Since $C$ is reduced, $C + I + G + (X - M_I)$ must fall, and the $C + I + G + (X - M_I)$ line will shift downward.

Still another reason why price level increases result in downward shifts in the $C + I + G + (X - M_I)$ line is as follows: *Increases in the price level tend to lower net exports because foreigners tend to respond to price increases by cutting back their purchases from us (and we purchase more from them).* For example, Europeans may be glad to buy American computers at existing prices, but they may buy Japanese computers if prices double in the United States. Since $(X - M_I)$ is reduced, $C + I + G + (X - M_I)$ must fall, and the $C + I + G + (X - M_I)$ line will shift downward.

Just as an increase in the price level will shift the $C + I + G + (X - M_I)$ line downward (say from position 1 to position 2 in Figure 7.2), so a decrease in the price level will shift it upward (say from position 1 to position 3 in Figure 7.2). Why? Because a decrease in the price level will lower interest rates, thus encouraging investment spending. Also, the real value of the currency and government bonds held by the public will rise, thus pushing up the consumption function. And net exports will tend to increase as foreigners step up their purchases from this country.

## How to Derive the Aggregate Demand Curve

Based on the analysis in the previous section, it is a simple matter to derive the aggregate demand curve—and to show how it is related to the $C + I + G + (X - M_I)$ line. Suppose that the price level is at its current level $OP_1$ which means that the $C + I + G + (X - M_I)$ line is in position 1 in the top panel of Figure 7.3. Clearly, the equilibrium level of real GNP is $OQ_1$, as shown there. What happens to real GNP if the price level rises to $OP_2$, which means that the $C + I + G + (X - M_I)$ line shifts to position 2 in the top panel in Figure 7.3? The equilibrium value of real GNP falls to $OQ_2$, as shown there. What happens to real GNP if the price level falls to $OP_3$, which means that the $C + I + G + (X - M_I)$ line shifts to position 3 in the top panel in Figure 7.3? The equilibrium value of real GNP rises to $OQ_3$, as shown there.

The bottom panel of Figure 7.3 shows the aggregate demand curve, which is derived from the shifts of the $C + I + G + (X - M_I)$ line in the top panel. To derive point $A$ on the aggregate demand curve (which shows that real GNP is $OQ_2$ when the price level is $OP_2$), recall that when the price level is $OP_2$, the $C + I + G + (X - M_I)$ line is in position 2—and hence the equilibrium value of real GNP is $OQ_2$, according to the top panel. To derive point $B$ on the aggregate demand curve (which shows that real GNP is $OQ_1$ when the price level is $OP_1$), recall that when the price level is $OP_1$, the $C + I + G + (X - M_I)$ line is in position 1—and hence the equilibrium value of real GNP is $OQ_1$, according to the top panel. To derive point $C$ on the aggregate demand curve (which shows that real GNP is $OQ_3$ when the price level is $OP_3$), recall that when the price level is $OP_3$, the $C + I + G + (X - M_I)$ line is in position 3—and hence the equilibrium value of real GNP is $OQ_3$, according to the top panel.

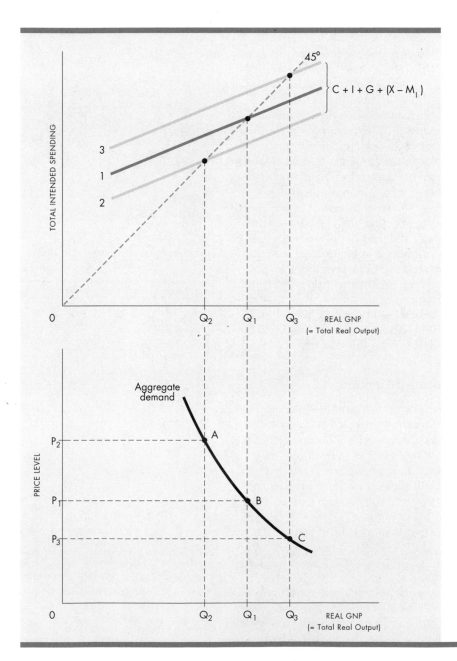

**Figure 7.3**
**Derivation of the Aggregate Demand Curve**
To derive Point $A$ on the aggregate demand curve, note that, if the price level equals $OP_2$, the $C + I + G + (X - M_I)$ line is in position 2, and equilibrium real GNP equals $OQ_2$. To derive point $B$, note that, if the price level equals $OP_1$, the $C + I + G + (X - M_I)$ line is in position 1, and equilibrium real GNP equals $OQ_1$.

### Reasons for the Aggregate Demand Curve's Shape

Take a close look at the bottom panel of Figure 7.3. Clearly, an increase in the price level (such as from $OP_1$ to $OP_2$) results in a reduction in total real output, and a decrease in the price level (such as from $OP_1$ to $OP_3$) results in a rise in total real output. Thus, based on our analysis in the previous section, we find that the quantity of real national output that is demanded is inversely related to the price level. In other words, the aggregate demand curve slopes downward to the right, as shown in the bottom panel of Figure 7.3. Basically, this is because increases in the price level lower the $C + I + G + (X - M_1)$ line, and decreases in the price level raise it.

In previous sections of this chapter, as well as in Chapter 5, we promised to explain why the aggregate demand curve slopes downward to the right. Our discussion of Figure 7.3 provides this explanation.

## THE AGGREGATE SUPPLY CURVE IN THE SHORT RUN ₂

Just as the aggregate demand curve is analogous to the demand curve for an individual product, so the *aggregate supply curve* is analogous to the supply curve for an individual product. As we know from Chapter 5, *the aggregate supply curve shows the level of real national output that will be supplied at each price level.* Aggregate supply curves can pertain to either the short run or the long run. In the short run, the prices of all inputs are assumed to be fixed; in the long run, they are permitted to adjust fully to eliminate the unemployment or shortage of inputs (like labor).

As can be seen in Figure 7.4, the short-run aggregate supply curve

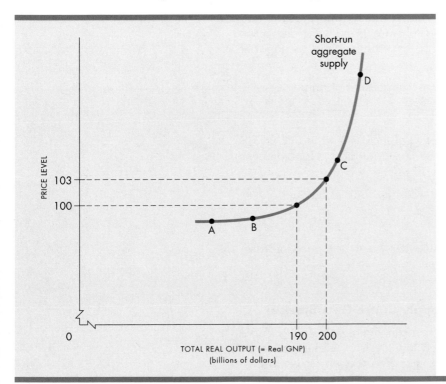

**Figure 7.4**
**Short-Run Aggregate Supply Curve**
The aggregate supply curve shows the level of total real output that will be supplied at each price level. If the price level is 100, a total real output of $190 billion will be supplied. If the price level is 103, a total real output of $200 billion will be supplied.

slopes upward to the right. In other words, when other things are held equal, the higher the price level, the larger the total output supplied will be; and the lower the price level, the smaller the total output supplied will be. This might be expected since the supply curve for an individual product also slopes upward to the right, as we saw in Chapter 3.

But just as we could not derive the aggregate demand curve simply by adding up the demand curves for all the individual commodities in the economy, so we cannot derive the aggregate supply curve by adding up the supply curves for all the individual commodities. If we did this, we would commit a grave error because the factors held constant in constructing an individual supply curve are not held constant in constructing an aggregate supply curve. In particular, in constructing an individual supply curve, the price of only one commodity is allowed to vary, whereas in constructing an aggregate supply curve, the price level (and thus every price) is allowed to vary.

## Why the Short-Run Aggregate Supply Curve Slopes Upward to the Right

To see why most economists believe that the short-run aggregate supply curve slopes upward to the right, let's begin by noting the obvious fact that firms are motivated to make profits. Because the profits earned by producing a unit of output equal the product's price minus the cost of producing it, increases in the product's price tend to increase the firm's profits. (Why? Because the wages of workers and the prices of raw materials and other inputs are fixed in the short run.) Thus, *since increases in product prices tend to increase the profit per unit resulting from the production of the product, they tend to induce firms to produce more output.*

As an illustration, consider the Montgomery Corporation, which produces computer software that sells for $12 per unit. Suppose that it uses one hour of labor to produce one unit of software. If the wage rate is $10 per hour, and if we suppose for simplicity that Montgomery has no other costs, its profit per unit of output is

$$\text{profit per unit of output} = \text{price} - \text{cost per unit of output}$$
$$= \$12 - \$10$$
$$= \$2.$$

Now suppose that the price of its software increases from $12 to $13 per unit. If the wage rate remains constant at $10 per hour, Montgomery's profit per unit of output increases to

$$\text{profit per unit of output} = \text{price} - \text{cost per unit of output}$$
$$= \$13 - \$10$$
$$= \$3.$$

Given that production is more profitable than before the price increase, Montgomery is likely to increase its output.

## Why the Short-Run Aggregate Supply Curve Gets Steeper

According to many economists, the short-run aggregate supply curve tends to be close to horizontal at relatively low levels of output, and tends to be steeper and steeper as output increases. To see why it is close to horizontal at relatively low output levels, note that there is likely to be considerable unutilized productive capacity under these conditions. If business picks up, firms are likely to increase their output by bringing this unutilized capacity back into operation. Since their costs per unit of output will not increase appreciably as their production rises, they will not raise price substantially. Thus the short-run aggregate supply curve will be close to horizontal.

On the other hand, at relatively high levels of output, production is pushing hard against capacity constraints, and it becomes increasingly difficult and costly for firms to increase their output further. Thus the short-run aggregate supply curve becomes steeper as output rises. Why? Because bigger and bigger increases in the price level are required to elicit a given additional amount of output. Moving from point *B* to point *C* to point *D* in Figure 7.4, the price level must go up by increasing amounts to elicit an additional billion dollars of real output. Eventually the short-run aggregate supply curve may become close to vertical.

Not all economists agree that the short-run aggregate supply curve has the shape indicated in Figure 7.4. As we shall see in Chapters 13 and 14, the new classical macroeconomists argue that the short-run aggregate supply curve may be vertical if the changes in the price level that occur are expected. A discussion of the arguments given by the new classical macroeconomists in this regard must be postponed to Chapters 13 and 14. All that you should note at this point is that the shape of the short-run aggregate supply curve is a matter of controversy.

## The Short-Run Aggregate Supply Curve in the Simple Keynesian Model

In the previous chapter, where we took up the simple Keynesian model to explain the level of national output, no mention was made of the short-run aggregate supply curve. *Because the price level was assumed to be fixed, the implicit assumption underlying this model was that the short-run aggregate supply curve is horizontal, as in the left-hand panel of Figure 7.5.* This model, proposed by Keynes in the Great Depression of the 1930s, is based on the idea that there are plenty of unemployed workers, equipment, and other resources. Since these resources can be used to produce additional output at about the same cost per unit of output as the

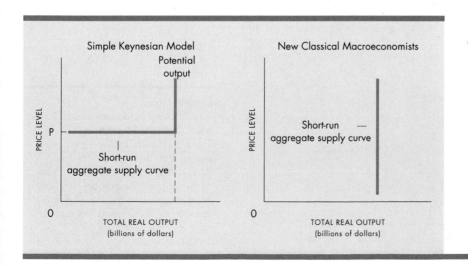

**Figure 7.5**
**Shape of Short-Run Aggregate Supply Curve, According to the Simple Keynesian Model and the New Classical Macroeconomists**
The shape of the short-run aggregate supply curve is a matter of controversy. According to the simple Keynesian model, its shape is as shown in the left panel; according to the new classical macroeconomists, its shape may be as shown in the right panel.

existing volume of output, firms do not have to receive higher prices for their products to be willing to expand production. And since wages and the prices of other resources are assumed to be fixed, there is little or no downward pressure on prices as output decreases. Eventually, however, if output is pushed up to its potential level, the short-run aggregate supply curve becomes vertical, as shown in the left-hand panel of Figure 7.5, because the economy will be working at full capacity.

It is interesting to compare the short-run aggregate supply curve, as envisaged by the simple Keynesian model, with the new classical macroeconomists' view of the short-run aggregate supply curve. As pointed out in the previous section, *the new classical* macroeconomists *believe that this curve may be vertical, as shown in the right-hand panel of Figure 7.5.* Clearly, there is a vast difference between these two models in this regard. As we shall see in subsequent chapters, this difference stems in considerable part from different assumptions regarding the degree of wage and price flexibility in the economy. The new classical macroeconomists assume that wages and prices are completely flexible, whereas the simple Keynesian model assumes that they are so inflexible that they do not go down even if there is substantial unemployment of resources. Both are regarded by many economists as relatively extreme assumptions.

## NATIONAL OUTPUT AND THE PRICE LEVEL

*In the short run, the equilibrium level of real national output and the equilibrium price level are given by the intersection of the aggregate demand curve and the short-run aggregate supply curve.* In Figure 7.6, the equilibrium level of real national output is $200 billion and the equilibrium price

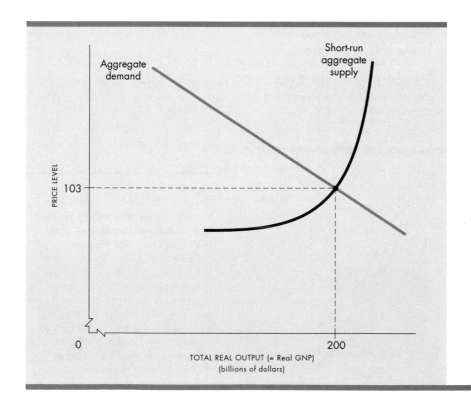

**Figure 7.6**
**Equilibrium Price Level and Total Real Output: Short Run**
The equilibrium level of total real output and the equilibrium price level are given by the intersection of the aggregate demand and supply curves. Here the equilibrium price level is 103 and the equilibrium level of total real output is $200 billion.

level is 103. The reasoning here is essentially the same as in Chapter 3, where we showed that the equilibrium price and output of a commodity are given by the intersection of the commodity's demand and supply curves. In the present case, an equilibrium can occur only at a price level and level of real national output where aggregate demand equals aggregate supply, as we know from Chapter 5.

## TEST YOURSELF

1. Give three reasons why, if the price level increases, the $C + I + G + (X - M_I)$ line will shift downward.

2. Why must an equilibrium occur only at a price level and level of real national output where aggregate demand equals aggregate supply?

3. Why does the short-run aggregate supply curve become steeper and steeper as total real output increases?

4. In what ways does the aggregate demand curve differ from the demand curve for cotton? In what ways does the aggregate supply curve differ from the supply curve for cotton?

## WHY SHIFTS OCCUR IN THE AGGREGATE DEMAND CURVE

In Chapter 3, we saw that shifts occur in the demand curve for an individual commodity. The same thing is true of the aggregate demand curve. A host of factors can shift the aggregate demand curve to the right or the left. If firms demand more plant and equipment, perhaps because the expected profitability of additional productive capacity goes up or because interest rates go down, this will shift the aggregate demand curve to the right. If the government spends more money on goods and services, this too will shift it to the right. Or if the government reduces taxes, thus providing consumers with more disposable income and encouraging them to spend more on consumers' goods, this too will shift it to the right, as we shall see in Chapter 9.

*Anything that increases the amount of total real output demanded (when the price level is held constant) will shift the aggregate demand curve to the right.* Thus developments abroad as well as at home can result in such a shift. For example, if the incomes of foreigners go up, this is likely to result in an increase in their demand for American goods and services—and thus shift the aggregate demand curve to the right. Also, as we shall see in subsequent chapters, if the government increases the money supply, this is likely to shift the aggregate demand curve to the right.

On the other hand, *anything that reduces the amount of total real output demanded (when the price level is held constant) will shift the aggregate demand curve to the left.* Thus, if firms demand less plant and equipment because the expected profitability of additional productive capacity goes down or because interest rates rise, this will shift the aggregate demand curve to the left. If the government spends less on goods and services, or if it raises taxes (thus discouraging consumer spending), this too will shift the aggregate demand curve to the left. And if the incomes of foreigners go down, this is still another reason why the aggregate demand curve may shift to the left.

# EFFECTS OF SHIFTS IN THE AGGREGATE DEMAND CURVE

In Chapter 3, we saw that shifts in the demand curve for an individual commodity result in changes in the price and output of this commodity. We now see that shifts in the aggregate demand curve result in changes in the price level and total real output.

## Effect of a Rightward Shift

Suppose that consumers or investors decide to *increase* their spending, perhaps because of a change in their expectations. (That is, they anticipate a marked improvement in economic conditions.) Since the level of total real output demanded at each price level increases, the aggregate demand curve shifts outward and to the right, as shown in Figure 7.7. What is the effect on the price level and on total output? *The answer depends on where the aggregate demand curve intersected the short-run aggregate supply curve before the shift in the aggregate demand curve.*

If the intersection occurred in the horizontal range of the short-run aggregate supply curve, the rightward shift of the aggregate demand curve will increase total real output, but will have no effect on the price level. (See panel A of Figure 7.7.) As pointed out above, this is the simple Keynesian case. However, if the intersection occurred in the range where the short-run aggregate supply curve is upward-sloping, the rightward shift of the aggregate demand curve will increase both the price level and total real output. (See panel B of Figure 7.7.) And if the intersection occurred in the range where the short-run aggregate supply curve is vertical, there will be an increase in the price level but no effect on output. (See panel C of Figure 7.7.)

**Figure 7.7**
**Effect of a Rightward Shift of the Aggregate Demand Curve**
Panel A shows that, in the horizontal range of the short-run aggregate supply curve, a rightward shift of the aggregate demand curve increases output, but not the price level. Panel B shows that, in the upward-sloping range of the short-run aggregate supply curve, a rightward shift of the aggregate demand curve increases both output and the price level. Panel C shows that, in the vertical range of the short-run aggregate supply curve, a rightward shift of the aggregate demand curve increases the price level, but not output.

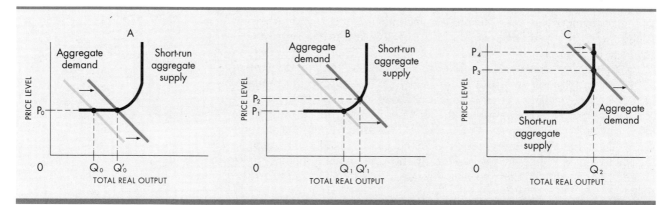

## Effect of a Leftward Shift

In contrast to the previous situation, suppose that consumers or investors decide to *reduce* their spending. Since the level of total real output demanded at each price level falls, the aggregate demand curve shifts inward and to the left, as shown in Figure 7.8. The effect of this shift depends on where the aggregate demand curve intersected the short-run aggregate supply curve before the shift occurred.

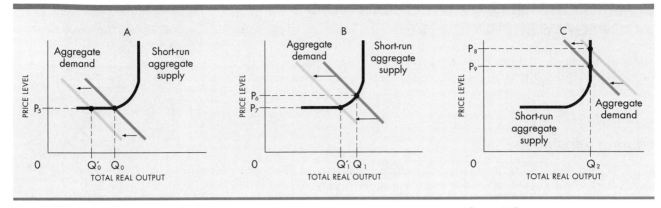

If the intersection occurred in the horizontal range of the short-run aggregate supply curve, the leftward shift of the aggregate demand curve will reduce total real output, but will have no effect on the price level (panel A of Figure 7.8). If the intersection occurred in the upward-sloping range of the short-run aggregate supply curve, this shift will reduce both the price level and total real output (panel B of Figure 7.8). If the intersection occurred in the vertical range of the short-run aggregate supply curve, this shift will reduce the price level but will not affect output (panel C of Figure 7.8).

## WHY SHIFTS OCCUR IN THE SHORT-RUN AGGREGATE SUPPLY CURVE

Shifts occur in the short-run aggregate supply curve as well as in the aggregate demand curve. In this section, we describe the reasons for such shifts; in the next section, we analyze their effects.

**THE WAGE RATE AND OTHER INPUT PRICES.** Input prices are held constant along a particular short-run aggregate supply curve. If they change, the curve shifts. Since the profit that a firm will make from a unit of output decreases as wage rates and other input prices go up, firms are likely to cut back on their output in response to increases in wage rates and other input prices. In other words, the aggregate supply curve is likely to shift to the *left* under these circumstances, as shown in Figure 7.9. On the other hand, if wage rates and other input prices go down, firms are likely to increase their output rate, since the profit that they will make from a unit of output will rise. In other words, the aggregate supply curve is likely to shift to the *right* under these circumstances.

**TECHNOLOGY AND PRODUCTIVITY.** If improvements in technology occur, firms can produce more with a given set of resources, the result being that the profit from a unit of output increases. Consequently, firms are induced to produce more, the result being that the short-run aggregate supply curve shifts to the *right*.

**AMOUNTS OF LABOR AND CAPITAL.** Clearly, the greater the amount of labor and capital available in an economy, the more that can be produced. Thus, as the labor force grows and as firms invest in more and more capital, the short-run aggregate supply curve shifts to the *right*, since a greater output will be produced at each price level.

**Figure 7.8**
**Effect of a Leftward Shift of the Aggregate Demand Curve**
Panel A shows that, in the horizontal range of the short-run aggregate supply curve, a leftward shift of the aggregate demand curve reduces output, but not the price level. Panel B shows that, in the upward-sloping range of the short-run aggregate supply curve, a leftward shift of the aggregate demand curve reduces both output and the price level. Panel C shows that, in the vertical range of the short-run aggregate supply curve, a leftward shift of the aggregate demand curve reduces the price level, but not output.

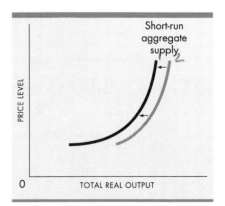

**Figure 7.9**
**Effect of an Increase in Wage Rates on the Short-Run Aggregate Supply Curve**
If wage rates (or other input prices) increase, the short-run aggregate supply curve tends to shift to the left.

# EFFECTS OF SHIFTS IN THE SHORT-RUN AGGREGATE SUPPLY CURVE

Shifts in the short-run aggregate supply curve, like those in the aggregate demand curve, result in changes in the price level and total real output, as indicated below.

## Effect of a Rightward Shift

Suppose that, because of increases in productive capacity or changes in technology, firms are willing and able to supply *more* goods and services (at any given price level) than in the past. Under these circumstances, the short-run aggregate supply curve shifts outward and to the right, as shown in Figure 7.10. What is the effect on the price level and on total output? If prior to this shift the aggregate demand curve intersected the short-run aggregate supply curve at a point where the latter was positively sloped, *the result will be an increase in total real output and a reduction in the price level*, as shown in Figure 7.10.

## Effect of a Leftward Shift

On the other hand, suppose that firms are willing and able to supply *less* goods and services (at any given price level) than in the past. For example, suppose that there is a worldwide shortage of important raw materials like oil or iron ore which results in increases in their prices. Given that this is the case, a given level of total real output can be produced only at a higher price level than was previously the case. That is, the short-run aggregate supply curve shifts upward and to the left, as shown in Figure 7.11. *The effect will be a reduction in total real output and an increase in the price level*, as shown in Figure 7.11.

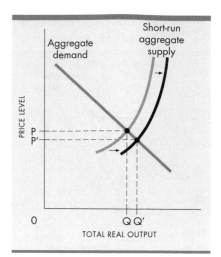

**Figure 7.10**
**Effect of a Shift to the Right in the Short-Run Aggregate Supply Curve**
If the short-run aggregate supply curve shifts to the right, the result will be increased real output (*OQ'* rather than *OQ*) and a lower price level (*OP'* rather than *OP*).

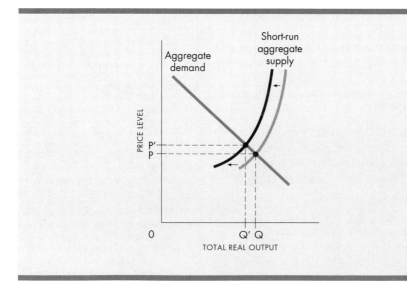

**Figure 7.11**
**Effect of a Shift to the Left in the Short-Run Aggregate Supply Curve**
If the short-run aggregate supply curve shifts to the left, the result will be reduced real output (*OQ'* rather than *OQ*) and a higher price level (*OP'* rather than *OP*).

## EXAMPLE 7.1    A RATCHET EFFECT ON AGGREGATE SUPPLY

Suppose that prices are rigid downward; that is, they can be increased but not decreased. The short-run aggregate supply curve (which is assumed here to have only a horizontal and a vertical range) is $P_1BS$, as shown at right. The aggregate demand curve shifts to the right (from $D$ to $D'$).

(a) Will the movement of the aggregate demand curve from $D$ to $D'$ affect the short-run aggregate supply curve? If so, how and why? (b) If the aggregate demand curve were to return to its original position (at $D$), would the short-run aggregate supply curve return to its original position? Why or why not? (c) Do the new classical macroeconomists assume that prices are rigid downward?

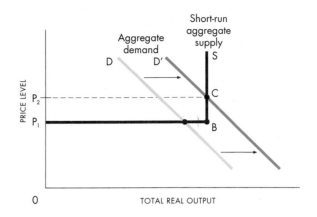

**Solution**

(a) Yes. The movement of the aggregate demand curve from $D$ to $D'$ results in an increase in the price level from $OP_1$ to $OP_2$. Since the price level rises in this way, firms will be unwilling to supply the old amounts at the old prices. To supply the same amount of output as they formerly supplied when prices were $OP_1$, they now insist on prices of $OP_2$. Thus the short-run aggregate supply curve will shift from $P_1BS$ to $P_2CS$. (b) No. Because prices are rigid downward, the short-run aggregate supply curve will remain at $P_2CS$ (at least for a considerable period of time). Thus there is a "ratchet effect" whereby rightward shifts in the aggregate demand curve push the short-run aggregate supply curve upward, but leftward shifts in the aggregate demand curve do not push it back to its original position.* (c) No. As pointed out on page 144, they assume that wages and prices are completely flexible.

* A ratchet is a device that permits a wheel to turn only one way.

## WHAT IF THERE IS AN INFLATIONARY GAP?

We must return now to a central point taken up in Chapter 5: *The equilibrium value of real national output may not equal its potential value. In other words, equilibrium national output may not attain the level that would prevail if there were full employment.* As we saw in Chapter 5, there frequently has been a gap between actual and potential GNP in the United States. Moreover, this gap can be positive or negative. Although actual GNP often has been less than potential GNP, there have been periods when actual GNP exceeded potential GNP, due to an increase in aggregate demand when full employment has already been reached. If the gap between actual and potential output is positive, we say that there is an *inflationary gap;* if it is negative, we say that there is *a recessionary gap.*

It is important to recognize that the economy, left to its own devices, will tend to move toward full employment if there is a recessionary or inflationary gap. To illustrate this fact, suppose that the situation is as shown in Figure 7.12, where the aggregate demand and supply curves intersect at $A$, a point to the right of the potential national output. Clearly, equilibrium national output exceeds potential national output, so there is an in-

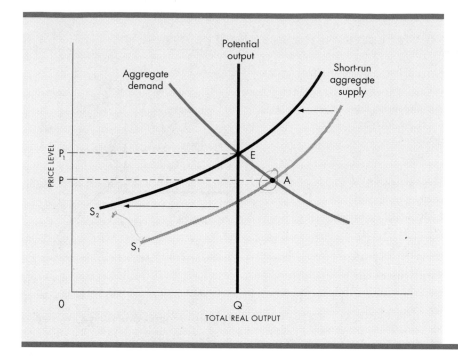

**Figure 7.12**
**The Economy's Response to an Inflationary Gap**
If the initial equilibrium is at point A, wage rates (and other input prices) will be bid up, with the result that the short-run aggregate supply curve will shift from $S_1$ to $S_2$. The economy will move toward full employment, but in the process there will be substantial inflation, with its attendant social costs. (The price level will increase from $OP$ to $OP_1$.)

flationary gap. In such a situation, jobs abound and labor is in short supply. Unemployment, while it exists, is less than the normal frictional level. (Recall from Chapter 5 that frictional unemployment occurs because people change jobs, move, and so on.)

The consequence is that wage rates are bid up, with the result that firms' costs rise. Thus the short-run aggregate supply curve is shifted to the left. Eventually, as shown in Figure 7.12, the short-run aggregate supply curve shifts from $S_1$ to $S_2$, thus pushing the equilibrium output down to the potential level. In other words, whereas the initial equilibrium point was A, it eventually is E.

How is this full-employment equilibrium eventually achieved? By inflation. Figure 7.12 shows that the price level increases from $OP$ to $OP_1$ when the economy makes the transition from point A to point E. As we saw in Chapter 5, such a bout of inflation can be a jarring social experience. Many economists believe that the government can help to avoid inflation of this sort. This topic is discussed at length in Chapters 9 and 12–14.

## WHAT IF THERE IS A RECESSIONARY GAP?

If equilibrium occurs below full employment, rather than above it, the economy will still tend to move toward full employment, as shown in Figure 7.13, but, according to many economists, this process may take a long time. Suppose that the initial equilibrium is at B, a point to the left of the potential national output. Because equilibrium national output is less than potential national output, there is a recessionary gap. Unemployment is high, and there will be a tendency for wage rates and other input prices to fall. If the short-run aggregate supply curve eventually shifts to the right from $S_3$ to $S_4$, the equilibrium output will be pushed up to the potential level at point C, and full employment will be achieved.

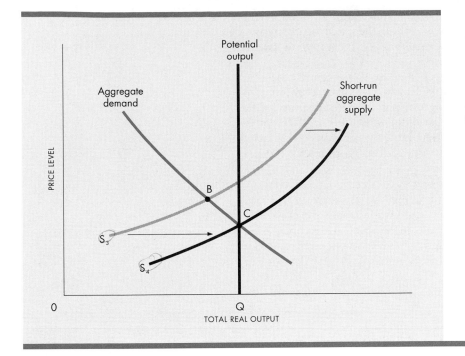

**Figure 7.13**
**The Economy's Response to a Recessionary Gap**
If the initial equilibrium is at point B, large-scale unemployment will tend to push wage rates (and other input prices) downward. If the high level of unemployment continues, the short-run aggregate supply curve eventually will shift from $S_3$ to $S_4$. The economy will move toward full employment, but in the process there will be high unemployment, with its attendant social costs

However, as just pointed out, many, but not all, economists believe that this process may take a very long time. Why? Because they maintain that wages (and some other input prices) tend to be very difficult to lower, due to minimum wage legislation and other government actions that have tended to put a floor under wage rates, as well as a psychological resistance among workers to wage reductions. Also, workers may feel that recessions will be short-lived and that they will be better off not to accept wage cuts.

For these reasons, many economists believe that the self-correcting process in Figure 7.13 may take longer than the public regards as acceptable—and longer than politicians can tolerate. Prolonged periods of high unemployment, as we saw in Chapter 5, entail large social costs. Many economists believe that the government can help to avoid unemployment of this sort. This topic is discussed in detail in subsequent chapters.

## THE AGGREGATE SUPPLY CURVE AND EQUILIBRIUM IN THE LONG RUN

As pointed out at the beginning of this chapter, whereas input prices are fixed in the short run, in the long run they can adjust fully to eliminate the unemployment or shortage of inputs (like labor). Thus, *once these adjustments have been made, full employment will occur, and real national output will be at its potential level*. If the potential output of a particular economy is 100 billion (1992) dollars, this will be the amount of output supplied regardless of the price level.

In other words, *the aggregate supply curve is vertical in the long run.* Why? Because in the long run, wages and the prices of nonlabor inputs adjust. For example, there is time for old labor contracts to expire and for new ones to be negotiated. Shortages of raw materials are resolved. Unemployed workers find jobs. In the long run, input prices change by the same proportion as product prices, with the result that there is no incentive for firms to alter their output levels. When the price of everything changes by the same proportion, the real value of everything is unchanged.

To see this, consider a firm that experiences a 10 percent increase in the price of its product. If this is due to a 10 percent increase in the general price level, this firm will in the long run pay 10 percent more for its inputs. Consequently, its profit per dollar of sales will be no different in the long run than it was before the 10 percent increase in the price level. Since this is the case, it has no incentive to produce more than it did before the increase in the price level.

Figure 7.14 shows the long-run aggregate supply curve for an economy with potential real GNP equal to *OQ*. It is a vertical line because the total quantity of goods and services produced when all inputs are efficiently and fully utilized does not depend on the price level. If the price level were to increase from 100 to 120 (and if wages and the prices of nonlabor inputs were to increase by the same proportion), the total quantity of goods and services produced would remain equal to *OQ*.

*In the long run, the equilibrium level of real national output and the equilibrium price level are given by the intersection of the aggregate demand curve and the long-run aggregate supply curve.* Thus, in Figure 7.14, the equilibrium value of real GNP is *OQ*, and the equilibrium value of the price level is *OP*. Note that *the aggregate demand curve affects only the price level, not the level of real output, in the long run. The level of output equals its potential level regardless of the price level.* In Chapter 16, which deals with economic growth, we will study the factors determining the level of potential output—or, what amounts to the same thing, the factors determining the location of the long-run aggregate supply curve.

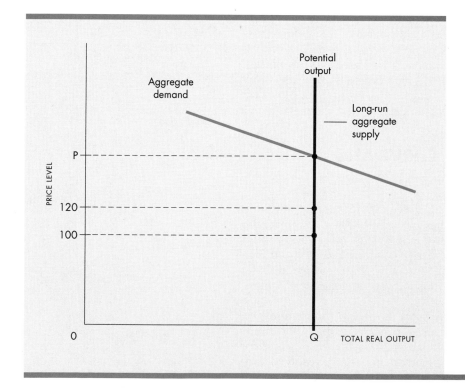

**Figure 7.14**
**Equilibrium Price Level and Total Real Output: Long Run**
In the long run, the aggregate supply curve is vertical. The equilibrium level of total real output and the equilibrium price level are given by the intersection of the aggregate demand and supply curves. Here the equilibrium price level is *OP* and the equilibrium level of total real output is *OQ*.

# TEST YOURSELF

1. What sorts of shifts in either the aggregate demand curve or the short-run aggregate supply curve (or both) would result in an increase in the price level but constant real output?

2. "One of the principal reasons why the short-run aggregate supply curve slopes upward to the right is that, as total real output increases, the quantity of money must increase as well, which means that the price level must rise, at least beyond some point." Do you agree? Why, or why not?

3. Suppose that the aggregate demand curve is $P = 120 - Q$, where $P$ is the price level and $Q$ is real output (in billions of dollars). If the short-run aggregate supply curve (which is a horizontal line in the relevant range) shifts upward from $P = 102$ to $P = 104$, what will happen to real output?

4. The aggregate demand curve in Country X shifts to the right, with the result that the price level rises. Do you think that this will affect Country X's short-run aggregate supply curve? Why, or why not?

5. Suppose that the Organization of Petroleum Exporting Countries raises oil prices by 50 percent in 1992. What effect will this have on the U.S. aggregate demand curve? On the short-run aggregate supply curve?

# SUMMARY

1. The aggregate demand curve shows the level of real national output that will be demanded at each price level. It slopes downward to the right because increases in the price level push up interest rates, which reduce investment. Also, increases in the price level shift the consumption function downward and reduce net exports.

2. The short-run aggregate supply curve shows the level of real national output that will be supplied at each price level. It slopes upward to the right because increases in product prices tend to increase the profit per unit from the production of a product. In the short run, input prices are assumed to be fixed.

3. The equilibrium level of real national output and the equilibrium price level are given by the intersection of the aggregate demand and supply curves. If the short-run aggregate supply curve is upward-sloping, a rightward shift of the aggregate demand curve will increase both output and the price level.

4. The short-run aggregate supply curve is likely to shift in response to changes in input prices and technology, among other things. A rightward shift of the aggregate supply curve is likely to increase national output and reduce the price level; a leftward shift of the aggregate supply curve is likely to reduce national output and increase the price level.

5. If actual national output exceeds potential output, we say that there is an inflationary gap; if it is less than potential output, we say that there is a recessionary gap. Left to its own devices, the economy will tend to eliminate such gaps, but many economists believe that the elimination of a recessionary gap may take longer than the public regards as acceptable—and longer than politicians can tolerate.

6. In the long run, the aggregate supply curve is vertical. Input prices, fixed in the short run, can adjust fully to eliminate the unemployment or shortage of inputs (like labor). They change by the same proportion as product prices, with the result that there is no incentive for firms to alter their output levels. The equilibrium value of real output in the long run equals potential output, regardless of the price level.

# CONCEPTS FOR REVIEW

**Aggregate demand curve**

**Short-run aggregate supply curve**

**Long-run aggregate supply curve**

**Inflationary gap**

**Recessionary gap**

# APPENDIX: THE EFFECTS OF CHANGES IN EXCHANGE RATES ON AGGREGATE DEMAND AND SUPPLY CURVES

You often read or hear that the dollar has gone up or down in value relative to the Japanese yen or the German mark. Economists refer to such developments as changes in exchange rates. *The exchange rate is the number of units of one currency that exchanges for a unit of another currency.* In 1991, one could exchange (at a bank) 135 Japanese yen for one dollar. Thus the exchange rate was 135 to 1, since it took 135 yen to purchase 1 dollar.

Exchange rates change over time. For example, the international value of the dollar decreased greatly between 1985 and 1988. In 1985, it exchanged for 238 yen; in 1988, it exchanged for 130 yen. Such changes in exchange rates can have big effects on the level of a country's net exports. Why? Because they influence how much a country's products cost abroad, as well as how much imported goods and services cost at home.

If the value of the dollar goes up relative to the Japanese yen, it takes more Japanese yen to buy an American product. In other words, American products become more expensive to the Japanese, with the result that our exports decline. At the same time, since a dollar exchanges for more yen, it takes fewer U.S. dollars to buy a Japanese product. In other words, Japanese products become cheaper in the United States, with the result that our imports increase. Thus, *if the value of the dollar goes up relative to the Japanese and other foreign currencies, our net exports will decline (because our exports will fall and our imports will rise).*

On the other hand, if the value of the dollar goes down relative to the Japanese yen, it takes fewer Japanese yen to buy an American product. In other words, American products become cheaper in Japan, with the result that our exports increase. At the same time, since a dollar exchanges for

## Foreign Exchange
### THURSDAY, SEPTEMBER 5, 1991

|  | Fgn. currency in dollars | | Dollar in fgn. currency | |
|---|---|---|---|---|
|  | Thu. | Wed. | Thu. | Wed. |
| f-Argent (Austral) | .000103 | .000103 | 9738.0 | 9738.0 |
| Australia (Dollar) | .7860 | .7850 | 1.2739 | 1.2739 |
| Austria (Schilling) | .0817 | .0817 | 12.24 | 12.24 |
| c-Belgium (Franc) | .0280 | .0280 | 35.70 | 35.70 |
| Brazil (Cruzeiro) | .0026 | .0026 | 383.15 | 383.15 |
| Britain (Pound) | 1.6930 | 1.6930 | .5907 | .5907 |
| 30-day fwd | 1.6864 | 1.6861 | .5930 | .5931 |
| 60-day fwd | 1.6794 | 1.6796 | .5955 | .5954 |
| 90-day fwd | 1.6743 | 1.6736 | .5973 | .5975 |
| Canada (Dollar) | .8768 | .8762 | 1.1405 | 1.1413 |
| 30-day fwd | .8748 | .8741 | 1.1431 | 1.1440 |
| 60-day fwd | .8727 | .8721 | 1.1459 | 1.1467 |
| 90-day fwd | .8707 | .8700 | 1.1485 | 1.1494 |
| y Chile (Peso) | .002772 | .002772 | 360.75 | 360.75 |

*Source: New York Times , September 5, 1991, p. D14.*

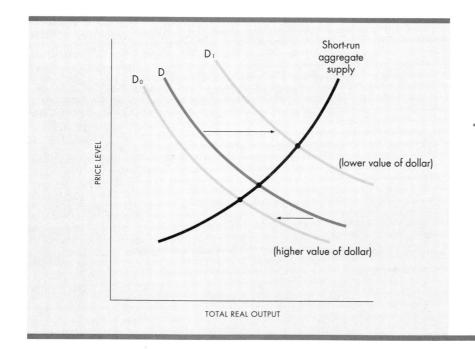

**Figure 7.15**
**Effect of Changes in Value of Dollar (Relative to Other Currencies) on U.S. Aggregate Demand Curve**
If the value of the dollar rises relative to other currencies, the aggregate demand curve shifts downward and to the left (from D to $D_0$). If the value of the dollar falls relative to other currencies, the aggregate demand curve shifts upward and to the right (from D to $D_1$).

fewer yen, it takes more U.S. dollars to buy a Japanese product. In other words, Japanese products become more expensive in the United States, with the result that our imports fall. Thus, *if the dollar goes down relative to the Japanese and other foreign currencies, our net exports will go up (because our exports will increase and our imports will fall.)*

One temporary complication: it takes time for exports and imports to adjust to changes in exchange rates. These lags result in the so-called *J-curve effect.* According to this effect, U.S. net exports will decline, rather than increase, in the period immediately after the value of the dollar goes down. This is because for a time everyone exports and imports approximately the same physical amount of goods as before, but imports cost more in terms of our currency, with the result that our net exports (in dollar terms) decline. However, as time goes on, imports fall and exports rise, so the expected increase in our net exports occurs.

Figure 7.15 shows the effects of changes in the exchange rate on the U.S. aggregate demand curve. As indicated in this figure, *an increase in the value of the dollar (relative to other currencies) shifts the U.S. aggregate demand curve downward and to the left.* This is because such an increase in the value of the dollar reduces our net exports, as we have just seen. Figure 7.15 also shows that *a decrease in the value of the dollar (relative to other currencies) shifts the U.S. aggregate demand curve upward and to the right.* This is because such a decrease in the value of the dollar increases our net exports, as we have just seen.

To determine the effect of exchange rate changes on real GNP and the price level, one must consider the effect of such changes on the short-run aggregate supply curve as well as the aggregate demand curve. Suppose that the dollar falls in value relative to the Japanese yen (and other currencies). The result is that Americans have to pay higher prices for imported goods, many of which are used as inputs in the production of American products. Since American firms will be led to charge higher prices for their own products (at any given level of output), *the U.S. short-run aggregate supply curve will tend to shift upward and to the left.* On the

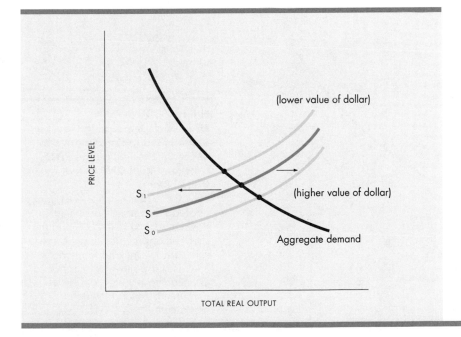

Figure 7.16
**Effect of Changes in Value of Dollar (Relative to Other Currencies) on U.S. Short-Run Aggregate Supply Curve**
If the value of the dollar rises, the short-run aggregate supply curve will shift downward and to the right (from $S$ to $S_0$). If the value of the dollar falls, the short-run aggregate supply curve will shift upward and to the left (from $S$ to $S_1$).

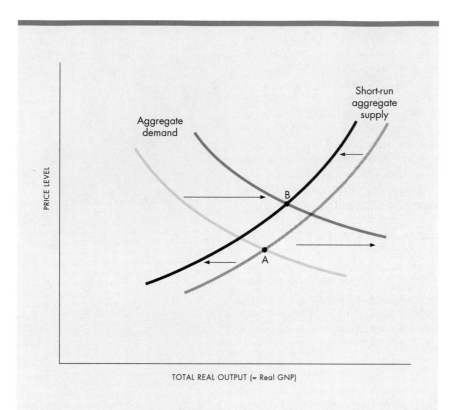

**Figure 7.17**
**Effect of a Reduction in the Value of the Dollar (Relative to Other Currencies) on the Price Level and Real GNP in the United States**
If the value of the dollar falls, the aggregate demand curve shifts upward and to the right, and the short-run aggregate supply curve shifts upward and to the left. The result is a movement from *A* to *B*, meaning a higher price level and (in this case) a higher total real output.

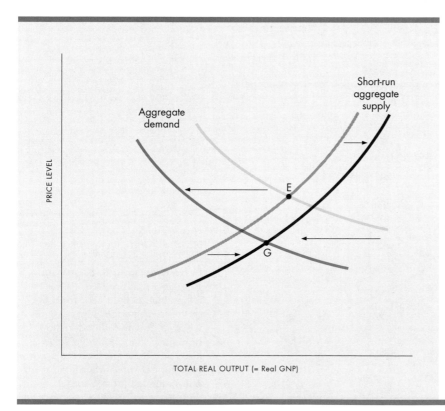

**Figure 7.18**
**Effect of an Increase in the Value of the Dollar (Relative to Other Currencies) on the Price Level and Real GNP in the United States**
If the value of the dollar rises, the aggregate demand curve shifts downward and to the left, and the short-run aggregate supply curve shifts downward and to the right. The result is a movement from *E* to *G*, meaning a lower price level and (in this case) a lower total real output.

other hand, *if the dollar rises in value, the U.S. short-run aggregate supply curve shifts downward and to the right,* as shown in Figure 7.16.

Taking account of the effect on both the aggregate demand and aggregate supply curves, Figure 7.17 shows that a *decrease in the value of the dollar is inflationary, although it may increase total real output in the United States.* Whether it increases total real output depends on whether (as in Figure 7.17) the aggregate demand curve shifts more than the short-run aggregate supply curve. (The evidence suggests this is true.) Figure 7.18 shows that *an increase in the value of the dollar tends to reduce the price level, although it may decrease total real output in the United States.* Whether it decreases total real output depends on whether (as in Figure 7.18) the aggregate demand curve shifts more than the short-run aggregate supply curve. (The available evidence suggests this is true.)

# BUSINESS FLUCTUATIONS

ARMED WITH THE BASIC theory presented in the previous chapter, we are now able to begin our discussion and analysis of the nature and causes of business fluctuations—the ups and downs of the economy. One of the principal reasons for presenting aggregate demand and supply curves is that they help us to understand business fluctuations. Business executives, government officials, and practically everyone else are interested in business fluctuations because they influence our welfare, and are intimately related to the twin economic evils of unemployment and inflation, discussed in Chapter 5.

In this chapter, we begin by defining business fluctuations and providing a brief overview of the business fluctuations in the United States during 1929–91. Then we discuss how variation in investment spending, government spending, and net exports, as well as other factors, can cause or aggravate business fluctuations. Finally, we describe the ways in which economists try to forecast business fluctuations—leading indicators, simple aggregate models, and econometric models—and we evaluate the track record of the leading economic forecasters. The treatment of business fluctuations in this chapter is by no means complete; it is only a brief introduction to this topic, which is taken up from a variety of points of view in subsequent chapters.

## ANATOMY OF THE BUSINESS CYCLE

To illustrate what we mean by business fluctuations—or the business cycle—let's look at how national output has grown in the United States since World War I. Figure 8.1 shows the behavior of real GNP (in constant dollars) in the United States since 1919. It is clear that output has grown considerably during this period. Indeed, GNP is more than 6 times what it was 70 years ago. It is also clear that this growth has not been steady. On the contrary, although the long-term trend has been upward, there have been periods—like 1919–21, 1929–33, 1937–38, 1944–46, 1948–49, 1953–54, 1957–58, 1969–70, 1973–75, January–July 1980, 1981–82, and a period beginning in late 1990—when national output has declined.

Recall that the potential GNP is the total amount of goods and services that could have been produced if there had been full employment. Figure 8.1 shows that national output tends to rise and approach (and perhaps exceed) its potential level (that is, its full-employment level), then falter and fall below this level, then rise to approach it once more, then fall

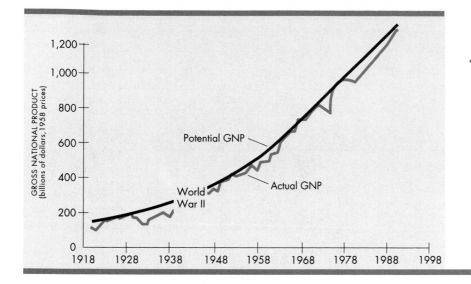

below it again, and so on. For example, output remained close to its potential level in the prosperous mid-1920s, fell far below this level in the depressed 1930s, and rose again to this level once we entered World War II. This movement of national output is sometimes called the **business cycle,** but it must be recognized that these cycles are far from regular or consistent. On the contrary, they are very irregular.

Each cycle can be divided into four phases, as shown in Figure 8.2. The **trough** is the point where national output is lowest relative to its potential level (that is, its full-employment level). **Expansion** is the subsequent phase during which national output rises. The **peak** occurs when national output is highest relative to its potential level. Finally, **recession** is the subsequent phase during which national output falls.[1]

Two other terms are frequently used to describe stages of the business cycle. A **depression** is a period when national output is well below its po-

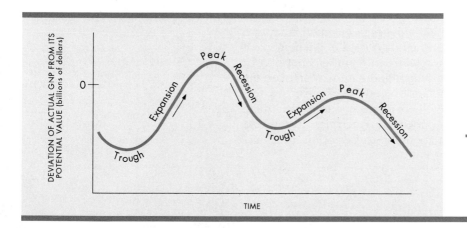

Figure 8.2
**Four Phases of Business Cycle**
Each cycle can be divided into four phases: trough, expansion, peak, and recession.

[1] More precisely, the peak and trough are generally defined in terms of deviations from the long-term trend of national output, rather than in terms of deviations from the potential (that is, the full-employment) level of national output. But the latter definition tends to be easier for beginners to grasp. Also, according to some people, a rough definition of a recession is at least two consecutive quarters of falling real GNP; it is not sufficient for output just to fall.

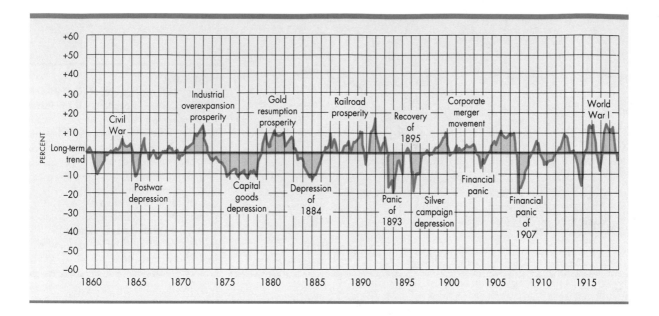

tential level; it is a severe recession. Depressions are, of course, periods of excessive unemployment. **Prosperity** is a period when national output is close to its potential level. Prosperity, if total spending is too high relative to potential output, can be a time of inflation. (Of course, in some business cycles, the peak may not be a period of prosperity because output may be below its potential level, or the trough may not be a period of depression because output may not be far below its potential level.)

From 1946 to 1990, peaks have occurred in 1948, 1953, 1957, 1960, 1969, 1973, 1980 (January), 1981, and 1990, while troughs have occurred in 1949, 1954, 1958, 1961, 1970, 1975, 1980 (July), and 1982 (November). Relative to the great Depression of the 1930s, none of these recessions has been very long or very deep (although the 1974–75 and 1981–82 recessions resulted in substantial unemployment).

Although business cycles have certain things in common, they are highly individualistic. (See Figure 8.3.) For certain classes of phenomena, it may be true that "if you've seen one, you've seen them all," but not for business cycles. They vary too much in length and nature. Moreover, the basic set of factors responsible for the recession and the expansion differs from cycle to cycle.[2] This means that any theory designed to explain them must be broad enough to accommodate their idiosyncrasies. In this and subsequent chapters, much will be said about the causes of business fluctuations.

---

[2] For example, there is some evidence that every so often, a business boom, or peak, takes place at about the same time as a boom in building construction; thus such a peak is buoyed further by this favorable conjuncture—and every so often, a trough is lowered by it. These long swings in building (and other phenomena), lasting 15 to 25 years, are called Kuznets cycles after Harvard's late Nobel laureate, Simon Kuznets, who devoted considerable study to them.

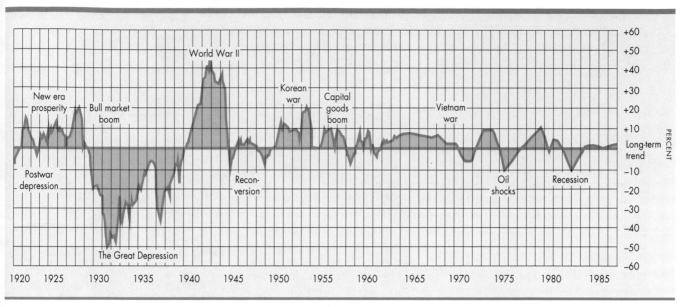

**Figure 8.3**
**Business Fluctuations in the United States, 1860–1987**
To construct this chart, a single index of economic activity was used. After fitting a trend line to it, the deviations of this index from its trend value were plotted. The results show the fluctuations in economic activity in the United States.

# BUSINESS FLUCTUATIONS DURING 1929–91: A BRIEF OVERVIEW

In the previous section, we described the general nature of business fluctuations. Now we turn to a description of the actual fluctuations that have occurred in the United States in recent decades. Our treatment is necessarily sketchy, since this is only a brief introductory discussion, but it should help to provide a useful background for subsequent chapters.

### The Great Crash

Let's begin with the late 1920s. During 1928 and 1929, the American economy was in the midst of a prosperity. As shown in Figure 8.1, gross national product was approximately equal to its potential value. Unemployment was low. Among the reasons for this prosperity was a relatively strong demand for machinery and equipment to produce new products (like the automobile, radio, telephone, and electric power) and to replace old machinery and equipment that had been worn out or outmoded during World War I and its aftermath.

The picture changed dramatically in 1929. After the stock market plummeted in October of that year, the economy headed down at a staggering pace. Real GNP fell by almost one-third between 1929 and 1933. Unemployment rose to an enormous 25 percent of the labor force by 1933. One important reason for this debacle was the severe contraction of gross private domestic investment. (Recall from Chapter 4 that gross private domestic investment is spending on tools, equipment, machinery, construction, and additional inventories.) Whereas gross private domestic investment was about $16 billion in 1929, it fell to about $1 billion in 1933. (The reasons for this decrease will be discussed in later chapters.) Another important factor was the decrease in the supply of money between 1929 and 1933. The money supply shrank from $26 billion in 1929 to $20 billion in 1933. This too tended to depress spending and output.

Put in terms of the aggregate demand and supply curves discussed in Chapter 7, the situation was as shown in Figure 8.4. For the reasons given in the previous paragraph, the aggregate demand curve shifted markedly to the left; and as would be expected on the basis of Figure 8.4, total real output and the price level fell between 1929 and 1933.

## World War II

The United States remained mired in the Great Depression until World War II (and the mobilization period that preceded the war). To carry out the war effort, the government expanded the money supply and spent huge amounts on military personnel and equipment. One result of this increase in spending was a substantial increase in real GNP, which rose by about 75 percent between 1939 and 1945. Another result was a marked reduction in unemployment, as the armed forces expanded and as jobs opened up in defense plants (and elsewhere). Still another result was the appearance of serious inflationary pressures. As the aggregate demand curve marched to the right, there was severe upward pressure on the price level as increases in spending pushed national output close to its maximum. (See Figure 8.5.) To counter this pressure, the government instituted price controls and other measures that kept a temporary lid on prices; but when these controls were lifted after the termination of the war, the price level increased dramatically. Between 1945 and 1948, the Consumer Price Index rose by about 34 percent.

## The Postwar Years

In 1948, the U.S. economy reached a peak, after which the unemployment rate increased to about 6 percent in 1949. But this recession was short-lived, and expansion continued. In 1953, another recession began, but it was relatively mild. After the trough was reached in 1954, GNP rose substantially during the next several years, only to fall back once more in the recession of 1957–58. The fifties were characterized by relatively slow growth of real GNP and by a rising unemployment rate, both of which were the cause of considerable concern.

## The Prosperous Sixties

As previous paragraphs have shown, the American economy experienced recurring fluctuations prior to 1960. During the 1960s, this pattern seemed to change, as the United States entered a period of expansion which was uninterrupted until 1969. There were a variety of reasons for this extremely long expansion, including the tax cut of 1964, which (according to most economists) increased after-tax income and stimulated consumer spending and investment. The increases in the money supply during this period are also given credit for this long expansion.

While unemployment was being squeezed to minimal levels, inflation was heating up. An important factor here was the government's spending on the Vietnam War, which was added to an already high level of expenditure on other goods and services, the result being that national output was at its maximum level in the late 1960s. Indeed, spending was so great that prices were pushed up at an increasingly alarming rate. And as prices rose, there was pressure for corresponding wage increases, which in turn pushed up firms' costs, and which were reflected in further price increases.

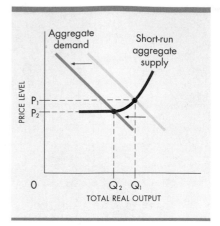

**Figure 8.4**
**Shift of the Aggregate Demand Curve, 1929–33**
A marked shift to the left in the aggregate demand curve was the principal reason for the onset of the Great Depression. (For simplicity, we assume here that the aggregate supply curve remained fixed.) Output fell drastically (from $OQ_1$ to $OQ_2$); the price level fell too (from $OP_1$ to $OP_2$).

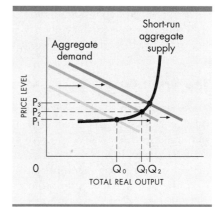

**Figure 8.5**
**Shifts of the Aggregate Demand Curve in World War II**
When we entered World War II, the aggregate demand curve shifted to the right as military expenditures mushroomed. Output increased (from $OQ_0$ to $OQ_1$ to $OQ_2$), and inflationary pressures mounted. (For simplicity, we assume that the aggregate supply curve remained fixed.) Much the same thing occurred during the Vietnam War.

By the end of the 1960s, inflation seemed to be the nation's foremost economic problem.

## The Turbulent Seventies

In August 1971, the government established controls on prices, wages, and rents. This was the first time such controls had been adopted by an American government in peacetime. Although these controls seemed to hold down prices for a while, the government regarded them as increasingly unworkable, and they were phased out in 1973 and 1974. In early 1974, the price of oil was quadrupled by the OPEC countries. This, together with a hike in farm prices, spearheaded a severe inflationary spurt. (The Consumer Price Index rose by 12 percent during 1974.)

The middle and late 1970s were characterized by **stagflation,** a combination of high unemployment and high inflation. (The term stagflation was coined by putting together *stag*nation and in*flation*.) What caused this turn of events? According to many economists, it was because the short-run aggregate supply curve shifted upward and to the left. In their view, the situation was like that in Figure 8.6. This shift in the short-run aggregate supply curve both reduced national output and increased the price level. Since a reduction in national output means high unemployment and an increase in the price level means inflation, it is easy to see that such a shift in the short-run aggregate supply curve might result in stagflation.

But why did the short-run aggregate supply curve shift upward and to the left during the 1970s? The following reasons are among those frequently cited: (1) Food prices shot up, beginning in late 1972, because of bad crops around the world (and the disappearance of Peruvian an-

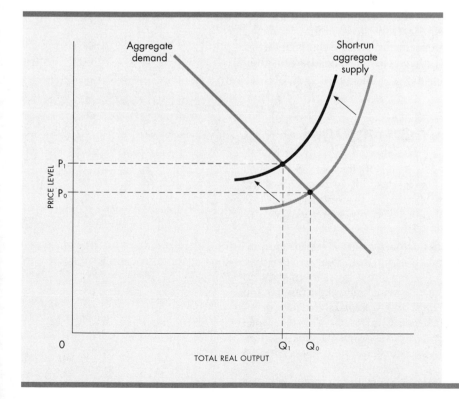

**Figure 8.6**
**Shift of the Short-Run Aggregate Supply Curve in the Seventies and Early Eighties**
According to many economists, the stagflation of the late 1970s was due in considerable part to a shift of the short-run aggregate supply curve upward and to the left due to marked shortages and price increases for oil, food, and other materials. Assuming for simplicity that the aggregate demand curve remained fixed, output fell from $OQ_0$ to $OQ_1$, and the price level rose from $OP_0$ to $OP_1$.

chovies, which caused a drop in the fish catch off the South American coast). (2) Many other raw-material prices increased rapidly, due to world-wide shortages. (3) As pointed out above, the price of crude oil increased greatly in 1974, 1979, and other years, due to the actions of Arab and other oil-producing countries. Because of these factors, a given level of GNP could be produced only at a higher price level than was previously the case. That is, the short-run aggregate supply curve shifted upward and to the left.

### The Eighties: Recession and Growth

In the latter part of 1981, the economy slumped into another recession, and the unemployment rate increased considerably. By the middle of 1982, it was over 9 percent, and unemployment, not inflation, seemed to be the nation's biggest economic problem. But this did not mean that inflation was quelled. The price level continued to rise, but at a less alarming rate.

November 1982 saw the trough of the recession. During 1983, real GNP grew by about 3.4 percent. Moreover, inflation continued to fall, the increase in the Consumer Price Index during 1983 being 3.2 percent. In 1984, the economy continued to show considerable strength, with real GNP growing at about 6.4 percent and inflation being held to about 4.3 percent. Throughout the rest of the 1980s, the growth of output continued, and became the longest peacetime expansion in U.S. history.

### The Nervous Nineties

During 1990, many business executives, government officials, and ordinary citizens were concerned that the economy was falling into a recession—and they were right. According to the Council of Economic Advisers, "After growing sluggishly for the first part of 1990, the economy entered a recession in the latter part of the year." During 1991, the government predicted that the recession would be short, but everyone recognized the fallibility of such predictions. On the inflation front, there was talk after Iraq invaded Kuwait that stagflation might crop up again, but inflation during 1991 remained moderate.

## VARIATION IN INVESTMENT SPENDING

What causes business fluctuations? A wide variety of factors, as we shall see. Although it would be premature to try to describe in detail all of the relevant factors, we take up a sampling of them in this and the next few sections. More complete discussions of these and other factors are provided in subsequent chapters.

One important factor causing business fluctuations is the variation in investment spending: Investment varies much more from year to year than does consumption expenditure. Figure 8.7 shows that investment goes up and down, while consumption climbs steadily with only slight bumps and dips. *The volatility of investment is an important factor in explaining the changes in national output over time.* Increases in investment tend to push the aggregate demand curve to the right, thus raising GNP. Decreases in investment tend to push the aggregate demand curve to the left, thus reducing GNP.

There are many reasons why investment in plant and equipment varies

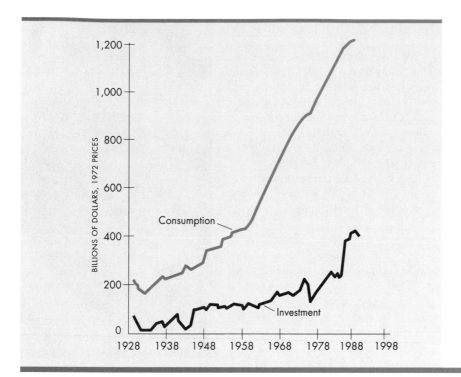

**Figure 8.7**
**Consumption Expenditure and Gross Private Domestic Investment, United States, 1929–90**
Investment varies more from year to year than does consumption spending.

so much over the course of the business cycle. As shown in the Appendix to this chapter, if sales are increasing at an increasing rate, investment is likely to rise. If sales are increasing at a decreasing rate, investment is likely to fall. Thus the rate of increase of sales is likely to influence investment—and since the rate of increase of sales varies greatly, so does the level of investment.

Another factor responsible for the variation in investment is the timing of innovations. For example, a new product may be invented, and large investments may be required to produce, distribute, and market it. Consider the computer industry. It took big investments to launch the personal computers that have become so common in offices and homes. As we shall see in the next section, some economists believe that business fluctuations are due in part to the timing of innovations.

## The Effects of Innovations and Random Economic Events

Major innovations do not occur every day. Neither do they occur at a constant rate. There are more in some years than in others, and sheer chance influences the number of innovations in a given year. Similarly, chance greatly influences the timing of many other types of events that bear on the level of output and investment. These include crop failures, hurricanes, and other such natural disasters, as well as man-made events, like strikes in major industries and financial panics, which also affect output and investment.

Let's suppose that these events—innovations and other occurrences that have a major effect on investment—occur more or less at random. Because so many factors influence the timing of each such event, we cannot predict how many will occur in a particular year. Instead, the number is subject to chance variation, like the number thrown in a dice game or the number of spades in a poker hand. In particular, suppose that the chance that one of these events occurs in one year is about the same as in another year.

If this is the case, economists—led by Norway's Nobel laureate, Ragnar Frisch—have shown that business cycles are likely to result. The basic idea is that the economy, because of its internal structure, is like a pendulum or rocking chair. *If it is subjected to random shocks—like pushing a rocking chair every now and then—it will move up and down.* These **random shocks** are the bursts of investment that arise as a consequence of a great new invention or of the development of a major new deposit of a vital resource like oil, or for some other such reason. These bursts play the role of the forces hitting the pendulum or the rocking chair. To a considerable extent, they may be due to noneconomic events or forces, but whatever their cause, they bang into the economy and shove it in one direction or another.

Of course, the occurrence of these shocks is not the whole story. *Business fluctuations in this model do not occur only because of the random events that affect investment. In addition, the economy must respond to— and amplify—the effects of these stimuli.* The economy must be like a rocking chair, not a sofa. (If you whack a sofa every now and then, you are likely to hurt your hand, but not to move the sofa much.) Frisch showed that the economy is likely to respond to, and amplify, these shocks. This model explains the fact, stressed in a previous section, that although cycles bear some family resemblance, no two are really alike. Thus the model has the advantage of not explaining more than it should. It does not imply that business fluctuations are more uniform and predictable than they are.

Ragnar Frisch

## INVENTORY CYCLES

The "minor" or "short" business cycle, lasting about two to four years, is sometimes called an **inventory cycle** because it has often been due largely to variations in inventories. This cycle proceeds as follows. Firms, having let their inventories decline during a business slowdown, find that they are short of inventories. They increase their inventories, which means that they produce more than they sell. This investment in inventories has a stimulating effect on national output. So long as the rate of increase of their sales holds up, firms continue to increase their inventories at this rate.[3] Thus inventory investment continues to stimulate the economy. But when their sales begin to increase more slowly, firms begin to cut back on their inventory investment. This reduction in inventory investment has a depressing effect on national output. As their sales decrease, firms cut back again on their inventory investment, further damping national output. Then when inventories are cut to the bone, the process starts all over again.

As an illustration, consider the recession of 1974–75. During the fourth quarter of 1974, inventories were still increasing at an annual rate of about $10 billion. Then because of a drop in sales, firms found themselves with excess inventories. They cut back their orders from suppliers, which in turn had to reduce output and employment. Inventories were reduced at

[3] The acceleration effect discussed in the chapter Appendix applies to inventories as well as to plant and equipment, since firms often try to maintain inventories equal to a certain percentage of sales. Thus the amount by which sales increase will affect the rate of investment in inventories as well as plant and equipment.

an annual rate of about $20 billion during early 1975. This inventory liquidation played a major role in the recession. Production plummeted. Fortunately, the reduction in inventories all but ceased in the second half of 1975, and production and employment picked up.

## VARIATION IN GOVERNMENT SPENDING

It should not be assumed that business fluctuations are solely or necessarily due to the behavior of the private sector. Particularly during and after wars, government spending has sometimes been a major destabilizing force. There were great bulges in government spending during World War II and lesser bulges during the Korean War and Vietnam War. These increases in spending produced strong inflationary pressures, as shown in Figure 8.8. The price level rose over 50 percent during and immediately after World War II, and major inflationary spurts also occurred during the wars in Korea and Vietnam.

Government spending has been a destabilizing force after, as well as during, wars. The recession in 1953–54 was caused primarily by the reduction in government expenditures when the Korean War came to a close. When hostilities terminated, government expenditures were reduced by more than $10 billion. Government spending sometimes has also had the same destabilizing effect in other than wartime or postwar situations. The recession in 1957–58 was aggravated by a drop in defense expenditures in late 1957. Faced with this drop, the defense contractors cut their inventories and expenditures for plant and equipment.

## THE POLITICAL BUSINESS CYCLE

Still another explanation of business fluctuations is based on the so-called political business cycle. According to a number of prominent economists, some business fluctuations, rather than being due to instability of spending

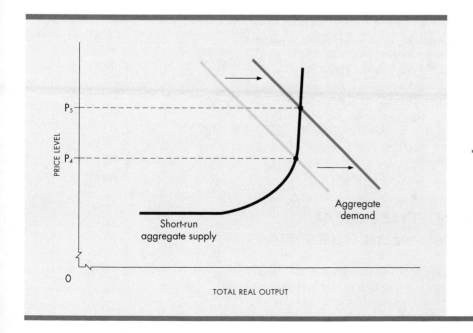

**Figure 8.8**
**Effects of Wartime Increases in Government Spending on the Price Level**
The great increases in government spending during wartime have shifted the aggregate demand curve to the right, and have produced strong inflationary pressures. Here the price level increases from $OP_4$ to $OP_5$.

by the private sector or to wartime or postwar changes in government expenditures, are caused by politicians' use of economic policy for their own political ends.

According to economists who have studied these political business cycles, the scenario runs roughly as follows. To begin with, a year or two before the election, the incumbent president (and representatives and senators whose eyes are fixed on the election) promotes an expansionary economic policy. That is, government expenditures are increased and taxes are cut, thus pushing the aggregate demand curve to the right. Also, the president may do his best to get the Federal Reserve to increase the money supply at a relatively rapid rate. Because of all this economic stimulus, the economy is in an expansion when the election comes around. The unemployment rate is relatively low—or, at least, it is falling. People's money incomes are rising. The voters are put in a mood to return the incumbents to office.

After the election, the inflationary impact of the expansionary economic policy becomes evident. If the economy was reasonably close to full employment when it was stimulated in this way, much of the increase in spending is likely to result in inflation, not higher real output. But in the short run, the effect on production and employment is much greater than the effect on the price level. Thus the inflationary effects of the expansionary pre-election economic policies become evident only after the election.

Not too long after the election, the president and Congress, faced with public outcries about the accelerated rate of inflation, assume an anti-inflationary posture. That is, they restrain the rightward shift of the aggregate demand curve. To do so, they cut back on the rate of increase of government spending and, if necessary, increase taxes. Also, the Federal Reserve is likely to reduce the rate of growth of the money supply. The result is a recession—but the incumbents are likely to call it a "slow-down," a "pause," or a "readjustment." After the recession has reduced the inflationary pressures, the stage is set for the process to start all over again, since it is close to a year or two before the next presidential election.

This description of the political business cycle is clearly oversimplified. For one thing, it is not easy for the president (or anyone else) to predict the timing of the effects of an expansionary policy. Yet this simple model seems to contain a certain amount of truth, both in the United States and in other countries. During election years, the American economy has been much more likely to be expanding than slowing down. Moreover, the available evidence seems to indicate that this is true in a wide variety of other democracies around the world. It appears unlikely that this difference in economic conditions between election and nonelection years could be due to chance.

## NET EXPORTS AND THE INTERNATIONAL TRANSMISSION OF BUSINESS FLUCTUATIONS

Changes in net exports can result in changes in GNP, as we saw in Chapter 6 (and the Appendix to Chapter 7). Thus they too can help to cause business fluctuations. Indeed, because of changes in net exports, business fluctuations often are transmitted from one country to another. To understand the role played by net exports, it is important to recall that net exports equal exports minus imports. Thus, to understand the determinants of net exports, we must look at the determinants of exports and imports.

*One of the most important determinants of imports is GNP itself.* As a country's GNP increases, so does its imports. (Recall Appendix 6.2 of Chapter 6.) For example, as America's GNP grew during the 1980s, American consumers and firms stepped up their purchases of Japanese videocassette recorders and German machine tools. Thus, since a country's exports are relatively insensitive to its own GNP, its net exports—which equal its exports minus its imports—tend to fall as its GNP increases.

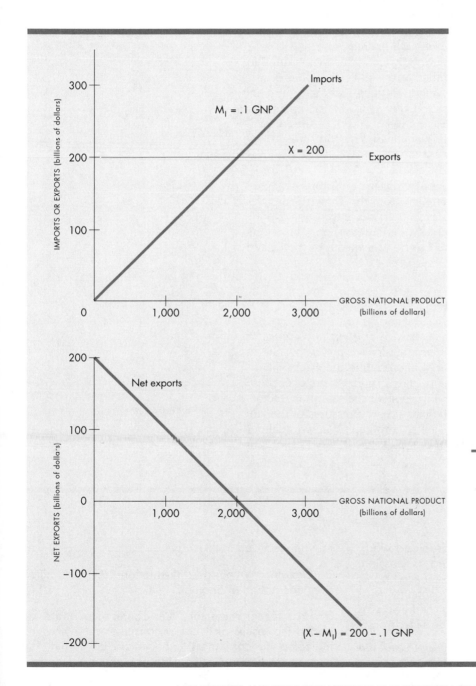

**Figure 8.9**
**The Relationship between Net Exports and Gross National Product**
If exports are $200 billion (regardless of GNP), and if imports are 10 percent of GNP, the upper panel shows the relationship between GNP, on the one hand, and exports and imports, on the other. The lower panel shows the relationship between GNP and net exports. As GNP increases, net exports decrease.

To illustrate, consider the country represented in Figure 8.9. According to the top panel of this figure, this country's exports equal $200 billion, regardless of the level of its GNP, and its imports equal 10 percent of its GNP. Thus, as shown in the bottom panel, its net exports—its exports minus its imports—go down as its GNP increases.

By the same token, *a country's exports tend to rise as the GNP of other countries increases.* For example, as the GNP of Japan or Germany goes up, its consumers and firms tend to buy more American goods and services. With rising incomes in Japan or Germany, our personal computers and software are in greater demand. Since our exports to Japan or Germany are the same as their imports from us, the fact that the level of our exports to them depends on their GNP is no news: it is another way of saying what we stressed in the previous paragraph—that a country (in this case Japan or Germany) imports more as its GNP increases.

At this point, it is easy to see how and why business fluctuations tend to be transmitted from one country to another. Suppose that a boom occurs in Europe or Japan. As GNP in these countries increases, their imports from the United States increase, as pointed out in this section. This increase in our net exports tends to increase our GNP, since it pushes our aggregate demand curve to the right. Thus our economy too tends to be stimulated. This is one way that a boom in Europe or Japan can be transmitted to the United States.

On the other hand, suppose that a recession occurs in Europe or Japan. As GNP in these countries falls, their imports from the United States decline, which means that our exports decline. This decline in our exports tends to reduce our GNP, which may push us into a recession. This is one way that a recession in Europe or Japan can be transmitted to the United States.

## MONETARY FACTORS

Finally, we must stress that *monetary factors are of great importance in causing business fluctuations.* By monetary factors we mean the rate at which the money supply grows, the rate of interest, and the availability of credit. As noted above, the Federal Reserve has major powers over these factors in the United States. In Chapter 12, we shall see that these factors figured significantly in slowing down the inflationary pressures of the late 1970s and early 1980s. Monetary factors are so important that we shall devote Chapters 10–12 entirely to them. In economics as in other aspects of life, money counts.

## TEST YOURSELF

1. In September 1990, there was widespread worry that the American economy was entering a recession. Allen Sinai, chief economist for the Boston Company, was reported as saying that "the economy was headed toward a recession before Iraq, and Iraq was just the nail in the coffin."[4] Why was Iraq's invasion of Kuwait regarded in this way?

2. Explain how business fluctuations are transmitted from one nation to another.

3. In a recent recession, the Conference Board reported the results of its latest consumer survey, which indicated that consumers' expectations concerning the economic future turned considerably more optimistic.

[4] "Growth Rate for Second Quarter Is Put at 0.4 Percent," *New York Times*, September 26, 1990.

How might this change in expectations help to pull the economy out of the recession occurring then? (*Hint:* Intentions to buy autos and appliances moved higher.)

4. "The government itself is frequently the cause of business fluctuations." Comment and evaluate.

# CAN BUSINESS FLUCTUATIONS BE FORECASTED?

How useful are modern economic theories in forecasting GNP? This is a perfectly reasonable question. After all, when you study solid state physics, you expect to come away with certain principles that will enable you to predict physical phenomena—for example, the effects of small but controlled amounts of impurities on the properties of metal. To the extent that economics is a science, you have a right to expect the same thing, since an acid test of any science is how well it predicts.

This question is also of great practical importance. Government officials are enormously interested in what GNP is likely to be in the next year or so, since they must try to anticipate whether excessive unemployment or serious inflationary pressures are developing. Business executives are equally interested, since their firms' sales, profits, and needs for equipment depend on GNP. For these reasons, forecasting is one of the principal jobs of economists in government and industry.

## Forecasting, No Exact Science

The first thing that must be said is that, *in forecasting as in most other areas, economics is not an exact science.* If economists tell you they can predict exactly what GNP will be next year, you can be pretty sure that they are talking through their hats. Of course, by luck, they may be able to predict correctly, but lucky guesses do not a science make. However, although economic forecasting is not perfectly accurate, economic forecasts are still useful. Since governments, firms, and private individuals must continually make decisions that hinge on what they expect will happen, there is no way that they can avoid making forecasts, explicit or implicit. The only question is how best to make them.

There is considerable evidence that, *even though forecasts based on economic models are sometimes not very good, they are better—on the average—than those made by noneconomists.* There is no substitute for economic analysis in accurate forecasting over the long haul. This really isn't very surprising. It would be strange if economists, whose profession it is to study and predict economic phenomena, were to do worse than those without this training—even if the others are tycoons or politicians. Further, it would be strange if government and industry were to hire platoons of economists at fancy prices—which they do—if they couldn't predict any better than anyone else.

Economists have no single method for forecasting GNP. They vary in their approaches just as physicians, for example, differ in theirs. But reputable economists tend to use one of a small number of forecasting techniques, each of which is described below. Of course, many economists do not restrict themselves to one technique, but rely on a combination of several, using one to check on another.

# LEADING INDICATORS

Perhaps the simplest way to forecast business fluctuations is to use **leading indicators,** which are certain economic series that typically go down or up before national output does. The National Bureau of Economic Research, founded by Wesley C. Mitchell (1874–1948), has carried out detailed and painstaking research to examine the behavior of various economic variables over a long period of time, in some cases as long as 100 years. The Bureau has attempted to find out whether each variable goes down before, at, or after the peak of the business cycle, and whether it turns up before, at, or after the trough. Variables that go down before the peak and up before the trough are called **leading series.** Variables that go down at the peak and up at the trough are called **coincident series.** And those that go down after the peak and up after the trough are called **lagging series.**

It is worthwhile examining the kinds of variables that fall into each of these three categories, since they give us important facts concerning the anatomy of the cycle. *Some important leading series are new orders for durable goods, average work week, building permits, stock prices, certain wholesale prices, and claims for unemployment insurance.* These are the variables that tend to turn down before the peak and turn up before the trough.[5] Coincident series include employment, industrial production, corporate profits, and gross national product, among many others. Some typical lagging series are retail sales, manufacturers' inventories, and personal income.

Wesley Mitchell

## How Leading Indicators Are Used, and with What Success

Economists sometimes use leading series as forecasting devices. There are good economic reasons why these series turn down before a peak or up before a trough. In some cases, they indicate changes in spending in strategic areas of the economy, while in others they indicate changes in business executives' and investors' expectations. Both to guide the government in determining its economic policies and to guide firms in their planning, it is important to try to spot turning points—peaks and troughs—in advance. This, of course, is the toughest part of economic forecasting. Economists sometimes use these leading indicators as evidence that a turning point is about to occur. *If a large number of leading indicators turn down, this is viewed as a sign of a coming peak. If a large number turn up, this is thought to signal an impending trough.* The Department of Commerce publishes a composite index that is a weighted average of about a dozen leading indicators, such as those listed in the previous paragraph. The behavior of this index is shown in Figure 8.10.

Unfortunately, the leading indicators are not very reliable. It is true that the economy has seldom turned down in recent years without a warning from these indicators. This is fine. But unfortunately these indicators have turned down on a number of occasions—1952 and 1962, for example—when the economy did not turn down subsequently. Thus they sometimes provide false signals. Also, in periods of expansion, they sometimes turn down too long before the real peak. And in periods of recession, they sometimes turn up only a very short while before the trough, so that they

[5] Of course, claims for unemployment insurance turn *up* before the peak and *down* before the trough.

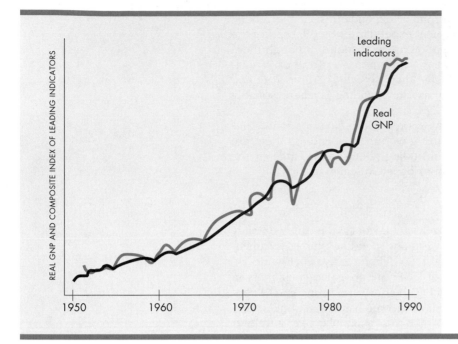

**Figure 8.10**
**Leading Indicators and Real GNP, United States, 1950–90**
Both GNP and the composite index of leading indicators are plotted against time, the scales of the two series being constructed so that they can readily be compared. As you can see, the leading indicators often give warnings of impending troughs or peaks. But sometimes they herald troughs or peaks that never occur.

give us little notice of the impending turning point. Nonetheless, these indicators are not worthless. They are watched closely and used to supplement other, more sophisticated forecasting techniques.

## SIMPLE AGGREGATE MODELS

Leading indicators are used primarily to spot turning points—peaks and troughs. They are of little or no use in predicting GNP. *One simple way of trying to forecast GNP is to treat certain components of total spending as given and to use these components to forecast the total.* This method is sometimes used by the president's Council of Economic Advisers, among others. For example, suppose that we decide to forecast investment spending, government expenditures, and net exports as a first step, after which we will use these forecasts to predict GNP. As we know from Chapter 4, investment spending is made up of three parts: expenditures on plant and equipment, residential construction, and changes in inventories. *To forecast expenditures on plant and equipment, the results of surveys of firms' expenditure plans for the next year are helpful.* The Department of Commerce and the Securities and Exchange Commission send out questionnaires (at the beginning of each year) to a large number of firms, asking them how much they plan to spend on plant and equipment during the year.

These surveys can help us forecast business expenditures on plant and equipment, but what about the other parts of investment spending—residential construction and changes in inventories? Lots of techniques are used to forecast them. *Some people use construction contracts and similar indicators as the basis for forecasts of residential construction. For inventory changes, some people watch surveys (like those that have been carried out by* Fortune *magazine and the Commerce Department) which ask companies about their inventory plans.*

Next, we need a forecast of government expenditures. At the federal level, it is possible to forecast government expenditures on the basis of the president's proposed budget or Congress's appropriations (although these forecasts can sometimes be quite wrong, as in the case of the early Vietnam War when expenditures were higher than expected). At the state and local level, it is often possible to extrapolate spending levels reasonably well.

Finally, we need a forecast of net exports, that is, exports minus imports. As in the case of investment and government spending, there are many ways to make such forecasts, including taking the average of the forecasts made by various government or private research groups.

## How Can GNP Be Forecasted?

Suppose that, having studied as many relevant factors as we can, we finally conclude that in our best estimate investment spending plus government expenditure plus net exports will equal $600 billion next year. How do we go from this estimate to an estimate of GNP? Suppose that consumers in the past have devoted about 90 percent of their disposable income to consumption expenditure, and that disposable income has been about 70 percent of GNP. Assuming that this will also be true again next year, it follows that consumption expenditure will equal 63 percent (90 percent times 70 percent) of GNP. In other words,

$$C = .63Y, \tag{8.1}$$

where $C$ is consumption expenditure and $Y$ is GNP. Also, by definition, $Y = C + I + G + (X - M_I)$, where $I$ is gross private investment, $G$ is government expenditure, and $(X - M_I)$ is net exports. Since $I + G + (X - M_I) = 600$, it follows that

$$Y = C + 600. \tag{8.2}$$

Substituting the right-hand side of Equation (8.1) for $C$,

$$Y = .63Y + 600,$$

or

$$Y - .63Y = 600$$
$$.37Y = 600$$
$$Y = \frac{600}{.37}$$
$$= 1,622.$$

Thus our forecast for GNP next year is $1,622 billion.

At this point, our job may seem to be over. But it really isn't; we must check this forecast in various ways. For example, it implies that consumption expenditures next year will be $1,022 billion. (Since $C = .63Y$, according to Equation (8.1), and $Y$ equals 1,622, $C$ must equal 1,022.) Does this seem reasonable? For example, how does it compare with the latest results of the survey of consumer buying plans carried out at the Survey Research Center at the University of Michigan? Also, the forecasted level of GNP must be compared with the productive capacity of the economy. Do we have the physical capacity to produce this much at stable prices? To what extent will the general price level be pushed upward? Moreover, our assumptions concerning investment and government spending must be re-examined in the light of our forecast of GNP. If GNP is $1,622 billion, is it reasonable to assume that $I$ will be the amount we initially forecasted? Or do we want to revise our forecast of investment? A great many steps must be carried out before we finally put forth a GNP forecast, if we are conscientious and professional in our approach. Moreover, even after the forecast is made, it is often updated as new information becomes available, so the process goes on more or less continuously.

## ECONOMETRIC MODELS

In recent years, more and more emphasis has been placed on econometric models. **Econometric models** *are systems of equations estimated from past data that are used to forecast economic variables.* Thirty years ago, econometric models were in their infancy. But now the president's Council of Economic Advisers, the Treasury, the Federal Reserve Board, and other parts of the federal government pay attention to the forecasts made by econometric models—and sometimes construct their own econometric models. Business firms too hire economists to construct econometric models for them, to forecast both GNP and their own sales.

The essence of any econometric model is that it blends theory and measurement. It is not merely a general, nonquantitative theory. Useful as such a theory may be, it does not in general permit quantitative or numerical forecasts. Nor is an econometric model a purely empirical result based on little or no theoretical underpinning. Although such results may also be useful, they generally are untrustworthy once the basic structure of the economic situation changes. Most econometric models designed to forecast GNP are built, at least in part, on the theoretical foundations described in previous chapters. In other words, they contain a number of equations, one of which is designed to explain consumption expenditures, one to explain investment expenditures, and so forth. The leading figure in the development of such models has been Nobel Laureate Lawrence Klein of the University of Pennsylvania. The principal model that he has constructed—or helped to construct—is known as the Wharton model.

## ECONOMETRIC FORECASTS: THE TRACK RECORD

How well can econometric models forecast? During the 1960s, the leading econometric models did well. The performance of the Wharton model in this period was particularly impressive. Its average error in forecasting GNP was only about $3 billion—or less than ½ of 1 percent. In this ball game, that is a very fancy batting average.

During the 1970s, the predictive performance of leading econometric models was poorer than in the previous decade. In particular, the average one-year forecast of the percentage change in GNP (in money terms) was off by 4.1 percentage points for the year ending in the first quarter of 1975. An important reason for this decline in performance was the difficulty in incorporating the effects of the Arab oil embargo, the drastic oil price increase, and the high inflation rate of 1973–74 into such models. The assumption underlying any econometric model is that the basic structure of the economy—the numbers in the equations of the model—will not change much. If this assumption does not hold, the model is in trouble. After all, any econometric model is powered by past data, not magic.

After 1975, economic forecasts became significantly more accurate than in 1974. The average one-year forecast of the percentage change in GNP (in real terms) was quite close to the actual figure during 1976–81. But 1981 was another year that forecasters would like to forget. They failed to foresee that real GNP would fall substantially in 1982. Afterward, their accuracy picked up again.

Economic forecasting remains a difficult and uncertain business, but economic forecasts must continue to be made. For example, in early 1990, the Council of Economic Advisers published forecasts of the percent increase in real GNP and in the price level during 1990. As shown in Table 8.1, the inflation forecast was more accurate than the forecast of real GNP growth.

---

## EXAMPLE 8.1    HOW GOOD WERE CHAIRMAN GREENSPAN'S FORECASTS?

Alan Greenspan

of increase of the price level were as follows:

| YEAR | PERCENT INCREASE IN REAL GNP | | PERCENT INCREASE IN PRICE LEVEL | |
|------|----------|--------|----------|--------|
|      | FORECAST | ACTUAL | FORECAST | ACTUAL |
| 1978 | 4.8 | 3.3 | 6.5 | 7.3 |
| 1979 | 2.5 | 2.5 | 7.6 | 8.9 |
| 1980 | −1.6 | −0.2 | 8.4 | 9.0 |
| 1981 | 1.1 | 1.9 | 9.4 | 9.7 |
| 1982 | −1.0 | −2.5 | 8.4 | 6.4 |
| 1983 | 1.9 | 3.6 | 6.2 | 3.9 |
| 1984 | 5.8 | 6.4 | 4.9 | 3.8 |
| 1985 | 3.6 | 2.7 | 4.5 | 3.3 |
| 1986 | 2.9 | 2.5 | 4.4 | 2.7 |
| 1987 | 2.4 | 2.9 | 2.9 | 3.0 |

Alan Greenspan, the chairman of the Federal Reserve Board, is a distinguished economist. In the Senate hearings prior to his confirmation, the accuracy of his forecasts was questioned by Senator William Proxmire of Wisconsin, who pointed out that Greenspan, when he served as chairman of former president Ford's Council of Economic Advisers, had published forecasts that overestimated the growth of GNP and underestimated the rate of inflation. When he left the Council of Economic Advisers, Greenspan returned to Townsend-Greenspan and Company, an economic forecasting firm, where his forecasts of the annual percent change in GNP (in 1982 dollars) and of the rate

(a) Did Greenspan anticipate the drop in real GNP in 1980 and 1982? (b) Did he foresee the increase in real GNP in 1983? (c) Did he anticipate the weaker (than in previous years) growth of the economy in 1985 and 1986? (d) Did he foresee the steep rise in inflation during 1978–80? (e) Did he anticipate the marked decline in inflation during the 1980s?

**Solution**

(a) Yes. (b) Yes. (c) Yes. (d) To a considerable extent, yes. (e) To some extent, but inflation declined faster than he forecasted it would.*

* For further discussion, see "Forecasts: Greenspan's Grades," *New York Times,* July 24, 1987.

---

## Table 8.1
## Forecasts of Real Growth of GNP and Inflation Rate in 1990, Council of Economic Advisers

| PERCENT CHANGE (FROM 1989 TO 1990) IN: | FORECAST (MADE IN EARLY 1990) | ACTUAL (PERCENT) |
| --- | --- | --- |
| Real GNP | 2.6 | 0.3 |
| Price level | 4.5 | 6.2 |

Source: Economic Report of the President, 1990 and 1991.

Despite the rather large errors in some economic forecasts, neither government nor industry can swear off forecasting. For decades, economic forecasting has played an important role in the decision-making process, both in government and industry. In recent years, George Bush has relied on economic forecasts prepared by the Council of Economic Advisers to help him formulate policies dealing with inflation, unemployment, and a host of other topics. Presidents Eisenhower, Kennedy, Johnson, Nixon, Ford, Carter, and Reagan also paid close attention to economic forecasts. So do most corporate presidents. *This isn't because these forecasts are always very good. It's because they are the best available.*

## TEST YOURSELF

1. "What goes up must come down. There is a cycle in economic activity just as in many other things, and one can use this cycle to forecast quite accurately." Comment and evaluate.

2. A leading business magazine reports that the leading indicators "are dead on center. This suggests that, although the downward trend of business has halted, there is still no clear upward thrust." Explain what this means.

3. "In forecasting, even the best economic insight is no match for a single bad assumption about policy-making in Washington." What does this mean? Do you agree? If so, what are the implications?

4. Suppose that investment spending plus government expenditure plus net exports will equal $700 billion next year, and that consumption expenditure will equal 65 percent of GNP. Forecast next year's GNP.

5. In Question 4, suppose that your estimate of investment expenditure plus government expenditure plus net exports is in error by $10 billion. If your other estimates are correct, how big an error will occur in your forecast of GNP?

## SUMMARY

1. National output tends to rise and approach its potential (that is, its full-employment) level for a while, then falters and falls below this level, then rises to approach it once more, and so on. These ups and downs are called business fluctuations, or business cycles.

2. Each cycle can be divided into four phases: trough, expansion, peak, recession. These cycles are very irregular and highly variable in length and amplitude. Unemployment tends to be higher at the trough than at the peak; inflation tends to be higher at the peak than at the trough.

3. A wide variety of factors can cause business fluctuations. One is the variation in investment spending, due in part to changes in the rate of increase (or decrease) of sales and to the timing of major innovations. The "minor" or "short" business cycle, lasting about two to four years, has often been due largely to variation in inventories.

4. The government's economic activities can help to cause business fluctuations. Particularly during and after wars, government spending has sometimes been a major destabilizing force. In addition, according to a number of prominent economists, some business fluctuations have been due to politicians' use of economic policy for their own political ends.

5. Changes in net exports can also help to cause business fluctuations, which often are transmitted from one country to another. For example, if a boom occurs in Europe or Japan, this will tend to increase our exports, and thus promote an increase in output in this country.

6. Although economics is by no means an exact science, economic forecasts are useful for many purposes. This does not mean that these forecasts are always very accurate. It means only that they are better than noneconomists' fore-casts. Economists have a number of techniques for forecasting. One makes use of leading indicators—variables that historically have turned up or down before GNP.

7. Another technique is based on the use of simple models plus surveys and other data. Investment, government expenditures, and net exports are sometimes estimated as a first step. Then, using the historical relationship between consumption and GNP, it is possible to forecast GNP.

8. Still another technique is based on econometric models, which are systems of equations estimated from past data. Econometric models have frequently done better than the average forecasts of general economists. However, it is important to recognize that econometric models—like any forecasting device in the social sciences—are quite fallible, as indicated by the large errors in the 1974 and 1981 fore-casts.

## CONCEPTS FOR REVIEW

| | | |
|---|---|---|
| Business cycle | Depression | Leading series |
| Trough | Prosperity | Coincident series |
| Expansion | Random shocks | Lagging series |
| Peak | Inventory cycle | Econometric models |
| Recession | Leading indicators | |

## APPENDIX: THE ACCELERATION PRINCIPLE

Changes in investment spending can cause business fluctuations, as we have seen. In this appendix, we study some of the factors that influence the level of investment spending. Specifically, we focus attention on the acceleration principle, a theory that says that investment is related to the rate of change of output. When output is increasing beyond previous levels, investment is required to increase the capacity to produce output. When output is falling, it may be unnecessary even to replace old capital as it is scrapped, let alone to spend money on new capital.

### The Acceleration Principle in Action: A Numerical Example

Suppose that the Johnson Shoe Corporation, a maker of women's shoes, requires 1 machine to make 50,000 pairs of shoes per year. Since each machine (and related plant and facilities) costs $2 million and each pair of shoes costs $20, it takes $2 worth of plant and equipment to produce $1 worth of output per year. In 1983, we suppose that the quantity of the firm's plant and equipment was exactly in balance with its output. In other words, the firm had no excess capacity; sales were $10 million and the actual stock of capital was $20 million. The firm's sales in subsequent years

**Table 8.2**
**Relationship between Sales and Investment, Johnson Shoe Corporation**

| YEAR | SALES | NEEDED STOCK OF CAPITAL | ACTUAL STOCK OF CAPITAL | REPLACEMENT INVESTMENT (MILLIONS OF DOLLARS) | NET INVESTMENT | GROSS INVESTMENT |
|------|-------|-------------------------|-------------------------|----------------------------------------------|----------------|------------------|
| 1983 | 10 | 20 | 20 | 1 | 0 | 1 |
| 1984 | 12 | 24 | 24 | 1 | 4 | 5 |
| 1985 | 14 | 28 | 28 | 1 | 4 | 5 |
| 1986 | 15 | 30 | 30 | 1 | 2 | 3 |
| 1987 | 16 | 32 | 32 | 1 | 2 | 3 |
| 1988 | 16 | 32 | 32 | 1 | 0 | 1 |
| 1989 | 15 | 30 | 31 | 0 | −1 | 0 |
| 1990 | 15 | 30 | 30 | 0 | −1 | 0 |
| 1991 | 15 | 30 | 30 | 1 | 0 | 1 |
| 1992 | 17 | 34 | 34 | 1 | 4 | 5 |

are shown in Table 8.2. For example, in 1984 its sales increased to $12 million; in 1985 they increased to $14 million; and so forth.

Table 8.2 also shows the amount the firm will have to invest each year in order to produce the amount it sells. Let's begin with 1984. To produce $12 million worth of product, the firm must have $24 million worth of capital. This means that it must increase its stock of capital from $20 million—the amount it has in 1983—to $24 million. In other words, it must increase its stock of capital by $4 million, which means that its net investment in plant and equipment must equal $4 million. But this is not the same as its gross investment—the amount of plant and equipment the firm must buy—because the firm must also replace some plant and equipment that wears out. Suppose that $1 million of plant and equipment wear out each year. Then gross investment in 1984 must equal net investment ($4 million) plus $1 million, or $5 million.

Next, let's look at 1985. The firm's sales in that year are $14 million. To produce this much output, the firm must have $28 million of capital, which means that it must increase its stock of capital by $4 million—from $24 million to $28 million. In addition, there is $1 million of replacement investment to replace plant and equipment that wear out in 1985. In all, the firm's gross investment must be $5 million. In 1986, the firm's sales are $15 million. To produce this output, this firm must have $30 million of capital, which means that it must increase its stock of capital by $2 million—from $28 million to $30 million. In addition, there is $1 million of replacement investment. In all, the firm's gross investment must be $3 million. Table 8.2 shows the results for subsequent years.

## Magnified Percentage Changes in Investment

From Table 8.2, it is clear that *changes in sales can result in magnified percentage changes in investment.* For example, between 1983 and 1984 sales went up by 20 percent, whereas gross investment went up by 400 percent. Between 1991 and 1992, sales went up by about 13 percent, whereas gross investment went up by 400 percent. The effect of a decrease in sales is even more spectacular because it tends to drive net investment to zero (or to negative values, as in 1989). Indeed, even gross investment may be driven to zero, as in 1989, if the firm wants to reduce the value of its plant and equipment. To accomplish this, the firm simply does not replace the plant and equipment that wear out.

## The Importance of the Rate of Change of Sales

Table 8.2 shows that *the amount of gross investment depends on the amount by which sales increase.* In particular, for gross investment to remain constant year after year, the annual increase of sales must also remain constant. You can see this in 1984 and 1985. In each of these years, since sales increased from the previous year by the same amount ($2 million), gross investment remained constant at $5 million per year. It is very important to note that *gross investment will fall when sales begin to increase by decreasing amounts.* The fact that sales are increasing does not ensure that gross investment will increase. On the contrary, if sales are increasing by decreasing amounts, gross investment will fall. This is a very important point, since it indicates that a reduction in the rate of growth of sales can be the kiss of death for investment, thus helping to cause a recession.

This effect of changes in sales on gross investment is often called the **acceleration principle,** since changes in sales result in accelerated, or magnified, changes in investment, and since an increase in investment results from an increase in the annual growth (an **acceleration**) of sales. The acceleration principle applies to kinds of investment other than plant and equipment. For example, it is easy to show that it applies to inventories (and housing) as well, since firms often try to maintain a certain amount of inventory for each dollar of sales—just as they often maintain a certain amount of plant and equipment for each dollar of sales.

# INTRODUCTION TO FISCAL POLICY

FACED WITH THE BUSINESS fluctuations described in the previous chapter, the government has tried in various ways to stabilize the economy—that is, to reduce unemployment and fight inflation. The government's power to spend and tax has been used for this purpose. For example, tax cuts have frequently been enacted to try to get the economy out of recessions. This chapter takes a first look at fiscal policy, in the context of the models we developed in Chapters 6 and 7. We begin by studying the effects of government spending and taxation on GNP, using the aggregate demand and supply curves provided in Chapter 7. With this theoretical background in mind, we take up the role of automatic stabilizers and discretionary fiscal policy in the United States in recent decades. Also, we discuss supply-side economics, which emphasizes the use of tax cuts to stimulate national output. Much more will be said about fiscal policy in Chapter 15, after we have studied monetary policy.

The White House

## STRATEGIES FOR DEALING WITH A RECESSIONARY GAP

To begin with, suppose that the economy is suffering from excessive unemployment, and that output is well below its potential level. Using the terminology introduced in Chapter 7, there is a **recessionary gap.** In particular, let's assume that the situation is as shown in the left-hand panel of Figure 9.1. As you can see, the equilibrium value of total real output is $OQ_1$, which is well below $OQ_0$, the economy's potential output. Given this situation, there are several ways in which output can be pushed up to its potential level—so full employment can be restored. One way is to wait for wage rates and other input prices to fall in response to the high unemployment rate, thus shifting the short-run aggregate supply curve to the right, as shown in the middle panel of Figure 9.1. Although some economists believe that such a strategy is feasible, most believe that it would take too long because, in their view, wages tend to be quite sticky. (Recall Chapters 5 and 7.) In Chapter 14, we will review the controversies and evidence on this score. For now, it is sufficient to say that governments frequently want to do what they can to hasten the movement toward full employment.

Another way to deal with the recessionary gap in the left-hand panel of Figure 9.1 is to wait for spending by the private sector to pick up, thus shifting the aggregate demand curve to the right, as shown in the right-hand panel of Figure 9.1. Here too the problem is that it may take a painfully long time for such a shift in the aggregate demand curve to

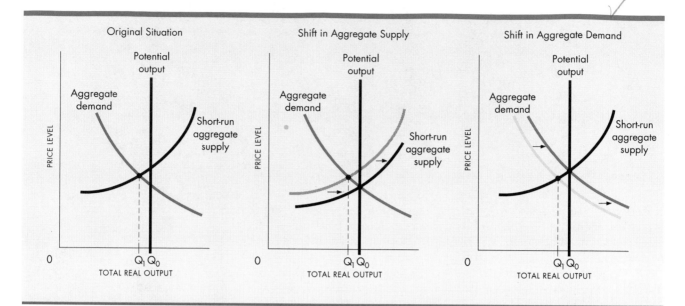

occur. As we have seen in Chapter 8, some recessions have gone on for years.

Still another strategy is for the government to increase its spending and/or to cut taxes, thus shifting the aggregate demand curve to the right. As in the case described in the previous paragraph, such a shift in the aggregate demand curve can push output up to its potential level, as shown in the right-hand panel of Figure 9.1. Governments eager to restore full employment often have used fiscal policy in this way. One problem has been that the stimulus resulting from their actions has sometimes been felt when spending by the private sector has picked up, the consequence being inflationary pressure because the aggregate demand curve has been pushed too far to the right. Much more will be said below and in subsequent chapters concerning the pros and cons of anti-recessionary fiscal policies.

## STRATEGIES FOR DEALING WITH AN INFLATIONARY GAP

Having described how fiscal policy has been used to deal with an economy suffering from excessive unemployment, let's turn to a case where an economy is suffering from serious inflation. As pointed out in Chapter 7, if the equilibrium value of real national output exceeds potential output, as shown in the left-hand panel of Figure 9.2, economists say that there is an *inflationary gap.* In a situation of this sort, there will be substantial inflationary pressures, and there are several ways in which the equilibrium value of real national output can be reduced so it no longer exceeds potential output—and so price stability can be restored.

One way is to allow market forces to take their course. As pointed out in Chapter 7, wages and other input prices will be bid up, thus shifting the short-run aggregate supply curve to the left. The result will be inflation, but when the price level increases to $OP_0$ in the middle panel of Figure 9.2, the inflation should stop.

Another way to deal with the inflationary gap in the left-hand panel of

**Figure 9.1**
**Alternative Ways of Dealing with a Recessionary Gap**
As shown in the left-hand panel, equilibrium output is $OQ_1$, which is well below the potential output of $OQ_0$. Thus there is a recessionary gap. One way to deal with this situation is to wait for wages and other input prices to fall, thus pushing the short-run aggregate supply curve to the right, as shown in the middle panel. Another way is to wait for an increase in private-sector spending to push the aggregate demand curve to the right, as shown in the right-hand panel. Still another way is for the government to shift the aggregate demand curve to the right (as in the right-hand panel) by increasing its own spending and/or by cutting taxes.

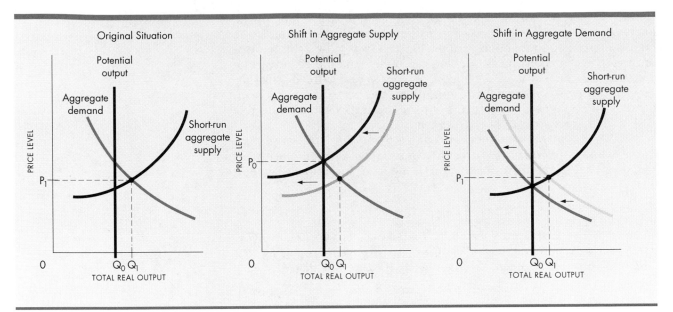

| Original Situation | Shift in Aggregate Supply | Shift in Aggregate Demand |

Figure 9.2 is to wait for spending by the private sector to recede, thus shifting the aggregate demand curve to the left, as shown in the right-hand panel of Figure 9.2. Unfortunately, however, such a reduction in aggregate demand may not occur in time to prevent the inflationary process in the middle panel of Figure 9.2 from taking place.

Still another strategy is for the government to cut its spending and/or raise taxes, thus shifting the aggregate demand curve to the left. As in the case described in the previous paragraph, such a shift in the aggregate demand curve can push output down to its potential level, as shown in the right-hand panel of Figure 9.2. Governments, eager to cut back inflationary pressures, often have used fiscal policy in this way. One problem is that the economic restraint resulting from their actions has sometimes been felt when spending by the private sector has receded, the consequence being that output has fallen below its potential level, and unemployment has risen. Much more will be said below and in subsequent chapters concerning the pros and cons of anti-inflationary fiscal policies.

## EXPANSIONARY FISCAL POLICY AND BUDGET DEFICITS

Having described how fiscal policy has been used in an attempt to stabilize the economy, we must add that expansionary fiscal policies—policies aimed at reducing recessionary gaps—frequently result in budget **deficits;** that is, government spending exceeds tax revenues. To meet the shortfall, the government has borrowed from the public. In other words, the government has sold bonds, notes, and other government IOUs of various kinds to the public. According to many economists, the government's demand for funds tends to raise interest rates, which is likely to reduce investment expenditures.

It is not hard to see why the government's demand for loanable funds will tend to raise interest rates. After all, the interest rate, as we saw in Chapter 5, is the price paid for borrowing money. If the government in-

**Figure 9.2**
**Alternative Ways of Dealing with an Inflationary Gap**
As shown in the left-hand panel, equilibrium output is $OQ_1$, which is well above the potential output of $OQ_0$. Thus there is an inflationary gap. One way to deal with this situation is to allow wages and other input prices to rise, thus pushing the short-run aggregate supply curve to the left, as shown in the middle panel. Another way is to wait for a decrease in private-sector spending to push the aggregate demand curve to the left, as shown in the right-hand panel. Still another way is for the government to shift the aggregate demand curve to the left (as in the right-hand panel) by cutting its own spending and/or by raising taxes.

creases the demand for loanable funds, the price of loanable funds—the interest rate—would be expected to rise. A thorough discussion of the budget deficit is postponed to Chapter 15, since you must study the role of money in the economy before you can understand the economics of the budget deficit. For now, the important point to bear in mind is that *the government must somehow finance whatever deficits it runs.* And according to most economists, its financing of these deficits is likely to affect real GNP and the performance of the economy.

Another important point to bear in mind is that *the deficit—or surplus, if one exists—is related to the amount that a nation saves and invests, as well as to its net exports.* To see that this is the case, recall from Chapter 6 that

$$\text{GNP} = C + I + G + (X - M_{\text{I}}), \tag{9.1}$$

where $C$ is consumption expenditure, $I$ is investment expenditure, $G$ is government expenditure, and $(X - M_{\text{I}})$ is net exports. Recognizing that GNP can only be consumed, saved, or taxed, it is also true that

$$\text{GNP} = C + S + T, \tag{9.2}$$

where $S$ is saving and $T$ is taxes. Thus

$$C + I + G + (X - M_{\text{I}}) = C + S + T. \tag{9.3}$$

Subtracting $C$ from both sides and rearranging terms,

$$(G - T) = (S - I) - (X - M_{\text{I}}). \tag{9.4}$$

Since the budget deficit equals $(G - T)$, this equation shows that the budget deficit must equal the difference between saving and investment—$(S - I)$—minus net exports—$(X - M_{\text{I}})$. Of course, we can also solve this equation for $(X - M_{\text{I}})$, the result being

$$(X - M_{\text{I}}) = (S - I) - (G - T). \tag{9.5}$$

Holding $(S - I)$ constant, net exports—$(X - M_{\text{I}})$—are inversely related to the budget deficit—$(G - T)$. This fact will play a significant role in Chapter 18, where we discuss the reasons why net exports in the United States have been negative in recent years. For an illustration of how these equations can be used, see Example 9.1.

## FISCAL POLICY: CLOSED VERSUS OPEN ECONOMIES

Fiscal policy has less impact on real GNP and the price level in an open economy than in a closed economy. To see why, suppose that our economy is closed (that is, no exports or imports), and that the government decides to use fiscal policy to stimulate the economy; that is, it cuts taxes or increases spending. The result is a shift to the right (from $D_1$ to $D_2$) in the aggregate demand curve, as shown in Figure 9.3. If our economy is closed, no more need be said. But since it is not closed, we must recognize that such a fiscal policy is likely to increase the value of the dollar relative to other currencies. For example, the price of a dollar (in Japanese yen) might rise from 135 to 140 yen.

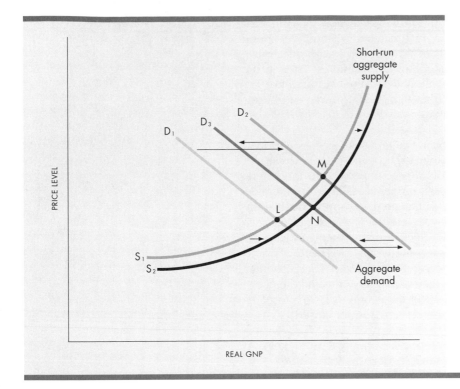

**Figure 9.3**
**Effect of Expansionary Fiscal Policy in an Open Economy**
An expansionary fiscal policy shifts the aggregate demand curve to the right (from $D_1$ to $D_2$), but it also is likely to increase interest rates, which tends to increase the value of the dollar. Thus the aggregate demand curve is shifted back to the left (from $D_2$ to $D_3$), and the aggregate supply curve is shifted to the right (from $S_1$ to $S_2$), the result being that the economy moves from $L$ to $N$ (rather than to $M$, which would have been the case if the economy were closed).

---

## EXAMPLE 9.1   HOW BUDGET DEFICITS ARE RELATED TO SAVING, INVESTMENT, AND NET EXPORTS

The following table provides some information concerning a small country:

|  | (BILLIONS OF DOLLARS) |
|---|---|
| Gross national product (this year) | 16.0 |
| Gross national product (full-employment level) | 20.0 |
| Government expenditures on goods and services | 1.8 |

According to experts on this country's economy, the government's tax receipts are equal to 10 percent of its GNP.

(a) Is the government of this country running a deficit or a surplus? (That is, are government expenditures greater than or less than tax receipts?) (b) Suppose that, when GNP is at its full-employment level of $20 billion, saving equals $1.8 billion, investment equals $1.0 billion, and net exports equal $0.5 billion. If tax rates cannot be changed, and if full em-ployment occurs, will there be a balanced budget? (That is, will government spending equal tax receipts?) (c) Under the circumstances in part (b), can you determine the level of government expenditures?

### Solution

(a) Government expenditures equal $1.8 billion. Tax receipts equal 10 percent of GNP, or $1.6 billion. Thus there is a deficit of $0.2 billion. (That is, spending exceeds receipts by $0.2 billion.) (b) From Equation (9.4), we know that the budget deficit equals saving less investment minus net exports. Since saving equals $1.8 billion, investment equals $1.0 billion, and net exports equal $0.5 billion, the budget deficit must equal $(1.8 - 1.0) - 0.5 = 0.3$ billions of dollars. Thus there will not be a balanced budget. (c) If GNP is at its full employment level of $20 billion, taxes must equal $2 billion. (Recall that taxes equal 10 percent of GNP.) Thus, if the budget deficit equals $0.3 billion, government expenditures must equal $2.3 billion.

To see why this is true, recall from the previous section that the government, when it adopts an expansionary fiscal policy, tends to spend substantially more than it receives in taxes, and borrows the difference. When the government borrows, it is likely to bid up interest rates in the United States, and foreign investors are likely to be attracted by these relatively high interest rates. To purchase the high-yielding American bonds and stocks, they must buy dollars. Thus the swollen demand for dollars pushes up their price.

This increase in the price of a dollar (in Japanese yen or German marks) shifts the aggregate demand curve to the left. Why? Because net exports fall since American goods become more expensive to foreigners, and since foreign goods become cheaper to Americans. Also, the increase in the value of the dollar shifts the short-run aggregate supply curve to the right because imported goods and services are cheaper. (Recall the Appendix to Chapter 7.) In Figure 9.3, the effect is to shift the aggregate demand curve from $D_2$ (its position if the economy was closed) to $D_3$, and to shift the short-run aggregate supply curve from $S_1$ to $S_2$. Thus, whereas the government's expansionary fiscal policy would have pushed the economy from point $L$ to point $M$ in Figure 9.3, if the economy were closed, it will push it from point $L$ to point $N$, if the economy is not closed.

Comparing point $N$ with point $M$, we find that fiscal policy has less effect on real GNP and the price level in an open economy than in a closed economy. The increased value of the dollar reduces the expansionary effect on real GNP because it decreases net exports, and it reduces the inflationary effect because imports are cheaper.

## MAKERS OF FISCAL POLICY

When you go to a ball game, you generally get a program telling you who on each team is playing each position. To understand the formulation and implementation of fiscal policy in the United States we need the same kind of information. Who are the people who establish our fiscal policy? Who decides that in view of the current and prospective economic situation, tax rates or government expenditures should be changed? This is not a simple question because lots of individuals and groups play important roles. In the Congress, the House and Senate Budget Committees—as well as the Congressional Budget Office—have been charged with important responsibilities in this area. Also, the Appropriations Committees, the House Ways and Means Committee, and the Senate Finance Committee have considerable influence. In addition, another congressional committee is of importance: the Joint Economic Committee of Congress. Established by the Employment Act of 1946, this committee goes over the annual Economic Report of the President on the state of the economy and, through its hearings, provides a major forum for review of economic issues.

In the executive branch of government, the most important person in the establishment of fiscal policy is, of course, the president. Although he must operate in the context of the tax and expenditure laws passed by Congress, he and his advisers are the country's principal analysts of the need for fiscal expansion or restraint. Needless to say, he doesn't pore over the latest economic data and make the decisions all by himself. The Office of Management and Budget, which is part of the Executive Office

Richard G. Darman, Director of the Office of Management and Budget

# THE COUNCIL OF ECONOMIC ADVISERS

Before World War II, there was relatively little place in the government for economists. The Treasury had a small number, the antitrust division of the Justice Department a handful, but there was no place for economists who aspired to give advice on broad policy matters. The Employment Act of 1946 changed that situation by creating a council to "gather timely and authoritative information . . . to develop and recommend to the President national economic policies . . . and to make and furnish studies . . . as the President may request."

But as demonstrated by the first chairman, Edwin Nourse, the act was really a hunting license for a chairman to peddle his good counsel. Nourse, who believed that the Council's role was to "interpret literal facts . . . without becoming involved in any way in the advocacy of particular measures," found that such services were rarely required by the president. It is hard to find any trace of the Nourse era on the economic policies of the late forties.

Even the election of John F. Kennedy, who was eager to increase the U.S. rate of economic growth, did not ensure the Council's future. Kennedy was inclined to fiscal conservatism and less interested in domestic than in foreign affairs. It was Walter Heller, the new chairman under Kennedy, who made the CEA an integral part of the New Frontier. The tax cut of 1964, which Heller sold to a president committed to balanced budgets, is a tribute to his success in making a body without formal powers or legislative prerogatives an integral part of the policy-making process.

The Council's influence has risen and ebbed in recent years with both the state of the economy and other pressures on the president. In 1966, as the Vietnam War intensified, the Council urged a tax increase; Lyndon Johnson, more attuned to the political considerations, did not take action on the proposal until 1967. The Council's position in the Nixon administration further exemplified this process. Led by Paul McCracken and Herbert Stein, the Council

Michael Boskin

championed restraint in fiscal and monetary policies early in Nixon's first term. But faced with mounting inflationary pressures, the Council members reluctantly joined other administration economists in setting up wage and price controls.

In the Reagan administration, the CEA's position became precarious after Martin Feldstein, its chairman until 1984 (when he returned to Harvard), clashed openly with administration officials about the dangers inherent in large federal deficits. For a time, President Reagan appointed no one to succeed Feldstein, and there was talk in early 1985 that the Council might be abolished. However, in February 1985, the president named Beryl Sprinkel, former under secretary of the treasury, as CEA chairman. In the Bush administration, Michael Boskin, on leave from Stanford University, has played a significant role, but the leading figure in economic policy making often has been Nicholas Brady, Secretary of the Treasury and an old friend of the president.

of the President, is a very powerful adviser to the president on expenditure policy, as is the Treasury Department on tax policy. In addition, there is the **Council of Economic Advisers,** which is part of the Executive Office of the President. Established by the Employment Act of 1946, its job is to help the president carry out the objectives of that act. During the past 45 years, the Council of Economic Advisers, headed by a series of distinguished economists who left academic and other posts to contribute to public policy, has become an important actor on the national economic policy stage.

# AUTOMATIC STABILIZERS

Now that we have met some of the major players, we must point out that, in their efforts to fight off serious unemployment or inflation, they get help from some **automatic stabilizers:** structural features of our system of taxes and transfer payments that tend to stabilize national output. Although these economic stabilizers cannot do all that is required to keep the economy on an even keel, they help a lot. As soon as the economy turns down and unemployment mounts, they give the economy a helpful shot in the arm. As soon as the economy gets overheated and inflation crops up, they tend to restrain it. These stabilizers are automatic because they come into play without the need for new legislation or administrative decisions.

## Tax Revenues

Changes in income tax revenues are an important automatic stabilizer. Our federal system relies heavily on the income tax. The amount of income tax collected by the federal government goes up with increases in GNP and goes down with decreases in GNP. This, of course, is just what we want to occur. When output falls off and unemployment mounts, tax collections fall off too, so disposable income falls less than GNP. This means less of a fall in consumption expenditure, which tends to brake the fall in GNP. When output rises too fast and the economy begins to suffer from serious inflation, tax collections rise too—which tends to brake the increase in GNP. Of course, corporation income taxes, as well as personal income taxes, play a significant role here.

## Unemployment Compensation and Welfare Payments

Unemployment compensation is paid to workers who are laid off, according to a system that has evolved over the past 50 years. When an unemployed worker goes back to work, he or she stops receiving unemployment compensation. Thus, when GNP falls off and unemployment mounts, the tax collections to finance unemployment compensation go down (because of lower employment), while the amount paid out to unemployed workers goes up. On the other hand, when GNP rises too fast and the economy begins to suffer from serious inflation, the tax collections to finance unemployment compensation go up, while the amount paid out goes down because there is much less unemployment. Again, this is just what we want to see happen. The fall in spending is moderated when unemployment is high, and the increase in spending is curbed when there are serious inflationary pressures. Various welfare programs have the same kind of automatic stabilizing effect on the economy.

# DISCRETIONARY FISCAL POLICY

In the past thirty years, the federal government frequently has changed tax rates—as well as expenditures—in an attempt to cope with unemployment and inflation. The following kinds of measures have been adopted.

**1. THE GOVERNMENT HAS VARIED TAX RATES.** When there has been considerable unemployment, the government sometimes has cut tax rates, as it did in 1975. Or if inflation has been the problem, the government sometimes has increased taxes, as it did in 1968 when, after considerable political maneuvering and buckpassing, the Congress was finally persuaded to put through a 10 percent tax surcharge to try to moderate the inflation caused by the Vietnam War. However, temporary tax changes are likely to have less effect than permanent ones, since, as pointed out in Chapter 6, consumption expenditure would be expected to be influenced less by transitory changes in income than by permanent changes.

**2. THE GOVERNMENT HAS VARIED ITS EXPENDITURE FOR GOODS AND SERVICES.** When increased unemployment seemed to be in the wind, it sometimes stepped up outlays on roads, urban reconstruction, and other public programs. Of course, these programs must be well thought out and socially productive. There is no sense in pushing through wasteful and foolish spending programs merely to make jobs. Or when, as in 1969, the economy has been plagued by inflation, the government sometimes has (as President Nixon ordered) stopped new federal construction programs temporarily.

**3. THE GOVERNMENT HAS VARIED WELFARE PAYMENTS AND OTHER TYPES OF TRANSFER PAYMENTS.** For example, when unemployment has been regarded as excessive, the federal government has sometimes helped the states to extend the length of time that the unemployed can receive unemployment compensation; this was expected to help reduce the unemployment rate.

## Problems in Formulating Effective Discretionary Fiscal Policy

While governments frequently carry out discretionary fiscal policies, it is important to recognize the many types of problems that can interfere with the effectiveness of such policies. *One of the big disadvantages of public works and similar spending programs is that they take so long to get started.* Plans must be made, land must be acquired, and preliminary construction studies must be carried out. By the time the expenditures are finally made and have an effect, the dangers of excessive unemployment may have given way to dangers of inflation, so that the spending, coming too late, may do more harm than good.

In recent years, there has been a widespread feeling that government expenditures should be set on the basis of their long-run desirability and productivity. The optimal level of government expenditure is at the point where the value of the extra benefits to be derived from an extra dollar of government expenditure is at least equal to the dollar of cost. This optimal level is unlikely to change much in the short run, and it would be

When Dwight Eisenhower took office in 1953, he inherited a prosperity that had been bubbling along since the postwar boom. But by August 1953, there were signs that the economy was headed for a recession. By 1954 the unemployment rate was 6 percent, the highest since the Great Depression. Although Eisenhower remained outwardly confident, there was concern behind the scenes about the deepening recession and a debate about what the government should do. Because the recession reduced tax revenues, the government was running a deficit, and some people felt that taxes should be raised to snuff out the deficit.

But President Eisenhower was getting other advice. In 1954 the Committee for Economic Development (composed largely of top business executives) urged the president to forget about balancing the budget and to leave the economy alone. As 1954 wore on and the Democrats and the labor unions demanded action, the economy stumbled, sputtered, then took off in an upward direction. The first Republican recession since 1929 had come and gone, and even dedicated Democrats had to admit that the nation had survived. But we survived by doing nothing. And in hindsight, nothing turns out to have been just the thing to do.

An important factor in promoting recovery was the existence of our economy's automatic stabilizers. The concept of automatic stabilizers had been brought to the Eisenhower administration by Arthur

Dwight Eisenhower

F. Burns, who chaired the Council of Economic Advisers. Ironically, in 1952 Congress had tried to kill the Council by cutting off its funding. By the end of 1954 it was clear that the Council, its chairman, and its stabilizing budget policy had passed a major test with honors.

N.B.

wasteful to spend more—or less—than this amount for stabilization purposes when tax changes could be used instead. Thus many economists believe that tax cuts or tax increases should be the primary fiscal weapons to fight unemployment or inflation.

However, *one of the big problems with tax changes is that it sometimes is difficult to get Congress to take speedy action.* There is often considerable debate over a tax bill, and sometimes it becomes a political football. Another difficulty with tax changes is that it generally is much easier to reduce taxes than it is to get them back up again. To politicians, lower taxes are attractive because they are popular, and higher taxes are dangerous because they may hurt a politician's chances of reelection. In discussing fiscal policy (or most other aspects of government operations, for that matter), to ignore politics is to risk losing touch with reality.

Further, economists warn that, to the extent that discretionary fiscal policy involves reacting to short-term economic developments with little consideration of longer-term consequences, the result may be more harm than good. This problem is discussed at length in Chapter 14. The point here is that changes in taxes and government spending aimed at stabilizing the economy in the short run may not be most effective in promoting the long-term health of the economy.

## TEST YOURSELF

1. If there is a recessionary gap, does the effect of fiscal policy on real GNP depend on the shape of the short-run aggregate supply curve? If so, is it true that fiscal policy has the greatest effect on real GNP when the short-run aggregate supply curve is vertical?

2. Explain why fiscal policy has less impact on real GNP and the price level in an open economy than in a closed economy.

3. Suppose that the consumption function in a particular economy is given by the following table:

| DISPOSABLE INCOME (BILLIONS OF DOLLARS) | CONSUMPTION EXPENDITURE (BILLIONS OF DOLLARS) |
| --- | --- |
| 400 | 350 |
| 500 | 425 |
| 600 | 500 |
| 700 | 575 |
| 800 | 650 |

If taxes are 20 percent of GNP, fill in the blanks below.

| GNP (BILLIONS OF DOLLARS) | CONSUMPTION EXPENDITURE (BILLIONS OF DOLLARS) |
| --- | --- |
| — | 350 |
| — | 425 |
| — | 500 |
| — | 575 |
| — | 650 |

4. A leading business magazine reports that saving falls short of investment in a particular country and that this country's net exports are positive. Is it possible that this country's government is experiencing a budget deficit? Why, or why not?

5. Use aggregate demand and supply curves to indicate how governments have used fiscal policy in their attempts to snuff out inflation.

## SUPPLY-SIDE ECONOMICS

In the late 1970s and 1980s, some economists advocated tax reductions in order to stimulate national output. Their views came to be known as ***supply-side economics,*** and received considerable attention when some of

Tax Cuts

them received high-level posts in the Reagan administration. They played an important role in formulating and helping to push through the very large tax cut passed in August 1981.

The reason for their being called *supply-side* economists was that they were concerned primarily with influencing aggregate supply. To stimulate rightward shifts of the aggregate supply curve, supply-siders favor the use of various financial incentives, particularly tax cuts. Why do they want to shift the aggregate supply curve to the right? Because this will increase total real output (without raising the price level). However, as shown in Figure 9.4, the increase in total real output will not be as large if the aggregate supply curve is relatively flat as it will be if it is vertical. In general, the supply-siders seem more inclined to accept the view that the aggregate supply curve is vertical (or close to it) than the Keynesian view that it is flat.

**TAX REDUCTIONS ON LABOR INCOME.** The supply-siders advocated cuts in taxes on labor income on the grounds that people will work longer and harder. Economists disagree over the magnitude of this effect. The available evidence seems to indicate that the hours worked by prime-age males would not be affected much by tax changes. But the amount of work done by married women seems more responsive to changes in tax rates. (If the tax rate is high, some married women feel that it is not worthwhile to take a job outside their home.)

**TAX REDUCTIONS ON CAPITAL INCOME.** Supply-siders also advocated reductions in taxes on dividends and interest income. In their view, such cuts would encourage additional saving. Although economists agree that saving and investment tend to promote the growth of an economy, there is considerable controversy over the extent to which saving is influenced by tax cuts. Early studies of consumption and saving found saving behavior to be relatively insensitive to changes in the rate of return that savers receive. (That is, if people can obtain a 10 percent annual return from their

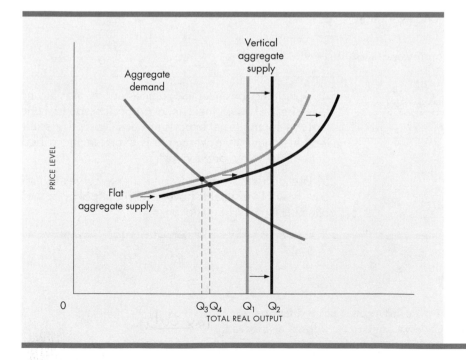

**Figure 9.4**
**Supply-Side Economics: The Effect of a Rightward Shift of the Aggregate Supply Curve**
Supply-side economists advocate tax reductions to shift the aggregate supply curve to the right. If the aggregate supply curve is vertical (or close to it), such a shift will increase total real output by a much greater amount (from $OQ_1$ to $OQ_2$) than if it is relatively flat (in which case total real output increases from $OQ_3$ to $OQ_4$).

savings in banks and elsewhere, they may not save much more than if they can obtain only 8 percent.) Recent studies, particularly by Michael Boskin, (chairman of George Bush's Council of Economic Advisers), challenge this conclusion, but critics respond that the 1981 tax cut did not increase the percent of total income devoted to saving.

**THE LAFFER CURVE.** According to some supply-siders, the tax burden prior to 1981 was so high that further increases in the marginal tax rate would have resulted in lower, not higher, total tax revenue. To explain why they believe this to be true, they used the ***Laffer curve,*** which relates the amount of income tax revenue collected by the government to the tax rate. According to Arthur Laffer (after whom the curve was named), tax revenues will be zero if the tax rate is zero. This is indisputable. Also, he points out that tax revenues will be zero if the tax rate is 100 percent. Why? Because if the government takes all the income in taxes, there is no incentive to earn taxable income.

According to the Laffer curve, the maximum tax revenue is reached when the tax rate is at some intermediate level between zero and 100 percent. In Figure 9.5, this level is *Oa.* According to Laffer, U.S. tax rates in the 1970s reached or exceeded this level. Many other economists deny this. Although they admit that a reduction in tax rates might have reduced the incentive to cheat on taxes and to find tax loopholes (as well as to encourage people to work harder and save more), they feel that Laffer's evidence is too weak to support his conclusions.

Some supply-siders asserted that the 1981 tax cut would result in such large increases in output and income that tax receipts would surge despite the reduction in tax rates. Thus they felt that federal revenues would not fall short of federal expenditures. In fact, however, federal revenues were about $200 billion less than federal expenditures in fiscal 1985, and large deficits persisted in subsequent years.

It seems fair to say that there is considerable uncertainty about the shape of the Laffer curve and where the United States is located on it. Even the existence and usefulness of such a curve is a matter of dispute.

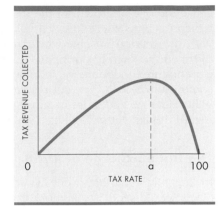

**Figure 9.5**
**The Laffer Curve**
Beyond point a, further increases in the tax rate result in less revenue collected. According to some economists like Arthur Laffer, U.S. tax rates in the 1970s were at this point. Other economists disagreed. There is considerable controversy over the shape and usefulness of the Laffer curve.

# FISCAL POLICY: FOUR CASE STUDIES

## The Tax Cut of 1964

With some knowledge of the players and the plays they can call, we can look now at four examples of fiscal policy in action. When the Kennedy administration took office in 1961, it was confronted with a relatively high unemployment rate—about 7 percent in mid-1961. By 1962, although unemployment was somewhat lower (about 6 percent), the president's advisers, led by the late Walter W. Heller, chairman of the Council of Economic Advisers, convinced the president to propose a tax cut to reduce unemployment further.

The proposed tax bill was a victory for Heller and the CEA. Even though it would mean a deliberately large deficit, the president had been convinced to cut taxes to push the economy closer to full employment. But Congress was not so easily convinced. Many members of Congress labeled the proposal irresponsible and reckless. Others wanted to couple tax reform with tax reduction. It was not until 1964, after President Kennedy's death, that the tax bill was enacted.

The effects of the tax cut are by no means easy to measure, in part be-

John F. Kennedy

cause the rate of growth of the money supply increased at the same time, which (as we shall see in Chapter 10) should also affect GNP. But in line with the theory presented in earlier sections, consumption expenditure did increase sharply during 1964. Moreover, the additional consumption expenditure undoubtedly induced additional investment. According to some estimates, the tax cut resulted in an increase in GNP of about $24 billion in 1965 and more in subsequent years. Most economists seemed to regard the tax cut of 1964 as a success.

## The Tax Surcharge of 1968

In late July 1965, President Lyndon Johnson announced that the United States would send 50,000 more troops to Vietnam. From fiscal 1965 to fiscal 1966, defense expenditures rose from $50 billion to $62 billion—a large increase in government expenditure, and one that took place at a time of relatively full employment. Such an increase in government expenditure would be expected to cause inflationary pressures. The Council of Economic Advisers recognized this danger, and recommended in late 1965 that the president urge Congress to increase taxes. Johnson was reluctant. The inflationary pressures mounted during 1966, and little was done by fiscal policy makers to quell them.

Even in 1967, Congress was unwilling to raise taxes. The case for fiscal restraint was, it felt, not clear enough. As for the president, he said, "It is not a popular thing for a President to do . . . to ask for a penny out of a dollar to pay for a war that is not popular either." Finally, in mid-1968, a 10 percent surcharge on income taxes, together with some restraint in government spending, was enacted. Economists tended to regard this increase in taxes as the right medicine, but it was at least two years too late, and its effects were delayed and insufficient.

## The Tax Cut of 1975

In late 1974, the unemployment rate began to mount. Whereas it was 5.5 percent in August, it reached 7.2 percent in December. Although economists were rather slow to recognize that the economy was slumping into a severe recession, by early 1975 it was felt that some stimulus was needed. Inflation, which President Ford had labeled "Public Enemy Number One" in the fall of 1974, continued to be a problem, but most policy makers felt that unemployment rates were reaching intolerable levels.

In early 1975, President Ford proposed a $16 billion tax cut. As his Council of Economic Advisers stated, its purpose was "to halt the decline in production and employment so that growth of output can resume and unemployment can be reduced."[1] Congress passed a $23 billion tax cut in March 1975, only a relatively few months before the recovery was well under way. The tax cut had less impact than some economists predicted because consumers did not spend, but instead saved, much of the tax reduction. This behavior by consumers is what the permanent-income hypothesis (in Chapter 6) would predict. Because the tax reduction was temporary, it had less effect on consumers' permanent income—and thus less effect on consumption expenditure—than if it was permanent.

---

[1] Council of Economic Advisers, *1975 Annual Report,* Washington, D.C.: Government Printing Office, 1975.

### The Tax Cut of 1981

President Reagan, when he entered office, was intent on lowering taxes. He argued that this would push the aggregate supply curve to the right, because it would encourage people and firms to work, invest, and take prudent risks, the result being more output and less inflationary pressure. When he pressed for a large tax reduction in 1981, he frequently cited the beneficial effects of the tax cut of 1964. His critics pointed out that economic conditions in 1981 were different from those in 1964. Nonetheless, a huge tax cut was passed in 1981. Since much of this tax cut went into effect in 1982 and later, it was hoped in 1982 that it would help lift the economy out of the recession that afflicted the United States then. But some observers, in Wall Street and elsewhere, were worried that it might rekindle inflation, which was relatively low in early 1982.

In fact, the economy began to expand in late 1982, and 1983 was a year of vigorous cyclical recovery. (Real GNP rose by about 6 percent, and the unemployment rate fell by 2.5 percentage points in 1983.) Moreover, the expansion, which did not increase inflation substantially, continued throughout 1984—and helped to reelect President Reagan. While the 1981 tax cut was only one of the relevant factors, it certainly helped to bring about the desired expansion (and the record deficits that will be discussed at length in Chapter 15).

President Reagan signing the 1981 tax cut bill

## RECENT AMERICAN EXPERIENCE WITH FISCAL POLICY

It should be evident by now that much more is known today about the impact of fiscal policy than at the time when the economy was staggered by the Great Depression. But this does not mean that economists have all (or nearly all) the answers. The hard choices faced by economists in the top councils of government can be demonstrated by a close inspection of the recent attempts to give the economy a smoother side.

### The Ford Years

Let's begin with the situation in the mid-1970s. In early 1974 the price of foreign oil was increased very substantially by the OPEC countries. This price increase, as well as considerable increases in farm prices, spearheaded an inflationary spurt. During 1974 consumer prices rose by about 12 percent! From the point of view of inflation, this was the worst year in decades. At the same time, the nation's real output fell, as the economy dropped into the most serious recession since World War II. The result was a marked increase in unemployment. By March 1975 the unemployment rate was 8.7 percent, as compared with 4.9 percent in December 1973.

Faced with a combination of excessive unemployment and excessive inflation, President Ford proposed a $16 billion tax cut, and, as we saw above, Congress passed a relatively ineffectual $23 billion tax cut in March 1975, shortly before the economy began to revive in mid-1975. Unemployment fell from 8.7 percent in March 1975 to 7.5 percent in March 1976, but stagflation (the combination of a high unemployment rate and a high rate of inflation) was by no means vanquished. On the contrary, both unemployment and inflation continued to be excessive.

## The Carter Years

In 1977 the federal government ran a deficit of about $50 billion; that is, expenditures exceeded receipts by this amount. And in January 1978 President Carter proposed personal tax reductions of $24 billion. But during 1978 the rate of inflation increased sharply, and approached double-digit levels. Since the inflation rate was higher than expected, the Carter administration scaled back its proposed tax cut to $20 billion, and Congress actually passed a $19 billion tax cut.

In the face of heightened inflation, fiscal policy did not attempt to rein in the economy very much. The deficit in 1978 was about $30 billion. There was a continuing debate within the administration over whether the inflation rate could be reduced substantially without a recession—and whether a recession was the proper medicine. In 1980, there was a very brief recession, but it did little to cool off inflation.

## The Reagan Years

When the Reagan administration took office in 1981, it was committed to cut both government expenditures and taxes. In August 1981 the administration pushed through Congress a huge tax cut for both individuals and businesses. At the same time, it reduced federal expenditures (relative to the level that former president Carter had proposed). However, the tax cuts were far in excess of the spending cuts, particularly since reductions in GNP in late 1981 also tended to reduce tax receipts. Thus the administration was faced with record deficits of over $100 billion in fiscal 1982 and about $200 billion in fiscal 1983. In early 1982 President Reagan said he would try to cut spending further in an attempt to soak up some of the red ink. But the economy was in a recession (with an unemployment rate of 9 percent) and there was little sympathy on Capital Hill for further spending cuts. Since inflation had fallen to well under double digits, unemployment once again seemed to be Public Enemy Number One.

In November 1982 the economy pulled out of the recession, and the expansion began. Economists of all schools, but particularly supply-side economists—who advocated the 1981 tax cut to increase incentives for work and saving, and thus to shift the aggregate supply curve to the right—gave the 1981 tax cut considerable credit for increasing real GNP and reducing unemployment. During 1983–86, all years of healthy expansion, the federal government ran huge deficits of about $200 billion per year. President Reagan vowed that he would not raise taxes, and proposed cuts in nonmilitary government expenditures, whereas the critics asked for tax increases and reductions in military spending. In 1986, Congress passed a major tax reform bill that lowered tax rates and broadened the tax base by reducing loopholes. In late 1987, after the sharp stock-market decline, President Reagan and congressional leaders met to try to find a mutually agreeable way to cut the huge deficits, but limited progress was made.

## The Bush Years

In November 1988, George Bush, then vice president, was elected to the presidency on a platform of "no new taxes." Many critics, here and abroad, doubted that the federal deficit could be reduced without additional tax revenue. During 1989 and 1990, the deficit continued to be about $200 billion. In late 1990, Congress and President Bush agreed to a

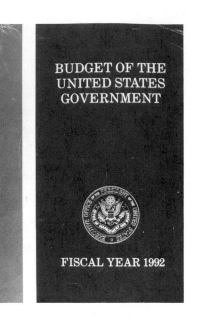

BUDGET OF THE UNITED STATES GOVERNMENT

FISCAL YEAR 1992

George Bush

fiscal package that would reduce the deficit, but by no means eliminate it. Included were additional taxes, including increased tax rates for high-income families and bigger taxes on cigarettes, beer, and wine. After an expansion of record length, the U.S. economy entered a recession in late 1990, and some observers questioned whether it was a good time to raise taxes.

In the early 1990s, one point above all was obvious: *The huge federal deficit dominated discussions of fiscal policy.* In Chapter 15, we will provide a detailed treatment of the deficit and its effects, as well as a more complete view of fiscal policy. Before this can be done, we must take up the role of money in the economy, the subject of the next several chapters.

## TEST YOURSELF

1. "It is tempting to use fiscal policy in a reactive fashion, employing frequent discretionary changes in taxes and spending to alter economic activity temporarily and to counteract each aggregate fluctuation."[2] What other strategies might be used?

2. "An important advantage of public works as a tool of fiscal policy is that they can be started quickly. An important advantage of tax rate changes is that they almost never get embroiled in partisan politics." Comment and evaluate.

[2] Council of Economic Advisers, *1990 Annual Report,* Washington, D.C.: Government Printing Office, 1990, p. 68.

3. "Even if the government spends a lot of money on a useless program, it will still create jobs, and hence be a good thing." Comment and evaluate.

4. According to the late Joseph Pechman of the Brookings Institution, "Among taxes, the federal individual income tax is the leading [automatic] stabilizer." Explain why, and discuss the significance of this fact. He also says that "on the expenditure side, the major built-in stabilizer is unemployment compensation." Again, explain why, and discuss the significance of this fact.

## SUMMARY

1. When the economy has suffered from high unemployment, and output has been below its potential level, the government often has pushed the aggregate demand curve to the right by increasing its spending and/or cutting taxes. When the economy has suffered from inflationary pressures, and equilibrium output has exceeded potential output, the government sometimes has pushed the aggregate demand curve to the left by cutting its spending and/or raising taxes.

2. Fiscal policy tends to have less effect on real GNP and the price level in an open economy than in a closed economy. An expansionary fiscal policy tends to increase the value of the dollar relative to other currencies, which reduces net exports. Also, the increase in the value of the dollar shifts the aggregate supply curve to the right because imported goods and services are cheaper.

3. Policy makers receive a lot of help in stabilizing the economy from our automatic stabilizers—automatic changes in

tax revenues, unemployment compensation, and welfare payments. However, the automatic stabilizers can only cut down on variations in unemployment and inflation, not eliminate them.

4. Discretionary programs have been used to supplement the effects of these automatic stabilizers. Such discretionary actions include changing tax rates, changing government expenditure on public works and other programs, and changing welfare payments and other such transfers. An important problem with some of these tools of fiscal policy is the lag in time before they can be brought into play.

5. Supply-side economists have advocated tax reductions to stimulate national output, the idea being that this would shift the aggregate supply curve to the right because it would increase incentives for work and savings. Supply-side economics played an important role in the arguments for the large tax cut in 1981.

6. A brief history of the fiscal policies adopted by Presidents Ford, Carter, Reagan, and Bush indicates the sorts of decisions made in the past. In the early 1990s, discussions of fiscal policy in the United States tended to center on the federal budget deficit, the topic of Chapter 15, where a more complete treatment of fiscal policy is provided.

## CONCEPTS FOR REVIEW

| | | |
|---|---|---|
| **Automatic stabilizers** | **Council of Economic Advisers** | **Laffer curve** |
| **Deficit** | **Supply-side economics** | |

# PART THREE

# MONEY, BANKING, AND STABILIZATION POLICY

# MONEY AND THE ECONOMY

ACCORDING TO THE MAXIM of an ancient Roman, "Money alone sets all the world in motion." Although a statement that leaves so little room for the laws of physics or astronomy may be a mite extravagant, no one would deny the importance of money in economic affairs. The quantity of money is a very significant factor in determining the health and prosperity of any economic system. Inadequate increases in the quantity of money may bring about excessive unemployment, while excessive increases in the quantity of money may result in serious inflation. To many economists, a discussion of business fluctuations and economic stabilization that ignores the money supply is like a performance of *Hamlet* that omits the prince.

In this chapter, we are concerned with the nature and value of money, as well as with the relationship between a nation's money supply and the extent of unemployment and inflation. In particular, we consider questions like: What is money? What determines its value? What factors influence the demand for money, and what factors influence its quantity? What is the relationship between the quantity of money and the price level? What is the relationship between the quantity of money and the level of gross national product? To understand the workings of our economy and the nature of our government's economic policies, you must be able to answer these questions.

> Sluggish growth in money and credit is attracting increasing concern from both Washington and Wall Street. Top White House economist Michael J. Boskin calls the problem of credit availability "the single biggest threat to a sustained recovery." Many private economists question the upturn's viability in the face of unusually weak money growth. And even Fed officials admit to surprise over the latest money numbers.

*Source: Business Week,* August 5, 1991, p. 17

## WHAT IS MONEY?

We begin by defining money. At first blush, it may seem natural to define it by its physical characteristics. You may be inclined to say that money consists of bills of a certain size and color with certain words and symbols printed on them, as well as coins of a certain type. But this definition would be too restrictive, since money in other societies has consisted of whale teeth, wampum, and a variety of other things. Thus it seems better to define money by its functions than by its physical characteristics. Like beauty, money is as money does.

### Medium of Exchange

*Money acts as a medium of exchange.* People exchange their goods and services for something called money, and then use this money to buy the goods and services they want. To see how important money is as a medium of exchange, let's suppose that it did not exist. To exchange the goods and services they produce for the goods and services they want to consume, people would resort to *barter,* or direct exchange. If you were a wheat farmer, you would have to go to the people who produce the meat, clothes, and other goods and services you want, and swap some of your wheat for each of these goods and services. Of course this would be a very cumbersome procedure, since it would take lots of time and effort to locate and make individual bargains with each of these people. To get some idea of the extent to which money greases the process of exchange in any highly developed economy, consider all the purchases your family made last year—cheese from Wisconsin and France, automobiles from Detroit, oil from Texas and the Middle East, books from New York, and thousands of other items from all over the world. Imagine how few of these exchanges would have been feasible without money.

### Standard of Value, Store of Value

*Money acts as a standard of value.* It is the unit in which the prices of goods and services are measured. How do we express the price of coffee or tea or shirts or suits? In dollars and cents. Thus money prices tell us the rates at which goods and services can be exchanged. If the money price of a shirt is $45 and the money price of a tie is $15, a shirt will exchange for 3 ties. Put differently, a shirt will be "worth" 3 times as much as a tie.

*Money acts as a store of value.* A person can hold on to money and use it to buy things later. You often hear stories about people who hoard a lot of money under their mattresses or bury it in their back yards. These people have an overdeveloped appreciation of the role of money as a store of value. But even those of us who are less miserly use this function of money when we carry some money with us, and keep some in the bank to make future purchases.

Finally, it should be recognized that money is a social invention. It is easy to assume that money has always existed, but this is not the case. Someone had to get the idea, and people had to come to accept it. Nor has money always had the characteristics it has today. In ancient Greece and Rome, money consisted of gold and silver coins. By the end of the seventeenth century, paper money was established in England; but this paper currency, unlike today's currency, could be exchanged for a stipulated amount of gold. Only recently has the transition been made to money that is not convertible into a fixed amount of gold or silver. But regardless of its form or characteristics, *anything that is a medium of exchange, a standard of value, and a store of value is* **money.**

## THE MONEY SUPPLY, NARROWLY DEFINED

In practice, it is not easy to draw a hard-and-fast line between what is money and what is not money, for reasons discussed below. But everyone agrees that coins, currency, demand deposits, and other checkable deposits are money. And the sum total of coins, currency, demand deposits, and other checkable deposits is called the money supply, narrowly defined.[1]

---

[1] In addition, travelers checks are included in the money supply, narrowly defined, since one can pay for goods and services about as easily with travelers checks as with cash. As indicated in Table 10.1, travelers checks are only about 1 percent of the money supply, narrowly defined. Since they are so small a percentage of the money supply, we ignore them in the following discussion.

## Coins and Currency

*Coins* are a small proportion of the total quantity of money in the United States. This is mainly because coins come in such small denominations. It takes a small mountain of pennies, nickels, dimes, quarters, and half-dollars to make even a billion dollars. Of course, the metal in each of these coins is worth less than the face value of the coin; otherwise people would melt them down and make money by selling the metal. In the 1960s, when silver prices rose, the government stopped using silver in dimes and quarters to prevent coins from meeting this fate.

*Currency*—paper money like the $5 and $10 bills everyone likes to have on hand—constitutes a second and far larger share of the total money supply than coins. Together, currency and coins outstanding totaled about $246 billion in 1990, as shown in Table 10.1. The Federal Reserve System, described in the next chapter, issues practically all of our currency in the form of Federal Reserve notes. Before 1933, it was possible to exchange currency for a stipulated amount of gold, but this is no longer the case. (The price of gold on the free market varies; thus the amount of gold one can get for a dollar varies too.) All American currency (and coin) is presently "fiat" money. It is money because the government says so and because the people accept it. There is no metallic backing of the currency anymore. But this does not mean that we should be suspicious of the soundness of our currency, since gold backing is not what gives money its value. (In fact, to some extent, cause and effect work the other way. The use of gold to back currencies has in the past increased the value of gold.) Basically, the value of currency depends on its acceptability by people. And the government, to insure its acceptability, must limit its quantity.

## Demand Deposits and Other Checkable Deposits

*Demand deposits*—bank deposits subject to payment on demand—are another part of the narrowly defined money supply. They are much larger than currency and coins, as shown in Table 10.1. At first you may question whether these demand deposits—or checking accounts, as they are commonly called—are money at all. In everyday speech, they often are not considered money. But economists include demand deposits as part of the money supply, and for good reason. After all, you can pay for goods and services just as easily by check as with cash. Indeed, the public pays for more things by check than with cash. This means that checking accounts are just as much a medium of exchange—and just as much a standard of value and a store of value—as cash. Thus, since they perform all of the functions of money, they should be included as money.

Other *checkable deposits* include negotiable order of withdrawal (NOW) accounts and other accounts that are very close to being demand deposits. A *NOW account* is essentially an interest-bearing checking account at banks, savings banks and other thrift institutions. First created in 1972 by a Massachusetts savings bank, such accounts became legal in more and more states, particularly in the northeast. In 1980, Congress passed a financial reform act that permitted federally chartered thrift institutions to have NOW accounts. Banking innovations like NOW accounts have blurred the distinction between checking and savings accounts. Since many savings and loan associations, mutual savings banks, and credit unions are now providing accounts against which checks can be drawn, it would make no sense to include as money only demand de-

### Table 10.1
### Money Supply, December 1990

| | AMOUNT (BILLIONS OF DOLLARS) |
|---|---|
| Demand deposits | 278 |
| Currency and coins[a] | 246 |
| Other checkable deposits[b] | 294 |
| Travelers checks[c] | 8 |
| Total | 826 |

[a]Only currency and coins outside bank vaults (and the Treasury and Federal Reserve) are included.
[b]Includes ATS and NOW balances at all institutions, credit union, share draft, and other minor items.
[c]See footnote 1.

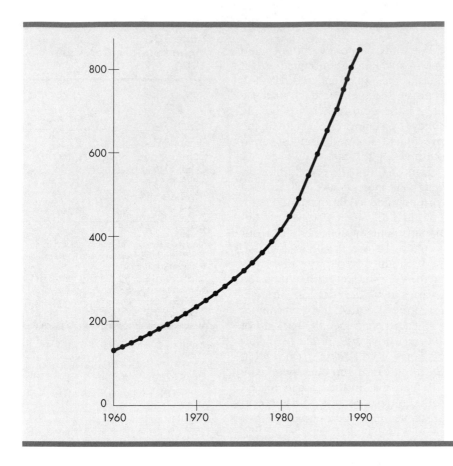

**Figure 10.1**
**Behavior of Money Supply
(Narrowly Defined), United
States, 1960–90**
The money supply, about $826 billion in 1990, has generally increased from year to year, but the rate of increase has by no means been constant.

posits in commercial banks. Instead, all such checkable deposits are included.

Figure 10.1 shows how the narrowly defined money supply—the sum total of coins, paper currency, demand deposits, and other checkable deposits—has behaved since World War II. You can see that the quantity of money has generally increased from one year to the next, and that the increase has been at an average rate of about 5 to 10 percent per year. However, the rate of increase of the quantity of money has by no means been constant. In some years, like 1990, the quantity of money increased by about 4 percent; in others, like 1986, it increased by over 10 percent. A great deal will be said later about the importance and determinants of changes in the quantity of money.

## THE MONEY SUPPLY, BROADLY DEFINED

The narrowly defined money supply (which includes coins, currency, demand deposits, and other checkable deposits) is not the only definition of the money supply that is used by economists. There is also the money supply, broadly defined, which includes savings and small time deposits (deposits under $100,000 with a specific maturity, for example, one year) and money market mutual fund balances and money market deposit accounts, as well as coins, currency, demand deposits, and other checkable deposits. The money supply, narrowly defined, is often called **M-1,** while the money supply, broadly defined, is often called **M-2**.

The traditional reason for excluding time and saving deposits from the narrow definition of money has been that, in most instances, you could not pay for anything with them. For example, suppose that you had a savings account at a commercial bank. You could not draw a check against it, as you could with a demand deposit. And to withdraw your money from the account, you might have to give the bank a certain amount of notice (although in practice this right might be waived and the bank would ordinarily let you withdraw your money when you desired). Nonetheless, since this savings account could so readily be transformed into cash, it was almost like a checking account. Not quite, but almost.

In recent years, the distinction between $M$-1 and some of the non-$M$-1 components of $M$-2 has tended to disappear. Consider money market deposit accounts and money market mutual funds, both of which are included in $M$-2 but not $M$-1. You may be able to write checks on your money market deposit account; and nonbank financial institutions like brokerage firms now offer money market mutual funds that are checkable, although they may be subject to minimum withdrawal restrictions or prior notice of withdrawal.

Besides time and savings accounts, many other assets can also be transformed into cash without much difficulty—though not quite as easily as time and savings deposits. For example, it is not difficult to convert government bonds into cash. There is no way to draw a hard-and-fast dividing line between money and nonmoney, since many assets have some of the characteristics of money. Consequently, there are still other definitions of the money supply that are more inclusive than $M$-2. But most economists feel that, although assets like government bonds have some of the properties of money, it would be stretching things too far to include them in the money supply. (For one thing, their price varies as interest rates change.)

Economists call such assets **_near-money,_** and recognize that the amount of near-money in the economy has an important effect on spending habits. There is some disagreement among economists as to exactly what is and what isn't near-money, but this needn't concern us here. The major point we want to make is that any dividing line between money and nonmoney must be arbitrary.

In this book, we shall use the narrow definition, $M$-1, when we refer to the money supply. But the choice is arbitrary.

# THE VALUE OF MONEY

Let's go back to one very important point that was mentioned briefly in a previous section. There is no gold backing for our money. In other words, there is no way that you can exchange a $10 bill for so many ounces of gold. (If you look at a $10 bill, you will see that it says nothing about what the government will give you in exchange for it.) Currency and demand (and other checkable) deposits are really just debts, or IOUs. Currency is the debt of the government, while demand deposits are the debts of the banks. Intrinsically, neither currency nor deposits have any real value. A $10 bill is merely a small piece of paper, and a deposit is merely an entry in a bank's accounts. And, as we have seen, even coins are worth far less as metal than their monetary value.

All this may make you feel a bit uncomfortable. After all, if our coins, currency, demand deposits, and other checkable deposits have little or no intrinsic value, doesn't this mean that they can easily become worthless? To answer this question, we must realize that basically, *money has value because people will accept it in payment for goods and services.* If your university will accept your check in payment for your tuition, and your grocer will accept a $20 bill in payment for your groceries, your demand deposit and your currency have value. You can exchange them for goods and services you want. And your university or your grocer accepts this money only because they have confidence that they can spend it for goods and services they want.

## Money's Value Depends on the Price Level

Thus money is valuable because it will buy things. But how valuable is it? For example, how valuable is $1? Clearly, *the value of a dollar is equivalent to what a dollar will buy. And what a dollar will buy depends on the price level.* If all prices doubled, the value of a dollar would be cut in half, because a dollar would be able to buy only half as many goods and services as it formerly could. On the other hand, if all prices were reduced by 50 percent, the value of a dollar would double, because a dollar would be able to buy twice as many goods and services as it formerly could. You often hear people say that today's dollar is worth only $.50. What they mean is that it will buy only half what a dollar could buy at some specified date in the past.

It is interesting and important to see how the value of the dollar, as measured by its purchasing power, has varied over time. Figure 10.2 shows how an index of the price level in the United States has changed since 1779. Over time, prices have fluctuated sharply, and some of the greatest fluctuations have resulted from wars. For example, the price level fell sharply after the Revolutionary War, and our next war—the War of 1812—sent prices skyrocketing, after which there was another postwar drop in prices. The period from about 1820 to about 1860 was marked by relative price stability, but the Civil War resulted in an upward burst followed by a postwar drop in prices. After a period of relative price stability from 1875 to 1915, there was a doubling of prices during World War I and the usual postwar drop. World War II saw an increase of about 40 percent, but there was no postwar drop in prices. Instead there has been continual inflation. During the past 20 years, the price level has tripled.

**THE VALUE OF MONEY IS INVERSELY RELATED TO THE PRICE LEVEL.** In inflationary times, the value of money decreases; the opposite is true when the price level falls (an infrequent phenomenon in the past four decades). Thus the wartime periods when the price level rose greatly were periods when the value of the dollar decreased greatly. The doubling of prices during World War I meant that the value of the dollar was chopped in half. Similarly, the postwar periods when the price level fell greatly were periods when the value of the dollar increased. The 50 percent decline in prices after the Civil War meant a doubling in the value of the dollar. Given the extent of the variation of the price level shown in Figure 10.2, it is clear that the value of the dollar has varied enormously during our history.

# INFLATION AND THE QUANTITY OF MONEY ✓

As we have seen, the value of money is reduced in periods of inflation. In runaway inflation, its value can be largely wiped out, as in Germany after

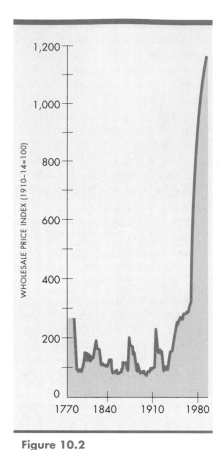

**Figure 10.2**
**Index of Wholesale Prices, United States, 1779–1990 (1910–14=100)**
The price level has fluctuated considerably, sharp increases generally occurring during wars. Since World War II, the price level has tended to go only one way—up. In the past 20 years, the price level has tripled.

World War I. (Recall Chapter 5.) Our own country suffered from runaway inflations during the Revolutionary War and the Civil War. You may have heard the expression that something is "not worth a continental." It comes from the fact that the inflated dollars in use during the Revolutionary War were called continentals.

Generally, such severe inflations have occurred because the government increased the money supply at an enormously rapid rate. It is not hard to see why a tremendous increase in the quantity of money will result in a runaway inflation. Other things held constant, increases in the quantity of money will result in increases in total intended spending, and once full employment is achieved, such increases in intended spending will cause more and more inflation.

Eventually, when the inflation is severe enough, households and businesses may refuse to accept money for goods and services because they fear that it will depreciate significantly before they have a chance to spend it. Instead, they may insist on being paid in merchandise or services. Thus the economy will turn to barter, with the accompanying inconveniences and inefficiency.

To prevent such an economic catastrophe, the government must manage the money supply responsibly. As we have stressed in previous sections, the value of money depends basically on the public's willingness to accept it, and the public's willingness to accept it depends on money's being reasonably stable in value. If the government increases the quantity of money at a rapid rate, thus causing a severe inflation and an accompanying precipitous fall in the value of money, public confidence in money will be shaken, and the value of money will be destroyed. The moral here is clear: *the government must restrict the quantity of money, and it must conduct its economic policies so as to maintain a reasonably stable value of money.*

## UNEMPLOYMENT AND THE QUANTITY OF MONEY

In the previous section, we were concerned primarily with what happens when the quantity of money grows too rapidly. As we have seen, the result is inflation. But this is only part of the story. The quantity of money can grow too slowly as well as too rapidly; and when this happens the result, according to most economists, is increased unemployment. If the money supply grows very slowly, or decreases, there will be a tendency for total intended spending to grow very slowly or decrease. This in turn will cause national output to grow very slowly or decrease, thus causing unemployment to increase.

According to many economists, the recession of 1974–75 was due partly to an inadequate growth of the money supply. The Federal Reserve, trying to stem the inflationary tide in 1974, cut back on the rate of increase of the money supply. Looking back over past business fluctuations, it appears that an inadequate rate of increase in the quantity of money was responsible, at least in part, for many recessions. Recall that in our discussion of business fluctuations in Chapter 8 we stressed the importance of monetary factors. In this chapter, as well as Chapters 11 to 14, we will study these factors in detail.

# DETERMINANTS OF THE QUANTITY OF MONEY

Judging from our discussion thus far, it is clear that to avoid excessive unemployment or excessive inflation, the quantity of money must not grow too slowly or too fast. But what determines the quantity of money? When the United States was on the gold standard, the amount of money in circulation was determined by the amount of monetary gold in the country. When gold flowed into the country, the money supply increased; when it flowed out, the money supply decreased. This is no longer the case, since we are no longer on the gold standard—and neither is any other major nation.

If gold doesn't determine the amount of money in circulation in the U.S., what does? The answer is that the supply of money is determined to a considerable degree by the Federal Reserve, which, as we have noted before, is our nation's central bank. Within limits, the Federal Reserve can and does control the quantity of money. But to some extent the private sector of the economy also determines the quantity of money. For example, the nation's commercial banks, through their lending (and other) decisions, can influence the money supply.[2] In the remainder of this chapter, we shall make the simplifying assumption that the money supply is governed solely by the Federal Reserve. In the following chapter, we shall see how the commercial banks also play an important role in this regard.

# THE DEMAND FOR MONEY ✓

We have discussed in general terms how changes in the quantity of money affect the tempo of economic activity. Now let's look in detail at how changes in the quantity of money affect gross national product. The first step in doing this is to discuss the demand for money. Why does a family or firm want to hold money? Certainly, a family can be wealthy without holding much money. We all know stories about very rich people who hold very little money, since virtually all of their wealth is tied up in factories, farms, and other nonmonetary assets. Given that people and firms obtain a much higher return from other kinds of assets than from money, why do they want to hold money, rather than other kinds of assets? Two of the most important reasons are the following.

**1. TRANSACTIONS DEMAND FOR MONEY.** To carry out most transactions, money is required. Thus people and firms have to keep some money on their person and in their checking accounts to buy things. The higher a person's income—in real terms—the more goods and services that person probably will want to purchase, and hence the more money he or she will want to hold for transaction purposes. For example, in 1991, when a doctor made about $100,000 a year, the average physician would want to keep more money on hand for transactions purposes than in the days— many years ago—when a doctor made perhaps $10,000 a year. Because ~e quantity of money demanded by a household or firm increases with

~~r~~ course, banks do not create money all by themselves. The public's preferences and ac-
~~...~~ as well as bank behavior, influence the amount of demand deposits. Also, commercial
may not be as unique in this respect as it appears at first sight.

its income, it follows that the total quantity of money demanded for transactions purposes in the economy as a whole is directly related to real gross national product. That is, the higher (lower) the level of real GNP, the greater (less) the quantity of money demanded for transactions purposes.

In addition, the total quantity of money demanded for transactions purposes is directly related to the price level. That is, the higher (lower) the price level, the greater (less) the quantity of money demanded for transactions purposes. Obviously, if the price level were to double tomorrow, you would want to keep more money on hand for transactions purposes. In order to purchase the same goods and services as before, you would need more money.

**2. PRECAUTIONARY DEMAND FOR MONEY.** Besides the transactions motive, households and firms like to hold money because they are uncertain concerning the timing and size of future disbursements and receipts. Unpredictable events often require money. People get sick, and houses need repairs. Also, receipts frequently do not come in exactly when expected. To meet such contingencies, people and firms like to put a certain amount of their wealth into money and near-money. In the economy as a whole, the total quantity of money demanded for precautionary purposes (like the quantity demanded for transactions purposes) is likely to vary directly with real GNP and the price level. If GNP goes up, households and firms will want to hold more money for precautionary purposes, because their incomes and sales will be higher than before the increase in GNP. If

---

# EXAMPLE 10.1 QUANTIFYING THE DEMAND FOR MONEY

Stephen Goldfeld of Princeton University has found that a 1 percent increase in real GNP or a 1 percent increase in interest rates[*] has had the following effect on the real quantity of money demanded (that is, the quantity of money demanded divided by the price level):

| | EFFECT OF 1 PERCENT INCREASE IN REAL GNP (PERCENT) | EFFECT OF 1 PERCENT INCREASE IN INTEREST RATE (PERCENT) |
|---|---|---|
| Short run | +0.19 | −0.045 |
| Long run | +0.68 | −0.160 |

(a) The short-run effects are the effects after three months; the long-run effects are the effects after a few years. Why are the effects in the long run greater than in the short run? (b) If real GNP increases by 10 percent, what is the effect on the real quantity of money demanded in the long run? (c) If the interest rate increases from 8 percent to 10 percent, what is the effect on the real quantity of money demanded in the short run? (d) Goldfeld also found that the quantity of

money demanded is proportional to the price level. Why do you think that this is the case?

## Solution

(a) Because it takes time for households and business firms to recognize and adapt to changing conditions. In the short run, they tend to be locked in to existing patterns of behavior, and it takes time to adjust. (b) The real quantity of money demanded will increase by about 6.8 percent. (c) Since the interest rate increases by 25 percent (from 8 to 10 percent), the real quantity of money demanded will fall by about 25 X .045, or 1.125 percent. (d) People demand money to pay for things. As the price level goes up, they require more money to pay for the same things. In other words, as the price level goes up, more money is demanded in order to have the same purchasing power as before.[*]

[*]For simplicity, only his results concerning the interest rate for time deposits are included. Also, see R. Hall and J. Taylor, *Macroeconomics*, third edition, New York: Norton, 1991.

the price level goes up, they will want to hold more money to offset the reduced purchasing power of the dollar.[3]

## The Interest Rate and the Demand Curve for Money

Up to this point, we have discussed why individuals and firms want to hold money. But we must recognize that there are disadvantages, as well as advantages, in holding money. One is that the real value of money will fall if inflation occurs. Another is that an important cost of holding money is the interest or profit one loses, since instead of holding money, one might have invested it in assets that would have yielded interest or profit. For example, the annual cost of holding $5,000 in money if one can obtain 6 percent on existing investments is $300, the amount of interest or profit forgone.[4]

With GNP constant, the amount of money demanded by individuals and firms is *inversely* related to the interest rate. *The higher the interest rate, the smaller the amount of money demanded. The lower the interest rate, the greater the amount of money demanded.* This is because the cost of holding money increases as the interest rate or yield on existing investments increases. For example, if the interest rate were 7 percent rather than 6 percent, the cost of holding $5,000 in money for one year would be $350 rather than $300. Thus, as the interest rate or profit rate increases, people try harder to minimize the amount of money they hold. So do firms. Big corporations like IBM or General Motors are very conscious of the cost of holding cash balances.

**Figure 10.3**
**The Demand for Money**
Holding the interest rate and the price level constant, the quantity of money demanded is *directly* related to real GNP, as shown in panel A. Holding the interest rate and real GNP constant, the quantity of money demanded is *directly* related to the price level, as shown in panel B. Holding real GNP and the price level constant, the quantity of money demanded is *inversely* related to the interest rate, as shown in panel C. This last relationship is known as the demand curve for money.

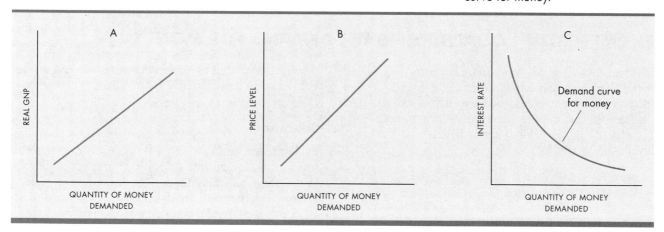

[3] Still another motive for holding money is the speculative motive. People like to hold some of their assets in a form in which they can be sure of its monetary value and can take advantage of future price reductions. The amount of money individuals and firms will keep on hand for speculative reasons will vary with their expectation concerning future price movements. In particular, if people feel that the prices of bonds and stocks are about to drop soon, they are likely to demand a great deal of money for speculative reasons. By holding money, they can obtain such securities at lower prices than at present.

[4] For simplicity, we assume here that money yields no interest or profit. This is not true because, as we saw earlier, the money supply includes some interest-bearing checkable deposits. But this makes no real difference to our argument. Even if money yields some interest, it yields a much smaller return than alternative investments like bonds. Thus there is an opportunity cost involved in holding money.

Figure 10.3 summarizes three important conclusions of our discussion in this and the previous section. Panel A of Figure 10.3 shows that, *holding the interest rate and the price level constant, the quantity of money demanded is directly related to real GNP.* As we explained in the previous section, the higher (lower) the level of real GNP, the greater (less) the quantity of money demanded. Panel B of Figure 10.3 shows that, *with the interest rate and real GNP constant, the quantity of money is directly related to the price level.* In other words, the higher (lower) the price level, the greater (less) the quantity of money demanded. Panel C of Figure 10.3 shows that, *with real GNP and the price level constant, the quantity of money demanded is inversely related to the interest rate.*[5] This latter relationship, described here, is called the **demand curve for money.**

---

## TEST YOURSELF

1. "Money, in and of itself, has no value whatsoever. It is valuable only because of what it can buy." Comment and evaluate.

2. Explain in detail why the following items are not money: (a) government bonds, (b) General Motors stock, (c) gold, (d) uranium.

3. Give some reasons why savings accounts should be regarded as money. Give some reasons why they should not. Which side of the argument do you find more convincing?

4. Why is the interest rate regarded as the ``price'' of holding money? What factors will shift the demand curve for money to the right? To the left?

---

# CHANGES IN THE MONEY SUPPLY AND NATIONAL OUTPUT

## Effects of a Change in the Money Supply: The Simple Keynesian Model

Now that we have investigated the demand for money, we are ready to show how changes in the quantity of money influence the value of GNP. To begin with, let's see how the money supply can be inserted into the simple Keynesian model (in Chapter 6), which assumes that the price level is fixed.

To begin with, let's trace the effects of an increase in the money supply from $200 billion to $250 billion. If the demand curve for money is as shown in panel A of Figure 10.4, the result will be a *decrease in the interest rate* from 8 percent to 6 percent. Why? Because, if the interest rate is 8 percent, people will demand only $200 billion of money, not the $250 billion that is supplied. Having more money on hand than they want, they will invest the excess in bonds, stocks, and other financial assets, with the result that the price of bonds, stocks, and other financial assets will rise.[6]

---

[5] However, the relationship between the quantity of money and the interest rate pertains only to the short run. In the long run, increases in the money supply, if they result in increased inflation, may *raise* interest rates, because lenders will require a greater return to offset the greater rate of depreciation of the real value of the dollar. Still, however, the real rate of interest—the rate of interest adjusted for inflation—may decline. For further discussion of this point, see page 281.

[6] For simplicity, we assume that when people have excess money balances, they use the money to buy financial assets. (Also, we assume that when people have smaller money balances than they want, they sell financial assets to get more money.) A more complete analysis is provided in Appendix A of this book. The results are essentially the same as those provided here.

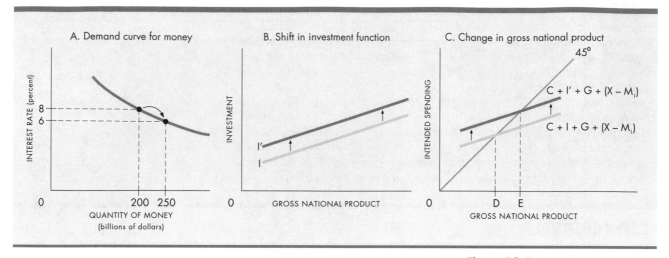

A. Demand curve for money

B. Shift in investment function

C. Change in gross national product

**Figure 10.4**
**Effect of an Increase in the Money Supply**
If the money supply increases from $200 billion to $250 billion, the interest rate drops from 8 percent to 6 percent (panel A). Because of the decrease in the interest rate, the investment function shifts upward (panel B), and the equilibrium level of GNP increases from *D* to *E* (panel *C* ).

*Such a rise in the price of bonds is equivalent to a fall in the rate of interest.* (To see why, suppose that a very long-term bond pays interest of $300 per year. If the price of the bond is $3,000, the interest rate on the bond is 10 percent. If the price of the bond rises to $4,000, the interest rate on the bond falls to 7 1/2 percent. Thus the increase in price amounts to a reduction in the interest rate.) When the interest rate has fallen to 6 percent, people will be willing to hold the $250 billion in money. At this interest rate, the quantity of money demanded will equal the quantity of money supplied.

The decrease in the interest rate from 8 percent to 6 percent affects the *investment function,* which is the relationship between GNP and intended investment spending.[7] Recall from Chapter 6 that the level of investment is inversely related to the interest rate. Because it is less costly to invest and because credit is more readily available[8] *the investment function will shift upward,* as shown in panel B of Figure 10.4. This occurs because at each level of gross national product, firms will want to invest more, since investment is more profitable (because of the cut in the interest rate) and funds are more readily available.[9] (Note that panel B assumes that, if the interest rate is held constant, investment is directly related to GNP. This is reasonable because, the greater the output of the economy, the greater the pressure on firms to invest in additional plant and equipment. In Chapter 6, we assumed for simplicity that investment was the same, regardless of GNP.)

This shift in the investment function then affects the equilibrium level

[7] Changes in the money supply, interest rates, and credit availability affect the consumption function, government spending, and net exports as well as the investment function. For example, *increases (decreases) in interest rates shift the consumption function and the level of government spending downward (upward).* These factors augment the effect of monetary policy described in the text. We focus attention on the investment function in Figure 10.4 merely because this simplifies the exposition.

[8] Note that it is not just a matter of interest rates. Availability of credit is also important. In times when money is tight, some potential borrowers may find that they cannot get a loan, regardless of what interest rate they are prepared to pay. In times when money is easy, people who otherwise might find it difficult to get a loan may be granted one by the banks. To repeat, both availability and interest rates are important.

[9] Many firms depend to a considerable extent on retained earnings to finance their investment projects. Thus, since they do not borrow externally, the effect on their investment plans of changes in interest rates and credit availability may be reduced. However, since changes in the interest rate reflect changes in the opportunity cost of using funds to finance investment projects, they still may have an appreciable effect on the investment function.

of gross national product. As shown in panel C of Figure 10.4, *the equilibrium level of gross national product will increase* from *D* to *E*, in accord with the principles discussed in Chapter 6. (Recall that the equilibrium value of GNP is at the point where the $C + I + G + (X - M_1)$ line intersects the 45-degree line.) Thus *the effect of the increase in the money supply is to increase gross national product.*

This, in simplified fashion, is how an increase in the money supply affects GNP, according to the simple Keynesian model.[10] To summarize, *the increase in the money supply results in a reduction in the interest rate, which results in an increase in investment, which results in an increase in GNP.* Of course, a decrease in the money supply has just the opposite effect. Specifically, *a decrease in the money supply results in an increase in the interest rate, which results in a decrease in investment, which results in a decrease in GNP.*[11]

## Effects of a Change in the Money Supply: No Assumption of a Constant Price Level

As emphasized repeatedly in earlier chapters, the simple Keynesian model discussed in the previous section assumes that the price level is fixed. If we relax this assumption, we must use the aggregate supply and demand curves described in Chapter 7. As in the previous section, suppose that the money supply increases from $200 billion to $250 billion, the result being that the interest rate falls from 8 to 6 percent and that the investment function shifts upward.[12] As indicated in Figure 10.5, the increase in investment spending pushes the aggregate demand curve to the right. This makes sense, since the quantity of total real output demanded (at the existing price level) goes up.

What will be the effect of this increase in the money supply? The answer depends heavily on the shape of the aggregate supply curve. If the economy is fully employed and the aggregate supply curve is vertical (or close to it), increases in the money supply will result in inflation, but little or no extra real output. However, if the intersection of the aggregate demand and supply curves prior to the increase in the money supply occurred in the upward-sloping range of the aggregate supply curve, as in Figure 10.5, the effect is an increase in real GNP from $OY_0$ to $OY_1$ and an increase in the price level from $OP_0$ to $OP_1$. Thus the increase in the money supply raises both total real output and the price level. (Of course, if the intersection occurred in the horizontal range of the aggregate supply curve, the situation would be like that discussed in the previous section, since the price level would be constant.)

Just as an increase in the money supply pushes the aggregate demand curve to the right, so a decrease in the money supply pushes it to the left.

---

[10] The alert reader will recognize that the increase in GNP in panel C will shift the demand curve for money in panel A of Figure 10.4. For simplicity, we ignore this feedback. It is included in the more complete model presented in Appendix A.

[11] Harking back to Chapter 7, we are in a better position to understand now why the aggregate demand curve slopes downward and to the right. An increase in the price level increases the transactions demand for money because the average money cost of each transaction tends to go up. Thus the demand curve for money shifts to the right, with the result that the interest rate increases. As indicated in this section, the higher interest rate results in reduced spending on output. Thus there is an inverse relationship between the price level and aggregate demand.

[12] Recall that for simplicity we assume in this and the previous section that changes in the money supply, interest rates, and credit availability influence only the investment function, not consumption expenditure, government spending, or net exports. See footnote 7.

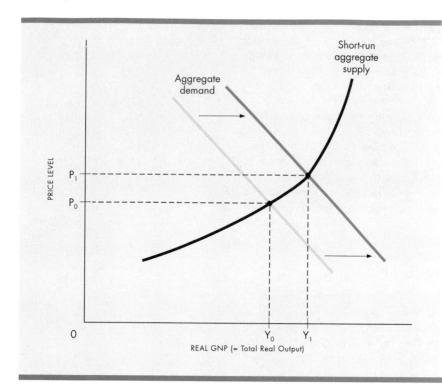

**Figure 10.5**
**Effect of an Increase in the Money Supply on Real GNP and the Price Level**
An increase in the money supply pushes the aggregate demand curve to the right, thus increasing real GNP from $OY_0$ to $OY_1$, and raising the price level from $OP_0$ to $OP_1$.

As pointed out in the previous section, a decrease in the money supply results in an increase in the interest rate, which results in a decrease in investment. Since the quantity of total real output demanded (at each price level) goes down, the aggregate demand curve shifts to the left. If the aggregate supply curve is vertical (or close to it), the result will be a reduction in the price level, but little or no cut in real output. But if the economy is operating in the upward-sloping range of the aggregate supply curve, the result will be a reduction in both the price level and real output.

## CLOSING A RECESSIONARY GAP

In recent decades, governments throughout the world have tried to manipulate the money supply in order to close (or at least reduce) recessionary and inflationary gaps. Suppose that the economy is in the short-run equilibrium position shown in Figure 10.6. There is a recessionary gap, as evidenced by the fact that the equilibrium level of real national output, $OQ_1$, is less than its potential level, $OQ_0$. (Recall that potential output is the amount of output that would be produced if there were full employment.) One way to deal with this situation is to leave things alone. As we know from previous chapters, a recessionary gap of this sort will eventually cure itself. As wages and prices eventually fall, the short-run aggregate supply curve will shift to the right, and the equilibrium level of real output will rise toward the potential level, $OQ_0$. Eventually the economy will move to point $A$, where the aggregate demand curve intersects the long-run aggregate supply curve, which is the vertical line at $OQ_0$. (If you are somewhat hazy concerning this process, review the middle panel of Figure 9.1).

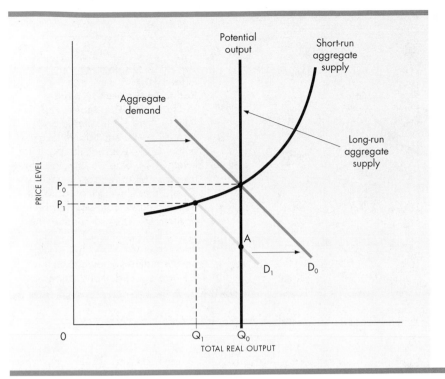

**Figure 10.6**
**Increasing the Money Supply to Close a Recessionary Gap**
Initially there is a recessionary gap, since the equilibrium level of output, $OQ_1$, is less than the potential level, $OQ_0$. One way to close this gap may be to increase the money supply, thus shifting the aggregate demand curve from position $D_1$ to position $D_0$. Although this increases output to its potential level, there are inflationary consequences: the price level increases from $OP_1$ to $OP_0$.

But as Keynes and his followers pointed out, this process may take a long time to work itself out—and the pain inflicted on the unemployed and others may be substantial. Thus many economists have recommended that governments increase the money supply to help close a recessionary gap. For example, in Figure 10.6, the government might increase the money supply so as to push the aggregate demand curve from its initial position ($D_1$) rightward to $D_0$, the result being that total real output will be raised from $OQ_1$ to its potential level, $OQ_0$. In this way, the recessionary gap will be closed.

However, one undesirable side effect is that the increase in the money supply raises the price level from $OP_1$ to $OP_0$. In other words, there are inflationary consequences. As pointed out in the previous section, the extent of the inflationary consequences depends on the steepness of the short-run aggregate supply curve. If the short-run aggregate supply curve is close to vertical, the inflationary consequences may be very great; but if the short-run aggregate supply curve is close to horizontal, they may be quite moderate. Much more will be said about the possible inflationary consequences of anti-recessionary policies in Chapter 13.

## CLOSING AN INFLATIONARY GAP

Turning from a recessionary gap to an inflationary gap, suppose that the economy is in the short-run equilibrium position shown in Figure 10.7. There is an inflationary gap, as indicated by the fact that the equilibrium level of real national output, $OQ_2$, is greater than the potential level, $OQ_0$. Here, as in the case of a recessionary gap, one way to deal with the situation is to leave things alone. As we know from previous chapters, an in-

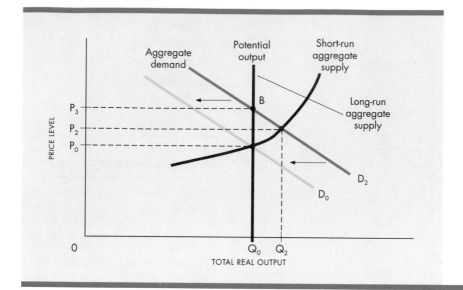

**Figure 10.7**
**Reducing the Money Supply to Close an Inflationary Gap**
Initially there is an inflationary gap, since the equilibrium level of output, $OQ_2$, exceeds the potential level, $OQ_0$. One way to close this gap may be to reduce the money supply, thus shifting the aggregate demand curve from position $D_2$ to position $D_0$. This will result in the price level equaling $OP_0$, which is lower than $OP_3$, which it would have equaled without the shift in the aggregate demand curve.

flationary gap of this sort will eventually cure itself. As wages and prices are bid up, the short-run aggregate supply curve shifts to the left. Eventually the economy will move to point $B$, where the aggregate demand curve intersects the long-run aggregate supply curve, and the equilibrium level of real national output equals the potential level, $OQ_0$. (For a review of this process, see the middle panel of Figure 9.2)

However, this leftward shift of the short-run aggregate supply curve will result in inflation until the price level rises to $OP_3$ in Figure 10.7. Given the many undesirable consequences of such inflation (detailed in Chapter 5), many economists have recommended that governments cut back on the money supply to help close an inflationary gap. For example, in Figure 10.7, the government might reduce the money supply so as to push the aggregate demand curve from its initial position ($D_2$) leftward to $D_0$, the result being that the price level will be $OP_0$, rather than $OP_3$. In this way, the government closes the inflationary gap.

Unfortunately, one side effect may be that unemployment will increase. Although this increase in unemployment will not be permanent, many economists believe that it can be substantial and prolonged. Much more will be said about this important topic in Chapter 13.

## MONETARISM

Some prominent economists, led by Milton Friedman of Stanford University's Hoover Institution, share a point of view known as monetarism; hence, they are called monetarists. During the 1950s and 1960s (and to a lesser extent during the 1970s and 1980s), there was a continuing (and sometimes bitter) controversy between the monetarists and the Keynesians. Monetarists regard the rate of growth of the money supply as the principal determinant of nominal GNP. (**Nominal GNP** means GNP in money, not real terms. In other words, nominal GNP is GNP measured in current, not constant, dollars.) At heart, the argument between the monetarists and the Keynesians was over what determines the level of output, employment, and prices. The Keynesians put more emphasis on the federal budget than did the monetarists; the monetarists put more emphasis

Milton Friedman

on the money supply than did the Keynesians. More will be said on this score in Chapter 14 and in Appendix A.

The monetarists have had a great impact on economic thought in the postwar period, even though theirs has been a minority view. Professor Friedman's most severe critics admit that his research in this area (which helped win him a Nobel prize) has been pathbreaking and important. According to his findings, *the rate of change of the money supply shows well-marked cycles that match closely those in economic activity in general and precede the latter by a long interval.* On the average, the rate of change of the money supply has reached its peak nearly 16 months before the peak in general business and has reached its trough over 12 months before the trough in general business.[13]

## THE VELOCITY OF MONEY

The monetarists revived interest in the so-called quantity theory of money, which was developed many years ago by such titans of economics as Alfred Marshall of Cambridge and Irving Fisher at Yale. To understand this theory, it is useful to begin by defining a new term: the velocity of circulation of money. The **velocity of circulation of money** is the rate at which the money supply is used to make transactions for final goods and services. That is, it equals the average number of times per year that a dollar is used to buy the final goods and services produced by the economy. In other words,

Irving Fisher

$$V = \frac{GNP}{M},$$ (10.1)

where $V$ is velocity, GNP is the nominal gross national product, and $M$ is the money supply. For example, if our nominal gross national product is $1 trillion and our money supply is $200 billion, the velocity of circulation of money is 5, which means that, on the average, each dollar of our money consummates $5 worth of purchases of gross national product.

Nominal gross national product can be expressed as the product of real gross national product and the price level. In other words,

$$GNP = P \times Q,$$ (10.2)

where $P$ is the price level—the average price at which final goods and services are sold—and $Q$ is gross national product in real terms. For example, suppose that national output in real terms consists of 200 tons of steel. If the price of a ton of steel is $100, then nominal GNP equals $P \times Q$, or $100 \times 200$, or $20,000.[14]

If we substitute $P \times Q$ for GNP in Equation (10.1), we have

$$V = \frac{P \times Q}{M},$$ (10.3)

That is, velocity equals the price level $(P)$ times the real GNP $(Q)$ divided by the money supply $(M)$. This is another way to define the velocity of circulation of money—a way that will prove very useful.

[13] Milton Friedman, testimony before the Joint Economic Committee, "The Relationship of Prices to Economic Stability and Growth," 85th Congress, 2d Session.

[14] Since real GNP is measured here in physical units (tons), $P$ is the price level. If real GNP had been measured in constant dollars, P would have been a price index. In either event, our conclusions would be basically the same.

# THE EQUATION OF EXCHANGE

Now that we have a definition of the velocity of circulation of money, our next step is to present the so-called equation of exchange. The **equation of exchange** is really nothing more than a restatement, in somewhat different form, of our definition of the velocity of circulation of money. To obtain the equation of exchange, all we have to do is multiply both sides of Equation (10.3) by $M$. The result is

$$MV = PQ. \qquad (10.4)$$

To understand exactly what this equation means, let's look more closely at each side. *The right-hand side equals the amount received for final goods and services during the period,* because $Q$ is the output of final goods and services during the period and $P$ is their average price. Thus the product of $P$ and $Q$ must equal the total amount received for final goods and services during the period—or nominal GNP. For example, if national output in real terms equals 200 tons of steel, and if the price of a ton of steel is $100, then $100 × 200—that is, $P × Q$—must equal the total amount received for final goods and services during the period.

*The left-hand side of Equation (10.4) equals the total amount spent on final goods and services during the period.* Why? Because the left-hand side equals the money supply—$M$—times the average number of times during the period that a dollar was spent on final goods and services—$V$. Consequently, $M × V$ must equal the amount spent on final goods and services during the period. For example, if the money supply equals $10,000 and velocity equals 2, the total amount spent on final goods and services during the period must equal $10,000 × 2, or $20,000.

Thus, since the *amount received for* final goods and services during the period must equal the *amount spent on* final goods and services during the period, the left-hand side must equal the right-hand side.

The equation of exchange—Equation (10.4)—is what logicians call a tautology. It holds by definition. Yet it is not useless. On the contrary, economists regard the equation of exchange as very valuable, because it sets forth some of the fundamental factors that influence GNP and the price level. This equation has been used by economists for many years. It is the basis for the crude quantity theory of money used by the classical economists, as well as the recent theories put forth by the monetarists.

# THE CRUDE QUANTITY THEORY OF MONEY AND PRICES

The classical economists discussed in Chapter 5 assumed that both $V$ and $Q$ were constant. They believed that $V$ was constant because it was determined by the population's stable habits of holding money, and they believed that $Q$ would remain constant at its full employment value.[15] On the basis of these assumptions, they propounded the **crude quantity theory** of money and prices, a theory that received a great deal of attention and exerted considerable influence in its day.

---

[15] In some cases, they did not really assume continual full employment. Instead, they were concerned with the long-run changes in the economy and compared the peaks of the business cycle, where full employment frequently occurs.

If these assumptions hold, it follows from the equation of exchange—Equation (10.4)—that the price level (P) must be proportional to the money supply (M), because V and Q have been assumed to be constant. (In the short run, the full-employment level of real gross national product will not change much.) Thus we can rewrite Equation (10.4) as

$$P = \left(\frac{V}{Q}\right)M, \tag{10.5}$$

where (V/Q) is a constant. So P must be proportional to M if these assumptions hold.

The conclusion reached by the crude quantity theorists—namely, *that the price level will be proportional to the money supply*—is very important, if true. To see how they came to this conclusion, one must recognize that they stressed the transaction motive for holding money. Recall from an earlier section that, based on this motive, one would expect the quantity of money demanded to be directly related to the level of nominal GNP. Further, the demand for money was assumed to be stable, and little or no attention was paid to the effect of the interest rate on the demand for money. Indeed, the crude quantity theorists went so far as to assume that the quantity of money demanded was *proportional* to the level of nominal GNP. This amounted to assuming that velocity was constant.

Suppose there is a 10 percent increase in the quantity of money. Why would the crude quantity theorists predict a 10 percent increase in the price level? To begin with, they would assert that, since the quantity of money has increased relative to the value of nominal GNP, households and firms now hold more money than they want to hold. Further, they would argue that households and firms will spend their excess money balances on commodities and services, and that the resulting increase in total intended spending will increase the nominal value, but not the real value of GNP (since full employment is assumed). In other words, the increase in aggregate demand will bid up prices. More specifically, they would argue that prices will continue to be bid up until they have increased by 10 percent, since only then will the nominal value of GNP be big enough so that households and firms will be content to hold the new quantity of money.

## Evaluation of the Crude Quantity Theory

The crude quantity theory is true to its name: it is only a crude approximation to reality. One important weakness is its assumption that velocity is constant. Another is its assumption that the economy is always at full employment, which we know from previous chapters to be far from true. But despite its limitations, the crude quantity theory points to a very important truth: If the quantity of money increases by a large percentage, the price level is very likely to increase greatly as well. Thus, if the money supply is increased tenfold, there will be a marked increase in the price level. If we take the crude quantity theory at face value, we would expect a tenfold increase in the price level; but that is a case of spurious accuracy. Perhaps the price level will go up only eightfold. Perhaps it will go up twelvefold. The important thing is that it will go up a lot.

Consider the runaway inflation that occurred in Germany after World War I. The German inflation occurred because the German government printed and spent large bundles of additional money. You often hear people warn of the dangers in this country of the government's "resorting to the printing presses" and flooding the country with a vast increase in the money supply. It is a danger in any country. And one great value of the crude quantity theory is that it predicts correctly what will occur as a consequence—rapid inflation.

## IS VELOCITY CONSTANT?

The crude quantity theory was based on two simplifying assumptions, both of which are questionable. One assumption was that real gross national product $Q$ remains fixed at its full-employment level. The other was that the velocity of circulation of money $(V)$ remains constant. A more sophisticated version of the quantity theory can be derived by relaxing the first assumption. This version of the quantity theory recognizes that the economy is often at less than full employment and consequently that real gross national product $Q$ may vary a good deal for this reason.

So long as velocity remains constant, the equation of exchange—Equation (10.4)—can be used to determine the relationship between gross national product in current dollars and $M$, even if $Q$ is allowed to vary. On the basis of the equation of exchange, it is obvious that $P \times Q$ should be proportional to $M$, if the velocity of circulation of money $V$ remains constant. Since $P \times Q$ is the nominal gross national product, it follows that, if this assumption holds, *the nominal gross national product should be proportional to the money supply*. In other words,

$$\text{GNP} = aM, \tag{10.6}$$

where GNP is the nominal gross national product and $V$ is assumed to equal a constant—$a$. Thus, if the money supply increases by 10 percent, the nominal value of GNP should increase by 10 percent. If the money supply increases by 20 percent, the nominal value of GNP should increase by 20 percent. And so forth.

If velocity is constant, this version of the quantity theory should enable us to predict nominal gross national product if we know the money supply. Also, if velocity is constant, this version of the quantity theory should enable us to control nominal gross national product by controlling the money supply. But is velocity constant? Since Equation (10.6) is based on this assumption, we must find out.

Figure 10.8 shows how the velocity of circulation of money has behaved since 1920. Obviously velocity has not been constant. Excluding the war years, it has generally been between 2.5 and 6.5 in the United States. It has changed rather slowly, although it has varied a good deal over the business cycle. Velocity tends to decrease during depressions and increase during booms. *All in all, one must conclude from Figure 10.8 that, although velocity has not varied enormously, it is not so stable that Equation (10.6) alone can be used in any precise way to forecast or control gross national product.*[16]

---

[16] It is important to note that the velocity figures in Figure 10.8 are based on the narrow definition of the money supply, $M$-1. If $M$-2 is used instead, velocity is more nearly constant. For example, between 1960 and 1976, velocity based on $M$-2 varied within a very narrow range. See Council of Economic Advisers, *1990 Annual Report*, Washington, D.C.: Government Printing Office, 1990, p. 82.

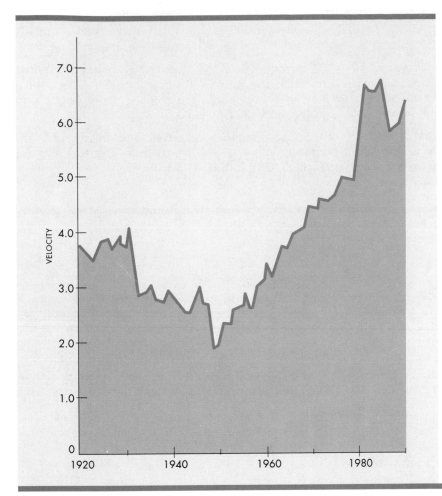

**Figure 10.8**
**Velocity of Circulation of Money, United States, 1920–90**
The velocity of circulation of money has generally been between 2.5 and 6.5, except during World War II.

However, this version of the quantity theory points out a very important truth, which is that *the money supply has an important effect on gross national product (in money terms). Increases in the quantity of money are likely to increase nominal GNP, while decreases in the quantity of money are likely to decrease nominal GNP.* Because velocity is not constant, the relationship between the money supply and gross national product is not as neat and simple as that predicted by Equation (10.6), but there is a relationship.

Consequently, monetarists often relax the assumption that $V$ is constant, and assert that it is possible to predict $V$ as a function of other variables, like the frequency with which people are paid, the level of business confidence, and the cost of holding money (the interest rate). According to some economists, one of Friedman's major contributions was to replace the constancy of $V$ with its predictability. However, during the 1980s, some leading monetarists admitted they were having lots of trouble in forecasting $V$.

Other economists feel that changes in $V$ reflect, rather than cause, changes in GNP. Indeed, some economists believe that changes in real GNP cause changes in the money supply, rather than the other way around. More will be said on this score in Chapter 14, where we discuss real business cycle models.

# TEST YOURSELF

1. If the value of GNP (in money terms) increases 10 percent and the money supply remains fixed, does velocity increase? Why, or why not? What are some of the factors that might cause an increase in velocity?

2. "The history of the United States is an account of one inflation after another. The currency is being debased further and further. Soon we may experience a runaway inflation." Comment and evaluate.

3. Describe how the quantity of money influences nominal and real GNP according to (a) the simple Keynesian model, (b) the crude quantity theory, and (c) the model in Figure 10.5.

4. Suppose that a bond pays annual interest of $100 forever. What is the interest rate if its price is (a) $1,000, (b) $2,000, (c) $3,000?

# SUMMARY

1. Money performs three basic functions. It serves as a medium of exchange, a standard of value, and a store of value. The money supply, narrowly defined, is composed of coins, currency, demand deposits, and other checkable deposits.

2. Besides the narrow definition of money, broader definitions include savings and time deposits (and other items like money market mutual fund shares). In addition, there are lots of other assets—for example, government bonds—that can be transformed without much difficulty into cash. It is not easy to draw a line between money and nonmoney, since many assets have some of the characteristics of money.

3. America's history has seen many sharp fluctuations in the price level. Generally, severe inflations have occurred because the government expanded the money supply far too rapidly. However, too small a rate of growth of the money supply can also be a mistake, resulting in excessive unemployment.

4. Most economists believe that the lower the interest rate, the greater the amount of money demanded. Thus increases in the quantity of money result in lower interest rates, which result in increased investment (and other types of spending), which pushes the aggregate demand curve to the right. Thus, if the short-run aggregate supply curve is upward sloping, increases in the money supply increase real GNP and the price level.

5. Governments often increase the money supply to try to close a recessionary gap, and reduce the money supply (or at least its rate of growth) to try to close an inflationary gap. Whereas increases in the money supply tend to push the aggregate demand curve to the right, reductions in the money supply tend to push it to the left.

6. The effect of an increase in the money supply depends on the shape of the aggregate supply curve. If this curve is nearly vertical, the effect will be a rise in the price level, but little or no increase in real output. If it is nearly horizontal, the effect will be an increase in real output with little or no rise in the price level.

7. The equation of exchange is $MV = PQ$, where $M$ is the money supply, $V$ is velocity, $P$ is the price level, and $Q$ is gross national product in real terms. The velocity of circulation of money is the rate at which the money supply is used to make transactions for final goods and services. Specifically, it equals GNP in money terms divided by the money supply.

8. If the velocity of circulation of money remains constant, GNP in money terms should be proportional to the money supply. Monetarists believe that changes in the money supply are the principal determinant of nominal GNP. In fact, velocity has by no means remained stable over time, but monetarists believe it is predictable.

# CONCEPTS FOR REVIEW

| | | |
|---|---|---|
| **Coins** | **M -1** | **Nominal GNP** |
| **Currency** | **M -2** | **Velocity of circulation** |
| **Demand deposits** | **Near-money** | **Equation of exchange** |
| **Checkable deposits** | **Demand curve for money** | **Crude quantity theory** |

# THE BANKING SYSTEM AND THE QUANTITY OF MONEY

ON JANUARY 7, 1991, THE front page of the *New York Times* trumpeted: "U.S. Is Taking over Northeast Bank to Head Off a Run." The Bank of New England, based in Boston and one of the nation's largest banks, was widely regarded as being in deep financial trouble. So were a substantial number of other big banks in the United States. In early January 1991, the federal government seized the Bank of New England, and announced that it would protect all depositors until the bank could be sold.

In this chapter, we look in detail at how commercial banks operate. We begin by discussing the Federal Reserve System and the functions of commercial banks. Then we describe the nature of commercial banks' loans and investments, as well as the important concept of reserves. After looking into legal reserve requirements we go on to describe how commercial banks create money—a very important and commonly misunderstood process. Finally, we take up the effects of currency withdrawals and desired excess reserves on our results. In the course of our discussion, you will find out why the Bank of New England went belly-up and why many observers are worried about the health of other banks.

## THE FEDERAL RESERVE SYSTEM

Any nation must exercise control over the quantity of money. In the United States, the Federal Reserve System is charged with this responsibility. The Federal Reserve System—or "Fed," as it is called by the *cognoscenti*—plays a central role in the economy as a whole. After a severe financial panic in 1907, when a great many banks failed, there was strong public pressure to do something to strengthen our banking system. At the same time, there was great fear of centralized domination of the nation's banks. The result—after six years of negotiation and discussion—was the establishment by Congress of the **Federal Reserve System** in 1913.

### Commercial Banks

As shown in Figure 11.1, the organization of the Federal Reserve System can be viewed as a triangle. At the base are the commercial banks. In 1980, Congress gave the Federal Reserve very substantial powers over all banks and over nonbank depository institutions, even those that did not belong to the Federal Reserve System.

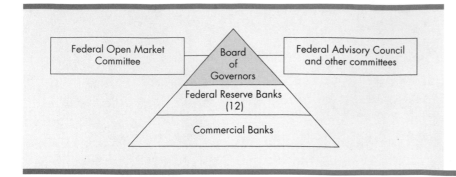

**Figure 11.1**
**Organization of the Federal Reserve System**
The Federal Reserve System contains the commercial banks, the 12 regional Federal Reserve Banks, and the Board of Governors, as well as the Federal Open Market Committee and various advisory councils and committees.

### Federal Reserve Banks

In the middle of the triangle in Figure 11.1 are the 12 Federal Reserve Banks, each located in a Federal Reserve district. The entire nation is divided into 12 Federal Reserve districts, with Federal Reserve Banks in New York, Chicago, Philadelphia, San Francisco, Boston, Cleveland, St. Louis, Kansas City, Atlanta, Richmond, Minneapolis, and Dallas. Each of these banks is a corporation owned by the commercial banks, but, despite this fact, the commercial banks do not in any sense act as owners of the Federal Reserve Bank in their district. Instead, each Federal Reserve Bank is a public agency. These Federal Reserve Banks act as "bankers' banks," performing much the same sorts of functions for commercial banks that commercial banks perform for the public. That is, they hold the deposits of banks and make loans to them. In addition, the Federal Reserve Banks perform a function no commercial bank can perform: They issue Federal Reserve notes, which are the nation's currency.

### The Board of Governors

At the top of the triangle in Figure 11.1 is the Board of Governors of the Federal Reserve System. Located in Washington, this board—generally called the Federal Reserve Board—has 7 members appointed by the president for 14-year terms. The board, which coordinates the activities of the Federal Reserve System, is supposed to be independent of partisan politics and to act to promote the nation's general economic welfare. It is responsible for supervising the operation of the money and banking system of the United States. The board is assisted in important ways by the Federal Open Market Committee, which establishes policy concerning the purchase and sale of government securities. The Federal Open Market Committee is composed of the board plus the presidents of five Federal Reserve Banks. The board is also assisted by the Federal Advisory Council, a group of 12 commercial bankers that advises the board on banking policy.

## FUNCTIONS OF THE FEDERAL RESERVE

The Federal Reserve Board, with the 12 Federal Reserve Banks, constitutes the central bank of the United States. Every major country has a central bank. England has the Bank of England, and France has the Bank of France. **Central banks** are very important organizations, whose most important function is to help control the quantity of money. One interesting feature of our central bank is that its principal allegiance is to Congress, not to the executive branch of the federal government. This came about because Congress wanted to protect the Fed from pressure by the president and the Treasury Department. Thus the Fed was supposed to be independent of the executive branch. In fact, although the Fed has sometimes locked horns with the president, it has generally cooperated with him and his administration, as we shall see in Chapter 12.

To repeat, a central bank's most important function is to control the money supply. But this is not its only function. A central bank also handles the government's own financial transactions, and coordinates and controls the country's commercial banks. Specifically, the Federal Reserve System is charged with the following responsibilities.

**BANK RESERVES.**   The Federal Reserve Banks hold deposits, or reserves, of the banks. As we shall see, these reserves play an important role in the process whereby the Fed controls the quantity of money.

**CHECK COLLECTION.**   The Federal Reserve System provides facilities for check collection. In other words, it enables a bank to collect funds for checks drawn on other banks.

**CURRENCY.**   The Federal Reserve Banks supply the public with currency through the issuance of Federal Reserve notes.

**GOVERNMENT FISCAL AGENT.**   The Federal Reserve Banks act as fiscal agents for the federal government. They hold some of the checking accounts of the U.S. Treasury, and aid in the purchase and sale of government securities.

**BANK SUPERVISION.**   Federal Reserve Banks supervise the operation of the commercial banks. More will be said about the nature of bank supervision and regulation later in the chapter, and much more will be said about the functions of the Federal Reserve in the next chapter.

## COMMERCIAL BANKS IN THE UNITED STATES

There are over 10,000 commercial banks in the United States. This testifies to the fact that, in contrast to countries like England, where a few banks with many branches dominate the banking scene, the United States has promoted the growth of a great many local banks. In part, this has stemmed from a traditional suspicion in this country of "big bankers." ("Eastern bankers" are a particularly suspect breed in some parts of the country.)

Commercial banks have two primary functions. First, *banks hold demand deposits and permit checks to be drawn on these deposits*. This function is familiar to practically everyone. Most people have a checking account in some commercial bank, and draw checks on this account. Second, *banks lend money to industrialists, merchants, homeowners, and other individuals and firms*. At one time or another, you will probably apply for a loan to finance some project for your business or home. Indeed, it is quite possible that some of the costs of your college education are being covered by a loan to you or your parents from a commercial bank.

In addition, commercial banks perform a number of other functions, such as holding time and savings accounts. You will recall that these accounts bear interest and, although technically one must give a certain amount of notice before withdrawal, in practice they can usually be withdrawn whenever their owner likes. Commercial banks also sell money orders and travelers checks, handle estates and trusts, rent safe-deposit boxes, and provide a variety of services for customers.

Needless to say, commercial banks are not the only kind of financial institution. Mutual savings banks and savings and loan associations hold savings and time deposits and various forms of checkable deposits; "consumer finance" companies lend money to individuals; insurance companies lend money to firms and governments; "factors" provide firms with working capital; and investment bankers help firms sell their securities to the public. All these types of financial institutions play an important role in the American economy. In general, they all act as intermediaries between savers and investors; that is, they all turn over to investors money that they received from savers.

## The Bank of America: A Case Study

We can learn something about banking in the United States from the history of a particular bank—the Bank of America, one of the nation's largest commercial banks. In 1904, Amadeo Peter Giannini, a 34-year-old son of an Italian immigrant, founded the Bank of Italy in the Italian district of San Francisco. Giannini was a man of enormous energy and drive. At the age of 12, he had gone to school by day, while working in his stepfather's produce firm for much of each night. At 19, he was a full-fledged member of the produce firm, and at 31 had become rich enough to retire from the produce business—and eventually to turn to banking.

Giannini showed the sort of entrepreneurial zeal in banking that would be expected from his previous track record. As an illustration, consider the following episode:

> In 1906, the city of San Francisco was rocked by earthquake and swept by fire. As the flames approached the little Bank of Italy, the young banker piled his cash and securities into a horsedrawn wagon and with a guard of two soldiers took them to his home at San Mateo, twenty miles from San Francisco, where he buried them in the garden; and then while the ruins of the city were still smoking he set up a desk in the open air down by the waterfront, put up a sign over the desk which read BANK OF ITALY, and began doing business again—the first San Francisco bank to resume.[1]

Clearly, Giannini was a banker who did not observe banker's hours.

Giannini's bank prospered and grew. By the time he was 50, it had over 25 branches. During the 1920s, he acquired more and more branches, until old-line California bankers began to realize that the Bank of Italy had become a factor to be reckoned with. They did their best to prevent its further expansion, but to no avail. A man who can turn an earthquake to his advantage is unlikely, after all, to submit to such pressures. Indeed, by 1929, Giannini had 453 banking offices in California alone, as well as a considerable number elsewhere. His was the fourth largest commercial bank in the country.

In 1930, Giannini's bank was renamed the Bank of America. The 1930s

Amadeo Peter Giannini

---

[1] Frederick Lewis Allen, *The Lords of Creation,* New York: Harper and Bros., 1935, p. 320. Much of this section is based on Allen's account.

were not particularly kind to it, any more than they were to the rest of the economy. But in the next 50 years, the Bank of America grew and grew. By 1983, it had deposits of about $90 billion, and was the largest commercial bank in the United States. However, earnings declined during the 1980s, and the bank incurred a loss in 1985, triggering a reorganization and down-sizing of its operations. (In 1990, it was behind Citibank and Chase Manhattan in assets, as shown in Table 11.1). Nonetheless, it has come a long way since the days of the open-air desk on the waterfront.

**Table 11.1**
**The Ten Largest Commercial Banks in the United States in Terms of Assets, 1990**

| BANK AND LOCATION | ASSETS (BILLIONS OF DOLLARS) |
| --- | --- |
| Citibank, New York | 231 |
| Chase Manhattan, New York | 107 |
| Bank of America, San Francisco | 99 |
| Morgan (J.P.), New York | 89 |
| Security Pacific, Los Angeles | 84 |
| Chemical New York, New York[a] | 72 |
| NCNB, Charlotte | 61 |
| Manufacturers Hanover, New York[a] | 60 |
| First Interstate Bancorp, Los Angeles | 59 |
| Bankers Trust, New York | 56 |

[a] Merger announced in 1991.

*Source: Business Week, 1990.*

# HOW BANKS OPERATE

The Bank of America, one of the biggest in the country, is hardly a typical commercial bank. It has had a remarkable history and a gifted founder. Many commercial banks are very small, as you would guess from the fact that there are over 10,000 of them in the United States. And there is a great deal of variation among banks in their operating procedures and styles. Some are principally for firms; they do little business with individuals. Others are heavily engaged in lending to consumers. Nonetheless, although it is difficult to generalize about the operations of commercial banks because they vary so much, certain principles and propositions generally hold.

1. *Banks generally make loans to both firms and individuals, and invest in securities of state, local, and federal governments.* The relationship between a business firm and its bank is often a close and continuing one. The firm keeps a reasonably large deposit with the bank for long periods of time, while the bank provides the firm with needed and prudent loans. The relationship between an individual and his or her bank is much more casual, but banks like consumer loans because they tend to be relatively profitable. In addition, besides lending to firms and individuals, banks have bought large quantities of government bonds (that is, long-term IOUs of state, local, and federal governments).

2. *Banks, like other firms, are operated to make a profit.* They don't do

it by producing and selling a good, like automobiles or steel. Instead, they perform various services, including lending money, making investments, clearing checks, keeping records, and so on. They manage to make a profit from these activities by lending money and making investments that yield a higher rate of interest than they must pay their depositors. For example, the Bank of America may be able to get 15 percent interest on the loans it makes, while it must pay only 9 percent interest to its depositors. (Commercial banks pay interest on some, but not all, deposits. Also, they provide services at less than cost to holders of deposits.) If so, it receives the difference of 6 percent, which goes to meet its expenses—and to provide it with some profits.

3. *Banks must constantly balance their desire for high returns from their loans and investments against the requirement that these loans and investments be safe and easily turned into cash.* Since a bank's profits increase if it makes loans or investments that yield a high interest rate, it is clear why a bank favors high returns from its loans and investments. But those that yield a high interest rate often are relatively risky, which means that they may not be repaid in full. Because a bank lends out its depositors' money, it must be careful to limit the riskiness of the loans and investments it makes. Otherwise it may fail.

Until about 50 years ago, banks used to fail in large numbers during recessions, causing depositors to lose their money. Even during the prosperous 1920s, over 500 banks failed per year. It is no wonder that the public viewed the banks with less than complete confidence. Since the mid-1930s, bank failures have been much rarer, in part because of tighter standards of regulation by federal and state authorities. For example, bank examiners audit the books and practices of the banks. In addition, confidence in the banks was strengthened by the creation in 1934 of the Federal Deposit Insurance Corporation, which insures over 99 percent of all commercial bank depositors. At present, each deposit is insured up to $100,000. Nonetheless, as pointed out at the beginning of this chapter, there was much more concern over the safety of the banks during the early 1990s than during the previous half-century.

## THE BALANCE SHEET OF AN INDIVIDUAL BANK

A good way to understand how a bank operates is to look at its balance sheet. The left-hand side of a firm's balance sheet shows the nature of its *assets;* the right-hand side of a firm's balance sheet shows the firm's *liabilities* (that is, its debts) and its *net worth* (the value of the firm's owners' claims against the firm's assets). Since a firm's net worth is defined as the difference between its assets and its liabilities, the sum of the items on the left-hand side of a balance sheet must equal the sum of the items on the right-hand side. (Much more will be said about balance sheets in Chapter 21.) Table 11.2 shows the Bank of America's balance sheet as of the end of 1990.

*The Left-Hand Side.* The left-hand side shows that the total assets of the Bank of America were $110.7 billion, and that these assets were made up as follows: $7.8 billion in cash, $6.9 billion in bonds and other securities, $85.8 billion in loans, and $10.2 billion in other assets. In particular, note that the loans included among the assets of the Bank of America are the loans it made to firms and individuals. As we have emphasized repeatedly, lending money is one of the major functions of a commercial bank.

*The Right-Hand Side.* The right-hand side of the balance sheet says that

**Table 11.2**
**Balance Sheet, Bank of America, December 31, 1990 (Billions of Dollars)**

| ASSETS | | LIABILITIES AND NET WORTH | |
|---|---|---|---|
| Cash | 7.8 | Deposits | 92.3 |
| Securities | 6.9 | Other liabilities | 12.0 |
| Loans | 85.8 | Net worth | 6.4 |
| Other assets | 10.2 | | |
| Total[a] | 110.7 | Total | 110.7 |

[a] This figure differs from that in table 11.1 because of differences in dating and concept.

*Source:* Bank of America.

the total liabilities—or debts—of the Bank of America were $104.3 billion, and that these liabilities were made up of $92.3 billion in deposits (both demand and time), and $12.0 billion in other liabilities. Note that the deposits at the Bank of America are included among its liabilities, since the Bank of America owes the depositors the amount of money in their deposits. It will be recalled from the previous sections that maintaining these deposits is one of the major functions of a commercial bank. Returning to the balance sheet of the Bank of America, the difference between its total assets and its total liabilities—$6.4 billion—is its net worth, which is the value of the bank's owners' claims against the bank's assets.

## Cash Less Than Deposits

One noteworthy characteristic of any bank's balance sheet is the fact that *a very large percentage of its liabilities must be paid on demand*. For example, if all the depositors of the Bank of America tried to withdraw their demand deposits, a substantial proportion of its liabilities would be due on demand. Of course, the chance of everyone wanting to draw out his or her money at once is infinitesimally small. Instead, on a given day some depositors withdraw some money, while others make deposits, and most neither withdraw nor deposit money. Consequently, any bank can get along with an amount of cash to cover withdrawals that is much smaller than the total amount of its deposits. For example, the Bank of America's cash equaled about one-twelfth of its total deposits. Note that "cash" here includes the bank's deposit with the Federal Reserve system and its deposits with other banks, as well as cash in its vault.

The Bank of America's practice of holding an amount of cash—including its deposits with the Federal Reserve and with other banks—that is much less than the amount it owes its depositors may strike you as dangerous. Indeed, if you have a deposit at the Bank of America, you may be tempted to go over and withdraw the money in your account and deposit it in some bank that does have cash equal to the amount it owes its depositors. But you won't be able to do this because *all banks hold much less cash than the amount they owe their depositors*. Moreover, this is a perfectly sound banking practice, as we shall see in the following sections.

# FRACTIONAL-RESERVE BANKING

To understand the crucial significance of **fractional-reserve banking,** as this practice is called, let's compare two situations—one where a bank must hold as reserves an amount equal to the amount it owes its depositors, another where its reserves do not have to match the amount it owes its depositors. In the first case, the bank's balance sheet might be as shown in Table 11.3, if demand deposits equal $2 million and net worth equals $500,000. The bank's loans and investments in this case are made entirely with funds put up by the owners of the bank. To see this, note that loans and investments equal $500,000, and that the bank's net worth also equals $500,000. Thus, if some of these loans are not repaid or if some of these investments lose money, the losses are borne entirely by the bank's stockholders. The depositors are protected completely because every cent of their deposits is covered by the bank's reserves.

Now let's turn to the case of fractional-reserve banking. In this case, the bank's balance sheet might be as shown in Table 11.4, if deposits

**Table 11.3**
**Bank Balance Sheet: Case Where Reserves Equal Demand Deposits (Millions of Dollars)**

| ASSETS | | LIABILITIES AND NET WORTH | |
|---|---|---|---|
| Reserves | 2.0 | Demand | |
| Loans and | | deposits | 2.0 |
| investments | 0.5 | Net worth | 0.5 |
| Total | 2.5 | Total | 2.5 |

**Table 11.4**
**Bank Balance Sheet: Fractional Reserves (Millions of Dollars)**

| ASSETS | | LIABILITIES AND NET WORTH | |
|---|---|---|---|
| Reserves | 0.4 | Demand | |
| Loans and | | deposits | 2.0 |
| investments | 2.1 | Net worth | 0.5 |
| Total | 2.5 | Total | 2.5 |

equal $2 million and net worth equals $500,000. Some of the loans and investments made by the bank are not made with funds put up by the owners of the bank, but with funds deposited in the bank by depositors. Thus, though depositors deposited $2 million in the bank, the reserves are only $400,000. What happened to the remaining $1.6 million? Since the bank (in this simple case) only has two kinds of assets, loans (and investments) and reserves, the bank must have lent out (or invested) the remaining $1.6 million.

### Origins of Fractional-Reserve Banking

The early history of banking is the story of an evolution from the first to the second situation. The earliest banks held reserves equal to the amounts they owed depositors, and were simply places where people stored their gold. But as time went on, banks began to practice fractional-reserve banking. It is easy to see how this evolution could take place. Suppose that you owned a bank of the first type. You would almost certainly be struck by the fact that most of the gold entrusted to you was not demanded on any given day. Sooner or later, you might be tempted to lend out some of the gold and obtain some interest. Eventually, as experience indicated that this procedure did not inconvenience your depositors, you and other bankers might make this practice common knowledge.

You might use several arguments to defend this practice. First, you would probably point out that none of the depositors had lost any money. (To the depositors, this would be a rather important argument.) Second, you could show that the interest you earned on the loans made it possible for you to charge depositors less for storing their gold. Consequently, you would argue that it was to the depositors' advantage (because of the savings that accrued to them) for you to lend out some of the gold. Third, you would probably argue that putting the money to work benefited the community and the economy. After all, in many cases, firms can make highly productive investments only if they can borrow the money, and by lending out your depositors' gold, you would enable such investments to be made.

### Legal Reserve Requirements

Arguments of this sort have led society to permit fractional-reserve banking. In other words, a bank is allowed to hold less in reserves than the amount it owes its depositors. But what determines the amount of reserves banks hold? For example, the Bank of America, according to Table 11.2, held cash equal to about 8 percent of its total deposits. Probably it could get away with holding much less in reserves, so long as there is no panic among depositors and it makes sound loans and investments. One reason why the Bank of America held this much cash is very simple. *The Federal Reserve System requires every commercial bank to hold a certain percentage of its deposits as reserves.* The Fed can set this percentage between the limits of 8 and 14 percent for checkable deposits (that is, deposits subject to direct or indirect transfer by check).[2] Also, on the affirmative action of five of the seven members of the Fed's board of gover-

[2] For up to about $40 million in checkable deposits, this percentage is 3 percent. Note too that *these reserve requirements apply to deposits in other thrift institutions (savings and loan associations, mutual savings banks, and credit unions), not just banks.*

nors, it can impose an additional reserve requirement of up to 4 percent. And in extraordinary circumstances the Fed can for 180 days set the percentage at any level it deems necessary. These are **legal reserve requirements;** they also exist for time deposits (of businesses and nonprofit institutions), but are lower than for checkable deposits.

Most of these reserves are held in the form of deposits by banks at their regional Federal Reserve Bank. Thus, for example, a great deal of the Bank of America's reserves are held in its deposit with the Federal Reserve Bank of San Francisco. In addition, some of any bank's reserves are held in cash on the bank's premises. However, its legal reserves are less than the "cash" entry on its balance sheet since its deposits with other banks do not count as legal reserves.

The most obvious reason why the Fed imposes these legal reserve requirements would seem to be to keep the banks safe, but in this case the obvious answer isn't the right one. Instead, *the most important reason for legal reserve requirements is to control the money supply.* It will take some more discussion before this becomes clear.

## THE SAFETY OF THE BANKS

We have just argued that the reserve requirements imposed by the Federal Reserve System exceed what would be required under normal circumstances to insure the safety of the banks. To support our argument, we might cite some authorities who claim that a bank would be quite safe if it only had reserves equal to about 2 percent of its deposits. Under these circumstances it would be able to meet its depositors' everyday demands for cash. Obviously this level of reserves is much lower than the legally required level.

### The Role of Bank Management

At the same time, one should recognize that high reserve requirements will not by themselves insure bank safety. For example, suppose that a bank lends money to every budding inventor with a scheme for producing perpetual-motion machines, and that it grants particularly large loans to those who propose to market these machines in the suburbs of Missoula, Montana. This bank is going to fail eventually, even if it holds reserves equal to 20 percent—or 50 percent, for that matter—of its demand deposits. It will fail simply because the loans it makes will not be repaid, and eventually these losses will accumulate to more than the bank's net worth. In other words, if the bank is sufficiently inept in making loans and investments, it will lose all the owners' money and some of the depositors' money besides.

The well-managed bank must make sensible loans and investments. In addition, it must protect itself against short-term withdrawals of large amounts of money. Although much-larger-than-usual withdrawals are not very likely to occur, the bank must be prepared to meet a temporary upswing in withdrawals. One way is to invest in securities that can readily be turned into cash. For example, the bank may invest in short-term government securities that can readily be sold at a price that varies only moderately from day to day. Such securities are often referred to as *secondary reserves.*

## The Role of Government

There can be no doubt that bank deposits are much safer today than they were 75 or 100 years ago. The reason is that the government has put its power squarely behind the banking system. It used to be that "runs" on the banks occurred with jarring frequency. Every now and then, depositors, frightened that their banks would fail and that they would lose some of their money, would line up at the tellers' windows and withdraw as much money as they could. Faced with runs of this sort, banks were sometimes forced to close because they could not satisfy all demands for withdrawals. (See page 231 for the famous case of the Knickerbocker Trust Company.) Needless to say, no fractional-reserve banking system can satisfy demands for total withdrawal of funds.

FDIC headquarters, Washington, D.C.

The situation now is quite different. The government—including the Federal Deposit Insurance Corporation (FDIC), the Fed, and other public agencies—has made it clear that it will not stand by and tolerate the sorts of panics that used to occur periodically in this country. The FDIC insures the accounts of depositors in practically all banks so that, even if a bank fails, the depositor will get his or her money back—up to $100,000. Also, the banks themselves are better managed and regulated. For example, bank examiners are sent out to look over the bankers' shoulders and see whether they are solvent. It is a far cry from the situation about 80 years ago that led to the creation of the Federal Reserve System.

## Problems during the Nineties

Nonetheless, this does not mean that bank regulation is all that it might be—or that the health of the banking industry is robust. On the contrary, in early 1991, there were persistent rumors and reports that many huge New York banks, as well as a variety of smaller banks elsewhere, were in serious financial troubles because many of their real estate loans went sour when the real estate market did not live up to expectations. Also, some banks had made risky investments in high-yield bonds and risky loans to developing countries like Argentina and Brazil. While these problems did not mean that your bank deposit was not insured (up to $100,000), it did mean that your bank might fail, with attendant losses to its owners, among others.

To bolster the profitability of the banks, the Bush administration suggested that they be allowed to establish out-of-state branches and to diversify into other fields like insurance. To increase the resources of the FDIC, it has been suggested that the insurance premiums that banks pay be increased. To make the banks sturdier, it has been suggested that capital requirements for banks be increased, thus providing an extra cushion to absorb larger losses before banks fail and force the FDIC to pay off depositors. These and other suggestions were part of the ferment resulting from the fragile health of many major U.S. banks in the 1990s.

## The Lending Decision: A Case Study

To get a better feel for the workings of a bank, let's look at an actual decision faced by Robert Swift, the assistant vice-president of the Lone Star National Bank of Houston, Texas. Mr. Swift received a call from Ralph Desmond, president of the Desmond Engineering Corporation. Mr. Desmond wanted to change his bank; he was dissatisfied with the amount

# THE FAILURE OF THE KNICKERBOCKER TRUST IN 1907

The Knickerbocker Trust in New York City was a successful bank at the turn of the century. The Knickerbocker Trust's main branch was at a fashionable Fifth Avenue address, where many well-to-do people (including the writer Mark Twain) kept their accounts. At its downtown office near Wall Street, the Knickerbocker Trust held some of the deposits of large corporations like General Electric and the Pennsylvania Railroad. In turn, the bank made loans to numerous growing businesses. Under its dynamic president, Charles T. Barney, the Knickerbocker held city bonds and invested in the development of the transit system, in new hotels along Fifth Avenue, and in elegant apartment buildings on the Upper West Side. Not all of the bank's loans paid off. But most did, and the bank prospered.

An opportunity then came along for Charles Barney to make a lot of money, if he was willing to take some major risks. Barney had connections with a speculator named Charles Morse. Morse and his partner, Frederick Heinze, formulated a scheme to manipulate the price of copper stock on Wall Street in 1907. The extent of Barney's involvement is debatable, but many believed he made behind-the-scenes arrangements for the Morse-Heinze combine, which, on October 15, 1907, tried and failed to squeeze the copper market, and the syndicate went under. There was no evidence that Barney had overcommitted loans to Morse, but there were rumors to this effect, and Barney, like any banker of the day, realized that gossip could lead to the death of his bank before any facts were proven. He knew that as the word spread that the Knickerbocker was in trouble, the depositors would start a run of withdrawals. Like any banker caught in that situation, Barney also knew that, if he could temporarily pull enough cash together, he might be able to calm his customers. If they were made to believe that the bank could make its payouts, his bank might be saved.

On Sunday, October 20, Charles Barney left his home on Park Avenue to try to borrow the cash he needed. He went to appeal to the only person who

**KNICKERBOCKER WILL NOT OPEN**

Conference of Bankers Deems it Unwise to Aid the Trust Company Further To-day.

**EIGHT MILLIONS WITHDRAWN**

could save him: J. P. Morgan. Morgan had helped tide over banks in trouble before, and he was one of the few men who had the reputation and resources to do it. Morgan had been friendly with Barney, and owned some Knickerbocker stock. But Morgan refused even to see him. For Barney, disaster was inescapable. Trying to forestall the rumors, the bank's board of directors on Monday forced Barney's resignation. It didn't help. The run on the Knickerbocker began. On Tuesday morning bank officials announced they had $8 million cash in their vaults, but most of it was gone before the end of the day. The Knickerbocker closed its doors. Those customers who hadn't withdrawn their money were out of luck for an unforeseeable future. The failure of the Knickerbocker Trust led to doubts about other banks, and snowballed into the Panic of 1907. Realizing that the ensuing bank failures could endanger the entire system—including his own holdings—J. P. Morgan subsequently stepped in, and under his leadership, a large reserve fund was pooled together. But by the time the panic was over, 246 banks had closed, and a disgraced, distraught Charles Barney had killed himself. Ironically, the Knickerbocker Trust was not all that bad a bank—it was to reopen five months later, and depositors got most of their money back.

N. B.

he could borrow from his present bank. He wanted to borrow $30,000 from the Lone Star to pay what he owed to his present bank, pay some bills coming up, and buy some material needed to fulfill a contract. Mr. Swift asked Mr. Desmond to come to his office with various financial statements regarding the Desmond Engineering Corporation and its prospects. These included recent income statements and balance sheets, as well as a variety of other data, including information indicating how rapidly the firm collected its bills and the quality of the debts owed the firm.

Mr. Swift forwarded Mr. Desmond's loan application to the credit department of the bank for further analyses. The credit department added comments on the Desmond Engineering Corporation's solvency and prospects. Besides being secured by a mortgage on some equipment owned by the Desmond Engineering Corporation, this loan was to be personally endorsed by Mr. Desmond and another principal stockholder in the firm. Consequently, Mr. Swift obtained information on the extent and nature of the personal assets of Mr. Desmond and the other stockholder. This information was used, together with all the other data on the firm, to determine whether the bank would make the loan. After a reasonable amount of time, Mr. Swift recommended the acceptance of Mr. Desmond's loan application. In his view, Mr. Desmond had a very good chance of repaying the loan.[3]

Note two things about this decision. First, if the bank grants Mr. Desmond the loan, it will create a demand deposit for him. In other words, it will create some money. Second, the bank can do this only if it has reserves exceeding the legal reserve requirements. Both of these points are important enough to dwell on for a while.

# TWO WAYS BANKS CANNOT CREATE MONEY

Genesis tells us that God created heaven and earth. Economists tell us that banks create money. To many people, the latter process is at least as mysterious as the former. Even bankers have been known to fall into serious error by claiming that they do not create money. Yet the way banks create money is a relatively simple process, which the next few sections will describe in detail. Suppose that someone receives $10,000 in newly printed currency and deposits it in his local bank. Before we see how the banks can create more than $10,000 from this deposit, we will describe two ways in which banks *cannot* create new money. Since people often jump to the conclusion that one or the other of these two processes is the correct one, it is a good idea to kill off these heresies at the outset.

## Case 1: Reserves Must Equal Deposits

Suppose that ours is not a fractional-reserve banking system. In other words, assume that every bank has to maintain reserves equal to its deposits. In this case, the bank receiving the $10,000 deposit cannot create any new money. You may be inclined to think that it can be done, but it can't. To see why not, consider the changes in the bank's balance sheet, shown in Table 11.5. When the $10,000 is deposited in the bank, the

[3] This case comes from Leonard Marks and Alan Coleman, *Cases in Commercial Bank Management,* New York: McGraw Hill. However, the outcome is purely conjectural.

**Table 11.5**
**Changes in Bank Balance Sheet, Where Reserves Equal Demand Deposits (Dollars)**

| ASSETS | | LIABILITIES AND NET WORTH | |
|---|---|---|---|
| Reserves | +10,000 | Demand deposits | +10,000 |
| Loans and investments | No change | Net worth | No change |
| Total | +10,000 | Total | +10,000 |

bank's deposits go up $10,000. Since the bank must hold $10,000 in reserves to back up the new $10,000 deposit, it must put the $10,000 it receives from the depositor into its reserves. Thus the bank's demand deposits go up by $10,000, and its reserves go up by $10,000. Since demand deposits are on the right-hand side of the balance sheet and reserves are on the left-hand side, the balance sheet continues to balance. *No new money is created. All that happens is that the depositor gives up $10,000 in one form of money—currency—and receives $10,000 in another form of money—a demand deposit.*[4]

## Case 2: Violation of Legal Reserve Requirements

Next, let's turn to the second way banks cannot create money. Suppose that we have a fractional-reserve banking system and that the legal reserve requirement is 16 2/3 percent. In other words, the bank must hold $1 in reserves for every $6 of demand deposits. Suppose that the bank decides to take the crisp, new $10,000 in currency that is deposited and add it to its reserves, thus increasing its reserves by $10,000. Then suppose it reasons (incorrectly) that it can increase its deposits by $50,000, since it has $10,000 in additional reserves. Why $50,000? Because the $10,000 in additional reserves will support $60,000 in demand deposits; and since the person who deposited the $10,000 has a demand deposit of $10,000, this means that it can create additional demand deposits of $60,000 minus $10,000, or $50,000.

The bank will create these additional demand deposits simply by making loans or investments. Thus when a person comes in to the bank for a loan, all the banker has to do is give her a demand deposit—a checking account—that didn't exist before. In other words, the banker can say to his staff, "Establish a checking account of $50,000 for Ms. Smith. We have just lent her this amount to buy a new piece of equipment to be used in her business." At first, this whole process looks a bit like black magic, perhaps even larceny. After all, how can checking accounts be established out of thin air? But they can, and are. In essence, this is how banks create money.

---

[4] Note that the $10,000 in currency which the depositor gives the bank is no longer counted as money once it is given to the bank. Only currency outside the vaults of all commercial banks (as well as outside the Treasury and the Federal Reserve Banks) is included in the money supply.

For simplicity, checkable deposits other than demand deposits are ignored here and below.

# WILL THE BANKS GO THE WAY OF THE SAVINGS AND LOAN INDUSTRY?

One of the biggest financial stories of the late 1980s and early 1990s was the collapse of the huge savings and loan industry. According to Charles Bowsher, the Comptroller General, the savings and loan debacle will cost as much as $500 billion in the next 40 years, or about $5,000 for each American household.[1] It is important to understand the nature, causes, and implications of this debacle because they shed substantial light on the way financial institutions work and on decisions that must be made by the American public concerning the future of our financial system. Equally important, some people worry that a similar fate may be in store for some of our biggest commercial banks.

The origins of the savings and loan industry can be traced back to the nineteenth century. Responding to the desire of American families to own their own homes, these savings institutions, often relatively small, received modest deposits and lent out the money in the form of long-term home mortgages. During the 1930s, the federal government established deposit insurance for savings and loan institutions as well as for commercial banks. The savings and loan industry was regulated by the Federal Home Loan Bank Board. According to many observers, the management of a savings and loan association was a relatively simple business. At one time, according to one wag, "Savings and loan executives lived by the 3-6-3 rule—pay 3 percent on deposits, charge 6 percent on mortgage loans, and tee off on the golf course at 3 o'clock."[2]

All of this changed drastically in the late 1970s when the Federal Reserve pushed interest rates sky-high to curb double-digit inflation. When interest rates rose, many depositors withdrew their money from savings and loan institutions, which were required by law to pay less than a government-set maximum rate of interest, which was relatively low. Congress responded by permitting the savings and loan institutions to pay higher interest rates, but this

Another savings and loan institution closed down

was not enough to get the stricken institutions out of financial trouble. Their basic problem was that they had invested their money in low-yielding mortgages that paid the same low rate of interest over the life of the mortgage, often 20 or 30 years. But to attract and keep deposits, they had to pay higher interest rates than their investments in these mortgages were earning.

By the early 1980s, nearly all savings and loan institutions were unprofitable. (See Table 1.) In an attempt to recoup their losses, many began to make short-term nonmortgage loans. Using little or no capital of their own, they invested large amounts in highly risky bonds (so-called "junk bonds"), in land development projects, and in office buildings. In 1986, land and real estate prices, particularly in the Southwest, dropped, as did the price of "junk bonds." The savings and loan industry's losses were over $10 billion in 1988 and about $20 billion in 1989.

[1] "How Capital Ignored Alarms on Savings," *New York Times,* June 6, 1990.
[2] Ibid.

**Table 1**
**Number of Insolvent Savings and Loan Institutions, and Total Income of Savings Institutions, 1977–88**

| YEAR | NUMBER OF INSOLVENT SAVINGS AND LOAN INSTITUTIONS | TOTAL INCOME (BILLIONS OF DOLLARS) |
|------|---------------------------------------------------|------------------------------------|
| 1977 | 14 | 3.2 |
| 1978 | 10 | 3.9 |
| 1979 | 15 | 3.6 |
| 1980 | 16 | 0.8 |
| 1981 | 53 | −4.6 |
| 1982 | 222 | −4.1 |
| 1983 | 281 | 1.9 |
| 1984 | 434 | 1.0 |
| 1985 | 449 | 3.7 |
| 1986 | 460 | 0.1 |
| 1987 | 505 | −7.8 |
| 1988 | 338 | −12.1 |

*Source:* L. Nakamura, "Closing Troubled Financial Institutions: What Are the Issues?" *Business Review of the Federal Reserve Bank of Philadelphia,* May–June 1990.

If many savings and loan institutions used little or no capital of their own, how did they get the money to invest? By paying relatively attractive interest rates on their government-insured deposits. Because these deposits were government insured, people were willing to put their money into savings and loans institutions, regardless of how unprofitable these institutions were or how risky the investments these institutions were making. After all, if a savings and loan institution went bust, the depositors were insured against loss by the federal government. Thus, if a savings and loan institution announced that it would pay a relatively high interest rate on deposits, it could attract deposits.

By the late 1980s, the federal government, which previously had tended not to focus on the problem, began to try to deal with it. Hundreds of insolvent savings and loan institutions were closed. A new federal agency, the Resolution Trust Corporation, was established to sell off the assets of these institutions. However, the proceeds will fall far short of the amount that the federal government owes the depositors to compensate for the loss of their insured deposits. As stated above, the cost to the government (including interest on the amount the government must borrow to meet this obligation) has been estimated to be as much as $500 billion.

This debacle can be attributed to a number of causes. In part, it was due to the inexperience and incompetence of some savings and loan executives, as well as to the fact that some were guilty of fraud. In part, it was due to the political influence of the savings and loan institutions, which contributed substantially to many prominent politicians, and to the weakness of the federal regulatory agencies, which allowed many savings and loan institutions to operate with very little investment put up by their owners and which did not intervene as quickly as they should have to deal with "problem" savings and loan institutions.

Also, according to many observers, a basic cause of this disaster was federal deposit insurance, which enabled failing savings and loan institutions to obtain funds to put into ill-advised and sometimes fraudulent schemes. Depositors, knowing that their deposits were federally insured, had little or no incentive to monitor the operations or performance of these institutions. A number of proposals have been made to reform the existing system of deposit insurance, which, of course, includes banks as well as savings and loan institutions. One proposal is that shareholders be forced to put up more equity capital and that financial institutions be limited in the extent to which they can engage in high-risk lending. Some say that all insured deposits should be invested only in government securities.

Another proposal is that financial institutions that have high-risk assets should pay higher premiums for deposit insurance than financial institutions with low-risk assets. All financial institutions are obliged to pay premiums for deposit insurance; at present, these premiums do not vary with the riskiness of their assets. Still another proposal is that deposits be insured up to a lower level than $100,000 (the current level) or that only a certain percentage (say 80 percent) of a person's deposits be insured.

While it is understandable and worthwhile for Congress to look for ways to make deposit insurance more effective, it is important to keep in mind that deposit insurance has played a central role in preventing runs on banks and other financial institutions. As stressed in this chapter, any bank, no matter how sound, is vulnerable to such runs, which were quite prevalent before the advent of deposit insurance. While improvements undoubtedly can be made in our system of deposit insurance, it would be tragic if we returned to the bad old days of bank runs. As the Council of Economic Advisers said in

1990, "The U.S. experience with bank panics in the late 19th and early 20th centuries was the motivation for the current system of deposit insurance. . . . This system has worked very well in preventing further panics. . . ."[3]

In the early 1990s, there were repeated warnings that some of the nation's largest commercial banks, such as New York's Chase Manhattan Bank, were in trouble. Assets in banks on the government's problem list—those whose financial viability is questioned—increased from about $225 billion in 1984 to over $400 billion in 1990. Some observers argued that, just as government regulatory agencies waited too long to close down insolvent savings and loan institutions, so they were waiting too long to close down insolvent banks. Also, there was a lot of grumbling that banks, like the savings and loan institutions, had put up too little of their own capital. Other experts claimed that the banks were in far better shape than the savings and loan institutions had been, and that the problems were being exaggerated. The situation was by no means clear, but lots of people seemed to have their fingers crossed.

[3] *Economic Report of the President* (Washington, D.C.: Government Printing Office, 1990), p. 100.

## Probing Deeper

1. In late 1990, the rating of the bonds of the Chase Manhattan Bank was lowered, reflecting the opinion of Wall Street that the bank was not in strong financial shape. Chase said that "problems with real estate loans" were largely responsible. What sort of problems was Chase having with its real estate loans?

2. In 1991, the Bush administration proposed that industrial companies be allowed to own banks. Also, banks would be permitted to perform new functions; for example, they would be allowed to sell insurance. What were the advantages claimed for these proposals?

3. The Bush administration also proposed that banks be able to open branches in other states without restrictions. What would this achieve, according to proponents?

4. According to some observers, the Bush administration's proposals were akin to the efforts in the early 1980s to help the ill-fated savings and loan industry. What were the basic problems of the savings and loan industry?

5. In dealing with the current problems of the banking industry, what lessons can the government (and others) learn from the savings and loan debacle?

## Where Is the Error?

But we prefaced this example by saying that it contains an error. The error is the supposition that the bank can create an additional $50,000 of demand deposits on the basis of the $10,000 deposit. To see why this won't work, consider the changes in the bank's balance sheet, shown in Table 11.6. After the bank received the $10,000 deposit, its demand deposits and its reserves both increased by $10,000, as shown in the first panel of Table 11.6. Then, as we noted above, the bank made a $50,000 loan and (in the process of making the loan) created $50,000 in new deposits, as shown in the second panel. So far, so good. The bank's balance sheet continues to balance—in accord with common sense and accounting (in that order). The bank's reserves are one-sixth of its demand deposits; they satisfy the legal reserve requirements established by the Fed.

**Table 11.6**
**Changes in Bank Balance Sheet: Fractional Reserves (Dollars)**

|  |  | ASSETS |  | LIABILITIES AND NET WORTH |  |
|---|---|---|---|---|---|
| Bank receives deposit | Reserves | +10,000 | | Demand deposits | +10,000 |
| | Loans and investments | No change | | Net worth | No change |
| | Total | +10,000 | | Total | +10,000 |
| Bank makes loan | Reserves | No change | | Demand deposits | +50,000 |
| | Loans and investments | +50,000 | | Net worth | No change |
| | Total | +50,000 | | Total | +50,000 |
| Ms. Smith spends $50,000 | Reserves | −50,000 | | Demand deposits | −50,000 |
| | Loans and investments | No change | | Net worth | No change |
| | Total | −50,000 | | Total | −50,000 |
| Total effect | Reserves | −40,000 | | Demand deposits | +10,000 |
| | Loans and investments | +50,000 | | Net worth | No change |
| | Total | +10,000 | | Total | +10,000 |

So what is the problem? None, unless the money lent by the bank is spent. If the woman who received the loan—Ms. Smith—never used the money she borrowed, the bank could act this way and get away with it. But people who borrow money are in the habit of spending it; why pay interest on money one doesn't use? Even if Ms. Smith, the recipient of this loan, spent the money, the bank could act in accord with this example and get away with it if the people who received the money from Ms. Smith deposited it in this same bank. But the chances of this occurring are very small. The equipment Ms. Smith plans to buy is likely to be produced by a firm in some other city; and even if it is located in the same city, the firm may well have an account at another bank.

To see the problem that results when the loan is spent, suppose that Ms. Smith spends the $50,000 on a machine produced by the Acme Corporation, which has an account at the First National Bank of Boston. She sends the Acme Corporation a check for $50,000 drawn on our bank. When the Acme Corporation receives Ms. Smith's check, it deposits this check to its account at the First National Bank of Boston, which, using the facilities of the Federal Reserve System, presents the check to our bank for payment. Our bank must then fork over $50,000 of its cash—its reserves—to the First National Bank of Boston. Consequently, once the $50,000 check is paid, the effect on our bank's balance sheet is as shown in the third panel of Table 11.6. Taken as a whole, the bank's demand deposits have increased by $10,000, and its reserves have decreased by $40,000, as shown in the bottom panel of Table 11.6.

At this point, the error in this example is becoming clear. *If the bank was holding $1 in reserves for every $6 in demand deposits before the $10,000 deposit was made, these transactions must cause the bank to violate the legal reserve requirements.* This may be proved as follows. Suppose that, before the $10,000 deposit, our bank had $X in demand deposits and

$\dfrac{X}{6}$ in reserves. Then, after the transactions described above, it must have ($X$ + \$10,000) in demand deposits and $\left(\$\dfrac{X}{6} - \$40,000\right)$ in reserves. Certainly, the reserves (which equal $\$\dfrac{X}{6} - \$40,000$) are now less than one-sixth of the demand deposits (which equal $X$ + \$10,000). This must be true whatever value $X$ has. (Try it and see.) Thus no bank can create money in this way because, if it did, it would violate the legal reserve requirements after the newly created demand deposits were used. (As we shall see later, a monopoly bank—that is, the only bank in the country—could create money like this, but monopoly banks do not exist in the United States.)

## TEST YOURSELF

1. Suppose that John Smith deposits \$50,000 in newly printed currency to his account at Bank A. What is the effect on Bank A's balance sheet?

| ASSETS (DOLLARS) | LIABILITIES AND NET WORTH (DOLLARS) |
|---|---|
| Reserves _____ | Demand deposits _____ |
| Loans and investments __ | Net worth _____ |
| Total _____ | Total _____ |

2. Suppose that Bank A lends the Bugsbane Music Box Company \$30,000. What is the effect on Bank A's balance sheet of both the deposit described in Question 1 and this loan? Fill in the blanks below.

| ASSETS (DOLLARS) | LIABILITIES AND NET WORTH (DOLLARS) |
|---|---|
| Reserves _____ | Demand deposits _____ |
| Loans and investments __ | Net worth _____ |
| Total _____ | Total _____ |

3. After the Bugsbane Music Box Company receives the \$30,000 loan, it uses the money to buy a new piece of equipment from the XYZ Tool Company. The XYZ Tool Company deposits Bugsbane's check on Bank A to its account at the Bank of America. What is the total effect on Bank A's balance sheet of the deposit described in Question 1, the loan in Question 2, and the purchase described here? Fill in the blanks below.

| ASSETS (DOLLARS) | LIABILITIES AND NET WORTH (DOLLARS) |
|---|---|
| Reserves _____ | Demand deposits _____ |
| Loans and investments __ | Net worth _____ |
| Total _____ | Total _____ |

4. If Bank A had the legally required amount of reserves prior to the transactions described in Questions 1, 2, and 3, and if the legal reserve requirement is that Bank A must hold \$1 in reserves for every \$5 in demand deposits, does Bank A have more reserves than are legally required after these transactions? If so, how much more?

## HOW BANKS CAN CREATE MONEY

Now that we have learned two ways that banks *cannot* create money, let's describe how they *can* create money. Imagine the following scenario. First, suppose once again that someone deposits \$10,000 of newly printed money in our bank, which we'll call Bank A. Second, suppose that Bank A lends Ms. Smith \$8,333, and that Ms. Smith uses this money to purchase some equipment from Mr. Jones, who deposits Ms. Smith's check in his account at Bank B. Third, Bank B buys a bond (a security that is an IOU of the firm or government that issues it) for $6,944 from Ms. Stone, who uses the money to pay Mr. Green for some furniture. Mr. Green deposits the check to his account at Bank C. Admittedly, this is a somewhat complicated plot with a substantial cast of characters, but life is like that.

## Money Creation at Bank A

The first step in our drama occurs when someone deposits $10,000 in newly printed money in Bank A. The effect of this deposit is shown in the first panel of Table 11.7: Bank A's demand deposits and its reserves both go up by $10,000. Now Bank A is far too smart to try to make a $50,000 loan, lest it wind up with less reserves than dictated by the legal reserve requirements. Instead, it makes a loan of $8,333, since this is the amount of its **excess reserves** (those in excess of legal requirements). Because of the $10,000 increase in its deposits, its legally required reserves increase by $ $\frac{10,000}{6}$, or $1,667. (Recall that $1 in reserves must be held for every $6 in deposits.) Thus, if it had no excess reserves before, *it now has excess reserves of $10,000 – $1,667, or $8,333.* When Ms. Smith asks one of the loan officers of the bank for a loan to purchase equipment, the loan officer approves a loan of $8,333, not $50,000. Ms. Smith is given a checking account of $8,333 at Bank A.

How can Bank A get away with this loan of $8,333 without winding up with less than the legally required reserves? The answer is given in the rest of Table 11.7. The second panel of this table shows what happens to Bank A's balance sheet when Bank A makes the $8,333 loan and creates a new demand deposit of $8,333. Obviously, both demand deposits and loans go up by $8,333. Next, look at the third panel of Table 11.7, which shows what happens when Ms. Smith spends the $8,333 on equipment.

## Table 11.7
## Changes in Bank A's Balance Sheet (Dollars)

| | ASSETS | | LIABILITIES AND NET WORTH | |
|---|---|---|---|---|
| Bank receives deposit | Reserves | +10,000 | Demand deposits | +10,000 |
| | Loans and investments | No change | Net worth | No change |
| | Total | +10,000 | Total | +10,000 |
| Bank makes loan | Reserves | No change | Demand deposits | + 8,333 |
| | Loans and investments | + 8,333 | Net worth | No change |
| | Total | + 8,333 | Total | + 8,333 |
| Ms. Smith spends $8,333 | Reserves | – 8,333 | Demand deposits | – 8,333 |
| | Loans and investments | No change | Net worth | No change |
| | Total | – 8,333 | Total | – 8,333 |
| Total effect | Reserves | + 1,667 | Demand deposits | +10,000 |
| | Loans and investments | + 8,333 | Net worth | No change |
| | Total | +10,000 | Total | +10,000 |

As pointed out above, she purchases this equipment from Mr. Jones. Mr. Jones deposits Ms. Smith's check to his account in Bank B which presents the check to Bank A for payment. After Bank A pays Bank B (through the Federal Reserve System), the result—as shown in the third panel—is that Bank A's deposits go down by $8,333 since Ms. Smith no longer has the deposit. Bank A's reserves also go down by $8,333 since Bank A has to transfer these reserves to Bank B to pay the amount of the check.

As shown in the bottom panel of Table 11.7, the total effect on Bank A is to increase its deposits by the $10,000 that was deposited originally and to increase its reserves by $10,000 minus $8,333, or $1,667. In other words, reserves have increased by one-sixth as much as demand deposits. This means that Bank A will meet its legal reserve requirements. To see this, suppose that before the deposit of $10,000, Bank A had demand deposits of $X$ and reserves of $\dfrac{X}{6}$. Then after the full effect of the transaction occurs on Bank A's balance sheet, Bank A's demand deposits will equal ($X$ + $10,000), and its reserves will equal $\left(\$\dfrac{X}{6} + \dfrac{\$10,000}{6}\right)$, since $1,667 = $10,000/6. Thus Bank A continues to hold $1 in reserves for every $6 in demand deposits, as required by the Fed.

It is important to recognize that *Bank A has now created $8,333 in new money*. To see this, note that Mr. Jones winds up with a demand deposit of this amount that he didn't have before; and this is a net addition to the money supply, since the person who originally deposited the $10,000 in currency still has his $10,000, although it is in the form of a demand deposit rather than currency.

## Money Creation at Bank B

The effects of the $10,000 deposit at Bank A are not limited to Bank A. Instead, as we shall see, other banks can also create new money as a consequence of the original $10,000 deposit at Bank A. Let's begin with Bank B. Recall from the previous section that the $8,333 check made out by Ms. Smith to Mr. Jones is deposited by the latter in his account at Bank B. This is a new deposit of funds at Bank B. As pointed out in the previous section, Bank B gets $8,333 in reserves from Bank A when Bank A pays Bank B to get back the check. Thus the effect on Bank B's balance sheet, as shown in the first panel of Table 11.8, is to increase both demand deposits and reserves by $8,333.

Bank B is in much the same position as was Bank A when the latter received the original deposit of $10,000. Bank B can make loans or investments equal to its excess reserves, which are $6,944. (The way we derive $6,944 is explained in the footnote below.)[5] Specifically, it decides to buy a bond for $6,944 from Ms. Stone, and credits her checking account at Bank B for this amount. Thus, as shown in the second panel of Table 11.8, the effect of this transaction is to increase Bank B's investments by $6,944 and to increase its demand deposits by $6,944. Ms. Stone writes a check for $6,944 to Mr. Green to pay for some furniture. Mr. Green de-

---

[5] Since Bank B's deposits increase by $8,333, its legally required reserves increase by $\dfrac{8,333}{6}$, or $1,389. Thus $1,389 of its increase is legally required, and the rest ($8,333 −$1,389=$6,944) is excess reserves.

**Table 11.8**
**Changes in Bank B's Balance Sheet (Dollars)**

| | ASSETS | | LIABILITIES AND NET WORTH | |
|---|---|---|---|---|
| Bank receives deposit | Reserves | +8,333 | Demand deposits | +8,333 |
| | Loans and investments | No change | Net worth | No change |
| | Total | +8,333 | Total | +8,333 |
| Bank buys bond | Reserves | No change | Demand deposits | +6,944 |
| | Loans and investments | +6,944 | Net worth | No change |
| | Total | +6,944 | Total | +6,944 |
| Mr. Green deposits money in Bank C | Reserves | −6,944 | Demand deposits | −6,944 |
| | Loans and investments | No change | Net worth | No change |
| | Total | −6,944 | Total | −6,944 |
| Total effect | Reserves | +1,389 | Demand deposits | +8,333 |
| | Loans and investments | +6,944 | Net worth | No change |
| | Total | +8,333 | Total | +8,333 |

posits the check in Bank C. Bank B's demand deposits and its reserves are decreased by $6,944 when it transfers this amount of reserves to Bank C to pay for the check. When the total effects of the transaction are summed up, Bank B, like Bank A, continues to meet its legal reserve requirements, since its increased reserves ($1,389) equal one-sixth of its increased demand deposits ($8,333).

*Bank B has also created some money—$6,944 to be exact.* Mr. Green has $6,944 in demand deposits that he didn't have before; and this is a net addition to the money supply since the person who originally deposited the currency in Bank A still has his $10,000, and Mr. Jones still has the $8,333 he deposited in Bank B.

## The Total Effect of the Original $8,333 in Excess Reserves

How big an increase in the money supply can the entire banking system support as a consequence of the original $8,333 of excess reserves arising from the $10,000 deposit in Bank A? Clearly, the effects of the original injection of excess reserves into the banking system spread from one bank to another, since each bank hands new reserves (and deposits) to another bank, which in turn hands them to another bank. For example, Bank C now has $6,944 more in deposits and reserves and so can create $5,787 in new money[6] by making a loan or investment of this amount. This process goes on indefinitely, and it would be impossible to describe each of the multitude of steps involved. Fortunately, it isn't necessary to do so. We can figure out the total amount of new money the entire banking system

---

[6] Why $5,787? Because it must hold $\frac{\$6,944}{6}$ = $1,157 as reserves to support the new demand deposit of $6,944. Thus it has excess reserves of $5,787, and it can create another new demand deposit of this amount.

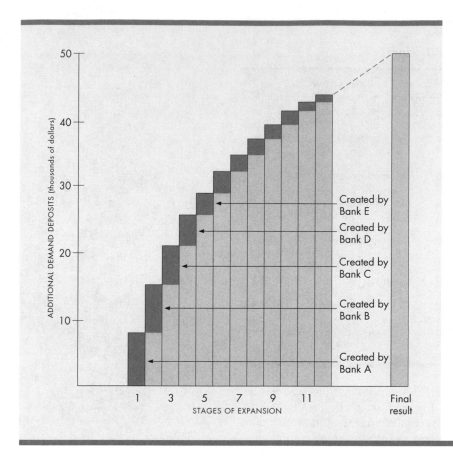

**Figure 11.2**
**Cumulative Expansion in Demand Deposits on the Basis of $8,333 of Excess Reserves and Legal Reserve Requirement of 16⅔ Percent**
The original deposit was $10,000, which resulted in excess reserves of $8,333. In the first stage of the expansion process, Bank A created an additional $8,333. In the second stage, Bank B created an additional $6,944.

Suppose Bank C lent $5,787 to Mr. White, who used the money to buy a truck from Mr. Black, who deposited Mr. White's check to his account at Bank D. If so, Bank C created an additional $5,787.

Suppose that Bank D lent Ms. Cohen $4,823 which Ms. Cohen used to buy some lumber from Mr. Palucci, who deposited Ms. Cohen's check to his account at Bank E. If so, Bank D created an additional $4,823.

The process goes on until the final result is $50,000 of additional demand deposits.

can support as a consequence of the original excess reserves at Bank A without going through all these steps.

We do this by computing how much new money each bank creates. Bank A creates $8,333, which is the amount of excess reserves provided by the $10,000 deposit. Then Bank B creates an additional $6,944, which is five-sixths of $8,333. Then Bank C creates an additional $5,787—five-sixths of $6,944 or (5/6)(5/6) $8,333, which is $(5/6)^2$ of $8,333. The amount of money created by each bank is less than that created by the previous bank, so that the total amount of new money created by the original injection of $8,333 of excess reserves—$8,333 + $6,944 + $5,787 + . . .—tends to a finite limit as the process goes on and on. Elementary algebra tells us what this sum of terms will be. *When the process works itself out, the entire banking system can support $50,000 in new money as a consequence of the original injection of $8,333 of excess reserves.*[7] For a further explanation of this fact, see Figure 11.2, which describes the cumulative expansion in demand deposits. (Table 11.9 show the amount of new demand deposits created at each stage of this process.)

We must note that the banking system as a whole has accomplished what we said in a previous section that an individual bank—Bank A—could not do. It has created an additional $50,000 of demand deposits on

---

[7] The proof of this is as follows. The total amount of new money supported by the $8,333 in excess reserves is $8,333 + $6,944 + $5,787 + . . ., which equals $8,333 + 5/6 × $8,333 + $(5/6)^2$ × $8,333 + $(5/6)^3$ × $8,333 + . . ., which equals $8,333 × $(1 + 5/6 + (5/6)^2 + (5/6)^3$ + . . .) = $8,333 × $\frac{1}{1-(5/6)}$ = $50,000, since $1 + 5/6 + (5/6)^2 + (5/6)^3 + . . . = \frac{1}{1-(5/6)}$.

**Table 11.9**
**Increase in Money Supply Resulting from $8,333 in Excess Reserves**

| SOURCE | AMOUNT (DOLLARS) |
|---|---|
| Created by Bank A | 8,333 |
| Created by Bank B | 6,944 |
| Created by Bank C | 5,787 |
| Created by Bank D | 4,823 |
| Created by Bank E | 4,019 |
| Created by Bank F | 3,349 |
| Created by Bank G | 2,791 |
| Created by Bank H | 2,326 |
| Created by Bank I | 1,938 |
| Created by Bank J | 1,615 |
| Created by other banks | 8,075 |
| Total | 50,000 |

the basis of the original $8,333 in excess reserves.[8] It seems perfectly reasonable that the banking system as a whole should be able to do this, since each $1 of reserves can back up $6 in demand deposits. But for the reasons discussed in a previous section, an individual bank cannot do it, unless, of course, it is a monopoly bank. If it is, it need have no fear of losing reserves to other banks, because there are no other banks; so it can behave this way. However, banking in the United States is not monopolized.

## THE EFFECT OF EXCESS RESERVES: A GENERAL PROPOSITION

If a certain amount of excess reserves is made available to the banking system, the banking system as a whole can increase the money supply by an amount equal to the amount of excess reserves multiplied by the reciprocal of the required ratio of reserves to deposits. In other words, to obtain the total increase in the money supply that can be achieved from a certain amount of excess reserves, multiply the amount of excess reserves by the reciprocal of the required ratio of reserves to deposits—or, what amounts to the same thing, *divide the amount of excess reserves by the legally required ratio of reserves to deposits.* Putting it in still another way, the banking system as a whole can increase the money supply by $(1/r)$ dollars—where $r$ is the required ratio of reserves to deposits—for every $1 in excess reserves.[9]

Suppose that the banking system gains excess reserves of $10,000 and that the required ratio of reserves to deposits is 1/6. To determine how much the banking system can increase the money supply, we must divide the amount of the excess reserves—$10,000—by the required ratio of reserves to deposits—1/6—to get the answer: $60,000. If the required ratio of reserves to deposits is 1/10, by how much can the banking system increase the money supply? Dividing $10,000 by 1/10, we get the answer: $100,000. Note that the higher the required ratio of reserves to deposits, the smaller the amount by which the banking system can increase the money supply on the basis of a given amount of excess reserves. More will be said about this in the next chapter.

Finally, an increase in reserves generally affects a great many banks at about the same time. For expository purposes, it is useful to trace through the effect of an increase in the reserves of a single bank—Bank A in our case. But usually this is not what happens. Instead, lots of banks experience an increase in reserves at about the same time. Thus they all have excess reserves at about the same time, and they all make loans or investments at about the same time. The result is that, when the people who borrow money spend it, each bank tends both to gain and lose reserves. Thus, on balance, each bank need not lose reserves. In real life the amount of bank money often **expands simultaneously** throughout the

---

[8] In addition, the banking system created the original $10,000 deposit, but this was not an increase in the quantity of money since $10,000 in currency in the hands of the public was exchanged for it.

[9] The total amount of money supported by $1 of excess reserves is $1 + (1 - r) + (1 - r)^2 + (1 - r)^3 + \ldots = \dfrac{1}{1 - (1 - r)} = \dfrac{1}{r}$. We reach this conclusion by the same method we used in footnote 7.

banking system until the legally required ratio of deposits to reserves is approached.

# THE EFFECT OF A DECREASE IN RESERVES

Up to this point, we have been talking only about the effect of an increase in reserves. What happens to the quantity of money if reserves decrease?

## A Numerical Example

Suppose that you draw $10,000 out of your bank and hold it in the form of currency, perhaps by sewing it in your mattress. Let us begin with the effect on your bank. Clearly, it will experience a $10,000 decrease in deposits (because of your withdrawal) and, at the same time, a $10,000 decrease in reserves. Thus, if it was holding $1 in reserves for every $6 in deposits before you withdrew the money, it now holds less than the legally required reserves. If its deposits go down by $10,000, its reserves must legally go down by $1,667, not $10,000, if the 6:1 ratio between deposits and reserves is to be maintained. To observe the legal reserve requirements, your bank must increase its reserves by $10,000 minus $1,667, or $8,333. That is, it has a *deficiency* of reserves (negative excess reserves) of $8,333. It has several ways to get this money, one being to sell securities. It may sell a municipal bond (an IOU of a municipal government) to Mrs. Cherrytree for $8,333. To pay for the bond, she writes a check on her bank, Bank Q, for the $8,333. Thus, as shown in Table 11.10, your bank's investments decrease by $8,333, and its reserves increase by $8,333 when Bank Q transfers this amount to your bank to pay for the check.

But this is not the end of the story. Because Bank Q has lost $8,333 in deposits and $8,333 in reserves, its reserves are now less than the legal minimum. To maintain the legally required reserves, its reserves should have gone down by $\frac{\$8,333}{6}$, or $1,389—not by $8,333. Thus Bank Q must increase its reserves by $8,333 minus $1,389, or $6,944. In other words, it has a deficiency of reserves of $6,944. To make up this deficiency, it sells a bond it holds for $6,944. But when the person who buys the bond gives Bank Q his check for $6,944 drawn on Bank R, Bank R loses $6,944 in deposits and $6,944 in reserves. Thus Bank R's reserves are now below the legal requirement. To maintain the legally required reserves, its reserves should have gone down by $\frac{\$6,944}{6}$, or $1,157—not by $6,944. So Bank R must increase its reserves by $6,944 minus $1,157, or $5,787. And on and on the process goes.

Let us consider the overall effect on the money supply of the $8,333 deficiency in reserves experienced by your bank. Bank Q's demand deposits decreased by $8,333, Bank R's demand deposits decreased by $6,944 (that is, 5/6 of $8,333), and so on. The total decrease in the money supply—$8,333 + $6,944 + . . .—tends to a finite limit as the process goes on and on. This limit is $50,000. Thus, *when the process works itself out, the entire banking system will reduce the money supply by $50,000 as a consequence of a $8,333 deficiency in reserves.*

**Table 11.10**
**Changes in Your Bank's Balance Sheet (Dollars)**

|  | ASSETS | | LIABILITIES AND NET WORTH | |
|---|---|---|---|---|
| You withdraw deposit | Reserves | −10,000 | Demand deposits | −10,000 |
| | Loans and investments | No change | Net worth | No change |
| | Total | −10,000 | Total | −10,000 |
| Bank sells bond and gets funds from Bank Q | Reserves | +8,333 | Demand deposits | No change |
| | Loans and investments | −8,333 | Net worth | No change |
| | Total | No change | Total | No change |
| Total effect | Reserves | −1,667 | Demand deposits | −10,000 |
| | Loans and investments | −8,333 | Net worth | No change |
| | Total | −10,000 | Total | −10,000 |

## A General Proposition

*More generally, if the banking system has a deficiency of reserves of a certain amount, the banking system as a whole will reduce demand deposits by an amount equal to the deficiency in reserves multiplied by the reciprocal of the required ratio of reserves to deposits.*

In other words, to obtain the total decrease in demand deposits resulting from a deficiency in reserves, *divide the deficiency by the legally required ratio of reserves to deposits.* Putting it another way, the banking system as a whole will reduce demand deposits by $(1/r)$ dollars—where $r$ is the required ratio of reserves to deposits—for every $1 deficiency in reserves. Although there is often a simultaneous contraction of money on the part of many banks, just as there is often a simultaneous expansion, this doesn't affect the result.

Let's apply this proposition to a particular case. Suppose that the banking system experiences a deficiency in reserves of $8,333 and that the required ratio of reserves to deposits is ⅙. Applying this rule, we must divide the deficiency in reserves—$8,333—by the required ratio of reserves to deposits—⅙—to get the answer, which is a $50,000 reduction in demand deposits. This answer checks with the result in the previous section.

Note that the effect if a $1 deficiency in reserves is equal in absolute terms to the effect of $1 in excess reserves. Both result in a $(1/r)$ change in demand deposits. Or, more precisely, this is the case if certain assumptions, discussed in the next sections, are true. To complete our discussion of how banks create money, we turn now to these assumptions.

## CURRENCY WITHDRAWALS

In discussing the amount of additional demand deposits that can be created by the banking system as a result of the injection of $8,333 of excess reserves, we made the important assumption that everyone who received the new demand deposits—from Mr. Green back to the person who originally deposited his money in Bank A—wants to keep this money in the form of demand deposits rather than currency. However, this clearly may not be the case. Some people who receive new demand deposits may choose to withdraw some part of this money as currency. For example, Mr. Green may decide to withdraw some of his new demand deposit in cash.

What effect will this withdrawal of currency have on the amount of demand deposits the banking system can create? To begin with, note that this withdrawal of currency from the entire banking system reduces the reserves of the banking system. Applying the results of the previous section, this means that the banking system can create less in demand deposits than it could if the currency had not been withdrawn. Specifically, the banking system can create an amount of demand deposits equal to the amount of excess reserves *left permanently with the banking system* divided by the required ratio of reserves to demand deposits.

Similarly, in discussing how much demand deposits will be reduced as a consequence of a deficiency in reserves, we made the important assumption that everyone who buys a security from a bank pays the bank by check. But some people may pay partly or in full with currency, and this will affect how much the amount of demand deposits must be reduced by the banking system. If somebody pays in currency to one of the banks, this restores some of the reserves that the banking system lost. Thus, applying the rule set forth in the previous section, the banking sys-

---

# EXAMPLE 11.1   CURRENCY HOLDINGS OF THE PUBLIC

The public is free to decide how much money it wants to hold in the form of currency (and coins) and how much it wants to hold in the form of demand deposits. Suppose that the relationship between the amount it wants to hold in currency (and coins) and the amount it wants to hold in demand deposits is as follows:

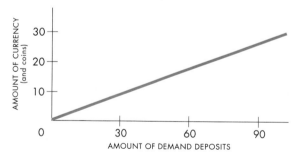

The reserve requirement is 20 percent, and commercial banks hold no excess reserves. For simplicity, assume that there are no checkable deposits other than demand deposits.

(a) If the Federal Reserve wants to reduce the quantity of money by $2 billion, how much of a decrease must occur in demand deposits? (b) To obtain this decrease in demand deposits, by how much must banks' legal reserves decline? (c) In fact, the ratio of currency (and coins) to demand deposits increased during the 1970s in the United States. Was this consistent with the above graph? (d) Some people attribute the rise in this ratio to an increase in tax evasion and the growth of the underground economy. Why?

## Solution

(a) The graph indicates that the public wants to hold $1 in currency (and coins) for every $3 in demand deposits. Thus, if demand deposits decrease by $1.5 billion, currency (and coin) will decrease by $0.5 billion, the total decrease in the money supply being $2.0 billion. (b) Since legal reserves equal 20 percent of demand deposits (because no excess reserves are held), legal reserves must decrease by $0.3 billion (that is, 20 percent of $1.5 billion) if demand deposits decrease by $1.5 billion. (c) No. (d) Because the underground economy tends to be based on the use of currency (which is not traceable) rather than deposits (which are traceable).

tem must reduce its demand deposits by less than if the bank had been paid by check.

In general, whether excess reserves are positive or negative, the change in demand deposits equals the excess reserves *left permanently with the banking system* divided by the required ratio of reserves to demand deposits. Thus *whether or not excess reserves have the maximum effect on demand deposits depends on how much of these reserves the public leaves in the banking system.*[10]

## EXCESS RESERVES

Another important assumption lies behind our discussion of the effects of an excess or deficiency of reserves on the amount of demand deposits. *We have assumed that no bank wants to hold excess reserves.* In other words, we have assumed that, whenever a bank has enough reserves to make a loan or investment, it will do so. Recall Bank A, which received a new deposit of $10,000. This new deposit enabled Bank A to increase its loans and investments by $8,333 without winding up with less than the legally required reserves. Thus we assumed that it would go ahead and make this much in additional loans and investments. In general, this seems to be a reasonable assumption, for the simple reason that loans and investments bring profits (in interest) into the bank while excess reserves bring none. During recent decades, banks have held relatively small amounts of excess reserves.

However, in the Great Depression of the 1930s, banks held large amounts of excess reserves. Why? Because the risks in lending and investment seemed great, and interest rates were very low. If a bank cannot find loans and investments it regards as attractive, it may decide to make no such loans or investments. After all, there isn't much profit to be made on a loan that is not repaid. Also, if interest rates are very low, the bank may feel that it isn't losing much by not lending money.

What difference does it make whether banks hold excess reserves? The answer is plenty. If, for example, Bank A decides to lend less than the full $8,333, this will mean that the injection of excess reserves will have a smaller effect on the amount of demand deposits than we indicated previously.[11] Similarly, if banks hold excess reserves, these reserves will offset what otherwise would be a deficiency. Thus *whether or not an injection or reduction of reserves has the maximum effect on demand deposits depends on the lending and investing policies of the bankers. If they do not lend out or invest as much as they can, the effect on demand deposits will be diminished accordingly.*

---

[10] Note too that people can convert demand deposits into time deposits, and vice versa. There are legal reserve requirements against time deposits, but they are lower than those against demand deposits. The conversion of demand deposits into time deposits will influence how much money can be supported by a certain amount of reserves. Thus the banking system can support an increase in the amount of demand deposits equal to the amount of excess reserves divided by the legally required ratio of reserves to demand deposits (no more, no less) only if there is no conversion of demand deposits into time deposits. In other words, we assume that all the demand deposits created by the banking system are converted into neither cash nor time deposits.

[11] Also, if a bank pays off some of its borrowings from the Fed, a $10,000 deposit may not increase its loans and investments by the full $8,333.

# TEST YOURSELF

1. "Banks do not create money. After all, they can only lend out money that they receive from depositors." Comment and evaluate.

2. Suppose that the legally required ratio of reserves to deposits is 1/10. If the banking system's reserves shrink by $50 million, by how much will the money supply change? What assumptions are you making about excess reserves and currency withdrawals?

3. "Demand deposits are increased by banks when they call in loans and sell investments." Comment and evaluate.

4. Describe the way in which the banking system can create money if there is a single monopoly bank in the nation.

5. Suppose that the legally required ratio of reserves to deposits is 1/10. If $100 million in excess reserves are made available to the banking system, by how much can the banking system increase the money supply? What is the answer if the legally required ratio of reserves to deposits is 1/6 rather than 1/10?

# SUMMARY

1. The Federal Reserve System is responsible for regulating and controlling the money supply. Established in 1913, the Federal Reserve System is composed of the commercial banks, 12 regional Federal Reserve Banks, and the Federal Reserve Board, which coordinates the activities of the system. The Federal Reserve is the central bank of the United States.

2. Commercial banks have two primary functions. First, they hold demand (and other checkable) deposits and permit checks to be drawn on them. Second, they lend money to firms and individuals. Most of our money supply is not coin and paper currency, but bank money—demand (and other checkable) deposits. This money is created by banks.

3. Whereas the earliest banks held reserves equal to deposits, modern banks practice fractional-reserve banking. That is, their reserves equal only a fraction of their deposits. The Federal Reserve System requires every commercial bank (and other thrift institution with checkable deposits) to hold a certain percentage of its deposits as reserves. The major purpose of these legal reserve requirements is to control the money supply.

4. The safety of bank deposits has been enhanced greatly by the government's stated willingness to insure and stand behind them. However, bank failures still occur, and bank regulation is not as stringent as it might be. Many observers are worried about the health of some major U.S. banks.

5. A bank creates money by lending or investing its excess reserves. If banks had to keep reserves equal to their deposits, they could not create money. A bank cannot lend or invest more than its excess reserves, unless it is a monopoly bank, because it will wind up with less than the legally required reserves.

6. The banking system as a whole can increase its demand deposits by an amount equal to its excess reserves divided by the legally required ratio of reserves to deposits. Thus, if excess reserves in the banking system equal a certain amount, the banking system as a whole can increase demand deposits by the amount of the excess reserves divided by the legally required ratio of reserves to deposits.

7. If there is a deficiency in reserves in the banking system, the system as a whole must decrease demand deposits by the amount of this deficiency divided by the legally required ratio of reserves to deposits. Demand deposits are decreased by banks' selling securities or refusing to renew loans, just as demand deposits are increased by banks' making loans and investments.

8. Our argument so far has assumed that when excess reserves were made available to the banking system, there was no withdrawal of part of them in the form of currency, and that when deficiencies in reserves occur, no currency is deposited in banks. If such changes in the amount of currency take place, the change in demand deposits will equal the excess reserves left permanently with the banking system divided by the legally required ratio of reserves to deposits.

9. We have also assumed that the banks want to hold no excess reserves. Since banks make profits by lending money and making investments, this assumption is generally sensible. But when loans are risky and interest rates are low—for example, in the Great Depression of the 1930s—banks have been known to hold large excess reserves. Clearly, an injection of excess reserves or a deficiency of reserves will not have their full, or maximum, effect on demand deposits if the banks do not lend and invest as much as possible.

# CONCEPTS FOR REVIEW

Federal Reserve
  System
Commercial banks
Simultaneous expansion

Central banks
Fractional-reserve
  banking

Legal reserve
  requirements
Excess reserves

# MONETARY POLICY

In recent years, monetary policy has been the subject of considerable controversy. For example, during the summer of 1990, when the economy seemed to be falling into a recession, many observers contended that the Federal Reserve should loosen up on the money supply and lower interest rates in order to stimulate aggregate demand. Others felt that such a move would be wrong because the increase in aggregate demand would raise the inflation rate. Without doubt, such controversies will continue in the future, since one thing is certain: Economists of practically all persuasions agree that monetary policy has a major impact on the economy.

In this chapter, we are concerned with a variety of basic questions about monetary policy. Who makes monetary policy? What sorts of tools can be employed by monetary policy makers? How does monetary policy affect our national output and the price level? What are some of the problems involved in formulating effective monetary policy? What has been the nature of monetary policy in the United States in recent decades?

## WHAT IS MONETARY POLICY?

*Monetary policy* is the exercise of the central bank's influence over the quantity of money and interest rates to promote the objectives of national economic policy. We described in Chapter 10 how the money supply affects gross national product and the price level. Increases in the money supply tend to push up real GNP and the price level, while decreases in the money supply tend to push them down. The extent to which the effect is on the price level rather than real GNP depends on the steepness of the short-run aggregate supply curve. The steeper it is, the greater the effect on the price level and the smaller the effect on real GNP. In the long run, increases in the money supply raise only the price level, not real GNP, and decreases in the money supply lower the price level, not real GNP.

When a recession seems imminent and business is soft, the central bank often increases the money supply and pushes down interest rates. That is, it "eases credit" or "eases money," as the newspapers put it. This tends to push the aggregate demand curve to the right, as we saw in Figure 10.6. On the other hand, when the economy is in danger of overheating and serious inflation threatens, the central bank often reins in the money supply and pushes up interest rates. That is, in newspaper terms, it "tightens credit" or "tightens money." This tends to push the aggregate

The Federal Reserve building, Washington, D.C.

demand curve to the left, thus curbing the upward pressure on the price level, as we saw in Figure 10.7.

In formulating monetary policy, the government's objectives generally are to attain or maintain reasonably full employment without excessive inflation. As we shall see, not all economists agree that the sorts of discretionary policies described in the previous paragraph are most likely to achieve these objectives, but we shall postpone a discussion of this controversy. Regardless of how you think the central bank should behave, it is important that you understand the ways in which it can increase or decrease the money supply.

*A country's monetary authorities can influence the money supply by managing the reserves of the banking system.* Suppose that the monetary authorities want to increase the money supply more rapidly than they would otherwise. How can they realize this objective? By providing the banks with plenty of excess reserves. As we saw in the previous chapter, excess reserves enable the banks to increase the money supply. Indeed, we learned that if there were no desired excess reserves and no currency withdrawals, the banks could increase the money supply by $6 for every $1 of excess reserves.[1] (The ways in which the monetary authorities can increase the reserves of the banking system—and thus provide excess reserves—are discussed at length in subsequent sections.)

On the other hand, suppose that the monetary authorities decide to cut back on the rate of increase of the money supply. To do so, they can slow down the rate of increase of bank reserves. As we saw in the previous chapter, this will force the banks to curtail the rate of growth of their demand deposits, by easing off on the rate of growth of their loans and investments. Indeed, if the monetary authorities go so far as to reduce the reserves of the banking system, this will tend to reduce the money supply. Under the assumptions made in the previous chapter, the banks must cut back the money supply by $6 for every $1 deficiency in reserves.

## MAKERS OF MONETARY POLICY

Who establishes our monetary policy? Who decides that, in view of the current and prospective economic situation, the money supply should be increased (or decreased) at a certain rate? As in the case of fiscal policy, this is not a simple question to answer; many individuals and groups play an important role. Certainly, however, *the leading role is played by the* **Federal Reserve Board** *and the* **Federal Open Market Committee.** The chairman of the Federal Reserve Board is the chief spokesman for the Federal Reserve System. The recent chairmen—Alan Greenspan, Paul A. Volcker, G. William Miller, Arthur F. Burns, and William McChesney Martin—undoubtedly have had considerable influence over monetary policy.

Although the Federal Reserve is responsible to Congress, Congress has established no clear guidelines for its behavior. Thus the Federal Reserve has had wide discretionary powers over monetary policy. But the Federal Reserve System is a huge organization, and it is not easy to figure out ex-

[1] This assumes that the legal reserve requirement is 16 2/3 percent. If the legal reserve requirement were 10 percent, a $10 increase in the money supply could be supported by $1 of excess reserves. Also, as pointed out in the previous chapter, a much smaller increase in the money supply may result from a dollar of reserves if banks want to hold excess reserves and if currency is withdrawn.

actly who influences whom and who decides what. Formal actions can be taken by a majority of the board and of the Federal Open Market Committee (which is composed of the 7 members of the board plus 5 of the presidents of the 12 regional banks). However, this obviously tells only part of the story.

To get a more complete picture, it is essential to note too that many agencies and groups other than the Fed have an effect on monetary policy, although it is difficult to measure their respective influences. The Treasury frequently has an important voice in the formulation of monetary policy. The Fed must take into account the problems of the Treasury, which is faced with the task of selling huge amounts of government securities each year. Also, congressional committees hold hearings and issue reports on monetary policy and the operations of the Federal Reserve. These hearings and reports cannot fail to have some effect on Fed policy. In addition, beginning in 1975, Congress has stipulated that the Fed must publish its long-term targets for growth in the money supply, the purpose being to establish somewhat more control over monetary policy. Finally, the president may attempt to influence the Federal Reserve Board. To keep the board as free as possible from political pressure, members are appointed for long terms—14 years—and a term expires every 2 years. But since members frequently do not serve out their full terms, a president may be able to name more than two members during each of his terms in office. (President Carter was able to name 4 members in his first few years in office.)

# THE FEDERAL RESERVE BANKS: $2$
# THEIR CONSOLIDATED BALANCE SHEET

As we know from the section before last, the Federal Reserve influences the money supply largely by controlling the quantity of bank reserves. To understand how the Federal Reserve can control the quantity of bank reserves, we must begin by examining the consolidated balance sheet of the 12 regional Federal Reserve Banks. Such a consolidated balance sheet is shown in Table 12.1. It pertains to October 30, 1990.

As shown in Table 12.1, the assets of the Federal Reserve Banks are largely of three kinds: gold certificates, securities, and loans to commercial banks. Each is explained below.

**Table 12.1**
**Consolidated Balance Sheet of the 12 Federal Reserve Banks, October 30, 1990 (Billions of Dollars)**

| ASSETS | | LIABILITIES AND NET WORTH | |
|---|---|---|---|
| Gold certificates[a] | 11 | Reserves of banks | 35 |
| Securities | 238 | Treasury deposits | 8 |
| Loans to commercial banks | 1 | Outstanding Federal Reserve notes | 256 |
| Other assets | 65 | Other liabilities and net worth | 16 |
| Total | 315 | Total | 315 |

[a]Cash is included here too.
Source: Federal Reserve Bulletin, 1991.

1. *Gold certificates* are warehouse receipts issued by the Treasury for gold bullion. For present purposes, this item is less important than securities or loans to commercial banks.

2. The *securities* listed on the Federal Reserve Banks' balance sheet are U.S. government bonds, notes, and bills. By buying and selling these securities, the Federal Reserve exercises considerable leverage on the quantity of bank reserves (as we shall see below).

3. The *loans to commercial banks* listed on the Federal Reserve Banks' balance sheet are loans of reserves that the Fed has made to commercial banks. As pointed out in the previous chapter, the Fed can make such loans if it wants to. The interest rate charged for such loans—the discount rate—is discussed below.

According to the right-hand side of the balance sheet in Table 12.1, the liabilities of the Federal Reserve Banks are largely of three kinds: outstanding Federal Reserve notes, Treasury deposits, and reserves of banks. Each is explained below.

1. The *outstanding Federal Reserve notes* are the paper currency that we use. Since these notes are debts of the Federal Reserve Banks, they are included among the Banks' liabilities.

2. *Treasury deposits* are the deposits which the U.S. Treasury maintains at the Federal Reserve banks. The Treasury draws checks on these deposits to pay its bills.

3. The *reserves of banks* have been discussed in some detail in the previous chapter. Although these reserves are assets from the point of view of the commercial banks, they are liabilities from the point of view of the Federal Reserve Banks.

## OPEN MARKET OPERATIONS

Table 12.1 shows that government securities constitute about 80 percent of the assets held by the Federal Reserve Banks. The market for government securities is huge and well developed, and the Federal Reserve is part of this market. Sometimes it buys government securities, sometimes it sells them. Whether it is buying or selling—and how much—can have a heavy impact on the quantity of bank reserves. Indeed, the most important means the Federal Reserve has to control the quantity of bank reserves (and thus the quantity of excess reserves) are **open market operations,** which is the name given to the purchase and sale by the Fed of U.S. government securities in the open market.

### Buying Securities

Suppose that the Federal Reserve buys $1 million worth of government securities in the open market, and that the seller of these securities is General Motors.[2] To determine the effect of this transaction on the quantity of bank reserves, let's look at the effect on the balance sheet of the Fed and on the balance sheet of the Chase Manhattan Bank, General Motors' bank.[3] In this transaction, the Fed receives $1 million in government secu-

---

[2] Large corporations often hold quantities of government securities.

[3] For simplicity, we assume that General Motors has only one bank, the Chase Manhattan Bank. Needless to say, this may not be the case, but it makes no difference to the point we are making here. We make a similar assumption regarding the investment firm of Merrill Lynch in the next section.

## Table 12.2
### Effect of Fed's Purchasing $1 Million of Government Securities (Millions of Dollars)

**A. Effect on Fed's balance sheet:**

| ASSETS | | LIABILITIES AND NET WORTH | |
|---|---|---|---|
| Government securities | +1 | Bank reserves | +1 |

**B. Effect on balance sheet of the Chase Manhattan Bank:**

| ASSETS | | LIABILITIES AND NET WORTH | |
|---|---|---|---|
| Reserves | +1 | Demand deposits | +1 |

rities and gives General Motors a check for $1 million. When General Motors deposits this check to its account at the Chase Manhattan Bank, the bank's demand deposits and reserves increase by $1 million.

Thus, as shown in Table 12.2, the left-hand side of the Fed's balance sheet shows a $1 million increase in government securities, and the right-hand side shows a $1 million increase in bank reserves. The left-hand side of the Chase Manhattan Bank's balance sheet shows a $1 million increase in reserves, and the right-hand side shows a $1 million increase in demand deposits. Clearly, *the Fed has added $1 million to the banks' reserves*. The situation is somewhat analogous to the $10,000 deposit at Bank A in the previous chapter.

## Selling Securities

Suppose that the Federal Reserve sells $1 million worth of government securities in the open market. They are bought by Merrill Lynch, Pierce, Fenner, and Smith, a huge brokerage firm. What effect does this transaction have on the quantity of bank reserves? To find out, let's look at the balance sheet of the Fed and the balance sheet of Merrill Lynch's bank, which we again assume to be the Chase Manhattan. When Merrill Lynch buys the government securities from the Fed, the Fed gives Merrill Lynch the securities in exchange for Merrill Lynch's check for $1 million. When the Fed presents this check to the Chase Manhattan Bank for payment, Chase Manhattan's demand deposits and reserves decrease by $1 million.

Thus, as shown in Table 12.3, the left-hand side of the Fed's balance sheet shows a $1 million decrease in government securities, and the right-

## Table 12.3
### Effect of Fed's Selling $1 Million of Government Securities (Millions of Dollars)

**A. Effect on Fed's balance sheet:**

| ASSETS | | LIABILITIES AND NET WORTH | |
|---|---|---|---|
| Government securities | −1 | Bank reserves | −1 |

**B. Effect on balance sheet of the Chase Manhattan Bank:**

| ASSETS | | LIABILITIES AND NET WORTH | |
|---|---|---|---|
| Reserves | −1 | Demand deposits | −1 |

hand side shows a $1 million decrease in reserves. The left-hand side of the Chase Manhattan Bank's balance sheet shows a $1 million decrease in reserves, and the right-hand side shows a $1 million decrease in demand deposits. Clearly, *the Fed has reduced the reserves of the banks by $1 million.*

### The Federal Open Market Committee

As indicated above, open market operations are the Fed's most important methods for controlling the money supply. The Federal Reserve adds to bank reserves when it buys government securities and reduces bank´reserves when it sells them. Obviously, the extent to which the Federal Reserve increases or reduces bank reserves depends in an important way on the amount of government securities it buys or sells. The greater the amount, the greater the increase or decrease in bank reserves.

The power to decide on the amount of government securities the Fed should buy or sell at any given moment rests with the Federal Open Market Committee. This group wields an extremely powerful influence over bank reserves and the nation's money supply. Every three or four weeks, the Federal Open Market Committee meets to discuss the current situation and trends, and gives instructions to the manager of the Open Market Account at the Federal Reserve Bank of New York, who actually buys and sells the government securities.

## CHANGES IN LEGAL RESERVE REQUIREMENTS

Open market operations are not the only means the Federal Reserve has to influence the money supply. Another way is *to change the legal reserve requirements.* In other words, *the Federal Reserve Board can change the amount of reserves banks must hold for every dollar of demand deposits.* In 1934, Congress gave the Federal Reserve Board the power to set—within certain broad limits—the legally required ratio of reserves to deposits for both demand and time deposits. From time to time, the Fed uses this power to change legal reserve requirements. For example, in 1958 it cut the legally required ratio of reserves to deposits in big city banks from 17½ percent to 16 ½ percent, and the ratio remained there until 1968, when it was raised to 17 percent. Table 12.4 shows the legal reserve requirements in 1991.

**Table 12.4**
**Legal Reserve Requirements of Depository Institutions, 1991**

| TYPE AND SIZE OF DEPOSITS | RESERVE REQUIREMENTS (PERCENT OF DEPOSITS) |
|---|---|
| Net transaction accounts | |
| Up to $41.1 million | 3 |
| Over $41.1 million | 12 |
| Nonpersonal time deposits | 0 |

*Source:* Federal Reserve *Bulletin*, February 1991.

## Effect of an Increase in Reserve Requirements

The effect of an increase in the legally required ratio of reserves to deposits is that banks must hold larger reserves to support the existing amount of demand deposits. This in turn means that banks with little or no excess reserves will have to sell securities, refuse to renew loans, and reduce their demand deposits to meet the new reserve requirements. For example, suppose that a bank has $1 million in reserves and $6 million in demand deposits. If the legal reserve requirement is 16 percent, it has excess reserves of $1 million minus $960,000 (.16 x $6 million), or $40,000. It is in good shape. If the legal reserve requirement is increased to 20 percent, this bank now needs $1.2 million (.20 x $6 million) in reserves. Since it only has $1 million in reserves, it must sell securities or refuse to renew loans.

Consider now what happens to the banking system as a whole. Clearly, an increase in the legally required ratio of reserves to deposits means that, with a given amount of reserves, the banking system can maintain less demand deposits than before. For example, if the banking system has $1 billion in total reserves, it can support $\frac{\$1 \text{ billion}}{.16}$, or $6.25 billion in demand deposits when the legal reserve requirement is 16 percent. But it can support only $\frac{\$1 \text{ billion}}{.20}$, or $5 billion in demand deposits when the legal reserve requirement is 20 percent. (See Table 12.5.)[4] Thus *increases in the legal reserve requirement tend to reduce the amount of demand deposits—bank money—the banking system can support.*

---

**Table 12.5**
**Consolidated Balance Sheet of All Banks, before and after an Increase (from 16 to 20 Percent) in the Legal Reserve Requirement (Billions of Dollars)**

A. Before the increase in the legal reserve requirement:

| ASSETS | | LIABILITIES | |
|---|---|---|---|
| Reserves | 1.00 | Demand deposits | 6.25 |
| Loans and investments | 7.25 | Net worth | 2.00 |
| Total | 8.25 | | 8.25 |

B. After the increase in the legal reserve requirement:

| ASSETS | | LIABILITIES | |
|---|---|---|---|
| Reserves | 1.00 | Demand deposits | 5.00 |
| Loans and investments | 6.00 | Net worth | 2.00 |
| Total | 7.00 | | 7.00 |

---

[4] We assume arbitrarily in Table 12.5 that the total net worth of the banks is $2 billion. Obviously, this assumption concerning the amount of total net worth makes no difference to the point we are making here. Also, for simplicity, we ignore checkable deposits other than demand deposits here and below.

## Effect of a Decrease in Reserve Requirements

What is the effect of a decrease in the legally required ratio of reserves to deposits? It means that banks must hold less reserves to support the existing amount of demand deposits, which in turn means that banks will suddenly find themselves with excess reserves. If the banking system has $1 billion in reserves and $10 billion in demand deposits, there are no excess reserves when the legal reserve requirement is 10 percent. But suppose the Federal Reserve lowers the legal reserve requirement to 9 percent. Now the amount of legally required reserves is $900 million ($10 billion x .09), so that the banks have $100 million in excess reserves—which means that they can increase the amount of their demand deposits. Thus *decreases in the legal reserve requirements tend to increase the amount of demand deposits—bank money—the banking system can support.*

Changes in legal reserve requirements are a rather drastic way to influence the money supply—they are to open market operations as a cleaver is to a scalpel, and so are made infrequently. For example, for about ten years—from April 1958 to January 1968—no change at all was made in legal reserve requirements for demand deposits in city banks. Nonetheless, the Fed can change legal reserve requirements if it wants to. And there can be no doubt about the potential impact of such changes. Large changes in reserve requirements can rapidly alter bank reserves and the money supply. When the Fed eased credit in December 1990, it eliminated the 3 percent reserve requirement on certificates of deposit held by corporations with maturities of less than 18 months—and quickly added billions of dollars to bank reserves.

# CHANGES IN THE DISCOUNT RATE

Still another way that the Federal Reserve can influence the money supply is through changes in the discount rate. As shown by the balance sheet of the Federal Reserve Banks (in Table 12.1), commercial banks can borrow from the Federal Reserve when their reserves are low (if the Fed is willing). This is one of the functions of the Federal Reserve. The interest rate the Fed charges the banks for loans is called the ***discount rate,*** and the Fed can increase or decrease the discount rate whenever it chooses. Increases in the discount rate discourage borrowing from the Fed, while decreases in the discount rate encourage it.

The discount rate can change substantially and fairly often (Table 12.6). Take 1980. The discount rate was increased from 12 to 13 percent in early 1980, then reduced to 12 percent in May, 11 percent in June, and 10 percent in July, after which it was raised back up to 13 percent by December 1980. When the Fed increases the discount rate (relative to other interest rates), it makes it more expensive for banks to augment their reserves in this way; hence it tightens up a bit on the money supply. On the other hand, when the Fed decreases the discount rate, it is cheaper for banks to augment their reserves in this way, and hence the money supply eases up a bit. Thus, in December 1990, the Fed, trying to stimulate a weak economy, reduced the discount rate from 7 to 6.5 percent.

The Fed is largely passive in these relations with the banks. It cannot make the banks borrow. It can only set the discount rate and see how many banks show up at the "discount window" to borrow. Also, the Fed will not allow banks to borrow on a permanent or long-term basis. They

**Table 12.6
Average Discount Rate, 1960–90**

| YEAR | DISCOUNT RATE (PERCENT) |
|------|-------------------------|
| 1960 | 3.53 |
| 1961 | 3.00 |
| 1962 | 3.00 |
| 1963 | 3.23 |
| 1964 | 3.55 |
| 1965 | 4.04 |
| 1966 | 4.50 |
| 1967 | 4.19 |
| 1968 | 5.17 |
| 1969 | 5.87 |
| 1970 | 5.95 |
| 1971 | 4.88 |
| 1972 | 4.50 |
| 1973 | 6.45 |
| 1974 | 7.83 |
| 1975 | 6.25 |
| 1976 | 5.50 |
| 1977 | 5.46 |
| 1978 | 7.46 |
| 1979 | 10.28 |
| 1980 | 11.77 |
| 1981 | 13.41 |
| 1982 | 11.02 |
| 1983 | 8.50 |
| 1984 | 8.80 |
| 1985 | 7.69 |
| 1986 | 6.33 |
| 1987 | 5.66 |
| 1988 | 6.20 |
| 1989 | 6.93 |
| 1990 | 6.98 |

Source: Economic Report of the President

are expected to use this privilege only to tide themselves over for short periods, not to borrow in order to relend at a profit. To discourage banks from excessive use of the borrowing privilege, the discount rate is kept relatively close to short-term market interest rates.

Most economists agree that changes in the discount rate have relatively little direct impact, and that the Fed's open market operations can and do offset easily the amount the banks borrow. Certainly changes in the discount rate cannot have anything like the direct effect on bank reserves of open market operations or changes in legal reserve requirements. *The principal importance of changes in the discount rate lies in their effects on people's expectations.* When the Fed increases the discount rate, it is generally interpreted as a sign that the Fed will tighten credit and the money supply. A cut in the discount rate is generally interpreted as a sign of easier money and lower interest rates.

## TEST YOURSELF

1. Suppose that the Federal Reserve buys $5 million worth of government securities from General Motors. Insert the effects in the blanks below.

Effects on Fed's balance sheet:

Securities _____ Bank reserves _____

Effects on balance sheet of General Motors' bank:

Reserves _____ Demand deposits _____

2. Suppose that the Federal Reserve sells $5 million worth of government securities to General Motors. What is the effect on the quantity of bank reserves?

3. "When the Fed increases legal reserve require-

ments, it loosens credit, because the banks have more reserves." Comment and evaluate.

4. If the Federal Reserve buys $500 million worth of government securities, will this tend to shift the aggregate demand curve to the right? To the left? Explain.

5. Suppose that you have $5,000 to invest. At a restaurant you overhear someone saying that the Fed is almost certain to increase the discount rate dramatically. If this rumor is correct, do you think that you should invest now, or wait until after the increase in the discount rate? Or doesn't it matter? Be sure to explain the reasons for your preference (or lack of it) in this regard.

## WHEN IS MONETARY POLICY TIGHT OR EASY?

Everyone daydreams about being powerful and important. It is a safe bet, however, that few people under the age of 21 daydream about being members of the Federal Reserve Board or the Federal Open Market Committee. Yet the truth is that the members of the board and the committee are among the most powerful people in the nation. Suppose you were appointed to the Federal Reserve Board. As a member, you would have to decide—month by month, year by year—exactly how much government securities the Fed should buy or sell, as well as whether and when changes should be made in the discount rate, legal reserve requirements, and the other instruments of Federal Reserve policy. How would you go about making your choices?

Obviously you would need lots of data. Fortunately, the Fed has a very large and able research staff to provide you with plenty of the latest information about what is going on in the economy. But what sorts of data should you look at? One thing you would want is some information on the extent to which monetary policy is inflationary or deflationary—that is, the extent to which it is *"easy"* or *"tight."* This is not simple to measure, but there is general agreement that the members of the Federal Reserve Board—and other members of the financial and academic communities—look closely at short-term interest rates and the rate of increase of the money supply.

## The Level of Short-Term Interest Rates

As indicated in Chapter 10, Keynesians have tended to believe that changes in the quantity of money affect aggregate demand via their effects on the interest rate. High interest rates tend to reduce investment, which in turn reduces GNP. Low interest rates tend to increase investment, which in turn increases GNP. Because of their emphasis on these relationships, Keynesians tend to view monetary tightness or ease in terms of the behavior of interest rates. High interest rates are interpreted as meaning that monetary policy is tight. Low interest rates are interpreted as meaning that monetary policy is easy.

According to many economists, the *real interest rate,* not the *nominal interest rate,* is what counts in this context. The *real* interest rate is the percentage increase in *real* purchasing power that the lender receives from the borrower in return for making the loan. The *nominal* interest rate is the percentage increase in *money* that the lender receives from the borrower in return for making the loan. The crucial difference between the real rate of interest and the nominal rate of interest is that the former is *adjusted for inflation* whereas the latter is not.

Suppose that a firm borrows $1,000 for a year at 12 percent interest, and that the rate of inflation is 9 percent. When the firm repays the lender $1,120 at the end of the year, this amount of money is worth only $1,120 ÷ 1.09, or about $1,030, when corrected for inflation. Thus the real rate of interest on this loan is 3 percent, not 12 percent (the nominal rate). Why? Because the lender receives $30 in constant dollars (which is 3 percent of the amount lent) in return for making the loan. The real rate of interest is of importance in investment decisions because it measures the real cost of borrowing money.[5]

## The Rate of Increase of the Money Supply

As indicated in Chapter 10, monetarists have tended to link changes in the quantity of money directly to changes in GNP. Consequently, they have tended to view monetary tightness or ease in terms of the behavior of the money supply. When the money supply is growing at a relatively slow rate (much less than 4 or 5 percent per year), this is interpreted as meaning that monetary policy is tight. A relatively rapid rate of growth in the money supply (much more than 4 or 5 percent per year) is taken to mean that monetary policy is easy.

Another measure stressed by the monetarists is the **monetary base,** which by definition equals bank reserves plus currency outside banks. The monetary base is important because the total money supply is dependent upon—and made from—it. A relatively slow rate of growth in the monetary base (much less than 4 or 5 percent per year) is interpreted

---

[5] Expressed as an equation, $i_r=i_n-p$, where $i_r$ is the real rate of interest, $i_n$ is the nominal rate of interest, and $p$ is the rate of inflation. In the example in the text, $i_n=12$ percent and $p=9$ percent; thus $i_r=3$ percent.

as a sign of tight money. A relatively rapid rate of growth (much more than 4 or 5 percent per year) is taken to mean that monetary policy is easy.

## SHOULD THE FED PAY MORE ATTENTION TO INTEREST RATES OR THE MONEY SUPPLY?

We have just seen that the level of interest rates and the rate of growth of the money supply are the two principal indicators of monetary tightness or ease. Unfortunately, the Fed may not be able to control them both. To see this, suppose that the existing money supply equals $300 billion, and that the public's demand curve for money shifts upward and to the right, as shown in Figure 12.1. That is, at each level of the rate of interest, the public demands a greater amount of money than heretofore. If the interest rate remains at 12 percent, the quantity of money demanded by the public will exceed $300 billion, the existing quantity supplied. Thus the level of interest rates will rise from 12 to 14 percent, as shown in Figure 12.1. Economists who favor the use of interest rates as an indicator are likely to warn that, unless interest rates are reduced, a recession will ensue.

The Fed can push the level of interest rates back down by increasing the quantity of money. The equilibrium value of the interest rate is the one where the quantity of money demanded equals the quantity of money supplied. (Recall Chapter 10.) If the demand curve for money remains fixed at its new higher level, the Fed can push the interest rate back down to 12 percent by increasing the quantity of money to $330 billion. With this quantity of money, the equilibrium interest rate is 12 percent, as shown in Figure 12.1. However, by doing so, the Fed no longer is increasing the money supply in accord with its previous objectives. Economists

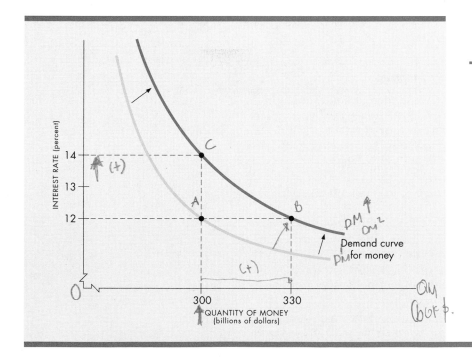

**Figure 12.1**
**Effect of a Shift in the Demand Curve for Money**
If the demand curve for money shifts upward and to the right, as shown here, the equilibrium value of the interest rate will increase from 12 to 14 percent, if the quantity of money supplied remains $300 billion. (Recall from Chapter 10 that the equilibrium value of the interest rate is the one where the quantity of money demanded equals the quantity supplied.) If the Fed wants to push the equilibrium level of the interest rate back to 12 percent, it must increase the quantity of money supplied to $330 billion.

who favor the use of the rate of growth of the money supply as an indicator are likely to warn that the Fed is increasing the money supply at too rapid a rate.

Thus the Fed is faced with a dilemma. If it does not push interest rates back down to this former level, some economists will claim it is promoting recession. If it does do so, other economists will claim it is promoting inflation. Unfortunately, it is very difficult for the Fed (or anyone else) to tell exactly how much weight should be attached to each of these indicators. In the 1950s and 1960s, the Fed paid much more attention to interest rates than to the rate of increase of the money supply. In the 1970s and 1980s, due to the growing influence of the monetarists, the Fed at times put more emphasis on the rate of growth of the money supply, although it continued to pay a great deal of attention to interest rates. In the late 1980s, the Fed seemed more inclined to use nominal GNP as a target variable, as we shall see below.

# THE SATURDAY NIGHT SPECIAL: A CASE STUDY

Let's continue to assume that you have been appointed to the Federal Reserve Board, and that the economy suddenly is confronted with what seems to be a dangerously inflationary situation. What sort of action would you recommend? One appropriate action might be to sell a considerable amount of government securities, which would reduce bank reserves. You might also recommend an increase in the discount rate or even an increase in legal reserve requirements. To see how well you were doing, you would watch the variables discussed in the previous sections. Specifically, you would look at the rate of increase of the money supply, as well as the rate of increase of the monetary base, and try to reduce both. At the same time you would try to increase interest rates.

Let's compare your recommendations with what the Fed really did in a similar situation. You will recall that in 1979 the inflation rate began to hit double digits. In the second quarter of 1979 the money supply began to rise sharply. Financial managers here and abroad issued statements that inflation was reaching dangerous levels. Fiscal policy was not used to curb this inflation. Consequently, much of the responsibility for fighting inflation fell to the Federal Reserve. What actions did it take?

On Saturday, October 6, 1979, the Federal Open Market Committee held a special meeting where the members were quartered in different hotels to avoid attracting public attention. Feeling that extraordinary measures were required, the committee raised reserve requirements and increased the discount rate from 11 to 12 percent, even though it was widely believed that the economy had entered a recession. At the same time, the committee indicated that it would try to reduce the rate of growth of the money supply. Some people on Wall Street called the announcement the Saturday Night Special, since it hit the financial community hard.

In the last quarter of 1979, the rate of growth of the money supply fell to about 5 percent. Interest rates rose sharply. The prime rate, which had been about 13 percent in September 1979, hit 20 percent in April 1980. However, inflationary pressures were still great. Between December 1979 and February 1980, the Consumer Price Index rose at an annual rate of 17 percent. Financial markets were demoralized. Since there was the risk of inflation getting even worse, and of interest rates therefore going through the roof, it was difficult, if not impossible, for market participants to determine what interest rate to set on new bonds. Consequently, the long-term bond market in large part suspended operations for a while.

It was hoped that the widely anticipated recession, which finally began in January 1980, would bring down the inflation rate, as well as interest rates. When asked whether monetary tightening would result in a recession, Federal Reserve Chairman Volcker is reported to have said, "yes, and the sooner the better." Apparently, policy makers felt that the most important thing was to reduce inflation, even if a slight or moderate recession ensued.

Clearly, the Fed did pretty much what you would have recommended. It cut down on the rate of increase of the money supply, and pushed up interest rates. Unfortunately, such actions may reduce real output (and increase unemployment), as well as cut the inflation rate. Some liberals criticized the Fed's actions on these grounds. Others, particularly conservatives, said that the Fed moved too slowly and not vigorously enough to quell inflation. In fact, inflation, while subsiding significantly, remained at historically high levels during the early 1980s. But in early 1982, it declined substantially.[6]

---

# EXAMPLE 12.1   HOW QUICKLY DOES MONETARY POLICY WORK?

An enormous amount of statistical and econometric research has been carried out to determine how quickly an unanticipated recession can be combated by monetary policy. According to Robert Gordon of Northwestern University, the total lag between the occurrence of such an unanticipated slowdown in economic activity and the impact of monetary policy is about 14 months. In other words, it takes about 14 months for the Federal Reserve to become aware of the slowdown, to take the appropriate actions, and to have these actions affect real GNP.

(a) On the average, how long do you think it takes for a slowdown to be reflected in the government's economic data? (b) How long do you think it takes for the Fed to pay attention to the signal and change monetary policy? (c) Once a change has been made in the rate of increase of the money supply, how long do you think it takes until real GNP is affected? (d) What problems result from the long lag between a change in economic conditions and the impact of monetary policy?

## Solution

(a)-(c) According to Gordon, the average lags are approximately as follows:[*]

| LAG | MONTHS |
| --- | --- |
| From slowdown to reflection in economic data | 2 |
| From reflection in economic data to change in money supply | 3 |
| From change in money supply to effect on real GNP | 9 |
| Total | 14 |

(d) By the time the effects of the expansionary monetary policy are felt, the economy may not need additional stimulus. Suppose that you were driving a car in which the wheels responded to turns of the steering wheel with a substantial lag. The problems would be analogous to those confronting the Fed.

[*]R. Gordon, *Macroeconomics*, Boston: Little, Brown, 1978, p. 471.

---

[6] Much of the material in this section is taken from T. Mayer, J. Duesenberry, and R. Aliber, *Money, Banking, and the Economy*, 3rd ed., New York: Norton, 1987; and W. Melton, *Inside the Fed*. Homewood, Illinois: Dow Jones-Irwin, 1985.

# MONETARY POLICY IN THE UNITED STATES

## The Carter Years

For a more complete—and more balanced—picture of monetary policy in the United States, let's look briefly at the history of monetary policy since the mid-1970s. In his 1976 presidential campaign, President Carter belabored Arthur F. Burns, the chairman of the Federal Reserve, for increasing the money supply too slowly, and once Carter became president, there was speculation that he and Burns might clash. During 1977 the narrowly defined money supply ($M$-1) grew by about 7 percent, and the broadly defined money supply ($M$-2) grew by about 9 percent. Interest rates increased somewhat. Velocity increased, as it had during 1976, apparently due in part to the adoption by corporations and individuals of methods to conserve on money balances. Monetary policy in 1977 was not restrictive.

In 1978 the rate of inflation once again approached double-digit levels. As many observers predicted, President Carter did not reappoint Arthur F. Burns as chairman of the Fed; instead, the job went to G. William Miller, an industrialist. In late 1978 the Fed, led by Miller, raised the discount rate to an all-time high of 9 ½ percent. Some reserve requirements were also increased. The narrowly defined money supply ($M$-1) grew by about 7 percent, and the broadly defined money supply ($M$-2) grew by about 4 percent in 1978.

In August 1979 Miller resigned as Fed chairman (to become secretary of the Treasury) and was succeeded by Paul Volcker, formerly president of the Federal Reserve Bank of New York. In his first months in office, Volcker was viewed as a more determined foe of inflation than his predecessor. Interest rates were pushed to record highs. Yet the rate of inflation, which was widely regarded as the nation's number-one economic problem, stubbornly remained at well above 10 percent.

## The Reagan Years

During 1981, the prime rate was pushed up to about 20 percent, and the general public as well as the financial community was getting the message that the Fed meant business in its fight against inflation. The widespread expectation that inflation would continue unchecked began to disappear. During 1982, the Consumer Price Index rose by about 4 percent, which was high relative to 20 years before, but low relative to the late 1970s. The money supply grew by about 8 or 9 percent in 1982 and 1983, and interest rates fell substantially. By early 1985, the prime rate was about 11 percent.

During 1985 and 1986, the money supply grew at a very rapid clip, reflecting the Federal Reserve's desire to extend the recovery. Interest rates fell substantially. In 1987, Alan Greenspan replaced Paul Volcker as Fed chairman. The Fed began to tighten money somewhat to prevent the dollar from falling further against other currencies, but after the stock market crash in October 1987, it loosened money again.

## The Bush Years

The American economy continued to grow during 1988 and 1989, but there was increased concern about inflation. In 1990, with the American

# P–STAR: A USEFUL GUIDE TO LONG-RUN INFLATION?

The Federal Reserve must try to anticipate what the price level will be a number of years in the future, as well as in the next few months. If it forecasts that the price level five years from now will be much higher than at present, the Fed is likely to tighten money and credit, since an unacceptably high rate of inflation seems likely. On the other hand, if it forecasts that the price level then will be below what it is now, the Fed is likely to loosen money and credit, since the nation seems to face deflation. But how can the Federal Reserve—or anyone else—forecast the price level five years hence?

In 1989, economists at the Fed announced that they had found a forecasting technique that they regarded as potentially valuable. To make long-range forecasts of the price level, they calculate $P^*$ (called $P$-star), which is defined as follows

$$P^* = \frac{M \times V^*}{Q^*}$$

where $M$ is the broadly defined money supply (called $M$-2 in Chapter 10) composed of $M$-1 plus savings deposits, small (less than $100,000) time deposits, and other items, $V^*$ is the average value of velocity (based on the $M$-2 definition of money), and $Q^*$ is real potential GNP.

Clearly, this formula is no more than a restatement of the equation of exchange: $MV = PQ$. If you divide both sides of the equation of exchange by $Q$, you get the above formula: $P = MV/Q$. Note that this formula uses $M$-2 rather than $M$-1 as the relevant definition of the money supply. This is because research indicates that velocity based on the $M$-2 definition has been much more stable in recent decades than velocity based on the $M$-1 definition. In the absence of any indication to the contrary, it seems sensible to assume in a long-range forecast that real output will be approximately equal to its potential level.

To use this formula, you have to estimate $M$-2, $Q^*$, and $V^*$. As we have seen, the Fed is concerned continually with the money supply, so it is in a reasonably good position to estimate $M$-2. To forecast $Q^*$, the Fed assumes that real potential GNP increases at 2.5 percent per year. Thus, if real potential GNP at present is known, it is easy to estimate the level of real potential GNP a given number of years hence,

The Federal Reserve Bank of New York

based on this assumption. As for $V^*$, the Fed assumes that $V^*$ will equal 1.65, which research indicates to be the average value of velocity in the past (based on the $M$-2 definition of money).

The Federal Reserve has been cautious in its discussion of $P$-star. It has indicated repeatedly that its use of this indicator is experimental and that a proper evaluation of this indicator will take many years. Some economists think that it is dangerous to rely on the stability of velocity over long periods of time; others are more optimistic. One thing is certain: the Fed is right in believing that it is too soon to tell whether $P$-star will be a star performer or a dud.[1]

---

[1] For further discussion, see J. Hallman, R. Porter, and D. Small, "$M$2 Per Unit of Potential GNP as an Anchor for the Price Level," *Federal Reserve Board Staff Study no. 157,* April 1989.

military buildup in Iraq and higher oil prices, the Fed feared that it might have to contend with serious inflationary pressures. At the same time, it was worried that the economy would fall into a recession. In late 1990, more and more economists and other observers felt that a recession had already begun. In response, the Fed lowered the discount rate and loosened money. While the concern over inflation had not gone away, the main thrust of Federal Reserve policy in early 1991 was toward stimulating the economy.

One interesting development in recent years has been that the Fed seems to have become more inclined to use nominal GNP as a target variable. In other words, it has tried to keep the rate of increase of nominal GNP within certain bounds. This reflects the fact that the Fed can only influence the aggregate demand curve: how the effects of shifts in the aggregate demand curve divide themselves between changes in real output and changes in the price level will depend on the shape of the short-run aggregate supply curve, which the Fed cannot control. Of course, this does not mean that over the longer run the Fed is not concerned with changes in the price level or in real output. But in the short run it seems to pay considerable attention to nominal GNP.

## PROBLEMS IN FORMULATING MONETARY POLICY

The Fed maintains a constant watch on the economy, checking for signs that the economy is sliding into a recession, being propelled into an inflationary boom, or growing satisfactorily. As we saw in Chapter 8, there is no foolproof way to forecast the economy's short-term movements. Recognizing the fallibility of existing forecasting techniques all too well, the Fed nonetheless uses these techniques as best it can to guide its actions.

Having come to some tentative conclusion about the direction in which the economy is heading, the Fed decides to what extent it should tighten or ease money. The answer depends on the Fed's estimates of when monetary changes will take effect and the magnitude of their impact, as well as on its forecasts of the economy's future direction. Also, the answer depends on the Fed's evaluation of the relative importance of full employment and price stability as national goals. If it regards full employment as much more important than price stability, it will probably want to err in the direction of easy money. On the other hand, if it thinks price stability is at least as important as full employment, it may want to err in the direction of tight money.

Once the Fed has decided what it wants to do, it must figure out how to do it. Should open market operations do the whole job? If so, how big must be the purchase or sale of government securities? Should a change be made in the discount rate, or in legal reserve requirements? How big a change? These are the operational questions the Fed continually must answer.

In answering these questions, the Fed must reckon with two very inconvenient facts, both of which make life difficult.

*1. There is often a long lag between an action by the Fed and its effect on the economy.* Although the available evidence indicates that monetary policy affects some types of expenditures more rapidly than others, it is

# IS THERE AN INDEPENDENT FEDERAL RESERVE? SHOULD THERE BE?

Some say the Fed is responsible to Congress. Its enabling legislation was passed by Congress in 1913, and it could presumably be reorganized should it sufficiently rouse Congress's wrath. But Congress moves with nothing if not deliberate speed, and it seldom has sought to influence the Federal Reserve through major new legislation. The president fills vacancies on the Board of Governors, but since terms on the board run for 14 years, presidents may have to wait until their second term to appoint a majority of the board.

In fact, as knowledgeable observers often agree, there are two groups that, without appearing prominently on the organization chart, exercise considerable influence over the policies of the Fed. One is the business community—a group with a definite interest in preserving the value of a dollar. The second is the board's professional staff of senior economists. Administrations come and go, but staff economists remain, and their uniquely detailed knowledge of the workings of the Fed assure them a hearing at 20th and Constitution.

Does it matter that the Fed is a focal point for the forces in the economy who fear inflation and are willing to accept somewhat higher unemployment in the hope prices will not rise as rapidly? It may matter less than the formal structure suggests. Virtually since its inception, the Federal Reserve has had a crop of antagonistic observers in Congress. Former Secretary of the Treasury John Connally compared one of the Fed's perennial congressional foes to a cross-eyed discuss thrower. "He'll never set any records for distance but he certainly keeps the crowd on its toes."

All chairmen of the Fed—such as Alan Greenspan, Paul Volcker, G. William Miller, and Arthur Burns in recent years—have been sensitive to the ultimate

The Federal Open Market Committee

vulnerability of the Fed's independence, and so have been reluctant to buck administration policy too dramatically. Whether the Federal Reserve's current procedures could survive a general call for more accountability is an open question. In early 1975, Congress passed a resolution that the Federal Reserve must publish its targets for growth in the money supply. But the extent to which this really tied the Fed's hands has been by no means clear. Some critics say that the targets have been adjusted frequently to agree with the actual growth of the money supply. In 1978, the Humphrey-Hawkins Act called for annual targets for the growth in the money supply, as well as semiannual reports to Congress concerning the Fed's performance in hitting the targets. But the money supply routinely grew at rates outside the targets. In the Reagan administration, some officials felt that the Fed's independence should be curtailed, but no such changes have been passed by Congress.

E.A.

not uncommon for the bulk of the total effects to occur a year or more after the change in monetary policy.[7] Thus the Fed may act to head off an imminent recession, but find that some of the consequences of its action are not felt until later, when inflation—not recession—is the problem. Conversely, the Fed may act to curb an imminent inflation, but find that the consequences of its action are not felt until some time later, when recession, not inflation, has become the problem. In either case, the Fed can wind up doing more harm than good.

*2. Experts disagree about which of the available measures—such as interest rates, the rate of increase of the money supply,[8] or the rate of increase of the monetary base—is the best measure of how tight or easy monetary policy is.* Fortunately, these measures often point in the same direction; but when they point in different directions, the Fed can be misled. During 1967–68, the Fed wanted to tighten money somewhat. Using interest rates as the primary measures of the tightness of monetary policy, it increased interest rates. However, at the same time, it permitted a substantial rate of increase in the money supply and the monetary base. By doing so, the Fed—in the eyes of many experts—really eased, not tightened money.

## MONETARY POLICY IN AN OPEN ECONOMY

In formulating monetary policy, the Federal Reserve must recognize the obvious fact that the United States is an open economy. International trade and finance are of great importance to the United States. If the Federal Reserve tightens money and raises interest rates, what will be the effect on the value of the dollar (relative to other currencies)?[9] Will the dollar become more valuable? (That is, will it exchange for more Japanese yen or German marks?) Or will it become less valuable? (That is, will it exchange for less Japanese yen or German marks?) Also, what will be the effect of the Federal Reserve's policies on American net exports? If the Federal Reserve tightens money and raises interest rates, will our net exports increase or decrease?

If the Fed tightens money and raises interest rates, investors all over the world will be attracted by the higher interest rates that they can obtain by investing in the United States. They will be more inclined to buy U.S. stocks, bonds, and other assets—and to do so, they will have to obtain dollars. The swollen demand for U.S. dollars will result in an increase in the dollar's value relative to other currencies. Further, the increase in its value will reduce our net exports because it will mean that our goods and services will become more expensive to foreigners, and foreign goods and services will become cheaper to us. Consequently, our exports will fall and our imports will rise, which means that our net exports will decrease. (Recall the discussion on page 186 of Chapter 9.)

On the other hand, if the Fed loosens money and lowers interest rates, investors will find the United States a less attractive place to invest. Thus

---

[7] Robert Gordon has estimated that, on the average, it takes about 9 months for a change in the money supply to affect real GNP. See Example 12.1.

[8] Also, there are problems in determining which measure of the money supply should be used. The Fed used *M*-1 until 1982, but subsequently turned to *M*-2 because it hoped that *M*-2 would be a more reliable measure.

[9] For an earlier discussion of exchange rates and their effects, see the Appendix to Chapter 7.

they will tend to sell U.S. stocks, bonds, and other assets, and invest the proceeds elsewhere—the result being a decrease in the value of the dollar relative to other currencies. Further, the decrease in its value will increase our net exports because it will mean that our goods and services will become cheaper to foreigners, and foreign goods and services will become more expensive to us. Consequently, our exports will rise and our imports will fall, which means that our net exports will increase.

Much more will be said on this topic in Chapters 17 and 18. For now, the important thing to note is that *the Federal Reserve must continually be concerned about what is going on in other countries like Germany and Japan; it cannot restrict its attention to domestic matters.* As pointed out by the Council of Economic Advisers in 1990, fluctuations in the value of the dollar and in our exports and imports "may jeopardize efficient resource allocation and, thus, economic growth."[10] The health of American industries that rely heavily on export markets, as well as those that compete with imports, can be affected seriously by the Fed's policies. As we have seen, tight money can reduce our exports and encourage imports. During recent decades, the Fed has paid increasing attention to the effects of its policies on the value of the dollar (relative to other currencies) and on our exports and imports.

## SHOULD THE FED BE GOVERNED BY A RULE?

Many monetarists, led by Milton Friedman, say that the Fed's attempts to "lean against the wind"—by easing money when the economy begins to dip and tightening money when the economy begins to get overheated—really do more harm than good. (The new classical macroeconomists, discussed in Chapter 14, say much the same thing.) In their view, the Fed actually intensifies business fluctuations by changing the rate of growth of the money supply. Why? Partly because the Fed sometimes pays too much attention to measures other than the money supply. But more fundamentally, it is because the Fed tends to overreact to ephemeral changes, and because the effects of changes in the money supply on the economy occur with a long and highly variable lag. In their view, this lag is so unpredictable that the Fed—no matter how laudatory its intent—tends to intensify business fluctuations.

According to Professor Friedman and his followers, the Fed should abandon its attempts to "lean against the wind." *They propose that the Fed conform to a rule that the money supply should increase at some fixed, agreed-upon rate, such as 4 or 5 percent per year. The Fed's job would be simply to see that the money supply grows at approximately this rate.* The monetarists do not claim that a rule of this sort would prevent all business fluctuations, but they do claim that it would work better than the existing system. In particular, they feel that it would prevent the sorts of major depressions and inflations we have experienced in the past. Without major decreases in the money supply (such as occurred during the crash of 1929–33), major depressions could not occur. Without major increases in the money supply (such as occurred during World War II), major inflations could not occur. Of course, it would be nice if monetary policy

[10] Council of Economic Advisers, *1990 Annual Report,* Washington, D.C.: Government Printing Office, 1990, p. 90.

could iron out minor business fluctuations as well, but in their view this simply cannot be done at present.

This proposal has received considerable attention from both economists and politicians. A number of studies have been carried out to try to estimate what would have happened if Friedman's rule had been used in the past. The results, although by no means free of criticism, seem to indicate that such a rule might have done better than discretionary action did in preventing the Great Depression of the 1930s and the inflation during World War II. But in the period since World War II, the evidence in favor of such a rule is less persuasive. Most economists seem to believe that it would be a mistake to handcuff the Fed to a simple rule of this sort. They think that a discretionary monetary policy or a feedback rule can outperform Friedman's rule.

A *feedback rule* specifies how monetary (or fiscal) policy will respond to the state of the economy. For example, a simple feedback rule might specify that the monetary authorities should increase the rate of growth of the money supply by 1 percentage point in response to each 1 percentage point increase of the unemployment rate, if the unemployment rate exceeds 6 percent. Given a particular change in the state of the economy, a feedback rule stipulates exactly what monetary (and fiscal) policies to undertake. In contrast, a *discretionary policy* allows the relevant policy makers to respond to economic events in whatever ways they regard as best.

Economists differ considerably in their views concerning the proper way to conduct monetary policy. Some believe that feedback rules or discretionary policies should be adopted. Others believe that the money supply should grow at a fixed rate. Our next two chapters will provide much more discussion of these important differences in point of view. For now, the important point to understand is that the monetary authorities, using open market operations and other techniques described in this chapter, can influence bank reserves, which in turn influence the money supply. As we have seen in previous chapters, most economists believe that changes in the money supply can have a powerful effect on output and the price level.

## TEST YOURSELF

1. "The Fed should keep interest rates low to promote prosperity. Unfortunately, however, it is dominated by bankers who like high interest rates because they increase bank profits." Comment and evaluate.

2. "The Fed is like a driver whose steering wheel takes about a minute to influence the car's wheels." Comment and evaluate.

3. Explain why the Federal Reserve may not be able to control both the level of interest rates and the rate of growth of the money supply. What problems does this cause?

4. According to economist Sherman Maisel, William McChesney Martin, former chairman of the Federal Reserve Board, felt "that the primary function of the Federal Reserve Board was to determine what was necessary to maintain a sound currency. . . .[To Martin] it is as immoral for a country today to allow the value of its currency to fall as it was for kings of old to clip coinage." Do you agree with Martin's views? Why, or why not?

# SUMMARY

1. Monetary policy is concerned with the money supply and interest rates. When a recession seems imminent and business is soft, the monetary authorities are likely to increase the money supply and reduce interest rates. On the other hand, when the economy is in danger of overheating and inflation threatens, the monetary authorities are likely to rein in the money supply and push up interest rates.

2. Although monetary policy is influenced by Congress, the Treasury, and other parts of the government and the public at large, the chief responsibility for the formulation of monetary policy lies with the Federal Reserve Board and the Federal Open Market Committee. To a very large extent, monetary policy operates by changing the quantity of bank reserves.

3. The most important tool of monetary policy is open market operations, which involve the buying and selling of government securities in the open market by the Federal Reserve. When the Fed buys government securities, this increases bank reserves. When the Fed sells government securities, this reduces bank reserves.

4. The Fed can also tighten or ease money by increasing or decreasing the discount rate or by increasing or decreasing legal reserve requirements.

5. As indicators of how tight or easy monetary policy is, the Fed has looked at the level of short-term interest rates, the rate of growth of the money supply, and the rate of growth of the monetary base. During the 1950s and 1960s, the Fed paid most attention to the first indicator; in the 1970s and early 1980s, the Fed increased the amount of attention paid to the last two. Recently, the Fed seems to have become more inclined to use nominal GNP as a target variable.

6. The Federal Reserve is faced with many difficult problems in formulating and carrying out monetary policy. There is often a long—and highly variable—lag between an action by the Fed and its effect on the economy. There is also considerable disagreement over the best way to measure how tight or easy monetary policy is.

7. There has been criticism of various kinds regarding the performance of the Federal Reserve. Often, the Fed is criticized for paying too little attention to the long lags between its actions and their effects on the economy. Some economists, led by Milton Friedman, believe that monetary policy would be improved if discretionary policy were replaced by a rule that the Fed should increase the money supply at some fixed, agreed-on rate, such as 4 or 5 percent per year.

# CONCEPTS FOR REVIEW

**Monetary policy**

**Federal Reserve Board**

**Federal Open Market Committee**

**Open market operations**

**Changes in legal reserve requirements**

**Discount rate**

**Easy money**

**Tight money**

**Monetary base**

# INFLATION, UNEMPLOYMENT, AND THE ROLE OF EXPECTATIONS

MONETARY POLICY IS A TOOL that is used by government officials in an attempt to stabilize the economy. When a recession occurs, the Fed is likely to increase the money supply, the objective being to reduce the unemployment rate. When the price level increases too rapidly, the Fed is likely to tighten money, the objective being to reduce the inflation rate. Both of these actions may have unfortunate side effects: An anti-recessionary policy may increase inflationary pressures, and an anti-inflationary policy may increase the unemployment rate. In this chapter, we study these sides effects and the controversies over their magnitude (and existence).

In addition, we look carefully at the role played by people's expectations in determining the effects of the government's anti-recessionary and anti-inflationary policies. As we shall see, the way in which individuals and firms form their expectations concerning the future of the economy is of central importance in this regard. In particular, we discuss the theory of rational expectations, which has been used by many leading economists in recent years.

Source: Business Week, May 13, 1991, p. 38.

## DEMAND-SIDE AND SUPPLY-SIDE INFLATION

Inflation is often triggered by rightward shifts of the aggregate demand curve. (See the left-hand panel of Figure 13.1.) This kind of inflation, called *demand-side inflation*, stems from the demand or spending behavior of the nation's consumers, firms, and government. We have had many inflations of this kind. The major inflations during the Revolutionary War and Civil War were basically caused by demand-side factors; and so, much more recently, was the inflation arising from the Vietnam War.

In those extreme cases where resources are fully utilized, the rise in the price level that occurs in demand-side inflation can be viewed as a matter of arithmetic: since national output is fixed, the rise in the price level must be proportional to the increase in total spending. For example, take the very simple case where a country produces only one good, corn. Suppose that the amount of money spent on this country's corn crop doubles, while the size of the corn crop is fixed. What will happen to the price of corn? It will double.

Besides demand-side inflation, which is due to rightward shifts of the aggregate demand curve, there is also *supply-side inflation*, which results from leftward shifts of the aggregate supply curve. (See the right-

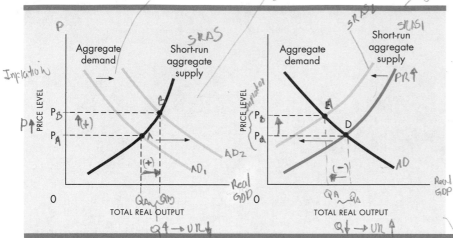

**Figure 13.1**
**Demand-Side and Supply-Side Inflation**
In the left-hand panel, the price level increases from $OP_0$ to $OP_1$ because of a rightward shift of the aggregate demand curve. This is a case of demand-side inflation. In the right-hand panel, the price level increases from $OP_0$ to $OP_2$ because of a leftward shift of the short-run aggregate supply curve. This is a case of supply-side inflation.

hand panel of Figure 13.1.) For example, when the oil-producing countries increased the price of crude oil in 1974 and 1979, this resulted in price increases in a wide variety of products that are made (directly or indirectly) from petroleum. Because these price increases were not offset by price reductions elsewhere in the economy, the overall price level increased (and at a very rapid rate) in 1974 and 1979.

Of course, the price hike for crude oil (and other materials) was by no means the sole reason for the inflation during the 1970s, but unquestionably it did play a noteworthy role in shifting the short-run aggregate supply curve upward and to the left, as shown in the right-hand panel of Figure 13.1. (Recall that this was pointed out in our discussion of stagflation in Chapter 8.) This was an example of supply-side inflation.

It is important to note that supply-side inflation of this sort is unlikely to continue for a long period of time unless the Fed "accommodates" or "validates" it by following policies that shift the aggregate demand curve to the right. (See Example 13.1.) If the aggregate demand curve does not shift, the inflation will die out. For example, in the right hand panel of Figure 13.1, the inflation will be over once the economy moves from point $D$ to point $E$. There will be no further increase in the price level.

## THE PHILLIPS CURVE

During the 1960s, economists placed a great deal of emphasis on the Phillips curve, named after A. W. Phillips of the London School of Economics, who first called attention to it. Subsequently, as we shall see, the Phillips curve collapsed. The reasons for its collapse, and the controversies over its existence and interpretation, are taken up in this and the following sections.

The **_Phillips curve_** shows the relationship between the annual rate of change of the price level in an economy and the unemployment rate in that economy.[1] For example, if the relationship is like that plotted in Fig-

---

[1] Originally, Phillips plotted data showing the relationship between the unemployment rate and the rate of change of wages, not prices. Thus the Phillips curve often is defined as the relationship between the rate of change of the wage level (not the price level) and the unemployment rate. But for present purposes, it is more convenient to adopt the definition in the text, which is often used by economists.

## EXAMPLE 13.1 ⟨ THE FED AND SUPPLY-SIDE INFLATION

Suppose that, due to decisions made by foreign governments like Saudi Arabia, the price of oil (in money, not real terms) is quadrupled. Since U.S. firms must increase prices if they are to be willing to produce the same output as before, the short-run aggregate supply curve will shift upward and to the left, as shown below:

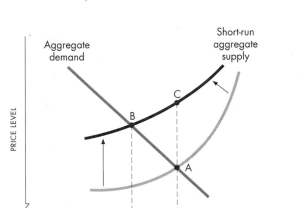

(a) If the Federal Reserve holds the money supply at its initial level, what will happen to real output and to unemployment? (b) Will the price (in real terms) of oil quadruple? (c) Suppose that the Federal Reserve, fearing a big rise in unemployment, increases the money supply. If the increase is large enough, can a decrease in real output be avoided? (d) If a decrease in real output is avoided in this way, what will be the effect on the price level?

### Solution

(a) As shown in the diagram at left, the economy will move from point A to Point B. Thus real output will fall from $OQ_0$ to $OQ_1$ and the decrease in real output will increase unemployment. (b) No, because the price level at point B is higher than at point A. Thus, although the money price of oil has quadrupled, the real price (i.e., the price in constant dollars) has less than quadrupled. (c) Yes. By increasing the money supply, the Fed can push the aggregate demand curve to the right. If it pushes it far enough to the right, it can make it intersect the new short-run aggregate supply curve at point C, where real GNP is at its original level, $OQ_0$. (d) The price level will rise considerably. As shown in the diagram, the price level at point C is much higher than at point A. The Fed, by enabling the action of the foreign governments to increase the price level without resulting in additional unemployment, is said to have *accommodated* the supply-side inflation.

---

ure 13.2, the inflation rate is inversely related to the unemployment rate. If the unemployment rate is 6 percent, the inflation rate will be 5 percent per year. To reduce the inflation rate to 2 percent, the unemployment rate must be increased to 9 percent.

If the Phillips curve in Figure 13.2 remains fixed, the government is faced with a fundamental choice. It can reduce unemployment only if it is willing to accept a higher rate of inflation, and it can reduce the rate of inflation only if it is willing to accept a higher rate of unemployment. For example, in Figure 13.2, if the unemployment rate is 7 percent and the inflation rate is 3 1/2 percent, the government would like to reduce unemployment, but if it reduces it to 6 percent, the inflation rate will jump to 5 percent. It would also like to reduce inflation, but if it cuts it to 2 percent, the unemployment rate will jump to 9 percent. This poses a problem for the government (and for society as a whole), since it would be desirable to reduce both inflation and unemployment.

Why should the Phillips curve be downward sloping to the right? In other words, why should the inflation rate be inversely related to the unemployment rate? If all inflation is demand-side inflation, some economists have explained such an inverse relationship in the following way. Suppose that the economy is in equilibrium at point A in Figure 13.3. If the aggregate demand curve shifts to the right from $D_0$ to $D_1$, total real output

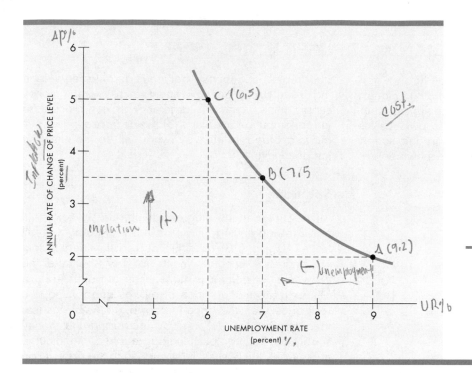

**Figure 13.2**
**The Phillips Curve**
If all inflation is demand-side inflation, one might expect the inflation
rate to be inversely related to the
unemployment rate. (Expected inflation is assumed to be constant.)

will increase from $100 billion to $110 billion, and the price level will increase from 100 to 105. On the other hand, suppose that the aggregate
demand curve shifts further to the right—from $D_0$ to $D_2$. Then total real
output will increase from $100 billion to $120 billion (rather than $110
billion), and the price level will increase from 100 to 110 (rather than
105).

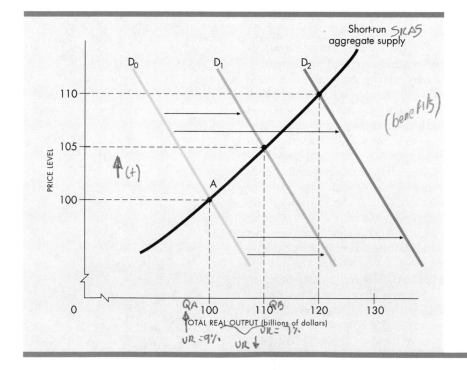

**Figure 13.3**
**Effects of Rightward Shifts in the
Aggregate Demand Curve (from
$D_0$ to $D_1$ or $D_2$) on Total Real
Output and the Price Level**
If the aggregate demand curve
shifts from $D_0$ to $D_2$, there will be
a greater increase in total real output and a greater increase in the
price level than if the aggregate
demand curve shifts from $D_0$ to
$D_1$. Specifically, total real output
increases from $100 billion to
$120 billion if the aggregate de-
mand curve shifts from $D_0$ to $D_2$,
but it increases only from $100 bil-
lion to $110 billion if the curve
shifts from $D_0$ to $D_1$. The price
level increases from 100 to 110 if
the aggregate demand curve shifts
from $D_0$ to $D_2$, but it increases
only from 100 to 105 if the curve
shifts from $D_0$ to $D_1$.

Clearly, the greater rightward shift of the aggregate demand curve (to $D_2$ rather than $D_1$) results in a bigger increase in output (to $120 billion rather than $110 billion), which means that the unemployment rate will be lower than if the aggregate demand curve shifts only to $D_1$. At the same time, the greater rightward shift of the aggregate demand curve results in a 10 percent inflation rate rather than a 5 percent inflation rate. (Recall that the price level increases from 100 to 110 if the aggregate demand curve shifts to $D_2$, whereas it increases from 100 to 105 if the aggregate demand curve shifts to $D_1$.) Hence, a lower unemployment rate is associated with a higher inflation rate.

## THE PHILLIPS CURVE COLLAPSES

During the 1960s, economists came to believe that the Phillips curve was a stable, predictable relationship. Panel A of Figure 13.4 shows the relationship between the inflation rate and the unemployment rate in the United States from 1955 to 1969. As you can see, there was a fairly close relationship between them in this period. Economists relied heavily on these data to buttress their belief that the Phillips curve really existed, and that it had the hypothesized shape. It is no exaggeration to say that the Phillips curve in Figure 13.4 (that is, the heavy line) had a major influence on both economic analysis and economic policy in the 1960s.

But then something unforeseen (by most economists) occurred. *The inflation and unemployment rates in the seventies and eighties did not conform at all closely to the relationship that prevailed in the sixties.* As shown in panel B of Figure 13.4, the points for 1970 to 1990 lie far above and to the right of the relationship that prevailed earlier. In other words, holding constant the unemployment rate, the inflation rate tended to be much higher in the seventies and eighties than in the sixties. Or, holding the inflation rate constant, the unemployment rate tended to be much higher in the seventies and eighties than in the sixties. Whichever way you look at it, this departure from the earlier relationship between inflation and unemployment was bad news.

Why did this departure from the earlier relationship occur? In part, it occurred because the inflation of the 1970s was to a considerable extent of the supply-side, not the demand-side, variety. Recall that, when we explained in the previous section why the Phillips curve might exist, we assumed that all inflation was demand-side inflation. Clearly, this was not true during the 1970s.

On the contrary, there was a shift to the left in the short-run aggregate supply curve due to price hikes in oil, agricultural products, and other raw materials. Because of this shift, both the inflation rate and the unemployment rate increased. And the rapid inflation of the seventies helped to bring on higher levels of unemployment. The oil price hikes acted like an excise tax levied on the consumer; they reduced the amount that consumers could spend on other things. The general inflation raised people's money incomes, thus pushing them into higher income tax brackets and increasing the amount they had to pay in taxes. (Similarly, the inflation swelled the paper profits of many firms, and increased their tax bills.) Because of the oil price increases and the effective increase in taxes, as well as other factors like the decline in the stock market, consumers cut back on their spending. Thus the equilibrium value of GNP fell.

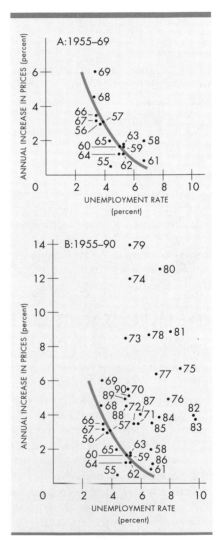

**Figure 13.4**
**Relationship between Inflation Rate and Unemployment Rate**
*Source: Economic Report of the President,* Washington, D. C.: Government Printing Office, 1979, 1982, 1985, 1988, and 1991.

## THE TRANSITORY NATURE OF THE TRADEOFF BETWEEN INFLATION AND UNEMPLOYMENT

Another reason for the collapse of the Phillips curve was that policy makers (and some economists) misinterpreted this curve and attempted to establish combinations of inflation and unemployment that were unsustainable. As we have seen in earlier chapters, the economy, left to its own devices, will tend to eliminate inflationary and recessionary gaps. By doing so, it will make certain points on the Phillips curve unsustainable. That is, if the government pushes the economy to any of these points, the economy will not stay there.

Leading economists like Milton Friedman and Edmund Phelps pointed out that the Phillips curve in Figure 13.2 is only a short-run relationship. They were not surprised that, holding constant the unemployment rate, the rate of inflation was higher in the 1970s than in the 1960s. In their view, expansionary monetary and fiscal policies that resulted in inflation would only reduce unemployment temporarily, with the result that the rate of inflation would tend to accelerate.

Their basic point was that *the Phillips curve in the long run is vertical.* That is, the unemployment rate in the long run will be the same, regardless of the inflation rate. There is a certain natural (or full-employment) rate of unemployment, which is determined by how long workers search before taking a new job. The more reluctant they are to take unattractive or low-paying jobs, the higher the natural rate of unemployment. Economists who stress the importance of structural unemployment argue that the natural rate of unemployment depends too on the rates at which changes in technology and tastes occur and the speed with which workers in declining industries can be retrained for jobs in expanding industries. In Chapter 5, we discussed these and other determinants of the natural rate of unemployment.

## THE IMPORTANCE OF EXPECTATIONS

Why will expansionary monetary and fiscal policies aimed at pushing the unemployment rate below its natural (or full-employment) level produce only temporary reductions in unemployment (but accelerating inflation)? To answer this question, it is essential to recognize that the short-run Phillips curve reflects people's expectations concerning the future rate of inflation. If people have come to expect a higher rate of inflation than in the past, this will shift the Phillips curve upward and to the right. To illustrate, let's compare two situations, one where workers and firms expect that prices will increase by 10 percent per year in the immediate future, the other where they expect no inflation at all. In the former case, unions will not be content to obtain less than a 10 percent increase in money wages, since a smaller increase would mean a cut in real wages. In the latter case, unions can afford to settle for a much more moderate increase in money wages, since none of the money wage increase is expected to be offset by inflation. Thus the rate of increase of wages—and hence the rate of increase of prices—is likely to be greater in the former than the latter case, if the unemployment rate is the same.

In summary, *the more inflation people expect, the further upward and out from the origin the short-run Phillips curve is likely to be. And the less inflation people expect, the further downward and close to the origin the*

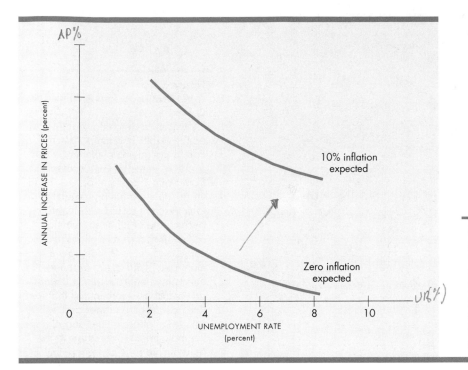

Figure 13.5
**Short-Run Phillips Curve, Given That the Expected Annual Inflation Rate Is 10 Percent or Zero**
If the expected annual inflation rate is 10 percent, the short-run Phillips curve is further upward and out from the origin than if the expected annual inflation rate is zero.

*short-run Phillips curve will be. Figure 13.5 illustrates this point; it shows how the short-run Phillips curve is likely to change position, depending on whether the expected annual inflation rate is 10 percent or zero.*

## HOW THE PHILLIPS CURVE SELF-DESTRUCTS: AN EXAMPLE

Having stressed the importance of people's expectations concerning the inflation rate, we can turn to the following example. Suppose that the natural rate of unemployment is 5 ½ percent, and that the government, not realizing that it is this high, uses expansionary monetary and fiscal policies to reduce unemployment to 4 percent. Because of the resulting increase in aggregate demand, the price level rises, *and if the level of money wages remains relatively constant,* firms' profits go up. Higher profits lead to expanded output and more employment. Thus the economy moves from point *C* (where it was before the government's expansionary policies) to point *D* in Figure 13.6. This movement is entirely in accord with the concept of the Phillips curve; a reduction in unemployment is gained at the expense of more inflation (6 percent rather than 4 percent).[2]

However, this movement is only temporary because workers adjust their expectations concerning inflation. Before the government's expansionary monetary and fiscal policies were adopted, the inflation rate was 4 percent, and this was (more or less) what workers expected. The move-

[2] To prevent confusion, note that we are not assuming that the short-run relationship between the inflation rate and the unemployment rate (curve 1 in Figure 13.6) is the same as the curve in Figure 13.2. Figure 13.6 pertains to one situation; Figure 13.2 pertains to an entirely different situation (perhaps another country or time period).

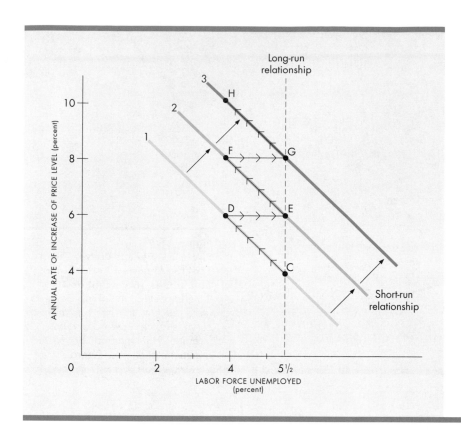

**Figure 13.6**
**A Vertical Long-Run Phillips Curve**
Expansionary monetary and fiscal policy results in a temporary reduction in the unemployment rate from 5 ½ to 4 percent ( a movement from point C to point D). But the increase in the inflation rate (from 4 to 6 percent) results in a higher expected rate of inflation, which shifts the short-run relationship from curve 1 to curve 2. If the government persists in trying to reduce the unemployment rate below the natural rate of 5 ½ percent, all that it will achieve is a higher and higher rate of inflation. In the long run, the unemployment rate returns to the natural rate (5 ½ percent in this case). Thus the long-run relationship between the unemployment rate and inflation rate is vertical.

ment from point C to point D means an increase in the inflation rate to 6 percent, which the workers do not expect. Although they are fooled at first, people *adapt* their expectations; that is, the rate of inflation they expect is adjusted upward toward the new 6 percent rate. As pointed out in the previous section, this increase in the expected amount of inflation will shift the short-run Phillips curve upward and out from the origin. The short-run relationship between the unemployment rate and the inflation rate will shift from curve 1 to curve 2 in Figure 13.6, and unemployment will return to 5 ½ percent, the natural rate. In other words, the economy will move from point D to point E. Faced with this new short-run curve, the government will raise the inflation rate to 8 percent if it persists in trying to maintain the unemployment rate at 4 percent. That is, it will have to move to point F in Figure 13.6.

## A Second Try

Suppose that the government continues to try to maintain a 4 percent unemployment rate. Since the inflation rate increases to 8 percent as a consequence, people once more begin to adapt their expectations to the new inflation rate. Workers, trying to compensate for the higher inflation rate, ask for bigger wage increases because they recognize that the inflation rate has risen. Once again, the short-run Phillips curve shifts upward and outward from the origin. The short-run relationship between the unemployment rate and the inflation rate will shift from curve 2 to curve 3 in Figure 13.6, and unemployment will return to 5 ½ percent, the natural rate. In other words, the economy will move from point F to point G. If

the government persists in trying to keep the unemployment rate at 4 percent, the economy will move next to point *H*, where the inflation rate is 10 percent.

### The Long-Run Relationship

The government, if it keeps trying to reduces the unemployment rate below the natural rate of 5 ½ percent, will continually fail to do so. All that it will achieve is a higher and higher rate of inflation. Thus the downward-sloping Phillips curve really does not exist, except in the short run, and governments that believe in its existence can cause considerable mischief. It is not possible for the economy to remain permanently at any point on the short-run curves in Figure 13.6 other than at the natural rate of unemployment (5 ½ percent in this case). Thus the long-run relationship between the unemployment rate and the inflation rate is a vertical line, as shown in Figure 13.6.

## TEST YOURSELF

1. "The inflations arising from the Revolutionary, Civil, and Vietnam wars were largely supply-side." Comment and evaluate.

2. According to Franco Modigliani, "Acceptance of the Phillips curve . . . implied . . . there was no longer a unique Full Employment but rather a whole family of possible equilibrium [employment] rates, each associated with a different rate of inflation." Explain what he means, and indicate whether you agree or not, and why.

3. Suppose that the relationship between the annual rate of change of the price level and the percent of the labor force unemployed is as shown in the following table:

| RATE OF CHANGE OF PRICE LEVEL (PERCENT PER YEAR) | UNEMPLOYMENT RATE (PERCENT) |
|---|---|
| 5 | 8 |
| 6 | 7 |
| 7 | 6 |
| 8 | 5 |

Plot the Phillips curve on a graph. Would Milton Friedman accept this curve as a long-run Phillips curve? Why, or why not?

4. During the 1980s, Americans began to expect lower and lower rates of inflation. Explain in detail the effects of this on the short-run relationship between the unemployment rate and the rate of inflation.

## FIGHTING INFLATION WITH MONETARY AND FISCAL POLICY: WHAT ARE THE COSTS?

In the previous section, we discussed the government's use of monetary and fiscal policy to reduce unemployment. As we saw, the government, if it tries continually to reduce unemployment below its natural rate, is likely to bring about more and more inflation. It will succeed in lowering the unemployment rate temporarily, which has obvious social benefits, as we saw in Chapter 5. But these benefits will be attained at the cost of increased inflation, which may be severe if the government tries to push the unemployment rate far below its natural rate. No matter how hard it tries, the government will not succeed in permanently lowering the unemployment rate below the natural rate.

Now we turn to the government's use of monetary and fiscal policy to reduce inflation. Since one administration after another has had to deal

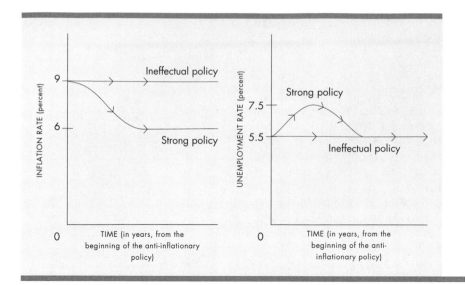

**Figure 13.7**
**Changes over Time in the Inflation Rate and the Unemployment Rate Following a Strong Anti-Inflationary Policy**
A restrictive monetary and fiscal policy will eventually reduce the inflation rate (from 9 to 6 percent in the left-hand panel), but it may also result in a temporary increase in the unemployment rate (from 5.5 to 7.5 percent in the right-hand panel). Liberals tend to believe that the increase in unemployment will be greater and longer-lasting than do conservatives.

with inflation, the government has had a great deal of practice in this regard, but much of it has been ineffectual. Despite tough talk against inflation, our nation's economic policy makers have tended to shy away from taking strong anti-inflationary actions. Why? Because even though the Phillips curve is vertical in the long run, they believe that it is downward sloping in the short run. In other words, they think that, if they push down the inflation rate, the result will be an increase in unemployment, which they would like to avoid for the reasons given in Chapter 5.

To see what is involved, let's compare what happens if a strong anti-inflationary policy is pursued with what happens if monetary and fiscal policy is not used in an effective way to restrain inflation. As shown in the left-hand panel of Figure 13.7, a restrictive monetary and fiscal policy—that is, an increase in interest rates, a tightening of the money supply, increases in taxes, and cuts in government spending—is likely to reduce the inflation rate, although it will take some time for this to occur. In the case shown in Figure 13.7, the inflation rate falls eventually from 9 to 6 percent.

But as shown in the right-hand panel of Figure 13.7, this restrictive policy is also likely to increase the unemployment rate, at least for a time. Tight monetary and fiscal policies are likely to throw some people out of work. In Figure 13.7, we assume arbitrarily that the unemployment rises temporarily from 5.5 to 7.5 percent. The extent to which unemployment rises is likely to depend on the shape of the short-run aggregate supply curve. If this curve is relatively steep, inflation may be curbed substantially with less of an increase in unemployment than if this curve is relatively flat.

## ARE THE BENEFITS WORTH THE COSTS?

There is a fundamental difference of opinion between liberal and conservative economists as to whether the benefits of such an anti-inflationary policy are worth its costs. Liberals (often Keynesians) tend to question

The expectations of people and firms concerning the rate of inflation influence many economic variables, not just the Phillips curve. In particular, *the nominal interest rate is influenced by whether people and firms expect a high rate of inflation or a low one.* (Recall that the nominal interest rate is unadjusted for the rate of inflation, whereas the real interest rate is adjusted for it.) To see why this is so, let's compare two economies, one where there is no inflation (and none is expected) and one where there is 6 percent inflation (and this amount of inflation is expected).

In the zero-inflation economy, suppose that the nominal interest rate is 5 percent. If the other economy is exactly the same as this one except for the fact that actual and expected inflation in the second economy is 6 percent, what is the nominal interest rate in the second economy? The answer is 11 percent. Lenders recognize that, if they are merely to get back the same amount of real purchasing power as they lend, they must charge 6 percent interest. (For example, if a lender charges 6 percent interest, he or she will get back $1,060 in principal and interest on a $1,000 loan at the end of one year; in real terms, this is no more—and no less—than the $1,000 he or she lent at the beginning of the year.) And besides the 6 percent interest, the lender must receive 5 per-

cent interest in order to earn the same real return as in the zero-inflation economy. Thus the total nominal interest rate must be 6 + 5 = 11 percent.

Clearly, the following equation must hold:

Nominal interest rate = Expected inflation rate + Real interest rate.

In other words, *lenders insist on a nominal interest rate that exceeds the real interest rate by an amount equal to the expected inflation rate.* To illustrate, consider the lenders in the previous paragraph. They insisted on a nominal interest rate of 11 percent, which equals the expected inflation rate (6 percent) plus the real interest rate (5 percent).

Holding the real interest rate constant, this equation leads us to believe that *the nominal interest rate is directly related to the expected inflation rate.* If the public expects the inflation rate to be *high,* the nominal interest rate is also likely to be *high.* If the public expects the inflation rate to be *low,* the nominal interest rate is also likely to be *low.* In fact, as shown in the graph below, there has been a direct relationship

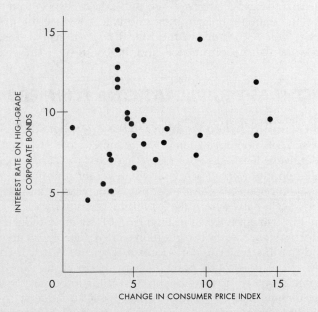

Source: *Economic Report of the President,* 1990 and 1991. Each dot pertains to a year, from 1965 to 1990.

whether the benefits exceed the costs; hence, they seldom are hawks in the nation's periodic wars against inflation. On the other hand, conservatives (often monetarists or new classical macroeconomists) generally are more convinced that the benefits exceed the costs. Consequently, they tend to lead the charge toward price stability.

On the other hand, the tables are turned when anti-recessionary policy is considered. Liberals, who tend to feel that the benefits of reducing unemployment exceed the costs (higher inflation), generally are the hawks in the nation's wars against unemployment, whereas conservatives tend to be less convinced that the benefits of a strong anti-recessionary policy are worth their costs. Obviously, there is no way to tell whether one group is right or wrong. A lot depends on your political views. If you regard unemployment as a greater social evil than inflation, you get one answer; if you believe that the reverse is true, you get the opposite answer.

But according to some economists, like Robert Lucas of the University of Chicago, an effective anti-inflationary policy really is much less costly than most people think—and much less costly than shown in Figure 13.7. In their view, what the government must do to conquer inflation is to influence the expectations of the public with respect to future inflation. The key to beating inflation, they say, is to convince the public that inflation really will be beaten. In the following sections, we discuss in detail the views of these economists—and the controversy they have stirred up.

## HOW ARE EXPECTATIONS FORMED?

In Figure 13.6, when we analyzed the case where the government wanted to reduce unemployment, we assumed that expectations are formed adaptively. That is, people were assumed to change their forecasts of the inflation rate to conform with whatever inflation rate currently exists. But many economists object that this assumption is naive. For example, let's consider a case where the government, rather than trying to reduce the unemployment rate (as in Figure 13.6), wants to reduce the inflation rate. Suppose that the short-run Phillips curve initially is curve 1 in Figure 13.8, and that the government adopts a restrictive policy that moves the economy from point A to point B, with the result that the inflation rate falls from 12 percent to 10 percent. According to our argument in Figure 13.6, people will now expect that inflation will continue at 10 percent.

But such expectations would be irrational, if the public is convinced that the government really is serious about fighting inflation. Instead, people, if rational, will expect that inflation will fall further to perhaps 6 percent, because of the government's policies.

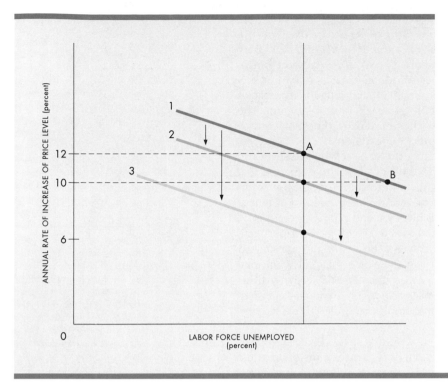

**Figure 13.8**
**The Phillips Curve if the Public Is Convinced the Government Is Serious about Fighting Inflation**
If the short-run Phillips curve is curve 1, and the government adopts an anti-inflationary policy that moves the economy from point A to point B, the inflation rate falls from 12 to 10 percent. If people expect it to remain at 10 percent, the short-run Phillips curve will shift to curve 2. But if people are convinced that the government means business, they will expect inflation to fall further (to 6 percent, if that is the government's aim), and the short-run Phillips curve will shift to curve 3.

This difference in expectations can be important. If people expect the inflation rate to fall to 6 percent, the short-run Phillips curve shifts downward much more rapidly than if people expect inflation to continue at 10 percent. Specifically, it shifts to curve 3 in Figure 13.8, whereas it would have shifted to curve 2 if people expected a 10 percent inflation rate. Thus it is much easier to tame inflation further because of the change in expectations. According to many economists, it is important that a government's anti-inflation policy be firm, consistent, and well understood. If firms, workers, and consumers are persuaded that the government will stick by its guns, and reduce inflation (even if it means heavy unemployment in the short run), they will relatively quickly moderate their wage and price demands, and inflation will soon be reduced. In other words, *the credibility of a government's anti-inflationary policy is of the utmost importance*. If such a policy is credible (and thus influences expectations), inflation will subside relatively quickly; if it is not credible, there may be great difficulties in bringing it down.

Without question, anti-inflation policy in the United States in the 1970s was not always credible. There was far more talk than action. In part, this was because government officials and their advisers were not convinced that people's expectations and behavior would change rapidly enough so that inflation could be licked without incurring considerable social costs (and perhaps political defeat at the polls).

## THE PHILLIPS CURVE UNDER CORRECT EXPECTATIONS

To see more clearly how people's expectations influence the social costs of a restrictive anti-inflationary policy, let's consider the extreme case where people and firms have correct expectations. Of course, this case is far from realistic, but it nonetheless is illuminating. *Whereas we formerly said that the short-run Phillips curve was downward-sloping, this is not true if people and firms have correct expectations. Instead, the Phillips curve is vertical in the short run as well as the long run.* Moreover, in contrast to our statements in earlier sections, there are not substantial costs associated with anti-inflationary policies since such policies do not have to result in increased unemployment. The purpose of this section is to show how these radically different conclusions would follow if the public had correct expectations.

To begin with, it is important to note that the reason why the short-run aggregate supply curve slopes upward to the right is that we assume that input prices are fixed *in money terms* in the short run. Suppose, for example, that labor is the only input, and that the hourly wage rate is constant at $9 per hour. As shown in column 4 of Table 13.1, the *real* wage rate goes down as the inflation rate goes up from 0 to 3 to 6 to 9 percent per year. Thus, if the inflation rate is 9 percent per year, the real wage rate a year from now is only $9 divided by 1.09, or $8.26. Since the real wage rate goes down as the inflation rate goes up, it is not hard to see why firms will produce more as the price level rises. After all, their costs in real terms are lower, so it is profitable to produce more under these circumstances.

But suppose, on the other hand, that workers have correct expectations concerning the future rate of inflation, and that they insist on wage increases that are great enough to offset expected inflation. If the expected inflation rate is 9 percent per year, they will insist now on obtaining a year from now an hourly wage rate of $9 times 1.09 or $9.81, as indicated in column 5 of Table 13.1. In contrast to the case where the money wage is constant, there will be no cut in the real wage rate due to inflation, and there will be no incentive for firms to increase output. Thus the short-run aggregate supply curve will be vertical, as shown in Figure 13.9. Increases in the price level will have no effect on total real output, even in the short run.

## Table 13.1
## Effects of Inflation on Real Wage Rate, Case Where the Money Wage Rate is Constant and Case Where the Money Wage Rate Increases to Offset Inflation (Which Is Expected)

| INFLATION RATE (PERCENT) | PRICE LEVEL NEXT YEAR[a] | CASE WHERE MONEY WAGE RATE IS CONSTANT | | CASE WHERE MONEY WAGE RATE INCREASES TO OFFSET INFLATION (WHICH IS EXPECTED) | |
|---|---|---|---|---|---|
| | | HOURLY MONEY WAGE NEXT YEAR | HOURLY REAL WAGE NEXT YEAR[b] | HOURLY MONEY WAGE NEXT YEAR | HOURLY REAL WAGE NEXT YEAR[b] |
| 0 | 100 | $9.00 | $9.00 | $9.00 | $9.00 |
| 3 | 103 | $9.00 | 8.74 | 9.27 | 9.00 |
| 6 | 106 | $9.00 | 8.49 | 9.54 | 9.00 |
| 9 | 109 | $9.00 | 8.26 | 9.81 | 9.00 |

[a] The price level this year is assumed to equal 100.
[b] The hourly real wage next year is expressed in this year's dollars. Thus it equals the hourly money wage next year divided by the ratio of next year's price level to 100. For example, if inflation is 3 percent and unexpected, the hourly real wage next year equals $9.00 divided by 103/100, or $8.74.

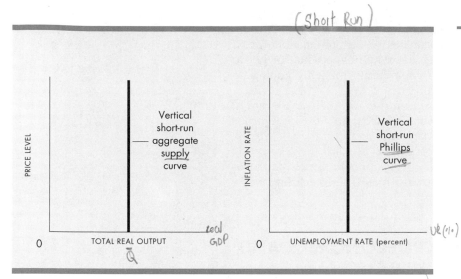

*(Short Run)*

Vertical short-run aggregate supply curve

Vertical short-run Phillips curve

PRICE LEVEL

TOTAL REAL OUTPUT — *real GDP*  $\bar{Q}$

INFLATION RATE

UNEMPLOYMENT RATE (percent) — *UR (%)*

0   0

**Figure 13.9**
**Short-Run Aggregate Supply Curve and Short-Run Phillips Curve under Correct Expectations**
Under correct expectations, both the short-run aggregate supply curve and the short-run Phillips curve are vertical. Since workers are compensated in advance for the expected rate of inflation, firms have no incentive to increase output as the price level rises. Thus the short-run aggregate supply curve is vertical, as shown in the left-hand panel, and the short-run Phillips curve is vertical, as shown in the right-hand panel.

If the short-run aggregate supply curve is vertical, so is the short-run Phillips curve. To see this, note once again that a vertical aggregate supply curve means that changes in the price level do not affect total real output. If this is the case, they also do not affect the unemployment rate, which means that the Phillips curve is vertical, as shown in Figure 13.9.

At this point, we have proved what we set out to prove in this section—that under correct expectations the short-run Phillips curve is vertical. Harking back to our discussion of the costs of an anti-inflationary monetary and fiscal policy, it is important to note that, if the short-run Phillips curve is vertical, there really is no need to experience the temporary increase in unemployment (shown in Figure 13.7) that, according to previous sections, would result from such a policy. However, while this result is interesting, it is of limited practical use since in fact firms and people do not have correct expectations.

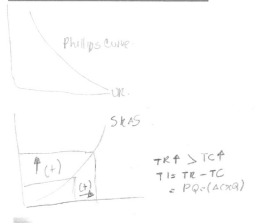

Phillips curve.

UR.

SRAS

↑ (+)   (+)

TR↑ > TC↑
TI= TR − TC
= PQ−(AC×Q)

## THE THEORY OF RATIONAL EXPECTATIONS

In recent years, many economists have assumed that firms and individuals have **rational expectations**. Put briefly, *a person's expectations (or forecast) of a particular economic variable are rational if the person makes the best possible use of whatever information is available.* This does not mean that the person's forecast is necessarily very accurate. As we saw in Chapter 8, it is far from easy to make very accurate economic forecasts. What it does mean is that the person does his or her homework and does not make stupid mistakes.

For example, if information is available concerning the size of the wage increases granted by the auto industry, and if this information is relevant in making forecasts of what the inflation rate will be, a person is assumed to obtain and take proper account of this information in making forecasts of the inflation rate. If the person does not do so, his or her expectations are not rational, according to the economist's definition.

The theory of rational expectations, formulated initially by Indiana University's John Muth, has had a great impact on economic analysis and policy. *Basically, what it says is that individuals and firms do not make systematic errors in forecasting the future.* For example, suppose that a

John Muth

person uses a model to forecast the inflation rate, and that experience indicates that this model always underestimates the actual inflation rate. If this person's expectations are rational, one would expect him or her to recognize this downward bias and to compensate for it by adding an amount to forecasts based on this model.

*On the average, forecasts, if they are rational, are correct.* To repeat, this does not mean that forecasters are always accurate. Instead, it means that, if we look at the results of a very large number of forecasts, we will find that the *average* forecasting error is zero. Unlike the forecasting model in the previous paragraph (which always underestimated the inflation rate), there is no downward or upward bias. The forecasting errors are random.

## THE NEW CLASSICAL MACROECONOMICS AND THE PHILLIPS CURVE UNDER RATIONAL EXPECTATIONS

Robert Lucas of the University of Chicago, one of the leaders of the new classical macroeconomists, was a pioneer in applying the theory of rational expectations to macroeconomics. *According to Lucas and his colleagues, the short-run Phillips curve is vertical.* To see how they come to this conclusion, note that, if the public has rational expectations, *the error in forecasting inflation*—namely, the difference between the *actual* rate of inflation and the *expected* rate of inflation—*is just a random number.* Why? Because as emphasized in the previous section, individuals and firms do not make systematic errors in forecasting the future. Thus, if expectations are rational, the errors in forecasting inflation are random— that is, they are unpredictable.

Further, *according to the new classical macroeconomists, output and employment are influenced by inflation only if inflation differs from what is expected.* As we saw in the section before last, the short-run aggregate supply curve and the short-run Phillips curve are both vertical when the public's expectations are correct. In the view of these economists, if workers do not tend to underestimate the prospective rate of inflation, the short-run aggregate supply curve does not tend to be upward-sloping to the right. Much more will be said about this proposition in the following chapter, where we provide a lengthy discussion of the new classical macroeconomics. All that you have to understand now is that, according to the new classical macroeconomists, increases in inflation that are expected will not reduce unemployment.

But based on the theory of rational expectations, *no change in the rate of inflation that is predictable can make the expected rate of inflation depart from the actual rate of inflation.* As we have seen, according to this theory, the public makes the best possible use of whatever information is available, and firms and individuals do not make systematic errors in forecasting the future. Thus a change in the rate of inflation that is predictable will be taken into account by the public in the formation of the public's expectations regarding inflation. It will not make the expected rate of inflation differ from the actual rate of inflation.

Putting the foregoing pieces together, Lucas and his colleagues conclude that unemployment will always tend to equal the natural rate of unemployment, except for unpredictable deviations from the natural rate that are due to forecasting errors. Consequently, the short-run Phillips curve tends to be vertical.

Returning once more to our discussion of the costs of an anti-inflationary monetary and fiscal policy, the bottom line is that Lucas and his colleagues argue that the key thing that the government must do is convince the public that it really will lower the inflation rate. If the government's policies are *credible*, inflation can, according to this argument, be reduced without a substantial increase in unemployment.

## CONTROVERSY AND EVIDENCE DURING THE 1980S

Whereas Lucas is convinced that an entrenched inflation can be quelled relatively quickly and painlessly, many other economists are skeptical of this conclusion. To a considerable extent, the argument revolves about the flexibility of prices and wages. As pointed out in previous chapters, the new classical macroeconomists tend to believe that prices and wages are flexible. In contrast, Keynesians—and the "new Keynesians" whose ideas are taken up in the next chapter—believe that prices and wages are "sticky"; in other words, they think that prices and wages are inflexible because of long-term contracts and other factors. Some say that there is a self-perpetuating momentum to wage increases during an entrenched inflation. Thus, even after the government adopts restrictive monetary and fiscal policies, these wage increases continue for a substantial period of time, with the result that unemployment mounts.

Based on the results of the government's strong anti-inflationary policies of the early 1980s, what do the facts indicate regarding the costs of such policies? The Fed's restrictive monetary policies, including the Saturday Night Special described on page 261, were instituted in 1979. Inflation fell from about 12 percent in 1980 to 9 percent in 1981 to 4 percent in 1982. The policy was more costly than anticipated by many conservatives. It produced a major recession that increased unemployment and lowered output substantially. But conservatives claim that it would have been far less costly if the Fed had taken a more unambiguous stand, and had announced its intentions more clearly.

On the other hand, many liberals seem to have exaggerated the length of time it would take to wring the entrenched inflation out of the economy. (Some said it might take 5 or 10 years.) In fact, inflation fell more rapidly than many liberals anticipated. They counter that this was due to the fact that, because the American steel and auto industries were in trouble, the auto and steel unions were in no position to press for continued large wage increases.

Taken as a whole, the evidence of the 1980s seems to indicate that a strong anti-inflationary monetary and fiscal policy is likely to be more costly than many conservatives say and less costly than many liberals say. Given the fact that such a policy is not costless, one moral is that the government should be very careful to avoid the high inflation rates that make such a policy seem necessary in the first place.

## TEST YOURSELF

1. Define what economists mean by rational expectations. Do you think that most people have rational expectations? If not, does this mean that theories based on the assumption of rational expectations are useless?

2. Explain why the short-run aggregate supply curve and the short-run Phillips curve are vertical if firms and individuals have correct expectations.

3. How do rational expectations differ from adaptive expectations, assumed on pages 278–79 and in Figure 13.6?

4. Are there costs in adopting a strong anti-recessionary monetary and fiscal policy? If so, what are they? Under what circumstances do you think that the benefits exceed the costs?

## SUMMARY

1. The Phillips curve shows the relationship between the rate of inflation and the unemployment rate. During 1955–69, there was a fairly close relationship between the inflation rate and the unemployment rate. But then something unforeseen by most economists occurred. The inflation and unemployment rates in the 1970s and 1980s did not conform at all closely to the relationship that prevailed in the 1960s. Both the unemployment rate and the inflation rate tended to be much higher in the 1970s and 1980s than in the 1960s.

2. According to Milton Friedman and others, the downward-sloping Phillips curve is only a short-run relationship. In the long run, they believe that it is vertical. In their view, expansionary policies that result in inflation will only reduce unemployment temporarily, with the result that the government, if it sets out to reduce unemployment to an amount below its natural rate, will generate higher and higher rates of inflation.

3. According to new classical macroeconomists like Robert Lucas, it is naive to assume that people change their forecasts of the inflation rate in accord with whatever inflation rate currently exists. If people believe that the government is serious about fighting inflation, the short-run Phillips curve will shift downward more rapidly. If people's expectations are rational in this way, it can be much easier to tame inflation.

4. The theory of rational expectations has had a great impact on economic analysis and policy. A person's expectations (or forecast) of a particular economic variable are rational if the person makes the best possible use of whatever information is available. This does not mean that the person's forecast is necessarily very accurate. However, it does mean that forecasts, if they are rational, are correct on the average. That is, forecasting errors are random.

5. The new classical macroeconomists argue that people and firms have rational expectations, and that the short-run aggregate supply curve and the short-run Phillips curve are vertical. Thus, in their view, anti-inflationary monetary and fiscal policies do not have to result in increased unemployment. American experience during the 1980s suggests that new classical macroeconomists (and monetarists) have tended to underestimate the increase in unemployment resulting from anti-inflationary policies, but that Keynesians have tended to overestimate it.

## CONCEPTS FOR REVIEW

**Demand-side inflation**

**Supply-side inflation**

**Short-run Phillips curve**

**Long-run Phillips curve**

**Rational expectations**

**Adaptive expectations**

**Wage and price controls**

**Incomes policy**

# APPENDIX: ATTEMPTS TO CURB INFLATION WITHOUT REDUCING AGGREGATE DEMAND

Much of this chapter has been concerned with the use of monetary and fiscal policy to combat inflation. Another way that the government can try to curb inflation is by adopting **wage and price controls.** During World War II—and other wartime emergencies—the government imposed controls of this sort. In other words, the government intervened directly in the marketplace to see that wages and prices did not increase by more than a certain amount. The economics profession has little enthusiasm for direct control of wages and prices.

Wage and price controls tend to result in a distorted allocation of resources because they do not permit the price system to work properly, the result being inefficiency and waste. Also, they impair our economic freedom, and are expensive to administer. In 1968, the Council of Economic Advisers stated that: "While such controls may be necessary under conditions of an all-out war, it would be folly to consider them as a solution to the inflationary pressures that accompany high employment under any other circumstance. . . ."

Consider the wage and price controls established by the Nixon administration from 1971 to 1974. According to many observers, the effects of these controls were largely cosmetic and short term. Without question, they interfered with the efficient workings of the price system, and were expensive to administer. Eventually, they were dropped. A detailed discussion of the nature and effects of these wage and price controls is provided in the next section.

## Wage and Price Controls under the Nixon Administration: A Case Study

Despite the disadvantages of price controls, the Nixon administration adopted them in the summer of 1971. Wholesale prices were rising then at about 5 percent per year. Collective bargaining agreements were reached calling for wage increases far in excess of productivity increases, and there was no question but that firms would boost prices in an attempt to cover the resulting increase in costs. In August 1971, President Nixon froze wages and prices for a three-month period. Then he appointed a 15-member Pay Board and a 7-member Price Commission, both of which were supervised by the government's Cost of Living Council.

The Pay Board was given the responsibility of administering wage controls, and the Price Commission was to administer price controls. In November 1971, these two bodies announced their initial policies. The Pay Board stated that pay increases had to be kept under 5.5 percent per year. A company could increase some employees' pay by more than this amount, but other employees would have to get less since total increases could not exceed this figure. The Price Commission ruled that price increases had to be kept under 2.5 percent. Both for prices and wages, exceptions could be made in some areas. Large firms were required to notify the Pay Board and Price Commission of intended wage or price increases.

From November 1971 to January 1973, this program of wage and price controls continued. Although it did not eliminate inflation, prices seemed to go up more slowly than before the freeze. (The Consumer Price Index went up by about 3 percent during 1972.) By early 1973, it appeared that controls might safely be relaxed. In January 1973, the Pay Board and the Price Commission became part of the Cost of Living Council, headed by Harvard's labor economist, John Dunlop. And controls were eliminated or relaxed for most prices and wages, with the major exceptions of the health, food, and construction industries. To a considerable extent, the Nixon administration phased out the first peacetime wage and price controls in our history.

Unfortunately, inflation occurred subsequently at a bewildering pace. During the first half of 1973, wholesale prices of farm products and processed foods and feeds rose at the unbelievable rate of 48 percent per year. At the same time, the prices of lumber, fuel, and other industrial goods rose at alarming rates. President Nixon responded by imposing a 60-day freeze on prices (but not wages), beginning in mid-June of 1973. This was only a breather, an interim measure designed to give the administration some time to deal with the serious inflationary pressures that were evident throughout the economy.

In August 1973, the administration announced that price increases could not exceed cost increases. This was the core of the new post-freeze program. But it soon became obvious that this new program was not proving effective, and that there was growing criticism and skepticism concerning price controls. In April 1974, Congress allowed the control authority to expire. This phase of the program was widely acknowledged to be a failure.

According to many observers, the price level rose, once controls were relaxed, to the level that it would have attained in any event, if there had been no controls. Thus it appears that the effects of the controls were short term and largely cosmetic.

## INCOMES POLICIES

Besides wage and price controls, there has been considerable interest, both here and abroad, in using incomes policies to help curb inflation without cutting back on aggregate demand. According to one common definition, an **incomes policy** contains three elements:

1. **AN INCOMES POLICY HAS SOME TARGETS FOR WAGES (AND OTHER FORMS OF INCOME) AND PRICES FOR THE ECONOMY AS A WHOLE.** For example, the target may be to stabilize the price level, or to permit the Consumer Price Index to increase by less than 2 percent per year, or to allow wage increases not exceeding a certain percentage.

2. **AN INCOMES POLICY GIVES PARTICULAR FIRMS AND INDUSTRIES SOME MORE DETAILED GUIDES FOR DECISION MAKING ON WAGES (AND OTHER FORMS OF INCOME) AND PRICES.** These guides are set in such a way that the overall targets for the entire economy will be fulfilled. For example, if the aim is price stability, these guides tell firms and unions what kinds of decisions are compatible with this target. To be useful, the guides must be specific and understandable enough to be applied in particular cases. There obviously is little point in telling firms and unions to avoid "inflationary" wage and price decisions if they don't know whether a particular decision is "inflationary" or not.

3. **AN INCOMES POLICY CONTAINS SOME MECHANISMS TO GET FIRMS AND UNIONS TO FOLLOW THE GUIDES.** An incomes policy differs from price and wage controls in that it seeks to induce firms and unions to follow these guides

voluntarily. But if it is to have any effect, clearly the government must be prepared to use certain forms of "persuasion" beyond gentle scolding. In fact, governments sometimes have publicly condemned decisions by firms and unions that were regarded as violating the guides. Government stockpiles of materials and government purchasing policies have also been used to penalize or reward particular firms and industries. Other pressures too have been brought to bear in an attempt to induce firms to follow the established guides. Thus the difference between an incomes policy and price and wage controls is one of degree and emphasis, not a clear-cut difference in kind.

An example of an incomes policy in the United States was the so-called Kennedy-Johnson guidelines, which said that the rate of increase of wage rates (including fringe benefits) should be equal to the rate of increase of output per hour of labor in the economy as a whole. These guidelines were established in 1961, and like many such incomes policies, they may have had a temporary dampening effect on inflation, but they were no permanent solution. Eventually they broke down.

Perhaps the most important reason why the guidelines broke down was that they could not deal with the strong demand-side inflation of the late 1960s. Even the strongest defenders of the guidelines are quick to point out that they are no substitute for proper monetary and fiscal policy. *If fiscal or monetary policy is generating strong inflationary pressures, such as existed in the late 1960s, it is foolish to think that guidelines can save the situation.* Perhaps they can cut down on the rate of inflation for a while; but in the long run, the dike is sure to burst. If the guidelines are voluntary, as in this case, firms and unions will ignore them, and the government will find it difficult, if not impossible, to do anything about it. *Even price and wage controls are no adequate antidote to strong inflationary pressures generated by an overly expansive fiscal or monetary policy. Such controls may deal temporarily with the symptoms of inflation, but over the long haul these inflationary pressures will have an effect.*

# CONTROVERSIES OVER STABILIZATION POLICY: THE NEW CLASSICAL MACROECONOMICS AND THE NEW KEYNESIANS

DURING THE PAST SEVERAL DECADES, there has been a continuing controversy among economists over the effects of monetary and fiscal policy on output and employment, as well as over the kinds of public policies that should be adopted. As we have seen, a variety of groups of economists—such as the Keynesians, the monetarists, the supply-siders, the new classical macroeconomists, and the new Keynesians—have contributed to this debate. This chapter discusses the views of two of these groups—the new classical macroeconomists and the new Keynesians. (Note that each of these groups is characterized by a considerable amount of disagreement. Thus new classical macroeconomists do not all see eye to eye, and neither do new Keynesians, even though the members of each group share many convictions and attitudes.) To put the views of each of these groups in proper perspective, we begin by looking briefly at the debates that occurred among economists in the 1960s and 1970s.

## MONETARISTS VERSUS KEYNESIANS: THE CENTRAL DEBATE OF THE 1960S AND 1970S

As stressed in Chapter 10, the principal debate of the 1960s and 1970s was between the monetarists and the Keynesians. This debate was not limited to the classroom and scholarly gatherings. It spilled over onto the pages of daily newspapers and aroused considerable interest in Congress and other parts of the government. At heart, the argument was over what determines the level of output, employment, and prices. The **Keynesians** put more emphasis on the federal budget than did the monetarists; the **monetarists** put more emphasis on the money supply than did the Keynesians. To understand this debate, we need to know something about the development of economic thought. Until the Great Depression of the 1930s, the prevailing theory was that GNP, expressed in real terms, would tend automatically to its full-employment level. (Recall from Chapter 5 the classical economists' reasons for this belief.) Moreover, the prevailing theory was that the price level could be explained by the crude quantity theory of money. In other words, the price level $(P)$ was assumed to be proportional to the quantity of money $(M)$ because $MV = PQ$, and both $Q$ (real GNP) and $V$ (the velocity of money) were thought to be essentially constant.

During the Great Depression of the 1930s, this body of theory seemed inadequate to many economists. GNP was not tending automatically toward its full-employment level. And the crude quantity theory seemed to have little value. In contrast, Keynes's ideas seemed to offer the theoretical guidance and policy prescriptions that were needed. Keynesians did not neglect the use of monetary policy entirely, but they felt that it should play a subsidiary role. Particularly in depressions, monetary policy seemed to be of relatively little value, since you can't push on a string. In other words, monetary policy can make money available, but it cannot ensure that it will be spent. To Keynesians, fiscal policy was of central importance.

During the 1940s, 1950s, and early 1960s, the Keynesian view was definitely predominant, here and abroad. But by the mid-1960s, it was being challenged seriously by the monetarists, led by Milton Friedman and his supporters. The monetarist view harked back to the pre-Keynesian doctrine in many respects. In particular, it emphasized the importance of the equation of exchange as an analytical device and the importance of the quantity of money as a tool of economic policy. The monetarist view gained adherents in the late 1960s, partly because of the long delay in passing the federal tax increase of 1968. The reluctance of the administration to propose and the reluctance of Congress to enact this tax increase vividly illustrated some of the difficulties in using fiscal policy for stabilization. Even more important was the fact that the tax increase, when finally enacted, failed to have the restrictive effect on GNP (in the face of expansionary monetary policy) that some Keynesians had predicted.

During the 1970s, as more and more evidence accumulated, many of the differences between the monetarists and Keynesians seemed to wane in importance. Most monetarists conceded that fiscal policy can affect output and the price level; most Keynesians conceded the same regarding monetary policy. Although it would be incorrect to say that no differences remained on this score, there seemed to be a growing recognition that the differences had narrowed considerably. Thus Milton Friedman, the leading monetarist, was quoted as saying, "We are all Keynesians now." And 1985 Nobel laureate Franco Modigliani, a leading Keynesian, responded in his 1976 presidential address to the American Economic Association by saying, "We are all monetarists now."

## SUPPLY-SIDE ECONOMICS

While the differences between the monetarists and the Keynesians were narrowing, a new group of economists, known as *supply-side economists*, entered the fray. Since we have already discussed supply-side economics at length in Chapter 9 (pages 191–93), there is no need for a long discussion here. As you will recall, supply-side economists, who rose to prominence in the late 1970s and 1980s, are concerned primarily with influencing aggregate supply, particularly through the use of various financial incentives such as tax reductions. Supply-side economics really is not new. Major economists of the eighteenth and nineteenth (as well as twentieth) centuries were concerned with the stimulation of aggregate supply. In the early 1980s, supply-side economists were very influential in the Reagan administration.

## THE NEW CLASSICAL MACROECONOMISTS

Another group that emerged in the 1970s were the **new classical macroeconomists**, led by Robert Lucas of the University of Chicago, Thomas Sargent of Stanford University, and Neil Wallace of the University of Minnesota. Their theory of macroeconomics was based on three assumptions. First, new classical macroeconomists assumed that markets cleared; in other words, prices of inputs and outputs varied so as to equate the quantity supplied to the quantity demanded. Second, they assumed that people and firms have imperfect information. Third, they assumed that the expectations of people and firms conform to the theory of rational expectations.

Robert Lucas

### Rational Expectations Revisited

As emphasized in the previous chapter, the theory of rational expectations has had a substantial impact on economic analysis and policy. Basically, what it says is that individuals and firms do not make systematic errors in forecasting the future. In other words, forecasts, *on the average*, are assumed to be correct. Of course, this does not mean that forecasters are always right. As we saw in Chapter 8, this is far from true. Instead, the new classical macroeconomists assume that forecasting errors are purely random. By assuming that people's expectations are on the average correct, they also assume in effect that these expectations are determined as part of the model and are genuinely forward-looking. Consequently, the announcement or anticipation that a particular event will occur results in immediate effects on the economy, even before the anticipated event actually occurs.

## UNEMPLOYMENT AND BUSINESS FLUCTUATIONS

According to the new classical macroeconomists, high rates of unemployment are not evidence of a gap between actual and potential output that can be reduced; instead, output fluctuations result from random forecasting errors. Markets are assumed to work efficiently; and firms, acting to maximize their profits, are assumed to make the best possible decisions. According to Lucas, since unemployed workers have the option of accepting pay cuts to get jobs, excess unemployment is essentially voluntary.

Fluctuations in aggregate demand are due principally to erratic and unpredictable government policy, in his view. Changes in the quantity of money induce cyclical fluctuations in the economy. But the power of policy changes to affect real GNP is limited. People come to learn the way in which policy is made, and only unanticipated government policy changes can have a substantial impact on output or employment. Once firms and individuals learn of any systematic rule for adjusting government policy to events, the rule will have no effect.

# THE LUCAS AGGREGATE SUPPLY CURVE

The new classical macroeconomists believe that national output will vary directly with the ratio of the actual to the expected price ratio. In other words, the aggregate supply curve is as shown in Figure 14.1. Such an aggregate supply curve is often called a **Lucas aggregate supply curve** (after Robert Lucas). It is important to note that this aggregate supply curve implies that *only unexpected changes in the price level will result in changes in aggregate supply.* For example, in Figure 14.1, aggregate supply equals *0Q* regardless of whether the price level is 100 or 110, if the price level is forecasted correctly. (Recall Chapter 13.)

To see why Lucas and others believe that this is the case, suppose that the economy is in equilibrium at full employment with stable prices and that actual and expected inflation rates are zero. Given this situation, let's assume that the government increases the money supply substantially, with the result that the prices of all commodities go up (say by 2 percent). The head of a firm producing these commodities mistakenly regards the increase in the price it receives as evidence that its commodity's price is going up relative to the prices of other goods. This is perfectly reasonable, given that he or she expects the inflation rate to be zero. Thus each firm increases output and employment. But when they realize that *all* prices have risen by 2 percent (say), they go back to their original output and employment levels since relative prices have not changed. All that has happened is that the price level has gone up by 2 percent.

On the other hand, suppose that the same situation occurs, but that firms and individuals expect a 2 percent inflation rate. Under these circumstances, when the government increases the money supply and the price of a firm's product rises by 2 percent, a firm will not interpret this as an increase in the relative price of its product. Since this price increase is no more than expected as a consequence of general inflation, there is no reason for firms to interpret it in this way. Thus, in accord with the Lucas aggregate supply curve, this change in the price level, because it is expected, does not lead to a change in national output—whereas the unexpected change in the price level discussed in the previous paragraph does induce changes in the national output.

## Figure 14.1
### The Lucas Aggregate Supply Curve

According to Robert Lucas, the level of real GNP depends upon the expected price level as well as the actual price level. Holding the expected price level constant, the level of real GNP is directly related to the actual price level, as in Chapter 7. But according to Lucas, increases in the expected price level shift the relationship between the actual price level and real GNP. Thus, if the expected price level increases from 100 to 110, this relationship shifts to the left, as shown in this graph. Note that, if the actual increase in the price level is expected, it has no effect on real GNP, which equals *0Q.*

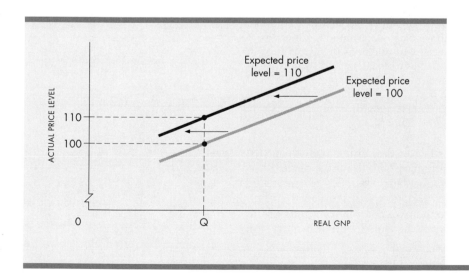

# CAN STABILIZATION POLICIES WORK?

Based on their theories, the new classical macroeconomists conclude that the *government cannot use monetary and fiscal policies to close recessionary and inflationary gaps in the way described in Chapters 9 and 12, because the models presented in those chapters do not recognize that the expectations of firms and individuals concerning their incomes, job prospects, sales, and other relevant variables are influenced by government policies.* If firms and individuals formulate their expectations rationally, they will tend to frustrate the government's attempts to use activist stabilization policies.

To illustrate what these economists are saying, suppose that the economy is in a recession and that the government, trying to close the recessionary gap in the ways described in Chapters 9 and 12, increases the amount that it spends on goods and services and increases the money supply. Because prices tend to move up while wages do not, profits tend to rise and firms find it profitable to expand. But this model is based on the supposition that labor is not smart enough to foresee that prices are going to go up and that labor's real wage is going to diminish. If labor does foresee this (that is, if its expectations are rational), it will insist on an increase in its money wage, which will mean that firms will not find it profitable to expand, and the government's anti-recession policy will not work as expected.

This point was discussed in the previous chapter, where we showed that (under the assumptions described there) the Phillips curve under rational expectations is vertical in the short run. (Recall pages 286–87.) The new classical macroeconomists have emphasized this point repeatedly.

# REACTIONS PRO AND CON

These views have received considerable attention in academic and policy circles. For example, in one of its annual reports, the Federal Reserve Bank of Minneapolis stated:

> The [new classical] view conjectures that some amount of cyclical swing in production and employment is inherent in the micro-level processes of the economy that no government macro policies can, or should attempt to, smooth out. Expected additions to money growth certainly won't smooth out cycles, if the arguments in this paper are correct. Surprise additions to money growth have the potential to make matters worse. . . . One strategy that seems consistent with the significant, though largely negative, findings of [the new classical macroeconomists] would have monetary policy focus its attention on inflation and announce, and stick to, a policy that would bring the rate of increase in the general price level to some specified low figure.[1]

Given the fact that the new classical macroeconomists have challenged the core of the theory underlying discretionary stabilization policies, it is not surprising that many economists, particularly liberals, have attacked their conclusions. Franco Modigliani, for instance, has claimed that their model is inconsistent "with the evidence; if it were valid, deviations of unemployment from the natural rate would be small and transitory—in

[1] Federal Reserve Bank of Minneapolis, *Rational Expectations—Fresh Ideas that Challenge Some Established Views of Policy Making*, Minneapolis, 1977, pp. 12–13.

which case [Keynes's] *General Theory* would not have been written."[2] Since Lucas's theory makes excess unemployment the result of purely unexpected events, one would think that unemployment would fluctuate randomly around its equilibrium level, if this theory is true. Critics point out that recessions sometimes last quite a long time.

Critics also claim that the new classical macroeconomics neglects the inertia in wages and prices. Contracts are written for long periods of time. Workers stick with firms for considerable periods. Consequently, wages and prices do not adjust as rapidly as is assumed by the new classical macroeconomists. According to the critics, most empirical analysis does not support the view that wages and prices adjust rapidly. On the contrary, wage and price movements show only slow and adaptive changes.

One of the most serious criticisms has centered on the new classical macroeconomists' contention that business fluctuations would be eliminated if firms and consumers had accurate current information about the aggregate price level. Given that the Consumer Price Index is widely disseminated with a relatively short lag, this does not seem very plausible. As Northwestern's Robert Gordon put it, "With monthly and even weekly data on the money supply available, people could make expectational errors about monetary changes lasting for only a few weeks, not nearly enough to explain business cycles lasting an average of four and one-half years in the postwar era, and twelve years for the period of high unemployment between 1929 and 1941."[3]

## REAL BUSINESS CYCLE MODELS

In contrast to the models described in the previous section, some new classical macroeconomists, such as Edward Prescott of the University of Minnesota, argue that business fluctuations are due predominantly to "real" rather than "monetary" factors. These economists, whose influence within the new classical camp has grown substantially in the late 1980s and early 1990s, are called **real business cycle theorists**. In their view, business fluctuations are the natural (indeed *efficient*) response of the economy to changes in technology and the availability of resources. Thus business fluctuations are due largely to shifts in the aggregate supply curve, not the aggregate demand curve.

To illustrate what they have in mind, consider Figure 14.2. Suppose that technological change shifts the long-run aggregate supply curve to the right, with the result that real GNP increases from $OY_0$ to $OY_1$. Then suppose that OPEC cuts back on the supply of oil, causing a shift of the aggregate supply curve to the left, with the result that real GNP falls from $OY_1$ to $OY_2$. These output fluctuations are due to shifts in the aggregate supply curve, not the aggregate demand curve. According to real business cycle models, this is the way that business fluctuations in the real world tend to occur.

What are the factors that shift the aggregate supply curve, thus causing business fluctuations? Among the most important are new products, new methods of production, new sources of raw materials, changes in the price of raw materials, and good or bad weather. (Recall Chapter 8.) These factors are sometimes called **supply shocks**. The effects of a *fa-*

Edward Prescott

[2] F. Modigliani, "The Monetarist Controversy, or, Should We Forsake Stabilization Policies," *American Economic Review*, March 1977, p. 6.
[3] R. Gordon, *Macroeconomics*, 5th ed. (Glenview, Illinois: Scott Foresman, 1990), p. 202.

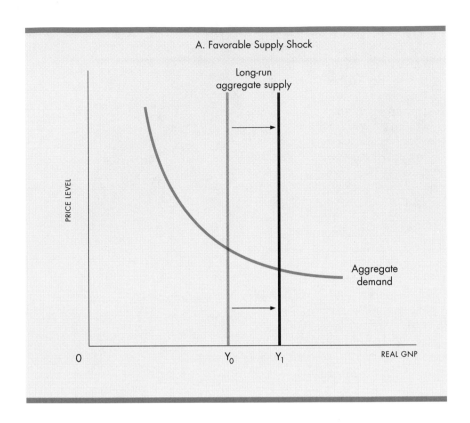

A. Favorable Supply Shock

Long-run
aggregate supply

PRICE LEVEL

Aggregate
demand

0          $Y_0$      $Y_1$          REAL GNP

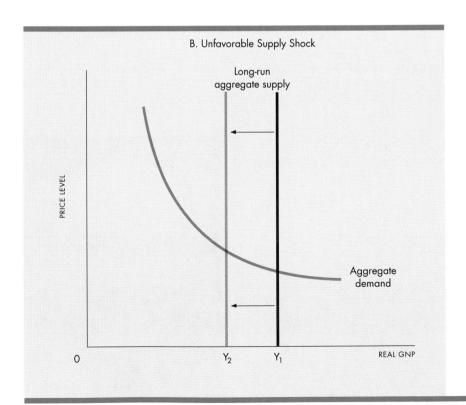

B. Unfavorable Supply Shock

Long-run
aggregate supply

PRICE LEVEL

Aggregate
demand

0          $Y_2$      $Y_1$          REAL GNP

**Figure 14.2**
**Favorable and Unfavorable Supply Shocks**
In panel A, a favorable supply shock (technological advance) shifts the aggregate supply curve to the right and increases real GNP from $OY_0$ to $OY_1$. In panel B, an unfavorable supply shock (oil cutback) shifts the aggregate supply curve to the left and decreases real GNP from $OY_1$ to $OY_2$.

*vorable* supply shock (that is, one that pushes the aggregate supply curve to the right) may persist for several years, after which an *unfavorable* supply shock (one that pushes the aggregate supply curve to the left) may be felt. For example, in Figure 14.2, the technological advance that increases real GNP from $OY_0$ to $OY_1$ is a favorable supply shock, which is succeeded by an unfavorable supply shock—the cutback of oil from OPEC—which reduces real GNP from $OY_1$ to $OY_2$.

As in the other new classical models discussed earlier in this chapter, real business cycle models assume that equilibrium is achieved in all markets. In other words, markets clear. Each firm produces the amount of output it desires, and hires the quantity of labor it wants. Workers get as much work as they want; there is no involuntary unemployment. Prices and wages respond flexibly to changing economic conditions. This is in contrast to the new Keynesian models, taken up in succeeding sections, which assume that there are many factors that prevent markets from clearing. Also, it is in contrast to the original Keynesian model which, as will be recalled from Chapter 5, assumed that wages were inflexible.

## THE EFFECT OF A SUPPLY SHOCK

To illustrate in more detail how supply shocks can cause business fluctuations, suppose that there is a temporary decline in agricultural productivity due to bad weather, and that this productivity decline reduces real income in agriculture. As Chapter 6 would lead us to expect, this cut in real income leads farmers to decrease their consumption of goods and services, but they do not decrease their consumption levels all at once. Instead, they spread the reduction of consumption over time. Thus a supply shock of this sort would be expected to spread from one sector of the economy to another. As farmers cut back their consumption levels, non-agricultural industries—like clothing and automobiles—may feel the pinch. Also, the effects of such a supply shock would be expected to persist for some time. Since farmers cut back their consumption spending gradually, the adverse effects on the sales of other industries—like clothing and automobiles—are likely to continue for some time.

An unfavorable supply shock—such as this decline in agricultural productivity—leads firms to want fewer workers at the prevailing wage. Thus, according to real business cycle models, real wages will fall, as the demand curves for labor shift to the left. The fact that these models predict that real wages will tend to fall when real GNP falls—and that real wages will tend to rise when real GNP rises—is in accord with past experience, according to some observers, but not according to others.[4]

## THE RELATIONSHIP BETWEEN MONEY AND OUTPUT

Proponents of real business cycle models believe that these models can explain the recent history of the U.S. economy reasonably well. If this is true, it is a remarkable achievement, given that so little attention is given to shifts in the aggregate demand curve. But many economists are skepti-

[4] R. Gordon, *op. cit.*; and C. Walsh, "New Views of the Business Cycle," *Business Review of the Federal Reserve Bank of Philadelphia*, January–February 1986.

cal, particularly because they are very uncomfortable with a theory that provides so little a role for monetary policy. As stressed in Chapter 10, there is a significant direct relationship between the money supply and real GNP. How do the proponents of real business cycle models explain this relationship?

In their view, changes in real GNP cause changes in the money supply, rather than the other way around. As output goes up or down during a business cycle, the volume of transactions does the same; and the demand for money tends to go up or down too. Also, according to the proponents of real business cycle models, an increase (or decrease) in the demand for money will bring about an increase (or decrease) in the supply of money. For example, they cite the Federal Reserve's operating procedures to help explain the close relationship between the money supply and real GNP after World War II:

> In most of this period, the Federal Reserve set short-term interest rate targets as a means of managing money growth. Under such a policy, if the demand for money increases, then the monetary authority attempts to counter the resulting higher interest rates by increasing reserves to the banking system, thus increasing the money supply. Given such an operating procedure, any disturbance that causes real output to vary would also cause the money stock to change in the same direction.[5]

## ENTHUSIASM AND SKEPTICISM

Proponents of real business cycle models say that these models enable economists to take a more integrated approach to business fluctuations and economic growth. At present, business fluctuations—the relatively short-term ups and downs of the economy—are often studied separately from economic growth, the relatively long-term, generally upward movement of the economy. According to real business cycle models, both business fluctuations and economic growth stem from factors that shift the long-run aggregate supply curve. Because some factors have only temporary effects, they result in business fluctuations, whereas other factors leave more permanent effects, and thus result in economic growth.

However, there is considerable skepticism that supply shocks of this sort are big enough to cause the business fluctuations we have experienced. As Robert Gordon of Northwestern University has put it:

Robert Gordon

> Skeptics doubt that any conceivable supply shock could explain why output fell one third in the Great Depression of the 1930s. Only the oil price shocks of the 1970s . . . qualify as a supply shock severe enough to explain the recessions that occurred in 1974–75 and 1980–82. Proponents of the real business cycle approach have failed to identify particular events in particular sectors that could be labeled supply shocks in earlier episodes like the Great Depression and postwar recessions before 1974. At an industry level, one would expect technology shocks to occur randomly. Highly distinctive technologies are used in different industries; for instance, an innovation that increases the speed of a Macintosh desktop computer has little effect on the productivity of coal miners. Favorable shocks in some industries would cancel out adverse shocks in other industries, which deepens the skepticism that (except for the oil shocks of the 1970s), the *average* effect of all the separate industry shocks could be large enough to explain actual booms and recessions.[6]

[5] C. Walsh, *ibid.*, p. 12.
[6] R. Gordon, *op. cit.*, pp. 205–6.

1. According to the new classical macroeconomists, all unemployment is voluntary. In their view, any unemployed worker has the opportunity to work, but refuses to do so because, given his or her expectations concerning inflation, the expected real wage rate is too low. Does this seem reasonable? Why, or why not?

2. Based on the Lucas aggregate supply curve, is it true that a large positive "price surprise"—that is, a large positive difference between the actual and expected price level—leads to firms' producing more output? Why, or why not?

3. Robert Gordon has stated that "the weakness of the new classical model lies not in the assumption of rational expectations, but rather in its assumption of continuous market clearing." What does continuous market clearing mean? Do you agree with Gordon? Why, or why not?

4. Critics of real business cycle theories question whether any conceivable supply shock could explain the huge drop in output in the Great Depression. (Real GNP fell by about 30 percent between 1929 and 1933.) What is a supply shock? Do you agree with the critics? Why, or why not?

## THE NEW KEYNESIANS

Just as there is a new classical macroeconomics, so there is a new Keynesianism. Like the original Keynesians, the new Keynesians do not believe that markets clear continuously; in other words, they do not believe that the quantity demanded of a good or input always equals the quantity supplied. Instead, they believe that, if there is a sudden shift in the demand or supply curve, prices will fail to adjust quickly enough to equate the quantity demanded to the quantity supplied. In their view, the economy can stay in a state of disequilibrium for years if prices adjust slowly enough.

As we know from previous sections, this is a quite different view from that held by the new classical macroeconomists, who assume that markets clear continuously because prices adjust quickly. The new Keynesians, like the old Keynesians, say that their view is the more realistic one. They argue that it is unrealistic to assume that workers who are unemployed during recessions are voluntarily unemployed. Ask such a worker, they say, whether he or she would refuse a job offer at the prevailing wage. In their view, it is very likely that he or she would say no, thus shedding doubt on whether the labor market actually clears. Turning to product markets, they ask whether a firm in a recession is selling all that it would desire. In their view, such a firm would be likely to say it was not, thus shedding doubt on whether the product market actually clears.

Like the new classical macroeconomists, the new Keynesians have adopted the theory of rational expectations. For example, MIT's Stanley Fisher has shown that, if the public has rational expectations, systematic monetary policy can stabilize the economy. But his theory assumes that wages are inflexible, whereas the new classical macroeconomists assume that they are flexible. This is a fundamental difference.

## HOW DO NEW KEYNESIANS DIFFER FROM OLD KEYNESIANS?

Both old and new Keynesians assume that prices or wages, or both, tend to adjust slowly in the short run, with the result that the quantity of output, more than price, tends to adjust to changes in aggregate demand. But whereas old Keynesians merely assumed that wages tend to be rigid and that prices are sticky, new Keynesians have developed theories that help to explain why such wage and price stability can be expected, given the rational behavior of individuals and firms. In other words, new Keynesians have tried to construct a microeconomic foundation for Keynesianism that old Keynesians failed to provide.

Basically, the focus of new Keynesians has been on the reasons for wage and price rigidities. As we shall see, some rigidities of this sort can be temporary: output adjusts slowly, but eventually gets to the unique optimal level. In other cases, however, these rigidities can be permanent: because the model has more than one equilibrium, the economy can be caused to move to an entirely different equilibrium with different levels of employment and output.

## MENU COSTS AND STICKY PRICES

To explain why prices adjust slowly, the new Keynesians assume that markets are not perfectly competitive. In other words, firms are assumed to have some control over the prices of their products. For many products, like computers, oil, or beer, this is a reasonable assumption. Going a step further, they also assume that a firm incurs costs when it changes its price. Such a cost is called a **menu cost**. Why? Because it is the same sort of cost that a restaurant incurs when it changes its prices—and thus must print new menus.

As an illustration, consider the Jefferson Company, a producer of a wide variety of hand tools. If it changes its price schedule, it must print new catalogs, spend a considerable amount to inform its customers of the price changes, change many aspects of its billing system, and so forth. Its accountants figure that it costs Jefferson $40,000 every time it changes its price schedule.

Suppose that there is an upward shift in the demand curve for Jefferson's product. Given this increase in demand, Jefferson's president suspects that it may be wise to raise the firm's prices. According to the firm's accountants, the firm's sales, costs, and profits will be as shown in Table 14.1, if it raises or does not raise its prices. Clearly, the president is right; Jefferson would make higher profits if it increased its prices. However, the figures in Table 14.1 do not take into account the $40,000 cost of changing prices. When these menu costs are taken into account, it is not profitable for Jefferson to increase its prices.

In the next few months, the upward shift in the demand curve for Jefferson's product continues, and its president wonders once again whether the firm should raise its prices. The firm's accountants estimate that its sales, costs, and profits will be as shown in Table 14.2, if it now raises or does not raise its prices. At this point, is it profitable for Jefferson to change its price schedule? The answer is yes, because Table 14.2 shows that the increase in profit—$260,000 − $210,000 = $50,000—is more than sufficient to cover the menu cost of $40,000.

**Table 14.1**
**Jefferson Company's Profit if It Raises or Does Not Raise Its Prices, Original Situation**

|  | PRICES ARE RAISED | PRICES ARE NOT RAISED |
|---|---|---|
| Sales | $1,095,000 | $1,070,000 |
| Costs | 840,000 | 850,000 |
| Profit | 255,000 | 220,000 |

**Table 14.2**
**Jefferson Company's Profit if It Raises or Does Not Raise Its Prices, Subsequent Situation**

|  | PRICES ARE RAISED | PRICES ARE NOT RAISED[a] |
|---|---|---|
| Sales | $1,120,000 | $1,080,000 |
| Costs | 860,000 | 870,000 |
| Profit | 260,000 | 210,000 |

[a] Note that, if prices are not raised, sales and costs differ from what they would have been in Table 14.1 if prices were not raised. This is because Table 14.2 pertains to a later situation than does Table 14.1

The point here is that, according to the new Keynesians, prices can be sticky because of the existence of menu costs. This is one way that they explain why prices adjust slowly, and why markets do not clear continually.

## LONG-TERM LABOR CONTRACTS AND STICKY WAGES

Like prices, wages can be sticky, according to the new Keynesians, and this is due in part to long-term labor contracts. In the United States, formal labor contracts prevail in heavily unionized industries like steel, automobiles, rubber, and electrical machinery. Those contracts influence the level of wages in other industries, since they tend to be imitated elsewhere. Many contracts extend for three years; the contract calls for specified increases in wage rates each year plus (in some instances) extra wage increases that offset whatever changes occur in the Consumer Price Index.

Not all contracts come up for renewal at the same time. Instead, as shown in Figure 14.3, some contracts come up for renewal each year. Assuming for simplicity that all contracts are negotiated at the beginning of the year, and that all last for three years, the contracts negotiated in 1991 cover 1991, 1992, and 1993; those negotiated in 1992 cover 1992, 1993, and 1994; and so on. One important consequence of these multi-year labor contracts is that wages adjust slowly, and with a substantial lag, to changes in aggregate demand.

Table 14.3 shows the scheduled wage adjustments in the first, second, and third years of union contracts during the 1980s. Take, for example, the case of 1983. New contracts in that year called for only a 4.5 percent wage increase, but because of the lingering effects of old contracts negotiated in 1981 and 1982, wage rates went up by far more. (As shown in Table 14.3, contracts negotiated in 1981 and 1982 called for 7.5 and 7.0 percent wage increases, respectively, in 1983.) Thus it was very difficult to reduce the rate of increase of wages quickly. Instead, wages adjusted gradually to changes in economic conditions.

Given that long-term contracts tend to slow the rate of adjustment of

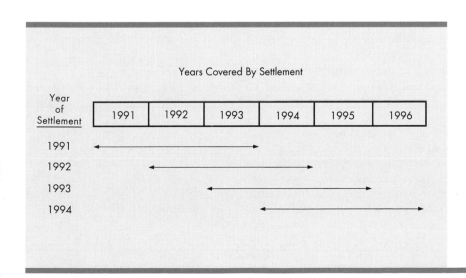

**Figure 14.3**
**Overlapping Three-Year Labor Contracts**
Not all contracts come up for renewal at the same time; instead they overlap, one consequence being that wages adjust slowly, and with a substantial lag, to changes in aggregate demand.

Table 14.3
**Wage Increases in First, Second, and Third Year of Union Contracts, United States, 1980–90**

| YEAR OF CONTRACT SETTLEMENT | YEAR WHEN WAGE ADJUSTMENT IS EFFECTIVE (PERCENTAGE INCREASE) | | | | | | | | | | |
|---|---|---|---|---|---|---|---|---|---|---|---|
| | 1980 | 1981 | 1982 | 1983 | 1984 | 1985 | 1986 | 1987 | 1988 | 1989 | 1990 |
| 1980 | 9.5 | 8.8 | 6.7 | | | | | | | | |
| 1981 | | 9.6 | 8.0 | 7.5 | | | | | | | |
| 1982 | | | 7.0 | 7.0 | 6.1 | | | | | | |
| 1983 | | | | 4.5 | 4.8 | 4.5 | | | | | |
| 1984 | | | | | 4.0 | 4.0 | 4.0 | | | | |
| 1985 | | | | | | 3.7 | 4.0 | 3.9 | | | |
| 1986 | | | | | | | 2.4 | 3.0 | 3.0 | | |
| 1987 | | | | | | | | 2.4 | 2.8 | 2.8 | |
| 1988 | | | | | | | | | 3.5 | 2.5 | 2.8 |

*Source:* D. Mitchell, "Shifting Norms in Wage Negotiation," *Brookings Papers on Economic Activity*, vol. 16, no. 2, 1985; and Gordon, *op. cit.*

wages, it is interesting to ask why workers and firms prefer to enter into such agreements. One reason is that each wage negotiation costs both workers and firms a considerable amount of time and money, since each side must prepare its case thoroughly. Thus both sides are happy if these negotiations only take place every few years. Also, if labor and management do not come to an agreement, a strike may occur, with substantial potential losses to both sides. Neither side really wants a strike (except in very unusual circumstances), and if there are wide time intervals between negotiations, there also are likely to be wide time intervals between strikes.

## IMPLICIT CONTRACTS

Another theory used by new Keynesians to explain wage rigidity focuses on **implicit contracts**, which are agreements between workers and firms that are not found in any formal, written contracts. Rather, they are informal or *implicit*. Workers and firms have many understandings that are not formalized in any written agreement. Indeed, it would be impossible to write down all of the understandings that grow up between labor and management.

According to this theory, workers are more inclined to shun risk than their employers, which seems reasonable given that the owners of firms have been willing to assume the risks of operating a business. In particular, workers are reluctant to assume the risks involved in allowing wage rates to adjust quickly to clear the labor markets, because this would mean that wage rates would vary considerably during business fluctuations. Under these circumstances, all workers would run the risk that their wages would vary over the business cycle.

Instead, according to implicit contract theory, wages are set based on long-term considerations, and do not go up and down during business

# EXAMPLE 14.1    CAN PROFIT-SHARING BE USED TO REDUCE UNEMPLOYMENT?

As we have stated repeatedly (beginning in Chapter 5), if wage rates are inflexible, involuntary unemployment is likely to occur. According to the new Keynesians, long-term union contracts are one of the factors that make wage rates downwardly inflexible, at least in the short run. Martin Weitzman of MIT has proposed a way to increase the downward flexibility of wage rates, thus reducing the amount of involuntary unemployment. Put baldly, the proposal is that some part of a worker's wage rate should be tied directly to his or her employer's profits; in other words, workers should get part of their compensation in the form of **profit sharing**.

Suppose that a worker receives $2 per hour in wages for every million dollars in profits of his or her employer. In addition, suppose that he or she receives a guaranteed hourly wage of $5, regardless of what the employer's profits may be. Then the following graph shows the relationship between the worker's hourly wage rate and the employer's annual profits:

Martin L. Weitzman

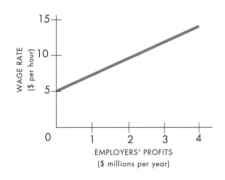

(a) If the employer earns profits of $4 million per year, what will the worker's hourly wage rate be? (b) If the employer earns profits of $1 million per year, what will the worker's hourly wage rate be? (c) Suppose that the employer's profits drop from $4 million to $1 million because of the onset of a recession. Is the employer as likely to lay off workers under the profit-sharing system described above as under the traditional wage-setting arrangement where the hourly wage rate is $10 (say), regardless of the employer's profits? (d) Some people argue that this sort of profit sharing distributes the burden of recession more equitably than the traditional wage-setting arrangement. In what way is the burden distributed differently? (e) Weitzman's proposal has been criticized by many groups, including unions. What concerns might workers and others have about the adoption of such a profit-sharing plan?

## Solution

(a) $13 per hour. (b) $7 per hour. (c) No. Since a worker will receive only $7 per hour during the recession, rather than $10 per hour, the employer is less likely to lay him or her off, because it is more likely that the worker's services are worth $7 per hour than $10 per hour. (d) Under profit sharing, all workers (covered by profit sharing) take a cut in pay during a recession, but fewer are laid off than under the traditional arrangement. Thus the burden is shared more equally than under the traditional arrangement, where most workers suffer no pay cut during a recession, but the minority who are laid off experience a severe reduction in earnings. (e) Some unions are concerned that the average wage rate (averaged over the various phases of the business cycle) may be much lower than under the traditional arrangement. Also, there is the question of whether workers will be willing to trade more jobs and greater stability of employment for a weaker and reduced wage guarantee.

* See Martin Weitzman, *The Share Economy*, Cambridge, Mass.: Harvard University Press, 1984.

fluctuations. Thus wages do not behave so as to clear markets, and employment will vary considerably. Firms in effect provide insurance for workers, who do not want their wages to vary over the business cycle. Responding to their workers' preferences, firms maintain relatively rigid wages, but at a level that allows them to increase their profits.

In particular, firms often lay off workers with the least seniority when it is necessary to lay off anyone. This means that workers with considerable seniority have a relatively good "insurance policy" against being laid off. Most workers may prefer a system of this sort (whereby a relatively few workers with little seniority are laid off when times get tough, but where the wages of those who are not laid off are quite rigid) to a system where wages are permitted to vary enough over the business cycle so that labor markets clear continually.

Critics note that, if workers are not willing to be bound by the prevailing implicit contracts, they may refuse unemployment after being laid off—by finding work elsewhere. Similarly, when the demand for labor grows, resulting in the rigid prevailing wage being lower than what other firms may be willing to pay for their services, workers may leave the firm and take jobs elsewhere. Further, it should be recognized that according to this theory, unemployment really is voluntary since all workers enter freely into the relevant implicit contracts recognizing that they are accepting the risk of unemployment.

## EFFICIENCY WAGES

Still another theory used by the new Keynesians to explain why wage rates may not clear labor markets is based on the concept of efficiency wages. Efficiency wage theory states that firms may find that they get more output per dollar (spent on wages) if they pay their workers more than the minimum amount. For example, the Monroe Company, which needs 100 workers, may be able to hire this number if it offers a wage of $10 per hour. However, it may decide to offer $12 an hour because the workers may be more careful and painstaking in their work if they are offered this higher wage.

Under many circumstances, managers encounter great difficulties in monitoring and evaluating how hard an employee is working. For example, a sales representative may be away from his or her office much of the time, and no manager may be able to keep tabs on what he or she is really doing. Under these circumstances, some employees may shirk. If the firm pays no more than the going wage, there may be little that its managers can do about such shirking, other than fire employees who are caught shirking. But this is unlikely to be a very effective threat since a fired employee can expect to get a job elsewhere at the same wage rate—the going wage.

On the other hand, if the firm pays substantially more than the going wage rate, workers will think twice before shirking since they will not want to endanger their jobs. Recognizing that it will be hard to find a job elsewhere that pays as well, they will work hard to keep their jobs, thus increasing the quality of their performance and reducing the firm's costs. So long as the cost reduction (before considering the larger wage bill) exceeds the increase in the amount spent on wages, the firm will increase its profits by paying the higher wage (commonly called an ***efficiency wage***).

This theory helps to explain why labor markets may not clear, since the efficiency wage may not clear the market. Also, according to some economists, firms do not cut wages during recessions because this might alienate workers, thus reducing their efficiency and increasing the likelihood of shirking. This too helps to explain why labor markets do not clear continually.

## THE INSIDER-OUTSIDER HYPOTHESIS

Some new Keynesian models involve more than one possible equilibrium, and the equilibrium actually achieved may not be the best one for society as a whole. In particular, consider the case of a labor union which has great power over the wage rate in a particular craft. The union is concerned with the well-being of its membership, but cares little about workers engaged in this craft who are not union members. Consequently, in its negotiations with firms, it tries to keep its members employed at an attractive wage level, but does not worry about non-union members.

According to Sweden's Assar Lindbeck and others, it is useful to think in terms of an "insider-outsider" theory of employment and unemployment. The "insiders" are the union members; the "outsiders" are those outside the union. The insiders have jobs and care little about the outsiders; indeed, they have an interest in keeping the outsiders where they are—out. In situations of this sort, the equilibrium level of unemployment may be higher than society as a whole would regard as optimal. Whereas the outsiders would like to obtain employment, the insiders do their best to keep them out.

## POLICY ACTIVISM: PRO AND CON

Much of the debate between the new Keynesians and the new classical macroeconomists is really over policy activism. The new Keynesians—like the old Keynesians—tend to be policy activists; they believe that discretionary monetary and fiscal policies are required to keep the economy on a reasonably even keel. The new classical macroeconomists tend to be very skeptical about how much stabilization policies of this sort can achieve. The debate over the pros and cons of policy activism has been going on for decades. While it is hazardous to try to summarize the views of each side (since there is considerable disagreement within each camp), the disagreements tend to be along the following lines.

**STABILITY OF PRIVATE SPENDING.** Many opponents of policy activism tend to believe that, if the government's economic policies did not destabilize the economy, private spending would be quite stable. One reason for this belief is the permanent-income hypothesis, discussed in Chapter 6. Personal consumption expenditures change relatively slowly as households adjust their estimates of their long-term income prospects. Policy activists, on the other hand, believe that business and consumer spending represent a substantial source of economic instability that should be offset by monetary and fiscal policy.

**FLEXIBILITY OF PRICES.** Even if intended private spending is not entirely stable, flexible prices tend to stabilize it, according to the non-activists. The

# THE DESIGN OF MACROECONOMIC POLICY: THE CEA CRITICIZES ITS PREDECESSORS

In 1990, President Bush's Council of Economic Advisers, in its annual report, criticized the discretionary policy making advocated almost 30 years before by President Kennedy's Council of Economic Advisers. Its statement is presented below. Of course, proponents of discretionary policy, whose views are summarized on pp. 310–11, take a different position on these issues.

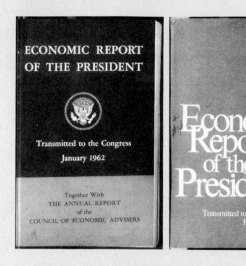

The power of monetary and fiscal policies to affect the economy has led some to advocate discretionary policymaking, with frequent changes in policy instruments, such as tax rates or expenditure programs, to influence near-term economic conditions. Indeed, a strong endorsement of discretionary policy was eloquently put forth in the 1962 *Annual Report of the Council of Economic Advisers* as a way to achieve the goals of the Employment Act of 1946—"maximum employment, production, and purchasing power." That *Report* argued that "discretionary policy is essential" and recommendations constituting a "far-reaching innovation in discretionary fiscal policy" were made.

In contrast, recent economic research and practical experience, while supporting the view that macroeconomic policy has powerful effects, lead to the conclusion that discretionary macroeconomic policies can be detrimental to good economic performance. Instead, policies should be designed to work well with a minimum of discretion, with a clear focus on the longer term, and with allowance for future contingencies. Government should credibly commit to follow such policies consistently. As argued below, this approach to policy design can best achieve the nation's economic goals.

In its extreme form, discretionary policy involves frequently reacting to short-term developments, with little attempt to consider and communicate intentions for future actions. Such a shortsighted policy approach gives little weight to the benefits of outlining a contingency plan and committing to that plan. For this reason, discretionary macroeconomic policies can actually be counterproductive. Most businesses and many households are forward-looking; expectations of future tax rates, inflation rates, and government spending programs affect their decisions. Frequent unanticipated government actions cause uncertainty for the private sector and interfere with long-term business and household planning.

Without commitment to a clear plan, strong incentives exist to change policies in an attempt to achieve short-term gain. Economists refer to this incentive as "time inconsistency," because policymakers have a natural incentive to alter previously adopted policies or to follow "inconsistent" policies. Such policy changes can have detrimental long-term effects. For example, programs of fiscal stimulus can lead, over time, to long-run government spending that exceeds the level implied by an assessment of the costs and benefits of the programs themselves. Analogous problems exist for monetary policy. For example, an incentive exists to employ short-term monetary policy to boost output above sustainable levels. Such actions can lead to increased inflation over a longer term. Because inflation takes more time to develop than the rise in economic activity, it may not be adequately taken into account in the public policy process.

The drawbacks to discretionary policy go beyond these disadvantages. Experience has shown that the ability of discretionary macroeconomic policies to move the economy in the right direction at the right time is quite limited. First, assessing the current state of the economy is difficult because economic data are subject to appreciable errors and are generally available only after a considerable lag. Second, economic forecasting is difficult and quite imprecise, limiting the ability of policymakers to anticipate swings in the economy.

Third, even if economic fluctuations are forecast correctly, determining the appropriate policy measures is difficult because the economy responds somewhat unpredictably to changes in fiscal and monetary policy. Finally, lags between a policy action and its ultimate effect on the economy imply that timely implementation of a discretionary change in policy frequently may not be possible. To be sure, discretionary policy changes might partly offset unusually large and sustained economic fluctuations. But, in general, the ability of discretionary macroeconomic policies to contribute to economic stability is quite limited.

The alternative to discretionary policies might be called systematic policies. A systematic policy specifies, as clearly as possible, *a plan for the instruments of policy,* be they the Federal budget, the growth rate of the monetary aggregates, or tax rates. For a systematic policy to improve economic performance, it must of course be well designed. In some cases a systematic policy might be very simple and specific, such as a promise not to raise marginal tax rates or a law that sets a target for the budget deficit for several years into the future. In the 1960s and 1970s, a rule that specified a fixed growth rate of the money supply was proposed and might have been appropriate; changes in the financial sector in the 1980s, however, have rendered such a simple rule unworkable. . . .

However, the concept of a systematic policy is much broader than a simple or even complex numerical formula for policy. In some cases it may not be possible to be so precise about a policy plan or its contingencies, and some judgment in interpreting or implementing the plan is necessary. Even in such cases, a systematic policy has significant advantages over a discretionary policy if it places some discipline or general guidelines on future changes in the policy instruments, and if policymakers commit to this discipline. Moreover, even the most carefully designed systematic policies may need to be revised occasionally in view of significant changes in economic structure.

Economic research and policy experience have led to a growing awareness of the importance of the *credibility* of policymakers to carry out a stated policy. Various definitions of policy credibility have been offered, but the following seems most useful: an announced policy is credible if the public believes that it will be implemented, and acts on those beliefs even in the face of occasional contradictory evidence. Policy credibility is not an all-or-nothing concept, and in many situations credibility can only be achieved gradually.

Policy credibility will often lead to economic performance that is superior to that in which policy is not credible. The more credible the policy, the more likely it is to improve performance. A credible disinflation plan initiated by the monetary authorities will bring down inflation more quickly and with less chance of recession than a plan with little credibility. . . .

policy activists reply that prices are relatively inflexible downward; in their view, the length of time that would be required for the economy to get itself out of a severe recession would be intolerably long. Their opponents seem more inclined than policy activists to believe that high unemployment will cause wages and input prices to fall, shifting the aggregate supply curve downward and increasing output in a reasonable period of time.

**RULES VERSUS ACTIVISM.** Opponents of policy activism tend to believe that, even if intended private spending is not entirely stable, and if prices are not entirely flexible, activist monetary and fiscal policies to stabilize the economy are likely to do more damage than good. As pointed out in Chapter 12, they sometimes favor a rule stipulating that the money supply should grow steadily at a constant rate, because of the difficulties in forecasting the future state of the economy and because of the long and variable time lag in the effect of changes in the quantity of money on output and prices. The policy activists, while admitting that monetary and fiscal policies have sometimes been destabilizing, are much more optimistic about the efficacy of such policies in the future.

# POLICY RULES AND TIME INCONSISTENCY

The new classical macroeconomists have stressed repeatedly the importance of the public's expectations regarding future policy. For this reason they think that one should distinguish between *rigid policy rules, feedback policy rules,* and *discretionary policy*. **A rigid policy rule** *specifies completely the behavior of the variable governed by the policy rule*. For example, Milton Friedman's suggestion that the money supply be set so that it grows at a fixed, agreed-on percentage rate is a rigid policy rule. Once the government established the percentage growth rate, the behavior of the money supply is completely specified. Regardless of what happens, the money supply must grow at this particular rate, so long as this policy rule is in force.

In contrast, *a* **feedback policy rule**, *as we saw in Chapter 12, allows the behavior of the variable governed by the policy rule to change, depending upon future circumstances*. For example, the government might specify that, if the unemployment rate exceeds 7 percent, the rate of increase of the money supply will be set at 8 percent, whereas if the unemployment rate does not exceed 7 percent, it will be set at 5 percent. In this case, the government does not specify the behavior of the money supply completely, since one cannot predict whether at a given time in the future the unemployment rate will be above 7 percent or not. But it does issue a well-defined formula indicating how the money supply will behave, depending upon future circumstances.

The new classical macroeconomists argue that feedback policy rules cannot affect real GNP. If the public knows the feedback rule in advance, any change in the money supply specified by the rule will be anticipated by the public. Thus Robert Lucas and his coworkers believe that such a rule will not be effective. Why? Because, according to Lucas, only unexpected changes in the price level will result in changes in aggregate supply. (Recall page 295.) Consequently, Lucas and his coworkers feel that a rigid policy rule of the sort proposed by monetarists like Milton Friedman is best. In their view, the adoption of such a rule would promote the credibility of monetary policy. In other words, the public would be convinced that the money supply really would grow in accord with this rigid policy rule.

**Discretionary policy**, *as we know from previous discussions, is policy that is formulated at the discretion of the policy makers*. According to the new classical macroeconomists, one of the big problems arising from discretionary policy is **time inconsistency**. Suppose, for example, that the government is trying to reduce the rate of inflation. Once it convinces the public that the inflation rate is really going to go down—that is, once it makes its disinflationary policy credible—policy makers may feel that it is in their interest to depart from their announced policy. For example, suppose that an election is coming up. If they nudge the rate of increase of the money supply up a bit, the resulting unexpected increase in the price level is likely to raise real GNP and reduce the unemployment rate, thus increasing their chances of an election victory. Of course, as the public becomes more and more used to being double-crossed in this way, it becomes harder and harder for the government to convince the public that any of its announced policies will really be carried out.[7]

---

[7] For some relevant discussion, see N. G. Mankiw, "A Quick Refresher Course in Macroeconomics," *Journal of Economic Literature*, December 1990.

# THE NEW KEYNESIAN RESPONSE

The new Keynesians take a quite different tack. They believe that changes in the attitudes and expectations of firms and consumers can cause substantial economic instability that should be offset by government stabilization policy. In contrast to the new classical macroeconomists, they do not favor rigid policy rules. For example, they point out that the growth of velocity in the United States since 1982 has been very erratic (recall page 219), which would seem to suggest that the growth rate of nominal GNP would have fluctuated considerably if a rigid rule calling for a constant growth of the money supply had been applied.

As we have seen, the new Keynesians put a great deal of emphasis on the fact that long-term wage and price contracts exist. Consequently, they are less concerned than the new classical macroeconomists with the credibility of the government's policies. Because wages and prices tend to be sticky, total real output tends to be affected by the actual behavior of the money supply and the price level, not just by unanticipated changes in the price level.

In recent years, activists have recognized more fully and more openly the many difficulties in formulating an effective economic stabilization policy. In the 1960s, there was considerable talk among activists about "fine-tuning" the economy; such optimism is long gone. Activists readily admit that there may be a long and variable lag between the time when a policy change occurs and when its effects are felt. Also, they recognize that it is very difficult to forecast what the state of the economy may be when the effects of a policy change occur.

Nonetheless, activists have not abandoned the attempt to formulate more effective discretionary stabilization policies. On the contrary, they continue to press for changes in monetary and fiscal policies that, in their eyes, would keep the economy on a more even keel. But they also tend to be cautious, certainly more cautious than thirty years ago, in their claims for what discretionary stabilization policies can achieve.

# DIVERGENT POLITICAL BELIEFS

One final and very important point: While economics is a science, not a mere reflection of the economist's political beliefs, it nonetheless is impossible to divorce an economist's views of the economy from his or her political feelings, where policy issues are involved. To a considerable extent, the differences between the policy activists and their opponents stem from divergent political beliefs. The policy activists tend to be optimistic concerning the extent to which the government can be trusted to formulate and carry out a responsible set of monetary and fiscal policies. They recognize that some politicians are willing to win votes in the next election by destabilizing the economy, but they nonetheless believe that discretionary action by elected officials will generally be more effective than automatic rules. Opponents of policy activism, on the other hand, are skeptical of the willingness of politicians to do what is required to stabilize the economy, rather than what is politically expedient. Since this aspect of the debate is difficult to resolve (in any scientific way), a complete resolution of this controversy is not likely any time soon.

## TEST YOURSELF

1. According to the new Keynesians, some unemployment is involuntary. In their view, some unemployed workers would like jobs at the going wage rate, but cannot find them. Does this seem reasonable? Why, or why not?

2. In Japan, labor contracts tend to extend for one year, not the three-year period that is common in the United States. Does this mean that wages are likely to be less rigid in Japan than in the Untied States? If so, of what significance is it?

3. If wages and prices were sticky before 1930, can this be attributed to long-term labor contracts between unions and firms? Why, or why not?

4. In 1914, Henry Ford reduced the length of the working day from 9 to 8 hours, and raised the minimum daily wage from $2.34 to $5.00. He afterward said that this ``was one of the finest cost-cutting moves we ever made.'' How is it possible that an increase in the wage rate can reduce costs? Was this in accord with efficiency wage theory? Why, or why not?

## SUMMARY

1. The principal debate of the 1960s and 1970s was between the Keynesians and the monetarists. The Keynesians put more emphasis than did the monetarists on the federal budget; the monetarists put more emphasis than did the Keynesians on the money supply. In the late 1970s, supply-side economists came to prominence, their emphasis being on tax cuts to push the aggregate supply curve to the right.

2. The new classical macroeconomists like Robert Lucas also came to prominence in the 1970s. Based on their assumptions, the new classical macroeconomists conclude that the government cannot use monetary and fiscal policies to close recessionary and inflationary gaps in the ways described in Chapters 9 and 12, because the models presented in those chapters do not recognize that the expectations of firms and individuals concerning their incomes, job prospects, sales, and other relevant variables are influenced by government policies. If firms and individuals formulate their expectations rationally,they will tend to frustrate the government's attempts to use activist stabilization policies.

3. According to real business cycle models, put forth by some new classical macroeconomists like Edward Prescott, business fluctuations are due largely to shifts in the aggregate supply curve. Among the most important factors shifting the aggregate supply curve are new products, new methods of production, new sources of raw materials, and good or bad weather. Real business cycle theorists tend to ignore monetary policy, and believe that changes in real GNP result in changes in the money supply, rather than the other way around.

4. The new Keynesians, like the old Keynesians, assume that prices and wages tend to be rigid in the short run, with the result that the quantity of output, more than price, tends to adjust to changes in aggregate demand. But whereas the old Keynesians merely assumed that wages and prices are sticky, the new Keynesians have developed theories that help to explain why such wage and price stickiness can be expected, given the rational behavior of individuals and firms.

5. According to the new Keynesians, prices tend to be sticky because of menu costs (costs incurred by firms when they change prices), and wages tend to be sticky because of long-term labor contracts. Based on the theory of implicit contracts, they conclude that wages are set based on long-term considerations. (Responding to workers' aversion to risk, firms maintain relatively rigid wages.) Based on efficiency wage theory, they say that firms often pay more than the minimum amount required to attract the required number of workers, because a higher wage will result in higher performance by workers.

6. The debate over the pros and cons of policy activism has been going on for decades. Opponents of policy activism tend to believe that activist monetary and fiscal policies to stabilize the economy are likely to do more damage than good. They have often favored a rigid policy rule stipulating that the money supply should grow at a constant rate. Policy activists, while admitting that discretionary monetary and fiscal policies have sometimes been destabilizing, are more optimistic about the efficacy of such policies in the future.

# CONCEPTS FOR REVIEW

New classical macroeconomics

Lucas aggregate supply curve

Real business cycle models

Supply shocks

New Keynesians

Menu costs

Implicit contracts

Profit sharing

Efficiency wages

Policy credibility

Rigid policy rule

Feedback policy rule

Discretionary policy

Time inconsistency

# THE BUDGET DEFICIT AND THE NATIONAL DEBT

THE BUDGET DEFICIT IS the difference between government expenditures and receipts. In 1991, the annual budget deficit was expected to reach the record-breaking level of $318 billion. Even to politicians who are used to dealing with huge amounts of money, this is a staggering sum. In this chapter, we focus on the government's budget deficit, our purpose being to determine whether it really should be the object of serious concern, and if so, why. Also, we discuss whether the national debt, which is the product of past deficits, is at a dangerously high level. Given the enormous amount of attention devoted to these topics in the newspapers and on television, you should find this discussion of great interest.

## ✓ HOW BIG ARE U.S. BUDGET DEFICITS?

To begin with, it is important to be clear regarding the size of the deficit. Obviously, the size of the deficit must be related to the size of the economy. A $200 billion deficit means one thing if a country's GNP is $100 billion, and quite another thing if its GNP is $10 trillion. Thus a deficit that would be huge for a tiny country like Monaco would be insignificant for a large country like the United States.

One way to relate the size of the deficit to GNP is to express the deficit as a percentage of GNP. Figure 15.1 shows that the deficit has increased from about 1 percent of GNP in the 1960s to about 2 percent in the 1970s to about 4 or 5 percent in the 1980s and early 1990s. Clearly, there has been a substantial increase in the deficit, relative to GNP.

However, not all economists believe that these measurements are correct. Robert Eisner of Northwestern University has argued that, when adjusted for inflation, the budget deficit is smaller than it appears when stated in nominal terms. (See page 316.) For these and other reasons, he believes that fiscal policy has not been as effective as it could be. For example, in his view, the reported deficit in 1980 of $61 billion was actually an adjusted surplus of almost $8 billion. However, Eisner's views are controversial, and have failed to comfort the many people who are concerned about the size and persistence of recent federal budget deficits.

## ✓ CONTROVERSIES OVER DEFICITS

Are budget deficits really such a bad thing? This is a question that has been raised repeatedly in the last decade. In 1984, there was a public fra-

**GOOD NEWS (SORT OF) FOR DEFICIT-BURDENED TAXPAYERS**

**W**orries about the record 1992 budget deficit—now estimated to hit $348 billion—have helped keep long-term interest rates up around 8.5%. But the deficit may be much easier to finance than expected, suggests economist Maury Harris of PaineWebber Inc. His reason: More than half of the deficit is ~~~~~~~~~~~~~~~~~~~~~~~~~~~

*Source: Business Week, August 5, 1991, p. 16.*

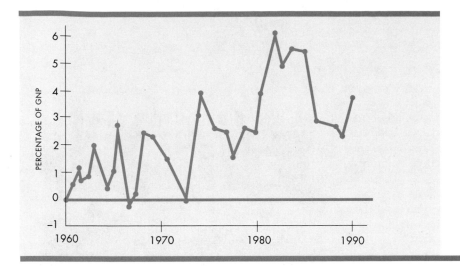

**Figure 15.1**
**Federal Deficit as a Percentage of GNP, 1960–90**
The federal deficit increased from about 1 percent of GNP in the 1960s to about 2 percent in the 1970s to about 4 or 5 percent in the 1980s and early 1990s.

cas within the Reagan administration over the need to reduce the deficit. According to Martin Feldstein, then chairman of President Reagan's Council of Economic Advisers, these deficits were very dangerous to the long-term health of the American economy. If they were allowed to continue, they would push up interest rates and result in a crowding-out of private investment on plant and equipment. Also, U.S. exports would be hurt because high U.S. interest rates would push up the value of the dollar relative to other currencies, thus making our exports more expensive to foreign purchasers. For these and other reasons, Feldstein (and many other economists) were extremely worried about the deficit.

In contrast, Donald Regan, who in 1984 was secretary of the Treasury, played down the importance of the deficit. In his view, deficits do not push up interest rates and they do not result in an overvaluation of the dollar relative to other currencies. In part, his arguments seemed to be based on studies carried out by some supply-side economists, including members of the Treasury staff. But most economists did not buy these arguments. If the government increases its demands for credit because of the very large deficits, the interest rate (which is the price of borrowing money) will rise.

## ARE BUDGET DEFICITS INFLATIONARY?

One reason why the public is concerned about deficits is that they are often thought to cause inflation. Whether or not this is the case depends on how the deficits are financed. One way the government can finance a deficit is to print new money. In other words, the Fed can increase the money supply, thus enabling the government to use the additional money to pay for the portion of its expenditures not covered by tax revenues. If deficits are financed in this way, and if the resulting increases in the money supply are substantial, the result may be inflation. This follows from the fact stressed repeatedly in previous chapters that substantial increases in the money supply may cause inflation.

But recent deficits in the United States have been financed largely by government borrowing. Every so often, the Treasury sells a few billion dollars worth of bonds, notes, or bills. To sell its securities, the Treasury

# HOW INFLATION DISTORTS THE DEFICIT

As the national debt has grown larger and larger, interest on the national debt has become a substantial part of the government's expenditures. In 1990, the federal government paid out $184 billion in interest on its bonds, notes, and other IOUs! However, many economists, led by Northwestern's Robert Eisner, argue that, when inflation is taken into account, these interest payments exaggerate the true amount that the government pays in interest.

To understand their argument, recall (from page 281) that the nominal rate of interest equals the expected rate of inflation plus the real interest rate. For example, if the real interest rate is 5 percent and the expected rate of inflation is 6 percent, the nominal interest rate is 11 percent. Eisner and others argue that *only the real interest that the government pays should be included as an expenditure item in the budget*. Why? Because it—and it alone—is the amount of real purchasing power paid by the government to lenders.

Suppose that the government borrows $1,000 for a year, and that the real rate of interest is 3 percent. If there is no inflation, at the end of the year the government must pay the lender the principal of $1,000 plus interest of $30, as shown in the table below. If the rate of inflation is 10 percent, the government must pay the lender $1,100 just to compensate the lender for inflation; in addition, it must pay the lender 3 percent × $1,100, or $33, in real interest. Thus, as shown in the table below, the government pays the lender $1,133 in all.

According to conventional government accounting, the interest cost—which is counted as an expenditure in the federal budget—is $30 if there is no inflation and $133 if the rate of inflation is 10 percent. From the point of view of conventional accounting, this

Robert Eisner

makes sense. After all, if you ignore inflation and say that $1,000 at the end of the period is sufficient to repay the debt, it follows that the interest cost is $30 if there is no inflation and $133 if there is an inflation rate of 10 percent. But if you take proper account of inflation, you realize that, if there is an inflation rate of 10 percent, only $33 of the $133 is real interest cost; the remaining $100 offsets the decrease in the real value of the principal of $1,000.

If the conventional accounting figures are adjusted so that only the real interest cost is counted as a government expenditure, the government's budget deficit is reduced by about $100 billion per year during the early 1990s, according to Eisner. While this is a significant reduction, it is not big enough to wipe out the deficit, which was about $220 billion in 1990. Nonetheless, it is important to recognize that inflation distorts the deficit figures in this way.[1]

[1] For further discussion, see R. Eisner, "Budget Deficits: Rhetoric and Reality," *Journal of Economic Perspectives,* Summer 1989. I am indebted to Eisner for comments and suggestions regarding this discussion.

|  | ZERO INFLATION RATE | INFLATION RATE = 10 PERCENT | |
|---|---|---|---|
|  |  | PRESENT GOVERNMENT ACCOUNTING | CORRECTED FOR INFLATION |
| Interest cost (which is *included* in the budget as a government expenditure) | $30 | $133 | $33 |
| Principal (which is *not included* in the budget as a government expenditure) | 1,000 | 1,000 | 1,100 |
| *Total amount* government must pay lender at end of year | $1,030 | $1,133 | $1,133 |

must offer potential buyers a high enough rate of return to make them an attractive investment. Suppose that the Treasury issues today $1 billion of one-year securities to cover a deficit of $1 billion. If the rate of interest is 10 percent, it must pay the $1 billion plus interest of $100 million at the end of one year. To pay this $1.1 billion to the holders of these securities, it must borrow $1.1 billion a year from now. If it again has to pay 10 percent interest, it will owe $1.21 billion (the principal of $1.1 billion plus $.11 billion in interest) a year hence. Thus the amount that the government has to borrow to finance a $1 billion deficit today grows over time.

However, so long as the government does not create new money to finance the deficit, the result need not be inflationary. But what if the government sells its securities to the Federal Reserve, rather than to households and firms? In this case, when the Fed purchases the securities from the government, it creates new money to buy them. (Recall from Chapter 12 that the Fed increases bank reserves when it buys government securities. But unlike the case considered on page 253, the Fed purchases the securities from the government, not from General Motors.) This increase in the money supply results in an increase in aggregate demand, which eventually pushes up the price level. Thus it makes a lot of difference who buys the government securities issued to finance a deficit. If they are not purchased by the Fed, there is no increase in the money supply; if the Fed purchases them, there is an increase in the money supply.

Going a step further, Thomas Sargent of Stanford University and Neil Wallace of the University of Minnesota have pointed out that, even if deficits are not financed right away by the creation of new money, they may have inflationary consequences. As pointed out in the paragraph before last, the interest payments resulting from a growing national debt can become very large. Suppose that investors become convinced that at some point in the reasonably near future the level of government debt will have become so big that the interest payments will constitute a disturbingly large proportion of the government's budget. If they think that the government will resort to the creation of new money at that time to finance all or part of the deficit, they are likely to fear that there will be substantial inflation then.

Thomas Sargent

Faced with this prospect, investors may insist on a relatively high interest rate on government securities to compensate them for the anticipated inflation, and they may try to hold less money, since the value of money is expected to fall. At the same time, they may increase their demand for goods, thus pushing up the price level now. The result is that, even though the deficit is not financed right away by the creation of new money, there may be inflation.

But if the deficit is kept within reasonable bounds, this situation need not occur. So long as the deficit is small enough so that investors remain convinced that the government is willing and able to keep the money supply under proper control, there need not be a problem of this sort. Even if the deficit is very large, it need not occur if people believe that deficits of this magnitude are only temporary and that in a relatively short time the budget will be brought into closer balance.

## DO BUDGET DEFICITS "CROWD OUT" PRIVATE INVESTMENT?

Another reason why people are concerned about large budget deficits is that they fear that the government's deficit spending may result in a sub-

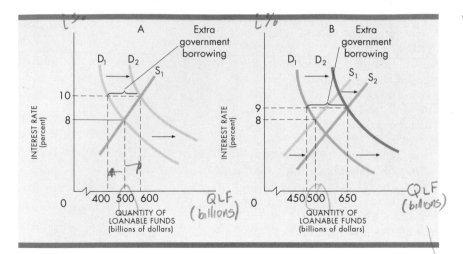

Figure 15.2
**How Government Borrowing
Can Crowd Out Private
Investment**
If the government enters the market
for loanable funds to finance its
$200 billion deficit, the demand
curve for loanable funds shifts to
the right from $D_1$ to $D_2$, the result
being that the interest rate rises
from 8 to 10 percent and the quantity of funds borrowed by the private sector drops from $500 billion
to $400 billion, as shown in panel
A. If the extra government expenditure increases national output (and
disposable income), the amount of
saving may increase, thus pushing
the supply curve to the right from
$S_1$ to $S_2$, as shown in panel B. The
result is that the interest rate rises
only to 9 percent, and the quantity
of funds borrowed by the private
sector falls only to $450 billion,
not $400 billion.

stantial cut in investment spending by the private sector. In other words,
they fear that government budget deficits may crowd out private investment. Why may this occur? Because large government borrowing may
push up the interest rate, which in turn may cut private investment.

To illustrate how ***crowding out*** can occur, consider panel A of Figure
15.2, which shows the private sector's demand curve and supply curve for
loanable funds. The demand curve for loanable funds, $D_1$, shows the total
quantity of loanable funds demanded by firms and households at each interest rate. (Recall from Chapter 6 that the interest rate is the price paid for
the use of loanable funds.) As would be expected, this demand curve
slopes downward to the right, indicating that the quantity of loanable
funds demanded goes up as the interest rate falls. The supply curve for
loanable funds, $S_1$, shows the total quantity of loanable funds supplied by
households, firms, and others at each interest rate. As would be expected,
this supply curve slopes upward to the right, indicating that the quantity
of loanable funds supplied goes up as the interest rate rises. The equilibrium level of the interest rate is 8 percent, where the quantity of loanable
funds demanded equals the quantity supplied, and the equilibrium
amount of funds borrowed for all purposes is $500 billion.

Now suppose that the government, which formerly did not have to
borrow, increases its spending by $200 billion, and that the spending in-
crease is financed entirely by borrowing. The result, as shown in panel A
of Figure 15.2, is that the demand curve for loanable funds shifts to the
right (from $D_1$ to $D_2$), reflecting the government's demand for the additional $200 billion of funds. Because of this shift of the demand curve, the
equilibrium interest rate rises to 10 percent, and the quantity of funds borrowed increases to $600 billion. But $200 billion of these funds go to the
government, which means that the private sector borrows only $400 bil-
lion. Thus the private sector borrows, and hence invests, $100 billion less
than it did before the government entered the market for loanable funds
to finance its $200 billion deficit.

However, this analysis may be incomplete. If the extra $200 billion of
government expenditure increases national output (and disposable income), the amount of saving may increase (in accord with our discussion
on page 111). Consequently, the supply curve for loanable funds may
shift to the right (from $S_1$ to $S_2$) as shown in panel B of Figure 15.2, the result being that the interest rate rises only to 9 percent, and the private sec-

where:
QLF: Quantity of loanable funds
$i$: interest rate.

Government borrowing
go up.

Private borrowing

Extra government
borrowing is $200billion

tor borrows, and hence invests, $450 billion (rather than $400 billion in panel A). Thus the private sector invests $50 billion (rather than $100 billion in panel A) less than it did before the government set out to borrow $200 billion. Under these circumstances, a smaller amount of private investment is crowded out than in panel A, where the increased government expenditure did not increase national output.

### Is Crowding Out Important?

Why does it matter if some private investment is crowded out? The answer is that, *if private investment is crowded out, the total amount of capital in the economy will be smaller than otherwise.* (Recall from Chapter 4 that net investment equals the change in the total amount of capital.) And a smaller capital stock means that our population will have fewer and poorer tools to work with—and thus less output. Consequently, large and persistent budget deficits really can harm future generations because they may result in a smaller total amount of capital being passed on to our descendants.

In fact, however, private investment in the United States has not fallen substantially in the face of the large deficits of the 1980s because foreigners have provided much of the funds. For example, the Japanese have purchased large amounts of our government securities. But what this means is that *future generations of Americans, while they will have a capital stock that is not much reduced, will owe a substantial amount to foreigners.* Obviously, when the government borrows from abroad, purchasing power is transferred from foreigners to us when the borrowing occurs, but purchasing power is transferred from us to foreigners when we pay interest on the debt and repay the principal.

Another effect of the high interest rates induced by large deficits has been an increase in the value of the dollar relative to other currencies. As pointed out in Chapter 12, this is because foreign investors have had to buy dollars in order to purchase U.S. securities, which (because of our high interest rates) have been attractive to them. Due to the swollen demand for dollars, the value of a dollar (relative to the Japanese yen or German mark) has tended to rise. One consequence of this has been that U.S. exports have tended to fall (because American goods have become more expensive relative to foreign goods) and U.S. imports have tended to rise (because foreign goods have become cheaper relative to American goods). Thus *large deficits have tended to depress our net exports.*

Finally, under certain circumstances, some economists believe that deficits can increase, not decrease, investment. This is known as the *crowding-in effect.* The idea is that, if the economy is experiencing considerable unemployment, the government's deficit spending may increase national output, which in turn may increase investment. Of course, the magnitude of this effect depends on how sensitive real GNP is to the extra government spending and on how sensitive investment by the private sector is to whatever increase occurs (on this account) in real GNP. If the economy is at or close to full employment, it is unlikely that this effect will occur, but if the economy is at the pit of a depression, this effect, according to some economists, may overwhelm the crowding-out effect.

## DO BUDGET DEFICITS MATTER? 4

Not all economists believe that deficits really matter. On the contrary, some, like Robert Barro of Harvard University, argue that it makes no dif-

Robert Barro

ference whether government expenditures are paid for by taxes or whether they are financed by government borrowing. The basic idea is that, if the government increases its spending and finances this increase by borrowing, the public realizes that taxes will have to be raised in the future to pay for this increase in spending, as well as to meet the interest payments on the debt that the government is issuing. Thus people will reduce their consumption at present in order to increase their saving; in this way they can built up sufficient wealth so that, when the higher taxes eventually are levied, they will be able to pay their taxes without a big drop in their levels of consumption.

The point here is that, *from the point of view of the taxpayer, the deficit financing of a government expenditure—that is, the financing of this expenditure by borrowing—can be regarded as a postponement of taxes.* While such a postponement increases the taxpayer's disposable income now, it reduces his or her disposable income later. If the taxpayer's consumption expenditure depended only on his or her current income (as in the case of the simple models in Chapter 6), the result would be an increase in consumption expenditure now. But as pointed out in Chapter 6, it is more reasonable to expect that the taxpayer's consumption expenditure depends on his or her permanent, rather than current, income. If that is true, and if this postponement of taxes does not alter the taxpayer's permanent income, it will have no effect on his or her expenditure decisions.

For this theory to hold, people must have a planning horizon that extends into the indefinite future. Only if this is true will a person take account of tax payments (and other consequences of government borrowing) that occur beyond his or her lifetime. According to Barro, a family's concern for its heirs will result in its planning horizon extending beyond the lifetimes of its adult members. If a family wants to make a bequest of a particular amount to its heirs, deficit financing of government spending may have no effect on a family's expenditure decisions even if the necessary future tax increases occur after the death of the family's adult members.

## Ricardian Equivalence

The basic idea that debt financing and taxes may be equivalent is not new. In the early nineteenth century, David Ricardo, one of the greatest figures in economics, put forth the same idea, which is often referred to as **Ricardian equivalence.** But Ricardo went on to question whether people are in fact so super-rational as to make calculations of this sort. Many other economists question whether debt financing and taxes really are equivalent. For one thing, families and firms sometimes cannot borrow all they want at the prevailing rate of interest—or at the rate of interest at which the government borrows. For another thing, families may not be as concerned about leaving bequests to their heirs as the theory supposes. (Thus they may feel that they can evade the future tax payments resulting from current government borrowing by the simple expedient of dying!)

In the early 1980s, when former president Ronald Reagan urged that taxes be cut substantially, some economists argued that Ricardian equivalence actually prevailed in the U.S. economy. Consequently, in their view, a tax reduction that increased the government's budget deficit would do no harm, since it would not drive up interest rates. The extra government debt would be financed by increased private saving. However, most economists did not buy this idea. According to the majority view, a large tax cut would raise aggregate demand, raise interest rates, and tend to crowd out private investment.

Given the strong assumptions that must be accepted if Ricardian equivalence is to hold, it is not surprising that many economists question whether it is relevant or useful in explaining the real world. Nonetheless, some studies, such as that by Paul Evans of Ohio State University, seem to suggest that it may be a useful approximation. To economists like Robert Gordon of Northwestern University, the tax cut of 1981 provided an interesting test case. From Chapter 9, you will recall that in August 1981 Congress enacted a large reduction in tax rates to occur in 1982–84. Had people acted in the forward-looking way Barro assumed, consumption expenditure would have been unchanged while saving would have increased to compensate for the future tax burden due to the extra government debt. In fact, however, the personal saving rate fell after 1981, which, as Gordon points out, seems to shed doubt on this theory.

## TEST YOURSELF

1. Explain how large budget deficits can discourage investment and inhibit the growth of a nation's capital stock.

2. Did the large deficits of the 1980s have a devastating effect on the rate of growth of the U.S. capital stock? If not, why not?

3. Can large deficits have an adverse effect on a nation's net exports? If so, how can this occur?

4. Describe and evaluate Robert Barro's views concerning the impact of the deficit financing of government expenditures on the economy. Was the behavior of saving in the United States after the tax cut of 1981 in accord with Ricardian equivalence?

## THE CYCLICALLY ADJUSTED BUDGET BALANCE

To see whether fiscal policy is expansionary (increasing aggregate demand) or contractionary (reducing aggregate demand), people often look at the size of the budget deficit. A large deficit often is viewed as more expansionary than a small one (or a surplus). However, this can be quite misleading since budget deficits can occur because the economy is at less than full employment (defined as the lowest sustainable unemployment rate compatible with reasonable price stability). A better measure of whether fiscal policy is expansionary or contractionary is the *cyclically adjusted budget balance,* which shows the difference between tax revenues and government expenditures that would result if gross national product were at its potential, not its actual, level.

To illustrate, let's go back several decades, and consider the situation in 1958 when the Eisenhower administration ran a deficit of about $10 billion. Basically, the reason for this deficit was that, with the unemployment rate at about 7 percent, there was a substantial gap between actual and potential output. Gross national product fell from 1957 to 1958, and, as a result, incomes and federal tax collections fell, and the government ran a deficit. But this $10 billion deficit was entirely due to the high level of unemployment the country was experiencing.

Had gross national product been at its potential level, there would

## SHOULD EISENHOWER HAVE TRIED TO BALANCE THE BUDGET?

1958 was a recession year in the United States. Tax revenues declined. Unemployment compensation payments rose. The budget deficit for the year approached $10 billion. According to many economists, the large deficit helped to get the recovery going, but when the recession was over President Eisenhower set out to recoup his losses by balancing the budget. As the president forged ahead with his plan for a budget surplus, voices were raised in warning. Some of these warnings came from a group of top business executives, the Committee for Economic Development.

Another person urging caution in the drive for a big surplus was Vice President Richard Nixon. During the recession of 1958, Nixon had urged a tax cut to stimulate the economy. His advice was not heeded. Now, as he prepared to run for president in 1960, he urged a more expansionary budget policy. Again his advice was rejected because the administration was more concerned about fighting inflation. Eisenhower in his last year in office was willing to take the political risk of pinching off growth. He assumed that the next administration would be able to carry on with the expansionary policy—a next administration that was expected to be Republican.

By the summer of 1960, the recovery had ground to a halt, stopping well short of the goal of full employment. As the ranks of the jobless increased,

Democratic presidential candidate John Kennedy was helped politically, while Richard Nixon watched the economy slide back into recession and victory slip through his fingers. Historians still argue whether it was the budget surplus and the unexpected recession that cost him the victory; but many economists seem to agree that a budget deficit in 1960 would have generated more jobs and more growth in the economy.

N. B.

have been a surplus of about $5 billion in 1958. Incomes and federal tax receipts would all have been higher. Government spending and the tax rates in 1958 were not such as to produce a deficit if output had been at its potential level. On the contrary, the cyclically adjusted budget balance shows that, if gross national product had been at its potential level, tax receipts would have increased so that federal revenues would have exceeded expenditure by about $5 billion. (For a discussion of the aftermath of the 1958 budget deficit, see the box on this page.)

It is important to distinguish between the cyclically adjusted budget and the actual budget. If the actual budget deficit is growing but the cyclically adjusted budget deficit is falling, most economists would feel that fiscal policy is not becoming more expansionary. As you can see in Figure

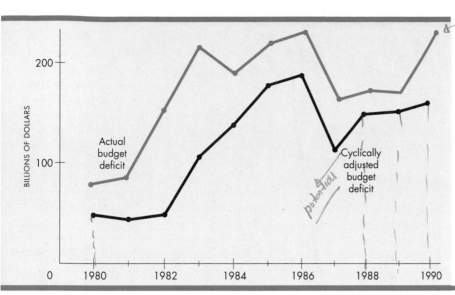

*(handwritten annotations: "5", "GST", "DO BB Matter?", "Essay Question", "potential")*

**Figure 15.3**
**Cyclically Adjusted and Actual Budget Deficits, 1980–90**
The cyclically adjusted budget balance shows the difference between tax revenues and government expenditures that would result if gross national product were at its potential level.

15.3, the cyclically adjusted budget deficit can differ substantially from the actual budget deficit. To understand whether fiscal policy is becoming more expansionary or contractionary, you must understand the difference.

## THE NATIONAL DEBT: SIZE AND GROWTH

As we have seen, when the federal government incurs a deficit, it generally borrows money to cover the difference. The **national debt**—com-

---

## EXAMPLE 15.1    INTERPRETING FEDERAL BUDGET DEFICITS

The actual deficits of the U.S. government in selected years are shown below:

| YEAR | (BILLIONS OF DOLLARS) |
| --- | --- |
| 1954 | 1.2 |
| 1961 | 3.4 |
| 1967 | 8.7 |
| 1968 | 25.2 |
| 1975 | 53.2 |
| 1980 | 73.8 |
| 1990 | 220.4 |

(a) Are all of these deficits the result of spendthrift government spending? (b) In 1954, 1961, 1975, and 1980, there were drops in GNP which helped to cause tax revenue to fall below government expenditure. From the above figures alone, can one determine the extent to which a particular government deficit is due to high government spending or a weak economy? (c) Were the deficits in 1967 and 1968 the result of a weak economy? What information would you obtain to answer this question?

### Solution

(a) No. In some years, like 1954, 1961, 1975, and 1980, at least part of the reason for the deficit was a weak economy due to recession. (b) No. What one needs to know is the cyclically adjusted budget deficit or surplus in each year. (c) No. The unemployment rate is of use in indicating whether the economy was weak. Since the unemployment rate was less than 4 percent in 1967 and 1968, the economy certainly was not weak in these years. The cyclically adjusted budget deficit or surplus would help to answer this question.

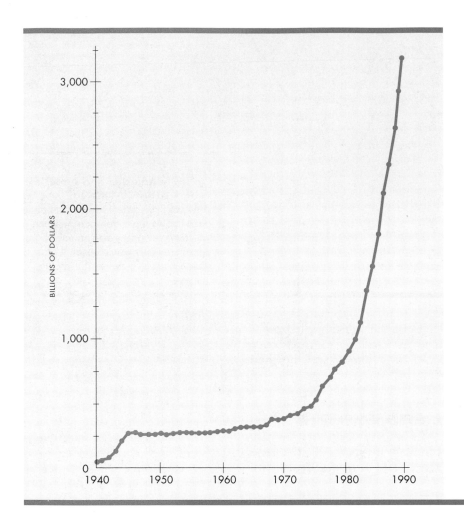

**Figure 15.4**
**Size of the National Debt, United States, 1940–90**
The national debt, about $3.2 trillion in 1990, has been growing rapidly due to huge government deficits.

posed of bonds, notes, and other government IOUs of various kinds—is the result of such borrowing. These IOUs are held by individuals, firms, banks, and public agencies. There is a large and very important market for government securities, which are relatively riskless and highly liquid. If you look at the *New York Times* or *Wall Street Journal*, for example, you can find each day the prices at which each of a large number of issues of these bonds, notes, and bills are quoted.

How large is the national debt? In 1990, as shown in Figure 15.4, it was about $3.2 trillion. Without question, this is a huge amount, but it is important to relate the size of the national debt to the size of our national output. After all, a $3.2 trillion debt means one thing if our annual output is $4 trillion, and another thing if our annual output is $400 billion. As a percent of output, the national debt was not much larger in 1990 than in 1939. In 1990, the debt was about 59 percent of output; in 1939, it was about 53 percent of output. The debt—expressed as a percentage of output—is shown in Figure 15.5. Although the figures do not seem to provide any cause for immediate alarm,[1] many economists have warned that

---

[1] Note too that much of the public debt is in the hands of government agencies, not held by the public. For example, in 1990 only about $2.4 trillion was held by the public.

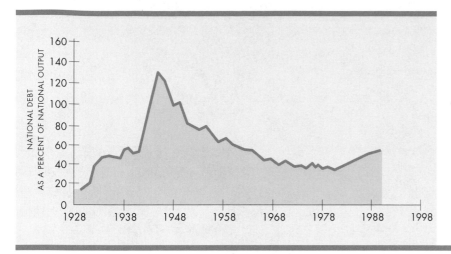

**Figure 15.5
National Debt as a Percent of National Output, United States, 1929–90**
As a percent of national output, the national debt declined steadily from World War II to about 1980. During the 1980s, it increased, but not very greatly.

there are problems in incurring large deficits of the kind that were responsible for the rapid rate of increase in the debt during the 1980s and early 1990s. These warnings have already been discussed in this chapter.

**A BURDEN ON FUTURE GENERATIONS.** Why have people been so agitated about the debt's size? One important reason has been that they have felt that the debt was a burden that was being thrust on future generations. To evaluate this idea it is important to recognize that a public debt is not like your debt or mine, which must be paid off at a certain time in the future. In practice, new government debt is issued by the government to pay off maturing public debt. There never comes a time when we must collectively reach into our pockets to pay off the debt. And even if we did pay it off, the same generation would collect as the one that paid. However, as stressed above, the deficits that create the debt can put a burden on future generations if they crowd out private investment, thus reducing the amount of capital turned over to future generations.

**EFFECTS OF EXTERNALLY HELD DEBT.** To the extent that the debt is held by foreigners, we must send goods and services overseas to pay the interest on it. This means that less goods and services are available for our citizens. Thus, if we finance a particular government activity by borrowing from foreigners, the cost may be transferred to future generations, since they must pay the interest. But from the point of view of the world as a whole, the current generation sacrifices goods and services, since the lending country forgoes current goods and services. Also, it must be recognized that, if the debt is incurred to purchase capital goods, they may produce enough extra output to cover the interest payments.

**REDISTRIBUTION OF INCOME AND EFFECTS ON INCENTIVES.** Taxes must be collected from the public at large to pay interest to the holders of government bonds, notes, and other obligations. To the extent that the bond-holders receiving the interest are wealthier than the public as a whole, there is some redistribution of income from the poor to the rich. To the extent that the taxes needed to obtain the money to pay interest on the debt reduce incentives, the result also may be a smaller national output.

# THE DEPARTMENT OF THE TREASURY AND THE NATIONAL DEBT

Average U.S. citizens have very little direct contact with the Department of the Treasury. If they work for the federal government, they receive a bimonthly check; if they are so fortunate as to have overpaid their income tax, they may receive a lovely green refund check. In fact, the processing of checks is (at least, to the nonrecipient economist) much less important than many other functions of the Treasury. Should the Congress or the president wish technical advice on the effect of a new tax measure, the Treasury Department will supply the analysis. In addition, it represents American interests in negotiations over international monetary arrangements with other countries; and, through the Internal Revenue Service and the Customs Service, it collects most federal taxes.[1]

But from an economist's point of view, one of the most interesting tasks the Treasury performs may be the management of the national debt. Imagine yourself with a debt of over $2 trillion (held by private investors), with billions coming due each week. Obviously, much of the Treasury's time must be spent scratching for new Peters in order to pay old Pauls. This may not sound like an easy task; and, in fact, it isn't. Over the years the Treasury has developed a bewildering array of devices—refinancing Series E bonds, U.S. savings bonds, short-term bills, long-term bonds—for coaxing new lenders to release their cash, or persuading old lenders to defer collection. One of the most important of these instruments is U.S. Treasury bills, which in 1990 amounted to about $500 billion. (Should you ever have a spare $10,000, the smallest denomination in which Treasury bills are sold, their current prices can be found in the financial pages of any major newspaper.)

Nicholas Brady, Secretary of the Treasury

Almost every month the Treasury must decide in what form the portion of the debt coming due should be refinanced. Are interest rates going up? If so, it might refinance by selling long-term bonds, locking up money at the present low rate. Will interest rates fall? If so, it might prefer the 90-day bill. Before an issue is floated, the Treasury gets a reading of market conditions from committees of the American Bankers Association and the Investment Bankers Association. But cost is not its only problem. The Treasury must also worry about the effect of its operations on financial markets and must have developed future refunding policies. In any case, an elaborate financial network of banks, big insurance companies, pension funds, and investment houses is always waiting to respond to the Treasury's next offering.

E. A.

---

[1] Moreover, faithful television fans may realize that, through its Bureau of Customs, the Treasury is responsible for controlling the importation of narcotics.

# THE POLITICAL ECONOMY OF BUDGET DEFICITS

One reason why it has been so difficult to reduce the government's large budget deficits is that politicians have been extremely reluctant to favor tax hikes, which seldom are popular with voters. Another reason is that Congress and the president have found it difficult to agree on the sorts of government expenditures that should be cut.

The Reagan administration was opposed to tax increases and in favor of spending reductions, but not cuts in defense spending. In 1987 and 1988, Democrats tried to pin the responsibility for the huge deficit on President Reagan, in particular because of his unwillingness to raise taxes or cut defense spending. After the decline in the stock market in October 1987, he agreed to a $9 billion tax increase and a $5 billion cut in defense spending, as part of an overall plan to reduce $30 billion from the 1987 deficit and $46 billion from the 1988 deficit. Many Democrats thought this was a step in the right direction, but far too small a step. Many Republicans felt that non-defense spending should be cut and that it was a mistake to consider tax increases or reductions in military spending.

During 1989 and 1990, as tensions between the United States and the Soviet Union seemed to decline, both Democrats and Republicans began to plan for a substantial reduction in defense expenditures. However, talk about a "peace dividend" subsided after Iraq invaded Kuwait, and the United States sent a large military force to the Persian Gulf to force Iraq out of Kuwait. (Recall our discussion on page 10 of the costs of the war against Saddam Hussein.)

In late 1990, President Bush, abandoning his opposition to new taxes, engaged in a long series of negotiations with Congress to try to reduce the deficit. The result was an increase in the income tax rate for highest-income families from 28 percent to 31 percent, a hike in taxes on cigarettes, beer, and wine, and other tax increases, as well as statements that spending cuts would occur. However, government forecasts indicated that the budget deficit was likely to be over $300 billion in 1991, due in part to the recession.

# ALTERNATIVE POLICIES REGARDING THE FEDERAL BUDGET

## Should the Budget Be Balanced Annually?

At least three policies concerning the government budget are worthy of detailed examination. The first policy says that *the government's budget should be balanced each and every year.* This is the philosophy that generally prevailed, here and abroad, until a few decades ago. Superficially, it seems reasonable. After all, won't a family or firm go bankrupt if it continues to spend more than it takes in? Why should the government be any different? However, the truth is that the government has economic capabilities, powers, and responsibilities that are entirely different from those of any family or firm, and it is misleading—sometimes even pernicious— to assume that what is sensible for a family or firm is also sensible for the government.

If this policy of balancing the budget is accepted, the government cannot use fiscal policy as a tool to stabilize the economy. Indeed, if the government attempts to balance its budget each year, it may make unemployment or inflation worse rather than better. For example, suppose that severe unemployment occurs because of a drop in national output. Since incomes drop, tax receipts drop as well. Thus, if the government attempts to balance its budget, it must cut its spending and/or increase tax rates, both of which may tend to lower, not raise, national output. On the other hand, suppose that inflation occurs because spending increases too rapidly. Since incomes increase, tax receipts increase too. Thus, for the government to balance its budget, it must increase its spending and/or decrease tax rates, both of which may tend to raise, not lower, spending.

Despite these considerations, there has been a considerable amount of political support for a constitutional amendment to mandate a balanced federal budget. No doubt, the federal government, through inappropriate fiscal or monetary policies, has frequently been responsible for excessive inflation or unemployment. As we saw in the previous chapter, some economists say that the real problem is how to prevent the government from creating disturbances, rather than how to use the government budget (and monetary policy) to offset disturbances arising from the private sector. But for the reasons discussed above, most economists would not go so far as to conclude that the government should balance its budget each year.

## Should the Budget Be Balanced over the Business Cycle?

A second budgetary philosophy says that *the government's budget should be balanced over the course of each "business cycle."* As we have seen in previous chapters, the rate of growth of national output tends to behave cyclically. It tends to increase for a while, then drop, increase, then drop. Unemployment also tends to ebb and flow in a similar cyclical fashion. According to this second budgetary policy, the government is not expected to balance its budget each year, but is expected to run a big enough surplus during periods of high employment to offset the deficit it runs during the ensuing period of excessive unemployment. This policy seems to give the government enough flexibility to run the deficits or surpluses that, according to many economists, may be needed to stabilize the economy, while at the same time allaying any public fear of a chronically unbalanced budget. It certainly seems to be a neat way to reconcile the government's use of fiscal policy to promote noninflationary full employment with the public's uneasiness over chronically unbalanced budgets.

Unfortunately, however, it does contain one fundamental flaw. There is no reason to believe that the size of the deficits required to eliminate excessive unemployment will equal the size of the surpluses required to moderate the subsequent inflation. Suppose that national output falls sharply, causing severe and prolonged unemployment; then regains its full-employment level only briefly; then falls again. In such a case, the deficits incurred to get the economy back to full employment are likely to exceed by far the surpluses run during the brief period of full employment. Thus there would be no way to stabilize the economy without running an unbalanced budget over the course of this business cycle. If this policy were adopted, and if the government attempted to balance the budget over the course of each business cycle, many economists believe that this might interfere with an effective fiscal policy designed to promote full employment with stable prices.

### Should We Worry about Balancing the Budget?

Finally, a third budgetary policy says that *the government's budget should be set so as to promote whatever attainable combination of unemployment and inflation seems socially optimal,* even if this means that the budget is unbalanced over considerable periods of time. Proponents of this policy argue that, although it may mean a continual growth in the national debt, the problems caused by a moderate growth in the national debt are small when compared with the social costs of unemployment and inflation.

## CHANGES IN PUBLIC ATTITUDES

Certainly, the history of the past fifty years has been characterized by enormous changes in the nation's attitude toward the government budget. Fifty years ago, the prevailing attitude was that the government's budget should be balanced. The emergence of the Keynesian theory of the determination of national output and employment shook this attitude, at least to the point where it became respectable to advocate a balanced budget over the business cycle, rather than in each year. In many circles, persistent deficits of moderate size were viewed with no alarm.

In the late 1970s and early 1980s, there was some movement back toward earlier views favoring balanced budgets. Conservatives emphasized the usefulness of the balanced budget as a device to limit government spending, which they regarded as excessive. The public tended to blame very high rates of inflation on large deficits. Although neither political party was prepared (even remotely) to renounce deficits, considerable lip service was paid to the desirability of a balanced budget. For example, in August 1982, the Senate approved a constitutional amendment requiring a balanced budget, while at the same time the government was running a deficit of over $100 billion!

## ATTEMPTS TO ELIMINATE THE DEFICIT

In recent years, some measures were adopted to help eliminate, or at least reduce, the federal budget deficit. Probably the most prominent was the Gramm-Rudman-Hollings Act. In addition, other measures, such as the line-item veto and the balanced budget amendment, have been proposed.

**GRAMM-RUDMAN-HOLLINGS ACT.** In 1985, the Congress passed the Balanced Budget and Emergency Deficit Control Act, which was often called the ***Gramm-Rudman-Hollings Act*** after the three legislators who sponsored the bill. Originally, the act specified that the budget deficit be cut (by about $40 billion per year) from about $200 billion in fiscal 1986 to zero in fiscal 1991. In 1987, the act was amended; the new schedule called for deficit reductions of about $36 billion per year from 1989 to 1993, the target being a zero deficit in 1993. In 1990, further major changes (described below) were made.

If no agreement was reached on a way to meet the target in a particular year, the act called for automatic spending cuts in a variety of government programs (but not Social Security or interest on the national debt). Thus the act seemed to say that the government either had to cut the deficit by rational action and negotiation, or the deficit would automati-

The sponsors of the Gramm-Rudman-Hollings bill

cally be cut by the formula specified in the act. At first glance, this seemed to be a forceful device to eliminate the deficit, but appearances can be deceiving.

For one thing, there were lots of gimmicks that the government used to make it appear that the deficit was being reduced when in fact little was being accomplished. For example, the act required only that the Office of Management and Budget issue a forecast that the target would be met in the next year, not that it actually be met. The result was that the forecasts were sometimes very optimistic, and that a variety of kinds of budgetary window dressing were applied to make the forecasted budget deficit look smaller than would really be the case.

Nonetheless, most experts seem to believe that the Gramm-Rudman-Hollings Act had some effect on the size of the federal deficit. Clearly, it did not succeed in reducing the deficit very substantially, but it was not completely irrelevant either. In 1990, a new system was adopted that attempted to limit spending rather than deficits. Different government programs received different limits or caps so that overspending in one category would trigger spending cuts in that category but not in others. The Office of Management and Budget was empowered to monitor program expenditures and to trigger cuts if necessary. Only time will tell whether this new system will have much effect on the budget deficit.

James Buchanan

**LINE-ITEM VETO.** At present, when Congress passes a bill regarding taxes and expenditures, the president must either sign it into law or veto the whole bill. He or she cannot delete particular parts. Some people believe that this should be changed. In their opinion, the president should be given a ***line-item veto***, which means that the president should be able to delete any particular item in the budget. But other people question whether the president would be willing to take the political heat generated if he or she cut specific expenditure programs in this way.

**BALANCED BUDGET AMENDMENT.** Still other people, such as Nobel laureates James Buchanan and Milton Friedman, favor an amendment to the Constitution of the United States requiring the federal government to balance its budget. In their view, this would enable Congress to resist more effectively the political pressures to spend what they regard as excessive amounts. Other people are dubious of the wisdom of such a policy, as we have seen earlier in this chapter.

## TEST YOURSELF

1. If the federal deficit rises, does this mean that fiscal policy is pushing real GNP upward? If the federal budget deficit falls, does this mean that fiscal policy is restraining real GNP? Explain.

2. What is the burden on U.S. citizens of U.S. government debt held by the Japanese or the Germans? Is this burden the same as that of U.S. government debt held by Iowans and Californians? Why, or why not?

3. What are the arguments in favor of balancing the federal budget each year? What are the arguments against such a policy? Should the federal budget be balanced over the business cycle rather than during each year?

4. What were the key provisions of the Gramm-Rudman-Hollings Act? How effective was it in reducing the federal deficit?

# SUMMARY

1. The budget deficit is the difference between government expenditures and receipts. In 1990, the U.S. budget deficit equaled about $220 billion; as a percentage of GNP, it was about 4 percent. Many, but not all, economists are concerned about the size and persistence of the deficit.

2. One reason why the public is concerned about deficits is that they are thought to cause inflation. If the government finances the deficit by increasing the money supply, this may well be the case. Even if deficits are not financed right away by the creation of new money, inflationary pressures could build up if the public becomes convinced that sometime in the near future the government will have to increase the money supply substantially to finance all or part of the deficit.

3. Many economists believe that the government's deficit spending may result in a significant cut in investment spending by the private sector. In other words, they fear that government budget deficits may "crowd out" private investment because government borrowing may push up the interest rate, which in turn may reduce private investment. In this way, government deficits may harm future generations because they may result in a smaller total amount of capital being passed on to our descendants.

4. Not all economists believe that deficits really matter. For example, according to Robert Barro, it makes no difference whether government expenditures are paid for by taxes or whether they are financed by government borrowing. From the point of view of the taxpayer, the financing of a government expenditure by borrowing can be regarded as a postponement of taxes. This idea, know as Ricardian equivalence, has been questioned on a variety of counts. It is an area of continuing controversy.

5. A large deficit is often viewed as being more expansionary than a small one (or a surplus). But this can be misleading because budget deficits may occur because the economy is at less than full employment. A better measure is the cyclically adjusted budget balance, which is the difference between tax revenues and government expenditures that would result if gross national product were at its potential, not its actual, level.

6. The national debt is the result of the federal government's borrowings to finance deficits. To the extent that the debt is held by foreigners, we must send goods and services overseas to pay the interest on it (as well, of course, as the principal). Although the size of the debt may be of consequence, it is not true that it somehow may lead to bankruptcy.

7. In recent years, some measures have been adopted which are aimed at eliminating, or at least reducing, the federal budget deficit. Probably the most prominent was the Gramm-Rudman-Hollings Act. In addition, other measures, such as the line-item veto and the balanced budget amendment, have been proposed.

# CONCEPTS FOR REVIEW

**Budget deficit**
**Crowding out**
**Ricardian equivalence**

**Cyclically adjusted budget balance**
**National debt**
**Balanced budget**

**Gramm-Rudman-Hollings Act**
**Line-item veto**
**Balanced budget amendment**

# ECONOMIC GROWTH

HAVING DISCUSSED BUSINESS fluctuations, and the views of various groups of economists concerning what the government can and can't do to stabilize the economy, we turn now to economic growth, which is the long-term increase in per capita output. Economists have long recognized that economic growth and business fluctuations are closely interrelated. Economic growth is due largely to increases in potential output—or, put differently, to rightward shifts in the long-run aggregate supply curve. In this chapter, we look closely at the factors responsible for these increases in potential output.

At the outset, it is important to recognize the importance of economic growth. Until fairly recently in human history, poverty was the rule, not the exception. As Sir Kenneth Clark puts it in his famous lectures on *Civilisation,*

> Poverty, hunger, plagues, disease: they were the background of history right up to the end of the nineteenth century, and most people regarded them as inevitable—like bad weather. Nobody thought they could be cured: St. Francis wanted to sanctify poverty, not abolish it. The old Poor Laws were not designed to abolish poverty but to prevent the poor from becoming a nuisance. All that was required was an occasional act of charity.[1]

To understand how the human condition has changed so much in the industrialized nations of the world, you must understand the process of economic growth. (A discussion of economic growth in less developed countries will be presented in Chapter 34.)

## WHAT IS ECONOMIC GROWTH?

There are two common measures of the rate of ***economic growth***. The first is the rate of growth of a nation's real gross national product, which tells us how rapidly the economy's total real output of goods and services is increasing. The second is the rate of growth of *per capita* real gross national product, which is a better measure of the rate of increase of a nation's standard of living. We shall use the second measure unless we state otherwise. Two aspects of the rate of growth of per capita real gross national product should be noted from the start.

---

[1] K. Clark, *Civilisation,* New York: Harper & Row, 1970.

1. *This measure is only a very crude approximation to the rate of increase of economic welfare.* For one thing, gross national product does not include one good that people prize most highly: leisure. For another, gross national product does not value at all accurately new products and improvements in the quality of goods and services, and does not allow properly either for noneconomic changes in the quality of life or for the costs of environmental pollution. Nor does gross national product take account of how the available output is distributed. Clearly, it makes a difference whether the bulk of the population gets a reasonable share of the output, or whether it goes largely to a favored few.

2. *Small differences in the annual rate of economic growth can make very substantial differences in living standards a few decades hence.* For example, per capita GNP in the United States was about $22,000 in 1990. If it grows at 2 percent per year, it will be about $26,800 (1990 dollars) in the year 2000, whereas if it grows at 3 percent per year, it will be about $29,600 (1990 dollars) in the year 2000. Thus an increase of 1 percentage point in growth rate means a $2,800 (or 10 percent) increase in per capita GNP in the year 2000. Even an increase of 1/4 of 1 percentage point can make a considerable difference. If the growth rate increases from 1 3/4 percent to 2 percent per year, per capita GNP in the year 2000 will increase from $26,200 to $26,800. Of course, this is no more than arithmetic, but that doesn't make it any less important.

# ECONOMIC GROWTH AND THE PRODUCTION POSSIBILITIES CURVE

To represent the process of economic growth, it is convenient to use the production possibilities curve which, as you will recall from Chapter 2, shows all efficient combinations of output an economy can produce. For example, suppose that a society produces only two goods: food and tractors. If this society has at its disposal a fixed amount of resources and if technology is fixed, the production possibilities curve (like the one in Figure 16.1) shows the maximum quantity of food that can be produced, given each amount of tractors produced.

### Shifts of the Production Possibilities Curve

*A nation's potential output increases when its production possibilities curve shifts outward,* as from position *A* to position *B* in Figure 16.2. This happens because the society can produce (and consume) more of one good without having to produce (and consume) less of the other good. Thus its productive capacity must be greater. If the production possibilities curve shifts outward, if the economy is efficient, and if population remains constant, per capita GNP increases and economic growth occurs. Moreover, the faster the production possibilities curve shifts outward, the greater the rate of economic growth.

### No Shift of the Production Possibilities Curve

Even if a nation's production possibilities curve does not shift outward, economic growth can occur if unemployment or inefficiency is reduced. If a nation allows some of its resources to be unemployed or underutilized because of an insufficiency of intended spending, this will cause the

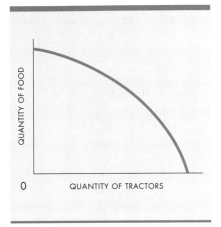

**Figure 16.1**
**Production Possibilities Curve**
The production possibilities curve shows all efficient combinations of output an economy can produce.

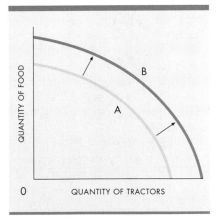

**Figure 16.2**
**Outward Shift of Production Possibilities Curve**
A nation's potential output increases when its production possibilities curve shifts outward from position *A* to position *B*.

economy to operate at a point *inside* the production possibilities curve rather than *on* the curve. The same thing will happen if a nation allocates its resources inefficiently. Clearly, a nation can achieve some economic growth by getting closer to the production possibilities curve through a reduction in unemployment or inefficiency.

## THE AGGREGATE PRODUCTION FUNCTION

A nation's potential output is directly related to the amount of resources it possesses and the extent to which they are used. These resources, or inputs, are of various kinds, including labor, capital, and land. The relationship between the amount used of each of these inputs and the resulting amount of potential output is often called the ***aggregate production function.***

Given that a nation's potential output depends on the amount of labor, capital, and land it uses, then the rate of growth of a nation's potential output must depend, in part at least, on the changes that occur in the amount of each of these inputs that is used. For example, if a nation invests heavily in additional capital, we would expect this to result in a substantial increase in potential output. Thus *a nation's rate of economic growth depends on the extent of the changes in the amounts of the various inputs used*. In addition, *a nation's rate of economic growth depends on the rate of technological change*. The aggregate production function is constructed on the assumption that technology is fixed. Changes in technology result in shifts in the production function, since more output is obtained from a given amount of resources.

## THE LAW OF DIMINISHING MARGINAL RETURNS

If a nation's land, labor, and capital increase, one would certainly expect its output to increase as well. But suppose the nation cannot increase the amount used of all of its resources at the same rate. Instead, suppose it can increase the quantity of one resource, say labor, while the amount of the other resources, like land, is held constant. In this situation, what will be the effect on output if the nation uses more and more of the resource that can be augmented? This is an important question, which occurs both in the present context and in the study of the production processes of the business firm.

To help answer it, economists have formulated the famous ***law of diminishing marginal returns,*** which states that, *if more and more of a resource is used, the quantities of other resources being held constant, the resulting increments of output will decrease after some point has been reached*. Before describing how it sheds light on the process of economic growth, we discuss the nature of this law.

Suppose that we obtain data concerning the amounts of output resulting from the utilization of various amounts of one resource, holding constant the amounts of other resources. For example, suppose that data are obtained concerning the amounts of output resulting from various amounts of labor, holding constant the amounts of capital and land. Then suppose that we determine the *extra* amount of output resulting from the addition of each *extra* unit of labor. According to the law of diminishing marginal returns, this extra amount of output will eventually *decrease,* as more and more labor is utilized with the fixed amounts of capital and land. In other words, beyond some point, *an additional unit of labor will add less and less to total output.*

## An Agricultural Example

To illustrate the workings of this law, consider Table 16.1, which shows the total output—or GNP—of a simple agricultural society under a set of alternative assumptions concerning the number of hours of labor used. For simplicity, we assume that this society produces only one product, corn, so that total output can be measured in bushels of corn. Also, we assume that the amount of land and capital that can be used is fixed in quantity. Column 1 in the table shows various alternative numbers of hours of labor that can be used with this fixed amount of land and capital. Column 2 shows the total output in each case.

Column 3 shows the additional output resulting from the addition of an extra hour of labor; this is called the **marginal product of labor.** For example, if the quantity of labor is between 2 million hours and 3 million hours, the marginal product of labor is 2.5 bushels per hour of labor, because each extra hour of labor results in an extra 2.5 bushels of output.

In Table 16.1, the marginal product of labor increases as more and more labor is used, but only up to a point. Beyond 4 million hours of labor, the marginal product of labor goes down as more and more labor is used. Specifically, the marginal product of labor reaches a maximum of 3.0 bushels per hour when between 3 and 4 million hours of labor are used. Then it falls to 2.0 bushels per hour when between 4 and 5 million hours of labor are used, remains at 2.0 bushels per hour when between 5 and 6 million hours of labor are used, and falls once again to 1.0 bushel per hour when between 6 and 7 million hours of labor are used.

Thus, as predicted by the law of diminishing marginal returns, *the marginal product of labor eventually declines.* Moreover, as shown in column 4 of Table 16.1, the **average product of labor,** which is defined as total output per hour of labor, also falls beyond some point as more and more labor is used with a fixed amount of other resources. This too stems from the law of diminishing marginal returns.

## Table 16.1
## The Law of Diminishing Marginal Returns

| (1) HOURS OF LABOR (MILLIONS) | (2) BUSHELS OF CORN (MILLIONS) | (3) MARGINAL PRODUCT OF LABOR (BUSHELS PER HOUR) | (4) AVERAGE PRODUCT OF LABOR (BUSHELS PER HOUR) |
|---|---|---|---|
| 1 | 1.5 | | 1.50 |
| | | 2.0 | |
| 2 | 3.5 | | 1.75 |
| | | 2.5 | |
| 3 | 6.0 | | 2.00 |
| | | 3.0 | |
| 4 | 9.0 | | 2.25 |
| | | 2.0 | |
| 5 | 11.0 | | 2.20 |
| | | 2.0 | |
| 6 | 13.0 | | 2.17 |
| | | 1.0 | |
| 7 | 14.0 | | 2.00 |
| | | 0.0 | |
| 8 | 14.0 | | 1.75 |

### Reasons for Diminishing Returns

It is easy to see why the law of diminishing marginal returns must be true. For example, imagine what would happen in the simple economy of Table 16.1 if more and more labor were applied to a fixed amount of land. Beyond a point, as more and more labor is used, the extra labor has to be devoted to less and less important tasks. If enough labor is used, it even becomes increasingly difficult to prevent the workers from getting in one another's way! For such reasons, one certainly would expect that, beyond some point, extra amounts of labor would result in smaller and smaller increments of output.

Finally, note two important things about this law. First, at least one resource must be fixed in quantity. The law of diminishing marginal returns does not apply to cases where there is a proportional increase in all resources. Second, technology is assumed to be fixed. The law of diminishing marginal returns does not apply to cases where technology changes.

## THOMAS MALTHUS AND POPULATION GROWTH

A nation's rate of economic growth depends on, among other things, how much the quantities of inputs of various kinds increase. To illuminate the nature of the growth process, we discuss the effect on the rate of economic growth of increasing each kind of input, holding the others constant. We begin by looking at the effects of changes in the quantity of labor. Economists have devoted a great deal of attention to the effects of **population growth** on the rate of economic growth. The classic work was done by Thomas Malthus (1776–1834), a British parson who devoted his life to academic research. The first professional economist, he taught at a college established by the East India Company to train its administrators—and was called "Pop" by his students behind his back. Whether "Pop" stood for population or not, Malthus's fame is based on his theories of population growth.

Malthus believed that the population tends to grow at a geometric rate. In his *Essay on the Principle of Population,* published in 1798, he pointed out the implications of such a constant rate of growth:

> If any person will take the trouble to make the calculation, he will see that if the necessities of life could be obtained without limit, and the number of people could be doubled every twenty-five years, the population which might have been produced from a single pair since the Christian era, would have been sufficient, not only to fill the earth quite full of people, so that four should stand in every square yard, but to fill all the planets of our solar system in the same way, and not only them but all the planets revolving around the stars which are visible to the naked eye, supposing each of them . . . to have as many planets belong to it as our sun has.[2]

In contrast to the human population, which tends to increase at a geometric rate,[3] the supply of land can increase slowly if at all. And land, par-

Thomas Malthus

---

[2] T. Malthus, *Essay on the Principle of Population,* as quoted by R. Heilbroner, *The Worldly Philosophers,* 5th ed., New York: Simon and Schuster, 1980, p. 71. For those who would like to read more concerning the history of economic thought, Heilbroner's book is highly recommended.

[3] Of course, it does not matter to Malthus's argument whether the population doubles every 25 years or every 40 years. The important thing is that it increases at a geometric rate.

# EXAMPLE 16.1    "BIRTH RIGHTS" AND POPULATION CONTROL

Some observers have suggested that a nation's population might be controlled through the use of the price system. For example, the government might say that each couple should be allowed two "free births." After that, the couple would have to buy a certificate granting the right to have an additional child. The government would issue a fixed amount of certificates or "birth rights," each certificate enabling a woman to have a child. The available certificates would be sold to the highest bidders.

(a) What would the supply curve for these certificates look like? (b) Using a diagram, show how the equilibrium price of a certificate would be determined. (c) What factors would determine the location and shape of the demand curve for certificates? (d) What social, political, and religious objections can you see to such a scheme?

are willing to pay for the right to have them. (d) Obviously, many people would feel that such a program would be a major violation of their freedom, particularly since there are strong religious feelings and beliefs involved. People who wanted children and who were too poor to pay for a certificate would certainly object strenuously. There is no serious support for such a system in the United States.

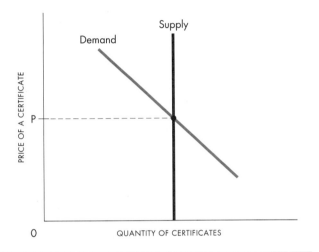

## Solution

(a) The supply curve would be a vertical line since the quantity of certificates supplied is fixed. (b) The diagram is as shown at right, and the equilibrium price is *OP*. (c) The demand curve would be influenced by how much people want children, and how much they

---

ticularly in Malthus's time, was the source of food. Consequently, it seemed to Malthus that the human population was in danger of outrunning its food supply: "Taking the whole earth," he wrote, ". . . and supposing the present population to be equal to a thousand millions, the human species would increase as the numbers, 1, 2, 4, 8, 16, 32, 64, 128, 256, and subsistence as 1, 2, 3, 4, 5, 6, 7, 8, 9. In two centuries, the population would be to the means of subsistence as 256 to 9; in three centuries as 4096 to 13, and in two thousand years the difference would be incalculable."[4]

## A Bleak Prospect

Certainly, Malthus's view of humanity's prospects was bleak, as he himself acknowledged (in a masterpiece of British understatement) when he wrote that "the view has a melancholy hue." Gone is the optimism of Adam Smith. According to Malthus, the prospect for economic progress was very limited. Given the inexorable increase in human numbers, the standard of living will be kept at a minimum level required to keep body and soul together. If it exceeds this level, the population will increase,

---

[4] T. Malthus, "The Principle of Population Growth," reprinted in E. Mansfield, *Principles of Macroeconomics: Readings, Issues, and Cases,* 4th ed. See also the full *Essay on the Principle of Population,* Philip Appleman, ed. New York; Norton, 1976, which contains critical commentary from Malthus's own time to the present.

driving the standard of living back down. On the other hand, if the standard of living is less than this level, the population will decline because of starvation. Certainly, the long-term prospects were anything but bright. Thomas Carlyle, the famous historian and essayist, called economics "the dismal science." To a considerable extent, economics acquired this bad name through the efforts of Parson Malthus.

Malthus's theory can be interpreted in terms of the law of diminishing marginal returns. Living in what was still largely an agricultural society, he emphasized the role of land and labor as resources, and assumed a relatively fixed level of technology. Since land is fixed, increases in labor—due to population growth—will eventually cause the marginal product of labor to get smaller and smaller because of the law of diminishing marginal returns. In other words, because of this law, the marginal product of labor will behave as shown in Figure 16.3, with the result that continued growth of the labor force will ultimately bring economic decline—that is, a reduction in output per worker. This happens because, as the marginal product of labor falls with increases in the labor force, the average product of labor will eventually fall as well—and the average product of labor is another name for output per worker.

Of course, Malthus recognized that various devices could keep the population down—war, famine, birth-control measures, among others. In fact, he tried to describe and evaluate the importance of various checks on population growth. For example, suppose that population tends to grow to the point where output per worker is at a subsistence level—just sufficient to keep body and soul together. If this is the case, and if the subsistence level of output per worker is *OA*, then the labor force will tend to equal *OP* in Figure 16.3. Why? Because, as noted above, Malthus believed that if the standard of living rises appreciably above *OA*, population will increase, thus forcing it back toward *OA*. On the other hand, if the standard of living falls below *OA*, some of the population will starve, thus pushing it back toward *OA*.

## Effects of Population Growth

Was Malthus right? Among some of the less developed nations of the world, his analysis seems very relevant today. During the past 40 years, the population of the less developed nations has grown very rapidly, in part because of the decrease in death rates attributable to the transfer of medical advances from the industrialized countries to the less developed countries. Between 1940 and 1970, the total population of Asia, Africa, and Oceania almost doubled. There has been a tendency for growing populations to push hard against food supplies in some of the countries of Africa, Latin America, and Asia; and the Malthusian model can explain important elements of the situation.

However, Malthus's theory seems far less relevant or correct for the industrialized countries. In contrast to his model, population has not increased to the point where the standard of living has been pushed down to the subsistence level. On the contrary, the standard of living has increased dramatically in all of the industrialized nations. The most important mistake Malthus made was to underestimate the extent and importance of technological change. Instead of remaining fixed, the marginal-product-of-labor curve in Figure 16.3 moved gradually to the right, as new methods and new products increased the efficiency of agriculture. In other words, the situation was as shown in Figure 16.4. Thus,

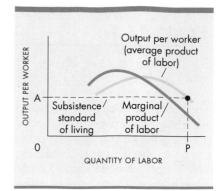

**Figure 16.3**
**Diminishing Marginal Returns and the Effect of Population Growth**
According to Malthus, the labor force will tend to *OP* because, if output per worker exceeds *OA*, population will increase, and if output per worker is less than *OA*, starvation will reduce the population.

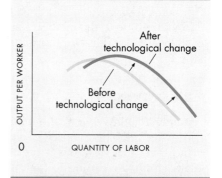

**Figure 16.4**
**Shift over Time in the Marginal Product of Labor**
Technological change has shifted the marginal-product-of-labor curve to the right.

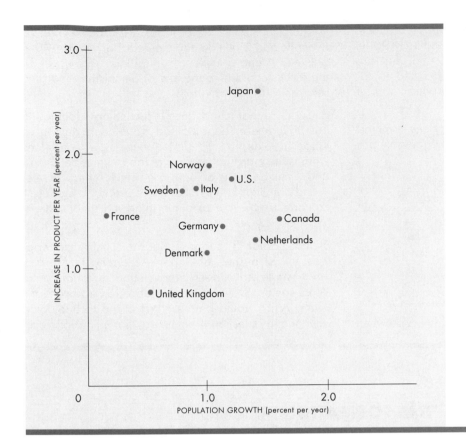

**Figure 16.5**
**Relationship between Population Growth and Increases in National Product per Capita, 11 Industrialized Nations, 1913–59**
In industrialized nations, there is little or no relationship between a nation's rate of population growth and its rate of economic growth.

as population increased, the marginal product of labor did not go down. Instead, technological change prevented the productivity of extra agricultural workers from falling.

Among the industrialized nations, have countries with relatively high rates of growth of population had relatively low—or relatively high—rates of economic growth? In general, there seems to be little or no relationship between a nation's rate of population increase and its rate of economic growth. Figure 16.5 plots the rate of population increase against the rate of growth of output per capita in 11 industrialized nations between 1913 and 1959. The results suggest that there is little or no relation between them; and the relationship that exists appears to be direct rather than inverse.

## TEST YOURSELF

1. Suppose that a society produces only two goods, food and tractors, and that its population possibilities curve in 1991 and 1992 is given at right.

If this society produces 4,000 tractors and 3 million tons of food in 1991 and 5,000 tractors and 3 million tons of food in 1992 (its population remaining constant), has any economic growth occurred between 1991 and 1992? If so, to what is it due?

| QUANTITY OF FOOD (MILLIONS OF TONS) | QUANTITY OF TRACTORS (THOUSANDS OF TRACTORS) |
| --- | --- |
| 0 | 9 |
| 1 | 8 |
| 2 | 7 |
| 3 | 5 |
| 4 | 3 |
| 5 | 0 |

2. Suppose that the society in Question 1 produces 6,000 tractors and 3 million tons of food in 1993 (its population remaining the same as in 1992), has any economic growth occurred between 1992 and 1993? If so, is it due entirely to a shift in the production possibilities curve? How can you tell?

3. Suppose that a society produces only one commodity, wheat, and that it has the following aggregate production function:

| HOURS OF LABOR (MILLIONS) | BUSHELS OF WHEAT (MILLIONS) |
|---|---|
| 0 | 0 |
| 1 | 2 |
| 2 | 4 |
| 3 | 6 |
| 4 | 7 |
| 5 | 7 |

What is the marginal product of labor when between 1 and 2 million hours of labor are used? When between 2 and 3 million hours of labor are used? When between 4 and 5 million hours of labor are used? Do the results conform to the law of diminishing marginal returns? Why, or why not?

4. Suppose that an advance in technology doubles the output that can be obtained from each amount of labor in Question 3. Under these new conditions, what is the marginal product of labor when between 1 and 2 million hours of labor are used? When between 4 and 5 million hours of labor are used? Do the results conform to the law of diminishing marginal returns? Why, or why not?

5. In Question 3, suppose that the subsistence wage was 1,400 bushels of wheat. According to Malthus, what would have been the equilibrium labor force? What factors would push the labor force toward this level? What would be the effect of the technological advance in Question 4 on the equilibrium labor force?

# DAVID RICARDO AND CAPITAL FORMATION

A contemporary and good friend of Malthus's who also contributed to the theory of economic growth was David Ricardo (1772–1823). Of all the titans of economics, he is probably least known to the general public. Smith, Malthus, Marx, and Keynes are frequently encountered names. Ricardo is not, although he made many brilliant contributions to economic thought. An extremely successful stockbroker who retired at the age of 42 with a very large fortune, he devoted much of his time to highly theoretical analyses of the economic system and its workings. In contrast to Malthus, who was reviled for his pessimistic doctrines, Ricardo and his writings were widely admired in his own time. He was elected to the House of Commons and was highly respected there.

### Ricardo on Income Distribution

Ricardo was concerned in much of his work with the distribution of income. Unlike Adam Smith, who paid much less attention to the conflict among classes, Ricardo emphasized the struggle between the industrialists—a relatively new and rising class in his time—and the landowners—the old aristocracy that resisted the rise of the industrial class. This clash was reflected in the struggle in Britain around 1800 over the so-called Corn Laws (*corn* being a general term covering all types of grain). Because of the increase of population, the demand for grain increased in Britain, causing the price of grain to rise greatly. This meant higher profits for the landowners. But the industrialists complained bitterly about the increase in the price of food, because higher food prices meant that they had to pay higher wages. As the price of grain increased, merchants began to import cheap grain from abroad. But the landowners, who dom-

David Ricardo

inated Parliament, passed legislation—the Corn Laws—to keep cheap grain out of Britain. In effect the Corn Laws imposed a high tariff or duty on grain.

According to Ricardo's analysis, the landlords were bound to capture most of the benefits of economic progress, unless their control of the price of grain could be weakened. As national output increased and population expanded, poorer and poorer land had to be brought under cultivation to produce the extra food. As the cost of producing grain increased, its price would increase too—and so would the rents of the landlords. The workers and the industrialists, on the other hand, would benefit little, if at all. As the price of grain increased, the workers would have to get higher wages—but only high enough to keep them at a subsistence level (since Ricardo agreed entirely with his friend Malthus on the population issue). Thus the workers would be no better off; and neither would the industrialists, who would wind up with lower profits because of the increase in wage rates.

Ricardo felt that the Corn Laws should be repealed and that free trade in grain should be permitted. In a beautiful piece of theoretical analysis that is still reasonably fresh and convincing more than a century after its publication, he laid out the basic principles of international trade and pointed out the benefits to all countries that can be derived by specialization and free trade. For example, suppose that England is relatively more efficient at producing textiles, and France is relatively more efficient at producing wine. Then, on the basis of Ricardo's analysis, it can be shown that each country is likely to be better off by specializing in the product it is more efficient at producing—textiles in England, wine in France—and trading this product for the one the other country specializes in producing. In the next chapter, we will discuss this argument in more detail; it is a very important part of economics.

## Ricardo's View of Capital Formation

Let's turn to the effect on economic growth of increases in physical capital, holding other inputs and technology fixed. Ricardo constructed some interesting theories concerning the effects of **capital formation**—i.e., investment in plant and equipment—on economic growth. Other things held constant, a nation's output depends on the amount of plant and equipment that it has and operates. Moreover, one can draw a curve showing the marginal product of capital—the extra output that would result from an extra dollar's worth of capital—under various assumptions about the total amount of capital in existence. This curve will slope downward to the right, as shown in Figure 16.6, because of the law of diminishing marginal returns. As more and more capital is accumulated, its marginal product eventually must decrease. For example, if $100 billion is the total investment in plant and equipment (or total capital), the extra output to be derived from an extra dollar of investment is worth $A; whereas if the total investment is increased to $150 billion, the economy must resort to less productive investments, and the extra output to be derived from an extra dollar of investment is only worth $B.

The curve in Figure 16.6 leads to the conclusion that investment in plant and equipment, although it will increase the growth rate up to some point, will eventually be unable to increase it further. As more and more is invested in new plant and equipment, less and less productive projects must be undertaken. Finally, when all the productive projects have been

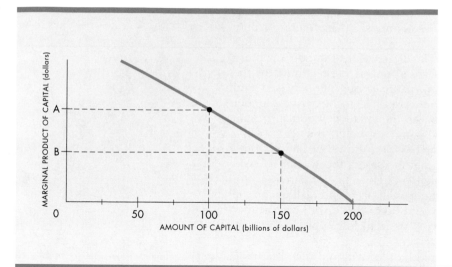

**Figure 16.6**
**Marginal Product of Capital**
This curve shows the marginal product of capital, under various assumptions concerning the total amount of capital. For example, if there is $100 billion of capital, the marginal product of capital is $A, whereas if there is $150 billion of capital, the marginal product of capital is $B.

carried out, further investment in plant and equipment will be useless. At this point—$200 billion of total capital in Figure 16.6—further investment in plant and equipment will not increase output at all.

This kind of analysis led Ricardo to the pessimistic conclusion that the economy would experience decreases in the profitability of investment in plant and equipment, and eventual termination of economic growth. Also, he expected increases in the ratio of capital to output, because he expected increases in the total amount of capital to be accompanied by decreases in the marginal product of capital.

To illustrate this, suppose that an economy's output equals $1 trillion and its total capital is $3 trillion. Suppose too that $100 billion of extra capital will result in $30 billion in extra output, another $100 billion of extra capital will result in $20 billion in extra output, and still another $100 billion in extra capital will result in $10 billion in extra output. Then the amount of capital per dollar of output will be (3,000 + 100)/(1,000 + 30) if $100 billion is invested, (3,000 + 200)/(1,000 + 50) if $200 billion is invested, and (3,000 + 300)/(1,000 + 60) if $300 billion is invested. Since the marginal product of capital is decreasing, the amount of capital per dollar of output is increasing—from 3 to 3.01 to 3.05 to 3.11.

## Was Ricardo Right?

Have we seen increases in the amount of capital per dollar of output, decreases in the profitability of investment in plant and equipment, and eventual termination of economic growth? No. Ricardo, like Malthus, was led astray by underestimating the extent and impact of future changes in technology. Suppose that, because of the development of major new products and processes, lots of new opportunities for profitable investment arise. Obviously, the effect on the curve in Figure 16.6 is to shift it to the right, because there are more investment opportunities than ever before above a certain level of productivity. But if this curve shifts to the right, as shown in Figure 16.7, we may be able to avoid Ricardo's pessimistic conclusions.

To see how this can occur, note that, if X in Figure 16.7 is the relevant curve in a particular year and if $100 billion is the total amount of capital,

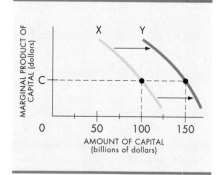

**Figure 16.7**
**Effects of Technological Change on the Marginal Product of Capital**
Technological change has shifted the marginal-product-of-capital curve to the right. (Actually, Ricardo's variable input was a combined dose of capital and labor.)

an extra dollar of investment in plant and equipment would have a marginal product of $C. A decade later, if Y is the relevant curve and if the total amount of capital has grown to $150 billion, the marginal product of an extra dollar of investment in plant and equipment is still $C. Thus there is no reduction in the productivity of investment opportunities despite the 50 percent increase in the total amount of capital. Because of technological change and other factors, productive and profitable new investment opportunities are opened up as fast as old ones are invested in.

The history of the United States is quite consistent with this sort of shift in investment opportunities over time. Even though we have poured an enormous amount of money into new plant and equipment, we have not exhausted or reduced the productivity or profitability of investment opportunities. The rate of return on investment in new plant and equipment has not fallen. Instead, it has fluctuated around a fairly constant level during the past 70 years. Moreover, the amount of capital per dollar of output has remained surprisingly constant. It has not increased.

# CAPITAL FORMATION AND ECONOMIC GROWTH

To see more clearly the role of investment in the process of economic growth, let's extend the simple model we discussed in Chapter 6. Suppose we ignore the government (and the rest of the world) and consider only the private sector of the economy. Suppose that the full-employment, noninflationary GNP this year is $1,000 billion, and that the consumption function is such that consumption expenditure is $900 billion if GNP is $1,000 billion. If intended investment this year is $100 billion, with the result that GNP is in fact $1,000 billion, *next year's full-employment GNP will increase because this year's investment will increase the nation's productive capacity*. In other words, this year's investment increases next year's full-employment GNP. The amount of the increase in full-employment GNP depends on the **capital-output ratio,** which is the number of dollars of investment (or extra capital goods) required to produce an extra dollar of output. For example, if the capital-output ratio is 2, $2 of investment is required to increase full-employment GNP by $1.

## Effect of Investment on Full-Employment GNP

Let's look more closely at the effect of investment on full-employment GNP. If the capital-output ratio is 2, full-employment GNP will increase by $50 billion as a consequence of the $100 billion of investment. Thus full-employment GNP next year is $1,050 billion. On the other hand, suppose that this year's investment is $200 billion rather than $100 billion, and that the consumption function is such that consumption expenditure is $800 billion rather than $900 billion if GNP is $1,000 billion. What will full-employment GNP be next year? If the capital-output ratio is 2, it will be $1,100 billion. Why? Because the $200 billion in investment will increase full-employment GNP by $100 billion—from $1,000 billion to $1,100 billion.

Thus the full-employment GNP will be larger if investment is $200 billion than if it is $100 billion. Similarly, the full-employment GNP will be larger if investment is $300 billion than if it is $200 billion. If the capital-output ratio is 2, the full-employment GNP will be $1,150 billion next year if investment is $300 billion. Why? Because the $300 billion in investment will increase full-employment GNP by $150 billion—from $1,000 to $1,150 billion.

In general, the greater the percent of GNP that the society devotes to investment this year, the greater will be the increase in its full-employment GNP. Thus, *so long as the economy sustains noninflationary full employment and the capital-output ratio remains constant, the rate of growth of national output will be directly related to the percent of GNP devoted to investment.*[5]

### Some Evidence Concerning the Effects of Investment

Certainly, this result seems sensible enough. If a country wants to increase its growth rate, it should produce more blast furnaces, machine tools, and plows, and less cosmetics, household furniture, and sports cars. But all this is theory. What do the facts suggest? Table 16.2 shows the rate of investment and the growth rate in six major industrialized nations of the non-Communist world in the 1970s. The investment rate was highest in Japan; so was the growth rate. The investment rates were lowest in the United States and the United Kingdom, and their growth rates were among the lowest. Of course, this does not prove that there is any simple cause-and-effect relationship between the investment rate and the growth rate, but it certainly is compatible with the view that investment influences growth.

As revealed in the historical record of the United States, between 1929 and 1947 the amount of U.S. plant and equipment increased at about the same rate as the labor force. On the other hand, between 1947 and 1965, the amount of U.S. plant and equipment increased much more rapidly than the labor force. These facts would lead one to expect that the rate of economic growth would be more rapid in the latter period; and, in keeping with the theory, this turns out to be true. Again, one must be cautious about interpreting such comparisons. Lots of other things besides the investment rate were different in 1947–65 than in 1929–47, and these other things, not the investment rate, may have been responsible for the difference in growth rates. However, it seems likely that the difference in investment rates was at least partially responsible.

## THE ROLE OF HUMAN CAPITAL

A nation's rate of economic growth is influenced by the rate at which it invests in human capital as well as physical capital. It may seem odd to speak of *human* capital, but every society builds up a certain amount of human capital through investments in formal education, on-the-job-training, and health programs. You often hear people talk about investing in their children's future by putting them through college. For the economy

**Table 16.2**
**Rate of Growth of Output (1978–80) and Investment as Percentage of Output (1970–77)**

| NATION | RATE OF GROWTH OF OUTPUT (PERCENT) | PERCENT OF OUTPUT INVESTED |
|---|---|---|
| | *Annual average* | |
| France | 2.8 | 18.8 |
| Germany | 3.3 | 18.7 |
| Canada | 2.4 | 19.3 |
| Japan | 5.0 | 26.7 |
| United Kingdom | 1.0 | 17.6 |
| United States | 2.6 | 14.5 |

*Source: Economic Report of the President.*

---

[5] It can be shown that the rate of growth of GNP equals $s/b$, where $s$ is the proportion of GNP that is saved (and invested), and $b$ is the capital-output ratio, assuming that both $s$ and $b$ are constant and that full employment is maintained. For example, if $b$ is 2 and $s = .10$, GNP will grow at 5 percent per year, since $.10/2 = .05$. This result is part of the so-called Harrod-Domar growth model developed by Sir Roy Harrod of Oxford and Evsey Domar of MIT Although useful, this result must be used with caution since it is based on highly simplified assumptions.

as a whole, the expenditure on education and public health can also be viewed—at least partly—as an investment, because consumption is sacrificed in the present in order to make possible a higher level of per capita output in the future.

The United States invests in human capital on a massive scale. In 1987, it devoted roughly $500 billion to gross investment in formal education. In addition, $100 billion was spent on worker training, excluding informal efforts to improve skills and performance. These enormous and rapidly growing investments in human capital have unquestionably increased the productivity, versatility, and adaptability of our labor force. They have certainly made a major contribution to economic growth.

Theodore Schultz

Income tends to rise with a person's education. Using this relationship to measure the influence of education on a person's productivity, some economists, notably the University of Chicago's Nobel laureate Theodore Schultz and Gary Becker, have tried to estimate the profitability, both to society and to the person, of an investment in various levels of education. Becker has tried to estimate the rate of return from a person's investment in a college education. According to his estimates, the typical urban white male received about a 10 percent return (after taxes) on his investment in tuition, room, books, and other college expenses (including the earnings he gave up by being in college rather than at work). This was a relatively high return—much higher, for example, than if the student (or his family) simply put the equivalent amount of money in a savings bank or in government bonds.

During the 1970s and early 1980s, rates of return from investments in schooling were estimated to be 10–13 percent for secondary education and 8–10 percent for higher education. However, because it is so difficult to adjust for differences among people in ability and effort, these results should be viewed with caution.

## THE ROLE OF TECHNOLOGICAL CHANGE

A nation's rate of economic growth depends on the rate of technological change, as well as on the extent to which quantities of inputs of various kinds increase. Indeed, the rate of technological change is perhaps the most important single determinant of a nation's rate of economic growth. Recall from Chapter 1 that technology is knowledge concerning the industrial and agricultural arts. Thus **technological change** consists of new methods of producing existing products; new designs that make it possible to produce goods with important new characteristics; and new techniques of organization, marketing, and management.

Consider the computer, one of the most important technological advances of the twentieth century. Computers have increased production, decreased waste, improved quality control, and reduced the chance of damage to equipment. In banking, for example, they have made possible much faster processes for sorting checks, balancing accounts, and computing service charges.

We have already seen that technological change can shift the curves in both Figures 16.4 and 16.7, thus warding off the law of diminishing marginal returns. But note that new knowledge by itself has little impact. *Unless knowledge is applied, it has little effect on the rate of economic growth.* A change in technology, when applied for the first time, is called an **innovation,** and the firm that first applies it is called an **innovator.** Innovation is a key stage in the process leading to the full evaluation and utilization of a new process or product. The innovator must be willing to take the risks involved in introducing a new and untried process, good, or service; and in many cases, these risks are high. Once a change in technology has been applied for the first time, the **diffusion process**—the process by which the use of the innovation spreads from firm to firm and from use to use—begins. How rapidly an innovation spreads depends heavily on its economic advantages over older methods or products. The more profitable the use of the innovation is, the more rapidly it will spread.

Joseph Schumpeter, Harvard's distinguished economist and social theorist, stressed the important role played by innovators in the process of economic growth. In Schumpeter's view, innovators are the mainspring of economic progress, the people with the foresight to see how new things can be brought into being and the courage and resourcefulness to surmount the obstacles to change. For their trouble, innovators receive profit; but this profit eventually is whittled down by competitors who imitate the innovators. The innovators push the curves in Figures 16.4 and 16.7 to the right, and once their innovations are assimilated by the economy, other innovators may shove these curves somewhat farther to the right. For example, one innovator introduces vacuum tubes, a later innovator introduces semiconductors; one innovator introduces the steam locomotive, a later innovator introduces the diesel locomotive. This process goes on and on—and is a main source of economic growth.

## The Computer: A Case Study

To get a better feel for the nature of technological change and the process of innovation, let's return to the important case of the computer. Many of the basic ideas underlying the computer go back to Charles Babbage, a brilliant nineteenth-century British inventor; but not until 1946 was the first electronic computer, the ENIAC, designed and constructed. John Mauchly and J. Presper Eckert, both professors at the Moore School of Electrical Engineering at the University of Pennsylvania, were responsible for the ENIAC's design and construction. The work was supported by the U.S. Army. John von Neumann, a famous mathematician at the Institute for Advanced Study at Princeton, added the important concepts of stored programming and conditional transfer.

After the war, Mauchly and Eckert established a small firm to produce electronic computers. Their firm was acquired by Remington Rand, which in 1951 marketed the Univac I, a machine used by the Census Bureau. The International Business Machines Corporation (IBM), the leading company in office machinery and data processing, which before this had been cautious about the potential market for computers, was spurred into action by Remington Rand's success. Once it entered the field, IBM's financial resources, strong marketing organization, and engineering strength enabled it to capture a very large share of the computer market, here and abroad. In the United States, IBM's share of the market grew to about 70 percent during the 1960s.

The computer has been an extremely important stimulus to economic growth. By 1990 computers were engaged in a host of activities in a wide variety of industries. These computers have had important effects on production techniques. For example, in the chemical, petroleum, and steel industries, computers were an important step in the evolution of control techniques. Computers helped to determine and enforce the best conditions for process operation, as well as acting as data loggers. They could also be programmed to help carry out the complex sequence of operations required to start up or shut down a plant.

Obviously, the computer has enabled us to produce more output from a given amount of resources. In other words, it has enabled us to push the production possibilities curve outward, thus increasing our rate of economic growth. But it must be recognized that the process by which the computer has had this effect has by no means been simple or straightforward. Many people in many countries were involved in the development of the basic ideas. Many organizations, public and private, funded the experimental work. Firms of various types were the innovators with respect to particular aspects of the modern computer. And countless individuals and organizations had to be willing to accept, work with, and invest in computers.

## DETERMINANTS OF TECHNOLOGICAL CHANGE

What determines the rate of technological change and the rate at which changes in technology are applied and spread? Clearly, *the nature and extent of a nation's scientific capability, and the size and quality of its educational system are of fundamental importance.* The first thing that must be said about the influence of a nation's scientific capability on its rate of technological change is that science and technology are two quite different things that have drawn together only recently. Until the twentieth century, it was not true that technology was built on science. Even today, many technological advances rely on little in the way of science. However, in more and more areas of the economy (such as aircraft, electronics, and chemicals), the rapid application of new technology has come to depend on a strong scientific base. Merely to imitate or adapt what others have developed, a firm in these areas needs access to high-caliber scientists.

A nation's educational system also has a fundamental influence on the rate of technological change. First, and perhaps most obviously, it determines how many scientists and engineers are graduated, and how competent they are. Clearly, the rate of technological change depends on the quantity and quality of scientific and engineering talent available in the society. Second, the educational system influences the inventiveness and adaptability of the nation's work force. Despite the closer links between technology and science, workers and independent inventors remain important sources of inventions in many areas. Third, the educational system also influences the rate of technological change and innovation via the training of managers.

*Industrial managers are a key agent in the innovative process.* We must emphasize that the proper management of innovation is much more than establishing and maintaining a research and development laboratory that produces a great deal of good technical output. In many industries, most important innovations are not based in any significant degree on the firms' research and development (R and D). And even when the basic idea does come from a firm's own R and D, the coupling of R and D with marketing and production is crucial. Many good ideas are not applied properly because the potential users do not really understand them, and many R and D projects are technically successful but commercially irrele-

# HAS THE UNITED STATES LOST ITS TECHNOLOGICAL EDGE?

Although it is very difficult to measure international differences in technological levels, the available evidence suggests that the United States long has been a leader in technology. Scattered impressionistic evidence indicates that this was true in many fields before 1850. After 1850, the available quantitative evidence indicates that productivity was higher in the United States than in Europe, that the United States had a strong export position in technically progressive industries, and that Europeans tended to imitate American techniques. The existence of such a gap in the nineteenth century would not be surprising, since this was a heyday of American invention. (Among the key American inventions of the period was the system of interchangeable parts.) Needless to say, the United States did not lead in all fields, but it appears that we held a technological lead in many important parts of manufacturing.

After World War II, there was a widespread feeling that this technological gap widened, due in part to the wartime devastation of many countries in Europe and elsewhere. In the 1960s, Europeans expressed considerable concern over the technology gap. They asserted that superior know-how stemming from scientific and technical achievements in the United States had allowed American companies to obtain large shares of European markets in fields like aircraft, space equipment, computers, and other electronic products. In 1966, Italy's foreign minister Amintore Fanfani went so far as to call for a "technological Marshall Plan" to speed the flow of American technology across the Atlantic. In response to this concern, the Organization for Economic Cooperation and Development (OECD) made a large study of the nature and causes of the technology gap. It concluded that a large gap existed in computers and some electronic components, but that no general or fundamental gap existed in pharmaceuticals, bulk plastics, iron and steel, machine tools (other than numerically controlled machine tools), nonferrous metals (other than tantalum and titanium), and scientific instruments (other than electronic test and measuring instruments). Thus the OECD studies indicated that the American technological lead was greatest in relatively research-intensive sectors of the economy.

The factors responsible for these technological

Bell Laboratories headquarters in Murray Hill, NJ

gaps were difficult to sort out and measure. A host of factors—the social climate, the educational system, the scientific community, the amount and quality of industrial research, the nature of domestic markets, the quality of management, and government policies, among others—influence a country's technological position. According to the OECD studies, the size and homogeneity of the American market was an important factor, but not a decisive one. Also, the large size of American firms was another factor, but not a decisive one. In addition, the large government expenditures on research and development (R and D) in the United States played an important role. Also, according to the OECD studies, a very important factor was that American firms had a significant lead in the techniques of management, including the management of R and D and the coupling of R and D with marketing and production.[1]

During the past twenty years, the U.S. technological lead has been reduced in a great many areas. Frequently, this lead no longer exists at all. The following table shows the difference between the annual rate of growth of output per hour of labor in the United States and in other major industrial nations during 1950–85. Clearly, productivity increased much more rapidly in practically all these other countries than in the United States. In industries like

[1] E. Mansfield et al., *Technology Transfer, Productivity, and Economic Policy,* New York: Norton, 1982.

steel and automobiles, the United States has yielded the technological lead to others, notably the Japanese. Even in relatively new industries born largely in the United States, such as semiconductors, many fault the American industries for lagging behind the Japanese.

Confronted with this trend, the federal govern-

---

**Difference between Annual Growth Rate of Manufacturing Output per Hour of Labor in Selected Foreign Countries and in the United States**

| COUNTRY | 1950–57 | 1957–66 | 1966–73 | 1973–79 | 1979–85 |
|---|---|---|---|---|---|
| (DIFFERENCE FROM THE UNITED STATES, IN PERCENTAGE POINTS) | | | | | |
| West Germany | 4.8 | 3.3 | 3.0 | 2.8 | 0.2 |
| France | 2.2 | 3.2 | 3.6 | 3.5 | 0.9 |
| Italy | 3.6 | 3.6 | 4.1 | 1.9 | 0.8 |
| Japan | 7.5 | 5.2 | 8.3 | 4.0 | 2.5 |
| United Kingdom | —0.8 | 0.5 | 2.2 | 0.2 | 0.9 |
| China | 1.4 | 1.3 | 2.2 | 0.8 | —1.4 |

*Source:* Panel on Technology and Employment, *Technology and Employment,* Washington, D.C.: National Academy Press, 1987, p. 83.

---

ment under both Democratic and Republican administrations has tried to establish appropriate policies. During President Reagan's administration, Congress established a 25 percent (later reduced to 20 percent) incremental tax credit for R and D. That is, a firm could reduce its income tax liability by an amount equal to 25 percent of the difference between its current R and D expenditure and the average amount of its R and D expenditure in the previous three years. The available evidence suggests that this R and D tax credit has had only a limited effect on industrial R and D spending, but it does appear to have increased it somewhat.

The Bush administration, like its predecessor, has avoided subsidizing specific new technologies. In the words of President Bush's Council of Economic Advisers, "The private sector has inherent advantages over government in identifying potentially useful new technologies. Private decisions are disciplined by careful market evaluations of their prospects. Government decisions, in contrast, are often influenced by noneconomic objectives and based on information supplied by self-interested parties, without regard to taxpayers' cost. Governments in the United States and elsewhere have shown themselves to be

less able than private businesses to pick specific technologies that will be commercially successful."[2]

Nonetheless, in response to pressure from Congress and from within the administration itself, the Bush administration began in 1991 to move in the direction of subsidizing civilian R and D. The White House Office of Science and Technology Policy published a list of critical technologies for industry. Recommendations were made that defense R and D be cut, and that civilian R and D be expanded. The emphasis seemed to be on technologies that would be applicable in a variety of areas and that were in a pre-competitive stage. It will take many years to determine what, if anything, will come out of this ferment.

Part of America's problem seems to be due to its apparent inability to match the Japanese as quick and effective users of technologies developed elsewhere. American firms, long accustomed to leading the world, do not monitor, imitate, and build on the technological advances of their rivals (here and abroad) as quickly and cheaply as do the Japanese. However, for innovations based on technologies developed largely within the innovating firm, there is no evidence that the Japanese can develop and introduce a new product or process more quickly or cheaply than the Americans.

## Probing Deeper

1. How can one tell whether the United States does, or does not, have a technological lead in a particular industry?

2. What factors determine whether the United States has such a lead?

3. What difference does it make to the American people if the United States loses whatever lead it had in a particular industry?

4. If it is true that the United States is losing its technological lead in a particular industry, why should the government intervene? (Can't the private sector be counted on to take the appropriate measures?)

5. Is the fact that an industry is in trouble, or that it is declining, or that it has difficulty competing with foreign firms an adequate justification for additional investment in R and D in this industry?

6. Are there advantages as well as disadvantages resulting from the reduction of America's technological lead? If so, what are they?

---

[2] *Economic Report of the President, 1990,* p. 117.

vant because they were not designed with sufficient comprehension of market realities. Typically, successful technological innovations seem to be stimulated by perceived production and marketing needs, not solely by technological opportunities. In other words, most of the time it takes a market-related impetus to prompt work on a successful innovation.

In addition, *the rate of technological change depends on the organization of industry and the nature of markets.* Although a certain amount of industrial concentration may promote more rapid technological change, increases in concentration beyond a moderate level probably reduce rather than increase the rate of technological change. The rate of technological change also depends on the scale and sophistication of available markets. The scale of the market determines how many units of a new product or process are likely to be sold, which in turn influences the cost per unit of developing and introducing an innovation. Finally, it is extremely important to note that a country that is not a technological leader can still achieve considerable technological change by borrowing and transferring technology from the leaders.

## Technological Change and Labor Productivity

It is difficult to measure the rate of technological change. Perhaps the most frequently used measure is the rate of growth of labor productivity: the rate of growth of output per hour of labor. Unfortunately, this measure is influenced by lots of other factors besides the rate of technological change. Nonetheless, despite its inadequacies, it is worthwhile to look briefly at how rapidly productivity has increased in the United States over the long run. Since about 1890, the nation's real output per hour of labor increased by about 2 percent per year—and these productivity gains were widely diffused, real hourly earnings growing about as rapidly, on the average, as output per hour of labor.

As indicated in Table 16.3, the rate of growth of labor productivity slowed considerably in the 1970s and 1980s. According to some ob-

**Table 16.3**
**Percent Change in Output per Hour of Labor, Nonfarm Business Sector, U.S., 1954–90**

| YEAR | PERCENT CHANGE[a] | YEAR | PERCENT CHANGE[a] |
|------|------|------|------|
| 1990 | –0.6 | | |
| 1988 | 2.2 | 1970 | 0.3 |
| 1986 | 1.6 | 1968 | 3.3 |
| 1984 | 3.1 | 1966 | 2.5 |
| 1982 | 0.2 | 1964 | 3.9 |
| 1980 | –0.7 | 1962 | 3.6 |
| 1978 | 0.6 | 1960 | 0.8 |
| 1976 | 3.2 | 1958 | 2.4 |
| 1974 | –2.5 | 1956 | 0.3 |
| 1972 | 3.7 | 1954 | 1.4 |

[a] Percent change from the previous year.
*Source: Economic Report of the President, 1985, 1988, and 1991.*

servers, this productivity slowdown has been due in part to a decline in the rate of innovation in the United States. In their opinion, the rate of introduction of new products and processes has fallen. It is true that the patent rate fell after about 1969, and that direct evidence of a fall in the rate of innovation has existed in some industries, like pharmaceuticals, where one can measure the number of major innovations that are carried out per unit of time. But in other industries, such as microelectronics, the rate of innovation has seemed hale and hearty.

## ENTREPRENEURSHIP AND THE SOCIAL ENVIRONMENT

Robotics in U.S. industry

Still another set of basic factors influencing a nation's level of potential output and its rate of economic growth is the economic, social, political, and religious climate of the nation. It is difficult, if not impossible, to measure the effect of these factors, but there can be no doubt of their importance. Some societies despise material welfare and emphasize the glories of the next world. Some societies are subject to such violent political upheavals that it is risky, if not foolish, to invest in the future. Some societies are governed so corruptly that economic growth is frustrated. And some societies look down on people engaged in industry, trade, or commerce. Obviously, such societies are less likely to experience rapid economic growth than others with a more favorable climate and conditions.

The relatively rapid economic growth of the United States was undoubtedly stimulated in part by the attitude of its people toward material gain. It is commonplace to note that the United States is a materialistic society, a society that esteems business success, that bestows prestige on the rich, that accepts the Protestant ethic (which, crudely stated, is that work is good), and that encourages individual initiative. The United States has been criticized over and over again for some of these traits—often by nations frantically trying to imitate its economic success. Somewhat less obvious is the fact that, because the United States is a young country whose people came from a variety of origins, it did not inherit many feudal components in the structure of society. This too was important.

The United States has also been characterized by great economic and political freedom, by institutions that have been flexible enough to adjust to change, and by a government that has encouraged competition in the marketplace. This has meant fewer barriers to new ideas. Also, the United States has for a long time enjoyed internal peace, order, and general respect for property rights. There have been no violent revolutions since the Civil War, and for many years we were protected from strife in other lands by two oceans—which then seemed much broader than they do now. All these factors undoubtedly contributed to rapid economic growth.

## THE GAP BETWEEN ACTUAL AND POTENTIAL OUTPUT

Up to this point, our discussion of economic growth has centered on the factors that determine how rapidly a nation's potential output grows—factors like technological change, increased education, investment in plant and equipment, and increases in the labor force. In other words, we have focused on the factors responsible for rightward shifts of the long-run aggregate supply curve. Although we have not paid much attention in this chapter to the gap between actual and potential output, this does not mean that increases in output per capita cannot be achieved by reducing this gap. Obviously, they can be.

However, only so much can be achieved by squeezing the slack out of the economy. For example, if there is a 7 percent unemployment rate, output per capita can be increased by perhaps 6 percent simply by reducing the unemployment rate to 5 percent. *But this is a one-shot improvement.* To get any further increase in output per capita, the nation must increase its potential output. This doesn't mean that it isn't important to maintain a high level of employment in the economy. Of course, it is, for reasons discussed at length in Chapter 5. But the point we are making is that, once the economy gets to full employment, no further increase in output per capita can occur by this route. If a nation wants further increases in output per capita over the long haul, it must influence the factors responsible for the rate of growth of potential output.

## ECONOMIC GROWTH AND THE STANDARD OF LIVING

In conclusion, it is important to stress once more that economic growth is of enormous importance to human beings throughout the world. Increases in output per capita mean increases in our standard of living. In the industrialized nations, the goal of rapid economic growth has become more controversial in recent decades, partly because some observers question the extent to which economic growth is worth its costs in social dislocation, pollution and so forth. (Much more will be said on this score in Chapter 33.) However, there is no indication that most nations have lost interest in further economic growth.

## TEST YOURSELF

1. Suppose that a society's full-employment GNP increases between 1991 and 1992 by $100 billion. During the same period, its corporations paid $20 billion in salaries to corporate executives, and it invested $200 billion. What is the capital-output ratio in this society? Will the capital-output ratio in this society always be the same? Why, or why not?

2. Suppose that a society's capital-output ratio is 3 and that it invests 10 percent of its GNP. If full employment is maintained, by what percentage will its GNP grow?

3. "Ricardo's pessimistic view of the prospects for economic growth stemmed from his assumptions concerning the capital-output ratio. If he had recognized that it was not fixed, he would have been closer to correct." Comment and evaluate.

4. Some studies indicate that what matters most to people is their income relative to others around them rather than the absolute level of their income. Would this fact tend to reduce the importance of growth as a means of helping the poor? Explain.

# SUMMARY

1. Economic growth is measured by the increase of per capita real gross national product, an index that does not measure accurately the growth of economic welfare, but is often used as a first approximation.

2. A nation's rate of economic growth depends on the increase in the quantity and quality of its resources (including physical and human capital) and the rate of technological change. In addition, the rate of economic growth depends on the extent to which a society maintains full employment and on the efficiency with which its resources are allocated and managed.

3. One factor that may influence a nation's rate of economic growth is the rate at which its population grows. In Malthus's view, population growth, unless checked in some way, ultimately meant economic decline, since output could not grow in proportion to the growth in population. The law of diminishing marginal returns ensured that beyond some point, increases in labor, holding the quantity of land constant, would result in smaller and smaller increments of output. However, Malthus underestimated the extent and importance of technological change, which offset the law of diminishing marginal returns.

4. Another factor that determines whether per capita output grows rapidly or slowly is the rate of expenditure on new plant and equipment. Without technological change, more and more of this sort of investment would result in increases in the amount of capital per dollar of output and decreases in the profitability of investment in plant and equipment, as Ricardo pointed out. But because of technological change, none of these things has occurred. According to the avail-

able evidence, a nation's rate of economic growth seems directly related to its rate of investment in plant and equipment.

5. To a considerable extent, economic growth here and abroad has resulted from technological change. A change in technology, when applied for the first time, is called an innovation, and the firm that first applies it is called an innovator. Innovation is a key stage in the process leading to the full evaluation and utilization of a new process or product. Unless knowledge is used, it has little effect on the rate of economic growth.

6. The rate of technological change and the rate at which new technology is applied depend on a number of factors, including the nature and extent of a nation's scientific capability, the size and quality of its educational system, the quality of its managers, the attitude and structure of its firms, the organization of its industries, and the nature of its markets.

7. Another factor with an important effect on a nation's rate of economic growth is the rate at which it invests in human capital. The United States invests in human capital on a massive scale, and these enormous and rapidly growing investments have unquestionably increased the productivity, versatility, and adaptability of our labor force.

8. Still another set of basic factors influencing the rate of economic growth is the economic, social, and political climate of the nation. Some societies despise material welfare, are subject to violent political upheavals, and are governed by corrupt groups. Such societies are unlikely to have a high rate of economic growth.

# CONCEPTS FOR REVIEW

Economic growth

Aggregate production function

Law of diminishing marginal
   returns

Marginal product of labor

Average product of labor

Population growth

Capital formation

Capital-output ratio

Technological change

Innovation

Innovator

Diffusion process

# PART FOUR

# INTERNATIONAL ECONOMICS

# INTERNATIONAL TRADE

PRACTICALLY ALL HUMAN beings realize that they are not islands unto themselves, and that they benefit from living with, working with, and trading with other people. Exactly the same is true of nations. They too must interact with one another, and they too benefit from trade with one another. No nation can be an island unto itself—not even the United States. To understand how the world economy functions, you must grasp the basic economic principles of international trade.

This chapter discusses many of the fundamental questions about international trade. What is the nature of American foreign trade? What are the effects of international trade? What determines the sorts of goods a nation will import or export? What are the advantages of free trade and the arguments against it? What are the social costs of tariffs and quotas, and what has been their history in the United States? What are some of the major issues regarding protectionism in the United States today? Some of these questions have occupied the attention of economists for hundreds of years; some are as current as today's newspaper.

## AMERICA'S FOREIGN TRADE

America's foreign trade, although small relative to our national product, plays a very important role in our economic life. Many of our industries depend on other countries for markets or for raw materials (like coffee, tea, or tin). Our **exports**—the things we sell to other countries—amount to about 10 percent of our gross national product. In absolute terms, our exports (and imports) are bigger than those of any other nation. Without question, our way of life would have to change considerably if we could not trade with other countries.

When we were a young country, we exported raw materials primarily. During the 1850s about 70 percent of our exports were raw materials and foodstuffs. But the composition of our exports has changed with time. More are now finished manufactured goods and less are raw materials. In the 1960s, about 60 percent of our exports were finished manufactured goods, and only about 20 percent were raw materials and foodstuffs. Table 17.1 shows the importance of machinery and industrial supplies in our merchandise exports. Table 17.2 indicates to whom we sell. Western Europe and Canada take about one-half of our exports, and Latin America takes over 10 percent.

What sorts of goods do we buy from abroad? About 10 percent of our

**Table 17.1**
**U.S. Merchandise Exports, 1990**

| PRODUCT | AMOUNT (BILLIONS OF DOLLARS) |
|---|---|
| Food, feed, and beverages | 35 |
| Industrial supplies and materials | 106 |
| Machinery | 120 |
| Automotive vehicles and parts | 37 |
| Aircraft | 32 |
| Other | 59 |
| Total | 389 |

*Source: Survey of Current Business, March 1991*

**Table 17.2**
**Percent of U.S. Exports, by Area, 1990**

| COUNTRY | PERCENT |
|---|---|
| Japan | 13 |
| Western Europe | 32 |
| Latin America | 16 |
| Canada | 17 |
| Eastern Europe | 1 |
| Other | 21 |
| Total | 100 |

*Source: See Table 17.1*

*imports* are agricultural commodities like coffee, sugar, bananas, and cocoa. Over 10 percent are petroleum and its products. But a considerable proportion is neither raw materials nor foodstuffs. Over one-half of our imports, as shown in Table 17.3, are manufactured goods like bicycles from England or color TVs from Japan. More than 40 percent of our imports come from Western Europe and Japan (see Table 17.4). But the pattern varies from product to product. Thus Canada is our leading foreign source for wood pulp and nonferrous metals, while Latin America is our leading source of imported coffee and sugar.

## ADVANTAGES OF TRADE

We have discussed the extent and nature of our trade with other countries, but not *why* we trade with other countries. Do we—and our trading partners—benefit from this trade? And if so, what determines the sorts of goods we should export and import? These are very important questions, among the most fundamental in economics. The answers are by no means new. They have been well understood for considerably more than a century, due to the work of such great economists as David Hume, David Ricardo, Adam Smith, and John Stuart Mill. Basically, the advantages of trade, both for individuals and for nations, stem from the fact that trade permits specialization, and specialization increases output, as we saw in Chapter 2.

To clarify the benefits of trade, consider the following example. Suppose that the United States can produce 2 computers or 5,000 cases of wine with 1 unit of resources. Suppose that France can produce 1 computer or 10,000 cases of wine with 1 unit of resources. Given the production possibilities in each country, are there any advantages in trade between the countries? And if so, what commodity should each country export, and what commodity should each country import? Should France export wine and import computers, or should it import wine and export computers?

To answer these questions, assume that the United States is producing a certain amount of computers and a certain amount of wine—and that France is producing a certain amount of computers and a certain amount of wine. If the United States shifts 1 unit of its resources from producing wine to producing computers, it will increase its production of computers by 2 computers and reduce its production of wine by 5,000 cases of wine. If France shifts 1 unit of resources from the production of computers to the production of wine, it will increase its production of wine by 10,000 cases and reduce its production of computers by 1 computer.

Table 17.5 shows the *net* effect of this shift in the utilization of resources on *world* output of computers and of wine. World output of computers increases (by 1 computer) and world output of wine increases (by 5,000 cases) as a result of the redeployment of resources in each country. Thus *specialization increases world output.*

Moreover, if world output of each commodity is increased by shifting 1 unit of American resources from wine to computers and shifting 1 unit of French resources from computers to wine, it follows that world output of each commodity will be increased further if each country shifts *more* of its resources in the same direction. This is because the amount of resources required to produce each good is assumed to be constant, regardless of how much is produced.

**Table 17.3**
**U.S. Merchandise Imports, 1990**

| PRODUCT | AMOUNT (BILLIONS OF DOLLARS) |
|---|---|
| Food, feed, and beverages | 27 |
| Petroleum and oil products | 62 |
| Other industrial supplies and materials | 82 |
| Capital goods | 117 |
| Automotive vehicles and parts | 86 |
| Consumer goods (excluding autos) | 106 |
| Other | 18 |
| Total | 498 |

*Source:* See Table 17.1

**Table 17.4**
**Percent of U.S. Imports, by Area, 1990**

| COUNTRY | PERCENT |
|---|---|
| Japan | 16 |
| Western Europe | 30 |
| Latin America | 15 |
| Canada | 15 |
| Eastern Europe | a |
| Other | 24 |
| Total | 100 |

a Less than one-half of one percent.
*Source:* See Table 17.1

Thus, in this situation, one country—the United States—should specialize in producing computers, and the other country—France—should specialize in producing wine. This will maximize world output of both wine and computers, permitting a rise in both countries' standards of living. Complete specialization of this sort is somewhat unrealistic, since countries often produce some of both commodities, but this simple example illustrates the basic principles involved.

# COMPARATIVE ADVANTAGE

The case just described is a very special one, since one country (France) has an absolute advantage over another (the United States) in the production of one good (wine), whereas the second country (the United States) has an absolute advantage over the first (France) in the production of another good (computers). What do we mean by the term **absolute advantage**? Country A has an **absolute advantage** over Country B in the production of a good when Country A can produce a unit of the good with less resources than can country B. Since the United States can produce a computer with fewer units of resources than France, it has an absolute advantage over France in the production of computers. Since France requires fewer resources than the United States to produce a given amount of wine, France has an absolute advantage over the United States in the production of wine.

But what if one country is more efficient in producing both goods? If the United States is more efficient in producing both computers and wine, is there still any benefit to be derived from specialization and trade? At first glance, you are probably inclined to answer no. But if this is your inclination, you should reconsider—because you are wrong.

## A Numerical Example

To see why specialization and trade have advantages even when one country is more efficient than another at producing both goods, consider the following example. Suppose the United States can produce 2 computers or 5,000 cases of wine with 1 unit of resources, and France can produce 1 computer or 4,000 cases of wine with 1 unit of resources. In this case, the United States is a more efficient producer of both computers and wine. Nonetheless, as we shall see, world output of both goods will increase if the United States specializes in the production of computers and France specializes in the production of wine.

Table 17.6 demonstrates this conclusion. If 2 units of American resources are shifted from wine to computer production, 4 additional computers and 10,000 fewer cases of wine are produced. If 3 units of French resources are shifted from computer to wine production, 3 fewer computers and 12,000 additional cases of wine are produced. Thus the combined effect of this redeployment of resources in both countries is to increase world output of computers by 1 computer and to increase world output of wine by 2,000 cases. Even though the United States is more efficient than France in the production of both computers and wine, world output of both goods will be maximized if the United States specializes in computers and France specializes in wine.

Basically, this is so because, although the United States is more efficient than France in the production of both goods, it has a greater ad-

**Table 17.5
Case of Absolute Advantage**

| | INCREASE OR DECREASE IN OUTPUT OF: | |
| | COMPUTERS | WINE (THOUSANDS OF CASES) |
|---|---|---|
| Effect of U.S.'s shifting 1 unit of resources from wine to computers | +2 | −5 |
| Effect of France's shifting 1 unit of resources from computers to wine | −1 | +10 |
| Net Effect | +1 | +5 |

**Table 17.6
Case of Comparative Advantage**

| | INCREASE OR DECREASE IN OUTPUT OF: | |
| | COMPUTERS | WINE (THOUSANDS OF CASES) |
|---|---|---|
| Effect of U.S.'s shifting 2 units of resources from wine to computers | +4 | −10 |
| Effect of France's shifting 3 units of resources from computers to wine | −3 | +12 |
| Net effect | +1 | +2 |

vantage in computers than in wine. It is twice as efficient as France in producing computers, but only 25 percent more efficient than France in producing wine. To derive these numbers, recall that 1 unit of resources will produce 2 computers in the United States, but only 1 computer in France. Thus the United States is twice as efficient in computers. On the other hand, 1 unit of resources will produce 5,000 cases of wine in the United States, but only 4,000 cases in France. Thus the United States is 25 percent more efficient in wine.

## Trade Depends on Comparative Advantage

Specialization and trade depend on comparative, not absolute, advantage. A nation has a ***comparative advantage*** in those products where its efficiency relative to other nations is highest. So long as a country has a comparative advantage in the production of some commodities and a comparative disadvantage in the production of others, it can benefit from specialization and trade. A country will specialize in products where it has a comparative advantage, and import those where it has a comparative disadvantage.

Consider the case of France and the United States in Table 17.6. The United States has a comparative advantage in the production of computers and a comparative disadvantage in the production of wine. France has a comparative advantage in the production of wine and a comparative disadvantage in the production of computers. Both countries can benefit if France specializes in wine and the United States specializes in computers.

## A Geometric Representation of Comparative Advantage

The principle of comparative advantage, like so many important economic concepts, can be displayed diagrammatically. Again, we suppose that in the United States 1 unit of resources will produce 2 computers or 5,000 cases of wine. Consequently, the ***production possibilities curve*** in the United States—the curve that shows the maximum number of computers that can be produced, given various outputs of wine—is the one in panel A of Figure 17.1. The United States must give up 1 computer for every additional 2,500 cases of wine that it produces; thus the slope of the American production possibilities curve is $-\dfrac{1}{2,500}$.[1]

Also, as in the previous section, we suppose that in France 1 unit of resources will produce 1 computer or 4,000 cases of wine. Thus the production possibilities curve in France is as shown in panel B of Figure 17.1. France must give up 1 computer for every additional 4,000 cases of wine it produces; thus the slope of France's production possibilities curve is $-\dfrac{1}{4,000}$.

Now suppose that the United States uses all its resources to produce computers and that France uses all its resources to produce wine. In other words, the United States operates at point $A$ on its production possibilities curve and France operates at point $B$ on its production possibilities curve.

---

[1] As we know from Chapter 2, the production possibilities curve shows the maximum amount of one commodity that can be produced, given various outputs of the other commodity. Since the United States must give up 1/2,500 computer for each additional case of wine that it produces, the slope must be —1/2,500.

Then suppose that the United States trades its computers for France's wine. *AC* in panel **A** of Figure 17.1 shows the various amounts of computers and wine the United States can end up with if it specializes in computers and trades them for French wine. *AC* is called the **trading possibilities curve** of the United States. The slope of *AC* is minus 1 times the ratio of the price of a case of wine to the price of a computer, since this ratio equals the number of computers the United States must give up to get a case of French wine. Similarly, the line *BD* in panel **B** of Figure 17.1 shows France's trading possibilities curve. That is, *BD* represents the various amounts of computers and wine France can wind up with if it specializes in wine and trades it for U.S. computers.

The thing to note about both panels of Figure 17.1 is that each country's trading possibilities curve—*AC* in panel **A**, *BD* in panel **B**—lies above its production possibilities curve. This means that *both countries can have more of both commodities by specializing and trading than by trying to be self-sufficient*—even though the United States is more efficient than France at producing both commodities. Thus Figure 17.1 shows what we said in the previous section: If countries specialize in products where they have a comparative advantage and trade with one another, each country can improve its standard of living.

## THE TERMS OF TRADE

The **terms of trade** are defined as the quantity of imported goods that a country can obtain in exchange for a unit of domestic goods. Thus, in Figure 17.1, the terms of trade are measured by the ratio of the price of a computer to the price of a case of wine—since this ratio shows how many cases of French wine the United States can get in exchange for an American computer. In Figure 17.1, we assume that this ratio equals 3,333:1. It is important to note that this ratio must be somewhere between 2,500:1 and 4,000:1. By diverting its own resources from computer production to wine production, the United States can exchange a computer for 2,500 cases of wine. Since this is possible, it will not pay the United States to trade a computer for less than 2,500 cases of wine. Similarly, since France can exchange a case of wine for 1/4,000 of a computer by diverting its own resources from wine to computers, it clearly will not be willing to trade a case of wine for less than 1/4,000 of a computer.

But where will the price ratio lie between 2,500:1 and 4,000:1? The answer depends on *world supply and demand for the two products*. The stronger the demand for computers (relative to their supply) and the weaker the demand for wine (relative to its supply), the higher the price ratio. On the other hand, the weaker the demand for computers (relative to their supply) and the stronger the demand for wine (relative to its supply), the lower the price ratio.

## INCOMPLETE SPECIALIZATION

Figure 17.1 shows that the United States should specialize completely in computers, and that France should specialize completely in wine. This result stems from the assumption that the cost of producing a computer or a case of wine is constant. If, on the other hand, the cost of producing each good increases with the amount produced, the result is likely to be incomplete specialization. In other words, although the United States will

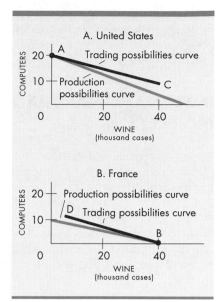

**Figure 17.1**
**Benefits of Specialization and Trade**
*AC* represents the various amounts of computers and wine that the United States can end up with, if it specializes in computers and trades them for French wine. The slope of *AC* equals −1 times the ratio of the price of a case of wine to the price of a computer, assumed to be $\frac{1}{3,333}$. *BD* represents the various amounts of computers and wine that France can wind up with, if it specializes in wine and trades for U.S. computers. *AC* lies above America's production possibilities curve and *BD* lies above France's production possibilities curve. Thus both countries can have more of both commodities by specializing and trading than by attempting to be self-sufficient.

continue to specialize in computers and France will continue to specialize in wine, each country will also produce some of the other good as well. This is a more likely outcome, since specialization generally tends to be less than complete.

## INTERNATIONAL TRADE AND INDIVIDUAL MARKETS

We have emphasized that nations can benefit by specializing in the production of goods for which they have a comparative advantage and trading these goods for others where they have a comparative disadvantage.[2] But how do a nation's producers know whether they have a comparative advantage or disadvantage in the production of a given commodity? They do not call up the local university and ask the leading professor of economics (although that might not always be such a bad idea). Instead, as we shall see in this section, the market for the good provides the required signals.

To see how this works, let's consider a new (and rather whimsical) product—bulletproof suspenders. Suppose that the Mob, having run a scientific survey of gunmen and policemen, finds that most of them wear their suspenders over their bulletproof vests. As a consequence, the Mob's gunmen are instructed to render a victim immobile by shooting holes in his suspenders (thus making his trousers fall down and trip him). Naturally, the producers of suspenders will soon find it profitable to produce a new bulletproof variety, an innovation which, it is hoped, will make a solid contribution to law and order. The new suspenders are demanded only in the United States and England, since the rest of the world wears belts. The demand curve in the United States is as shown in panel A of Figure 17.2, and the demand curve in England is as shown in panel B. Suppose further that this product can be manufactured in both the United States and England. The supply curve in the United States is as shown in panel A, and the supply curve in England is as shown in panel B.

Take a closer look at Figure 17.2. Note that prices in England are expressed in pounds (£) and prices in the United States are expressed in dollars ($). This is quite realistic. Each country has its own currency, in which prices in that country are expressed. In early 1991, £1 was equal to about $1.85. In other words, you could exchange a pound note for $1.85—or $1.85 for a £1 note. For this reason, the two panels of Figure 17.2 are lined up so that a price of $3.70 is at the same level as a price of £2, $5.55 is at the same level as £3, and so on.

---

[2] The principle of comparative advantage is useful in explaining and predicting the pattern of world trade, as well as in showing the benefits of trade. For example, consider the exports of Great Britain and the United States. Robert Stern of the University of Michigan compared British and American exports of 39 industries. In 21 of the 24 industries where our labor productivity was more than three times that of the British, our exports exceeded British exports. In 11 of the 15 industries where our labor productivity was less than three times that of the British, our exports were less than British exports. Thus, in 32 out of 39 industries, the principle of comparative advantage, as interpreted by Stern, predicted correctly which country would export more. This is a high batting average, since labor is not the only input and labor productivity is an imperfect measure of true efficiency. Moreover, as we shall see in subsequent sections, countries raise barriers to foreign trade, preventing trade from taking place in accord with the principle of comparative advantage.

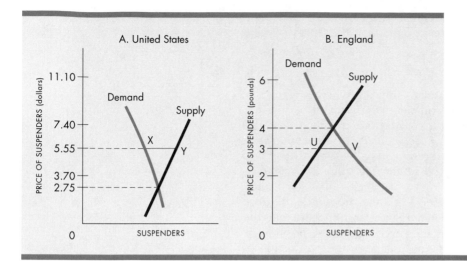

**Figure 17.2**
**Determination of Quantity Imported and Exported under Free Trade**
Under free trade, price will equal $5.55 or £3. The United States will export XY units, the English will import UV units, and XY = UV.

## No Foreign Trade

To begin with, suppose that bulletproof suspenders cannot be exported or imported, perhaps because of a very high tariff (tax on imports) imposed on them in both the United States and England. (One can readily imagine members of both Congress and Parliament defending such a tariff on the grounds that a capacity to produce plenty of bulletproof suspenders is important for national defense.) If this happens, the price of bulletproof suspenders will be $2.75 in the United States and £4 in England. Why? Because, as shown in Figure 17.2, these are the prices at which each country's demand curve intersects its supply curve.

## Foreign Trade Permitted

Next, suppose that international trade in this product is permitted, perhaps because both countries eliminate the tariff. Now what will happen? Since the price is lower in the United States than in England, people can make money by sending this product from the United States to England. After all, they can buy it for $2.75 in this country and sell it for £4 (=$7.40) in England. But they will not be able to do so indefinitely. As more and more suspenders are supplied by the United States for the English market, the price in the United States must go up (to induce producers to produce the additional output) and the price in England must go down (to induce consumers to buy the additional quantity).

When an equilibrium is reached, *the price in the United States must equal the price in England.* If this did not happen, there would be an advantage in increasing American exports (if the price in England were higher) or in decreasing American exports (if the price in the United States were higher). Thus only if the prices are equal can an equilibrium exist.

At what level will this price—which is common in both countries—tend to settle? Obviously, *the price must end up at the level where the amount of the good one country wants to export equals the amount the other country wants to import.* In other words, it must settle at $5.55 or £3. Otherwise, the total amount demanded in both countries would not equal the total amount supplied in both countries. And any reader who has mastered the material in Chapter 3 knows that such a situation cannot be an equilibrium.

### The Signal of Market Forces

At this point, we can see how market forces indicate whether a country has a comparative advantage or a comparative disadvantage in the production of a certain commodity. *If a country has a comparative advantage, it turns out — after the price of the good in various countries is equalized and total world output of the good equals total world demand for it — that the country exports the good under free trade and competition.* In Figure 17.2, it turns out — as we've just seen — that the United States is an exporter of bulletproof suspenders under free trade, because the demand and supply curves in the United States and England take the positions they do. The basic reason why the curves take these positions is that the United States has a comparative advantage in the production of this good. Thus, to put things in a nutshell, a nation's producers can tell (under free trade) whether they have a comparative advantage in the production of a certain commodity by seeing whether it is profitable for them to export it. If they can make a profit, they have a comparative advantage.[3]

## ECONOMIES OF SCALE AND LEARNING

Specialization and trade may be advantageous even if there is no difference among countries in the efficiency with which they can produce goods and services. In a case like this, although no nation has a technological advantage over any other, specialization and trade may still be of benefit, because there may be economies of scale in producing some commodities. Thus, if one country specializes in one good and another country specializes in another good, firms can serve the *combined* markets of both countries, which will make their costs *lower* than if they could only reach their domestic markets. This is a major argument for forming an international economic association like the European Common Market, discussed later in this chapter. (Also, it is a major argument for the steps taken in the early 1990s to remove trade barriers within the Common Market.)

Another reason for specialization is that it may result in learning. It is well known that the cost of producing many articles goes down as more and more of the articles are produced. In the aircraft and machine tool industries, producers are well aware of the reduction in costs from learning. The unit costs of a new machine tool tend to be reduced by 20 percent for each doubling of cumulated output, due to improved efficiency through individual and organizational learning. If such learning is an important factor in an industry, there are advantages in having one nation's producers specialize in a certain good. Specialization can reduce costs to a lower level than if each nation tries to be self-sufficient. Longer production runs cut costs since *the more a producer makes, the lower the unit costs.*

---

[3] In reality things are not quite so simple. For one thing, high transport costs are often involved in moving goods from one country to another. These costs can impede trade in certain commodities. Also, tariffs or quotas can be enacted by governments to interfere with free trade. Much more will be said on this score in later sections.

# INNOVATION AND INTERNATIONAL TRADE

International trade also arises because of technological change. Suppose that a new product is invented in the United States and an American firm begins producing and selling it in the American market. It catches on, and the American innovator decides to export the new product to Europe and other foreign markets. If the new product meets European needs and tastes, the Europeans will import it from the United States; and later, when the market in Europe gets big enough, the American firm may establish a branch plant in Europe. For a time at least, European firms do not have the technological know-how to produce the new product, which is often protected to some extent by patents.

Trade of this sort is based on a *technology gap* between countries. Consider the plastics industry. After the development of a new plastic, there generally has been a period of 15 to 25 years when the innovating country has had a decisive advantage and has been likely to lead in per capita production and exports. It has had a head start, as well as the benefits of patents and commercial secrecy. Production has been licensed to other countries,but often on a limited scale and only after a number of years. Soon after the patents expire, a different phase begins. Imitation is easier, technical know-how spreads more readily, direct technical factors lose importance, and such other factors as materials costs become much more important. Industry from other countries may challenge the innovator in export markets, and sometimes in the innovator's home market as well, although the innovating firm still benefits to some extent from its accumulated knowledge and experience and its ongoing research and development.[4]

# MULTINATIONAL FIRMS

One of the most remarkable economic phenomena of the last 30 years has been the growth of **multinational firms**—firms that make direct investments in other countries and produce and market their products abroad. For example, Coca-Cola is produced and bottled all over the world. Most multinational firms are American, but companies like Shell in petroleum and Hoffman-La Roche in drugs are examples of foreign-based multinational firms. The available data indicate that the multinational firms have grown by leaps and bounds, and that their shipments have become a bigger proportion of international trade.

The reasons why firms have become multinational are varied. In some cases, firms have established overseas branches to control foreign sources of raw materials. In other cases, they have invested overseas in an effort to defend their competitive position. Very frequently, firms have established foreign branches to exploit a technological lead. After exporting a new product (or a cheaper version of an existing product) to foreign markets, firms have decided to establish plants overseas to supply these markets. Once a foreign market is big enough to accommodate a plant of minimum efficient size, this decision does not conflict with economies of

---

[4] Besides differences in technology, another reason for trade is a difference in national tastes. If Country A likes beef and Country B likes pork, it may pay both countries to produce beef and pork, and Country A may find it advantageous to import beef from Country B and Country B may find it advantageous to import pork from Country A.

scale. Moreover, transport costs often hasten such a decision. Also, in some cases, the only way a firm can introduce its innovation into a foreign market is through the establishment of overseas production facilities.

### Effects of Multinational Firms

By carrying its technology overseas, the multinational firm plays a very important role in the international diffusion of innovations. A firm with a technological edge over its competitors often prefers to exploit its technology in foreign markets through wholly owned subsidiaries rather than through licensing or other means. To some extent, this is because of difficulties in using ordinary market mechanisms to buy and sell information. The difficulties of transferring technology across organizational, as well as national, boundaries also contribute to the decision. For these and other reasons, the innovating firm may find it advantageous to transfer its technology to other countries by establishing subsidiaries abroad.

One of the most important effects of the multinational firm has been to integrate the economies of the world more closely into a worldwide system. In other words, multinational firms have tended to break down some of the barriers between nations. Besides speeding the diffusion of new technology, they have linked the capital markets of many countries and promoted the international transfer of important managerial labor.

Particularly in the less developed countries, there has been an impassioned debate over the pros and cons of the multinational firm, which sometimes is viewed with suspicion by the nation-states in which it operates. These nation-states feel that their sovereignty is threatened by the great power of the multinational firm over their national economies. And the tragedy at Bhopal, India, where thousands of people were killed in 1984 by an accident at a plant owned by a major multinational firm—Union Carbide Corporation—has caused further conflict of this sort. (In 1988, an Indian judge ordered Union Carbide to pay about $200 million in compensation to the victims.) Also some observers are wary of multinational firms because of the possibility that they will attain undesirable monopoly power.

## TEST YOURSELF

1. Suppose that the United States can produce 3 computers or 3,000 cases of wine with 1 unit of resources, while France can produce 1 computer or 2,000 cases of wine with 1 unit of resources. Will specialization increase world output?

2. Suppose that the United States has 100 units of resources while France has 50 units. Based on the data in Question 1, draw the production possibilities curve in each country. Without international trade, what will be the ratio of the price of a computer to the price of a case of wine in each country?

3. Given the information in Questions 1 and 2, how will firms in France and the United States know whether they should produce wine or computers? Must the government instruct them on this score? Why, or why not?

4. Under the circumstances described in Questions 1 and 2, will each country specialize completely in the production of one or the other good? Why, or why not? What factors result in incomplete specialization in the real world?

# TARIFFS AND QUOTAS

## What Is a Tariff?

Despite its advantages, not everyone benefits from free trade. On the contrary, the well-being of some firms and workers may be threatened by foreign competition; and they may press for a **tariff**, a tax the government imposes on imports. The purpose of a tariff is to cut down on imports in order to protect domestic industry and workers from foreign competition. A secondary reason for having tariffs is to produce revenue for the government.

To see how a tariff works, consider the market for wristwatches. Suppose that the demand and supply curves for wristwatches in the United States are as shown in panel A of Figure 17.3, and that the demand and supply curves for wristwatches in Switzerland are as shown in panel B. Clearly, Switzerland has a comparative advantage in the production of wristwatches, and under free trade the price of a wristwatch would tend toward $10 in the United States and toward 14 Swiss francs in Switzerland. (Note that 1.4 Swiss francs are assumed to equal 1 dollar.) Under free trade, the United States would import 10 million wristwatches from Switzerland.

Now if the United States imposes a tariff of $10 on each wristwatch imported from Switzerland, the imports will completely cease. Any importers who buy watches in Switzerland at the price (when there is no foreign trade) of 10 Swiss francs—which equals about $7—must pay a tariff of $10; this makes their total cost about $17 per watch. But this is more than the price of a watch in the United States when there is no foreign trade (which is $15). Consequently, there is no money to be made by importing watches—unless Americans can be persuaded to pay more for a Swiss watch than for an identical American watch.

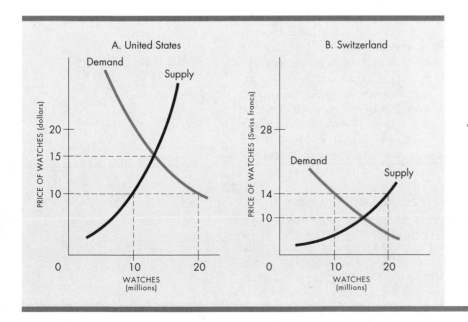

**Figure 17.3**
**Effect of a Tariff on Swiss Watches**
Under free trade, price would equal $10, or 14 Swiss francs. If a tariff of $10 is imposed on each watch imported from Switzerland, there will be a complete cessation of imports. Price in the United States will increase to $15, and price in Switzerland will fall to 10 Swiss francs.

## The Social Costs of Tariffs

What is the effect of the tariff? The domestic watch industry receives a higher price—$15 rather than $10—than it would without a tariff. And the workers in the domestic watch industry may have more jobs and higher wages than without the tariff. The victim of the tariff is the American consumer, who pays a higher price for wristwatches. Thus the domestic watch industry benefits at the expense of the rest of the nation. But does the general public lose more than the watch industry gains? In general, the answer is yes. The tariff reduces the welfare of the nation as a whole.

The tariff in Figure 17.3 is a *prohibitive tariff*—a tariff so high that it stops all imports of the good in question. Not all tariffs are prohibitive. (If they were, the government would receive no revenue at all from tariffs.) In many cases, the tariff is high enough to stop some, but not all, imports; and, as you would expect, the detrimental effect of a nonprohibitive tariff on living standards is less than that of a prohibitive tariff. But this does not mean that nonprohibitive tariffs are harmless. On the contrary, they can do lots of harm to domestic consumption and living standards.

The detrimental effects of tariffs have long been recognized, even in detective stories. Thus, in the course of solving the mystery concerning the Hound of the Baskervilles, Sherlock Holmes expressed his enthusiastic approval of a newspaper editorial that read as follows:

> You may be cajoled into imagining that your own special trade or your own industry will be encouraged by a protective tariff, but it stands to reason that such legislation must in the long run . . . lower the general conditions of life on this island.

Of course, Holmes considered this point elementary (my dear Watson) but worth hammering home.

## What Is a Quota?

Besides tariffs, other barriers to free trade are *quotas*, which many countries impose on the amount of certain commodities that can be imported annually. The United States sets import quotas on sugar and exerts pressure on foreigners to get them to limit the quantity of steel and textiles that they will export to us. To see how a quota affects trade, production, and prices, let's return to the market for wristwatches. Suppose the United States places a quota on the import of wristwatches: no more than 6 million wristwatches can be imported per year. Figure 17.4 shows the effect of the quota. Before it was imposed, the price of wristwatches was $10 (or 14 Swiss francs), and the United States imported 10 million wristwatches from Switzerland. The quota forces the United States to reduce its imports to 6 million.

What will be the effect on the U.S. price? The demand curve shows that, if the price is $12, American demand will exceed American supply by 6 million watches; in other words, we will import 6 million watches. Thus, once the quota is imposed, the price will rise to $12, since *this is the price that will reduce our imports to the amount of the quota*. A quota—like a tariff—increases the price of the good. (Note too that the price in Switzerland will fall to 12 francs. Thus the quota will reduce the price in Switzerland.)

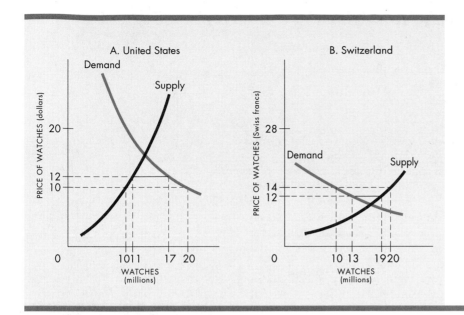

**Figure 17.4
Effects of a Quota on Swiss Watches**
Before the quota is imposed, the price is $10, or 14 Swiss francs. After a quota of 6 million watches is imposed, the price in the United States rises to $12, and the price in Switzerland falls to 12 Swiss francs.

## The Social Costs of Quotas

Both a quota and a tariff reduce trade, raise prices, protect domestic industry from foreign competition, and reduce the standard of living of the nation as a whole. But most economists tend to regard quotas with even less enthusiasm than they do tariffs. Under many circumstances, a quota insulates local industry from foreign competition even more effectively than a tariff does. Foreigners, if their costs are low enough, can surmount a tariff barrier; but if a quota exists, there is no way they can exceed the quota. Moreover, a (nonprohibitive) tariff provides the government with some revenue, while quotas do not even do that. The windfall price increase from a quota accrues to the importer who is lucky enough or influential enough—or sufficiently generous with favors and bribes—to get an import license. (However, if the government auctions off the import licenses, it can obtain revenue from a quota.)

## Export Subsidies and Other Nontariff Barriers to Free Trade

Finally, ***export subsidies,*** another means by which governments try to give their domestic industry an advantage in international competition, are also a major impediment to free trade. Such subsidies may take the form of outright cash disbursements, tax exemptions, preferential financing or insurance arrangements, or other preferential treatment for exports. Export subsidies, and other such measures, frequently lead to countermeasures. Thus, to counter foreign export subsidies, the U.S. government has imposed duties against such subsidies on goods sold here.

Other nontariff barriers to free trade include licensing requirements and unreasonable product quality standards. By granting few licenses (which are required in some countries to import goods) and by imposing unrealistically stringent product quality standards, governments discourage imports.

# ARGUMENTS FOR TARIFFS AND QUOTAS

Given the disadvantages to society at large of tariffs and other barriers to free trade, why do governments continue to impose them? There are many reasons, some sensible, some irrational.

## The National Defense Argument

One of the most convincing arguments is the desirability of maintaining a domestic industry for purposes of *national defense*. Thus, even if the Swedes had a comparative advantage in producing airplanes, we would not allow free trade to put our domestic producers of aircraft out of business if we felt that a domestic aircraft industry was necessary for national defense. Although the Swedes are by no means unfriendly, we would not want to import our entire supply of such a critical commodity from a foreign country, where the supply might be shut off for reasons of international politics. (Recall the Arab oil embargo of 1973.)

This is a perfectly valid reason for protecting certain domestic industries, and many protective measures are defended on these grounds. To the extent that protective measures are in fact required for national defense, economists go along with them. The restrictions entail social costs (some of which were described in previous sections), but these costs may well be worth paying for enhanced national security. The trouble is that many barriers to free trade are justified on these grounds when in fact they protect domestic industries only tenuously connected with national defense. Moreover, even if there is a legitimate case on defense grounds for protecting a domestic industry, subsidies are likely to be a more straightforward and efficient way to do so than tariffs or quotas.

## Other Arguments for Tariffs

Besides national defense, several other arguments for tariffs or quotas can make sense.

**1. TARIFFS OR OTHER FORMS OF PROTECTION CAN BE JUSTIFIED TO FOSTER THE GROWTH OR DEVELOPMENT OF YOUNG INDUSTRIES.** Suppose that Japan has a comparative advantage in the production of a certain semiconductor, but Japan does not presently produce this item. It may take Japanese firms several years to become proficient in the relevant technology, to engage in the learning described in a previous section and to take advantage of the relevant economies of scale. While this industry is "growing up," Japan may impose a tariff on such semiconductors, thus shielding its young industry from competition it cannot yet handle. This "infant industry" argument for tariffs has a long history; Alexander Hamilton was one of its early exponents. Needless to say, it is *not* an argument for *permanent* tariffs, since infant industries are supposed to grow up—and the sooner the better. (Moreover, a subsidy for the industry would probably be better and easier to remove than a temporary tariff, according to many economists.)

**2. TARIFFS SOMETIMES MAY BE IMPOSED TO PROTECT DOMESTIC JOBS AND TO REDUCE UNEMPLOYMENT AT HOME.** In the short run the policy may succeed, but we must recognize that other nations are likely to retaliate by enacting or increasing their own tariffs, so that such a policy may not work very well in the long run. A more sensible way to reduce domestic unem-

# STRATEGIC TRADE POLICY

Paul Krugman

Avinash Dixit

In recent years, an influential band of young economists, led by MIT's Paul Krugman and others, have argued that, in today's world, nations may find it worthwhile to engage in strategic trade policies to secure higher incomes for their residents. Thus, if only two highly profitable firms can exist in a particular industry, it may make sense for countries to use subsidies or tariffs to raise the probability that one of their firms will be one of the fortunate pair. Or if certain high-technology industries result in large technological benefits to the rest of the economy, it may make sense to use subsidies or tariffs to promote and protect these sectors.

Of course, all of this departs from the conventional economic view that nations are best off by promoting free trade. As Krugman indicates,

> The new approaches open up the possibility that there may be 'strategic' sectors after all. Because of the important roles now being given to economies of scale, advantages of experience, and innovation as explanations of trading patterns, it seems more likely that . . . labor or capital will sometimes earn significantly higher returns in some industries than in others. Because of the increased role of technological competition, it has become more plausible to argue that certain sectors yield important [social benefits], so producers are not in fact paid the full social value of their production.
>
> What all this means is that the extreme pro-free-trade position—that markets work so well that they cannot be improved on—has become untenable. In this sense the new approaches to international trade

provide a potential rationale for a turn by the United States toward a more activist trade policy.[1]

However, these new approaches raise a great many unanswered questions. How can one identify strategic sectors? It is very difficult to specify the industries where the returns to capital and labor are very high and where public policy could raise GNP by encouraging them to go into the sector. Also, it is very difficult to measure the extent of the social benefits that will result from various kinds of investments. To what extent will these new approaches be used by interest groups to advocate policies that will not benefit the country as a whole? Given the vagueness of the criteria for identifying strategic sectors, many groups could use these ideas to justify protection for themselves and their allies.

Because of such questions, many economists, such as Princeton's Avinash Dixit, are skeptical concerning the usefulness of strategic trade policy. According to Dixit, "The idea that free trade promotes the general interest, and that departures from it are motivated by various special interests, . . . still stands and continues to govern the overwhelming majority of the volume of world trade. . . ."[2] Nonetheless, there can be no doubt that the proponents of strategic trade policy have had a substantial impact on economists and policy makers.

---

[1] Paul Krugman (ed.), *Strategic Trade Policy and the New International Economics*, Cambridge, Mass.: MIT Press, 1986, p. 15.
[2] Ibid., p. 302.

ployment is to use the tools of fiscal and monetary policy described in Chapters 9 and 12 rather than tariffs. If workers are laid off by industries that cannot compete with foreign producers, proper monetary and fiscal policy, together with retraining programs, should enable these workers to switch to other industries that can compete.

**3. TARIFFS SOMETIMES MAY BE IMPOSED TO PREVENT A COUNTRY FROM BEING TOO DEPENDENT ON ONLY A FEW INDUSTRIES.** Consider a Latin American country that is a major producer of bananas. Under free trade, this country might produce bananas and little else, putting its entire economy at the mercy of the banana market. If the price of bananas fell, the country's national income would decrease drastically. To promote industrial diversification, this country may establish tariffs to protect other industries—for example, certain types of light manufacturing. In a case like this, the tariff protects the country from having too many eggs—or bananas (if you want to avoid mixing a metaphor)—in a single basket.

**4. TARIFFS MAY SOMETIMES IMPROVE A COUNTRY'S TERMS OF TRADE—THAT IS, THE RATIO OF ITS EXPORT PRICES TO ITS IMPORT PRICES.** The United States is a major importer of bananas. If we impose a tariff on bananas, thus cutting down on the domestic demand for them (because the tariff will increase their price), the reduction in our demand is likely to reduce the price of bananas abroad. Consequently, foreign producers of bananas will really pay part of the tariff. However, other countries may retaliate; and if all countries pursue such policies, few, if any, are likely to find themselves better off.

## Frequently Encountered Fallacies

Although, as we have just seen, tariffs can be defended under certain circumstances, many of the arguments for them frequently encountered in political oratory and popular discussions are misleading. Although no field of economics is free of popular misconceptions and fallacies, this one is particularly rich in pious inanities and thunderous non sequiturs.

**FALLACY 1.** One frequently encountered fallacy is that, if foreigners want to trade with us, they must be benefiting from the trade. Consequently, according to this argument, we must be giving them more than we get— and it must be in our interest to reduce trade. This argument is entirely erroneous in its assumption that trade cannot be beneficial to *both* trading partners. On the contrary, as we have seen, the heart of the argument for trade is that it can be mutually beneficial.

**FALLACY 2.** Another fallacy one often encounters in polite conversation— and not-so-polite political debate—is that a tariff is required to protect our workers from low-wage labor in other countries. According to this argument, since American labor (at $10 an hour) clearly cannot compete with foreign labor (some of which works at extremely low wage levels), we have no choice but to impose tariffs. If we do not, cheap foreign goods will throw our high-priced laborers out of work. This argument is wrong on two counts. First, *high wages do not necessarily mean high unit costs of production*. Because the productivity of American workers is high, unit labor costs in the United States are roughly in line with those in other countries. (Unit labor cost equals the wage rate divided by labor productivity. Thus unit labor cost may be no higher here than abroad, even though the wage rate here is much higher, if labor productivity here is also much higher than abroad.) Second, *if our costs were out of line with those of other countries, there should be a change in exchange rates, which would tend to bring them back into line.* As we shall see in Chapter 18, exchange rates should move to bring our exports and imports into balance.

**FALLACY 3.**    Still another fallacy that makes the rounds is that it is better to "buy American" because then we have both the goods that are bought and the money, whereas if we buy from foreigners we have the goods but they have the money. Like some jokes, this fallacy has an ancient lineage—and one that borders on respectability, since Abraham Lincoln is supposed to have subscribed to it. Basically, the flaw is the implicit assumption that money is somehow valued for its own sake. In reality, all foreigners can do with the money is buy some of our goods, so that really we are just swapping some of our goods for some of theirs. If such a trade is mutually advantageous, fine.

## Why So Much Nonsense?

Why do politicians (both Democrats and Republicans) sometimes utter these fallacies? No doubt an important reason is simply ignorance. There is no law that prevents people with little understanding of economics from holding public office. But this may not be the only reason. Special-interest groups—particular industries, unions, and regions—have a lot to gain by getting the government to enact protective tariffs and quotas. And Congress and the executive branch of the government are often sensitive to the pressures of these groups, which wield considerable political power.

Faced with a choice between helping a few powerful, well-organized groups and helping the general public—which is poorly organized and often ignorant of its own interests—politicians frequently tend to favor the special-interest groups. After all, these groups have a lot to gain and will remember their friends, while the general public—each member of which loses only a relatively small amount—will be largely unaware of its losses anyhow. Having decided to help these groups, representatives or senators may not exert themselves unduly to search out or expose the weakness in some of the arguments used to bolster their position. Thus there is the story of a well-known senator who, about to deliver a certain oration, wrote in the margin of one section of his speech: "Weak point here. Holler like hell."

Finally, it is important to recognize once again that, although the majority of citizens benefit from free trade, some are likely to be hurt by it. A reduction in the tariff on shoes is likely to hurt people who own and work in American shoe factories. If our domestic shoe industry cannot compete with foreign producers, workers will be laid off and plants will close. The result will be a considerable loss to domestic shoe producers and workers. Most people believe that society as a whole, which benefits from free trade, should help the minority that is victimized by it. To promote this objective, the United States established "adjustment assistance" for firms or workers who, because of government agreement to reduce barriers to free trade, have suffered idleness or unemployment due to an increase in imports. Workers can enter retraining programs and can obtain allowances to help pay for moving to other jobs. (However, such benefits were reduced substantially in the early 1980s.)

# TARIFFS IN THE UNITED STATES

How high are American tariffs, now and in the past? In our early years, we were a very protectionist nation. The argument for protecting our young industry from the competition of European manufacturers was the "infant industry" argument, which, as we saw above, can be perfectly sensible. However, our own industries understandably found it advantageous to prolong their childhood for as long as possible—and to press for continuation of high tariffs. During the nineteenth century and well into the twentieth, the industrial Northeast was particularly strong in its support of tariffs. Furthermore, the Republican party, which generally held sway in American politics between the Civil War and the New Deal, favored a high tariff. Thus, as shown in Figure 17.5, the tariff remained relatively high from about 1870 until the early 1930s. With the exception of the period around World War I, average tariff rates were about 40 to 50 percent. With the enactment of the Smoot-Hawley Tariff of 1930, the tariff reached its peak—about 60 percent. Moreover, these tariff rates understate the extent to which the tariff restricted trade: Some goods were completely shut out of the country by the tariff, and do not show up in the figures.

With the Democratic victory in 1932, a movement began toward freer trade. The Trade Agreements Act of 1934 allowed the president to bargain with other countries to reduce barriers to trade. He was given the power to lower U.S. tariffs by as much as 50 percent. In 1945, he was given the power to make further tariff reductions. Between 1934 and 1948, tariff rates fell substantially, as shown in Figure 17.5. By 1948, the United States was no longer a high-tariff country; the average tariff rate was only about 10 percent.[5]

## The Kennedy Round and the European Community

During the 1950s, there were no further decreases in the tariff—but there were no substantial increases either. The movement toward freer trade was continued by President Kennedy in 1962, and during the 1960s, the "Kennedy Round" negotiations took place among about 40 nations in an

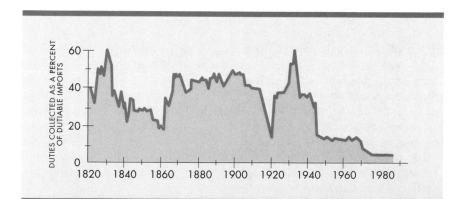

**Figure 17.5**
**Average American Tariff Rates**
The tariff generally remained high from about 1870 to the early 1930s; in recent decades it has decreased substantially.

[5] In 1947, the United States and 22 other nations signed the *General Agreement on Tariffs and Trade* (GATT), which calls for all participating countries to meet periodically to negotiate bilaterally on tariff cuts. Any tariff cut negotiated in this way will be extended to all participating nations.

attempt to reduce tariffs. In 1967, the United States agreed to cut tariffs by about one-third on a great many items.

The negotiations during the 1960s were prompted by the establishment of the **European Economic Community**—or **"Common Market."** The EEC was composed originally of Belgium, France, West Germany, Holland, Italy, and Luxembourg; and in the late 1970s, Britain, Denmark, and Ireland joined. When the EEC was formed, the member countries agreed to reduce the tariff barriers against one another's goods—but not against the goods of other nations, including the United States.

The formation and success of the Common Market—and the likelihood that other European countries would join—posed a problem for the United States. The Common Market is a large and rich market, with over 200 million people and a combined gross national product in the trillions of dollars. With the reduction of tariff barriers *within* the Common Market, trade *among* the members of the Common Market increased rapidly, and prices of many items were cut. But American exporters were less than ecstatic about all of this, because the members of the Common Market still maintained their tariff barriers against American goods. While the "Kennedy Round" negotiations succeeded in reducing some of the tariff barriers between the United States and the Common Market, important tariff barriers remained, particularly for agricultural products.

## The Tokyo and Uruguay Rounds

In 1973, over 100 nations met in Tokyo to plan a new round of trade negotiations. The aim was to make progress toward the reduction of both tariffs and nontariff barriers to trade. (In recent years, tariffs have been replaced to some extent by nontariff barriers to trade.) After over 5 years of difficult negotiations, an agreement was approved in April 1979. This agreement called for the industrial nations to reduce tariffs on thousands of goods by an average of about 33 percent during an 8-year period. It also tried to reduce export subsidies, phony technical standards for imports (used to keep out foreign goods), and barriers to international bidding for government contracts.

In 1986, a new round of negotiations, called the Uruguay Round, began. An attempt was made to curtail domestic subsidies for farmers, which distort international trade, as well as to reduce nontariff barriers to trade. Also, the industrialized countries like the United States tried to get the poorer countries like India and Brazil to protect intellectual property rights (like patents and copyrights) more effectively. The negotiations did not fulfill these objectives. In December 1990, the trade officials participating in the negotiations gave up, and suspended the talks. But international discussions of these issues continued.

Important trade legislation was passed by the Congress in 1988. Reacting to the huge trade deficits of the 1980s, the U.S. government set out to require "fair" trade. The 1988 Trade Acts empower the government to retaliate against nations that erect substantial and numerous "unfair trade barriers." Also, 60-day notice is required for plant shutdowns, and aid for workers displaced by plant closings is increased.

In Europe, there was an emphasis in the early 1990s on removing barriers to intra-European free trade. For example, European governments have tended to favor firms from their own countries when they have awarded construction or defense contracts. In 1985, the member states of the European Community—or Common Market—undertook to remove such barriers to free trade by 1992. Some American firms fear that, while the removal of such barriers will encourage more intra-European trade, there may be a tendency for the Europeans to maintain barriers against products from outside Europe.

## Increased Protectionism

Recent years have seen a marked increase in protectionist feelings in the United States. As Western Europe and Japan have become more formidable competitors abroad and at home, many industries have pressed for quotas and higher tariffs. The automobile, steel, and textile industries have been among the most frequent petitioners for protection. In 1981, the Japanese agreed to limit import of Japanese autos into the United States to 1.68 million per year; by 1988, the quota was increased to 2.3 million per year. The United States stopped asking for the restraints in 1985, but Japan "voluntarily" decided to keep them. (See page 375.)

In the mid-1980s, hundreds of petitions were filed by industry and labor, asking the federal government to protect them from imports. In considerable part, this was due to the very strong dollar. As we shall see in the following chapter, the dollar's value relative to other currencies rose markedly during the early 1980s, the result being that foreign goods became much cheaper to American buyers. Also, in some industries like semiconductors, the quality of foreign goods sometimes exceeded that of American suppliers. Faced with very stiff competition from imports, American firms asked the government for protection.

---

# EXAMPLE 17.1    THE EFFECTS OF A TARIFF ON SHOES

The quantity of shoes demanded in the United States at each price of a pair of shoes is shown below. In addition, the quantities of shoes supplied by American producers and by foreign producers at each price are shown too.

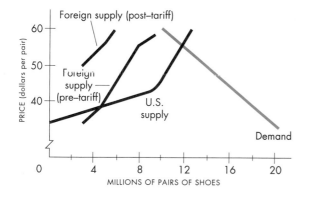

(a) Assuming that the market for shoes is competitive, what is the equilibrium price of a pair of shoes in the United States? (b) What proportion of the U.S. market goes to foreign producers of shoes? (c) Suppose that the United States imposes a tariff of $15 per pair of shoes. How many pairs of shoes will foreign producers now supply if the price is (1) $50, (2) $55, (3) $60? (Note that a $50 price together with a $15 tariff means that the price to the foreign producer is $50 – $15, or $35.) (d) After the imposition of the tariff, what is the equilibrium price? (e) After the imposition of the tariff, what proportion of the U.S. market goes to foreign producers of shoes? (f) How much revenue does the U.S. government get from this tariff?

## Solution

(a) $45, since at this price U.S. supply (10 million pairs) plus foreign supply (6 million pairs) equals the quantity demanded (16 million pairs). (b) 6/16. (c) 3 million pairs (since this is what would have been supplied at a price of $35 without the tariff), 5 million pairs (since this is what would have been supplied at a price of $40 without the tariff), 6 million pairs (since this is what would have been supplied at a price of $45 without the tariff). (d) $50, since at this price U.S. supply (11 million pairs) plus foreign supply (3 million pairs) equals the quantity demanded (14 million pairs). (e) 3/14. (f) 3 million x $15, or $45 million.

# RESTRICTIONS ON U.S. IMPORTS OF JAPANESE AUTOS

When the first Japanese cars arrived on the West Coast in the 1970s, no one saw them as a threat to American jobs. Although they were cheaper and more fuel-efficient than American-made cars, most Americans couldn't be bothered; with gasoline at thirty cents a gallon, the difference in cost between a car that got thirty miles per gallon and one that got ten was not very great, even for someone who drove a lot.

But all this changed with the Arab oil embargo of 1973. As gas prices climbed, Americans took another look at small foreign cars. With expensive American labor and outmoded facilities on one side, and Japanese efficiency and management techniques on the other, Japan seemed to be winning the war in the showroom

Workers rally to fight foreign competition

While imports may create as many jobs as they consume in the long run, in the short run many smokestack industry workers can be left permanently unemployed or underemployed. Worried American workers wanted protection, and they found a strong advocate in Representative John Dingell, one of the leaders of an emerging protectionist movement in Congress. Dingell spoke with President Reagan and Trade Representative William Brock, and urged that if voluntary restrictions on Japanese auto imports weren't adopted, Congress would impose mandatory ones. Faced with this choice, the Japanese agreed in negotiations to voluntary restrictions.

The restrictions worked. As the number of Japanese auto imports dropped between 1981 and 1982, domestic auto industry employment rose. But the cost of saving hundreds of *thousands* of American jobs was restricted choice and higher prices for hundreds of *millions* of American consumers. Hefty dealer markups were imposed on the scarcer but still-popular imports, and as sticker prices rose on Toyotas and Datsuns, General Motors, Ford, and Chrysler found that they could raise prices too.

The combined price paid by consumers for trade restrictions is very high; it has been estimated that each job protected from foreign competition with quotas or tariffs costs consumers about $160,000 in higher prices—more than enough to support the holder of that job. While trade restrictions may save jobs in the short run, they lock inefficiencies into the American economy and merely delay needed efforts to divert people and assets into areas of the economy in which the United States has a competitive advantage—and which therefore offer long-term employment and profit possibilities.

N.B.

In the late 1980s and early 1990s, although the value of the dollar fell substantially, protectionist pressure continued. As indicated in earlier sections of this chapter, the American consumer is the loser when protectionist measures are adopted. Robert Crandall of the Brookings Institution has estimated that auto import quotas have resulted in about a $400 per car increase in the price of U.S. cars and a $1,000 per car increase in the price of Japanese imports, the total annual cost to American consumers being over $4 billion. According to Crandall, "The cost per job saved, therefore, was nearly $160,000 per year. Employment creation at this cost is surely not worth the candle."[6] (Some other industries where the cost per job saved has exceeded $100,000 are book manufacturing, dairy products, and steel.)[7]

Most economists feel that this upsurge in protectionism is an unfortunate development. Although they understand that it will be difficult to beat back the protectionist tide, they hope that this upsurge of protectionist spirit will be short-lived, and that developments here and abroad in the 1990s will enable us and our trading partners to move closer to the realization of the benefits of free trade.

## TEST YOURSELF

1. According to Hendrik Houthakker, "Our workers get high real income not because they are protected from foreign competition, but because they are highly productive, at least in certain industries." Do you agree? Why, or why not?

2. According to Richard Cooper, "Technological innovation can undoubtedly strengthen the competitive position of a country in which the innovation takes place, whether it be one which enlarges exports or displaces imports." Give examples of this phenomenon, and discuss various ways that one might measure the effects of technological innovation on a country's competitive position.

3. "The principle of comparative advantage doesn't work. The U.S. exports electronic computers to Japan and imports electronic consumer goods like TV sets from Japan." Comment and evaluate.

4. Would you favor a high tariff on imported steel if you were (a) an automobile worker, (b) a steel worker, (c) an automobile buyer, (d) a plastics worker? Explain your reasoning in each case.

## SUMMARY

1. International trade permits specialization, and specialization increases output. This is the advantage of trade, both for individuals and for nations.

2. Country A has an absolute advantage over Country B in the production of a good when Country A can produce a unit of the good with less resources than can Country B. Trade can be mutually beneficial even if one country has an absolute advantage in the production of all goods.

3. Specialization and trade depend on comparative, not absolute, advantage. A nation is said to have a comparative advantage in those products where its efficiency relative to other nations is highest. Trade can be mutually beneficial if a country specializes in the products where it has a comparative advantage and imports the products where it has a comparative disadvantage.

4. If markets are relatively free and competitive, producers will automatically be led to produce in accord with comparative advantage. If a country has a comparative advantage in the production of a certain good, it will turn out—after the price of the good in various countries is equalized and total

[6] R. Crandall, "Import Quotas and the Automobile Industry," *The Brookings Review,* Summer 1984, p. 16.
[7] G. Hufbauer, D. Berliner, and K. Eliot, *Trade Protection in the United States: 31 Case Studies,* Washington, D.C.: Institute for International Economic Studies, 1986.

world output of the good equals total world demand—that this country is an exporter of the good under free trade.

5. Specialization may occur because of economies of scale and learning. Also, some countries develop new products and processes, which they export to other countries until the technology becomes widely available.

6. A tariff is a tax imposed by the government on imports, the purpose being to cut down on imports in order to protect domestic industry and workers from foreign competition. Tariffs benefit the protected industry at the expense of the general public, and, in general, a tariff costs the general public more than the protected industry (and its workers and suppliers) gains.

7. Quotas are another barrier to free trade. They too reduce trade, raise prices, protect domestic industry from foreign competition, and reduce the standard of living of the nation as a whole.

8. Tariffs, quotas, and other barriers to free trade can sometimes be justified on the basis of national security considerations. Moreover, tariffs and other forms of protection can sometimes be justified to protect infant industries, to prevent a country from being too dependent on only a few industries, and to carry out other national objectives. But many arguments for tariffs are fallacious.

9. In our early years, we were a very protectionist country. Our tariffs remained relatively high until the 1930s, when a movement began toward free trade. Between 1934 and 1948, our tariff rates dropped substantially. Again during the 1960s, there was a significant reduction in our tariffs. But more recently, as some of our industries (like steel) have been hit hard by imports, there has been a tendency to push for more protectionist measures. Since 1980, the protectionist tide has been very strong.

10. Although it has equaled only about 10 percent of our gross national product, foreign trade is of very considerable importance to the American economy. Many of our industries rely on foreign countries for raw materials or for markets, and our consumers buy many kinds of imported goods. In absolute terms, our exports and imports are larger than those of any other nation.

# CONCEPTS FOR REVIEW

**Exports**
**Imports**
**Absolute advantage**
**Comparative advantage**
**Production possibilities curve**

**Trading possibilities curve**
**Terms of trade**
**Multinational firm**
**Tariff**
**Prohibitive tariff**

**Quota**
**Export subsidy**
**European Economic Community**
**(Common Market)**

# EXCHANGE RATES AND THE BALANCE OF PAYMENTS

IN RECENT YEARS, THE VALUE of the dollar in terms of foreign currencies has varied considerably from one period of time to another. For example, in 1985 a dollar was worth about 3 German marks, whereas in 1991 it was worth only about 1.6 German marks. If you were a tourist who visited Germany in both years, this change was of obvious importance to you because it meant that you got less German money for your dollars in 1991 than in 1985. If you were an exporter or importer, it was no less important; and if you were an economic policy maker, it was also of great relevance, as we shall see.

To understand why this decrease occurred in the value of the dollar, as well as to explore a variety of other related topics in international finance, we must consider several questions: What are exchange rates and how are they determined? How are international business transactions carried out? Should there be fixed or flexible exchange rates? What is a balance-of-payments deficit, and what is its significance? What problems have afflicted the international monetary system in recent years? These questions, which are both fundamental and timely, are taken up in this chapter.

## INTERNATIONAL TRANSACTIONS AND EXCHANGE RATES

Suppose you want to buy a book from a German publisher, and that book costs 20 marks. (The German currency consists of marks, not dollars.) To buy the book, you must somehow get marks to pay the publisher, since this is the currency in which the publisher deals. Or, if the publisher agrees, you might pay in dollars; but the publisher would then have to exchange the dollars for marks, since its bills must be paid in marks. Whatever happens, either you or the publisher must somehow exchange dollars for marks, since international business transactions, unlike transactions within a country, involve two different currencies.

If you decide to exchange dollars for marks to pay the German publisher, how can you make the exchange? The answer is simple. You can buy German marks at a bank, just as you might buy lamb chops at a butcher shop. Just as the lamb chops have a price (expressed in dollars), so the German marks have a price (expressed in dollars). The bank may tell you that each mark you buy will cost you $.65. This makes the **ex-**

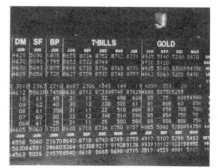

Exchange rate board showing international currencies

*change rate* between dollars and marks 0.65 to 1, since it takes 0.65 dollars to purchase 1 mark.

In general, *the exchange rate is simply the number of units of one currency that exchanges for a unit of another currency.* The obvious question is: What determines the exchange rate? Why is the exchange rate between German marks and American dollars what it is? Why doesn't a mark exchange for 25 cents, rather than 65 cents? This basic question will occupy us in the next several sections.

# EXCHANGE RATES UNDER THE GOLD STANDARD

As a starter, let's see how exchange rates were determined under the **gold standard,** which prevailed before the 1930s. *If a country was on the gold standard, a unit of its currency was convertible into a certain amount of gold.* Before World War I the dollar was convertible into one-twentieth of an ounce of gold, and the British pound was convertible into one-quarter of an ounce of gold. Thus, since the pound exchanged for 5 times as much gold as the dollar, the pound exchanged for $5. The currency of any other country on the gold standard was convertible into a certain amount of gold in the same way; and *to see how much its currency was worth in dollars, you divided the amount of gold a unit of its currency was worth by the amount of gold (one-twentieth of an ounce) a dollar was worth.*

Gold bricks stored in a bank vault.

Why did the exchange rate always equal the ratio between the amount of gold a foreign currency was worth and the amount of gold a dollar was worth? Why did the price of a British pound stay at $5 before World War I? To see why, suppose that the price (in dollars) of a pound rose above this ratio—above $5. Instead of exchanging their dollars directly for pounds, Americans would have done better to exchange them for gold and then exchange the gold for pounds. By this indirect process, Americans could have exchanged $5 for a pound, so they would have refused to buy pounds at a price above $5 per pound.

Similarly, if the price of a pound fell below $5, the British would have refused to sell pounds, since they could have obtained $5 by converting the pound into gold and the gold into dollars. Thus, *because Americans would refuse to pay more than $5, and the British would refuse to accept less, for a pound, the price of a pound had to remain at about $5.* (In practice, the pound could be a few cents above or below $5, because it costs money to transport gold in order to carry out the conversion.)

## Balance between Exports and Imports

But what ensured that this exchange rate, dictated by the gold content of currencies, would result in a rough equality of trade between countries? If one pound exchanged for $5, perhaps the British might find our goods so cheap that they would import a great deal from us, while we might find their goods so expensive that we would import little from them. Under these circumstances, the British would have to ship gold to us to pay for the excess of their imports from us over their exports to us, and eventually they could run out of gold. Could this happen? If not, why not? These questions occupied the attention of many early economists. The classic answers were given by David Hume, the Scottish philosopher, in the eighteenth century.

Hume pointed out that under the gold standard a mechanism ensured that trade would be brought into balance and that neither country would run out of gold. This mechanism was as follows. If, as we assumed, the British bought more from us than we bought from them, they would have to send us gold to pay for the excess of their imports over their exports. As their gold stock declined, their price level would fall. (Recall the quantity theory of money.) As our gold stock increased, our price level would rise. Thus, because of our rising prices, the British would tend to import less from us; and because of their falling prices, we would tend to import more from them. Consequently, the trade between the two countries would tend toward a better balance. Eventually when enough gold had left Britain and entered the United States, prices here would have increased enough, and prices in Britain would have fallen enough, to put imports and exports in balance.

# THE FOREIGN EXCHANGE MARKET

The gold standard is long gone; and after many decades of fixed exchange rates (discussed in a later section), the major trading nations of the world began to experiment with flexible exchange rates in early 1973. Let's consider a situation where exchange rates are allowed to fluctuate freely, like the price of any commodity in a competitive market. In a case of this sort, exchange rates—like any price—are determined by supply and demand. There is a market for various types of foreign currency—German marks, British pounds, French francs, and so on—just as there are markets for various types of meat.

In the case of the German mark, the demand and supply curves may look like those shown in Figure 18.1. The demand curve shows the amount of German marks that people with dollars will demand at various prices of a mark. The supply curve shows the amount of German marks that people with marks will supply at various prices of a mark. Since the amount of German currency supplied must equal the amount demanded in equilibrium, *the equilibrium price (in dollars) of a German mark is given by the intersection of the demand and supply curves.* In Figure 18.1, this intersection is at $.65.

## The Demand and Supply Sides of the Market

Let's look in more detail at the demand and supply sides of this market. On the *demand* side are people who want to import German goods (like the book you want to buy) into the United States, people who want to travel in Germany (where they'll need German money), people who want to build factories in Germany, and others with dollars who want German currency. The people on the *supply* side are those who want to import American goods into Germany, Germans who want to travel in the United States (where they'll need American money), people with marks who want to build factories in the United States, and others with marks who want American currency.

*When Americans demand more German cameras or Rhine wine (causing the demand curve to shift upward and to the right), the price (in dollars) of the German mark will tend to increase.* Thus, if the demand curve

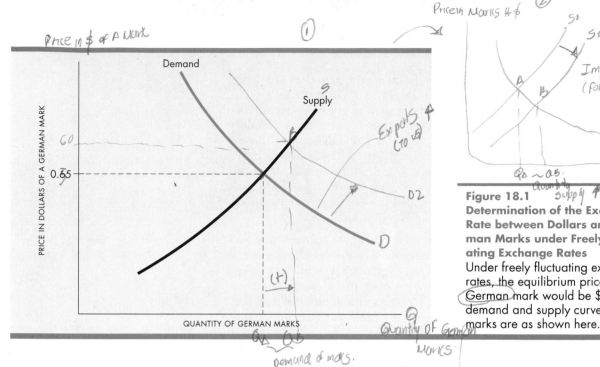

**Figure 18.1**
**Determination of the Exchange Rate between Dollars and German Marks under Freely Fluctuating Exchange Rates**
Under freely fluctuating exchange rates, the equilibrium price of a German mark would be $.65 if the demand and supply curves for marks are as shown here.

for marks shifts as shown in Figure 18.2, the result will be an increase in the equilibrium price (in dollars) of a mark from $.65 to $.70. Conversely, *when the Germans demand more American cars or computers (resulting in a shift of the supply curve downward and to the right), the price (in dollars) of the German mark will tend to decrease.*

To see why an increase in German demand for American cars or computers shifts the supply curve downward and to the right, recall that the supply curve shows the amount of marks that will be supplied at each price of a mark. Thus a shift downward and to the right in the supply curve means that more marks will be supplied at a given price (in dollars) of the mark. Given the posited increase in German demand for American goods, such a shift in the supply curve would be expected.

## Appreciation and Depreciation of a Currency

Two terms frequently encountered in discussions of the foreign exchange market are ***appreciation*** and ***depreciation.*** When Country A's currency becomes more valuable relative to Country B's currency, Country A's currency is said to appreciate relative to that of Country B, and Country B's currency is said to depreciate relative to that of Country A. In Figure 18.2, the mark appreciated relative to the dollar and the dollar depreciated relative to the mark. This use of terms makes sense. Since the number of dollars commanded by a mark increased, the mark became more valuable relative to the dollar and the dollar became less valuable relative to the mark.

Note that such a change in exchange rates would not have been possible under the gold standard. Unless a country changed the amount of gold that could be exchanged for a unit of its currency, exchange rates were fixed under the gold standard. Sometimes governments did change the amount of gold that could be exchanged for their currencies. For example, in 1933 the United States increased the price of gold from $21 an ounce to $35 an ounce. When a country increased the price of gold, this was called a ***devaluation*** of its currency.

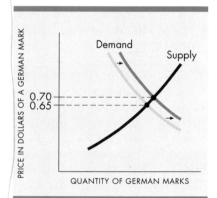

**Figure 18.2**
**Effect of Shift in Demand Curve for German Marks**
Because of the demand curve's shift to the right, the equilibrium price of a German mark increases from $.65 to $.70.

## Determinants of Exchange Rates

In a previous section, we have seen that flexible exchange rates are determined by supply and demand. But what are some of the major factors determining the position of these supply and demand curves? Under flexible exchange rates, the exchange rate between any two currencies will reflect differences in the price levels in the two countries, and differences in economic growth rates and interest rates. Consider the exchange rate between the American dollar and the German mark. If the United States has a higher inflation rate, a higher rate of economic growth, and a lower interest rate than Germany, the dollar will tend to depreciate relative to the mark, for the reasons discussed in the following paragraphs.

**RELATIVE PRICE LEVELS.** In the long run, the exchange rate between any two currencies may be expected to reflect differences in the price levels in the two countries. (This is the so-called *purchasing-power parity* theory of exchange rate determination.) To see why, suppose that Germany and the United States are the only exporters or importers of automobiles, and that automobiles are the only product they export or import. If an automobile costs $8,000 in the United States and 20,000 marks in Germany, what must be the exchange rate between the dollar and the mark? Clearly, a mark must be worth 0.40 dollars, because otherwise the two countries' automobiles would not be competitive in the world market. If a mark were set equal to 0.60 dollars, this would mean that a German automobile would cost $12,000 (that is, 20,000 times $.60), which is far more than what an American automobile would cost. Thus foreign buyers would obtain their automobiles in the United States.

Based on this theory, one would expect that, *if the rate of inflation in Country A is higher than Country B, Country A's currency is likely to depreciate relative to Country B's.* Suppose that costs double in the United States but increase by only 25 percent in Germany. After this burst of inflation, an automobile costs $16,000 (that is, 2 times $8,000) in the United States and 25,000 marks (that is, 1.25 times 20,000 marks) in Germany. Thus, based on the purchasing-power parity theory, the new value of the mark must be 0.64 dollars, rather than the old value of 0.40 dollars. (Why 0.64 dollars? Because this is the exchange rate that makes the new cost of an automobile in the United States, $16,000, equivalent to the new cost of an automobile in Germany, 25,000 marks.) Because the rate of inflation is higher in the United States than in Germany, the dollar depreciates relative to the mark.

**RELATIVE RATES OF GROWTH.** Although relative price levels may play an important role in the long run, other factors tend to exert more influence on exchange rates in the short run. In particular, *if one country's rate of economic growth is higher than the rest of the world, its currency is likely to depreciate.* If a country's economy is booming, this tends to increase its imports. If there is a boom in the United States, Americans will tend to import a great deal from other countries. If a country's imports tend to grow faster than its exports, its demand for foreign currency will tend to grow more rapidly than the amount of foreign currency that is supplied to it. Consequently, its currency is likely to depreciate.

**RELATIVE INTEREST-RATE LEVELS.** If the rate of interest in Germany is higher than in the United States, banks, multinational corporations, and other investors in the United States will sell dollars and buy marks in order to invest in the high-yielding Germany securities. Also, German investors (and others) will be less likely to find American securities attractive. Thus the mark will tend to appreciate relative to the dollar, since the demand curve for marks will shift to the right and the supply curve for marks will shift to the left. In general, *an increase in a country's interest rates leads to an appreciation of its currency, and a decrease in its interest rates leads to a depreciation of its currency.* In the short run, interest-rate differentials can have a major impact on exchange rates, since there is a huge amount of funds that are moved from country to country in response to differentials in interest rates.

### The Adjustment Mechanism under Flexible Exchange Rates

Under flexible exchange rates, what insures a balance in the exports and imports between countries? The situation differs from that described by David Hume, since Hume assumed the existence of the gold standard. Under flexible exchange rates, the balance is achieved through changes in exchange rates. Suppose that for some reason Britain is importing far more from us than we are from Britain. This will mean that the British, needing dollars to buy our goods, will be willing to supply pounds more cheaply. In other words, the supply curve for British pounds will shift downward and to the right, as shown in Figure 18.3. This will cause the price of a pound to decline from $P_1$ dollars to $P_2$ dollars. Or, from Britain's point of view, the price (in pounds) of a dollar will have been bid up by the swollen demand for imports from America.

Because of the increase in the price (in pounds) of a dollar, our goods will become more expensive in Britain. Thus the British will tend to reduce their imports of our goods. At the same time, since the price (in dollars) of a pound has decreased, British goods will become cheaper in the United States, and this will stimulate us to import more from Britain. Consequently, as our currency appreciates in terms of theirs — or, to put it another way, as theirs depreciates in terms of ours — the British are induced to import less and export more. Thus there is an automatic mechanism (just as there was under the gold standard) to bring trade between countries into balance.

## FIXED EXCHANGE RATES

Although many economists believed that exchange rates should be allowed to fluctuate, very few exchange rates really did so in the period from the end of World War II up to 1973. Instead, *most exchange rates were fixed by government action and international agreement.* Although they may have varied slightly about the fixed level, the extent to which they were allowed to vary was small. Every now and then, governments changed the exchange rates, for reasons discussed below; but for long periods of time, they remained fixed.

If exchange rates remain fixed, the amount demanded of a foreign currency may not equal the amount supplied. Consider the situation in Figure 18.4. If $A$ is the demand curve for German marks, the equilibrium price of a mark is $.40. But suppose the fixed exchange rate between dollars and marks is 0.35 to 1 — that is, each mark exchanges for $.35. Unless the government intervenes, more German marks will be demanded at a

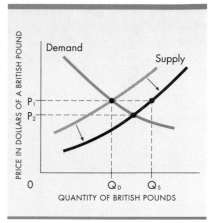

**Figure 18.3**
**Adjustment Mechanism**
If Britain imports more from us than we do from Britain, the supply curve for British pounds will shift downward and to the right, resulting in a decline of the price of the pound from $P_1$ to $P_2$ dollars. If Britain tries to maintain the price at $P_1$ dollars, the British government will have to exchange dollars for $(Q_S - Q_D)$ pounds.

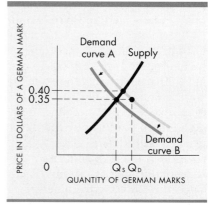

**Figure 18.4**
**Fixed Exchange Rate**
The equilibrium price of a German mark is $.40, if $A$ is the demand curve. If $.35 is the fixed exchange rate, the U.S. government may try to shift the demand curve for marks from $A$ to $B$, thus bringing the equilibrium exchange rate into equality with the fixed exchange rate.

price of \$.35 per mark than will be offered. Specifically, the difference between the quantity demanded and the quantity supplied will be $Q_D - Q_S$. Unless the government steps in, a black market for German marks may develop, and the real price may increase toward \$.40 per mark.

## Types of Government Intervention

To maintain exchange rates at their fixed levels, governments can intervene in a variety of ways. For example, they may reduce the demand for foreign currencies by reducing defense expenditures abroad, by limiting the amount that their citizens can travel abroad, and by curbing imports from other countries. Thus, in the case depicted in Figure 18.4, the American government might adopt some or all of these measures to shift the demand curve for German marks downward and to the left. If the demand curve can be pushed from $A$ to $B$, the equilibrium price of a German mark can be reduced to \$.35, the fixed exchange rate. For the time being, there will no longer be any mismatch between the quantity of marks demanded and the quantity supplied.

When exchange rates are fixed, mismatches of this sort cannot be eliminated entirely and permanently. To deal with such temporary mismatches, governments enter the market and buy and sell their currencies in order to maintain fixed exchange rates. Take the case of post–World War II Britain. At times the amount of British pounds supplied exceeded the amount demanded. Then the British government bought up the excess at the fixed exchange rate. At other times, when the quantity demanded exceeded the amount supplied, the British government supplied the pounds desired at the fixed exchange rate. As long as the equilibrium exchange rate was close to (sometimes above and sometimes below) the fixed exchange rate, the amount of its currency the government sold at one time equaled, more or less, the amount it bought at another time.

But in some cases governments have tried to maintain a fixed exchange rate far from the equilibrium exchange rate. The British government tried during the 1960s to maintain the price (in dollars) of the pound at \$2.80, even though the equilibrium price was about \$2.40. The situation was as shown in Figure 18.5. Since the quantity of British pounds supplied exceeded the quantity demanded at the price of \$2.80, the British government had to buy the difference. That is, it had to buy $(Q_S - Q_D)$ pounds with dollars. Moreover, it had to keep on exchanging dollars for pounds in these quantities for as long as the demand and supply curves remained in these positions. Such a situation could not go on indefinitely, since the British government eventually had to run out of dollars. How long it could go on depended on how big Britain's reserves of gold and foreign currency were.

# BALANCE-OF-PAYMENTS DEFICITS AND SURPLUSES

Under a system of fixed exchange rates, economists and financial analysts look at whether a country has a balance-of-payments deficit or surplus to see whether its currency is above or below its equilibrium value. What is a **balance-of-payments deficit?** What is a **balance-of-payments surplus?** It is important that both of these terms be understood.

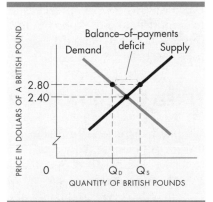

**Figure 18.5**
**Balance-of-Payments Deficit**
Because the British pound is overvalued at \$2.80, the quantity of pounds demanded ($Q_D$) is less than the quantity supplied ($Q_S$). The shortfall—that is, ($Q_S - Q_D$) pounds—is the balance-of-payments deficit.

## Balance-of-Payments Deficit

If a country's currency is *overvalued* (that is, if its price exceeds the equilibrium price), the quantity supplied of its currency will exceed the quantity demanded. Let's return to the case where the price of the British pound was set at $2.80. Under these circumstances, the quantity supplied of pounds exceeds the quantity demanded by $(Q_S - Q_D)$ pounds, as shown in Figure 18.5. This amount—$(Q_S - Q_D)$ pounds—is Britain's balance-of-payments deficit. (See Figure 18.5.) As pointed out in the previous section, it is the number of pounds that Britain's central bank, the Bank of England, must purchase. To pay for these pounds, the Bank of England must give up some of its *reserves* of foreign currencies or gold.

In a situation of this sort, there may be a "run" on the overvalued currency. Suppose that speculators become convinced that the country with the balance-of-payments deficit cannot maintain the artificially high price of its currency much longer because its reserves are running low. Because they will suffer losses if they hold on to a currency that is devalued, the speculators are likely to sell the overvalued currency (in Figure 18.5, the British pound) in very large amounts, thus causing an even bigger balance-of-payments deficit for the country with overvalued currency. Faced with the exhaustion of its reserves, the country is likely to be forced to allow the price of its currency to fall.

## Balance-of-Payments Surplus

If a country's currency is *undervalued* (that is, if its price is less than the equilibrium price), the quantity demanded of its currency will exceed the quantity supplied. During the early 1970s, the price of the German mark was set at $.35, even though its equilibrium price was about $.40. As shown in Figure 18.6, the quantity of marks demanded exceed the quantity supplied by $(Q'_D - Q'_S)$ marks under these circumstances. This amount—$(Q'_D - Q'_S)$ marks—is Germany's balance-of-payments surplus. (See Figure 18.6.) Germany can keep the price of the mark at $.35 only if it provides these $(Q'_D - Q'_S)$ marks in exchange for foreign currencies and gold. By doing so, it increases its reserves.

Whereas a country with an overvalued currency is likely to be forced by the reduction in its reserves to reduce the price of its currency, a country with an undervalued currency is unlikely to be forced by the increase in its reserves to increase the price of its currency. And a country with an undervalued currency often is reluctant to increase the price of its currency because of political pressures by its exporters (and their workers) who point out that such a revaluation would make the country's goods more expensive in foreign markets and thus would reduce its exports. Consequently, when exchange rates were fixed, countries with undervalued currencies were less likely to adjust their exchange rates than countries with overvalued currencies.

## Measuring Deficits and Surpluses

If we are given the demand and supply curves for a country's currency, it is a simple matter to determine the deficit or surplus in its balance of payments. All that we have to do is subtract the quantity demanded of the currency from the quantity supplied. However, since we do not observe these demand and supply curves in the real world, this method of deter-

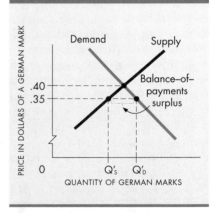

**Figure 18.6**
**Balance-of-Payments Surplus**
Because the German mark is undervalued at $.35, the quantity of marks demanded $(Q'_D)$ is greater than the quantity supplied $(Q'_S)$. The surplus—that is, $(Q'_D - Q'_S)$ marks—is the balance-of-payments surplus.

mining the deficit or surplus, while fine in principle, is not practical. The available data show only the total amount of the country's currency bought and the total amount of the country's currency sold. Since each unit of the country's currency that is bought must also be sold, it is evident that the total amount bought must equal the total amount sold. Given that this is the case, how can one identify and measure a balance-of-payments deficit or surplus?

The answer lies in the transactions of the country's central bank. If the central bank's purchases or sales of currency make up for the difference between the quantity demanded and the quantity supplied, it will purchase currency if there is a balance-of-payments deficit and sell currency if there is a balance-of-payments surplus. The amount it purchases or sells measures the size of the deficit or surplus. In other words, the official transactions of this country's government with other governments are used to measure the deficit or surplus. Roughly speaking, this is how a balance-of-payments deficit or surplus has been measured. However, beginning in May 1976, the U.S. government stopped publishing figures on the deficit or surplus in our balance of payments. Under the current regime of flexible exchange rates, changes in demand and supply for foreign exchange generally show up as changes in exchange rates, rather than in the transactions of the central bank. Thus figures regarding the deficit or surplus in our balance of payments have lost much of their previous meaning.

## THE BALANCE-OF-PAYMENTS ACCOUNTS

Although the U.S. government no longer calculates the deficit or surplus in our balance of payments, it does publish our **balance-of-payments accounts**, which are an important record of *the flow of payments between the United States and other countries*. There are two types of items in the balance-of-payments accounts: debit items and credit items. **Debit items** are items for which we must pay foreigners—items that use up our foreign currency. **Credit items** are items for which we are paid by foreigners—items that provide us with a stock of foreign currency. If a French importer buys an American car to sell in France, this is a credit item in the U.S. balance-of-payments accounts because a foreigner—the French importer—must pay us for the car. On the other hand, if an American importer buys some French wine to sell in the United States, this is a debit item in the U.S. balance-of-payments accounts. We must pay the foreigner—the French winemaker—for the wine.

It is essential to understand at the outset that *the balance-of-payments accounts always balance*. The total of credit items must always equal the total of debit items, because the sum of the debit items is the total value of goods, services, and assets we received from foreigners. These goods, services, and assets must be paid for with credit items, since credit items provide the foreign currency required by foreigners. Since the debit items must be paid for by the credit items, *the sum of the credit items must equal the sum of the debit items*.

Let's consider the U.S. balance-of-payments accounts in 1989, shown in Table 18.1. Debit items are negative; credit items are positive. The entire balance-of-payments accounts are divided into two parts, the current account and the capital account, each of which is described below.

**Table 18.1**
**United States Balance-of-Payments Accounts, 1989**

|  | CREDIT | DEBIT |
|---|---|---|
|  | (BILLIONS OF DOLLARS) | |
| Current Account | | |
| Merchandise exports | 362 | |
| Merchandise imports | | 475 |
| Net travel and transportation receipts | 1 | |
| Investment income (and other services) | 26 | |
| Net military transactions | | 6 |
| Unilateral transfers | | 14 |
| Capital account | | |
| Change in U.S. assets abroad | | 102 |
| Change in foreign assets in U.S. | 189 | |
| Change in U.S. reserve assets | | 24 |
| Change in foreign official assets in the U.S. | 7 | |
| Statistical discrepancy | 35 | |
| Total[a] | 620 | 620 |
| Balance on goods and services = $389 billion − $481 billion = −$92 billion | | |
| Balance on current account = $389 billion − $495 billion = −$106 billion | | |

[a]Because of rounding, numbers may not sum to total. Also, both the balance on goods and services and the balance on current account contain small rounding errors.

## The Current Account

The current account in Table 18.1 summarizes America's international trade in currently produced goods and services. It contains entries pertaining to six types of international transactions.

**MERCHANDISE EXPORTS.** During 1989, the United States exported about $362 billion worth of merchandise. This is a credit item since it represents payments to us by foreign purchasers of American goods.

**MERCHANDISE IMPORTS.** During 1989, the United States imported about $475 billion worth of merchandise. This is a debit item since it requires payments to manufacturers abroad.

**NET TRAVEL AND TRANSPORTATION RECEIPTS.** Travel and transportation services must be accounted for in the balance-of-payments accounts, since they entail payments by one country to another. When a British vessel carries our merchandise, we must pay for this service. Or when an American tourist stays at the George V Hotel in Paris, we must pay for this service—and judging from the George V's rates, pay dearly at that. You will recall from the previous discussion that credit items supply us with foreign currency while debit items use up our foreign currency. Thus it is clear that when foreign carriers transport our goods or people, this is a debit item, but when we carry other countries' goods or people, this is a credit item in our balance of payments. Similarly, expenditures by American tourists traveling abroad are debit items, but money spent here by foreign tourists is a credit item. Table 18.1 shows that, during 1989, the United States had a credit balance of about $1 billion with regard to travel and transportation.

**INVESTMENT INCOME AND OTHER SERVICES.** This item includes, among other things, the flow of profits from U.S. firms in foreign countries to their headquarters in the United States, minus the flow of profits from foreign firms in the United States to their headquarters abroad. When the Ford Motor Company's British subsidiary sends its profits home, this provides us with foreign currency, and thus is a credit item. When Ciba-Geigy's American subsidiary sends its profits to the firm's headquarters in Switzerland, this uses up our foreign currency and thus is a debit item. In addition, this item includes interest we pay foreigners for money lent to us, and interest paid to us for money we lent foreigners. Interest we pay foreigners is a debit item, since it uses up our foreign currency, while interest paid to us by foreigners is a credit item. Table 18.1 shows that, during 1989, the United States had a credit balance of about $26 billion with regard to investment income and other services.

**NET MILITARY TRANSACTIONS.** Besides the transactions made by private citizens, the government's transactions must be included too in our balance-of-payments accounts. The United States government supports a vast network of military bases around the world. We also engage in a host of other government activities abroad (like the Peace Corps), and all these programs affect our balance of payments. Frequently, they result in debit items since they involve payments abroad. Money spent by U.S. military authorities stationed in Wiesbaden, Germany, to buy supplies from local German companies is a debit item. However, we also earn a large amount of foreign currency by selling armaments to foreign nations; these transactions result in credit items. Table 18.1 shows that, during 1989, the U.S. had a debit balance of about $6 billion with regard to military transactions.

If we add up the foregoing five entries (merchandise exports, merchandise imports, net travel and transportation receipts, investment income and other services, and net military transactions), we get the so-called *balance on goods and services*. This balance, shown in Table 18.1, equaled about—$92 billion, which means that foreigners spent about $92 billion less on our goods and services than we spent on foreign goods and services.

**UNILATERAL TRANSFERS.** This final item in the current account includes the amount that residents of the United States send abroad minus the amount that Americans residing abroad send home. If an American working in St. Louis sends part of her pay to her relatives in Italy, this is a debit item since it uses up our foreign currency. In addition, the amount that the government sends abroad for foreign aid is also counted as a unilateral transfer. Table 18.1 shows that, during 1989, the United States had a debit balance of about $14 billion with regard to unilateral transfers.

If all six entries in the current account are totaled, we get the so-called *balance on current account*. This balance, shown in Table 18.1, equaled about—$106 billion, which means that we had a deficit of about $106 billion on current account. Any deficit of this sort must be offset by a surplus in the rest of the balance-of-payments accounts (that is, in the capital account) because, as stressed above, the total of the debit items must equal the total of the credit items.

## The Capital Account

The capital account in Table 18.1 summarizes America's international transactions associated with capital investments (but not the income from these investments, since it is included in the current account). It contains entries pertaining to four types of international transactions.

**CHANGE IN U.S. ASSETS ABROAD.** When Americans buy plants in foreign countries, or purchase the securities of foreign firms, or make deposits in foreign banks, such transactions require that we use foreign currency, since we will be buying foreign assets. Thus these transactions result in debit items. During 1989, as shown in Table 18.1, the total debit balance due to the increase in both U.S. private and government assets abroad was about $102 billion.

**CHANGE IN FOREIGN ASSETS IN THE U.S.** When Saudi Arabians buy American firms or farmland, or purchase U.S. Treasury securities, or make deposits in the Bank of America, such transactions provide us with foreign currency, since foreigners use their currency to purchase our assets. Thus these transactions result in credit items. Table 18.1 shows that, during 1989, increases in foreign assets in the U.S. resulted in a credit balance of about $189 billion.

**CHANGE IN U.S. RESERVE ASSETS.** The U.S. government holds reserve assets, such as gold and foreign currencies. When we transfer some of these reserves to a foreign government, we can exchange them for dollars or foreign currencies. Thus a decrease in our reserves is a credit item. Prior to 1971, the U.S. government offset many of the debit items in its balance-of-payments accounts by transferring gold to other governments. That is, it helped to finance the deficits in its balance of payments in this way. Since 1971, the U.S. government no longer has been willing to transfer gold to foreign governments, but it has used other reserve assets such as foreign currencies. As shown in Table 18.1, there was a $24 billion increase in reserves in 1989.

**CHANGE IN FOREIGN OFFICIAL ASSETS IN THE U.S.** Increases in foreign official assets in the United States are increases in dollars held by foreign governments, generally in the form of U.S. Treasury bills. Since such increases provide us in effect with foreign currency, they are credit items. For many years, they have helped in a major way to finance deficits in the U.S. balance of payments. During 1989, increases in foreign official assets in the United States resulted in a credit balance of about $7 billion.

All of the entries in both the current and capital account are subject to error. To some extent, this may be due to faulty and incomplete data collection, but a more important reason for the errors and omissions in the balance-of-payments accounts is that the United States finds it difficult to keep track of all the movements of goods, services, and money to and from other countries. Table 18.1 shows that, because of this *statistical discrepancy*, the government underestimated the credit items during 1989 by about $35 billion.

Finally, when we get down to the bottom of the balance-of-payments accounts, we find that the total of the credit items equals the total of the debit items. (Both are $620 billion.) As pointed out above, logic assures us that this equality will always prevail, since we must pay in cash or IOUs for what we get from other nations.

## The Balance of Trade

The newspapers often mention the balance of trade. The ***balance of merchandise trade*** refers only to a part of the balance-of-payments accounts. A nation is said to have a *favorable* balance of merchandise trade if its exports of merchandise are more than its imports of merchandise, and an *unfavorable* balance of merchandise trade if its exports of merchandise are less than its imports of merchandise. As Table 18.1 shows, the United States had an unfavorable balance of merchandise trade of about $113 billion in 1989. Until 1970, the United States generally had a favorable balance of trade, but in recent years this seldom has been the case.

Although the balance of merchandise trade is of interest, it tells us only part of what we want to know about a country's transactions with other countries. As shown in Table 18.1, there is much more to the balance of payments than a comparison of merchandise exports with merchandise imports. Moreover, a "favorable" balance of trade is not necessarily a good thing, since imports, not exports, contribute to a nation's standard of living.

## TEST YOURSELF

1. Suppose that the demand curve for German marks is as follows:

| QUANTITY DEMANDED (BILLIONS OF MARKS) | PRICE(IN DOLLARS) OF A MARK |
| --- | --- |
| 20 | 0.20 |
| 15 | .30 |
| 10 | .40 |
| 5 | .50 |

Plot this demand curve on a graph. What sorts of groups, organizations, and individuals are part of the demand side of this market.

2. Suppose that the supply curve for German marks is as shown at top right. Plot this supply curve on the same graph as the demand curve in Question 1. What sorts of groups, organizations, and individuals are part of the supply side of this market?

| QUANTITY SUPPLIED (BILLIONS OF MARKS) | PRICE (IN DOLLARS) OF A MARK |
| --- | --- |
| 8 | 0.20 |
| 9 | .30 |
| 10 | .40 |
| 11 | .50 |

3. Based on the information in Questions 1 and 2, what is the equilibrium value of the exchange rate, if it is completely flexible? Why? Is the exchange rate between the U.S. dollar and the German mark completely flexible at present?

4. Suppose that the exchange rate is fixed, and that the price (in dollars) of a mark is set at $0.30. Based on the data in Questions 1 and 2, will the quantity of marks demanded equal the quantity supplied? What sorts of government actions will have to be taken?

## EXCHANGE RATES: PRE–WORLD WAR II EXPERIENCE

Now that we are familiar with a balance-of-payments deficit and surplus (and the balance-of-payments accounts), we can begin to see how various types of exchange rates have worked out. What has been our experience with the gold standard? With fixed exchange rates? With flexible exchange rates?

During the latter part of the nineteenth century, the gold standard seemed to work very well, but serious trouble developed after World

War I. During the war, practically all of the warring nations went off the gold standard to keep people from hoarding gold or from sending it to neutral countries. After the war, some countries tried to re-establish the old rates of exchange. Because the wartime and postwar rates of inflation were greater in some countries than in others, under the old exchange rates the goods of some countries were underpriced and those of other countries were overpriced. According to the doctrines of David Hume, this imbalance should have been remedied by increases in the general price level in countries where goods were underpriced and by reductions in the general price level in countries where goods were overpriced. But wages and prices proved to be inflexible, and, as one would expect, it proved especially difficult to adjust them downward. When the adjustment mechanism failed to work quickly enough, the gold standard was abandoned.

During the 1930s, governments tried various schemes. This was the time of the Great Depression, and governments were trying frantically to reduce unemployment. Sometimes a government allowed the exchange rate to be flexible for a while, and when it found what seemed to be an equilibrium level, fixed the exchange rate there. Sometimes a government depreciated the value of its own currency relative to those of other countries in an attempt to increase employment by making its goods cheap to other countries. When one country adopted such policies, others retaliated, causing a reduction in international trade and lending, but little or no benefit for the country that started the fracas.

## THE GOLD EXCHANGE STANDARD

In 1944, the Allied governments sent representatives to Bretton Woods, New Hampshire, to work out a more effective system for the postwar era. It was generally agreed that competitive devaluations, such as occurred in the 1930s, should be avoided. Out of the Bretton Woods conference came the **International Monetary Fund** (IMF), which was set up to maintain a stable system of fixed exchange rates and to insure that when exchange rates had to be changed because of significant trade imbalances, disruption was minimized.

The system developed during the postwar period was generally labeled the **gold-exchange standard,** as opposed to the gold standard. Under this system, the dollar—which had by this time taken the place of the British pound as the world's key currency—was convertible (for official monetary purposes) into gold at a fixed price. And since other currencies could be converted into dollars at fixed exchange rates, other currencies were convertible indirectly into gold at a fixed price.

During the early postwar period, the gold-exchange standard worked reasonably well. However, it was not too long before problems began to develop. As noted in a previous section, when exchange rates are fixed, a U.S. balance-of-payments deficit is evidence of pressure on the dollar in foreign exchange markets. During the period from 1950 to 1972 (the last full year when exchange rates were fixed), the United States showed a chronic deficit in its balance of payments. This chronic deficit caused considerable uneasiness and concern, both here and abroad.

In March 1973, representatives of the major trading nations met in Paris to establish a system of fluctuating exchange rates, thus abandoning the Bretton Woods system of fixed exchange rates. This was a major break with the past, and one that was greeted with considerable apprehension

International Monetary Fund head-quarters

as well as hope. However, the major trading nations did not go so far as to establish completely flexible exchange rates. Instead, the float was to be managed. Central banks would step in to buy and sell their currency. Thus the United States agreed that "when necessary and desirable" it would support the value of the dollar. Also, some European countries decided to maintain fixed exchange rates among their own currencies, but to float jointly against other currencies.

## FIXED VERSUS FLEXIBLE EXCHANGE RATES

Why, until 1973, did most countries fix their exchange rates, rather than allow them to fluctuate? One important reason was the feeling that flexible exchange rates might vary so erratically that it might be difficult to carry out normal trade. Thus American exporters of machine tools to Britain might not know what British pounds would be worth six months from now, when they would collect a debt in pounds. According to the proponents of fixed exchange rates, fluctuating rates would increase uncertainties for people and firms engaged in international trade and thus reduce the volume of such trade. Moreover, they argued that the harmful effects of speculation over exchange rates would increase if exchange rates were flexible, because speculators could push a currency's exchange rate up or down, and destabilize the exchange market. Further, they argued that flexible exchange rates might promote more rapid inflation, because countries would be less affected by balance-of-payments discipline.

Many economists disagreed, feeling that flexible exchange rates would work better. They asked why flexible prices are used and trusted in other areas of the economy, but not in connection with foreign exchange. They pointed out that a country would have more autonomy in formulating its fiscal and monetary policy if exchange rates were flexible, and they claimed that speculation regarding exchange rates would not be destabilizing. But until 1973, the advocates of flexible exchange rates persuaded few of the world's central bankers and policy makers.

## HOW WELL HAVE FLOATING EXCHANGE RATES WORKED?

From 1973 to date, exchange rates have been flexible, not fixed. As noted above, there has been some intervention by central banks to keep the movement of exchange rates between broad bounds, but this intervention generally has not been very great. The result has been considerable volatility in exchange rates. The exchange rate between the dollar and the German mark has sometimes varied by 2 percent or more from one day to the next, and by 15 percent or more over a period of several months. As shown in Figure 18.7, the value of the dollar (in terms of other major currencies) has gyrated substantially during the past 20 years.

Unquestionably, the variations in exchange rates, some of which are erratic and without fundamental economic significance, have made international transactions more difficult. Thus Renault, the French auto manufacturer, is reported to have hesitated to launch an export drive into the U.S. market because of the erratic behavior of the dollar-franc exchange rate.

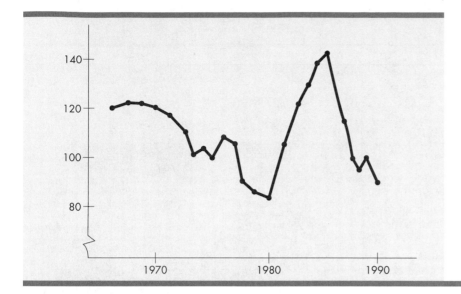

**Figure 18.7**
**Value of U.S. Dollar in Terms of Major Foreign Currencies, 1967–90 (March 1973 = 100)**
The value of the dollar (in terms of other major currencies) has varied considerably in recent decades.
*Source: Economic Report of the President,* 1991.

During the 1970s, the value of the dollar fell considerably, as shown in Figure 18.7. Between September 1977 and March 1978, and again between June and October 1978, the value of the dollar fell by about 10 percent, due in part to our unfavorable balance of trade (because we pursued a more expansionary policy than our major trading partners) and to interest rates being higher abroad than here.

During the early 1980s, the dollar staged a spectacular rebound. Between 1980 and 1985, its value rose by about 60 percent. In large part, this was due to the fact that inflation in the United States seemed to have moderated, real interest rates here were higher than in other countries (partly the result of huge government borrowing to finance its deficits), and the rates of return from investments here seemed relatively high. This marked appreciation of the dollar hurt American exporters, since their goods became very expensive to foreigners, but it helped to keep a lid on inflation, since imported goods were relatively cheap, and many American firms could not raise their own prices very much without losing business to imported goods.

In the late 1980s, the dollar took a dive, losing practically all of the value it had gained in the early 1980s. In part, this was due to lower interest rates in the United States and to the feelings of speculators that the dollar was overvalued. Also, according to many economists it was partly because a number of governments sold dollars and bought other currencies in order to bring down the dollar's value. In other words, there was some coordination of major governments' policies to try to reduce the value of the dollar. (See page 394.)

## SHOULD THE VALUE OF THE DOLLAR BE STABILIZED?

According to some economists like John Williamson of the Institute for International Economics, governments should do more to stabilize the value of the dollar. They argue that governments should buy and sell currencies so as to keep exchange rates within certain ***target zones,*** as well as co-

John Williamson

# INTERNATIONAL POLICY COORDINATION

In September 1985, government officials from Japan, West Germany, and the United States began meeting secretly in New York's Plaza Hotel to see whether they could resolve a potentially painful political issue. All parties agreed that the U.S. dollar was overvalued. But bringing it down would alter trade balances and affect economies all over the world. The goal was a "soft landing" for the dollar. Could it be accomplished? According to many economists, the answer was yes, but only through *international policy coordination*.

Proponents of international policy coordination make the following sorts of arguments. First, a coordinated and concerted effort to reduce tensions in the world economy should be more effective than a piecemeal or independent approach. Second, policy coordination should increase the likelihood that policy goals in various countries are compatible. Third, a united approach may make it possible for governments to take action on politically painful policies. In addition, economists like John Williamson of the Institute of International Economics point to the Plaza Accord, and claim that it really worked.

But there also are limits to policy coordination. For one thing, there may be disagreement among governments over objectives. For example, in the late 1980s Europeans and Japanese wanted the United States to take bold steps to reduce its deficit. In turn, the Americans could not understand why the Europeans tolerated such high unemployment rates. Also, policy coordination may be hampered by disputes among nations over who will get the lion's share of the benefits resulting from policy coordination. Further, there are financial limits to policy coordination. For example, central banks have only limited amounts of reserves to use for the stabilization of exchange rates.

One opponent of international policy coordination is Harvard's Martin Feldstein, former chairman of the Council of Economic Advisers. He believes that attempts to stabilize the value of the dollar will not work, in part because domestic policy controversies within the United States will not be resolved by

Secretary of State James Baker announces the Plaza Accord

international agreements, and because no U.S. official can assure other countries that the United States really will carry out particular actions (because of the constitutional separation of powers).

In the 1980s, tensions in the world economy prompted calls for policy coordination. Only some of these efforts seem to have borne fruit. Attempts to reduce the volatility of exchange rates have brought about very close cooperation among monetary authorities with some effectiveness, according to many economists. Not only was the Plaza Accord of 1985 regarded as a success by many economists; so was the European Monetary System (EMS), established in 1979, which was aimed at stabilizing intra-European exchange rates. However, success at coordinating fiscal policies has been much more elusive, given the intractability of the U.S. budget deficit. Also, coordination of tax and spending policies is severely constrained by domestic political considerations. Nonetheless, while the payoffs from cooperation have been limited so far, there is a general sense in some quarters that the alternatives to cooperation are much less appealing, and that attempts to coordinate policy should continue.

N. B.

ordinate monetary and fiscal policies. Under the Louvre accord of 1987, the biggest countries tried to stabilize their currencies within certain ranges that were agreed upon, but these ranges were not published as formal targets. In late 1987, when the U.S. government objected to the policies of some of the other countries, it ignored this accord and permitted the dollar to drop.

Other economists like Harvard's Martin Feldstein feel that it would be a mistake to try to stabilize the value of the dollar. In their view, attempts of this sort would mean that monetary and fiscal policies would have to be diverted from their proper roles, thus sacrificing the traditional goals of price stability and high employment. And if the value of the dollar were stabilized, it "would mean harmful distortions in the balance of trade and in the international flow of capital."[1]

Although flexible exchange rates have been in operation for about 20 years, the truth is that a clear assessment of their success—or lack of it— is hard to make because we don't know what would have occurred if some other system of exchange rates had been adopted. Clearly, flexible exchange rates have not lived up to the claims of some of their proponents, but neither have they been as disastrous as some of their opponents claimed. So far, they've enabled us to muddle through, although not without substantial problems.

Martin Feldstein

# THE INTERNATIONAL MONETARY FUND

Having described our experience with the gold standard, fixed exchange rates, and flexible exchange rates, we must look more closely at the role of the International Monetary Fund. As pointed out above, representatives of 16 countries met in 1944 in Bretton Woods, New Hampshire, to try to establish a new international monetary system. Out of these historic conferences came a system that survived—with some crises and changes— for almost 30 years. A cornerstone of this system was the International Monetary Fund (IMF), established by 40 nations to insure reasonable stability of exchange rates. The Fund was composed initially of about $30 billion of gold and currency, contributed by the member countries. It has been enlarged greatly since then, and membership has grown to over 100 countries.

Bretton Woods, New Hampshire

### The IMF under Fixed Exchange Rates

The IMF had three purposes. First, it provided a permanent mechanism for consultation by various countries on international financial problems. Second, it tried to promote the stability of exchange rates and to avoid competitive depreciation of currencies. Third, it was empowered to make temporary loans to member countries to give them time to correct disequilibria in their balances of payments, thus promoting smoother international financial adjustments.

Note that the Fund was built on a philosophy of fixed exchange rates. The men who met at Bretton Woods were impressed with the problems of flexible exchange rates, at least as they were used in the 1930s, and agreed that exchange rates should be reasonably stable. Of course, they

[1] M. Feldstein, "The Case Against Trying to Stabilize the Dollar," *American Economic Review*, May 1989.

recognized that from time to time changes in certain exchange rates would be required. (Among the people at Bretton Woods was John Maynard Keynes, which suggests that the conferees were hardly financial babes in the woods.) But changes in exchange rates should, they felt, be made only in response to persistent disequilibria. In this respect, the spirit behind the IMF differed substantially from the old gold standard. Whereas the IMF recognized that exchange rates should sometimes change, the gold standard emphasized exchange stability under all circumstances.

## The IMF under Flexible Exchange Rates

The role of the IMF in the international monetary system had to be altered considerably when flexible exchange rates were adopted. In 1976, the IMF Board of Governors adopted an amendment to the IMF Articles of Agreement. This amendment formalized a number of major changes in the functioning of the IMF. To considerable extent, it ratified the changes that already had occurred.

Specifically, this amendment permitted each country belonging to the IMF to choose its own preferred exchange-rate arrangement. A country could allow the value of its currency to be determined entirely by supply and demand. Or it could fix the exchange rate between its currency and that of some other country. Or it could adopt some other arrangement. All that the country had to undertake to do was to foster orderly economic and financial conditions and to avoid preventing the effective adjustment of balance-of-payments problems. Although the reintroduction of a system of "stable but adjustable" exchange rates was mentioned as a possibility in the amendment, such a change would require a "high majority" of the voting power and could be vetoed by the United States (which had 20 percent of the votes).

## SDRs and Gold

The leading Western economic powers agreed in 1968 to allow the International Monetary Fund to establish *special drawing rights (SDRs)*. These SDRs were a new kind of reserve asset, which could be used by member countries much as they used gold in the past. New SDRs can be created by a vote of 85 percent of the IMF's membership. Unlike garden-variety IMF loans, SDRs do not have to be repaid to the IMF, but their allocation among countries must be in accordance with IMF quotas. SDRs are sometimes called "paper gold."

"Paper gold" is backed by nothing other than the member countries' pledge to accept it in exchange for currencies. It is much like our domestic money—which, as we know from Chapter 10, is not convertible into gold or silver. In 1970, over $3 billion worth of "paper gold" was created by the IMF. The United States received about $900 million, the United Kingdom received about $400 million, and France and Germany about $200 million each. More SDRs were issued in later years. For example, by early 1976 about $7.7 billion of SDRs had been created, of which the United States got about $2.8 billion. However, while many economists have favored the expanded reliance on SDRs, many of the world's bankers have been suspicious of "paper gold". Because of their limited acceptance, SDRs have remained of subsidiary financial importance.

The trend during the 1970s was toward a declining role for gold in the

# ARE FOREIGNERS BUYING UP THE UNITED STATES AT BARGAIN PRICES?

Few events in recent years have generated as much controversy as the sale of Columbia Pictures to Sony Corporation and the sale of Rockefeller Center to Mitsubishi Estate. At the heart of this controversy are three basic fears: 1) that foreigners are buying up the United States at bargain prices, 2) that foreigners are gaining control of the United States, and 3) that foreigners are "hollowing out" the U.S. economy.

Fear of foreign investment is not new in the United States. Before 1914, Americans—then as now the world's largest debtor nation—complained about British investment in railways, mines, and land. Yet, thanks in part to the growth encouraged by that investment, America soon switched to being the world's largest investor itself. Now, once again, Americans fear and resent foreign ownership. However, this time, the focus of the bad feelings is on the Japanese.

The data suggest that fears of a foreign takeover of the United States, especially by the Japanese, are grossly exaggerated. In the United States, foreign-controlled firms own about 10 percent of the assets, employ about 4 percent of the work force, and account for about 10 percent of the sales. These percentages are roughly what they are in Europe (but much larger than in Japan). Of the total investment made by foreigners in the United States, roughly two-thirds has originated in Europe, with the British accounting for a very large share. Only about 15 percent (so far) has come from Japan. While Japanese direct foreign investment in the United States has grown substantially in recent years, it still only accounts for about 1.5 percent of total U.S. assets.

Foreigners have invested in the United States for a variety of reasons. One reason, though by no means the most important, has been the depreciation of the dollar since 1985. However, while a cheaper dollar reduces the price of U.S. assets to foreigners to "bargain" levels, it also reduces the value of the income from those assets. Thus other more fundamental reasons lie behind the recent surge in direct foreign investment. These include the attraction of the huge North American market, the acceleration of global integration, and attempts to circumvent trade barriers.

There is also little evidence that foreign firms are

Rockefeller Center

exploiting the U.S. economy by stealing valuable technologies and exporting high value-added jobs. On the contrary, the evidence suggests that, with few exceptions, foreign firms are net importers of technology and that the average skill level and pay in foreign-owned firms is higher than the national average.

In response to public fears about foreign ownership, there have been numerous suggestions in the U.S. Congress (and state legislatures) that foreign investment be curbed. While such suggestions have some political appeal, they could be economically harmful because they could limit the supply of capital in the United States, thus raising its price. Some politicians have argued that because other countries restrict the inflow of capital, we should do the same. However, because other countries are short-sighted enough to limit the inflow of money and jobs is not a good excuse for our matching their folly. The best bet for the United States in the long run is to push for continued liberalization of international capital flows because we will remain one of the major beneficiaries.

N. B.

# AMERICA'S CHRONIC TRADE DEFICIT

You probably know that the United States has been importing more than it has been exporting in recent years; in other words, it has been experiencing a trade deficit. What is less well known is that this trade deficit was not very large until the early 1980s. Our current account deficit—the excess of imports of goods and services over exports, plus net transfer payments made to foreign residents—rose from $9 billion in 1982 to about $143 billion in 1986. The deterioration of the U.S. trade balance was not confined to certain sectors. Between 1982 and 1986, the U.S. merchandise trade balance worsened in 9 of 10 major product classifications. Also, our bilateral trade balances with practically all of our major trading partners, such as Japan, worsened during this period. During the late 1980s, our trade deficit seemed to decline, but remained large, as shown in Figure 1 (located below in the left-hand column).

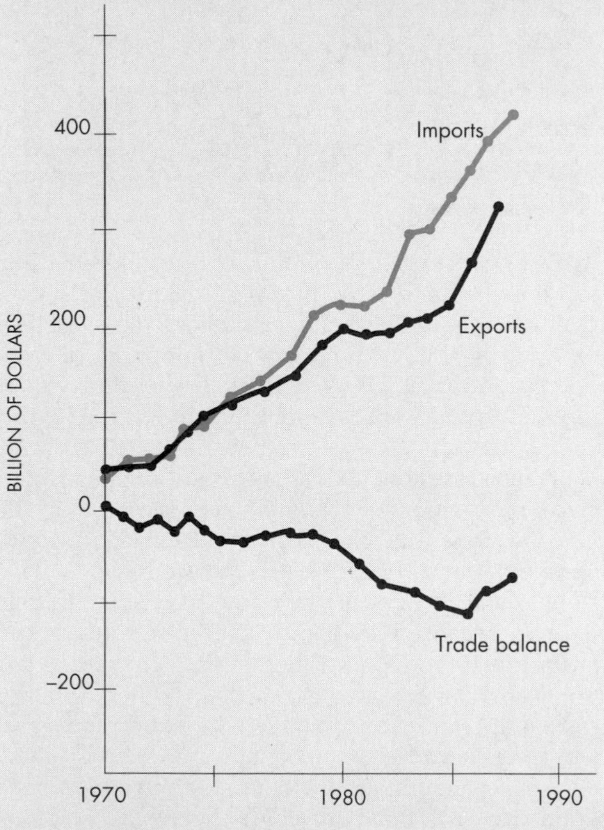

One reason for this huge trade deficit is that the American economy grew more rapidly during this period than did the economies of most foreign countries. As stated by the Council of Economic Advisers,

> The U.S. deficit on goods and services signifies that total expenditures on goods and services in the United States (domestic demand) exceed U.S. production of goods and services (GNP), and that the United States is importing the difference. Intuitively, the strong U.S. recovery—especially in terms of domestic demand—has boosted expenditures on imports as well as on domestically produced goods. Relatively weak growth abroad, however, has limited the expansion of U.S. export markets.[1]

Another important factor responsible for the trade deficit was the enormous federal budget deficit. As we know from Equation 9.5 on page 184,

$$(X - M_I) = (S - I) - (G - T),$$

where $X$ is exports, $M_I$ is imports, $S$ is saving, $I$ is investment, $G$ is government spending, and $T$ is taxes. Multiplying both sides of this equation by minus one, we find that

$$(M_I - X) = (I - S) + (G - T).$$

Since $G - T$ equals the federal budget deficit, it is clear that the trade deficit—which equals $(M_I - X)$—is directly related to the federal budget deficit. Consequently, the fact that the federal budget deficit was very large during this period (see Chapter 15) was one reason why the trade deficit was so big.

Still another reason for the large trade deficit was the very strong dollar during this period. Recall from Figure 18.7 that the value of the dollar increased greatly during the early 1980s, reducing our exports

**Figure 1**
**U.S. Imports, Exports, and Trade Balance, 1970–89**
*Source: Economic Report of the President,* 1991.

[1]*Annual Report of the Council of Economic Advisers,* Washington, D.C.: Government Printing Office, 1987, p. 102.

398     EXCHANGE RATES AND THE BALANCE OF TRADE (CH. 18)

and raising our imports. Obviously, this increased the trade balance. When the dollar fell in the late 1980s, many economists hoped that the trade deficit would fall more sharply than in fact it did.

Putting these and other factors together, an official of the Federal Reserve has explained our current account deficit in the following terms:

> The explanation of the behavior of the U.S. current account during the 1980s that emerges from the empirical literature is one in which the fundamental cause is the macroeconomic policy mix pursued in the United States and its major trading partners. At the beginning of the decade, the anti-inflation stance of U.S monetary policy drove real interest rates and the dollar upward. However, the dollar's strength had little effect on the current account since the ensuing U.S. recession dampened the demand for imports. Starting in about 1982, the strongly expansionary course of U.S. fiscal policy began to impart additional upward impetus to U.S. interest rates and the dollar while at the same time fostering a recovery in U.S. economic activity and U.S. demand for imports. The result was a sharp deterioration in the current account in 1983-1984, which was exacerbated by the restrictive posture taken by fiscal authorities in the major foreign industrial countries and the economic problems of the heavily indebted developing countries. The widening of the U.S. current account deficit meant that foreigners in effect were financing more and more of the U.S. government budget deficit, thereby allowing the U.S. private sector to maintain higher levels of consumption and investment expenditures than it otherwise could have.
>
> Steps toward tightening U.S. fiscal policy, starting in 1985, appear to have played a role in reversing the course of the dollar and the current account. Another instrumental factor seems to have been financial market concerns about the longer-run sustainability of the U.S. external position and the recognition that at some point some adjustment would be necessary.
>
> The attempts to *quantify* the various causes of the U.S. current account deficit are, of course, rough, and as one might expect, the results are far from unanimous across models. Nevertheless, the conclusion that one can draw from the empirical literature is that less than half of the deterioration in the current account was associated with the relative strength of U.S. economic activity compared with that abroad, and more than half was associated with the loss of price competitiveness of U.S. goods and services, owing largely to the strong appreciation of the dollar in the first half of the 1980s.
>
> The pace of economic activity at home and abroad as well as the course of the dollar were proximate causes only. Various econometric models indicate that expansionary U.S. fiscal policy coupled with restrictive fiscal policy in the major foreign industrial countries and the anti-inflation stance of U.S. monetary policy can explain a sizable amount of the developments in economic activity and exchange rates. There nevertheless remains a significant portion—perhaps one-third—of the rise in the dollar that remains unexplained, and which perhaps reflects a speculative bubble, and therefore some of the weakening in the U.S. current account is also unexplained.
>
> The models also have been used to investigate the seemingly puzzling persistence of the current account deficit in the face of the dollar's steep decline since early 1985. Several points can be made with regard to the persistence of the deficit. First, in the absence of the dollar's fall, the nominal current account balance probably would have been weaker than the rates actually recorded. Second, the persistence is not too surprising in that the econometric models do not predict a rapid turnaround: trade volumes react with a fairly substantial lag (usually distributed over two years) to changes in prices, and the dollar prices of imports also respond with a lag (again typically distributed over two years) to changes in exchange rates. Moreover, much of the dollar's initial decline represented simply a reversal of its surge at the end of 1984 and early 1985, which probably was not reflected in prices or trade volumes anyway. Finally, the dollar's depreciation between early 1985 and the end of 1987 was more-or-less continuous so that a series of so-called J-curve effects—a weakening of the current account as import prices in dollars rise before import volumes decline in response—would tend to mask the improvement in the underlying current account position for a while. There have been some special (and unpredicted) factors as well, such as the vagaries of the oil market.[2]

## Probing Deeper

1. Should the United States be concerned about a large trade deficit of this sort? Why, or why not?

2. What can the United States do to reduce the trade deficit?

3. According to the Council of Economic Advisers, "The insulation from foreign competition that the weak dollar provided . . . in the United States in the 1970s left many . . . [U.S.] industries poorly prepared to deal with . . . competition [from imports] in the 1980s." Why?

4. The Council of Economic Advisers argues that "the shift in monetary policy from one of perceived ease and accommodation to an actual and ultimately perceived anti-inflationary stance in the early 1980s was likely critical to the reversal during 1981 and 1982 of the real depreciation of the dollar that had occurred in the late 1970s." Why?

[2] D. Howard, "Implications of the U.S. Current Account Deficit," *Journal of Economic Perspectives,* Fall 1989.

international monetary system. In 1976, it was agreed that gold would no longer be a medium of settlement in International Monetary Fund transactions. But it is still possible for countries to trade in gold. There is now a free market where anyone can buy or sell gold. The price of gold varies substantially from month to month. Since gold is viewed by many as a hedge against inflation, its price tends to rise as fears of inflation mount. Confronted by very high rates of inflation in the early 1980s, some Americans proposed a return to the gold standard. President Reagan appointed an official commission to examine the proposal, which did not receive widespread support.

## INTERNATIONAL LENDING

Before concluding this chapter, we must discuss international capital movements in somewhat more detail. The factors underlying international transactions with regard to goods and services are clear enough. We saw in the previous chapter why countries find it profitable to import and export goods and services. But we need to know more about the reasons why nations lend to one another. What factors are responsible for the fact (shown vividly in the balance-of-payments accounts in Table 18.1) that one nation invests in another?

If the world were free of political problems and nationalist fervor, the answer would be easy. Because different parts of the world are endowed with different amounts and quantities of land and other resources, and have different population densities and amounts of capital, the rate of return to be derived from investments will vary from place to place. Consequently, nations where savings rates are high and investment opportunities are relatively poor will invest their capital in nations where the investment opportunities are better.

Such international lending helps both the lender and the borrower. The lender receives a higher rate of return than it would otherwise, and the borrower gains by having more capital to work with, so that the borrower's output and wages are higher than they would be otherwise. So long as the lender receives a relatively high return from the borrowing country, there is no reason why it should ask for repayment. It may continue to lend money to the borrowing country for years and years. England, for instance, was a net lender to the United States for about a century. To pay interest to the lender, the borrowing country must sell the lender more goods than it buys, thus building up a credit in its balance of payments that it can use to finance the interest, which is a debit item.

But the world is not free of political problems and nationalist fervor. Wars occur, governments topple, devastating inflations take place, property is confiscated. Only a fool contemplates investment in another country without taking some account of these and other risks; and because these risks are present, international lending that would otherwise be profitable and beneficial—and would take place if only economic considerations were involved—is sometimes stymied. Suppose that you had $1 million to invest, and that you could invest it at 15 percent interest in a country with an unstable government, where the chances were substantial that your investment would be confiscated and that you would get back only a fraction of the $1 million. Would you make the loan? Maybe; maybe not. Unfortunately, such risks discourage many international loans that would otherwise be advantageous to both lender and borrower.

## TEST YOURSELF

1. Should the federal government buy and sell currencies in order to stabilize the value of the dollar? Why should we care whether the value of the dollar increases or decreases?

2. Under what circumstances would you be willing to invest $10,000 (if you had $10,000) in (a) El Salvador, (b) Poland, (c) Japan, (d) India? What interest rate would you expect? What guarantees would you expect? Why?

3. "Under flexible exchange rates, reserves play a much less important role than under fixed exchange rates." What does this mean? Do you agree? Why, or why not?

4. Should the United States try to eliminate a trade deficit? Why, or why not? What factors were responsible for the large U.S. trade deficit in the 1980s and early 1990s?

## SUMMARY

1. An important difference between international business transactions and business transactions within a country is that international business transactions involve more than one currency. The exchange rate is the number of units of one currency that exchanges for a unit of another currency.

2. Before the 1930s, many major countries were on the gold standard, which meant that their currency was convertible into a certain amount of gold, and that the relative gold content of currencies determined exchange rates.

3. From 1945 to 1973, when exchange rates became more flexible, most exchange rates were fixed by government action and international agreement. They were allowed to vary slightly, but only slightly, about the official rate. The amount demanded of a foreign currency did not always equal the amount supplied. To maintain exchange rates at the official levels, governments entered the market and bought and sold their currencies as needed. They also intervened by curbing imports, limiting foreign travel, and other measures.

4. Under a system of fixed exchange rates, a country will have a balance-of-payments deficit if its currency is overvalued and a balance-of-payments surplus if its currency is undervalued. A balance-of-payments deficit is the difference between the quantity supplied and quantity demanded of the currency. A balance-of-payments surplus is the difference between the quantity demanded and quantity supplied of the currency.

5. The United States experienced a chronic balance-of-payments deficit during the 1950s, 1960s, and 1970s. This deficit—the result of the growing productivity of other economies, our large investments abroad, and our military and foreign aid expenditures abroad—was financed by reductions in our gold stock and by foreigners' acceptance of our short-term debt. In 1973, the system of fixed exchange rates was abandoned.

6. Under a system of flexible exchange rates, the market for foreign exchange functions like any other free market, the exchange rate being determined by supply and demand.

Under such a system, exchange rates tend to move in a way that removes imbalances among countries in exports and imports. The price of a country's currency tends to fall (rise) if its inflation rate and growth rate are relatively high (low) or if its interest rate is relatively low (high).

7. A country's balance-of-payments accounts measure the flow of payments between it and other countries. Debit items result in a demand for foreign currency, whereas credit items supply foreign currency. The total of the debit items must equal the total of the credit items because the total of the debit items is the total amount of goods, servces,

and assets we received from foreigners, and these goods, services, and asets must be paid for with credit items.

8. The balance of merchandise trade refers only to part of the balance of payments. A nation is said to have a favorable (unfavorable) balance of merchandise trade if its exports of merchandise exceed (are less than) its imports of merchandise. During the 1980s and early 1990s, the United States had a very unfavorable balance of merchandise trade. The reasons for this trade deficit have been discussed at length in this chapter.

## CONCEPTS FOR REVIEW

| | | |
|---|---|---|
| Exchange rate | Balance-of-payments surplus | International Monetary Fund |
| Gold standard | Balance-of-payments accounts | Gold-exchange standard |
| Appreciation | Debit items | Target zones |
| Depreciation | Credit items | International policy coordination |
| Devaluation of currency | Balance of merchandise trade | Special drawing rights (SDRs) |
| Balance-of-payments deficit | | |

# PART FIVE

# CONSUMER BEHAVIOR AND BUSINESS DECISION MAKING

# MARKET DEMAND AND PRICE ELASTICITY

IN OCTOBER 1990, APPLE COMPUTER launched a new product, the Macintosh Classic, which sold very well. In other words, market demand for the Classic was high. In a capitalist economy, market demand is a fundamental determinant of what is produced and how. It is no exaggeration to say that firms spend enormous time and effort trying to cater to, estimate, and influence market demand.

In this chapter, we discuss the factors influencing the market demand curve for a commodity, as well as the measurement of market demand curves and their role in decision making by private business firms and government agencies. We consider questions like: How can we measure market demand curves? How sensitive is the quantity demanded of various products to changes in price? What factors underlie the market demand curve for a commodity? These are important questions, from both a theoretical and a practical point of view.

## MARKET DEMAND CURVES

Let's review what a market demand curve is. We saw in Chapter 3 that a commodity's market demand curve shows how much of the commodity will be purchased during a particular period of time at various prices. Figure 19.1 ought to be familiar; it is the ***market demand curve*** for wheat in the early 1990s, which figured prominently in our discussion of the price system in Chapter 3. Among other things, it shows that during the early 1990s about 2.6 billion bushels of American wheat would have been purchased per year if the price was $2.00 per bushel, that about 2.5 billion bushels would have been purchased per year if the price was $2.40 per bushel, and that about 2.4 billion bushels would have been purchased if the price was $2.80 per bushel.

Since the market demand curve reflects what consumers want and are willing to pay for, when the market demand curve for wheat shifts upward to the right, this indicates that consumers want more wheat at the existing price. On the other hand, when the curve shifts downward to the left, this indicates that consumers want less wheat at the existing price. Such shifts in the market demand curve for a commodity trigger changes in the behavior of the commodity's producers. When the market demand curve shifts upward to the right, the price of wheat will tend to rise, thus inducing farmers to produce more wheat, because they will find that, given the price increase, their profits will increase if they raise their out-

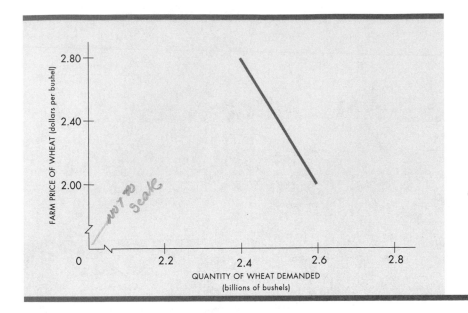

**Figure 19.1**
**Market Demand Curve for Wheat, Early 1990s**
This curve shows how much wheat would be purchased per year at various prices.

put levels. The same process occurs in other parts of the economy. Shifts in the demand curve reflecting the fact that consumers want more (less) of a commodity set in motion a sequence of events leading to more (less) production of the commodity.

## Measuring Market Demand Curves

To be of practical use, market demand curves must be based on careful measurements. Let's look briefly at some of the techniques used to estimate the market demand curve for particular commodities. At first glance, a quick and easy way to estimate the demand curve might seem to be interviewing consumers about their buying habits and intentions. However, although more subtle variants of this approach sometimes may pay off, simply asking people how much they would buy of a certain commodity at particular prices does not usually seem very useful, since off-the-cuff answers to such questions are rarely very accurate. Thus marketing researchers and econometricians interested in measuring market demand curves have been forced to use more complex procedures.

One such procedure is the ***direct market experiment.*** Although the designs of such experiments vary greatly and are often quite complicated, the basic idea is simple—to see the effects on the quantity demanded of actual variations in the price of the product. (Researchers attempt to hold other market factors constant or to take into account whatever changes may occur.) The Parker Pen Company conducted an experiment to estimate the demand curve for their ink, Quink. They increased the price from $.15 to $.25 in four cities, and found that the quantity demanded was quite insensitive to the price. Experiments like this are frequently made to try to estimate a product's market demand curve.

Still another technique is to use statistical methods to estimate demand curves from historical data on price and quantity purchased of the commodity. For example, one might plot the price of slingshots in various periods in the past against the quantity sold, as shown in Figure 19.2. Judging from the results, curve *D* in Figure 19.2 seems a reasonable ap-

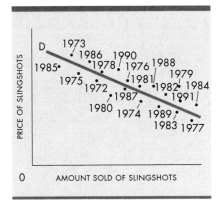

**Figure 19.2**
**Estimated Demand Curve for Slingshots**
One very crude way to estimate the market demand curve is to plot the amount sold of a commodity in each year against its price in that year, and draw a curve that seems to fit the points reasonably well. However, this technique is generally too crude to be reliable.

proximation to the demand curve. Although this simple analysis provides some insight into how statistical methods are used to estimate demand curves from historical data, it is a vast oversimplification. For one thing, the market demand curve may have shifted over time, so that curve $D$ is not a proper estimate. Fortunately, modern statistical techniques recognize this possibility and allow us to estimate the position and shape of this curve (at each point in time) in spite of it.

Hundreds, perhaps thousands, of studies have been made to estimate the demand curves for particular commodities. In view of the importance of the results for decision making, this is not surprising. To illustrate the role played by such studies in the formulation of public policy, let's consider the following case involving the Boston and Maine Railroad.

## Railroad Transportation in Metropolitan Boston: A Case Study

When the Boston and Maine Railroad wanted to discontinue passenger commuter service into Boston (because it felt such service was unprofitable), the Mass Transportation Commission of Massachusetts contracted with the Boston and Maine to establish a demonstration project to estimate the effect of lowering fares on the quantity of commuter tickets sold. The Boston and Maine was requested not to file a petition for the discontinuance of commuter service into Boston until after the experiment. During the experiment, which lasted about a year, fares were reduced about 28 percent on the average. The result was, of course, an increase in the number of tickets sold. However, the more important thing to the railroad and the commission was the *extent* to which the fare cut would increase the number of tickets sold. *How great* would be the resulting increase in the number of tickets sold? This was the important question because to increase the railroad's profits, a fare cut had to increase the railroad's revenues more than it increased its costs. And unless the price cut increased the number of tickets sold by a greater percentage than the reduction in price, it would not increase the railroad's revenues at all.

A comparison of the Boston and Maine's commuter revenues showed that this large fare reduction resulted in only a 0.6 percent increase in the railroad's revenues. Thus the price reduction increased the railroad's revenues by little or nothing. Since the reduction in fares increased the railroad's costs — because it was more costly to handle the larger volume of traffic — and increased its revenues scarcely at all, it did not increase the railroad's profits. Thus, after the experiment, the Boston and Maine decided to continue with its petition to terminate commuter service. (Eventually, however, public subsidies were instituted to keep the service going.)

This is a fairly typical example of a direct market experiment designed to obtain information on relevant aspects of a market demand curve. Note the problems experiments of this sort must face. First, *the experiment can be very costly if it alienates customers or reduces the firm's profits.* Second, *it is difficult to hold other relevant variables constant.* For example, the effect of price changes was mixed up, to some extent, with the effect of increased service in the Boston and Maine case. Third, *it is hard to conduct an experiment of this sort over a long enough period to estimate long-run effects.* Thus, in the Boston and Maine case, the effect of the fare reduction on the number of tickets sold might have been much greater if the

# EXAMPLE 19.1    SPECULATION AND THE DEMAND CURVE

In many markets speculators buy and sell, hoping to make money in the process. Suppose that the demand and supply curves for corn this year and next year are as shown below. Speculators, seeing that the price of corn is likely to rise (from $OA$ to $OH$), decide to buy corn this year and sell it next year. Thus, including the speculators, the demand curve shifts to the right this year, and the supply curve shifts to the right next year, as shown below:

**Solution**

(a) Yes. Without the speculators, much less corn would be consumed next year than this year. With them, consumption of corn is relatively constant. (b) Yes. The value (price times quantity) of the corn sold this year is increased considerably (from area $OABS_0$ to area $OCES_0$). The value of the corn sold next year does not change very much, based on the diagram. (It is area

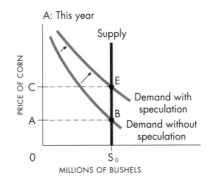

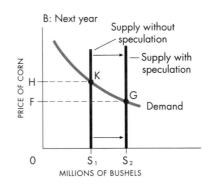

(a) In this case, do speculators even out the consumption of corn over time, thus avoiding famine-feast cycles? (b) In this case, do speculators raise the total value of the corn sold in the two periods? (c) In this case, speculators guessed correctly that the price of corn would rise. If they guess incorrectly, can they make more uneven the consumption of corn over time? (d) Once speculation is included in the analysis, does the demand curve for a product depend on its expected future price?

$OHKS_1$ without speculation and area $OFGS_2$ with speculation.) Thus the total value of the corn sold in the two periods is raised. (c) Yes. (d) Yes. If there is a general feeling that the price of a product is going to increase substantially, the demand curve for this product may shift to the right.

---

experiment had lasted longer. Nonetheless, despite these problems, experiments of this sort can produce useful evidence on the location and shape of a product's market demand curve. They are an important supplement to statistical analysis of historical data to estimate market demand curves.

## THE PRICE ELASTICITY OF DEMAND

The quantity demanded of some commodities, like beef in Figure 19.3, is fairly sensitive to changes in the commodity's price. That is, changes in price result in significant changes in quantity demanded. On the other hand, the quantity demanded of other commodities, like cotton in Figure

19.3, is very insensitive to changes in the price. Large changes in price result in small changes in the quantity demanded.

To promote unambiguous discussion of this subject, we must have some measure of the sensitivity of quantity demanded to changes in price. The measure customarily used for this purpose is the **price elasticity of demand,** *defined as the percentage change in quantity demanded resulting from a 1 percent change in price.*[1] For example, suppose that a 1 percent reduction in the price of slingshots results in a 2 percent increase in quantity demanded. Then, using this definition, the price elasticity of demand for slingshots is 2. (Convention dictates that we give the elasticity a positive sign even though the change in price is negative and the change in quantity demanded is positive.) The price elasticity of demand is likely to vary from one point to another on the market demand curve. For example, the price elasticity of demand for slingshots may be higher when a slingshot costs $1.00 than when it costs $0.25.

Note that the price elasticity of demand is expressed in terms of *relative*—i.e., proportional or percentage—changes in price and quantity demanded, not *absolute* changes in price and quantity demanded. Thus, in studying the slingshot market, we looked at the *percentage* change in quantity demanded resulting from a 1 *percent* change in price. This is because absolute changes depend on the units in which price and quantity are measured. Suppose that a reduction in the price of good *Y* from $100 to $99 results in an increase in the quantity demanded from 200 to 210 pounds per month. If price is measured in dollars, the quantity demanded of good *Y* seems quite sensitive to price changes, since a decrease in price of "1" results in an increase in quantity demanded of "10." On the other hand, if price is measured in cents, the quantity demanded of good *Y* seems quite insensitive to price changes, since a decrease in price of "100" results in an increase in quantity demanded of "10." By using relative changes, we do not encounter this problem. Relative changes do not depend on the units of measurement. Thus the percentage reduction in the price of good *Y* is 1 percent, regardless of whether price is measured in dollars or cents. And the percentage increase in the quantity demanded of good *Y* is 5 percent, regardless of whether it is measured in pounds or tons.

## Calculating the Price Elasticity of Demand

The price elasticity of demand is a very important concept and one that economists use often, so it is worthwhile to spend some time explaining exactly how it is computed. Suppose that you have a table showing various points on a market demand curve. For example, Table 19.1 shows the quantity of wheat demanded at various prices, as estimated by Professor Karl Fox of Iowa State University during the early 1960s.[2] Given these data, how do you go about computing the price elasticity of demand for wheat? Since the price elasticity of demand for any product generally

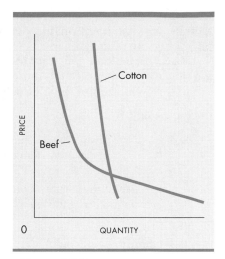

**Figure 19.3**
**Market Demand Curves, Beef and Cotton**
The quantity demanded of beef is much more sensitive to price than is the quantity demanded of cotton.

**Table 19.1**
**Market Demand for Wheat, Early 1960s**

| FARM PRICE OF WHEAT (DOLLARS PER BUSHEL) | QUANTITY OF WHEAT DEMANDED (MILLIONS OF BUSHELS) |
|---|---|
| 1.00 | 1,500 |
| 1.20 | 1,300 |
| 1.40 | 1,100 |
| 1.60 | 900 |
| 1.80 | 800 |
| 2.00 | 700 |
| 2.20 | 675 |

*Source:* K. Fox, V. Ruttan, and L. Witt, *Farming, Farmers, and Markets for Farm Goods.* New York: Committee for Economic Development, 1962.

---

[1] What if price does not change by 1 percent? Then the price elasticity of demand is defined as the *percentage change in quantity demanded divided by the percentage change in price*. This definition will be used in the next section. Put in terms of symbols, the price elasticity of demand equals $\dfrac{-\Delta Q}{\Delta P} \times \dfrac{P}{Q}$, where $P$ is price, $\Delta P$ is the change in price, $Q$ is quantity demanded, and $\Delta Q$ is the change in the quantity demanded.
[2] Note that Table 19.1 pertains to the early 1960s whereas Figure 19.1 pertains to the early 1990s. Consequently, the demand curves are quite different, as you can see.

varies from point to point on its market demand curve, you must first determine at what point on the demand curve you want to measure the price elasticity of demand.

Let us assume that you want to estimate the price elasticity of demand for wheat when the price of wheat is between $2.00 and $2.20 per bushel. To do this, you can use the following formula:

price elasticity =

$$\frac{\text{percentage change}}{\text{in quantity demanded}} \div \frac{\text{percentage change}}{\text{in price}} =$$

$$\frac{\text{change in quantity demanded}}{\text{original quantity demanded}} \div \frac{\text{change in price}}{\text{original price}}.$$

Table 19.1 shows that the quantity demanded equals 700 million bushels when the price is $2.00, and that it equals 675 million bushels when the price is $2.20. But should we use $2.00 and 700 million bushels as the original price and quantity? Or should we use $2.20 and 675 million bushels as the original price and quantity? If we choose the former,

price elasticity =

$$-\frac{675 - 700}{700} \div \frac{2.20 - 2.00}{2.00} = .36.$$

The price elasticity of demand is estimated to be .36. (The minus sign at the beginning of this equation is due to the fact, noted above, that convention dictates that the elasticity be given a positive sign.)

But we could just as well have used $2.20 and 675 million bushels as the original price and quantity. If this had been our choice, the answer would be

price elasticity =

$$-\frac{700 - 675}{675} \div \frac{2.00 - 2.20}{2.20} = .41,$$

which is somewhat different from the answer we got in the previous paragraph.

To get around this difficulty, the generally accepted procedure is to use the average values of price and quantity as the original price and quantity. In other words, we use as an estimate of the price elasticity of demand:

price elasticity =

$$\frac{\text{change in quantity demanded}}{\text{sum of quantities}/2} \div \frac{\text{change in price}}{\text{sum of prices}/2}.$$

This is the so-called **_arc elasticity of demand._** In the specific case we are considering, the arc elasticity is

price elasticity =

$$-\frac{(675 - 700)}{\left(\frac{675 + 700}{2}\right)} \div \frac{2.20 - 2.00}{\left(\frac{2.20 + 2.00}{2}\right)} = .38.$$

This is the answer to our problem.

# DETERMINANTS OF THE PRICE ELASTICITY OF DEMAND

Many studies have been made of the price elasticity of demand for particular commodities. Table 19.2 reproduces the results of some of them. Note the substantial differences among products. For example, the estimated price elasticity of demand for women's hats is about 3.00, while for cotton it is only about 0.12. Think for a few minutes about these results, and try to figure out why these differences exist. If you rack your brains for a while, chances are that you will agree that the following factors are important determinants of whether the price elasticity of demand is high or low.

**NUMBER AND CLOSENESS OF AVAILABLE SUBSTITUTES.** *If a commodity has many close substitutes, its demand is likely to be highly elastic,* i.e., the price elasticity is likely to be high. If the price of the product increases, a large proportion of its buyers will turn to the close substitutes that are available. If its price decreases, a great many buyers of substitutes will switch to this product. Naturally, the closeness of the substitutes depends on how narrowly the commodity is defined. In general, one would expect that, as the definition of the product becomes narrower and more specific, the product has more close substitutes and its price elasticity of demand is higher. Thus the demand for a particular brand of oil is more price elastic than the overall demand for oil, and the demand for oil is more price elastic than the demand for fuel as a whole. If a commodity is defined so that it has perfect substitutes, its price elasticity of demand approaches infinity. Thus, if one farmer's wheat is exactly like that grown by other farmers and if the farmer raises the price slightly (to a point above the market level), the farmer's sales will be reduced to nothing.

**IMPORTANCE IN CONSUMERS' BUDGETS.** It is often asserted that the price elasticity of demand for a commodity is likely to depend on the importance of the commodity in consumers' budgets. The elasticity of demand for commodities like pepper and salt may be quite low. Typical consumers spend a very small portion of their income on pepper and salt, and the quantity they demand may not be influenced much by changes in price within a reasonable range. However, although a tendency of this sort is often hypothesized, there is no guarantee that it always exists.

**LENGTH OF THE PERIOD.** Every market demand curve pertains, you will recall, to a certain time interval. In general, *demand is likely to be more sensitive to price over a long period than over a short one.* The longer the period, the easier it is for consumers and business firms to substitute one good for another. If, for example, the price of oil should decline relative to other fuels, oil consumption in the month after the price decline would probably increase very little. But over a period of several years, people would have an opportunity to take account of the price decline in choosing the type of fuel to be used in new and renovated houses and businesses. In the longer period of several years, the price decline would have a greater effect on the consumption of oil than in the shorter period of one month.[3]

---

[3] For durable goods like automobiles, the price elasticity of demand may be smaller over a long period than a short one. If the price of autos increases, the quantity demanded is likely to fall substantially because many people will postpone buying a new car. But as time goes on, the quantity of autos demanded will tend to rise as old autos wear out.

**Table 19.2**
**Estimated Price Elasticities of Demand for Selected Commodities, United States**

| COMMODITY | PRICE ELASTICITY |
|---|---|
| Women's hats | 3.00 |
| Gasoline | 0.30 |
| Sugar | 0.31 |
| Corn | 0.49 |
| Cotton | 0.12 |
| Hay | 0.43 |
| Potatoes | 0.31 |
| Oats | 0.56 |
| Barley | 0.39 |
| Buckwheat | 0.99 |
| Refrigerators | 1.40 |
| Airline travel | 2.40 |
| Radio and TV sets | 1.20 |
| Legal services | 0.50 |
| Pleasure boats | 1.30 |
| Canned tomatoes | 2.50 |
| Newspapers | 0.10 |
| Tires | 0.60 |
| Beef | 0.92 |
| Shoes | 0.40 |

# HENRY FORD AND THE PRICE ELASTICITY OF DEMAND FOR AUTOS

In 1905 the average automobile produced in the United States cost more than the average Datsun seventy years later. Many of the firms in the auto industry were warmed-over buggy makers who hand-crafted rich men's toys. But change was in the air. *Motor Age*, the industry's first trade magazine, prophesied that "the simple car is the car of the future—. A golden opportunity awaits some bold manufacturer of a simple car."

It remained for Henry Ford, the son of a Wisconsin farmer, to translate these words into a car—the Model T. Ford, commenting on his rural youth, declared, "It was life on the farm that drove me into devising ways and means to better transportation." Turning from the kid glove and checkbook set, he saw the potential market—at the right price—for car sales in the agricultural community.

The Model T was introduced in 1909. A few numbers indicate its phenomenal progress.

Henry Ford in his first automobile, 1903

| YEAR | PRICE (DOLLARS) | CARS SOLD |
|------|-----------------|-----------|
| 1909 | 900 | 58,022 |
| 1914 | 440 | 472,350 |
| 1916 | 360 | 730,041 |

However, all good things come to an end. By the twenties, Ford's unwillingness to alter the Model T in any fashion (cosmetic or mechanical), as well as increased competition from other manufacturers, and the development of trade-in and installment buying (which reduced the price elasticity of demand for automobiles) brought the Model T to an end. But the record profits of the Ford Motor Company between 1910 and 1920 vindicated Henry Ford in his belief that "it is better to sell a large number of cars at a reasonably small margin than to sell fewer cars at a larger margin of profit. Bear in mind that when you reduce the price of the car without reducing the quality you increase the possible number of purchases. There are many men who will pay $360 for a car who would not pay $440. I figure that on the $360 basis we can increase the sales to 800,000 cars for the year—less profit on each car, but more cars, more employment of labor and in the end, we get all the profit we ought to make." Needless to say, price reductions do not always result in higher profits. But in his appraisal of the auto market between 1910 and 1920, Henry Ford seemed right.

E.A.

# PRICE ELASTICITY AND TOTAL MONEY EXPENDITURE

Many important decisions hinge on the price elasticity of demand for a commodity. In this section, we show how the price elasticity of demand determines the effect of a price change on the total amount spent on a commodity. As a first step, we must define three terms: price elastic, price inelastic, and unitary elasticity. The demand for a commodity is **price elastic** if the price elasticity of demand is *greater than* 1. The demand for a commodity is **price inelastic** if the price elasticity of demand is *less than* 1. And the demand for a commodity is of **unitary elasticity** if the price elasticity of demand *equals* 1. As indicated below, the effect of a price change on the total amount spent on a commodity depends on whether the demand for the commodity is price elastic, price inelastic, or of unitary elasticity. Let's consider each case.

## Case 1: Demand Is Price Elastic

In this case, if the price of the commodity is *reduced*, the total amount spent on the commodity will *increase*. To see why, suppose that the price elasticity of demand for compact discs is 2 and that the price of the compact discs is reduced by 1 percent. Because the price elasticity of demand is 2, the 1 percent reduction in price results in a 2 percent increase in quantity of compact discs demanded. Since the total amount spent on compact discs equals the quantity demanded times the price, the 1 percent reduction in price will be more than offset by the 2 percent increase in quantity demanded. The result of the price cut will be an increase in the total amount spent on compact discs.

On the other hand, if the price of the commodity is *increased,* the total amount spent on the commodity will *fall*. For example, if the price of compact discs is raised by 1 percent, this will reduce the quantity demanded by 2 percent. The 2 percent reduction in the quantity demanded will more than offset the 1 percent increase in price, the result being a decrease in the total amount spent on compact discs.

## Case 2: Demand Is Price Inelastic

In this case, if the price is *reduced,* the total amount spent on the commodity will *decrease*. To see why, suppose that the price elasticity of demand for corn is 0.5 and the price of corn is reduced by 1 percent. Because the price elasticity of demand is 0.5, the 1 percent price reduction results in a ½ percent increase in the quantity demanded of corn. Since the total amount spent on corn equals the quantity demanded times the price, the ½ percent increase in the quantity demanded will be more than offset by the 1 percent reduction in price. The result of the price cut will be a decrease in the total amount spent on corn.

On the other hand, if the price of the commodity is *increased,* the total amount spent on the commodity will *increase*. For example, if the price of corn is raised by 1 percent, this will reduce quantity demanded by ½ percent. The 1 percent price increase will more than offset the ½ percent reduction in quantity demanded, the result being an increase in the total amount spent on corn.

**Table 19.3**
**Effect of an Increase or Decrease in the Price of a Commodity on the Total Expenditure on the Commodity**

| COMMODITY'S PRICE ELASTICITY OF DEMAND | EFFECT ON TOTAL EXPENDITURE OF: | |
| --- | --- | --- |
| | PRICE DECREASE | PRICE INCREASE |
| Price elastic (which means that elasticity is greater than 1) | Increase | Decrease |
| Price inelastic (which means that elasticity is less than 1) | Decrease | Increase |
| Unitary elasticity (which means that elasticity equals 1) | No change | No change |

## Case 3: Demand Is of Unitary Elasticity

In this case, a price increase or decrease results in no difference in the total amount spent on the commodity. Why? Because a price decrease (increase) of a certain percentage always results in a quantity increase (decrease) of the same percentage, so that the product of the price and quantity is unaffected.

Table 19.3 summarizes the results of this section. It should help you review our findings.

## TEST YOURSELF

1. Professor Kenneth Warner of the University of Michigan has estimated that a 10 percent increase in the price of cigarettes results in a 4 percent decline in the quantity of cigarettes consumed. For teenagers, he estimated that a 10 percent price increase results in a 14 percent decline in cigarette consumption. Based on his estimates, what is the price elasticity of demand for cigarettes? Among teenagers, what is the price elasticity of demand? Why is the price elasticity different among teenagers than for the public as a whole?

2. Suppose that each of the four corners of an intersection contains a gas station, and that the gasoline is essentially the same. Do you think that the price elasticity of demand for each station's gasoline is above or below 1? Why? Do you think that it is less than or greater than the price elasticity of demand for all gasoline in the U.S.?

3. The Bugsbane Music Box Company is convinced that an increase in its price will reduce the total amount of money spent on its product. Can you tell from this whether the demand for its product is price elastic or price inelastic?

4. Suppose that the relationship between the price of aluminum and the quantity of aluminum demanded is as follows:

| PRICE (DOLLARS) | QUANTITY |
|---|---|
| 1 | 8 |
| 2 | 7 |
| 3 | 6 |
| 4 | 5 |
| 5 | 4 |

What is the arc elasticity of demand when price is between $1 and $2? Between $4 and $5?

## THE FARM PROBLEM AND THE PRICE ELASTICITY OF DEMAND

To illustrate the importance of the price elasticity of demand, let's consider American agriculture. One of the most difficult problems for farmers is that, under a free market, farm incomes vary enormously between good times and bad, the variation being much greater than for nonfarm incomes. This is so because farm prices vary a great deal between good times and bad, whereas farm output is much more stable than industrial output. Why is agriculture like this?

The answer lies in considerable part with the price elasticity of demand for farm products. Food is a necessity with few good substitutes. Thus we would expect the demand for farm products to be price inelastic. And as Table 19.2 suggests, this expectation is borne out by the facts. Given that the demand curve for farm products is price inelastic—and that the quantity supplied of farm products is also relatively insensitive to price—it follows that relatively small shifts in either the supply curve or the demand curve result in big changes in price. This is why farm prices are so unsta-

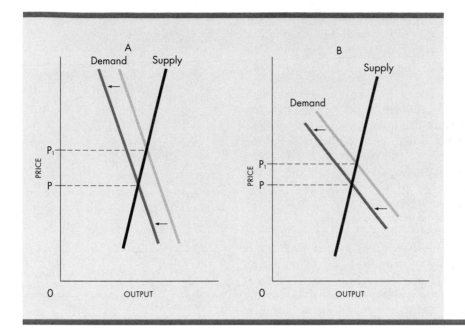

**Figure 19.4**
**Instability of Farm Prices and Incomes**
Because the demand curve in panel A is much less elastic than in panel B, a small shift in the demand curve has a much bigger impact on price in panel A than in panel B.

ble. Panel A of Figure 19.4 shows a market where the demand curve is much more inelastic than in panel B. As you can see, a small shift to the left in the demand curve results in a much larger drop in price in panel A than in panel B.

## Price Elasticity and the Brannan Plan

This is not the only role the price elasticity of demand plays in our farm problems. Many other questions involve it. Consider the plan proposed after World War II by Charles Brannan who served as President Truman's secretary of agriculture. The plan was later supported in somewhat modified form by Ezra Taft Benson, secretary of agriculture in the Eisenhower administration. But it drew fire from many farmers, and not until 1973, after nearly three decades of controversy, was the plan approved by Congress.

According to the **Brannan plan,** a floor is established under the price received by farmers. Suppose that the market price is below this target level. If the target level is $3 in Figure 19.5, and if the output that farmers can grow (without violating government restrictions) is $OQ_3$, this plan lets the competitive market alone, so that the output of $OQ_3$ is sold at a price of $2. Then according to this plan, the government issues subsidy checks to farmers to cover the difference between the market price ($2) and the target price ($3).

The cost to the Treasury under the Brannan plan is ($3 − $2) × $OQ_3$. Why? Because the Treasury pays a subsidy of ($3 − $2) per bushel, and $OQ_3$ bushels are grown; thus the total subsidy is ($3 − $2) × $OQ_3$. Before the Brannan plan was adopted, the government supported the price at $3, and bought the amount—($OQ_3$ − $OQ_2$)—that private buyers would not purchase at that price. The cost to the Treasury under this system is $3 × ($OQ_3$ − $OQ_2$). Why? Because the Treasury buys ($OQ_3$ − $OQ_2$) bushels at $3 per bushel.

An important question is: Will the cost to the U.S. Treasury under the

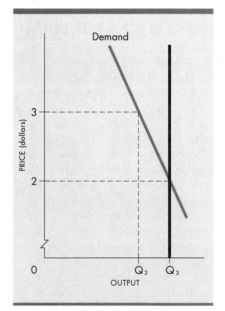

**Figure 19.5**
**Effect of the Brannan Plan**
Under the Brannan plan, the competitive market would be let alone, so that, if output were $OQ_3$, the price would be $2. Then the government would pay farmers the difference between this price and the target price, $3.

Brannan plan be greater than under the previous system? The answer can be shown to depend on the price elasticity of demand. As demonstrated in footnote 4, the cost under the Brannan plan is greater than under the previous system [4] if $\$2 \times OQ_3 < \$3 \times OQ_2$. But since $\$2 \times OQ_3$ is the total money expenditure at a price of $2 and $\$3 \times OQ_2$ is the total money expenditure at a price of $3, it follows from the previous section that $\$2 \times OQ_3$ will be less than $\$3 \times OQ_2$ if the price elasticity of demand is less than 1. (Why? Because the total amount spent on a commodity will be less at a lower price [such as $2] than at a higher price [such as $3] if demand is price inelastic.) Thus, since the elasticity of demand for farm products is in fact less than 1, the cost to the Treasury will be greater under the Brannan plan than under a system whereby the price is supported at $3, with the government clearing the market of the farm products not purchased by the private sector at that price.[5]

Our purpose here is not to decide whether the Brannan plan is good or bad. To make such a decision, we would have to take account of many factors besides the cost to the Treasury. (In Chapter 31, a detailed examination of our nation's farm programs is provided.) Instead, our point is that the price elasticity of demand is an important concept in discussing the effects of the Brannan plan, just as in discussing the instability of farm income and prices. Moreover, as we shall see in subsequent sections, the price elasticity of demand is equally as important in problems concerning the industrial sector of the economy as in problems concerning agriculture.

## INDUSTRY AND FIRM DEMAND CURVES

Up to this point, we have been dealing with the market demand curve for a commodity. *The market demand curve for a commodity is not the same as the market demand curve for the output of a single firm that produces the commodity, unless, of course, the industry is composed of only a single firm.* If the industry is composed of more than one firm, as is usually the case, the demand curve for the output of each firm producing the commodity will usually be quite different from the demand curve for the commodity. The demand curve for the output of Farmer Brown's wheat is quite different from the market demand curve for wheat.

*In particular, the demand curve for the output of a particular firm is generally more price elastic than the market demand curve for the commodity,* because the products of other firms in the industry are close substitutes for the product of this firm. As pointed out earlier, products with many close substitutes have relatively high price elasticities of demand.

If there are many, many firms selling a homogeneous product, the individual firm's demand curve becomes *horizontal,* or essentially so. To see this, suppose that 100,000 firms sell a particular commodity and that each of these firms is of equal size. If any one of these firms were to triple

[4] The cost to the government under the Brannan plan is $(\$3 - \$2) \times OQ_3 = \$3 \times OQ_3 - \$2 \times OQ_3$, while the cost under the other system is $\$3 \times (OQ_3 - OQ_2) = \$3 \times OQ_3 - \$3 \times OQ_2$. Thus the difference in cost between the Brannan plan and the other system is $\$3 \times OQ_2 - \$2 \times OQ_3$, which means that the cost under the Brannan plan would be greater than under the other system if $\$2 \times OQ_3 < \$3 \times OQ_2$.

[5] Note that this result does not depend on our choice of $3 as the target price and of $2 as the market price. Regardless of what the target price and market price may be, this result will hold, if the price elasticity of demand is less than 1.

its output and sales, the total industry output would change by only .002 percent—too small a change to have any perceptible effect on the price of the commodity. Consequently, each firm can act as if variations in its output—within the range of its capabilities—will have no real impact on market price. In other words, the demand curve facing the individual firm is horizontal, as in Figure 19.6.

## INCOME ELASTICITY OF DEMAND

So far this chapter has dealt almost exclusively with the effect of a commodity's price on the quantity demanded of it in the market. But price is not, of course, the only factor that influences the quantity demanded of the commodity. Another important factor is the level of money income among the consumers in the market. The sensitivity of the quantity demanded to the total money income of all of the consumers in the market is measured by the ***income elasticity of demand,*** *which is defined as the percentage change in the quantity demanded resulting from a 1 percent increase in total money income (all prices being held constant).*

A commodity's income elasticity of demand may be positive or negative. For many commodities, increases in income result in increases in the amount demanded. Such commodities, like steak or caviar, have positive income elasticities of demand. For other commodities, increases in income result in decreases in the amount demanded. These commodities, like margarine and poor grades of vegetables, have negative income elasticities of demand. However, be careful to note that the income elasticity of demand of a commodity is likely to vary with the level of income under consideration. For example, if only families at the lowest income levels are considered, the income elasticity of demand for margarine may be positive.

*Luxury items tend to have higher income elasticities of demand than necessities.* Indeed, one way to define luxuries and necessities is to say that luxuries are commodities with high income elasticities of demand, and necessities are commodities with low income elasticities of demand.

### Empirical Studies

Many studies have been made to estimate the income elasticity of demand for particular commodities, since, like the price elasticity of demand, it is of great importance to decision makers. In making long-term forecasts of industry sales, for example, firms must take the income elasticity of demand into account. Thus, if the income elasticity of demand for a product is high, and if incomes increase considerably during the next 20 years, the product's sales will tend to increase greatly during that period. On the other hand, if the income elasticity of demand for a product is close to zero, one would expect the product's sales not to increase very much on account of such increases in income.

To illustrate the findings of empirical studies in this area, consider the following results: The income elasticity of demand has been estimated, according to one well-known study, to be 0.37 for eggs, 0.34 for cheese, 0.42 for butter, 1.00 for liquor, −0.20 for margarine, 0.07 for milk and cream, and 1.48 for restaurant consumption of food. Certainly, these estimates seem reasonable. One would expect the income elasticity of demand to be negative for margarine, because consumers tend to view mar-

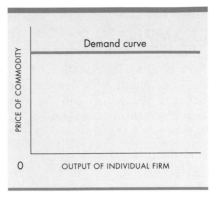

**Figure 19.6**
**Demand Curve for Output of an Individual Firm: The Case of a Great Many Sellers of a Homogeneous Commodity**
If there are many firms selling a homogeneous product, the demand curve facing an individual firm is horizontal.

## EXAMPLE 19.2    THE DEMAND FOR "SUDS"

According to Thomas Fogarty and Kenneth Elzinga, the price elasticity of demand for beer in the United States is about 0.8, and the income elasticity of demand for beer is about 0.4.

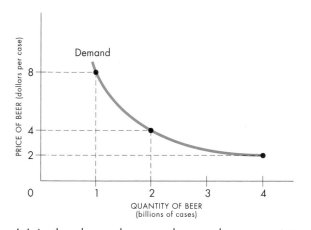

(a) Is the demand curve shown above consistent with their findings? Why, or why not? (b) If the price of a case of beer increases, will this result in an increase or decrease in the amount of money spent per year on beer? (c) If consumer income increases by 15 percent, while the price of beer remains constant, what will be the effect on the amount of money spent per year on beer? (d) Holding the prices of other goods and income constant, do you think that the market demand curve for beer varies from month to month? From state

to state? If so, why? (e) If Budweiser lowers the price of its beer by 1 percent, can it expect to increase the quantity it sells by 0.8 percent? Why, or why not? (f) A number of years ago, Budweiser was selling for 58 cents per case more than its rivals in the St. Louis market and had 12 percent of the market. About a year later, Budweiser sold its beer at the same price as its rivals and had 39 percent of the market. Suppose that other brewers held their price constant at $2 per case during this period, and that the total amount of beer sold in this market was constant during this period. What was the price elasticity of demand for Budweiser beer in this market?

### Solution

(a) No. According to this demand curve, the price elasticity of demand for beer is 1, since the amount spent on beer is the same ($8 billion) regardless of the price. (b) Increase. (c) It will increase by about 6 percent. (d) Yes, because of differences among months and states in temperature, tastes, and other factors. (e) No. Because Budweiser is only one firm in the market, the percentage increase in the quantity it sells is likely to be greater than 0.8 percent, if other firms hold their price constant. (f) $-(.39X - .12X)/.255X \div (\$2.00 - \$2.58)/\$2.29 = 4.2$. ($X$ is the total amount of beer sold in this market then.)

---

garine as an inferior good, and as their incomes rise, they tend to switch from margarine to butter. Also, it is not surprising that the income elasticity of demand for milk and cream is close to zero, since people tend to view milk and cream as necessities, particularly for children. In addition, it is quite reasonable that the income elasticity of demand for liquor and restaurant consumption of food is higher than for the other commodities. Liquor and restaurant meals tend to be luxury items for most people.

## CROSS ELASTICITY OF DEMAND

Besides the price of the commodity and the level of total money income—the factors discussed primarily in previous sections of this chapter—the quantity demanded of a commodity also depends on the prices of other commodities. Suppose the price of butter is held constant. The amount of butter demanded will be influenced by the price of margarine.

The **cross elasticity of demand,** *defined as the percentage change in the quantity demanded of one commodity resulting from a 1 percent change in the price of another commodity, is used to measure the sensitivity of the former commodity's quantity demanded to changes in the latter commodity's price.*

Pairs of commodities are classified as **substitutes** or **complements,** depending on the sign of the cross elasticity of demand. *If the cross elasticity of demand is positive, two commodities are substitutes.* Butter and margarine are substitutes because a decrease in the price of butter will result in a decrease in the quantity demanded of margarine—many margarine eaters really prefer the "higher-priced spread." *On the other hand, if the cross elasticity of demand is negative, two commodities are complements.* For example, gin and tonic may be complements since a decrease in the price of gin may increase the quantity demanded of tonic. The reduction in the price of gin will increase the quantity demanded of gin, thus increasing the quantity demanded of tonic since gin and tonic tend to be used together.

Many studies have been made of the cross elasticity of demand for various pairs of commodities. After all, it frequently is very important to know how a change in the price of one commodity will affect the sales of another commodity. For example, what would be the effect of a 1 percent increase in the price of pork on the quantity demanded of beef? According to one study, the effect would be a .28 percent increase in the quantity demanded of beef—since this study estimates that the cross elasticity of demand for these two commodities is 0.28. What effect would a 1 percent increase in the price of butter have on the quantity demanded of margarine? According to the same study, the effect would be a .81 percent increase in the quantity demanded of margarine—since this study estimates that the cross elasticity of demand for these two commodities is 0.81.

## TEST YOURSELF

1. Is each of the following statements true, partly true, or false? Explain. (a) If a good's income elasticity of demand is less than one, an increase in the price of the good will increase the amount spent on it. (b) The income elasticity of demand will have the same sign regardless of the level of income at which it is measured. (c) If Mr. Miller spends all of his income on steak (regardless of his income or the price of steak), Mr. Miller's cross elasticity of demand between steak and any other good is zero.

2. What is the sign of the cross elasticity of demand for each of the following pairs of commodities: (a) tea and coffee, (b) tennis rackets and tennis balls, (c) whiskey and gin, (d) fishing licenses and fishing poles, (e) nylon rugs and wool rugs?

3. On page 410, we saw the quantity of Model T's sold increased from about 472,000 to about 730,000 when its price was reduced from $440 in 1914 to $360 in 1916. How can this fact be reconciled with recent studies which indicate that the price elasticity of demand for automobiles is about 1.2 to 1.5?

4. According to the U.S. Department of Agriculture, the income elasticity of demand for coffee is about 0.23. If incomes rose by 1 percent, what effect would this have on the quantity demanded of coffee?

# SUMMARY

1. The market demand curve, which is the relationship between the price of a commodity and the amount of the commodity demanded in the market, is one of the most important and frequently used concepts in economics. The shape and position of a product's market demand curve depend on consumers' tastes, consumer incomes, the price of other goods, and the number of consumers in the market.

2. The market demand curve for a commodity is not the same as the demand curve for the output of a single firm that produces the commodity, unless the industry is composed of only one firm. In general, the demand curve for the output of a single firm will be more elastic than the market demand curve for the commodity. Indeed, if there are many firms selling a homogeneous commodity, the individual firm's demand curve becomes horizontal.

3. There are many techniques for measuring demand curves, such as interview studies, direct experiments, and the statistical analysis of historical data.

4. The price elasticity of demand, defined as the percentage change in quantity demanded resulting from a 1 percent change in price, measures the sensitivity of the amount demanded to changes in price. Whether a price increase results in an increase or decrease in the total amount spent on a commodity depends on the price elasticity of demand.

5. The income elasticity of demand, defined as the percentage change in quantity demanded resulting from a 1 percent increase in total money income, measures the sensitivity of the amount demanded to changes in total income. Luxury items are generally assumed to have higher income elasticities of demand than necessities.

6. The cross elasticity of demand, defined as the percentage change in the quantity demanded resulting from a 1 percent change in the price of another commodity, measures the sensitivity of the amount demanded to changes in the price of another commodity. If the cross elasticity of demand is positive, two commodities are substitutes; if it is negative, they are complements.

# CONCEPTS FOR REVIEW

| | | |
|---|---|---|
| Market demand curve | Price elastic | Income elasticity of demand |
| Direct market experiment | Price inelastic | Cross elasticity of demand |
| Price elasticity of demand | Unitary elasticity | Substitute |
| Arc elasticity of demand | Brannan plan | Complement |

# GETTING BEHIND THE DEMAND CURVE: CONSUMER BEHAVIOR

CRATE & BARREL, A SELLER OF moderately priced tableware, experienced sales during the 1990 Christmas season that were over 14 percent higher than the year before. Apparently, this was due to many consumers who, feeling the financial pinch of the recession that occurred then, decided to buy moderately priced items. To a considerable extent consumers, voting with their pocketbooks, are the masters of our economic system. No wonder, then, that economists spend much of their time describing and analyzing how consumers act. In this chapter, we present the basic model economists use to analyze consumer behavior.

Product display in a Crate & Barrel store

## CONSUMER EXPENDITURES

### The Martins of Jacksonville

Since we are concerned here with consumer behavior, perhaps the best way to begin is to look at the behavior of a particular consumer. It is hard to find any consumer who is "typical." There are hundreds of millions of consumers in the United States, and they vary enormously. Nonetheless, it is instructive to look at how a particular American family—the Martins of Jacksonville, Florida[1]—spends its money. The Martins are about 40 years old, are both married for the second time, and have three children (by his first marriage). They own their own home, and both work. Mr. Martin is a computer programmer, and Mrs. Martin is a product manager at American Transtech. Together the Martins make about $66,000 a year.

How do the Martins spend their money? For most consumers, we cannot answer this question with any accuracy, because the people in question simply do not tell anyone what they do with their money. But because the Martins and their buying habits were scrutinized in an article in a national magazine, it is possible to describe quite accurately where their money goes. As shown in Table 20.1, the Martins, who own their own home, spend about $1,000 a month—about 18 percent of their income—on housing. In addition, they spend about $300 a month—about 5 percent of their income—on food and drink. Also, they spend about $700 a month—about 13 percent of their income—on child support and education.

In addition, as shown in Table 20.1, the Martins spend about $700 a

---

[1] This case study comes from a national magazine. The name of the family has been changed, but the facts are real.

## Table 20.1
### Monthly Spending Pattern of Mr. and Mrs. Martin of Jacksonville, Florida

| ITEM | AMOUNT (DOLLARS) | PERCENT OF INCOME |
|------|-----------------|-------------------|
| Housing | 1,000 | 18 |
| Food and drink | 300 | 5 |
| Child support and education | 700 | 13 |
| Entertainment and clothing | 700 | 13 |
| Medical, dental, and insurance expenses | 200 | 4 |
| Transportation | 200 | 4 |
| Other expenditures | 800 | 15 |
| Taxes and saving | 1,600 | 29 |
| Monthly income | 5,500 | 100[a] |

[a] Because of rounding errors, the percentages do not sum to 100.

month—about 13 percent of their income—on entertainment and clothing. Medical, dental, and insurance expenses consume about $200 a month—about 4 percent of income; another $200 a month—again, about 4 percent of their income—is spent on transportation. Finally, the Martins allocate about $800 a month—about 15 percent of their income—to other expenditures, and about $1,600 a month—about 29 percent of their income—to taxes and savings.

This, in a nutshell, is how the Martins spend their money. The Martins exchange their resources—mostly labor—in the resource markets for $66,000 a year. They take this money into the product markets and spend about three-fourths of it for the goods and services described above. The remaining one-fourth of their income goes for taxes and saving. The Martins, like practically every family, keep a watchful eye on where their money goes and what they are getting in exchange for their labor and other resources. As stressed in Chapter 2, the basic purpose of our economic system is to satisfy the wants of consumers.

## AGGREGATE DATA FOR THE UNITED STATES

How does the way that the Martins spend their money compare with consumer behavior in general? In Table 20.2, we provide data on how all consumers allocated their aggregate income in 1990. These data tell us much more about the typical behavior of American consumers than our case study of the Martins. Note first of all that American households paid about 15 percent of their income in taxes. In addition, American households saved about 4 percent of their income. In other words, they refrained from spending 4 percent of their income on goods and services; instead, they put this amount into stocks, bonds, bank accounts, or other such channels for saving. Also, about 2 percent of their income went for interest payments to banks and other institutions from which they had borrowed money.

American consumers spent the remaining 79 percent of their income on goods and services. Table 20.2 makes it clear that they allocated much of their expenditures to housing, food and drink, and transportation.

## Table 20.2
### Allocation of Income by U.S. Households, 1990

| | PERCENT OF TOTAL[a] |
|---|---|
| Personal taxes | 15 |
| Personal saving | 4 |
| Interest payments | 2 |
| Consumption expenditures | |
| Autos and parts | 5 |
| Furniture and household equipment | 4 |
| Other durable goods | 2 |
| Food and drink | 13 |
| Clothing and shoes | 5 |
| Gasoline and oil | 2 |
| Other nondurable goods | 6 |
| Housing | 12 |
| Household operations | 5 |
| Transportation | 3 |
| Medical costs | 10 |
| Other services | 13 |
| Total income | 100 |

[a] Because of rounding errors, figures do not sum to total.
*Source: Survey of Current Business*, January 1991.

Spending on housing, household operations, and furniture and other durable household equipment accounted for about 21 percent of American consumers' total income. Spending on food and beverages accounted for about 13 percent of total income. Spending on automobiles and parts, gasoline and oil, and other transportation accounted for about 10 percent of total income. Thus taxes, savings, housing, food and drink, and transportation accounted for about two-thirds of the total income of all households in the United States.

The data in Table 20.2 make it obvious that the Martin family is not very typical of American consumers. For example, it spends a much larger percentage of its income on entertainment and education than do consumers as a whole. To some degree, this is because the Martins are more affluent than most American families, but this is only part of the reason. To a large extent, it simply reflects the fact that people want different things. Looking around you, you see considerable diversity in the way consumers spend their money. Take your own family as an example. It is a good bet that your family spends its money quite differently than the nation as a whole. If your parents like to live in a big house, your family may spend much more than the average on housing. Or if they like to go to sports events, their expenditures on such entertainment may be much higher than average.

## A MODEL OF CONSUMER BEHAVIOR

Why do consumers spend their money the way they do? The economist answers this question with the aid of a **model of consumer behavior,** which is useful both for analysis and for decision making. To construct this model, the economist obviously must consider the tastes of the consumer. As Henry Adams put it, "Everyone carries his own inch-rule of taste, and amuses himself by applying it, triumphantly, wherever he travels." Certainly one would expect that the amount a consumer purchases of a particular commodity is influenced by his or her tastes. Some people like beef, others like pork. Some people like the opera, others would trade a ticket to hear Luciano Pavarotti for a ticket to the Dallas Cowboys game any day of the week. Three assumptions, which seem reasonable for most purposes, underlie the economist's model of consumer preferences.

*1.* We assume that *consumers, when confronted with two alternative market baskets, can decide whether they prefer the first to the second, the second to the first, or whether they are indifferent between them.* For example, suppose Mrs. Martin is confronted with a choice between a market basket containing 3 chocolate bars and a ticket to the movies and another market basket containing 2 chocolate bars and a record of the Tabernacle Choir singing Chopin's Minute Waltz. Despite the rather bizarre composition of these two market baskets, we assume that she can somehow decide whether she prefers the first market basket to the second, the second market basket to the first, or whether she is indifferent between them.

*2.* We assume that *the consumer's preferences are transitive.* The meaning of transitive in this context is simple enough. Suppose that Mrs. Martin prefers an ounce of Chanel No. 5 perfume to an ounce of Blue Grass perfume, and that she prefers an ounce of Blue Grass perfume to an ounce of Sortilège perfume. Then, if her preferences are transitive, she must prefer an ounce of Chanel No. 5 perfume to an ounce of Sortilège perfume.

Alfred Marshall (1842–1924) played a major role in the construction of consumer demand theories, and was a pioneer in many other areas of economics as well. His *Principles of Economics* (1890), which had eight editions, was a leading economics text for many years.

The reason for this assumption is clear. If the consumer's preferences were not transitive, the consumer would have inconsistent or contradictory preferences. Although some people may have preferences that are not transitive, this assumption seems to be a reasonable first approximation—for the noninstitutionalized part of the population at least.

*3.* We assume that *the consumer always prefers more of a commodity to less.* For example, if one market basket contains 3 bars of soap and 2 monkey wrenches and a second contains 3 bars of soap and 3 monkey wrenches, it is assumed that the second market basket is preferred to the first. To a large extent, this assumption is justified by the definition of a commodity as something the consumer desires.[2] This does not mean that certain things are not a nuisance. If one market basket contains 3 bars of soap and 2 rattlesnakes, we would not be at all surprised if the consumer did *not* prefer this market basket to one containing 3 bars of soap and no rattlesnakes. But to such a consumer, a rattlesnake would not be desired—and thus would not be a commodity. Instead, the absence of a rattlesnake would be desired—and would be a commodity.

## Total Utility

In Chapter 2, we pointed out that a model, to be useful, must omit many unimportant factors, concentrate on the basic factors at work, and simplify in order to illuminate. So that we focus on the important factors at work here, let's assume that there are only two goods, food and clothing. This is an innocuous assumption, since the results we shall obtain can be generalized to include cases where any number of goods exists. For simplicity, food is measured in pounds, and clothing is measured in number of pieces of clothing.

Consider Mrs. Martin, making choices for her family. Undoubtedly, she regards certain market baskets—that is, certain combinations of food and clothing (the only commodities)—to be more desirable than others. She certainly regards 2 pounds of food and 1 piece of clothing to be more desirable than 1 pound of food and 1 piece of clothing. For simplicity, suppose that it is possible to measure the amount of satisfaction that she gets from each market basket by its utility. A **utility** *is a number that represents the level of satisfaction that the consumer derives from a particular market basket.* For example, the utility attached to the market basket containing 2 pounds of food and 1 piece of clothing may be 10 utils, and the utility attached to the market basket containing 1 pound of food and 1 piece of clothing may be 6 utils. (A util is the traditional unit in which utility is expressed.)

## Marginal Utility

It is important to distinguish between total utility and marginal utility. The total utility of a market basket is the number described in the previous paragraph, whereas *the* **marginal utility** *measures the additional satisfaction derived from an additional unit of a commodity.* To see how marginal utility is obtained, let's take a close look at Table 20.3. The total

[2] An individual's desire for a particular good during a particular period of time is not infinite but in the aggregate human wants seem to be insatiable. Besides the basic desires for food, shelter, and clothing, which must be fulfilled to some extent if the human organism is to survive, wants arise from cultural factors. Advertising and the emulation of social leaders stimulate and extend a person's wants.

**Table 20.3**
**Total Utility and Marginal Utility Derived by the Martins from Consuming Various Amounts of Food per Day[a]**

| POUNDS OF FOOD | TOTAL UTILITY/utils | MARGINAL UTILITY |
|---|---|---|
| 0 | 0 | |
| 1 | 3 | 3 (=3–0) |
| 2 | 7 | 4 (=7–3) |
| 3 | 9 | 2 (=9–7) |
| 4 | 10 | 1 (=10–9) |

[a] This table assumes that no clothing is consumed. If a nonzero amount of clothing is consumed, the figures in this table will probably be altered since the marginal utility of a certain amount of food is likely to depend on the amount of clothing consumed.

utility the Martin family derives from the consumption of various amounts of food is given in the middle column of this table. (For simplicity, we assume for the moment that the Martins consume only food.) The marginal utility, shown in the right-hand column, is the extra utility derived from each amount of food over and above the utility derived from 1 less pound of food. Thus it equals the difference between the total utility of a certain amount of food and the total utility of 1 less pound of food.

For example, as shown in Table 20.3, the *total* utility of 3 pounds of food is 9 utils, which is a measure of the total amount of satisfaction that the Martins get from this much food. In contrast, the *marginal* utility of 3 pounds of food is the extra utility obtained from the third pound of food—that is, the total utility of 3 pounds of food less the total utility of 2 pounds of food. Specifically, as shown in Table 20.3, it is 2 utils. Similarly, the *total* utility of 2 pounds of food is 7 utils, which is a measure of the total amount of satisfaction that the Martins get from this much food. In contrast, the *marginal* utility of 2 pounds of food is the extra utility from the second pound of food—that is, the total utility of 2 pounds of food less the total utility of 1 pound of food. Specifically, as shown in Table 20.3, it is 4 utils.

### The Law of Diminishing Marginal Utility

Economists generally assume that, as a person consumes more and more of a particular commodity, there is, beyond some point, a decline in the extra satisfaction derived from the last unit of the commodity consumed. For example, if the Martins consume 2 pounds of food in a particular period of time, it may be just enough to meet their basic physical needs. If they consume 3 pounds of food in the same period of time, the third pound of food is likely to yield less satisfaction than the second. If they consume 4 pounds of food in the same period of time, the fourth pound of food is likely to yield less satisfaction than the third. And so on.

This assumption or hypothesis is often called the **law of diminishing marginal utility.** This law states that, *as a person consumes more and more of a given commodity (the consumption of other commodities being held constant), the marginal utility of the commodity eventually will tend to decline.* The figures concerning the Martin family in Table 20.3 are in accord with this law, as shown in Figure 20.1, which plots the marginal utility of food against the amount consumed. Once the consumption of food exceeds about 1 1/2 pounds, the marginal utility of food declines.

## THE EQUILIBRIUM MARKET BASKET

Preferences alone do not determine the consumer's actions. *Besides knowing the consumer's preferences, we must also know his or her income and the prices of commodities to predict which market basket he or she will buy.* The consumer's money income is the amount of money he or she can spend per unit of time. A consumer's choice of a market basket is constrained by the size of his or her money income. For example, although Mr. Martin may regard a Hickey Freeman as his favorite suit, he may not buy it because he may have insufficient funds (as the bankers delicately put it). Also, the market basket the consumer chooses is influenced by the prices of commodities. If the Hickey Freeman suit were offered by a discount store at $100, rather than its list price of $850, Mr. Martin might purchase it after all.

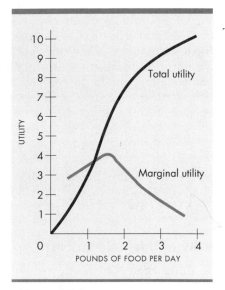

**Figure 20.1**
**Total and Marginal Utility from Food Consumption, Martin Family**
The marginal utility of the first pound of food (which, according to Table 20.3, equals 3 utils) is plotted at the midpoint between 0 and 1 pounds of food. The marginal utility of the second pound of food (which, according to Table 20.3, equals 4 utils) is plotted at the midpoint between 1 and 2 pounds of food. The marginal-utility curve connects these and other points showing the marginal utility of various amounts of food consumed.

Beyond some point, the marginal utility curve of any commodity would be expected to fall, according to the law of diminishing marginal utility (which states that, as a person consumes more and more of a given commodity, the marginal utility of the commodity eventually will tend to decline). In the case shown here, the marginal utility curve falls when the Martin family's consumption of food exceeds about 1 1/2 pounds per day.

Given the consumer's tastes, economists assume that he or she attempts to maximize utility. In other words, *consumers are assumed to be rational in the sense that they choose the market basket—or more generally, the course of action—that is most to their liking.* As previously noted, consumers cannot choose whatever market basket they please. Instead, they must maximize their utility subject to the constraints imposed by the size of their money income and the nature of commodity prices.

The optimal market basket, the one that maximizes utility subject to these constraints, is the one where the consumer's income is allocated among commodities so that, for every commodity purchased, the marginal utility of the commodity is proportional to its price. For example, consider the Martin family. For them, the optimal market basket is the one where

$$\frac{MU_F}{P_F} = \frac{MU_C}{P_C} \qquad (20.1)$$

where $MU_F$ is the marginal utility of food, $MU_C$ is the marginal utility of clothing, $P_F$ is the price of a pound of food, and $P_C$ is the price of a piece of clothing.

## Why Is This Rule Correct?

To understand why the rule in Equation (20.1) is correct, it is convenient to begin by pointing out that $MU_F \div P_F$ is the marginal utility of the *last dollar's worth* of food and that $MU_C \div P_C$ is the marginal utility of the *last dollar's worth* of clothing. To see why this is so, take the case of food. Since $MU_F$ is the extra utility of the *last pound* of food bought, and since $P_F$ is the price of this *last pound,* the extra utility of the *last dollar's worth* of food must be $MU_F \div P_F$. For example, if the last pound of food results in an extra utility of 4 utils and this pound costs $2, then the extra utility from the last dollar's worth of food must be $4 \div 2$, or 2 utils. In other words, the marginal utility of the last dollar's worth of food is 2 utils.

Since $MU_F \div P_F$ is the marginal utility of the last dollar's worth of food and $MU_C \div P_C$ is the marginal utility of the last dollar's worth of clothing, what Equation (20.1) really says is that *the rational consumer will choose a market basket where the marginal utility of the last dollar spent on all commodities purchased is the same*. To see why this must be so, consider the numerical example in Table 20.4, which shows the marginal utility the Martins derive from various amounts of food and clothing. Rather than measuring food and clothing in physical units, we measure them in Table 20.4 in terms of the amount of money spent on them.

Given the information in Table 20.4, how much of each commodity should Mrs. Martin buy if her money income is only $4 (a ridiculous assumption but one that will help to make our point)? Clearly, the first dollar she spends should be on food since it will yield her a marginal utility of 20. The second dollar she spends should also be on food since a second dollar's worth of food has a marginal utility of 16. (Thus the total utility derived from the $2 of expenditure is $20 + 16 = 36$.)[3] The marginal utility of the third dollar is 12 if it is spent on more food—and 12 too if it is spent on clothing. Suppose that she chooses more food. (The total util-

---

[3] Since the marginal utility is the extra utility obtained from each dollar spent, the total utility from the total expenditure must be the sum of the marginal utilities of the individual dollars of expenditure.

**Table 20.4**
**Marginal Utility Derived by the Martins from Various Quantities of Food and Clothing**

| COMMODITY | DOLLARS WORTH | | | | |
|---|---|---|---|---|---|
| | 1 | 2 | 3 | 4 | 5 |
| | MARGINAL UTILITY (UTILS) | | | | |
| Food | 20 | 16 | 12 | 10 | 7 |
| Clothing | 12 | 10 | 7 | 5 | 3 |

ity derived from the $3 of expenditure is 20 + 16 + 12 = 48.) What about the final dollar? Its marginal utility is 10 if it is spent on more food and 12 if it is spent on clothing; thus she will spend it on clothing. (The total utility derived from all $4 of expenditure is then 20 + 16 + 12 + 12 = 60.)

Thus Mrs. Martin, if she is rational, will allocate $3 of her income to food and $1 to clothing. This is the **equilibrium market basket,** the market basket that maximizes consumer satisfaction. The important thing to note is that this market basket demonstrates the principle set forth earlier in Equation (20.1). As shown in Table 20.4, the marginal utility derived from the last dollar spent on food is equal to the marginal utility derived from the last dollar spent on clothing. (Both are 12.) Thus this market basket has the characteristic described above: the marginal utility of the last dollar spent on all commodities purchased is the same. In the next section, we show that this will always be the case for market baskets that maximize the consumer's utility. If it were not true, the consumer could obtain a higher level of utility by changing the composition of his or her market basket.

## Further Proof of the Budget Allocation Rule

In the previous section, we stated the proposition that the consumer, to maximize utility, will choose a market basket where the marginal utility of the last dollar spent on all commodities purchased is the same. In this section, we show that, if this budget allocation rule is not followed, the consumer cannot be maximizing utility. This is offered as further proof of the proposition in the previous section. For simplicity, we assume that the consumer buys only two commodities, food and clothing.

Suppose that the marginal utility of the last dollar spent on food is 5 utils whereas the marginal utility of the last dollar spent on clothing is 3 utils. The consumer is not maximizing utility, because spending $1 more on food will increase total utility by 5 utils,[4] and spending $1 less on clothing will reduce total utility by 3 utils. Thus the transfer of $1 of expenditure from clothing to food will increase total utility by 2 utils— which means that the consumer currently isn't maximizing utility. More generally, a transfer of expenditure from clothing to food will always increase a consumer's utility so long as the marginal utility of the last dollar spent on food exceeds the marginal utility of the last dollar spent on clothing. Thus *the consumer will not be maximizing utility if the marginal utility of the last dollar spent on food exceeds the marginal utility of the last dollar spent on clothing.*

Suppose that the situation is reversed, the marginal utility of the last dollar spent on food being 3 utils and the marginal utility of the last dollar spent on clothing being 5 utils. The consumer is not maximizing utility, because spending $1 more on clothing will increase total utility by 5 utils,[5] and spending $1 less on food will reduce total utility by 3 utils. Thus the transfer of $1 of expenditure from food to clothing will result in a net increase of utility of 2 utils—which means that the consumer currently isn't maximizing utility. More generally, a transfer of expenditure from food to clothing will always increase total utility so long as the

[4] We assume here that the extra utility from an *extra* dollar spent on food equals the extra utility from the *last* dollar spent on food. This is an innocuous assumption.
[5] We assume here that the extra utility from an *extra* dollar spent on clothing equals the extra utility from the *last* dollar spent on clothing. This, like the assumption in footnote 4, is innocuous.

# EXAMPLE 20.1    THE DIAMOND-WATER PARADOX

In 1991, flawless diamonds frequently sold for over $10,000 per carat, while water sold for about 2 cents per hundred gallons. For centuries, people have been fascinated by this fact. Diamonds, after all, are hardly essential to life, whereas water *is* essential. How is it, then, that people are willing to buy diamonds at a price that seems so much higher than that of water? Suppose that the typical consumer's marginal utility curves for diamonds and water are as shown below:

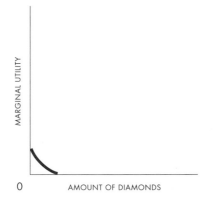

carat of diamonds will be 500,000 times as great as the marginal utility of a hundred gallons of water? (d) Describe in your own words why people are willing to buy diamonds at a price that seems so much higher than that of water.

**Solution**

(a) No. If the consumer is maximizing utility, the

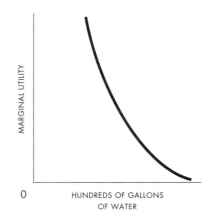

(a) If the price per carat of a diamond is 500,000 times as great as the price per hundred gallons of water, and if the consumer buys both diamonds and water, does it follow that the total utility that the consumer receives from the diamonds is 500,000 times as great as the total utility received from the water? (b) Does it follow that the marginal utility of a carat of diamonds is 500,000 times as great as the marginal utility of a hundred gallons of water? (c) If the consumer buys a great deal of water and practically no diamonds, is it possible that the marginal utility of a

*marginal* utility of a carat of diamonds must be 500,000 times as great as the *marginal* utility of a hundred gallons of water. But there is no reason to believe that this is true of the *total* utilities. (b) Yes. (c) Yes. (d) They buy practically no diamonds and very large quantities of water. The marginal utility of diamonds is so much higher than the marginal utility of water that the marginal utility of the last dollar spent on diamonds is equal to the marginal utility of the last dollar spent on water.

marginal utility of the last dollar spent on clothing exceeds the marginal utility of the last dollar spent on food. Thus *the consumer will not be maximizing utility if the marginal utility of the last dollar spent on clothing exceeds the marginal utility of the last dollar spent on food.*

In the previous paragraph, we showed that the consumer will *not* be maximizing utility if the marginal utility of the last dollar spent on food *is less than* the marginal utility of the last dollar spent on clothing. In the paragraph before last, we showed that the consumer will *not* be maximizing utility if the marginal utility of the last dollar spent on food *exceeds* the marginal utility of the last dollar spent on clothing. It follows that the consumer will be maximizing utility only when the marginal utility of the last dollar spent on food *equals* the marginal utility of the last dollar spent on clothing. This is what we set out to prove.

1. Suppose that the total utility attached by Ms. Johnson to various quantities of hamburgers consumed (per day) is as follows:

| NUMBERS OF HAMBURGERS | TOTAL UTILITY (UTILS) |
|---|---|
| 0 | 0 |
| 1 | 5 |
| 2 | 12 |
| 3 | 15 |
| 4 | 17 |
| 5 | 18 |

Between 3 and 4 hamburgers, what is the marginal utility of a hamburger? Between 4 and 5 hamburgers, what is the marginal utility of a hamburger? Do these results conform to the law of diminishing marginal utility?

2. If Ms. Johnson is maximizing her satisfaction, and if the marginal utility of a hot dog is twice that of a bottle of beer, what must the price of a hot dog be if (a) the price of a bottle of beer is $.75, (b) the price of a bottle of beer is $1? (Assume that Ms. Johnson consumes both beer and hot dogs.)

3. "A good's price is related to its marginal utility, not its total utility. Thus a good like water or air may be cheap, even though its total utility is high." Comment and evaluate.

4. If the marginal utility of one good is 3 and its price is $1, while the marginal utility of another good is 6 and its price is $3, is the consumer maximizing his or her satisfaction, given that he or she is consuming both goods? Why, or why not?

# THE CONSUMER'S DEMAND CURVE

In analyzing consumer behavior, economists often use the concept of an **individual demand curve.** Like the market demand curve (discussed at length in Chapter 19), the individual demand curve is the relationship between the quantity demanded of a good and the good's price. But whereas the market demand curve shows the quantity demanded in the *entire market* at various prices, the individual demand curve shows the quantity demanded by a *particular consumer* at various prices. Applying the theory of consumer behavior presented earlier in this chapter, one can derive a particular consumer's demand curve for a particular good. To see how this can be done, let's turn to Mrs. Martin and show how we can derive the relationship between the price of food and the amount of food she will buy per week.

Assuming that food and clothing are the only goods, that Mrs. Martin's weekly income is $400, and that the price of clothing is $40, per piece of clothing, we confront Mrs. Martin with a variety of prices of food. First, we confront her with a price of $1 per pound of food. How much food will she buy? Next, we confront her with a price of $2 per pound of food. How much food will she buy? The theory of consumer behavior shows how, under each of these sets of circumstances, she will allocate her income between food and clothing. (From Equation (20.1), we know that she will choose an allocation where the marginal utility of the last dollar spent on food will equal the marginal utility of the last dollar spent on clothing.) Suppose that she will buy 200 pounds of food when the price is $1 per pound, and 100 pounds of food when the price is $2 per pound. These are two points on Mrs. Martin's individual demand curve for food—those corresponding to prices of $1 and $2 per pound. Figure 20.2 shows these two points, *X* and *Y*.

It is no trick to obtain more points on her individual demand curve for

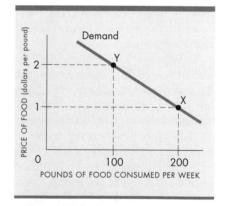

**Figure 20.2**
**Mrs. Martin's Individual Demand Curve for Food**
The consumer's individual demand curve for a commodity shows the amount of the commodity the consumer will buy at various prices. (Point *X* and *Y* on Mrs. Martin's individual demand curve for food are derived in Figure 20.13.)

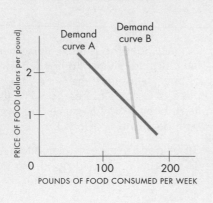

**Figure 20.3**
**Hypothetical Individual**
**Demand Curves**
If Mrs. Martin values food so much that she is determined to buy much the same amount regardless of its price, her individual demand curve for food may look like demand curve *B*; but if she is less determined to maintain her family's food consumption, her individual demand curve for food may look like demand curve *A*.

food. All that we have to do is confront her with other prices of food, and see how much food she buys at each price. Plotting the amount of food she buys against the price, we obtain new points on her individual demand curve for food. Connecting up all these points, we get her complete individual demand curve for food, shown in Figure 20.2.

## Factors Influencing the Demand Curve

*The location and shape of an individual demand curve depend on the tastes of the consumer.* For example, if Mrs. Martin values food so much that she is determined to maintain her family's consumption of this commodity regardless of its price, her individual demand curve for food may look like demand curve *B* in Figure 20.3. But if she is less determined to maintain her family's food consumption, it may look like demand curve *A* in Figure 20.3.

*Besides the consumer's tastes, other factors determining the location and shape of the consumer's individual demand curve are the income of the consumer and the prices of other goods.* For example, Mrs. Martin's individual demand curve for food in Figure 20.2 is based on the assumption that her income is $400 per week and that the price of a piece of clothing is $40. If her income or the price of clothing changes, her individual demand curve for food will change as well. Figure 20.4 shows how her individual demand curve for food may change if her income increases from $300 to $500 per week (assuming that the price of a piece of clothing remains fixed at $40). Figure 20.5 shows how her individual demand curve for food may change if the price of a piece of clothing increases from $40 to $50 (assuming that her income remains constant at $500 per week).

In Chapter 3, we learned the importance of distinguishing between *changes in the quantity demanded* and *changes in demand*. This is just as true for individual consumers as for the market as a whole. The shifts in Mrs. Martin's demand curve for food shown in Figures 20.4 and 20.5 are *changes in demand*. In other words, they are changes in the relationship between the quantity demanded and price. Even if there is no change in demand—that is, even if there is no shift in the demand curve—the quantity demanded may change because of a change in price. For exam-

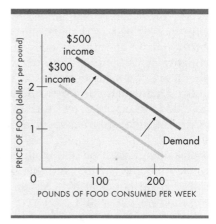

**Figure 20.4**
**Effect of a Change in Income**
**(from $300 to $500 per Week)**
**on Mrs. Martin's Individual De-**
**mand Curve for Food**
If Mrs. Martin's income increases from $300 to $500 per week (and if the price of a piece of clothing remains at $40), her demand curve will shift upward and to the right.

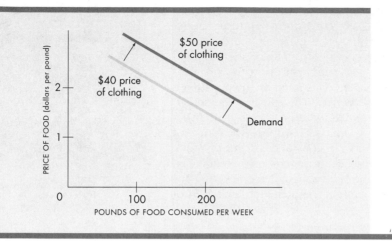

Figure 20.5
**Effect of a Change in the Price of a Piece of Clothing (from $40 to $50) on Mrs. Martin's Individual Demand Curve for Food**
If the price of a piece of clothing increases from $40 to $50 (and if her income remains at $500 per week), her demand curve for food will shift upward and to the right.

ple, in Figure 20.2, the quantity of food demanded by Mrs. Martin increases from 100 to 200 pounds per week if the price of food declines from $2 to $1 per pound. Yet Mrs. Martin's demand curve for food is unchanged in Figure 20.2, so there is no increase in demand. Instead, there has been a *movement along* Mrs. Martin's demand curve from point *Y* to point *X*. The quantity of food demanded by Mrs. Martin has changed even though her demand for food has *not* changed.

## WHY DO INDIVIDUAL DEMAND CURVES GENERALLY SLOPE DOWNWARD?[6]

Individual demand curves almost always slope downward to the right. That is, consumers almost always respond to an increase in a commodity's price by reducing the amount of it they consume. Or, put the other way around, a commodity's price almost always must be reduced to persuade the consumer to buy more of it. One way to explain this fact is by an appeal to the law of diminishing marginal utility, which (as we've seen) states that, as a person consumes more and more of a particular commodity, the commodity's marginal utility declines. *Since the marginal utility — the extra utility derived from an extra unit of the commodity — declines, the price the consumer is willing to pay for an extra unit of the commodity must decline too.* This explanation relies on the assumption that marginal utility is measurable. Another way to explain the same thing makes no such assumption. According to this explanation, an increase in a commodity's price has two kinds of effects on the consumer—a substitution effect and an income effect.

### Substitution Effect

*If the price of a commodity increases, the **substitution effect** of this price increase is the change in the quantity demanded of the commodity result-*

---

[6] This section is optional. Some instructors may want to skip it. The reader can go to the next section without losing the thread of the argument.

*ing from the commodity's becoming more expensive relative to other commodities, if the consumer's level of utility is held constant.* Suppose that the price of chicken increases. Because of this price increase, the consumer may not be able to achieve as high a level of utility as he or she achieved before the price increase. Nonetheless, let's see what effect the price increase would have on the amount of chicken consumed by the consumer, *even if his or her level of utility were unchanged.* This effect is the substitution effect. *The substitution effect of a price increase always is a reduction in the quantity demanded of the commodity.* Suppose the price of chicken increases, while other prices and the consumer's level of utility are held constant. Because chicken becomes more expensive relative to other goods, the consumer will substitute other goods for chicken. Thus the substitution effect would be a *reduction* in the quantity demanded of chicken.

## Income Effect

If the price of a commodity increases, the consumer's level of utility may be reduced, as pointed out above. *The **income effect** of the price increase is the change in the quantity demanded of the commodity due to this change in the consumer's utility level.* If an increase in the price of chicken cuts the consumer's level of utility by a particular amount, which in turn reduces the quantity of chicken demanded by the consumer, this reduction in the quantity demanded is the income effect. *The income ef-*

---

## EXAMPLE 20.2    MEAT AND CONSUMER'S SURPLUS

It is important to recognize that consumers generally would be willing to pay more than in fact they pay for a particular good. Suppose that a consumer's demand curve for meat is as shown below, and that the price of a pound of meat is $2.

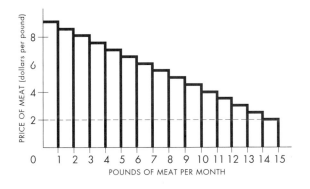

(a) What is the maximum amount that the consumer would pay for the first pound of meat per month? By how much does this exceed the actual price? (b) What

is the maximum amount that the consumer would pay for the second pound of meat per month? By how much does this exceed the actual price? (c) What is the maximum amount that the consumer would pay for the 15 pounds of meat consumed per month? By how much does this exceed the actual amount paid? (d) Returning to Example 20.1, do you think that the actual amount paid for water is much less than the maximum amount that would be paid? Does this help to explain the diamond-water paradox?

### Solution

(a) $9. $7. (b) $8.50. $6.50. (c) $82.50. $52.50. (d) Yes. Yes, the actual amount paid for water is not a good indicator of the importance to the consumer (that is, the total utility) of water, since the actual amount paid is much less than the maximum amount that would be paid for it. *Economists use the term, **consumer's surplus,** to mean the difference between the maximum amount that the consumer would pay and what he or she actually pays.* For example, the consumer's surplus for the first pound of meat is $7.

---

*fect of a price increase can be either a reduction or increase in the quantity demanded.* For some commodities, like steak and probably chicken, a reduction in the consumer's utility level will result in the consumer's demanding *less* of them; thus the income effect of a price increase is a *reduction* in the quantity demanded of these commodities. For other commodities like margarine and poorer grades of food products, a reduction in the consumer's utility level may result in the consumer's demanding *more* of them; thus the income effect of a price increase is an *increase* in the quantity demanded of these commodities.

### The Total Effect of a Price Increase

The *total* effect of a price increase is the *sum* of the income effect and the substitution effect. That is, the total change in the quantity demanded is the change in the quantity demanded due to the change in the consumer's utility level (the income effect) plus the change in the quantity demanded that would have occurred even if the consumer's utility level had not changed (the substitution effect). If (as is frequently the case) the income effect of a price increase is a reduction in the quantity demanded, the demand curve must slope downward. Why? Because both the income effect and the substitution effect are reductions in the quantity demanded, so the total effect of a price increase must be a reduction in the quantity demanded. Even if the income effect of a price increase is an increase in the quantity demanded, the demand curve may slope downward. Why? Because the increase in the quantity demanded due to the income effect may be more than offset by the substitution effect, which is always a reduction in the quantity demanded. Thus the demand curve will slope upward only in those *rare* cases where the income effect is an increase in the quantity demanded and where the income effect is big enough to offset the substitution effect.

## DERIVING THE MARKET DEMAND CURVE

In previous sections, we have described how each consumer's individual demand curve for a commodity can be derived, given the consumer's tastes and income, as well as the prices of other commodities. Suppose that we have obtained the individual demand curve for each of the consumers in the market. How can these individual demand curves be used to derive the market demand curve?

The answer is simple. *To derive the market demand curve, we obtain the horizontal sum of all the individual demand curves.* In other words, to find the total quantity demanded in the market at a certain price, we add up the quantities demanded by the individual consumers at that price.

Table 20.5 shows the individual demand curves for food of four families: the Walters, Joneses, Smiths, and Kleins. For simplicity, suppose that these four families constitute the entire market for food. (This assumption can easily be relaxed; it just makes things simple.) Then the market demand curve for food is shown in the last column of Table 20.5. Figure 20.6 shows the families' individual demand curves for food, as well as the resulting market demand curve. To illustrate how the market demand

## Table 20.5
## Individual Demand Curves and Market Demand Curve for Food

| PRICE OF FOOD (DOLLARS PER POUND) | JONES | KLEIN | SMITH | WALTER | MARKET DEMAND |
|---|---|---|---|---|---|
| | | | (HUNDREDS OF POUNDS PER MONTH) | | |
| 1.00 | 50.0 | 45.0 | 5.0 | 2.0 | 102 |
| 1.20 | 43.0 | 44.0 | 4.2 | 1.8 | 93 |
| 1.40 | 36.0 | 43.0 | 3.4 | 1.6 | 84 |
| 1.60 | 30.0 | 42.0 | 2.6 | 1.4 | 76 |
| 1.80 | 25.0 | 41.4 | 2.4 | 1.2 | 70 |
| 2.00 | 20.0 | 41.0 | 2.0 | 1.0 | 64 |

curve is derived from the individual demand curves, suppose that the price of food is $1 per pound. Then the total quantity demanded in the market is 102 hundreds of pounds per month, since this is the sum of the quantities demanded at this price by the four families. (As shown in Table 20.5, this sum equals 50.0 + 45.0 + 5.0 + 2.0, or 102.)

Since individual demand curves for a commodity almost always slope downward to the right it follows that *market demand curves too almost always slope downward to the right.* (Why? Because, as stressed above, the market demand curve is the horizontal sum of all of the individual demand curves.) However, as emphasized in Chapter 19, the shape and location of the market demand curve vary greatly from commodity to commodity and from market to market. Market demand curves, like people, do not look alike.

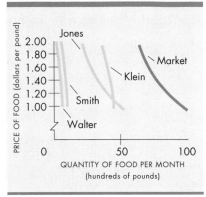

### Figure 20.6
### Individual Demand Curves and Market Demand Curve for Food
The market demand curve is the horizontal sum of all the individual demand curves.

## TEST YOURSELF

1. Suppose that there are five people who are the only members of a particular market. The amount that each person will buy of the product in question (at each price) is shown below. Determine five points on the market demand curve for the product.

| PRICE (DOLLARS) | FIRST PERSON | SECOND PERSON | THIRD PERSON | FOURTH PERSON | FIFTH PERSON |
|---|---|---|---|---|---|
| | | QUANTITY DEMANDED | | | |
| 1 | 5 | 4 | 2 | 8 | 7 |
| 2 | 4 | 4 | 2 | 7 | 6 |
| 3 | 3 | 4 | 1 | 6 | 5 |
| 4 | 2 | 3 | 0 | 5 | 4 |
| 5 | 1 | 3 | 0 | 5 | 2 |

2. Some people judge the quality of a good by its price. If a consumer does this, how does it affect the model presented in this chapter? (*Hint:* Is utility independent of price?)

3. Bill Thompson would be willing to pay 30 cents for the first apple he consumes per day and 24 cents for the second apple he consumes per day. The current price of an apple is 24 cents. How great is Bill Thompson's consumer's surplus? What does this number mean? How might such a number be used?

4. Mrs. Moriarty (the Professor's wife) learns that the price of turkey has fallen. (a) What is the substitution effect? Do you think that it will be positive or negative? Why? (b) What is the income effect? Do you think that it will be positive or negative? Why? (c) Do you think that the Moriarty family's demand curve for turkey slopes downward to the right? Why, or why not?

# RECENT DEVELOPMENTS IN ECONOMICS: THE ROLE OF TIME IN CONSUMPTION DECISIONS

In recent years, economists, led by Gary Becker of the University of Chicago, have begun to view a household as similar to a firm, in the sense that a household uses inputs of various kinds to produce outputs, like meals or recreation. Some of the inputs that the household uses are food, chairs, tables, and beds, but another input of great importance is *time*. The consumer has only a limited amount of time, and this time limitation, as well as his or her limited income, must be taken into account in making decisions.

To illustrate the importance of time to the consumer, take the case of a haircut. The cost to the consumer of a haircut is not only the $8 he must pay the barber; it is also the value of the time it takes for the barber to cut his hair, and, often more important, the value of the time he must wait before the barber is free to begin to cut his hair. Similarly, the cost of a vacation in Florida is not just the amount of money that must be paid for air tickets, hotels, meals, and entertainment; it is also the value placed on the reduced amount of time available to engage in non-vacation activities.

How does the economist measure the value of the time that is used up in consuming a particular item like a vacation? By the opportunity cost of the time. Thus the value of the time spent on the Florida vacation is the value of that time in its best alternative use. For example, if the consumer could have used this time to earn $100 a day, and if this would have been the best alternative use of this time to the consumer, then the value of the time spent on this vacation is $100 per day to this consumer.

Some economists have calculated the elasticity of demand for particular services with respect to the time they consume. In other words, they have estimated the percentage reduction in quantity demanded resulting from a 1 percent increase in the time taken by the service. For example, Jan Acton of

Gary Becker

the RAND Corporation studied the relationship between the number of visits to free sources of medical care by Brooklyn residents and the length of time, on the average, that such residents had to spend traveling and waiting for service. He found that a 1 percent increase in travel time was associated with slightly less than a 1 percent fall in number of visits.

Of course, the value of time is not the same for all people. For example, the alternative cost of time to a teenager is generally lower than for an adult. This helps to explain the fact that teenagers frequently are more willing than adults to wait in line for tickets to various kinds of sports and musical events. Further, it has been suggested that the rise of fast-food chains has been due to an increase in the opportunity cost of time. Because of the increase in wage rates, there has been a rise in the value of time, according to this argument.

# SUMMARY

1. The amount of a particular commodity a consumer purchases is clearly influenced by his or her preferences. The model of consumer behavior assumes that the consumer's preferences are transitive and that commodities are defined so that more of them is preferred to less.

2. Utility is a number that represents the level of satisfaction derived by the consumer from a particular market basket. Market baskets with higher utilities are preferred over market baskets with lower utilities.

3. The model of consumer behavior recognizes that preferences alone do not determine the consumer's actions. The choices open to the consumer are dictated by the size of his or her money income and the nature of commodity prices. These factors, as well as the consumer's preferences, determine his or her choice.

4. If the consumer maximizes utility, his or her income is allocated among commodities so that, for every commodity purchased, the marginal utility of the commodity is proportional to its price. In other words, the marginal utility of the last dollar spent on each commodity is made equal for all commodities purchased.

5. The individual demand curve shows the quantity of a good demanded by a particular consumer at various prices of the good. The individual demand curve for practically all goods slopes downward to the right. Its location depends on the consumer's income and tastes and the prices of other goods.

6. To derive the market demand curve, we obtain the horizontal sum of all the individual demand curves of the people in the market. Since individual demand curves for a commodity almost always slope downward to the right, it follows that market demand curves too almost always slope downward to the right.

# CONCEPTS FOR REVIEW

Model of consumer
 behavior
Utility
Marginal utility
Law of diminishing
 marginal utility

Equilibrium market
 basket
Individual demand curve
Substitution effect
Consumer's surplus
Income effect

*Indifference curve
*Budget line

* This concept is presented in the Appendix to this chapter.

# APPENDIX: HOW INDIFFERENCE CURVES CAN BE USED TO ANALYZE CONSUMER BEHAVIOR

In this Appendix, we show how the theory of consumer behavior can be used in cases where one is not willing to assume that marginal utility is measurable. Generally, it is exceedingly difficult to formulate meaningful measures of a person's extra satisfaction from an extra amount of a particular good. We shall show that the theory remains useful even if such measures cannot be obtained. Once again, we assume for simplicity that there are only two goods, food and clothing, since this allows us to use simple two-dimensional diagrams to illustrate the model. Since there are only

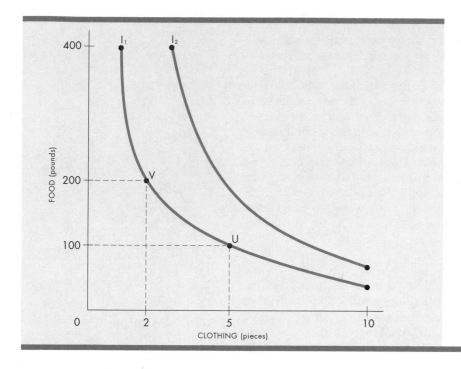

**Figure 20.7**
**Two of Mrs. Martin's**
**Indifference Curves**
$I_1$ and $I_2$ are two of Mrs. Martin's
indifference curves. Each shows
market baskets that are equally desirable to Mrs. Martin. For example, she is indifferent between 200
pounds of food and 2 pieces of
clothing (point V) and 100
pounds of food and 5 pieces of
clothing (point U).

these two commodities, we can represent every possible combination of
goods purchased by a consumer by a point in Figure 20.7, which measures the amount of food purchased along the vertical axis and the
amount of clothing purchased along the horizontal axis.

## Indifference Curves

An ***indifference curve*** *contains points representing market baskets
among which the consumer is indifferent.* To illustrate, consider Mrs. Martin, making choices for her family. Certain market baskets—that is, certain combinations of food and clothing (the only commodities)—will be
equally desirable for her. For example, she may be indifferent between a
market basket containing 100 pounds of food and 5 pieces of clothing
and a market basket containing 200 pounds of food and 2 pieces of clothing. These two market baskets can be represented by two points, *U* and
*V*, in Figure 20.7. In addition, other market baskets—each of which can
be represented by a point in Figure 20.7—are just as desirable to Mrs.
Martin as those represented by points *U* and *V*. If we connect all of these
points, we get a curve that represents market baskets that are equally desirable to the consumer. In our case, Mrs. Martin is indifferent among all
of the market baskets represented by points on curve $I_1$ in Figure 20.7. $I_1$
is therefore called an indifference curve.

There are three important things to note about any consumer's indifference curves:

*1. Any consumer has lots of indifference curves, not just one.* If Mrs.
Martin is indifferent among all the market baskets represented by points
on $I_2$ in Figure 20.7, $I_2$ is another of her indifference curves. Moreover,
one thing is certain. She prefers any market basket on $I_2$ to any market
basket on $I_1$, since $I_2$ includes market baskets with as much clothing and
more food (or as much food and more clothing) than the market baskets

on $I_1$. (Remember that commodities are defined so that more of them is preferred to less.) Consequently, it must always be true that market baskets on higher indifference curves like $I_2$ must be preferred to market baskets on lower indifference curves like $I_1$.

2. *Every indifference curve must slope downward to the right,* to reflect the fact that commodities are defined so that more of them is preferred to less. If one market basket has more of one commodity than a second market basket, it must have less of the other commodity than the second market basket—assuming that the two market baskets are to yield equal satisfaction to the consumer. You can prove this to yourself. Suppose that you have a choice between two snacks and that you are indifferent between them. One snack consists of 1 piece of apple pie and 2 glasses of milk. The other consists of 2 pieces of apple pie and a certain number of glasses of milk. If you prefer more apple pie to less, and if you prefer more milk to less, can the number of glasses of milk in the latter snack be as large as 2? Clearly, the answer is no.

3. *Indifference curves cannot intersect.* If they did, this would contradict the assumption that more of a commodity is preferred to less. For example, suppose that $I_1$ and $I_2$ in Figure 20.8 are two indifference curves and that they intersect. If this is the case, the market basket represented by point $D$ is equivalent in the eyes of the consumer to the one represented by point $E$, since both are on indifference curve $I_1$. Moreover, the market basket represented by point $F$ is equivalent in the eyes of the consumer to the one represented by point $E$, since both are on indifference curve $I_2$. And this means that the market basket represented by point $F$ must be equivalent in the eyes of the consumer to the one represented by point $D$. (Remember that consumer preferences are assumed to be transitive!) But this is impossible because market basket $F$ contains the same amount of food and 6 more pieces of clothing than does market basket $D$. Since more of a commodity is preferred to less, market basket $F$ must be preferred to market basket $D$.

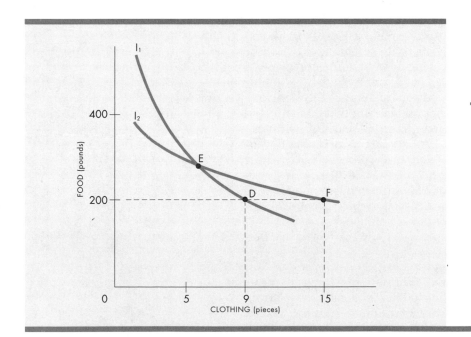

**Figure 20.8**
**Intersecting Indifference Curves: A Contradiction**
Indifference curves cannot intersect. If they did, the consumer would be indifferent between $D$ and $E$, since both are on indifference curve $I_1$; and between $F$ and $E$, since both are on indifference curve $I_2$. But this implies that he or she must be indifferent between $D$ and $F$, which is impossible since $F$ contains the same amount of food and 6 more pieces of clothing than $D$.

## Indifference Curves and Utility

To continue building this new version of our model of consumer behavior, we need to return to the concept of utility. Since all market baskets on a particular indifference curve yield the same satisfaction to the consumer, they all must have the same utility. For example, all market baskets on indifference curve $I_1$ in Figure 20.7 must have the same utility. Moreover, market baskets on higher indifference curves must have higher utilities than market baskets on lower indifference curves. For example, all market baskets on indifference curve $I_2$ in Figure 20.7 must have higher utilities than market baskets on indifference curve $I_1$.

Given a group of indifference curves for a certain consumer, it is easy to establish an index of the utility obtained from any market basket by this consumer. *All that we have to do is attach a number to each indifference curve, this number being larger for higher indifference curves than for lower indifference curves. The utility index for any market basket is then the number attached to the indifference curve on which this market basket is located.* The resulting utility index shows at a glance which market baskets the consumer will pick over other market baskets. The rational consumer will, of course, try to pick the market basket that maximizes this index of utility.

Note that this utility index is not unique. Any set of numbers that increases as one goes from successively lower to higher indifference curves will constitute a suitable set of indices. Thus no assumption is made that we can obtain a meaningful measure of marginal utility. But it is possible to construct a utility index of this sort, so long as the three basic assumptions underlying the theory of consumer demand (described in the earlier section on "A Model of Consumer Behavior") are met.

## The Budget Line

The consumer wants to maximize his or her utility, which means that he or she wants to achieve the highest possible indifference curve. But whether or not a particular indifference curve is attainable depends on the consumer's money income and on commodity prices. Exactly what constraints are imposed on the consumer by the size of his or her money income and the nature of commodity prices? To make things concrete, let's return to Mrs. Martin. Suppose that her total income is $400 per week, and that she can spend this amount only on two commodities, food and clothing. Needless to say, it is unrealistic to assume that there are only two commodities in existence, but, to repeat what was said earlier, this makes it easier to present the model, and the results can easily be generalized to cases where more than two commodities exist. (Also, the assumption that her income is $400 is arbitrary, but this assumption can readily be relaxed.)

Given these conditions, the answer to how much of each commodity Mrs. Martin can buy depends on the price of a pound of food and the price of a piece of clothing. Suppose the price of a pound of food is $1 and the price of a piece of clothing is $40. Then if she spent all of her income on food, she could buy 400 pounds of food per week. On the other hand, if she spent all of her income on clothing, she could buy 10 pieces of clothing per week. Or she could, if she wished, buy some food and some clothing. There are a large number of combinations of amounts of

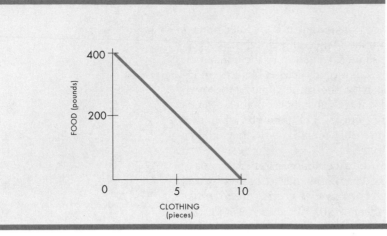

**Figure 20.9**
**Mrs. Martin's Budget Line**
The consumer's budget line shows
the market baskets that can be purchased, given the consumer's income and prevailing commodity
prices. This budget line assumes
that Mrs. Martin's income is $400
per week, that the price of a
pound of food is $1, and that the
price of a piece of clothing is $40.

food and clothing that she could buy, and each such combination can be represented by a point on the line in Figure 20.9. This line is called her budget line. *A consumer's **budget line** shows the market baskets that he or she can purchase, given the consumer's income and prevailing market prices.*

The consumer's budget line will shift if changes occur in the consumer's money income or in commodity prices. In particular, an increase in money income means that the budget line rises, and a decrease in money income means that the budget line falls. This is illustrated in Figure 20.10, which shows Mrs. Martin's budget line at money incomes of $200, $400, and $600 per week. As you can see, her budget line moves upward as her income rises.

Commodity prices too affect the budget line. A decrease in a commodity's price causes the budget line to cut this commodity's axis at a point farther from the origin. Figure 20.11 shows Mrs. Martin's budget line when the price of a pound of food is $1 and when it is $2. You can see that the budget line cuts the vertical, or food, axis farther from the origin when the price of food is $1 per pound.

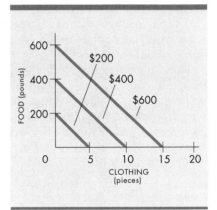

**Figure 20.10**
**Mrs. Martin's Budget Line at Money Incomes of $200, $400, and $600 per Week**
The higher the consumer's money income, the higher the budget line. Holding commodity prices constant, the budget line's slope remains constant.

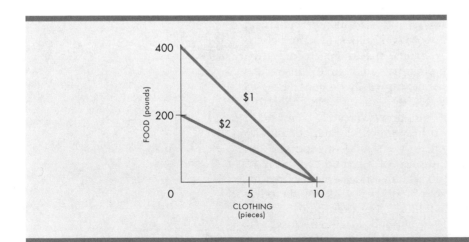

**Figure 20.11**
**Mrs. Martin's Budget Line at Food Prices of $1 and $2 per Pound**
Holding constant Mrs. Martin's money income at $400 per week and the price of a piece of clothing at $40, the budget line cuts the vertical axis farther from the origin when the price of food is $1 than when it is $2.

## The Equilibrium Market Basket

With information on the consumer's indifference curves and budget line, we are in a position to determine the consumer's equilibrium market basket—the market basket that, among all those that the consumer can purchase, yields the maximum utility. The first step is to combine the indifference curves with the budget line on the same graph. Figure 20.12 brings together Mrs. Martin's indifference curves (from Figure 20.7) and her budget line (Figure 20.9). Given the information assembled in Figure 20.12, it is a simple matter to determine her equilibrium market basket. *Her indifference curves show what she wants:* specifically, she wants to attain the highest possible indifference curve. Thus, she would rather be on indifference curve $I_2$ than on indifference curve $I_1$, and on indifference curve $I_3$ than on indifference curve $I_2$. But, as we have pointed out repeatedly, she cannot choose any market basket she likes. *The budget line shows which market baskets her income and commodity prices permit her to buy.* Thus she must choose some market basket on her budget line.

Consequently, *the consumer's choice boils down to choosing that market basket on the budget line that is on the highest indifference curve. This is the equilibrium market basket.* For example, Mrs. Martin's equilibrium market basket is clearly at point $G$ in Figure 20.12; it consists of 200 pounds of food and 5 pieces of clothing per week. This is her equilibrium market basket because any other market basket on the budget line is on a lower indifference curve than point $G$ is. But will the consumer choose this market basket? Admittedly, it may take some time and fumbling for the consumer to find out that this is the best market basket for him or her under the circumstances. Consumers, after all, do make mistakes. But they also learn, and eventually one would expect a consumer to come very close to acting in the predicted way.

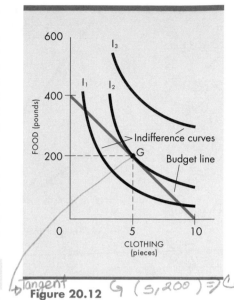

**Figure 20.12**
**Mrs. Martin's Equilibrium Market Basket**
Mrs. Martin's equilibrium market basket is at point $G$, containing 200 pounds of food and 5 pieces of clothing. This is the point on her budget line that is on the highest indifference curve, $I_2$, she can attain.

## Deriving the Individual Demand Curve

Finally, we show how indifference curves can be used to derive the consumer's demand curve. In particular, let's return to the case of Mrs. Martin, and show how her demand curve for food can be derived.

Assuming that food and clothing are the only goods, that Mrs. Martin's weekly income is $400, and that the price of clothing is $40 per piece of clothing, Mrs. Martin's budget line is budget line 1 in Figure 20.13, when the price of food is $1 per pound. Thus, as we saw in Figure 20.2, Mrs. Martin will buy 200 pounds of food per week under these conditions.

If, however, the price of food increases to $2 per pound, her income and the price of clothing remaining constant, her budget line will be budget line 2 in Figure 20.13, and she will attain her highest indifference curve, $I_1$, by choosing the market basket corresponding to point $U$, a market basket containing 100 pounds of food per week. Thus, if the price of food is $2 per pound, she will buy 100 pounds of food per week.

We have derived two points on Mrs. Martin's individual demand curve for food—those corresponding to prices of $1 and $2 per pound. Figure 20.2 shows these two points, $X$ and $Y$. To obtain more points on her individual demand curve for food, all we have to do is assume a particular price of food, construct the budget line corresponding to this price (holding her income and the price of clothing constant), and find the market basket on this budget line that is on her highest indifference curve. Plot-

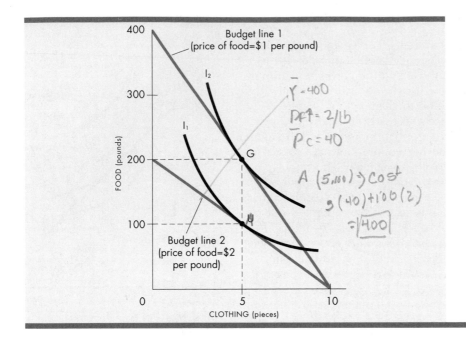

Handwritten annotations on figure:

$\bar{Y} = 400$

$P_f = 2/lb$

$\bar{P}_C = 40$

A $(5, 100) \rightarrow$ cost

$5(40) + 100(2)$

$= |400|$

**Figure 20.13**
**Effect of Change in Price of Food on Mrs. Martin's Equilibrium Market Basket**
If the price of a pound of food is $1, Mrs. Martin's budget line is such that her equilibrium market basket is at point *G*, where she buys 200 pounds of food per week. If the price of a pound of food is $2, Mrs. Martin's budget line is such that her equilibrium market basket is at point *U*, where she buys 100 pounds of food per week.

ting the amount of food in this market basket against the assumed price of food, we obtain a new point on her individual demand curve for food. Connecting up all these points, we get her complete individual demand curve for food, shown in Figure 20.2.

*Prices go down*

# A GUIDED TOUR OF THE BUSINESS FIRM

IT IS HARD TO OVERSTATE the importance of business firms in the American economy. They produce the bulk of our goods and services, hire most of the nation's workers, and issue stocks and bonds that represent a large percentage of the nation's wealth. Judged by any yardstick—even less complimentary ones like the responsibility for environmental pollution—business firms are an extremely important part of the American economy. In this chapter, we discuss the various types of business firms, such as proprietorships and corporations. Then we describe the various types of securities—common stock, bonds, and so forth—issued by firms, and discuss the workings of the stock market. Next, we take up the motivation and structure of firms, as well as their technology. Finally, we provide some essential elements of accounting. This material is a necessary introduction to the workings of the business enterprise, absolutely essential to anyone who works for, manages, or invests in a firm.

## THE IBM CORPORATION: A CASE STUDY

To begin with, let's look in some detail at one of America's biggest firms: the IBM Corporation. A description of its history and vicissitudes should give you a better feel for what firms do and the sorts of problems they face.

IBM world headquarters

### Electronic Computers: Coming from Behind

The IBM Corporation operated under the strong leadership of Thomas Watson, Sr., until his death in 1956. Watson joined the Computing-Tabulating-Recording Corporation in 1914, and renamed it International Business Machines in 1924. The firm became a very successful and fast-growing office-equipment company. In the late 1940s and early 1950s, the first electronic computers were developed, but IBM did not then appreciate the commercial potential of such equipment. According to Watson's son:

> During these really earth-shaking developments in the accounting machine industry, IBM slept soundly. We had put the first electronically-operated punched card calculator on the market in 1947. We clearly knew that electronic computing even in those days was so fast that the machine waited 9/10 of every card cycle for the mechanical portions of the machine to feed the next card. In spite of this, we didn't jump to the obvious conclusion that if we could feed data

more rapidly, we could increase speeds by 900 percent. Remington Rand and Univac drew this conclusion and were off to the races.

Finally we awoke and began to act. We took one of our most competent operating executives with a reputation for fearlessness and competence and put him in charge of all phases of the development of an IBM large-scale electronic computer. He and we were successful.

How did we come from behind? First, we had enough cash to carry loads of engineering, research, and production, which were heavy. Second, we had a sales force which enabled us to tailor our machine very closely to the market. Finally, and most important, we had good company morale. All concerned realized that this was a mutual challenge to us as an industry leader. We had to respond with all that we had to win, and we did.[1]

## Snow White and the Seven Dwarfs

Although IBM was a slow starter, it soon became the dominant producer of electronic computers. By 1956, it had over 80 percent of the market. According to many observers, its success was due particularly to its marketing skills. In the 1960s, it became known as Snow White, while its rivals—Burroughs, Univac, NCR, Control Data, Honeywell, GE, and RCA—were referred to as the Seven Dwarfs. In the 1970s, after GE and RCA left the computer industry, only five dwarfs remained.

On January 17, 1969, the federal government brought a massive antitrust case against IBM, accusing it of monopolistic practices. The case went on for thirteen years. According to IBM's former chairman, Frank Cary, "The suit was a tremendous cloud that was over the company. . . . It couldn't help influencing us in a whole variety of ways. Ending it lifted a huge burden from management's shoulders." In January 1982, the Justice Department dropped the case, saying that it was "without merit."

After the settlement of the case, IBM proceeded to sell aggressively and to enter new markets. Some observers worried that it was becoming too big and powerful; others felt that it had plenty of competition from the Japanese, among others.

## The IBM Personal Computer

One of IBM's most dramatic moves in the early 1980s was its entrance into the personal computer market. The job of overseeing the development of IBM's personal computer (PC) was entrusted to a twelve-member group, which worked for about a year on the project. The group broke with tradition by making the PC's technical specifications available to other firms, thus allowing outsiders to write software and make peripheral equipment for the PC that would extend its appeal. Within a few months after its introduction, the IBM PC was setting the standard for the industry. By 1983, IBM had garnered about 28 percent of the market for personal computers.

However, IBM is not invincible. During the mid-1980s, it was rocked by competition from Digital Equipment Corporation and imitators of its PCs, among others. From 1986 to 1988, it fought back by streamlining management, speeding up product introductions, and cutting spending where possible. In the first quarter of 1991, its earnings plunged by about 50 percent. While it attributed this to the recession, some analysts cited delays in introducing new products as another factor.

The first IBM personal computer

[1] T. Belden and M. Belden. *The Lengthening Shadow: The Life of Thomas J. Watson,* Boston: Little, Brown, 1962.

# AMERICAN FIRMS, BIG AND SMALL

IBM is an economic colossus—a huge organization with over 300,000 employees. Of course it is not typical of American business firms. If we broaden our focus to take in the entire population of business firms in the United States, the first thing we note is their tremendous number; according to government statistics, there are over 10 million. The vast majority of these firms, as one would expect, are very small. There are lots of grocery stores, gas stations, auto dealers, drugstores, clothing shops, restaurants, and so on. You see hundreds of them as you walk along practically any downtown city street. But these small firms, although numerous, do not control the bulk of the nation's productive capacity. The several hundred largest firms have great economic power, measured by their sales, assets, employment, or other such indices. The small firms tend to be weak and short-lived. Although some prosper, many small firms go out of business after only a few years of existence.

# PROPRIETORSHIPS

Most of the nation's business firms are proprietorships. A proprietorship is a legal form of business organization—the most common form and also the simplest. Specifically, a **_proprietorship_** is a firm owned by a single individual. For example, the corner drugstore may well be one. If so, it has a single owner—say, Bill Randolph. He hires the people he needs to wait on customers, deliver orders, do the bookkeeping, and so forth. He borrows, if he can, whatever money he feels he needs. He reaps the profits, or incurs the losses. All his personal assets—his house, his furniture, his car—can be taken by creditors to meet the drugstore's bills; that is, he has unlimited liability for the debts of the business.

**PROS.** What Lincoln said about the common man or woman applies as well to proprietorships: God must love them, or He wouldn't have created so many of them. If proprietorships didn't have advantages over other legal forms of business organization under many sorts of circumstances, there wouldn't be so many of them. What are these advantages? First, _owners of proprietorships have complete control over their businesses._ They don't have to negotiate with partners or other co-owners. They are the boss—and the only boss. Anyone who has been in a position of complete authority knows the joy it can bring. Many proprietors treasure this feeling of independence. Second, _a proprietorship is easy and inexpensive to establish:_ all you have to do is hang out your shingle and announce you are in business. This too is a great advantage.

**CONS.** But proprietorships have important disadvantages as well—and for this reason, they are seldom found in many important industries. One disadvantage is that _it is difficult for a proprietor to put together enough financial resources to enter industries like automobiles, steel, or computers._ No one in the world has enough money to establish, by himself or herself, a firm of IBM's present size. Another disadvantage is that _proprietors are liable for all of the debts of the firm._ If their business fails, their personal assets can be taken by their creditors, and they can be completely wiped out.

# PARTNERSHIPS

A **partnership** is somewhat more complicated than a proprietorship. As its name implies, it is a form of business organization where two or more people agree to own and conduct a business. Each partner agrees to contribute some proportion of the capital and labor used by the business, and to receive some proportion of the profits or losses. There are a variety of types of partnerships. In some cases, one or more of the partners may be "silent partners," who put up some of the money, but have little or nothing to do with the operations of the firm. The partnership is a common form of business organization in some industries and professions, like the law.

**PROS.** A partnership has certain advantages. Like a proprietorship, *it can be established without great expense or legal red tape.* (However, if you ever go into a partnership with someone, you would be well advised to have a good lawyer draw up a written agreement establishing such things as the salaries of each partner and how profits are to be shared.) In addition, a partnership can avoid some of the problems involved in a proprietorship. *It can usually put together more financial resources and specialized know-how than a proprietorship*—and this can be an important advantage.

**CONS.** But the partnership also has certain drawbacks. First, *each partner is liable without limit for the bills of the firm.* For example, even if one partner of a law firm has only a 30 percent share of the firm, he or she may be called upon to pay all the firm's debts if the other partners cannot do so. Second, *there is some red tape in keeping a partnership in existence.* Whenever a partner dies or withdraws, or whenever a new partner is admitted, a new partnership must be established. Third, like the proprietorship, *the partnership is not a very effective way to obtain the large amounts of capital required for some modern industries.* A modern automobile plant may cost $500 million, and not many partnerships could assemble that much capital. For these reasons, as well as others discussed in the next section, the corporation has become the dominant form of business organization.

# CORPORATIONS

A far more complicated form of business organization than either the proprietorship or partnership, the **corporation** is a fictitious legal person, separate and distinct from its owners. A corporation is formed by having lawyers draw up the necessary papers stating (in general terms) what sorts of activities the owners of the corporation intend to engage in. The owners of the corporation are the stockholders. **Stock,** pieces of paper signifying ownership of the corporation, is issued to the owners, generally in exchange for their cash. Ordinarily, each **share** of stock gives its owner one vote. The corporation's **board of directors,** which is responsible for setting overall policy for the firm, is elected by the stockholders. The firm's owners can, if they are dissatisfied with the company's policies or think they have better opportunities elsewhere, sell their stock to someone else, assuming, of course, that they can find a buyer.

**PROS.** The corporation has many advantages over the partnership or proprietorship. In particular, *each of the corporation's owners has limited,*

*not unlimited, liability.* If I decide to become one of the owners of IBM and if a share of IBM stock sells for $110 a share, I can buy ten shares of IBM stock for $1,100. And I can be sure that, if IBM falls on hard times, I cannot lose more than the $1,100 I paid for the stock. There is no way that I can be assessed beyond this. Moreover, *the corporation, unlike the partnership or proprietorship, has unlimited life.* If several stockholders want to withdraw from the firm, they simply sell their stock. The corporation goes on, although the identity of the owners changes. For these reasons, *the corporation is clearly a better device for raising large sums of money than the partnership or proprietorship.* This is an enormous advantage of the corporation, particularly in industries like automobiles and steel, which could not otherwise finance their operations.

CONS.   Without question, the corporation is a very important social invention. It permits people to assemble the large quantities of capital required for efficient production in many industries. Without limited liability and the other advantages of the corporation, it is doubtful that the opportunities and benefits of large-scale production could have been reaped. However, this does not mean that the corporate form will work for all firms. In many cases, a firm requires only a modest amount of capital, and there is no reason to go to the extra trouble and expense of establishing a corporation. Moreover, one disadvantage of the corporation is **double taxation of income,** since corporations pay income taxes—and the tax rate is often about one-third of every extra dollar earned. Thus every dollar earned by a corporation and distributed to stockholders is taxed twice by the federal government—once when it is counted as income by the corporation, and once when the remainder is counted as income by the stockholders.

# CORPORATE SECURITIES

The corporation raises money by issuing various kinds of securities; of these, three kinds—common stock, preferred stock, and bonds—are particularly significant. Each of these types of securities is important to the workings of the corporation and to the public's investment decisions.

COMMON STOCK.   *Common stock* is the ordinary certificate of ownership of the corporation. Holders of common stock are owners of the firm. They share in the firm's profits—if there are any profits. At frequent intervals, the board of directors of the firm may declare a dividend of so much per share for the common stockholders. For example, the common stockholders of IBM received dividends of $4.84 per share in 1990. **Dividends** are thus the income the owners of common stock receive. (In addition, of course, common stockholders may make money by selling their stock for more than they paid for it; such income is called **capital gains.**) Common stock is generally regarded as more risky than preferred stock or bonds, for reasons that will be explained.

PREFERRED STOCK.   *Preferred stock* is a special kind of certificate of ownership that pays at most a stated dividend. For example, consider the General Motors Corporation, the huge auto maker. Owners of one type of General Motors preferred stock receive $5 a share per year, as long as the firm makes enough to pay this dividend. To protect the owners of preferred stock, it is stipulated that no dividends can be paid on the common stock unless the dividends on the preferred stock are paid in full. Since

# BUYING AND SELLING COMMON STOCKS

Over 30 million Americans own common stocks, which indicates that you don't have to be wealthy to be an investor. Suppose that you are interested in buying IBM stock. To determine its current price, you need only look at the financial pages of any major newspaper. For example, on April 2, 1991, the *Wall Street Journal* showed the following information concerning IBM common stock:

| 52-week | | | | Sales | | | | Net |
|---|---|---|---|---|---|---|---|---|
| High | Low | Stock | Div | 100s | High | Low | Last | Change |
| 139 ¾ | 96 ¼ | IBM | 4.84 | 14230 | 114 ¼ | 111 ⅞ | 112 ¼ | −1 ⅝ |

Reading from left to right, $139.75 and $96.25 are the highest and lowest prices of IBM stock in the previous year, and $4.84 is the level of IBM's dividends in the previous year. The last five figures show the number of shares sold (1,423,000), the highest price (114.25), the lowest price (111.87 ½ ), and the final price (112.25) of a share on the previous day, as well as the change in the price from the day before (down $1.62 ½ per share).

To determine whether IBM common stock is a good buy, you would be well advised to look at IBM's recent earnings record and to obtain as much information as you can concerning the firm's earning prospects. This is because, as a firm's earnings (per share of common stock) go up, the price of its stock tends to go up too. Some economists and business analysts have gone so far as to publish formulas by which one can determine, on the basis of forecasts of what a firm's earnings will be, how much the stock is worth. They believe that one should buy if the current price of the stock is below this measure of the stock's intrinsic value and sell if the price is above it.

In contrast, other economists believe that the movement of stock prices has more to do with psychology than with financial valuation of this sort. As John Maynard Keynes put it, "[Most persons] are concerned, not with what an investment is really worth to a man who buys it 'for keeps,' but with what the market will value it at, under the influence of mass psychology, three months or a year hence. . . . For it

is not sensible to pay 25 for an investment of which you believe the prospective yields to justify a value of 30, if you also believe that the market will value it at 20 three months hence." As Princeton's Burton Malkiel observes, "This theory might . . . be called the 'greater-fool theory.' It's perfectly all right to pay three times what a stock is worth as long as later on you can find some innocent to pay five times what it's worth."[1]

There is no simple, foolproof way to determine whether IBM common stock is a good buy. Since even the most astute traders on Wall Street frequently do no better than one could do by buying the Dow-Jones average, you would do well to approach the stock market with caution. More than one economic savant has lost his or her shirt.

[1] B. Malkiel, *A Random Walk down Wall Street*, 5th ed., New York: Norton, 1990, p. 32.

the common stockholders cannot receive their dividends unless the preferred stock's dividends have been paid, common stock is obviously more risky than preferred stock. But by the same token, the amount preferred stockholders have to gain if the company prospers is less than the amount common stockholders have to gain, since however high its profits may be, the firm will pay only the stated dividend—for example, $5 per share per year in the case of General Motors—to the owners of preferred stock.

BONDS. Bonds are quite different from both common and preferred stocks. **Bonds** are debts of the firm; in other words, they are IOUs issued by the firm. In contrast to stockholders, the bondholders are not owners of a firm: they are its creditors, and receive interest, not dividends. Specifically, a bond is a certificate bearing the firm's promise to pay the interest every six months until the bond matures, at which time the firm also promises to pay the bondholders the principal (the amount they lent the firm) as well. Often bonds are sold in $1,000 denominations. For example, one type of bond issued by IBM is a 9 3/8 percent bond, due in 2004. The owner of each such bond receives $93.75 per year in interest, and IBM promises to pay him or her the principal of $1,000 when the bond falls due in 2004. A firm must pay the interest on the bonds and the principal when it is due, or it can be declared bankrupt. In other words, the bondholders are legally entitled to receive what is due them before the stockholders can get anything.

Thus, from the point of view of the investor, bonds are generally considered less risky than preferred stock, and preferred stocks are considered less risky than common stock. But we have ignored another fact: inflation. The tendency for the price level in the United States to increase over time has meant that bondholders have been paid off with dollars that were worth less than those they lent. For this reason, together with the fact that owners of common stocks reaped substantial capital gains during the 1960s and early 1970s, many investors tended to favor common stocks. Indeed, during the 1960s, a "cult of equities" developed; these were the years when it appeared that stock prices were headed only one way—even higher. It became very fashionable to buy common stock. But in the middle 1970s, the public's infatuation with common stocks seemed to fade, as stock prices fell; and the 1980s and early 1990s have seen considerable variation in stock prices. To understand why the value of stocks can gyrate so considerably, it is necessary to look briefly at the workings of the stock market.

## THE STOCK MARKET

In general, large corporations do not sell stock directly to the investor. Instead, the investor buys stock on the stock market. Two major stock exchanges in the United States are the New York Stock Exchange and the American Stock Exchange, both in New York City. On these and similar exchanges in other cities, the common stocks of thousands of corporations are bought and sold.

PRICE FLUCTUATIONS. The price of each common stock fluctuates from day to day, indeed from minute to minute. Basically, the factors responsible for these price fluctuations are the shifts in the demand curve and supply curve for each kind of common stock. For example, if a strike breaks out

at a General Motors plant, this may cause the demand curve for General Motors stock to shift downward to the left, since the strike is liable to mean lower profits for General Motors. Because of this downward, or leftward, shift in the demand curve, the price of General Motors common stock will tend to fall, as in fact happened during a recent United Auto Workers strike.

**THE GREAT CRASH.**    When stock prices tumble substantially, old investors think back to the Great Crash of 1929. The 1920s witnessed a feverish interest in investing in the stock market. Along with raccoon coats, Stutz Bearcats, and the Charleston, common stocks were the rage. Both the professionals on Wall Street and the neophytes on Main Street bought common stocks and more common stocks. Naturally, as the demand curves for common stocks shifted upward to the right, their prices rose, thus whetting the appetites of investors for still more common stocks. This upward spiral continued until 1929, when the bubble burst. Suddenly the prices of common stocks fell precipitously—and continued to drop during the early 1930s. The most famous average of industrial stock prices, the Dow-Jones average, fell from 381 in 1929 to 41 in 1933. Many investors, large and small, were wiped out.

**STOCKS COME BACK.**    The Great Crash made investors wary of common stocks for many years. But by the 1960s confidence in them was fully restored, and there certainly was no tendency for investors to shy away from them. In the 1970s and 1980s, the stock market remained a major outlet for savings. However, this does not mean that stock prices did not fluctuate. On October 19, 1987, the Dow-Jones average of stock prices fell by about 20 percent, the largest loss on a single day in history. Dubbed Black Monday by journalists, this day saw 600 million shares of stock change hands, as investors lost about $500 billion, at least on paper. This crash illustrated vividly and painfully what sensible observers knew all along: the stock market goes up and it goes down. During 1986, the stock market increased dramatically (by over 23 percent); in late 1987, investors lost a substantial proportion of these gains.

Judging from historical experience, the public's taste for common stocks seems to be justified. Studies show that, during the course of a lifetime, the typical investor would have done better to invest in common stocks than in the best-quality bonds, because stock prices have tended to rise. This tended to apply in a great many cases, even for investors who lived through the Great Crash. And it has certainly been borne out over the past 50 years. Thus, although common stocks are riskier in some respects than bonds or preferred stocks, they seem to have performed better, on the average, at least in recent times.

## Making Money on Stocks

During periods when the average of stock prices is going up, such as the 1920s and much of the 1950s and 1960s (as well as in more recent bull markets), it is relatively easy to be a financial wizard, whether by luck or calculation. A much more exacting test of your financial acumen is how well you can pick which stocks will outperform the averages. If you can predict that increases will occur in a certain firm's profits, and if other people don't predict the same thing, you may be able to pass this test. However, the sobering truth is that "playing the stock market" is much more an art than a science. The stock market is affected by psychological

# USING DIVERSIFICATION TO REDUCE RISK

Stocks are a risky investment; that is, you cannot be at all sure of how much money you will make or lose on them. *One way that professional investors reduce risk is by diversification: they invest in a number of stocks, and avoid putting all of their eggs in a single basket.* To see how diversification can reduce risk, consider the following simple example. Suppose that you can buy stock in only two firms, an overcoat manufacturer and a sportswear producer. If next year's weather is mild, stock in the sportswear producer will earn 20 cents per dollar invested, while stock in the overcoat manufacturer will earn nothing. If next year's weather is not mild, stock in the overcoat manufacturer will earn 20 cents per dollar invested, while stock in the sportswear producer will earn nothing.

Based on previous experience, there is a 50-50 chance that next year will be mild—and a 50-50 chance that it will not be mild. *Thus an investment in either one of these stocks is quite risky.* For example, if you buy stock in the overcoat manufacturer, there is a 50-50 chance that you will receive 20 cents per dollar invested, since this is the chance that the weather will not be mild. On the other hand, there is also a 50-50 chance that you will receive nothing, since this is the chance that the weather will be mild.

A simple and effective way to reduce this risk is to diversify. Rather than buying only one stock or the other, suppose that you put half of your money into each stock. *After diversifying in this way, you can be sure of getting 10 cents per dollar invested.* Why? Because if next year is not mild, you will receive 20 cents per dollar invested from your overcoat stock and nothing from your sportswear stock; thus your return from both stocks combined is 10 cents per dollar invested. Similarly, if next year is mild, you will receive 20 cents per dollar invested from your sportswear stock and nothing from your overcoat stock; thus your return from both stocks combined is 10 cents per dollar invested.

The reason why risk is eliminated through diversification is that the stocks of the two firms are affected differently by different weather conditions. Since the one firm's stock always does well when the other firm's stock does poorly, diversification can, as we have seen, do away with risk. But this is a very unusual situation. Ordinarily, it is possible to reduce, but not eliminate, risk through diversification. This is because there generally is not a simple inverse relationship (like that assumed above) between the returns from various firms' stocks.

In recent decades, economists have devoted considerable attention to financial topics of this sort. In 1990, three American economists—Harry Markowitz, Merton Miller, and William Sharpe—received the Nobel Prize in economics for their work in this area.

Harry Markowitz

Merton Miller

William F. Sharpe

as well as economic considerations. Moreover, when you try to spot stocks that will increase in price, you are pitting your knowledge and experience against those of skilled professionals with big research staffs and with friends and acquaintances working for the companies in question. And even these professionals can do surprisingly poorly at times.

Do economists have a nose for good investments? John Maynard Keynes was an extremely successful speculator who made millions of dollars. Other economists have been far less successful. Certainly, a knowledge of basic economics is not sufficient to enable you to make money on the stock market, but insofar as the market reflects economic realities, a knowledge of basic economics should be helpful.

# THE GIANT CORPORATION

Much of the trading on the stock market centers around the relatively small number of giant corporations that control a very substantial percentage of the total assets and employment in the American economy. And well it might, for the largest 100 manufacturing corporations control about half of this country's manufacturing assets. These firms have tremendous economic and political power. They include the giant automobile manufacturers (General Motors, Ford), the big oil firms (Exxon, Amoco, Mobil, Chevron, Atlantic-Richfield), the big computer and office machinery producers (IBM, Hewlett Packard, Xerox), the leading tobacco firms (American Brands, RJR Nabisco, Philip Morris), the electrical equipment producers (General Electric, Westinghouse), and many others.

## Management

Usually, the president is the chief operations officer in the firm, although sometimes the chairman of the board of directors fills this role. As for the board of directors, some members are chosen for their reputations and contacts, while others are chosen for their knowledge of the firm, the industry, or some profession or specialty.

The board generally contains at least one representative of the financial community, and a university president or former government official is often included to show that the firm is responsive to broad social issues. Members of IBM's board include Harold Brown, a former secretary of defense, and Nanneri Keohane, president of Wellesley College.

The board of directors is concerned with overall policy. Since it meets only a few times a year, it seldom becomes involved in day-to-day decisions; and it usually goes along with management's policies, so long as management retains the board's confidence.

## Separation of Ownership from Control

An interesting and important feature of the large corporation is the fact that it is owned by many people, practically all of whom have little or no detailed information about the firm's operations. The owners of IBM number over 800,000, but most of them know relatively little about what is going on in the firm. Moreover, because of the wide diffusion of ownership, working control of a large corporation can often be maintained by a group with only one-fifth or less of all the voting stock. The result is a *sep-*

*aration of ownership from control.* In other words, the owners control the firm in only a limited and somewhat sporadic sense.

So long as a firm's management is not obviously incompetent or corrupt, it is difficult for insurgent stockholders to remove the management from office. Most stockholders do not go to the annual meetings to vote for members of the firm's board of directors. Instead, they receive *proxies,* which, if returned, permit the management to exercise their votes. Usually enough shareholders mail in their proxies to give management the votes it needs to elect a friendly board of directors. In recent years, the Securities and Exchange Commission, which oversees and regulates the financial markets, has attempted to make the giant corporations more democratic by enabling insurgent groups to gain access to mailing lists of stockholders and so forth. But there is still a noteworthy and widespread separation of ownership from control.

## TEST YOURSELF

1. The Exxon Corporation built a new olefins plant (costing $500 million) in Baytown, Texas. Is this plant a firm? Why or why not? Do you think that a proprietorship would be likely to build and own such a plant? Why, or why not?

2. Assume that a partnership wanted to enter the automobile industry. What problems would such a legal form of organization impose upon the potential entrants? Are any of the Big Three in the U.S. automobile industry (General Motors, Ford, and Chrysler) partnerships?

3. Explain why each of the following statements is true or false. (a) The University of Texas is a firm. (b) Massachusetts General Hospital is a firm. (c) A firm must be owned by more than one person. (d) The owner of a firm must participate in its management.

4. On April 1, 1991, the common stock of Exxon Corporation closed at $57.50 per share. What effect would each of the following have on its price? (a) A marked increase in the demand for gasoline. (b) A prolonged strike at a major Exxon refinery. (c) Price ceilings on gas and oil.

5. Explain why bondholders do not vote for a corporation's board of directors and why common stockholders are not guaranteed a particular dividend rate.

## MOTIVATION OF THE FIRM

What determines the behavior of the business firm? As a first approximation, *economists usually assume that firms attempt to maximize* **profits,** which are defined as the difference between the firm's revenue and its costs. In other words, economists generally assume that firms try to make as much money as possible. This assumption certainly does not seem unreasonable; most business executives appear to be interested in making money. Nonetheless, the assumption of profit maximization oversimplifies the situation. Although business executives certainly want profits, they are interested in other things as well. Some firms claim that they want to promote better cultural activities or better racial relations in their community. At a less lofty level, other firms say that their aim is to increase their share of the market. Whether or not one takes these self-proclaimed goals very seriously, it is clear that firms are not interested *only* in making money—

often for the same reason that Dr. Johnson gave for not becoming a philosopher: "because cheerfulness keeps breaking in."[2]

**INTRAFIRM POLITICS.** In a large corporation, there are some fairly obvious reasons why firms may not maximize profits. Various groups within such firms develop their own party lines, and intrafirm politics is an important part of the process determining firm behavior. Whereas in a small firm it may be fairly accurate to regard the goals of the firm as being the goals of the proprietor, in the large corporation the decision on the goals of the firm is a matter of politics, with various groups within the organization struggling for power. In addition, because of the separation of ownership from control, top management usually has a great deal of freedom as long as it seems to be performing reasonably well. Under these circumstances, the behavior of the firm may be dictated in part by the interests of the management group, resulting in higher salaries, more perquisites, and a bigger staff for their own benefit than would otherwise be the case.

**RISK AND UNCERTAINTY.** Also, in a world full of risk and uncertainty, it is difficult to know exactly what profit maximization means, since the firm cannot be sure that a certain level of profit will result from a certain action. Instead, the best the firm can do is to estimate that a certain probability distribution of profit levels will result from a certain action. Under these circumstances, the firm may choose less risky actions even though they have a lower expectation of very high profits than other actions. In a world where ruin is ruinous, this may be perfectly rational policy.

### Profit Maximization Is the Standard Assumption

Nonetheless, profit maximization remains the standard assumption in economics. As we agreed in our discussion of model building in Chapter 2, to be useful, models need not be exact replicas of reality. Economic models based on profit maximization have been very useful indeed. For one thing, they help to show how the price system functions. For another, in the real world, they suggest how a firm should operate if it wants to make as much money as possible. Even if a firm does not want to maximize profit, these theories can be utilized. For example, they can show how much profit the firm is forgoing by taking certain courses of action. In recent years, the theory of the profit-maximizing firm has been studied more and more for the sake of determining profit-maximizing rules of business behavior.

## TECHNOLOGY, INPUTS, AND THE PRODUCTION FUNCTION

The decisions a firm should make in order to maximize its profits are determined by the current state of technology. Technology, it will be recalled from Chapter 1, is the sum total of society's knowledge concerning the industrial arts. Just as consumers are limited by their income, firms are limited by the current state of technology. If the current state of technol-

---

[2] This quote is taken from R. Solow, "The New Industrial State, or Son of Affluence," *The Public Interest*, Fall 1967. Since footnotes are so often used to cite dreary material, it seems worthwhile to use them occasionally to cite humor as well.

# THE PRINCIPAL-AGENT PROBLEM

Although economists generally assume as a first approximation that firms maximize profit, they realize that this does not always occur. One factor that can interfere with profit maximization is the so-called principal-agent problem. In a large corporation, the managers very seldom own the firm. Instead, a firm's managers are agents who work for the firm's owners, who are the principals. *The principal-agent problem is that the managers may pursue their own objectives, even though this decreases the profits of the owners.*

Consider William Moran, a manager and part-owner of the Media Company. If he were the sole owner of this firm, an extra dollar of benefits (large staff, company-paid travel, and so on) that he receives from the firm would reduce his profits by one dollar. That is, the cost of these benefits would come entirely out of his own pocket. However, if he were to own only one-fifth of the firm, an extra dollar of benefits would reduce his profits by only 20 cents. Hence, only one-fifth of the cost of these benefits would come out of his pocket.

*William Moran is likely to increase the amount of benefits he receives if the cost to him of a dollar's worth of benefits is 20 cents rather than a dollar.* Since the other owners pick up four-fifths of the bill, why not take an extra "business" trip to Acapulco or the Riviera? If he had to pay the full cost, he would settle for a vacation in the Catskills, but since he only pays 20 percent of the full cost, he finds it worthwhile to take the extra "business" trip.

*If a manager is not an owner or part-owner of the firm, this problem becomes even more serious.* Because the cost of the benefits he or she receives is borne entirely by the owners, the manager has an incentive to increase these benefits very substantially. Since the owners of the firm find it hard to distinguish between those benefits that bolster profits and those that do not do so, the manager has some leeway. However, if the manager tries to cheat the owners in too blatant a fashion, the owners may fire the manager.

Recognizing the existence of this principal-agent problem, people avoid investing in a firm where managers behave in this way. If no one is willing to invest and if the managers have to put up their own funds to finance the business, they will be much less

likely to take "business" trips to Acapulco or the Riviera (or even the Catskills). Conceivably, owners could make managers sign contracts making the managers responsible for paying for the excessive benefits they receive, but since this would make it necessary for the owners to monitor the managers' activities in minute detail (and would cause enormous ill-will among the managers), it would not be a practical solution.

*To deal with this problem, firms often establish contracts that give the managers an incentive to reduce such benefits and to pursue objectives that are reasonably close to profit maximization.* Thus the firm's owners might give the managers a financial stake in the success of the firm. Many corporations have adopted stock-option plans, whereby managers can purchase shares of common stock at less than market price. These plans give managers an incentive to promote the firm's profits and to act in accord with the owners' interests. There is some evidence that these plans do have an effect. For example, according to one recent study, if managers own between 5 and 20 percent of a firm, the firm is likely to perform better (in terms of profitability) than if they own less than 5 percent.[1]

[1] R. Morck, A. Shleifer, and R. Vishny, "Management Ownership and Corporate Performance: An Empirical Analysis," *Journal of Financial Economics*, March 1988.

ogy is such that we do not know how to produce more than 40 bushels of corn per year from an acre of land if 2 workers are hired, then this is as much as the firm can produce from this combination of land and labor. In making its decisions, the firm must take this into account.

## Inputs

In constructing a model of the profit-maximizing firm, economists must somehow represent the state of technology and include it in their model. As a first step toward this end, we must define an **input.** Perhaps the simplest definition of an input is that it is anything the firm uses in its production process. Some of the inputs of a farm producing corn might be seed, land, labor, water, fertilizer, various types of machinery, as well as the time of the people managing the farm.

## Production Function

Having defined an input, we can now describe how economists represent the state of technology. The basic concept economists use for this purpose is the production function.

For any commodity, *the **production function** is the relationship between the quantities of various inputs used per period of time and the maximum quantity of the commodity that can be produced per period of time.* More specifically, the production function is a table, a graph, or an equation showing the maximum output rate that can be achieved from any specified set of usage rates of inputs. The production function summarizes the characteristics of existing technology at a given point in time. It reflects the technological constraints the firm must reckon with.

To see more clearly what we mean by a production function, consider the Milwaukee Machine Company, a hypothetical machine shop that produces a simple metal part. Suppose that we are dealing with a period of time that is so short that the firm's basic plant and equipment cannot be altered. For simplicity, suppose that the only input whose quantity can be altered in this period is the amount of labor used by the machine shop. Suppose that the firm collects data showing the relationship between the quantity of its output and the quantity of labor it uses. This relationship, given in Table 21.1, is the firm's production function. It shows that, when 1 worker is employed, 100 parts are produced per month; when 2 workers are employed, 210 parts are produced per month; and so on. Information concerning a firm's production function is often obtained from the firm's engineers, as well as its artisans and technicians. Much more will be said about production functions in later chapters. All that we want to do here is to introduce the concept of the production function.

**Table 21.1**
**Production Function, Milwaukee Machine Company**

| QUANTITY OF LABOR USED PER MONTH (NUMBER OF WORKERS EMPLOYED) | OUTPUT PER MONTH (NUMBER OF PARTS) |
| --- | --- |
| 0 | 0 |
| 1 | 100 |
| 2 | 210 |
| 3 | 315 |
| 4 | 415 |
| 5 | 500 |

# ELEMENTS OF ACCOUNTING: THE FIRM'S BALANCE SHEET

Having touched on the firm's technology, we must return to the motivation of the firm. In a previous section, we stated that economists generally assume that firms attempt to maximize profits. Viewed as a first approximation, this assumption does not seem too hard to swallow, but exactly what do we mean by profit? This is an important question, of interest to business executives and investors as well as to economists. The accounting profession provides the basic figures that are reported in the newspapers and in a firm's annual reports to its stockholders. If IBM reports that it made a particular amount last year, this figure is provided by IBM's accountants. How do the accountants obtain this figure? What are its limitations?

Basically, accounting concepts are built around two very important statements: the balance sheet and the income statement. A *firm's* **balance sheet** *shows the nature of its assets, tangible and intangible, at a certain point in time.*

## Left-Hand Side of the Balance Sheet

Let us return to the Milwaukee Machine Company. Its balance sheet might be as shown in Table 21.2. The left-hand side of the balance sheet shows the assets of the firm as of December 31, 1991. **Current assets** are assets that will be converted into cash relatively quickly (generally within a year), whereas **fixed assets** generally will not be liquidated quickly. The firm has $20,000 in cash, $120,000 in inventory, $160,000 in equipment, and $180,000 in buildings. At first glance, these figures may seem more accurate than they are likely to be. It is very difficult to know how to value various assets. For example, should they be valued at what the firm paid for them, or at what it would cost to replace them? More will be said about these problems below.

**Table 21.2**
**Balance Sheet, Milwaukee Machine Company, as of December 31,1991**

| ASSETS (DOLLARS) | | LIABILITIES AND NET WORTH (DOLLARS) | |
|---|---|---|---|
| Current assets | | Current liabilities | |
| Cash | 20,000 | Accounts payable | 20,000 |
| Inventory | 120,000 | Notes payable | 40,000 |
| Fixed assets | | Long-term liabilities | |
| Equipment | 160,000 | Bonds | 160,000 |
| Buildings | 180,000 | | |
| | | Net worth | |
| | | Preferred stock | 100,000 |
| | | Common stock | 100,000 |
| | | Retained earnings | 60,000 |
| Total | 480,000 | Total | 480,000 |

## Right-Hand Side of the Balance Sheet

The right-hand side of the firm's balance sheet shows the claims by creditors on the firm's assets and the value of the firm's ownership. In Table 21.2, the Milwaukee Machine Company has total liabilities—or debts—of $220,000. There is $60,000 in **current liabilities,** which come due in less than a year; and $160,000 in **long-term liabilities,** which come due in a year or more. Specifically, there is $20,000 in **accounts payable,** which are bills owed for goods and services that the firm bought; $40,000 in **notes payable,** short-term notes owed to banks, finance companies, or other creditors; and $160,000 in **bonds payable,** or bonds outstanding.

## Left-Hand Side = Right-Hand Side

The difference between the value of a firm's assets and the value of its liabilities is its **net worth,** which is the value of the firm's owners' claims against the firm's assets. In other words, the value of the firm to its owners is the total value of its assets less the value of the debts owed by the firm. Since

total value of assets − total liabilities = net worth,

it follows that

total value of assets = total liabilities + net worth.

That is, *the sum of the items on the left-hand side of the balance sheet must equal the sum of the items on the right-hand side.* This, of course, must be true because of the way we define net worth.

In the case of the Milwaukee Machine Company, the firm's net worth—the difference between its assets and its liabilities—is $260,000. Specifically, there is $100,000 worth of preferred stock and $100,000 worth of common stock; there is also $60,000 in retained earnings. **Retained earnings** is the total amount of profit that the stockholders have reinvested in the business. In other words, the stockholders of the Milwaukee Machine Company have reinvested $60,000 of their profits in the business. Rather than withdrawing this sum as dividends, they have kept it invested in the firm.

## THE FIRM'S INCOME STATEMENT

*A firm's **income statement** shows its sales during a particular period, its costs incurred in connection with these sales, and its profits during this period.* Table 21.3 shows the Milwaukee Machine Company's income statement during the period January 1, 1992, to December 31, 1992. Sales during this period were $240,000. The cost of manufacturing the items made during this period was $110,000 which includes $30,000 for materials, $40,000 for labor, $34,000 for depreciation (discussed below), and $6,000 for miscellaneous operating expenses.

However, because the firm has reduced its inventory from $120,000 to $110,000 during the period, the cost of manufacturing the items *made* during the period does not equal the cost of manufacturing the items *sold* during the period. To find the *cost of goods sold*—which is the amount that logically should be deducted from sales to get the profits made from the sale of these goods—we must add the decrease in the value of inventory to the total manufacturing cost. (Why? Because the firm sold more items than it produced during this period. Thus the cost of the items it sold equals the cost of the items it produced during this period plus the cost of the items it sold from its inventory. Since the cost of the items it sold from its inventory equals the decrease in the value of its inventory, the cost of the items it sold equals the cost of the items it produced during this period plus the decrease in inventory.) Putting it another way, we must add the beginning inventory and subtract the closing inventory, as shown in Table 21.3. The resulting figure for cost of goods sold is $120,000.

But manufacturing costs are not the only costs the firm incurs. To estimate the firm's profits, we must also deduct from sales its selling and ad-

**Table 21.3**
**Income Statement, Milwaukee Machine Company,**
**January 1, 1992, to December 31, 1992 (dollars)**

| | | |
|---|---:|---:|
| Net sales | | 240,000 |
| Manufacturing cost of goods sold | | 120,000 |
|    Materials | 30,000 | |
|    Labor | 40,000 | |
|    Depreciation | 34,000 | |
|    Miscellaneous operating costs | 6,000 | |
|    Total | 110,000 | |
|      Plus beginning inventory | 120,000 | |
|      Less closing inventory | −110,000 | |
|    Adjusted total | 120,000 | |
| Selling and administrative costs | | 20,000 |
| Fixed interest charges and state and | | |
|    local taxes | | 10,000 |
| Net earnings before income taxes | | 90,000 |
| Corporation income taxes | | 40,000 |
| Net earnings after taxes | | 50,000 |
| Dividends on preferred stock | | 4,000 |
| Net profits of common stockholders | | 46,000 |
| Dividends paid on common stock | | 20,000 |
| Addition to retained earnings | | 26,000 |

ministrative expenses, its interest charges, and its state and local taxes, as well as its federal income taxes. Table 21.3 shows that the Milwaukee Machine Company's after-tax earnings during 1992 were $50,000. This is the amount left for the owners of the business. The income statement also shows what the owners do with what is left. Table 21.3 shows that the Milwaukee Machine Company used $4,000 to pay dividends to holders of preferred stock. When this was done, the holders of common stock were free to distribute some of the profits to themselves. According to Table 21.3, they distributed $20,000 to themselves in dividends on the common stock, and plowed the rest—$26,000—back into the business as retained earnings.

## Depreciation

Before leaving the income statement, we should explain one element of manufacturing cost—*depreciation.* While the other elements of manufacturing cost are self-explanatory, this one is not. The idea behind depreciation is that the buildings and equipment will not last forever; eventually they will have to be replaced. Clearly, it would be foolish to charge the entire cost of replacing them to the year when they are replaced. Instead, a better picture of the firm's true profitability will be drawn if the cost of replacing them is spread gradually over the life of buildings and equipment, thus recognizing that each year's output has a hand in wearing them out. One frequently used technique is so-called *straight-line depreciation,* which spreads the cost of buildings and equipment (less their scrap value) evenly over their life. Thus, if the Milwaukee Machine Company buys a piece of equipment for $20,000 and if it is expected to last ten years (its scrap value being zero), it would charge depreciation of $2,000 per year for this machine (for ten years after its purchase). The

$34,000 charge for depreciation in Table 21.3 is the sum of such charges. Clearly, this is only a rough way to estimate the true depreciation charges, but it is good enough for many purposes.

### Economic versus Accounting Profits

The previous section described the nature of profit, as defined by accountants. This is the concept on which practically all published figures in business reports are based. But economists define profits somewhat differently.

*To economists, profit is the amount that a firm's owners receive over and above what they could make from the capital and labor they provide, if this capital and labor were used outside the firm.* In this way, the opportunity costs of their capital and labor are taken into account. Also,

---

## EXAMPLE 21.1     HOW TO DEPRECIATE A BASEBALL CLUB

Suppose that you decide to buy the Philadelphia Phillies for $80 million. There are some important tax advantages you should understand. According to Bill Veeck, former owner of the Chicago White Sox, "It is almost impossible not to make money on a baseball club when you are buying it new, because, unless you are inordinately successful, you pay no income tax." In particular, half of the purchase price of the team can be regarded as the cost of the players, which are depreciable assets like machinery or breeding cattle. Suppose that you regard 5 years as being the "useful life" of the players, and that you use straight-line depreciation.

(a) How much depreciation (of the players) can you deduct from the Phillies' receipts each year to figure your profits? (b) Suppose that you pay $10 million in cash and borrow the remaining $70 million to pay for the Phillies. If you pay 10 percent interest, how much interest expense do you deduct from the Phillies' receipts each year to figure your profits? (c) Suppose that this year the Phillies' receipts equal $44 million and their operating expenses (excluding depreciation of the players and the interest on your loan) equal $30 million. Must you pay any income tax? (Assume that you have no income from sources other than the Phillies.)

### Solution

(a) Since the cost of the players can be regarded as one-half of the purchase price of the team, it equals one-half of $80 million, or $40 million. Since the life of the players is 5 years, annual depreciation equals $40 million divided by 5, or $8 million. (b) $70 million times 10 percent, or $7 million. (c) Your income from the Phillies is as follows:

| | |
|---|---|
| Earnings(before depreciation and interest) | $14 million |
| Less depreciation | −8 million |
| Less interest | −7 million |
| | −$1 million |

Since you incurred a loss (because of the depreciation of the players), you pay no income tax.

---

economists do not assume that the firm attempts to maximize the current, short-run profits measured by the accountant. Instead they assume that the firm will attempt to maximize the sum of profits over a long period of time.[3]

Suppose that the owners of the Milwaukee Machine Company, who receive profits but no salary or wages, put in long hours for which they could receive $30,000 in 1992 if they worked for someone else. Also suppose that if they invested their capital somewhere other than in this firm, they could obtain a return of $22,000 on it in 1992. Under these circumstances, economists would say that the firm's after-tax profits in 1992 were $50,000 − $30,000 − $22,000, or − $2,000, rather than the $50,000 shown in Table 21.3. In other words, the economists' concept of profit includes only what the owners make above and beyond what their labor and capital employed in the business could have earned elsewhere. In this case, that amount is negative.

---

## EXAMPLE 21.2    HOW MUCH DOES A HOT DOG VENDOR MAKE?

Louie Stathopoulos sells hot dogs out of a steel cart under an umbrella in the Wall Street area in New York City. On a sunny day, he sells the following numbers of hot dogs, sodas, knishes, and sausages per day, his price and cost per unit being shown below.

| ITEM | NUMBER SOLD | PRICE | COST |
|---|---|---|---|
| Hot Dog | 125 | $1 | 36¢ |
| Soda | 75 | 60¢ | 33¢ |
| Knish | 20 | 75¢ | 33¢ |
| Sausage | 10 | $1 | 40¢ |

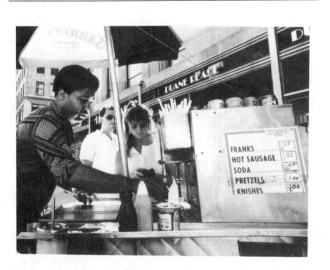

He pays $40 per day for ice, $3 for propane, $13 for rent, and $2 for insurance. His cart cost $4,500, and will have to be replaced after about 1,000 days of use.[*]
(a) What are Mr. Stathopoulos's total sales on a sunny day? (b) What is his total cost, including depreciation? (c) What is his accounting profit? (d) He works from 6 A.M. to 9 P.M. on a sunny day. If he could earn $4 per hour at another job, is he earning an economic profit? (e) If it rains, he sells about 70 percent less than the above amounts. Does he earn a positive economic profit on a rainy day?

### Solution

(a) 125 × $1 + 75 × 60¢ + 20 × 75¢ + 10 × $1 = $195. (b) 125 × 36¢ + 75 × 33¢ + 20 × 33¢ + 10 × 40¢ + $58 (for ice, propane, rent, and insurance) + $4.50 (for straight-line depreciation of his cart) = $142.85. (c) $195 − $142.85 = $52.15. (d) Working 15 hours per day, he could earn 15 × $4, or $60, at another job. Thus he is not earning an economic profit. (e) No, since he will earn even less per hour of work than on a sunny day.

[*] These are actual figures for Mr. Stathopoulos's business. See "Selling the Sidewalk Frank," *New York Times*, July 26, 1987.

---

[3] The profits earned at various points in time should be *discounted* before being added together, but, for simplicity's sake, we neglect this point here. For some relevant discussion, see Chapter 29.

To a considerable extent, the differences between the concepts used by the accountant and the economist reflect the difference in their functions. The accountant is concerned with controlling the firm's day-to-day operations, detecting fraud or embezzlement, satisfying tax and other laws, and producing records for various interested groups. On the other hand, the economist is concerned primarily with decision making and rational choice among prospective alternatives. Although the figures published on profits almost always conform to the accountant's, not the economist's, concept, the economist's concept is the more relevant one for many kinds of decisions. (And this, of course, is recognized by sophisticated accountants.) For example, suppose the owners of the Milwaukee Machine Company are trying to decide whether they should continue in business. If they are interested in making as much money as possible, the answer depends on the firm's profits as measured by the economist, not the accountant. If the firm's economic profits are greater than (or equal to) zero, the firm should continue in existence; otherwise, it should not. Thus the Milwaukee Machine Company should not stay in existence if 1992 is a good indicator of its future profitability.

## TEST YOURSELF

1. Which of the following are inputs in the steel industry? (a) coke, (b) iron ore, (c) labor, (d) land, (e) capital, (f) water, (g) oxygen, (h) food eaten by Bethlehem Steel's workers.

2. Changes in the tax law have allowed firms to depreciate assets more quickly. For example, they can depreciate some types of assets over 3 years, rather than 5 years. If a firm depreciates an asset more quickly, will its accounting profits in the first year after it buys the asset be increased or decreased?

3. Suppose that a firm's balance sheet is as follows:

| ASSETS (DOLLARS) | | LIABILITIES AND NET WORTH (DOLLARS) | |
| --- | --- | --- | --- |
| Current assets | | Current liabilities | |
| Cash | 200,000 | Accounts payable | 100,000 |
| Inventory | 300,000 | Notes payable | _____ |
| Fixed assets | | Long-term liabilities | |
| Equipment | _____ | Bonds | 400,000 |
| Buildings | 800,000 | | |
| | | Net worth | 400,000 |
| Total | 2,000,000 | Total | _____ |

Fill in the three blanks. What is the total amount that the firm owes? How much have the owners contributed? What is the difference between current assets and fixed assets?

4. Suppose that a firm's accounting profits for 1992 are $20,000. The firm is a proprietorship, and the owner worked 500 hours managing the business during 1992, for which she received no compensation other than the profits. If she could have gotten $10 an hour working for someone else, how much were her economic profits during 1992? Suppose that she also contributed $50,000 in capital to the firm, and that she could have obtained 6 percent interest on this capital if she had invested it elsewhere. In this case, how much were her economic profits?

## SUMMARY

1. There are three principal types of business firms: proprietorships, partnerships, and corporations. The corporation has many advantages over the other two—limited liability, unlimited life, and greater ability to raise large sums of money. Nonetheless, because the corporation also has disadvantages, many firms are not corporations.

2. The corporation raises money by issuing various kinds of securities, of which three kinds—common stock, preferred stock, and bonds—are particularly important.

3. A relatively small number of giant corporations control a very substantial proportion of the total assets and employment in the American economy. In the large corporation, ownership and control tend to be separated.

4. As a first approximation, economists generally assume that firms attempt to maximize profits. In large part, this is because it is a close enough approximation to reality for many of the most important purposes of economics. Also, economists are interested in the theory of the profit-maximizing firm because it provides rules of behavior for firms that do want to maximize profits.

5. To summarize the characteristics of existing technology at a given point in time, the economist uses the concept of the production function, which shows the maximum output rate of a given commodity that can be achieved from any specified set of usage rates of inputs.

6. Accounting concepts are built around two very important statements: the balance sheet and the income statement. The balance sheet shows the nature of the firm's assets and liabilities at a given point in time. The difference between its assets and its liabilities is its net worth, which is the value of the firm's owners' claims against its assets.

7. A firm's income statement shows its sales during a particular period, its costs incurred in connection with these sales, and its profits during the period.

8. Economists define profits somewhat differently than accountants do. In defining profit, economists deduct the amount the owners could receive from the capital and labor they provide, if this capital and labor were used outside the firm. Also, economists are interested in longer periods than those to which accounting statements apply. Although the profit figures that are published almost always conform to the accountant's concept, the economist's concept is the more relevant one for many kinds of decisions.

## CONCEPTS FOR REVIEW

| | | |
|---|---|---|
| **Proprietorship** | **Dividends** | **Balance sheet** |
| **Partnership** | **Preferred stock** | **Current assets** |
| **Corporation** | **Bonds** | **Fixed assets** |
| **Board of directors** | **Profits** | **Net worth** |
| **Double taxation of income** | **Input** | **Income statement** |
| **Common stock** | **Production function** | **Depreciation** |

# OPTIMAL INPUT DECISIONS BY BUSINESS FIRMS

FIRMS MUST CONSTANTLY TRY to determine whether they are using the most appropriate techniques. Take the steel industry. In 1991, Weirton and National Steel decided to use continuous casting, which transforms molten metal directly into slabs, to make all their steel. Nucor Corporation uses continuous casting to produce steel slabs 2 inches thick, cutting energy costs by 20–40 percent and slashing labor hours per ton of output in half. No decision a firm makes is more important than its choice of production technique.

In this chapter, we shall take a closer look at the decision-making process within the firm. Our discussion builds on the previous chapter, which dealt with the organization, motivation, and technology of the firm. We look in more detail at the firm's technology, and focus particular attention on the following central question: If a firm attempts to maximize profits, what production technique—that is, what combination of inputs—should it choose to produce a particular quantity of output? Two points should be noted at the outset. First, when finding the optimal input combination, we take as given the quantity of output that the firm will produce. In subsequent chapters, we shall discuss how the firm should choose this quantity. Second, just as one purpose of Chapters 19 and 20 was to show how a product's market demand curve can be derived, so an important purpose of Chapters 22 through 24 is to show how a product's market supply curve can be derived. In this chapter, we present some of the concepts and findings that are required for this purpose.

## THE PRODUCTION FUNCTION REVISITED

If the Bethlehem Steel Corporation decides to produce a certain quantity of steel, it can do so in many ways. It can use open-hearth furnaces, or basic oxygen furnaces, or electric furnaces; it can use various types of iron ore; and it can use various types of coke. Which of these many ways will maximize Bethlehem Steel's profits? The management of Bethlehem Steel—and every business firm—devotes considerable time and energy to answering this kind of question. Let's restate it in the economist's terms. Given that a firm is going to produce a certain quantity of output, what production technique—i.e., what combination of inputs—should it choose to maximize its profits?

As a first step toward answering this question, it is wise to review the

concept of the production function, taken up in the previous chapter. As you will recall, *the **production function** shows the most output that existing technology permits the firm to extract from each quantity of inputs.* Consider the hypothetical case of a wheat farm with 1 acre of land. The relationship between the amount of labor used per year by this farm and the farm's output is shown in Table 22.1. This is the farm's production function. It shows that the farm can produce 30 bushels of wheat per year if 1 unit of labor is used, 70 bushels of wheat per year if 2 units of labor are used, and so on.

*The production function summarizes the characteristics of existing technology at a given point in time;* it shows the technological constraints that a firm must reckon with. Like it or not, the most that the wheat farm in Table 22.1 can produce, if it uses 2 units of labor, is 70 bushels per year. This is the best that existing technology permits. Perhaps future advances in technology will permit such a farm (with 2 units of labor) to produce more than 70 bushels per year, but this presently cannot be done.

### A Crude-Oil Pipeline: A Case Study

To illustrate what a production function looks like in a real case, let's consider a crude-oil pipeline that transports petroleum from oil fields and storage areas over hundreds of miles to major urban and industrial centers. We begin by noting that the output of such a pipeline is the amount of oil carried per day, and that the two principal inputs are the diameter of the pipeline and the horsepower applied to the oil carried. Both inputs are important. The bigger the diameter of the pipe, the more oil the pipeline can carry, holding constant the horsepower applied. And the greater the horsepower applied, the more oil the pipeline can carry, holding constant the diameter of the pipeline.

The production function shows the maximum output rate that can be derived from each combination of input rates. Thus, in this case, the production function shows the maximum amount of oil carried per day as a function of the pipeline's diameter and the amount of horsepower applied. On the basis of engineering estimates, one can derive the production function for crude-oil pipelines. Leslie Cookenboo of the Exxon Corporation derived such a production function, assuming that the pipeline carries Mid-Continent crude, has ¼-inch pipe throughout the lines, has lines 1,000 miles in length with a 5 percent terrain variation, and no net gravity flow in the line.[1] Some of his results are shown in Table 22.2. For example, the production function shows that if the diameter of the pipeline is 22 inches and the horsepower is 40,000, the pipeline can carry 215,000 barrels per day. Certainly, any firm operating a pipeline or considering the construction of one is vitally interested in such information. The production function plays a strategic role in the decision making of any firm.

## TYPES OF INPUTS

As pointed out in the previous chapter, an input is anything that the firm uses in its production process. In analyzing production processes, we

[1] L. Cookenboo, "Production Functions and Cost Functions: A Case Study," in E. Mansfield (ed.), *Managerial Economics and Operations Research,* 5th ed., New York: Norton, 1987.

**Table 22.1**
**Relationship between Labor Input and Output on 1-Acre Wheat Farm**

| NUMBER OF UNITS OF LABOR | BUSHELS OF WHEAT PRODUCED PER YEAR |
|---|---|
| 0 | 0 |
| 1 | 30 |
| 2 | 70 |
| 3 | 100 |
| 4 | 125 |
| 5 | 145 |

**Table 22.2**
**Production Function, Crude-Oil Pipeline**

| LINE DIAMETER (INCHES) | HORSEPOWER (THOUSANDS) | | | | |
|---|---|---|---|---|---|
| | 20 | 30 | 40 | 50 | 60 |
| | *Output rate (thousands of barrels per day)* | | | | |
| 14 | 70 | 90 | 95 | 100 | 104 |
| 18 | 115 | 140 | 155 | 165 | 170 |
| 22 | 160 | 190 | 215 | 235 | 250 |
| 26 | 220 | 255 | 290 | 320 | 340 |

suppose that all inputs can be classified into two categories: fixed and variable.

*A **fixed input** is one whose quantity cannot change during the period of time under consideration.* This period will vary. It may be six months in one case, six years in another case. Among the most important inputs often included as fixed are the firm's plant and equipment—that is, its factory and office buildings, its machinery, its tooling, and its transportation facilities. In the simple example of the wheat farm in Table 22.1, land is a fixed input since its quantity is assumed to be fixed at 1 acre.

*A **variable input** is one whose quantity can be changed during the relevant period.* It is generally possible to increase or decrease the number of workers engaged in a particular activity (although this is not always the case, since they may have long-term contracts). Similarly, it frequently is possible to alter the amount of raw material that is used. In the case of the wheat farm in Table 22.1, labor clearly is a variable input since its quantity can be varied from 0 to 5 units.

## THE SHORT RUN AND THE LONG RUN

Whether an input is considered variable or fixed depends on the length of the period under consideration. The longer the period, the more inputs are variable, not fixed. Although the length of the period varies from case to case, economists have found it very useful to focus special attention on two time periods: the short run and the long run. *The **short run** is defined as the period of time in which at least one of the firm's inputs is fixed.* More specifically, since the firm's plant and equipment are among the most difficult inputs to change quickly, *the short run is generally understood to mean the length of time during which the firm's plant and equipment are fixed.* On the other hand, *the **long run** is that period of time in which all inputs are variable.* In the long run, the firm can make a complete adjustment to any change in its environment.

To illustrate the distinction between the short run and the long run, let's consider the General Motors Corporation. Any period of time during which GM's plant and equipment cannot be altered freely is the short run. A period of one year is certainly a case of the short run, because in a year GM could not vary the quantity of its plant and equipment. It takes longer than a year to construct an automotive plant, or to alter an existing plant to produce a new kind of automobile. For example, the tooling phase of the model changeover cycle has often taken about 2 years. Also, because some of its existing contracts with suppliers and workers extend for more than a year, GM cannot vary all its inputs in a year without violating these contracts. On the other hand, any period of time during which GM can vary the quantity of all inputs is the long run. A period of 50 years is certainly a case of the long run. Whether a shorter period of time—10 years, say—is a long-run situation depends on the problem at hand. If all the relevant inputs can be varied, it is a long-run situation; if not, it is a short-run situation.

A useful way to look at the long run is to consider it a *planning horizon.* While operating in the short run, the firm must continually be planning ahead and deciding its strategy in the long run. Its decisions concerning the long run determine the sort of short-run position the firm will occupy in the future. Before a firm makes the decision to add a new type of product to its line, the firm is in a long-run situation (with regard

General Motors headquarters

to the new product), since it can choose among a wide variety of types and sizes of equipment to produce the new product. But once the investment is made, the firm is confronted with a short-run situation, since the type and size of equipment is, to a considerable extent, frozen.

## AVERAGE PRODUCT OF AN INPUT

In order to determine which production technique—that is, which combination of inputs—a firm should use, it is necessary to define the average product and marginal product of an input. *The **average product** of an input is the firm's total output divided by the amount of input used to produce this amount of output.* The average product of an input can be calculated from the production function. Consider the wheat farm in Table 22.1. The average product of labor is 30 bushels per unit of labor when 1 unit of labor is used, 35 bushels per unit of labor when 2 units are used, 33⅓ bushels per unit of labor when 3 units are used, and so forth.

## MARGINAL PRODUCT OF AN INPUT

As the amount of labor used on the farm increases, so does the farm's output, but the amount of extra output from the addition of an extra unit of labor varies depending on how much labor is already being used. The extra output from the addition of the first unit of labor is $30 - 0 = 30$ bushels per unit of labor. The extra output due to the addition of the second unit of labor is $70 - 30 = 40$ bushels per unit of labor. And the extra output from the addition of the fifth unit of labor is $145 - 125 = 20$ bushels per unit of labor. *The **marginal product** of an input is the addition to total output due to the addition of the last unit of input, the quantity of other inputs used being held constant.* Thus the marginal product of labor is 30 bushels when between 0 and 1 units of labor are used, 40 bushels when between 1 and 2 units of labor are used, and so on.

The concept of marginal product is analogous to that of marginal utility, which we discussed in Chapter 20. Recall that marginal utility is the extra utility resulting from an additional unit of a commodity. Substitute "output" for "utility" and "an input" for "a commodity" in the previous sentence, and you get a perfectly valid definition of marginal product. Economics is chock full of marginal "thises" and marginal "thats," and it is important that you become aware of their general family traits.

Table 22.3 shows the average and marginal products of labor at various levels of utilization of labor; Figure 22.1 shows the same thing graphically. The data in both Table 22.3 and Figure 22.1 concerning the average and marginal products of labor are derived from the production function. Given the production function, shown in Table 22.1 and reproduced in Table 22.3, the average and marginal products at each level of utilization of labor can be determined in the way we have indicated.

In Figure 22.1, as in the case of most production processes, the average product of the variable input—labor in this case—rises, reaches a maximum, and then falls. The marginal product of labor also rises, reaches a maximum, and falls. This too is typical of many production processes. Why do average product and marginal product behave in this way? Because of the law of diminishing marginal returns, to which we now turn.

**Table 22.3**
**Average and Marginal Products of Labor, 1-Acre Wheat Farm**

| NUMBER OF UNITS OF LABOR | TOTAL OUTPUT (BUSHELS PER YEAR) | MARGINAL PRODUCT (BUSHELS PER UNIT OF LABOR) | AVERAGE PRODUCT (BUSHELS PER UNIT OF LABOR) |
|---|---|---|---|
| 0 | 0 | | — |
| | | 30 | |
| 1 | 30 | | 30 |
| | | 40 | |
| 2 | 70 | | 35 |
| | | 30 | |
| 3 | 100 | | 33⅓ |
| | | 25 | |
| 4 | 125 | | 31¼ |
| | | 20 | |
| 5 | 145 | | 29 |

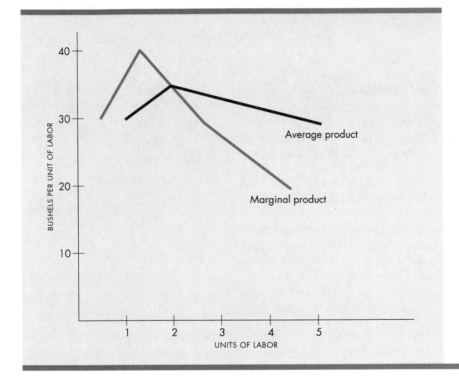

**Figure 22.1**
**Average and Marginal Products of Labor, 1-Acre Wheat Farm**
The marginal product of the first unit of labor (which, according to Table 22.3, equals 30 bushels per unit of labor) is plotted at the midpoint between 0 and 1 units of labor. The marginal product of the second unit of labor is plotted at the midpoint between 1 and 2 units of labor. The marginal product curve connects these and other points showing the marginal product of various amounts of labor.

The average product curve shows the average product of labor when various amounts of labor are used. As the graph shows, both the average product and the marginal product of labor rise, reach a maximum, and then fall.

# THE LAW OF DIMINISHING MARGINAL RETURNS

Perhaps the best-known—and certainly one of the least understood—laws of economics is the so-called *law of diminishing marginal returns.* Put in a single sentence, this law states that *if equal increments of an input are added, the quantities of other inputs being held constant, the resulting increments of product will decrease beyond some point;* that is, the marginal product of the input will diminish.

Suppose that a small factory that manufactures a metal automobile component has eight machine tools. If this firm hires only one or two workers, total output and output per worker will be quite low. These workers will have a number of quite different tasks to perform, and the advantages of specialization will be sacrificed. Workers will spend considerable time switching from one machine to another, and many of the eight machine tools will be idle much of the time. What happens as the firm increases its work force? As more and more workers are added, the marginal product (that is, the extra product) of each will tend to rise, as the work force grows to the point where it can man the fixed amount of equipment effectively. However, if the firm continues to increase the number of workers, the marginal product of a worker will eventually begin to decrease. Why? Because workers will have to wait in line to use the fixed number of machine tools, and because the extra workers will have to be assigned to less and less important tasks: Eventually, if enough workers are hired (and utilized within the plant), they may get in each other's way to such an extent that production may grind to a halt.

Returning to the wheat farm discussed in the previous section, Table 22.3 shows that the law of diminishing marginal returns applies in this case too. The third column of this table indicates that, beyond 2 units of labor, the marginal product of labor falls. Certainly, it seems entirely reasonable that, as more and more of a variable input (in this case, labor) is combined with a fixed amount of another input (in this case, land), the additional output to be derived from an additional unit of the variable input will eventually decrease. In the case of a 1-acre wheat farm, one would expect that, as more and more labor is added, the extra workers' functions eventually would become less and less important and productive.

The law of diminishing marginal returns plays a major part in determining the firm's optimal input combination and the shape of the firm's cost functions, as we shall see in this and the next chapter. To prevent misunderstanding and confusion, several points about this law should be stressed. First, *it is assumed that technology remains fixed.* If technology changes, the law of diminishing marginal returns cannot predict the effect of an additional unit of input. Second, *at least one input must be fixed in*

---

# EXAMPLE 22.1    PRODUCTION THEORY IN THE MILKING SHED

According to the U.S. Department of Agriculture, the relationship between a cow's total output of milk and the amount of grain it is fed is as follows:

| AMOUNT OF GRAIN (POUNDS) | AMOUNT OF MILK (POUNDS) |
| --- | --- |
| 1,200 | 5,917 |
| 1,800 | 7,250 |
| 2,400 | 8,379 |
| 3,000 | 9,371 |

Forage input is assumed to be fixed at 6,500 pounds of hay.

(a) What is the average product of grain when each amount is used? (b) Should a milk producer feed a cow the amount of grain that will maximize its average product? Why, or why not? (c) What is the marginal product of grain when between 1,200 and 1,800 pounds are fed; when between 1,800 and 2,400 pounds are fed; and when between 2,400 and 3,000 pounds are fed? (d) Does this production function exhibit diminishing marginal returns?

**Solution**

(a) At 1,200 pounds, it is 4.93; at 1,800 pounds, it is 4.03; at 2,400 pounds, it is 3.49; and at 3,000 pounds, it is 3.12 pounds of milk per pound of grain. (b) No, because this generally will not maximize profit, as we shall see in subsequent discussions. (c) 2.22, 1.88, and 1.65 pounds of milk per pound of grain. (d) Yes. The marginal product of grain decreases as more of it is used.

*quantity,* since the law of diminishing marginal returns is not applicable to cases where there is a proportional increase in all inputs. Third, *it must be possible to vary the proportions in which the various inputs are utilized.* This is generally possible in industry and agriculture.

## TEST YOURSELF

1. Suppose that a firm has the following production function:

| HOURS OF LABOR PER YEAR (THOUSANDS) | OUTPUT PER YEAR (THOUSANDS) |
|---|---|
| 0 | 0 |
| 1 | 2 |
| 2 | 8 |
| 3 | 12 |
| 4 | 14 |
| 5 | 15 |

Plot on a graph the marginal product of labor at various levels of utilization of labor.

2. Using the data in Question 1, plot the average product of labor at various levels of utilization of labor.

3. A tool and die shop has three types of inputs: labor, machines, and materials. It cannot obtain additional machines in less than 6 months. In the next month, do you think that labor is a fixed or variable input? Do you think that machines are a fixed or variable input? Explain.

4. The tool and die shop in Question 3 expands its use of all three types of inputs. The owner of the shop worries that by doing so the firm may encounter diminishing marginal returns. Is this a legitimate concern? Why, or why not?

## THE OPTIMAL INPUT DECISION

Now we are in a position to answer the question posed at the beginning of this chapter: Given that a firm is going to produce a particular quantity of output, what production technique—i.e., what combination of inputs—should it choose to maximize profits? Note first that if the firm maximizes its profits, it must minimize the cost of producing this quantity of output. This seems obvious enough. But what combination of inputs (that will produce the required quantity of output) will minimize the firm's costs?

A firm will minimize cost by combining inputs in such a way that the marginal product of a dollar's worth of any one input equals the marginal product of a dollar's worth of any other input used. Another way to say the same thing is: *The firm will minimize cost by combining inputs in such a way that, for every input used, the marginal product of the input is proportional to its price.* Why does this say the same thing? Because the marginal product of a dollar's worth of an input equals the marginal product of the input divided by its price. If the marginal product of a unit of labor is 40 units of output, and if the price of labor is $8,000 per unit, the marginal product of a dollar's worth of labor is 40 ÷ 8,000 = .005 units of output. Thus, if the firm is combining inputs so that the marginal product of a dollar's worth of any one input equals the marginal product of a dollar's worth of any other input used, it must at the same time be combining inputs so that, for every input used, the marginal product of the input is proportional to its price.

Consider the wheat farm cited above. Suppose that the farm can vary the amount of labor it uses. Table 22.4 shows the marginal product of each input when various combinations of inputs (all combinations being

### Table 22.4
**Determination of Optimal Input Combination**

| AMOUNT OF INPUT USED LABOR (UNITS) | LAND (ACRES) | MARGINAL PRODUCT LABOR | LAND | MARGINAL PRODUCT ÷ PRICE OF INPUT LABOR | LAND | TOTAL COSTS (DOLLARS) |
|---|---|---|---|---|---|---|
| 0.5 | 7.0 | 50 | 5 | 50 ÷ 8,000  *0.006* | 5 ÷ 2,000 | 18,000 |
| 1.0 | 4.1 | 40 | 10 | 40 ÷ 8,000  *0.005* | 10 ÷ 2,000 | 16,200 |
| 1.5 | 3.0 | 30 | 30 | 30 ÷ 8,000  *0.00?* | 30 ÷ 2,000 | 18,000 |
| 2.5 | 2.0 | 20 | 50 | 20 ÷ 8,000  *0.003* | 50 ÷ 2,000 | 24,000 |

able to produce the specified quantity of output) are used. Suppose that the price of labor is $8,000 per unit and that the annual price of using land is $2,000 per acre. (We assume that the firm takes the prices of inputs as given and that it can buy all it wants of the inputs at these prices.) For each combination of inputs, Table 22.4 shows the marginal product of each input divided by its price. Based on our rule, the optimal input combination is 4.1 acres of land and 1 unit of labor, since this is the only combination (capable of producing the required output) where the marginal product of labor divided by the price of labor equals the marginal product of land divided by the price of land. (See Table 22.4.)

Is this rule correct? Does it really result in a least-cost combination of inputs? Let's look at the cost of the various input combinations in Table 22.4. The first combination (0.5 units of labor and 7 acres of land) costs $18,000; the second combination (1.0 units of labor and 4.1 acres of land) costs $16,200; and so on. An examination of the total cost of each input combination shows that the input combination chosen by our rule—1.0 units of labor and 4.1 acres of land—is indeed the least-cost input combination, the one for the profit-maximizing firm to use.

## A MORE GENERAL PROOF OF THE RULE

One example really does not prove that the rule results in minimum costs; it only demonstrates that it does so in this particular case. In this section, we prove that this rule generally is valid. To do so, we show that, if this rule is violated (and the firm combines inputs so that the marginal product of a dollar's worth of one input does *not* equal the marginal product of a dollar's worth of some other input used), the firm is not minimizing its costs. Specifically, we take the case of the wheat farm, and proceed in two steps. (1) We show that if the marginal product of a dollar's worth of labor is *greater* than the marginal product of a dollar's worth of land, the firm is not minimizing costs. (2) We show that if the marginal product of a dollar's worth of labor is *less* than the marginal product of a dollar's worth of land, the firm is not minimizing costs.

Suppose that *the marginal product of a dollar's worth of labor is greater than the marginal product of a dollar's worth of land.* Since the marginal product of a dollar's worth of labor is greater than the marginal product of a dollar's worth of land, it must follow that the wheat farm can increase its output, *without increasing its costs,* if it substitutes a dollar's worth of labor for a dollar's worth of land. Suppose that the marginal product of a dollar's worth of labor is 2 bushels of wheat, whereas the marginal product of a dollar's worth of land is 1 bushel of wheat. Then, if it substitutes a

$$\frac{MP \text{ or Labor}}{P \text{ or Labor}} = \frac{MP \text{ Land}}{P \text{ Land}}$$

# HOW TO MAKE MONEY IN REAL ESTATE BY LOGIC ALONE

One of the most common errors made by decision makers is that they do not ignore sunk costs. What is a sunk cost? It is a cost that has been incurred in the past and that cannot be altered or affected by any action the decision maker can take. For example, suppose that a real estate investor signs an agreement to buy a lot. The purchase price is $20,000. He makes a $5,000 down payment and will pay the remaining $15,000 in six months. Under the terms of the agreement, he will not secure title to the lot until he has paid the entire $20,000. If he fails to make the remaining payment of $15,000, the agreement states that he will lose his down payment, but he is not liable for the unpaid balance.

After buying this lot, and making the $5,000 down payment, the real estate investor travels to another city where he finds a lot which is just as desirable from his point of view as the one he has bought. Because the real estate market in this city is depressed, the price of this lot is $14,000. The real estate investor wishes that he had seen this lot before purchasing the other one, but feels that there is nothing he can do. He only wants one such lot and, if he were to back out of the purchase agreement he signed, he would lose $5,000. Clearly, he doesn't want to incur such a loss!

But the real estate investor is committing a cardinal sin: he is not ignoring a sunk cost. Regardless of

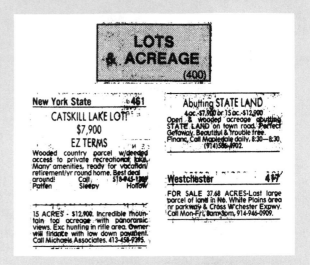

which lot he purchases, he loses the $5,000. Thus the $5,000 is a sunk cost. The real question is whether he will pay an *additional* $15,000 for the lot on which he has paid the down payment or whether he will pay an *additional* $14,000 for the lot he has seen more recently. Put in this way, there is no doubt about the proper course of action: he should ignore the $5,000 sunk cost, and buy the lot for $14,000. In this way, the total cost (including the sunk cost) is $19,000, which is less than the price of the lot he originally intended to purchase.

---

dollar's worth of labor for a dollar's worth of land, the wheat farm can increase its output by 1 bushel of wheat without increasing its costs. (Why? Because the addition of an extra dollar's worth of labor increases output by 2 bushels, while the subtraction of the dollar's worth of land reduces output by 1 bushel—and the net effect is an increase in output of 1 bushel.) Thus, since the firm can increase its output without increasing its costs, it must be able to reduce its costs, if it maintains the same output. In other words, it must not be minimizing its costs.

Suppose that *the marginal product of a dollar's worth of labor is less than the marginal product of a dollar's worth of land.* Since the marginal product of a dollar's worth of labor is less than the marginal product of a dollar's worth of land, it must follow that the wheat farm can increase its output, *without increasing its costs,* if it substitutes a dollar's worth of land for a dollar's worth of labor. Suppose that the marginal product of a dollar's worth of labor is 1 bushel of wheat, whereas the marginal product of a dollar's worth of land is 2 bushels of wheat. Then, if it substitutes a dollar's worth of land for a dollar's worth of labor, the wheat farm can increase its output by 1 bushel of wheat without increasing its costs. (Why? Because the addition of an extra dollar's worth of land increases output by 2 bushels, while the subtraction of a dollar's worth of labor reduces output by 1 bushel—and the net effect is an increase in output of 1 bushel.) Thus, since the firm can increase its output without increasing its costs, it must be able to reduce its costs, if it maintains the same output. In other words, it must not be minimizing its costs.

Since the firm is not minimizing the cost of producing its current output when the marginal product of a dollar's worth of labor is greater than, or less than, that of a dollar's worth of land, it must be true that *the firm is minimizing its cost only when the marginal product of a dollar's worth of labor equals that of a dollar's worth of land*. This is what we set out to prove.

## PRODUCING KANSAS CORN: A CASE STUDY

If by now you wonder about the practical payoff from this sort of analysis, consider how a distinguished agricultural economist, Earl Heady of Iowa State University, used these methods to help farmers make better production decisions. Table 22.5 shows the various amounts of land and fertilizer that will produce 82.6 bushels of corn on Kansas Verdigras soil. As you can see, this amount of corn can be produced if 1.19 acres of land and no fertilizer are used, or if 1.11 acres of land and 20 pounds of fertilizer are used, or if .99 acres of land and 60 pounds of fertilizer are used, and so forth.

The third column of Table 22.5 shows the ratio of the marginal product of a pound of fertilizer to the marginal product of an acre of land, when each of these input combinations is used. For example, when 1.19 acres of land and no fertilizer are used, this ratio equals .0045. Based on the rule discussed in previous sections, a firm, if it minimizes costs, must set this ratio equal to the ratio of the price of a pound of fertilizer to the price of an acre of land. Why? Because the rule discussed above stipulates that the firm should choose an input combination so that

$$\frac{\text{marginal product of fertilizer}}{\text{price of fertilizer}} = \frac{\text{marginal product of land}}{\text{price of land}}.$$

So if we multiply both sides of this equation by the price of fertilizer, and divide both sides by the marginal product of land, we get

$$\frac{\text{marginal product of fertilizer}}{\text{marginal product of land}} = \frac{\text{price of fertilizer}}{\text{price of land}}.$$

Thus, to minimize costs, a firm should set the ratio in the third column of Table 22.5 equal to the ratio of the price of fertilizer to the price of land.

Heady and his coworkers, having obtained the results in Table 22.5, used this technique to determine the optimal input combination farmers should use to minimize their costs.[2] The optimal input combination de-

---

[2] It is assumed that a certain amount of labor is used, this amount being proportional to the number of acres of land.

**Table 22.5
Combinations of Fertilizer and Land Required to Produce 82.6 Bushels of Corn, and Ratio of Marginal Products at Each Such Combination**

| AMOUNT OF INPUT USED | | MARGINAL PRODUCT OF FERTILIZER ÷ MARGINAL PRODUCT OF LAND |
|---|---|---|
| FERTILIZER (POUNDS) | LAND (ACRES) | |
| 0 | 1.19 | .0045 |
| 20 | 1.11 | .0038 |
| 40 | 1.04 | .0030 |
| 60 | 0.99 | .0019 |
| 80 | 0.96 | .0010 |
| 100 | 0.95 | .0003 |

In 1985 the Coca-Cola company made a well-publicized change in its formula for Coke. The company touted the change with a huge marketing campaign. In fact, the formula for Coke had been quietly changed six years earlier.

Because of worldwide shortages, the price of beet and cane sugar jumped from 19 cents per pound in September 1978 to 26 cents per pound in January 1979. While such a price hike does not dramatically affect most sugar buyers, for Coke it was catastrophic. A change of 1 cent per pound in sugar prices can cause a $20 million swing in Coke's operating profits. The bottling empire is America's largest sugar buyer, taking a million tons per year or about 10 percent of all the sugar sold in the United States.

Because of the efficiencies of corn production in this country, a sweetener made by refining corn into sugar makes high-fructose corn sweeteners about 10 percent cheaper than beet and cane sugar when prices are normal. By using a 55 percent fructose sweetener, Coca-Cola can realize substantial cost savings, particularly when sugar prices are abnormally high. Coke publicly announced the switch to corn sweeteners in January 1979, but other than sugar producers and traders, no one seemed to notice. Eight months later, 7-Up followed suit and decided to increase its use of corn sweeteners, and Pepsi also considered such a move.

The response of the soft drink companies to the high price of sugar is typical of any firm faced with a high-priced input. Firms try to reduce the use of expensive inputs in order to maintain profits or to avoid having to raise the price of their products (and risk losing sales to competitors). The higher the price of an input, the more incentive there is for a profit-maximizing firm to conserve on its use of that input.

N.B.

pends on the price of land and the price of fertilizer. Suppose that a pound of fertilizer costs .003 times as much as an acre of land. Under these circumstances, the minimum-cost input combination would be 40 pounds of fertilizer and 1.04 acres of land—since, as shown in Table 22.5, this is the input combination where the ratio of the marginal product of fertilizer to the marginal product of land is .003. No matter what the ratio of the price of fertilizer to the price of land may be, the least-cost input combination can be derived this way.

Such results are of considerable practical value to farmers. Moreover, the same kind of analysis can be used by organizations in other sectors of the economy. not just agriculture. Studies of how the Defense Department could reduce its costs have utilized concepts and techniques of essentially this sort. In a more peaceful vein, this same kind of analysis has been used in various kinds of manufacturing firms. For example, steel firms have made many such studies to determine least-cost ways to produce steel, and auto firms have made similar studies to reduce their own costs.

## TEST YOURSELF

1. Suppose that a cost-minimizing firm in a perfectly competitive market uses two inputs: labor and capital. If the marginal product of capital is twice the marginal product of labor, and if the price of a unit of labor is $4, what must be the price of a unit of capital?

2. In Figure 22.1 the marginal product of labor equals its average product when the latter is a maximum. Do you think that this is generally the case? Why, or why not? (*Hint:* if the marginal product of an extra amount of labor exceeds the average product, will the average product increase? If it is less than the average product, will the average product decrease?)

3. A firm uses two inputs: capital and labor. The firm's chief engineer says that its output depends in the following way on the amount of labor and capital it uses:

$$Q = 3L + 4C,$$

where $Q$ is the number of units of output produced per day, $L$ is the number of units of labor used per day, and $C$ is the amount of capital used per day. Does this relationship seem sensible? Why, or why not?

4. In the previous problem, suppose that the price of using a unit of labor per day is $50 and the price of using a unit of capital per day is $100. What is the optimal input combination for the firm, if the relationship in the previous problem is valid? Does this seem reasonable? Why, or why not?

## SUMMARY

1. Inputs can be classified into two categories: fixed and variable. A fixed input is one whose quantity cannot be changed during the period of time under consideration. A variable input is one whose quantity can be changed during the relevant period.

2. Whether an input is considered variable or fixed depends on the length of the period under consideration. The longer the period, the more inputs are variable, not fixed. The short run is defined as the period of time in which some of the firm's inputs (generally its plant and equipment) are fixed. The long run is the period of time in which all inputs are variable.

3. The average product of an input is the firm's total output divided by the amount of input used to produce this amount of output. The marginal product of an input is the addition to total output due to the addition of the last unit of input, the quantity of other inputs used being held constant.

4. The law of diminishing marginal returns states that if equal increments of an input are added (and the quantities of other inputs are held constant), the resulting increments of product will decrease beyond some point; that is, the marginal product of the input will diminish.

5. To minimize its costs, a firm must choose its input combination so that the marginal product of a dollar's worth of any one input equals the marginal product of a dollar's worth of any other input used. Put differently, the firm should combine inputs so that, for every input used, the marginal product of the input is proportional to its price.

## CONCEPTS FOR REVIEW

| | | |
|---|---|---|
| **Production function** | **Short run** | **Marginal product** |
| **Fixed input** | **Long run** | **Law of diminishing marginal** |
| **Variable input** | **Average product** | **returns** |
| * **Isoquant** | ***Isocost curve** | |

* This concept is presented in the Appendix to this chapter.

# APPENDIX: ISOQUANTS, ISOCOST CURVES, AND THE OPTIMAL INPUT COMBINATION

In this Appendix, we present a somewhat different way of finding a firm's optimal input combination. This approach is based on the use of isoquants and isocost curves.

## Isoquants

In the case of a crude-oil pipeline, a given amount of oil can be carried per day either by using a large diameter of pipe and relatively small horsepower or by using a smaller diameter of pipe and greater horsepower. Similar opportunities to vary inputs to achieve a given output rate exist in practically all industries. To describe these opportunities, economists use the concept of an isoquant. An **isoquant** *is a curve showing all possible efficient combinations of inputs capable of producing a certain quantity of output*. An *inefficient* combination of inputs is one that includes more of at least one input, and as much as other inputs, as some other combination of inputs that can produce the same quantity of output. Inefficient combinations cannot minimize costs or maximize profits. On a wheat farm, it may be possible to produce 1 unit of output with 2 units of land and 3 units of labor. It may also be possible to produce 1 unit of output with 3 units of land and 3 units of labor. The second input combination—which is inefficient—cannot be the least-cost input combination, so long as land has a *positive* price. Only *efficient* input combinations are worth bothering with in the present circumstances, and they alone are included in an isoquant.

There is an isoquant pertaining to each level of production. Figure 22.2 shows some isoquants for a wheat farm. These isoquants show the various combinations of inputs that can produce 100, 200, and 300 bushels of wheat per period of time. Consider the isoquant for 100 bushels of wheat per period of time. According to this isoquant, the farm can attain this output rate if $OL_1$ units of labor and $OD_1$ units of land are used per period of time. Alternatively, this output rate can be attained with $OL_2$ units of labor and $OD_2$ units of land—or $OL_3$ units of labor and $OD_3$ units of land—per period of time.

The shape and position of a firm's isoquants are derived from the firm's production function. Indeed, one way to represent the firm's production function is by showing its isoquants. Thus the firm's isoquants, like its production function, show the firm's technological possibilities—the various efficient input-output combinations that can be achieved with existing technology. The shape of an isoquant is typically like that shown in Figure 22.2; that is, it slopes downward to the right, but *its slope becomes less and less steep*.

To illustrate what isoquants in an actual firm look like, consider once again our crude-oil pipeline. Figure 22.3 shows the isoquants corresponding to 100,000, 200,000, and 300,000 barrels of crude oil carried per day. For example, the isoquant corresponding to 100,000 barrels per day shows all the combinations of line diameter and horsepower that permit a pipeline to carry 100,000 barrels per day (for 1,000 miles). Note that each of these isoquants slopes downward to the right. Moreover, comparing these isoquants with Table 22.2, you can readily see that, if Table 22.2 contained more detailed data on the production function, it would be simple to derive the isoquants from the data regarding the production func-

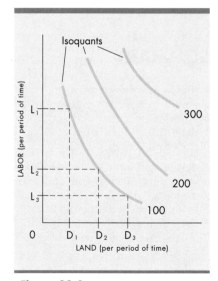

**Figure 22.2**
**Isoquants, Wheat Farm**
An isoquant shows all possible efficient combinations of inputs capable of producing a certain quantity of output. These isoquants show the various combinations of inputs that can produce 100, 200, and 300 bushels of wheat per period of time. For example, 100 bushels of wheat can be produced with $OL_1$ units of labor and $OD_1$ units of land, with $OL_2$ units of labor and $OD_2$ units of land, or with $OL_3$ units of labor and $OD_3$ units of land.

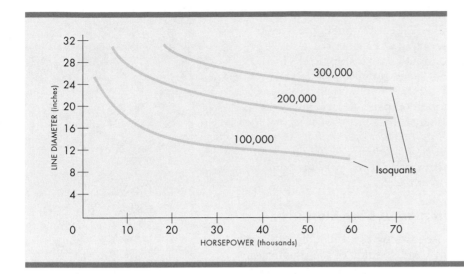

**Figure 22.3**
**Isoquants for 100,000, 200,000
and 300,000 Barrels of Crude
Oil Carried per Day, Crude-Oil
Pipeline**
This graph shows the isoquants in
an actual case. Note that they are
shaped as economic theory would
predict.

tion in Table 22.2. How? By determining from this more detailed version of Table 22.2 the various input combinations that can produce each output rate. For example, to derive the isoquant corresponding to 100,000 barrels of crude oil carried per day, one could determine from such a table the various input combinations that can produce this output rate.

## Isocost Curves and the Optimal Input Decision

To determine the combination of inputs that will minimize the firm's costs, one can use the isoquant concept. All input combinations that can efficiently produce the specified level of output can be represented by the isoquant corresponding to this level of output. For example, the isoquant in Figure 22.4 shows all the input combinations a wheat farm can use to produce a certain amount of wheat. The optimal input combination must lie on this isoquant, but where? A simple way to determine the optimal input combination is to draw a number of **isocost curves,** as shown in Figure 22.4. *Each isocost curve shows the input combinations the firm can obtain for a given expenditure.* Consider the isocost curves corresponding to expenditures of $12,000, $16,200, and $20,000, shown in Figure 22.4.

In Figure 22.4 the price of labor is $8,000 per unit, and the annual price of using land is $2,000 per acre. Given the price of each input, it is a simple matter to draw each isocost curve. Take the case of the isocost curve corresponding to annual expenditures of $12,000. If this expenditure were devoted entirely to labor, 1 ½ units of labor could be hired. Thus this isocost curve must cut the horizontal axis in Figure 22.4 at 1 ½ units of labor. Similarly, if this expenditure were devoted entirely to land, 6 acres of land could be hired. Thus this isocost curve must cut the vertical axis at 6 acres of land. Finally, if we connect the point where the isocost curve cuts the vertical axis to the point where it cuts the horizontal axis, we obtain the entire isocost curve.

Given both the isoquant and the isocost curves, one can readily determine the input combination that will minimize the firm's costs. This input combination corresponds to *that point on the isoquant that lies on the lowest isocost curve*—in other words, point *A* in Figure 22.4. Input combinations on lower isocost curves (like that corresponding to $12,000) that lie

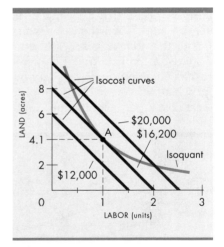

**Figure 22.4**
**Least-Cost Input Combination**
The least-cost input combination is at point *A*, where 4.1 acres of land and 1 unit of labor are used. The isoquant shows all input combinations that can be used to produce the required amount of wheat, and the isocost curves show the input combinations costing $12,000, $16,200, and $20,000, respectively.

below *A* are cheaper than *A*, but cannot produce the desired output. Input combinations on isocost curves (like that corresponding to $20,000) that lie above *A* will produce the desired output at a higher cost than *A*.

What is the relationship between the input combination determined in this way and the input combination determined by means of the rule described on page 468? Reassuringly enough, these input combinations will always be the same, since the rule described on page 468 will always give the same answer as the geometric technique. In general, *if you find the combination of inputs where the marginal product of a dollar's worth of any one input equals the marginal product of a dollar's worth of any other input used, this will give you the same answer as if you find the point on the isoquant that lies on the lowest isocost curve.*

## Finding the Optimal Input Combination: A Case Study

To illustrate the use of isoquants and isocost curves to identify optimal input combinations, let's go back to Earl Heady's study of the production of corn, discussed on page 471. Figure 22.5 shows an isoquant that Heady and his coworkers estimated from the production of corn on Kansas Verdigras soil. This isoquant shows the amounts of land and fertilizer that will produce 82.6 bushels of corn. It indicates that this amount of corn can be produced if 1.19 acres of land and no fertilizer are used, or if 1.11 acres of land and 20 pounds of fertilizer are used, or if .99 acres of land and 60 pounds of fertilizer are used, and so forth. (The same data are shown in Table 22.5.)

After estimating isoquants of this sort, Heady and his coworkers derived the optimal input combination farmers should use to minimize their costs. Suppose that a pound of fertilizer costs .003 times as much as an acre of land. Then the isocost curves would be as shown in Figure 22.5. Under these circumstances, the minimum-cost combination would be 40 pounds of fertilizer and 1.04 acres of land. (This finding agrees with the results obtained on page 472, where we took up this same case.) No matter what the ratio of the price of fertilizer to the price of land may be, the least-cost input combination can be derived this way.

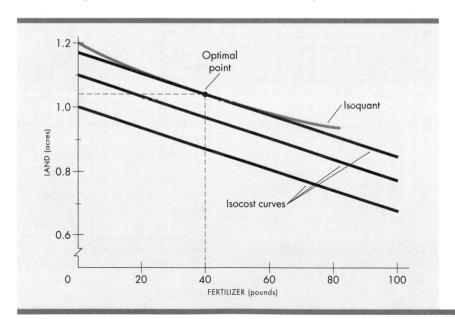

**Figure 22.5**
**Isoquant for the Production of 82.6 Bushels of Corn in Kansas**
This graph shows how economic analysis has been used to help farmers make better production decisions. Given the assumed conditions, the optimal input combination would be 40 pounds of fertilizer and 1.04 acres of land.

# COST ANALYSIS

WELL OVER 10 MILLION people subscribe to cable television. An important question facing both government officials and the cable operators themselves is whether it is efficient for more than one firm to provide cable television in a particular city. Does the cost per subscriber of providing cable television go down markedly as a firm gains more and more subscribers? If so, it is less costly for a single firm to provide cable television than to have two or more firms share the market. But since this single firm would have substantial power over the price it charges subscribers, some have argued that, if costs go down markedly, this single firm should be regulated in various ways by government agencies.

This example illustrates the major role played by a firm's costs in many issues facing the government and the public at large—as well, of course, as the firms themselves. In this chapter, we discuss the nature of costs, describe the various cost functions of the firm, and indicate some of the ways that these cost functions can be measured and used. Among the major questions taken up are: What do we mean by a firm's costs? How do various types of costs vary with the firm's output rate? Of what significance or use are the relationships between a firm's output and its various types of cost? These questions are of the utmost importance, both for the managers of a firm and for society as a whole.

## WHAT ARE COSTS?

The previous chapter discussed how we can determine the input combination that minimizes costs. But what do we mean by costs?

Although this question may seem foolishly simple, it is in fact tricky. *Fundamentally, the cost of a certain course of action is the value of the best alternative course of action that could have been adopted instead.* The cost of producing automobiles is the value of the goods and services that could be obtained from the resources used currently in automobile production if these resources were no longer used to produce automobiles. In general, the costs of inputs to a firm are their values in their most valuable alternative uses. As we pointed out in Chapter 1, this is the so-called **opportunity cost,** or **alternative cost** doctrine.

Suppose that a firm's owner devotes 50 hours a week to the firm's business, and that, because he is the owner, he pays himself no salary.

According to the usual rules of accounting, as we saw in Chapter 21, the costs of his labor are not included in the firm's income statement. But according to the economist's opportunity cost doctrine, the cost of his labor is by no means zero! Instead, this cost equals whatever amount he could obtain if he worked 50 hours a week for someone else. Both economists and sophisticated accountants agree that opportunity costs are the relevant costs for many types of problems, and that failure to use the proper concept of cost can result in serious mistakes.

Costs for the individual firm are the necessary payments to the owners of resources to get them to provide these resources to the firm. To obtain these resources as inputs, the firm must bid them away from alternative uses. The payments made to the owners of these resources may be either explicit or implicit costs. If a payment is made to a supplier, laborer, or some other resource owner besides the firm's owner, this is an explicit cost, which is paid for in an explicit way. But if a resource is owned by the firm's owner, there may be no explicit payment for it, as in the case of the labor of the owner who paid himself no salary. *The costs of such owner-supplied resources are called **implicit costs.*** As we stressed above, such implicit costs equal what these resources could bring if they were used in their most valuable alternative employments. And the firm's profits (or losses), as defined by the economist, are the difference between the firm's revenues and its total costs, both explicit and implicit.

## SHORT-RUN COST FUNCTIONS

In the previous chapter, we showed how to determine the least-cost combination of inputs to produce any quantity of output. With this information at our disposal, it is easy to determine the minimum cost of producing each quantity of output. *Knowing the (minimum) cost of producing each quantity of output, we can define and measure the firm's **cost functions,** which show how various types of costs are related to the firm's output.* A firm's cost functions will vary, depending on whether they are based on the short or long run. In the short run, the firm cannot vary the quantities of plant and equipment it uses. These are the firm's fixed inputs, and they determine the scale of its operations.

### Total Fixed Cost

Three kinds of costs are important in the short run—total fixed cost, total variable cost, and total cost. ***Total fixed cost*** *is the total expenditure per period of time by the firm for fixed inputs.* Since the quantity of the fixed inputs is unvarying (by definition), the total fixed cost will be the same whatever the firm's level of output. Among the firm's fixed costs in the short run are property taxes and interest on bonds issued in the past. If the firm has contracts with suppliers and workers that cannot be renegotiated (without dire consequences) in the short run, the expenses involved in meeting these contracts are also fixed costs.

To inject a whimsical note into a subject not otherwise noted for its amusement value, consider a hypothetical firm—the Bugsbane Music Box Company. This firm produces a high-priced line of music boxes that, when opened, play your favorite aria, show tune, or hymn, and emit a deadly gas that kills all insects, rodents, or pests—and, alas, occasionally

## Table 23.1
### Fixed, Variable, and Total Costs, Bugsbane Music Box Company

| NUMBER OF MUSIC BOXES PRODUCED PER DAY | TOTAL FIXED COST | TOTAL VARIABLE COST (DOLLARS) | TOTAL COST |
|---|---|---|---|
| 0 | 300 | 0 | 300 |
| 1 | 300 | 60 | 360 |
| 2 | 300 | 110 | 410 |
| 3 | 300 | 160 | 460 |
| 4 | 300 | 200 | 500 |
| 5 | 300 | 260 | 560 |
| 6 | 300 | 360 | 660 |
| 7 | 300 | 510 | 810 |
| 8 | 300 | 710 | 1,010 |
| 9 | 300 | 1,060 | 1,360 |

a frail Chihuahua—within a 50-foot radius. Table 23.1 shows that Bugsbane's fixed costs are $300 per day; the firm's total fixed cost function is shown in Figure 23.1.

## Total Variable Cost

***Total variable cost*** *is the firm's total expenditure on variable inputs per period of time.* Since higher output rates require greater utilization of variable inputs, they mean a higher total variable cost. Thus, if Bugsbane increases its daily production of music boxes, it must increase the amount it spends per day on metal (for the components), wood (for the outside of the boxes), labor (for the assembly of the boxes), and other variable inputs. Table 23.1 shows Bugsbane's total variable costs at various output rates; Figure 23.2 shows the firm's total variable cost function.

Up to the output rate of 4 music boxes per day, total variable cost increases at a decreasing rate; beyond that output rate, total variable cost increases at an increasing rate. It is important to understand that this characteristic of the total variable cost function results from the operation of the law of diminishing marginal returns. At small output rates, increases in the utilization of variable inputs may bring about increases in their productivity, causing total variable cost to increase with output, but at a decreasing rate. Beyond a point, however, there are diminishing marginal returns from the variable input, with the result that total variable costs increase at an increasing rate.

## Total Cost

***Total cost*** *is the sum of total fixed cost and total variable cost.* Thus, to obtain the Bugsbane Company's total cost at a given output, we need only add its total fixed cost and its total variable cost at that output. The result is shown in Table 23.1, and the corresponding total cost function is shown in Figure 23.3. Since the total cost function and the total variable cost function differ by only a constant amount (equal to total fixed cost), they have the same shape, as shown in Figure 23.4, which brings together all three of the total cost functions (or cost curves as they are often called).

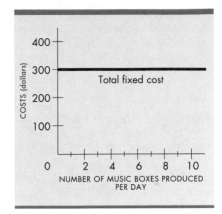

**Figure 23.1**
**Total Fixed Cost, Bugsbane Music Box Company**
The total fixed cost function is always a horizontal line, since fixed costs do not vary with output.

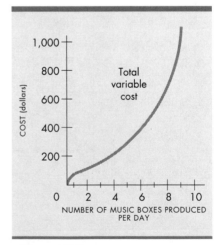

**Figure 23.2**
**Total Variable Cost, Bugsbane Music Box Company**
Total variable cost is the total expenditure per period of time on variable inputs. Due to the law of diminishing marginal returns, total variable cost increases first at a decreasing rate, then at an increasing rate.

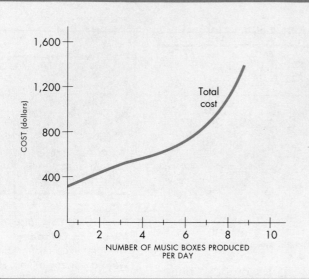

**Figure 23.3**
**Total Cost, Bugsbane Music Box Company**
Total cost is the sum of total fixed cost and total variable cost. It has the same shape as the total variable cost curve, since they differ by only a constant amount (equal to total fixed cost).

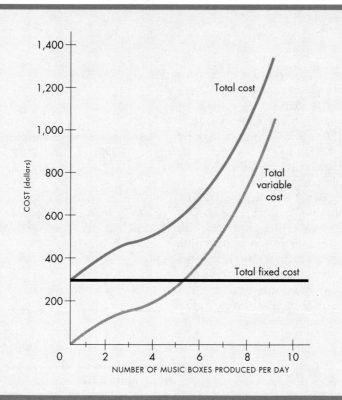

**Figure 23.4**
**Fixed, Variable, and Total Costs, Bugsbane Music Box Company**
All three cost functions, presented in Figures 23.1–23.3, are brought back for a curtain call.

## AVERAGE COST IN THE SHORT RUN

The president of Bugsbane unquestionably cares about the average cost of a music box as well as the total cost incurred; so do economists. *Average cost tells you how much a product costs per unit of output.* There are three average cost functions, one corresponding to each of the three total cost functions.

**Table 23.2**
**Average Fixed Cost, Average Variable Cost, and Average Total Cost, Bugsbane Music Box Company**

| NUMBER OF MUSIC BOXES PRODUCED PER DAY | AVERAGE FIXED COST | AVERAGE VARIABLE COST (DOLLARS) | AVERAGE TOTAL COST |
|---|---|---|---|
| 1 | 300(= 300 ÷ 1) | 60(= 60 ÷ 1) | 360(= 360 ÷ 1) |
| 2 | 150(= 300 ÷ 2) | 55(= 110 ÷ 2) | 205(= 410 ÷ 2) |
| 3 | 100(= 300 ÷ 3) | 53(= 160 ÷ 3) | 153(= 460 ÷ 3) |
| 4 | 75(= 300 ÷ 4) | 50(= 200 ÷ 4) | 125(= 500 ÷ 4) |
| 5 | 60(= 300 ÷ 5) | 52(= 260 ÷ 5) | 112(= 560 ÷ 5) |
| 6 | 50(= 300 ÷ 6) | 60(= 360 ÷ 6) | 110(= 660 ÷ 6) |
| 7 | 43(= 300 ÷ 7) | 73(= 510 ÷ 7) | 116(= 810 ÷ 7) |
| 8 | 38(= 300 ÷ 8) | 89(= 710 ÷ 8) | 126(= 1010 ÷ 8) |
| 9 | 33(= 300 ÷ 9) | 118(= 1060 ÷ 9) | 151(= 1360 ÷ 9) |

## Average Fixed Cost

Let's begin with ***average fixed cost***, *which is simply the total fixed cost divided by the firm's output.* Table 23.2 and Figure 23.5 show the average fixed cost function for the Bugsbane Music Box Company. Average fixed cost must decline with increases in output, since it equals a constant—total fixed cost—divided by the output rate.

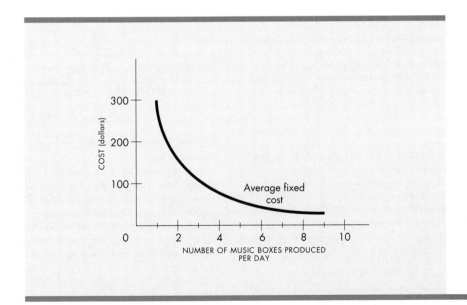

**Figure 23.5**
**Average Fixed Cost, Bugsbane Music Box Company**
Average fixed cost is total fixed cost divided by the firm's output. Since it equals a constant (total fixed cost) divided by the output rate, it must decline with increases in output.

## Average Variable Cost

The next type of average cost is ***average variable cost,*** *which is total variable cost divided by output.* For Bugsbane, the average variable cost function is shown in Table 23.2 and Figure 23.6. At first, increases in the output rate result in decreases in average variable cost, but beyond a point, they result in higher average variable cost. This is because the law of diminishing marginal returns is in operation. As more and more of the variable inputs are utilized, the extra output they produce declines be-

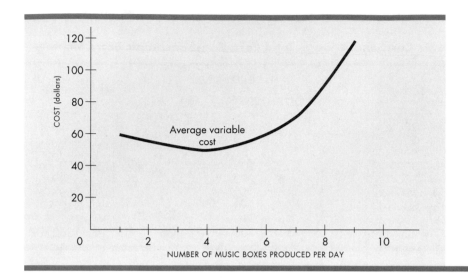

**Figure 23.6**
**Average Variable Cost, Bugs-bane Music Box Company**
Average variable cost is total variable cost divided by the firm's ouput. Beyond a point (in this case, 4 music boxes per day), average variable cost rises with increases in output because of the law of diminishing marginal returns.

yond some point, so that the amount spent on variable input per unit of output tends to increase.

## Average Total Cost

The third type of average cost is ***average total cost,*** *which is total cost divided by output.* For Bugsbane, the average total cost function is shown in Table 23.2 and Figure 23.7. At any level of output, *average total cost equals average fixed cost plus average variable cost.* This is easy to prove:

$$\text{average total cost} = \frac{\text{total cost}}{\text{output}} = \frac{\text{total fixed cost} + \text{total variable cost}}{\text{output}}$$

since total cost = total fixed cost + total variable cost. Moreover,

$$\frac{\text{total fixed cost} + \text{total variable cost}}{\text{output}} =$$

$$\frac{\text{total fixed cost}}{\text{output}} + \frac{\text{total variable cost}}{\text{output}}$$

and the right-hand side of this equation equals average fixed cost plus average variable cost. Thus we have proved what we set out to prove.

The fact that average total cost is the sum of average fixed cost and average variable cost helps explain the shape of the average cost function. If, as the output rate goes up, both average fixed cost and average variable cost decrease, average total cost must decrease too. But beyond some point, average total cost must increase because increases in average variable cost eventually more than offset decreases in average fixed cost. However, average total cost achieves its minimum after average variable cost, because the increases in average variable cost are for a time more than offset by decreases in average fixed cost. All the average cost functions are shown in Figure 23.9 on page 484.

## MARGINAL COST IN THE SHORT RUN

No one can really understand the operations of a business firm without understanding the concept of ***marginal cost,*** *the addition to total cost re-*

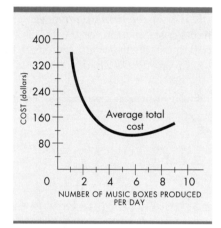

**Figure 23.7**
**Average Total Cost, Bugsbane Music Box Company**
Average total cost is total cost divided by output. It equals average fixed cost plus average variable cost. When output is 4 music boxes or less per day, both average fixed cost and average variable cost are decreasing, so average total cost must *decrease* too. When output is 5 or 6 music boxes per day, average total cost *decreases* because the fall in average fixed cost more than offsets the rise in average variable cost. When output exceeds 6 music boxes per day, the rise in average variable cost more than offsets the fall in average fixed cost, so average total cost increases.

## Table 23.3
### Calculation of Marginal Cost, Bugsbane Music Box Company

| NUMBER OF MUSIC BOXES PRODUCED PER DAY | TOTAL COST (DOLLARS) | MARGINAL COST |
|---|---|---|
| 0 | 300 | |
| | | 60(=360 – 300) |
| 1 | 360 | |
| | | 50(=410 – 360) |
| 2 | 410 | |
| | | 50(=460 – 410) |
| 3 | 460 | |
| | | 40(=500 – 460) |
| 4 | 500 | |
| | | 60(=560 – 500) |
| 5 | 560 | |
| | | 100(=660 – 560) |
| 6 | 660 | |
| | | 150(=810 – 660) |
| 7 | 810 | |
| | | 200(=1,010 – 810) |
| 8 | 1,010 | |
| | | 350(=1,360 – 1,010) |
| 9 | 1,360 | |

*sulting from the addition of the last unit of output.* To see how marginal cost is calculated, look at Table 23.3, which shows the total cost function of the Bugsbane Music Box Company. When output is between 0 and 1 music box per day, the firm's marginal cost is $60, since this is the *extra cost* of producing the first music box per day. In other words, $60 equals marginal cost in this situation because it is the difference between the total cost of producing 1 music box per day ($360) and the total cost of producing 0 music boxes per day ($300).

In general, marginal cost will vary depending on the firm's output level. Thus Table 23.3 shows that at Bugsbane marginal cost is $50 when the firm produces between 1 and 2 music boxes per day, $100 when the firm produces between 5 and 6 music boxes per day, and $350 when the firm produces between 8 and 9 music boxes per day. Table 23.3—and Figure 23.8, which shows the marginal cost function graphically—indicates that marginal cost, after decreasing with increases in output at low output levels, increases with further increases in output. In other words, *beyond some point it becomes more and more costly for the firm to produce yet another unit of output.*

### Increasing Marginal Cost and Diminishing Returns

The reason why marginal cost increases beyond some output level is to be found in the law of diminishing marginal returns. *If (beyond some point) increases in variable inputs result in less and less extra output, it follows that a larger and larger quantity of variable inputs must be added to produce an extra unit of output. Thus the cost of producing an extra unit of output must increase.*

To illustrate how diminishing marginal returns result in increasing marginal cost, let's return for a moment to the wheat farm in Tables 22.1 and 22.3. (For convenience, the data regarding this farm are reproduced in Table 23.4.) If it is producing 70 bushels of wheat, it requires an extra 1/30 unit of labor to produce an extra bushel—since Table 23.4 shows that the marginal product of a unit of labor is 30 bushels. But if it is producing 100 bushels of wheat, an extra 1/25 unit of labor is needed to produce an extra bushel, since Table 23.4 shows that the marginal product of a unit of labor is 25 bushels. Thus more of the variable input (specifically, 1/25 unit of labor rather than 1/30 unit of labor) is required to produce an

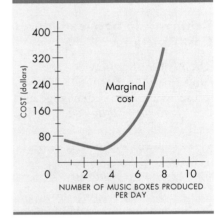

**Figure 23.8**
**Marginal Cost, Bugsbane Music Box Company**
Marginal cost is the addition to total cost arising from the addition of the last unit of output. The marginal cost of the first unit of output (which, according to Table 23.3, is $60) is plotted at the midpoint between 0 and 1 units of output. The marginal cost of the second unit of output is plotted at the midpoint between 1 and 2 units of output. The marginal cost function connects these and other points showing the marginal cost of various amounts of output. Beyond a point (in this case, between 3 and 4 music boxes per day), marginal cost increases because of the law of diminishing marginal returns.

**Table 23.4**
**Average and Marginal Products of Labor, 1-Acre Wheat Farm**

| NUMBER OF UNITS OF LABOR | TOTAL OUTPUT | MARGINAL PRODUCT (BUSHELS PER UNIT OF LABOR) | AVERAGE PRODUCT |
|---|---|---|---|
| 0 | 0 | | — |
| 1 | 30 | 30 | 30 |
| 2 | 70 | 40 | 35 |
| 3 | 100 | 30 | 33⅓ |
| 4 | 125 | 25 | 31¼ |
| 5 | 145 | 20 | 29 |

extra bushel of wheat. And *since more and more of the variable input is required to produce an extra unit of output, the cost of producing an extra unit of output increases as output rises.*

## Relationship between Marginal Cost and Average Cost Functions

The relationship between the marginal cost function and the average cost functions must be noted. Figure 23.9 shows the marginal cost curve together with the three average cost curves. *The marginal cost curve intersects both the average variable cost curve and the average total cost curve*

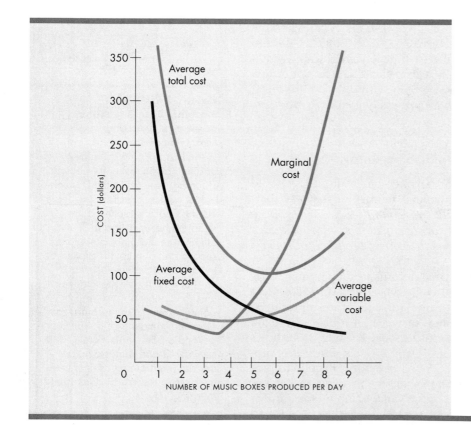

**Figure 23.9**
**Average Fixed Cost, Average Variable Cost, Average Total Cost, and Marginal Cost, Bugsbane Music Box Company**
All of the curves presented in Figures 23.5–23.8 are brought together for review. Note that the marginal cost curve intersects both the average variable cost curve and the average total cost curve at their minimum points.

*at their minimum points*. The reason for this is simple. If the extra cost of a unit of output is greater (less) than the average cost of the units of output already produced, the addition of the extra unit of output clearly must raise (lower) the average cost of production. Thus, if marginal cost is greater (less) than average cost, average cost must be rising (falling). And if this is so, average cost can be a minimum only when it equals marginal cost. (The same reasoning holds for both average total cost and average variable cost, and for the short and long runs.)

To make sure that you understand this point, consider the following numerical example. Suppose that the average total cost of producing 4 units of output is $10, and that the marginal cost of the fifth unit of output is less than $10. Will the average total cost be less for 5 units of output than for 4 units? It will be less, because the fifth unit's cost will pull down the average. On the other hand, if the marginal cost of the fifth unit of output had been greater than $10, the average total cost for 5 units of output would have been greater than for 4 units of output, because the fifth unit's cost would pull up the average. Thus *average total cost will fall when it is above marginal cost, and it will rise when it is below marginal cost.* Consequently, *when it is a minimum, average total cost must equal marginal cost*, as shown in Figure 23.9.

---

## EXAMPLE 23.1    THE COSTS OF A SMALL MACHINE SHOP

A machine shop has the following relationship between cost and output:

| OUTPUT (THOUSANDS OF UNITS OF OUTPUT PER YEAR) | TOTAL FIXED COST (DOLLARS PER YEAR) | TOTAL VARIABLE COST (DOLLARS PER YEAR) |
|---|---|---|
| 0 | 64,000 | 0 |
| 400 | 64,000 | 20,000 |
| 440 | 64,000 | 23,000 |
| 480 | 64,000 | 27,000 |
| 520 | 64,000 | 32,000 |

(a) Included in the fixed cost is $5,600 in interest on the owner's investment in the machine shop. If the owner owns the shop completely (and does not have to pay interest to anyone else), should this item still be included? (b) Suppose that the owner and his wife do all the work, and that the opportunity cost of their labor is the same, regardless of the shop's output. Is their labor cost a fixed or variable cost? (c) What is the marginal cost of a unit of output when output is between 480 and 520 thousands of units per year? (d) At which of the above output levels is average total cost a minimum? Is this the output that the owner should choose?

**Solution**

(a) Yes, because if he sold this shop, he could lend out the proceeds and get $5,600 in interest. Thus this is the opportunity cost of the owner's investment in the shop. (b) It is a fixed cost. (c) ($32,000 − $27,000) ÷ 40,000 = 12.5 cents. (d) 520 thousand units. In general, as we shall see in the following chapter, the owner, wanting to maximize profit, should not choose the output in the short run that minimizes average total cost.

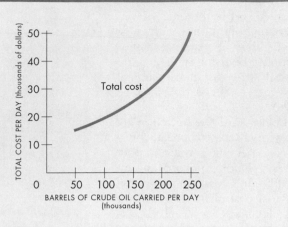

**Figure 23.10**
**Total Cost Function, Crude-Oil Pipeline, 18-Inch Diameter**
This graph shows the total cost function in an actual case. Note that it is shaped as economic theory would predict.

# SHORT-RUN COST FUNCTIONS OF A CRUDE-OIL PIPELINE: A CASE STUDY

Cost functions are not academic toys, but eminently practical analytical devices that play a major role in decision making by business executives and government agencies. To illustrate the nature and use of short-run cost functions, we will take up the real-world case of crude-oil pipelines where we left off (in the previous chapter). In the short run, it is reasonable to assume that the diameter of a pipeline is fixed. Given the production function in Table 22.2, it is easy to figure out the total cost of carrying various amounts of oil per day, with a pipeline of a given diameter. In other words, we assume that the company that owns the pipeline can vary the horsepower by varying the number and type of pumping stations, but that the diameter of the pipeline is fixed.[1] Under these circumstances, if the diameter of the pipeline is 18 inches, what will the pipeline's cost functions look like?

Figures 23.10 and 23.11 answer this question. Figure 23.10 shows the ***total cost function*** for an 18-inch pipeline—the total daily cost of operating it, given that it carries various amounts of crude oil per day. If the pipeline carries 200,000 barrels of oil per day, the total daily cost is $33,000; if the amount of oil is increased to 250,000 barrels per day, the total daily cost rises to $48,000.

Figure 23.11 shows the ***average total cost function*** for an 18-inch pipeline—the total daily cost per barrel for the pipeline, given that it carries various amounts of crude oil per day. According to Figure 23.11, the total daily cost per barrel for this pipeline to carry 200,000 barrels per day is $.16 ½, and the total daily cost per barrel for it to carry 250,000 barrels per days is $.19 ⅕. Figure 23.11 also shows the ***marginal cost function*** for such a pipeline—the additional daily cost of carrying an extra barrel of crude oil per day. When this pipeline is carrying 200,000 barrels per day, the marginal cost runs to about $.23.

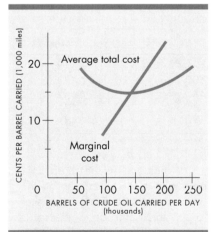

**Figure 23.11**
**Average Total Cost Function and Marginal Cost Function Crude-Oil Pipeline, 18-inch Diameter**
This graph shows the average cost and marginal cost functions in an actual case. Note that their shape follows economic theory.

[1] Because the number and type of pumping stations must be altered, Leslie Cookenboo refers to this as the "intermediate run." See Cookenboo, *op. cit.*

To the operators of the pipeline, a knowledge of these cost functions can mean the difference between profit and loss. For example, suppose that the operators of a particular 18-inch pipeline are thinking about increasing the amount of oil the pipeline will carry per day. Specifically, suppose that the pipeline can now carry 200,000 barrels per day and that the operators are thinking about adding enough horsepower so that it can carry 250,000 barrels per day. Suppose that, according to the best estimates available, the pipeline can get $5 million in additional revenue each year if it carries the additional 50,000 barrels per day. Should the operators increase in this way the amount of oil the pipeline can carry?

If they want to increase profits, they should decide against this increase in the amount of horsepower. According to the total cost function in Figure 23.10, the pipeline's daily costs would increase by $15,000 per day if horsepower were increased so that 250,000, rather than 200,000 barrels of oil could be carried per day, while the extra oil carried would increase daily revenues by $5 million ÷ 365, or about $14,000 per day. Thus the extra costs would exceed the extra revenue, which means that the pipeline's profit would be reduced by increasing the amount of horsepower. In making decisions of this sort (and they must make them repeatedly!), managers must rely heavily on information about the relevant cost functions.

## TEST YOURSELF

1. Suppose that a firm's short-run total cost function is as follows:

| OUTPUT(NUMBER OF UNITS PER YEAR) | TOTAL COST PER YEAR (DOLLARS) |
| --- | --- |
| 0 | 20,000 |
| 1 | 20,100 |
| 2 | 20,200 |
| 3 | 20,300 |
| 4 | 20,500 |
| 5 | 20,800 |

What are the firm's total fixed costs? What are its total variable costs when it produces 4 units per year?

2. In Question 1, what is the firm's marginal cost when between 4 and 5 units are produced per year? Does marginal cost increase beyond some output level?

3. In Question 1, what is the firm's average cost when it produces 1 unit per year? 2 units per year? 3 units per year? 4 units per year? 5 units per year?

4. Fill in the blanks below:

| TOTAL OUTPUT | TOTAL FIXED COST | TOTAL VARIABLE COST | AVERAGE TOTAL COST (DOLLARS) | AVERAGE FIXED COST | AVERAGE VARIABLE COST |
| --- | --- | --- | --- | --- | --- |
| 0 | 500 | — | | | |
| 1 | 500 | 20 | — | — | — |
| 2 | 500 | — | 300 | — | — |
| 3 | 500 | — | — | — | 133⅓ |
| 4 | 500 | 1,100 | — | — | — |

5. In Question 4, does marginal cost increase with increases in output? Explain.

## LONG-RUN COST FUNCTIONS

### The Long-Run Average Cost Function

We have held to the last one additional kind of cost function that plays a very important role in economic analysis. This is the firm's **long-run average cost function,** *which shows the minimum average cost of produc-*

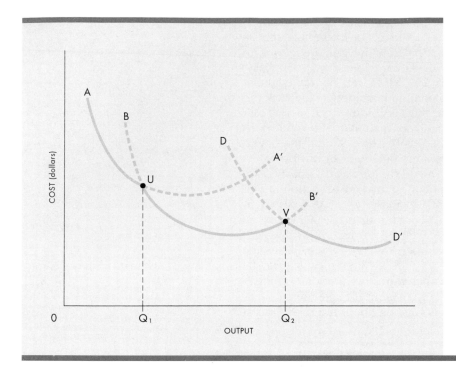

**Figure 23.12**
**Short-Run Average Cost Curves and Long-Run Average Cost Curve**
The short-run average total cost functions for three plants—small, medium, and large—are *AA'*, *BB'*, and *DD'*. The long-run average cost function is *AUVD'*, if these are the only three types of plants that can be built.

*ing each output level when any desired type or scale of plant can be built.* Unlike the cost functions discussed in the previous sections, this cost function pertains to the long run—*to a period long enough so that all inputs are variable and none is fixed.* As pointed out in the previous chapter, a useful way to look at the long run is to consider it a *planning horizon.* The firm must continually be planning ahead and trying to decide its strategy in the long run.

Suppose a firm can build plants of three sizes—small, medium, and large. The short-run average total cost functions corresponding to these plants are *AA'*, *BB'*, and *DD'* in Figure 23.12. If the firm is still in the planning stage of plant construction, it can choose whichever plant has the lowest costs. Consequently, the firm will choose the small plant if it believes its output rate will be smaller than $OQ_1$, the medium plant if it believes its output rate will be above $OQ_1$, but below $OQ_2$, and the large plant if it believes that its output rate will be above $OQ_2$. Thus the long-run average cost curve is *AUVD'*. And if, as is generally the case, there are many possible types of plants, the long-run average cost curve looks like *LL'* in Figure 23.13. (Only a few of the short-run average cost curves are shown in Figure 23.13.)

The usefulness of the long-run average cost function can be illustrated by the familiar case of crude-oil pipelines. Figure 23.14 shows the long-run average cost function for these pipelines, as well as selected short-run average cost functions (corresponding to diameters of 8, 10, 12, 14, 16, 18, 20, 24, 26, 30, and 32 inches). Note that long-run average cost—that is, cost per barrel—decreases as more and more oil is carried per day, at least up to 400,000 barrels per day. Thus it appears that costs are reduced when the greatest possible quantities of oil are transported in large-diameter pipelines.

This fact is important in evaluating the effects of various kinds of mar-

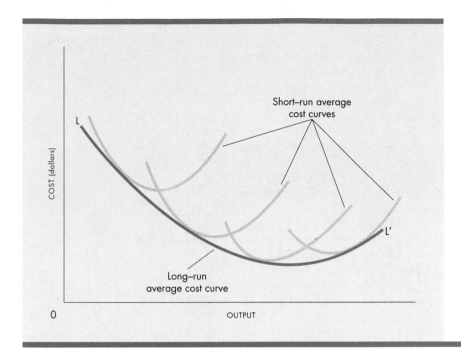

**Figure 23.13**
**Long-Run Average Cost Curve**
If many possible types of plants can be built, the long-run average cost function is *LL'*.

ket structure in the pipeline industry. *If long-run average costs decrease with increases in output up to an output representing all, or nearly all, of the market, it is wasteful to force competition in such an industry, since costs would be greater if the industry output were divided among a number of firms than if it were produced by only one or two firms.* More will be said on this score in Chapter 25.

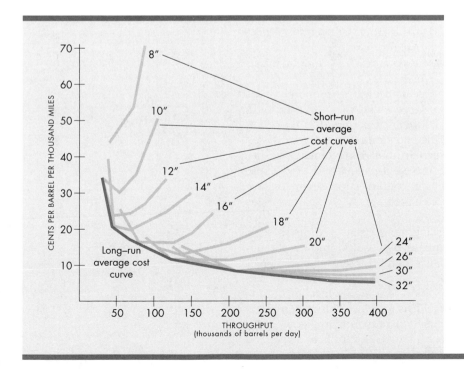

**Figure 23.14**
**Costs per Barrel of Operating Crude-Oil Trunk Pipeline**
This graph shows the long-run average cost curve (and the relevant short-run average cost curves) in an actual case. Note that in this range at least, long-run average cost decreases as output increases.

# RETURNS TO SCALE

What determines the shape of the long-run average cost function in a particular industry? Its shape must depend upon the characteristics of the production function—specifically, upon whether there are increasing, decreasing, or constant returns to scale. To understand what these terms mean, consider a long-run situation and suppose that the firm increases the amount of all inputs by the same proportion. What will happen to output? *If output increases by a larger proportion than each of the inputs, this is a case of* **increasing returns to scale**. *If output increases by a smaller proportion than each of the inputs, this is a case of* **decreasing returns to scale**. *If output increases by the same proportion as each of the inputs, this is a case of* **constant returns to scale**.

At first glance it may seem that constant returns should prevail: After all, if two factories are built with the same equipment and use the same type and number of workers, it would seem obvious that they can produce twice as much output as one such factory. But things are not that simple. If a firm doubles its scale, it may be able *to use techniques that could not be used at the smaller scale*. Some inputs are not available in small units; for example, we cannot install half a numerically controlled machine tool. Because of indivisibilities of this sort, increasing returns to scale may occur. Thus, although one could double a firm's size by simply building two small factories, this may be inefficient. One large factory may be more efficient than two smaller factories of the same total capacity because it is large enough to use certain techniques and inputs that the smaller factories cannot use.

Another reason for increasing returns to scale stems from certain *geometrical relations*. For example, since the volume of a box that is $3 \times 3 \times 3$ feet is 27 times as great as the volume of a box that is $1 \times 1 \times 1$ foot, the former box can carry 27 times as much as the latter box. But since the area of the six sides of the $3 \times 3 \times 3$-foot box is 54 square feet and the area of the six sides of the $1 \times 1 \times 1$-foot box is 6 square feet, the former box only requires 9 times as much wood as the latter. Greater *specialization* also can result in increasing returns to scale. As more men and machines are used, it is possible to subdivide tasks and allow various inputs to specialize.

Decreasing returns to scale can also occur; the most frequently cited reason is *the difficulty of coordinating a large enterprise*. It can be difficult even in a small firm to obtain the information required to make important decisions; in a large firm, the difficulties tend to be greater. It can be difficult even in a small firm to be certain that management's wishes are being carried out; in a larger firm these difficulties too tend to be greater. Although the advantages of a large organization seem to have captured the public fancy, there are often very great disadvantages as well.

Whether there are increasing, decreasing, or constant returns to scale in a particular situation must be settled case by case. Moreover, the answer is likely to depend on the particular range of output considered. There frequently are increasing returns to scale up to some level of output, then perhaps constant returns to scale up to a higher level of output, beyond which there may be decreasing returns to scale. This pattern is responsible for the *U*-shaped long-run average cost function in Figure 23.13. At relatively small output levels, there are increasing returns to scale, and long-run average cost decreases as output rises. At relatively high output

## EXAMPLE 23.2    ECONOMIES OF SCALE IN CABLE TELEVISION?

According to a study reported to the U.S. House of Representatives, the long-run average cost function of a firm providing cable television to households is as follows:

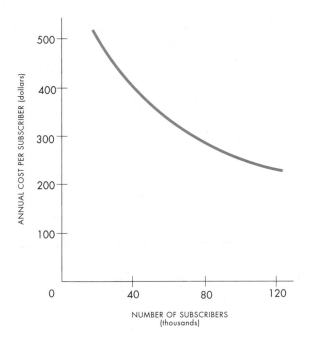

(a) Do there appear to be **economies of scale** in the cable television business? In other words, does long-run average cost fall with increases in output? (b)

If so, why do you think that this is the case? (c) According to the authors of this study, long-run marginal cost in this business tends to be less than long-run average cost. Is this true? If so, why? (d) Would you expect that a large number of firms would provide cable television in a particular city? Why, or why not?

### Solution

(a) Yes. Long-run average costs fall as the number of subscribers (a rough measure of output) increases. (b) A firm providing cable television must invest in a substantial amount of equipment—satellite dishes, towers, antennas, and cable distribution facilities—before it can service its first customer. The investment required to service additional customers is minor compared to this initial investment. Thus, in the long run (when any desired type or scale of plant can be built), the average cost of servicing a subscriber goes down as the number of subscribers goes up. (c) It is true because (as pointed out on page 485) if average cost decreases with increased output, marginal cost must be less than average cost. (d) No. Because there are economies of scale, one would expect that many communities would have only one firm providing cable television—and this in fact is true.*

*For further discussion, see J. Gomez-Ibanez and J. Kalt, eds., *Cases in Microeconomics*, Englewood Cliffs, N.J.: Prentice Hall,

---

levels, there are decreasing returns to scale, and long-run average cost increases as output rises.

As we shall see in the following section, this *U*-shaped pattern is not found in all industries. Within the range covered by the available data, there is little or no evidence in many industries that long-run average cost increases as output rises. But this may be because the data do not cover a wide enough range. Eventually, one would expect long-run average cost to rise because of problems of coordination, increased red tape, and reduced flexibility. Firms as large as General Motors or IBM are continually bedeviled by the very real difficulties of enormous size.

## MEASUREMENT AND APPLICATION OF COST FUNCTIONS

### Measurement of Cost Functions

Countless studies have been made to estimate cost functions in particular firms and industries. Many of these have been based on the relationship

# CAN AMERICAN FIRMS COMPETE?

The 1980s were a very bruising decade for many American manufacturers. Whereas 20 years ago, American firms were regarded, both here and abroad, as models of efficiency, they have been twitted recently of growing fat and lazy. As *Business Week* put it, "While the Japanese were developing remarkably higher standards for a whole host of products, from consumer electronics to cars and machine tools, many U.S. managers were smugly dozing at the switch."[1] As evidence, the critics point to the fact that plants in the United States have been having a very difficult time producing goods of comparable quality at as low a cost as their foreign rivals.

To illustrate, consider the important case of automobiles. According to the National Research Council, the Japanese could produce a small car and ship it to the United States at an overall cost that was $700–$1,500 below the production cost of American producers. Obviously, this is an enormous difference. Moreover, the Japanese cars tended to be of higher quality. Even in 1987, after American firms had taken numerous steps to improve quality, the number of problems reported by owners of new cars was about 35 percent greater for American than Japanese cars.[2]

The following is a brief summary of the reasons for this Japanese cost and quality advantage, according to an influential report by the National Research Council:

> Popular accounts of the emergence of Japanese producers as first-rate, worldwide competitors tend to emphasize the impact of new automation technology (e.g., robotics), strong support of the central government (i.e., "Japan, Inc."), and influence of Japanese culture (i.e., a dedicated work force). There is no doubt that these factors have played some role. Yet, it is our view that the sources of the Japanese advantage are not to be found in such factors. Rather, they are rooted in a commitment to manufacturing excellence and a strategy that uses manufacturing as a competitive weapon.
>
> The key to Japan's lead . . . appears to be the interaction of the material control system, maintenance practices, and employee involvement. The key to the

[1]"The Push for Quality," *Business Week*, June 8, 1987, p.131.
[2]Ibid., p. 139.

material control system is the concept of "just in time" production. Often called "Kanban" (after the production cards or tickets used to trigger production), the system is designed so that materials, parts, and components used at a given step in production are produced or delivered just before they are needed. Thus, stages in the process (including suppliers) are tightly coupled, with very little work-in-process inventory. Suppliers must therefore make frequent deliveries of parts, and lot sizes must be small to accommodate product variety.

It is the Japanese view that reduction of decoupling inventory exposes "the real problems"—waste of time and materials, imbalance in operations, defective parts, equipment operating improperly, and so forth. ([The table on the facing page] provides comparative data on inventory levels. These data show that dramatically less inventory is used by Japanese firms in the production of automobiles. This is true whether one looks at the process as a whole or at specific plants.)

With smaller buffer stocks the production system will simply not work if there are frequent or lengthy breakdowns. Thus, the just-in-time approach exposes opportunities for reducing waste and solving problems, while at the same time creating pressure for maximizing uptime and minimizing defects. Maintenance programs, preventive and scheduled, are therefore pursued vigorously. Plants operate with only two shifts, and equipment is maintained during nonproduction time. The result is a much lower rate of machine failure and breakdown.

Pressure for defect elimination is reflected in relationships with suppliers and in work practices on the line. "Just in time" production does not allow for extensive inspection of incoming parts. Suppliers must, therefore, achieve highly demanding quality levels, consistently and reliably. The major Japanese manufacturers work closely with outside vendors to make sure that responsibility for quality is felt and acted upon at the source of product. This same approach—quality control at the source—is used in production on the line, where workers have the authority to stop the operation if they spot defects or other production problems. Worker-initiated line stops are central to the concept of Jidoka: making problems visible to everyone's eye and stopping the line if trouble occurs; all thoughts, methods, and tools to avoid stops are Jidoka.

The basic thrust of the Kanban system and the concept of Jidoka are to eliminate waste, expose problems, and conserve resources. This is not simply a different technique of controlling production, but a very different way of managing the production process. It is clear that these systems interact with other factors in our list of productivity determinants. Separating their effects from the effects of quality systems and job structure, for example, is somewhat arbitrary. The Kanban-Jidoka system uses fewer inspectors, and its success requires broader and deeper jobs. . . .

Indeed, it appears that job structure plays an important role in explaining observed productivity differentials. We have already noted two features of the Japanese system (maintenance practices and Jidoka) in which jobs are designed to involve workers in a variety of tasks. The effects of structure, and the differences in management style and practices that go with it (fewer layers of management, more managing from the bottom up), extend to other aspects of production. Quality circles or "small group involvement activities" deal with such questions as layout, process methods, and automation. Such involvement appears to be an important factor in obtaining relatively high levels of commitment and motivation.

The nature of worker-management relations in Japan is further suggested by much lower levels of unexcused absence than that found in the United States. . . . In general, absenteeism influences costs, not only through redundant labor but also through fringe costs of the absent group as well as indirect effects such as scrap, reduced learning, and so forth. It appears that absenteeism may actually account for as much as 10–12 percent of the cost gap.

. . . [It] is clear that work-force management must be a significant factor in explaining the Japanese cost advantage. Likewise, an attempt to explain quality differences would certainly accord a major influence to the work force and its management. It seems evident,

---

## Inventory Comparisons—U.S. and Japan

| LEVEL/PROCESS | JAPAN | | UNITED STATES |
|---|---|---|---|
| 1. *Plant and Process Inventories* Assembly plant component inventories (equivalent units of production) | | | |
| Heaters | 1 | hour | 5 days |
| Radiators | 2 | hours | 5 days |
| Brake drums | 1.5 | hours | 3 days |
| Front-wheel-drive transfer case in process parts storage by operation (number of parts) | | | |
| Mill | 7 | | 240 |
| Drill | 11 | | 200 |
| Ream and chamfer | 13 | | 196 |
| Drill | 24 | | 205 |
| Mill, washer, test | 10 | | 40 |
| Assemble | 6 | | 96 |
| Finish | 7 | | 87 |
| Total | 79 | | 1064 |
| 2. *Company Inventories* Work in process inventories per vehicle | | | |
| 1979 | $80.2 | | $536.5 |
| 1980 | $74.2 | | $584.3 |
| Work in process turns[a] | | | |
| 1979 | 40.0 | | 12.1 |
| 1980 | 46.1 | | 13.4 |

[a] Defined as cost of goods sold divided by work in process inventories.

*Source:* 1.—Industry sources (data provided by panel members); 2.—Annual reports for representative producers.

---

therefore, that in concert with different systems of production management and control, the work force plays a central role in the Japanese competitive advantage.[3]

## Probing Deeper

1. Do all firms, like the Japanese, use manufacturing as a "competitive weapon"? What other sorts of "competitive weapons" exist?

2. The table shows that inventory levels have tended to be lower in Japanese than in American

[3] National Research Council, "The Japanese Cost and Quality Advantages in the Auto Industry," in E. Mansfield, ed., *Managerial Economics and Operations Research,* 5th ed., New York: Norton, 1987, pp. 34, 39–42.

auto firms. Why has this tended to reduce cost?

3. Why do the Japanese believe that the production of goods in small lots often tends to increase product quality?

4. Why does absenteeism of labor increase a firm's costs? If it is true, as estimated above, that absenteeism may account for 10–12 percent of the difference in cost between Japan and the United States, what can American firms do about it?

5. The National Research Council report tends to play down the importance of advanced automation in accounting for Japan's relatively low costs. Can managerial changes reduce costs in the absence of increased automation?

6. According to *Business Week*, the typical American factory spends about 20–25 percent of its costs to find and fix mistakes. How can a firm go about reducing such costs?

over time between cost and output. Figure 23.15 shows the total costs of a hypothetical firm in various years plotted against the firm's output in these years. Based on the data, a reasonable approximation to the firm's total cost function might be the curve that is drawn in Figure 23.15. However, there are a number of difficulties in this simple procedure. For one thing, the firm's cost function may not have remained fixed throughout this period. For another, accounting data on costs may not be as accurate as one would like.[2] For these and other reasons, economists and statisticians have devised more sophisticated techniques to estimate cost functions.

To illustrate the sorts of results that have been obtained, Figure 23.16 shows the total cost function, average total cost function, and marginal cost function for a leather belt shop. Note that the total cost function appears linear, that is, a straight line, in the relevant range.

These results were obtained over 40 years ago by one of the pioneers in this field, Joel Dean of Columbia University. Since that time, a great deal of evidence has been amassed on the shape of the cost functions of individual firms and industries. Two findings are particularly worth noting. First, *within the range of observed data, the long-run average cost*

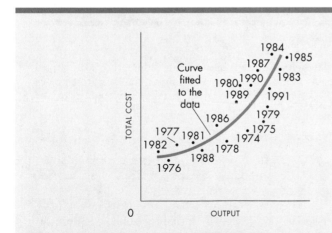

**Figure 23.15**
**Relationship between Total Cost and Output: Time Series for a Particular Firm**
One very crude way to estimate the total cost curve is to plot total cost in each year against total output in that year, and draw a curve, like the one shown in the diagram, that fits the points reasonably well. However, this technique is generally too crude to be reliable.

[2] Some of the difficulties are that the depreciation of an asset is often determined by the tax laws rather than economic criteria, many inputs are valued at historical, rather than opportunity cost, and accountants sometimes use arbitrary allocations of overhead and joint costs.

*curve in many industries seems to be L-shaped* (as in Figure 23.17), *not U-shaped* (as in Figure 23.13). That is, there is little or no evidence that it turns upward, rather than remains horizontal, at high output levels. As pointed out in the previous section, this may be due in part to the limited range of the data. Second, *many empirical studies indicate that marginal cost in the short run tends to be constant in the relevant output range*. However, this really does not contradict our assertions in previous sections, because the data used in these studies often do not cover periods when the firm was operating at peak capacity.

## Break-Even Charts

Estimated cost functions are used in a variety of ways by firms and government agencies. As an illustration, consider **break-even charts**. To construct a break-even chart, *the firm's total revenue must be plotted on the same chart with its total cost function*. It is generally assumed that the price the firm receives for its product will not be influenced by the amount it sells, so that total revenue is proportional to output. Thus the total revenue curve is a straight line through the origin. Also, it is generally assumed that the firm's average variable cost and marginal cost are constant *in the relevant output range*, meaning that the firm's total cost function is also assumed to be a straight line.

Panel A of Figure 23.18 shows the break-even chart for an actual cable manufacturing firm. The sales price of each unit of its output was $200. The firm's fixed costs were $50,000 per month and its average variable cost per unit of output was $20. The break-even chart shows the monthly profit or loss that will result from each sales level. Panel A (Figure 23.18) shows that the firm would have lost $14,000 per month if it had sold 200 units per month. On the other hand, it would have made a profit of $22,000 per month if it had sold 400 units per month. The chart also shows the **break-even point,** *the output level that must be reached if the firm is to avoid losses*. In panel A, the break-even point is 278 units of output per month.

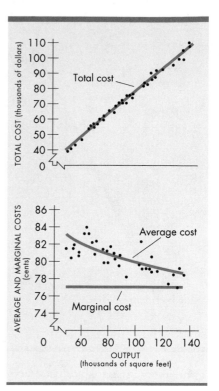

**Figure 23.16**
**Total, Average, and Marginal Cost Functions of a Leather Belt Shop**
This graph shows the short-run total, average, and marginal cost curves in an actual case. Note that marginal cost is constant in this case, but the data pertain only to a limited range of output levels.

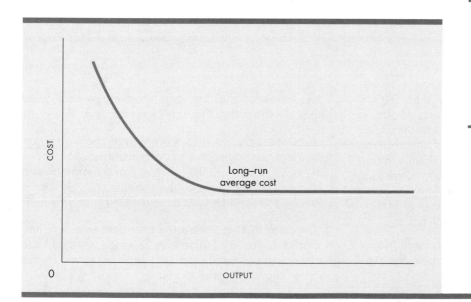

**Figure 23.17**
**Apparent Shape of Many Long-Run Average Cost Curves**
Within the range of observed data, there is little or no evidence in many industries that the long-run average cost curve turns upward, rather than remains horizontal, at high output levels. But the range of observed data is limited.

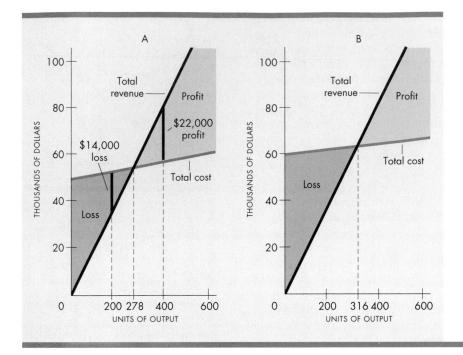

**Figure 23.18**
**Break-Even Chart, Cable Manufacturing Firm**
In panels A and B, the sales price of each unit of output is $200. In panel A, the firm's fixed costs are $50,000 per month, and its average variable cost per unit of output is $20. In panel B, the firm's fixed costs are $60,000 per month, and its average variable cost per unit of output is $10. In panel A, the firm's break-even point is 278 units of output per month, whereas in panel B it is 316 units of output per month.

Break-even charts are used very extensively by firms and other groups to estimate the effect of the sales rate on costs, receipts, and profits. A firm may use a break-even chart to determine the effect on profits of a projected increase in sales, or how many units of a particular product it must sell in order to break even. For instance, the cable manufacturing firm wanted to find out, among other things, how its break-even point would be affected if it installed new equipment that would increase its fixed costs to $60,000 per month and reduce its average variable cost to $10. Panel B of Figure 23.18 shows that, under these circumstances, the firm's break-even point would be 316, rather than 278, units of output per month. This information is, of course, of considerable value to the firm. It means that if the firm installs the new equipment, it must sell at least 316 units of output per month to stay in the black.

## TEST YOURSELF

1. Explain why each of the following statements is true, partly true, or false. (a) "Decreasing returns to scale occur when increased scale allows efficiencies of various sorts." (b) "The law of diminishing marginal returns is inconsistent with increasing returns to scale." (c) "John Maynard Keynes said, 'In the long run we are all dead.' He was right. What is important for the determination of the optimal number of firms in an industry is the short-run average cost function."

2. As the electronics industry has grown more mature and new technologies have been developed, the costs of many electronic products have fallen dramatically. Is this evidence that the long-run average cost curve slopes downward to the right? Explain.

3. A business analyst uses a break-even chart which assumes that her firm's total cost is a linear function of output (as in Figure 23.18). If the firm's marginal cost increases sharply as its output increases, is this break-even chart likely to be very accurate? Why, or why not?

4. Suppose that you were the president of a firm that operates a crude-oil pipeline. Describe in detail the various ways in which the cost functions given in this chapter might be useful to you.

# SUMMARY

1. The cost of a certain course of action is the value of the best alternative course of action that could have been pursued instead. This is the doctrine of opportunity, or alternative, cost.

2. Three kinds of total cost functions are important in the short run—total fixed cost, total variable cost, and total cost. In addition, there are three kinds of average cost functions (corresponding to each of the total cost functions)—average fixed cost, average variable cost, and average total cost.

3. Marginal cost—the addition to total cost due to the addition of the last unit of output—is of enormous significance in the firm's decision making process. Because of the law of diminishing marginal returns, marginal cost tends to increase beyond some output level.

4. The firm's long-run average cost curve shows the minimum average cost of producing each output level when any desired type or scale of plant can be built. The shape of the long-run average cost curve is determined in part by whether there are increasing, decreasing, or constant returns to scale.

5. Suppose that a firm increases the amount of all inputs by the same percentage. If output increases by more than this percentage, this is a case of increasing returns to scale. If output increases by less than this percentage, this is a case of decreasing returns to scale. If output increases by this percentage, this is a case of constant returns to scale.

6. If long-run average costs decrease with increases in output up to an output representing all, or nearly all, of the market, it is wasteful to force competition in such an industry, since costs would be greater if the industry output were divided among a number of firms than if it were produced by only one or two firms.

7. Cost functions play a very important practical role in economics and management. There have been countless studies to estimate cost functions in particular firms and industries, based on engineering and accounting data.

8. Cost functions can be used to help solve important sorts of managerial problems, as well as problems of public policy. We have shown how estimates of cost functions have been used to construct break-even charts, commonly employed by firms to promote better decisions.

# CONCEPTS FOR REVIEW

**Opportunity cost**

**Alternative cost**

**Implicit cost**

**Cost functions**

**Total fixed cost**

**Total variable cost**

**Total cost**

**Average fixed cost**

**Average variable cost**

**Average total cost**

**Marginal cost**

**Total cost function**

**Average total cost function**

**Marginal cost function**

**Long-run average cost function**

**Increasing returns to scale**

**Decreasing returns to scale**

**Constant returns to scale**

**Break-even chart**

**Break-even point**

**Economies of scale**

# PART SIX

# MARKET STRUCTURE AND ANTITRUST POLICY

# PERFECT COMPETITION

EVEN A COUNTRY AS RICH as the United States cannot afford to waste resources, particularly when much of the world is hungry. One of the important determinants of how a society's resources are used is how its markets are organized. Thus, if the market for wheat contained few sellers rather than many, it would certainly use resources quite differently. Or if 20 firms, rather than one, provided local telephone service in Chicago, resources would be used differently. Economists do not have any simple formulas that will eliminate all social waste. But based on existing models and evidence, they believe that some forms of market organization tend to minimize social waste, whereas other forms seem to promote it.

In this chapter, we examine the way resources are allocated and prices are set under **perfect competition.** This type of market organization—or market structure, as it is often called—is a polar case which seldom, if ever, occurs in a pure form in the real world. But it is an extremely useful model that sheds much light on a market structure's effects on resource allocation. Anyone who wants to understand how markets work in a capitalistic economy—or why our public policies toward business are what they are—must understand perfect competition, as well as the other market structures taken up in the next two chapters.

## MARKET STRUCTURE AND ECONOMIC PERFORMANCE

Many economists have come to the conclusion, based on their studies of the workings of markets, that certain kinds of market organization are better, from society's point of view, than others. This is a much stronger statement than merely saying, as we did in the previous section, that market structure influences market behavior. This statement is based on some set of values and preferences, explicit or implicit, and on certain economic models that predict that "better" behavior is more likely if markets are organized in certain ways than in other ways. Although there is considerable controversy on this score, many economists believe that, from society's point of view, market structures should be as close as possible to perfect competition (for reasons given in the next three chapters).

Economists have generally found it useful to classify markets into four broad types: **perfect competition, monopoly, monopolistic competition,** and **oligopoly.** Each of these terms describes a particular type of

**Table 24.1**
**Types of Market Structure**

| MARKET STRUCTURE | EXAMPLES | NUMBER OF PRODUCERS | TYPE OF PRODUCT | POWER OF FIRM OVER PRICE | BARRIERS TO ENTRY | NONPRICE COMPETITION |
|---|---|---|---|---|---|---|
| Perfect competition | Parts of agriculture are reasonably close | Many | Standardized | None | Low | None |
| Monopolistic competition | Retail trade | Many | Differentiated | Some | Low | Advertising and product differentiation |
| Oligopoly | Autos, steel, machinery | Few | Standardized or differentiated | Some | High | Advertising and product differentiation |
| Monopoly | Public utilities | One | Unique product | Considerable | Very high | Advertising |

market structure or organization. Table 24.1 provides a capsule description of each of these types. Before looking in detail at each of them, we must go over this table to see how these market structures differ.

**NUMBER OF FIRMS.** The economist's classification of market structures is based to an important extent on the number of firms in the industry that supplies the product. In perfect competition and monopolistic competition, there are *many* sellers, each of which produces only a small part of the industry's output. In monopoly, on the other hand, the industry consists of only a *single* seller. Oligopoly is an intermediate case where there are a *few* sellers. Thus Consolidated Edison, if it is the only supplier of electricity in a particular market, is a monopoly. And since there is only a small number of computer manufacturers, the market for computers is an oligopoly.

**CONTROL OVER PRICE.** Market structures differ considerably in the extent to which an individual firm has control over price. A firm under perfect competition has *no control* over price. For example, a wheat farm (which is close to being a perfectly competitive firm) has no control over the price of wheat. On the other hand, a monopolist is likely to have *considerable control* over price. Thus, in the absence of public regulation, Consolidated Edison would have considerable control over the price of electricity in New York City. A firm under monopolistic competition or oligopoly is likely to have *more* control over price than a perfectly competitive firm and *less* control over price than a monopolist.

**TYPE OF PRODUCT.** These market structures also differ in the extent to which the firms in an industry produce standardized (that is, identical) products. Firms in a perfectly competitive market all produce *identical* products. Thus Farmer Brown's corn is essentially the same as Farmer Smith's. In a monopolistic competitive industry like dress manufacturing, firms produce *somewhat different* products. One firm's dresses differ in style and quality from another firm's dresses. In an oligopolistic industry, firms *sometimes*, but not always, produce identical products. And in a monopolistic industry, there can be *no difference* among firms in their products, since there is only one firm.

**BARRIERS TO ENTRY.** The ease with which firms can enter the industry differs from one market structure to another. In perfect competition, barriers to entry are *low*. Thus only a small investment is required to enter many parts of agriculture. Similarly, there are *low* barriers to entry in monopolistic competition. But in oligopolies such as autos and steel, there tend to be *very considerable* barriers to entry because it is so expensive to build an auto or steel plant (and for many other reasons too). In monopoly, entry is blocked; once entry occurs, the monopolist is an ex-monopolist.

**NONPRICE COMPETITION.** These market structures also differ in the extent to which firms compete on the basis of advertising and differences in product characteristics, rather than price. In perfect competition, there is *no* nonprice competition. In monopolistic competition, there is *considerable emphasis* on nonprice competition. Thus dress manufacturers compete by trying to develop better styles and by advertising their product lines. Oligopolies also tend to rely *heavily* on nonprice competition. For example, auto firms try to increase their sales by building better and more attractive cars and by advertising. Monopolists also engage in advertising, although this advertising is not directed at reducing the sales of other firms in the industry, since no other firms exist.

Table 24.1 provides a useful summary of some of the key characteristics of each market structure. Before proceeding further, study it carefully.

## PERFECT COMPETITION

When business executives speak of a highly competitive market, they often mean one in which each firm is keenly aware of its rivalry with a few others and in which advertising, styling, packaging, and other such commercial weapons are used to attract business away from them. In contrast, the basic feature of the economist's definition of perfect competition is its *impersonality*. Because there are so many firms in the industry, no firm views another as a competitor, any more than one small tobacco farmer views another small tobacco farmer as a competitor. A market is perfectly competitive if it satisfies the following three conditions.

**HOMOGENEITY OF PRODUCT.** The first condition is that *the product of any one seller must be the same as the product of any other seller*. This condition ensures that buyers do not care from which seller they purchase the goods, so long as the price is the same. This condition is met in many markets. As pointed out in the previous section, Farmer Brown's corn is likely to be essentially the same as Farmer Smith's.

**MANY BUYERS AND SELLERS.** The second condition is that there must be a large number of buyers and sellers. *Each participant in the market, whether buyer or seller, must be so small in relation to the entire market that he or she cannot affect the product's price.* That is, all buyers and sellers must be "price takers," not "price makers." As we know from Chapter 19, a firm under perfect competition faces a *horizontal demand curve*, since variations in its output—within the range of its capabilities—will have no effect on market price.

**MOBILITY OF RESOURCES.** The third condition is that *all resources must be able to switch readily from one use to another, and consumers, firms, and* *resource owners must have complete knowledge of all relevant economic and technological data.*

No industry in the real world, now or in the past, satisfies all these conditions completely; thus no industry is perfectly competitive. Some agricultural markets may be reasonably close, but even they do not meet all the requirements. But this does not mean that it is useless to study the behavior of a perfectly competitive market. The conclusions derived from the model of perfect competition have proved very helpful in explaining and predicting behavior in the real world. Indeed, as we shall see, they have permitted a reasonably accurate view of resource allocation in many important segments of our economy.

## THE OUTPUT OF THE FIRM

What determines the output rate in the short run of a perfectly competitive firm? Since the firm is perfectly competitive, it cannot affect the price of its product, and it can sell any amount it wants at this price. Since we are concerned with the short run, the firm can expand or contract its output rate by increasing or decreasing its utilization of its variable, but not its fixed, inputs. The situation in the long run will be reserved for a later section.

### What Is the Profit at Each Output Rate?

To see how a firm determines its output rate, suppose that your aunt dies and leaves you her business, the Allegro Piano Company. Once you take over the business, your first problem is to decide how many pianos (each of which has a price of $1,000) the firm should produce per week. Having a good deal of economic intuition, you instruct your accountants to estimate the company's *total revenue* (defined as price times output) and total costs (as well as fixed and variable costs) at various output levels. They estimate the firm's total revenue at various output rates and its total cost function (as well as its total fixed cost function and total variable cost function), with the results shown in Table 24.2. Subtracting the total cost at a given output rate from the total revenue at this output rate, you ob-

**Table 24.2**
**Costs and Revenues, Allegro Piano Company**

| OUTPUT PER WEEK (PIANOS) | PRICE | TOTAL REVENUE (PRICE X OUTPUT) | TOTAL FIXED COST (DOLLARS) | TOTAL VARIABLE COST | TOTAL COST | TOTAL PROFIT |
|---|---|---|---|---|---|---|
| 0 | 1,000 | 0 | 1,000 | 0 | 1,000 | −1,000 |
| 1 | 1,000 | 1,000 | 1,000 | 200 | 1,200 | − 200 |
| 2 | 1,000 | 2,000 | 1,000 | 300 | 1,300 | 700 |
| 3 | 1,000 | 3,000 | 1,000 | 500 | 1,500 | 1,500 |
| 4 | 1,000 | 4,000 | 1,000 | 1,000 | 2,000 | 2,000 |
| 5 | 1,000 | 5,000 | 1,000 | 2,000 | 3,000 | 2,000 |
| 6 | 1,000 | 6,000 | 1,000 | 3,200 | 4,200 | 1,800 |
| 7 | 1,000 | 7,000 | 1,000 | 4,500 | 5,500 | 1,500 |
| 8 | 1,000 | 8,000 | 1,000 | 7,200 | 8,200 | − 200 |

tain the total profit at each output rate, which is shown in the last column of Table 24.2.

## Finding the Maximum-Profit Output Rate

As the output rate increases from 0 to 4 pianos per week, the total profit *rises*. As the output rate increases from 5 to 8 pianos per week, the total profit *falls*. Thus the *maximum* profit is achieved at an output rate between 4 and 5 pianos per week.[1] (Without more detailed data, one cannot tell precisely where the maximum occurs, but this is close enough for present purposes.) Since the maximum profit is obtained at an output of between 4 and 5 pianos per week, this is the output rate you choose.

Figure 24.1 gives a somewhat more vivid picture of the firm's situation by plotting the relationship between total revenue and total cost, on the one hand, and output on the other. At each output rate, the vertical distance between the total revenue curve and the total cost curve is the amount of profit the firm earns. Below an output rate of about 1 piano per week and above a rate of about 8 pianos per week, the total revenue curve lies *below* the total cost curve, indicating that profits are negative—that is, there are losses. Both Table 24.2 and Figure 24.1 show that the output rate that will maximize the firm's profits is between 4 and 5 pianos per week. At this output rate, the firm will make a profit of over $2,000 per week, which is more than it can make at any other output rate.

There is an alternative way to analyze the firm's situation. Rather than

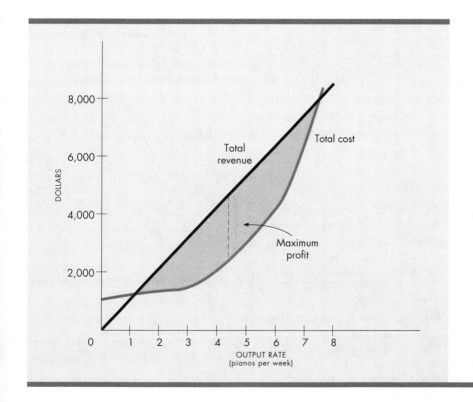

**Figure 24.1**
**Costs, Revenues, and Profits, Allegro Piano Company**
Profit equals the vertical distance between the total revenue curve and the total cost curve. This distance is maximized when the output rate is between 4 and 5 pianos per week. At this output rate, profit (measured by the vertical distance) is somewhat more than $2,000.

---

[1] This assumes that the output rate can be varied continuously and that there is a single maximum. These are innocuous assumptions.

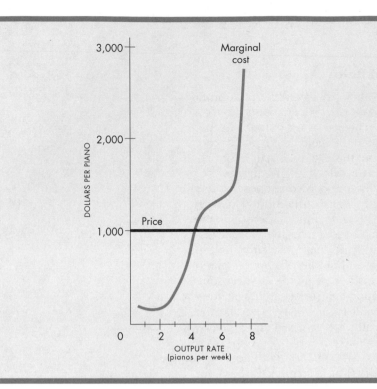

**Figure 24.2**
**Marginal Cost and Price, Allegro Piano Company**
At the profit-maximizing output rate of between 4 and 5 pianos per week, marginal cost (which is $1,000 when the output rate is between 4 and 5) equals price ($1,000). Recall from Figure 23.8 that marginal cost is plotted at the mid-point of the range of output to which it pertains.

looking at total revenue and total cost, let's look at price and marginal cost. Table 24.3 and Figure 24.2 show the product price and marginal cost of each output rate. It turns out that the maximum profit is achieved at the output rate where price equals marginal cost. In other words, both Table 24.3 and Figure 24.2 indicate that price equals marginal cost at the profit-maximizing output rate of between 4 and 5 pianos per week. This raises a question. Will price usually equal marginal cost at the profit-maximizing output rate, or is this merely a coincidence?

## The Golden Rule of Output Determination

Readers familiar with television scripts and detective stories will have recognized that the question just posed can only be answered in one way without ruining the plot. The equality of marginal cost and price at the profit-maximizing output rate is no mere coincidence. It will usually be true if the firm takes the price of its product as given. Indeed, the Golden Rule of Output Determination for a perfectly competitive firm is: *Choose the output rate at which marginal cost is equal to price.*

To determine the profit-maximizing output rate of a firm, compare the extra revenue with the extra cost of each additional unit of output. If the extra revenue (which equals price in the case of perfect competition) is greater than the extra cost (which equals marginal cost), the extra unit should be produced; otherwise, it should not be produced. For example, let's reconsider the Allegro Piano Company. Should this firm produce the first piano? Yes, because (according to Table 24.3) the extra revenue ($1,000) exceeds the extra cost ($200). Should it produce a second piano? Yes, because the extra revenue ($1,000) exceeds the extra cost ($100).

**Table 24.3**
**Marginal Cost and Price, Allegro Piano Company**

| OUTPUT PER WEEK (PIANOS) | MARGINAL COST (DOLLARS) | PRICE |
|---|---|---|
| 0 | | 1,000 |
| 1 | 200 | 1,000 |
| 2 | 100 | 1,000 |
| 3 | 200 | 1,000 |
| 4 | 500 | 1,000 |
| 5 | 1,000 | 1,000 |
| 6 | 1,200 | 1,000 |
| 7 | 1,300 | 1,000 |
| 8 | 2,700 | 1,000 |

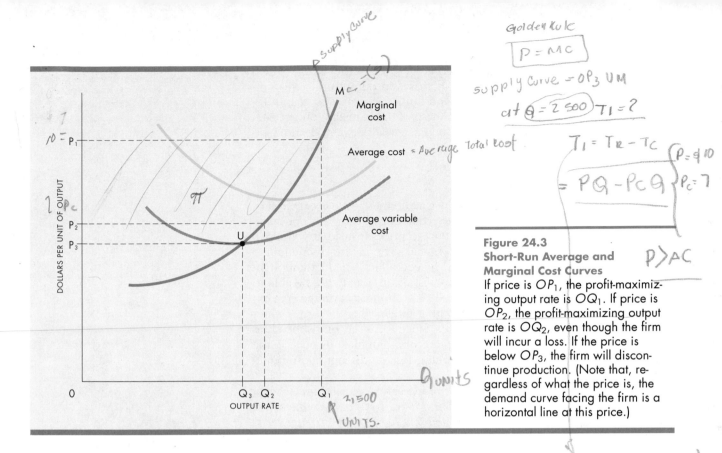

**Handwritten annotations (in figure margins):**

P Supply Curve

$10 = P_1$

P_c

$2$

P_2

P_3

DOLLARS PER UNIT OF OUTPUT

π

U

MC = (?)

Marginal cost

Average cost = Average Total cost

Average variable cost

0   Q_3  Q_2        Q_1   2,500

OUTPUT RATE    units

Q units

↑ UNITS.

Golden Rule
$$P = MC$$

supply Curve = OP_3 UM

at $Q = 2500$   $T_1 = ?$

$T_1 = T_R - T_C$   $\begin{cases} P = \$10 \\ P_c = 7 \end{cases}$

$= PQ - P_c Q$

$P > AC$

**Figure 24.3**
**Short-Run Average and Marginal Cost Curves**
If price is $OP_1$, the profit-maximizing output rate is $OQ_1$. If price is $OP_2$, the profit-maximizing output rate is $OQ_2$, even though the firm will incur a loss. If the price is below $OP_3$, the firm will discontinue production. (Note that, regardless of what the price is, the demand curve facing the firm is a horizontal line at this price.)

$= 10 (2,500) - 7(2,500)$

$= 25,000 - 17,500$

$= \$7,500$

$P < AC \rightarrow -T_1$

at $Q = 2,000$ Units $\begin{cases} P_s = 5 \\ P_c = 7 \end{cases}$

$\pi = T_R - T_C$

$= P_s Q - P_c Q$

$= 5(2,000) - 7(2000)$

$= 10,000 - 14,000$

$= \$4,000$   Loss

---

Should it produce a sixth piano? No, because the extra revenue ($1,000) is less than the extra cost ($1,200).

To prove that a perfectly competitive firm will maximize profit by producing the output where price equals marginal cost, consider Figure 24.3, which shows a typical short-run marginal cost function. Suppose that the price is $OP_1$. At any output rate less than $OQ_1$, price is greater than marginal cost.[2] This means that increases in output will increase the firm's profits since they will add more to total revenues than to total costs. Why? Because, as we have seen, an extra unit of output adds an amount equal to price to total revenue and an amount equal to marginal cost to total cost. Thus, since price exceeds marginal cost, an extra unit of output adds more to total revenue than to total cost.

At any output rate above $OQ_1$, price is less than marginal cost. This means that decreases in output will increase the firm's profits since they will subtract more from total costs than from total revenue. This happens because one less unit of output subtracts an amount equal to price from total revenue and an amount equal to marginal cost from total cost. Thus, since price is less than marginal cost, one less unit of output subtracts more from total cost than from total revenue. (Such a case occurs when the Allegro Piano Company is producing 7 pianos per week. As shown in Table 24.3, the extra cost of producing the seventh piano is $1,300, while the extra revenue it brings in is $1,000. So it pays the Allegro Piano Company to produce less than 7 pianos per week.)

Since increases in output will increase profits if output is less than $OQ_1$, and decreases in output will increase profits if output is greater than $OQ_1$,

---

[2] Except perhaps for an irrelevant range where marginal cost decreases with increases in output.

it follows that profits must be maximized at $OQ_1$, the output rate at which price equals marginal cost. After all, if increases in output up to this output ($OQ_1$) result in increases in profit and further increases in output result in decreases in profit, $OQ_1$ must be the profit-maximizing output rate. For the Allegro Piano Company, this output rate is between 4 and 5 pianos per week, as we saw above.

### Does It Pay to Be a Dropout?

All rules—even the Golden Rule we just mentioned—have exceptions. Under some circumstances, the perfectly competitive firm will not maximize its profits if it sets marginal cost equal to price. Instead, it will maximize profits only if it becomes an economic dropout by discontinuing production. Let's demonstrate that this is indeed a fact. The first important point is that even if the firm is doing the best it can, it may not be able to earn a profit. If the price is $OP_2$ in Figure 24.3, short-run average cost exceeds the price, $OP_2$, at all possible output rates. Thus the firm cannot earn a profit whatever output it produces. Since the short run is too short for the firm to alter the scale of its plant, it cannot liquidate its plant in the short run. Its only choice is to produce at a loss or discontinue production.

Under what conditions will the firm produce at a loss, and under what conditions will it discontinue production? *If there is an output rate where price exceeds average variable cost, it will pay the firm to produce, even though price does not cover average total cost. If there is no such output rate, the firm is better off to produce nothing at all*. This is true because even if the firm produces nothing, it must pay its fixed cost. Thus, if the loss resulting from production is less than the firm's fixed cost, the firm is better off producing than not producing. On the other hand, if the loss resulting from production is greater than the firm's fixed cost, the firm is better off not to produce.

In other words, *the firm will find it advantageous to produce if total losses are less than total fixed cost*. Since

$$\text{total losses} = \text{total cost} - \text{total revenue},$$

this will be the case if

$$\text{total cost} - \text{total revenue} < \text{total fixed cost}.$$

If we subtract total fixed cost from both sides of this inequality, and if we add total revenue to both sides, we find that the firm is better off to produce if

$$\text{total cost} - \text{total fixed cost} < \text{total revenue}.$$

Dividing each side of this inequality by output (and recognizing that total revenue = price × output), we find that the firm is better off to produce if

$$\text{average variable cost} < \text{price},$$

since average variable cost equals average total cost minus average fixed cost.

Once again, we have proved what we set out to prove—that the firm will maximize profits by producing *nothing* if there is no output rate at which price exceeds average variable cost. If such an output rate does exist, the Golden Rule applies: The firm will set its output rate at the point where marginal cost equals price.

## Dropping Out: Illustrative Cases

To illustrate the conditions under which it pays a firm to drop out, suppose that the cost functions of the Allegro Piano Company are as shown in Table 24.4. In this case, there exists no output rate such that average variable cost is less than price—which, you will recall, is $1,000 per piano. Thus, according to the results of the last paragraphs, the Allegro Piano Company should discontinue production under these conditions. The wisdom of this course of action is shown by the last column of Table 24.4, which demonstrates that the profit-maximizing—or, what amounts to the same thing, the loss-minimizing—output rate is zero.

Sometimes, as in the present case, the best thing to produce is nothing. The situation is analogous to the common experience of leaving a movie after the first ten minutes indicate that it is not going to be a good one, even though the admission price is not refundable. One ignores the fixed costs (the admission price) and, finding that the variable cost (the pleasure gained from activities that would be forgone by seeing the rest of the show) is going to exceed the benefits of staying, one leaves.

### Table 24.4
### Costs and Revenues, Allegro Piano Company

| OUTPUT PER WEEK (PIANOS) | PRICE | TOTAL REVENUE | TOTAL FIXED COST | TOTAL VARIABLE COST (DOLLARS) | AVERAGE VARIABLE COST | TOTAL COST | TOTAL PROFIT |
|---|---|---|---|---|---|---|---|
| 0 | 1,000 | 0 | 1,000 | 0 | — | 1,000 | −1,000 |
| 1 | 1,000 | 1,000 | 1,000 | 1,200 | 1,200 | 2,200 | −1,200 |
| 2 | 1,000 | 2,000 | 1,000 | 2,600 | 1,300 | 3,600 | −1,600 |
| 3 | 1,000 | 3,000 | 1,000 | 4,200 | 1,400 | 5,200 | −2,200 |
| 4 | 1,000 | 4,000 | 1,000 | 6,000 | 1,500 | 7,000 | −3,000 |
| 5 | 1,000 | 5,000 | 1,000 | 8,000 | 1,600 | 9,000 | −4,000 |
| 6 | 1,000 | 6,000 | 1,000 | 10,200 | 1,700 | 11,200 | −5,200 |
| 7 | 1,000 | 7,000 | 1,000 | 12,600 | 1,800 | 13,600 | −6,600 |
| 8 | 1,000 | 8,000 | 1,000 | 15,200 | 1,900 | 16,200 | −8,200 |

Several years ago, some sour cherry producers left cherries on their trees unpicked for essentially this reason. A warm spring created a bumper crop so big that the prices dropped sharply. For some producers, average variable costs exceeded price at all possible output levels. The consequence, as our theory would predict, was that producers began to close down. For example, in western New York, some cherry growers considered "bulldozing their orchards and going out of business," in the words of a Williamson, New York, farmer.

## THE MARKET SUPPLY CURVE

In Chapter 3, we described some of the factors underlying a commodity's market supply curve, but we could not go into much detail. Now we can, because our Golden Rule of Output Determination underlies the market supply curve. As a first step, let's derive the *firm's supply curve*, which shows how much the firm will want to produce at each price.

## The Firm's Supply Curve

Since the firm takes the price of its product as given (and can sell all it wants at that price), we know from the previous sections that the firm will choose the output level at which price equals marginal cost. Or if the price is below the firm's average variable cost curve at every output level, the firm will produce nothing. These results are all we need to determine the firm's supply curve.

Suppose that the firm's short-run cost curves are as shown in Figure 24.3. The marginal cost curve must intersect the average variable cost curve at the latter's minimum point, $U$. If the price of the product is less than $OP_3$, the firm will produce nothing, because there is no output level where price exceeds average variable cost. If the price of the product exceeds $OP_3$, the firm will set its output rate at the point where price equals marginal cost. Thus, if the price is $OP_1$, the firm will produce $OQ_1$; if the price is $OP_2$, the firm will produce $OQ_2$; and so forth. Consequently, *the firm's supply curve is exactly the same as the firm's marginal cost curve for prices above the minimum value of average variable cost ($OP_3$).* For prices at or below the minimum value of average variable cost, the firm's supply curve corresponds to the price axis, the desire to supply at these prices being uniformly zero. Thus the firm's supply curve is $OP_3UM$.

## DERIVING THE MARKET SUPPLY CURVE

Our next step is to derive the market supply curve from the supply curves of the individual firms. If one assumption holds, the **market supply curve** *can be regarded as the horizontal summation of the supply curves of all the firms producing the product.* If there were 3 firms in the industry and their supply curves were as shown in Figure 24.4, the market supply curve would be the horizontal summation of their 3 supply curves. Thus,

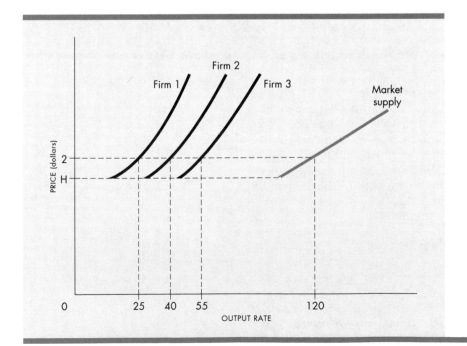

**Figure 24.4**
**Horizontal Summation of Short-Run Supply Curves of Firms**
If each of the three firms' supply curves is as shown here (and if each firm supplies nothing if the price is below $OH$), the market supply curve is the horizontal summation of the firms' supply curves, assuming that input prices are not influenced by the output of the industry. If the price is $2, firm 1 will supply 25 units, firm 2 will supply 40 units, and firm 3 will supply 55 units; thus, the total amount supplied is 120 units.

# EXAMPLE 24.1    HOW MUCH MERCURY DO WE HAVE?

According to the U.S. Bureau of Mines, the quantity of mercury reserves in the United States at selected price levels of mercury is as follows:

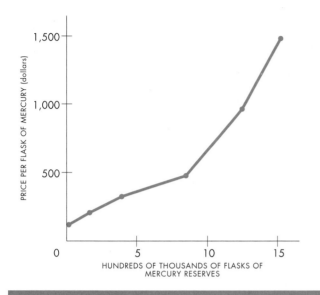

(a) Is this the supply curve for mercury? Why, or why not? (b) Does this curve show how much mercury will be supplied per period of time? (c) Why is the quantity of reserves sensitive to price? (d) Does it appear that, as price increases, beyond some point increasing price begins to lose its power to elicit substantially larger supplies? Is this reasonable? Why, or why not?

## Solution

(a) No. This curve shows how much mercury will be available (not produced) at various prices. (b) No. (c) Because, at higher mercury prices, it becomes profitable to obtain mercury from relatively high-cost sources; whereas at lower mercury prices this is not the case. (d) Yes. This is reasonable because beyond some point it becomes increasingly expensive to find and obtain an extra flask of mercury.

---

since these 3 supply curves show that firm 1 would supply 25 units of output at a price of $2 per unit, that firm 2 would supply 40 units at this price, and that firm 3 would supply 55 units at this price, the market supply curve shows that 120 units of output will be supplied if the price is $2 per unit. Why? Because the market supply curve shows the *total* amount of the product that all of the firms together would supply at this price—and 25 + 40 + 55 = 120. If there were only 3 firms, the market would not be perfectly competitive, but we can ignore this inconsistency. Figure 24.4 is designed to illustrate the fact that the market supply curve is the horizontal summation of the firm supply curves, at least under one important assumption.

The assumption underlying this construction of the short-run market supply curve is that *increases or decreases in output by all firms simultaneously do not affect input prices*. This is a convenient simplification, but it is not always true. Although changes in the output of one firm alone often cannot affect input prices, the simultaneous expansion or contraction of output by all firms may well alter input prices, so that the individual firm's cost curves—and supply curve—will shift. For instance, an expansion of the whole industry may bid up the price of certain inputs, with the result that the cost curves of the individual firms will be pushed upward. In the aerospace industry, a sudden expansion of the industry might well increase the price of certain inputs like the services of aerospace scientists and engineers.

If, contrary to the assumption underlying Figure 24.4, input prices *are* increased by the expansion of the industry, one can still derive the short-run market supply curve by seeing how much the industry will supply in the short run at each price of the product. But it is incorrect to assume that the market supply curve is the horizontal summation of the firm supply curves. More will be said in the chapter Appendix about the effects of industry output on input prices.

### Determinants of the Location and Shape of the Market Supply Curve

Based on the preceding discussion, we now can identify the basic determinants of the location and shape of a commodity's short-run market supply curve. If increases or decreases in output by all firms do not affect input prices, the short-run market supply curve is the horizontal summation of the firm supply curves. Thus its location and shape are derived from the location and shapes of the marginal cost curves of the firms in the industry, since these marginal cost curves determine the firm supply curves. From previous chapters, we know that the location and shape of each marginal cost curve depend on *the size of the firm's plants, the level of input prices, and the state of technology* in particular. Thus these factors play a major role in determining the location and shape of the market supply curve. Also, its location and shape in the short run are determined by the *number of firms* in the industry. The market supply curve in Figure 24.4 would be located farther to the right if there were more firms in the industry. In addition, its location and shape are determined by *the effect of industry output on input prices.*

*The short-run market supply curve generally slopes upward and to the right because marginal cost curves (in the relevant range) generally slope upward to the right.* If industry output does not affect input prices, the market supply curve is the horizontal sum of the firms' marginal cost curves (in the range where they are rising). Consequently, since each of the marginal cost curves slopes upward and to the right (in this range), this is also true of their horizontal sum, the short-run market supply curve.

## TEST YOURSELF

1. Suppose that the total costs of a perfectly competitive firm are as follows:

| OUTPUT RATE | TOTAL COST (DOLLARS) |
|---|---|
| 0 | 40 |
| 1 | 60 |
| 2 | 90 |
| 3 | 130 |
| 4 | 180 |
| 5 | 240 |

If the price of the product is $50, what output rate should the firm choose?

2. Suppose that the firm in Question 1 experienced an increase of $30 in its fixed costs. Plot its new total cost function. What effect will this increase in its fixed costs have on the output it will choose?

3. After the increase in fixed costs described in Question 2, what does the firm's marginal cost curve look like? Plot it on a graph. Does it differ from what it was before the increase in fixed costs? Why, or why not?

4. After the increase in fixed costs described in Question 2, what output rate would the firm choose if the price of its product were $40? $50? $60? $70?

# THE PRICE ELASTICITY OF SUPPLY

Market supply curves vary in their shape. For some commodities, the quantity supplied is very sensitive to changes in the commodity's price. For others, the quantity supplied is not at all sensitive to changes in price. To measure the sensitivity of quantity supplied to changes in price, economists use the **price elasticity of supply,** *which is defined as the percentage change in quantity supplied resulting from a 1 percent change in price.* Suppose that a 1 percent reduction in the price of slingshots results in a 1.5 percent reduction in the quantity supplied. Then the price elasticity of supply for slingshots (in the neighborhood of the existing price) is 1.5. The price elasticity of supply is likely to vary from one point to another on the market supply curve. Thus the price elasticity of supply for slingshots may be higher when the price of a slingshot is $2 than when it is $1.

The same factors that influence the location and shape of the market supply curve also determine the price elasticity of supply. But to these factors previously mentioned—the number of plants, input prices, and the nature of technology, among others—another important factor should be added—the length of the time period to which the supply curve pertains. *Market supply curves, like market demand curves, tend to be more price elastic if the time period is long rather than short.* Consider the market for watermelons. If we are dealing with a very short period—a few hours or a day—the supply of watermelons may be fixed, as shown in Figure 24.5. That is, the market supply curve may be perfectly inelastic, the price elasticity of supply being zero, because the period is too short to grow any more watermelons or transport any more watermelons into the market.

Suppose now that we lengthen the period of time to a year or so. In this period, farmers can alter the size of their watermelon crop in response to variations in price. Thus the price elasticity of supply will be higher than in the very short period of a few hours or a day. In this longer period, the price elasticity of supply has been estimated to be about .30; and the supply curve may be as shown in Figure 24.5.

Finally, suppose that we lengthen the period further—to 10 years. In this period, farmers will take land out of watermelon production or put

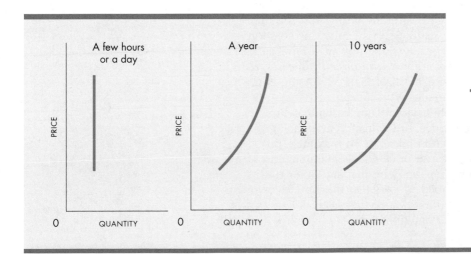

**Figure 24.5**
**Market Supply Curves for Watermelons, Periods of Varying Length**
The left-hand panel shows the market supply curve in a period of a few hours or a day. The middle panel refers to a year or so. The right-hand panel refers to 10 years.

land into watermelon production. Indeed, they can make all reasonable adjustments to changes in price. So the price elasticity of supply will be higher than in a period of a year or so—and much higher than in a period of a few hours or a day. The supply curve may be as shown in Figure 24.5.

## PRICE AND OUTPUT: THE MARKET PERIOD

How much of a particular product will be produced if the market is perfectly competitive, and what will the price be? The answers depend on the length of the time period. To begin with, let's consider the relatively short period of time when the supply of the relevant good is *fixed*. This period of time is called the **market period.** In the market period, as in the short and long runs, the price of a good in a perfectly competitive market is determined by the market demand and market supply curves. However, in the market period, the market supply curve is a vertical line, as shown in Figure 24.6.

Thus, in the market period, output is unaffected by price. In Figure 24.6, output is *OQ*—and regardless of price, it cannot be changed. The equilibrium price depends on the position of the demand curve. Price is *OP₁* if the demand curve is *A*, and *OP₂* if the demand curve is *B*.

*The role of the price as a rationing device is particularly obvious in the market period, where this is the major function of price.* Consumers who are willing to pay a relatively high price get some of the product; others do without. The allocation of jam in the prisoner-of-war camp and the allocation of tickets to *A Chorus Line*, both taken up in Chapter 3, are among the examples you have encountered earlier of how price rations output in the market period. These cases can be regarded as taking place in the market period because the supply is fixed in each case.

## PRICE AND OUTPUT: THE SHORT RUN

Let's turn now to the short run, the period during which each firm's plant and equipment are fixed. What determines the price and output of a good in a perfectly competitive market in the short run? The answer once again is the market demand and market supply curves. However, the position and shape of these curves will generally be different in the short run than in the market period. In particular, the market supply curve in the short run will not be a vertical line; it will generally slope upward to the right, as in panel B of Figure 24.7. Thus, *in the short run, price influences, as well as rations, the amount supplied.* In panel B of Figure 24.7, the equilibrium price and output in the short run are *OP* and *OQ*.

Panel A of Figure 24.7 shows the behavior of an individual firm in short-run equilibrium. Since *OP* is the price, the demand curve facing the firm is a horizontal line at *OP*, as shown in panel A. To maximize profit, the firm produces an output of *Oq*, because price equals marginal cost at this output. In short-run equilibrium, firms may be making either profits or losses. In the particular case described in panel A, the firm earns a profit equal to the shaded area shown there. Since the profit per unit of output equals *CP*, total profit equals *CP* multiplied by *Oq*, which is this shaded area.

Taken together, the two panels in Figure 24.7 bring out the following

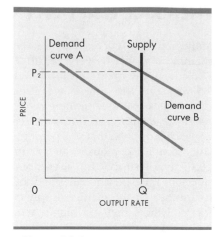

**Figure 24.6**
**Price Determination in the Market Period**
In the market period, supply is fixed at *OQ*. Equilibrium price is *OP₁* if the demand curve is demand curve *A*, and *OP₂* if the demand curve is demand curve *B*.

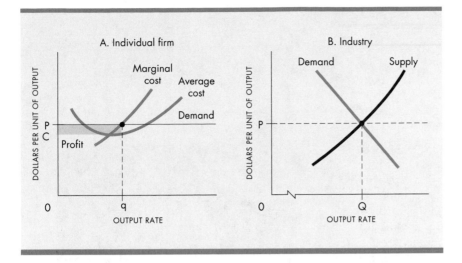

**Figure 24.7**
**Short-Run Competitive Equilibrium**
In the short run, equilibrium price is *OP*, and the equilibrium output of the industry is *OQ*, since (as shown in panel B) the industry demand and supply curves intersect at this price and output. The demand curve facing the individual firm is a horizontal line at *OP* (as shown in panel A). Each firm produces *Oq* units of the product, since this is the output that maximizes its profits. The output of the industry (*OQ*) is the sum of the outputs (*Oq*) of the individual firms. In short-run equilibrium, firms may be making either profits or losses. In this particular case, the individual firm earns a profit equal to the shaded area in panel A. (Why? Because the profit *per unit of output* equals the price [*OP*] minus average cost [*OC*], or the vertical distance *CP*. To obtain the firm's *total profit*, this distance must be multiplied by the firm's output [*Oq*], the result being the shaded area.) If firms were making losses rather than profits, the demand curve confronting each firm would intersect the marginal cost curve at a point below (rather than above) the average cost curve.

important point. To the *individual* firm, the price of the product is taken as given. If the price is *OP*, the firm in panel A reacts to this price by setting an output rate of *Oq* units. It cannot alter the price; it can only react to it. But *as a group* the reactions of the firms are a major determinant of the price of the product. The supply curve in panel B shows the total amount that the entire group of firms will supply at each price. It summarizes the reactions of the firms to various levels of the price. Put briefly, the equilibrium price is viewed by the individual firm as being beyond its control; yet the supply decisions of all firms taken as a group are a basic determinant of the equilibrium price.

## PRICE AND OUTPUT: THE LONG RUN

In the long run, what determines the output and price of a good in a perfectly competitive market? In the long run, a firm can change its plant size, which means that established firms may *leave* an industry if it has below-average profits, or that new firms may *enter* an industry with above-average profits. Suppose that textile firms can earn up to (but no more than) a 15 percent rate of return by investing their resources in other industries. If they can earn only 12 percent by keeping these resources invested in the textile industry, they will leave the textile industry. On the other hand, if a rate of return of 18 percent can be earned by investing in the textile industry, firms in other industries, attracted by this relatively high return, will enter the textile industry.

### Equilibrium: Zero Economic Profit

Equilibrium is achieved in the long run when enough firms—no more, no less—are in the industry so that **economic profits**—*defined as the excess of a firm's profits over what it could make in other industries*—are *zero*. This condition is necessary for long-run equilibrium because, as we have seen, new firms will enter the industry if there are economic profits, and existing firms will leave if there are economic losses. This process of entry and exit is the key to long-run equilibrium. It is discussed repeatedly in this and subsequent sections.

In the past decade or two, economists have begun to use laboratory experiments to understand better how markets work. In an experimental market, the subjects (often college students) trade a commodity (e.g., a scrap of paper) that has no intrinsic value. Buyers make a profit by purchasing the commodity from sellers and reselling it to the experimenter. For example, the rules of the experiment may state that the experimenter will redeem the first unit of the commodity for $2.00, the second unit for $1.50, the third unit for $1.00, and so on. Sellers make a profit by buying units from the experimenter and selling them to the buyers. For example, the experimenter may provide the seller with the first unit of the commodity for $0.25, the second unit for $0.75, the third unit for $1.00, and so on.

The way in which the market is organized varies from experiment to experiment. Frequently, they are organized as double auctions, which are characterized by public bids to buy units of the commodity and public offers to sell units of it. Any participant is free to accept whatever terms he or she wants. Typically, bids are made verbally. An auctioneer, when hearing a bid or offer, writes it on the blackboard. The last bid and offer remain standing until accepted, cancelled, or replaced.

Based on the work of Caltech's Charles Plott, Arizona's Vernon Smith, and other leaders in this new field, auctions of this type tend to converge to the competitive equilibrium even with relatively few traders. In other words, if one constructs a market demand curve (based on the amount of the commodity that each buyer will purchase at a given price in order to maximize profit) and a market supply curve (based on the amount of the commodity that each seller will sell at a given price in order to maximize profit), the actual price in the experiment gen-

Charles Plott

erally moves toward the level at which the market demand curve intersects the market supply curve.

This, of course, is an interesting test of the basic model considered in this chapter, which seems to come through with flying colors. Laboratory experiments have also been carried out to test and extend the models of monopoly, monopolistic competition, and oligopoly discussed in succeeding chapters. Without question, such experiments have been and will be useful in a variety of ways. However, as the leading experimenters are quick to point out, one must be very careful in extrapolating behavior from a very simple laboratory setting to a complex industrial environment. The real world is, of course, a lot more complicated than these simple experiments.

Note that the existence of economic profits or losses in an industry brings about a shift in the industry's short-run supply curve. If there are economic profits, new firms will enter the industry, and so shift the short-run supply curve to the right. On the other hand, if there are economic losses in the industry (i.e., if the industry's profits are less than could be obtained elsewhere), existing firms will leave the industry, causing the short-run supply curve to shift to the left. Only if economic profits are zero will the number of firms in the industry—and the industry's short-run supply curve—be stable. Putting this equilibrium condition another way, *the long-run equilibrium position of the firm is at the point where its long-run average costs (i.e., average total costs) equal price.* If price exceeds average total costs, economic profits are being earned; and if price is less than average total costs, economic losses are being incurred.

## Equilibrium: Maximum Economic Profit

Going a step further, *long-run equilibrium requires that price equal the lowest value of long-run average total costs.* In other words, firms must be producing at the *minimum point* on their long-run average cost curves, because to maximize their profits they must operate where price equals long-run marginal costs,[3] and at the same time they also have to operate where price equals long-run average cost. But if both these conditions are satisfied, long-run marginal cost must equal long-run average cost—since both equal price. And we know that long-run marginal cost equals long-run average cost only at the point at which long-run average cost is a minimum.[4] Consequently, if long-run marginal cost equals long-run average cost, the firm must be producing at the minimum point on the long-run average cost curve.

This equilibrium position is illustrated in Figure 24.8. When all adjust-

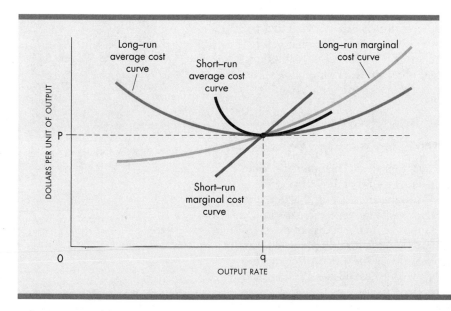

**Figure 24.8**
**Long-Run Equilibrium of a Perfectly Competitive Firm**
In long-run equilibrium, output is *Oq* and the firm's plant corresponds to the short-run average and marginal cost curves shown here. At *Oq*, long-run marginal cost equals short-run marginal cost equals price; also, long-run average cost equals short-run average cost equals price. These conditions ensure that the firm is maximizing profits and that economic profits are zero.

[3] The reasons why marginal cost must be equal to price, if profits are to be maximized, are given in earlier sections of this chapter.
[4] The previous discussion of this point on p. 485 concerned short-run cost functions, but the argument applies just as well to long-run cost functions.

ments are made, price equals *OP*. The equilibrium output of the firm is *Oq*, and its plant corresponds to the short-run average and marginal cost curves in Figure 24.8. At this output and with this plant, long-run marginal cost equals short-run marginal cost equals price. This ensures that the firm is maximizing profit. Also, long-run average cost equals short-run average cost equals price. This ensures that economic profits are zero. Since the long-run marginal cost and long-run average cost must be equal, the firm is producing at the minimum point on its long-run average cost curve.

To illustrate the process of entry and exit in an industry that has approximated perfect competition, let's consider the bituminous coal industry. Entry into this industry has been relatively easy, but exit has been relatively difficult, for at least two reasons. First, it is costly to shut down a mine and reopen it later. Second, because of corrosion and water damage, it is hard to shut down a mine for longer than two years unless it is to be abandoned entirely. For these reasons, mines tend to stay open and produce even though short-term losses are incurred. In the period before World War II, the demand for coal fell substantially, but while the industry suffered substantial losses, mines were slow to close down. Nonetheless, the competitive process had its way. Slowly, but surely, the number of mines fell markedly in response to these losses. Thus, despite the barriers to rapid exit, firms eventually left the industry, just as the model would predict.

## THE ALLOCATION OF RESOURCES UNDER PERFECT COMPETITION: A MORE DETAILED VIEW

At this point, it is instructive to describe the process by which a perfectly competitive economy—one composed of perfectly competitive industries—would allocate resources. In Chapters 2 and 3, we stressed that the allocation of resources among alternative uses is one of the major functions of any economic system. Equipped with the concepts of this and previous chapters, we can now go much further in describing how a perfectly competitive economy shifts resources in accord with changes in tastes, technology, and other factors.

### Consumers Turn from Corn to Wheat

To be specific, suppose that a change occurs in tastes. Consumers become more favorably disposed toward wheat and less favorably disposed toward corn than in the past.[5] In the short run, the increase in the demand for wheat increases the price of wheat, and results in some increase in the output of wheat. However, the output cannot be increased very substantially because the industry's capacity cannot be expanded in the short run. Similarly, the fall in the demand for corn reduces the price of corn, and results in some reduction in output. But the output will not be curtailed greatly because firms will continue to produce as long as they can cover variable costs.

---

[5] Since we assume here that the markets for wheat and corn are perfectly competitive, it is also assumed that there is no government intervention in these markets.

## Prices Signal Resource Reallocation

The change in the relative prices of wheat and corn tells producers that a reallocation of resources is called for. Because of the increase in the price of wheat and the decrease in the price of corn, wheat producers are earning economic profits and corn producers are showing economic losses. This will trigger a new deployment of resources. If some variable inputs in corn production can be used as effectively in the production of wheat, they may be switched from corn production to wheat production. Even if no variable inputs are used in both wheat and corn production, adjustments can be made in various interrelated markets, with the result that wheat production gains resources and corn production loses resources. When short-run equilibrium is attained in both the wheat and corn industries, the reallocation of resources is not yet complete since there has not been enough time for producers to build new capacity or liquidate old capacity. In particular, neither industry is operating at minimum average cost. The wheat producers are operating at greater than the output level where average cost is a minimum; and the corn producers are operating at less than this level.

## Effects in the Long Run

What will happen in the long run? The shift in consumer demand from corn to wheat will result in greater adjustments in production and smaller adjustments in price than in the short run. In the long run, existing firms can leave corn production and new firms can enter wheat production. Because of short-run economic losses in corn production, some corn land and related equipment will be allowed to run down, and some firms engaged in corn production will be liquidated. As firms leave corn production, the supply curve shifts to the left, causing the price to rise above its short-run level. The transfer of resources out of corn production will stop when the price has increased, and costs have decreased, to the point where losses are avoided.

While corn production is losing resources, wheat production is gaining them. The prospect of positive economic profits in wheat production will cause new firms to enter the industry. The increased demand for inputs will raise input prices and cost curves in wheat production, and the price of wheat will be depressed by the movement to the right of the supply curve because of the entry of new firms. Entry ceases when economic profits are no longer being earned. At this point, when long-run equilibrium is achieved, more resources will be used in the industry than were used in the short run. (Note that, if corn land and equipment can be converted to the production of wheat, some of the "entry" may occur through existing farmers' shifting of their crop mix toward wheat and away from corn.)

Finally, long-run equilibrium is established in both industries, and the reallocation of resources is complete. It is important to note that this reallocation can affect industries other than wheat and corn. If corn land and equipment can be easily adapted to the production of wheat, corn producers can simply change to wheat production. If not, the resources used in corn production are converted to some use other than wheat, and the resources that enter wheat production come from some use other than corn production.

# EXAMPLE 24.2    HOW MANY APPLES SHOULD BE PRODUCED?

Suppose that the demand and supply curves for apples are as shown below:

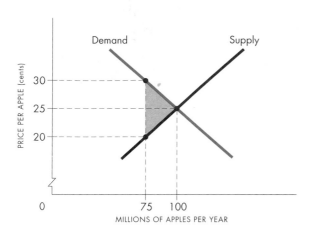

(a) If 75 million apples are produced per year, how much would an additional apple cost to produce? How much would an additional apple be worth to consumers? (b) Under these circumstances, is it socially worthwhile to increase apple production? Why, or why not? (c) If 100 million apples are produced per year, how much would an additional apple cost to produce? How much would an additional apple be worth to consumers? (d) If 100 million apples are produced, is it socially worthwhile to increase apple production? Explain. (e) How great is the loss to society if 75 million, rather than 100 million, apples are produced?

## Solution

(a) 20 cents, since the supply curve shows marginal cost. 30 cents, because the demand curve shows the maximum amount consumers would pay for an extra apple. (b) Yes, because the extra social cost of producing an extra apple is less than the extra social ben-

efit from doing so. Consumers would be glad to pay producers to produce extra apples. (c) 25 cents. 25 cents. (d) No, since the extra social cost of producing an extra apple is no less than the maximum amount that consumers would pay for an extra apple. If private benefits and costs do not differ from social benefits and costs, 100 million apples is the optimal output level. It would not be socially worthwhile to exceed or fall short of it. (e) The vertical distance from the demand curve to the supply curve is the difference between the social benefit and the social cost of an *extra* apple. (For example, if 75 million apples are produced, the social benefit of an extra apple exceeds its social cost by 30 − 20 = 10 cents.) Thus the difference between the social benefit and social cost of the *extra 25 million apples* equals the sum of these vertical distances for all of the extra apples. This sum equals the shaded area in the above diagram, which amounts to 25 million × 5 cents = $1.25 million. This is the loss to society.

# BITUMINOUS COAL: A CASE STUDY

To illustrate how resources are allocated in the long run, we will look in more detail at the bituminous coal industry. Although it does not have all the characteristics of a perfectly competitive industry, it has had enough of them so that the perfectly competitive model has predicted many aspects of its behavior reasonably well. From the turn of the century until about 1923, the bituminous coal industry expanded rapidly. Between 1903 and 1923, the price of coal increased from $1.24 to $2.68 per ton, in considerable part because of the marked upward shift to the right of the demand curve for coal, an important fuel in this period of general industrial growth. In addition, the high prices of the period were sometimes the result of temporary shortages caused by strikes and insufficient railroad transportation. Thus temporary upward shifts to the left of the supply curve for coal, as well as shifts of the demand curve, were responsible for the increases in price.

Given the very high coal prices of 1917–23, coal mining was very profitable. Indeed, after-tax income in 1920 was about 20 percent of invested capital for all bituminous coal companies—and much higher for particular companies. These high profits signaled that more resources should be invested in the industry. And just as the perfectly competitive model would predict, more resources were invested; the number of bituminous coal firms increased by over 130 percent in nine key states between 1903 and 1923, and the industry's capacity grew by over 50 percent between 1913 and 1923.

Unfortunately, the demand for coal dropped considerably from 1923 to 1933, plunging the industry into a severe economic crisis. The downward shift to the left of the demand curve for coal during the early 1930s was due in considerable part to the fall in national output during the Great Depression. It was accompanied by a marked decrease in the price of coal. From $2.68 in 1923, the price per ton fell to $1.34 in 1933. Needless to say, this tremendous drop meant losses for bituminous coal producers. Indeed, in every year between 1925 and 1940, the bituminous coal industry as a whole showed losses.

These economic losses signaled that resources should be withdrawn from the bituminous coal industry and used elsewhere in the economy where they could be more valuably employed. And as the perfectly competitive model would predict, resources were in fact taken out of bituminous coal. Between 1923 and 1933, there was a reduction of over 40 percent in the number of coal companies operating in nine key states. And the industry's capacity fell by almost 40 percent between 1923 and 1933. Despite the difficulties in exit that we described in a previous section, the competitive process had its way. Its signals were heeded. Consequently, the industry began to move closer and closer to a position of long-run equilibrium, and although the industry remained on the nation's sick list, it began to show much smaller losses. By the onset of World War II, many of the basic adjustments had occurred.

In the postwar period, many important changes have taken place in the bituminous coal industry. Strip mining has become much more important relative to underground mining. The federal government has passed new legislation setting stricter safety requirements for coal. The energy crisis of the 1970s focused new attention on our great coal resources. But from the point of view of the present chapter, perhaps the most interesting development is the increased dominance of the industry by relatively few large firms—and the fact that many big coal companies have been purchased by the major oil firms. About half of the country's 10 biggest coal companies were bought up during the 1960s. Some observers worry that the bituminous coal industry, which tended to be relatively competitive in the past, may be less so in the future.

# TEST YOURSELF

1. If the price elasticity of supply for corn is about 0.1 in the short run, as estimated by Marc Nerlove of the University of Pennsylvania, a 1 percent increase in the price of corn would have approximately what impact on the quantity supplied?

2. In Example 24.2, suppose that 125 million apples are produced per year. Under these circumstances, is it socially desirable to reduce apple production? Explain.

3. Suppose that the demand curve for onions is $P = 10 - 3Q$, where $P$ is the price of a pound of onions and $Q$ is the quantity demanded (in millions of pounds). If the supply of onions in the market period is $3\frac{1}{6}$ million pounds, what is the equilibrium price of onions in the market period? What does the supply curve for onions look like in the market period?

4. In the short run, suppose that the demand curve for onions is as given in Question 3, and that the supply curve is $P = Q/3$. What is the equilibrium price of onions in the short run? What does the supply curve of onions look like in the short run?

# SUMMARY

1. Economists generally classify markets into four types—perfect competition, monopoly, monopolistic competition, and oligopoly. Perfect competition requires that the product of any seller be the same as the product of any other seller, that no buyer or seller be able to influence the price of the product, and that resources be able to switch readily from one use to another.

2. If it maximizes profit, a perfectly competitive firm should set its output rate in the short run at the level where marginal cost equals price, so long as price exceeds average variable cost. If there is no output rate at which price exceeds average variable cost, the firm should discontinue production.

3. The firm's supply curve coincides with its marginal cost curve for prices exceeding the minimum value of average variable cost. For prices that are less than or equal to the minimum value of average variable cost, the firm's supply curve coincides with the price axis.

4. As a first approximation, the market supply curve can be viewed as the horizontal summation of the supply curves of all the firms producing the product. This assumes that increases or decreases in output by all firms simultaneously do not affect input prices.

5. The market supply curve of a product is determined by the size of the firms' plants, the level of input prices, the nature of technology, and the other factors determining the shape of the firms' marginal cost curves, as well as by the effect of changes in the industry output on input prices and by the number of firms producing the product.

6. The sensitivity of the quantity supplied to changes in price is measured by the price elasticity of supply, defined as the percentage change in quantity supplied resulting from a 1 percent change in price. In general, the price elasticity of supply is greater if the time interval is long rather than short.

7. Price and output under perfect competition are determined by the intersection of the market supply and demand curves. In the market period, supply is fixed; thus price plays the role of the allocating device. In the short run, price influences as well as rations the amount supplied.

8. In the long run, equilibrium is achieved under perfect competition when enough firms—no more, no less—are in the industry so that economic profits are eliminated. In other words, the long-run equilibrium position of the firm is at the point where its long-run average cost equals price. But since price must also equal marginal cost (to maximize profit), it follows that the firm must be operating at the minimum point on the long-run average cost curve.

9. In a perfectly competitive economy, prices are the signals that are used to guide the reallocation of resources in response to changes in consumer tastes, technology, and other factors.

# CONCEPTS FOR REVIEW

**Perfect competition**
**Monopoly**
**Monopolistic competition**
**\*Constant cost industry**

**Oligopoly**
**Firm's supply curve**
**Market supply curve**
**\*Increasing cost industry**

**Price elasticity of supply**
**Market period**
**Economic profits**
**\*Decreasing cost industry**

\* This concept is presented in the Appendix to this chapter.

# APPENDIX: CONSTANT, INCREASING, AND DECREASING COST INDUSTRIES

Perfectly competitive industries can be categorized into three types—constant cost industries, increasing cost industries, and decreasing cost industries.

## Constant Cost Industries

*In a **constant cost industry** an expansion of output does not result in a change in input prices.* Figure 24.9 shows the long-run equilibrium in a constant cost industry. Panel A shows the short- and long-run cost curves of a typical firm in the industry. Panel B shows the demand and supply curves for the industry as a whole. It is assumed that the industry is in long-run equilibrium, with the result that the price line is tangent to the long-run (and short-run) average cost curve at its minimum point. The price is *OP*.

Let's assume that the demand curve shifts upward and to the right, as shown in panel B. In the short run, with the number of firms fixed, the

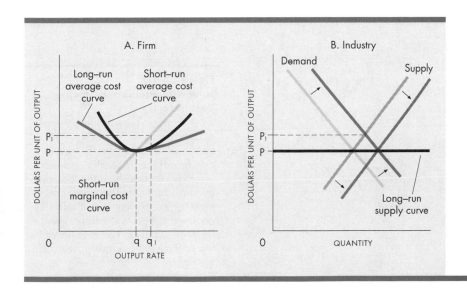

**Figure 24.9**
**Long-Run Equilibrium: Constant Cost Industry**
If the demand curve shifts upward and to the right, the price will increase in the short run from *OP* to *OP₁*. Each firm will expand output from *Oq* to *Oq₁*, and entry will occur, thus shifting the supply curve downward and to the right. The long-run supply curve in a constant cost industry is horizontal.

price of the product will rise from $OP$ to $OP_1$; each firm will expand output from $Oq$ to $Oq_1$; and each firm will be making economic profits since $OP_1$ exceeds the short-run average costs of the firm at $Oq_1$. The consequence is that firms will enter the industry and shift the short-run supply curve to the right. In a constant cost industry, the entrance of the new firms does not affect the costs of the existing firms. The inputs used by this industry are used by many other industries as well, and the appearance of the new firms in this industry does not bid up the price of inputs (and consequently raise the costs of existing firms). In the long run, the price settles back to $OP$, the level of (minimum) long-run average cost. Thus *a constant cost industry has a horizontal long-run supply curve.* Since output can be varied by varying the number of firms producing $Oq$ units at an average cost of $OP$, the long-run supply curve is horizontal at $OP$.

## Increasing Cost Industries

Most economists seem to regard increasing, not constant, cost industries as the most prevalent of the three types. *An **increasing cost industry** is one where the price of inputs increases with the amount the industry uses.* The situation in such an industry is shown in Figure 24.10. The original conditions are the same as those in Figure 24.9, and we suppose again that the demand curve shifts upward and to the right, with the result that the price of the product increases and firms earn economic profits, thus attracting new entrants. More and more inputs are required by the industry, and in an increasing cost industry the price of inputs increases with the amount the industry uses. Consequently, the cost of inputs increases for the established firms as well as the new entrants. The long-run average cost curve of each firm is pushed up, as shown in panel A. The short-run supply curve shifts downward and to the right, as shown in panel B. Thus the new equilibrium price is $OP_2$ and each firm produces $Oq_2$ units. *An increasing cost industry has a positively sloped long-run supply curve,* as shown in Figure 24.10. That is, after long-run equilibrium is achieved, increases in output require increases in the price of the product.

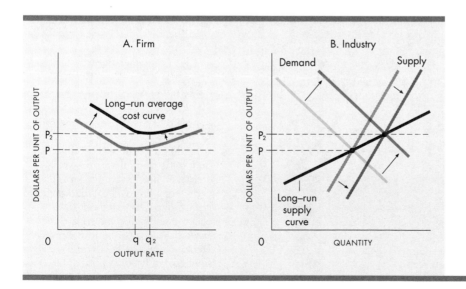

**Figure 24.10
Long-Run Equilibrium: Increasing Cost Industry**
If the demand curve shifts upward and to the right, the price will increase in the short run. Entry will occur, and the price of inputs will increase, thus pushing the long-run average cost curve upward. The short-run supply curve will shift downward and to the right. The long-run supply curve in an increasing cost industry slopes upward to the right.

## Decreasing Cost Industry

Decreasing cost industries are the most unusual situation, although quite young industries may sometimes fall into this category. *In a **decreasing cost industry,** the expansion of the industry results in a decrease in the costs of the established firms.*[6] Thus *a decreasing cost industry has a negatively sloped long-run supply curve.* That is, after long-run equilibrium is reached, increases in output are accompanied by decreases in price.

Whether an industry is a constant cost industry, an increasing cost industry, or a decreasing cost industry is an empirical question that must be settled case by case. In trying to determine whether a particular industry is an increasing or constant cost industry, one important consideration is whether or not it is a relatively large user of certain inputs. Because the automobile industry uses a great deal of the nation's steel, an expansion of the automobile industry might well cause an increase in the price of steel; but an expansion of the paper-clip industry, which uses very little of the nation's steel, would be unlikely to raise the price of steel.

---

[6] Certain *external economies,* which are cost reductions that occur when an industry expands, may be responsible for the existence of decreasing cost industries. An example of such an external economy is an improvement in transportation that is due to the expansion of an industry and that reduces the costs of each firm in the industry.

# MONOPOLY AND ITS REGULATION

AT THE OPPOSITE EXTREME from perfect competition is monopoly. Under a monopolistic market structure, what sorts of behavior can we expect? How much of the product will be produced, and at what level will its price be set? What are the social disadvantages of monopoly? In what ways have government commissions attempted to regulate industries whose market structures approximate monopoly? These are some of the major questions dealt with in this chapter.

To begin with, recall what is meant by **monopoly:** *a market where there exists one, and only one, seller.* Monopoly, like perfect competition, seldom corresponds more than approximately to conditions in real industries, but it is a very useful model. In several respects, monopoly and perfect competition stand as polar opposites. The firm in a perfectly competitive market has so many rivals that competition becomes entirely impersonal. The firm is a price taker, an inconspicuous seller in a sea of inconspicuous sellers. Under monopoly, on the other hand, the firm has no direct competitors at all; it is the sole supplier.

However, even the monopolist is affected by certain indirect and potential forms of competition. Suppose a firm managed to obtain a monopoly on wheat production. It would have to worry about competition from corn and other agricultural commodities that could be substituted for wheat. Moreover, the wheat monopolist would also have to take into account the possibility that new firms might arise to challenge its monopoly if it attempted to extract conspicuously high profits. Thus even the monopolist is subject to some restraint imposed by competitive forces.

## CAUSES OF MONOPOLY

There are many reasons why monopolies, or market structures that closely approximate monopoly, may arise.

PATENTS.    A firm may acquire a monopoly over the production of a good by having patents on the product or on certain basic processes used in its production. The patent laws of the United States give an inventor the exclusive right to make a certain product or to use a certain process for 17 years. The purpose of the patent system is to encourage invention and innovation and to discourage industrial secrecy. Many firms with monopoly power achieved it in considerable part through patents. For example, the United Shoe Machinery Company became the sole supplier of certain important kinds of shoemaking equipment through control of basic patents. United Shoe was free to dominate the market until 1954, when, after prosecution under the antitrust laws, the firm was ordered to license its patents. And in 1968, when this remedy seemed insufficient, a divestiture program was agreed upon.

**CONTROL OF INPUT.** A firm may become a monopolist by obtaining control over the entire supply of a basic input required to manufacture a product. The International Nickel Company of Canada controls about nine-tenths of the proven nickel reserves in the world. Since it is hard to produce nickel without nickel, the International Nickel Company obviously has a strong monopoly position. Similarly, the Aluminum Company of America (Alcoa) kept its dominant position for a long time by controlling practically all the sources of bauxite, the ore used to make aluminum. However, as we shall see in Chapter 27, Alcoa's monopoly was broken in 1945 when the Supreme Court decided that Alcoa's control of practically all the industry's output violated the antitrust laws.

**GOVERNMENT ACTION.** A firm may become a monopolist because it is awarded a market franchise by a government agency. The government may give a particular firm the franchise to sell a particular product in a public facility. Or it may give a particular company the right to provide a service, such as telephone service, to people in a particular area. In exchange for this right, the firm agrees to allow the government to regulate certain aspects of its operation. The form of regulation does not matter here; the important point for now is that the monopoly is created by the government.

**DECLINING COST OF PRODUCTION.** A firm may become a monopolist because the average costs of producing the product reach a minimum at an output rate that is large enough to satisfy the entire market (at a price that is profitable). In a case like this, a firm obviously has an incentive to expand until it produces all the market wants of the good. (Its costs fall as it continues to expand.) Thus competition cannot be maintained in this case. If there are a number of firms in the industry, the result is likely to be economic warfare—and the survival of a single victor, the monopolist.[1]

Cases where costs behave like this are called ***natural monopolies.*** When an industry is a natural monopoly, the public often insists that its behavior be regulated by the government. For example, electric power is an industry where there seem to be great economies of scale—and thus decreasing average costs. Fuel consumed per kilowatt hour is lower in larger power generating units, and there are economies in combining generating units at a single site. Because of these factors, there has been little attempt to force competition in the industry, since it would be wasteful. Instead, as we describe later, the market for electric power in a particular area tends to be a regulated monopoly.[2]

The likelihood that the long-run average cost curve will decrease up to a point that satisfies the entire market depends on the size of the market. The smaller the market, the more likely it is. In Figure 25.1, the industry is a natural monopoly if the demand curve is *A,* but not if it is *B.* In a large

---

[1] Note that economies of scale are different from the external economies discussed in note 6 of the previous chapter. The individual firm has no control over external economies.

[2] However, it is worth noting that technological developments in this industry may permit more competition in the future.

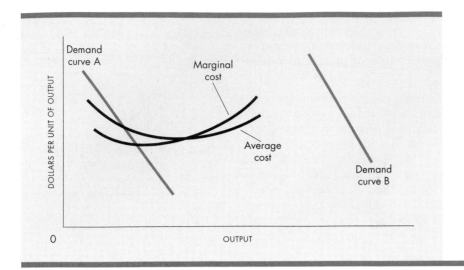

**Figure 25.1**
**Natural Monopoly**
The industry is a natural monopoly if the demand curve is *A*, but not if it is *B*.

market like the United States, it is much less likely that an industry will be a natural monopoly than in a small market like Belgium or Denmark. One of the advantages claimed for the reduction in trade barriers among West European countries in 1992 was that it would create a larger market that could support more efficient production and more competitive industries. For now, the important point to recognize is that, just as stagnant marshes are the breeding ground for mosquitos, so small, insulated markets are the breeding ground for monopoly.

## DEMAND CURVE AND MARGINAL REVENUE UNDER MONOPOLY

Before we can make any statements about the behavior of a monopolistic market, we must point out certain important characteristics of the demand curve facing the monopolist. Since the monopolist is the only seller of the commodity, the demand curve it faces is the market demand curve for the product. Since the market demand curve is almost always downward-sloping to the right, the monopolist's demand curve must also be downward-sloping to the right. This is quite different from perfect competition, where the firm's demand curve is horizontal. To illustrate the situation faced by a monopolist, consider the hypothetical case in Table 25.1. The price at which each quantity (shown in column 1) can be sold by the monopolist is shown in column 2. The firm's **total revenue**—its total dollar sales volume—is shown in column 3. Obviously, column 3 is the product of the first two columns. Column 4 contains the firm's **marginal revenue,** *defined as the addition to total revenue attributable to the addition of one unit to sales.* (Thus, if *R(q)* is total revenue when *q* units are sold and *R(q – 1)* is total revenue when *(q – 1)* units are sold, the marginal revenue between *q* units and *(q – 1)* units is *R(q) – R(q – 1)*.)

Marginal revenue is very important to the monopolist. We can estimate it from the figures in the first three columns of Table 25.1. The marginal revenue between 1 and 2 units of output per day is $180 – $100, or $80; the marginal revenue between 2 and 3 units of output per day is $240 – $180, or $60; the marginal revenue between 3 and 4 units of output per

**Table 25.1**
**Demand and Revenue of a Monopolist**

| QUANTITY | PRICE | TOTAL REVENUE (DOLLARS) | MARGINAL REVENUE |
|---|---|---|---|
| 1 | 100 | 100 | 80 |
| 2 | 90 | 180 | 60 |
| 3 | 80 | 240 | 40 |
| 4 | 70 | 280 | 20 |
| 5 | 60 | 300 | 0 |
| 6 | 50 | 300 | –20 |
| 7 | 40 | 280 | –40 |
| 8 | 30 | 240 | |

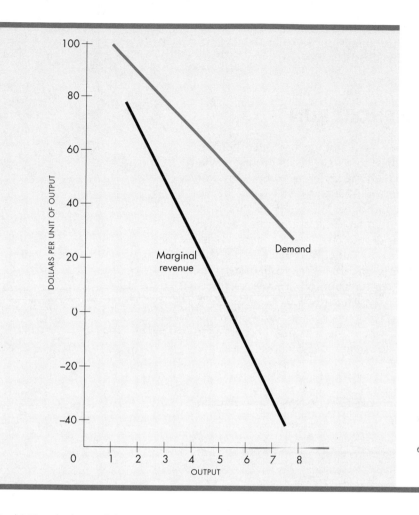

**Figure 25.2**
**Marginal Revenue and**
**Demand Curves**

The demand curve comes from Table 25.1. Each value of marginal revenue is plotted at the midpoint of the range of output to which it pertains. Since the demand curve is downward-sloping, marginal revenue is always less than price, for reasons discussed in the text. Note that the value of marginal revenue is related to the price elasticity of demand. At outputs where demand is price elastic, marginal revenue is *positive*; at outputs where it is price inelastic, marginal revenue is *negative*, and at outputs where it is of unitary elasticity, marginal revenue is zero.

day is $280 − $240, or $40; and so on. The results are shown in column 4 of the table (and are plotted in Figure 25.2). Note that marginal revenue is analogous to marginal cost (and marginal utility and marginal product, for that matter). Recall that marginal cost is the extra cost resulting from an extra unit of production. Substitute "revenue" for "cost" and "sales" for "production" in the previous sentence, and what do you get? A perfectly acceptable definition of marginal revenue.

*Marginal revenue will always be less than price if the firm's demand curve is downward-sloping* (as it is under monopoly and other market structures that are not perfectly competitive). In Table 25.1, the extra revenue from the second unit of output is $80 whereas the price of this unit is $90. *The basic reason is that the firm must reduce the price of all units of output, not just the extra unit, in order to sell the extra unit.* Thus, in Table 25.1, the extra revenue from the second unit of output is $80 because, while the price of the second unit is $90, the price of the first unit must be reduced by $10 in order to sell the second unit. Thus the extra revenue (that is, marginal revenue) from selling the second unit of output is $90 − $10, or $80, which is less than the price of the second unit.

Similarly, the marginal revenue from selling the third unit of output ($60, according to Table 25.1) is less than the price at which the third unit can be sold ($80, according to Table 25.1). Why? Because, to sell the third unit of output, the price of the first two units of output must be reduced by $10 each (that is, from $90 to $80). Thus the extra revenue (that is, marginal revenue) from selling the third unit is not $80, but $80 less the $20 reduction in the amount received for the first two units.

## PRICE AND OUTPUT: THE SHORT RUN

We are now in a position to determine how output and price behave under monopoly. If the monopolist is free to maximize its profits, it will choose the price and output rate at which the difference between total revenue and total cost is greatest. Suppose that the firm's costs are as shown in Table 25.2 and that the demand curve it faces is as shown in Table 25.1. Based on the data in these two tables, the firm can calculate the profit that it will make at each output rate. To do so, it subtracts its total cost from its total revenue, as shown in Table 25.3. What output rate will maximize the firm's profit? According to Table 25.3, profit *rises* as its output rate increases from 1 to 3 units per day, and profit *falls* as its output rate increases from 4 to 8 units per day. Thus the *maximum* profit is achieved at an output rate between 3 and 4 units per day.[3] (Without more detailed data, one cannot tell precisely where the maximum occurs, but this is close enough for present purposes.) Figure 25.3 shows the same thing graphically.

**Table 25.2**
**Costs of a Monopolist**

| QUANTITY | TOTAL VARIABLE COST | TOTAL FIXED COST (DOLLARS) | TOTAL COST | MARGINAL COST |
|---|---|---|---|---|
| 0 | 0 | 100 | 100 | |
| 1 | 40 | 100 | 140 | 40 |
| 2 | 70 | 100 | 170 | 30 |
| 3 | 110 | 100 | 210 | 40 |
| 4 | 150 | 100 | 250 | 40 |
| 5 | 200 | 100 | 300 | 50 |
| 6 | 260 | 100 | 360 | 60 |
| 7 | 350 | 100 | 450 | 90 |
| 8 | 450 | 100 | 550 | 100 |

What price will the monopolist charge? To maximize its profit, it must charge the price that results in its selling the profit-maximizing output, which in this case is between 3 and 4 units per day. Thus, according to Table 25.1, it must charge between $70 and $80 per unit. Why? Because if it charges $70, it will sell 4 units per day; and if it charges $80, it will sell 3 units per day. Consequently, to sell the profit-maximizing output of between 3 and 4 units per day, it must charge a price of between $70 and $80 per unit.

[3] This assumes that the output rate can vary continuously and that there is a single maximum. These are innocuous assumptions.

**Table 25.3**
**Profits of a Monopolist**

| QUANTITY | TOTAL REVENUE | TOTAL COST | TOTAL PROFIT |
|---|---|---|---|
| | | (DOLLARS) | |
| 1 | 100 | 140 | −40 |
| 2 | 180 | 170 | 10 |
| 3 | 240 | 210 | 30 |
| 4 | 280 | 250 | 30 |
| 5 | 300 | 300 | 0 |
| 6 | 300 | 360 | −60 |
| 7 | 280 | 450 | −170 |
| 8 | 240 | 550 | −310 |

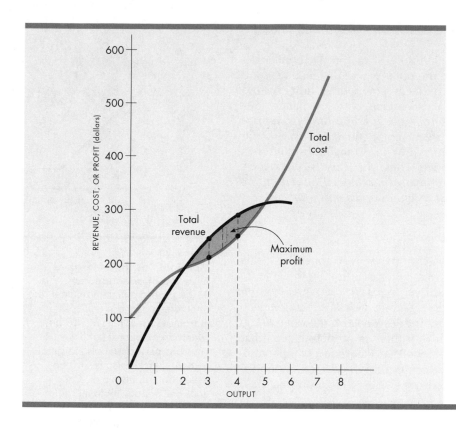

**Figure 25.3**
**Total Revenue, Cost, and Profit of a Monopolist**
The output rate that will maximize the firm's profit is between 3 and 4 units per day. At this output rate, profit (which equals the vertical distance between the total revenue and total cost curves) is over $30 per day. Based on the demand curve for its product (shown in Table 25.1), the firm must set a price of between $70 and $80 to sell between 3 and 4 units per day.

## The Golden Rule of Output Determination

In Chapter 24, we set forth the Golden Rule of Output Determination for a perfectly competitive firm. We can now formulate a Golden Rule of Output Determination for a monopolist: *set the output rate at the point where marginal revenue equals marginal cost.* Table 25.4 and Figure 25.4 show that this rule results in a maximum profit in this example. It is evident from Table 25.4 that marginal revenue equals marginal cost at the profit-maximizing output of between 3 and 4 units per day. Figure 25.4 shows the same thing graphically.

Why is this rule generally a necessary condition for profit maximization? At any output rate at which marginal revenue *exceeds* marginal cost, profit can be increased by *increasing* output, since the extra revenue will exceed the extra cost. At any output rate at which marginal revenue is *less than* marginal cost, profit can be increased by *reducing* output, since the decrease in cost will exceed the decrease in revenue. Thus, since profit will *not* be a maximum when marginal revenue exceeds marginal cost or falls short of marginal cost, *it must be a maximum only when marginal revenue equals marginal cost.*

## The Monopolist's Equilibrium Position

Figure 25.5 shows the equilibrium position of a monopolist in the short run. Short-run equilibrium will occur at the output, *OQ*, where the marginal cost curve intersects the marginal revenue curve (the curve that shows the firm's marginal revenue at each output level). And if the monopolist is to sell *OQ* units per period of time, the demand curve shows

**Table 25.4**
**Marginal Cost and Marginal Revenue of a Monopolist**

| QUANTITY | TOTAL PROFIT | MARGINAL COST | MARGINAL REVENUE |
|---|---|---|---|
| | | (DOLLARS) | |
| 1 | −40 | | |
| | | 30 | 80 |
| 2 | 10 | | |
| | | 40 | 60 |
| 3 | 30 | | |
| | | 40 | 40 |
| 4 | 30 | | |
| | | 50 | 20 |
| 5 | 0 | | |
| | | 60 | 0 |
| 6 | −60 | | |
| | | 90 | −20 |
| 7 | −170 | | |
| | | 100 | −40 |
| 8 | −310 | | |

that it must set a price of *OP*. Thus the equilibrium output and price are *OQ* and *OP*, respectively.

It is interesting to compare the Golden Rule of Output Determination for a monopolist (set the output rate at the point where marginal revenue equals marginal cost) with that for a perfectly competitive firm (set the output rate at the point where price equals marginal cost). The latter is really the same as the former because, *for a perfectly competitive firm, price equals marginal revenue.* Since the perfectly competitive firm can sell all it wants at the market price, each additional unit sold increases the firm's total revenue by the amount of the price. Thus, *for both the monopolist and the perfectly competitive firm, profits are maximized by setting the output rate at the point where marginal revenue equals marginal cost.*

## When Will a Monopolist Shut Down?

From the previous chapter, we know that perfectly competitive firms sometimes find it preferable to shut down rather than follow this rule. Is this true for monopolists as well? The answer is yes. *Just as perfectly competitive firms will discontinue production if they will lose more money by producing than by shutting down, so monopolists will do the same thing, and for the same reasons.* In other words, if there is no output such that price exceeds average variable cost, monopolists, like perfect competitors, will discontinue production. This makes sense. If by producing, monopolists incur greater losses than their fixed costs, they will "drop out," i.e., produce nothing.

## Two Misconceptions

Finally, note two misconceptions concerning monopoly behavior. First, it is sometimes said that monopolists will charge "as high a price as they can get." This is nonsense. The monopolist in Table 25.1 could charge a higher price than $70 to $80, but to do so would be foolish since it would

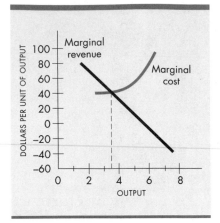

**Figure 25.4**
**Marginal Cost and Marginal Revenue of a Monopolist**
At the profit-maximizing output rate of between 3 and 4 units per day, marginal cost (which is $40 between an output rate of 3 and 4 units per period) equals marginal revenue (which also is $40 between an output rate of 3 and 4 units per period). Both marginal cost and marginal revenue are plotted at the midpoints of the ranges of output to which they pertain. (See Figures 23.8 and 25.2.)

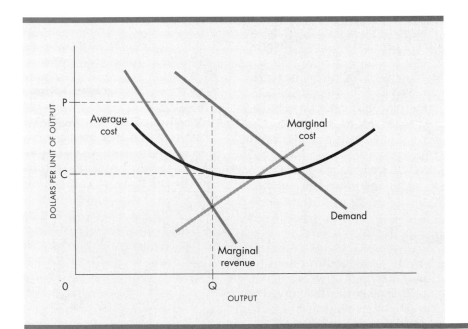

**Figure 25.5**
**Equilibrium Position of a Monopolist**
The monopolist sets its output rate at *OQ*, where the marginal revenue curve intersects the marginal cost curve. At this output, price must be *OP*. And profit per unit of output equals *CP*, since average cost equals *OC*.

result in lower profits. Second, it is sometimes said that monopolists will seek to maximize their profit per unit of output. This too is nonsense, since monopolists are interested in their total profits and their return on capital, not on the profit per unit of output. Rational monopolists will not sacrifice their total profits to increase their profit per unit of output.

## PRICE AND OUTPUT: THE LONG RUN

*In contrast to the situation under perfect competition, the long-run equilibrium of a monopolistic industry may not be marked by the absence of economic profits.* If a monopolist earns a short-run economic profit, it will not be confronted in the long run with competitors, unless the industry ceases to be a monopoly. The entrance of additional firms into the industry is incompatible with the existence of monopoly. Thus the long-run equilibrium of an industry under monopoly may be characterized by economic profits.

On the other hand, if the monopolist incurs a short-run economic loss, it will be forced to look for other, more profitable uses for its resources. One possibility is that the firm's existing plant is not optimal and that it can earn economic profits by appropriate alterations to its scale and characteristics. If so, the firm will make these alterations in the long run and remain in the industry. However, *if there is no scale of plant that will enable the firm to avoid economic losses, it will leave the industry in the long run.* The mere fact of having a monopoly over the production of a certain commodity does not mean that the firm must be profitable. A monopoly over the production of cut-glass spittoons would be unlikely to catapult a firm into financial glory—or even allow it to avoid losses.

## PERFECT COMPETITION AND MONOPOLY: A COMPARISON

At the beginning of the previous chapter, we said that a market's structure would be likely to affect the behavior of the market; in other words, a market's structure would influence how much was produced and the price that would be set. If we could perform an experiment in which an industry was first operated under conditions of perfect competition and then under conditions of monopoly (assuming that the demand for the industry's product and the industry's cost functions would be the same in either case),[4] we would find that the equilibrium price and output would differ under the two sets of conditions.

### Higher Price and Less Output under Monopoly

Specifically, if the product demand curve and the industry's cost functions are the same, *the output of a perfectly competitive industry tends to be greater and the price tends to be lower than under monopoly.* We see this in Figure 25.6, which shows the industry's demand and supply curves, if it is perfectly competitive. Since price and output under perfect competition are given by the intersection of the demand and supply curves, $OQ_C$ is

[4] However, the cost and demand curves need not be the same. For example, the monopolist may spend money on advertising, thus shifting the demand curve. It should be recognized that the assumption that they are the same is stronger than it appears at first glance.

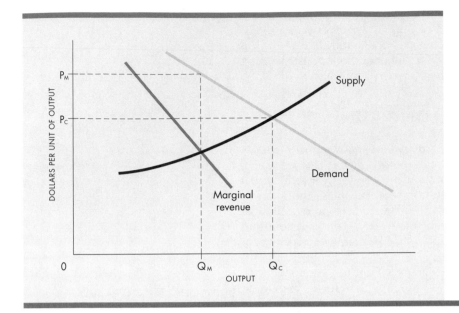

**Figure 25.6
Comparison of Long-Run
Equilibria: Perfect Competition
and Monopoly**
Under perfect competition, $OQ_C$ is
the industry output and $OP_C$ is the
price. Under monopoly, $OQ_M$ is
the industry output, $OP_M$ is the
price. Clearly, output is higher and
price is lower under perfect competition than under monopoly.

the industry output and $OP_C$ is the price. But what if all of the competitive firms are bought up by a single firm, which operates as a pure monopolist? Under these conditions, what formerly was the industry's supply curve is now the monopolist's marginal cost curve.[5] And what formerly was the industry's demand curve is now the monopolist's demand curve. Since the monopolist chooses the output where marginal cost equals marginal revenue, the industry output will be $OQ_M$ and the price will be $OP_M$. Clearly, $OQ_M$ is less than $OQ_C$, and $OP_M$ is greater than $OP_C$ — which is what we set out to prove.

Of course, all this is theory. But there is plenty of evidence that monopolists restrict output and charge higher prices than under competition. Take the case of tungsten carbide, which sold for $50 per pound until a monopoly was established in 1927 by General Electric. Then the price went to between $225 and $453 per pound, until the monopoly was broken by the antitrust laws in 1945. The price then dropped back to between $27 and $45 per pound.[6] This case was extreme, but by no means unique. For centuries people have observed that when monopolies are formed, output tends to be restricted, and price tends to be driven up.

## Monopoly and Resource Allocation

Moreover, it has long been felt that the allocation of resources under perfect competition is socially more desirable than under monopoly. Society

[5] The monopolist will operate the various plants that would be independent under perfect competition as branches of a single firm. The marginal cost curve of a multiplant monopoly is the horizontal sum of the marginal cost curves of the individual plants. (To see why, suppose that a monopoly has two plants, A and B. The total amount that the monopoly can produce at a particular marginal cost is the sum of (1) the amount plant A can produce at this marginal cost, and (2) the amount plant B can produce at this marginal cost.) From the previous chapter, we know that this is also the supply curve of the industry if the plants are operated as separate firms under perfect competition.
[6] W. Adams, *The Structure of American Industry*, 5th ed., New York: Macmillan, 1977, p. 485.

might be better off if more resources were devoted to producing the monopolized good in Figure 25.6, and if the competitive, not the monopolistic, output were produced. For example, in the *Wealth of Nations,* published about 200 years ago, Adam Smith stressed that when competitive forces are thwarted by "the great engine . . . of monopoly," the tendency for resources to be used "as nearly as possible in the proportion which is most agreeable to the interest of the whole society" is thwarted as well.

Why do many economists believe that the allocation of resources under perfect competition is more socially desirable than that under monopoly? This is not a simple question, and like most hard questions can be answered at various levels of sophistication. Put most simply, many economists believe that firms under perfect competition are induced to produce quantities of goods that are more in line with consumer desires, and that firms under perfect competition are induced to use the least costly methods of production. In the following section, we shall indicate in detail why they believe that these things are true. In Chapter 27 (and in Appendix D), we provide a much more complete discussion of the pros and cons of monopoly and competition.

# EXAMPLE 25.1    ANOTHER NEWSPAPER FOR HAVERHILL?

In Haverhill, Massachusetts, one newspaper had been published for over a century. Then, another newspaper was founded. In the Haverhill market, suppose that the market demand curve for the town's newspapers, and the demand curve facing each newspaper, were as shown below. Also, each newspaper's cost curves and marginal revenue curve are given below. (Note: In this special case, the firm's demand curve is the same as a monopolist's marginal revenue curve.)

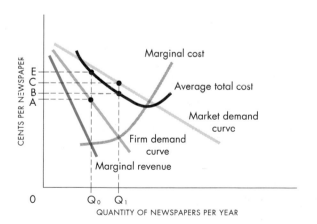

QUANTITY OF NEWSPAPERS PER YEAR

(a) If both firms stay in business, how much will each lose? (b) If only one of them stays in business,

can it make a profit? How big a profit? (c) Is this a case of natural monopoly? (d) If entry by one firm may drive the other out of business, is this illegal?

## Solution

(a) Each firm will produce $OQ_0$ newspapers, since this is the output where marginal revenue equals marginal cost. To sell this output, each sets a price of $OA$, since this is the price on the firm's demand curve corresponding to the sale of $OQ_0$ newspapers. At an output of $OQ_0$ newspapers, each firm's average total cost equals $OE$. Thus it loses $(OE - OA)$ cents per newspaper sold, and since it sells $OQ_0$ newspapers per year, its total annual loss is $OQ_0 \times (OE - OA)$ cents. (b) The monopolist will produce $OQ_1$ newspapers, since this is the output where its marginal revenue equals marginal cost. (Recall that in this case the firm's demand curve is the same as the monopolist's marginal revenue curve.) To sell this output, it must charge a price equal to $OC$ cents per newspaper. Since its average total cost is $OB$ cents per newspaper, it makes a profit of $(OC - OB)$ cents per newspaper sold, and its total annual profit is $OQ_1 \times (OC - OB)$ cents. (c) Yes. (d) This question was taken to court by these newspapers. The decision was that it was not illegal.

## TEST YOURSELF

1. If you were the president of a firm that has a monopoly on a certain product, would you choose an output level where demand for the product was price inelastic? Explain.

2. Suppose that a monopolist's demand curve is as follows:

| QUANTITY DEMANDED (PER YEAR) | PRICE (DOLLARS) |
| --- | --- |
| 8 | 1,000 |
| 7 | 2,000 |
| 6 | 3,000 |
| 5 | 4,000 |
| 4 | 5,000 |
| 3 | 6,000 |
| 2 | 7,000 |
| 1 | 8,000 |

Plot the firm's marginal revenue curve.

3. Suppose that the monopolist in Question 2 has fixed costs of $10,000 and an average variable cost of $4,000. The average variable cost is the same for outputs of 1 to 10 units per year. What output rate will the firm choose? What price will it set?

4. Plot the marginal cost curve of the firm in Question 3. Where does this curve intersect the marginal revenue curve you drew in Question 2?

5. Suppose that the firm in Question 3 experienced a 50 percent increase in both its fixed and average variable costs. If the demand curve in Question 2 remains valid, what effect will this cost increase have on the output rate and price that the firm will choose?

## THE CASE AGAINST MONOPOLY

Many people oppose monopolies on the grounds that they "gouge" the consumers by charging a higher price than would otherwise exist—a price that can be sustained only because monopolists artificially limit the supply. In other words, these people claim that monopolists reap higher profits than would be possible under perfect competition and that these profits are at the expense of consumers, who pay higher prices than under perfect competition. Is their claim accurate? As we have just seen, a monopolist will reap higher profits than under perfect competition and consumers will pay higher prices under monopoly than under perfect competition. But is this bad?

To the extent that the monopolist is rich and the consumers are poor, we are likely to answer yes. Also, to the extent that the monopolist is less deserving than the consumers, we are likely to answer the same thing. But suppose the monopolist is a selfless philanthropist who gives to the poor. Is monopoly still socially undesirable? The answer remains yes, because *monopoly imposes a burden on society by misallocating resources. In the presence of monopoly, the price system cannot be relied on to direct the allocation of resources to their most efficient use.*

### The Misallocation of Resources

To see more precisely how monopoly interferes with the proper functioning of the price system, suppose that all industries other than the shoe industry are perfectly competitive. The shoe industry, however, has been monopolized. How does this cause a misallocation of resources? Under fairly general circumstances, a good's price can be taken as a measure of the social value of an extra unit of the good. Thus, if the price of a pair of socks is $1, the value to the consumer of an extra pair of socks can be taken to be $1. Moreover, under fairly general circumstances, a good's marginal cost can be taken as a measure of the cost to society of an extra unit of the good. Thus, if the marginal cost of a pair of shoes is $30, the cost to society of producing an extra pair of shoes can be taken to be $30.

In perfectly competitive industries, price is set equal to marginal cost, as we saw in Chapter 24. Thus each of the competitive industries produces up to the point where the social value of an extra unit of the good (which equals price) is set equal to the cost to society of producing an extra unit of the good (which equals marginal cost). This is the amount each of these industries should produce—the output rate that will result in an optimal allocation of resources.

## Why Is the Competitive Output Optimal?

To see that this is the optimal output rate, consider what happens when an industry produces up to the point where the social value of an extra unit of the good is *more* than the cost to society of producing an extra unit. This isn't the socially optimal output rate because a one-unit increase in the output rate will increase the social value of output by more than the social cost of production, which means that it will increase social welfare. Thus, since a one-unit increase in the output rate will increase social welfare, the existing output rate cannot be optimal. (Recall Example 24.2.)

Next, consider what happens when an industry produces up to the point where the social value of an extra unit of the good is *less* than the cost to society of producing the extra unit. This isn't the socially optimal output rate because a one-unit decrease in the output rate will decrease the social value of output by less than the social cost of production, which means that it will increase social welfare. Thus, since a one-unit decrease in the output rate will increase social welfare, the existing output rate cannot be optimal.

Putting together the results of the previous two paragraphs, it follows that the socially optimal output rate must be at the point where the social value of an extra unit of the good *equals* the social cost of producing an extra unit of the good. Why? Because if the output rate is not optimal when the social value of an extra unit of the good exceeds or falls short of the cost to society of producing the extra unit, it must be optimal only when the two are equal.

## The Monopolist Produces Too Little

Now let's return to the shoe industry—the sole monopolist.[7] Is the shoe industry producing the optimal amount of shoes? The answer is no. Like any monopolist, it produces at the point where marginal revenue equals marginal cost. Thus, since marginal revenue is *less* than price (as was proved above), the monopolist produces at a point where price is *greater* than marginal cost. Consequently, *the monopolistic industry produces at a point where the social value of an extra unit of the good (which equals price) is greater than the cost to society of producing the extra unit (which equals marginal cost).* As we saw in a previous paragraph, this means that the monopolist's output rate is too small. A one-unit increase in the output of shoes will increase the social value of output by more than the

[7] Are puns really the lowest form of humor?

social cost of production. (The situation is similar to that in Example 24.2 when 75 million apples are produced.)

In summary, *monopoly results in a misallocation of resources since too little is produced of the monopolized good.* Here lies the economist's principal complaint against monopoly: it results in a misallocation of resources. Too little is produced of the monopolized good. Society is less well off—in terms of its own tastes and potentialities—than it could be. The price system, which would not lead to, or tolerate, such waste if all industries were perfectly competitive, is not allowed to perform as it should. (These inefficiencies caused by monopoly are described further and in more detail in Appendix D.)

### Income Distribution, Efficiency, and Technological Change

Misallocation of resources is only part of the economist's brief against monopoly. As we have already pointed out, *monopoly redistributes income in favor of the monopolists*. In other words, monopolists can fatten their own purse by restricting their output and raising their price. Admittedly, there is no scientific way to prove that monopolists are less deserving than the rest of the population, but it is also pretty difficult to see why they are more deserving.

In addition, *since monopolists do not have to face direct competition, they are likely to be less diligent in controlling costs and in using resources efficiently*. As Sir John Hicks put it, "The best of all monopoly profits is a quiet life." Certainly we all dream at times of being able to take life easy. It would be strange if monopolists, having succeeded in insulating themselves from direct competition, did not take advantage of the opportunity—not open to firms in perfectly competitive markets—to relax a bit and worry less about pinching pennies. For this reason, economists fear that, to use Adam Smith's pungent phrase, "Monopoly . . . is a great enemy to good management."

Further, *it is often claimed that monopolists are slow to innovate and adopt new techniques and products*. This lethargy stems from the monopolist's freedom from direct competition. Innovation tends to be disruptive, while old ways, like old shoes, tend to be comfortable. The monopolist may be inclined, therefore, to stick with "time-honored" practices. Without question, competition is an important spur to innovation and to the rapid diffusion of innovations. But there are well-known arguments on the other side as well. Some economists argue that substantial monopoly power promotes innovation and technological change. Much more will be said on this score in Chapter 27.

## PUBLIC REGULATION OF MONOPOLY

One way that society has attempted to reduce the harmful effects of monopoly is through **public regulation.** Suppose that the long-run cost curve in a particular industry is such that competition is not feasible. In such a case, society may permit a monopoly to be established. But a commission or some other public body is also established to regulate the monopoly's behavior. Among the many such regulatory commissions in the United States are the Federal Energy Regulatory Commission, the Federal Communications Commission, and the Interstate Commerce Commission. They regulate the behavior of firms with monopoly power in the

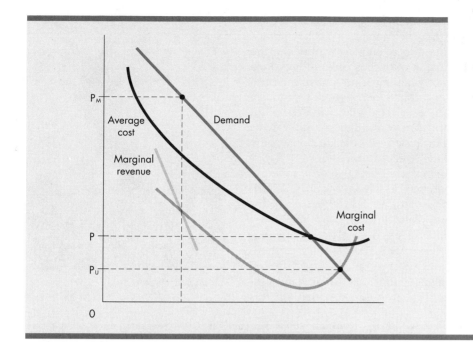

**Figure 25.7**
**Regulation of Monopoly**
The price established by a commission might be $OP$, where the demand curve intersects the average total cost curve. (Costs here include what the commission regards as a fair profit per unit of output.) In the absence of regulation, the monopolist would set a price of $OP_M$ (because it would set its output at the point where marginal revenue equals marginal cost). Since $OP$ is less than $OP_M$, regulation has reduced price in this instance, but not to the point where price equals marginal cost (as in perfect competition). For price to equal marginal cost, price would have to equal $OP_U$. (For a discussion of marginal-cost pricing, see the Appendix to this chapter.)

electric power, communication, transportation, and other industries. These industries are big as well as important, taking in about 10 percent of the national output. Thus we need to know how these commissions operate and make decisions on prices and other matters.

*Regulatory commissions often set the price — or the maximum price — at the level at which it equals average total cost, including a "fair" rate of return on the firm's investment.* In Figure 25.7, the price would be established by the commission at *OP*, where the demand curve intersects the average total cost curve (which includes what the commission regards as a fair profit per unit of output). Needless to say, there has been considerable controversy over what constitutes a fair rate of return. Frequently, commissions have settled on 8 to 10 percent. In addition, there has been a good deal of controversy over what should be included in the company's "investment" on which the fair rate of return is to be earned. A company's assets can be valued at **historical cost** or at **reproduction cost**—at what the company paid for them or at what it would cost to replace them. If the price level does not change much, these two approaches yield much the same answer. But if prices are rising—as they have been during most of the past 40 years—replacement cost will be greater than historical cost, with the result that the company will be allowed higher profits and rates if replacement cost is used. Most commissions now use historical cost.[8]

## DOES REGULATION AFFECT PRICES?

The regulatory commissions and the principles they use have become extremely controversial. *Many observers feel that the commissions are lax,*

---

[8] The use of marginal-cost pricing by regulated industries is discussed in the Appendix to this chapter.

and that they tend to be captured by the industries they are supposed to regulate. Regulated industries, recognizing the power of such commissions, invest considerable time and money in attempts to influence the commissions. The public, on the other hand, often has only a foggy idea of what the commissions are doing, and of whether or not it is in the public interest. According to some critics like Ralph Nader, "Nobody seriously challenges the fact that the regulatory agencies have made an accommodation with the businesses they are supposed to regulate—and they've done so at the expense of the public." For these and other reasons, some economists believe that regulation has little effect on prices.

It is difficult to isolate and measure the effects of regulation on the average level of prices. Some well-known economists have conducted studies which suggest that regulation has made little or no difference in this regard. Nobel laureate George Stigler and Claire Friedland of the University of Chicago compared the levels of rates charged for electricity by regulated and unregulated electric power companies. They found that there was no significant difference between the average rates charged by the two sets of firms. Other economists challenge Stigler's and Friedland's interpretation of their factual findings, and much more research on this

George J. Stigler

# EXAMPLE 25.2    PRICE DISCRIMINATION IN DENTISTRY

An isolated town of 5,000 inhabitants in the Rocky Mountains is looking for a dentist. To simplify matters, we divide the town's inhabitants into two categories: the rich and the poor. The demand curve for dental care among each type of inhabitant is shown below. Adding the two demand curves horizontally, we find that the total demand curve for dental care is *DAB*.

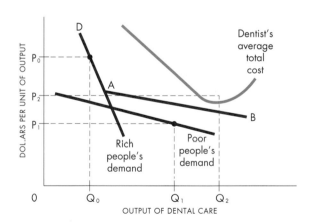

(a) If a dentist charges the same price to all inhabitants (rich or poor), can the dentist cover his or her average total costs? (b) If the dentist charges the rich a higher price than the poor, can the dentist cover his or her average total costs? (c) *Price discrimination* occurs when a producer sells the same commodity or service

at more than one price. Thus the dentist in (b) is engaging in price discrimination. In fact, do physicians and dentists engage in price discrimination? (d) In some instances, is it true that a good or service cannot be produced without price discrimination? (e) Is this always the case?

## Solution

(a) No. The total demand curve lies below the average total cost curve. Thus, regardless of what output the dentist chooses, price would be less than average total cost. (b) Yes. If the dentist charges rich people a price of $OP_O$, he or she can sell $OQ_O$ units of dental care to them. If he or she charges poor people a price of $OP_1$, he or she can sell $OQ_1$ units of dental care to them. Thus the total output, which equals $OQ_2$ brings an average price of $OP_2$, which is greater than average total cost. (c) Yes. (d) Yes, the situation depicted in the graph is an example. Without price discrimination, this dentist could not cover his or her costs. (e) No. It is important to note that price discrimination frequently occurs in situations where the good or service could be produced without it. Price discrimination is used in these situations to increase the profits of the producer. (From the point of view of society as a whole, price discrimination frequently is objectionable because it violates the conditions for optimal resource allocation described in Appendix D.)

topic is needed. Nonetheless, it seems fair to conclude that, although the simple model of the regulatory process presented in previous sections would predict that regulated prices would be lower, on the average, than unregulated prices (of the same item), the evidence in support of this prediction is much weaker than might be supposed.

Whether or not regulation has a significant effect on the *average* level of prices, it certainly has an effect on *particular* prices charged by regulated firms. In some cases, it has reduced the price of a product. There seems to be general agreement that the Federal Energy Regulatory Commission kept the price of natural gas (in interstate commerce) below what this price would have been during the 1970s in the absence of regulation. In other cases, it has increased the price of a product. Some observers believe that prior to the deregulation of the airlines in the late 1970s, the Civil Aeronautics Board (CAB) increased the airplane fare between New York and Washington. As evidence of this, they compared at that time this fare with the fare from San Francisco to Los Angeles, which was not subject to CAB regulation since the trip was entirely within California. Although the distance from San Francisco to Los Angeles is almost twice as great as that from New York to Washington, the fare from San Francisco to Los Angeles was less than that from New York to Washington.

Federal Energy Regulatory Committee headquarters, Washington, D.C.

## THE DEREGULATION MOVEMENT: THE CASE OF THE AIRLINES

As pointed out above, considerable controversy has centered on the regulatory process, with many observers feeling that the commissions are lax and that they tend to be captured by the industries they are supposed to regulate. The regulatory process in a variety of industries, such as airlines, railroads, and trucking, has been criticized severely. For example, the Civil Aeronautics Board (CAB), which was established in 1938, and which regulated the prices charged by the interstate scheduled airlines as well as entry into the industry, was criticized during the 1970s for preventing price competition among airlines and for permitting little new entry. According to the General Accounting Office (a federal government agency), airline fares would have been 20 to 50 percent lower in the absence of CAB regulation.

In the late 1970s and early 1980s, there was a dramatic movement toward deregulation in the United States. A variety of industries, including airlines, railroads, trucking, and financial institutions, were affected. In the case of the airlines, the seeds for deregulation were sown in the 1970s with the appointment of Alfred Kahn, a Cornell economist, as chairman of the CAB. During the late 1970s, airlines were allowed to institute discount fares, and entry restrictions were relaxed. Eventually, Congress passed legislation that phased out the CAB's powers. The power to regulate routes terminated at the end of 1981, and the power to regulate rates terminated at the end of 1982.

During the late 1980s and early 1990s, the deregulation of the airlines became controversial, for at least two reasons. First, since deregulation brought lower fares, it also brought a rise in airline passenger traffic, which in turn helped to produce more congestion in airports and more delayed flights. Second, while deregulation initially stimulated an increase in the number of airlines, the airline industry subsequently became much

Alfred Kahn

more concentrated, as a number of firms merged. Thus Texas Air took over Eastern (and People Express) in 1986; and Northwest acquired Republic. In 1989, more than 90 percent of the domestic market was controlled by eight airlines. Deregulation was one of the factors blamed for this increase in concentration, which some observers regarded as excessive.

Nonetheless, there is no evidence that the airline industry is going to be regulated again. Economists point out that deregulation has raised the airline industry's efficiency by increasing the number of passengers per plane, encouraging the airlines to get more productivity out of their workers, and improving the match between types of equipment and types of market. Also, deregulation has resulted in the consumer's being offered a much greater variety of combinations of price and service quality. Most observers seem to conclude that, although deregulation has not been an unalloyed blessing, it has resulted in many economic advantages.

Long lines at an airport ticket counter

## EFFECTS OF REGULATION ON EFFICIENCY

As previous chapters have stressed, competitive markets provide considerable incentives for a firm to increase its efficiency. Firms that are able to push their costs below those of their competitors reap higher profits than their competitors. As a simple illustration, suppose that firms A and B both have contracts to produce 100 airplanes, and that the price they will get for each airplane is $25,000. Firm A's management, which is diligent, imaginative, and innovative, gets the cost per airplane down to $10,000, and thus makes a healthy profit of $1,500,000. Firm B's management which is lazy, unimaginative, and dull, lets the cost per airplane rise to $30,000, and thus loses $500,000. Clearly, firm A is rewarded for its good performance, while firm B is penalized for its poor performance.

### No Incentive for Efficiency

One of the primary purposes of regulators is to prevent a monopoly from earning excessive profits. The firm is allowed only a "fair" rate of return on its investment. One problem with this arrangement is that the firm is guaranteed this rate of return, regardless of how well it performs. If the regulators decide that the Sleepy Hollow Electric and Gas Company should receive a 10 percent rate of return on its investment, this is the rate of return it will receive regardless of whether the Sleepy Hollow Electric and Gas Company is managed well or poorly. Why is this a problem? Because unlike the competitive firms discussed in the previous paragraph, there is no incentive for the firm to increase its efficiency.

The available evidence indicates that, if a firm is guaranteed a fixed amount of profit for a job (regardless of how efficiently it does this job), the firm will tend to be less efficient than if the amount of profit it receives is directly related to its efficiency. The Department of Defense has found that, when it bought goods or services on a cost-plus-fixed-fee basis, these goods and services were not produced as cheaply as when it bought them in a competitive market. This is reasonable. It takes time, energy, and lots of trouble to make a firm more efficient. Why should a firm's managers bother to induce added efficiency if the firm's profits are the same, regardless of how efficient or inefficient it is?

## Regulatory Lag and Incentive for Efficiency

The regulatory process is characterized by long delays. In many regulated industries, a proposed rate increase or decrease may be under consideration for months before a decision is made by the commission. In cases where such a price change is strongly contested, it may take years for the required hearings to occur before the commission and for appeals to be made subsequently to the courts. Such a delay between a proposed price change and its ultimate disposition is called a **regulatory lag.** Long regulatory lags are often criticized by those who would like the regulatory process to adapt more quickly to changing conditions and to provide more timely decisions. But one advantage of regulatory lags is that they result in some rewards for efficiency and penalties for inefficiency.

To see why this is so, consider a regulated company whose price is set so that the firm can earn a rate of return of 10 percent (which is what the commission regards as a "fair" rate of return). The firm develops and introduces some improved manufacturing processes which reduce the firm's costs, thus allowing it to earn 13 percent. If it takes 18 months for the commission to review the prices it approved before and to modify them to take account of the new (lower) cost levels, the firm earns a higher rate of return (13 percent rather than 10 percent) during these 18 months than if it had not developed and introduced the improved manufacturing processes. This is a reward for efficiency.

On the other hand, suppose that this firm makes several serious blunders which result in a substantial increase in its costs; thus the firm earns only a rate of return of 6 percent. If it takes 18 months for the commission to review the prices it set before and to modify them to take account of the changes in firms' cost levels, this firm earns a lower rate of return (6 percent rather than 10 percent) during these 18 months than if it had not made these blunders. This is a penalty for inefficiency.

Although regulatory lag does restore some of the incentives for efficiency (and some of the penalties for inefficiency), it would be a mistake to believe that it results in as strong a set of incentives as does competitive markets. One of the basic problems with regulation is that, *if a regulatory commission prevents a firm from earning higher-than-average profits, there may be relatively little incentive for the firm to increase its efficiency and innovate.*

## TEST YOURSELF

1. Compare the long-run equilibrium of a perfectly competitive industry with that which would occur if all the firms were to be merged in a single monopolistic firm. Is there any reason for society to prefer one equilibrium over the other?

2. "No firm has a monopoly since every good competes to some extent with every other good. Thus there is no good that is completely sealed off from competition." Comment and evaluate.

3. "Firms with relatively high profits are bound to be monopolists. If they were competitive, the entry of new firms into the industry would drive economic profits down to zero. Thus the easiest and best way to determine whether a firm is a monopolist is to look at its profits." Comment and evaluate.

4. According to the Council of Economic Advisers, "although exit from an industry via bankruptcy is a normal characteristic of efficient competitive markets, the bankruptcy of a regulated firm tends to be viewed as a sign of regulatory failure." What problems are likely to result from this attitude?

# SUMMARY

1. A pure monopoly is a market with one, and only one, seller. Monopolies may occur because of patents, control over basic inputs, and government action, as well as decreasing average costs up to the point where the market is satisfied.

2. If average costs reach their minimum at an output rate large enough to satisfy the entire market, perfect competition cannot be maintained; and the public often insists that the industry (a natural monopoly) be regulated by the government.

3. Since the monopolist is the only seller of the product, the demand curve facing the monopolist is the market demand curve, which slopes downward (rather than being horizontal as in perfect competition).

4. The unregulated monopolist will maximize profit by choosing the output where marginal cost equals marginal revenue, marginal revenue being defined as the addition to total revenue attributable to the addition of one unit to sales. This rule for output determination also holds under perfect competition, since price equals marginal revenue under perfect competition.

5. If monopolists cannot prevent losses from exceeding fixed costs, they, like perfect competitors, will discontinue production. In contrast to the case in perfect competition, the long-run equilibrium of a monopolistic industry may not be marked by the absence of economic profits.

6. The output of a monopoly tends to be smaller and the price tends to be higher than under perfect competition.

Economists tend to believe that society would be better off if more resources were devoted to the production of the good than under monopoly, the competitive output often being regarded as best.

7. One way that society has attempted to reduce the harmful effects of monopoly is through public regulation. Commissions often set price at the level at which it equals average total cost, including a "fair rate of return" on the firm's investment.

8. There has been a great deal of controversy over the practices of the regulatory commissions. Many economists have viewed them as lax or ill-conceived. In many areas, like transportation, they have been concerned as much with the regulation of competition as with the regulation of monopoly; and, according to many studies, their decisions have resulted in substantial costs and inefficiencies.

9. Regulatory commissions try to prevent a monopoly from earning excessive profits; the firm is allowed only a "fair rate of return" on its investment. One difficulty with this arrangement is that, since the firm is guaranteed this rate of return (regardless of how well or poorly it performs), there is no incentive for the firm to increase its efficiency. Although regulatory lag results in some incentives of this sort, they often are relatively weak.

10. In some industries (like airlines, trucking, and railroads), the late 1970s and early 1980s saw a strong movement toward deregulation. More recently, there have been fewer dramatic changes along this line.

# CONCEPTS FOR REVIEW

**Monopoly**

**Natural monopoly**

**Total revenue**

**Marginal revenue**

**Public regulation**

**Historical cost**

**⁺Marginal cost pricing**

**Reproduction cost**

**Price discrimination**

**Regulatory lag**

* This concept is presented in the Appendix to this chapter.

# APPENDIX: MARGINAL COST PRICING

In this and the previous chapter, we indicated that, under the assumptions made here, the conditions for optimal resource allocation are satisfied under perfect competition. (See Appendix D for a more detailed discussion of this point.) Economists interested in the functioning of planned, or socialist, economies have pointed out that a price system also could be used to increase social welfare in such economies. Also, it has been argued that government-owned enterprises and public utilities in capitalist economies should set price equal to marginal cost, just as perfectly competitive firms do. In this Appendix, we discuss marginal cost pricing, and how it might be used by government-owned or regulated monopolists, as well as by socialist economies.

## Socialist Economies

It is often argued that rational economic organization could be achieved in a socialist economy that is decentralized, as well as under perfect competition. The socialist government might solve the system of equations that is solved automatically in a perfectly competitive economy, and obtain the prices that would prevail under perfect competition. Then the government might publish this price list, together with instructions for consumers to maximize their satisfaction and for producers to maximize profit. (Of course, the wording of the instructions to consumers might be a bit less heavy-handed than "Maximize your satisfaction!")

Under a socialist system of this sort, the government does not have to become involved in the intricate and detailed business of setting production targets for each plant. It need only compute the proper set of prices. In following the rules to maximize "profits," plant managers will choose the proper production levels. Thus decentralized decision making, rather than detailed centralized direction, could be used, thus reducing administrative costs and bureaucratic disadvantages—or so, at least, the theorists say.

## Government-Owned or Regulated Monopolies

The prices the government would publish, like those prevailing in a perfectly competitive economy, would equal marginal cost. Many economists have recommended that government-owned enterprises in basically capitalist economies also adopt *marginal cost pricing,* i.e., that they set price equal to marginal cost. Taking the case of a bridge where the marginal cost (the extra cost involved in allowing an additional vehicle to cross) is zero, Harold Hotelling argued in a famous article that the socially optimal price for crossing the bridge is zero, and that its costs should be defrayed by general taxation. If a toll is charged, the conditions for optimal resource use are not met.[9]

Marginal cost pricing has fascinated economists during the fifty years that have elapsed since Hotelling's article, but there are a number of problems in the application of this idea. One of the most important is that if the firm's average costs decrease with increases in its scale of output (as is frequently the case in public utilities), it follows from the discussion in

[9] Harold Hotelling, "The General Welfare in Relation to Problems of Taxation and of Railway and Utility Rates," *Econometrica,* 1938.

Chapter 23 that marginal cost must be less than average cost, with the consequence that the firm will not cover its costs if price is set equal to marginal cost.[10] This means that marginal cost pricing must be accompanied by some form of subsidy if the firm is to stay in operation—and the collection of the funds required for the payment of the subsidy may also violate the conditions for optimal resource allocation. This subsidy also means that there is a change in the income distribution favoring users of the firm's output and penalizing nonusers.

## The Common Sense of Marginal Cost Pricing

To illustrate the reasoning that underlies marginal cost pricing, consider the case of water supplies. What determines the level at which the price of water should be set?

> Suppose that at a certain moment in time [consumers are willing to pay] $30 per unit. Then, if the community as a whole can acquire and transport another unit of water for say, $20, it would clearly be desirable to do so; in fact, any of the individual customers to whom the unit of water is worth $30 would be happy to pay the $20 cost, and none of the other members of the community would be made worse off thereby. We may say that, on efficiency grounds, additional units should be made available so long as any members of the community are willing to pay the additional or marginal costs incurred. . . . So the . . . rule is to make the price equal to marginal cost and equal for all customers.[11]

Unfortunately, it seems that water-pricing practices do not often conform to this rule. Some types of water users are commonly charged lower prices than other types of water users, although the marginal cost of the water is the same. According to a study carried out at the RAND Corporation,

> In Los Angeles, for example, there is an exceptionally low rate for irrigation use. Domestic, commercial, and industrial services are not distinguished as such, but they are differentially affected by the promotional volume rates. More serious, because much more common, is the system of block rates, with reductions [in price] for larger quantities used. . . . [This system leads] to wasteful use of water by large users, since small users would value the same marginal unit of water more highly if delivered to them. . . . The customer paying the lower price will on the margin be utilizing water for less valuable purposes than it could serve if transferred to the customer paying the higher price.

[10] Recall from Chapter 23 that an increase in output results in a reduction in average cost only when marginal cost is less than average cost. Since the firm's receipts will cover its costs only if price is at least equal to average cost, it follows that, under these circumstances, the firm cannot cover its costs if it sets price equal to marginal cost.
[11] Hirshleifer, Milliman, and DeHaven, "The Allocation of Water Supplies," in E. Mansfield (ed.), *Microeconomics: Selected Readings,* 4th ed., New York: Norton, 1982.

# OLIGOPOLY, GAME THEORY, AND MONOPOLISTIC COMPETITION

CONSIDER THE COMPUTER, soap, electrical equipment, steel, oil, and motorcycle industries, all of which are taken up in this chapter. None of these industries is perfectly competitive or monopolistic. Although perfect competition and monopoly are very useful models that shed much valuable light on the behavior of markets, they are polar cases. Economists have developed other models that portray more realistically the behavior of many modern industries. Oligopoly models, with their emphasis on strategic behavior, have proved useful in analyzing industries like computers, oil and motorcycles. In these industries, there are few firms, and the rivalry among them has many of the characteristics of a game. Thus game theory has been utilized to study decision making by these firms.

In this chapter, we focus attention on theories of oligopoly and strategic behavior. Game theory, which has contributed a great deal in recent years to our understanding of these topics, is considered at length. In addition, we take up the theory of monopolistic competition, which helps to explain market behavior in such industries as retail trade. We examine how resources are allocated and prices are set under oligopoly and monopolistic competition. We also compare the behavior of oligopolistic and monopolistically competitive markets with the behavior of perfectly competitive and monopolistic markets.

## OLIGOPOLY

*Oligopoly* (domination by a few firms) is a common and important market structure in the United States; many industries, like steel, automobiles, oil, and electrical equipment, are oligopolistic. An example of an oligopolist is IBM, described in Chapter 21. *The key characteristic of oligopoly is interdependence, actual and perceived, among firms.* Each oligopolist formulates its policies with an eye to their effect on its rivals. Since an oligopoly contains a small number of firms, any change in one firm's price or output influences the sales and profits of its competitors. Moreover, since there are only a few firms, each must recognize that changes in its own policies are likely to result in changes in the policies of its rivals as well.

What factors are responsible for oligopoly? First, in some industries, *low production costs cannot be achieved unless a firm is producing an output equal to a substantial portion of the total available market,* with the consequence that the number of firms will tend to be rather small. Second, *there may be economies of scale in sales promotion* in certain industries, and this too may promote oligopoly. Third, entry into some industries may be blocked by the requirement that a firm build and maintain a large, complicated, and expensive plant, or have access to patents or scarce raw materials. Only a few firms may be in a position to obtain all these necessary prerequisites for membership in the club.

## Economies of Scale

To illustrate the effects of *economies of scale*, consider the market for central office switches. Central office switches are the main computers that run local telecommunications networks. Because it costs over $1 billion to develop a modern central office switch, no single European country is big enough to support such a development project. Switch manufacturers must compete in international markets to obtain the very large sales needed to reduce their average costs to the point where they can make a profit. Due to the great economies of scale in this industry, only a small number of firms can survive.[1]

The automobile industry is a good example of *economies of scale in sales promotion.* To be effective, advertising must often be carried out on a large scale, the result being that the advertising cost per unit of output decreases with increases in output, at least up to some point. Also, car buyers like to deal with firms with a large, dependable dealer network. Since it takes a lot of money to establish such a network, and since the better dealers are attracted by the more popular brands, the smaller automobile manufacturers are at a substantial disadvantage.

## Barriers to Entry

In addition, the automobile industry offers a good example of *barriers to entry due to large financial requirements.* An automobile plant of minimum efficient size costs hundreds of millions of dollars to build and put into operation. This is an enormous amount of money, beyond the reach of practically all individuals. It takes the help of major financial interests and financial institutions to break into the automobile business. Since World War II, no new domestic firms have obtained a foothold in the American automobile industry.

The *availability of raw materials* can also be a barrier to entry. Such is the case in the steel industry, where a few big firms have most of the available iron ore, partly through foresight and partly because they were the only organizations that could afford to spend the vast sums required to obtain the ore. Also, *patents* can be a very big barrier to entry. The electric light industry is a famous example. General Electric was able to dominate the industry from 1892 to 1930 through the acquisition of the basic Edison patents and then the acquisition of patents on many of the improvements.

AT&T switching station

---

[1] J. Hausman, "Joint Ventures, Strategic Alliances, and Collaboration in Telecommunications," *Regulation,* Winter 1991.

# COLLUSION AND CARTELS

In oligopolistic industries, collusion is much more likely than under perfect competition or monopolistic competition. ***Collusion*** *occurs when firms get together and agree on price and output.* Conditions in oligopolistic industries tend to promote collusion, since the number of firms is small and the firms recognize their interdependence. *The advantages of collusion to the firms seem obvious: increased profits, decreased uncertainty, and a better opportunity to prevent entry.* Not all collusion is disguised from the public or secret. In contrast to illicit collusion, a ***cartel*** is an open, formal collusive arrangement among firms. In many countries in Europe, cartels have been common and legally acceptable. In the United States, most collusive arrangements, whether secret or open cartels, were declared illegal by the Sherman Antitrust Act, which was passed in 1890, but this does not mean that such arrangements do not exist.

For example, consider the electrical equipment industry. Widespread collusion to fix prices occurred among American electrical equipment manufacturers during the 1950s, and when the collusion was uncovered a number of high executives were tried, convicted, and sent to jail. Moreover, collusion of this sort is not limited to a single industry—or a single country. Some cartels, like that in quinine in the early 1960s or in crude oil in the 1970s to 1990s, are international in scope.

# PRICE AND OUTPUT OF A CARTEL

If a cartel is established to set a uniform price for a particular product, what price will it charge? As a first step, the cartel must estimate the marginal cost curve for the cartel as a whole. Then it must find the output where its marginal cost equals its marginal revenue, since this output maximizes the total profit of the cartel members. In Figure 26.1, this output is *OQ*. Thus, if it maximizes cartel profits, the cartel will choose a price of *OP*, which is the monopoly price. In short, *the cartel acts like a monopolist with a number of plants or divisions, each of which is a member firm.*

How will the cartel allocate sales among the member firms? If its aim is to maximize cartel profits, it will allocate sales to firms in such a way that the sum of the firms' costs is minimized. But this allocation is unlikely to occur in reality. The allocation process is a bargaining process, and firms with the most influence and the shrewdest negotiators are likely to receive the largest sales quotas, even though this decreases the total profits of the cartel. Moreover, high-cost firms are likely to receive larger sales quotas than would be the case if total cartel profits were maximized, since they would be unwilling otherwise to stay in the cartel. In practice, it appears that cartels often divide markets geographically or in accord with a firm's level of sales in the past.

### The Electrical Conspiracy

To illustrate how firms collude, consider the electrical equipment manufacturers we mentioned above. During the 1950s, there was widespread collusion among about 30 firms selling turbine generators, switchgear, transformers, and other products with total sales of about $1.5 billion per

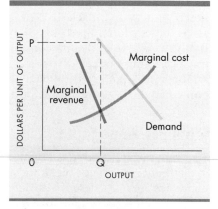

**Figure 26.1**
**Price and Output of a Cartel**
The marginal cost curve shows the marginal cost for the cartel as a whole. Based on the demand curve for the industry's product, the cartel can derive the marginal revenue curve. The output that maximizes the total profit of the cartel members is *OQ*. The corresponding price is *OP*.

year. Representatives of these firms got together and agreed upon prices for many products. The available evidence indicates that both prices and profits tended to be increased by the collusive agreements—or at least until the firms were prosecuted under the antitrust laws by the Department of Justice. The following statement by F. M. Scherer is a good description of some of the procedures used by these firms:

> Some of the most elaborate procedures were devised to handle switchgear pricing. As in the case of generators, book prices served as the initial departure point. Each seller agreed to quote book prices in sales to private buyers, and meetings were held regularly to compare calculations for forthcoming job quotations. Sealed-bid competitions sponsored by government agencies posed a different set of problems, and new methods were worked out to handle them. Through protracted negotiation, each seller was assigned a specific share of all sealed-bid business, e.g., General Electric's share of the high voltage switchgear field was set at 40.3 per cent in late 1958, and Allis-Chalmers' at 8.8 per cent. Participants then coordinated their bidding so that each firm was low bidder in just enough transactions to gain its predetermined share of the market. In the power switching equipment line, this was achieved for a while by dividing the United States into four quadrants, assigning four sellers to each quadrant, and letting the sellers in a quadrant rotate their bids. A "phases of the moon" system was used to allocate low-bidding privileges in the high voltage switchgear field, with a new seller assuming low-bidding priority every two weeks. The designated bidder subtracted a specified percentage margin from the book price to capture orders during its phase, while others added various margins to the book price. The result was an ostensibly random pattern of quotations, conveying the impression of independent pricing behavior.[2]

## BARRIERS TO COLLUSION

The fact that oligopoly often can lead to collusion is not new. Nor is it newly understood. Back in 1776, Adam Smith warned that "people of the same trade seldom meet together even for merriment and diversion, but the conversation ends in a conspiracy against the public, or in some contrivance to raise prices." However, it must be borne in mind that collusive arrangements are often difficult to accomplish and maintain for long. In particular, there are several important barriers to collusion.

### Legal Problems

The antitrust laws forbid outright collusion and price fixing. This does not mean that firms do not break those laws; witness the electrical equipment manufacturers just described. But the antitrust laws are an important obstacle to collusion.

### Technical Problems

Collusion is often difficult to achieve and maintain because an oligopoly contains an unwieldy number of firms, or the product is quite heterogeneous, or the cost structures of the firms differ considerably. It is clear that a collusive agreement will be more difficult to achieve and maintain if there are a dozen oligopolists than if there are three or four. Moreover, if

[2] F. M. Scherer, *Industrial Market Structure and Economic Performance,* p. 160.

the products sold by the oligopolists differ substantially, it will probably be more difficult for them to find a common price strategy that will be acceptable to all. Similarly, if the firms' cost structures differ, it will be more difficult to get agreement, since the low-cost firms will be more inclined to cut price. For example, National Steel, after introducing low-cost continuous strip mills in the 1930s, became a price cutter in the steel industry.

## Cheating

There is a constant temptation for oligopolists to cheat on any collusive agreement. If other firms stick to the agreement, any firm that cheats—by cutting its price below that agreed to under the collusive arrangement—can take a lot of business away from the other firms and increase its prof-

---

## EXAMPLE 26.1  THE END OF THE COZY MILK OLIGOPOLY IN NEW YORK

On July 4, 1987, Governor Mario Cuomo of New York, together with the state legislature, put through a bill to terminate a half-century of restrictions on milk sales in the state. This bill ended rules that blocked milk dealers in one county from selling in another county, and that denied milk licenses to dealers whose entry into the state was deemed "destructive" to the New York market. Prior to the passage of the 1987 bill, five major dealers dominated the sale of milk in New York City. According to the *New York Times*, the old state rules were used by state administrators to deny licenses to potential entrants that might reduce price. What precipitated the 1987 bill rescinding these rules was the entrance of a New Jersey firm, Farmland Dairies, into the New York City market in December 1986, after a federal court gave it permission to begin deliveries in the city.

(a) After Farmland entered the New York City milk market, do you think that the price of milk changed? If so, how? (b) According to the state attorney general, Robert Abrams, the old rules "encouraged and facilitated" price fixing by the New York dairies. How did the old rules do this? (c) Farmland's president, Marc Goldman, said that Farmland's production costs were only several cents a gallon less than in New York; yet the price dropped between 30 and 71 cents per gallon in New York supermarkets after Farmland's entry. Why did the price drop by so much more than the cost differential? (d) Members of Local 584 of the teamsters charged that many of their milk truck drivers would lose their jobs because of deregulation of the milk industry. The Milk Industry Council, which represents milk dealers, said that many small milk dealers would be put out of business. Doesn't this mean that it was socially unwise to enact the 1987 bill?*

### Solution

(a) Yes. The retail cost of a gallon of milk fell from $2.42 to $1.98, saving consumers about $100 million a year. (b) They kept out entrants, and helped keep only a few dairies in existence. (c) Because the profit margin—the difference between price and unit production cost—was reduced. (d) No. Consumers gained because of the lower price. The gains to consumers are likely to have exceeded the losses to the existing dealers and their employees.

* For further discussion, see "Albany Set to End Milk Rules." *New York Times*, July 4, 1987.

its substantially, at least in the short run. This temptation is particularly great when an industry's sales are depressed and its profits are low. Every firm is hungry for business, and it is difficult to resist. Moreover, one firm may be driven to cheating because it hears that another firm is doing so, with the eventual result that the collusive agreement is torn apart.

To illustrate the problems of maintaining a collusive agreement, let's return to the electrical equipment manufacturers. As the *Wall Street Journal* summed it up,

> One of the great ironies of the conspiracies was that no matter how hard the participants schemed,no matter how friendly their meetings and communications might be, there was an innate tendency to compete. Someone was always violating the agreements to get more business and this continually called for new illegal plans. For example, price-cutting in sales of power switching equipment to government agencies was getting out of hand in late 1958. This led to the "quadrant" system of dividing markets [described in the previous section].

As one executive of General Electric complained, "No one was living up to the agreements and we . . . were being made suckers. On every job someone would cut our throat; we lost confidence in the group." Given that these agreements were illegal, it is remarkable that such a complaint was uttered with a straight face.

## PRICE LEADERSHIP

In order to coordinate their behavior without outright collusion, some industries contain a ***price leader.*** It is quite common in oligopolistic industries for one or a few firms to set the price and for the rest to follow their lead. Two types of price leadership are the dominant-firm model and the barometric-firm model. *The **dominant-firm** model applies to cases where the industry has a single large dominant firm and a number of small firms.* The dominant firm sets the price for the industry, but it lets the small firms sell all they want at that price. *The **barometric-firm** model applies to cases where one firm usually is the first to make changes in price that are generally accepted by other firms in the industry.* The barometric firm may not be the largest, or most powerful, firm. Instead, it is a reasonably accurate interpreter of changes in basic cost and demand conditions in the industry as a whole. According to some authorities, barometric price leadership often occurs as a response to a period of violent price fluctuation in an industry, during which many firms suffer and greater stability is widely sought.

In the past, the steel industry was a good example of price leadership of the dominant-firm variety. The largest firm in the industry was U.S. Steel (now USX Corporation), which was formed in 1901 by the merger of a number of companies. Judge Elbert Gary, the first chairman of the board of U.S. Steel, sought the cooperation of the smaller firms in the industry. He inaugurated a series of so-called "Gary dinners," attended by all the major steel producers, which made declarations of industry policy on pricing and other matters. Since any formal pricing agreements would have been illegal, they made no such agreements. But, generally speaking, U.S. Steel set the pricing pattern and other firms followed. Moreover, this relationship continued long after Judge Gary had gone to his reward. According to Walter Adams of Michigan State University, U.S. Steel typi-

## EXAMPLE 26.2    HOW OTHER SOURCES OF OIL INFLUENCE OPEC'S PRICE

The Organization of Petroleum Exporting Countries (OPEC) is a cartel that includes many of the world's leading oil producers, such as Saudi Arabia, Nigeria, Venezuela, Indonesia, and others. Nonetheless, OPEC does not supply all the world's oil. Important oil producers outside OPEC include the United States, Mexico, Canada, Britain, Norway, and Australia. Suppose that the supply curve for non-OPEC oil and the world demand curve for oil are as shown below:

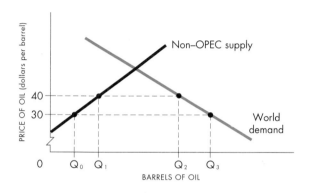

(a) If the price of oil is $30 per barrel, what is the quantity demanded of OPEC oil? (b) If the price of oil is $40 per barrel, what is the quantity demanded of OPEC oil? (c) From the above graph, how can we determine the demand curve for OPEC oil? (d)Given the demand curve for OPEC oil, how can we determine the price that would maximize OPEC's profit?

### Solution

(a) $(OQ_3-OQ_0)$ barrels of oil. (b) $(OQ_2-OQ_1)$ barrels of oil. (c) To determine the quantity of OPEC oil demanded at each price, subtract the quantity of non-OPEC oil supplied at that price from the quantity of oil demanded in the world as a whole at that price. (d) Find the marginal revenue curve corresponding to the demand curve for OPEC oil, and determine the output at which this marginal revenue curve intersects OPEC's marginal cost curve. The profit-maximizing price is the one that results in OPEC's selling this quantity of output.

cally set the price "and the other companies follow in lockstep—both in their sales to private customers and in their secret bids on government contracts."[3]

## NONPRICE COMPETITION

Oligopolists often compete aggressively through advertising and the development of new and different products. This is an important characteristic of oligopoly. In contrast to the case of perfect competition, **nonprice competition** plays a central role in oligopoly. It is worthwhile, therefore, to note a few salient points about the advertising and product development strategies of oligopolists.

### Advertising

Advertising is a very big business. Tens of billions of dollars are spent on it in the United States. One important purpose of advertising is to convince the consumer that one firm's product is better than another's. In industries where there is less physical differentiation of the product, advertising expenditures often are larger than in industries where the product varies more. Thus the cigarette, liquor, and soap industries spend over

[3] W. Adams, *The Structure of American Industry*, New York: Macmillan, 1961, p. 168.

10 percent of their gross revenues (excluding excise taxes) on advertising whereas the automobile industry spends less than 1 percent of its gross revenues on advertising.

The social desirability of much of this advertising is debatable, and much debated. While advertising can serve an important purpose by keeping the consumer better informed, some advertising is more misleading than informative. Unfortunately, it is difficult to make reliable estimates of the extent to which oligopolists may be overinvesting, from society's point of view, in advertising.[4]

### Product Development

The development of new and improved products is also a very big business in the United States. In 1991, industry spent over $78 billion on research and development. In many industries, R and D is a central part of oligopolistic competition. For example, a spectacular case occurred in the motorcycle industry in Japan in the early 1980s. Honda, the industry leader, was being pressed by Yamaha, a rival firm whose share of the market was rising. It responded by introducing 81 new motorcycle models within 18 months (and by cutting prices as well). In January 1983, Yamaha's president admitted defeat: "We cannot match Honda's product development and sales strength. . . . I would like to end the Honda-Yamaha war."

It is important to add, however, that much of industry's R and D is aimed at fairly minor improvements in products and processes. Moreover, a good deal of the engineering efforts of many important industries is aimed largely at style changes, not basic improvements in the product. A case in point is the automobile industry, which spends many billions of dollars per year to produce the model changes that are familiar to car buyers throughout the land.[5] From society's point of view, some observers question whether such huge expenditures are justifiable.

Perhaps the main reason why some oligopolists would rather compete through advertising and product differentiation than through price is that a firm's rivals can easily and quickly match a price reduction, whereas they may find it difficult to match a clever advertising campaign or an attractive product improvement. Eastman Kodak had to work over six years to develop the instant camera it introduced in 1976 to compete with Polaroid's instant camera. Thus many oligopolists tend to feel that they have a better chance of improving their long-run profits at the expense of their rivals in the arena of nonprice competition than by price cutting.

## THE THEORY OF CONTESTABLE MARKETS

During the late 1970s and early 1980s, the theory of contestable markets was born. This theory has received considerable attention. Because it is so new, it is very difficult to predict how significant it will eventually turn out to be. But it has had enough influence to warrant discussion.

---

[4] See W. Comanor and T. Wilson, *Advertising and Market Power,* Cambridge: Harvard University Press, 1975.
[5] For example, see L. White, *The Automobile Industry Since 1945,* Cambridge, Mass.: Harvard University Press, 1971. Earlier data were presented by Frank Fisher, Zvi Griliches, and Carl Kaysen.

What is a **contestable market?** It is a market into which entry is absolutely free, *and exit is absolutely costless.* Any firm can leave the market without impediment, and can get back whatever costs it incurred in entering. *The key characteristic of a contestable market is its vulnerability to hit-and-run entry.* A firm can enter such a market, make a quick profit, and leave without cost, if this seems to be the most profitable course of action.

Just as a perfectly competitive market is only a model, so the same is true of a contestable market. Nonetheless, models of this sort can be very useful and suggestive. At least three characteristics of a contestable market are worth noting. First, it can be shown that *profits are zero in equilibrium in a contestable market.* If profits were positive, a firm could enter the market, undercut the price of the firm with profits, and make a profit, after which it could leave the market if this seemed desirable. Thus profits will be eroded by such price cutting until they are zero. This is true regardless of how few firms exist in the contestable market. Because each is subject to such hit-and-run tactics, profits are eliminated.

Second, the organization of a contestable market is efficient in the sense that *the average cost of production is as low as possible.* Again because of the possibility of hit-and-run entry, firms in such a market must maintain their costs at the lowest possible level in the long run. If they do not do so, more efficient firms will enter, undercut their price, and force them to reduce their costs or withdraw from the market.

Third, if a contestable market contains two or more sellers, *their prices, in equilibrium, must equal their marginal costs.* As pointed out in Chapter 25, there are fundamental reasons why economists favor markets in which price equals marginal cost. One reason why perfect competition is favored by so many economists is that price equals marginal cost. Thus it is very interesting that this desirable feature of perfect competition exists as well in contestable markets.

In the past, it has often been presumed that these three outcomes—zero profits, minimum cost, and price equal to marginal cost—would be very unlikely to occur when there are few sellers. The theory of contestable markets implies that this is not necessarily the case. However, many critics say that this theory is based on very unrealistic assumptions concerning entry and exit. In particular, they point out that entry often is not free and that exit seldom is costless.

## TEST YOURSELF

1. Suppose that a cartel consists of four firms, each of which has a horizontal marginal cost curve. For each firm, marginal cost equals $4. Suppose that the marginal revenue curve for the cartel is $MR = 10 - 2Q$, where $MR$ is marginal revenue (in dollars) and $Q$ is the cartel's output per year (in thousands of units). What output rate will the cartel choose?

2. According to the Senate Subcommittee on Antitrust and Monopoly, "Some system of marketing quotas, whether overt or carefully hidden, must underlie any price-fixing agreement." Comment and evaluate.

3. Discuss the incentives that each firm in Question 1 would have to cheat on the collusive agreement described there.

4. Explain why the average cost of production will be as low as possible in a contestable market. What is the significance of this fact?

# THE THEORY OF GAMES

As pointed out at the beginning of this chapter, the rivalry among oligopolists has many of the characteristics of a game. As in a game, in oligopoly each firm must take account of its rivals' reactions to its own actions. For this reason, an oligopolistic firm cannot tell what effect a change in its output will have on the price of its product and on its profits unless it can guess how its rivals will respond to the change. To understand game theory, you have to know what a **game** is. It is a competitive situation where two or more persons pursue their own interests and no person can dictate the outcome. Poker is a game, and so is a situation in which two firms are engaged in competitive advertising campaigns. A game is described in terms of its players, rules, payoffs, and information conditions. These elements are common to all conflict situations.

## Definitions of Terms

More specifically, a **player,** whether a single person or an organization, is a decision-making unit. Each player has a certain amount of resources, and the **rules of the game** describe how these resources can be used. Thus the rules of poker indicate how bets can be made and which hands are better than others. A **strategy** is a complete specification of what a player will do under each contingency in the playing of the game. Thus a corporation president might tell her subordinates how she wants an advertising campaign to start, and what should be done at subsequent times in response to various actions of competing firms. The game's outcome clearly depends on each player's strategies. A player's **payoff** varies from game to game. It is win, lose, or draw in checkers, and various sums of money in poker.

# A SIMPLE TWO-PERSON GAME

For simplicity we will restrict our attention to *two-person games*: those with only two players. The relevant features of a two-person game can be shown by constructing a **payoff matrix**. To illustrate, consider the case of two big soap producers, Procter & Gamble and Lever Brothers. Suppose that these two firms are about to stage rival advertising campaigns and that each firm has a choice of strategies. Procter & Gamble can choose to concentrate on either television ads or magazine ads; Lever Brothers has the same choice. Table 26.1 shows what will happen to the

**Table 26.1**
**Payoff Matrix: Procter & Gamble and Lever Brothers**

| POSSIBLE STRATEGIES FOR P & G | POSSIBLE STRATEGIES FOR LEVER BROTHERS | |
| --- | --- | --- |
| | CONCENTRATE ON TV | CONCENTRATE ON MAGAZINES |
| Concentrate on TV | P & G's profit: $3 million<br>Lever's profit: $2 million | P & G's profit: $4 million<br>Lever's profit: $3 million |
| Concentrate on magazines | P & G's profit: $2 million<br>Lever's profit: $3 million | P & G's profit: $3 million<br>Lever's profit: $4 million |

profits of each firm when each combination of strategies is chosen. If both firms concentrate on TV ads, Procter & Gamble gains $3 million and Lever Brothers gains $2 million. If Procter & Gamble concentrates on TV ads and Lever Brothers concentrates on magazine ads, Procter and Gamble gains $4 million and Lever Brothers gains $3 million. And so on.

## Procter & Gamble's Viewpoint

Given the payoff matrix in Table 26.1, there is a definite optimal choice (called a **dominant strategy**) for each firm. To see that this is the case, let's begin by looking at the situation from Procter & Gamble's point of view. If Lever Brothers concentrates on TV ads, Procter & Gamble will make more money ($3 million rather than $2 million) if it concentrates on TV rather than magazines. If Lever Brothers concentrates on magazines, Procter & Gamble will make more money ($4 million rather than $3 million) if it concentrates on TV rather than magazines. Thus, regardless of the strategy chosen by Lever Brothers, Procter & Gamble will do best to concentrate on TV.

## Lever Brothers' Viewpoint

Now let's look at the situation from the point of view of Lever Brothers. If Procter & Gamble concentrates on TV ads, Lever Brothers will make more money ($3 million rather than $2 million) if it concentrates on magazines rather than TV. If Procter & Gamble concentrates on magazines, Lever Brothers will make more money ($4 million rather than $3 million) if it concentrates on magazines rather than TV. Thus, regardless of the strategy chosen by Procter and Gamble, Lever Brothers will do best to concentrate on magazines.

## The Solution of the Game

At this point, the solution of this game is clear. *Procter & Gamble will concentrate on TV ads and Lever Brothers will concentrate on magazine ads.* This is the best that either firm can do.

## Noteworthy Features of This Game

Several points should be noted concerning this game. First, in this game, both players have a **dominant strategy**—a strategy that is its best choice regardless of what the other player does. Not all games have a dominant strategy for each player.

Second, in this game the best strategy for each player is the same regardless of whether the players choose their strategies simultaneously or whether one of the players goes first. For example, Procter & Gamble will choose to concentrate on TV regardless of whether it picks its strategy before, after or at the same time as Lever Brothers. As we shall see, this is not true for all games. In some games, a player's best strategy depends on the timing of the player's move.

# THE PRISONERS' DILEMMA

The theory of games enables us to reach a deeper understanding of the conditions under which oligopolists are likely to cheat on a collusive

**Table 26.2**
**Payoff Matrix: National Robot and Robotica, Inc.**

| POSSIBLE DECISIONS BY ROBOTICA | POSSIBLE DECISIONS BY NATIONAL ROBOT | |
| --- | --- | --- |
| | STICK BY AGREEMENT | CHEAT |
| Stick by agreement | Robotica's profit: $6 million<br>National's profit: $6 million | Robotica's profit: $3 million<br>National's profit: $7 million |
| Cheat | Robotica's profit: $7 million<br>National's profit: $3 million | Robotica's profit: $4 million<br>National's profit: $4 million |

agreement. Suppose that the only two producers of robots—National Robot and Robotica, Inc.—form a cartel. Each firm can either stick by the cartel agreement or cheat. There are four possible outcomes, depending on which decision each firm makes. They are shown in Table 26.2, which is the payoff matrix showing the profit levels of each firm, depending on the decisions made by both.

What should National do? If Robotica sticks by the agreement, it appears that the better strategy for National is to cheat, since National's profits will be greater than if it sticks by the agreement. If Robotica cheats, the better strategy for National seems to be to cheat as well, since National's profits will be higher than if it sticks by the agreement. Thus it appears that National *will choose the strategy of cheating, since regardless of which strategy Robotica adopts, National seems better off by cheating than by sticking by the agreement.* In other words, cheating seems to be the dominant strategy.

What should Robotica do? If National sticks by the agreement, the better strategy for Robotica seems to be to cheat, since Robotica's profits will be greater than if it sticks by the agreement. If National cheats, the better strategy for Robotica appears to be to cheat as well, since Robotica's profits will be higher than if it sticks by the agreement. Thus it seems that Robotica *will choose the strategy of cheating, since regardless of which strategy National adopts, Robotica is better off by cheating than by sticking by the agreement.* Again, cheating seems to be the dominant strategy.

Consequently, in this situation, it appears that both firms will cheat. However, it is important to note that National and Robotica, because they do not trust each other to stick by their agreement, wind up with lower profits than if they both were to stick by the agreement ($4 million versus $6 million).

The type of game considered in Table 26.2 is often called the **prisoners' dilemma** because it is similar to a situation where two persons are arrested after committing a crime. The police lock each person in a separate room and offer each the following deal. "If you confess while your partner does not confess, you will get a 2-year jail term, while he will get 12 years." Each person knows that if they both confess, each will get 10 years (not 12 years because they cooperated with the police). If neither confesses, each will get only 3 years because the evidence against them is weak. In a case of this sort, each will be likely to confess, even though they will do worse than if they could bring themselves to trust each other.

EXAMPLE 26.3    WHAT WILL BE ON THE COVERS OF *NEWSWEEK* AND *TIME*?

Every week, *Time* and *Newsweek*, two leading news magazines, must each pick a story to emphasize on their covers. Suppose that there are two possibilities for next week's cover: a terrorist attack on a U.S. ambassador or a military agreement between the United States and the Soviet Union. Suppose that the editor of each magazine wants to maximize readership, and that the number of people reading each magazine depends as follows on which story is featured on the cover of each magazine:

| TIME'S CHOICE | NEWSWEEK'S CHOICE TERRORIST ATTACK | U.S.–U.S.S.R. AGREEMENT |
|---|---|---|
| Terrorist attack | *Newsweek*: 6 million readers<br>*Time*: 10 million readers | *Newsweek*: 7 million readers<br>*Time*: 9 million readers |
| U.S.–U.S.S.R. agreement | *Newsweek*: 6 million readers<br>*Time*: 9 million readers | *Newsweek*: 5 million readers<br>*Time*: 8 million readers |

a) Does *Time* have a dominant strategy? If so, what is it? (b) Does *Newsweek* have a dominant strategy? If so, what is it? (c) If you were *Newsweek*'s editor, what story would you expect *Time* to put on its cover? Why? (d) Given the answer to part (c), what choice would you make if you were the editor of *Newsweek*? (e) What do you think will be on the cover of each magazine? Why?

**Solution**

(a) Yes. Regardless of whether *Newsweek* has the terrorist attack or the U.S.–U.S.S.R. agreement on its cover, *Time* has a higher readership if it exhibits the terrorist attack on its cover. (b) No. If *Time* has the terrorist attack on its cover, *Newsweek* will get more readers by putting the U.S.–U.S.S.R. agreement on its cover. If *Time* has the U.S.–U.S.S.R. agreement on its cover, *Newsweek* will get more readers by putting the terrorist attack on its cover. (c) *Time* would be expected to put the terrorist attack on its cover because this is its dominant strategy, as pointed out in the answer to part (a). (d) Given that *Time* would be expected to put the terrorist attack on its cover (since this is its dominant strategy), the editor of *Newsweek* would be expected to put the U.S.–U.S.S.R. agreement on its cover, because this would produce a higher readership (7 million vs. 6 million). (e) Based on the foregoing analysis, *Time* would be expected to put the terrorist attack on its cover, and *Newsweek* would be expected to put the U.S.–U.S.S.R. agreement on its cover.[*]

[*] For further discussion, see A. Dixit and B. Nalebuff, *Thinking Strategically*, New York: W. W. Norton, 1991.

The situation in Table 26.2 is similar because, if the two firms could trust each other, both would enjoy higher profits.

# WHAT IF THE GAME IS REPEATED?

In some cases, a game is played only once; in others, it is repeated over and over. If National and Robotica must decide continually whether to cheat or not, the analysis in the previous section may not be correct. Suppose that National refuses to cheat the first time that it must make a decision and that it continues to stick by the agreement so long as Robotica does so. But if Robotica fails even once to cooperate, National will revert forever to the safe policy of cheating. Suppose that Robotica adopts exactly the same policy. What will be the result? Both firms will make a $6 million profit. If either one cheats, it will raise its profit to $7 million for a short period of time, but afterward its profit will fall permanently to $4 million because its rival will cheat as well. Consequently, if the game is repeated indefinitely, it will not be in the interest of either firm to cheat.[6]

Of course, this assumes that each firm can quickly detect whether the other firm is cheating. In fact, this may not be so easy. In some cases, trade associations have been authorized to collect detailed data regarding each firm's sales and prices. In this way, an attempt has been made to detect cheating quickly. The more promptly cheating is detected, the less profitable it tends to be.

Michigan's Robert Axelrod has argued that a good strategy for each player in a game of this sort is "**tit for tat**," which means that each player should do on this round whatever the other player did on the previous round. If National adopts a tit-for-tat strategy, it should abide by the agreement on the first round. If Robotica also abides by it, National should continue to do so, but once Robotica cheats, National should retaliate by cheating as well. Empirical studies suggest that some cartel members actually seem to have adopted tit-for-tat strategies in the past.

## WHEN IS A THREAT CREDIBLE?

Oligopolists like General Motors or Ford often send signals to one another indicating their motives, intentions, and objectives. Some signals are threats. Suppose, for example, that the Medea Company learns that the Pocono Corporation, its principal rival, is about to lower its price. Medea may announce its intention of lowering its own price substantially, thus signaling to Pocono that it is willing to start a price war if Pocono carries out its price reduction. In addition, some of Medea's managers may see to it that this message gets transmitted indirectly to some of Pocono's managers.

However, not all threats are credible. For example, if the payoff matrix is as shown in Table 26.3, Medea's threat is not very credible. (For simplicity, we assume in Table 26.3 that price can be set at only two levels—"high" and "low.") If Pocono sets a high price, Medea makes $5 million if it sets a high price and $3 million if it sets a low price. If Pocono sets a low price, Medea loses $1 million if it sets a high price and $2 million if it sets a low price.

### Table 26.3
### Payoff Matrix: Medea Company and Pocono Corporation

| POSSIBLE STRATEGIES FOR MEDEA | POSSIBLE STRATEGIES FOR POCONO | |
| --- | --- | --- |
| | LOW PRICE | HIGH PRICE |
| Low Price | Medea's profit: −$2 million<br>Pocono's profit: $2 million | Medea's profit: $3 million<br>Pocono's profit: −$1 million |
| High Price | Medea's profit: −$1 million<br>Pocono's profit: $6 million | Medea's profit: $5 million<br>Pocono's profit: $4 million |

[6] Stanford's D. Kreps, P. Milgrom, J. Roberts, and R. Wilson, among others, have carried out important research on this topic.

Hence, it certainly seems unlikely that Medea will carry out its threat to reduce its price to the low level, since, as we've just seen, Medea will make more (or lose less) money by keeping its price at the high level than by reducing it to the low level. This is true, regardless of whether Pocono reduces its price. Thus, if Pocono can be certain that Medea will do what maximizes its profit, it can regard Medea's threat as an idle gesture.

But things are not quite so simple. If Medea can convince Pocono that it will *not* do what maximizes its profit, it can make its threat credible. Thus, if it can convince Pocono that, if Pocono sets the low price, it will match it, *even though this reduces Medea's own profits*, Pocono may decide not to set the low price. Why? Because Pocono's profits are higher ($4 million versus $2 million) if it maintains a high price (and Medea does the same) than if Pocono sets a low price (and Medea does the same).

How can Medea convince Pocono that it will reduce its price, even though this seems to be irrational? For one thing, its managers may develop a reputation of doing what they say, "regardless of the costs." They may exhibit a well-publicized taste for facing down opponents and for refusing to back down, regardless of how crazy they may seem. Confronted with the "irrational" Medea Company, the Pocono Corporation may decide not to cut price. However, if Medea cannot convince Pocono of its "irrationality," Pocono will justifiably regard Medea's threat to reduce price as not being credible.

## MAKING RESISTANCE CREDIBLE

Oligopolists generally try to discourage firms from entering their market. As we have seen in previous sections, the entry of new firms tends to decrease the profits of existing firms. Take the case of the Berwyn Corporation, which faces the threat of entry by the Roanoke Company. Table 26.4 shows the profits of each firm, depending on whether or not Roanoke enters the market and on whether or not Berwyn resists Roanoke's entry by cutting its price and increasing its output (thus reducing Roanoke's profits if it enters).[7]

**Table 26.4**
**Payoff Matrix, before the Berwyn Corporation Makes Its Resistance Credible**

| POSSIBLE STRATEGIES FOR BERWYN CORPORATION | POSSIBLE STRATEGIES FOR ROANOKE COMPANY | |
| --- | --- | --- |
| | ENTER | DO NOT ENTER[a] |
| Resist Entry | Berwyn's profit: $2 million Roanoke's profit: $4 million | Berwyn's profit: $4 million Roanoke's profit: $6 million |
| Do Not Resist Entry | Berwyn's profit: $3 million Roanoke's profit: $8 million | Berwyn's profit: $4 million Roanoke's profit: $6 million |

[a] See Footnote 7.

[7] If Roanoke does not enter the market, there is no difference between Berwyn's resisting and not resisting, since there is nothing to resist. Consequently, Berwyn's profit figures in Table 26.4 are the same regardless of which strategy Berwyn is assumed to pursue.

The first move in this game is up to Roanoke, which must decide whether or not to enter. If it enters, Berwyn must decide whether or not to resist. Given the payoff matrix in Table 26.4, Berwyn, if it is "rational," will not resist because its profits will be lower ($2 million rather than $3 million) if it resists than if it does not resist. Since Roanoke knows that this is the case, it will enter, since its profits will be higher ($8 million rather than $6 million) if it enters than if it does not enter. Needless to say, Berwyn may threaten to resist, but this threat is not credible (if Berwyn is "rational") because, as we have just seen, Berwyn would lower its profits by resisting.

To make this threat credible, Berwyn may alter the payoff matrix in Table 26.4. Suppose that it builds lots of excess production capacity so that, if Roanoke enters, it can increase its output enormously and push price down to the point where Roanoke will lose money. Since it is expensive to keep excess capacity on hand, Berwyn's profit if it does not resist entry is now lower than before it built the extra capacity. The new payoff matrix is shown in Table 26.5. Now if Roanoke enters, Berwyn's profits are higher ($1.5 million versus $1 million) if it resists Roanoke's entry than if it does not resist. Consequently, Berwyn's threat to resist becomes credible. Under these circumstances, Roanoke will not enter because its profits will be $7 million higher ($6 million rather than –$1 million) if it does not enter than if it enters.

**Table 26.5**
**Payoff Matrix, after the Berwryn Corporation Makes Its Resistance Credible**

| POSSIBLE STRATEGIES FOR BERWYN CORPORATION | POSSIBLE STRATEGIES FOR ROANOKE COMPANY | |
| --- | --- | --- |
| | ENTER | DO NOT ENTER[a] |
| Resist Entry | Berwyn's profit: $1.5 million<br>Roanoke's profit: –$1 million | Berwyn's profit: $3 million<br>Roanoke's profit: $6 million |
| Do Not Resist Entry | Berwyn's profit: $1 million<br>Roanoke's profit: $8 million | Berwyn's profit: $3 million<br>Roanoke's profit: $6 million |

[a] See Footnote 7.

Note a very interesting fact about Berwyn's successful attempt to deter Roanoke from entering: *Berwyn has convinced Roanoke not to enter by reducing its own profits if it does not resist entry.* In this way, Berwyn has committed itself irrevocably to fight. If Roanoke enters, Berwyn is ready to fight (by raising output greatly and by pushing price down) and has an incentive to fight (because its profits are greater than if it does not fight). By committing itself in this way to resist entry, it has gained an advantage.

However, as pointed out in the previous section, there are other ways that Berwyn can convince Roanoke not to enter. If Berwyn has imposed enormous losses on every firm that has tried to enter in the past, and has a reputation for "irrational" opposition to entry, Roanoke may decide that it wants no part of a struggle with Berwyn. Consequently, Berwyn may find it worthwhile to foster such a reputation by hammering every entrant that appears, because the longer-term gains from the prevention of entry may exceed the short-term losses from these wars.

## THE ADVANTAGES OF BEING FIRST

Wal-Mart merchandise on display

In many cases, the firm that makes the first move has a big advantage. Take the case of Wal-Mart stores, a chain of discount retail stores. Sam Walton, the company's founder, set up hundreds of such stores in small towns in the Southwest. Since the market in each such town was too small to support more than one discount store, his strategy was to be the first to do so. That is, he had a preemptive strategy—a strategy of establishing stores before his rivals did so.

Suppose that Wal-Mart and a rival firm are both considering the establishment of a discount store in a particular small town, and that the relevant payoff matrix is shown in Table 26.6. If Wal-Mart enters the town but its rival does not, Wal-Mart will make $10 million and its rival will make nothing. If its rival enters the town but Wal-Mart does not, its rival will make $10 million and Wal-Mart will make nothing. If both Wal-Mart and its rival enter the town, both will lose $5 million because the town is too small to support two discount stores.

How this game will turn out depends on which firm acts first. If Wal-Mart acts first, it can enter and be reasonably sure that its rival will not do the same (because its rival would lose $5 million if it entered). On the other hand, if its rival acts first, it can enter and be confident that Wal-Mart would not do so (because Wal-Mart would lose $5 million if it entered). In a case like this, the prize goes to the swift and the nimble. In oligopoly as in boxing, it often pays to be fast on your feet.

**Table 26.6**
**Payoff Matrix: Wal-Mart and Its Rival**

| POSSIBLE STRATEGIES FOR WAL-MART STORES | POSSIBLE STRATEGIES FOR WAL-MART'S RIVAL | |
|---|---|---|
| | ENTER THE TOWN | DO NOT ENTER THE TOWN |
| Enter the Town | Wal-Mart's profit: −$5 million<br>Rival's profit: −$5 million | Wal-Mart's profit: $10 million<br>Rival's profit: zero |
| Do Not Enter the Town | Wal-Mart's profit: zero<br>Rival's profit: $10 million | Wal-Mart's profit: zero<br>Rival's profit: zero |

## COMPARISON OF OLIGOPOLY WITH PERFECT COMPETITION

We have seen that economists have constructed a number of types of models of oligopoly behavior—the cartel models, price leadership models, contestable market models, various game theoretic models, and others—but there is no agreement that any of these models is an adequate general representation of oligopoly behavior. For this reason, it is difficult to estimate the effects of an oligopolistic market structure on price, output, and profits. Nonetheless, if a perfectly competitive industry were turned overnight into an oligopoly, it is likely that changes would occur.

*1. Price would probably be higher than under perfect competition.* The difference between the oligopoly price and the perfectly competitive price will depend on the number of firms in the industry and the ease of entry. The larger the number of firms and the easier it is to enter the industry, the closer the oligopoly price will be to the perfectly competitive level.

*2.* If the demand curve is the same under oligopoly as under perfect competition, it also follows that *output will be less under oligopoly than under perfect competition.* However, it is not always reasonable to assume that the demand curve is the same in both cases, since the large expenditures for advertising and product differentiation incurred by some oligopolies may tend to shift the demand curve to the right. Consequently in some cases both price and output may tend to be higher under oligopoly than under perfect competition.

*3. Oligopolistic industries tend to spend more on advertising, product differentiation, and style changes than do perfectly competitive industries.* The use of some resources for these purposes is certainly worthwhile, since advertising provides buyers with information, and product differentiation allows greater freedom of choice. Whether oligopolies spend too much for these purposes is by no means obvious. However, there is a widespread feeling among economists, based largely on empirical studies (and hunch), that in some oligopolistic industries such expenditures have been expanded beyond socially optimal levels.

*4.* One might expect on the basis of the models presented in this chapter that the *profits earned by oligopolists would be higher, on the average, than the profits earned by perfectly competitive firms.* This conclusion is supported by some statistical evidence. In an early study, Joe Bain of the University of California found that firms in industries in which the largest few firms had a high proportion of total sales tended to have higher rates of return than firms in industries in which the largest few firms had a small proportion of total sales. Nonetheless, this is a controversial topic.[8]

## MONOPOLISTIC COMPETITION

The key feature of **monopolistic competition** is **product differentiation.** In contrast to perfect competition, where all firms sell an identical product, firms under monopolistic competition sell somewhat different products. We are talking here about what sometimes may appear to be subtle differences—Macy's dresses as compared to Wanamaker's dresses, or McDonald's Big Mac versus Burger King's Whopper—but they are significant in economic analysis.

One sector of the economy where product differentiation occurs frequently is retail trade. Producers try to make their product a little different, by altering the product's physical make-up, the services they offer, and other such variables. Other differences—which may be spurious—are based on brand name, image making, advertising claims, etc. In this way, the producers have some monopoly power, but it usually is small, because the products of other firms are very similar.

In perfect competition, the firms included in an industry are easy to de-

[8] For some relevant discussion, see L. Weiss, "The Concentration-Profits Relationship and Antitrust," in H. Goldschmid, H. M. Mann, and J. F. Weston, *Industrial Concentration, The New Learning,* Boston: Little Brown, 1974.

termine because they all produce the same product. But if product differentiation exists, it is no longer easy to define an industry, since each firm produces a somewhat different product. Nevertheless, it may be useful to group together firms that produce similar products and call them a ***product group.*** We can formulate a product group called "toothpaste" or "toilet soap" or "chocolate bars." The process by which we combine firms into product groups is bound to be somewhat arbitrary, since there is no way to decide how close a pair of substitutes must be to belong to the same product group. But it is assumed that meaningful product groups can be established.

Besides product differentiation, other conditions must be met for an industry to qualify as a case of monopolistic competition. First, *there must be a large number of firms in the product group.* In other words, the product must be produced by perhaps 50 to 100 or more firms, with each firm's product a fairly close substitute for the products of the other firms in the product group. Second, *the number of firms in the product group must be large enough so that each firm expects its actions to go unheeded by its rivals and is unimpeded by possible retaliatory moves on their part.* If there is a large number of firms, this condition will normally be met. Third, *entry into the product group must be relatively easy, and there must be no collusion, such as price fixing or market sharing, among firms in the product group.* If there is a large number of firms, collusion generally is difficult, if not impossible.[9]

## PRICE AND OUTPUT UNDER MONOPOLISTIC COMPETITION

Under monopolistic competition, what determines how much output a firm will produce, and what price it will charge? If each firm produces a somewhat different product, it follows that the demand curve facing each firm slopes downward to the right. That is, if the firm raises its price slightly it will lose some, but by no means all, of its customers to other firms. And if it lowers its price slightly, it will gain some, but by no means all, of it competitors' customers. This is in contrast to perfect competition, where the demand curve facing each firm is horizontal.

Figure 26.2 shows the short-run equilibrium of a monopolistically competitive firm. The firm in the short run will set its price at $OP_0$ and its output rate at $OQ_0$, since this combination of price and output will maximize its profits. We can be sure that this combination of price and output maximizes profit because marginal cost equals marginal revenue at this output rate. Economic profits will be earned because price, $OP_0$ exceeds average total costs, $OC_0$, at this output rate.

What will the equilibrium price and output be in the long run? One condition for long-run equilibrium is that *each firm be making no economic profits or losses,* since entry or exit of firms will occur otherwise — and entry and exit are incompatible with long-run equilibrium. Another condition for long-run equilibrium is that *each firm be maximizing its profits.* At what price and output will both these conditions be fulfilled?

[9] For the theory of monopolistic competition, we are indebted largely to Edward Chamberlin of Harvard University, whose path-breaking book on the subject first appeared in 1933. See E. Chamberlin *The Theory of Monopolistic Competition*, Cambridge, Mass.: Harvard University Press, 1933.

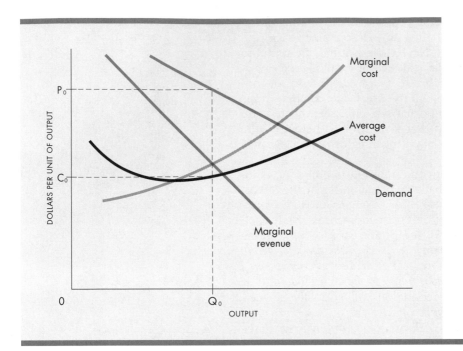

**Figure 26.2**
**Short-Run Equilibrium:**
**Monopolistic Competition**
The firm will set price at $OP_0$ and its output rate at $OQ_0$ since marginal cost equals marginal revenue at this output. It will earn a profit of $C_0P_0$ per unit of output.

Figure 26.3 shows that the long-run equilibrium is at a price of $OP_1$ and an output of $OQ_1$. The zero-economic-profit condition is met at this combination of price and output since the firm's average cost at this output equals the price, $OP_1$. And the profit-maximization condition is met since the marginal revenue curve intersects the marginal cost curve at this output rate.

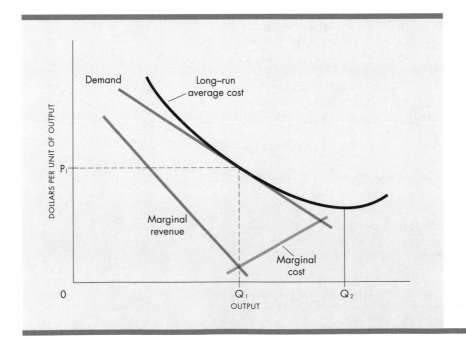

**Figure 26.3**
**Long-Run Equilibrium:**
**Monopolistic Competition**
The long-run equilibrium is at a price of $OP_1$ and an output of $OQ_1$. There are zero profits since long-run average cost equals price. Profits are being maximized since marginal cost equals marginal revenue at this output.

## Excess Capacity and Product Diversity

A famous conclusion of the theory of monopolistic competition is that *a firm under this form of market organization will tend to operate with excess capacity.* In other words, the firm will construct a plant smaller than the minimum-cost size of plant and operate it at less than the minimum-cost rate of output. Why? Because, as shown in Figure 26.3, the long-run average cost curve must be tangent in long-run equilibrium to the demand curve. (This tangency condition insures that, if the firm produces the profit-maximizing output, it obtains a zero economic profit, in accord with the conditions for long-run equilibrium.) Thus, since the demand curve is *downward-sloping,* the long-run average cost curve must also be *downward-sloping* at the long-run equilibrium output rate. Consequently, the firm's output must be less than $OQ_2$, the output rate at which long-run average costs are minimized, since the long-run average cost curve slopes downward only at output rates less than $OQ_2$.

This is an interesting conclusion, since it suggests that monopolistically competitive industries will be overcrowded with firms. There may be too many firms (from society's point of view), each of which is smaller than required to minimize its unit costs. However, one must be careful to recognize that, if there were fewer firms, there would be less diversity of products. Whether the apparently excessive number of firms is really excessive (from society's viewpoint) depends on whether, if there were fewer firms, the reduction in unit costs would outweigh the loss to consumers due to less product diversity.

# COMPARISONS WITH PERFECT COMPETITION AND MONOPOLY

Market structure is important because it influences market behavior. We need to know how the behavior of a monopolistically competitive industry differs from that of a perfectly competitive industry or a monopoly. Suppose that there exists a magician who can transform an industry's structure by a wave of a wand. (John D. Rockefeller was a real-life magician who transformed the structure of the oil industry in the late 1800s—but he seemed to favor mergers, mixed with some ungentlemanly tactics, over wands.) Suppose that the magician makes an industry monopolistically competitive, rather than perfectly competitive or monopolistic. What difference would it make in the behavior of the industry? Or, to take a less fanciful case, what difference would it make if government action or technological change resulted in such a change in an industry's market structure? It is difficult to say how the industry's behavior would be affected, because output would be heterogeneous in one case and homogeneous in the other, and its cost curves would probably vary with its organization. But many economists seem to believe that differences of the following kind can be expected.

*1. The firm under monopolistic competition is likely to produce less, and charge a higher price, than under perfect competition.* The demand curve confronting the monopolistic competitor slopes downward to the right. Consequently, as we saw in the previous chapter, marginal revenue must be less than price. Thus, under monopolistic competition, marginal cost must also be less than price, since marginal revenue must equal marginal cost at the firm's profit-maximizing output rate. But if marginal cost is less than price, the firm's output rate must be smaller—and the price higher—than if marginal cost equals price, which is the case under perfect competition. On the other hand, *relative to monopoly, monopolistically competitive firms are likely to have lower profits, greater output, and lower price.* The firms in a product group might obtain positive economic profits if they were to collude and behave as a monopolist. Such an increase in profits would benefit the producers. Consumers would be worse off because of the higher prices and smaller output of goods.

*2.* As noted in the previous section, *a firm under monopolistic competition may be somewhat inefficient because it tends to operate with excess capacity.* Each firm builds a smaller-than-minimum-cost plant and produces a smaller-than-minimum-cost output. More firms exist than if there were no excess capacity, resulting in some overcrowding of the industry. Inefficiencies of this sort would not be expected under perfect competition. However, these inefficiencies may not be very great, since the demand curve confronting the monopolistically competitive firm is likely to be highly elastic; and the more elastic it is, the less excess capacity the firm will have.

*3. Firms under monopolistic competition will offer a wider variety of styles, brands, and qualities than firms under perfect competition. Moreover, they will spend much more on advertising and other selling expenses than a perfectly competitive firm would.* Whether this diversity is worth its cost is hard to say. Some economists are impressed by the apparent waste in monopolistic competition. They think it results in too many firms, too many brands, too much selling effort, and too much spurious product differentiation. But if the differences among products are real and are understood by consumers, the greater variety of alternatives available under monopolistic competition may be very valuable to consumers. The proper evaluation of the social advantages and disadvantages of product differentiation is a problem economists have only partially solved.[10]

## TEST YOURSELF

1. In Table 26.1, suppose that Procter & Gamble's profit if it concentrates on TV and if Lever Brothers concentrates on magazines is $1 million, rather than $4 million. If the rest of the payoff matrix is unchanged, do Procter & Gamble and Lever Brothers still have dominant strategies? Explain.

2. Under the conditions given in Question 1, can Procter & Gamble predict what strategy Lever Brothers will adopt? (Hint: Does Lever Brothers have a dominant strategy?) If its prediction is correct, what strategy should Procter & Gamble choose?

3. In a previous section, it was asserted that, if the demand curve confronting a monopolistically competitive firm is highly elastic, the firm is likely to have less excess capacity than if it is relatively inelastic. Explain why this is true.

4. Explain how a firm's output and price are determined under monopolistic competition in (a) the short run and (b) the long run.

---

[10] Before leaving the subject of monopolistic competition, it should be recognized that Professor Chamberlin's theory has been subjected to considerable criticism. As a case in point, the definition of the product group is ambiguous. See G. Stigler, *Five Lectures on Economic Problems*, London: Longmans Green, 1949.

# SUMMARY

1. Oligopoly is characterized by a small number of firms and a great deal of interdependence, actual and perceived, among them. Oligopoly is a common market structure in the United States.

2. Conditions in oligopolistic industries tend to promote collusion. A cartel is an open, formal, collusive arrangement. A profit-maximizing cartel will act like a monopolist with a number of plants or divisions, each of which is a member firm. In practice, it appears that the members of a cartel often divide markets geographically or in accord with each firm's level of sales in the past.

3. Price leadership is quite common in oligopolistic industries, one or a few firms apparently setting the price and the rest following their lead. Two types of price leadership are the dominant-firm model and the barometric-firm model.

4. A contestable market is a market where entry is absolutely free and where exit is absolutely costless. Under these stringent assumptions, it appears that there will be zero profits, minimum cost, and price equal to marginal cost.

5. Game theory is often used to analyze oligopolistic markets. For example, the prisoners' dilemma sheds light on the factors determining whether firms will cheat on a cartel agreement. We also showed how game theory can be employed to determine when a threat is credible, to indicate how to discourage entry, and to show the nature of first-mover advantages.

6. Relative to perfect competition, it seems likely that both price and profits will be higher under oligopoly. Moreover, oligopolistic industries will tend to spend more on advertising, product differentiation, and style changes than perfectly competitive industries.

7. Monopolistic competition occurs where there are many sellers whose products are somewhat different. The demand curve facing each firm slopes downward to the right. The conditions for long-run equilibrium are that each firm is maximizing profits and that economic profits are zero.

8. The firm under monopolistic competition is likely to produce less, and charge a higher price, than under perfect competition. Relative to pure monopoly, monopolistically competitive firms are likely to have lower profits, greater output, and lower prices. Firms under monopolistic competition will offer a wider variety of styles, brands, and qualities than will firms under perfect competition.

# CONCEPTS FOR REVIEW

| | | |
|---|---|---|
| **Oligopoly** | **Dominant firm** | **Payoff matrix** |
| **Economies of scale** | **Barometric firm** | **Prisoner's dilemma** |
| **Barriers to entry** | **Nonprice competition** | **Tit for tat** |
| **Collusion** | **Contestable markets** | **Monopolistic competition** |
| **Cartel** | **Game theory** | **Dominant strategy** |
| **Price leadership** | **Strategy** | |

# INDUSTRIAL ORGANIZATION AND ANTITRUST POLICY

MONOPOLY AND MONOPOLIST have long been dirty words—or at least slightly derogatory ones. The public has tended to view monopolists with suspicion at least since Adam Smith's famous attack on monopolies in the eighteenth century. Smith preached and generations of economists since have taught that a monopolist charges a price in excess of the price that would prevail under perfect competition. For reasons given in Chapter 25, this is likely to result in a misallocation of society's resources. One way that society has attempted to deal with problems caused by monopoly is through public regulation, discussed in Chapter 25. Another way is through antitrust policy, discussed in the present chapter.

In this chapter we begin by discussing the case against oligopoly and monopolistic competition, after which we take up the defense of monopoly power made by some economists. Then, after describing the extent of industrial concentration in the United States, we discuss the nature, history, and effectiveness of antitrust policy in the United States, together with the problems in constructing standards for antitrust policy. Finally, we describe some laws in this country that restrict, rather than promote, competition.

## THE CASE AGAINST OLIGOPOLY AND MONOPOLISTIC COMPETITION

**COMPLAINTS AGAINST OLIGOPOLY.**  In Chapter 25, we discussed the case against monopoly. Although economists are more concerned about monopoly than about oligopoly or monopolistic competition, this does not mean that they give either oligopoly or monopolistic competition a clean bill of health. Even though oligopoly has aroused less public indignation and opposition than out-and-out monopoly, an oligopoly can obviously be just as deleterious to social welfare. After all, *if oligopolists engage in collusion, open or tacit, their behavior with regard to price and output may resemble a monopolist's.* Only if there is real competition among the oligopolists can we expect price to be pushed closer to marginal cost under oligopoly than under monopoly. If oligopolists "cooperate" and "maintain orderly markets," the amount of social waste may be no less than under monopoly.

**COMPLAINTS AGAINST MONOPOLISTIC COMPETITION.**  Monopolistic competition can also be a socially wasteful form of market organization. As we saw in Chapter 26, monopolistically competitive markets may be characterized by overcrowding and excess capacity. In addition, price under monopolistic competition—as well as under monopoly and oligopoly—will exceed marginal cost, although the difference between price and marginal cost may be smaller than under monopoly or oligopoly. Thus monopolistic competition, like monopoly and oligopoly, results in a misallocation of resources. The argument leading to this conclusion is exactly like that given in Chapter 25 (and Appendix D) for monopoly. Also, monopolistic competition, as well as oligopoly, may allow waste arising from too much being spent (from society's point of view) on product differentiation, advertising, and other selling expenses. (On the other hand, the diversity of products may benefit consumers enough to offset these disadvantages of monopolistic competition, as pointed out in Chapter 26.)

**THE BOTTOM LINE.** The moral is that many economists look with disfavor on serious departures from perfect competition, whether these departures are in the direction of monopoly, oligopoly, or monopolistic competition. Judged against the perfectly competitive model, all may lead to social waste and inefficiency. However, monopoly is generally presumed to be the greatest evil, with the result that economists usually look with most disfavor on markets dominated by one, or a very few, sellers—or buyers.[1]

## THE DEFENSE OF MONOPOLY POWER

Joseph Schumpeter

Not all economists agree that monopoly power is a bad thing. On the contrary, some respected voices in the economics profession have been raised to praise monopoly, not bury it. In discussing the social problems due to monopoly in Chapter 25, we assumed that the rate of technological change is independent of an industry's market structure. Some economists like Joseph Schumpeter have challenged this assumption. *They assert that the rate of technological change is likely to be higher in an imperfectly competitive industry (i.e., monopoly, oligopoly, etc.) than in a perfectly competitive industry.* Since the rate of technological change affects productivity and living standards, in their view a perfectly competitive economy is likely to be inferior in a dynamic sense to an economy containing many imperfectly competitive industries.

**ARGUMENTS AGAINST PERFECT COMPETITION.** These economists point out that firms under perfect competition have fewer resources to devote to research and experimentation than do firms under imperfect competition. Because profits are at a relatively low level, it is difficult for firms under perfect competition to support large expenditures on research and development. Moreover, they argue that unless a firm has sufficient control over the market to reap the rewards from an innovation, the introduction of the innovation may not be worthwhile. If competitors can imitate the innovation very quickly, the innovator may be unable to make any money from it.

**REJOINDERS TO THE CRITICS.** Defenders of perfect competition retort that there is likely to be less pressure for firms in imperfect markets to introduce new techniques and products, since such firms have fewer competitors. Moreover, firms in imperfect markets are better able to drive out

[1] Monopsony, where a single buyer exists, is taken up in Chapter 28.

entrants who, uncommitted to present techniques, are likely to be relatively quick to adopt new ones. (Entrants, unlike established producers, have no vested interest in maintaining the demand for existing products and the profitability of existing equipment.) Also, there are advantages in having a large number of independent decision-making units. There is less chance that an important technological advance will be blocked by the faulty judgment of a few men or women.

It is very difficult to obtain evidence to help settle this question, if it is posed in this way, since perfect competition is a hypothetical construct that does not exist in the real world. However, it does seem unlikely that a perfectly competitive industry (if such an industry could be constructed) would be able in many areas of the economy to carry out the research and development required to promote a high rate of technological change. Moreover, if entry is free and rapid, firms in a perfectly competitive industry will have little motivation to innovate. Although the evidence is not at all clear-cut, at least this much can be granted the critics of perfect competition.

## MONOPOLY POWER, BIG BUSINESS, AND TECHNOLOGICAL CHANGE

But some economists go much further than the assertion that a certain amount of market imperfection will promote a more rapid rate of technological change. *They say that an industry composed of or dominated by a few large companies is the best market structure for promoting rapid technological change.* Harvard's John Kenneth Galbraith has said that the "modern industry of a few large firms [is] an almost perfect instrument for inducing technical change."[2] And in some circles, it is accepted as an obvious fact that giant firms with their financial strength and well-equipped laboratories are absolutely necessary to maintain a rapid rate of technological change.

Suppose that, for a market of given size, we could replace the largest firms by a larger number of somewhat smaller firms—and thus reduce the extent to which the industry is dominated by the largest firms. Is there any evidence that this would decrease the rate of technological change, as is sometimes asserted? The evidence currently available is much more limited than one would like, but the available studies—based on detailed data concerning research expenditures, patents, important inventions and innovations, and the diffusion of innovations—do not indicate that such a decrease in industrial concentration would reduce the rate of technological change in most industries.

Specifically, the available studies do not show that total research and development expenditures in most industries would decrease if the largest firms were replaced by somewhat smaller ones. Nor do they indicate that the research and development expenditures carried out by the largest firms are generally more productive (or more ambitious or more risky) than those carried out by somewhat smaller firms. Moreover, they do not suggest that greater concentration of an industry results in a faster diffusion of innovations. However, if innovations require a large amount of capital, they do suggest that the substitution of a larger number of

---

[2] John Kenneth Galbraith, *American Capitalism,* Boston: Houghton Mifflin, 1952, p. 91.

smaller firms for a few large ones may lead to slower commercial introduction of the innovations.[3]

Thus, *contrary to the allegations of Galbraith and others, there is little evidence that industrial giants are needed in most industries to ensure rapid technological change and rapid utilization of new techniques.* This does not mean that industries composed only of small firms would necessarily be optimal for the promotion and diffusion of new techniques. On the contrary, there seem to be considerable advantages in a diversity of firm sizes. Complementarities and interdependencies exist among large and small firms. There is often a division of labor. Smaller firms may focus on areas requiring sophistication and flexibility and cater to specialized needs, while bigger firms concentrate on areas requiring large production, marketing, or technical resources. However, there is little evidence in most industries that firms considerably smaller than the biggest firms are not big enough for these purposes.

## HOW MUCH MONOPOLY POWER IS OPTIMAL?

The discussion in previous sections make it clear that the case against monopoly power is not open and shut. On the contrary, a certain amount of monopoly power is inevitable in practically all real-life situations, since perfect competition is a model that can only be approximated in real life. Moreover, a certain amount of monopoly power may be needed to promote desirable technological change. The difficult problem is to determine how much monopoly power is optimal under various circumstances (and how this power is to be measured). Some economists (like Galbraith) are convinced that a great deal of monopoly power is both inevitable and desirable. Others believe the opposite. And the economic arguments are not strong enough to resolve the differences of opinion.

## CONCENTRATION OF ECONOMIC POWER

*Some critics of monopoly power and big business are concerned with the centralization of power in the hands of a relatively few firms.* Although this is only partly an economic matter, it is obviously relevant to public policy makers. Economic power in the United States is distributed very unevenly; a few hundred corporations control a very large share of the total assets of the nonfarm economy. Moreover, within particular industries, there is considerable concentration of ownership and production, as we shall see in the next sections. This concentration of power has been viewed with concern by observers like A. A. Berle, who asserted that the largest several hundred firms "each with its own dominating pyramid within it—represent a concentration of power over economies which makes the medieval feudal system look like a Sunday School party. In sheer economic power this has gone far beyond anything we have yet seen."

It is important to note that this distrust of power leads to a distrust of giant firms, whether or not they have substantial monopoly power. Even

---

[3] Edwin Mansfield, Anthony Romeo, Mark Schwartz, David Teece, Samuel Wagner, and Peter Brach, *Technology Transfer, Productivity, and Economic Policy,* New York: Norton, 1982, and the references cited there.

if General Motors had little power over prices, it would still have considerable economic—and political—power because of its sheer size. Note too that a firm's size is not necessarily a good indicator of the extent of its monopoly power. A small grocery store in a remote community may be a monopolist, but a large merchandising firm with many rivals may have little monopoly power.

Let's look at the 100 biggest manufacturing firms in the United States. Recognizing that bigness is not the same as monopoly power, what percentage of the nation's assets do these firms control, and is this percentage increasing or decreasing over time? According to the latest available figures, the 100 largest manufacturing firms control over half of all manufacturing assets in the United States, and this percentage seems to have increased considerably since the end of World War II.

# INDUSTRIAL CONCENTRATION IN THE UNITED STATES

Economists and policy makers are interested in market structure because it influences market performance. But how can one measure an industry's market structure? How can one tell how close an industry is to being a monopoly or a perfectly competitive industry?

The **market concentration ratio,** which shows the percentage of total sales or production accounted for by the 4 largest firms, is a measure of how concentrated an industry is. The higher the market concentration ratio, the more concentrated the industry is in a very few hands. Basing this measure on 4 firms is arbitrary. You can use 5, 6, 7, or any number of firms you like. But the figures issued by the government are generally based on 4 firms. Also, this measure has important limitations, discussed below.

Consider Table 27.1, which shows the market concentration ratios for selected industries. These ratios vary widely from industry to industry. At one extreme, the automobile industry is a tight oligopoly, with the concentration ratio about as high as it can get: 92 percent. At the other extreme, there is very little industrial concentration in the commercial printing industry; its concentration ratio is only 6 percent.

Most economists who have studied trends in industrial concentration seem to agree that remarkably little change has occurred in the past 70 years in the average level of concentration in the United States. Also, the available evidence seems to indicate that the levels of market concentration are lower in the United States than in other major industrialized countries, with the possible exception of Great Britain and Japan.

Finally, it is important to recognize that the concentration ratio is only a rough measure of an industry's market structure. Certainly, to provide a reasonably adequate description, it must be supplemented with data on the extent and type of product differentiation in the industry, as well as on barriers to entry. Moreover, even with these supplements, it is still a crude measure. (Among other things, it takes no account of competition from foreign suppliers.) Nonetheless, the concentration ratio has proved to be a valuable tool to economists.

**Table 27.1
Concentration Ratios in
Selected Manufacturing
Product Markets, 1982[a]**

| INDUSTRY | MARKET SHARE OF 4 LARGEST FIRMS (PERCENT) |
|---|---|
| Automobiles | 92 |
| Photographic equipment | 74 |
| Tires | 66 |
| Aircraft | 64 |
| Blast furnaces and steel plants | 42 |
| Electronic computing equipment | 43 |
| Petroleum refining | 28 |
| Bread and cake | 34 |
| Pharmaceuticals | 26 |
| Radio and TV equipment | 22 |
| Newspapers | 22 |
| Commercial printing | 6 |

[a]As of late 1991, these were the most recent data available.
Source: Statistical Abstract of the United States.

# THE ANTITRUST LAWS

National policies are too ambiguous and rich in contradictions to be summarized neatly and concisely. Consequently, it would be misleading to say that the United States has adopted a policy of promoting competition and controlling monopoly. To a large extent, it certainly is true that "competition is our fundamental national policy," as the Supreme Court said in 1963. But it is also true that we have adopted many measures to promote monopoly and to limit competition, as we shall see in subsequent sections (and as has already been pointed out in Chapter 25). On balance, however, we probably have gone further in promoting competition than other major industrialized countries, and the principal pieces of legislation designed to further this objective are the **antitrust laws.**

## The Sherman Act

In 1890, the first antitrust law, the Sherman Act, was passed by Congress. Although the common law had long outlawed monopolistic practices, it appeared to many Americans in the closing years of the nineteenth century that legislation was required to discourage monopoly and to preserve and encourage competition. The formation of "trusts"—monopolistic combines that colluded to raise prices and restrict output—brought the matter to a head. The heart of the Sherman Act lies in the following two sections:

> Sec. 1. Every contract, combination in the form of trust or otherwise, or conspiracy, in restraint of trade or commerce among the several states or with foreign nations, is hereby declared to be illegal. Every person who shall make any such contract or engage in any such combination or conspiracy, shall be deemed guilty of a misdemeanor. . . .
>
> Sec. 2. Every person who shall monopolize, or attempt to monopolize or combine or conspire with any other person or persons, to monopolize any part of the trade or commerce among the several States, or with foreign nations shall be deemed guilty of a misdemeanor.

## The Clayton Act

The first 20 years of experience with the Sherman Act were not very satisfying to its supporters. The ineffectiveness of the Sherman Act led in 1914 to passage by Congress of two additional laws—the Clayton Act and the Federal Trade Commission Act. The Clayton Act tried to be more specific than the Sherman Act in identifying certain practices that were illegal because they would "substantially lessen competition or tend to create a monopoly." In particular, the Clayton Act outlawed unjustified **price discrimination,** a practice whereby one buyer is charged more than another buyer for the same product. It also outlawed the use of a **tying contract,** which makes the buyers purchase other items to get the product they want. Further, it outlawed mergers that substantially lessen competition; but since it did not prohibit one firm's purchase of a competitor's plant and equipment, it really could not stop mergers. In 1950, this loophole was closed by the Celler-Kefauver Anti-Merger Act.

### The Federal Trade Commission Act

The Federal Trade Commission Act was designed to prevent undesirable and unfair competitive practices. Specifically, it created a Federal Trade Commission to investigate unfair and predatory practices and to issue cease-and-desist orders. The act stated that "unfair methods of competition in commerce are hereby declared unlawful." However, the commission—composed of 5 commissioners, each appointed by the president for a term of 7 years—was given the unenviable task of defining exactly what was "unfair." Eventually, the courts took away much of the commission's power; but in 1938, the commission acquired the function of outlawing untrue and deceptive advertising. Also, the commission has authority to carry out economic investigations of the structure and conduct of American business.

## THE ROLE OF THE COURTS

The antitrust laws, like any laws, are enforced in the courts. Typically, charges are brought against a firm or group of firms by the Antitrust Division of the Department of Justice, a trial is held, and a decision is reached by the judge. In key cases, appeals are made that eventually reach the Supreme Court. The real impact of the antitrust laws depends on how the courts interpret them. And the judicial interpretation of these laws has changed considerably over time.

The first major set of antitrust cases took place in 1911 when the Standard Oil Company and the American Tobacco Company were forced to give up a large share of their holdings of other companies. In these cases, the Supreme Court put forth and used the famous **rule of reason**—that only unreasonable combinations in restraint of trade, not all trusts, required conviction under the Sherman Act. In 1920, the rule of reason was used by the Supreme Court in its finding that U.S. Steel had not violated the antitrust laws even though it had tried to monopolize the industry—since the Court said it had not succeeded. Moreover, U.S. Steel's large size and its potential monopoly power were ruled beside the point since "the law does not make mere size an offense. It . . . requires overt acts."

During the 1920s and 1930s the courts, including the conservative Supreme Court, interpreted the antitrust laws in such a way that they were as toothless as a new-born babe. Although Eastman Kodak and International Harvester controlled very substantial shares of their markets, the Court, using the rule of reason, found them innocent on the grounds that they had not built up their near-monopoly position through overt coercion or predatory practices. Moreover, the Court reiterated that mere size was not an offense, no matter how great the unexerted monopoly power might be.

In the late 1930s, this situation changed very greatly, with the prosecution of the Aluminum Company of America (Alcoa). This case, decided in 1945 (but begun in 1937), reversed the decisions in the *U.S. Steel* and *International Harvester* cases. Alcoa had achieved its 90 percent of the market by means that would have been considered "reasonable" in the earlier cases—keeping its price low enough to discourage entry, building capacity to take care of increases in the market, and so forth. (Recall our discussion of Alcoa in Chapter 25.) Nonetheless, the Court decided that Alcoa, because it controlled practically all the industry's output, violated

Alcoa headquarters

the antitrust laws. Thus, to a considerable extent, *the Court used market structure rather than market conduct as a test of legality.*

## THE ROLE OF THE JUSTICE DEPARTMENT

The Justice Department, Washington, D.C.

The impact of the antitrust laws is determined by the vigor with which the Antitrust Division of the Justice Department prosecutes cases. If the Antitrust Division does not prosecute, the laws can have little effect. Like the judicial interpretation of the laws, the extent to which the Justice Department has prosecuted cases has varied from one period to another. Needless to say, the attitude of the political party in power has been an important determinant of how vigorously antitrust cases have been prosecuted. When the Sherman Act was first passed, it was of singularly little value. For example, President Grover Cleveland's attorney general did not agree with the law and would not prosecute under it. "Trust-busting" was truly a neglected art until President Theodore Roosevelt devoted his formidable energies to it. In 1903, he established the Antitrust Division of the Justice Department. Moreover, his administration started the major cases that led to the *Standard Oil, American Tobacco,* and *U.S. Steel* decisions.

Subsequently, there was a long lull in the prosecution of antitrust cases, reflecting the Supreme Court's rule-of-reason doctrine and a strong conservative tide in the nation. The lull continued for about 25 years, until 1937, when there was a significant upsurge in activity on the antitrust front. Led by Thurman Arnold, the Antitrust Division entered one of the most vigorous periods of antitrust enforcement to date. Arnold went after the glass, cigarette, cement, and other industries, the most important case being that against Alcoa. The Antitrust Division attempted in this period to reopen cases that were hopeless under the rule-of-reason doctrine. With the change in the composition of the Supreme Court, Arnold's activism turned out to be effective.

## LANDMARK DECISIONS SINCE WORLD WAR II

The 1960s and 1970s generally were a period of vigorous antitrust activity, with at least five notable developments.

1. *One of the biggest cases in the history of antitrust occurred in 1961 when, as you will recall from the previous chapter, the major electrical equipment manufacturers were convicted of collusive price agreements.* Executives of General Electric, Westinghouse, and other firms in the industry admitted that they met secretly in hotels and communicated by mail in order to maintain prices, share the market, and eliminate competition. Some of the executives were sentenced to jail on criminal charges, and the firms had to pay large amounts to customers to make up for the overcharges. In particular, 1,800 triple damage suits against the firms resulted in payments estimated at between $400 and $600 million. Even the most zealous antitrusters will admit that this was no slap on the wrist!

2. *Following the enactment of the Celler-Kefauver Anti-Merger Act, horizontal mergers—mergers of firms making essentially the same good—became increasingly likely to run afoul of the antitrust laws.* In 1962, Chief Justice Earl Warren went so far as to say that a merger that resulted in a firm having 5 percent of the market might be undesirable. In the *Von's*

*Grocery* case in 1965, the Court disallowed a merger between two supermarkets that together had less than 8 percent of the Los Angeles market. (In this case, the Court emphasized the trend toward increasing concentration in grocery retailing in Los Angeles.) Also, vertical mergers—mergers of firms that supply or sell to one another—have been viewed with a jaundiced eye by the courts. For example, in the *Brown Shoe* case, the Supreme Court said that the merger of Brown with R. G. Kinney would mean that other shoe manufacturers would be frozen out of a substantial part of the retail shoe market.

3. *A leading problem confronting the Justice Department in the 1960s was conglomerate mergers—mergers of firms in unrelated industries.* Conglomerate firms like Litton Industries, International Telephone, and Ling-Temco-Vought were regarded very highly by investors during the 1960s. Inspired by their apparent success, other firms began to merge with firms in other industries in order to become conglomerates themselves. Supporters of these mergers claimed that they enabled weak companies to be revitalized by superior management, bigger research facilities, and so on. However, this merger movement was opposed by many other observers on the grounds that conglomerates were obtaining too much power in the economy. To some extent, this problem diminished in importance after the conglomerates began to show relatively disappointing earnings in the late 1960s. But the Justice Department continued to keep a watchful eye on conglomerate mergers. In 1967 it succeeded in preventing a conglomerate merger between Procter & Gamble, the big soap manufacturer, and Clorox, a maker of liquid bleach. And in 1971 it made some attempt to force ITT to divest itself of the Hartford Fire Insurance Company, but the case was dropped.

4. *In 1982, a government antitrust suit (begun in 1974) against the American Telephone and Telegraph Company (AT&T) was settled.* According to the settlement, AT&T divested itself of 22 companies that provide most of the nation's local telephone service, and kept its Long Lines division, Western Electric, and the Bell Laboratories. While many observers worried that one result was likely to be an increase in local telephone rates, there was also considerable feeling that, after the telephone industry was restructured in this way, AT&T would be a leaner and more dynamic firm. One immediate effect of this divestiture was a great deal of confusion among customers and costly adjustments within AT&T, but subsequently many observers believed that it was resulting in faster introduction of new technologies and services and lower long-distance phone rates.

5. *The Antitrust Division sued IBM Corporation under Section 2 of the Sherman Act in January 1969, thus starting one of the biggest and costliest antitrust cases in history.* The government charged that IBM held a monopoly and that the firm's 360 line of computers was introduced in 1965 in a way that eliminated competition. IBM's defense was that its market position stemmed from its innovative performance and economies of scale, that its pricing was competitive, and that its profit rate really had not been high. Once the trial began in 1975, it took the government almost three years to present its case. In early 1982, on the same day that it settled the antitrust case against AT&T, the Reagan administration dropped the IBM case. It said the case was "without merit and should be dismissed."

AT&T headquarters, Basking Ridge, NJ

## THE GROWTH OF PRIVATE ANTITRUST SUITS

Recent decades have seen a great increase in the number of private antitrust suits. You may have thought that only governments can bring antitrust suits, but this is not true. Private parties can and do bring damage suits—and if they win, they get triple damages plus their reasonable costs. By the 1970s, the number of private antitrust cases (over 1,000 per year) far exceeded the number of government antitrust cases, and in some cases the judgments were very large. The growth of private antitrust suits has raised many questions. For one thing, firms have sometimes brought suit against their rivals, claiming that their rivals have violated the antitrust laws, when in fact this has not been true. Instead, their rivals have simply been more efficient and imaginative than these firms have been. Nonetheless, this legal ploy can be an effective way for an otherwise unsuccessful firm to try to strike back at its more successful rivals. Some people think that winners of antitrust suits should get less than triple damages; in this way, the incentive for such suits would decline.

## THE WAVE OF CORPORATE TAKEOVERS DURING THE 1980S

To understand the nature of antitrust policy during the 1980s, you must know that there was a rash of merger activity in that decade. Among other examples, General Electric took over RCA, and Chevron took over Gulf Oil. In terms of the value of the acquired firms, the volume of acquisitions was unprecedented. Moreover, a distinguishing characteristic of this recent wave of mergers was the frequency with which the acquiring firm by-passed the target corporation's management and tried to purchase a controlling interest directly from the target's stockholders.

An intense debate has taken place concerning the social costs and benefits of this wave of takeovers. On the one hand, it is clear that mergers can have substantial economic benefits. For example, they can result in economies of scale, as well as the more appropriate valuation of particular resources. Even hostile takeovers can be good for the economy if a more efficient management replaces a less efficient one. But there is no assurance that a merger will necessarily be socially beneficial. Once taken over, some firms may operate less efficiently, not more so, than before.

F. M. Scherer and David Ravenscraft have used accounting data in an attempt to shed light on this question. They conclude that

> there is no evidence that the acquiring companies managed their acquired assets either clearly worse or clearly better than the average of the industries to which the acquiring lines belonged. This finding of "no significant change" is at odds with the hypothesis that takeovers increase efficiency and pre-tax profits. If the takeover premium was paid in the expectation of increased profitability, tenderers must have systematically overestimated their ability to manage the target firm's operations better than the prior incumbents.[4]

[4] F. M. Scherer, "Takeovers: Present and Future Dangers," *The Brookings Review*, Winter 1986, p. 18. Also, see W. Adams and J. Brock, "The New Learning and the Euthanasia of Antitrust," *California Law Review*, October 1986.

As would be expected, those who feel that the takeover wave has been beneficial have attacked these conclusions. Thus Douglas Ginsburg and John Robinson argue that accounting studies,

> particularly those that attempt to measure profitability, suffer from serious methodological problems that limit their relevance for policy purposes. For example, they do not take into account the real market values of acquired assets — only the accounting valuations, which may significantly understate their value. They generally encounter great difficulty in allocating beneficial externalities that the purchase may generate for the acquirer, such as a target's tax-loss carry-forward. Moreover, unlike the studies based on stock price data, accounting studies have not yielded consistent significant results. As a result, the interpretation and value of these studies is highly uncertain.[5]

## ANTITRUST IN THE REAGAN AND BUSH YEARS

Antitrust policy changed in 1981 when President Reagan took office. His Antitrust Division believed that a fair number of activities that had been deemed antitrust violations in the past not only were legal, but also were beneficial to the economy. According to this view, business decisions should be free of antitrust interference unless they are unequivocally anticompetitive. Given the huge costs (about $1 billion to IBM, according to some estimates) of the IBM case, and the feeling among some economists that economies of scale were sometimes underestimated, it is not surprising that such a change in emphasis and direction occurred. But economists who favor an aggressive antitrust policy tended to regard this change with suspicion.

During the 1980s, antitrust officials felt that they should attack conspiracies to fix prices, but they were less concerned than their predecessors about many kinds of mergers.[6] (For example, little attention was paid to mergers between firms in different industries.) There was also more sympathy for the view that big firms often are more efficient than small ones, and that it is therefore a mistake to try to limit their growth. While some believe that antitrust enforcement was too lax, the Reagan administration argued that it was enforcing the laws in ways that advanced rather than hindered competition and consumer welfare.

In the Bush administration, there was more activity on the antitrust front. In 1990, the Justice Department filed suit against the American Institute of Architects charging that it unreasonably restrained price competition among architects. Also, it initiated an investigation into whether some leading colleges and universities had violated the antitrust laws. Further, the Federal Trade Commission complained that Capital Cities-ABC Inc. and the College Football Association had illegally conspired to limit the

[5] D. Ginsburg and J. Robinson, "The Case Against Federal Intervention in the Market for Corporate Control," *The Brookings Review,* Winter 1986, p. 13. Also, see A. Schleifer and R. Vishny, "The Takeover Wave of the 1980s," *Science,* August 17, 1990.

[6] In 1982, the Justice Department announced the following merger guidelines: (1) If the Herfindahl-Hirschman index (after the merger) is less than 1,000, the Justice Department is unlikely to challenge any merger. (2) If this index is between 1,000 and 1,800, a merger that changes the index by less than 100 points probably will not be challenged. (3) If this index is greater than 1,800, a merger that changes the index by less than 50 points will probably not be challenged. (The Herfindahl-Hirschmann index equals the sum of the squared market shares of the firms in the market. For example, if two firms exist in a market, and each firm has 50 percent of the market, this index equals $50^2 + 50^2 = 5,000$.)

number of football games shown on television. Many observers feel that the Bush administration focused more attention on the antitrust laws than did the Reagan administration.

---

## TEST YOURSELF

1. "Perfect competition results in optimal efficiency and an optimal distribution of income. This is why the United States opts for a perfectly competitive economy." Comment and evaluate.

2. "The real impact of the antitrust laws depends on judicial interpretation." Comment and evaluate.

3. Suppose that an industry is composed of five firms. The market share of each firm is given in the table at right. What is the concentration ratio for this industry?

| FIRM | MARKET SHARE (PERCENT) |
|------|------------------------|
| A | 10 |
| B | 10 |
| C | 20 |
| D | 25 |
| E | 35 |

4. Suppose that firm E loses half of its sales to firm C. If the sales of the other firms remain constant, what is the effect on the concentration ratio in Question 3?

---

## STANDARDS FOR ANTITRUST POLICY

There are at least two fairly distinct approaches to antitrust policy. *The first looks primarily and directly at* **market performance**—*the industry's rate of technological change, efficiency, and profits, the conduct of individual firms, and so on.* Advocates of this approach argue that, in deciding antitrust cases, one should review in detail the performance of the firms in question to see how well they have served the economy. If they have served well they should not be held in violation of the antitrust laws simply because they have a large share of the market. This test, as it is usually advocated, relies heavily on an evaluation of the technological "progressiveness" and "dynamism" of the firms in question. Although this approach seems quite sensible, it has a number of disadvantages. In particular, it is very difficult to tell at present whether a particular industry's performance is "good" or "bad." Economists simply do not have the sorts of measuring rods that would be required to obtain reasonably accurate and well-accepted readings on an industry's performance. In view of the vagueness of the criteria and the practical realities of the antitrust environment, adopting this approach would probably invite nonenforcement of the laws.

*The second approach emphasizes the importance of an industry's* **market stucture**—*the number and size distribution of buyers and sellers in the market, the ease with which new firms can enter, and the extent of product differentiation.* According to this approach, one should look to market structure for evidence of undesirable monopolistic characteristics. The basic idea behind this approach, as George Stigler puts it, is that "an industry which does not have a competitive structure will not have competitive behavior." This approach, too, has lots of critics. Many economists and lawyers feel that the relationship between market structure and market performance is so weak that it is a mistake to choose, more or less arbitrarily, some level of concentration and to say that, if concentration exceeds this level, market performance is likely to be undesirable.

## THE EFFECTIVENESS OF ANTITRUST POLICY

How effective have the antitrust laws been? Obviously it is difficult to tell with any accuracy, since there is no way to carry out an experiment in which American history is rewritten to show what would have happened if the antitrust laws had not been on the books. Many experts seem to feel that the antitrust laws have not been as effective as they might—or should—have been, largely because they do not have sufficient public support and there is no politically powerful pressure group pushing for their enforcement.

But this does not mean that the antitrust laws have had no effect. As Edward Mason of Harvard University pointed out, their effectiveness is due "not so much to the contribution that particular judgments have made to the restoring of competition as it is to the fact that the consideration of whether or not a particular course of action may or may not be in violation of the antitrust acts is a persistent factor affecting business judgment, at least in large firms."[7] This same idea is summed up in the old saying that the ghost of Senator Sherman sits as an *ex officio* member of every firm's board of directors.

Some indication of the effects of our antitrust laws can perhaps be obtained by looking at experience in other countries, since Britain, Germany, and many other European countries (as well as Japan) took a very tolerant view of monopoly power for a long time. After World War II, there was pressure to break up some of the powerful combines in Germany and Japan, but this pressure has been somewhat relaxed more recently—although antitrust practices seem to be gaining ground in the European Common Market. Foreign experience seems to indicate that the antitrust laws have helped prevent American firms from adopting many restrictive and predatory practices common elsewhere.

## THE PABST CASE: ANTITRUST IN ACTION

Perhaps the most effective way to learn certain things about the antitrust field is to try to decide an actual antitrust case. Suppose that, over the protests of the American Bar Association, you are appointed a district court judge and that your first job is to hear a case (actually brought by the government some years ago) to prevent Pabst Brewing Company from acquiring the Blatz Brewing Company. According to the government, the effect of this merger "may be substantially to lessen competition, or to tend to create a monopoly" in the production and sale of beer in the state of Wisconsin, the three-state area of Wisconsin, Illinois, and Michigan, and the United States.

*A fundamental issue in any case of this sort is the definition of market and industry boundaries.* Market boundaries must be broad enough to include all relevant competitors but not so broad as to include products that

PABST QUALITY.
IT'S A TRADITION THAT KEEPS GROWING.

---

[7] Edward Mason, Preface to Carl Kaysen and Donald Turner, *Antitrust Policy* (and reprinted in E. Mansfield, *Monopoly Power and Economic Performance,* 4th ed. New York: Norton, 1978).

are not reasonable substitutes. The delineation of market and industry boundaries—in terms of "line of commerce" and "section of the country"—is bound to involve judgment, there being no simple, mechanical rule to settle it.

In the *Pabst* case, both the government and Pabst agreed "that the line of commerce involved the production, sale, and distribution of beer and that the continental United States is a relevant geographic market." However, there was disagreement over the government's use of Wisconsin and the three-state area of Wisconsin, Illinois, and Michigan as separate geographical markets. Pabst and Blatz claimed that there was no good reason to single out these particular areas as distinct markets. The government, on the other hand, claimed that they were distinct markets because the two firms competed most intensively in these areas. Pabst was the nation's eleventh largest seller of beer; its sales were 2.67 percent of the national market and about 11 percent of the sales in Wisconsin. Blatz was the nation's thirteenth largest seller of beer, its sales being 2.04 percent of the national market and about 13 percent of the sales in Wisconsin. Thus, *if you look at the smaller geographical area (Wisconsin and the three-state area), the two firms account for a substantial proportion of the market—about 24 percent in Wisconsin. But if you look at the national market as a whole, they account for a small proportion—less than 5 percent.*

As the district judge how should you decide the case? Should you agree with the government that Wisconsin and the three-state area are relevant markets? Or should you agree with Pabst and Blatz that they are not relevant markets in themselves, but just parts of a market? Moreover, if you agree with the government concerning the market definition, should you also agree that two firms with a total of 24 percent of Wisconsin sales should not be allowed to merge? Or if you agree with Pabst and Blatz concerning the market definition, should you allow a merger between two firms that together account for about 5 percent of the national market? It is a tough problem, isn't it? To demonstrate just how tough it is, the district judge decided one way, while the Supreme Court decided the other way. The district court, agreeing with Pabst and Blatz that Wisconsin and the three-state area should not be treated as distinct relevant areas, dismissed the government's complaint. But the district court's decision was reversed by the Supreme Court, which agreed with the government's position that the smaller areas should be treated as relevant, distinct markets.

The antitrust field is characterized by many complexities and uncertainties, as well as by legal and economic vagueness and ambiguity. This case illustrates how difficult it is even to decide what the relevant market is!

## THE PATENT SYSTEM

In a previous section, we pointed out that our national economic policies are by no means free of contradiction. In particular, although many of our policies are designed to promote competition and limit monopoly, one should not assume that all of them are meant to promote these objectives. On the contrary, quixotic as it may seem, some are designed to do just the opposite—to restrict competition. Among the most important of these policies are our laws concerning patents, which grant inventors exclusive control over the use of their inventions for 17 years. That is, inventors are given a temporary monopoly over the use of their inventions.

## The Pros

Since Congress passed the original patent act in 1790, the arguments used to justify the existence of the patent laws have not changed very much. First, *these laws are regarded as an important incentive to induce the inventor to put in the work required to produce an invention.* Particularly in the case of the individual inventor, it is claimed that patent protection is a strong incentive. Second, *patents are regarded as a necessary incentive to induce firms to carry out the further work and make the necessary investment in pilot plants and other items that are required to bring the invention to commercial use.* If an invention became public property when made, why should a firm incur the costs and risks involved in attempting to develop, debug, and perfect it? Another firm could watch, take no risks, and duplicate the process or product if it were successful. Third, it is argued that because of the patent laws, *inventions are disclosed earlier than otherwise, the consequence being that other inventions are facilitated by the earlier dissemination of the information.* The resulting situation is often contrasted with the intense secrecy about processes that characterized the medieval guilds and which undoubtedly retarded technological progress and economic growth.

## The Cons

Not all economists agree that the patent system is beneficial. A patent represents a monopoly right, although, as many inventors can testify, it may be a very weak one. Critics of the patent system stress the social costs arising from the monopoly. After a new process or product has been discovered, it may cost very little for other persons who could make use of this knowledge to acquire it. The patent gives the inventor the right to charge a price for the use of the information, with the result that the knowledge is used less widely than is socially optimal. Critics also point out that patents have been used to create monopoly positions, which were sustained by other means after the original patents had expired. They cite as examples the aluminum, shoe machinery, and plate-glass industries. In addition, the cross-licensing of patents often has been used by firms as a vehicle for joint monopolistic exploitation of their market.

Critics also question the extent of the social gains arising from the system. They point out that the patent system was designed for the individual inventor, but that over the years most research and development has been institutionalized. They assert that patents are not really important as incentives to the large corporation, since it cannot afford to fall behind in the technological race, whether or not it receives a patent. Also, they say that because of long lead times, most of the innovative profits from many innovations can be captured before imitators have a chance to enter the market, whether or not the innovator is granted a patent. Finally, they claim that firms keep secret what inventions they can, and patent those they cannot.

These questions concerning the effects and desirability of the patent system have proven extremely difficult to settle. But most observers seem to agree that, despite its faults, it is hard to find a realistic substitute for the patent system.

# OTHER POLICIES DESIGNED TO RESTRICT COMPETITION

The reasons why laws are enacted to restrict, rather than promote, competition are not difficult to understand. People want competition for the other guy, but not for themselves. Moreover, certain sectors of the economy seem to need help, and have the political muscle to get it—partly in the form of laws designed to take some of the competitive heat off them.

## Robinson-Patman Act

A case of this sort is retail trade, where the small independent retailers felt threatened by the advent of the chain store. The chain stores were able to reduce the costs of distribution below those of the smaller retailers, with the result that the total number of grocery stores and drugstores fell considerably in the 1920s and 1930s. The small retailers charged that their smaller numbers were due to the predatory tactics of the chain stores. They took their charges to Congress and succeeded in getting the Robinson-Patman Act enacted in 1936.

The Robinson-Patman Act says that sellers must not discriminate in price among purchasers of similar grade and quality where the effect might be to drive competitors out of business. The act was aimed at preventing price discrimination in favor of chain stores that buy goods in large quantities. Most economists do not regard the Robinson-Patman Act with enthusiasm because it attempts to keep competitors in existence even if they are inefficient. (The social virtues of the competitive system do not lie in maintaining a lot of inefficient small businessmen in operation.) Moreover, most observers seem to believe that the act has had the effect of reducing the vigor of price competition in retail trade.

## Miller-Tydings Act

Another law designed to limit competition in U.S. retail trade was the Miller-Tydings Act of 1937, which exempted from the antitrust laws the use of resale price maintenance agreements in states permitting such agreements. *Resale price maintenance agreements* permitted manufacturers of a trademarked or branded item to establish the retail price of the item by contracts with retailers. Moreover, the Miller-Tydings Act permitted the manufacturer to bind *all* retailers in a state to a contract simply by signing such a contract with *any one* of the retailers in the state. The result was to reduce the amount of price competition in retail trade. In 1975, Congress passed a bill nullifying such agreements.

## Other Policies Limiting Competition

Finally, you should recognize that policies designed to limit competition are found in many other areas besides retail trade. Our national farm policies have been aimed at keeping the prices of agricultural products at a level exceeding what they would be under competition. In Chapter 28, we shall see that the government has promoted the growth of strong labor unions, which try to raise wages above competitive levels. In the field of international trade, the Webb-Pomerene Act of 1918 allowed American exporters to get together to form export trade associations,

# EXAMPLE 27.1    RESALE PRICE MAINTENANCE AND COSMETICS

Until 1975, resale price maintenance agreements allowed manufacturers of a trademarked item to establish a floor under the retail price of the item. Suppose that the manufacturer of a cosmetic established $OP$ as its minimum retail price, and that $D_0$ is the demand curve for this cosmetic at a particular drugstore. The drugstore's average costs are also shown in the diagram.

(a) Only the solid portion of demand curve $D_0$ is relevant to the drugstore. Why? (b) Can the drugstore make a profit on the sale of the cosmetic? (c) Will there be a change in the number of drugstores selling the cosmetic? What sort of a change? Why? (d) As changes occur in the number of drugstores selling the cosmetic, the demand curve eventually moves to $D_1$. Why? At this point, can a drugstore make a profit on the sale of the cosmetic?

## Solution

(a) Because the drugstore cannot sell the cosmetic at a price less than $OP$ without running afoul of the resale price maintenance agreements. (b) Yes. If it sells between $OQ_0$ and $OQ_1$ ounces of the cosmetic, the price it receives will exceed its average cost. (c) Yes. Because profits are made on this cosmetic, other stores will begin to sell it, the result being that the number of stores selling it will increase. (d) Because more and more stores sell the cosmetic, the total volume is spread more thinly among the stores. In other words, the demand curve facing a particular drugstore shifts to the left. When the demand curve reaches $D_1$, a drugstore can no longer make a profit from the sale of the cosmetic. Thus entry ceases.*

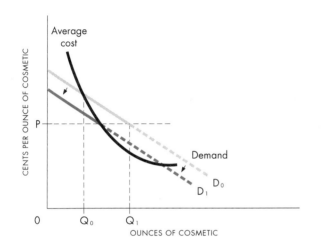

* For further discussion, see L. Weiss, Case Studies in American Industry, New York: Wiley, 1980.

which, according to some observers, may have tended to reduce competition. Even in the bituminous coal industry, which we looked at in some detail in Chapter 24, Congress passed the Bituminous Coal Act of 1937 to establish minimum prices and reduce "cutthroat" competition, though in 1943 the act was not renewed.

Thus it is erroneous to think that the United States has opted decisively for competition. On the contrary, although the antitrust laws are clearly designed to promote competition and limit monopoly, a number of other laws are designed to do just the opposite. In many of the industries where laws designed to restrict competition have been enacted—for example, agriculture, retail trade, and bituminous coal—the basic problem has been that too many people and too much capital were tied up in the industry. Economists generally believe that it would be wiser to encourage people and capital to leave these industries than to attempt to limit competition. (More will be said on this score in Chapter 31, where we discuss American farm policies.)

# TEST YOURSELF

1. "The antitrust laws effectively protect the large business from social pressure or regulation by maintaining the myth that the market does the regulating instead." Do you agree? Why, or why not?

2. General Motors and Toyota are two of the world's largest auto manufacturers. Several years ago, they proposed a joint venture to assemble a small car in California. The Federal Trade Commission approved this joint venture. Why wasn't this venture in violation of the antitrust laws?

3. Chief Justice Hughes observed, "Good intentions will not save a plan otherwise objectionable, but knowledge of actual intent is an aid in the interpretation of facts and prediction of consequence." Relate this to the construction of standards for antitrust policy.

4. What are the arguments in favor of the patent system? What are the arguments against it? Is there currently considerable political support for the abolition of the patent system?

# SUMMARY

1. A monopolistic industry produces too little of the monopolized good. Society is less well off than it could be. Oligopoly can be as bad as monopoly if oligopolists engage in collusion; and even if they don't collude, inefficiencies are likely to result. Monopolistic competition can also be a socially wasteful form of market organization.

2. In defense of monopoly power, some economists have asserted that the rate of technological change is likely to be greater in an imperfectly competitive industry than under perfect competition. It does seem unlikely that a perfectly competitive industry would be able—and have the incentive—to carry out the research and development required to promote a rapid rate of technological change in many sectors of the economy.

3. On the other hand, there is little evidence that giant firms are needed to ensure rapid technological change in a great many sectors of the economy. The technological contributions of smaller firms are much greater than is commonly recognized.

4. Economic power in the United States is distributed very unevenly; 100 corporations control about half the total manufacturing assets of the economy. Moreover, many individual industries are dominated by a few firms. This concentration of power is viewed with concern by some economists and lawyers.

5. In 1890, the Sherman Act was passed. It outlawed any contract, combination, or conspiracy in restraint of trade and made it illegal to monopolize or attempt to monopolize. In 1914, Congress passed the Clayton Act, and the Federal Trade Commission was created. A more recent antitrust development was the Celler-Kefauver Anti-Merger Act of 1950.

6. The real impact of the antitrust laws depends on the interpretation placed on these laws by the courts. In its early cases, the Supreme Court put forth and used the famous rule of reason—that only unreasonable combinations in restraint of trade, not all trusts, required conviction under the Sherman Act. The situation changed greatly in the 1940s when the Court decided that Alcoa, because it controlled practically all of the nation's aluminum output, was in violation of the antitrust laws.

7. In the Reagan administration, antitrust officials felt that they should attack conspiracies to fix prices, but they were much less concerned than their predecessors about many kinds of mergers, which took place in very large numbers during the 1980s. According to many observers, the Bush administration focused more attention on the antitrust laws than did the Reagan administration.

8. Many observers seem to feel that the antitrust laws have not been as effective as they might—or should—have been, largely because they do not have sufficient public support. At the same time, many feel that the evidence, although incomplete and unclear, suggests that the antitrust laws have had a nonnegligible effect on business behavior and markets.

9. Not all our laws are designed to promote competition and restrict monopoly. On the contrary, some laws are designed to do just the opposite. The patent system confers a temporary monopoly on inventors. And the Robinson-Patman Act and many other laws have been designed to restrict competition. The truth is that, despite some protests to the contrary, our nation is by no means fully committed to promoting competition and preventing monopoly.

## CONCEPTS FOR REVIEW

Market concentration
  ratio
Antitrust laws
Price discrimination

Tying contract
Rule of reason
Market performance
Market structure

Patent system
Resale price
  maintenance agreements

# PART SEVEN

# DISTRIBUTION OF INCOME

# DETERMINANTS OF WAGES

EVERYONE HAS A HEALTHY—indeed, sometimes an unhealthy—interest in income. Organizations as holy as the church and as unholy as the Mob exhibit an interest in this subject. Surely we all need to look carefully at the social mechanisms underlying the distribution of income in our society. Most income is in the form of wages and salaries; that is, it is labor income. What determines the price paid for a particular kind of labor? Why is the wage rate for surgeons frequently in the neighborhood of $100 an hour, while the wage rate for relatively unskilled labor is frequently in the neighborhood of $5 or $6 an hour? Or why is the wage rate of a secretary higher in 1992 than in 1960?

Economists frequently classify inputs into three categories—labor, capital, and land. The disadvantage of this simple classification is that each category contains an enormous variety of inputs. Consider the services of labor, which include the work of a football star like Joe Montana, a salesman like Willy Loman, and a knight like Don Quixote. But it does have the important advantage of distinguishing between different classes of inputs. In this chapter, we are concerned with the determinants of the price of labor. The next chapter will deal with the determinants of the prices of capital and land, as well as profits.

## THE LABOR FORCE AND THE PRICE OF LABOR

At the outset it is important to note that, to the economist, labor includes a great deal more than the organized labor that belongs to trade unions. The secretary who works at IBM, the young account executive at Merrill Lynch, the auto mechanic at your local garage, the professor who teaches molecular biology, all put forth labor. About two-thirds of the people employed are white-collar workers (such as salespeople, doctors, secretaries, or managers) and service workers (such as waiters, bartenders, or cooks), while only about one-third are blue-collar workers (such as carpenters, mine workers, or foremen) and farm workers. Moreover, as shown in Table 28.1, many more people work in the service industry and in retail trade than in manufacturing.

## Table 28.1
## Employment on Nonagricultural Payrolls, by Major Industry, 1990

| INDUSTRY | EMPLOYMENT (MILLIONS) |
|---|---|
| Mining | 1 |
| Construction | 5 |
| Manufacturing | 19 |
| Transportation and public utilities | 6 |
| Wholesale trade | 6 |
| Retail trade | 20 |
| Finance, insurance, and real estate | 7 |
| Services | 28 |
| Federal government | 3 |
| State and local government | 15 |
| Total | 110 |

Source: Economic Report of the President, 1991.

It is also worthwhile to preface our discussion with some data concerning how much people actually get paid. As shown in Table 28.2, average weekly earnings vary considerably from one industry to another. For example, in 1990, workers in manufacturing averaged about $442 a week, while construction workers averaged $524 a week, and workers in retail trade averaged $195 a week. Also, average weekly earnings vary considerably from one period to another. Table 28.2 shows that average weekly earnings in manufacturing in 1965 were only $108, as contrasted with $442 in 1990. In subsequent sections, we shall investigate the reasons for these differences in wages, both among industries and among periods of time.

More broadly, we shall be concerned in subsequent sections with the price of labor, which includes a great many forms of remuneration other than what are commonly regarded as wages. As noted above, economists include as labor the services performed by professional people (such as lawyers, doctors, and professors) and self-employed people (such as electricians, mechanics, and barbers). Thus the amount such people receive per unit of time is included here as a particular sort of price of labor, even though these amounts are often called fees or salaries rather than wages.

Finally, it is important to distinguish between *money* wages and *real* wages. Whereas the money wage is the amount of money received per unit of time, the real wage is the amount of real goods and services that can be bought with the money wage. The real wage depends on the price level for goods and services as well as on the magnitude of the money wage. Particularly during the late 1970s and early 1980s, the inflation we experienced meant that real wages increased less than money wages; thus the increases in earnings in Table 28.2 exaggerate the increase in real wages. In subsequent sections, since we shall assume that product prices are held constant, our discussion will be in terms of real wages.

## Table 28.2
## Average Weekly Earnings, Selected Industries, 1955–90 (Dollars)

| YEAR | MANUFAC- TURING | CONSTRUC- TION | RETAIL TRADE |
|---|---|---|---|
| 1955 | 76 | 91 | 49 |
| 1960 | 90 | 113 | 58 |
| 1965 | 108 | 138 | 67 |
| 1970 | 134 | 195 | 82 |
| 1975 | 190 | 265 | 108 |
| 1980 | 289 | 368 | 147 |
| 1985 | 386 | 464 | 175 |
| 1990 | 442 | 524 | 195 |

# THE EQUILIBRIUM WAGE AND EMPLOYMENT UNDER PERFECT COMPETITION

## The Firm's Demand Curve for Labor

Let's begin by discussing the determinants of the price of labor under perfect competition. That is, we assume that firms take the prices of their products, as well as the prices of all inputs, as given; and we assume that owners of inputs take input prices as given. Under these circumstances, what determines how much labor an individual firm will hire (at a specified wage rate)? Once we answer this question, we can derive a firm's demand curve for labor. A ***firm's demand curve for labor*** is the relationship between the price of labor and the amount of labor utilized by the firm. That is, it shows, for each price, the amount of labor that the firm will use.

## The Profit-Maximizing Quantity of Labor

Let us assume that we know the firm's production function, and that labor is the only variable input. Given the production function, we can determine the marginal product of labor when various quantities are used. The results of such a calculation are as shown in Table 28.3. If the price of the firm's product is $10, let's determine the value to the firm of each additional worker it hires per day.[1] According to Table 28.3, the firm achieves a daily output of 7 units when it hires the first worker; and since each unit is worth $10, this brings the firm's daily revenues up to $70. By hiring the second worker, the firm increases its daily output by 6 units; and since each unit is worth $10, the resulting increase in the firm's daily revenues is $60. Similarly, the increase in the firm's daily revenues from hiring the third worker is $50, the increase from hiring the fourth worker is $40, and so on.

*A firm should hire more workers as long as the extra workers result in at least as great an addition to revenues as they do to costs.* While this is a relatively simple idea, when stated this baldly, it nonetheless is very important. Consider the firm in Table 28.3. If the price of a worker is $50 per day, it is profitable for this firm to hire the first worker since this adds $70 to the firm's daily revenues but only $50 to its daily costs. Also, it is profitable to hire the second worker, since this adds $60 to the firm's daily revenues but only $50 to its daily costs. The addition of the third worker does not reduce the firm's profits. But beyond 3 workers per day, it does not pay the firm to hire more labor. (The addition of a fourth worker adds $50 to the firm's daily costs but only $40 to its daily revenues.)

## The Value of the Marginal Product of Labor

Thus the optimal number of workers per day for this firm is 3. Table 28.3 shows that this is the number of workers at which the value of the marginal product of labor is equal to the price of labor. What is the ***value of the marginal product of labor?*** It is the marginal product of labor multiplied by the product's price. In Table 28.3, the value of the marginal

**Table 28.3**
**The Firm's Demand for Labor under Perfect Competition**

| NUMBER OF WORKERS PER DAY | TOTAL OUTPUT PER DAY | MARGINAL PRODUCT OF LABOR | VALUE OF MARGINAL PRODUCT (DOLLARS) |
|---|---|---|---|
| 0 | 0 | | |
| | | 7 | 70 |
| 1 | 7 | | |
| | | 6 | 60 |
| 2 | 13 | | |
| | | 5 | 50 |
| 3 | 18 | | |
| | | 4 | 40 |
| 4 | 22 | | |
| | | 3 | 30 |
| 5 | 25 | | |

[1] For simplicity, we assume that the number of workers that the firm hires per day must be an integer, not a fraction. This assumption is innocuous, and can easily be relaxed.

product of labor is $70 when between 0 and 1 workers are used per day. Why? Because the marginal product of labor is 7 units of output, and the price of a unit of output is $10. Thus this product—7 times $10—equals $70.

To maximize profit, the value of the marginal product of labor must be set equal to the price of labor, because if the value of the marginal product is greater than labor's price, the firm can increase its profit by increasing the quantity used of labor; while if the value of the marginal product is less than labor's price, the firm can increase its profit by reducing the quantity used of labor. Thus *profits must be at a maximum when the value of the marginal product is equal to the price of labor.*

Given the results of this section, it is a simple matter to derive the firm's demand curve for labor. Specifically, its demand curve must be the value-of-marginal-product schedule in the last column of Table 28.3. If the daily wage of a worker is between $51 and $60, the firm will demand 2 workers per day; if the daily wage of a worker is between $41 and $50, the firm will demand 3 workers per day; and so forth. Thus *the firm's demand curve for labor is its value-of-marginal-product curve,* which shows the value of labor's marginal product at each quantity of labor used. This curve is shown in Figure 28.1[2]

## THE MARKET DEMAND CURVE FOR LABOR

In previous sections, we were concerned with the demand curve of a single firm for labor. But many firms, not just one, are part of the labor market, and the price of labor depends on the demands of all of these firms. The situation is analogous to the price of a product, which depends on the demands of all consumers. *The **market demand curve for labor** shows the relationship between the price of labor and the total amount of labor demanded in the market. That is, it shows, for each price, the amount of labor that will be demanded in the entire market.* The market demand curve for labor, like any other input, is quite analogous to the market demand curve for a consumer good, which we discussed in detail in Chapter 19.

But there is at least one important difference. *The demand for labor and other inputs is a **derived demand,** since inputs are demanded to produce other things, not as an end in themselves.* This fact helps to explain why the price elasticity of demand is higher for some inputs than for others. In particular, the larger the price elasticity of demand for the product the input helps produce, the larger the price elasticity of demand for the input. (In addition, the price elasticity of demand for an input is likely to be greater in the long run than in the short run, and greater if other inputs can readily be substituted for the input in question.)

## THE MARKET SUPPLY CURVE FOR LABOR

We have already seen that a product's price depends on its market supply curve as well as its market demand curve. This is equally true for labor.

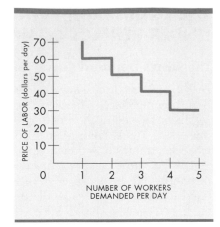

**Figure 28.1**
**The Firm's Demand Curve for Labor under Perfect Competition**
The firm's demand curve for labor is the firm's value-of-marginal-product curve, which shows the value of labor's marginal product at each quantity of labor used. The data for this figure come from Table 28.3.

---

[2] Strictly speaking, the firm's demand curve is the same as the curve showing the value of the input's marginal product only if this input is the only variable input. For a discussion of the more general case, see my *Microeconomics: Theory and Applications,* 7th ed., New York: Norton, 1991, Chapter 12.

# EXAMPLE 28.1 THE VALUE OF WATER'S MARGINAL PRODUCT: THE IMPORTANT CASE OF CALIFORNIA

In this chapter, we have stressed that, to maximize profit, competitive firms should hire labor up to the point where the value of labor's marginal product is equal to the price of labor. This rule for profit maximization applies to any input, not just to labor. In other words, to maximize profit, competitive firms should hire any input up to the point where the value of the input's marginal product is equal to the input's price.

Water is an important input in California's agricultural industries, particularly during the drought that afflicted the state during 1990 and 1991. The value of the marginal product of an extra acre-foot of water in the production of various California crops has been estimated to be as follows:

| | | | |
|---|---|---|---|
| Lemons | $62.00 | Grain hay | $31.37 |
| Cotton | 55.98 | Celery | 20.77 |
| Onions | 51.50 | Asparagus | 17.40 |
| Oranges | 46.86 | Peaches | 10.59 |
| Tomatoes | 32.75 | Lima beans | 8.83 |

(a) If an extra acre-foot of water were used to produce lemons, what would be the value of the extra lemons produced? (b) If an extra acre-foot of water were used to produce lima beans, what would be the value of the extra lima beans produced? (c) If a firm produces both lemons and lima beans, would the firm increase its profits if it could transfer (at no cost) an acre-foot of water from its lima bean production to its lemon production? Why or why not? (d) If California's agricultural producers are maximizing profit, is the price of water the same for lemon producers as for lima bean producers? Why or why not?

## Solution

(a) $62.00. (b) $8.83. (c) Yes. The extra acre-foot of water would result in an extra $62.00 worth of lemons. By reducing the amount of water devoted to lima beans by one acre-foot, the value of the lima bean production would fall by $8.83. Thus the net effect would be an increase in profit of $62.00 – $8.83 = $53.17. (Note that this assumes that the firm can *costlessly* divert an acre-foot of water from lima bean production to lemon production. This may not be true.

For example, the firm's lemons may be grown in an area far removed from its lima beans.) (d) No. As pointed out above, if firms are maximizing profit (and if they are perfectly competitive), they are purchasing water up to the point where the value of water's marginal product is equal to the price of water. Thus, since the value of water's marginal product differs between lemons and lima beans, one would expect that the price of water to lemon producers is different from the price of water to lima bean producers.[*]

[*] For further discussion, see J. Gomez-Ibanez and J. Kalt, eds., *Cases in Microeconomics*, Englewood Cliffs, N.J.: Prentice Hall, 1990. Of course, this brief discussion is highly simplified and abstracts from many institutional and other aspects of California water pricing.

Its **market supply curve** is *the relationship between the price of labor and the total amount of labor supplied in the market.* When individuals supply labor, they are supplying something they themselves can use, since the time that they do not work can be used for leisure activities. (As Charles Lamb, the English essayist, put it, "Who first invented work, and bound the free and holiday-rejoicing spirit down . . . to that dry drudgery at the desk's dead wood?"[3]) Because of this fact, the market supply curve for labor, unlike the supply curve for inputs supplied by business firms, may be **backward bending,** particularly for the economy as a whole. That is, *beyond some point, increases in price may result in smaller amounts of labor being supplied.*

An example of a backward-bending supply curve is provided in Figure 28.2. What factors account for a curve like this? Basically, the reason is that as the price of labor is increased, individuals supplying the labor become richer. And when they become richer, they want to increase their amount of leisure time, which means that they want to work less. Even though the amount of money per hour they give up by not working is greater than when the price of labor was lower, they nonetheless choose to increase their leisure time. This sort of tendency has shown up quite clearly in the last century. As wage rates have increased and living standards have risen, the average work week has tended to decline.

Note that there is no contradiction between the assumption that the supply curve of labor or other inputs *to an individual firm* is horizontal under perfect competition and the fact that the *market* supply curve for the input may not be horizontal. For example, unskilled labor may be available to any firm in a particular area at a given wage rate in as great an amount as it could possibly use. But the total amount of unskilled labor supplied in this area may increase relatively little with increases in the wage rate. The situation is similar to the sale of products. As we saw in Chapter 19, any firm under perfect competition believes that it can sell all it wants at the existing price. Yet the total amount of the product sold in the entire market can ordinarily be increased only by lowering the price.

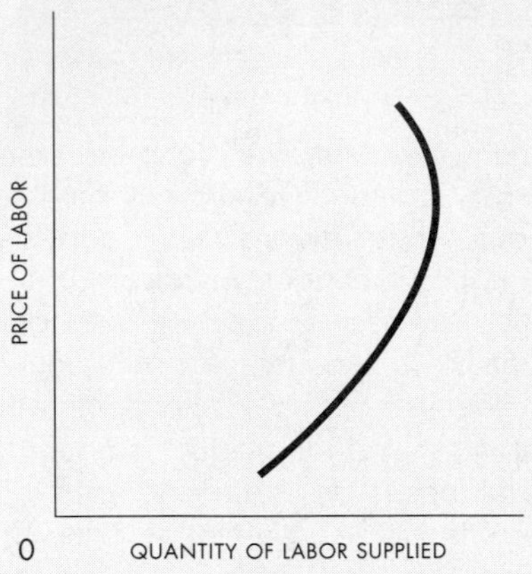

**Figure 28.2**
**Backward-Bending Supply Curve for Labor**
Beyond some point, increases in the price of labor may result in smaller amounts of labor being supplied. The reason for a supply curve of this sort is that, as the price of labor increases, the individuals supplying the labor become richer and want to increase their amount of leisure time.

## EQUILIBRIUM PRICE AND QUANTITY OF LABOR

Labor's price (or wage rate) is determined under perfect competition in essentially the same way that a product's price is determined—by supply and demand.

*The price of labor will tend toward equilibrium at the level where the quantity of labor demanded equals the quantity of labor supplied.* Thus, in Figure 28.3, the equilibrium price of labor is *OP.* If the price were higher than *OP,* the quantity supplied would exceed the quantity demanded and there would be downward pressure on the price. If the price were lower than *OP,* the quantity supplied would fall short of the quantity demanded and there would be upward pressure on the price. By the same token, *the equilibrium amount of labor utilized is also given by the intersection of the market supply and demand curves.* In Figure 28.3, *OQ* units of labor will be utilized in equilibrium in the entire market.

---

[3] The answer to Lamb's question is perhaps to be found in Genesis 3:19.

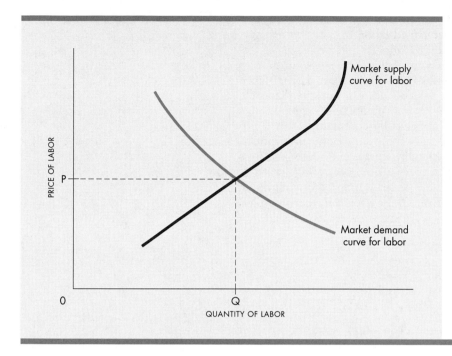

**Figure 28.3**
**Equilibrium Price and Quantity of Labor**
The equilibrium price of labor is *OP*, and the equilibrium quantity of labor used is *OQ*.

Graphs such as Figure 28.3 are useful, but it is important to look behind the geometry, and to recognize the factors that lie behind the demand and supply curves for labor. Consider the market for surgeons and that for unskilled labor. As shown in Figure 28.4, the demand curve for the services of surgeons is to the right of the demand curve for unskilled labor (particularly at high wage rates). Why is this so? Because an hour of a surgeon's services is worth more to people than an hour of an unskilled laborer's services. In this sense, surgeons are more productive than unskilled laborers. Also, as shown in Figure 28.4, the supply curve for the services of surgeons is far to the left of the supply curve for unskilled

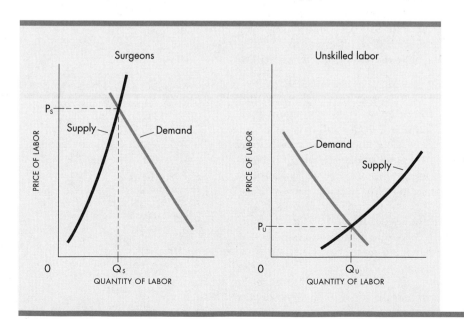

**Figure 28.4**
**The Labor Market for Surgeons and Unskilled Labor**
The wage for surgeons is higher than for unskilled labor because the demand curve for surgeons is farther to the right and the supply curve for surgeons is farther to the left than the corresponding curves for unskilled labor.

labor. Why is this so? Because very few people are licensed surgeons, whereas practically everyone can do unskilled labor. In other words, surgeons are much more scarce than unskilled laborers.

For these reasons, surgeons receive a much higher wage rate than do unskilled laborers. As shown in Figure 28.4, the equilibrium price of labor for surgeons is much higher than for unskilled labor. If unskilled laborers could quickly and easily turn themselves into competent surgeons, this difference in wage rates would be eliminated by competition, since unskilled workers would find it profitable to become surgeons. But unskilled workers lack the training and often the ability to become surgeons. Thus surgeons and unskilled labor are examples of **noncompeting groups.** Wage differentials can be expected to persist among noncompeting groups because people cannot move from the low-paid to the high-paid jobs. But this is not the only reason for wage differentials, as we shall see in the next section.

## WAGE DIFFERENTIALS

Everyone realizes that, even in the same occupation, some people get paid more than others. Why is this true?

**DIFFERENCES IN ABILITY OR SKILL.**   One reason for such wage differentials is that people differ in productive capacity; thus each worker differs from the next in the value of his or her output. Under these circumstances, the difference in wages paid to workers equals the difference in their marginal products' value. Consider the case of two lathe operators—Roberta and Leo. Roberta works for firm X and Leo works for firm Y. Roberta (together with the appropriate tools and materials) can produce output worth $2,000 per month and Leo (with the same tools and materials) can produce output worth $1,900 per month. In equilibrium, Roberta will earn $100 more per month than Leo. If the difference in wages were less than $100, Leo's employer would find it profitable to replace Leo with Roberta, since this would increase the value of output by $100 and cost less than $100. If the difference were more than $100, Roberta's employer would find it profitable to replace Roberta with Leo; although this would reduce the value of output by $100, it would reduce costs by more than $100.

**DIFFERENCES IN TRAINING.**   Besides differences in productive capacity and ability, there are many more reasons for wage differentials. Even if all workers were of equal ability, these differentials would still exist to offset differences in the characteristics of various occupations and areas. Some occupations require large investments in training, while other occupations require a much smaller investment in training. Chemists must spend about eight years in undergraduate and graduate training. During each year of training, they incur direct expenses for books, tuition, and the like, and they lose the income they could make if they were to work rather than go to school. Clearly, if their net remuneration is to be as high in chemistry as in other jobs they might take, they must make a greater wage when they get through than persons of comparable age, intelligence, and motivation whose job requires no training beyond high school. The difference in wages must be at least sufficient to compensate for their investment in extra training.

**OTHER DIFFERENCES.** Similarly, members of some occupations must bear larger occupational expenses than others. A psychologist may have to buy testing materials and subscribe to expensive journals. For net compensation to be equalized, such workers must be paid more than others. Also, some jobs are more unstable than others. Some types of construction workers are subject to frequent layoffs and have little job security, whereas many government employees (but not the top ones) are assured stable and secure employment. If the former jobs are to be as attractive as the latter, they must pay more. In addition, other differences among jobs must be offset by wage differentials if the net remuneration is to be equalized. For instance, there are differences among regions and communities in the cost of living. (Living costs are generally lower in small towns than in big cities.)

## THE ALL-VOLUNTEER ARMY: A CASE STUDY

In recent years, there has been considerable controversy concerning the advantages and disadvantages of an all-volunteer army, the system used in this country since the early 1970s. Senator Sam Nunn, head of the Armed Services Committee, has advocated a return to the draft; others like former President Reagan have opposed such a step. Many economists have argued that recruiting an all-volunteer army is more efficient and equitable than relying on the draft, which through a complicated system of deferments and exemptions, as well as a lottery system, selected a certain number of young men for military service. Proponents of an all-volunteer army point out (1) that it is more compatible with freedom of choice than the draft, (2) that military personnel are used more effectively because the price of such personnel is a more realistic indicator of its value in alternative uses, and (3) that the cost of military personnel is distributed more equitably among the members of society. Under the draft a small group of draftees bore a large share of the cost, because they received less in wages than would have been required to induce them to volunteer.

Other economists and social observers oppose an all-volunteer army. They argue (1) that the present system can hardly be expected to produce the necessary military personnel in a full-scale war, (2) that an army of "paid mercenaries" might constitute a political danger by attempting to gain improper power, and (3) that an all-volunteer army relies disproportionately on the black population, since young blacks constitute a much larger percentage of those without civilian jobs than their white counterparts. In early 1991, whereas blacks were about one-eighth of the adult population, they were about one-fourth of the troops engaged in the war against Iraq in the Persian Gulf.[4]

How did the all-volunteer army come into being? In 1964, President Johnson asked that a study be made to determine whether it would be possible to shift from reliance on the draft to a system in which defense needs would be met entirely by volunteers. A team of economists attempted to learn what it would cost. Essentially they applied the kind of analysis described in this chapter. The basic approach was to estimate the supply curve for labor to the Department of Defense.

[4] *New York Times,* January 25, 1991, p. A12.

Figure 28.5 shows the relationship between the proportion of the male population that enlists and the level of military pay (as a percent of civilian pay), the unemployment rate being held constant at two alternative levels. As would be expected, the number of enlistments increases with the level of military pay and the unemployment rate. Using this supply curve, which was estimated by the economists, one could determine (for given values of the unemployment rate) the level of military pay that was required to bring forth the number of extra enlistments needed to eliminate the draft.

According to the economists, a 60 to 90 percent increase in enlistments was needed to eliminate the draft. To bring forth these extra enlistments, they estimated on the basis of the supply curve that first-term military pay for enlisted personnel had to be increased by about 110 percent (if the unemployment rate were 5.5 percent). Using 1964 military earnings as a base, increases in first-term pay for enlisted personnel had to be about $3,000 to attract enough volunteers to maintain a defense force of 2.65 million. Multiplying 2.65 million volunteers by the average increase in pay, the economists estimated that the increased cost to the Defense Department would be about $5 billion per year.[5] This estimate was very crude, as the economists stressed, since many noneconomic factors influenced the enlistment rate, and the data and underlying assumptions were rough.

By 1973, the draft was no longer being used to obtain military personnel. Whether it will be reactivated in the near future is hard to say. (In 1986, a study for the Joint Chiefs of Staff concluded that a return to the draft would increase costs.) For present purposes, the important point is that economic analysis, based on the fundamental concepts in this chapter, has played a very significant role in the discussion and resolution of this major issue. And in the future as in the past, you can be sure that economists will continue to play a significant role in this area.

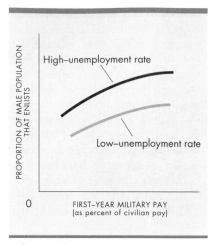

**Figure 28.5**
**Relationship between Military Pay and Number of Enlistments**
Holding the unemployment rate constant, the proportion of the male population that enlists is directly related to the level of military pay (as a percent of civilian pay). Using this supply curve, economists determined the level of military pay required to bring forth the extra enlistments needed to eliminate the draft.

## SIGNALING IN THE LABOR MARKET

Economists like Stanford's Michael Spence have called attention to the importance of signaling in the labor market. To see what signaling is, suppose for simplicity that there are two distinctly different types of workers (high ability and low ability) that an employer can hire. The marginal product of high-ability workers is greater than that of low-ability workers. However, the employer cannot be sure whether a particular worker is high-ability or low-ability until after the worker has been hired. This is because it takes time on the job for the employer to determine the capabilities and productivity of the worker.

*If the employer regards the educational level of a job applicant as a signal, or indicator, of the worker's ability, it may pay workers to invest in their education in order to signal the employer that they in fact are able.* Of course, Mary Stuart, in getting an education, may not think of herself

Michael Spence

---

[5] Note that the average increase in pay is less than the average increase in first-term pay. The way S. Altman and A. Fechter, who carried out the study, proceed from the latter to the former is described in their work. Also, note that the costs to the Defense Department, which are estimated here, may be quite different from the social costs of switching to an all-volunteer army.

as signaling. She will invest in education if there is sufficient return, which will depend on how much more the employer is willing to pay for highly educated than for poorly educated workers.

Assuming that the difficulty (and thus the cost) of attaining a higher educational level is less for high-ability than for low-ability people, it is clear that high-ability people will have more incentive than low-ability people to get high levels of education. Thus the employer's belief that educational level is an effective indicator, or signal, of ability and productivity will be reinforced by experience. Consequently, the employer will continue to find it profitable to offer a higher wage to job applicants with relatively high levels of education, since such applicants are more likely to be high-ability people. Thus high-ability individuals will continue to find it economically worthwhile to invest relatively heavily in their educations.

An important thing to note is that, to the individual, it appears that higher education is a prerequisite to a high-paying job. After all, under these circumstances, the employer pays more for people with more education. Also, to an outside observer, it appears that education enhances the productivity of the worker. This seems to be true because the better-educated people have higher productivity and earn bigger wages than the less-educated people. In fact, however, *even if education has no effect on productivity and is only a signal of a person's ability, there will be a direct relationship between a person's education, on the one hand, and his or her productivity and wages, on the other.* Of course, this is not to say that education doesn't affect productivity; without question, it does enhance a person's productivity. But this doesn't deny that it also serves as a signal.

## PRINCIPAL-AGENT PROBLEMS IN THE LABOR MARKET

Frequently, it is difficult for an employer to measure how hard a particular employee is working. For example, sales representatives often spend considerable periods of time traveling from one potential customer to another, and it is not easy for their employers to know whether they are working hard or not. In cases of this sort, there may be a principal-agent problem of the sort discussed in Chapter 21. The worker is, of course, an *agent* who works for the employer, who is the *principal*. What is the principal-agent problem? *The worker may pursue his or her own goals, and neglect the goals of the employer.*

As an illustration, take the case of Richard Ryan, a sales representative for a chemical firm. To keep things simple, suppose that he can generate only three possible levels of monthly receipts for his employer: $20,000, $10,000, or $6,000. If he works hard, he generates $20,000 per month in receipts for his employer if he is lucky, but only $10,000 if he is unlucky. If he does not work hard, he generates $10,000 per month if he is lucky, but only $6,000 if he is unlucky. (Ryan's salary has not been subtracted from these figures; to obtain the net receipts to his employer, it must be subtracted.) Thus, if Mr. Ryan generates receipts of $10,000 in a particular month, there is no way that his employer can tell whether he worked hard and was unlucky, or whether he did not work hard and was lucky. Even if his employer took the trouble to monitor his behavior (which could be prohibitively expensive), there may be no accurate method of gauging how hard he worked.

# INCENTIVE SYSTEMS: BONUS PAYMENTS VERSUS A FIXED WAGE

Mr. Ryan's employer would like to establish incentives to get him to work hard because this will increase the firm's profits. One way to do this is to establish a bonus system. Suppose that Ryan receives a fixed monthly wage (say $3,000), regardless of the size of the receipts he generates for his employer. Clearly, this payment scheme will not induce him to work hard, since he will receive no more pay if he works hard than if he doesn't work hard. Thus, unless he likes work for its own sake, he will not work hard. If there is a 50–50 chance that he will be lucky in any month (and a 50–50 chance that he will be unlucky), his employer can expect that he will generate, on the average, 0.5 ($10,000) + 0.5 ($6,000) = $8,000 in receipts per month. Deducting his wage of $3,000 from this gross figure, his employer receives, on the average, net receipts of $5,000 per month. (See Table 28.4.)

On the other hand, suppose that Ryan receives a bonus if he generates a large volume of receipts. To be specific, let's assume that he gets a low wage (say $2,000) if he generates $6,000 or $10,000 in receipts in a particular month, but a much higher wage (say $6,000) if he generates receipts of $20,000 in that month. Since there is a 50–50 chance that he will be lucky in any month (and a 50–50 chance that he will be unlucky), he can expect, on the average, to receive 0.5 ($2,000) + 0.5 ($6,000) = $4,000 per month if he works hard. (Why? Because he will receive $2,000 during those months when he is unlucky and $6,000 during those months when he is lucky.) On the other hand, if he does not work hard, he is certain to receive $2,000 per month. (Why? Because regardless of whether he is lucky or unlucky, he will generate only $6,000 or $10,000 in receipts, which means he will receive $2,000 per month.)

Mr. Ryan now has an incentive to work hard, since his monthly wage is much higher if he works hard than if he doesn't. His employer can expect that Ryan will generate, on the average, 0.5 ($10,000) + 0.5 ($20,000)

## Table 28.4
**Richard Ryan's Expected Monthly Income and His Employer's Expected Monthly Net Receipts, if He Receives a Fixed Wage and if He Receives Bonus Payments**

| METHOD OF PAYMENT | IF HE WORKS HARD | IF HE DOES NOT WORK HARD | RYAN'S MAXIMUM EXPECTED INCOME [a] | EMPLOYER'S EXPECTED NET RECEIPTS |
|---|---|---|---|---|
| Fixed monthly wage of $3,000 | $3,000 | $3,000 | $3,000 | $8,000 – $3,000 = $5,000 |
| $6,000 monthly payment if he generates $20,000 in receipts; $2,000 monthly payment otherwise | $4,000 | $2,000 | $4,000 | $15,000 – $4,000 = $11,000 |

[a] This is his expected income if he works hard or his expected income if he does not work hard, whichever is higher (if they differ).

= $15,000 in receipts per month. Subtracting his average wage of $4,000 per month from this gross figure, his employer receives average net receipts of $11,000 per month, which is greater than if he paid Ryan a fixed monthly wage of $3,000. (See Table 28.4.) Clearly, both Ryan and his employer are better off under this bonus system than if Ryan received the fixed monthly wage.

## THE MORAL OF THE TALE

The case of Richard Ryan illustrates an important point: *A bonus payment system can be used by firms to help induce workers to further the aims of the firm when there is no way to measure directly the amount of effort that a worker puts out.* Other incentive systems can be used as well. For example, Mr. Ryan's employer could have instituted a profit-sharing system whereby Ryan would have earned a basic wage plus a certain percentage of the profits in excess of a particular amount. If properly designed, this type of system can also provide an incentive for Ryan to work hard—and to increase the firm's profit.

## TEST YOURSELF

1. Suppose that a perfectly competitive firm's production function is as follows:

| QUANTITY OF LABOR (YEARS) | OUTPUT PER YEAR (THOUSANDS OF UNITS) |
|---|---|
| 0 | 0 |
| 1 | 3.0 |
| 2 | 5.0 |
| 3 | 6.8 |
| 4 | 8.0 |
| 5 | 9.0 |

The firm is a profit maximizer, and the labor market is competitive. Labor must be hired in integer numbers and for a year (no more, no less). If the firm hires 4 years of labor, and if the price of a unit of the firm's product is $3, one can establish a range for what the annual wage prevailing in the labor market must be. What is the maximum amount it can be? What is the

minimum amount? Why? Do these numbers seem realistic? Why, or why not?

2. Based on the data in Question 1, plot the marginal product of labor at various utilization rates of labor. Also, plot the value of labor's marginal product at each quantity of labor used.

3. "It is foolish to believe that a bonus payment system can increase a firm's profits. After all, such a system will increase a worker's wage; thus it must increase the firm's costs and reduce its profits." Comment and evaluate.

4. Suppose that the marginal product of skilled labor to a perfectly competitive firm is 2 units and the price of skilled labor is $8 an hour, while the marginal product of unskilled labor is 1 unit and the price of unskilled labor is $5.50 an hour. Is the firm minimizing its costs? Explain. (*Hint:* Regard skilled labor and unskilled labor as two separate inputs, and apply the cost-minimization rule in Chapter 22.)

## MONOPSONY

In previous sections, we have assumed that perfect competition exists in the labor market. In some cases, however, **monopsony** exists instead. *A monopsony is a market structure where there is a single buyer.* Thus a single firm may hire all the labor in an isolated "company town," such as exists in the coal-mining regions of West Virginia and Kentucky. What determines the price of labor under monopsony? Suppose the firm's demand curve for labor and the supply curve of labor are as shown in Figure 28.6. Because the firm is the sole buyer of labor, it takes into account the fact that to acquire more labor it must pay a higher wage to *all* workers, not just the extra workers. For example, if the firm wants to increase the number of workers it employs from 5 to 6, it may have to pay the sixth an hourly wage of $9. If the supply curve of labor slopes upward to the right, this wage is more than was required to obtain the first 5 workers. Since the firm must pay all workers the same wage to avoid labor unrest, it must raise the wages of the first 5 workers to the level of the sixth, if it hires the sixth worker. Thus *the cost of hiring the sixth worker exceeds the wage that must be paid this worker.*

The supply curve for labor in Figure 28.6 shows the cost of hiring an additional worker, if workers already employed do *not* have to be paid a higher wage when the additional worker is hired. Thus this supply curve does *not* show the true additional cost to the monopsonist of hiring an additional worker, for the reasons given in the previous paragraph. Instead, curve *A*, which includes wages that must be paid to the workers already employed, shows the true additional cost. For the reasons given above, curve *A* lies above the supply curve.

If profit is maximized, the monopsonistic firm will hire labor up to the point at which the extra cost of adding an additional laborer (shown by curve *A*) equals the extra revenue from adding the additional laborer (shown by the demand curve). Thus the quantity of labor purchased will be *OM* and the price of labor will be *OC* in Figure 28.6. In contrast, under

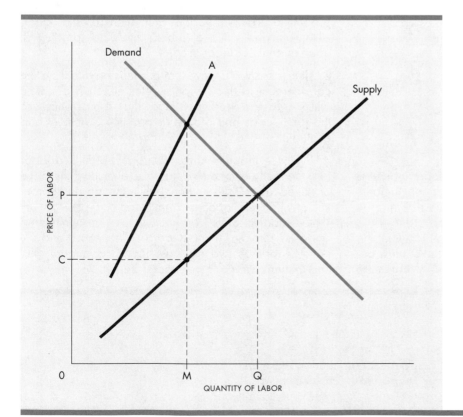

**Figure 28.6**
**Equilibrium Wage and Quantity of Labor under Monopsony**
The monopsonistic firm, if it maximizes profit, will hire laborers up to the point where the extra cost of adding an extra laborer, shown by curve A, equals the extra revenue from adding the extra laborer, shown by the demand curve for labor.

perfectly competitive conditions the equilibrium quantity and price would be at the intersection of the demand and supply curves. That is, the quantity of labor purchased would be *OQ* and the price of labor would be *OP*.

What is the effect of monopsony on the wage rate and the amount of labor hired? In general, *the wage rate, as well as the quantity hired, is lower under monopsony than under perfect competition.* This is the case in Figure 28.6, and it will generally hold true. This makes sense. One would expect a monopsonist, free from the pressures of competition, to pay workers less than would be required under perfect competition.

## LABOR UNIONS

About 1 in 6 nonfarm workers in the United States belongs to a union, and the perfectly competitive model does not apply to these workers any more than it does to monopsonistic labor markets. The biggest unions are the National Education Association, the Teamsters, and the Food and Commercial Workers, each with 1.3 million members or more. Next come the State, County, and Municipal Employees, the United Auto Workers, and the Electrical Workers, each with over a million members.

The **national unions**[6] are of great importance in the American labor movement. The supreme governing body of the national union is the convention, which is held every year or two. The delegates to the convention have the authority to set policy for the union. However, considerable power is exercised by the national union's officers.

A national union is composed of **local unions,** each in a given area or plant. Some local unions have only a few members, but others have thousands. The local union, with its own president and officers, often plays an important role in collective bargaining. The extent to which the local unions maintain their autonomy varies from one national union to another. In industries where markets are localized (like construction and printing), the locals are more autonomous than in industries where markets are national (like steel, automobiles, and coal).

Finally, there is the **AFL-CIO,** a federation of national unions created by the merger of the American Federation of Labor and the Congress of Industrial Organizations in 1955. The AFL-CIO does not include all national unions. The United Mine Workers refused to join the AFL-CIO, and the Auto Workers left it in 1968. (The Teamsters were kicked out in the mid-1950s because of corruption, but in 1987 they were allowed to rejoin.) The AFL-CIO is a very important spokesman for the American labor movement; but because the national unions in the AFL-CIO have given up relatively little of their power to the federation, its authority is limited.

The AFL-CIO is organized along the lines indicated in Figure 28.7. The constitution of the AFL-CIO puts supreme governing power in the hands of a biennial convention. The national unions are represented at these conventions on the basis of their dues-paying membership. Between conventions, the AFL-CIO's business is directed by its president (Lane Kirkland in 1991) and secretary-treasurer, as well as by various committees and councils composed of representatives of various national unions or people elected at the convention. The AFL-CIO contains seven trade and industrial departments, such as building trades, food and beverage trades,

[6] Sometimes they are called international unions because some locals are outside the United States—for example, in Canada.

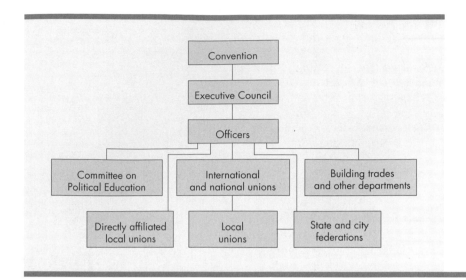

maritime trades, and so forth. Also, as indicated by Figure 28.7, a few local unions are not affiliated with a national union, but are directly affiliated with the AFL-CIO.

## RECENT TRENDS IN UNION MEMBERSHIP

In recent decades, union membership has decreased as a percent of the labor force. In 1955, about one-fourth of the labor force belonged to unions; now the proportion is only about one-sixth. To some extent, this has been due to dissension within the labor movement and to a diminution of the zeal that characterized the movement in earlier years. Also, rightly or wrongly, unions have lost a certain amount of public sympathy and respect because of racial discrimination, unpopular strikes, evidence of corruption, and the belief that they are responsible in considerable part for supply-side inflation. But these factors only partly explain this lack of growth. In addition, important changes in the labor force have tended to reduce union membership.

Specifically, the increasing proportion of *white-collar workers* in the labor force seems to have raised important problems for unions. To date, unions have made relatively little progress in organizing white-collar workers. One reason for this lack of progress is that white-collar employees tend to identify with management. Also, the increasing proportion of *women* in the labor force seems to raise important problems for unions. It is sometimes claimed that female workers are harder to organize because they do not stay in the labor force very long and because they are concentrated in jobs—clerical and sales positions—that are difficult to organize. Nonetheless, the majority of the Retail Clerks, the Clothing Workers, and the International Ladies' Garment Workers have been women.

However, even though union membership has not been growing in recent years, it would be a mistake to jump to the conclusion that the American labor movement is of little or no importance. For one thing, membership is not a very good measure of power. A small union can sometimes bring an enormous amount of pressure to bear if it is located strategically in the economy.

# EXAMPLE 28.2    CAN A UNION INCREASE EMPLOYMENT?

In many isolated areas, a single firm is the only employer of a certain kind of labor. Suppose that a textile firm is in this position, and that its demand curve for labor, as well as the supply curve for labor, are shown below. Curve A shows the extra cost to the firm of adding an extra laborer.

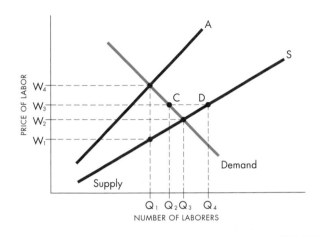

(a) How many laborers will the firm hire, and how much will each be paid? (b) Suppose that a union enters the market and that it sets a wage of $OW_3$. What now is the supply curve for labor? (c) How many laborers will the firm hire now? Is employment higher than before the union entered? (d) Will there be involuntary unemployment now?

## Solution

(a) The firm will hire $OQ_1$ laborers and pay a wage of $OW_1$, in accord with our discussion of monopsony. (b) It is $W_3DS$, because the firm cannot pay a wage below $OW_3$ under the assumed circumstances. (c) The firm will hire $OQ_2$ workers, since the extra cost of hiring an extra worker equals $OW_3$ so long as less than $OQ_4$ workers are hired. Employment is higher than before the union entered (when it was $OQ_1$). (d) Yes. At a wage of $OW_3$, $OQ_4$ workers will seek employment but only $OQ_2$ workers will be hired. Thus ($OQ_4 - OQ_2$) workers will be involuntarily unemployed.

# HOW UNIONS INCREASE WAGES

Unions wield considerable power, and economists must include them in their analysis if they want their models of the labor market to reflect conditions in the real world. We shall now see how this is done. Let us begin by supposing that a union wants to increase the wage rate paid its members. How can it accomplish this objective? In other words, how can it alter the market supply curve for labor, or the market demand curve for labor, so that the price of labor—its wage—will increase?

1. *The union may try to shift the supply curve of labor to the left.* It may shift the supply curve, as shown in Figure 28.8, with the result that the price of labor will increase from $OP$ to $OP_1$. How can the union cause this shift in the supply curve? Craft unions have frequently forced employers to hire only union members, and then restricted union membership by high initiation fees, reduction in new membership, and other devices. In addition, unions have favored legislation to reduce immigration, shorten working hours, and limit the labor supply in other ways.

2. *The union may try to get the employers to pay a higher wage, while allowing some of the supply of labor forthcoming at this higher wage to find no opportunity for work.* In Figure 28.9, the union may exert pressure on the employers to raise the price of labor from $OP$ to $OP_1$. At $OP_1$, not all of the available supply of labor can find jobs. The quantity of labor supplied is $OQ_2$, while the amount of labor demanded is $OQ_1$. The effect is the same as in Figure 28.8, but in this case the union does not limit the supply directly. It lets the higher wage reduce the opportunity for work.

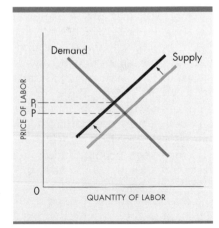

**Figure 28.8**
**Shift of Supply Curve for Labor**
A union may shift the supply curve to the left by getting employers to hire only union members and then restricting union membership, or by other techniques.

Strong industrial unions often behave in this fashion. Having organized practically all the relevant workers and controlling the labor supply, the union raises the wage to $OP_1$. This is a common and important case.

3. *The union may try to shift the demand curve for labor upward and to the right.* If it can bring about the shift described in Figure 28.10, the price of labor will increase from $OP$ to $OP_2$. To cause this shift in the demand for labor, the union may resort to **featherbedding.** That is, it may try to restrict output per worker in order to increase the amount of labor required to do a certain job. (To cite but one case, the railroad unions have insisted on much unnecessary labor.) Unions also try to shift the demand curve by helping the employers compete against other industries, or by helping to make Congress pass legislation that protects the employers from foreign competition.

# COLLECTIVE BARGAINING

**Collective bargaining** is the process of negotiation between the union and management over wages and working conditions. Representatives of the union and management meet periodically to work out an agreement or contract; this process generally begins a few months before the old labor contract runs out. Typically, each side asks at first for more than it expects to get, and compromises must be made to reach an agreement. The union representatives take the agreement to their members, who must vote to accept or reject it. If they reject it, they may vote to strike or to continue to negotiate.

Collective bargaining agreements vary greatly. Some pertain to only a single plant while others apply to an entire industry. However, an agreement generally contains the following elements. It specifies the extent and kind of recognition that management gives the union, the level of wage rates for particular jobs, the length of the work week, the rate of overtime pay, the extent to which seniority will determine which workers will be first to be laid off, the nature and extent of management's prerogatives, and how grievances between workers and the employer will be handled.

Historically, industries and firms have extended recognition to unions by accepting one of three arrangements—the closed shop, the union shop, or the open shop. In a **closed shop,** workers must be union members before they can be hired. This gives the union more power than if there is a **union shop,** in which the employer can hire nonunion workers who must then become union members in a certain length of time after being hired. In an **open shop,** the employer can hire union or nonunion labor, and nonunion workers need not, once employed, join the union. The closed shop was banned by the Taft-Hartley Act, passed in 1947. The Taft-Hartley Act also says that the union shop is legal unless outlawed by state laws; and in about 20 states there are "right to work" laws that make the union shop illegal. Needless to say, these right-to-work laws are hated by organized labor, which regards them as a threat to its security and effectiveness.

## Basic Forces at Work

Collective bargaining is a power struggle. At each point in their negotiations, both the union and the employer must compare the costs (or bene-

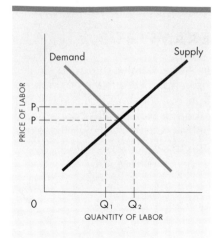

**Figure 28.9**
**Direct Increase in Price of Labor**
A union may get the employer to raise the wage from $OP$ to $OP_1$ and let the higher wage reduce the opportunity for work. This is commonly done by strong industrial unions.

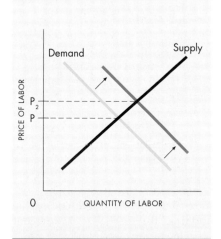

**Figure 28.10**
**Shift in Demand Curve for Labor**
A union may shift the demand curve for labor to the right by featherbedding or other devices, thus increasing the wage from $OP$ to $OP_2$.

fits) of agreeing with the other party with the costs (or benefits) of continuing to disagree. The costs of disagreement are the costs of a **strike,** while the costs of agreement are the costs of settling on terms other than one's own. These costs are determined by basic market forces. For example, during periods when demand is great, employers are more likely to grant large wage increases because the costs of disagreement seem higher (a strike will prove more costly) than those of settlement. The outcome of the negotiations will depend on the relative strength of the parties. The strength of the employers depends on their ability to withstand a strike. The strength of the unions depends on their ability to keep out nonunion workers and to enlist the support of other unions, as well as on the size of their financial reserves.

## UNION CONCESSIONS IN THE 1980S

In the 1980s, many important unions cut back on their wage requests. In the automobile industry, American firms found it difficult to compete with their Japanese rivals, and many experts attributed this partly to the very high wages in the U.S. auto industry. In the trucking industry, unionized firms found it increasingly difficult to compete with nonunion firms. More and more union members in industries like autos, trucking, steel, rubber, and the airlines began to worry about the effects of hefty wage increases on whether or not they would have jobs. The climate for collective bargaining was quite different than in earlier decades.

To illustrate, consider the labor negotiations in the auto industry in 1987. An important issue in these negotiations was the reform in work rules. After seeing productivity increases of 20 percent or more at some plants that adopted Japanese-style manufacturing systems, which organize workers in teams, auto executives pressed for the reduction of rigid union job classifications and work rules. Some union officials agreed, but because work rules are set in local, not national, negotiations, and because

Table 28.5
**Workers Accepting Concessions in Labor Settlements as a Percent of Workers Negotiating in the Year, by Union, 1975–88**

| UNION | 1975 | 1980 | 1985 | 1988 |
|---|---|---|---|---|
| United Food and Commercial Workers | —ᵃ | 0 | 46 | 73 |
| United Auto Workers | 6 | 12 | 97 | 100 |
| International Brotherhood of Electrical Workers | 0 | 0 | 40 | 60 |
| Service Employees | 13 | 0 | 26 | 18 |
| Carpenters and Joiners | 0 | 0 | 77 | —ᵃ |
| Steelworkers | 0 | 5 | 91 | —ᵃ |
| Communications Workers of America | 0 | 0 | 27 | —ᵃ |
| Association of Federal, State, County and Municipal Employees | 0 | 0 | 22 | —ᵃ |

ᵃ No contracts negotiated in year.
Source: Linda Bell, "Union Concessions in the 1980s," *Quarterly Review of the Federal Reserve Bank of New York,* Summer 1989.

some union members have strongly resisted such changes, reform has not been easy.

Let's define a union concession as a wage reduction (or no wage increase), a reduction in cost-of-living adjustments in pay, a relaxation of work rules, the adoption of a "two-tier" wage structure (where newly hired workers are paid at a lower rate than existing workers), or the substitution of profit-sharing (and related) plans for a wage increase. In the late 1980s, a majority of workers in unions like the United Auto Workers, Steelworkers, Carpenters, Electrical Workers, and Food and Commercial Workers accepted concessions in their new contracts (Table 28.5). In 1975 or 1980, such concessions were rare.

## TEST YOURSELF

1. "The unions should not be exempt from the antitrust laws." Comment and evaluate.

2. Suppose that a perfectly competitive firm suddenly becomes a monopsonist in the market for labor. Do you think that it would pay a lower, higher, or the same wage rate as it did before? Why?

3. Suppose that you were the president of a small firm that hired nonunion labor. How would you go about estimating the marginal product of a certain worker, or of certain types of workers? Would it be easy? If not, does this mean that the theory of wage determination is incorrect or useless?

4. Describe the various ways that labor unions can influence the wage rate. Do you think that they attempt to maximize the wage rate? If not, what do you think their objectives are?

## SUMMARY

1. Assuming perfect competition, a firm will employ each type of labor in an amount such that its marginal product times the product's price equals its wage. In other words, the firm will employ enough labor so that the value of the marginal product of labor equals labor's price.

2. The firm's demand curve for labor—which shows, for each price of labor, the amount of labor the firm will use—is the firm's value-of-marginal-product curve (if labor is the only variable input). The market demand curve for labor shows the relationship between its price and the total amount of labor demanded in the market.

3. Labor's price depends on its market supply curve as well as on its market demand curve. Labor's market supply curve is the relationship between the price of labor and the total amount of labor supplied in the market. (Labor's market supply curve may be backward bending.)

4. An input's price is determined under perfect competition in essentially the same way that a product's price is determined—by supply and demand. The price of labor will tend in equilibrium to the level at which the quantity of labor demanded equals the quantity of labor supplied. By the same

token, the equilibrium amount of labor utilized is also given by the intersection of the market supply and demand curves.

5. If there are qualitative differences among workers, the differential in their wages will reflect the differential in their marginal products. Also, even if all workers were of equal ability, there would still be differences in wage rates to offset differences among occupations in the cost of training and stability of earnings, and geographical differences in the cost of living.

6. Workers may invest in their own education to signal employers that they are able. Even if education has no effect on productivity and is only a signal of a person's ability, there will be a direct relationship between a person's education, on the one hand, and his or her productivity and wages, on the other. (Of course, this is not to say that education generally has no effect on productivity.)

7. A worker may pursue his or her own interests, and neglect the goals of the employer. To help induce workers to promote the aims of the firm (when it is very hard to measure the amount of effort that a worker puts forth), bonus payment systems are often instituted by employers.

8. There are several ways that unions can increase wages—by shifting the supply curve of labor to the left, by shifting the demand curve for labor to the right, and by influencing the wage directly.

9. Collective bargaining is the process of negotiation between union and management over wages and working conditions. The union's power is based to a considerable extent on its right to strike. In the 1980s, there were many union concessions.

## CONCEPTS FOR REVIEW

**Firm's demand curve for labor**

**Value of the marginal product of labor**

**Market demand curve for labor**

**Derived demand**

**Market supply curve for labor**

**Noncompeting groups**

**Monopsony**

**National union**

**Local union**

**AFL-CIO**

**Backward-bending supply curve**

**Featherbedding**

**Collective bargaining**

**Closed shop**

**Union shop**

**Open shop**

**Strike**

# INTEREST, RENT, AND PROFITS

NOT ALL INCOME is received in the form of wages. The school teacher who has a savings account at the Bank of America receives income in the form of *interest*. The widow who rents out 100 acres of rich Iowa land to a farmer receives income in the form of *rent*. And the engineer who founds and owns a firm that develops a new type of electronic calculator receives income in the form of *profit*. All of these types of income—interest, rent, and profit—are forms of property income. That is, they are incomes received by owners of property. In this chapter, we are concerned with the determinants of interest, rent, and profit. Also, we try to explain the social functions of each of these types of property income.

## THE NATURE OF INTEREST

Charles Lamb, the English essayist, said, "The human species, according to the best theory I can form of it, is composed of two distinct races, the men who borrow and the men who lend." Whether or not such a cleavage exists, most of the human species, at one time or another, are borrowers or lenders of money. Thus practically everyone is familiar with **interest**, which is a payment for the use of money. More specifically, *the rate of interest is the amount of money one must pay for the use of a dollar for a year*. Thus, if the interest rate is 8 percent, you must pay 8 cents for the use of a dollar for a year.

Everyone who borrows money pays interest. Consumers pay interest on personal loans taken out to buy appliances, mortgages taken out to buy houses, and many other types of loans. Firms pay interest on bonds issued to purchase equipment and on short-term bank loans taken out to finance inventories. And governments pay interest on bonds issued to finance schools, highways, and other public projects.

Interest rates vary, depending on the nature of the borrower and the type of loan. One of the most important determinants of the rate of interest charged borrowers is the *riskiness* of the loan. If lenders have doubts about their chances of getting their money back, they will charge a higher interest rate than if they are sure of being repaid. Thus small, financially rickety firms have to pay higher interest rates than large blue-chip firms; and the large, well-known firms have to pay higher interest rates than the federal government. Another factor that influences the interest rate is the *cost of bookkeeping and collection*. If a firm makes many small loans and must hound the borrowers to pay up, these costs are a great deal larger

than if it makes one large loan. Consequently the interest rate that must be charged for such small loans is often considerably higher than for bigger loans.

Despite the diversity of interest rates encountered at any point in time in the real world, it is analytically useful to speak of the **pure rate of interest,** which is the interest rate on a riskless loan. The rate of interest on U.S. government bonds—which are about as safe as one can get in this world—comes close to being a pure rate of interest. Actual interest rates will vary from the pure rate, depending on the riskiness of the loan together with other factors, but the configuration of actual interest rates will tend to move up and down with the pure interest rate.

## THE DETERMINATION OF THE INTEREST RATE

### The Demand for Loanable Funds

Since the interest rate is the price paid for the use of loanable funds, it—like any price—is determined by demand and supply. The **demand curve for loanable funds** shows the quantity of loanable funds demanded at each interest rate. The demand for loanable funds is a demand for what these funds will buy. Money is not wanted for its own sake, since it cannot build factories or equipment. Instead, it can provide command over resources—labor and equipment and materials—to do things like build factories or equipment.

As shown in Figure 29.1, the demand curve slopes downward to the right, indicating that more loanable funds are demanded at a lower rate of interest than at a higher rate of interest. A very large demand for loanable funds stems from firms who want to borrow money to invest in capital goods like machine tools, buildings, and so forth. At a particular point in time a firm has available a variety of possible investments, each with a

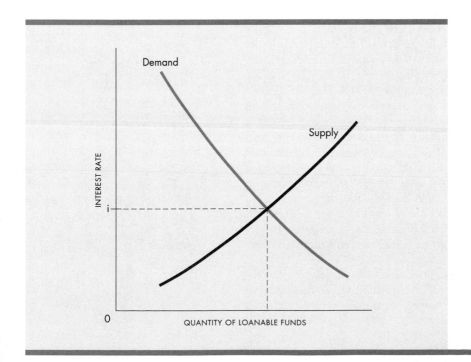

**Figure 29.1**
**Determination of Equilibrium Rate of Interest**
The interest rate is determined by the demand and supply of loanable funds, the equilibrium level of the interest rate being $Oi$.

certain rate of return, which indicates its profitability or net productivity. At higher interest rates, a firm will find it profitable to borrow money for fewer of these projects than if interest rates are lower.

To be more specific, *an asset's **rate of return** is the interest rate earned on the investment in the asset.* Suppose that a piece of equipment costs $10,000 and yields a permanent return to its owner of $1,500 per year.[1] (This return allows for the costs of maintaining the machine.) The rate of return on this piece of capital is 15 percent. Why? Because if an investment of $10,000 yields an indefinite annual return of $1,500, the interest rate earned on this investment is 15 percent.

If a firm maximizes profit, it will borrow to carry out investments where the rate of return, adjusted for risk, exceeds the interest rate. For example, it is profitable for a firm to pay 10 percent interest to carry out a project with a 12 percent rate of return, but it is not profitable to pay 15 percent interest for this purpose. (More will be said on this score in a subsequent section.) Consequently, the higher the interest rate, the smaller the amount that firms will be willing to borrow.

Large demands for loanable funds are also made by consumers and the government. Consumers borrow money to buy houses, cars, and many other items. The government borrows money to finance the building of schools, highways, housing, and many other types of public projects. As in the case of firms, the higher the interest rate, the smaller the amount that consumers and governments will be willing to borrow. Adding the demands of firms, consumers, and government together, we find the aggregate relationship at a given point in time between the pure interest rate and the amount of funds demanded—which is the demand curve for loanable funds. For the reasons given above, this demand curve looks like a demand curve should. It is downward-sloping to the right.

## The Supply of Loanable Funds

The **supply curve for loanable funds** is the relationship between the quantity of loanable funds supplied and the pure interest rate. The supply of loanable funds comes from households and firms that find the available rate of interest sufficiently attractive to get them to save. In addition, the banks play an extremely important role in influencing the supply of loanable funds. Indeed, banks can actually create or destroy loanable funds (but only within limits set by the Federal Reserve System, our central bank.)

The equilibrium value of the pure interest rate is given by the intersection of the demand and supply curves. In Figure 29.1 the equilibrium rate of interest is *Oi*. Factors that shift the demand curve or supply curve for loanable funds tend to alter the interest rate. If people become more willing to postpone consumption to future time periods, the supply curve for loanable funds will shift to the right, and the interest rate will decline. Or if inventions result in very profitable new investment possibilities, the demand curve will shift to the right and the interest rate will increase. (See Figure 29.2.)

However, this is only part of the story. Because of the government's influence on both the demand and supply sides of the market for loanable funds, the interest rate at any point in time is to a considerable extent a

---

[1] It is unrealistic to assume that the yield continues indefinitely, but it makes it easier to understand the principle involved.

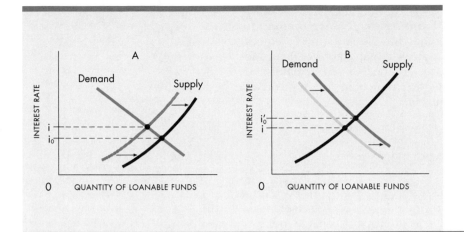

**Figure 29.2**
**Effects on the Equilibrium Interest Rate of Shifts in the Demand or Supply Curves for Loanable Funds**
If people become more willing to postpone consumption to future time periods, the supply curve will shift to the right, and the equilibrium interest rate will fall from $i$ to $i_0$.

If very profitable new investment opportunities are opened up, the demand curve will shift to the right, and the equilibrium interest rate will rise from $i$ to $i'_0$.

matter of public policy. A nation's monetary policy can have a significant effect on the level of the interest rate. More specifically, when the Federal Reserve pursues a policy of easy money, this generally means that interest rates tend to fall in the short run because the Fed is pushing the supply curve for loanable funds to the right. On the other hand, when the Federal Reserve pursues a policy of tight money, interest rates generally tend to rise in the short run because the Fed is pushing the supply curve for loanable funds to the left. (See Figure 29.3.)

The government is also an important factor on the demand side of the market for loanable funds, because it is a big borrower. During the 1980s and early 1990s, it borrowed huge amounts to finance the mammoth federal deficits. In 1990, total federal debt (excluding the debt of state and local governments) held by the public was about $2 trillion.

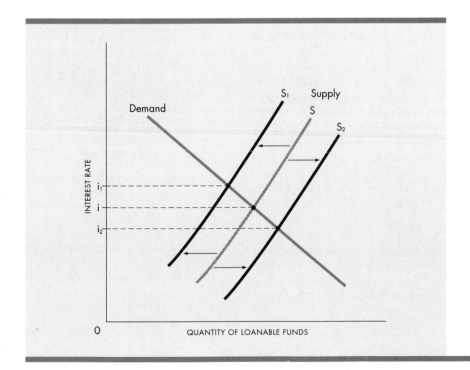

**Figure 29.3**
**Effects on the Equilibrium Interest Rate of Federal Reserve Policies Influencing the Supply Curve for Loanable Funds**
When the Federal Reserve pushes the supply curve to the right (from $S$ to $S_2$), the equilibrium interest rate falls from $i$ to $i_2$. When the Federal Reserve pushes the supply curve to the left ($S$ to $S_1$), the equilibrium interest rate increases from $i$ to $i_1$.

Finally, note that the equilibrium level of the pure interest rate can be determined by John Maynard Keynes's **liquidity preference theory,** as well as by the loanable funds theory described in this section. The liquidity preference theory focuses attention on all money, not just loanable funds, and says that the interest rate is determined by the demand and supply of all money in the economy. The two approaches are not contradictory; rather, they complement one another.

# FUNCTIONS OF THE INTEREST RATE

Interest has often been a relatively unpopular and somewhat suspect form of income. Even Aristotle, who was hardly noted for muddle-headedness, felt that money was "barren" and that it was improper to charge interest. And in the Middle Ages, church law outlawed usury, even though interest continued to be charged. In real life and in fiction, the money lender is often the villain, almost never the hero. Yet it is perfectly clear that *interest rates serve a very important function. They allocate the supply of loanable funds.*

At a given point in time, funds that can be used to construct new capital goods are scarce, and society faces the problem of allocating these scarce funds among alternative possible uses. One way to allocate the loanable funds is through freely fluctuating interest rates. When such funds are relatively scarce, the interest rate will rise, with the result that only projects with relatively high rates of return will be carried out since the others will not be profitable. On the other hand, when such funds are relatively plentiful, the interest rate will fall, and less productive projects will be carried out because they now become profitable.

## Choosing the Most Productive Projects

The advantage of using the interest rate to allocate funds is that only the most productive projects are funded. To see why, assume that all investments are riskless. *If firms can borrow all the money they want (at the prevailing interest rate), and if they maximize their profits, they will buy all capital goods and accept all investment opportunities where the rate of return on these capital goods or investment opportunities exceeds the interest rate at which they can borrow.*[2] The reason for this is clear enough. If one can borrow money at an interest cost that is less than the rate of return on the borrowed money, clearly one can make money. Thus, if you borrow $1,000 at 3 percent per year interest and buy a $1,000 machine that has a rate of return of 4 percent per year, you receive a return of $40 per year and incur a cost of $30 per year. Since you make a profit of $10 per year, it obviously pays to buy this machine.

At a particular point in time, there is a variety of possible capital goods that can be produced and investment projects that can be carried out. Their rates of return vary a great deal; some goods or projects have much higher rates of return than others. Suppose that we rank the capital goods or projects according to their rates of return, from highest to lowest. If

---

[2] We assume here that the investment opportunities are independent in the sense that the rate of return from each opportunity is not influenced by whether some other opportunity is accepted.

only a few of the goods or projects can be accepted, only those at the top of the list will be chosen. But as more and more can be accepted, society and private investors must go further and further down the list, with the consequence that projects with lower and lower rates of return will be chosen. How many of these capital goods and investment projects will be carried out? As noted above, firms will continue to invest as long as the rate of return on these goods or projects exceeds the interest rate at which they can borrow. Thus it follows that *the most productive projects—all those with rates of return exceeding the interest rate—will be carried out.*

### Socialism and the Interest Rate

Although interest is sometimes represented as a product of greedy capitalists, even socialist and Communist economies must use something like an interest rate to help allocate funds. After all, the socialists and Communists face the same sort of allocation problem that capitalists do. And when they try to screen out the less productive projects and to accept only the more productive ones, they must use the equivalent of an interest rate in their calculations, whether they call it that or not. (However, they do not pay interest income.) In the Soviet Union there have been published acknowledgments that a misallocation of resources resulted from decisions made in earlier years when interest rates—or their equivalent—were ignored. At present, Soviet decision makers use what amounts to interest rates in their calculations to determine which capital investments should be made and which should not.

Finally, besides its role in allocating the supply of loanable funds, the interest rate plays another important part in our economy: *It influences the level of investment, and thus the level of gross national product.* Increases in the interest rate tend to reduce aggregate investment, thereby reducing total spending, whereas decreases in the interest rate tend to increase aggregate investment, thereby increasing total spending. Through its monetary policies, the government attempts to influence the interest rate (and the quantity of money) so that total spending pushes gross national product toward its full-employment level with reasonably stable prices.

## CAPITAL BUDGETING

The principles discussed in the previous section can be applied to individual firms as well as entire societies. In particular, they help to indicate how a firm should make decisions on the choice of investment projects. Suppose that the Bugsbane Music Box Company believes that it will have $10 million from internal sources—primarily retained earnings and depreciation allowances—to invest next year. *To decide which investment projects to accept, it should estimate the rate of return from each one.* Suppose that it finds that it can invest $2 million in projects with rates of return of 30 percent, that it can invest $4 million in projects with rates of return of 25 percent, and so on, as shown in Table 29.1. Applying the principles just discussed, Bugsbane can maximize its profits by allocating the $10 million available from internal sources as follows: All projects yielding rates of return of 20 percent or more should be accepted; and all projects yielding less than 20 percent should not be undertaken. In other words, the projects with the highest rates of return—and with a total cost of $10 million—should be chosen.

This is a very useful step toward solving the firm's problem, but it assumes that the firm is unable or unwilling to borrow. If this is true, then nothing more needs to be said. But, as shown in Table 29.1, the firm has investment opportunities yielding 15 percent per year that it is not undertaking. It would pay the firm to undertake these projects even it it had to pay 10 or 12 percent interest—or anything less than 15 percent, for that matter. If the firm can borrow all the money it wants (within reason), but must pay 12 percent interest, what investment opportunities should it accept? All whose rate of return exceeds 12 percent. Thus, looking at Table 29.1, we see that the firm should invest its $10 million from internal sources and borrow an additional $6 million in order to undertake projects totaling $16 million.

This is an extremely simple case, but it illustrates how the interest rate and the concept of an asset's rate of return are used in practical business situations. **Capital budgeting**—the term applied to this area—has become an extremely important part of a firm's operations, as managers have relied more and more on economic concepts in allocating their firms' resources. Unaided hunch and intuition will no longer do in most major firms. Instead, most big firms insist that the prospective rate of return be estimated for each proposed investment, and that, making allowances for differences in risk, funds be allocated to the projects with the highest rate of return.[3] It is often difficult to make such estimates, but if funds are to be allocated rationally, it is essential that an analysis of this sort be carried out, formally or on the back of an envelope.

| Table 29.1 | |
|---|---|
| **Investment Opportunities for Bugsbane Music Box Company** | |
| RATE OF RETURN (PERCENT) | AMOUNT OF MONEY THE FIRM CAN INVEST AT GIVEN RATE OF RETURN (DOLLARS) |
| 30 | 2 million |
| 25 | 4 million |
| 20 | 4 million |
| 15 | 6 million |
| 10 | 7 million |

## CAPITAL AND ROUNDABOUT METHODS OF PRODUCTION

Labor and land are often called the **primary inputs** because they are produced outside the economic system. Labor is created by familiar biological processes (which usually are not economically oriented, one would hope), and land is supplied by nature. **Capital,** on the other hand, *consists of goods that are created for the purpose of producing other goods.* Factory buildings, equipment, raw materials, inventories—all are various types of capital. In contrast to labor and land, capital is an input produced by the economic system itself.[4] A machine tool is capital; so is a boxcar or an electric power plant. These inputs are produced by firms, and they are purchased and used by firms. But they are not final consumption goods; instead, they are used to produce the final goods and services consumed by the public.

Our economy devotes a considerable amount of its productive capacity to the production of capital. The giant electrical equipment industry produces generators used by the electric power industry. The machine tool industry produces the numerically controlled tools used by the automo-

---

[3] In practice, firms often base their decisions on discounted cash flow rather than rates of return. The present discussion is necessarily simplified. For a more complete treatment, see E. Mansfield, *Managerial Economics*, New York: W. W. Norton, 1990.

[4] Obviously, this distinction requires qualification. After all, land can be improved, and the quality of labor can be enhanced (by training and other means). Thus land and labor have some of the characteristics of capital since to some extent they can be "produced"—or at least enhanced—by the economic system.

bile, aircraft, and hundreds of other industries. The result in many sectors of the economy is a *roundabout method of production.* Consider the stages that lead to the manufacture of an automobile. Workers dig iron ore to be used to make pig iron to be used to make steel to be used to make machine tools to be used to make cylinders to be used to make a motor to be used to make the automobile.

## WHY CAPITAL?

Why does the economy bother to produce capital? After all, it may seem unnecessarily circuitous to construct capital to produce the goods and services consumers really want. Why not produce the desired goods and services—and *only* the desired goods and services—directly? Why produce plows to help produce agricultural crops? Why not forget about the plows and just produce the crops the consumers want? The answer is that the other inputs—labor and land—can produce more of the desired consumer goods and services when they are used in combination with capital than when they are used alone. A given amount of labor and land can produce more crops when used in combination with plows than when used alone.

The production and use of lots of capital make the other inputs—labor and land—more productive. But this does not mean that any society would be wise to increase without limit its production and use of capital. After all, the only way a society can produce more capital is to produce less goods and services of direct use to consumers. (For society as a whole, there are no free lunches, if resources are used fully and efficiently.) As the production of capital increases, consumers must cut further and further into their level of consumption at the present time in order to increase their capacity to produce in the future. Beyond a point, the advantage of having more in the future is overbalanced by the disadvantage of having less now. At this point, a society should stop increasing its production of capital goods.

The process by which people give up a claim on present consumption goods in order to receive consumption goods in the future is called **saving.** Just as a child may (infrequently) give up a lollipop today in order to get a lollipop and a candy cane next week, so an entire society may give up the present consumption of automobiles, food, tobacco, clothing, and so forth in order to obtain more of such goods and services later on.[5]

## CAPITALIZATION OF ASSETS

In a capitalist economy, each capital good has a market value. How can we determine what this value is? How much money is a capital good worth? To keep things reasonably simple, suppose that you can get 5 per-

---

[5] In a more poetic vein, this process of saving has been described as follows by William M. Thackeray:

  Though small was your allowance,
    You saved a little store;
  And those who save a little
    Shall get a plenty more.

If it does nothing else, the foregoing helps explain why Thackeray is better known as a novelist than a poet.

cent on various investments open to you; specifically, you can get 5 percent by investing your money in the stock of a local firm. That is, for every $1,000 you invest, you will receive a permanent return of $50 a year—and this is the highest return available. Now suppose that you have an opportunity to buy a piece of equipment that will yield you a permanent return of $1,000 per year. This piece of equipment is worth $1,000 ÷ .05 = $20,000 to you. Why? Because this is the amount you would have to pay for any other investment open to you that yields an equivalent amount—$1,000—per year. (If you must invest $1,000 for every $50 of annual yield, $20,000 must be invested to obtain an annual yield of $1,000.)

In general, if a particular asset yields a permanent amount—X dollars—each year, how much is this asset worth? In other words, how much should you be willing to pay for it? If you can get a return of $100 \times r$ percent per year from alternative investments, you would have to invest $X \div r$ dollars in order to get the same return as this particular asset yields. Consequently, this asset is worth

$$\frac{\$X}{r}.$$

This process of computing an asset's worth is called **capitalization.**

Thus, if the rate of return on alternative investments had been 3 percent rather than 5 percent in the example above, the worth of the piece of equipment would have been $1,000 ÷ .03 = $33,333 (since $X$ = $1,000 and $r$ = .03). This is the amount you would have to pay for any other investment open to you that yields an equivalent amount—$1,000—per year. To see this, note that, if you must invest $1,000 for every $30 (not $50, as before) of annual yield, $33,333 (not $20,000, as before) must be invested to obtain an annual yield of $1,000.

## EFFECTS ON AN ASSET'S VALUE OF CHANGES IN THE RATE OF RETURN ON OTHER INVESTMENTS

Note one important point about an asset's capitalized value. Holding constant an asset's annual returns, the asset's worth is higher the lower the rate of return available on other investments. Thus the piece of equipment discussed above was worth $33,333 when you could get a 3 percent return on alternative investments, but only $20,000 when you could get a 5 percent return on alternative investments. This makes sense. After all, the lower the rate of return on alternative investments, the more you must invest in them in order to obtain annual earnings equivalent to those of the asset in question. Thus the more valuable is the asset in question.

This principle helps to explain why in securities markets bond prices fall when interest rates rise, and rise when interest rates fall. As we saw in Chapter 21, a bond is a piece of paper that states that the borrower will pay the lender a fixed amount of interest each year (and the principal when the bond comes due). Suppose that this annual interest is $100, and that the interest rate equals $100 \times r$ percent per year. Then, applying the results of the previous paragraphs, this bond will be worth $100 \div r$ dollars, if the bond is due a great many years hence. Suppose the interest rate is 5 percent. Then it is worth $2,000. But if the interest rate rises to 10 percent,

# WHAT DOES THAT DREAM HOUSE REALLY COST?

The biggest investment you'll probably ever make is in a house. The ordinary procedure is for a house buyer to take out a mortgage, often from a savings and loan association or a bank. A mortgage is a loan; the house itself becomes security (or collateral) for the loan. If you fail to meet the mortgage payments, the lender can foreclose the mortgage, which means that the lender is entitled to take possession of the house.

To figure out how much your payments must be each month, the lender determines how much you must pay so that, when the mortgage terminates, you will have repaid the amount you borrowed and paid the stipulated interest on your debt. The size of the monthly mortgage payment depends on three things—(1) the amount you borrow, (2) how long the mortgage extends, and (3) the interest rate. The more that you borrow, the higher your monthly payment, holding all other things equal. And the higher the interest rate and the shorter the period of the mortgage, the higher your monthly payment.

To be more specific, look at the accompanying table, which shows the monthly payment per $1,000 borrowed. As you can see, the monthly payment is $9.66 per $1,000 borrowed, if the mortgage extends for 20 years and the interest rate is 10 percent. Thus, if you take out a $60,000 mortgage (at 10 percent for 20 years), the monthly payment is 60 times $9.66, or $579.60.

As noted above, much of the monthly payment is used to repay part of the principal of the loan. The rest goes for interest on the portion of the loan that is not yet repaid. Over the lifetime of a mortgage, a very substantial amount is paid by the borrower for interest. If you take out a 20-year, $60,000 mortgage at an interest rate of 10 percent, you will pay $79,104 in interest over the life of the mortgage. And the higher the interest rate, the bigger the amount that you will pay in interest. Thus, if the interest rate is 9 1/2 percent (rather than 10 percent), you will pay $74,352 (rather than $79,104) in interest over the life of a 20-year, $60,000 mortgage. As you can see, *a difference of 1/2 percent point in the interest rate increases the total interest payments by about $5,000!*

## Monthly Mortgage Payments (per $1,000 borrowed)

| INTEREST RATE | LENGTH OF MORTGAGE (YEARS) | | | |
| --- | --- | --- | --- | --- |
| | 15 | 20 | 25 | 30 |
| (percent) | | (dollars) | | |
| 7 | 8.99 | 7.76 | 7.07 | 6.66 |
| 7½ | 9.28 | 8.06 | 7.39 | 7.00 |
| 8 | 9.56 | 8.37 | 7.72 | 7.34 |
| 8½ | 9.85 | 8.68 | 8.06 | 7.69 |
| 9 | 10.15 | 9.00 | 8.40 | 8.05 |
| 9½ | 10.45 | 9.33 | 8.74 | 8.41 |
| 10 | 10.75 | 9.66 | 9.09 | 8.78 |

it will be worth only $1,000; and if the interest rate falls to 4 percent, it will be worth $2,500. Securities dealers make these sorts of calculations all the time, for they recognize that the value of the bond will fall when interest rates rise, and rise when interest rates fall.

## THE PRESENT VALUE OF FUTURE INCOME

In the previous section, we determined the value of an asset that yields a perpetual stream of earnings. Now let's consider a case where an asset will provide you with a single lump sum at a certain time in the future. Suppose that you are the heir to an estate of $100,000, which you will receive in two years. How much is that estate worth now?

*To answer this question, the first thing to note is that a dollar now is worth more than a dollar later.* Why? Because one can always invest money that is available now and obtain interest on it. If the interest rate is 6 percent, *a dollar received now is equivalent to $1.06 received a year hence.* Why? Because if you invest the dollar now, you'll get $1.06 in a year. Similarly, *a dollar received now is equivalent to $(1.06)^2$ dollars two years hence.* Why? Because if you invest the dollar now, you'll get 1.06 dollars in a year; and if you reinvest this amount for another year at 6 percent, you'll get $(1.06)^2$ dollars.

With this in mind, let's determine how much an estate of $100,000 (to be received two years hence) is worth now. If the interest rate is 6 percent, each dollar received two years hence is worth $1 \div (1.06)^2$ dollars now. Thus, if the interest rate is 6 percent, the estate is worth $100,000 \div (1.06)^2$ dollars now. Since $(1.06)^2 = 1.1236$, it is worth

$$\frac{\$100,000}{1.1236} = \$89,000.$$

In general, *if the interest rate is $100 \times r$ percent per year, a dollar received now is worth $(1 + r)^2$ dollars two years from now.* Thus, whatever the value of the interest rate may be, the estate is worth

$$\frac{\$100,000}{(1 + r)^2}.$$

**Table 29.2**
**Present Value of a Future Dollar**

| NUMBER OF YEARS HENCE (THAT DOLLAR IS RECEIVED) | INTEREST RATE (PERCENT) | | | |
|---|---|---|---|---|
| | 4 | 6 | 8 | 10 |
| | (cents) | | | |
| 1 | 96.2 | 94.3 | 92.6 | 90.9 |
| 2 | 92.5 | 89.0 | 85.7 | 82.6 |
| 3 | 89.0 | 83.9 | 79.4 | 75.1 |
| 4 | 85.5 | 79.2 | 73.5 | 68.3 |
| 5 | 82.3 | 74.7 | 68.1 | 62.0 |
| 10 | 67.6 | 55.8 | 46.3 | 38.5 |
| 15 | 55.5 | 41.7 | 31.5 | 23.9 |
| 20 | 45.6 | 31.1 | 21.5 | 14.8 |

The principle that a dollar now is worth more than a dollar later is of fundamental importance. If you don't understand it, you don't understand a basic precept of the world of finance. Although the example considered in previous paragraphs pertains only to a two-year period, this principle remains valid no matter how long the period of time we consider. Table 29.2 shows the present value of a dollar received at various points of time in the future. As you can see, its present value declines with the length of time before the dollar is received (so long as the interest rate remains constant).

## TEST YOURSELF

1. Suppose that the demand curve for loanable funds is as follows:

| QUANTITY DEMANDED (BILLIONS OF DOLLARS) | INTEREST RATE (PERCENT) |
| --- | --- |
| 50 | 4 |
| 40 | 6 |
| 30 | 8 |
| 20 | 10 |

Plot the demand curve on a graph. Describe the various kinds of borrowers that are on the demand side of the market for loanable funds.

Suppose that the supply curve for loanable funds is as follows:

| QUANTITY SUPPLIED (BILLIONS OF DOLLARS) | INTEREST RATE (PERCENT) |
| --- | --- |
| 20 | 4 |
| 25 | 6 |
| 30 | 8 |
| 35 | 10 |

Plot the supply curve on the same graph you used to plot the demand curve. What is the equilibrium rate of interest? If usury laws do not permit interest rates to exceed 6 percent, what do you think will happen in this market?

2. Describe the social functions of the interest rate. Do you agree with Aristotle that it is improper to charge interest?

3. Suppose that you can get 10 percent per year from alternative investments and that, if you invest in a particular business, you will get $1,000 per year indefinitely. How much is this investment worth to you?

4. If a firm can borrow money at 10 percent per year and will accept only (riskless) investments that yield 12 percent per year or more, is the firm maximizing profit? Explain.

## RENT: NATURE AND SIGNIFICANCE

Besides interest, another type of property income is rent. To understand rent, one must understand what economists mean by land. **Land** is defined by economists as *any input that is fixed in supply, its limits established by nature.* Thus, since certain types of minerals and natural resources are in relatively fixed supply, they are included in the economist's definition of land. Suppose that the supply of an input is completely fixed. Increases in its price will not increase its supply and decreases in its price will not decrease its supply. Following the terminology of the classical economists of the nineteenth century, *the price of such an input is* **rent**. Note that rent means something quite different to an economist than to the man in the street, who considers rent the price

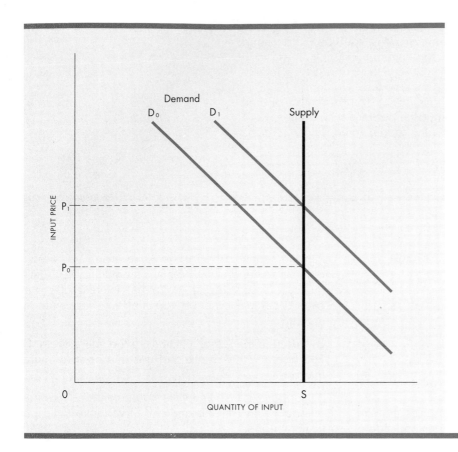

**Figure 29.4**
**Rent**
Rent is the price of an input in fixed supply. Since its supply curve is vertical, the price of such an input is determined entirely by the demand curve for the input. If the demand curve is $D_0$, the rent is $OP_0$; if the demand curve is $D_1$, the rent is $OP_1$.

of using an apartment or a car or some other object owned by someone else.

If the supply of an input is fixed, its supply curve is a vertical line, as shown in Figure 29.4. Thus the price of this input, its rent, is determined entirely by the demand curve for the input. If the demand curve is $D_0$, the rent is $OP_0$; if the demand curve is $D_1$, the rent is $OP_1$. Since the supply of the input is fixed, the price of the input can be lowered without influencing the amount supplied. Thus *a rent is a payment above the minimum necessary to attract this amount of the input.*[6]

Why is it important to know whether a certain payment for inputs is a rent? Because a reduction of the payment will not influence the availability and use of the inputs if the payment is a rent; whereas if it is not a rent, a reduction of the payment is likely to change the allocation of resources. If the government imposes a tax on rents, there will be no effect on the supply of resources to the economy.

---

[6] In recent years, there has been a tendency among economists to extend the use of the word *rent* to encompass all payments to inputs above the minimum required to make these inputs available to the industry or to the economy. (See Example 29.1.) To a great extent these payments are costs to individual firms; the firms must make such payments to attract and keep these inputs, which are useful to other firms in the industry. But if the inputs have no use in other industries, these payments are not costs to the industry as a whole (or to the economy as a whole) because the inputs would be available to the industry whether or not these payments are made.

### The Views of Henry George

In 1879, Henry George (1839–97) published a book, *Progress and Poverty,* in which he argued that rents should be taxed away by the government. In his view, owners of land were receiving substantial rents simply because their land happened to be well situated, not because they were doing anything productive. Since this rent was unearned income and since the supply of land would not be influenced by such a tax, George felt that it was justifiable to tax away such rent. Indeed, he argued that a tax of this sort should be the only tax imposed by the government.

Critics of George's views pointed out that land can be improved, with the result that the supply is not completely price inelastic. Moreover, they argued that if land rents are unearned so are many other kinds of income. In addition, they pointed out that it was unrealistic to expect such a tax to raise the needed revenue. George's single-tax movement gained a number of adherents in the last decades of the nineteenth century, and he even made an unsuccessful bid to become mayor of New York. Arguments in favor of a single tax continue to surface from time to time.

Henry George

### Rent: An Example

To make the concept of rent more concrete, consider the following example. There is a lot at the corner of Third Avenue and Winchester Street in a California suburb; this property is on the edge of the town. What will be the rent for this lot? It has various possible uses. It could be the location of a store or restaurant, a small farm, a site for an apartment building, or used for some other purpose. In each possible use, this lot has a certain value as an input.

In a competitive market, this lot will tend to rent for an amount equal to its value in its most productive use. That is, if the value of its marginal product is highest when it is used as the location for a store, a store will be built on it, and the lot will command a rent equal to the value of its marginal product. In this way, the lot will be drawn into the use that seems to yield the highest returns to the renter. From society's point of view, this has much to recommend it, since the use that yields the highest returns is likely to be the one consumers value most highly.

Classical economists viewed rent as a differential that had to be paid for the utilization of better rather than poorer land. They argued as follows. If land becomes scarce, the better lands will receive a nonzero price before the poorer lands. The rent on any acre will rise to the point where it is equal to the difference in productivity between this acre and an acre of no-rent land. Why? Because, as we saw in Chapter 28, the price differential between two inputs will equal the differential in their marginal products.

## PROFITS

Besides interest and rent, another important type of property income is profit. Profit is not new to us. In Chapter 21, we discussed at some length the economist's concept of profit and how it varies from the accountant's concept. According to accountants, profit is the amount of money the owner of a firm has left after paying wages, interest, and rent—and after providing proper allowance for the depreciation of buildings and equip-

# EXAMPLE 29.1    EXODUS OF SCIENTISTS AND ENGINEERS FROM TEACHING

D. Allan Bromley, President Bush's science adviser, has pointed out that, in mathematics, physics, and engineering, many college teachers have been leaving their jobs to work in industry.

(a) Why do you think that this has been occurring? (b) What might be the effect of such a trend on the size and quality of *future* supplies of scientists and engineers? (c) If society feels that more scientists of a particular type are needed, one way of achieving an increase in supply is to shift the supply curve for this type of scientist to the right, as shown in the graph below. How can the government effect such a shift? (d) Suppose that the supply curve does not shift to the right. If the demand curve for this type of scientist shifts to the right, as shown in the graph, does this result in some scientists of this sort receiving a higher salary than they would be willing to work for? If so, is this a rent?

### Solution

(a) Because new Ph.D.'s have been offered higher salaries by industry than by universities. (b) If the quality and number of college teachers were reduced, there might well be an adverse effect on the size and quality of future supplies of scientists and engineers. (c) By scholarship and other programs subsidizing the training of such scientists. (d) If the supply curve does not shift to the right, the equilibrium salary increases from $OW_0$ to $OW_1$, and those scientists who were willing to work for a salary of $OW_0$ receive a windfall of $(OW_1 - OW_0)$. Thus it is a rent in the sense that it is a payment above the minimum necessary to attract this amount of this input. But it is not a rent in the sense that the supply curve is vertical. (See footnote 6.)

ment. Economists dissent from this view; their position is that the opportunity costs of the labor, capital, and land contributed by the owner should also be deducted.

## Profit Statistics

Available statistics concerning profits are based on the accountant's concept, not the economist's. Before taxes, corporation profits average about 5-10 percent of gross national product. Profits—expressed as a percent of either net worth or sales—vary considerably from industry to industry and from firm to firm. (For example, the drug industry's profits in the postwar period have frequently been about 15-20 percent of net worth—considerably higher than in most other manufacturing industries.) Also, profits vary greatly from year to year, and are much more erratic than wages. They fall more heavily in recessions and rise more rapidly in recoveries than wages do. Table 29.3 shows profit as a percent of stockholders' equity in manufacturing in the United States in 1983–90.

To some extent, the measured differences in profits among firms come about because the profit figures are not corrected for the value of the inputs contributed by the owners. Because they are smarter and more resourceful, some owners provide managerial labor of a much higher quality than other owners do. Profits arising from this fact are, at least in part, wages for superior management. Similarly, some owners put up a lot of the capital and work long hours. Profits arising from these sources are, at least in part, interest on capital and wages for time spent working in the firm.

## Innovation, Uncertainty, and Monopoly Power

Why do profits—as economists define them—exist? Three important factors are innovation, uncertainty, and monopoly power. Suppose that an economy was composed of perfectly competitive industries, that entry was completely free, and that no changes in technology—no new processes, no new products, or other innovations—were permitted. Moreover, suppose that everyone could predict the future with perfect accuracy. Under these conditions, there would be no profits, because people would enter industries where profits exist, thus reducing these profits eventually to zero, and leave industries where losses exist, thus reducing these negative profits eventually to zero. This sort of no-profit equilibrium has already been discussed in Chapter 24.

But in the real world, innovations of various kinds are made. For example, Du Pont introduces a new product like nylon, or Henry Ford introduces the assembly line, or Marconi introduces the radio. The people who carry out these bold schemes are the ***innovators,*** those with vision and the daring to back it up. The innovators are not necessarily the inventors of new techniques or products, although in some cases the innovator and the inventor are the same. Often the innovator takes another's invention, adapts it, and introduces it to the market. According to economists like the late Joseph Schumpeter of Harvard, profits are the rewards earned by innovators. The profits derived from any single innovation eventually erode with competition and imitation, but other innovations replace them, with the result that profits from innovation continue to be made.

In the real world, uncertainty also exists. Indeed, one of the real hazards in attempting to be an innovator is the ***risk*** involved. According to a theory set forth several decades ago by Frank Knight of the University of Chicago, all economic profit is due to uncertainty. Profit is the reward for risk bearing. Assuming that people would like to avoid risk, they will prefer relatively stable, sure earnings to relatively unstable, uncertain earnings—*if the average level of earnings is the same.* Consequently, to induce people to take the risks involved in owning businesses in various industries, a profit—a premium for risk—must be paid to them. This is similar to the higher wages that, according to the previous chapter, must be paid for jobs where earnings are unstable or uncertain.

Still another reason for the existence of profits is the fact that markets

| | ALL MANU- FACTURING CORPOR- | DURABLE GOODS | NON- DURABLE GOODS |
|---|---|---|---|
| YEAR | ATIONS | INDUSTRIES | INDUSTRIES |
| | (percent) | | |
| 1983 | 10.6 | 8.1 | 12.7 |
| 1984 | 11.9 | 11.3 | 12.4 |
| 1985 | 10.1 | 9.2 | 11.0 |
| 1986 | 9.5 | 7.5 | 11.5 |
| 1987 | 12.8 | 11.9 | 13.7 |
| 1988 | 16.1 | 14.3 | 17.9 |
| 1989 | 13.6 | 11.1 | 16.2 |
| 1990 | 11.2 | 7.2 | 15.0 |

**Table 29.3
Annual Profit (After Taxes) as a Percentage of Stockholders' Equity, United States, 1983–90**

*Source: Economic Report of the President, 1991. The 1990 figures pertain to the third quarter.*

Frank Knight

are not perfectly competitive. Under perfect competition, there will be a tendency in the long run for profits to disappear. But, as we have seen, this will not be the case if an industry is a monopoly or oligopoly. Instead, profits may well exist in the long run in such imperfectly competitive industries. And, as we know from Chapter 27, much of our entire economy is composed of imperfectly competitive industries. Monopoly profits are fundamentally the result of "contrived scarcities." Since a firm's demand curve is downward-sloping if competition is imperfect, it pays the firm to take account of the fact that the more it produces, the smaller the price it will receive. In other words, the firm realizes that it will spoil the market if it produces too much. Thus it pays firms to limit their output, and this contrived scarcity is responsible for the existence of the profits they make as a consequence.

## THE FUNCTIONS OF PROFITS

To many people, profit seems to be "something for nothing." They do not recognize the innovative or risk-bearing functions of the owners of the firm, and consequently see no reason for the existence of profits. Other people, aware that profits arise because of imperfect competition, ignore the other functions of profit and regard it as entirely the ill-gotten gain of fat monopolists, often smoking big cigars and properly equipped with a rapacious leer. But no group is more hostile to profits than the followers and disciples of Karl Marx. According to Marx, laborers in a capitalist system receive a wage that is barely enough to cover the minimum amount of housing, food, clothing, and other commodities needed for survival. The difference between the amount the employers receive for their products and the amount they pay the laborers that produce them is "surplus value." And, according to Marx, this "surplus value," which includes what we would call profit, is a measure of, and consequence of, exploitation of labor by owners of firms.

Marx's views and those of others who look on profits with suspicion and even distaste are rejected by most economists, who feel that profits play a legitimate and very important role in a capitalistic system. In such a system, consumers, suppliers of inputs, and firms try to advance their own interests. Workers try to maximize their earnings, capitalists look for the highest interest returns, landlords try to get the highest rents, and firm owners seek to maximize their profits. At first glance, this looks like a chaotic, dog-eat-dog situation, but, as we have seen, it actually turns out to be an orderly and efficient system—if competition is present.

## PROFITS AND LOSSES: MAINSPRINGS OF A CAPITALISTIC SYSTEM

Profits and losses are mainsprings of any capitalistic system. They signal where resources are needed and where they are too abundant. When there are economic profits in an industry, this is the signal for resources to flow into it; when economic losses exist in an industry, this is the signal for resources to leave it. In addition, profits are very important incentives for innovation, for betting on the future, and for efficiency.

Consider Genentech, a major biotechnology firm. For an entrepreneur like Robert Swanson of Genentech, profits are the bait society dangles be-

# DIVERSIFIABLE RISK, NONDIVERSIFIABLE RISK, AND THE CAPITAL ASSET PRICING MODEL

Profit, as we have seen, is a reward for risk bearing. Some kinds of risk can be eliminated by diversification (as we saw on page 449); other kinds cannot. Risk that can be eliminated in this way is called *diversifiable* risk; risk that cannot be eliminated in this way is called *nondiversifiable* risk. Suppose that you are investing in the stock market. *Nondiversifiable risk is the risk that the general level of the stock market will go down because of a recession or for some other reason.* Because the prices of stocks of various companies tend to go up or down together, this kind of risk cannot be eliminated by diversification.

In contrast, *risk due to factors that are specific to a particular company can be eliminated by diversification.* For instance, DuPont's stock may be adversely affected by a new product's being introduced by Union Carbide, or Bethlehem Steel's stock may go down because of a strike. This kind of risk can be eliminated by diversification, because whereas some companies are hurt by new products or strikes during a given period, other companies gain from them. Consequently, if one purchases a considerable number of stocks representing a variety of industries, the effects of such factors are likely to be very small, on the average. Why? Because they will tend to cancel each other out.

In recent decades, the capital asset pricing model developed by economists like William Sharpe of Stanford and John Lintner of Harvard has played an important role on Wall Street, as well as in academic thinking. This theory builds on the long-accepted proposition that investors must receive a higher expected return to induce them to accept higher risk. Thus, if stock in Ford is riskier than stock in General Motors, the expected return from Ford's stock must be greater than that from General Motors' stock. Otherwise, investors would not buy Ford's stock.

In contrast to older doctrine, this theory emphasizes that *not all of the risk in a particular stock must be taken into account in determining how high this stock's expected return must be to compensate the investor for risk bearing.* Surprising as it may seem, *only the nondiversifiable risk is relevant.* Why? Because the diversifiable risk can be eliminated by diversification. Since the diversifiable risk can be avoided so easily, you cannot obtain a higher expected return by assuming this risk. People won't pay you for bearing unnecessary risks.

fore him and his firm to get them to take the risks involved in developing and marketing a new product like Activase, Genentech's gene-spliced heart drug introduced in late 1987. The profits that Genentech earns from this drug will be used to support its new ventures into other areas of biotechnology. The level of profits (or losses) in various fields of biotechnology will signal where more resources are needed and where they would be redundant.

The importance of profits in a free-enterprise economy is clear enough. However, this does not mean that all profits are socially justified or that the system as a whole cannot be improved. Monopoly profits may not be socially justified, and a competitive system, despite its advantages, may produce many socially undesirable effects—for example, an undesirable income distribution. Much more will be said on this score in the next chapter.

# THE FUNCTIONAL DISTRIBUTION OF INCOME

In this and the previous chapter, we have been concerned with wages, interest, rent, and profit. How is the total income of the nation as a whole divided among these categories? In other words, what proportion of all income goes to employees? What proportion goes for interest? For rent? For profits? In this section, we take up these questions.

Table 29.4 shows the proportion of national income going for (1) wages and salaries, (2) proprietors' income, (3) corporate profits, (4) interest, and (5) rent.[7] It is clear that wages and salaries are by far the largest of these five income categories. In 1990, about three-fourths of national income went for wages and salaries (including employer contributions to Social Security and pensions). Moreover, this is an understatement of the

**Table 29.4**
**Percentage Shares of National Income, 1900–90**

| PERIOD | WAGES AND SALARIES | PROPRIETORS' INCOME | CORPORATE PROFITS (PERCENT) | INTEREST | RENT | TOTAL |
|--------|--------|--------|--------|--------|------|-------|
| 1900–09 | 55 | 24 | 7 | 5 | 9 | 100 |
| 1910–19 | 54 | 24 | 9 | 5 | 8 | 100 |
| 1920–29 | 60 | 18 | 8 | 6 | 8 | 100 |
| 1930–39 | 67 | 15 | 4 | 9 | 5 | 100 |
| 1939–48 | 65 | 17 | 12 | 3 | 3 | 100 |
| 1949–58 | 67 | 14 | 13 | 3 | 3 | 100 |
| 1963–70 | 70 | 12 | 11 | 4 | 3 | 100 |
| 1990 | 73 | 9 | 7 | 11 | —[a] | 100 |

[a] Less than 1 percent.
Source: I. Kravis, "Income Distribution: Functional Share." *International Encyclopedia of the Social Sciences*, New York: Macmillan, 1968, and *Annual Reports of the Council of Economic Advisers*. These figures may not be entirely comparable over time, but they are sufficiently accurate for present purposes.

[7] The concept of rent on which these figures are based is different from the one presented in this chapter, but this does not affect the conclusions presented below.

share of employee compensation in national income, because part of proprietors' income is really wages. As we pointed out in an earlier section, a portion of what the proprietor of the corner drugstore or the local shoestore makes is compensation for the proprietor's labor, not profit as defined by the economist.

The figures in Table 29.4 indicate a marked reduction over time in the proportion of national income going to proprietors, and a marked increase over time in the proportion going for wages and salaries. Part of this shift is due to the fact that the corporation has become a more dominant organizational form, with the result that many people who would have been individual proprietors owning their own small businesses 50 years ago now work as employed managers for corporations. Another fact that may help to explain this shift is the long-term shift from agriculture (where labor's share of income is low) to manufacturing and services (where labor's share is higher).

Some economists are impressed by the constancy of the share of national income going to labor. Using definitions that are somewhat different than those underlying Table 29.4, they come up with numbers indicating that labor's share has not varied much over time. Other economists, using somewhat different definitions, conclude that labor's share has varied considerably. But one thing is for sure. There is no evidence that a bigger share of the economic pie is going to capitalists in the form of interest, rent, or profits. Perhaps the figures in Table 29.4 exaggerate the extent to which labor's share has increased, but there is certainly no evidence that it has decreased.

## TEST YOURSELF

1. Assume that you inherit $1,000, which will be paid to you in two years. If the interest rate is 8 percent, how much is this inheritance worth now? Why?

2. "The supply curve for iron ore is horizontal, so its price is a rent." Comment.

3. "Based on the available data concerning changes over time in labor's share of total income in the United States, it is evident that labor is getting so powerful that it is receiving more and more of the total. This is an important reason for the shortage of capital in the United States." Comment and evaluate.

4. Suppose that a candidate for president proposes that all profits be taxed away. Would you support this proposal? Why, or why not?

## SUMMARY

1. Interest is a payment for the use of money. Interest rates vary a great deal, depending on the nature of the borrower and the type and riskiness of the loan. One very important function of interest rates is to allocate the supply of loanable funds.

2. The pure interest rate—the interest rate on riskless loans—is, like any price, determined by the interaction of supply and demand. However, because of the influence of the government on both the demand and supply sides of the market, it is clear that the pure interest rate is to a considerable extent a matter of public policy.

3. Capital is composed of inputs produced by the economic system itself. Our economy uses very roundabout methods of production and devotes a considerable amount of its productive capacity to the production of capital.

4. If more and more capital is produced during a particular period, consumers must cut further and further into their consumption during that period. This process is called saving.

5. In a capitalist system, each capital good has a market value that can be determined by capitalizing its earnings.

Holding constant an asset's annual return, the asset's worth is higher, the lower the rate of return available on other investments.

6. Any piece of capital has a rate of return, which indicates its net productivity. An asset's rate of return is the interest rate earned on the investment in the asset. If firms maximize profits, they must carry out all projects where the rate of return exceeds the interest rate at which they can borrow.

7. Rent is the return derived by inputs that are fixed in supply. Since the supply of the input is fixed, its price can be lowered without influencing the amount supplied. Thus, if the government imposes taxes on rents, there will be no effect on the supply of resources to the economy.

8. Another important type of property income is profits. Available statistics on profits are based on the accountant's concept, not the economist's, with the result that they include the opportunity costs of the labor, capital, and land contributed by the owners of the firm. Profits play a very important and legitimate role in a free enterprise system.

9. Two of the important factors responsible for the existence of profits are innovation and uncertainty. Profits are the rewards earned by innovators and a payment for risk-bearing. Still another reason for the existence of profits is monopoly power; due to contrived scarcity, profits are made by firms in imperfectly competitive markets.

## CONCEPTS FOR REVIEW

| | | |
|---|---|---|
| Interest | Supply curve for loanable funds | Capitalization |
| Rate of interest | Liquidity preference theory | Land |
| Pure rate of interest | Capital budgeting | Rent |
| Demand curve for loanable funds | Primary inputs | Innovator |
| | Capital | Risk |
| Rate of return | Saving | Capital asset pricing model |
| Diversifiable risk | Nondiversifiable risk | |

# INCOME INEQUALITY AND POVERTY

ON SEPTEMBER 27, 1991 the front-page headline of the *New York Times* read, "Poverty Rate Rose Sharply Last Year as Incomes Slipped." The fact is that some Americans are poor—so poor that they suffer from malnutrition—and while poverty may not be a sin, it is no less an inconvenience to the poor. Given the affluence of American society, one is led to ask why poverty exists and whether it cannot be abolished by proper public policies. The purpose of this chapter is to examine these questions.

## HOW MUCH INEQUALITY OF INCOME?

We don't have to be very perceptive social observers to recognize that there are great differences in income levels in the United States. But our idea of what the distribution of income looks like depends on the sort of family and community we come from. A child brought up in Lake Forest, a wealthy suburb of Chicago, is unlikely to be as aware of the incidence of poverty as a child brought up on Chicago's poor South Side. For a preliminary glimpse of the extent of ***income inequality*** in the United States, scan Table 30.1, which shows the percentage of all families in the United States that were situated in various income classes in 1989. According to the table, the bottom fifth of the nation's families received an income of less than $16,003 in 1989. On the other hand, the top fifth of the nation's families received an income of $59,550 or more in 1989.

It may come as a surprise to some that so large a percentage of the nation's families made less than $16,003. The image of the affluent society projected in the Sunday supplements and on some television programs is strangely out of tune with these facts. Yet, to put these figures in world perspective, it should be recognized that Americans are very rich relative to other peoples. This fact is shown clearly by Table 30.2, which gives for various countries the 1988 level of income per person, which is the total income of each nation divided by its population. The United States is among the leaders in this table.

## WHY INEQUALITY?

Nonetheless, recognizing that our poor are better off than the bulk of the population in many other countries, the fact remains that there is substantial inequality of income in this country. Why is this the case? Based

**Table 30.1**
**Percentage Distribution of Families, by Income, 1989**

| MONEY INCOME (DOLLARS) | PERCENT OF ALL FAMILIES | PERCENT OF TOTAL INCOME RECEIVED | PERCENT OF FAMILIES WITH THIS AND LOWER INCOMES | PERCENT OF INCOME RECEIVED BY FAMILIES WITH THIS AND LOWER INCOMES |
|---|---|---|---|---|
| Under 16,003 | 20 | 5 | 20 | 5 |
| 16,003–28,000 | 20 | 11 | 40 | 16 |
| 28,000–40,800 | 20 | 17 | 60 | 33 |
| 40,800–59,550 | 20 | 24 | 80 | 57 |
| 59,550–98,960 | 15 | 25[a] | 95 | 82 |
| 98,960 and over | 5 | 18 | 100 | 100 |
| Total | 100 | 100 | | |

[a] Because of rounding errors, the figures in this column do not sum to 100. To make the total equal 100, this number was changed slightly. For present purposes, this is of no importance.
*Source:* Department of Commerce.

**Table 30.2**
**Selected Countries Grouped by Approximate Level of Income per Capita, 1988**

I. Countries with income per capita exceeding $10,000

| United States | Denmark | Sweden |
|---|---|---|
| Australia | France | Japan |
| Canada | Germany | Switzerland |

II. Countries with income per capita between $2,500 and $10,000

| Uruguay | Greece | Yugoslavia |
|---|---|---|
| Ireland | Hong Kong | Thailand |
| Soviet Union | Spain | Venezuela |
| Algeria | Iran | Mexico |
| Brazil | Malaysia | Turkey |

III. Countries and regions with income per capita less than $2,500

| India | El Salvador | Most of Africa |
|---|---|---|
| Indonesia | Haiti | Much of Asia |

All figures are expressed in 1988 dollars.
*Source:* R. Summers and A. Heston, "The Penn World Table (Mark 5): An Expanded Set of International Comparisons," *Quarterly Journal of Economics,* May 1991.

on our discussion of labor and property incomes in previous chapters, this question is not hard to answer. One reason is that some people possess greater abilities than others. Since Mark Davis and Darryl Strawberry have extraordinary skill as baseball players, it is easy to understand why they make a lot of money (over $3.6 million each in 1991 alone).[1] Another reason is differences in the amount of education and training people receive. Thus physicians or lawyers must receive a higher income

[1] *New York Times,* April 10, 1991, p. B8.

than people in occupations requiring little or no training. (Otherwise it would not pay people to undergo medical or legal training.) Still another reason is that some people own large amounts of property. Thus, because of a shrewd choice of ancestry, the Fords, Rockefellers, and Mellons get high incomes from inherited wealth. Still other reasons are that some people have managed to obtain monopoly power, and others have had an extraordinary string of good luck.

## A MEASURE OF INCOME INEQUALITY

To what extent has income inequality in the United States changed? Some people say that because of the advent of the "welfare state" the nation has moved rapidly toward greater equality of income. Others say that the rich are getting richer and the poor are getting poorer. Who is right? To answer this question, we need some way to measure the degree of income inequality. The most commonly used technique is the **Lorenz curve,** which plots the percentage of people, going from the poorest up, on the horizontal axis, and the percentage of total income they get on the vertical axis.

The Lorenz curve based on the figures in Table 30.1 is shown in Figure 30.1. To see how this diagram was constructed, note that in Table 30.1 families with incomes under $16,003 accounted for 20 percent of all families, but only 5 percent of all income. Thus, plotting 20 percent on the horizontal axis against 5 percent on the vertical axis, we get point A. The table also indicated that families with incomes under $28,000 accounted for 40 percent of all families, but only 16 percent of all income. Plotting these figures in the same way, we get point B. Connecting up all points like A and B, we obtain the Lorenz curve in Figure 30.1

**CASE 1: NO INEQUALITY.** Two extreme cases must be understood to see how the Lorenz curve is used. First, suppose that *incomes were the same for all families* (or whatever kinds of recipients are under consideration). Then the Lorenz curve would be a straight line connecting the origin of the diagram with its upper right-hand corner. That is, it would be OP in Figure 30.1. To see this, note that, if incomes are distributed equally, the lowest 10 percent of the families receive 10 percent of the total income, the lowest 20 percent of the families receive 20 percent of the total income, and so forth. Plotting 10 percent on the horizontal axis against 10 percent on the vertical axis, 20 percent on the horizontal axis against 20 percent on the vertical axis, and so forth, one gets a Lorenz curve of OP.

**CASE 2: COMPLETE INEQUALITY.** Suppose that *incomes were distributed completely unequally*—that is, one person has all of the income and the rest have none. In this case, the Lorenz curve would lie along the horizontal axis from O to M and along the vertical line from M to P. It would be OMP in Figure 30.1. Why? Because the lowest 10 percent of the families have zero percent of the total income, the lowest 20 percent of the families have zero percent of the total income, and so, in fact, do the lowest 99 percent of the families. Plotting 10 percent on the horizontal axis against zero percent on the vertical axis, 20 percent on the horizontal axis against zero percent on the vertical axis, and so on, one gets a Lorenz curve that lies along the horizontal axis from O to M. But since 100 percent of the families must receive 100 percent of the income, the Lorenz curve must then jump up from M to P.

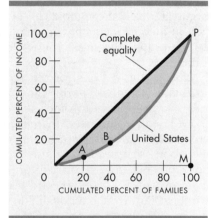

**Figure 30.1**
**Lorenz Curve for Family Income, United States, 1989**
OP is the Lorenz curve if income were distributed equally. The shaded area between this hypothetical Lorenz curve and the actual Lorenz curve is a measure of income inequality.

These two cases make it clear that *the shaded area in Figure 30.1*—the deviation of the actual Lorenz curve from the Lorenz curve corresponding to complete equality of income—*is a measure of income inequality.* The larger this shaded area, the greater the extent of income inequality. Figure 30.2 shows the Lorenz curve for the income distributions in three countries—*D, E,* and *F.* As reflected in the Lorenz curves, income inequality is greater in *F* than in *E,* and greater in *E* than in *D.* Why? Because the area between the actual Lorenz curve and the Lorenz curve corresponding to complete equality is greater in *F* than in *E,* and greater in *E* than in *D.*

## TRENDS IN INCOME INEQUALITY

Let us now return to the question posed at the beginning of the previous section: To what extent has income inequality in the United States changed? Figure 30.3 shows the Lorenz curves for the income distributions in 1929 and 1962. These curves make it clear that there was a considerable reduction in income inequality. The share of income going to the top 20 percent declined by one-fifth between 1929 and 1962. This change, described by some writers as an "income revolution," did not occur gradually throughout the period. Instead, essentially all the reduction in income inequality occurred before the end of World War II. Without question, this was a notable change in the American economic landscape.

One of the reasons for the reduction in income inequality between 1929 and the end of World War II was the increased importance of wages and salaries relative to other sources of income. Wages and salaries are more equally distributed than income from self-employment and property. Also, many public programs were established to provide income for the poor. (The details of these programs are described below.) In addition, the shift from substantial prewar unemployment to the full employment of World War II narrowed wage differentials among various types of workers. Further, the inequality in the distribution of wealth was reduced during this period.

During the 1980s there was an increase in income inequality. The share of total before-tax income received by the 20 percent of American families with highest incomes rose during this period, while the share received by the 20 percent with lowest incomes fell. However, this increase in income inequality was much too small to offset the reduction before and after World War II.

## EFFECTS OF THE TAX STRUCTURE ON INCOME INEQUALITY

So far we have looked at the distribution of before-tax income. But we must also consider the effect of the tax system on income inequality.

A tax is ***progressive*** if the rich pay a higher proportion of their income for the tax than do the poor. A tax is ***regressive*** if the rich pay a smaller proportion of their income for the tax than do the poor.

Needless to say, people who feel that the tax system should promote a redistribution of income from rich to poor favor progressive, not regressive taxes. Obviously, the personal income tax is progressive, since the

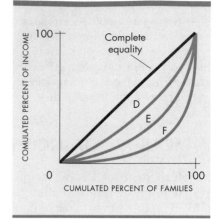

**Figure 30.2**
**Lorenz Curves for Countries D, E, and F**
Income inequality is greater in country F than in country E, and greater in country E than in country D.

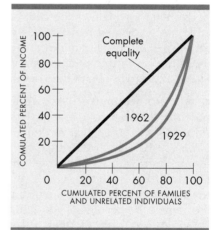

**Figure 30.3**
**Changes over Time in Lorenz Curves for Family Income in the United States**
Income inequality in the United States decreased between 1929 and 1962, as indicated by the Lorenz curves.

tax rate is greater for high-income people than for low-income people. Other progressive taxes are inheritance or estate taxes. (The federal government levies a gift tax to prevent wealthy people from circumventing the estate tax by giving their money away before death.) This is applauded by reformers who oppose accumulation and preservation of inherited wealth. But, as in the case of the personal income tax, the portion of an estate subject to taxes can be reduced through clever use of various loopholes, all quite legal. Thus the estate tax is not as progressive as it looks.

Not all taxes are progressive; examples of regressive taxes are not hard to find. General sales taxes of the sort used by most states and some cities are regressive, since high-income people pay a smaller percentage of their income in sales taxes than do low-income people. The Social Security tax is also regressive. It is difficult to tell whether the corporation income tax is progressive or regressive. At first glance, it seems progressive because the owners of corporations—the stockholders—tend to be wealthy people; and to the extent that the corporate income tax is paid from earnings that might otherwise be paid to the stockholders, one might conclude that it is progressive. But this ignores the possibility that the corporation may pass the tax on to the consumer by charging a higher price; in this case the tax may not be progressive.

# EXAMPLE 30.1    ECONOMIC EFFECTS OF ILLEGAL ALIENS

During the early 1980s, the number of illegal aliens in the United States was estimated to be between 2 and 12 million. In 1986, Congress, attempting to curb illegal immigration, passed the Immigration Reform and Control Act. Suppose that the value-of-marginal-product curve for labor in the U.S. market is as follows:

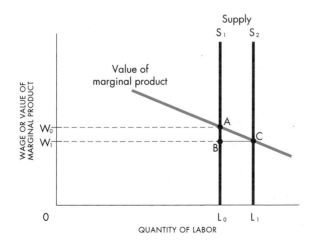

(a) If $S_1$ is the supply curve for labor *without* immigration of illegal aliens, what would be total labor income under these circumstances? (b) If $S_2$ is the supply curve for labor *with* immigration of illegal aliens, what would be the total labor income of the native U.S. population under these circumstances? (c) Will the owners of U.S. capital and land benefit from this immigration? Why or why not? (d) Why does La Raza Unidad, a farm labor union representing many Spanish-speaking American citizens, oppose such immigration?

## Solution

(a) Total labor income will equal the area of rectangle $OW_0 AL_0$, since it will equal the wage ($OW_0$) times the quantity of labor employed ($OL_0$). (b) Since the total supply of native U.S. labor is $OL_0$, total labor income will equal the area of rectangle $OW_1 BL_0$, since it will equal the wage ($OW_1$) times $OL_0$. (c) Yes. The value of the marginal product of the extra ($OL_1—OL_0$) workers exceeds their wage, $OW_1$, as can be seen in the graph on the left. Also, the owners of U.S. capital and land benefit from the fact that they can pay native U.S. labor a lower wage. (d) One reason may be that such immigration lowers the wage received by American citizens engaged in farm labor.

## Who Pays the Taxes and Receives the Transfer Payments

To get a better picture of the extent to which the government—in terms of both the money it spends and the taxes it levies—takes from the rich and gives to the poor, studies have been carried out to determine how much people in various income brackets pay in taxes and receive in transfer payments (Social Security, welfare payments, food stamps, Medicare, and Medicaid). The results of one important study of this sort are shown in Figure 30.4. As you can see, the effect of taxes (federal, state, and local) and transfers is to reduce income inequality. However, this is due largely to the fact that transfer payments go mainly to the poor. Taken by itself, the tax system is only mildly progressive or slightly regressive, depending on the study's assumptions. Moreover, there is evidence that the tax system was less progressive (or more regressive) in 1985 than in 1966.[2]

Estimates of this sort are interesting, but it is difficult to predict the **incidence** of some taxes—that is, it is difficult to know who *really* pays them. The incidence of certain taxes is relatively easy to determine. For example, it is generally accepted that the personal income tax is paid by the person whose income is taxed. But there are other cases—such as the corporation income taxes we just mentioned—where it is difficult to tell how much of the tax burden the firm shifts to the consumer.[3] For these and other reasons, there is considerable controversy over the extent to which the spending and taxing activities of the government really are progressive or regressive.

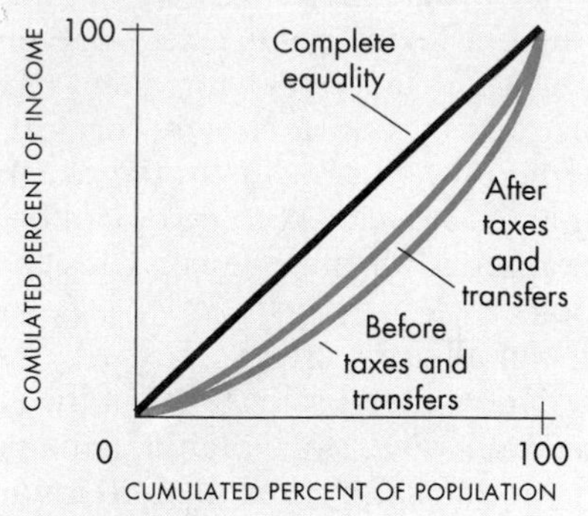

**Figure 30.4**
**Effect of Federal Income Tax and Transfer Payments on Lorenz Curve, United States**
In the United States, inequality of income after taxes and transfers is less than inequality of income before taxes and transfers.

# INCOME INEQUALITY: THE PROS AND CONS

## The Case against Income Inequality

Many distinguished social philosophers have debated the merits and demerits of making the income distribution more equal. We cannot consider all the subtler points, but those who favor greater equality make four main arguments.

*1. They say that inequality of income lessens total consumer satisfaction because an extra dollar given to a poor man provides him with more extra satisfaction than the loss of a dollar takes away from a rich man.* According to A. C. Pigou, "It is evident that any transference of income from a relatively rich man to a relatively poor man of similar temperament, since it enables more intense wants to be satisfied at the expense of less intense wants, must increase the aggregate sum of satisfactions."[4]

---

[2] J. Pechman, *Who Paid the Taxes, 1966–85?*, Washington, D.C.: Brookings Institution, 1985. Based on different assumptions about tax incidence, E. Browning and W. Johnson have concluded that the tax system is more progressive than Pechman concludes.

[3] To see how the burden of a tax can be shifted, consider the effects of an *excise* tax—a tax imposed on each unit sold of a particular product. The federal government imposes excise taxes on liquor and tobacco, among many other products. The immediate effect of these taxes is to raise the price of the commodity since the supply curve will be shifted upward and to the left. (See pp. 685–88.) If demand is price inelastic, most of the burden of the tax is shifted to the consumer. Under these circumstances, firms sell almost as many units of the product as before the tax was imposed, despite the higher price induced by the tax. On the other hand, if supply is relatively inelastic, the burden is borne mainly by the producer. Usually, the aim of excise taxes is to put the burden on consumers. In the case of liquor and tobacco there clearly is a feeling that drinking and smoking smack of sin, and sinners should pay, in this world and the next.

[4] A. C. Pigou, *Economics of Welfare*, 4th ed., London: Macmillan, 1948, p. 89.

# EQUAL PAY FOR WORK OF "COMPARABLE WORTH"

Women's earnings tend to be considerably lower than men's, the percentage gap being about 25 percent for persons 25–34 years of age and almost 37 percent for persons 35–44 years of age. A striking fact about female employment is that, although women can be found in virtually all occupations, they predominate overwhelmingly in a few like nursing and secretarial work. In 1986, women constituted 94 percent of registered nurses, 98 percent of secretaries, and 85 percent of waiters and waitresses in the United States.

Some believe that these jobs are underpaid because they tend to be filled by women, and to eliminate what they regard as a major inequity, they argue for "equal pay for work of comparable worth." The idea is to compare the worth of one occupation with that of another occupation, and to press for equal wage rates for them if they are judged to be of equal worth. Thus, if a nurse does work that is of equal worth to that of an accountant, nurses should get the same wage as accountants.

To measure the worth of an occupation, many proponents of "comparable worth" propose the use of a job evaluation point system. In 1983, a federal court found the state of Washington guilty of discrimination because it paid male-dominated occupations more than "comparable" female-dominated occupations. To determine what occupations were comparable, every state job was evaluated in terms of "accountability," "knowledge and skills," "mental demands," and "working conditions." A committee decided how many points to give each occupation on each of these criteria, and two occupations were regarded of comparable worth if they got the same total number of points.

An enormous amount of controversy has engulfed this decision, which said that Washington should raise women's wages and grant restitution for past injuries to them. Although higher courts reversed this decision, many politicians have supported the idea that an occupation's wage rate should be determined in this way by "comparable worth." In 1989, a law was enacted in Ontario, Canada, that says that employers must assess jobs in which at least 60 percent of the employees are women, and use such a job evaluation system to see how much women should be paid.

Many economists are opposed to the use of such job evaluation systems to set wage rates. In their view, the proper determinants of wage rates are the supply and demand curves discussed in Chapter 28, which together set wage rates in competitive markets. To ignore these supply and demand curves is to run the risk that some occupations will have shortages while others will have too many people. Certainly, job evaluation systems of this sort may reduce economic efficiency. However, proponents of these job evaluation systems emphasize equity, not efficiency; in their view, these systems will promote equity.

A problem in this very appealing argument is its assumption that the rich man and the poor man have the same capacities to gain enjoyment from income. Most economists believe that there is no scientific way to make such comparisons (as emphasized in Appendix D). They deny that the satisfaction one person derives from an extra dollar of income can be measured against the satisfaction another person derives from an extra dollar. Although such comparisons may be drawn, they rest on ethical, not scientific, grounds.

*2. It is argued that income inequality is likely to result in unequal opportunities for young people to gain advanced education and training.* The children of the rich can get an education, while the children of the poor often cannot. The result is that some able and productive people may be denied an education simply because their parents are poor. This is a waste of resources.

*3. It is argued that income inequality is likely to lead to political inequality.* The rich may well influence legislation and political decisions more heavily than the poor, and there is likely to be one kind of justice for the rich and another kind for the poor.

*4.* In the past few years, the arguments for income equality have been carried a step forward by John Rawls, the Harvard philosopher. He says that, *if people were framing a constitution for society without knowing what their class position would be, they would opt for equality.* And he argues that "all social values . . . are to be distributed equally unless an unequal distribution is to the advantage of society's least privileged group." Although Rawls's book, *A Theory of Justice,* has had considerable impact, many economists have pointed out that his prescription for society might not appeal to people who were willing to take risks. Suppose that you were framing a social constitution and that you could establish a society that guaranteed every family $30,000 a year (no more, no less) or one where 99 percent of all families would receive $40,000 and 1 percent would receive $24,000. You might choose the latter kind of society because, although there is a small chance that you would do worse than in the egalitarian case, the chance of doing better seems worth this risk.

## The Case for Income Inequality

In general, people who favor income inequality make five arguments.

*1. They argue that income inequality is needed to give people an incentive to work and create.* After all, if everyone receives the same income, why bother to increase your production, or to try to invent a new process, or to work overtime? Whatever you do, your income will be the same. This is an important point, though it overlooks the fact that nonmonetary incentives like pride in a job well done can be as important as monetary incentives.

*2. Advocates of income inequality claim that it permits greater savings, and thus greater capital formation.* Although this seems reasonable, it is not hard to cite cases where countries with greater inequality of income invest less, not more, than countries with less inequality of income. Thus some Middle Eastern countries with great income inequality have not had relatively high investment rates.

*3. Advocates of income inequality say that the rich have been important patrons of new and high-quality products that benefit the entire society.* They argue that there are social advantages in the existence of certain people with the wherewithal to pioneer in consumption and to support art and culture. In their view, a completely egalitarian society would be a rather dull affair.

   4. *Advocates of income inequality point out that even if everyone received the same income, the poor would not be helped a great deal, because the wealthy are relatively few.* If the riches of the rich were transferred to the poor, each person would get only a little, because there are so many poor and so few rich.

   5. According to Harvard's Robert Nozick and others, *one must look at the justice of the process leading to the distribution of income and wealth in order to determine whether a certain degree of income inequality is unfair.* For example, suppose that an entertainer carries out a series of shows that are very successful, and that she makes a lot of money. The process by which she makes this money is entirely legitimate. (People voluntarily pay for the tickets to her shows—and enjoy every minute of them!) Thus, according to this view, the resulting inequality of income is not unfair.


## The Tradeoff between Equality and Efficiency

Measures taken to reduce inequality are likely to decrease economic efficiency. In other words, if we reduce inequality, we may well cut society's total output. Why? Because, as pointed out in the previous section, people are likely to have less incentive to produce if their incomes are much the same regardless of how much they produce. This does not mean that all measures designed to reduce income inequality are bad. What it does mean is that, if you want to reduce income inequality, you should be sensitive to the effects on output. In particular, you should try to find policies that will attain a given reduction in inequality at a minimum cost in terms of reduced output.

   Consider, for example, the effects of very high income tax rates. Although it is sometimes argued that the tax rate for people making several hundred thousand dollars a year should be 80 or 90 percent, one important problem with such proposals is that they might well reduce the amount of work done and output produced. Why put in that extra week of work if Uncle Sam takes 80 or 90 percent of your earnings?

   In view of the strong feelings of many advocates and opponents of reduced income inequality, it is not surprising that they sometimes make extreme statements about the nature of the tradeoff between equality and efficiency. Some egalitarians deny that there is any tradeoff at all. They claim that inequality can be reduced without any cut in output. Some opponents of reductions in income inequality assert that there will be a catastrophic fall in output if the existing income distribution is tampered with. Although far too little is known about the quantitative character of this tradeoff, there seems to be general agreement among economists that the truth lies somewhere between these two extremes.

   People vary considerably in their evaluation of how much society should pay (in terms of decreased total output) for a particular reduction in income inequality. The late Arthur Okun of the Brookings Institution suggested that, to characterize your own feelings on this score, it is useful to view money as a liquid and to visualize a bucket which carries money from the rich to the poor.[5] The bucket is leaky, so only part of what is

---

[5] Arthur Okun, *Equality and Efficiency,* Washington, D.C.: Brookings Institution, 1975. For an excerpt from this book, see E. Mansfield, *Principles of Microeconomics: Readings, Issues, Cases,* 4th ed., New York: Norton, 1983.

taken from the rich can be given to the poor. If the leak is very small, a dollar taken from the rich may result in 99 cents going to the poor. Many people would accept a loss of this magnitude. If the leak is very large, a dollar taken from the rich may result in only 5 cents going to the poor. Few people would accept this big a loss. How big a loss would you accept? The larger the leak that you would find acceptable, the more willing you are to accept output losses in order to attain decreases in income inequality.

The argument between the advocates and opponents of reduced income inequality involves much more than economics. Whether you favor greater or less income inequality depends on your ethical and political beliefs. It is not a matter economics alone can settle. What economists can do is assess the degree of income inequality in a country and suggest ways to alter the gap between the haves and have-nots in accord with the dictates of the people or their leaders. In recent decades, economists in and out of government have devoted much effort to designing programs aimed at reducing poverty. To understand these programs, we must discuss what poverty is, and who the poor are.

## WHAT IS POVERTY?

Some people are fond of saying that everything is relative. Certainly this is true of poverty. Relative to the Mellons or Rockefellers, practically all of us are poor; but relative to the homeless who sleep in railroad and bus terminals, practically all of us are rich. Moreover, poverty is certainly subjective. Consider the average young executive making $50,000 a year. After a bad day at the office or a particularly expensive family shopping spree, he is likely to tell anyone who will listen that he is as poor as a church mouse.

There is no well-defined income level that can be used in all times and places as a touchstone to define poverty. Poverty is partly a matter of how one person's income stacks up against that of others. What most people in America today regard as stark poverty would have seemed like luxury to many Americans of 200 years ago—and would seem like luxury in parts of Asia and Africa today. Consequently, one must be careful not to define poverty in such a way that it cannot be eliminated—and then try to eliminate it. If poverty is defined as being in the bottom 10 percent of the income distribution, how can a war against poverty ever be won? Regardless of what measures are taken, there will always be a bottom 10 percent of the income distribution, unless all income inequality is eliminated (which is highly unlikely).

Perhaps the most widely accepted definition of **poverty** in the United States today is the one developed by the Social Security Administration, which began by determining the cost of a *minimal* nutritionally sound food plan (given by the Department of Agriculture). Then, since low-income families spend about one-third of their incomes on food, this food cost was multiplied by 3 to obtain an income level that was used as a criterion for poverty. Families with less income were regarded as "living below the poverty level."

Based on such computations, a family of four (including two children) needed an income of about $13,359 to make it barely over the Social Security Administration's poverty line in 1990. Although one could quarrel with this figure on various counts, most people probably would agree that families with income below this level are poor.[6]

## Two Case Studies

Particular cases of poverty are generally more illuminating and impressive than discussions in the abstract. Consider the following two actual cases in New York City (the names are fictitious).

THE SMITH FAMILY.    The Smiths—Christopher, 47, and Irene, 35—opened a small restaurant after years of saving. Within a month, Christopher had a severe heart attack and was laid up in the hospital. The Smiths lost the restaurant, and Irene went to work as a nurse's aide to supplement her husband's small disability benefits. After about a year of working and trying to take care of her husband and two children—John, 13, and Deborah, 12—Irene collapsed from the strain and had to enter a mental hospital. While she was away, a relative took care of Christopher and the children. After getting out of the hospital, Irene learned that her husband had cancer and required expensive surgery. She became so upset that the doctor called in one of the city's charity agencies, which tried to help this troubled and impoverished family as best it could.

THE JONES FAMILY.    Jean Jones, 35, is trying to raise seven children. Her husband, an unskilled laborer, never made much money. He drank a lot, terrified Mrs. Jones and the children with his abuse, and was an unfaithful husband. Four years ago, Mrs. Jones separated from him. She gets along as best she can on public assistance, but is having a difficult time. Two of the children have been arrested for theft; two others are in trouble in school; and one daughter is pregnant out of wedlock. Mrs. Jones feels beaten. In recent months, through the help of neighbors, she has consulted a community service bureau where the social workers have given her help and encouragement. But she obviously needs a great deal of aid if she and her family are to get their heads above water.

Neither of these cases is typical. Since they were cited by the *New York Times* as being among New York's 100 neediest cases, it is fair to say that their plight is probably worse than that of the great bulk of America's poor. But they provide some idea of just how bad things can get; and one has to be hardhearted indeed not to feel compassion for people like the Smiths and Mrs. Jones.

# INCIDENCE AND CAUSES OF POVERTY

Because college students tend to come from relatively well-off families, they often are unaware of the number of families in the United States whose incomes fall below the Social Security Administration's poverty line. According to estimates made by the federal government in 1990, about 13 percent of the population in the United States was below this line. In absolute terms, this means that over 30 million people were

---

[6] The basic figures come from the Department of Commerce's *Current Population Reports,* which explain in detail the way in which these figures are derived. The method described in the text is crude, but it provides results that are quite close to those of more complicated methods. Since 1969, the poverty line has been calculated on the basis of the Consumer Price Index, not the price of food.

poor—usually not as poor as the Smiths or Mrs. Jones, but poor enough to fall below the criterion described above.

Over the long run, the incidence of poverty (measured by this criterion) generally has been declining in the United States. In 1947, about 30 percent; in 1960, about 20 percent; and in 1990, about 13 percent of the people were poor by this definition. This is what we would expect. As the average level of income rises, the proportion of the population falling below the poverty line (which is defined by a relatively fixed dollar amount of income) will tend to decrease. But the fact that poverty has been declining in the long run does not mean that this process is going on as fast as it should. Many observers feel, as we shall see in subsequent sections, that poverty could and should be eradicated more rapidly.

Naturally, the poor are not confined to any particular demographic group, but some types of families are much more likely than others to be below the poverty line. In particular, *blacks are much more likely to be poor than whites.* In 1989, 31 percent of blacks were poor, whereas 10 percent of whites were poor. Also, *families headed by females are much more likely to be poor than families headed by males.* In addition, very large families—7 persons and over—are much more likely than others to be poor.

To a considerable extent, the reasons why families are poor lie beyond the control of the families themselves. About one-third of the poor adults have suffered a disability of some sort, or the premature death of the family breadwinner, or family dissolution. Some have had to face a smaller demand for their occupation (because of technological or other change) or the decline of their industry or geographical area. Some have simply lived "too long"—their savings have given out before their minds and bodies did. Another instrumental factor in making some families poor is discrimination of various kinds. The most obvious type is racial, but others exist as well—discrimination based on sex, religion, age, residence, education, and seniority. In addition, some people are poor because they have very limited ability or little or no motivation. These factors should not be overlooked.

Finally, there is sometimes a tendency for poverty to be self-perpetuating. Families tend to be poor year after year, and their children tend to be poor. Because the families are poor, the children are poorly educated, poorly fed, and poorly cared for, and poverty is transmitted from one generation to the next. It is a vicious cycle.

## TEST YOURSELF

1. Suppose that the following data pertain to the income distribution in the nation of Upper Usher in 1991:

| INCOME (DOLLARS) | PERCENT OF FAMILIES WITH INDICATED INCOME |
|---|---|
| 2,000 | 40 |
| 4,000 | 30 |
| 6,000 | 20 |
| 10,000 | 10 |

Plot the Lorenz curve for this nation in 1991.

2. In 1992, suppose that the income distribution in Upper Usher is as follows:

| INCOME (DOLLARS) | PERCENT OF FAMILIES WITH INDICATED INCOME |
|---|---|
| 2,000 | 20 |
| 4,000 | 40 |
| 6,000 | 35 |
| 10,000 | 5 |

Plot the 1992 Lorenz curve, and compare it with the

1991 curve. Did income inequality in this nation increase or decrease between 1991 and 1992?

3. Persons or families are classified as poor on the basis of their current money income. Should the following items also be taken into account? (a) The assets of the person or family; (b) the existence of rich relatives of the person or family; (c) the person's or family's income over a period of years, not a single year.

# SOCIAL INSURANCE

## Old-Age Insurance

Until about 50 years ago, the federal government played little or no role in helping the poor. Private charity was available in limited amounts, and the state and local governments provided some help, but the general attitude was "sink or swim." Self-reliance and self-support were the watchwords. The Great Depression of the 1930s, which changed so many attitudes, also made a marked change in this area. In 1935, with the passage of the Social Security Act, the federal government established a social insurance system providing compulsory old-age insurance for both workers and self-employed people, as well as unemployment insurance. By 1990, about 40 million Americans were receiving about $20 billion per month in benefits from the resulting system of old-age and survivors' insurance.

Every wage earner covered under the Social Security Act pays a tax, which in 1991 amounted to 7.65 percent of the first $53,400 of his or her annual earnings. The employer also pays a tax, which is equal to that paid by the employee. The amount that one can expect to receive each month in **old-age insurance** benefits depends on one's average monthly earnings. Also, the size of the benefits depends on the number of years one has worked. In 1991, if you retired at 65 and if you had steady lifetime earnings of about $40,000 per year, you would receive about $1,000 per month. If you retire at 65, the monthly benefits are greater than if you retire at 62. These benefits are a retirement annuity. In other words, they are paid to the wage earner from the date of retirement to the time he or she dies. In addition, when a wage earner dies, **Social Security** provides payments to his or her spouse, to dependent parents, and to children until they are about 18 years of age. Further, payments are made to a wage earner (and dependents), if he or she is totally disabled and unable to work.

## Controversies over Social Security

There are a number of controversial aspects of the Social Security program.

*1. If you work past the retirement age of 65, you can be penalized considerably*. For every three dollars in wages that you earn above and beyond $9,720 in 1991, you lose one dollar in Social Security benefits. Thus, since you must pay taxes on your earnings, you get to keep well under two-thirds of every extra dollar that you earn in wages (over $9,720 per year). But you can earn any amount of interest or dividends or pensions without your Social Security benefits being reduced. To some observers, this is unfair discrimination against older people who want to hold down jobs.

*2. The Social Security tax is regressive,* since those with annual earnings above $53,400 pay a smaller proportion of their income in Social Security taxes than do those with annual earnings below $53,400. For this and other reasons, many observers believe that the system is not as generous to the poor as it should be.

*3. Some people are disturbed that the Social Security system is not really an ordinary insurance system at all.* An ordinary insurance program must have assets that are sufficient to finance all of the benefits promised to the people in the program. This is not the case for Social Security. But this does not mean that you won't receive your Social Security benefits. What it does mean is that the Social Security system is a means of transferring income each year from the working young and middle-aged to the retired old people. It will be up to future Congresses to determine what these benefits will be. (In 1983, Congress made a number of important changes: for example, up to half of the Social Security benefits of the well-to-do are now taxable under the personal income tax.) Only time will tell how much you will receive.

*4. Some people are disturbed that Social Security is mandatory.* Milton Friedman is concerned that the government interferes with an individual's freedom to plan for the future by forcing him or her to be a member of the Social Security system. (Workers might be able to obtain larger pensions by investing the money that they contribute to Social Security in investments of their own choosing.) Other observers retort that without a mandatory system, some workers would make inadequate provision for their old age and might become public charges.

*5. Some people are concerned that Social Security is an impediment to saving and capital formation.* Martin Feldstein, former chairman of President Reagan's Council of Economic Advisers, feels that Americans save relatively little because they depend on Social Security to take care of their old age. This, he believes, tends to depress capital formation in the United States, since savings can be used to build factories, expand old plants, and add in various ways to the nation's stock of capital. He favors a slowdown in the rate of growth of Social Security, and more reliance on private pensions and personal savings.

## Medicare, Unemployment Insurance, Other Programs

In 1965, the Congress extended the Social Security program to include **Medicare,** a compulsory hospitalization insurance plan plus a voluntary insurance plan covering doctors' fees for people over 65. The hospitalization insurance pays for practically all the hospital costs of the first 90 days of each spell of illness, as well as some additional costs. The voluntary plan covers about 80 percent of doctors' fees after the first $100. The cost of the compulsory insurance is included in the taxes described above, as well as a 1.45 percent tax on annual earnings between $53,400 and $125,000. In 1992, the federal government paid out about $114 billion for Medicare.

Besides instituting old-age, survivors, and medical insurance, the Social Security Act also encouraged the states to set up systems of **unemployment insurance.** Such systems now exist in all states, financed by taxes on employers. Once an insured worker is unemployed, he can obtain benefits after a short waiting period, generally a week. The average weekly benefits differ from state to state; in December 1990 they ranged from about $220 in Massachusetts and New Jersey to about $115 in Mississippi and Tennessee. In most states, there is a 26-week ceiling on the duration of benefits. Clearly, unemployment insurance is another important device to keep people from falling below the poverty line.[7]

Finally, in 1974, a program was created to replace federal grants to the states to help the aged, the blind, and the disabled. This program, called the **Supplemental Security Income Program,** established a uniform national minimum income for people in these categories who are unable to work. (Also, many states supplement these federal payments.) In 1990, about 5 million people received over $15 billion from this program.

## ANTIPOVERTY PROGRAMS

According to the English poet and essayist Samuel Johnson, "A decent provision for the poor is the true test of civilization." There is general agreement that our social insurance programs, although useful in preventing and alleviating poverty, are not an adequate or complete anti-poverty program. For one thing, they focus largely on the elderly, which means that they do not aid many poor people. They do not help the working poor; and even for the unemployed, they provide only limited help for a limited period of time.

Consequently, the government has started a number of additional programs specifically designed to help the poor, although many of them are aimed more at the symptoms of poverty than at its basic causes. There are programs that provide goods and services to the poor. The biggest of these programs is **Medicaid,** which pays for the health care of the poor. The federal government's 1989 disbursements for this program were about $30 billion. In 1990, Congress passed legislation extending Medicaid coverage to more and more children; by 2003, all poor children up to the age of 18 will be covered by Medicaid.

The **food programs,** which have distributed food to needy families, are also of major significance in this regard. (Before 1973, this food generally came from surpluses due to the farm programs described in Chapter 31.) The federal government has given **stamps** that can be used to buy food to local agencies, which have sold them (at less than the equivalent of market prices) or have given them to low-income families. In 1989, the cost of this program to the federal government was about $13 billion.

Not all antipoverty programs give particular commodities to the poor; some programs provide them with cash. These are what people generally have in mind when they refer to **welfare.** There are advantages to cash payments. They allow a family to adapt its purchases to its own needs and circumstances. There are obvious disadvantages too, since the money may be spent on liquor and marijuana rather than on food and milk. The most important single program of cash payments gives **aid to families with dependent children.** In 1988, this program paid out more than $16 billion.

To qualify for this program, a family must contain dependent children who are without the support of a parent (usually the father) through death, disability, or absence (and in some states, through unemployment

---

[7] In 1991, some observers worried that fewer workers were eligible for unemployment insurance than in the past, because states had tightened requirements. For example, workers sometimes had to work longer and earn more to be eligible. Other people felt that the tightening of requirements was justified.

as well). The amount paid to a family under this program varies from state to state, since each state administers its own program and sets it own schedule of payments—as well as contributes part of the cost of the program, with the federal government providing the balance. In 1988, the average monthly payment was about $550 in states like Massachusetts and New York and about $115 in states like Mississippi and Alabama. To determine eligibility, the family's affairs are examined; and while receiving aid the family may be under the surveillance of a social worker who supervises its housekeeping and child care.

In 1988, Congress passed a welfare reform act, which was aimed at increasing the extent to which welfare recipients work or participate in job-training programs. This is called "workfare," the idea being that able-bodied adults should work in order to be eligible for welfare benefits. In general, the 1980s saw a reduced emphasis by the federal government on many welfare programs. The Reagan administration felt that income assistance should be confined to those that were undeniably needy; others would be taken care of by a strong private economy.

## The Negative Income Tax

There is widespread dissatisfaction with current antipoverty—or welfare—programs. The cost of these programs has risen alarmingly; the programs themselves are judged by many experts to be inefficient; and, in some people's view, the welfare recipients are subjected to unnecessary meddling and spying. Moreover, there is little incentive for many people to get off welfare. Both Republicans and Democrats seem to agree that current welfare programs need improvement. What changes might be made? One suggestion that has received serious consideration is the negative income tax, an idea proposed by Stanford University's Milton Friedman (an adviser to presidential candidate Barry Goldwater in 1964 and to President Nixon) and Yale's James Tobin (an adviser to President Kennedy).

A **negative income tax** would work as follows: Just as families with reasonably high incomes *pay* taxes, families with low incomes would *receive* a payment. In other words, the poor would pay a *negative* income tax. Figure 30.5 illustrates how a negative income tax might work; it shows the amount a family of four would pay—or receive—in taxes, depending on its income. According to Figure 30.5, $6,000 is the **break-even income**—the income at which a family of four neither pays nor receives income taxes. Above $6,000, a family pays taxes. Thus a family with an income of $9,000 pays $750 in taxes. Below $6,000 a family receives a payment. Thus a family with an income of $1,500 is paid $2,250.

There are several advantages of a negative income tax.

1. It would give people on welfare more incentive to work. As indicated in Figure 30.5, for every extra dollar it earns, the family receives only 50 cents less from the government under this kind of negative income tax. Thus the family gets to keep half of every extra dollar (up to $6,000) it earns, which is a larger portion of this extra dollar than has been true under the present system.

2. There would be no intrusion into the internal affairs of families on welfare and no regulations that cut off welfare payments if the husband remains with his family. In the past, the welfare system has given families an incentive to break up, and encroached on the dignity of poor people.

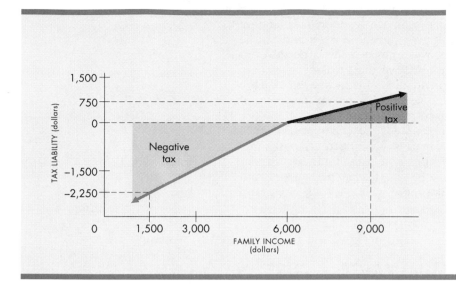

**Figure 30.5**
**Example of Negative Income Tax**
A family with more than $6,000 in income pays taxes. Thus a family with an income of $9,000 pays $750 in taxes. A family with an income less than $6,000 receives a payment. Thus a family with an income of $1,500 is paid $2,250.

3. It might cost less to administer the negative income tax than the present system, and differences among states in benefits might be reduced.

Despite these advantages, many citizens remain skeptical about the negative income tax. For one thing, they are antagonistic to the idea of

## EXAMPLE 30.2   WHY NOT CURE POVERTY WITH A CHECK?

If the United States government were to mail checks to all poor families to raise their incomes to the poverty level, these checks would amount to less than 1 percent of our gross national product. Suppose that the government decides to solve the poverty problem in this way.

(a) If the poverty level is $15,000 per year, what is the relationship between a family's income before subsidy and its income after subsidy? (b) Up to $15,000, does a family's earnings influence its income after subsidy? (c) For people whose pre-subsidy earnings are below the poverty level, what would be the effect of this program on the incentive to work? (d) For people whose pre-subsidy earnings are slightly above the poverty level, what would be the effect of this program on the incentive to work? (e) Would the cost of this program be greater than the amount of the checks mailed to the poor?

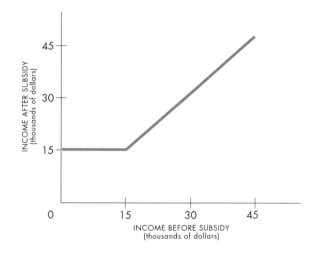

### Solution

(a) This relationship is shown in the figure at right. (b) No. (c) Because they can get $15,000 without working, some would be likely to quit working, or to work less hard. (d) Because they can get almost as much as their current income without working, some would be likely to quit working, or to work less hard. (e) Yes. There would be the additional costs due to the diminished incentives to work. For reasons discussed above, people would work less, and fewer goods and services would be produced.

giving people an income without requiring any work in return. They also are unwilling to transfer large amounts from rich to poor. This amount would depend on how high the break-even income was set and on the negative tax rates. In the late 1960s, it was estimated that a negative income tax would have meant that those above the break-even income level would transfer about $25 billion to those below the break-even level. Despite the attractive features of a negative income tax, a transfer of this magnitude proved unacceptable in many quarters.

Also, some economists regard the results of the experiments with a negative income tax in Seattle and Denver to have been disappointing. These experiments, carried out with a sample of households, seem to indicate that under a (generous) negative income tax people work significantly less, apparently because they are more willing to quit work, and less willing to search hard for a new job.

## INCREASES IN THE MINIMUM WAGE: A CURE FOR POVERTY?

At first glance, it may appear that the government can eradicate poverty by raising the minimum wage. In the United States, the minimum wage goes back over half a century. In 1938, the Congress passed the Fair Labor Standards Act, which established a minimum wage of 25 cents per hour. With inflation and changes in social attitudes and values, the minimum wage has been increased repeatedly. In 1991, it equaled $4.25 per hour.

Despite occasional claims to the contrary, the truth is that *increases in the minimum wage cannot cure poverty.* The effects of a minimum wage are demonstrated in Figure 30.6, which shows the demand and supply curves for unskilled labor in a competitive labor market. Without the minimum wage, the equilibrium wage rate is $4.00 per hour, and $OL_2$ hours of labor are hired. If a minimum wage of $5.00 per hour is put into effect,

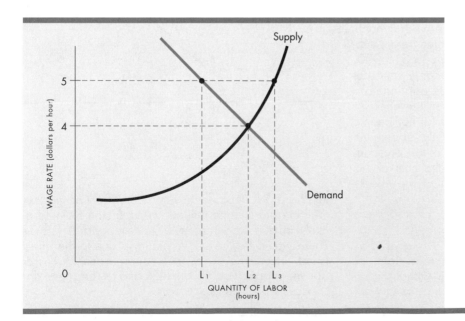

**Figure 30.6**
**Effect of a Minimum Wage**
Without the minimum wage, the equilibrium wage is $4 per hour, and $OL_2$ hours of labor are hired. With a minimum wage of $5 per hour, only $OL_1$ hours of labor are hired.

employers will cut back on the amount of labor that they hire. Rather than employing $OL_2$ hours of labor, they will employ only $OL_1$ hours of labor. Unemployment will be created. Whereas workers would like to work $OL_3$ hours, they will only be able to work $OL_1$ hours. Not all of this unemployment will be reflected in the government's unemployment statistics, since some people who are unable to find jobs may give up looking for work (and thus not be counted in the government's figures).

Clearly, the unskilled workers who keep their jobs are better off because of the minimum wage; they get $5 an hour rather than $4 an hour. But those who lose their jobs or are unable to find jobs are worse off. In general, one would expect that *the least skilled and most disadvantaged would be the ones that would be hardest hit by the minimum wage.* In particular, many economists believe that the minimum wage pushes up the unemployment rate among black teenagers. To soften the effect on teenagers, Congress established a training wage of about $3.60 per hour in 1991 for workers from 16 to 19 years old in their first job. (This training wage can be paid to a particular worker for no more than six months.) It is too soon to tell how effective this new training wage will be.

## THE WAR ON POVERTY: SOME FINAL VOLLEYS

Before concluding this chapter, it is worthwhile pointing out that there are considerable differences of opinion among politicians and economists concerning the severity of the poverty problem in the United States. The official government statistics concerning the incidence of poverty do not recognize the fact that many people below the official poverty line receive non-cash benefits from the government, such as food stamps, subsidized school lunches, public housing, Medicaid, and Medicare. These benefits accounted in 1980 for more than two out of every three dollars of government assistance. According to the U.S. Bureau of the Census, the percentage of the U.S. population below the poverty line is much smaller than the official statistics indicate, when these government non-cash benefits are taken into account. Specifically, the figure according to official statistics has been about 10 percent. When underreporting of incomes is taken into consideration, some economists conclude that only about 4 percent of the population have fallen below the poverty line in recent years. Based on these statistics, some observers claim that the war on poverty in the United States has been won.

On the other hand, many economists argue that the official poverty line established by the government is too low, the result being that a substantial number of poor people are not classified as poor in the official statistics. In 1990, the House of Representatives voted to give $600,000 to the National Academy of Sciences to study this issue. Whether or not the official statistics underestimate the poverty problem, it seems self-evident that a problem does exist. After all, even if only 4 percent fall below the poverty line, this means that about 10 million people are poor. Moreover, a disproportionately large number of children are being raised in poverty. According to the official statistics, one child in five lives in a family with income below the poverty line. Unquestionably, it is difficult to design and implement effective and efficient policies to alleviate poverty, but our society has no reasonable alternative than to try.

## TEST YOURSELF

1. Many people feel that Aid to Families with Dependent Children should be transformed into a vehicle for education, training, and work. In what sense is work the solution to dependency? Can training and job placement enable long-term welfare recipients to break out of poverty and dependency?

2. "The Social Security system is actuarially unsound. The amounts currently collected in Social Security taxes do not equal the amounts currently paid out in benefits. We cannot keep this up!" Comment and evaluate.

3. According to some economists, Social Security should be voluntary, not mandatory. Present the arguments on each side of this issue in as much detail as you can.

4. Do the official government statistics concerning poverty recognize that many people below the poverty line receive non-cash benefits from the government? If not, does this mean that these statistics are useless? Explain.

## SUMMARY

1. Lorenz curves are used to measure the extent of income inequality. They make it clear that there was a considerable reduction in income inequality in the United States between the late 1920s and the end of World War II.

2. Many factors are responsible for existing income differentials. Some people are abler, better educated, or luckier than others. Some people have more property, or more monopoly power, than others.

3. Critics of income inequality argue that it lessens total consumer satisfaction because an extra dollar given to the poor provides them with more extra satisfaction than the loss of a dollar taken away from the rich. Also, they argue that income inequality leads to social and political inequality.

4. Defenders of income inequality point out that it is scientifically impossible to make interpersonal comparisons of utility, and argue that income inequality is needed to provide incentives for people to work and create, and that it permits greater capital formation.

5. There is no well-defined income level that can be used in all times and all places to determine poverty. Perhaps the most widely accepted definition of poverty in the United States today is the one developed by the Social Security Administration, according to which about 13 percent of the population in the United States—over 30 million people—fell below the poverty line in recent years.

6. Black families, families headed by a female, and very large families are more likely than others to be poor. To a considerable extent, the reasons for their poverty lie beyond the control of the poor people. About one-third of poor adults have suffered a disability of some sort, or the premature death of the family breadwinner, or family dissolution. Most heads of poor families do not have jobs.

7. Because private charity is judged to be inadequate, the nation has authorized its government to carry out various public programs to aid the poor. There are programs to provide them with goods and services—Medicaid and food-stamp programs, for instance. Other programs, like aid to families with dependent children, give them cash. When these programs are taken into account, the percentage of the population falling below the poverty line is reduced considerably.

8. There is widespread dissatisfaction with existing antipoverty—or welfare—programs. They are judged to be inefficient; their costs have been increasing at an alarming rate; and they provide little incentive for people to get off welfare. One suggestion to remedy these problems is a negative income tax. In most of the forms put forth it involves a transfer of income that seems presently to be beyond the realm of political feasibility.

## CONCEPTS FOR REVIEW

| | | |
|---|---|---|
| Income inequality | Old-age insurance | Food programs |
| Lorenz curve | Social Security | Welfare |
| Progressive tax | Medicare | Aid to families with dependent |
| Regressive tax | Unemployment insurance | children |
| Tax incidence | Supplemental Security Income | Negative income tax |
| Poverty | Program | Break-even income |

# PART EIGHT

# GOVERNMENT AND THE ECONOMY

# THE ECONOMIC ROLE OF THE GOVERNMENT

TO STATE THAT THE UNITED STATES is a mixed capitalist system, in which both government decisions and the price system play important roles, is hardly to provoke a controversy. But going a step beyond takes us into areas where viewpoints often diverge. The proper functions of government and the desirable size and nature of government expenditures and taxes are not matters on which all agree. Indeed, the question of how big government should be, and what its proper functions are, is hotly debated by conservatives and liberals throughout the land.

## LIMITATIONS OF THE PRICE SYSTEM

Despite its many advantages, the price system suffers from limitations. Because these limitations are both prominent and well known, no one believes that the price system, left to its own devices, can be trusted to solve all society's basic economic problems. To a considerable extent, the government's role in the economy has developed in response to the limitations of the price system, which are described below.

DISTRIBUTION OF INCOME.   There is *no* reason to believe that the distribution of income generated by the price system is *fair* or, in some sense, *best*. Most people feel that the distribution of income generated by the price system should be altered to suit humanitarian needs; in particular, that help should be given to the poor. Both liberals and conservatives tend to agree on this score, although there are arguments over the extent to which the poor should be helped and the conditions under which they should be eligible for help. But the general principle that the government should step in to redistribute income in favor of the poor is generally accepted in the United States today.[1]

PUBLIC GOODS.   Some goods and services *cannot be provided through the price system because there is no way to exclude citizens from consuming the goods whether they pay for them or not.* For example, there is no way to prevent citizens from benefiting from national expenditures on defense, whether they pay money toward defense or not. Consequently, the

---

[1] Also, because the wealthy have more "dollar votes" than the poor, the sorts of goods and services that society produces will reflect this fact. Thus luxuries for the rich may be produced in larger amounts and necessities for the poor may be produced in smaller amounts than some critics regard as sensible and equitable. This is another frequently encountered criticism of the price system.

price system cannot be used to provide such goods; no one will pay for them since they will receive them whether they pay or not. Further, these goods, like the quality of the environment and national defense (and others cited below), *can be enjoyed by one person without depriving others of the same enjoyment*. Such goods are called **public goods.** The government provides many public goods. Such goods are consumed collectively, or jointly, and it is inefficient to try to price them in a market. They tend to be indivisible; thus they frequently cannot be split into pieces and be bought and sold in a market.

**EXTERNAL ECONOMIES AND DISECONOMIES.** In cases where *the production or consumption of a good by one firm or consumer has adverse or beneficial uncompensated effects on other firms or consumers, the price system will not operate effectively*. An **external economy** is said to occur when consumption or production by one person or firm results in uncompensated benefits to another person or firm. A good example of an external economy exists where fundamental research carried out by one firm is used by another firm. (To cite one such case, there were external economies from the Bell Telephone Laboratories' invention of the transistor. Many electronics firms, such as Texas Instruments and Fairchild, benefited considerably from Bell's research.) Where external economies exist, it is generally agreed that the price system will produce too little of the good in question and that the government should supplement the amount produced by private enterprise. This is the basic rationale for much of the government's huge investment in basic science. An **external diseconomy** is said to occur when consumption or production by one person or firm results in uncompensated costs to another person or firm. A good example of an external diseconomy occurs when a firm dumps pollutants into a stream and makes the water unfit for use by firms and people downstream. Where activities result in external diseconomies, it is generally agreed that the price system will tolerate too much of the activity and that the government should curb it. For example, as we shall see in Chapter 33, the government, in keeping with this doctrine, has involved itself in environmental protection and the reduction of air and water pollution.[2]

## WHAT FUNCTIONS SHOULD THE GOVERNMENT PERFORM?

There are wide differences of opinion on the proper role of government in economic affairs. Although it is generally agreed that the government should redistribute income in favor of the poor, provide public goods, and offset the effects of external economies and diseconomies, there is considerable disagreement over how far the government should go in these areas, and what additional areas the government should be responsible for. Some people feel that "big government" is already a problem; that government is doing too much. Others believe that the public sector of the economy is being under-nourished and that government should be allowed to do more. This is a fundamental question, and one that involves a great deal more than economics.

[2] The effects of external economies and diseconomies can also be taken care of by legal arrangements that assign liabilities for damages and compensate for benefits. However, such arrangements often are impractical or too costly to be used.

**CONSERVATIVE VIEW.** On the one hand, conservatives, such as Stanford University's Nobel laureate, Milton Friedman, believe that the government's role should be limited severely. They feel that economic and political freedom is likely to be undermined by excessive reliance on the state. Moreover, they tend to be skeptical about the government's ability to solve the social and economic problems at hand. They feel that the prevailing faith in the government's power to make a substantial dent in these problems is unreasonable, and they call for more and better information concerning the sorts of tasks government can reasonably be expected to do—and do well. They point to the slowness of the government bureaucracy, the difficulty in controlling huge government organizations, the inefficiencies political considerations can breed, and the difficulties in telling whether government programs are successful or not. On the basis of these considerations, they argue that the government's role should be carefully circumscribed.

**LIBERAL VIEW.** To such arguments, liberals like Nobel laureate Paul Samuelson of the Massachusetts Institute of Technology respond with telling salvos of their own. Just as conservatives tend to be skeptical of the government's ability to solve important social and economic problems, so liberals tend to be skeptical about the price system's ability to solve these problems. They point to the limitations of the price system, discussed above, and they assert that the government can do a great deal to overcome these limitations, by regulating private activity and by subsidizing and providing goods and services that the private sector produces too little of. Liberals tend to be less concerned than conservatives about the effects on personal freedom of greater governmental intervention in the economy. They point out that the price system also involves coercion, since the fact that the price system awards the available goods and services to those who can pay their equilibrium price can be viewed as a form of coercion. In their view, people who are awarded only a pittance by the price system are coerced into discomfort and malnutrition.[3]

## ESTABLISHING "RULES OF THE GAME"

Although there is considerable disagreement over the proper role of the government, both conservatives and liberals agree that it must do certain things. The first of these is to establish the "rules of the game"—that is, a legal, social, and competitive framework enabling the price system to function as it should. Specifically, *the government must see to it that contracts are enforced, that private ownership is protected, and that fraud is prevented.* Clearly, these matters must be tended to if the price system is to work properly. Also, *the government must maintain order (through the establishment of police and other forces), establish a monetary system (so that money can be used to facilitate trade and exchange), and provide standards for the weight and quality of products.*

As an example of this sort of government intervention, consider the Pure Food and Drug Act. This act, originally passed in 1906 and subsequently amended in various ways, protects the consumer against improper and fraudulent activities on the part of producers of foods and

---

[3] See P. Samuelson, "The Economic Role of Private Activity," and G. Stigler, "The Government of the Economy," in E. Mansfield, *Principles of Microeconomics: Readings, Issues, and Cases,* 4th ed.

drugs. It prohibits the merchandising of impure or falsely labeled food or drugs, and it forces producers to specify the quantity and quality of the contents on labels. These requirements strengthen the price system. Without them, the typical consumer would be unable to tell whether food or drugs are pure or properly labeled. Unless consumers can be sure that they are getting what they pay for, the basic logic underlying the price system breaks down. Similar regulation and legislation have been instituted in fields other than food and drugs—and for similar reasons.

## MAINTAINING A COMPETITIVE FRAMEWORK

Besides establishing a legal and social framework that will enable the price system to do its job, *the government must also see to it that markets remain reasonably competitive.* Only if they are will prices reflect consumer desires properly. If, on the other hand, markets are dominated by a few sellers (or a few buyers), prices may be "rigged" by these sellers (or buyers) to promote their own interests. For example, if a single firm is the sole producer of aluminum, it is a safe bet that this firm will establish a higher price than if there were many aluminum producers competing among themselves.

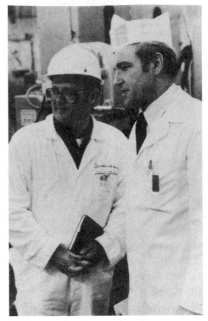

FDA inspectors

As previous chapters have indicated, the unfortunate thing about prices determined in noncompetitive markets—rigged prices, if you will—is that they give incorrect signals concerning what consumers want and how scarce resources and commodities are. Producers, responding to these incorrect signals, do not produce the right things in the right quantities. Consumers respond to these incorrect signals by not supplying the right resources in the right amounts, and by not consuming the proper amounts of the goods that are produced. Thus the price system is not permitted to function properly in the absence of reasonable competition.

To try to encourage and preserve competition, the Congress, as we have seen, has enacted a series of **antitrust laws,** such as the Sherman Antitrust Act and the Clayton Act, and it has established the Federal Trade Commission. The antitrust laws make it illegal for firms to collude or to attempt to monopolize the sale of a product. Both conservative and liberal economists, with some notable exceptions, tend to favor the intent and operation of the antitrust laws.

## REDISTRIBUTION OF INCOME

We have already noted, particularly in Chapter 30, the general agreement that the government should redistribute income in favor of the poor. In other words, *it is usually felt that help should be given to people who are ill, handicapped, old and infirm, disabled, and unable for other reasons to provide for themselves.* To some extent, the nation has decided that income—or at least a certain minimum income—should be divorced from productive services. Of course, this doesn't mean that people who are too lazy to work should be given a handout. It does mean that people who cannot provide for themselves should be helped. To implement this principle, various payments are made by the government to needy people—including the aged, the handicapped, the unemployed, and pensioners.

These **welfare payments** are to some extent a "depression baby," for

# SEMATECH: SHOULD THE GOVERNMENT SUBSIDIZE SEMICONDUCTORS?

In 1987, America's semiconductor manufacturers, facing intense competition from the Japanese, set out to establish a program based on Pentagon money and industry collaboration to reestablish their world leadership—or in the case of some firms, their viability—in the production and design of advanced computer chips. The project, known as SEMATECH, called for research on advanced manufacturing techniques. The Pentagon and industry would put up equal amounts of money, and there would be close cooperation between the semiconductor manufacturers and their customers and suppliers.

Semiconductor chips are the hearts of computers and telecommunications devices that play a central role in military guidance systems, as well as other defense-related products. The Defense Science Board Task Force on Semiconductor Dependency regarded the decline in the U.S. semiconductor industry vis-à-vis the Japanese as "an unacceptable threat" that damages the technology base that is important to American national security. Claiming that the U.S. military establishment had become too dependent on Japanese chips, it stated that: "The Japanese cannot be relied upon to transfer leadership semiconductor technology to U.S. systems suppliers for military uses."

In December 1987, Congress appropriated $100 million to SEMATECH, almost half its annual budget. SEMATECH is sponsored by 14 major semiconductor manufacturers including IBM, Intel, and Texas Instruments. It has three primary missions: to do research and development on advanced semiconductor manufacturing techniques, to test them on a demonstration production line, and to transfer the techniques to American producers. The 14 members of the research consortium will have first call on SEMATECH's results. In early 1988, the decision was made to locate SEMATECH in Austin, Texas, but there was some grumbling by Pentagon officials that the operating plan for SEMATECH was too vague. In July 1988, after considerable difficulty in obtaining a chief executive, Robert Noyce, former vice chairman of Intel Corporation, took the position, but died soon afterward. His successor was William Spencer, formerly senior technical officer at Xerox.

SEMATECH headquarters

According to Spencer, new technology is not SEMATECH's major achievement. In his view, "the biggest thing coming out of SEMATECH is the way equipment suppliers, semiconductor manufacturers, and systems houses are working together. . . .[I]f we don't pull together and do business differently, we're going to go out of business."[1]

Although Congress has been persuaded to subsidize semiconductor research and development in this way, many observers wonder whether the government should use taxpayers' money to help bail out industries in trouble. Also, some people question whether firms in so competitive an industry are really willing to cooperate. Each firm might be inclined to get what information it could from its rivals, but disclose as little as possible. Economists and others will look closely at SEMATECH's performance, since many fundamental questions are involved. Certainly, SEMATECH is a far cry from garden-variety free enterprise.

[1] "SEMATECH May Give America's Middleweights a Fighting Chance," *Business Week*, December 10, 1990, p. 186.

they grew substantially during the Great Depression of the 1930s, when relief payments seemed to be a necessity. But they also represent a feeling shared by a large segment of the population that human beings should be assured that, however the wheel of fortune spins and whatever number comes up, they will not starve and their children will not be deprived of a healthy environment and basic schooling. Of course, someone has to pay for this. Welfare payments allow the poor to take more from the nation's output than they produce. In general, the more affluent members of society contribute some of their claims on output to pay for these programs, their contributions being in the form of taxes. By using its expenditures to help certain groups and by taxing other groups to pay for these programs, the government accomplishes each year, without revolt and without bayonets, a substantial redistribution of income.

## STABILIZING THE ECONOMY

It is also generally agreed that *the government should promote the maintenance of reasonably full employment with reasonably stable prices.* Capitalist economies have tended to alternate between booms and depressions in the past. The Great Depression of the 1930s hit the American economy—and the world economy—a particularly devastating blow, putting millions of people out of work and in desperate shape. As we have seen in Chapters 5-15, there are important differences of opinion among economists regarding the extent to which the government can stabilize the economy. But it is generally agreed that the government should do what it can to avoid serious recessions and to maintain employment at a high level.

Also, the government must try to maintain a reasonably stable price level. No economy can function well if prices are gyrating wildly. Through its control of the money supply and its decisions regarding expenditures and taxation, the government has considerable impact on the price level, as well as on the level of employment. Unfortunately, during the 1970s in particular, the government was not very successful in maintaining price stability. According to many economists, the government's own policies (described in Chapters 9 and 12) contributed to this inflation.

## PROVIDING PUBLIC GOODS

As we have indicated, the government provides many public goods. Let's consider the nature of public goods in more detail.

**WHAT IS A PUBLIC GOOD?** One hallmark of a public good is that it can be consumed by one person without diminishing the amount that other people consume of it. Public goods tend to be relatively indivisible; they often come in such large units that they cannot be broken into pieces that can be bought or sold in ordinary markets. *Once such goods are produced, there often is no way to bar certain citizens from consuming them.* Whether or not citizens contribute toward their cost, they benefit from them. As pointed out in a previous section, this means that the price system cannot be used to handle effectively the production and distribution of such goods.

# WHY THE TENNESSEE VALLEY AUTHORITY?

TVA dam at Fort Loudon

The Great Mississippi Flood of 1927 left 800,000 homeless and focused national attention on the federal government's responsibility for flood control. Such control had been considered for years on the Tennessee River. Senator Norris of Nebraska campaigned for federal support for river control in the 1920s and 1930s, but his attempts were unsuccessful—largely because local utilities feared that by building dams, the federal government would be providing not only flood control but electric power as well.

The debate continued until in 1933 the Roosevelt administration created the Tennessee Valley Authority (TVA). The TVA was foremost a construction project that would create jobs in a depressed economy, but it was also created for regional development that would yield benefits for many years to come. In addition to its responsibility for flood control and for improving the navigability of the Tennessee's waters, the TVA built housing, worked on agricultural development, and provided electric power to the depressed area. And the local utilities challenged the TVA all the way.

By 1954 the TVA was well established and requested funds from Congress to build a steam-driven electric plant. Congress rejected the proposal because it did not feel that the TVA should be expanded further into a federal power facility not exclusively hydroelectric, nor should it be made into an even larger business.

Why is it proper for the government to provide for flood control, but not proper for it to build steam-driven electric power plants? The rationale for the government to provide a service is a breakdown of the free market—that is, when the private sector will not provide the proper quantity of certain goods and services. Congress accepted the idea that flood control and navigation were public goods, and that, insofar as electrification was a by-product of flood control, it was reasonable for the government to provide this service too. But the proposed steam-driven electrical generators could have been as easily provided by the private sector as by the government.

N.B.

**NATIONAL DEFENSE: A PUBLIC GOOD.** National defense is a public good. The benefits of expenditure on national defense extend to the entire nation. Extension of the benefits of national defense to an additional citizen does not mean that any other citizen gets less of these benefits. Also, there is no way of preventing citizens from benefiting from them, whether they contribute to their cost or not. Thus there is no way to use the price system to provide for national defense. Since it is a public good, national defense, if it is to reach an adequate level, must be provided by the government. Similarly with flood control, environmental protection, and a host of other such services.

**DECISION MAKING REGARDING PUBLIC GOODS.** Essentially, deciding how much to produce of a public good is a political decision. The citizens of the United States elect senators and members of Congress who decide how much should be spent on national defense, and how it should be spent. These elected representatives are responsive to special-interest groups, as well as to the people as a whole. Many special-interest groups lobby hard for the production of certain public goods. For example, an alliance of military and industrial groups presses for increased defense expenditures, and other interested groups promote expenditures on other functions.

The tax system is used to pay for the production of public goods. In

# EXAMPLE 31.1    THE ECONOMICS OF URBAN BLIGHT

During the past 40 years, the federal government has promoted and encouraged the redevelopment of the inner core of our major cities. Consider two adjacent urban properties. Suppose that the two owners, Mr. Lombardi and Mr. Moore, are each trying to determine whether to invest $100,000 to redevelop their properties. If they do not invest the $100,000 in redevelopment, each can get a 10 percent return from other forms of investment. The rate of return on the $100,000 investment by each owner (which depends on whether the other owner redevelops his property as well) is shown below:

|  | OTHER OWNER REDEVELOPS | OTHER OWNER DOES NOT REDEVELOP |
|---|---|---|
|  | rate of return (percent) | |
| Redevelop | 12 | 5 |
| Do not redevelop | 15 | 10 |

(a) If Mr. Lombardi redevelops his property, is Mr. Moore better off by redeveloping his property as well? (b) If Mr. Lombardi does not redevelop his property, is Mr. Moore better off by redeveloping his property? (c) Will either owner redevelop his property? (d) In a

situation of this sort, can social gains be achieved by government intervention?

**Solution**

(a) No, because the rate of return Mr. Moore receives if he redevelops is 12 percent, whereas the rate of return he receives if he does not redevelop is 15 percent (because his property benefits from Mr. Lombardi's investment in redevelopment even though he pays nothing). (b) No, because the rate of return Mr. Moore receives if he redevelops is only 5 percent (because little is accomplished so long as Mr. Lombardi does not redevelop too), whereas the rate of return he receives if he does not redevelop is 10 percent (which is what he can obtain from other investments). (c) No. Consider Mr. Moore. As pointed out in (a) and (b), whether or not Mr. Lombardi redevelops, Mr. Moore receives a higher return if he does not redevelop than if he does. Thus he will not redevelop. Neither will Mr. Lombardi, for the same reasons. (d) Yes. From society's point of view, or from the point of view of the two owners acting together as a unit, redevelopment may be desirable. If carried out properly, government intervention may bring this about.

effect, the government says to each citizen, "Fork over a certain amount of money to pay for the expenses incurred by the government." The amount a particular citizen is assessed may depend on his or her income (as in the income tax), the value of all or specific types of his or her property (as in the property tax), the amount he or she spends on certain types of goods and services (as in the sales tax), or on still other criteria. In the 1990s, the tax system has often been the object of enormous controversy. More will be said about the tax system, and the controversies swirling around it, in a later section of this chapter and in the next chapter.

# EXTERNALITIES

It is generally agreed that *the government should encourage the production of goods and services that entail external economies and discourage the production of those that entail external diseconomies.* Take the pollution of air and water. When a firm or individual dumps wastes into the water or air, other firms or individuals often must pay all or part of the cost of putting the water or air back into a usable condition. Thus the disposal of these wastes entails external diseconomies. Unless the government prohibits certain kinds of pollution, or enforces air and water quality standards, or charges polluters in accord with the amount of waste they dump into the environment, there will be socially undesirable levels of pollution.

**EFFECTS OF EXTERNAL DISECONOMIES.** To see how such externalities affect the social desirability of the output of a competitive industry, consider Figure 31.1, where the industry's demand and supply curves are contained in the left-hand panel. As shown there, the equilibrium output of the industry is $OQ_0$. If the industry results in no external economies or diseconomies, this is likely to be the socially optimal output. But what if the industry results in external diseconomies, such as the pollution described above? Then the industry's supply curve does not fully reflect the true social costs of producing the product. The supply curve that reflects these social costs is $S_1$, which, as shown in the middle panel of Figure 31.1, lies to the left of the industry's supply curve. The optimal output of the good is $OQ_1$, which is less than the competitive output, $OQ_0$.

What can the government do to correct the situation? There are a variety of ways that it can intervene to reduce the industry's output from $OQ_0$

**Figure 31.1**
**Effect of External Economies and Diseconomies on the Optimal Output of a Competitive Industry**
The optimal output is $OQ_0$ if neither external economies nor diseconomies are present. If there are external diseconomies, curve $S_1$ reflects the true social costs of producing the product, and $OQ_1$ is the optimal output. If there are external economies, curve $D_1$ reflects the true social benefits of producing the product, and $OQ_2$ is the optimal output.

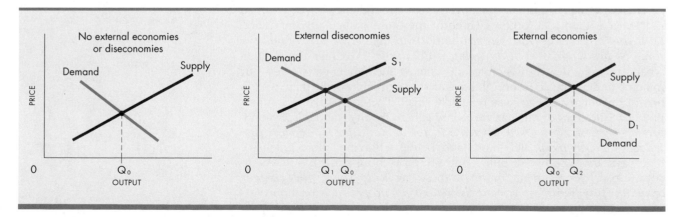

to $OQ_1$. For example, it can impose taxes on the industry, as we shall see in Chapter 32. If these taxes are of the right type and amount, they will result in the desired reduction of output.

**EFFECTS OF EXTERNAL ECONOMIES.** What if the industry results in external economies? For example, what if the manufacture of one industrial product makes it cheaper to produce other products? Then the industry's demand curve underestimates the true social benefits of producing the product. The demand curve that reflects these social benefits correctly is $D_1$, which, as shown in the right-hand panel of Figure 31.1, lies to the right of the industry's demand curve. The optimal output of the good is $OQ_2$, which is greater than the competitive output, $OQ_0$.

As in the case where the industry results in external diseconomies, the government can intervene in various ways to change the industry's output. But in this case, the object is to increase, not decrease, its output. To accomplish this, the government can, among other things, grant subsidies to the industry. If they are of the right type and amount, they can be used to increase the industry's output from $OQ_0$ to $OQ_2$.

# SIZE AND NATURE OF GOVERNMENT ACTIVITIES

## How Big Is the Government?

Up to this point, we have been concerned primarily with the reasons why the government must intervene in our economy—and the types of role it should play—but we have made little or no attempt to describe its role in quantitative terms. It is time now to turn to some of the relevant facts. One useful measure of the extent of the government's role in the American economy is the size of government expenditures, both in absolute terms and as a percent of our nation's total output.

The sum total of government expenditures—federal, state, and local— was about $1.8 trillion in 1990. Since the nation's total output was about $5.5 trillion, this means that government expenditures were about one-third of our total output. The ratio of government expenditures to total output in the United States has not always been this large, as Figure 31.2 shows. In 1929, the ratio was about 10 percent, as contrasted with over 30 percent in 1990. (Of course, the ratio of government spending to total output is smaller now than during World War II, but in a wartime economy, one would expect this ratio to be abnormally high.)

There are many reasons why government expenditures have grown so much faster than total output. Three of these are particularly important. First, *the United States did not maintain anything like the kind of military force in pre-World War II days that it does now.* In earlier days, when weapons were relatively simple and cheap, and when we viewed our military and political responsibilities much more narrowly than we do now, our military budget was relatively small. The cost of being a superpower in the days of nuclear weaponry is high by any standards. Second, *there has been a long-term increase in the demand for the services provided by government,* like more and better schooling, more extensive highways, more complete police and fire protection, and so forth. As incomes rise, people want more of these services. Third, **government transfer payments**—*payments in return for no products or services*— *have grown very substantially.* For example, various types of welfare payments have risen, and Social Security payments increased from about $20 billion in 1965 to about $250 billion in 1990. Since transfer payments do not entail any reallocation of resources from private to public goods, but a transfer of income from one private citizen or group to another. Figure 31.2 is, in some respects, an overstatement of the role of the public sector.

## What the Federal, State, and Local Governments Spend Money On

There are three levels of government in the United States—federal, state, and local. The state governments spend the least, while the federal government spends the most. This was not always the case. Before World War I, the local governments spent more than the federal government. In those days, the federal government did not maintain the large military establishment it does now, nor did it engage in the many programs in health, education, welfare, and other areas that it currently does. Figure 31.2 shows that federal spending is now a much larger percentage of the total than it was 60 years ago. Table 31.1 shows how the federal government spends its money. *About one-fourth of the federal expenditures goes for the defense and other items connected with international relations and national security. About one-half goes for Social Security, Medicare, welfare (and other income security) programs, health, and education. The rest goes to support farm, transportation, housing, and other such programs, as well as to pay interest on the federal debt and to run Congress, the courts, and the executive branch of the federal government.*

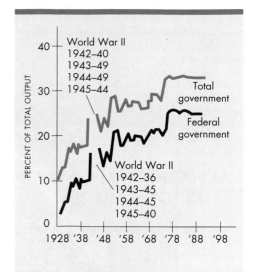

**Figure 31.2
Government Spending as a Percent of Total Output, United States**
Government expenditures—federal, state, and local—totaled about $1.8 trillion in 1990. These expenditures, which include transfer payments, have grown more rapidly than total output in this period.

**Table 31.1
Federal Expenditures, Fiscal 1992**

| PURPOSE | AMOUNT (BILLIONS OF DOLLARS) | PERCENT OF TOTAL | PURPOSE | AMOUNT (BILLIONS OF DOLLARS) | PERCENT OF TOTAL |
|---|---|---|---|---|---|
| National defense | 295 | 20 | Transportation | 33 | 2 |
| International affairs | 18 | 1 | Community and | | |
| Energy | 4 | a | regional | | |
| Veterans' benefits | 33 | 2 | development | 6 | a |
| General science, | | | Interest | 206 | 14 |
| space, and | | | General government | 13 | 1 |
| technology | 17 | 1 | Income security | 185 | 13 |
| Agriculture | 15 | 1 | Administration of | | |
| Education, training, | | | justice | 14 | 1 |
| employment, and | | | Medicare | 114 | 8 |
| social services | 46 | 3 | Social security | 289 | 20 |
| Health | 81 | 6 | | | |
| Natural resources | | | Offsetting receipts | –41 | –3 |
| and environment | 20 | 1 | Total[b] | 1,446 | 100 |
| Commerce and | | | | | |
| housing credit | 93 | 6 | | | |

[a] Less than ½ of 1 percent.
[b] Because of rounding errors, the figures may not sum to totals.
*Source: Economic Report of the President.* 1991. These are estimates made in 1990.

What about the local and state governments? On what do they spend their money? Table 31.2 shows that *the biggest expenditure of the state and local governments is on schools.* Traditionally, schools in the United States have been a responsibility of local governments—cities and towns. *State governments spend most of their money on education; welfare, old age, and unemployment benefits; and highways.* (Besides supporting education directly, they help localities to cover the cost of schooling.) In addition, the local and state governments support hospitals, redevelopment programs, courts, and police and fire departments.

## CHANGES IN VIEW OF GOVERNMENT RESPONSIBILITIES

We have already seen that government expenditures in the United States have grown considerably, both in absolute amount and as a percentage of our total output. Up to about 1975, this growth in government expenditures was part of a general trend in the United States toward a more extensive role of government in the economy. Two hundred years ago, there was considerable suspicion of government interference and meddling, freedom was the watchword, and governments were viewed as potential tyrants. In the nineteenth century, the United States prospered mightily under this *laissez-faire* system, but gradually—and not without considerable protest—the nation began to interpret the role of the government differently.

### Increases in Government Role

Responding to the dangers of noncompetitive markets, states were given the power to regulate public utilities and railroads. The Interstate Commerce Commission was established in 1887 to regulate railroads operating across state lines; and the Sherman Antitrust Act was passed in 1890 to curb monopoly and promote competition. To help control recurring business fluctuations and financial panics, banking and finance were regulated. In 1913, the Federal Reserve System was established as a central bank controlling the member commercial banks. In 1933, the Federal Deposit Insurance Corporation was established to insure bank deposits. And in 1934, the Securities and Exchange Commission was established to watch over the financial markets.

In addition, the government's role in the fields of labor and welfare expanded considerably. For example, in the 1930s minimum-wage laws were enacted, old-age pensions and unemployment insurance were established, and the government became an important force in collective bargaining and labor relations. Furthermore, the power of government was used increasingly to ensure that citizens did not fall below a certain economic level. Food-stamp programs and programs to provide aid to dependent children were established. *In general, the broad trend in the United States in the century up to about 1975 or 1980 was for the government to be used to a greater and greater extent to achieve social objectives.*

### Recent Changes in Attitude

However, during the 1970s and early 1980s there was a pronounced change in the public's attitude toward the government. People seemed

**Table 31.2**
**Expenditures of State and Local Governments, United States, 1988–89**

| TYPE OF EXPENDITURE | AMOUNT (BILLIONS OF DOLLARS) | PERCENT OF TOTAL |
|---|---|---|
| Education | 264 | 35 |
| Highways | 58 | 8 |
| Public welfare | 98 | 13 |
| Other | 342 | 45 |
| Total[a] | 762 | 100 |

[a] Because of rounding errors, the figures may not sum to totals.
*Source: Economic Report of the President, 1991.*

# THE SAGA OF THE B-1 BOMBER

About $300 billion of federal spending goes for defense. Decisions concerning how much to spend on what kinds of weapons systems are enormously complex and involve a mixture of military, political, and economic considerations. To illustrate some of these considerations, take the case of the B-1 bomber. As early as 1954, the Air Force began to think about a replacement of the B-52 bomber, but both Presidents Kennedy and Johnson were not impressed with the need for it, since they felt that strategic missiles would be more efficient and accurate than a new manned bomber.

Nonetheless, the Air Force and its contractors did not give up on the idea of the new bomber, and even after President Carter blocked the production of such a bomber in 1977, they continued to push for it. Moreover, the Armed Services Committee of the House of Representatives approved more than $300 million for research and development on this airplane between 1977 and 1980. Within the Pentagon, a group of Air Force officers, led by General Kelly Burke, worked hard to make the bomber a reality. When the Reagan administration was elected in 1980, the political climate was much more favorable, and in January 1982 Congress voted approval of the B-1 program.

To help build political support for the B-1 program, Rockwell, the builder of the B-1, farmed out the airplane's production among thousands of subcontractors. For example, the prototype engines were built in Lynn, Massachusetts; the actuators were built in Kalamazoo, Michigan; and so on. Nearly every member of Congress had a firm in his or her district that had a stake in the B-1 program.

The B-1 program was estimated to cost about $20 billion. But the costs of weapons systems are often underestimated, since this makes it easier to sell them to Congress. For a long time, the B-1 systems program office at Wright-Patterson Air Force Base made two different cost estimates; according to one report, "one [estimate] showed what we'd said the B-1 would cost. The other showed what we really thought it would cost."[1]

Whether the B-1 is an effective weapons system

has been the subject of great controversy. Some argue that it is slow, sluggish, and limited in range. There are problems, which may never be fully corrected, in the plane's electronic defensive systems. According to Congressional critics, these and other problems have resulted from the Air Force's assuming the role of prime contractor. In 1987, the House Armed Services Committee concluded that "the United States Air Force has been a greater threat to the success of the B-1 bomber than has the Soviet Union."[2]

The amount of resources devoted to military programs of this sort is nothing less than mammoth. (In the case of the B-1, the cost of 100 airplanes is about $25 billion!) Few people would question the need for a strong and effective national defense, but there is a widespread feeling that the weapons acquisition process is not as efficient as it might be. In September 1987, one of the first B-1 bombers crashed in southern Colorado, and in December 1987 the Strategic Air Command suspended low-level flights for these new bombers, thus provoking more controversy concerning this already controversial military procurement program. Another crash occurred in 1988. And when war broke out in the Persian Gulf in 1991, critics pointed out that the B-1 was not being used there.

[1] "Is the B-1 a Plane Whose Time Has Come?," *Philadelphia Inquirer*, March 18, 1984.

[2] "Turbulent History Still Buffets B-1 Program," *New York Times*, September 29, 1987, and "Low-Level Flights of B-1 Are Halted," *New York Times*, December 4, 1987. Also, see "The Military's New Myths," *New York Times*, January 30, 1991.

more inclined to question the government's capacity to solve the difficult social problems that confront our nation. In part, this seemed to be due to the apparent failure of large and expensive government programs initiated to solve a variety of social ills, such as poverty. In part, it seemed to reflect a general cynicism concerning government and politicians. One public-opinion poll after another showed that the public was irritated by the payment of what it regarded as excessively high taxes.

In 1978, California's voters supported Proposition 13 by nearly a 2-to-1 margin. Proposition 13 called for a 57 percent cut in the property tax and decreed that no local tax may increase by more than 2 percent per year. Californians were angry at the rapid increase in their property taxes during the 1970s. One Los Angeles family bought a house for $64,000 in 1968 and its property tax then was $1,800. By 1976, it had increased to $3,500, and without Proposition 13, it soon would have gone to $7,000. Californians supported Proposition 13 as a way to offset past increases and limit future increases in the property tax.

In the 1980 elections, Ronald Reagan won the presidency in part by promising to get government "off the backs" of citizens. In his first years in office, he cut back the rate of growth of federal expenditure and reduced many government programs. In 1984, he ran again on a platform that emphasized the reduction of government's role (but an increase in defense expenditure). Again he won. And in 1988, George Bush won with a similar platform. How long this sort of public attitude will persist is hard to say, but while it lasts, conservatives tend to be happy and liberals tend to be concerned.

## WHAT THE FEDERAL, STATE, AND LOCAL GOVERNMENTS RECEIVE IN TAXES

To get the money to cover most of the expenditures discussed in previous sections, governments collect taxes from individuals and firms. As Table 31.3 shows, *at the federal level the **personal income tax** is the biggest single money raiser*. It brings in almost one-half of the tax revenue collected by the federal government. The next most important taxes at the federal level are the social insurance (Social Security) taxes. Other noteworthy taxes are the corporation income tax, excise taxes (levied on the sale of tobacco, liquor, imports, and certain other items), and death and gift taxes. (Even when the Grim Reaper shows up, the Tax Man is not far behind.)

*At the local level, on the other hand, the most important form of taxation and source of revenue is the **property tax.*** This is a tax levied primarily on real estate. Other important local taxes—although dwarfed in importance by the property tax—are local sales taxes and local income taxes. Many cities—for example, New York City—levy a sales tax, equal to a certain percent—4 percent in New York City—of the value of each retail sale. The tax is simply added on to the amount charged the customer. Also, many cities—for example, Philadelphia and Pittsburgh—levy an income (or wage) tax on their residents and even on people who work in the city but live outside it. *At the state level, **sales (and excise) taxes** are the biggest money raisers,* followed by income taxes and highway-user taxes. The latter include taxes on gasoline and license fees for vehicles and drivers. Often they exceed the amount spent on roads, and the balance is used for a variety of nonhighway uses. (See Table 31.4.)

**Table 31.3**
**Federal Receipts by Tax, Fiscal 1992**

| TYPE OF TAX | AMOUNT (BILLIONS OF OF DOLLARS) | PERCENT OF TOTAL |
|---|---|---|
| Personal income tax | 530 | 45 |
| Corporation income tax | 102 | 9 |
| Social insurance taxes | 429 | 37 |
| Excise taxes | 48 | 4 |
| Estate and gift taxes | 13 | 1 |
| Other revenues | 43 | 4 |
| Total[a] | 1,165 | 100 |

[a] Because of rounding errors, the figures may not sum to totals.
*Source: Economic Report of the President, 1991. These are estimates made in 1990.*

**Table 31.4**
**State and Local Tax Revenues, by Source, 1988–89**

| SOURCE | REVENUES (BILLIONS OF DOLLARS) | PERCENT OF TOTAL |
|---|---|---|
| General sales tax | 166 | 25 |
| Property tax | 143 | 22 |
| Personal income tax | 98 | 15 |
| Corporate income tax | 26 | 4 |
| Other taxes | 228 | 34 |
| Total[a] | 661 | 100 |

[a] Because of rounding errors, the figures may not sum to totals.
*Source: Economic Report of the President, 1991.*

## TEST YOURSELF

1. "I believe the government should do only that which private citizens cannot do for themselves, or which they cannot do so well for themselves." Interpret and comment. Indicate how one might determine in practice what the legitimate functions of government are, according to this proposition.

2. "The ideal public policy, from the viewpoint of the state, is one with identifiable beneficiaries, each of whom is helped appreciably, at the cost of many unidentifiable persons, none of whom is hurt much." Interpret and comment. Indicate how this proposition might be used to help predict government behavior.

3. Explain why national defense is a public good but a rifle is not a public good.

4. "I cannot get the amount of national defense I want and you, a different amount." Explain. Is this true of all public goods?

5. According to the 1991 *Economic Report of the President,* the federal government will spend about $17 billion on general science, space, and technology in fiscal 1992. Why should the government support each of these activities?

## THE ROLE OF GOVERNMENT IN AMERICAN AGRICULTURE

Thus far, we have been discussing the government's role in the American economy in rather general terms. Now we turn to a particular example of the economic programs carried out by our government—the nation's farm programs. It is important to recognize at the outset that these farm programs are not being held up as a representative sample of what the government does. There are a host of other government economic programs—poverty programs, urban programs, defense programs, research programs, education programs, transportation programs, fiscal programs, monetary programs, and many more. Most of these programs are discussed at some point in this book.

Agriculture is an enormously important sector of the American economy. Even though its size has been decreasing steadily—and this contraction has been going on for many decades—agriculture still employs almost 3 million Americans. Its importance, moreover, cannot be measured entirely by its size. You need only think about how difficult it would be to get along without food to see the strategic role agriculture plays in our economic life. Also, when it comes to technological change, agriculture is one of the most progressive parts of the American economy. The efficiency of American agriculture is admired throughout the world.

## THE FARM PROBLEM

Nonetheless, it is widely acknowledged that American agriculture has had serious problems. Historically, the clearest indication of these problems has been shown by a comparison of the average income of American farmers with the average income among the rest of the population. Frequently, the average income of farm families has been 20 percent or more below the average income of nonfarm families. Moreover, a substantial proportion of the rural population has been poor. Thus the National Advisory Commission on Rural Poverty found that "rural poverty is so widespread, and so acute, as to be a national disgrace." Of course, this does not mean that all farmers are poor: on the contrary, many do very well indeed. But a substantial percentage of the nation's farmers has been poor by any standard.

This farm problem is nothing new. During the first two decades of the twentieth century, farmers enjoyed relatively high prices and relatively high incomes. But in 1920, the country experienced a sharp depression that jolted agriculture as well as the rest of the economy. Whereas the Roaring Twenties saw a recovery and boom in the nonfarm sector of the economy, agriculture did not recover as completely, and the 1930s were dreadful years; the Great Depression resulted in a sickening decline in farm prices and farm incomes. World War II brought prosperity to agriculture, but in the postwar period, farm incomes continually have been well below nonfarm incomes. In 1973 to 1975, prosperity returned to the farms, but the late 1970s and 1980s saw renewed complaints by farmers about prices and incomes. All in all, agriculture has had difficulties for many decades.

## Causes of the Farm Problem

The simple models of market behavior presented in previous chapters—the models involving market demand curves and market supply curves—can be used to explain the basic causes of the problems that have tended to besiege agriculture.

**CHARACTERISTICS OF DEMAND AND SUPPLY.** Let's start with the market demand curve for farm products. If you think about it for a moment, you will agree that this market demand curve must have two important characteristics. First, *its shape must reflect the fact that food is a necessity and that the quantity demanded will not vary much with the price of food.* Second, *the market demand curve for food is unlikely to shift to the right very much as per capita income rises,* because consumption of food per capita faces natural biological and other limitations.

Next, consider the market supply curve for farm products. Again, you should be aware of two important characteristics of this market supply curve. First, *the quantity of farm products supplied tends to be relatively insensitive to price,* because the farmers have only limited control over their output. (Weather, floods, insects, and other such factors are very important.) Second, because of the rapid technological change emphasized in a previous section, *the market supply curve has been shifting markedly and rapidly to the right.*

**DECLINE IN RELATIVE FOOD PRICES.** If you understand these simple characteristics of the market demand curve and market supply curve for farm products, it is no trick at all to understand why we have had the sort of farm problem just described. Figure 31.3 shows the market demand and market supply curves for farm products at various points in time. As you would expect, the market demand curve for farm products shifts rather slowly to the right as incomes (and population) grow over time. Specifically, the market demand curve shifted from $D$ in the first period to $D_1$ in the second period to $D_2$ in the third period. On the other hand, the mar-

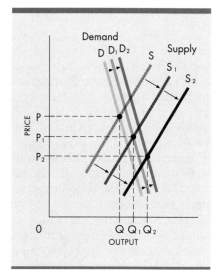

**Figure 31.3**
**Shifts over Time in Market Demand and Supply Curves for Farm Products**
The market demand curve has shifted rather slowly to the right (from $D$ to $D_1$ to $D_2$), whereas the market supply curve has shifted rapidly to the right (from $S$ to $S_1$ to $S_2$), with the result that the equilibrium price has declined (from $OP$ to $OP_1$ to $OP_2$).

ket supply curve for farm products shifted rapidly to the right as technology improved over time. Specifically, it shifted from $S$ in the first period to $S_1$ in the second period to $S_2$ in the third period.

What was the consequence of these shifts in the market demand and supply curves for food products? Clearly, *the equilibrium price of food products fell (relative to other products)*. Specifically, the equilibrium price fell from $OP$ to $OP_1$ to $OP_2$ in Figure 31.3. This price decrease was, of course, a large part of the farm problem. If we correct for changes in the general level of prices (which have tended to rise over time), there was, in general, a declining trend in farm prices. That is, agricultural prices generally fell, relative to other prices, in the last 60 years. Moreover, *given this fall in farm prices, farm incomes tended to fall, because, although lower prices were associated with greater amounts sold, the price reduction was much greater than the increase in quantity sold,* as shown in Figure 31.3.[4]

This simple supply-and-demand model explains the fact that, in real terms, farm prices and farm incomes have tended to fall in the United States. Certainly there is nothing mysterious about these trends. Given the nature and characteristics of the market demand curve and market supply curve for farm products, our simple model shows that these trends are as much to be expected as parades on the Fourth of July.

## Slow Exit of Resources

However, one additional fact must be noted to understand the farm problem: *people and nonhuman resources have been relatively slow to move out of agriculture in response to these trends*. As we have pointed out repeatedly in previous chapters, the price system uses such trends—lower prices and lower incomes—to signal producers that they should use their resources elsewhere. Farmers have been loath to move out of agriculture (even though they often could make more money elsewhere)—and this has been a primary cause of the farm problem that has existed over most of the past 50 years. If more people and resources had left farming, agricultural prices and incomes would have risen, and farm incomes would have come closer to nonfarm incomes. (Poor education and race were, of course, significant barriers to migration.)

Nonetheless, even though farmers have been slow to move out of agriculture, they have left the farm in the long run. In 1930 the farm population was about 30 million, or 25 percent of the total population; in 1950, it was about 23 million or 15 percent of the total population; and in 1989, it was about 5 million, or 2 percent of the total population. Thus the price system has had its way. Resources have been moving out of agriculture in response to the signals and pressures of the price system. This movement of people and nonhuman resources unquestionably has contributed to greater efficiency and production for the nation as a whole. But during most of the past 50 years, we have continued to have a "surplus" of farmers—and this has been the root of the farm problem.

---

[4] The amount farmers receive is the amount they sell times the price. Thus, in Figure 31.3, the amount farmers receive in income is $OP \times OQ$ in the first period, $OP_1 \times OQ_1$ in the second period, and $OP_2 \times OQ_2$ in the third period. Clearly, since the price is decreasing much more rapidly than the quantity is increasing, farm incomes are falling.

# GOVERNMENT AID TO AGRICULTURE

Traditionally, farmers have had a disproportionately large influence in Congress; and faced with declining economic fortunes, they appealed to the government for help. They extolled the virtues of rural life, emphasized that agriculture is a competitive industry, and claimed that it was unfair for their prices to fall relative to the prices they have had to pay. In addition, they pointed out that the movement of resources out of agriculture has entailed large human costs, since this movement, although beneficial to the nation as a whole, has been traumatic for the farm population. For reasons of this sort, they argued that the government should help farmers; and in particular, that the government should act to bolster farm prices and farm incomes.

## The Concept of Parity

Their voices were heard. In the Agricultural Adjustment Act of 1933, Congress announced the concept of parity as the major objective of American farm policy. This concept acquired great importance—and must be clearly understood. Put in its simplest terms, the concept of **parity** says that a farmer should be able to exchange a given quantity of his output for as much in the way of nonfarm goods and services as he could at some time in the past. For example, if a farmer could take a bushel of wheat to market in 1912 and get enough money to buy a pair of gloves, today he should be able to get enough money for a bushel of wheat to buy a pair of gloves.

To see what the concept of parity implies for farm prices, suppose that the price of gloves triples. Obviously, if parity is to be maintained, the price of wheat must triple too. Thus the concept of parity implies that farm prices must increase at the same rate as the prices of the goods and services farmers buy. Of course, farmers buy lots of things besides gloves, so in actual practice the parity price of wheat or other farm products is determined by the changes over time in the average price of all the goods and services farmers buy.

Two major points should be noted about parity. First, to use this concept, one must agree on some base period, such as 1912 in the example above, during which the relationship of farm to nonfarm prices is regarded as equitable. Obviously, the higher farm prices were relative to nonfarm prices in the base period, the higher farm prices will be in subsequent periods if parity is maintained. It is interesting to note that 1910–14 was used for many years as the base period. Since this was a period of relatively high farm prices and of agricultural prosperity, the farm bloc must have wielded considerable political clout on this issue. Second, note that the concept of parity is an ethical, not a scientific proposition. It states what the relative economic position of a bushel of wheat ought to be—or more precisely, it states one particular view of what the relative economic position of a bushel of wheat should be. Based on purely scientific considerations, there is no way to prove (or disprove) this proposition, since it is based on one's values and political preferences. Using the terminology of Chapter 1, it is a proposition in normative, not positive economics.

# PRICE SUPPORTS AND SURPLUS CONTROLS

During the four decades up to the 1970s, the concept of parity was the cornerstone of a system of government price supports. In many cases, the government did not support farm prices at the full 100 percent of parity. For example, Congress may have enacted a bill saying that the secretary of agriculture could establish a price of wheat, corn, cotton, or some other product that is between 65 and 90 percent of parity. But whatever the exact level of the price supports, the idea behind them was perfectly simple: it was to maintain farm prices above the level that would result in a free market.

Using the simple supply-and-demand model developed in previous chapters, we can see more clearly the effects of these price supports. The situation is shown in Figure 31.4. A support price, $OP'$, was set by the government. Since this support price was above the equilibrium price, $OP$, the public bought *less* of farm products ($OQ_2$ rather than $OQ$) and paid a *higher* price for them. Farmers gained from the price supports, since the amount they received for their crop under the price support was equal to $OP' \times OQ_1$, a greater amount than what they would have received in a free market, which was $OP \times OQ$.

Note, however, that since the support price exceeded the equilibrium price, the quantity supplied of the farm product, $OQ_1$, exceeded the quantity demanded, $OQ_2$. That is, *there was a surplus of the farm product in question*, which the government had to purchase, since no one else would. These surpluses were an embarrassment, both economically and politically. They showed that society's scarce resources were being utilized to produce products consumers simply did not want at existing prices. Moreover the cost of storing these surpluses was very large indeed: in some years, these storage costs alone hit the $1-billion mark.

## Policies to Cut Surpluses

To help reduce these surpluses, the government followed two basic strategies. First, *it tried to restrict output of farm products*. In particular, the government established an acreage allotment program, which said that farmers had to limit the number of acres they planted in order to get price supports on their crops. The Department of Agriculture estimated how much of each product would be demanded by buyers (other than the government) at the support price, and tried to cut back the total acreage planted with this crop to the point where the quantity supplied equaled the quantity demanded. These output restrictions did not eliminate the surpluses, because farmers managed to increase the yields from acreage they were allowed to plant, but undoubtedly they reduced the surpluses. With these restrictions, the situation was as shown in Figure 31.5, where $OQ_3$ was the total output that could be grown on the acreage that could be planted with the crop. Because of the imposition of this output control, the surplus—which the government had to purchase—was reduced from $(OQ_1 - OQ_2)$ to $(OQ_3 - OQ_2)$. Farmers continued to benefit from price supports because the amount they received for their crop—$OP' \times OQ_3$—was still greater than they would have received in a free market, because the amount demanded of farm products was not very sensitive to their price.

Second, *the government tried to shift the demand curve for farm products to the right*. An effort was made to find new uses for various farm

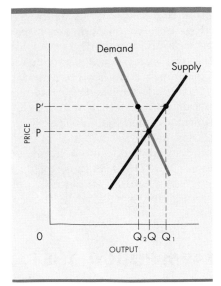

**Figure 31.4**
**Effects of Farm Price-Support Program**
The support price, $OP'$, is above the equilibrium price, $OP$, so the public buys $OQ_2$, farmers supply $OQ_1$ units of output, and the government buys the difference $(OQ_1 - OQ_2)$.

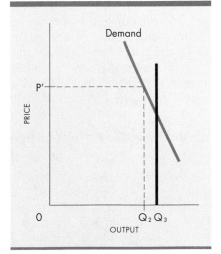

**Figure 31.5**
**Effects of Price Supports and Output Restrictions**
The government restricts output to $OQ_3$, with the result that it buys $(OQ_3 - OQ_2)$ units of output.

products. Also, various antipoverty programs, such as the food-stamp program, used our farm surpluses to help the poor. In addition, the government tried to expand the export markets for American farm products. Western Europe and Japan increased their demand for food, and the Communist countries purchased our farm products to offset their own agricultural deficiencies. Moreover, the less developed countries were permitted by Public Law 480 to buy our farm products with their own currencies, rather than dollars. The result was a reduction in farm surpluses, as shown in Figure 31.6. Since the market demand curve for farm products shifted to the right, the surplus was reduced from $(OQ_3 - OQ_2)$ to $(OQ_3 - OQ_4)$. Because of these demand-augmenting and output-restricting measures, surpluses during the late 1960s and early 1970s were considerably smaller than they were during the late 1950s and early 1960s.

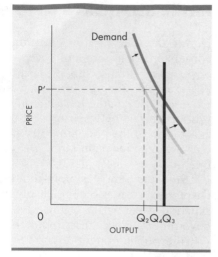

**Figure 31.6**
**Effects of Price Supports, Output Restrictions, and a Shift to the Right in the Demand Curve for Farm Products**
By shifting the demand curve to the right, the government reduces the surplus from $(OQ_3 - OQ_2)$ to $(OQ_3 - OQ_4)$ units of output.

# FARM POLICY: THE PAST TWENTY YEARS

In 1973, farm prices increased markedly, due partly to very great increases in foreign demand for American agricultural products. This increase in foreign demand was due to poor harvests in the Soviet Union, Australia, Argentina, and elsewhere, as well as to devaluations of the dollar. (In 1972–73, the Soviet Union alone bought over $1 billion of grain—on terms that provoked considerable controversy in the United States.) As a result, farm incomes reached very high levels, farm surpluses disappeared, and for the first time in 30 years the government was trying to stimulate farm production rather than restrict it.

Taking advantage of this new climate, Congress passed a new farm bill which ended price supports. This bill, the Agriculture and Consumer Protection Act of 1973, aimed at reducing government involvement in agriculture and at a return to freer markets. Specifically, agricultural prices were allowed to fluctuate freely in accord with supply and demand. However, the government made cash payments to farmers if prices fell below certain "target" levels established by the law. These target levels were above the prices that generally prevailed in the past, but they were below the high levels of prices prevailing in 1973.[5] A program of this kind was originally proposed in 1949 by Charles F. Brannan, who was secretary of agriculture under President Harry Truman. (Recall Chapter 19.)

### Increases in Government Involvement

During 1976 and 1977 U.S. farmers harvested bumper crops, with the result that prices fell considerably. The price of wheat, which had been about $3.50 per bushel in 1975, fell to about $2.30 per bushel in 1977. Farmers protested, and exerted political pressure for increased government price and income supports. In 1977 Congress passed the Food and Agricultural Act, which contained flexible price-support levels and income supports. No longer was there much talk about a return to freer markets. Instead, the emphasis seemed to be on more support for farm prices and incomes.

The early 1980s were a time of recession, and farmers (with large debts

---

[5] Actually, the provisions of the law were more complicated than this, but for present purposes, this simplified description is sufficient.

incurred for expansion in the 1970s) were battered by low farm prices and higher costs. Target prices were raised by Congress in the 1981 farm bill. Due in part to the increased value of the dollar relative to other currencies in the early 1980s (recall Chapter 18), which pushed up the price to foreigners of American farm products, our exports of farm products were hurt. In 1984, the price of wheat fell to about $3.50 a bushel, which was about a dollar below the target price. More and more farmers began to default on loans and to go bankrupt.

The Reagan administration, while originally opposed to large-scale government intervention in agriculture, responded with aid. In 1985, Congress passed a farm bill that lowered the price of American farm products in export markets. Government stocks of farm products were given to exporters to be provided free (as bonuses) to foreigners who bought our farm products. Also, target prices were reduced, but farm incomes were supported by deficiency payments (that are based on the discrepancy between the target price and the market price). During the late 1980s, the situation on the nation's farms improved, although 1988 saw a drought in the Corn Belt (and the summer of 1989 was dry in some winter-wheat states).

By the early 1990s, optimism began to spread throughout many parts of American agriculture. According to Gary Benjamin of the Federal Reserve Bank of Chicago, "Land values have recovered, and farm debts have declined 30 percent from the peak of 1983."[6] But many observers are concerned about the government's large role in agriculture. As Mark Drabenstott of the Federal Reserve Bank of Kansas City put it in 1991, "What is very bothersome is that after three years of a strong recovery, agriculture is still so dependent on government payments."[7] In 1988 alone, the federal government spent over $50 billion on agriculture.

At a rally to defend the small farmer from falling prices

## EVALUATION OF GOVERNMENT FARM PROGRAMS

It is obviously hard to evaluate the success of the government's farm programs. Farmers will certainly take a different view of price supports and other measures than their city cousins. Nonetheless, from the point of view of the nation as a whole, these farm programs have received considerable criticism. To understand these criticisms, we must hark back to our discussion earlier in this chapter of the proper functions of government, and ask what justification there is for the government's intervening in this way in agriculture. Perhaps the most convincing justification is that the government ought to help the rural poor. As we saw previously, most people agree that the government should redistribute income in this way.

**HAVE THE POOR BEEN HELPED?** Unfortunately, however, *our farm programs have done little for the farmers most in need of help*, because the amount of money a farmer has gotten from these programs has depended on how much he or she produced. Thus the big farmers have gotten the lion's share of the subsidies—and they, of course, needed help least. (The crown prince of Liechtenstein, as a partner in a Texas rice farm, received a subsidy of more than $2 million.) On the other hand, the small farmers,

[6] *New York Times,* May 18, 1990, p. D16.
[7] Ibid.

the farmers who are mired most deeply in poverty, have received little from these programs. Recognizing this fact, many observers have pointed out that, if these programs are really aimed at helping the rural poor, it would be more sensible to channel the money to them through direct subsidies, than to finance programs where much of the benefits goes to prosperous commercial farmers.

**HAS THE FARM PROBLEM BEEN SOLVED?**    It must also be recognized that *our farm programs have not dealt with the basic causes of the farm problem.* In the past at least, we have had too many people and resources in agriculture. This, as we stressed in previous sections, is why farmers' incomes have tended to be low. Yet the government's farm programs have been directed more toward supporting farm prices and incomes (and stabilizing a sector of the economy that historically has been unstable), rather than toward promoting the needed movement of people and resources out of agriculture. Indeed, some people would say that the government's farm programs have made it more difficult for the necessary adjustments to take place.

Given these defects, many proposals have been made to alter our farm programs. In the view of many observers, agriculture should return to something more closely approximating free markets, and the price system should be allowed to work more freely. The changes that occurred in the early 1970s were a step in that direction, but more recently the government has still been intervening heavily in agriculture.

We began this chapter by stressing the fact that the price system breaks down under some circumstances, and that the government must intervene. It is also worth stressing that the government sometimes intervenes when it shouldn't—and that even when it should intervene, it sometimes does so in a way that wastes resources. *This, of course, doesn't mean that the government should play no part in the American economy. On the contrary, the government must—and does—play an important role. What it does mean is that, just as the price system is no all-purpose cure-all, neither is the government.*

## TEST YOURSELF

1. Suppose that the demand and supply curves for paper are as shown at right. If paper production results in serious pollution of rivers and streams, is the socially optimal output of paper less than, greater than, or equal to *OQ*? Does the supply curve reflecting the true social costs of producing paper lie to the right or to the left of the supply curve shown at right? Why?

2. Suppose that paper production results in some important uncompensated benefits to other industries. If there are major external economies of this sort (and if paper production no longer results in any pollution), is the socially optimal output of paper less than, greater than, or equal to *OQ* in Question 1? Does the demand curve reflecting the true social benefits from paper output lie to the right or to the left of the demand curve shown in Question 1? Why?

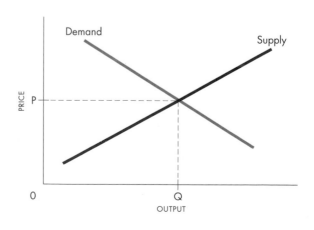

3. Explain the nature of America's farm problem. To what extent have government policies solved the problem?

4. Suppose that the demand curve for corn is as follows:

| PRICE (DOLLARS PER BUSHEL) | QUANTITY DEMANDED PER YEAR (MILLIONS OF BUSHELS) |
|---|---|
| 1 | 70 |
| 2 | 65 |
| 3 | 60 |
| 4 | 55 |
| 5 | 50 |
| 6 | 45 |

If the government supports the price of corn at $4 per bushel, and if it restricts output to 60 million bushels per year, how much corn will the government have to buy each year? If the government stopped supporting the price of corn, what would its price be?

5. The Council of Economic Advisers, in their 1987 Annual Report, said that "The Food Security Act of 1985 and its predecessors have helped to create many new problems that affect the U.S. agricultural sector, and have failed adequately to solve many old problems. The fundamental flaw is that Federal farm subsidies are linked directly to farm production.... [That is,] farmers are paid subsidies (explicit or implicit) that are proportional to their output...." Why is this a flaw?

6. "The sharp increases in the price of wheat during the mid-1970s were due primarily to shifts in the supply curve for wheat." Comment.

# SUMMARY

1. The price system, despite its many virtues, suffers from serious limitations. There is no reason to believe that the distribution of income generated by the price system is equitable or optimal. Also, there is no way for the price system to handle public goods properly, and because of external economies or diseconomies, the price system may result in too little or too much of certain goods being produced.

2. To a considerable extent, the government's role in the economy has developed in response to these limitations of the price system. There is considerable agreement that the government should redistribute income in favor of the poor, provide public goods, and offset the effects of external economies and diseconomies. Also, it is generally felt that the government should establish a proper legal, social and competitive framework for the price system, and that it should promote the maintenance of relatively full employment with reasonably stable prices.

3. Beyond this, however, there are wide differences of opinion on the proper role of government in economic affairs. Conservatives tend to be suspicious of "big government" while liberals are inclined to believe that the government should do more.

4. Government spending is now much larger, both in absolute terms and as a percent of total output, than it was in the early decades of this century. (It is now about one-third of our total output.) To a large extent, this increase has been due to our greater military responsibilities, as well as to the fact that, as their incomes have risen, our citizens have demanded more schools, highways, and other goods and services provided by government. Also, government transfer payments like Social Security and Medicare have grown substantially.

5. To get the money to cover most of these expenditures, governments collect taxes from individuals and firms. At the federal level, the most important form of taxation is the personal income tax; at the local level, the property tax is very important; and at the state level, sales (and excise) taxes are the biggest money raisers.

6. One example of the role of government in the American economy is the farm program. American agriculture has been plagued by relatively low incomes. In general, the demand for farm products has grown slowly, while rapid technological change has meant that the people and resources currently in agriculture could supply more and more farm products. Because people and resources did not move out of agriculture as rapidly as the price system dictated, farm incomes tended to be relatively low.

7. In response to political pressures from the farm blocs, the government set in motion a series of programs to aid farmers. A cornerstone of these programs was the concept of parity, which said that the prices farmers receive should increase at the same rate as the prices of the goods and services farmers buy. The government instituted price supports to keep farm prices above their equilibrium level. But since the support prices exceeded the equilibrium prices, there was a surplus of the commodities that the government had to purchase and store. To help reduce these surpluses, the government tried to restrict the output of farm products and expand the demand for them.

8. These farm programs received considerable criticism. From the point of view of income redistribution, they suffered from the fact that they did little for the farmers most in need of help. As tools of resource allocation, they suffered because they dealt more with the symptoms of the farm

problem than with its basic causes. In 1973, price supports were ended, but the government pledged to make cash payments to farmers if farm prices fall below certain target levels. During the late 1970s, 1980s, and early 1990s, the government continued to intervene heavily in agriculture.

9. The government's farm programs illustrate the fact that government intervention, like the price system, has plenty of limitations. Neither the price system nor government intervention is an all-purpose cure-all.

## CONCEPTS FOR REVIEW

| | | |
|---|---|---|
| **Public goods** | **Welfare payments** | **Property tax** |
| **External economy** | **Government transfer payments** | **Sales tax** |
| **External diseconomy** | **Personal income tax** | **Parity** |

# GOVERNMENT EXPENDITURES AND TAXATION

IN 1991, THE DEPARTMENT OF EDUCATION suggested that it might revise its student financial aid program to favor more heavily students from poor families over those in the middle class. Whether you favor or oppose such a revision, this illustrates the fact that the government influences our economic lives and fortunes in countless ways. At this point, we must look in detail at how decisions are made concerning the level and distribution of government expenditures. Also, we must describe the theory of public choice. These topics are of central importance in understanding the public sector of our economy. In addition, we must discuss the principles of taxation, as well as the characteristics of the major taxes used to support government activities in the United States.

## GOVERNMENT EXPENDITURES

Determining how much the federal government should spend is a mammoth undertaking, involving literally thousands of people and hundreds of thousands of hours of labor. Decisions on expenditures are part of the budgetary process. The ***budget*** is a statement of the government's anticipated expenditures and revenues. The federal budget is for a fiscal year, from October 1 to September 30. About 15 months before the beginning of a particular fiscal year, the various agencies of the federal government begin to prepare their program proposals for that year. Then they make detailed budget requests which the president, with his Office of Management and Budget, goes over. Since the agencies generally want more than the president wants to spend, he usually cuts down their requests.

In January (preceding the beginning of the fiscal year), the president submits his budget to Congress, which then spends many months in intensive deliberation and negotiation. Congressional committees concerned with particular areas like defense or education recommend changes in the president's budget. The Congressional Budget Office, headed in 1991 by Robert Reischauer, makes various types of economic analyses to help senators and representatives evaluate alternative programs. The process by which decisions are reached is influenced by the push and shove of partisan politics, as well as by economic factors. Eventually, however, decisions regarding the expenditures of the huge federal government are made.

### Benefit-Cost Analysis

How much should the government spend on various activities and services? Basically, the answer must be provided by the nation's political processes. For example, with regard to the provision of public goods, voting by ballot must be resorted to in place of dollar voting. . . .Decision making by voting becomes a substitute for preference revelation through the market. The results will not please everybody, but they will approximate—more or less perfectly, depending on the efficiency of the voting process and the homogeneity of preferences—the community's preferences.[1]

Under certain circumstances, particular types of economic analysis can prove helpful to the policy makers and citizens who must determine how much the government should spend on various programs. Let's begin by supposing that we can measure the benefits and costs of each such program. What is the optimal amount to spend on each one?

A particular government program is worthwhile if the benefits from the program exceed its costs. To see whether the program should be expanded or contracted, compare the extra benefit from the change in the program's scope to the extra cost. Spending on the program should be pushed to the point where the extra benefit from an extra dollar spent is at least equal to the dollar of cost. This will ensure that the amount spent on each government program yields a benefit at least as great as the value of output forgone in the private sector. This will also make sure that one government program is not being expanded at the expense of other programs that would yield greater benefits if they were expanded instead.

To illustrate, consider the construction of a dam. The alternative policies are to build a low dam or a high dam. Table 32.1 shows the annual costs and benefits associated with each of these policies. Clearly, the high dam should be built because the extra cost involved ($150,000 more than for the low dam) is more than outweighed by the extra benefits received ($200,000 more than for the low dam). Note, however, that this is a very simple case. In general, data on costs and benefits are not laid out so straightforwardly. Instead, there are very wide bands of uncertainty about the relevant costs and benefits.

The principle that extra benefit should be compared with extra cost is valuable—and, as we shall see in the next section, widely applicable—but it can solve only a small part of the problem of allocating resources in the public sector. Why? Because it is impossible to measure the benefits from defense or police protection or the courts in dollars and cents. Only in certain cases can benefits be quantified at all precisely. And it is not only a question of the amount of the benefits and costs; it is also a question of who benefits and who pays. Nonetheless, it is difficult to see how rational choices can be made without paying attention to costs and benefits—even if they are measured imprecisely, and are by no means the whole story.

**Table 32.1**
**Benefit-Cost Analysis for Constructing a Dam**

| ALTERNATIVE POLICIES | ANNUAL COST (DOLLARS) | ANNUAL BENEFIT (DOLLARS) |
| --- | --- | --- |
| Build a low dam | 600,000 | 650,000 |
| Build a high dam | 750,000 | 850,000 |

## Upward Bound: A Case Study[2]

Despite the difficulties involved, in recent years more and more **benefit-cost analyses** have been carried out to help guide public policy. For example, consider the following study, by the Greenleigh Associates, of Upward Bound, a U.S. Office of Economic Opportunity program begun in the 1960s to select and give underprivileged young people a special col-

[1] Richard and Peggy Musgrave, *Public Finance in Theory and Practice*, New York: McGraw-Hill, 1973, p. 8.
[2] This section is based on E. Gramlich, *Benefit-Cost Analysis of Government Programs*. Englewood Cliffs, N.J.: Prentice-Hall, 1981, pp. 162-65. The figures pertain to white males.

# MEDICAL CARE: CAN BENEFIT-COST ANALYSIS BE USED?

One of the most pressing problems facing the American economy is the seemingly inexorable rise in the costs of medical care. Corrected for inflation, per capita personal health care expenditures have risen at over 4 percent per year since 1950. According to official forecasts, the United States will devote about 15 percent of its total output to health care by the year 2000. This is a huge amount, and there are good reasons to think it is excessive, but despite the fact that government agencies (as well as leading corporations and others) have tried in a variety of ways to curb medical costs, they have continued to grow.

The reasons why health costs are likely to be excessive are described very well by Henry Aaron of the Brookings Institution and William Schwartz of Tufts University:

Henry Aaron

> Standard economic theory suggests that spending on health care is excessive. According to this doctrine, when people pay less than the full cost of what they buy, they will consume more than is socially optimal unless their consumption benefits not only themselves but others. This line of argument suggests that insurance induces excessive health expenditures because people pay for only part of the cost of care.
>
> Patients in 1987 paid, on the average, only about 10 cents of each dollar devoted to hospital care, a share that has changed negligibly for two decades. And they pay about 26 cents of each dollar paid to physicians, a share that has fallen steadily. Although these averages conceal large differences among patients, the fully insured (or those who have exceeded ceilings on patient outlays) and physicians acting in the patients' interests have the incentive to seek any service, however costly, that provides any benefits at all. Because of insurance, these decisions impose large costs on others.[1]

Given these effects of health insurance (for example, Blue Cross, much of it paid for by employers), it is not hard to see why medical costs have risen so greatly. The most important factor is the advance of medical technology, including open-heart surgery, magnetic resonance imaging, organ transplants, anti-ulcer drugs, and a host of others. These new tech-

niques are very expensive to develop and apply. Another important factor is that output per hour of labor in hospitals has not risen very rapidly. It is difficult to increase the efficiency of nurses and orderlies. Still another factor is the aging of the population. Obviously, older people tend to require more health care than do younger people.

Confronted with this growth in costs of medical care, the federal government has sought in various ways to slow it down. For example, in 1984, the Health Care Financing Administration (HCFA) started to pay hospitals fixed sums for Medicare patients (patients insured under a government program for the aged described on page 642) based on diagnoses at the time of their admission to the hospital. Formerly, HCFA had reimbursed hospitals for whatever costs (covered by the Medicare program) they incurred. Under the new system, hospitals ordinarily receive the same amount no matter what they spend. Based on preliminary evidence, this new system has slowed the growth of medical costs, although how much of this is due to poorer quality care, rather than increased efficiency, is hard to say.

According to leading experts, the potential savings from cutting out useless medical procedures are huge. Health maintenance organizations (HMO's)

---

[1] H. Aaron and W. Schwartz, "Rationing Health Care: The Choice Before Us," *Science,* January 26, 1990.

say that they lower the costs of medical care through greater efficiency and the elimination of useless services (primarily extra hospital days). For example, one study found that an HMO provided health care for about 25 percent less than did organizations paid on a fee-for-service basis for fully insured patients. (However, for patients that paid a substantial share of the costs, the fee-for-service care was no more costly than the HMO.)

Economists have suggested that more competition among health care providers can help to cut the rate of growth of the costs of health care. There have been proposals that only part of employer-financed health insurance premiums be excluded from an employee's income in computing his or her income tax, thus making the employee more conscious of the costs of medical care. Also, it has been suggested that data be developed and disseminated regarding the quality and cost of care provided by various hospitals and physicians. Such data could help patients and their employers to avoid hospitals and physicians that are high-cost relative to the quality of care they provide.

Benefit-cost analysis can also be of use, as illustrated by an example given by Louise Russell of Rutgers University.

Louise Russell

Suppose that a community's board of health has $300,000 to spend on a new health program and three possible programs on which to spend it. The programs are mutually exclusive and each will use the full $300,000—it is not possible to do a little of all of them. Program A will save 100 years of life, program B 10 years, and program C 1 year. Thus the cost per year of life saved is $3,000 for program A, $30,000 for program B, and $300,000 for program C. In each case the estimates of lifesaving are based on impeccable scientific evidence; there is no doubt that the programs are effective and that they will have the effect estimated. As will be evident later, real and respectable medical interventions vary as much in their cost per year of life saved as do these hypothetical programs.

If the object is to improve health as much as possible with the money, the choice seems obvious—program A, which will save 100 years of life. If program B is chosen, only 10 years will be saved with the same money, and the 100 years that could have been saved with A will be lost. Thus the opportunity cost of choosing program B is the loss of the opportunity to do program A and of the 100 years it could save. More generally, the opportunity cost of using resources in one way is the loss of the benefits they could have achieved had they been put to their next best use. By contrast, the opportunity cost of program A is much lower—the 10 years of life that would be saved if the money were spent instead on program B.

It is desirable to keep the opportunity cost of our choices as low as possible. Although the choice that does so is obvious in the example, choices in real life are usually more difficult. First, better health is an important objective, but not the only one, and more objectives make it more difficult to decide which alternative is best. Second, it is harder to give up real opportunities, even for better ones, than hypothetical opportunities. Third, and of critical importance, it is often not easy to determine the true opportunity cost of a decision.[2]

To illustrate how benefit-cost analysis can be used, consider Table 1, which shows that, if all women are given a Pap test for cancer every three years (from the age of 20 to the age of 75), the cost per year of life saved (compared with no testing) is about $14,000. On the other hand, if the test is carried out every two years, the cost per year of life saved (compared with no testing) is about $450,000. And if the test is carried out every year, the cost per year of life saved (compared with no testing) is over $1 million. Clearly, society must question whether annual testing of this sort is a good use of its resources, or whether the opportunity costs are too high.

Why does the cost per year of life go up so rapidly for more frequent testing? Because cervical

[2] L. Russell, "Some of the Tough Decisions Required by a National Health Plan," *Science,* November 17, 1989.

**Table 1**
**Cost per Year of Life Saved by Pap Smear Test Conducted Every 3 Years, Every 2 Years, and Every Year**

| FREQUENCY OF TEST | COST PER YEAR OF LIFE (1986 DOLLARS) |
|---|---|
| Every 3 years | $14,300 |
| Every 2 years | 451,200 |
| Every year | 1,144,000 |

Source: L. Russell, *op. cit.*

cancer develops slowly and can readily be treated in its early stages. Thus there is only a small additional health benefit from testing annually rather than testing every three years. And since testing annually requires tripling the total cost of testing, the cost per year of life saved is a great deal higher if tests are conducted annually rather than every three years.

As shown in Table 2, the United States devotes a

**Table 2**
**Health Care Outlays as a Percentage of Total Output, 1986**

| COUNTRY | PERCENTAGE |
|---|---|
| Australia | 7.2 |
| Canada | 8.5 |
| Denmark | 6.1 |
| France | 8.5 |
| Germany (West) | 8.1 |
| Italy | 6.7 |
| Japan | 6.7 |
| The Netherlands | 8.3 |
| New Zealand | 6.9 |
| Norway | 6.8 |
| Sweden | 9.1 |
| Switzerland | 8.0 |
| United Kingdom | 6.2 |
| United States | 11.1 |

Source: H. Aaron and W. Schwartz, *op. cit.*

larger percentage of its total output to health care than any other developed country. Yet life expectancies in other industrialized countries typically match or exceed our own. Given the many questions that have been raised concerning the efficiency of health care provision in the United States, and given the good reasons for believing that health costs are excessive, it seems likely that health cost containment will be one of the big domestic economic issues of the 1990s. The government has a major stake in this issue, as illustrated by the fact that federal expenditures on Medicare alone exceeded $100 billion in 1992.

**Probing Deeper**

1. Why do patients pay only about 10 cents of each dollar spent on hospital care? Who pays the rest?

2. What are the advantages of the government's paying fixed amounts to hospitals for Medicare patients with particular illnesses, rather than reimbursing hospitals for whatever costs they incurred? What are the potential problems?

3. Why do economists tend to favor more competition among health care providers?

4. What problems arise in applying benefit-cost analysis in the field of medical care?

5. Suppose that the cost of saving a particular person's life is $1 million. Using benefit-cost analysis, should this life be saved?

lege preparatory education. The study surveyed over 7,000 people who entered the Upward Bound program in 1966 to 1968. It tried to estimate the costs and benefits from the program.

On the average, the cost per person in the program was determined to be about $3,400. To estimate the benefits, each person in the program was compared with his or her older sibling with respect to earnings in the years subsequent to the program. In other words, the older siblings were viewed as a "control" group that could be used to indicate how much a person would have made if he or she had not taken part in the program. Based on such a comparison, it appeared that the benefits to society were about $7,000 per person in the program. That is, the extra earnings of such a person—used as an estimate of the value of the extra output he or she produced due to the program—was estimated to be about $7,000.

Since the benefits exceeded the costs, it appeared that the program was worthwhile. Of course, there are many difficulties in this and other such analyses, and they should be viewed with caution. Nonetheless, this study is an interesting example of a benefit-cost analysis.

"Project Double Discovery" class sponsored through Upward Bound

### Other Examples

Benefit-cost analyses have proved useful in many areas of government. In particular, they have been used for many years in the Department of Defense. Decisions to develop one weapons system rather than another, or to procure a certain amount of a given weapon, have been based in part on such studies. Other areas where benefit-cost analyses have been used extensively are water projects (irrigation, flood control, hydroelectric, and other projects), transportation projects, and urban renewal, recreation, and health projects. For example, in water projects, benefit-cost analysis has frequently been used by the Corps of Engineers and others to determine whether it is worthwhile to spend additional money on flood control, and if so, how much extra expenditure is justified.

# SCOPE AND EFFICIENCY OF GOVERNMENT ACTIVITIES

It is not easy to decide how large government expenditures should be. As we saw in Chapter 31, opinions differ widely on the proper role of government in economic affairs, and it is often impossible to measure the costs and benefits of government programs with dependable accuracy. Thus economists differ considerably in their opinions concerning the optimal size of government expenditures. Some, like Harvard's John Kenneth Galbraith, believe that the public sector of the economy has been deprived of needed resources, whereas the private sector has catered to relatively unimportant wants. Others, like Stanford's Milton Friedman, believe that government spending is far too large, and that it should be trimmed greatly.

To a considerable extent, this argument is over the proper *scope* of government. To see what we mean, assume that we can divide all goods into publicly provided goods and privately provided goods, and that Figure 32.1 shows the society's production possibilities curve. In other words, as you recall from Chapter 2, Figure 32.1 shows the maximum amount of publicly provided goods that can be produced, given each quantity produced of privately provided goods. What Galbraith and Fried-

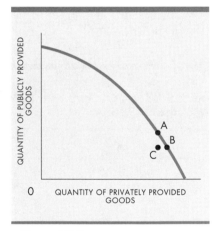

**Figure 32.1**
**Production Possibilities Curve, Publicly Provided and Privately Provided Goods**
At point B, society produces less publicly provided goods and more privately provided goods than at point A. Thus a movement from point A to point B reduces government expenditures by reducing the *scope* of government services. At point C, society is producing inefficiently, and a movement from point C to point B or point A can be attained by increasing the *efficiency* of government (and/or private) operations.

man (among others) disagree about is the point that society should choose on the production possibilities curve. Should society choose point *A* (where more publicly provided goods and less privately provided goods are produced) or point *B* (where less publicly provided goods and more privately provided goods are produced)? Galbraith would be likely to choose point *A;* Friedman would be likely to choose point *B.*

But there is another important question: How can we attain a point *on* the production possibilities curve, rather than one (like point *C*) that is *inside* it? As we know from Chapter 2, inefficiency will result in society's being on a point inside the production possibilities curve. Thus, to attain a point on the production possibilities curve, government officials (and others) must do their best to eliminate inefficiency. By doing so, society can get more from the available resources. For example, it can attain points *A* or *B* rather than point *C.* Whether society wants to use its added efficiency to attain point *A* or point *B* is then a political question. However, regardless of how this question is decided, society is better off to eliminate inefficiency.

# THE THEORY OF PUBLIC CHOICE

According to many economists interested in the theory of public choice, there are a variety of factors that induce the government to make decisions that are not efficient from an economic point of view. Thus, just as the price system suffers from the limitations cited in Chapter 31, so the government has shortcomings as a mechanism for promoting economic welfare. These factors, discussed below, often result in expanded government expenditures.

## Special-Interest Groups

It is no secret that politicians try to stay in office. In some cases, they must decide whether or not to adopt a policy which benefits a small number of people each of whom will gain a great deal at the expense of a very large number of people each of whom will lose very little. The small group of gainers (the special-interest group) is likely to be well organized, well financed, and vocal. The large group of losers is likely to be unaware of its losses and indifferent to the outcome of this decision, since each member of this group has little at stake. In a case of this sort, a politician will be inclined to adopt the policy favoring the special-interest group. Why? Because the politician, if he or she does not adopt this policy, will lose the support of this group. On the other hand, by adopting this policy, the politician is unlikely to lose the support of the large group of people that are hurt by it because they are much more interested in other issues where they have more at stake.

There are many cases where politicians have adopted policies favoring special-interest groups, even though the total gains to the special-interest group are less than the total losses to other segments of society. Whereas such policies are unsound economics, they have been regarded as good politics. One example is the enactment of tariffs and quotas that reduce domestic competition and result in consumers' paying higher prices. According to many observers, another example is the farm programs described in Chapter 31. Government services that benefit special-interest groups often are expanded, to the detriment of society at large.

## Bureaucratic Inefficiency

Many observers contend that government agencies are less efficient than private firms. As we have seen in previous chapters, the price system establishes strong incentives for firms to minimize their costs. If firms can lower their costs, they can increase their profits, at least temporarily. Government officials, on the other hand, often have less incentive to reduce costs. Indeed, it is sometimes claimed that there is an incentive to increase costs since an agency's power and influence are directly related to the size of its budget. Unfortunately, we do not have a great deal of evidence concerning whatever differences exist between the efficiency of government agencies and of private firms, due largely to the difficulties in measuring the efficiency or inefficiency of government agencies. For example, how efficient is the Environmental Protection Agency? Because it is so difficult to measure EPA's output, and because it is so difficult to find a standard against which to measure its performance, this question is exceedingly difficult to answer.

One area where there has been evidence of inefficiency has been the development and production of new weapons by the Department of Defense and its contractors. There have been spectacular overruns in development and production costs. For example, the cost of the Lockheed C5A transport plane increased from the original estimate of $3.4 billion to an actual figure of $5.3 billion. To some extent, such cost increases reflect the fact that new weapons systems tend to push the state of the art, so that unexpected problems must be expected. But, in addition, the firms that develop and produce these weapons systems often submit unrealistically low bids to get a contract, knowing that they are likely to get approval for cost increases later on. According to some observers, like Merton J. Peck of Yale University and F. M. Scherer of Harvard University, these cost overruns have also been due to inadequate attention to the efficient utilization of technical, production, and administrative resources.

## Nonselectivity

Another point made by public choice theorists is that, when citizens vote for their elected officials, they vote for a "bundle" of political programs. For example, in a particular election, the two candidates may be John Brown, who favors increased defense spending, reduced capital gains taxes, and a tougher policy against organized crime, and Jane Smith, who opposes all of these things. If you favor increased defense spending and a tougher policy against organized crime, but oppose reduced capital gains taxes, there is no way that you can elect a candidate that mirrors your preferences. All that you can do is vote for the candidate whose bundle of programs is closest to your preferences.

In contrast, citizens, when making choices in the marketplace, are better able to pick a set of goods and services that is in accord with their preferences, since they do not have to buy items that they do not want. If you want a green shirt and a purple tie (for formal occasions, of course), you can buy them without having to buy a pair of socks as well. Since citizens cannot be so selective with regard to goods and services in the public sector, public-choice theorists hold that the provision of such goods and services tends to be inefficient.

To conclude this brief section on the theory of public choice, it is important to recognize that no one is accusing government officials of being stupid, lazy, or corrupt. Some undoubtedly are, but this is true of business executives (and college professors) as well. The point is that the incentives faced by government officials and the nature of the political process result in decision making that can be suboptimal from an economic point of view. This helps to explain why the government, like the price system, can bungle the job of organizing the nation's economic activities. Neither is a panacea.

## TEST YOURSELF

1. Suppose that the government is trying to determine whether it should build a road from A to B, or whether it should build one that goes from B to C as well. The annual costs and benefits from the two alternative projects are as follows:

|  | ROAD FROM A TO B | ROAD FROM A TO B TO C |
|---|---|---|
| Annual cost (millions of dollars) | 10 | 15 |
| Annual benefit (millions of dollars) | 20 | 22 |

Which project, if any, should the government accept? Why?

2. Do cost overruns for weapons programs prove that the military contractors are inefficient? Why, or why not? Can you think of circumstances where a cost overrun is entirely due to the Department of Defense?

3. Suppose that if it produces the indicated amount of private goods, the maximum amount of public goods that a society can produce is as follows:

| QUANTITY OF PRIVATE GOODS | QUANTITY OF PUBLIC GOODS |
|---|---|
| 0 | 12 |
| 1 | 11 |
| 5 | 6 |
| 8 | 1 |
| 10 | 0 |

If this society produces 5 units of private goods and 5 units of public goods, is it being as efficient as it could be? If not, can we tell whether the inefficiency occurs in the public or private sector? And if so, how?

4. Suppose that you were given the job of making benefit-cost analyses to determine which kinds of new energy technologies (such as coal gasification, coal liquefaction, solar energy, and fusion) the Department of Energy should invest in. What are the most important problems you would face?

## TAXATION AND GOVERNMENT REVENUES

### The Federal Tax Legislative Process

It is one thing for the federal government to decide how much to spend and on what; it is another to raise the money to underwrite these programs. This section describes how the federal government decides how much to tax. Of course, this problem is not solved from scratch every year. Instead, the government takes the existing tax structure as given and changes it from time to time as seems desirable. Frequently the major initiative leading to a change in the tax laws comes from the president, who requests tax changes in his State of the Union message, his budget message, or a special tax message. Much of the spadework underlying his proposals will have been carried out by the Treasury Department, particularly the Treasury's Office of Tax Analysis, Office of the Tax Legislative Counsel, and Internal Revenue Service.

The proposal of a major tax change generally brings about considerable public debate. Representatives of labor, industry, agriculture, and other economic and social groups present their opinions. Newspaper articles, radio shows, and television commentators analyze the issues. By the time Congress begins to look seriously at the proposal, the battle lines between those who favor the change and those who oppose it are generally pretty clearly drawn. The tax bill incorporating the change is first considered by the Ways and Means Committee of the House of Representatives, a very powerful committee composed of members drawn from both political parties. After public hearings, the committee goes into executive session and reviews each proposed change with its staff and with the Treasury staff. After careful study, the committee arrives at a bill it recommends—though this bill may or may not conform to what the president asked for. Then the bill is referred to the entire House of Representatives for approval. Only rarely is a major tax bill recommended by the committee turned down by the House.

Next, the bill is sent to the Senate. There it is referred to the Finance Committee, which is organized like the House Ways and Means Committee. The Finance Committee also holds hearings, discusses the bill at length, makes changes in it, and sends its version of the bill to the entire Senate, where there frequently is considerable debate. Ultimately, it is brought to a vote. If it does not pass, that ends the process. If it does pass (and if it differs from the House version of the bill, which is generally the case), then a conference committee must be formed to iron out the differences between the House and Senate versions. Finally, when this compromise is worked out, the result must be passed by both houses and sent to the president. The president rarely vetoes a tax bill, although it has occasionally been done.

# PRINCIPLES OF TAXATION

According to the English political philosopher, Edmund Burke, "To tax and to please, no more than to love and to be wise, is not given to men." What constitutes a rational tax system? Are there any generally accepted principles to guide the nation in determining who should pay how much? The answer is that there are some principles most people accept, but they are so broad and general that they leave plenty of room for argument and compromise. Specifically, two general principles of taxation command widespread agreement.

**BENEFIT DISTRIBUTION.** The first principle is that *people who receive more from a certain government service should pay more in taxes to support it.* Certainly few people would argue with this idea. However, it is frequently difficult, if not impossible, to apply. For example, there is no good way to measure the amount of the benefits received by a particular taxpayer from many public services, such as police protection.

**ABILITY-TO-PAY PRINCIPLE.** The second principle is that *people should be taxed so as to result in a socially desirable redistribution of income.* In practice, this has ordinarily meant that the wealthy have been asked to pay more than the poor. This idea, too, has generally commanded widespread assent—although this, of course, has not prevented the wealthy from trying to avoid its application to them.

## Applications of These Principles

It follows from these principles that if two people are in essentially the same circumstances (their income, purchases, utilization of public services are the same), then they should pay the same taxes. This is an important rule, innocuous though it may seem. It says that equals should be treated equally—*whether one is a Republican and the other is a Democrat, or whether one is the president's friend and the other is his enemy, or whether one has salary income and the other has property income; they should be treated equally.* Certainly, this is a basic characteristic of an equitable tax system.

It is easy to relate most of the taxes in our tax structure to these principles. For example, the first principle—the benefit principle—is the basic rationale behind taxes on gasoline and license fees for vehicles and drivers. Those who use the roads are asked to pay for their construction and upkeep. Also, the property tax, levied primarily on real estate, is often supported on these grounds. It is argued that property owners receive important benefits—fire and police protection, for example—and that the extent of the benefits is related to the extent of their property.

The personal income tax is based squarely on the second principle: ability to pay. A person with a large income pays a higher proportion of income in personal income taxes than does a person with a smaller income. In 1990, if a couple's income (after deductions and exemptions) was $15,000, their federal income tax was $2,254, whereas if their income was $50,000, their federal income tax was $9,782. Also, estate and inheritance taxes hit the rich much harder than the poor.

The principles cited above are useful and important, but they do not take us very far toward establishing a rational tax structure. They are too vague and leave too many questions unanswered. If I use about the same amount of public services as you do, but my income is twice yours, how much more should I pay in taxes? Twice as much? Three times as much? Fifty percent more? These principles throw no real light on many of the detailed questions that must be answered by a real-life tax code.

## THE PERSONAL INCOME TAX

The federal **personal income tax** brings in about $500 billion a year. Yet many people are perhaps unaware of just how much they are contributing because it is deducted from their wages each month or each week, so that they owe little extra when April 15 rolls around. (Indeed, they may even be due a refund.) This pay-as-you-go scheme reduces the pain but, of course, it does not eliminate it; taxes are never painless.

**THE TAX SCHEDULE.** Obviously, how much a family has to pay in personal income taxes depends on the family's income. The tax schedule (as of 1990) is as shown in Table 32.2. The second column shows how much a couple would have to pay if their income was the amount shown in the first column. At an income of $30,000, their income tax would be $4,504; at an income of $50,000, their income tax would be $9,782. Clearly, the percentage of income owed in income tax increases as income increases, but this percentage does not increase indefinitely. The percentage of income going for personal income taxes never exceeded about 30 percent in 1990, no matter how much money the couple made. (See Table 32.2.)

**THE MARGINAL TAX RATE.** It is instructive to look further at how the "tax bite" increases with income. In particular, let's ask ourselves what proportion of an *extra* dollar of income the couple will have to pay in personal

**Table 32.2**
**Federal Personal Income Tax, Couple without Children, 1990**

| INCOME—AFTER DEDUCTIONS AND PERSONAL EXEMPTIONS (DOLLARS) | PERSONAL INCOME TAX (DOLLARS) | AVERAGE TAX RATE (PERCENT) | MARGINAL TAX RATE (PERCENT) |
|---|---|---|---|
| 3,000 | 454 | 15 | 15 |
| 15,000 | 2,254 | 15 | 15 |
| 30,000 | 4,504 | 15 | 15 |
| 50,000 | 9,782 | 20 | 28 |
| 500,000 | 141,148 | 28 | 28 |

income taxes. In other words, what is the ***marginal tax rate:*** the tax on an extra dollar of income? The fourth column of Table 32.2 shows that in 1990 the marginal tax rate was 15 percent if the couple's income was $15,000 or $30,000, and 28 percent if it was $50,000 or $500,000. (In 1991, the marginal tax rate for the highest-income families was higher than in 1990.)

**EFFECT ON INCOME INEQUALITY.** Clearly, the personal income tax tends to reduce the inequality of after-tax income, since the rich are taxed more heavily than the poor. Nonetheless, the personal income tax does not bear down as heavily on the rich as one might surmise from Table 32.2. This is because there are perfectly legal ways for people to avoid paying taxes on their incomes. For example, interest paid by state and local governments on their bonds is not taxable at all by the federal government. However, because of changes in the tax laws during the 1980s, many of the loopholes have been closed. This does not mean, of course, that there is no illegal tax evasion, such as underreporting of income, fake expenses, and imaginary dependents. But evasion is much less important than legal tax avoidance, despite Will Rogers's quip that the income tax has made more liars among the American public than golf.

## THE CORPORATE INCOME TAX

The federal government imposes a tax on the incomes of corporations as well as of people. If a corporation's profits exceed $335,000, the corporate income tax equals 34 percent of its profits.[3] Thus a corporation with annual profits of $1 million would pay $340,000 in corporate income tax. The ***corporate income tax*** involves double taxation. The federal government taxes a corporation's earnings both through the corporate income tax (when the corporation earns the profits) and through the personal income tax (when the corporation's earnings are distributed to the stockholders as dividends).

It is generally agreed that the personal income tax is paid by the person whose income is taxed; he or she cannot shift this tax to someone else. But the incidence of the corporate income tax is not so clear. To some extent, corporations may pass along some of their income tax bill to

[3] If corporation's profits are less than $335,000, the corporate income tax equals 15 percent of the first $50,000 of annual profits, 25 percent of the next $25,000 of annual profits, 34 percent of the next $25,000, and 39 percent of the next $235,000.

customers in the form of higher prices or to workers in the form of lower wages. Some economists feel that a corporation shifts much of the tax burden in this way; others disagree. This is a controversial issue that has proved very difficult to resolve.

## THE PROPERTY TAX AND THE SALES TAX

The **property tax** is the fiscal bulwark of our local governments. The way it works is simple enough. Most towns and cities estimate the amount they will spend in the next year or two, and then determine a property tax based on the assessed property values in the town or city. If there is $500 million in assessed property values in the town and the town needs to raise $5 million, the tax rate will be 1 percent of assessed property value. In other words, each property owner will have to pay 1 percent of the assessed value of his or her property. There are well-known problems in the administration of the property tax. First, assessed values of property often depart significantly from actual market values; the former are typically much lower than the latter. And the ratio of assessed to actual value is often lower among higher-priced pieces of property; thus wealthier people tend to get off easier. Second, there is widespread evasion of taxes on **personal property**—securities, bank accounts, and so on. Many people simply do not pay up. Third, the property tax is not very flexible: assessments and rates tend to change rather slowly.

The **sales tax,** of course, is a bulwark of state taxation. It provides a high yield with relatively low collection costs. Most of the states have some form of general sales tax, the rate being usually between 3 and 6 percent. For example, New York state has a 4 percent sales tax, and California has a 4¾ percent sales tax. Retailers add to the price of goods sold to consumers an amount equal to 3 to 6 percent of the consumer's bill. This extra amount is submitted to the state as the general sales tax. Some states exempt food purchases from this tax, and a few exempt medical supplies. Where they exist, these exemptions help reduce the impact of the sales tax on the poor; but in general the sales tax imposes a greater burden relative to income on the poor than on the rich, for the simple reason that the rich save a larger percentage of their income. Practically all of a poor family's income may be subject to sales taxes; a great deal of a rich family's income may not be, because it is not spent on consumer goods, but is saved.

Who really pays the property tax or the sales tax? To what extent can these taxes be shifted to other people? The answer is not as straightforward as one might expect. For the property tax, the owner of unrented residential property swallows the tax, since there is no one else to shift it to. But the owner of rented property may attempt to pass along some of the tax to the tenant. In the case of a general sales tax, it is generally concluded that the consumer pays the tax. But if the tax is imposed on only a single commodity, the extent to which it can be shifted to the consumer depends on the demand and supply curves for the taxed commodity. The following section explains in some detail why this is the case.

## TAX INCIDENCE

Suppose that a sales or excise tax is imposed on a particular good, say beer. In Figure 32.2, we show the demand and supply curves for beer be-

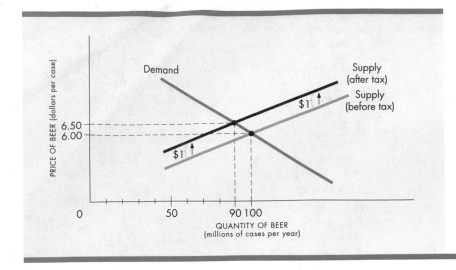

**Figure 32.2**
**Effect of a $1.00 Tax on a Case of Beer**
The tax shifts the supply curve upward by $1.00. Since the demand curve is unaffected, the equilibrium price of beer increases from $6.00 to $6.50 per case.

fore the imposition of the tax. With no tax, the equilibrium price of a case of beer is $6, and the equilibrium quantity is 100 million cases. If a tax of $1 is imposed on each case produced, what is the effect on the price of each case? Or to see it from the beer guzzler's perspective, how much of the tax is passed on to the consumer in the form of a higher price?

Since the tax is collected from the sellers, *the supply curve is shifted upward by the amount of tax,* as shown in Figure 32.2. For example, if the pretax price had to be $5 a case to induce sellers to supply 75 million cases of beer, the posttax price would have to be $1 higher—or $6 a case—to induce the same supply. Similarly, if the pretax price had to be $6 a case to induce sellers to supply 100 million cases of beer, the posttax price would have to be $1 higher—or $7 a case—to induce the same supply. The reason why the sellers require $1 more per case to supply the pretax amount is that they must pay the tax of $1 per case to the government. Thus, to wind up with the same amount as before (after paying the tax), they require the extra $1 per case.

**WHO PAYS THE TAX?**    Figure 32.2 shows that, after the tax is imposed, the equilibrium price of beer is $6.50, an increase of $.50 over its pretax level. Consequently, in this case, half of the tax is passed on to consumers, who pay $.50 per case more for beer. And half of the tax is swallowed by the sellers, who receive (after they pay the tax) $.50 per case less for beer. But it is not always true that sellers pass half of the tax on to consumers and absorb the rest themselves. On the contrary, in some cases, consumers may bear almost all of the tax (and sellers may bear practically none of it), while in other cases consumers may bear almost none of the tax (and sellers may bear practically all of it). The result will depend on how sensitive the quantity demanded and the quantity supplied are to the price of the good.

**SENSITIVITY OF DEMAND TO PRICE.**    In particular, holding the supply curve constant, *the less sensitive the quantity demanded is to the price of the good, the bigger the portion of the tax that is shifted to consumers.* To illustrate this, consider Figure 32.3, which shows the effect of $1 per case tax on beer in two markets, one (panel B) where the quantity demanded is much more sensitive to price than in the other case (panel A). As is evi-

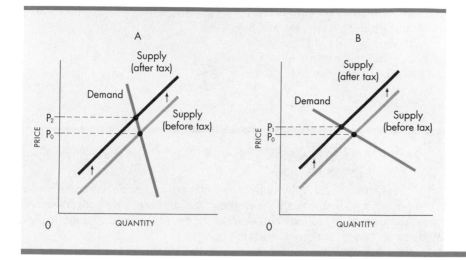

Figure 32.3
**Effect on Tax Incidence of the Sensitivity of the Quantity Demanded to Price**
The supply curve is the same in panel A as in panel B. The quantity demanded is more sensitive to price in panel B than in panel A. Before the tax the equilibrium price is $OP_0$ in both panels. After the tax the equilibrium price is $OP_2$ in panel A and $OP_1$ in panel B. The increase in price to the consumer is greater if the quantity demanded is less sensitive to price (panel A) than if it is more sensitive (panel B).

dent, the price increase to consumers resulting from the tax is much greater in panel A than in panel B—and the amount of the tax that is absorbed by producers is much less in panel A than in panel B.

**SENSITIVITY OF SUPPLY TO PRICE.** It can also be shown that, holding the demand curve constant, *the less sensitive the quantity supplied is to the price of the good, the bigger the portion of the tax that is absorbed by producers.* To illustrate this, consider Figure 32.4, which shows the effect of a $1-per-case tax on beer in two markets, one (panel A) where the quantity supplied is much more sensitive to price than in the other (panel B). As is evident, the price increase to consumers resulting from the tax is much bigger in panel A than in panel B—and the amount of the tax that is absorbed by producers is much smaller in panel A than in panel B.

**EFFECT OF TAX ON QUANTITY.** Finally, note that the tax reduces the equilibrium quantity of the good that is taxed—beer in this case. One reason why governments impose taxes on goods like cigarettes and liquor is that

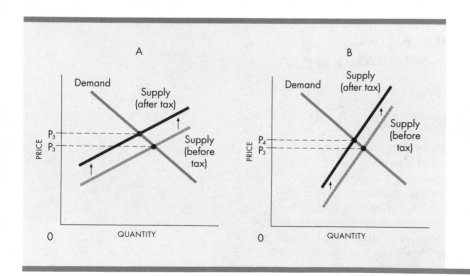

Figure 32.4
**Effect on Tax Incidence of the Sensitivity of the Quantity Supplied to Price**
The demand curve is the same in panel A as in panel B. The quantity supplied is more sensitive to price in panel A than in panel B. Before the tax the equilibrium price is $OP_3$ in both panels. After the tax the equilibrium price is $OP_5$ in panel A and $OP_4$ in panel B. The increase in price to the consumer is greater if the quantity supplied is more sensitive to price (panel A) than if it is less sensitive (panel B).

y are regarded (in some circles at least) as socially undesirable. Clearly, the more sensitive the quantity demanded and quantity supplied are to price, the larger the reduction in the equilibrium quantity. Thus, if the government imposes a tax of this sort to reduce the quantity consumed of the good, the effect will be greater if both the quantity demanded and the quantity supplied are relatively sensitive to price.

---

## EXAMPLE 32.1    SHOULD INCOME OR CONSUMPTION BE TAXED?

As the American economy approaches the twenty-first century, many economists warn that we are not saving enough. To help remedy this, some have suggested that the income tax might be replaced by a tax on consumption expenditure. For example, a family's taxes might depend in the following way on the total amount it spends on consumption of food, clothing, and other such items:

| CONSUMPTION EXPENDITURE (DOLLARS) | TAX (DOLLARS) |
|---|---|
| 5,000 | 1,000 |
| 10,000 | 2,500 |
| 20,000 | 5,000 |
| 50,000 | 15,000 |
| 100,000 | 40,000 |

(a) Suppose that the Jones family and the Moran family both earn $25,000 a year, but that the Joneses save 10 percent of their income, whereas the Morans save nothing. Will they pay the same tax? (b) According to proponents of a consumption tax, it will encourage people to save. Do you agree? Why, or why not?

(c) Why should the United States be interested in increasing the amount that people save? (d) What objections can you see to the replacement of the income tax by a consumption tax?*

### Solution

(a) No. The Morans will pay a larger tax than the Joneses because they spend more on consumption than the Joneses. (b) It seems likely that it would encourage saving because the future consumption that can be obtained for a given sacrifice of present consumption will be greater than under an income tax. (c) As pointed out in Chapter 1, saving enables society to invest in new plant and equipment, which will promote more rapid productivity increase. In recent years, the U.S. rate of productivity increase has been relatively low. (d) There are a plethora of difficulties in making such a fundamental change in the tax system. To take but one example, consider retired people who have paid income taxes all their working lives. It would not be equitable to subject them to a consumption tax.

* For further discussion, see J. Pechman, ed., *Options for Tax Reform*, Washington, D.C.: Brookings, 1984.

---

## ALTERNATIVE WAYS OF FINANCING GOVERNMENT EXPENDITURES—AND THEIR EFFECTS

To complete the present discussion of public finance, it is important to recall from Chapter 15 that there are three ways that the federal government can finance any expenditure. The first way is to *raise taxes* to cover the expenditure. The effect of this method of financing the expenditure is straightforward: purchasing power is transferred from the people paying the extra taxes to the government. Thus the costs are borne by the taxpayer. The second way is to *borrow the money* from willing lenders. In this case, too, the effect is straightforward: purchasing power is transferred from the lenders to the government. The current costs of the government programs are borne by the lenders, who receive interest subsequently in return.

The third way the federal government can finance any expenditure is to create new money. In other words, it can print extra currency (or create new money in other ways, as we have seen in Chapters 12–15). If the economy is already at full employment, this procedure is likely to cause inflation. The increase in the price level will mean that households and firms will have to buy less than would otherwise have been the case. At the same time, the government will use the new money to finance its expenditure (and obtain the resources it wants). Thus purchasing power is transferred from the consumers and firms whose incomes and receipts do not keep pace with inflation to the government. One disadvantage of this means of finance is that these consumers and firms are often the weakest and least able to bear this burden.

If the economy is not at full employment, the opportunity costs of government programs may be much less than if the economy is at full employment. Recall from Chapter 1 that the opportunity cost of using resources in a particular way is the value of the output that could have been obtained if these resources had been used in some other way. Clearly, if the resources used in a particular government program would have been unemployed if this program had not been started, society is giving up very little by using these resources in this program. Why? Because they would have been idle otherwise. On the other hand, if there is full employment, these resources would not have been idle, and the opportunity costs of the program would be the value of what they could produce elsewhere.

## TEST YOURSELF

1. Suppose that the supply curve for gin is as follows:

| PRICE OF GIN (DOLLARS PER QUART) | QUANTITY SUPPLIED (MILLIONS OF QUARTS) |
| --- | --- |
| 4 | 5 |
| 5 | 6 |
| 6 | 7 |
| 7 | 8 |
| 8 | 9 |
| 9 | 10 |

Plot the supply curve on graph paper. Suppose that the government imposes a tax of $2 per quart on gin, and that the tax is collected from the sellers. Plot the posttax supply curve on graph paper.

2. Under the circumstances described in Question 1, suppose that the quantity of gin demanded is 7 million quarts, regardless of the price (so long as it is between $4 and $9 per quart). What will be the equilibrium price of gin before the tax, and after it? How much of the tax is passed on to the consumer?

3. Under the circumstances described in Question 1, suppose that the demand curve for gin is a horizontal line at $6 per quart. If this is the case, what will be the equilibrium price of gin before the tax, and after it? How much of the tax is passed on to the consumer?

4. Can you be sent to jail for tax avoidance? If a person's marginal income tax rate is 25 percent and he receives $100 in tax-free income, how much does this equal in before-tax income?

## SUMMARY

1. The spending decisions of the federal government take place in the context of the budgetary process. The president submits his budget, which is a statement of anticipated expenditures and revenues, to Congress, which votes appropriations. The Ways and Means Committee of the House of Representatives and the Senate Finance Committee play important roles in the federal tax legislative process.

2. Basically, the amount that the government spends on various activities and services must be decided through the nation's political processes. Voting by ballots must be substituted for dollar voting. In making such decisions, it is important to distinguish between changes in government expenditure that alter the scope of government and changes in government expenditure due to changes in efficiency.

3. Spending on each government program should be pushed to the point where the extra benefit from an extra dollar spent is at least equal to the dollar of cost. In some areas, benefit-cost analyses have proved useful in determining which of a variety of projects can accomplish a particular goal most economically, and whether any of them is worth carrying out. However, accurate measurement of the relevant benefits and costs is frequently difficult.

4. Just as the price system suffers from limitations, so does the government. Special-interest groups sometimes gain at the expense of society as a whole. Government agencies sometimes have little incentive to increase efficiency. Citizens find it difficult to be selective in their choice of goods and services in the public sector. In recent years, economists seem to have put more emphasis on these (and other) limitations of the public sector.

5. It is generally agreed that people who receive more in benefits from a certain government service should pay more in taxes to support it. It is also generally agreed that people should be taxed so that the result is a socially desirable redistribution of income, and that equals should be treated equally. But these general principles, although useful, cannot throw light on many of the detailed questions a real-life tax code must answer.

6. The personal income tax is a very important source of federal revenues, the sales tax is an important source of state revenues, and the property tax is an important source of local revenues.

## CONCEPTS FOR REVIEW

| | | |
|---|---|---|
| **Budget** | **Ability-to-pay principle** | **Property tax** |
| **Benefit-cost analysis** | **Personal income tax** | **Sales tax** |
| **Benefit principle** | **Marginal tax rate** | **Tax incidence** |
| | **Corporate income tax** | |

# GOVERNMENT AND THE ENVIRONMENT

IN 1990, SECTIONS OF Long Island Sound were described as "a dead sea, with oxygen-starved waters sometimes fatal to shellfish and devoid of fin fish. Beaches throughout the 600 miles of coastline have been closed for hundreds of days a year, and sewage pollution has wiped out tens of thousands of acres of shellfish beds."[1] Unfortunately, Long Island Sound is not an isolated case. Environmental pollution is an important problem in the United States, and one which the government is trying to help solve.

Without question, the public is genuinely concerned about environmental problems. However, in the effort to clean up the environment, choices are not always clear, nor solutions easy. In this chapter, we consider the economic aspects of environmental decay, the purpose being to indicate the extent of our environmental problems, the factors that are responsible for them, and the sorts of public policies that have been adopted to help deal with them.

## OUR ENVIRONMENTAL PROBLEMS

### Water Pollution

To see what we mean by environmental pollution, let's begin with one of the most important parts of mankind's environment: our water supplies. As a result of human activities, large amounts of pollutants are discharged into streams, lakes, and the sea. Chemical wastes are released by industrial plants and mines, as well as by farms and homes when fertilizers, pesticides, and detergents run off into waterways. Oil is discharged into the waters by tankers, sewage systems, oil wells, and other sources. Organic compounds enter waterways from industrial plants and farms, as well as from municipal sewage plants; and animal wastes, as well as human wastes, contribute substantially to pollution.

Obviously, we cannot continue to increase the rate at which we dump wastes into our streams, rivers, and oceans. A river or ocean, like everything else, can bear only so much. The people of New Jersey know this well. In the summer of 1987, many New Jersey beaches were closed, when hundreds of dead dolphins, raw sewage, and even used syringes washed ashore. Of course, this is an extreme case, but many of our rivers,

[1] *New York Times*, June 6, 1990.

including the Hudson and the Ohio, are badly polluted. Water pollution is a nuisance and perhaps a threat.

## Air Pollution

If clean water is vital to human survival, so too is clean air. Yet the battle being waged against air pollution in most of our major cities has not been won. Particles of various kinds are spewed into the air by factories that utilize combustion processes, grind materials, or produce dust. Motor vehicles release lead compounds from gasoline and rubber particles worn from tires, helping to create that unheavenly condition known as smog. Citizens of Los Angeles are particularly familiar with smog, but few major cities have escaped at least periodic air pollution. No precise measures have been developed to gauge the effects of air pollution on public health and enjoyment, but some rough estimates suggest that perhaps 25 percent of all deaths from respiratory disease could be avoided by a 50 percent reduction in air pollution.[2]

One of the most important contributors to air pollution is the combustion of fossil fuels, particularly coal and oil products: by-products of combustion comprise about 85 percent of the total amount of air pollutants in the United States. Most of these pollutants result from impure fuels or inefficient burning. Among the more serious pollutants are sulphur dioxide, carbon monoxide, and various oxides of nitrogen. The automobile is one of the principal sources of air pollution.

The battle for clean air goes on in cities throughout the United States. During 1983–85, air pollution, as measured by the number of carbon monoxide molecules per million molecules of air, was highest (among cities with 1 million or more inhabitants) in Los Angeles, Denver, Phoenix, Newark (N.J.), New York, Minneapolis, Boston, Baltimore, Washington, and Chicago. Clearly, the pollution problem is not confined to a few regions; it is a national problem.

# THE IMPORTANT ROLE OF EXTERNAL DISECONOMIES

The reason why our economic system has tolerated pollution of the environment lies largely in the concept of external diseconomies, which we mentioned in Chapter 31. An **external diseconomy** occurs when one person's (or firm's) use of a resource damages other people who cannot obtain proper compensation. When this occurs, a market economy is unlikely to function properly. The price system is based on the supposition that the full cost of using each resource is borne by the person or firm that uses it. If this is not the case and if the user bears only part of the full costs, then the resource is not likely to be directed by the price system into the socially optimal use.

Consider electric power companies, which frequently do not pay the full cost of disposing of wastes in the atmosphere. They charge an artificially low price, and the public is induced to use more electric power than is socially desirable. Similarly, since the owners of automobiles do not pay the full cost of disposing of exhaust and other wastes in the atmosphere,

---

[2] See L. Lave and E. Seskin, *Air Pollution and Human Health,* Baltimore: published for Resources for the Future by the Johns Hopkins University Press, 1977.

they pay an artificially low price for operating an automobile, and the public is induced to own and use more automobiles than is socially desirable.

To understand why divergences between private and social costs can cause the price system to malfunction, we might begin by reviewing briefly how resources are allocated in a market economy. As we saw in Chapter 3, resources are used in their socially most valuable way because they are allocated to the people and firms who find it worthwhile to bid most for them, assuming that prices reflect true social costs. Under these circumstances, a firm that maximizes its profits will produce the socially desirable output and use the socially desirable amount of labor, capital, and other resources. Under these circumstances, there is no problem.

Suppose, however, that because of the presence of external diseconomies people and firms do not pay the true social costs for resources. For example, suppose that some firms or people can use water and air for nothing, but that other firms or people incur costs as a consequence of this prior use. In this case, the **private costs** of using air and water differ from the **social costs:** *the price paid by the user of water and air is less than the true cost to society.* In a case like this, users of water and air are guided in their decisions by the private cost of water and air—by the prices they pay. Since they pay less than the true social costs, water and air are artificially cheap to them, so that they will use too much of these resources, from society's point of view.

Note that the divergence between private and social cost occurs if, and only if, the use of water or air by one firm or person imposes costs on other firms or persons. Thus, if a paper mill uses water and then treats it to restore its quality, there is no divergence between private and social cost. But when the same mill dumps harmful wastes into streams and rivers (the cheap way to get rid of its by-products), the towns downstream that use the water must incur costs to restore its quality. The same is true of air pollution. If an electric power plant uses the atmosphere as a cheap and convenient place to dispose of wastes, people living and working nearby may incur costs as a result, since the incidence of respiratory and other diseases may increase. In such cases, there may be a divergence between private and social cost.

We said above that pollution-causing activities that result in external diseconomies represent a malfunctioning of the market system. At this point, the nature of this malfunctioning should be clear. *Firms and people dump too much waste material into the water and the atmosphere. The price system does not provide the proper signals because the polluters are induced to use our streams and atmosphere in this socially undesirable way by the artificially low price of disposing of wastes in this manner. Moreover, because the polluters do not pay the true cost of waste disposal, their products are artificially cheap, so that too much is produced of them.*

## DIRECT REGULATION BY GOVERNMENT

Pollution is caused by defects in our institutions, not by malicious intent, greed, or corruption. In cases where waste disposal causes significant external diseconomies, economists generally agree that government intervention may be justifiable. But how can the government intervene? Perhaps the simplest way is **direct regulation,** through the issuance of certain enforceable rules for waste disposal. For example, the government can prohibit the burning of trash in furnaces or incinerators, or the dumping of certain materials in the ocean; and make any person or firm that violates these restrictions subject to a fine, or perhaps even imprisonment. Also, the government can ban the use of chemicals like DDT, or require that all automobiles meet certain regulations for the emission of air pollutants. Further, the government can establish quality standards for air and water.

At present, our nation relies heavily on direct regulation to reduce pollution. However, economists agree that direct regulation suffers from some serious disadvantages:

1. Such regulations have generally taken the form of general, across-the-board rules. For example, if two factories located on the same river dump the same amount of waste material into the river, such regulations would probably call for each factory to reduce its waste disposal by the same amount. Unfortunately, although this may appear quite sensible, it may in fact be very inefficient. Suppose that it is much less costly for one factory to reduce its waste disposal than for the other. In such a case, it would be more efficient to ask the factory that could reduce its wastes more cheaply to cut down more on its waste disposal than the other factory. For reasons of this sort, *pollution reductions are likely to be accomplished at more than minimum cost, if they are accomplished by direct regulation.*

2. *To formulate such regulations in a reasonably sensible way, the responsible government agencies must have access to much more information than they are likely to obtain or assimilate.* Unless the government agencies have a detailed and up-to-date familiarity with the technology of hundreds of industries, they are unlikely to make sound rules. Moreover, unless the regulatory agencies have a very wide jurisdiction, their regulations will be evaded by the movement of plants and individuals from localities where regulations are stiff to localities where they are loose. In addition, the regulatory agencies must view the pollution problem as a whole, since piecemeal regulation may simply lead polluters to substitute one form of pollution of another. For example, New York and Philadelphia have attempted to reduce water pollution by more intensive sewage treatment. However, one result has been the production of a lot of biologically active sludge that is being dumped into the ocean—and perhaps causing problems there.

## EFFLUENT FEES

The government can also intervene by establishing effluent fees. An **effluent fee** is a fee a polluter must pay to the government for discharging waste. In other words, a price is imposed on the disposal of wastes into the environment; and the more firms or individuals pollute, the more they must pay. The idea behind the imposition of effluent fees is that they can bring the private cost of waste disposal closer to the true social costs. Faced with a closer approximation to the true social costs of their activities, polluters will reduce the extent to which they pollute the environment. Needless to say, many practical difficulties are involved in carrying out this seemingly simple scheme, but many economists believe that this is a better way than direct regulation to deal with the pollution problem.

The use of effluent fees has the following advantages over direct regulation. First, *it obviously is socially desirable to use the cheapest way to*

A wastewater treatment plant

*achieve any given reduction in pollution. A system of effluent fees is more likely to accomplish this objective than direct regulation, because the regulatory agency cannot have all the relevant information* (as we noted above), *whereas polluters, reacting in their own interest to effluent fees, will tend to use the cheapest means to achieve a given reduction in pollution.*

To see why this is the case, consider a particular polluter. Faced with an effluent fee—that is, a price it must pay for each unit of waste it discharges—the polluter will find it profitable to reduce its discharge of waste so long as the cost of doing so is less than the effluent fee it saves. Thus, if this firm can reduce its discharge of wastes relatively cheaply, it will be induced to make such a reduction by the prospect of increased profits. On the other hand, if it cannot reduce its discharge of wastes at all cheaply, it will not make such a reduction, since the costs will exceed the saving in effluent fees. Thus a system of effluent fees induces firms that can reduce waste disposal more cheaply to cut down more on their waste disposal than firms where such a reduction is more expensive. This means that a given reduction of pollution will occur at a relatively low cost.

*Another advantage of effluent fees is that they do not require government agencies to have the detailed technological expertise often required by direct regulation.* After all, when effluent fees are used, all the government has to do is meter the amount of pollution a firm or household produces (which admittedly is sometimes not easy) and charge accordingly. It is left to the firms and households to figure out the most ingenious and effective ways to cut down on their pollution and save on effluent fees. This too is a spur to inventive activities aimed at developing more effective ways to reduce pollution. Also economists favor the use of effluent fees because financial incentives are likely to be easier to administer than direct regulation.

While economists tend to favor the use of effluent fees, they are not always against direct regulation. Some ways of disposing of certain types of waste are so dangerous that the only sensible thing to do is to ban them. For example, a ban on the disposal of mercury or arsenic in places where human beings are likely to consume them—and die—seems reasonable enough. In effect, the social cost of such pollution is so high that a very high penalty—imprisonment—is put on it. In addition, of course, economists favor direct regulation when it simply is not feasible to impose effluent fees—for example, in cases where it would be prohibitively expensive to meter the amount of pollutants emitted by various firms or households.

## The Ruhr: A Case Study

Let's consider a well-known case of effluent fees in use: the Ruhr valley in Germany. The Ruhr is one of the world's most industrialized areas. It contains about 10 million people and about 4,300 square miles. Water supplies in the Ruhr are quite limited. Five small rivers supply the area. The amazing amount of waste materials these rivers carry is indicated by the fact that the average annual natural low flow is less than the volume of effluent discharged into the rivers. Yet the local water authorities have succeeded in making this small amount of water serve the needs of the firms and households of this tremendous industrial area, and at the same time the streams have been used for recreation. Moreover, all this has been

View of the Ruhr valley, Germany

done at a remarkably low cost. The success of water management in the Ruhr seems to be due in considerable part to institutional arrangements that allowed the German water managers to plan and operate a relatively efficient regional system. Collective water quality improvement measures are used. Water quality is controlled by waste treatment in over 100 plants, regulation of river flow by reservoir, and a number of oxidation lakes in the Ruhr itself.

Effluent fees are an integral part of the institutional arrangements governing water quality. The amount a firm has to pay depends upon how much waste—and what kind—it pumps into the rivers. A formula has been devised to indicate how much a polluter must pay to dispose of a particular type of waste. In simple terms, the formula bases the charge on the amount of clean water needed to dilute the effluent in order to avoid harm to fish. Using this formula, the local authorities can determine, after testing the effluent of any firm, the amount the firm should pay. Specifically, the amount depends on the amount of suspended materials that will settle out of the effluent, the amount of oxygen consumed by bacteria in a sample of effluent, the results of a potassium permanganate test, and the results of a fish toxicity test. You need not understand the nature or specific purposes of these measurements and tests. The important thing is that you understand their general aim—which is to measure roughly the amount of pollution caused by various kinds of wastes. Having made these measurements and tests, the local authorities use their formula to determine how much a firm must pay in effluent fees.

## TRANSFERABLE EMISSIONS PERMITS

Another way that the government can reduce pollution is to issue *transferable emissions permits*. These permits, each of which allows the holder of the permit to generate a certain amount of pollution, are limited in total number. They are sold by the government to the highest bidders. Thus the price of a permit is set by supply and demand, as indicated in Chapter 3. If there is a great demand for such permits, and if the total number is small, the price of a permit will be high. If there is a weak demand for such permits, and if the total number is large, the price of a permit will be low.

One advantage of transferable emissions permits is that the authorities can predict how much pollution there will be. After all, the total amount of pollution cannot exceed the amount authorized by the total number of permits issued. In contrast, if an effluent fee is adopted, it is difficult to predict how much pollution will result, since this depends on how polluters respond to the particular level of the effluent fee that is chosen. For this reason, transferable emissions permits are often preferred over effluent fees.

## TAX CREDITS FOR POLLUTION-CONTROL EQUIPMENT

Still another way for the government to intervene is to establish *tax credits* for firms that introduce pollution-control equipment. There are, of course, many types of equipment that a plant can introduce to cut down on pollution—for example, "scrubbers" for catching poisonous gases, and electrostatic precipitators for decreasing dust and smoke. But such pollution-control equipment costs money, and firms are naturally reluctant to spend money on purposes where the private rate of return is so low.

To reduce the burden, the government can allow firms to reduce their tax bill by a certain percentage of the amount they spend on pollution-control equipment. A typical suggestion is that the government offer a *tax credit* equal to 20 percent of the cost of pollution-control equipment. In this way, the government would help defray some of the costs of the pollution-control equipment by allowing a firm that installed such equipment to pay less taxes than if no such tax inducements existed.

However, such schemes have a number of disadvantages:

*1. Subsidies to promote the purchase of particular types of pollution-control equipment may result in relatively inefficient and costly reductions in pollution.* After all, other methods that don't involve special pollution-control equipment—such as substituting one type of fuel for another—may sometimes be a more efficient way to reduce pollution.

*2. Subsidies of this sort may not be very effective.* Even if the subsidy reduces the cost to the firm of reducing pollution, it may still be cheaper for the firm to continue to pollute. In other words, subsidies of this sort make it a little less painful for polluters to reduce pollution; but unlike effluent fees, they offer no positive incentive.

*3. It seems preferable on grounds of equity for the firms and individuals that do the polluting—or their customers—to pay to clean up the mess that results.* Effluent fees work this way, but with tax credits for pollution-control equipment, the government picks up part of the tab by allowing the polluter to pay lower taxes. In other words, the general public, which is asked to shoulder the additional tax burden to make up for the polluters' lower taxes, pays part of the cost. But is this a fair allocation of the costs? Why should the general public be saddled with much of the bill?

## HOW CLEAN SHOULD THE ENVIRONMENT BE?

One of the most fundamental questions about pollution control is: How clean do we want the air, water, and other parts of our environment to be? At first glance, it may seem that we should restore and maintain a pristine pure environment, but this is not a very sensible goal, since the costs of achieving it would be enormous. The Environmental Protection Agency has estimated that the cost of achieving zero discharge of pollutants would be hundreds of billions of dollars—a truly staggering sum.

Fortunately, however, there is no reason to aim at so stringent a goal. *It seems obvious that, as pollution increases, various costs to society increase as well.* Some of these costs were described at the beginning of this chapter. For example, we pointed out that increases in air pollution result in increased deaths, and that increases in water pollution reduce the recreational value of rivers and streams. Suppose that we could get accurate data on the cost to society of various levels of pollution. Of course, it is extremely difficult to get such data, but if we could, we could determine the relationship between the amount of these costs and the level of pollution. It would look like the hypothetical curve in Figure 33.1. The greater the level of pollution, the higher these costs will be.

But these costs are not the only ones that must be considered. *We must also take into account the costs of controlling pollution.* In other words,

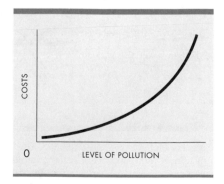

**Figure 33.1**
**Costs to Society of Pollution**
The costs to society of pollution increase with the level of pollution.

we must look at the costs to society of maintaining a certain level of environmental quality. These costs are not trivial, as we saw at the beginning of this section. To maintain a very low level of pollution, it is necessary to invest heavily in pollution-control equipment and to make other economic sacrifices.[3] If we could get accurate data on the cost to society of controlling pollution, we could find the relationship between the amount of these costs and the level of pollution. It would look like the hypothetical curve in Figure 33.2; the lower the level of pollution, the higher these costs will be.

## A Goal of Zero Pollution?

At this point, it should be obvious why we should not try to achieve a zero level of pollution. *The sensible goal for our society is to minimize the sum of the costs of pollution and the costs of controlling pollution.* In other words, we should construct a graph, as shown in Figure 33.3, to indicate the relationship between the sum of these two types of costs and the level of pollution. Then we should choose the level of pollution at which the sum of these two types of costs is a minimum. Thus, in Figure 33.3, we should aim for a pollution level of *A*. There is no point in trying for a lower level; such a reduction would cost more than it would be worth. For example, the cost of achieving a zero pollution level would be much more than it would be worth. Only when the pollution level exceeds *A* is the extra cost to society of the additional pollution greater than the cost of

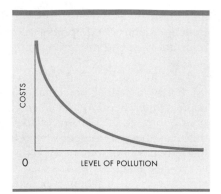

**Figure 33.2**
**Costs to Society of Pollution Control**
The more pollution is reduced, the higher are the costs to society of pollution control.

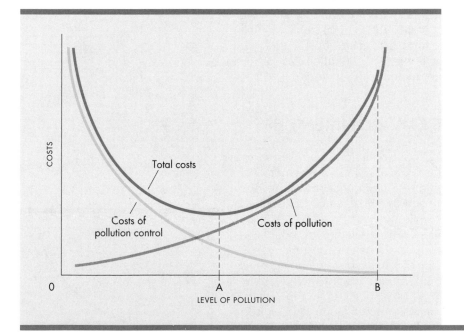

**Figure 33.3**
**Determining Optimal Level of Pollution**
The optimal level of pollution is at point *A*, since this is where the total costs are a minimum. Below point *A*, the cost to society of more pollution is less than the cost of preventing it. Above point *A*, the cost to society of more pollution is greater than the cost of preventing it.

[3] It is important to recognize that the costs of pollution control extend far beyond the construction of more and better water treatment plants, or the more extensive control of gas emission, or other such steps. A serious pollution-control program can put firms out of business, put people out of work, and bring economic trouble to entire communities. Further, a pollution-control system can result in a redistribution of income. For example, automobiles, electric power, and other goods and services involving considerable pollution are likely to increase in price relative to other goods and services involving little pollution. To the extent that polluting goods and services play a bigger role in the budgets of the poor than of the rich, pollution controls hurt the poor and help the rich.

## EXAMPLE 33.1    HOW TO REDUCE THE COSTS OF CLEANING UP

According to estimates made by Allen Kneese and Charles Schultze, the cost of achieving a one-pound reduction in the amount of pollutants emitted at a petroleum refinery and a beet-sugar plant are as shown below:

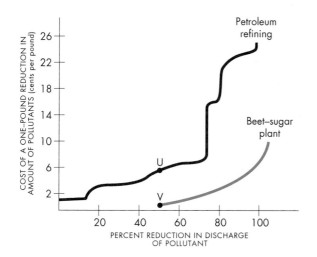

(a) Suppose that it is decided that the total amount of pollutants discharged by both plants should be reduced by 50 percent. If the government decrees that each plant should cut its discharge by 50 percent, what would be the cost of a one-pound reduction at each plant? (b) Can you suggest a way in which this total reduction in pollution can be achieved more efficiently? (c) To achieve this reduction most efficiently, which plant (the petroleum refinery or the beet-sugar plant) should reduce its discharge by the greater percentage? (d) Would an effluent fee achieve this reduction at less cost than the regulation in (a)?

### Solution

(a) The petroleum refinery would operate at point U, where the cost of a one-pound reduction in pollution is 6 cents. The beet-sugar plant would operate at point V, where the cost of a one-pound reduction would be 1 cent. (b) Since the beet-sugar plant can reduce pollution at less cost than the petroleum refinery (1 cent per pound rather than 6 cents per pound), it should cut its pollution more and the petroleum refinery should cut its pollution less. (c) The beet-sugar plant, for the reasons given in (b). (d) Yes. If an effluent fee were established, the cost of a one-pound reduction in pollution would tend to be the same at both plants. *

* See A. Kneese and C. Schultze, *Pollution, Prices, and Public Policy*, Washington, D.C.: The Brookings Institution, 1975; and W. Baumol and W. Oates, *Economics, Environmental Policy, and the Quality of Life*, Englewood Cliffs, N.J.: Prentice-Hall, 1979.

preventing it. For example, the cost of allowing pollution to increase from A to B is much greater than the cost of prevention.

It is easy to draw hypothetical curves, but not so easy actually to measure these curves. Unfortunately, no one has a very clear idea of what the curves in Figure 33.3 really look like—although we can be sure that their general shapes are like those shown there. Thus no one really knows just how clean we should try to make the environment. Under these circumstances, expert opinion differs on the nature and extent of the programs that should be carried out. Moreover, political considerations and pressures enter in. But one thing is for sure: we will continue to live with some pollution—and that, for the reason just given, will be the rational thing to do.

## POLLUTION-CONTROL PROGRAMS IN THE UNITED STATES

In recent decades, there has been considerable growth in government programs designed to control pollution. To take but one example, federal expenditures to reduce water pollution increased in the period from the mid-1950s to 1970 from about $1 million to $300 million annually. To curb water pollution, the federal government has for years operated a system of grants-in-aid to state, municipal, or regional agencies to help construct treatment plants; and grants are made for research on new treatment methods. In addition, the 1970 Water Quality Improvement Act authorized grants to demonstrate new methods and techniques and to establish programs to train people in water control management. (The federal government has also regulated the production and use of pesticides.) The states, as well as the federal government, have played an important role in water pollution control. They have set standards for allowable pollution levels, and many state governments have provided matching grants to help municipalities construct treatment plants.

In 1969, the Congress established a new agency—the Council on Environmental Quality—to oversee and plan the nation's pollution control programs. Modeled to some extent on the Council of Economic Advisers, the Council on Environmental Quality, which has three members, is supposed to gather information on considerations and trends in the quality of the environment, review and evaluate the federal government's programs in this area, develop appropriate national policies, and conduct needed surveys and research on environmental quality. The tasks assigned to the council are obviously important ones.

In 1970, the federal government established another new agency, the Environmental Protection Agency (EPA). Working with state and local officials, this agency establishes standards for desirable air and water quality, and devises rules for attaining these goals. The 1970 Clean Air Amendments directed EPA to establish minimum ambient standards for air quality, and it set limits on the emission of carbon monoxide, hydrocarbons, and nitrous oxides from automobiles. But after a number of clashes between EPA and the auto makers, the EPA relaxed the deadlines when these limits were supposed to be met. In 1972 amendments to the Water Pollution Act authorized EPA to set up effluent standards for both privately and publicly owned plants. A stated goal of the amendments was to eliminate the discharge of pollutants into water by 1985, but, for reasons discussed in the previous section, this goal was unrealistically stringent.

## DIRECTIONS OF ENVIRONMENTAL POLICY SINCE 1975

In the late seventies and early eighties, policy makers became increasingly concerned that regulatory agencies like EPA had been paying too little attention to the costs involved in reducing pollution. For example, a government study found that a relaxation of EPA's 1977 standard for water-pollution control in the steel industry *with no change in its more stringent 1983 standard* would allow savings in capital costs of $200 million. As President Carter's Council of Economic Advisers pointed out, "In making regulatory decisions on the speed of attaining standards, we should explicitly make a qualitative judgment about whether the gains from earlier attainment are worth the costs." Also, some experts, like Lester Lave of Carnegie-Mellon University and Gilbert Omenn of the Brookings Institution, concluded from their studies that the Clean Air Act was not very effective. In their view, "the application of pollution controls to existing plants and older cars has been limited, and costs have been excessive,

Lester Lave

# WHAT SHOULD BE DONE ABOUT GLOBAL WARMING?

According to many world political leaders, there is an urgent need to take action to halt global warming. Scientists have long known that certain gases, notably carbon dioxide, in the atmosphere trap solar energy and heat our planet. (See Figure 1.) Many leading scientists now believe that these gases are being generated faster than the biosphere can neutralize their effects, and that as a consequence the global climate is warming up. Because of this "greenhouse effect," it has been estimated that the earth's global mean temperature could increase by about 5 degrees by the end of the next century, with the result that the sea level may increase by about 2 feet.

Faced with this situation, 68 nations (including the United States, Japan, and the Soviet Union) agreed in late 1989 that carbon dioxide emissions would have to be curbed, and a United Nations report called for a 60 percent cut in "greenhouse" gas emissions. Because fuel combustion is the primary source of carbon dioxide emissions, lower energy consumption would probably be required to curb carbon dioxide resulting from fossil fuel consumption. As pointed out by the Council of Economic Advisers,

A variety of policy tools, including user charges, correction of market failures, regulatory standards, expanded funding for research on and development of substitutes for fossil fuels and other sources of greenhouse emissions, and efforts to reduce and reverse deforestation, could be used to slow the buildup of greenhouse gases in the atmosphere. These approaches are relevant for nearly all greenhouse gases, not just carbon dioxide. While international attention has naturally focused on carbon dioxide as the single largest contributor to the greenhouse effect, control costs must also be considered in the design of any strategy to reduce net emissions of greenhouse gases. A cost-effective strategy may involve a focus on other gases or on sinks that absorb greenhouse emissions. Different approaches may be suitable for different countries.

*A fee, charge, or tradable allowances system for greenhouse gas emissions based on an index of the global climate impacts of each greenhouse gas would provide a least-cost reduction in such emissions.* A fee or a tradable allowances scheme would lead firms and individuals to consider the social cost of greenhouse emissions in their private decisions. An emission charge or the need to consider the value of allowances would affect decisions ranging from the choice among alternative technologies for generating electricity, to the energy efficiency of cars, buildings, and industrial equipment, to the demand for automobile travel. Because market-based approaches are flexible and provide incentives that affect decisions at all points along the production-consumption chain and across all industries, they automatically focus on those activities where emissions reductions can be achieved at least cost.[1]

Alan Manne of Stanford University and Richard Rickels of the Electric Power Research Institute have carried out a detailed study to estimate the economic costs of constraining carbon dioxide emissions.[2] In particular, they look at what would happen to world output if these emissions were stabilized at current levels, and then gradually reduced by 20 percent by the year 2020. Based on their results, the economic costs would be huge. In particular, gross national

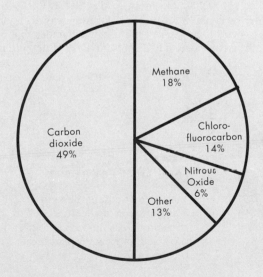

**Figure I**
**Gases Creating the Greenhouse Effect, 1989**
*Source*: New York Times, November 19, 1989.

---

[1] *Economic Report of the President*, Washington, D.C.: Government Printing Office, 1990, p. 218.
[2] A. Manne and R. Rickels, "CO2 Emission Limits: An Economic Analysis for the U.S.A."

Alan Manne

product would be reduced by about 3 percent in the United States and by about 1 to 2 percent in Europe and Japan. The present value of the cumulative loss over the next century for the United States alone would be about $1 trillion. Because the United States relies relatively heavily on coal as an energy source, the impact would be greater than in Europe or Japan. Moreover, the cost would be great in China, which wants to exploit its rich coal supplies to promote its economic development.

Given that the costs will be greater in some countries than in others, there has been considerable concern over the chances of obtaining a broad, enforceable agreement among countries to limit carbon dioxide emissions. Unless the Soviet Union, Eastern Europe, and the less developed countries (like

China) are willing to commit themselves to such an agreement, there will be only a modest benefit from limitations of this sort in the United States, Western Europe, and Japan. Particularly in the less developed countries, where the rate of growth of energy use is double the world average, it may be difficult to obtain strong enforcement of any agreement. (See Figure 2.)

Confronted by these daunting potential costs and problems, many leading economists have suggested that it would be wise to wait until more is known before adopting strong measures. To support this view, they point out that scientists are sharply split in their views concerning the likelihood of global warming. Some scientists, like Richard Lindzen of Massachusetts Institute of Technology, argue that current forecasts of global warming "are so inaccurate and fraught with uncertainty as to be useless to policy makers."[3] Others argue that if the warming is modest, as they think likely, it could result in benefits such as longer growing seasons in temperate zones and more rain in dry areas.

Given these basic uncertainties, the Council of Economic Advisers concludes as follows:

The highest priority in the near term should be to improve understanding in order to build a foundation for sound policy decisions. Until such a foundation is in place, there is no justification for imposing major costs on the economy to slow the growth of greenhouse gas emissions. Policies that may result in slower growth in greenhouse emissions, but can also be fully justified on other grounds, are the best short-run way to address this potential problem while the uncertainties that exist today are reduced. Being justified on other grounds

[3] "Skeptics Are Challenging Dire 'Greenhouse' Views," *New York Times*, December 13, 1989.

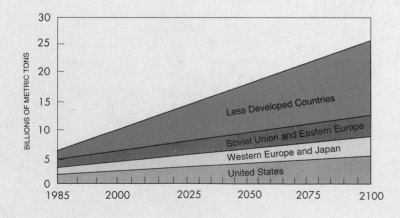

**Figure 2**
**Carbon Dioxide Emissions by Region**
The share of carbon dioxide emissions from the less developed countries (like China and India) is projected to grow rapidly. The U.S. share is projected to decline.
*Source*: Environmental Protection Agency. *Policy Options for Stabilizing Global Climate* (Rapidly Changing World Scenario).

means that a program yields non-greenhouse benefits commensurate with its costs; it cannot mean simply having some non-greenhouse benefits. The adoption of many small programs, each of which would fail a standard cost-benefit test, could significantly slow economic growth and eliminate jobs.

Because the intense research currently underway may reveal that it is desirable to slow the growth of greenhouse gas emissions, it is useful to consider the elements of what would be an economically rational strategy to do so. Any strategy to limit aggregate emissions without worldwide participation would be likely to fail. A cost-effective policy must provide for comprehensive coverage of both sources and sinks of all major greenhouse gases. It must also provide appropriate incentives for emissions reductions and deal directly with market failures. Carbon dioxide emissions, in particular, could be reduced at much lower cost through the use of emissions fees than through government-imposed standards for energy efficiency.[4]

## Probing Deeper

1. Why would a fee or tradable allowance system (which involves the use of transferable emissions permits) "provide a least-cost reduction in [greenhouse gas] emissions"?

2. Why could the "adoption of many small programs, each of which would fail a standard cost-benefit test, . . . significantly slow economic growth . . ."?

3. Why would any "strategy to limit aggregate emissions without worldwide participation...be likely to fail"?

4. Why must any effective strategy cover all greenhouse gases?

5. Why could "carbon dioxide emission, in particular, . . . be reduced at much lower cost through the use of emissions fees than through government-imposed standards for energy efficiency"?

[4] *Economic Report of the President, op. cit.*, p. 224. In 1991, the National Academy of Sciences issued a report calling for national energy-efficient building codes, an increase in overall mileage standards for new automobiles to 32.5 miles per gallon from 27.5, more Federal support for reforestation and mass transit, and the development of a new generation of nuclear power plants. This report added further fuel to the controversies in this area.

largely because Congress has failed to confront [many of] the difficult issues . . ."

During the 1980s, environmentalists and others charged that the Reagan administration was dismantling, or at least emasculating, EPA. Anne Gorsuch resigned in 1983 as head of EPA, as criticism of the agency continued to build. James Watt, former Secretary of the Interior, also angered environmentalists. Administration officials retorted to such criticism by claiming that they were trying to promote and restore balance between environmental objectives and economic growth. In 1985, a political battle raged over the superfund, the fund authorized by federal legislation to clean up sites where chemical wastes have been dumped. Environmentalists wanted a fund of $10 billion; the Reagan administration proposed $5 billion. Some observers wanted the oil and chemical firms to contribute more to the fund, while these firms bitterly opposed such a move.

The Bush administration seemed more interested in new environmental initiatives than the Reagan administration. In late 1990, major changes were made in the Clean Air Act. To protect the ozone that shields the earth from harmful ultraviolet radiation, production of chlorofluorocarbons and carbon tetrachloride will be phased out through the 1990s and outlawed by January 1, 2000. Also, the law calls for tighter restrictions on the pollutants causing urban smog and on automobile exhausts (beginning in the 1994 model year), as well as new limits on coal-burning power plants that are aimed at reducing emissions of sulfur dioxide and nitrogen oxide—both regarded as causes of acid rain. Some economists estimated that compliance with this new legislation could cost about $30 billion per year. Whether the benefits exceed the costs will not be known for many years.

Some people believe that public policy is moving too rapidly in this area; others believe that it is moving too slowly. It is not easy to determine how fast or how far we should go in attempting to reduce pollution. Those who will bear the costs of reducing pollution have an understandable tendency to emphasize (and perhaps inflate) the costs and discount the benefits of such projects. Those who are particularly interested in enjoying nature and outdoor recreation—like the Sierra Club—are understandably inclined to emphasize (and perhaps inflate) the benefits and discount the costs of such projects. Politics inevitably plays a major role in the outcome of such cases. The citizens of the United States must indicate, through the ballot box as well as the market place, how much they are willing to pay to reduce pollution. We must also decide at what level of government the relevant rules are to be made. Since many pollution problems are local, it often seems sensible to determine the appropriate level of environmental quality locally. (However, there are obvious dangers in piecemeal regulation, as pointed out above.)

## TEST YOURSELF

1. Suppose that the paper industry emits wastes into rivers and streams, and that municipalities or firms downstream must treat the water to make it usable. Do the paper industry's private costs equal the social costs of producing paper? Why, or why not?

2. Suppose that each ton of paper produced results in pollution that costs municipalities and firms downstream $1.00, and that a law is passed that requires the paper industry to reimburse the municipalities and firms downstream for these costs. Prior to this law, the supply curve for paper was:

| PRICE OF PAPER (DOLLARS PER TON) | QUANTITY SUPPLIED (MILLION TONS) |
| --- | --- |
| 1.00 | 10.0 |
| 2.00 | 15.0 |
| 2.50 | 17.5 |
| 3.00 | 20.0 |
| 4.00 | 25.0 |

After the law takes effect, what will be the quantity supplied at each price?

3. In Question 2, which output—the one prevailing before the industry has to reimburse others, or the one prevailing afterward—is socially more desirable? Why?

4. If the demand curve for paper is as shown below, what will be the equilibrium output of paper before and after the paper industry has to reimburse the municipalities and firms downstream (as indicated in Question 2)?

| PRICE OF PAPER (DOLLARS PER TON) | QUANTITY DEMANDED (MILLION TONS) |
| --- | --- |
| 1.00 | 30.0 |
| 2.00 | 25.0 |
| 3.00 | 20.0 |
| 3.50 | 17.5 |
| 4.00 | 15.0 |

5. Suppose that the social cost (in billions of dollars) due to pollution equals $5P$, where $P$ is the level of pollution, and that the cost (in billions of dollars) of pollution control equals $10 - 2P$. What is the optimal level of pollution? Is this a typical case?

## SUMMARY

1. One of the major social issues of the 1990s is environmental pollution. To a considerable extent, environmental pollution is an economic problem. Waste disposal and other pollution-causing activities result in external diseconomies.

2. Firms and individuals that pollute the water and air (and other facets of the environment) often pay less than the true social costs of disposing of their wastes in this way. Part of the true social cost is borne by other firms and individuals,

who must pay to clean up the water or air, or who must live with the consequences.

3. Because of the divergence of private from social costs, the market system does not result in an optimal allocation of resources. Firms and individuals create too much waste and dispose of it in excessively harmful ways. Because the polluters do not pay the full costs of waste disposal, their products are artificially cheap, with the result that too much is produced of them.

4. The government can intervene in several ways to help remedy the breakdown of the market system in this area. One way is to issue regulations for waste disposal and other activities influencing the environment. Another is to establish effluent fees, charges a polluter must pay to the government for discharging wastes. Still another way is to issue transferable emissions permits. In recent decades, there has been considerable growth in government programs designed to control pollution.

5. It is extremely difficult to determine how clean the environment should be. Of course, the sensible goal for society is to permit the level of pollution that minimizes the sum of the costs of pollution and the costs of controlling pollution; but no one has a very clear idea of what these costs are, and to a large extent the choices must be made through the political process.

## CONCEPTS FOR REVIEW

**External diseconomy**

**Private costs**

**Social costs**

**Direct regulation**

**Effluent fees**

**Transferable emissions permits**

**Tax credits**

# PART NINE

# THE LESS DEVELOPED
# COUNTRIES AND
# ALTERNATIVE ECONOMIC
# SYSTEMS

# THE LESS DEVELOPED COUNTRIES

FRESH FROM A RAID ON the well-stocked family refrigerator or comfortably placed in front of a television set, the average American finds it difficult to believe that hunger is a major problem in the world. Yet it is. The industrialized countries—like the United States, Western Europe, Japan, and the USSR—are really just rich little islands surrounded by seas of poverty in Asia, Africa, and much of Latin America. This chapter deals with the problems of these so-called "less developed countries" (LDCs): the poor countries of the world. We take up several questions. Which countries are poor and why? How badly do they need additional capital? How great is the danger of overpopulation? To what extent do they lack modern technology? How can they stimulate their rate of economic growth? What can the United States do to help them? These questions are crucial, both to the people in the less developed countries and to us.

## LESS DEVELOPED COUNTRIES: DEFINITIONS AND CHARACTERISTICS

### What Is a Less Developed Country?

Economics abounds with clumsy terms. A profession responsible for cross elasticity of demand and average propensity to consume cannot claim a prize for elegant language. The term **less developed country** is not a model of clarity. For a country to be less developed it must be poor, but *how* poor? Any answer has to be arbitrary. We shall define any country with a per capita income of under $5,000 (1988 dollars) as less developed. Although the $5,000 cutoff point is arbitrary, it certainly is low enough so that any country unfortunate enough to qualify is most certainly poor.

Table 34.1 shows that many countries have a per capita income of under $5,000. Thus much of the world is, by this definition, less developed. Indeed, the staggering fact is that well over half of the world's population lives in the less developed countries. Indeed, hundreds of millions of people live in countries where per capita income is less than $2,500.[1]

---

[1] The figures in Table 34.1 are not comparable with many of the other per capita income figures in this book, but the differences in concept need not concern us here. The important point is that these figures are designed to be comparable from one country to another in Table 34.1.

**Table 34.1**
**Countries Classified by Level of Per Capita Income, 1988**[a]

A. *Countries with per capita income of $5,000 or more*

| | | | |
|---|---|---|---|
| Australia | Finland | Luxembourg | Soviet Union |
| Austria | France | Netherlands | Sweden |
| Belgium | Germany | New Zealand | Switzerland |
| Canada | Iceland | Norway | United Kingdom |
| Denmark | Japan | Singapore | United States |

B. *Countries with per capita income of $2,500 to $4,999*

| | | | |
|---|---|---|---|
| Algeria | Chile | Iraq | Peru |
| Argentina | Colombia | Malaysia | Syria |
| Botswana | Gabon | Panama | Thailand |
| Brazil | Iran | Paraguay | Turkey |

C. *Countries with per capita income of less than $2,500*

| | | | |
|---|---|---|---|
| Afghanistan | Ethiopia | Kenya | Sudan |
| Bangladesh | Ghana | Madagascar | Tanzania |
| Burma | Haiti | Nepal | Uganda |
| China | India | Pakistan | Zaire |
| El Salvador | Indonesia | Sri Lanka | Zambia |

[a]All figures are expressed in 1988 dollars.
*Source:* R. Summers and A. Heston, "The Penn World Table (Mark 5): An Expanded Set of International Comparisons, 1950–88", *Quarterly Journal of Economics*, May 1991.

Imagine what life might be like if you grew up in a country with per capita income of less than $2,500 per year. Chances are that you would be illiterate. You would probably work on a farm with meager tools and little technology. You would have few possessions (and sometimes only enough food to keep body and soul together) and be likely to die young.

The unpleasant fact is that this harsh existence is the lot of a great many earth dwellers. This does not mean that the less developed countries do not have rich citizens. Indeed they do. But the rich are a tiny minority surrounded by masses of poor people. Nor does it mean that many of these people do not live in cities. Bombay is a city that is home to millions of inhabitants, most of them poor.

## Nationalism, Rising Expectations, and a Persistent Gap

It must also be recognized that many of the less developed countries have gained their political independence since World War II. Before World War II, the major European powers had substantial empires. The British had colonies all over the globe. In the postwar period, many countries have achieved independence. These new countries are often fiercely nationalistic. They resent what they regard as exploitation at the hands of the former European colonists and demand power and status. Although weak individually, together they represent a force that must be reckoned with.

Moreover, because of better communications and altered religious and cultural beliefs, the expectations and demands of people in less developed countries have changed enormously. Years ago, they were more likely to accept a life of privation and want, since their eye was on the next world. Now the emphasis has shifted to this world, and to material comforts—and getting them quickly. People in less developed countries have become aware of the high standards of living in the industrialized societies, and they want to catch up as fast as they can.

**Table 34.2**
**Percentage Growth in Output Per Capita, 1960–73, 1973–80, and 1980–88, Fourteen Less Developed Countries**

| COUNTRY | 1960–73 | 1973–80 | 1980–88 |
|---|---|---|---|
| Argentina | 2.3 | 0.1 | –1.7 |
| Brazil | 7.1 | 4.0 | –0.2 |
| China | 2.3 | 3.7 | 7.8 |
| Colombia | 3.0 | 2.8 | 0.9 |
| Egypt | 3.5 | 8.4 | 1.5 |
| India | 0.2 | 0.0 | 2.8 |
| Indonesia | 1.9 | 6.7 | 2.3 |
| Nigeria | 1.8 | 1.1 | –5.3 |
| Pakistan | 1.9 | 1.3 | 4.0 |
| Sudan | –0.7 | 2.7 | –2.5 |
| Tanzania | 3.2 | 3.0 | –0.5 |
| Turkey | 3.5 | 2.0 | 2.3 |
| Tunisia | 3.5 | 4.5 | –0.2 |
| Zaire | 3.2 | –6.8 | 0.2 |

*Source:* See Table 34.1.

Although the available data on the less developed countries are not as accurate as one would like, these countries generally seemed to increase their per capita output in the 1960s and 1970s; in the 1980s, however, many of them experienced a decline in per capita output (Table 34.2). For this and other reasons, *the gap between income per capita in the less developed countries and in the developed countries seems to have been increasing, not decreasing, in recent decades.* This is a disturbing fact. Apparently, the gap between rich and poor will not decrease, unless recent trends are altered.

## A Closer Look at the Less Developed Countries

The less developed countries vary enormously. Some, like China, are huge; others, like Paraguay, are small. Some have lots of people jammed into every square mile of land; others, like Brazil, have relatively few people spread over lots of land. Some, like Iraq, have important natural resources (notably oil); others have few resources. Some, like India, have had great civilizations many, many centuries old; others have had ruder histories. Nonetheless, although it is not easy to generalize about the less developed countries, many of them, besides suffering from relatively low productivity, have the following characteristics:

**STRESS ON AGRICULTURE.** The less developed countries generally devote most of their resources to food production. Agriculture is by far their largest industry. This contrasts markedly with industrialized countries like the United States, where only a small percentage of output is food. Moreover, food makes up most of the goods consumed in less developed countries. They are so poor that the typical family has very little besides food, a crude dwelling, some simple clothing, and other such necessities.

**DUAL ECONOMY.** Many less developed countries have two economies, existing side by side. One of these is a ***market-oriented economy*** much like that in developed countries. This economy is generally found in the big cities, where there may be some modern manufacturing plants, as well as government agencies, wholesale and retail outlets, and services for the small number of rich people in the country. Coexisting with this relatively modern economy is a **subsistence economy** based largely on barter, innocent of all but the crudest technology and capable of producing little more—and sometimes less—than a subsistence wage for the inhabitants. This subsistence economy often includes most of the rural areas. It has little or no capital, few decent roads, only the most rudimentary communications. Unfortunately, this is the economy in which the bulk of the population exists.

**POLITICAL PROBLEMS.**  Some of the less developed countries have relatively weak, unstable governments. Thus the climate for long-term investment and planning is relatively poor in such countries. Moreover, some governments are controlled by a small group of wealthy citizens or by other groups with a vested interest in resisting social change. Corruption among government officials is encountered too often, and honest officials are sometimes not very well trained or experienced in their duties. To some extent these problems stem from the relative youth of many of these countries. But whatever the reasons, they hamper the effect of government on economic development.

**INCOME INEQUALITY.**  Most of the less developed countries have a relatively high degree of income inequality. Indeed, there is much more income inequality than in the industrialized countries. Typically, a few landowners or industrialists in a less developed country are rich, sometimes enormously rich. But all outside this tiny group are likely to be very poor. The middle class, so important in the industrialized countries, is very small in most less developed countries.

## BARRIERS TO DEVELOPMENT AND THE NEED FOR CAPITAL FORMATION

Why are the less developed economies so poor, and what can they do to raise their income levels? These are very difficult questions, both because the answers vary from country to country and because the answers for any single country are hard to determine. A variety of factors generally is responsible for a country's poverty, and these factors are so intermeshed that it is difficult to tell which are most important. Nonetheless, certain factors stand out; among these is the lack of capital in less developed countries.

Without exception, the people in the less developed countries have had relatively little capital to work with. There have been few factories, machine tools, roads, tractors, power plants, miles of railroad, and so on. If you visited one of these countries, you would be struck by the absence of mechanical aids to production. Workers use their hands, legs, and simple tools, often as their ancestors did long ago.

There are several reasons why the less developed countries have not accumulated much capital. First, a country must usually reduce consumption to accumulate capital, but for the less developed countries, with their very low income levels, a reduction in consumption can be painful. Equally important, much of the saving that does go on in less developed countries is not utilized very effectively. Second, there are important barriers to domestic investment, such as the smallness of local markets, the

Tobacco farming in Paraguay

lack of skilled labor, and the lack of qualified entrepreneurs (faced with the right incentives) who are willing and able to take the risks involved in carrying out investment projects. Third, fear that property will be confiscated deters industrialized countries from investing in the less developed countries. As we pointed out above, many of the less developed countries are relatively young nations, filled with nationalistic fervor and fearful of becoming economically dependent. They are suspicious of foreign investment in their countries—and in some cases are quite capable of confiscating foreign-owned property. Needless to say, this does not make foreigners particularly anxious to invest in some of them.

## Methods to Increase Investment

Recognizing their need for additional capital, the less developed countries have used three principal methods to increase investment. First, they have *taxed away part of the nation's resources and used them for investment purposes or made them available to private investors*. Second, they have tried to *mobilize "surplus labor" from agriculture to carry out investment projects*. Third, they have *increased government spending on investment projects without increasing taxes, thus producing inflation*. Although effective within limits, each of these methods has important limitations. Taxes may dull incentives and in any event are often evaded; "surplus labor" is difficult to transfer and utilize; and a little inflation may soon develop into a big inflation. (As shown in Table 34.3, the rate of inflation in some less developed countries during the 1980s was impressive indeed.) Besides these three methods, a country can *use **foreign aid** to increase investment*. It too has its problems and limitations, but it is hard to see how many less developed countries can scrape up the capital they need without it.

## The Importance of Investments in Machinery

Recent studies suggest that the amount that a country invests in machinery has an important influence on its rate of economic growth. During 1965–80, countries that invested relatively heavily in equipment (like Japan) tended to grow faster than countries (like Argentina) that invested relatively little in equipment.[2] Investments in structures seem to have had far less effect on a country's rate of economic growth than investments in equipment. One reason why countries with high economic growth rates tend to invest more in equipment than countries with low economic growth rates is that the former countries have lower equipment prices than the latter countries do. According to some economists, the less developed countries should adopt policies to channel more of their scarce investment funds into machinery rather than construction projects.

# THE POPULATION EXPLOSION

Another very important reason why per capita income is so low in some (but by no means all) less developed countries is that they suffer from overpopulation. Many less developed countries have sizably increased

[2] J. B. De Long and L. Summers, "Equipment Investment and Econmic Growth", *Quarterly Journal of Economics*, May 1991.

**Table 34.3**
**Percentage Increase of the Domestic Price Level, 1980–87**

| COUNTRY | PERCENT INCREASE |
|---|---|
| Brazil | 58,122 |
| Colombia | 338 |
| Ghana | 1,444 |
| India | 86 |
| Malaysia | 27 |
| Pakistan | 61 |
| Peru | 10,985 |
| Philippines | 168 |
| Sri Lanka | 105 |
| Thailand | 34 |
| Turkey | 420 |

*Source:* United Nations. Note that these figures show the percentage increase over the entire period, not the average annual increase.

**Table 34.4**
**Annual Rates of Growth of Population, Less Developed and Developed Countries, 1950–67 and 1970–80 (Percentages)**

| LESS DEVELOPED COUNTRIES | | | DEVELOPED COUNTRIES | | |
| --- | --- | --- | --- | --- | --- |
| COUNTRY | 1950–67 | 1970–80 | COUNTRY | 1950–67 | 1970–80 |
| Brazil | 3.1 | 2.9 | France | 1.1 | 0.6 |
| Colombia | 3.2 | 2.8 | Germany | 1.2 | 0.1 |
| Egypt | 2.5 | 2.3 | Italy | 0.7 | 0.6 |
| Ghana | 2.7 | 2.9 | Japan | 1.1 | 1.2 |
| India | 2.2 | 2.1 | United Kingdom | 0.5 | 0.1 |
| Malaysia | 3.0 | 2.6 | United States | 1.6 | 1.1 |
| Pakistan | 2.4 | 3.1 | Average | 1.0 | 0.6 |
| Peru | 2.6 | 2.8 | | | |
| Philippines | 3.2 | 2.7 | | | |
| Sri Lanka | 2.5 | 1.7 | | | |
| Thailand | 3.0 | 2.7 | | | |
| Turkey | 2.7 | 2.4 | | | |
| Average | 2.8 | 2.6 | | | |

Source: A. Madison, *Economic Progress and Policy in Developing Countries*, New York: Norton, 1970; and United Nations.

their total output, but because of rapid population growth, output per capita has increased relatively little. Suppose that a less developed country's total output grows at 4 percent per year. If its population remains constant, output per capita will also grow at 4 percent per year. But if its population increases at 3 percent per year, output per capita will grow at only 1 percent per year.

Table 34.4 shows the rate of population growth during 1950–80 in a variety of less developed countries, as well as some major developed countries. The rate has been higher, without exception, in the less developed countries than in the developed ones. The most important reason is that modern methods of preventing and curing diseases have been introduced into the LDCs, thus reducing the death rate, particularly among children. It used to be that, although the birth rate in the less developed countries was higher than in the developed countries, the death rate was also higher, so that the rate of population growth was about the same in the less developed countries as in the developed ones. But in recent years, the death rate in the LDCs has been reduced, whereas the birth rate has remained high. The result has been a ***population explosion.*** Thus in parts of Latin America the population is doubling every 20 years.

This growth of sheer numbers, which recalls the work of Thomas Malthus (Chapter 16), is only part of the problem. The populations of the less developed countries also tend to be illiterate and ill-nourished. Thus they do not have the skills required to absorb much modern technology. In addition, many workers have little or nothing to do. They live with their relatives and occasionally hold a job. Although they may not be included in the official unemployment figures, they represent a case of *disguised unemployment*. In sum, the population of many less developed countries is large (relative to the available capital and natural resources), fast-growing, of relatively poor economic quality, and poorly utilized.

## Policy Responses to Population Problems

The less developed countries have responded to the population explosion in at least two ways. Where birth control is opposed on religious or cultural grounds, the LDCs often concentrate on the widespread unemployment that results from population increase. The rapidly expanding labor force cannot be employed productively in agriculture, since there is already a surplus of farm labor in many LDCs, and the capital stock is not increasing rapidly enough to employ the growing numbers in industry. Governments faced with serious unemployment of this sort often are induced to *create public works programs and other projects to make jobs, even if these projects do not really promote economic growth.* In recent years, they have also sometimes initiated self-employment programs.

Some LDCs also responded to the population explosion by *attempting to lower the birth rate through the diffusion of contraceptive devices and other birth control techniques.* However, many people now believe that high birth rates often are due to a desire to have large families, and that a reduction in birth rates will require education of potential parents. Some countries, such as China, have established economic incentives for families to limit the number of children. Progress has been slow, but in some countries like South Korea, birth control programs seem to have had a noteworthy effect.

Besides trying to cope with or influence the growth rate of their populations, the LDCs have also tried to increase the economic quality of their human resources. In other words, *they have been investing in human capital.* Such an investment seems warranted; educational and skill levels in many less developed countries have been quite low. Table 34.5 shows that in ten major less developed countries, the average percentage of public expenditure devoted to education has been substantial—indeed, not very different from in the United States. In many LDCs, the proportion of children in school is substantially higher than it used to be. This is certainly a step in the right direction, although enrollment in school is only a crude measure of the quality of the labor force. In order to absorb and utilize, and eventually develop, modern technology, the LDCs must continue to invest in a more productive labor force.

# TECHNOLOGY: A CRUCIAL FACTOR

Still another very important reason why per capita income is so low in the less developed countries is that these countries use rudimentary and often backward technology. In previous chapters, we have seen that to a considerable extent the increase in per capita income in the developed countries has resulted from the development and application of new technology. Too often, the less developed countries still use the technology of their forefathers—the agricultural and manufacturing methods of long, long ago. Why is this the case? Why don't the less developed countries copy the advanced technology of the industrialized countries, following the examples of the Japanese and Russians, among others, who promoted their economic development during the twentieth century by copying Western technology?

## Problems in Adopting Modern Technology

One barrier to the use of modern technology is lack of capital. Modern petroleum refining technology, to choose one, cannot be used without

**Table 34.5**
**Percentage of Total Public Expenditure Devoted to Education**

| COUNTRY | PERCENTAGE |
| --- | --- |
| Brazil | 21 |
| Colombia | 21 |
| Ghana | 20 |
| India | 26 |
| Pakistan | 5 |
| Peru | 22 |
| Philippines | 9 |
| Sri Lanka | 10 |
| Thailand | 21 |
| Turkey | 21 |
| Average | 18 |

*Source:* United Nations.

lots of capital, which the less developed countries find difficult to scrape up. But many technological improvements do not require substantial capital. Indeed, some technological improvements are capital-saving. That is, they reduce the amount of capital needed to produce a given amount of output.

A second reason why the less developed countries find it difficult to copy and use modern technology is that they lack both a skilled labor force and entrepreneurs. Imagine the difficulties in transplanting a complicated technology—for example, that involved in steel production—from the United States to a less developed country where there are few competent engineers, fewer experienced and resourceful managers, and practically no laborers with experience in the demanding work required to operate a modern steel plant.

Even more fundamental is the fact that much of our advanced Western technology is really not very well suited to circumstances in the less developed countries. Because the industrialized countries have relatively great amounts of capital and relatively little labor, they tend to develop and adopt technology that substitutes capital for labor. But this technology may not be appropriate for less developed countries where there is little capital and lots of labor. Thus *it is very important that the less developed countries pick and choose among the technologies available in the industrialized countries, and that they adapt these technologies to their own conditions.* Mindless attempts to ape the technologies used in the industrialized countries can result in waste and failure.

## Technological Change in the LDCs

In agriculture, important technological advances have taken place in the less developed countries in recent years. In particular, new types of seeds have been developed, increasing the yields of wheat, rice, and other crops. Some of this research was supported by the Rockefeller and Ford Foundations. The resulting increase in agricultural productivity has been so impressive that many observers call it a *"green revolution."* There is no question that wheat and rice production has increased greatly in countries like Mexico, the Philippines, Iran, Sri Lanka, India, and Pakistan. Plenty of opportunity remains for improvements in livestock yields as well, but religious beliefs and traditional prejudices are sometimes an important barrier to change.

In industry, most of the new technology adopted by the less developed countries is taken from the developed countries. Very little attempt is being made to devise new technologies more appropriate to conditions in the less developed countries, both because the less developed countries do not have the engineering and scientific resources to develop them, and because such attempts have not been very successful in the past. In countries where the private sector finds it unprofitable to carry out research and development, government research institutes sometimes try to fill the void, but these institutes frequently devote too much of their limited resources to projects not closely related to economic development. In addition, productivity centers have been created in some countries to teach managers and supervisory personnel how to make better use of a new technology. Such centers have helped promote the diffusion of new technology in Mexico and Taiwan, among other countries.

# THE CLASH OVER THE PROTECTION OF INTELLECTUAL PROPERTY

During the early 1990s, there has been a battle between the industrialized countries and the less developed countries over the protection of intellectual property (which is the product of creative effort) like patents or copyrights. The less developed countries, to the annoyance of the industrialized countries, have done relatively little to prevent their firms from utilizing foreign technology, even if this technology is patented. (Recall our discussion of the patent system in Chapter 27.) Their feeling is that the protection of intellectual property would give inventors and innovators an undesirable monopoly on advanced technology that could be used to extract high prices, as well as to impose unwarranted restrictions on the use of the technology. They deny that the protection of intellectual property would do much to aid their own development; instead, they argue that it would tend to prolong the period during which their per capita income is relatively low.

A proposition often advanced by the less developed countries is that knowledge should be made available at minimal cost to everyone since it is a common property of all. Because the development of the relatively impoverished countries of the world is a goal that benefits everyone, they say that the technology they need should be given to them at a low cost. Thus they often have relatively weak laws to protect intellectual property and less than diligent enforcement of the laws that exist.

As would be expected, the industrialized countries have expressed strong disagreement with these views. They argue that intellectual property rights must be respected to provide a fair return to the private investors who take the substantial risks involved in developing and commercializing a new technology. Unless such returns are forthcoming, the incentives for inventive and innovative activity will be impaired, to the detriment of all nations, rich or poor.

To illustrate the situation, consider South Korea, a country that has grown economically to the point where, by many definitions, it is no longer a less developed country. Chemical and pharmaceutical firms headquartered in the industrialized countries have complained that South Korea's patent protection has been inadequate. A revised Patent Act has been passed by South Korea which covers chemicals and pharmaceuticals, extends the patent term from 12 to 15 years, and doubles infringement penalties. Nonetheless, many observers seem to believe that South Korea will enforce the stronger patent protection sporadically, the threat of actions against its exports being important in this regard. In 1987–88, South Korea extended copyright protection to a wider range of works, and joined the Universal Copyright Convention.

Another case in point is Taiwan. Foreign firms have asserted that Taiwan's patent protection for chemicals and pharmaceuticals has been inadequate, and that there has been no unfair competition law dealing with false advertising, imitative product packaging, and inaccurate marks of origin. In 1987–88, a revised patent law was passed which extends full patent protection to chemical and pharmaceutical products. Also, firms unregistered in Taiwan can pursue trademark infringement cases in local courts, and copyright protection has been extended to computer software. Nonetheless, monetization of penalties allows offenders to continue to buy their way out of jail, and violators can file "invalidation claims" to delay court cases, making plaintiffs defend the legality of their patent and\or trademark.[1]

---

[1] For further discussion, see E. Mansfield, "Intellectual Property Rights, Technological Change, and Economic Growth," in M. Bloomfield and C. Walker (eds.), *Intellectual Property Rights and Capital Formation in the Next Decade*, University Press of America, 1988.

## ENTREPRENEURSHIP AND SOCIAL INSTITUTIONS

Yet another important reason why per capita income is so low in the less developed countries is that they lack entrepreneurs and favorable social institutions. This point was noted in a previous section but needs more discussion. In some LDCs there is a rigid social structure. One "knows one's place" and stays in it, people distrust and resist change, and things are done in the time-honored way they have always been done (as far as anyone can remember). No wonder these countries lack entrepreneurs! The basic social and political institutions discourage entrepreneurship. Moreover, these institutions also are at least partially responsible for the ineffective utilization of savings, relatively high birth rates, and difficulties in transferring technology noted above.

The governments of many less developed countries are relatively weak and unstable. It is difficult enough for any government to give these countries an effective tax system and a rational program of public expenditures, including proper provision for the highways, public utilities, communications, and other "social overhead capital" they need. But the problems are made even more difficult when the government is weak, unstable, and perhaps somewhat corrupt. Further, the population's value systems and attitudes sometimes do little to promote economic development. Willingness to work hard, punctually, and regularly, and an awareness of the future benefits of present sacrifice are sometimes absent.

## LACK OF NATURAL RESOURCES

Finally, it should also be pointed out that some of the LDCs have little in the way of natural resources. Moreover, technological change has made some of their resources less valuable, as in the case of synthetic rubber, which affected the market for natural rubber, an important natural resource of Malaya. But this is not true of all the less developed countries. Iran and Indonesia, among others, are endowed with oil, which (as members of the OPEC cartel) they are using to try to promote their affluence. In any event, the skimpiness of natural resources in some less developed countries does not mean that they are condemned to poverty. Neither Denmark nor Switzerland is endowed with great natural resources, but both are prosperous.

The important thing is how a country uses what it has. International trade allows a country to compensate, at least in part, for its deficiencies in natural resources. Thus, although some of the less developed countries have been dealt a poor hand by Mother Nature, this lack alone does not explain their poverty. They might have been more prosperous with more natural resources; but even with what they have, they might have done much better.

There are several ways for them to use their resources more effectively. In many of the less developed countries, a peasant may farm several strips of land that are very small and distant from one another, working a small patch here and a small patch there. Obviously, this procedure is very inefficient. If these small plots could be put together into larger farms, output and productivity could be increased. In other LDCs, huge farms are owned by landlords and worked by tenant farmers. This system too tends to be inefficient, because the tenant farmers have little incentive to increase productivity (since the extra output will accrue to the landlord) and the landlords have little incentive to invest in new technology (since they often fear that the tenant farmers will not know how to use the new equipment).

Land reform is a very lively—indeed an explosive—issue in many less developed countries, and one of the issues the Communists have frequently tried to exploit. Recall that agriculture is a very important part of the economy of most of the less developed countries. Thus the land is the

## EXAMPLE 34.1  ECONOMIC DEVELOPMENT WITH AN UNLIMITED LABOR SUPPLY

According to a famous theory put forth by Nobel Laureate W. Arthur Lewis of Princeton University, the supply curve of unskilled labor in some less developed countries is a horizontal line, as shown below. In other words, unlimited supplies of unskilled labor are available in this country at the existing wage rate, $OW$. Suppose that the value of the marginal product of each amount of unskilled labor in this country is as shown below. For example, the value of the marginal product (which equals the price of the product times labor's marginal product) is $L_1B$ when $OL_1$ workers are employed.

W. Arthur Lewis

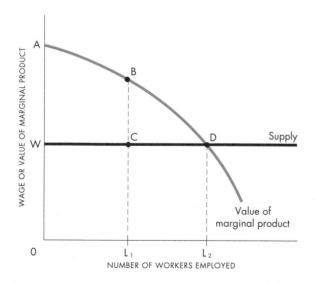

(a) How many unskilled workers will be employed in the country? (b) How much profit will be realized by hiring the $OL_1{}^{th}$ worker? (c) If firms invest their profit (from hiring the first, second, . . . , $OL_2{}^{th}$ workers) in plant and equipment, what effect will this have on the value-of-marginal-product curve? (d) If the value-of-

marginal-product curve shifts, will this affect the equilibrium wage rate?

### Solution

(a) $OL_2$ workers, since this is the point where the supply curve intersects the value-of-marginal-product curve. So long as the value of the marginal product of an extra worker exceeds his or her wage, it pays firms to hire the extra worker. Thus extra workers will be hired up to the point where employment is $OL_2$. (b) The profit earned from the hiring of each extra worker equals the difference between the value of this worker's marginal product and this worker's wage. Thus the profit realized by hiring the $OL_1{}^{th}$ worker equals $L_1B$ minus $OW$, or $CB$. (c) The value-of-marginal-product curve will shift to the right. With more plant and equipment, the marginal product of a particular amount of labor will increase. (d) No, because the value-of-marginal-product curve will still intersect the supply curve at a wage of $OW$.

major form of productive wealth. No wonder there is a bitter struggle in some countries over who is to own and work it.

## THE ROLE OF GOVERNMENT

There are several opinions on the role the governments of the less developed countries should play in promoting economic growth. Some people go so far as to say that these countries would fare best if they allowed market forces to work with a minimum of government interference. But the less developed countries themselves generally seem to believe that such a free enterprise system would produce results too slowly, if at all. Thus the prevailing view in the less developed countries is that the government must intervene—and on a large scale.

In some less developed countries—China, for example—the government exercises almost complete control over the economy. As we shall see in Chapter 35, China's economy is planned. The government makes the basic decisions on what is produced, how it is produced, and who gets it. But even in the non-Communist LDCs, such as India, the government makes many decisions on what sorts of investment projects will be undertaken, and it controls foreign exchange. And, needless to say, the government has the responsibility for providing the important social overhead capital—roads, public utilities, schools, and so on—that is so badly needed.

Further, the government may also foster social and political change. As the late Nobel laureate Simon Kuznets put it, "The problem of strategy is essentially the problem of how fast you can change an inadequate set of social and political institutions, without provoking a revolution internally, or losing allies and partners externally. The question is to know what institutions you want to change, and how."

Most economists would agree that the government has a very important role to play in promoting economic development. But there is a tendency to put less weight on the government's role than in the past. Experience has made it clear that some of the less developed countries are plagued by incompetent and corrupt government officials and by a plethora of bureaucratic red tape. Moreover, many governments have gone on spending sprees that have resulted in serious inflation. Even those who are very mistrustful of free markets find it difficult to put their complete faith in such governments, well-intentioned though they may be. Recent years have seen more and more emphasis on self-interest and individual action as contributors to growth. (If Adam Smith is peering down from the Great Beyond, he probably is smiling in agreement.) But this in no way denies the fact that governments have a key role to play.

## TEST YOURSELF

1. Between 1950 and 1967, the annual rate of growth of per capita national product was 5.3 percent in Taiwan, and 1.6 percent in India. Suggest as many hypotheses as you can to explain this difference.

2. In 1950, gross nonresidential investment was 9.8 percent of national product in Taiwan, and 7.4 percent of national product in India. In 1966, it was 16.7 percent of national product in Taiwan, and 13.8 percent of national product in India. Does this help to explain the difference in Question 1? Why, or why not?

3. Between 1950 and 1967, the annual rate of growth of population was 3.1 percent in Taiwan and

2.2 percent in India. Does this help to explain the difference in Question 1? Why, or why not?

4. Explain why the less developed countries have not adopted the advanced technology used in industrialized countries.

## BALANCED GROWTH

An important issue facing the governments of most less developed countries is the extent to which they want to maintain a balance between the agricultural and industrial sectors of the economy. That is, how much more rapidly should they expand industry than agriculture? According to some economists, less developed countries should invest heavily in industry, since the long-term trend of industrial prices is upward, relative to agricultural prices. In addition, advocates of unbalanced growth argue that the development of certain sectors of the economy will result in pressures for development elsewhere in the economy. Advocates of this approach point to the Soviet Union, which stressed industrialization in its growth strategy.

Other economists argue that industry and agriculture should be expanded at a more nearly equal rate. Successful industrial expansion requires agricultural expansion as well, because industry uses raw materials as inputs and because, as economic growth takes place, the people will demand more food. **Balanced growth** has other advantages. Various sectors of the economy are closely linked and an attempt to expand one sector in isolation is unlikely to succeed. Proponents of balanced growth deny that the long-term trend of industrial prices is upward, relative to agricultural prices. And to illustrate the wisdom of their approach, they cite as examples the United States and Britain, where industry and agriculture both expanded in the course of the development process.

### Increases in Industrialization

Without question, many less developed countries have expanded industry relative to agriculture. In some cases, such as India and Pakistan, it is generally agreed that more balance—more emphasis on agriculture—would have been preferable. Moreover, in many cases, the allocation of resources within industry could certainly have been improved. Countries sometimes put too much emphasis on substituting their own production—even when it is not efficient—for imports. Thus Chile prohibited the import of fully assembled cars to promote domestic production, but Chile's automobile plants were uneconomic.

One reason why the less developed countries tend to push industrialization is that they see heavy industrialization in the wealthier countries. The United States, Western Europe, Japan, and the USSR have lots of steel plants, oil refineries, chemical plants, and other kinds of heavy industry. It is easy for the less developed countries to jump to the conclusion that, if they want to become richer, they must become heavily industrialized too. It certainly seems sensible enough—until you think about the theory of comparative advantage. After all, if the less developed countries have a comparative advantage in areas other than heavy industry, they may do better to put more of their resources where their comparative advantage lies.

Another reason why the leaders of some less developed countries are fascinated by steel plants, airlines, and other modern industries is that they think such industries confer prestige on their countries and themselves. Such prestige may be costly. Given their current situation, many of these countries might be well advised to invest much of their scarce resources in promoting higher productivity in agriculture, where they have a comparative advantage. We are not saying that many of these countries should not attempt to industrialize. We *are* saying that some of them have pushed industrialization too far—and that many have pushed it in uneconomic directions.

## DEVELOPMENT PLANNING IN LESS DEVELOPED COUNTRIES

The governments of many LDCs have established **development plans** to specify targets or goals for the economy. In some countries, these goals are set forth in very specific, detailed form; in others, they are more generally formulated. An important purpose of these plans is to allocate scarce resources, such as capital, in order to achieve rapid economic growth (or whatever the country's social objectives may be). Thus, in India, estimates have been made of the amount of capital that would be generated internally, as well as the capital that could be imported from abroad. Then the plan attempted to set a system of priorities for the use of this capital.

Some plans are merely window dressing, full of bold words and little else. But others are the result of careful investigation and hard work. To be useful, a plan must set realistic goals, which take proper account of the country's resources, available capital, and institutions. An unrealistically ambitious plan, if actually put into effect, is likely to lead to inflation, while a plan that is too easily satisfied is likely to mean a less than optimal rate of economic growth.

A useful plan should specify the policies to be used to reach the plan's goals, as well as the goals themselves. It should also forecast carefully how the various components of gross national product will change over time, the extent to which inflationary pressures will develop, the adequacy of the supply of foreign exchange, and the effects of the development program on various regions and parts of the population.

Planning techniques have benefited from the application of many tools of modern economic analysis, among them linear programming and input–output analysis. Linear programming can be used to determine how resources should be allocated to maximize output, and input-output analysis can determine how much capacity there must be in various industries to satisfy certain consumption targets (see Appendices B and C of this book). These modern tools have undoubtedly helped in formulating development plans, but their importance should not be exaggerated. It would be a great mistake to think that making a good plan is merely a job for an electronic computer.

If the plan is realistic, it can be a useful tool, but unless it is implemented properly, it will achieve very little for the economy. How well it is implemented will depend on the government's ability to marshal resources through taxation and foreign aid, to work effectively with the private sector, and to pick productive public investment projects. In some countries, like India, "the plan" has sometimes become a political symbol, but in many others, planning has been politically less visible. Countries

# EXAMPLE 34.2    THE PUSH TOWARD INDUSTRIALIZATION

Governments of less developed countries sometimes force industrialization, even though many of their people would prefer a different strategy. Suppose that a particular country's production possibilities curve is as shown below:

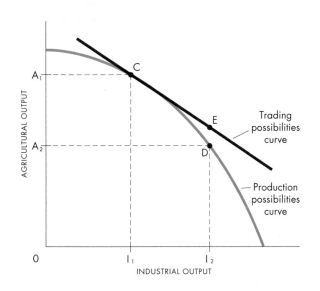

This country's government wants to increase its industrial output from $OI_1$ to $OI_2$.

(a) If its industrial output is increased in this way (and if the society remains on this production possibili-ties curve), what will be the cost to consumers? (b) How can the government push the society from point C to point D on the production possibilities curve? (c) Suppose that this country can trade its agricultural output for industrial goods in world markets, and that its trading possibilities curve (recall Chapter 17) is as shown at left. Is there a way to reduce the cost of obtaining the extra $(OI_2—OI_1)$ of industrial goods? If so, what is it? (d) If the price of agricultural goods rises relative to the price of industrial goods in world markets, how will this affect the trading possibilities curve? Will it affect the cost of obtaining the extra $(OI_2—OI_1)$ of industrial goods? If so, how?

## Solution

(a) Agricultural output will have to be reduced from $OA_1$ to $OA_2$. (b) It can subsidize production of industrial goods and tax consumption of agricultural goods. Or it can intervene directly to increase industrial output and reduce agricultural output. (c) The country can move from point C to point E by trading its agricultural goods for industrial goods in world markets. Since point E lies above point D, the cost (that is, the reduction in agricultural goods) of the extra industrial goods is less than at point D. (d) It will reduce the slope of the trading possibilities curve, which will be closer to horizontal. The cost of obtaining the extra industrial goods will fall, since point E will be raised.

---

where economic growth has been most rapid seem to have viewed "the plan" less as holy writ, and planning has tended to be more modest and low-keyed.

# PLANNING IN ACTION: THE CASE OF INDIA

Perhaps the best way to understand the operation of development plans is to look at the nature of a particular country's plans and the extent to which they have been fulfilled. Consider the interesting case of India, which has had a series of five-year plans.[3]

**FIRST FIVE-YEAR PLAN.** The First Five-Year Plan was for 1951–56. Its targets were to increase net investment in India from 5 to 6.75 percent of national income, to reduce income inequality, to cut the rate of population increase to 1 percent per year, and to lay the groundwork for a doubling of per capita output in a generation. To achieve these targets, the govern-

[3] It is worthwhile emphasizing that the development strategies of *small* LDCs, because of their necessarily greater reliance on foreign trade, must be quite different from that of *large* LDCs, like India.

ment relied heavily on capital formation. In particular, it sought to carry out many of the investment projects that had been discussed and planned under the British for 50 years or more. The First Five-Year Plan was accompanied by moderate growth. Per capita output grew by about 1.7 percent per year, and net investment rose from 5 to 8 percent of national income.

**SECOND FIVE-YEAR PLAN.**  At the beginning of 1956, the Indian Planning Commission published its Second Five-Year Plan, which called for much heavier investments—and more emphasis on investment in industry and mining, rather than agriculture and power—than the First Plan. Moreover, the Second Plan relied more heavily on deficit financing than did the First Plan, and devoted much more attention to the expansion of employment opportunities, since unemployment was a considerable problem. Unfortunately, the Second Plan ran into severe difficulties. One big problem was the loss of foreign exchange, as imports grew much more rapidly—and exports less rapidly—than expected. But perhaps more important was the fact that output did not grow as rapidly as the plan called for. By the end of the Second Five-Year Plan, all sectors of the economy, other than the service sector, were producing less than the planned targets. Nonetheless, per capita output grew about 1.8 percent per year.

**THIRD FIVE-YEAR PLAN.**  India's Third Five-Year Plan—for 1961-66—involved bigger investments and somewhat more emphasis on agriculture than the Second Plan. Responding to the fact that agricultural imports had been much higher than expected under the Second Plan, the Third Plan called for more investment in agriculture. Unfortunately, however, agricultural production during the Third Plan did not come up to expectations. Indeed, India might have experienced a serious famine in 1966 if it had not received substantial food imports from the United States. During the course of the Third Plan, India did increase the percentage of national income devoted to investment from 11 to 14 percent, but a substantial proportion of its investment was financed by foreign aid. Unfortunately, India's output grew by one-sixth, instead of the planned one-third, during the Third Plan, and there was little or no increase in per capita output.

**FOURTH FIVE-YEAR PLAN.**  Although the failure of the Third Plan was due in considerable measure to India's involvement in two wars and two bad harvests, it nonetheless shook many Indians' confidence in the planning process. There was a three-year delay before the Fourth Five-Year Plan was unveiled, and its political significance was played down. The Fourth Plan shifted the emphasis to agricultural development, including irrigation and fertilizers; it stressed a large birth control program; and it called for a 5 1/2 percent increase per year in national output, as well as further increases in investment. The Fourth Plan put somewhat more emphasis on the price system and somewhat less on detailed planning. In practice, however, the latter changes seemed slow to occur.

**FROM 1975 TO 1991.**  In 1975, when the late Prime Minister Indira Gandhi declared a national emergency, she claimed that many of the stern measures taken at that time were designed to help improve India's economic condition. She put forth a 20-Point Economic Program which emphasized the reduction of inflation, the encouragement of agriculture, and the reduction of the birth rate. Mrs. Gandhi's program of sterilization (sometimes forced) caused considerable resentment, and was one factor in her defeat at the polls in 1977. India's Janata party, which won the election over Mrs. Gandhi, promised to limit the role of centralized economic

Bokaro power station on the Konar River, India

planning, and to emphasize agriculture and labor-intensive manufacturing in rural areas. In line with this objective, the Sixth Five-Year Plan, put forth in 1978, allocated 20 to 25 percent of the total investment outlay to labor-intensive industrial projects. However, many observers questioned whether the plan's targets were entirely realistic.

During the early 1980s, the Indian economy continued to experience problems. Many industrial goals were not met. India's oil import bill ate up 80 percent of its export earnings. The Indians went to the International Monetary Fund and the World Bank for massive loans. The Seventh Five-Year Plan, put forth in 1984, called for total investment of $320 billion (including $180 billion of public investment) and an annual rate of economic growth of about 5 percent. In 1987, India experienced a drought (described as the worst of the century) which ruined the summer crops in much of the country and the economic growth rate fell to 1-2 percent.

In 1991, India's foreign exchange resources were strained by the war between the United States (and its allies) and Iraq, because of disrupted oil supplies and other factors. Prime Minister P.V. Narasimha Rao said India would welcome new foreign investment and try to remove "the cobwebs" that hindered its economy. Although India was staggering under a foreign debt burden of more than $70 billion, its officials vowed that it would not default on its loans. Clearly, the Indian economy has been buffeted by many difficulties.

Inspecting maize field production during India's "green revolution"

## CHOOSING INVESTMENT PROJECTS IN LESS DEVELOPED COUNTRIES

A crucial problem that any less developed country must face is how the available capital should be invested. Countless investment projects could be undertaken—roads, irrigation projects, power plants, improvements in agricultural equipment, and so on. Faced with this menu of alternatives, how should a country choose?

A procedure often used is to accept projects resulting in high output per unit of capital invested. That is, projects are ranked by the ratio of the value of the output they produce to the capital they require. If a project yields $2 million worth of output per year and requires $1 million of capital, its ratio would be 2. Projects with high values of this ratio are accepted. This procedure, which is crude but sensible, is based on the correct idea that capital is the really scarce resource in many of the less developed countries. It is aimed at maximizing the output to be derived from a certain amount of capital. However, a better technique for choosing projects is the concept of rate of return, which is used by profit-maximizing firms to choose among alternative investment opportunities.

A less developed country, like a firm, can compute the rate of return from each investment opportunity. That is, it can estimate the rate of interest that will be obtained from each investment. Then it, like a firm, should choose the projects with the highest rates of return.[4] For example, suppose that a less developed country must decide which of two irrigation projects to carry out. Government analysts estimate that the rate of return is 30 percent for the first project and 18 percent for the second pro-

[4] More sophisticated criteria are presented in more advanced texts. Even for a firm, the above criterion is oversimplified, although, for important classes of problems, it generally gives the correct answer.

ject. Based on these results, it appears that the first project is the better investment.

In computing the rate of return from each investment project, it is necessary to attach values to the resources it uses and to the returns it produces. At first glance, it may seem adequate to use market prices of inputs and outputs as these values. Thus, if unskilled labor's market price is $.10 an hour, this would be the value attached to unskilled labor. Unfortunately, there are some important pitfalls in using market prices in this way. In particular, *market prices of inputs in the less developed countries often do not indicate social costs properly*. Although the market price of unskilled labor may be $.10 an hour, there may be lots of unskilled labor doing essentially nothing in the countryside, with the result that the social cost—the true opportunity cost—of using such labor is zero, not $.10 an hour. Moreover, *the market prices of some outputs may not indicate their social worth*. Because of tariffs and quotas, domestic prices may differ significantly from world prices, which may be closer to the appropriate price for some analyses of this sort.

Thus, when computing each project's rate of return, it is important to make proper adjustments so that inputs are valued at their social cost and outputs are valued at their social worth. This is easier said than done, but even crude adjustments in the right direction can be worthwhile.

# FOREIGN AID

The plight of the less developed countries is of concern to Americans, both because it is good morality and good policy to help them. From the point of view of humanitarianism, the United States and the other rich nations have a moral responsibility to help the poor nations. From the point of view of our self-interest, the promotion of growth in the less developed countries should help to preserve and encourage political and international stability and to make them more effective trading partners.

How can the United States be of help? With regard to many of their problems, we can do relatively little. But one thing that we can do is to provide badly needed capital. Responding to that need, we have given and lent a substantial amount of capital to the less developed countries in the past 30 years.

## U.S. Aid Programs

American financial assistance took several forms in the period after World War II. In the immediate postwar period, the primary objective was to help the populations of the war-ravaged countries and to get the European economies back on their feet. The United Nations Relief and Rehabilitation Administration (UNRRA) provided $4 billion of food, clothing, and medical services, about three-quarters of which was financed by the United States. In addition, other forms of relief, aid, and loans were extended. In all, the United States provided about $17 billion in aid between the war's end and 1948, about half in loans and about half in grants.

By the early 1950s, Europe's economy was in pretty good shape, but this did not spell the end of our foreign aid programs. On the contrary, much of our aid shifted toward the less developed nations. Table 34.6 shows the total amount the United States spent on foreign aid between

## Table 34.6
## U.S. Foreign Economic and Military Aid Program, 1946–88

| YEAR | ECONOMIC LOANS | ECONOMIC GRANTS | MILITARY LOANS | MILITARY GRANTS | TOTAL |
|------|------|------|------|------|------|
| | | | (BILLIONS OF DOLLARS) | | |
| 1946-52 | 8.5 | 22.7 | — | 3.8 | 35.0 |
| 1953-61 | 5.9 | 18.2 | 0.2 | 24.1 | 48.3 |
| 1962-65 | 8.3 | 8.7 | 0.4 | 8.1 | 25.6 |
| 1966-69 | 7.1 | 9.3 | 1.2 | 9.6 | 27.1 |
| 1970 | 1.4 | 2.3 | 0.1 | 3.0 | 6.8 |
| 1971 | 1.3 | 2.1 | 0.7 | 3.9 | 8.1 |
| 1972 | 1.6 | 2.3 | 0.6 | 4.8 | 9.2 |
| 1973 | 1.4 | 2.7 | 0.6 | 5.2 | 9.9 |
| 1974 | 1.2 | 2.8 | 1.4 | 3.7 | 9.0 |
| 1975 | 1.7 | 3.2 | 0.8 | 1.6 | 7.2 |
| 1976 | 1.8 | 2.1 | 1.4 | 1.3 | 6.6 |
| 1976TQ[a] | 0.8 | 1.1 | 0.5 | 0.2 | 2.6 |
| 1977 | 2.1 | 3.5 | 1.4 | 0.8 | 7.8 |
| 1978 | 2.5 | 4.1 | 1.6 | 0.8 | 9.0 |
| 1979 | 1.9 | 5.2 | 5.2 | 1.6 | 13.8 |
| 1980 | 2.0 | 5.6 | 1.4 | 0.7 | 9.7 |
| 1981 | 1.5 | 5.8 | 2.5 | 0.7 | 10.6 |
| 1982 | 1.4 | 6.7 | 3.1 | 1.1 | 12.3 |
| 1983 | 1.6 | 7.0 | 3.9 | 1.7 | 14.2 |
| 1984 | 1.6 | 7.4 | 4.4 | 2.1 | 15.5 |
| 1985 | 1.6 | 10.7 | 2.4 | 3.4 | 18.1 |
| 1986 | 1.3 | 9.6 | 2.0 | 3.9 | 16.7 |
| 1987 | 1.1 | 8.2 | 1.0 | 4.1 | 14.5 |
| 1988 | 0.9 | 7.9 | 0.8 | 4.1 | 13.6 |

[a] Transition quarter, July-September 1976. In the earlier data, the year ends June 30; in the later data, it ends September 30.

1946 and 1988. During this period, we spent over $300 billion—a huge sum by any standard. About 40 percent of these expenditures have been for military purposes, about 60 percent have been for economic purposes. No nation has ever contributed as much to the economic development of poorer countries as we have.

Much of this aid has been in the form of loans or grants that must be spent on American goods and services. Also, much of it consisted of our giving away part of what were then surplus stocks of food. (Recall the agricultural programs discussed in Chapter 31.)

In addition, the United States has established various kinds of technical assistance programs designed to help the less developed countries borrow some of our technology, administrative techniques, medical knowledge, educational methods, and so on. The emphasis frequently is on training people from the less developed countries to the point where they can teach others in their own country. Often the costs of these programs are shared by the United States and by the recipient of the aid. Most observers seem to believe that these technical assistance programs have been worthwhile and successful.

## Other U.S. Assistance to LDCs

Some other aspects of American policy are also important, although they are not aid programs. For one thing, the United States and other developed countries can help the LDCs by reducing trade barriers, thus allowing them to increase their national incomes through trade. However, it seems unlikely that trade alone can substitute for aid, and the situation is clouded by the trade barriers the LDCs themselves have been erecting to protect their own industry. Another way that the United States can help is through private investment. American corporations have invested many billions of dollars in the less developed countries. To the less developed countries, this is a significant source of capital.

Besides providing capital, the multinational corporations have also been a source of needed technology. However, these firms have faced much more difficult problems in transmitting technology to less developed countries than to industrialized countries. Many of the techniques of the multinational firms are not very well suited to the less developed countries, with their plentiful unskilled labor, few skills, and little capital. Moreover, there is sometimes little incentive for multinational firms to adapt their products, production techniques, and marketing methods to the conditions present in developing countries. And when they do manage to make a technological transplant, its effects are often restricted to narrow segments of the economy. Still further, it should be noted that the multinational firms are often viewed with some suspicion and fear by the host governments.

## Controversies over Foreign Aid

For many years, foreign aid has been a controversial subject in the United States. Many critics argue that the money could better be spent at home to alleviate domestic poverty. They claim that other industrialized countries—like Germany and Japan—should contribute a bigger share of the aid to the less developed countries. And they assert that our aid programs have not had much impact on the less developed countries so far. Liberals object to our giving aid to governments charged with serious violation of human rights. Conservatives are disturbed that some aid channeled through international organizations may go to Marxist governments.

Many suggestions have been made for ways to improve the effectiveness of our foreign aid. One prominent suggestion is that we go further in concentrating the bulk of our aid on a relatively few countries—those that really want to do what is necessary to develop, that can use the money well, and that are important from the point of view of size and international politics. Obviously, adopting this suggestion means reducing aid to some other countries. Another suggestion is that, rather than impose political conditions on aid, we should give money with no strings attached. This suggestion entails a great deal more than economics. To evaluate it, one must decide what the goals of foreign aid should be. To what extent should it be aimed at raising the standard of living of the world's population, whatever the effect on the United States? To what extent should it be aimed at furthering American goals and American foreign policies? In practice, foreign aid has been bound up closely with our foreign policy. Given the political facts of life, it is difficult to see how it could be otherwise.

# CAN ARGENTINA, BRAZIL, AND MEXICO PAY THEIR DEBTS?

During the 1980s, the financial pages of the newspapers (and the front pages and editorials as well) were full of stories concerning the very severe debt problems of Argentina, Brazil, and Mexico (which together owed over $200 billion). In 1982, Mexico announced that it was unable to meet its obligations to foreign creditors. The U.S. government responded by mounting a rescue operation involving banks (to whom much of the debt was owed) and the International Monetary Fund. Subsequently, Brazil and Argentina also found it necessary to look for debt relief from their creditors, and ways were found to keep them afloat, at least temporarily.

The major American banks have lent an enormous amount of money to these countries. For example, Manufacturers Hanover, a major New York bank, lent over $1 billion—40 percent of its capital—to Argentina alone. During the 1970s, the banks increased their loans to these countries at a rapid rate. Because their exports were growing fast, the banks felt that these countries would be able to earn the dollars to pay off the loans. However, during 1980-82, the real rate of interest increased, thus increasing the interest payments on these loans. Moreover, the 1980-82 world recession reduced the export earnings of the debtor countries. Because of these and other factors, including major mistakes made by the debtor nations themselves, each of these nations was unable to meet its financial obligations.

Should these countries be granted new loans? According to some observers, this is throwing good money after bad, since the loans will never be repaid. In their opinion, the debt should be written off, at least in part. But others have argued that the problem is only temporary, and that continued lending is justified. Among other things, they stress the importance of avoiding unnecessary damage to the economies of the debtor nations. The banks to whom the debts are owed are anxious, of course, to collect as much as they can, while the debtor countries want to have the interest rates and fees on the loans reduced.

Should these debts be forgiven, at least in part? According to William Cline of the Institute for International Economics,

> none of the four key debtor countries—Mexico, Brazil, Argentina, or Venezuela—can be described as insolvent

and in need of bankruptcy treatment. Brazil's current suspension of bank payments results not from external shock but from internal mismanagement [in 1986]. . . . Not only is there no immediate need for widespread debt relief, but its long-term benefits are also doubtful. Debt forgiveness is incompatible with improving the debtor country's creditworthiness and returning the country to normal access to international capital markets.[1]

On the other hand, others like Harvard's Jeffrey Sachs argue that "the continued insistence on full debt payments could threaten the new democracies in Argentina, Brazil, Peru, and elsewhere that are saddled with the financial overhang of the preceding military regimes."[2] In his view, "the existing debt: (1) poses an enormous fiscal burden for most of the debtor countries, and thereby contributes to high inflation and macroeconomic instability; and (2) scares off potential new creditors, who might be willing to lend for profitable new projects were it not for the huge stock of old debt."[3]

In 1989, the Bush administration put forth the Brady Initiative (named after Treasury Secretary

[1] William Cline, "A Quick Fix That Would Be Harmful," *New York Times,* August 9, 1987, p. 2F.
[2] Jeffrey Sachs, "It's the Right Time to Offer Real Relief," *New York Times,* August 9, 1987, p. 2F.
[3] Jeffrey Sachs, "International Policy Coordination: The Case of the Developing Country Debt Crisis," in M. Feldstein (ed.), *International Economic Cooperation,* NBER Summary Report, 1987, p. 21.

Nicholas Brady), which emphasizes the reduction of this debt and of the interest costs by the commercial banks. According to the Council of Economic Advisers, "the Brady Initiative provides a framework for negotiated debt and debt-service reduction, on a case-by-case basis, to countries committed to implementing requisite economic reforms [aimed at stimulating the countries' economic growth]."[4] In 1989, agreements of this sort were worked out with Mexico, the Philippines, and Costa Rica.

[4] Council of Economic Advisers, *Annual Report,* Washington, D.C.: Government Printing Office, 1990.

# THE WORLD BANK

Another source of capital is the ***World Bank.*** In 1944, late in World War II, the major economic powers agreed to establish the International Bank for Reconstruction and Development, also known as the World Bank. Although its first loans were for postwar reconstruction, the bank's principal function now is to make long-term loans to the less developed countries—in Latin America, Asia, and elsewhere. They desperately need capital, while the rich, economically advanced countries have capital to lend. The World Bank's purpose was to channel funds from rich nations to poor, thus supplementing private investment, which was often scared off by the apparent risks. More specifically, the major economic powers contributed a certain amount of money to form the bank, with each country's share determined by its economic size. About one-third of the total was put up by the United States. The Soviet Union helped organize the World Bank, but later declined to join.

Now about 50 years old, the World Bank still makes loans to people or governments with sound investment projects who have been unable to get private financing. Moreover, by floating its own bond issues it can lend money above and beyond what was originally put up by the major powers. In other words, the World Bank sells its own IOUs, which are considered safe by investors because they are guaranteed by member countries. In addition, it helps less developed countries get loans from private lenders by insuring the loans. That is, the World Bank can tell the lender that if the loan goes sour, it will see that the lender is paid back.

This movement of capital from the capital-rich nations to the capital-poor nations should prove beneficial for both rich and poor. The poor countries are enabled to carry out projects that will result in economic returns high enough to pay off the lender with interest and have some net benefits left over. The rich countries are enabled to invest their capital at a higher rate of return than they could obtain at home. Thus both parties benefit, as long as the loans are economically sound.

The World Bank has established the ***International Development Agency*** to make "soft" loans, as well as the ***International Finance Corporation,*** which lends to foreign development banks. An increased percentage of the bank's financing has been channeled through these two agencies.

World Bank "Equal Access" program in the Upper Volta

The bank's activities have grown substantially; in 1965, its loan authorizations were about $1 billion; in 1974, they were about $4 billion; and in 1979 its loans exceeded $10 billion. Nonetheless, despite its achievements, many economists believe that in the past the World Bank has sometimes been too conservative and that it should have been willing to take bigger risks. Since the late 1960s, when Robert McNamara became its head, the bank has become less conservative in this respect.

By 1984, a substantial proportion of its loans were aimed at helping the LDCs with their balance-of-payments problems; and there were reports of a clash between A. W. Clausen (who succeeded McNamara as head of the bank) and the Reagan administration over whether such loans should be restricted. In the administration's view, the bank should concentrate on the provision of financing for development projects. Subsequently, Clausen was replaced by Barber Conable, a former New York congressman and University of Rochester professor, who upgraded the bank's image in Congress and obtained a large infusion of capital to support lending and technical assistance programs. In 1991, President Bush named Lewis Preston, a retired banker, to be Conable's successor.

## TEST YOURSELF

1. "It is always a good idea for less developed countries to substitute their own production for imports. This is the only way they can become economically independent." Comment and evaluate.

2. "A substantial economic advance in the less developed countries may require modification in the available stock of material technology, and probably even greater innovations in political and social structure." What does this mean? If it is correct, what are the implications for the less developed countries? For the developed countries?

3. "Foreign aid for economic development has a chance to be successful only within relatively narrow limits which are raised by cultural and political conditions impervious to direct outside influence." Do you agree? If this is correct, what are the implications for the less developed countries? For the developed countries?

4. Why don't some market prices of inputs correspond closely to social costs in less developed countries? Give examples. What implications does this have for the economic analysis of investment projects in LDCs?

## SUMMARY

1. A country is defined here as a less developed country if its per capita income is less than $5,000. Well over half of the world's population live in the less developed countries, which include many of the countries in Asia, Africa, and Latin America. In recent years, there has been a great increase in the expectations and material demands of the people in these countries.

2. The less developed countries vary greatly, but they generally devote most of their resources to the production of food, are composed of two economies (one market-oriented, the other subsistence), and often have relatively weak, unstable governments and a relatively high degree of income inequality.

3. One obvious reason why income per capita is so low is that the people in the less developed countries have so little capital to work with. The less developed countries, with their low incomes, do not save much, they lack entrepreneurs, and the climate for investment (domestic or foreign) often is not good.

4. Some less developed countries suffer from overpopulation; and as total output has increased, these gains have been offset by population increases. Modern medical techniques have reduced the death rate, while the birth rate has remained high. The result is a population explosion.

5. Another very important reason why per capita income is so low in these countries is that they often use backward

technology. The transfer of technology from one country to another is not as easy as it sounds, particularly when the recipient country has an uneducated population and little capital. Also, these countries lack favorable social institutions and sometimes have few natural resources.

6. An important issue facing the governments of most less developed countries is the extent to which they want to promote a balance between the agricultural and industrial sectors of the economy. Without question, the LDCs are expanding industry relative to agriculture. In some cases, such as India and Pakistan, more balance—less emphasis on industry, more on agriculture—would have been preferable. Moreover, some countries have put too much emphasis on substituting their own production for imports, even when their own production is uneconomic.

7. Many of the less developed countries have established development plans that specify targets or goals for the economy and policies designed to attain them. One criterion often used to determine whether a given investment project should be accepted or rejected is the ratio of the value of the output produced to the capital used. Only projects with high values of this ratio are accepted.

8. A more sophisticated criterion is the rate of return from the project, the method used by firms in capital budgeting. When computing each project's rate of return, it is important that inputs be valued at their social cost and that outputs be valued at their social worth.

9. The United States has been involved in a number of major aid programs to help the less developed countries. In recent years, these aid programs have sometimes come under attack, because of a feeling in Congress and elsewhere that they have not been working well. The World Bank also has channeled major amounts of capital into the less developed countries.

## CONCEPTS FOR REVIEW

**Less developed country**

**Market-oriented economy**

**Subsistence economy**

**Foreign aid**

**Population explosion**

**Green revolution**

**Balanced growth**

**Development plan**

**World Bank**

# THE COMMUNIST COUNTRIES AND MARXISM

IN THE 1990s, countries that have had communist regimes, such as the Soviet Union and China, have been in a state of serious economic turmoil, as some forces push them toward more liberalization and decentralization, and other forces push them in the opposite direction. Due in part to this turmoil, everybody talks and reads about **communism.** You hear the word frequently on television and see it frequently in the newspapers, but if you really know what it means, you are in the minority. It is a safe bet that most people have only a vague and distorted idea of what communism is, although about a third of the world's population has lived under Communist rule. The Soviet Union, China, Yugoslavia, Cuba, and many other countries have been Communist. You should know something about the nature of communism to understand what is going on in a large part of the world.

In this chapter we describe and analyze the nature and workings of the economic system in various countries that have had communist governments. After a brief discussion of the doctrines of Karl Marx, the intellectual father of communism, we describe how the Soviet economy has worked. Since economic planning has played a major role in its functioning, the USSR's planning system is described in some detail. Next, we turn to the economy of China, and to some of the major differences between communism and democratic socialism. Finally, we describe briefly the nature of radical economics, a recent, and still very small, movement in the United States that draws heavily on Marx's views.

## THE DOCTRINES OF KARL MARX

### The Class Struggle

The name Karl Marx probably makes you think of revolutionaries meeting by candlelight in damp cellars to plot the overthrow of nineteenth-century European governments. If this is the picture you associate with the name, you are quite right! Karl Marx was a revolutionary who wanted the masses to revolt against the existing social order. In 1848, he and Friedrich Engels published the famous *Communist Manifesto,* the spirit of which is given by its closing lines:

> Communists . . . openly declare that their ends can be attained only by the forcible overthrow of all existing social conditions. Let the ruling classes tremble at a Communist revolution. The proletarians have nothing to lose but their chains. They have a world to win. Workers of the world, unite!

This is stirring language, no doubt about it. But why did Marx preach revolution, and what goals do the communists want to achieve?

To understand their aims, it is helpful to look at Marx's famous treatise, *Capital* (the first part of which was published in 1867), which states much of his economic and political thought. According to Marx, the fundamental causes of political and social change are socioeconomic factors. Changes in the ways goods and services are produced and distributed — and in the ways in which people enter into "productive relations" with one another (the feudal lord with the serf under feudalism, or the capitalist with the worker under capitalism) — are responsible for the great political and social movements of history. History can be viewed as a series of class struggles. In ancient times, the struggle was between masters and slaves. In feudal times, it was between lords and serfs. And in modern times, it is between the **capitalists,** who own the means of production, and the workers, or **proletariat.**

According to Marx, every economic system — ancient, feudal, or modern — develops certain defects or internal contradictions, which eventually cause it to give way to a new system. As the old system begins to weaken, the new system gains strength. Thus the feudal system grew out of the ancient system, and the modern system grew out of the feudal system. In Marx's view, *the struggle between the capitalists and the proletariat will eventually result in the defeat of the capitalists. This will set the stage for a new economic system — socialism, a transitional phase toward communism.* Communism, according to Marx, is the ultimate, perfect form of economic system.

Karl Marx

## The Theory of Value and Wages

The reasons for Marx's belief that in modern times there must be a struggle between capitalists and workers lie in his theory of value and wages. *According to Marx, the **value** of any commodity — that is, its price relative to other commodities — is determined by the amount of labor time used in its manufacture.* In other words, if a shirt requires twice as much labor time to produce as a tie, its price is twice that of a tie. By labor time, Marx meant both the amount of labor used in making a commodity and the amount of labor time "congealed" in the machinery used to make the commodity. According to Marx, wages tend to equal the lowest level consistent with the subsistence of the workers, because capitalists, driven by the profit motive, pay the lowest wage they can.

Combining his theory of value and his theory of wages, Marx concluded that workers produce a **surplus value** — a value above and beyond the subsistence wage they receive — which is taken by the capitalists. This surplus value arises because the capitalists make the workers labor for longer hours than are required to produce an amount of output equal to their wage. Consider the worker who may be made to work 10 hours a day, even though her output in 6 hours equals the value of her wage. The output produced in the remaining 4 hours is surplus value.

According to Marx, surplus value is what makes the capitalist world tick. Indeed, the reason why capitalists engage in production is to make this surplus value, which they steal from the workers. Capitalists also use some of it to purchase new capital. Thus capital formation, in Marx's view, comes about as a consequence of surplus value. If the capitalist class is exploiting the workers in the way Marx visualized, it is not difficult to see why he felt that a class struggle between capitalists and workers was inevitable, and even easier to see why he was on the workers' side.

## Marx's Vision of the Future

In Marx's view, capitalism would eventually reveal certain fundamental weaknesses that would hasten its demise. As more and more capital is accumulated, Marx felt that the profit rate would be driven down, that unemployment would increase (because of a rise in technological unemployment), that business cycles would become more severe (depressions becoming more devastating), and that monopoly would grow more widespread. As these developments imposed greater and greater hardships on the working class, the chance of revolution would increase. Eventually the workers, recognizing that they "have nothing to lose but their chains," would throw off the yoke of capitalism.

However, Marx did not visualize an immediate progression to communism. Instead, he saw socialism as a way station on the road to communism. *Socialism would be a "dictatorship of the proletariat."* The workers would rule. Specifically, they would control the government, which, according to Marx, is merely a tool of the propertied class under capitalism. Moreover, the socialist government would own the means of production—the factories, mines, and equipment. Under socialism each person would receive an amount of income related to the amount he or she produced.

Finally, after an unspecified length of time, Marx felt that socialism would give way to communism, his ideal system. Communism would be a classless society, everyone working, and no one owning capital or exploiting the other person. Under communism, the state would become obsolete and wither away. The principle of income distribution would be "from each according to his ability, to each according to his needs." Marx was a visionary and a social prophet, and communism was his promised land, the ultimate goal for which he prodded the workers to revolt—and the land into which the forces of history would ultimately propel them.

## Criticisms of Marx

Since Marx's doctrines have captured the imagination of huge numbers of people, and hundreds of millions have marched under his banners, it is clear that Marx was a remarkable success as a social philosopher and political activist. But what about Marx the economist? Most economists feel that his economic theories have basic flaws, and that many of his economic predictions have gone badly astray. Although there is almost universal admiration for the power and originality of his mind, few economists in the non-Communist world buy his economic doctrines.

Specifically, there are the following problems with his theories:

*1. His labor theory of value simply will not hold water.* As we have seen in previous chapters, the price of a commodity depends on non-labor costs as well as labor costs. In particular, capital, land, and entrepreneurship contribute to production. Moreover, the price of a commodity depends on the demand for it as well as on its costs. (You will recall that price is determined by the intersection of the demand curve and the supply curve.)

*2. Marx's subsistence theory of wages has long been discredited.* It simply isn't true that wages are set at the subsistence level. Far from being barely sufficient to keep the worker alive, wages in the United States are high enough to provide the typical worker with a car, television, travel, and a variety of other conveniences. Further, Marx's prediction that the working class would experience greater and greater misery has not been fulfilled. On the contrary, the standard of living of workers in the West has increased at a remarkable rate in the century since Marx wrote *Capital*.

*3. His prediction that the rate of profit would fall has been wrong.* Instead, the rate of profit has moved up and down, with no clear trend in either direction. And his prediction of greater warfare between capitalists and workers has not materialized either. On the contrary, workers have tended to buy shares in corporations, thus joining the capitalist class. And the lines of demarcation between the working class and the capitalist class have been blurred, not accentuated, by time.

Nonetheless, despite these and other flaws in his theories, Marx was a very important figure in economics. He recognized some of the most important problems of capitalism—in particular the problems of unemployment, income inequality, and monopoly power—and analyzed these problems forcefully and originally. One need not agree with his ideas, or sympathize with some of his followers, to recognize his remarkable talents.

# THE SOVIET ECONOMY

## Communism in the USSR

The economy of the Soviet Union provides an important example of the application of Marxian theories. By the beginning of the twentieth century, **Marxism** was an international political force of some significance. In 1917, a Marxist-oriented party established itself in Russia. This was the first time any major country went communist. With V. I. Lenin at its helm, the Communist party overthrew the Russian government in November 1917, and set up the Union of Soviet Socialist Republics several years later. The stated goal of the party was to establish Marxian socialism—and eventually communism—in the USSR. When Lenin died in 1924, his place was taken by Josef Stalin, who ruled until his death in 1953. Since the USSR became by far the most economically advanced and the militarily strongest Communist country, we need to understand how its economy has worked.

Two characteristics of the Soviet economy should be stressed at the outset:

*1. Although Marx seemed to want the state to wither away, the Soviet government was for many years a remarkably hardy perennial.* The Kremlin's influence over Russian life is well known. Power has been centralized in the hands of a relatively few top officials who have made the big decisions about what is produced, how it is to be produced, and who is to receive how much. This contrasts with capitalist economies like ours, where these decisions are made largely in the marketplace.

*2. In accord with Marx's views, most productive resources in the Soviet Union have been publicly owned.* The government has owned the factories, mines, equipment, and so on. This too is quite different from the situation in the United States, where most productive resources are privately owned. Specifically, the Soviet government has owned practically all industry, most retail and wholesale stores, and most urban housing. Some farms have been government-owned, but most have been collective farms. The principal case of private ownership in the Soviet Union has been the small strip of land each family on a collective farm is allowed to work for itself. In addition, people have been allowed to own furniture, clothing, utensils, and sometimes houses.

## SOVIET ECONOMIC PLANNING

The Soviet Union's central planners have decided what the country will produce. How have they gone about making these decisions, what steps have they followed, and who has been involved in this process? Before trying to answer these questions, it is important to recognize that the procedures followed by the central planners have changed from time to time as they have recognized their mistakes and tried to rectify them. Planning and controlling a vast economy like the Soviet Union's is enormously complicated. In the period immediately after the Russian Revolution of 1917, the Communists made some whopping mistakes, but, as time went on, the planners became better able to carry out their jobs.

This is the general procedure that evolved. First, the principal officials of the Communist party made the fundamental decisions as to how much output would be allocated for consumption and how much for investment, which industries would be expanded and which would be cut back. Once these decisions were made, people at a lower level decided the details concerning how various plants should be operated. Then these decisions were transmitted to and carried out by managers, engineers, and workers. This decision-making process was clearly very centralized. During the 1960s, the Soviets began to experiment with greater decentralization, delegating more of the planning to the individual plants and industries, and doing less of it centrally. But these reforms met with resistance, as we shall see below.

Several groups have been involved in planning. The top officials of the Communist party have set the overall goals for the economy. These goals have generally been enunciated in a *five-year plan,* showing where the economy should be in five years. For example, in the Soviet Union's Twelfth Five-Year Plan (for 1986–90), one goal was to increase investment in the energy sector by about 35 percent (about 7 percent per year). When the broad goals have been decided, the detailed production plans have been drawn up by *Gosplan,* the State Planning Commission. Gosplan has obtained enormous amounts of data from the ministries responsible for the performance of particular industries. These data describe production capacities of various productive units and available productive resources. On this basis, Gosplan has made up a tentative production plan.

Once Gosplan's tentative plan has been formulated, a host of other groups have entered the picture. A number of ministries, each concerned with a particular industry, have reported to Gosplan in the Soviet administrative hierarchy. These ministries have reviewed Gosplan's tentative plan, as have individual plant managers. The purpose of this evaluation has been to make sure that the plan is realistic and feasible. Some plant managers have argued that the amount they are asked to produce is too high or that the amount of labor and materials they are allocated is too low. Negotiations take place, and suggestions for revision are sent back to Gosplan. Eventually Gosplan has produced the final five-year plan.

## Economic Planning: A Simple Illustration

The job faced by the Soviet planners has been difficult and complex. Unless you have some appreciation of how tough it has been, you cannot understand the difficulties any planned economy must face. Suppose you are handed the job of planning the performance of a small economy consisting of a chemical industry, a coal industry, and an electric power industry. To produce electric power, one needs coal, chemicals, electric power, and labor as inputs. To produce coal, one needs electric power, coal, and labor as inputs. To produce chemicals, one needs chemicals and labor as inputs. Suppose that the country's political rulers have said that in five years they want the country to consume $100 million of electric power, $50 million of coal, and $50 million of chemicals.

It is not easy to decide what production targets to establish for each industry. For one thing the output set for one industry must depend on the output set for another industry because each industry uses another's output. Thus, if you are not careful, one industry will be unable to achieve its target because another industry has produced too little. Suppose that each industry uses the products of the other industries in the proportions shown in Table 35.1. (The second column of figures, for example, states that every dollar's worth of coal requires $.30 worth of electric power, $.10 worth of coal, and $.60 worth of labor.) Under these circumstances, what should the production targets be? The answer isn't obvious. Try it and see. (It can be shown that the production targets must be as follows. In five years, $144 million of coal, $159 million of electric power, and $818 million of chemicals must be produced. For a proof, see pp. A16–A17.)

This illustration gives you some inkling of the problems faced by the Soviet planners—but only an inkling. Our illustration has only three industries, while in fact the Russians have had to deal with thousands. In the illustration, the input-output coefficients (in Table 35.1) were assumed known. In fact, these coefficients change over time and are not very accurately known. In this simple illustration, we can work out the production target for each industry, using straightforward mathematical techniques. The Soviet planning problem is so much bigger and more complicated that it is impossible, even with the most sophisticated mathematical techniques and the biggest computers, to solve their planning problem the way we could solve it for the three-industry economy.

**Table 35.1
Amount of Each Input Used
per Dollar of Output**

| TYPE OF INPUT | TYPE OF OUTPUT | | |
| --- | --- | --- | --- |
| | ELECTRIC POWER | COAL | CHEMICALS |
| | (DOLLARS) | | |
| Electric | 0.1 | 0.3 | 0.0 |
| Coal | 0.5 | 0.1 | 0.0 |
| Chemicals | 0.2 | 0.0 | 0.9 |
| Labor | 0.2 | 0.6 | 0.1 |
| Total | 1.0 | 1.0 | 1.0 |

# PRIORITIES AND PERFORMANCE

To make the planning problem more tractable, the Soviets have set higher priorities for certain production goals than for others. Thus they may set a goal for the production of houses and a goal for the production of missiles, but the production of missiles may be given higher priority. If trouble has arisen in meeting this production goal, the planners have taken resources away from the housing industry to make sure the higher-priority goal is achieved. This makes the planner's job a little easier, but does not guarantee that the economy will be very efficient.

The best-laid plans can go awry. To try to prevent this, the Russians have had a number of important organizations to check on the performances of plants and managers. First, there has been the **Gosbank,** the state-run banking system. When the plan has been published, the Gosbank has given the managers of each plant enough money to buy the resources—labor, materials, and so on—allocated to their plant. If the managers have run out of money, they have used more resources than the plan called for. Also, when the managers have sold the plant's output, the receipts have had to be deposited in the Gosbank. If the deposit has been less than the value of output specified in the plan, it has been clear that the plant has produced less than the plan called for. In this way, the Gosbank has kept close tabs on the performance of various plants. Second, the *State Control Commission* has had inspectors who go over the records of the Gosbank. Third, officials of the Communist party have been expected to report poor performance to the party bosses.

## Soviet Managers and Workers

The Soviet economy has been a **command economy**—people have been told what to do. The managers of an industrial plant have been told that to fulfill the plan, they must produce a certain amount, their **quota.** Moreover, they have been authorized to spend a specific amount on wages (they have been free to hire labor in the labor market), and to buy a specified amount of raw materials and equipment. Their job has been to carry out these orders, but they have not been told *how* to run their plant. That has been up to them. The Soviets have introduced managerial incentives not too different from those in the West. If managers have been resourceful and diligent, they may have been able to exceed their quota. In this case the Soviets—like good capitalists—have rewarded them with extra pay, and perhaps a promotion. If they have been lazy, foolish, or unlucky, they may have fallen short of their quota, which may have led to a pay cut or disgrace.

However, because managers have generally been judged on whether they have met their quotas, certain problems have arisen. Managers have tried to underestimate what their plants could produce in order to get easy quotas. They have tried to hoard and conceal materials and labor so that they would appear to use less resources than they did. And they have sometimes allowed the quality of their product to decline in order to meet their quota. Moreover, managers have been loath to introduce new methods or other innovations because of the risks involved. If a new method did not pan out, it could mean Siberia for the manager. It was better to play it safe, even though this hurt productivity over the long run.

Soviet workers have had considerable freedom to determine where they work. However, farm workers have not been allowed to leave the farms, and personnel have not been allowed to leave certain projects of great importance to the government. To get work of the right kind done to fulfill the plan, the planners have set up wage differentials to induce people to do the needed work. This is quite similar to the incentives that prevail under capitalism. In addition, however, other pressures have been used to get people to work hard and in accord with the plan. The government has provided awards to workers who do very well. The labor unions, which are really part of the state, have pushed for higher productivity. And people who perform poorly have been fined. Nonetheless, labor problems of various kinds have existed. There have been many complaints that Soviet workers have been unnecessarily late and absent from their jobs, and that labor turnover has been very high.

# PRICES IN THE USSR

As we have seen in earlier chapters, prices in a market economy allocate resources to promote the goals and satisfactions of the consumers. Obviously, prices in the Soviet Union have not functioned like this. On the contrary, they have been set by the government to promote the goals of the state. Note that there are two fundamental differences here between the United States and the Soviet Union. Prices are set largely by the market in the United States; they have been set by the government in the USSR. And prices should promote the goals of consumers in the United States, but have promoted the goals of the government in the USSR.

## Prices to Producers

More specifically, how have prices been set—and how have they been used—in the Soviet Union? The answer varies depending on whether one adopts the point of view of a producer or a consumer. First, consider a producer—a plant producing shoes, say. The government has set the price of the shoes, as well as the prices of the labor, materials, and other inputs the producer uses. The government has tried to set these prices so that a firm of average efficiency will run neither a profit nor a loss. Thus the system of prices has been used to see whether a producer is relatively efficient or relatively inefficient. If a plant makes a profit, this has been evidence that it is efficient; a loss has been evidence that it is inefficient.

This is no different from capitalism. But in the USSR, prices of inputs have not reflected the relative scarcity of inputs, as they do in capitalistic economies. Moreover, the price system in the USSR has not determined the output of each commodity, as it does under capitalism. Instead, as we saw in the previous section, government planning has determined target output levels.

## Prices to Consumers

Next, let's consider the prices consumers must pay. The function performed by these prices has been quite different from that performed by the prices that producers must pay. While the prices facing producers have been used to gauge the producers' efficiency (and how well they perform according to the plan), the prices facing consumers have been used to ration the consumer goods that are produced. Thus the price of a commodity to the producer has been likely to be quite different from its price to the consumer. For example, the price of a pair of shoes may have been 10 rubles to the producer and 20 rubles to the consumer. Why 20 rubles to the consumer? Because 20 rubles was the price the government felt would equate the amount demanded with the amount being produced.

Consumer prices have been set with an eye toward raising the planned revenue needed for investment. The gap between the price to the consumer and the price to the producer is the ***turnover tax.*** The turnover tax rate—100 percent in the case of the shoes, since the difference between the two prices, 10 rubles, is the same as the price to the producer—has varied considerably from commodity to commodity. It has provided a good deal of the Soviet government's revenue, and has been a way to reduce inflationary pressures and make consumer spending fit in with the government's economic plan.

# THE DISTRIBUTION OF INCOME

At this point, recall that one of the fundamental tasks of any economic system is to distribute the society's output among the people. Do citizens in the Soviet Union receive income in accord with their needs, as Marx envisioned? The answer clearly is no. The Soviet planners have set incomes in accord with the type of work people do, how hard they work, and how productive they are. The result is a great deal of income inequality in the Soviet Union. If we look only at income from labor, the extent of income inequality has been about as great there as in the United States. However, for all types of income (including interest, dividends, and capital gains, none of which exist in the Soviet Union), there has been more income inequality in the United States.

It is important to recognize that about three-fourths of all Soviet industrial workers have been paid according to *piece rates.* The amount these workers receive has been determined by how much output they turn out. Thus, to a much greater extent than in the United States, income has been tied directly to a person's production. This has been an important reason for the considerable income inequality in the USSR. Moreover, the Soviet labor unions have not played the same role American unions do. Whereas wage differentials in the United States have often been narrowed by union pressures, such pressures have not been exerted by unions in the USSR. It is very interesting, and understandable, that the Communists have emphasized monetary incentives to coax people to produce more.

## Income Differentials

In the Soviet Union, as in the United States, occupations differ greatly in pay and status, Distinguished Soviet scientists and professors, leading ballet and opera stars, and important government officials and industrial managers are at the top of the heap. Their incomes have been perhaps 20 times as high as that of an unskilled laborer, and they have had the good housing, the plush vacations, the cars, and other luxuries that are scarce in the Soviet Union. The unskilled and semiskilled workers have gotten the lowest incomes in the Soviet Union, as they do elsewhere. This doesn't mean, however, that various occupations cannot change their position in the salary scale. On the contrary, the Soviet planners have pushed wages for various types of work up or down in order to get the labor required to help fulfill the plan.

To put a floor under the living standards of the poor, the Soviet government has provided many free services, including education and health care. Also, the government has provided other services at a very low price. For example, very low-rent housing—most of it government owned—has been available. These programs have reduced income inequality by supplementing the incomes of the poor. The turnover tax, discussed above, has been used to finance these programs.

# SOVIET ECONOMIC GROWTH

A nation's rate of economic growth is often used as an indicator of its performance. Has the Soviet economy been growing more rapidly than the economies of the United States and other non-Communist countries? Be-

# EXAMPLE 35.1 · A PEEK BEHIND SOVIET PRICE TAGS

Consider two goods, X and Y, produced and sold in the Soviet Union. The average production cost, factory profit margin, turnover tax, wholesalers' margin, and retail margin of each good is shown below (in rubles):

|  | GOOD X | GOOD Y |
|---|---|---|
| Average cost of production | 100 | 100 |
| Factory's profit margin | 5 | 5 |
| Factory wholesale price | 105 | 105 |
| Turnover tax | 50 | 15 |
| Wholesaler's margin | 5 | 5 |
| Retail margin | 10 | 10 |
| Retail price | 170 | 135 |

(a) Do consumers value an extra unit of good X more or less than an extra unit of good Y? (b) Is the cost of producing a unit of good X more or less than that of producing a unit of good Y? (c) Given that the ratio of retail price to cost of production is so much higher for good X than for good Y, will the planners increase the output of good X relative to that of good Y? (d) Why is the turnover tax higher for good X than for good Y?

## Solution

(a) They value an extra unit of good X more than an extra unit of good Y, since they are willing to pay 170 rubles for an extra unit of good X but only 135 rubles for an extra unit of good Y. (b) The cost is 100 rubles for both a unit of good X and a unit of good Y. (c) Not if this is counter to their objectives. Output levels have been determined to promote the goals of the state (d) Because the government has felt that it must be higher for good X in order to equate the amount demanded with the amount being produced.

fore trying to answer this question, it is essential to recognize that the United States is far in front of the Soviet Union economically. Although accurate comparisons are difficult, per capita gross national product in the Soviet Union is only a fraction (less than one-half, according to many estimates) of that in the United States. When comparing the growth rates of the two countries, keep this fact in mind.

**THE FIFTIES.**    In the 1950s, the Soviet Union achieved a very rapid rate of economic growth. American observers watched with some uneasiness as the Soviet gross national product increased at about 7 percent per year, while our own increased much more slowly. This remarkable Soviet performance was partly responsible for President Kennedy's decision in the early 1960s to attempt to increase our own growth rate. One important reason for the rapid Soviet growth was the heavy investment by the Russians in plant and equipment. Investment constituted about 30 percent of gross national product, in contrast to about 15 percent in the United States. Soviet planners kept a tight lid on consumption. Indeed, consumption per capita grew little, if at all, from the late 1920s to the late 1950s. Soviet consumers were not allowed to increase their standard of living. The increases in production went primarily to build factories and equipment and to build military power. Other reasons for the high Soviet growth rate were the fact that the Soviets could—and did—borrow Western technology, and that the Soviet system did not tolerate unemployment.

**THE SIXTIES AND SEVENTIES.**    In the 1960s and 1970s, the Soviet growth rate seemed to slump. This, together with the fact that many people began to place somewhat less emphasis on the growth rate as a measure of economic performance, resulted in less concern in the United States over the Soviet growth rate, less pressure for government measures to increase our growth rate, and less talk about "growthmanship." According to leading

Kremlin watchers, an important reason for the decline in the Soviet growth rate was the greater emphasis on consumption in the post-Stalin Soviet Union. The Communist leaders began to allocate more to the consumer, and this increase in consumption goods meant a decrease in the production of investment goods, which in turn lowered the growth rate.

**THE EIGHTIES AND NINETIES.** According to the best available estimates, the Soviet growth rate remained relatively low during the 1980s, a fact which caused considerable concern among Soviet leaders. In 1990, there actually was a decline in real Soviet GNP, as everyone (including the Soviets) said that the Soviet economy was in trouble. For example, although the Soviet Union is the world's largest oil producer, its oil output fell because of outmoded drilling methods and strikes at equipment plants. Unemployment was up, and inflation hit 10 percent annually. In 1991, Soviet leaders solicited economic aid from the West.

At this point, it should be clear that the social mechanisms determining the rate of economic growth in the Soviet Union have been entirely different from those that determine the rate of economic growth in the United States. In the Soviet Union, the central planners have attempted to determine the growth rate by their decisions on the rate of investment in various industries, the amount spent on research and development, and the rate of expansion of the educational system. In the United States, on the other hand, decision making is decentralized. The American growth rate is determined largely by countless decisions by consumers and producers attempting to reach their own goals.

Soviet industry in the 1980s

# EVALUATION OF THE SOVIET ECONOMY

### Soviet Economic Performance

In previous sections, we've described the salient features of the Soviet economy. Now let's try to evaluate its performance. Needless to say, any such evaluation must be incomplete. And since we look at the Soviet economy through American eyes, it is sure to be biased—at least in the eyes of the Soviets (and of many Chinese, Cubans, and others). But we cannot avoid trying to make such an evaluation, despite the many formidable problems involved.

**FREEDOM.** One's evaluation of the Soviet economy must depend fundamentally on the value one places on freedom. The USSR has been a command economy; to us, its economy has not been free. The planners have decided what is produced, how it is produced, and who is to get what. Such an economy may sometimes be able to push industrialization and economic growth at a rapid rate, but at a great cost in economic freedom.

**EQUITY.** It is difficult to say much about the equity of the income distribution, since there is no scientifically valid way to say that one income distribution is better than another. This is an ethical question, which people must answer for themselves. Perhaps the most interesting aspect of the income distribution in the Soviet Union is that it contains so much inequality. There is less difference between the Soviet Union and the Western industrialized countries in the extent of income inequality than one might expect. Thus those who favor more income equality may find less to say for the Soviet economy than might be expected.

**EFFICIENCY.** The Soviet economy, while it has worked reasonably well at times in the past, has turned in a dreadful performance during the 1990s. Many of its problems are well known. First, incentives for innovation have been weak. Managers, fearful of not meeting their quotas, have often resisted new techniques. Second, since the planners, not the market, have dictated what will be produced, goods consumers do not want sometimes have been produced. The link between consumers and producers has not been as firm as in the Western economies. Third, the use of production quotas and targets has led to inefficiency. Thus, if the quota for a pencil factory is expressed in terms of number of pencils, the manager of the factory may reduce the quality or size of the pencils in order to meet the quota. Fourth, since input prices have not reflected relative scarcities, they have given improper signals to producers. Fifth, the Soviet Union has had many setbacks in agriculture. In 1989 and 1990, it continued to import grain, even in the face of substantial harvests. Soviet agriculture has seemed to suffer from the fact that many farms are too big, and that there have been too few incentives for efficiency.[1]

# GORBACHEV'S 1987 ECONOMIC PROPOSALS

On June 25, 1987, Mikhail Gorbachev, the Soviet leader, called for radical changes in the Soviet economy. In a speech to a meeting of the Communist Party's Central Committee, he said that the economy should be reorganized to eliminate the day-to-day management of the economy by powerful agencies like Gosplan, the central planning agency. Instead, these agencies should only set overall guidelines for the economy and ensure that key institutions, such as the military, would receive adequate resources. Put simply, he asserted that factories should no longer have to produce in accord with the plan handed down by Moscow.

Mikhail Gorbachev

Equally radical was his call for an end to the elaborately controlled and subsidized price system in the Soviet Union. He argued that "the whole of our pricing system, including wholesale, purchasing, and retail prices and tariffs, needs to be rebuilt as a package." Under his proposed reforms, factories would deal with each other and sign contracts based on negotiated prices, rather than prices set at the top. They would be encouraged to compete with one another.

Further, it appeared that job security, a central tenet of Soviet socialism, would be less complete. According to the new plan, unnecessary or lazy employees could be laid off, and inefficient enterprises could be closed. Also, there was talk of the reduction of subsidies for meat, bread, dairy products, and housing. In state stores in Moscow and other cities, meat has sold at less than half the cost of production. According to Gorbachev, the Soviet Union has devoted more than $115 billion a year to subsidies.

Yet another major proposal was that workers have the chance to get rich. Gorbachev argued that "no limit" should be established on a worker's pay, so long as it really is earned. Needless to say, this was a bold proposal in a society where large disparities in income have been widely resented.

---

[1] Responding to this situation, the United States, as well as Canada, Australia, and other countries, has sold many billions of dollars of grain to the Soviets.

# PRESSURES FOR ECONOMIC REFORM

According to knowledgeable observers, the 1987 reforms did not have a major impact on the Soviet economic system. For example, although factories were now free to sign contracts with other industrial enterprises, the state could still place an order with a factory and make sure that its order got top priority—because it kept control of the raw materials. Thus a factory making diesel engines could sell its engines to anyone, but only one customer could pay for the engines with consignments of steel—the state. No other source of steel existed.

In 1988, the Soviet Union legalized cooperatives, small businesses that are as close as the nation has come to free enterprise. Between 1988 and 1990, their output grew at a very rapid rate. According to some estimates, by 1990 their output constituted about 5 percent of the Soviet Union's gross national product, and the number of persons working at least part-time in cooperatives reached about 4.5 million. Some cooperative entrepreneurs have incurred hostility because of their comparatively flamboyant lifestyles, and there have been official attempts to confiscate the profits of these new businesses.

During 1989 and 1990, Gorbachev seemed to come closer to advocating a transition to free markets. In March 1990, the Soviet Parliament passed an ownership law which permitted individuals to own small businesses and also permitted companies to be sold to workers in the form of stock. Another law allowed a family to lease its farm for life and to will it to their children. But Gorbachev was unwilling to accept the idea of private property, as understood in the West, and he repeatedly stated that his people were not willing to accept the amount of unemployment and the extent of income inequality that genuinely free markets would entail. (Recall his statements on page 55.)

Also, the fact that many Soviet households had accumulated very large amounts of Soviet currency (during the long period when they had waited for scarce goods to become available) was a problem because, if prices were freed and if appliances and other desired consumption goods were offered for sale, the demand might be so great that inflation would result. This problem was related to the fact that the Soviet government had run large deficits which were financed by pumping billions of rubles into the economy. In early 1991, the Soviet government confiscated all 50-ruble and 100-ruble notes, thus cutting the currency in circulation by perhaps 20 to 30 percent. Also, retail prices for staple goods were increased; for example, the price of bread tripled.

As the Soviet people came to understand more clearly how much lower their standard of living was than in the West, there was increased pressure for economic reform. But any real acceptance of free markets faced resistance and a lack of comprehension from government ministries that would have no reason for existence in a market economy, as well as from conservatives and some military leaders who feared disorder and reductions in their own budgets and prestige. Western (and some Soviet) economists tended to regard the economic reforms proposed in 1990 as being only limited half-measures.

According to many leading economists, what was required was that factories and apartments be sold by the state to private individuals, that state monopolies be broken up, that the formation of new business enterprises be encouraged, that prices be freed, and that more unemployment and disparity of wealth be tolerated. In late 1991, the Soviet Union seemed to be disintegrating into a number of independent republics. Major economic changes seemed inevitable, but their precise nature was hard for experts to predict.

---

## TEST YOURSELF

1. In recent years, has the Soviet Union's rate of economic growth tended to decline? Has its rate of productivity growth (that is, the rate of growth of output relative to input) tended to decline as well? If so, why?

2. Describe the system of economic planning in the Soviet Union. To what extent is this system to be found in the writings of Karl Marx?

3. Discuss the differences between the United States and the Soviet Union in the way in which prices have been determined. What are some of the most important economic effects of these differences?

4. Has the state "withered away" in the Soviet version of communism? Explain. What have been some of the problems in Soviet planning?

---

## THE CHINESE ECONOMY

In 1949, another of the world's major powers—China—joined the Communist ranks. With Mao Zedong at its head, the Communist army entered Beijing (then Peking), the capital of a nation containing one-fourth of the world's population. China was a poor country, with little capital, little technology, and little education—a less developed country par excellence, despite its ancient civilization. Further, the Communists inherited an economy marred by many years of war with the Japanese. The country needed as much economic growth as possible, and quickly.

### The First Five-Year Plan

The Chinese Communists responded with a ruthless drive toward industrialization. China's Five-Year Plan of 1952–57 emphasized investment in heavy industry like steel and machinery and some expansion of light industry. It also called for a massive reorganization of agriculture, involving collective ownership of some farms and transfer of land from the rich to the poor. To permit the high rate of investment called for by the plan, the Chinese government pared consumption to the bone. The Chinese people were asked to work long and hard—for little return in goods and services.

Most observers agree that the plan achieved its goal of rapid economic growth. Even though China's population increased considerably, output per capita increased by about 4 or 5 percent per year during the 1950s. This was an enormous achievement for a country whose economy had been stagnant for centuries. To accomplish these objectives, China adopted measures that seem stern even when compared with the Soviet Union. (China, like the USSR, operated a command economy, but this did not prevent the development of considerable tension between them. To buttress its own position, each nation claimed that the other had abandoned the true faith of Marxism.)

## The Great Leap Forward

Having succeeded in pushing the economy ahead in the Five-Year Plan of 1952–57, in 1958 China's leaders launched a more ambitious plan, called the Great Leap Forward. Its aim was to increase per capita output by 25 percent. The large number of underemployed workers in China were to be swept into the employed labor force, and there was to be a great increase in investment. It all sounded very impressive on paper, but it turned out to be a disaster. Despite all the slogans and propaganda, the plan was unrealistic. Literally millions of people were asked to produce steel in primitive furnaces in their back yards. The result was a lot of unusable scrap metal. Also, poor planning directed millions of workers to produce other goods of little or no value. And too many people were ordered to leave agriculture and enter factories, with the result that far too little food was produced.

By 1960, the Great Leap Forward was obviously a failure of catastrophic proportions, and China's leaders had little choice but to alter their policies. In 1961, they published their new economic plan, which called for more emphasis on agriculture and less on industry. Industries that contributed to agricultural productivity—like the tractor industry—would receive more capital, while less would be devoted to industries that did not affect agriculture. Also, higher priority was given to the production of consumer goods for the peasants. Despite the new emphasis, the gains in agricultural production and efficiency seem to have been modest during the 1960s. Apparently, the Great Leap Forward had wreaked so much havoc that it was difficult to get agriculture moving ahead.

Workers in a farm-equipment factory

## The Cultural Revolution

The so-called Cultural Revolution that began in 1968 saw large-scale political disorders in Communist China. Because the data on Chinese economic performance are meager and unreliable, even the experts find it difficult to estimate the effects of this social turmoil on the economy. But by 1971, it seemed likely that the economy had recovered in large part from the economic disorders arising from the Cultural Revolution. According to estimates by Thomas Rawski, Chinese industrial production in 1971 was perhaps double what it had been in 1963.

## Movements Toward Decentralization, and Back Again

During the late 1970s and early 1980s, China began to move toward a more decentralized economic system where market forces were allowed to play an important role. In December 1978, China's Central Committee approved a new system of incentives for China's 800 million peasants, under which those that produced more were rewarded. The result was a sharp increase in farm output, and China's communes began to break up as individual households became the basic agricultural unit. According to some estimates, per capita food consumption increased by about 50 percent between 1978 and 1987.

In October 1984, China announced sweeping changes in its urban economy. About a million state-owned enterprises were to be given greater independence—and the necessity to compete to survive. Extensive government subsidies for consumer products like food and clothing were to be phased out, central planning was to be limited, and the prices of many products and services were to be determined by supply and demand. By late 1987, many dramatic changes had occurred, although China remained a Communist country.

In 1988, the Chinese government announced a series of stringent measures intended to reduce sharply the role of the free market in economic affairs, and controls were re-imposed on the prices of many commodities. According to China's Communist party chief, these changes occurred because of three problems: inflation, "unfair" distribution of wealth, and corruption in party and governmental institutions. In 1989, industrial output in China grew by only about 7 percent, as compared with 18 percent in the previous year, and the inflation rate fell to under 10 percent. In June 1989, the Chinese government sent tanks into Tiananmen Square in Beijing to crush a rising democracy movement. This event signaled a further step back from liberalization. In 1990, there were reports of slow economic growth in China, but no indications that China's leaders were interested in putting more emphasis on free markets.

# DEMOCRATIC SOCIALISM

We have described two brands of communism—Russian and Chinese. And in previous chapters, we have described capitalism. Now we must stress that there are other types of economic systems besides capitalism and communism. One of the most important of these is **democratic socialism,** which has included France's and Sweden's socialist governments and Britain's Labor government, among others. In many ways, the democratic socialist economies occupy a middle ground between our more capitalist system and the Communist systems. They generally favor government ownership of heavy industry like coal and steel (although the fervor for nationalization of such industries has died down in recent years); heavy taxation of the rich; and extensive welfare programs (social security, medical care, and so on); as well as a certain amount of economic planning, rather than the unfettered play of market forces.

But in contrast to the Communists, the democratic socialists generally do not favor violent revolution. Instead, they believe that democratic means should be used to obtain power. A good example is the British Labor government, which came into office after World War II. During the 1920s and 1930s, the Labor party had worked within the existing political system and gained strength. Finally, after the war it got its hands on the reins. Since then the Labor party has remained a major influence in British politics (although it has been in and out of office). As it has gathered further experience, its goals have changed somewhat. Thus, because government ownership of industry seems to have been inefficient, the socialists are much more tolerant of private property, and less interested in nationalizing industry, than they were 40 years ago.

## Changes in the United States

To a considerable extent, the more capitalist countries—like the United States—have taken over many of the socialist programs. The United States has moved a long way toward heavy taxation of the rich and toward extensive welfare programs. If Calvin Coolidge could be retrieved from the Great Beyond—and if Silent Cal could be induced to comment—he surely would be impressed (and perhaps dismayed) by how far the United States has traveled toward socialism since his presidency in the 1920s. Even though *planning* is viewed with suspicion in the United States, the government has become more and more involved in various aspects of our economic life, as we have seen in earlier chapters. The adoption by essentially capitalistic countries of many of their programs has taken some of the appeal—and some of the vitality and direction—from the socialists.

## RADICAL ECONOMICS

In the United States in recent decades, a new force in economics has appeared: ***radical economics.*** The radical economists draw heavily on the views of Karl Marx. Looking at the urban, racial, environmental, and poverty problems of today, they argue that the conventional tools of economics are too biased toward maintaining the *status quo* to analyze many of these problems properly. They challenge the methods and assumptions of conventional economics, criticize conventional economists for neglecting many important social problems, and question the reasonableness of many of our society's economic goals.

The analytical framework underlying radical economics consists largely of the following hypotheses. First, following Marx, the radical economists argue that the structure of any society is determined principally by the society's dominant mode of production, and that the most distinctive features of the mode of production under capitalism is the use of the wage-contract, the dominance of impersonal markets, and the private ownership of capital. Second, according to the radical economists, the pressure under capitalism for capital accumulation and riches tends to create a momentum in and of itself, which creates important contradictions and social problems. Third, according to the radical economists, the United States has reached a state of economic development where class struggles are not necessary or rational, since there is enough productive capacity so that all citizens can share adequately in wealth and leisure. To solve existing social problems, the radicals argue that the basic institutions of our society must change. In their eyes, nothing less will suffice.

The flavor of the radical position is well conveyed by this quotation from David Gordon:

> Radicals criticize capitalist society essentially because it evolves irrationally. Its basic mode of production and the structures of its institutions create conflicts which do not need to exist. In the language of economics, it forces "trade-offs" that are not necessary. Fundamentally, radicals argue, capitalism forces a conflict between the aggregate wealth of society (and obviously the enormous wealth of some individuals) and the freedom of most individuals. In another, truly democratic, humanist and socialist society, radicals argue, conditions could be forged in which increases in aggregate social wealth complemented the personal freedom of all individuals. Edwards and MacEwan mention some of the other unnecessary conflicts created (or sustained) by capitalist societies: "income growth versus a meaningful work environment, employment versus stable prices, private versus social costs, public versus private consumption, and income versus leisure." Other conflicts can be specified, but the criticisms gain force in the context of the radical vision of a "better" society. It should be emphasized in discussing the radical vision that many modern socialist radicals, though socialist, do not view most modern socialist countries with great approval. To many Western radicals, the purposes and the realities of the socialist

revolution in Cuba provide the closest manifest approximation to their ideals. Che Guevara, in many ways a more important ideologue of that revolution than Fidel Castro, has often expressed those ideals most eloquently.[2]

## Response to Radical Economics

As you would expect, the economics profession has responded in a variety of ways to the emergence of radical economics, with its relatively small number of followers. Some economists have chosen to ignore them, while others, like Nobel laureate Robert Solow of M.I.T., have responded sharply. In Solow's view,

> Radical economics may conceivably be the wave of the future, but I do not think that it is the wave of the present. In fact, to face the issue head on, I think that radical economics as it is practiced contains more cant, not less cant; more role-playing, not less role-playing; less facing of the facts, not more facing of the facts, than conventional economics. In short, we neglected radical economics because it is negligible. There is little evidence that radical political economics is capable of generating a line of normal science, or even that it wants to.[3]

Since radical economists are still engaged in the work that will tell whether theirs is really a contribution to science, it is premature to attempt to evaluate the accuracy or importance of their efforts. Admittedly, they have attracted considerable attention, despite the smallness of their numbers, but attention and agreement are two different things. The vast majority of the economics profession unquestionably would disagree with their conclusions. Most economists do not believe that capitalism should be replaced. Nor do they agree with the radicals' view of how our society works, or with their indictment of conventional economics.

## DOES CAPITALISM HAVE A FUTURE?

Most economists today do not seem to believe that our modern version of capitalism is about to wither on the vine. On the contrary, capitalism seems to be gaining ground, particularly in Eastern Europe, while socialism seems stagnant at best. This is particularly noteworthy, since at the end of World War II, many distinguished non-Marxist economists and social seers, as well as the Marxists, were predicting the demise of capitalism and the rise of socialism. One of the most significant developments of the past 45 years has been the extent to which these prophecies have fallen flat on their faces.

Contrary to Marx's predictions, capitalism does not seem on the wane. The essentially capitalistic economies of the world have shown a tremendous vitality, have grown at a relatively rapid rate, and have avoided any deep depressions (although inflation has proved to be a persistent difficulty). This is a great achievement, and one that should be recognized and appreciated. It does not mean that we do not have many problems. On the contrary, much of this book has been devoted to the discussion of our important social problems. But it does mean that our modern version of capitalism seems to be more than holding its own.

[2] D. Gordon, *Problems in Political Economy: An Urban Perspective.* Boston: Heath, 1971, p. 7.
[3] R. Solow, "The State of Economics," *American Economic Review,* May 1971.

# TEST YOURSELF

1. "In a field where controlled experimentation is impossible, the relative performance of India and China gives some idea of whether a Communist or a democratic system results in faster economic development." Comment and evaluate.

2. Several years ago, there were complaints in Chinese newspapers that the centralized system of job allocation was unable to find work for all the entrants into the labor force. According to some estimates, about 20 million people were waiting for job assignments. Does this amount to what would be called unemployment in the West? Explain.

3. According to some critics, like Assar Lindbeck, whereas either markets or centralized power can be used to organize a modern economy, the radical economists are against both. How then can an economy like ours be organized?

4. Compare the economic systems of the Soviet Union and China. To what extent have they departed from Marx's teachings? To what extent are their economic institutions much the same? What are the major differences in the way economic decisions are made? Which of them seems to be performing better economically?

# SUMMARY

1. Karl Marx viewed history as a series of class struggles, the present class struggle being between the capitalists, who own the means of production, and the workers. In Marx's view, capitalists and workers struggle because the workers are exploited. Marx, who subscribed to a labor theory of value, believed that the workers create a surplus value, the difference between the value of what they produce and the subsistence wage they receive. Capital formation, in Marx's view, comes about as a consequence of this surplus value.

2. According to Marx, the lot of the workers would inevitably get worse. Consequently, capitalism would eventually be overthrown and succeeded by socialism, then by communism. Socialism would be a "dictatorship of the proletariat." After an unspecified period of time, Marx felt that socialism would give way to communism, which would be characterized by a classless society, the withering away of the state, and the distribution of income according to the principle: "From each according to his ability, to each according to his needs."

3. The Soviet Union, the first country to embrace Marxian socialism, has had a command economy where power has been concentrated in the hands of a relatively few Communist officials who have made the big decisions on what is to be produced, how it is to be produced, and who is to receive how much. The government has owned the factories, mines, equipment, and other means of production—and has been the primary locus of power.

4. The top Soviet officials have established the overall goals for the economy. The detailed production plans to realize these broad goals have been drawn up by Gosplan, the State Planning Commission. In the 1990s, there were intense pressures for economic reform, as the Soviet Union seemed to be disintegrating into independent republics.

5. In the Soviet Union, the government, not the market, has set prices. Prices facing producers have been set in such a way that a firm of average efficiency will make neither a profit nor a loss. Prices facing consumers have been set to ration the consumer goods produced and to raise the planned revenue needed for investment. The difference between the price to the consumer and the price to the producer is the turnover tax.

6. Another type of Communist system is found in China, which is a very poor country despite its ancient civilization. China's first Five-Year Plan was an ambitious drive toward industrialization that seemed to achieve its objectives, but Mao's Great Leap Forward was a disaster that set back the country's economic development. During the 1970s and 1980s, China began to move toward a more decentralized economic system where market forces were permitted to play an important role; but more recently, it has reduced sharply the role of the free market in its economy.

7. In the United States, radical economics, which is based largely on Marxism, has entered the scene in recent decades. The radical economists challenge the methods and assumptions of conventional economics, and advocate basic institutional change. Many economists question whether radical economics is a contribution to science at all. At present, it is difficult to say, since radical economics is relatively new.

8. The essentially capitalist economies of the world have shown great vitality in the postwar period. They have grown at a relatively rapid rate, and have managed to avoid any deep depressions. Contrary to many predictions of over 40 years ago by some distinguished social seers, our modern version of capitalism seems to be more than holding its own in the world of today, although it obviously is beset by many serious problems.

# CONCEPTS FOR REVIEW

Communism

Capitalist

Proletariat

Socialism

Value

Surplus value

Marxism

Five-Year Plan

Gosplan

Gosbank

Command economy

Quota

Turnover tax

Piece rates

Democratic socialism

Radical economics

# DIGGING DEEPER INTO THE ECONOMIST'S TOOL BOX

IN THIS FINAL SECTION of the book, we present four appendices, each of which contains important material that is sometimes considered too advanced for the elementary course. Appendix A takes up *IS* and *LM* curves, with particular reference to the Keynesian-monetarist controversy. Appendix B is concerned with linear programming. Appendix C deals with general equilibrium analysis and input-output models. Appendix D is concerned with welfare economics, optimal resource allocation and perfect competition.

## APPENDIX A: *IS* AND *LM* CURVES[1]

To enlarge the simple Keynesian model of national output determination in Chapter 6 to include monetary factors, we use *IS* and *LM* curves, originated by Oxford's Nobel laureate, Sir John Hicks. Before describing how *IS* and *LM* curves are constructed, it is important to be clear concerning the basic assumptions that are being made. First, it is assumed that the price level is fixed, and that the public has a fixed demand curve for real money balances, a fixed consumption function, and a fixed investment function. Second, the money supply is fixed by the monetary authorities, and does not vary with GNP or the interest rate. Third, tax rates are fixed, and fiscal policy takes the form of varying government expenditure.

Sir John Hicks

### The *IS* Curve: Definition and Derivation

*The* IS *curve shows, for each possible level of the interest rate, the level of GNP that will satisfy the equilibrium condition that intended spending on output must equal GNP.* (If this equilibrium condition is a bit hazy, review Chapter 6.) This equilibrium condition is equivalent to saying that the public must be spending the intended amount relative to its income. (We put a great deal of stress on this equilibrium condition in Chapter 6.) To construct the *IS* curve, it is essential to recognize two things. First, the level of intended investment is inversely related to the interest rate. (In other words, for reasons described in Chapter 6, the higher the rate of interest, the lower the amount of intended investment, as shown in panel A of Figure A.1.) Second, the level of intended investment (as well as consumption, government expenditure, and net exports) will determine the

[1] To understand this Appendix, the reader should be familiar with Chapters 6 to 15.

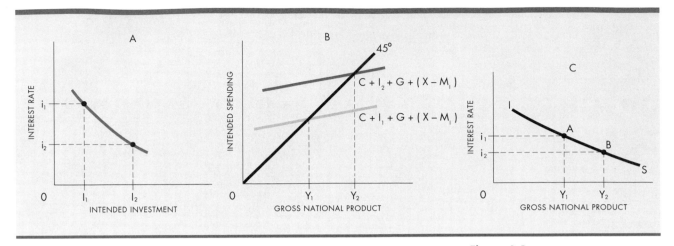

equilibrium level of GNP. (See panel B of Figure A.1.) Thus, since the interest rate determines the level of intended investment, and the level of intended investment determines the equilibrium level of GNP, there will be a relationship between the level of the interest rate and the equilibrium level of GNP. This relationship is the *IS* curve, shown in panel C of Figure A.1.

To see more precisely what the *IS* curve is, it is useful to derive some points on such a curve. Let's derive two points—*A* and *B*—on the *IS* curve in panel C of Figure A.1. To derive point *A*, note that, if the interest rate is $i_1$, intended investment will be $I_1$, according to panel A of Figure A.1. And if intended investment is $I_1$, total intended spending at each level of GNP will be shown by the $C + I_1 + G + (X - M_I)$ line in panel B of Figure A.1, with the result that the equilibrium level of GNP will be $Y_1$. Thus, if the interest rate is $i_1$, the equilibrium level of GNP is $Y_1$—which explains the coordinates of point *A*.

To explain point *B*, note that if the interest rate is $i_2$, intended investment will be $I_2$, according to panel A of Figure A.1. And if intended investment is $I_2$, total intended spending at each level of GNP will be as shown by the $C + I_2 + G + (X - M_I)$ line in panel B of Figure A.1, with the result that the equilibrium level of GNP will be $Y_2$. Thus, if the interest rate is $i_2$, the equilibrium level of GNP is $Y_2$—which explains the coordinates of point *B*.

Note that *the* IS *curve slopes downward to the right.* That is, the lower the interest rate, the higher the level of GNP on the *IS* curve. For example, when the interest rate fell from $i_1$ to $i_2$ in Figure A.1, panel A, intended investment increased from $I_1$ to $I_2$. And when intended investment rose from $I_1$ to $I_2$, the equilibrium level of GNP increased from $Y_1$ to $Y_2$, as shown in panel B of Figure A.1. More generally, since the level of intended investment is inversely related to the interest rate, but directly related to the equilibrium level of GNP, it follows that the interest rate must be inversely related to the level of GNP on the *IS* curve.

## The *LM* Curve: Definition and Derivation

*The* LM *curve shows, for each possible level of the interest rate, the level of GNP that will satisfy the equilibrium condition that the public be satisfied to hold the existing quantity of money.* Chapter 10 stressed the importance

**Figure A.1**
**Derivation of the *IS* Curve**
If the interest rate is $i_1$, intended investment is $I_1$. If the interest rate is $i_2$, intended investment is $I_2$.

If intended investment is $I_1$, equilibrium GNP is $Y_1$. If intended investment is $I_2$, equilibrium GNP is $Y_2$.

The *IS* curve shows, for each level of the interest rate, the level of GNP that will satisfy the equilibrium condition that intended spending on output must equal GNP. Points *A* and *B* are derived in the panels above, which show that equilibrium GNP equals $Y_1$ if the interest rate is $i_1$ and $Y_2$ if the interest rate is $i_2$.

of this equilibrium condition. Clearly, the quantity of money demanded for transactions purposes is dependent upon the value of GNP. Further, the quantity of money demanded is dependent on the rate of interest. Thus, as stressed in Chapter 10, the total quantity of money demanded by the public is dependent both on the value of GNP and on the interest rate.

More specifically, the total quantity of money demanded by the public is *directly* related to the value of GNP and *inversely* related to the interest rate. (Recall the discussion in Chapter 10.) As GNP increases (and incomes rise), people want to keep more money on hand to carry out the larger volume of transactions. Thus the quantity of money demanded by the public is directly related to the value of GNP (as shown in panel A of Figure A.2). On the other hand, the higher the interest rate, the more costly it is to hold money (because the more interest is forgone by holding money rather than buying bonds or other securities). Thus the higher the interest rate, the smaller the amount of money that is demanded. In other words, the quantity of money demanded by the public is inversely related to the interest rate. (This is shown in panel A of Figure A.2 by the fact that, if GNP is held constant, the quantity of money demanded increases as *i* decreases.)

Let's derive two points, *C* and *D*, on the *LM* curve, shown in panel B of Figure A.2. Recall that any *LM* curve is based on the supposition that the money supply is *fixed*, and that the money supply must be just equal to the quantity of money demanded (for an equilibrium to occur). The *LM* curve in panel B of Figure A.2 shows, for each interest rate, the value of GNP that will result in the public's demanding this fixed amount of money, say $1 trillion. If the relationships in panel A of Figure A.2 hold, the quantity of money demanded will equal $1 trillion if the interest rate is 4 percent and GNP is $Y_3$. Thus, if the interest rate is 4 percent, GNP (on this *LM* curve) must be $Y_3$—which explains the coordinates of point *C*. Panel A of Figure A.2 shows that the quantity of money demanded will also equal $1 trillion if the interest rate is 6 percent and the GNP is $Y_4$. Thus, if the interest rate is 6 percent, GNP (on this *LM* curve) must be $Y_4$—which explains the coordinates of point *D*.

Note that to maintain the quantity of money demanded equal to the fixed money supply ($1 trillion in this case), an increase in the interest rate must be accompanied by an increase in GNP. Why? Because, holding GNP constant, an increase in the interest rate will reduce the quantity of money demanded, as shown in panel A of Figure A.2. Thus, unless GNP is increased, the quantity of money demanded will be less than the fixed money supply. To bring it back into equality with the fixed money supply, and thus to maintain the equilibrium on which the *LM* curve is based, GNP must be increased. Similarly, a decrease in the interest rate must be accompanied by a decrease in GNP, if the quantity of money demanded is to equal the fixed money supply. For these reasons, *the* LM *curve slopes upward to the right*. That is, the higher the interest rate, the higher the level of GNP that satisfies the equilibrium condition underlying the *LM* curve.

## The Equilibrium Level of GNP

As pointed out in an earlier section, a full-scale equilibrium requires *both* that households and firms be spending the intended amounts relative to their incomes *and* that they be satisfied to hold the existing amount of

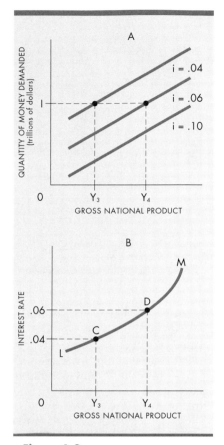

**Figure A.2**
**Derivation of the *LM* Curve**
Holding constant the interest rate, *i*, the quantity of money demanded increases as GNP increases. Holding constant GNP, the quantity of money demanded increases as the interest rate decreases. If *i* = .04 and GNP = $Y_3$, the quantity of money demanded equals $1 trillion. If *i* = .06 and GNP = $Y_4$, the quantity of money demanded equals $1 trillion. These correspond to points *C* and *D* in panel B.

The *LM* curve shows, for each possible level of the interest rate, the level of GNP that will satisfy the equilibrium condition that the quantity of money demanded equals the supply of money. Points *C* and *D* are derived in panel A.

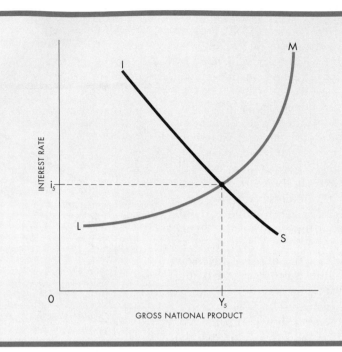

**Figure A.3**
**Determination of Equilibrium**
**GNP and Interest Rate**
The equilibrium level of GNP (and
of the interest rate) must be at the
intersection of the *IS* and *LM*
curves. The equilibrium GNP
equals $Y_5$, and the equilibrium
interest rate equals $i_5$.

money. In other words, both the equilibrium condition underlying the *IS*
curve and the equilibrium condition underlying the *LM* curve must be satisfied. For this to be so, the equilibrium conbination of GNP and interest
rate must be at a point lying both on the *IS* curve (which means that it satisfies the equilibrium condition underlying this curve) and on the *LM*
curve (which means that it satisfies the equilibrium condition underlying
this curve).

*If we plot the* IS *and* LM *curves on the same diagram, as in Figure A.3,*
*the equilibrium combination of GNP and interest rate must therefore be*
*the one that is given by the intersection of the two curves.* Only this combination lies on both curves, and thus satisfies both equilibrium conditions.
For example, in Figure A.3, the equilibrium level of GNP must be $Y_5$, and
the equilibrium level of the interest rate must be $i_5$. This is the only combination of GNP and the interest rate that will satisfy both equilibrium
conditions, given that the money supply, the public's demand curve for
money, its consumption function, its investment function, and government expenditures, taxes, and net exports remain fixed.

### Effects of Fiscal Policy on the *IS* Curve

*The* IS *curve will shift to the right if government expenditures increase or*
*taxes decrease.* The reason why these factors shift the *IS* curve to the right
is that, holding the interest rate constant, each of these factors increases
the level of GNP that satisfies the equilibrium condition underlying the *IS*
curve.

To see why this is so, take as an example the effect of a \$10 billion in-
crease in government expenditures in Figure A.1. Before the increase occurs, what is the equilibrium level of GNP corresponding to an interest
rate of $i_1$? As we saw in Figure A.1, it is $Y_1$. But after the increase occurs, it
is no longer $Y_1$. Due to the increased government expenditure, the $C + I +$

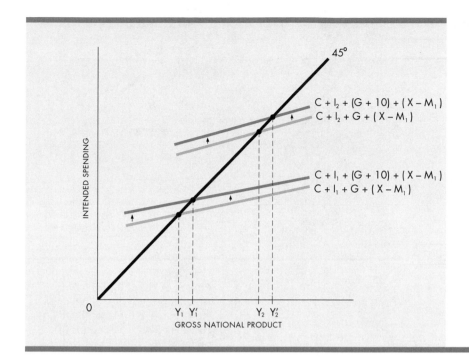

INTENDED SPENDING

45°

$C + I_2 + (G + 10) + (X - M_1)$
$C + I_2 + G + (X - M_1)$

$C + I_1 + (G + 10) + (X - M_1)$
$C + I_1 + G + (X - M_1)$

0          $Y_1$ $Y_1'$          $Y_2$ $Y_2'$
GROSS NATIONAL PRODUCT

**Figure A.4**
**Effect of a $10 Billion Increase in Government Expenditures on *IS* Curve**
If government expenditures are increased by $10 billion, and the interest rate is $i_1$, equilibrium GNP increases from $Y_1$ to $Y_1'$. If the interest rate is $i_2$, it increases from $Y_2$ to $Y_2'$. Since the level of GNP on the *IS* curve corresponding to any level of the interest rate is increased, the effect of the increase in government expenditures must be to shift the *IS* curve to the right.

$G + (X - M_I)$ line in panel B of Figure A.1 is raised from $C + I_1 + G + (X - M_I)$ to $C + I_1 + (G + 10) + (X - M_I)$, as shown in Figure A.4. Thus the equilibrium level of GNP is increased to $Y_1'$, as shown in Figure A.4. Similarly, if the interest rate is $i_2$, the equilibrium level of GNP is increased from $Y_2$ to $Y_2'$. Since the level of GNP on the *IS* curve corresponding to each level of the interest rate is increased, the effect of the increase in government expenditure is to shift the *IS* curve to the right.

## Effects of Monetary Policy on the *LM* Curve

*The* LM *curve will shift to the right if the monetary authorities increase the money supply, and it will shift to the left if they decrease the money supply.* To see why, consider first an increase in the money supply. Under such circumstances, if the interest rate stays the same, GNP must increase in order to bring the quantity of money demanded into equality with the new money supply. Why? Because the quantity of money demanded, if it is to equal the new money supply, must increase, and an increase in GNP will be required to produce such an increase in the quantity of money demanded. Thus, since the level of GNP where this equality holds (the interest rate being unchanged) is greater than before, the effect of the increase in the money supply must be to shift the *LM* curve to the right.

Next, consider a decrease in the money supply. If the interest rate stays the same, GNP must decrease in order to bring the quantity of money demanded into equality with the new money supply. Why? Because decreases in GNP will decrease the quantity of money demanded, which is required if the quantity of money demanded is to equal the diminished money supply. Thus, since the level of GNP where this equality holds (the interest rate being unchanged) is smaller than before, the effect of the decrease in the money supply must be to shift the *LM* curve to the left.

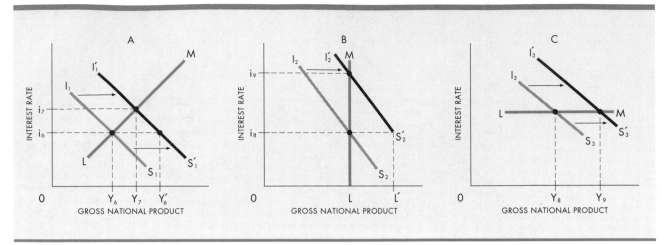

## Effects of Fiscal Policy on GNP

To understand the arguments in the past between Keynesians and monetarists over the effects of fiscal policy on GNP, it is useful to consider three alternative assumptions:

1. Let's assume that the economy is operating at a point where *the* LM *curve is neither close to being vertical nor close to being horizontal.* Under these circumstances, what are the effects of an expansionary fiscal policy (that is, an increase in government expenditures or a cut in taxes)? Since it shifts the *IS* curve to the right, an expansionary fiscal policy will increase both GNP and the interest rate, if the *LM* curve has such a shape. Panel A of Figure A.5 shows that this is the case. A shift to the right of the *IS* curve (such as from $I_1 S_1$ to $I_1' S_1'$) increases both GNP (from $Y_6$ to $Y_7$) and the interest rate (from $i_6$ to $i_7$).

2. Let's assume that the economy is operating at a point where *the* LM *curve is close to being vertical.* Indeed, to make things simple, let's assume that it is vertical. If so, an expansionary fiscal policy results in an increase in the interest rate, but no increase in GNP. For example, in panel B of Figure A.5, a shift to the right of the *IS* curve (such as from $I_2 S_2$ to $I_2' S_2'$) increases the interest rate (from $i_8$ to $i_9$), but not GNP. This is the so-called *classical range* of the *LM* curve, where fiscal policy cannot increase GNP.

3. Let's assume that the economy is operating at a point where *the* LM *curve is horizontal (or nearly so).* If so, an expansionary fiscal policy results in an increase in GNP, but no increase in the interest rate. For example, in panel C of Figure A.5, a shift to the right of the *IS* curve (such as from $I_3 S_3$ to $I_3' S_3'$) increases GNP (from $Y_8$ to $Y_9$), but not the interest rate. This is sometimes called the *liquidity-trap range.*

Although both a perfectly vertical and a perfectly horizontal *LM* curve are polar extremes, they are useful in indicating the differences that existed between the monetarists and the Keynesians. *The monetarists tended to believe that the* LM *curve is close to vertical, whereas the Keynesians tended to believe that it is much closer to horizontal.* Given their different views concerning the shape of the *LM* curve, it is easy to see why they came to quite different conclusions concerning the effects of fiscal policy on GNP. Clearly, the monetarists, based on their assumptions, tended to

**Figure A.5**
**Effects of Fiscal Policy**
An expansionary fiscal policy shifts the *IS* curve to the right. If the *LM* curve is upward sloped (as in panel A), the result of an expansionary fiscal policy will be an increase in both GNP and the interest rate. If the *LM* curve is vertical (as in panel B), the result will be an increase in the interest rate, but no increase in GNP. If the *LM* curve is horizontal (as in panel C), the result will be an increase in GNP, but no increase in the interest rate. The monetarists tended to believe that the *LM* curve is close to vertical, whereas the Keynesians tended to believe that it is closer to horizontal.

conclude that fiscal policy has less impact on GNP than the Keynesians were willing to accept.[2]

## Effects of Monetary Policy on GNP

To understand the arguments in the past between Keynesians and monetarists over the effects of monetary policy on GNP, it is useful to consider three alternative assumptions:

1. Let's assume that the economy is operating at a point where *the IS curve is neither close to being horizontal nor close to being vertical.* Under these circumstances, what are the effects of an expansionary monetary policy (that is, an increase in the money supply)? Since it shifts the *LM* curve to the right, an expansionary monetary policy will increase GNP and reduce the interest rate, if the *IS* curve has this shape. Panel A of Figure A.6 shows that this is the case. A shift to the right of the *LM* curve (from $L_1M_1$ to $L_1'M_1'$) increases GNP (from $Y_{10}$ to $Y_{11}$) and reduces the interest rate from $i_{10}$ to $i_{11}$).

2. Let's assume that the economy is operating at a point where *the IS curve is horizontal (or very nearly so).* If so, expansionary monetary policy results in an increase in GNP, but little or no decrease in the interest rate. For example, in panel B of Figure A.6, a shift to the right of the *LM* curve (from $L_2M_2$ to $L_2'M_2'$) increases GNP (from $Y_{12}$ to $Y_{13}$), but does not reduce the interest rate.

3. Let's assume that the economy is operating at a point where *the IS curve is close to being vertical.* If so, an expansionary monetary policy results in a decrease in the interest rate, but little or no increase in GNP. For example, in panel C of Figure A.6, a shift to the right of the *LM* curve (from $L_3M_3$ to $L_3'M_3'$) decreases the interest rate (from $i_{12}$ to $i_{13}$), but does not affect GNP.

Although both a perfectly horizontal and a perfectly vertical *IS* curve

**Figure A.6**
**Effects of Monetary Policy**
An increase in the money supply shifts the *LM* curve to the right. If the *IS* curve is downward sloped (as in panel A), an increase in the money supply will increase GNP and reduce the interest rate. If the *IS* curve is horizontal (as in panel B), it will increase GNP, but have no effect on the interest rate. If the *IS* curve is vertical (as in panel C), it will reduce the interest rate, but have no effect on GNP. The monetarists tended to believe that the *IS* curve is closer to horizontal, whereas some Keynesians tended to believe that it is closer to vertical.

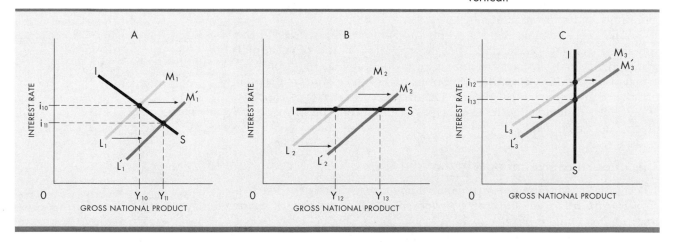

[2] The crowding-out effect, cited earlier in Chapter 15, is measured by the difference between (1) the equilibrium value of GNP if the interest rate remained at its original level, and (2) the equilibrium level of GNP at the new interest rate. In panel A of Figure A.5, the crowding-out effect equals $Y_6'—Y_7$; in panel B, it equals $L'—L$; and in panel C, it equals zero.

are polar extremes, they are useful in indicating the differences between the monetarists and the Keynesians. *Some Keynesians believed that the* IS *curve is close to vertical, whereas the monetarists believed that it is closer to horizontal.* Given their different views concerning the shape of the *IS* curve, it is easy to see why they came to different conclusions concerning the effects of monetary policy on GNP. Clearly, the monetarists, based on their assumptions, tended to conclude that monetary policy has a greater impact on GNP than the Keynesians were willing to accept.

# APPENDIX B: LINEAR PROGRAMMING[3]

In this Appendix, we look at the firm's production problems from a somewhat different angle—that of **linear programming.** Linear programming is the most famous of the mathematical programming methods that have come into existence since World War II. It is a technique that permits decision makers to solve maximization and minimization problems where there are certain constraints on what can be done. First used shortly after World War II to help schedule the procurement activities of the United States Air Force, linear programming has become an extremely important part of economic analysis and a very powerful tool for solving managerial problems. Its remarkable growth has been helped along by the development of computers, which can handle the many computations required to solve large linear programming problems.

There are at least two reasons why it is important to re-examine the theory of the firm in terms of linear programming:

1. The programming analysis is more fundamental in one respect than the conventional analysis presented up to this point. The conventional theory is based on the production function, which assumes that the efficient production processes have been determined and given to economists before they attack the problem. But in the real world, economists are usually confronted with a number of *feasible* production processes, and it is very difficult to tell which ones—or which combinations—are *efficient.* The choice of the optimal combination of production processes is an extremely important decision, and it can be analyzed more fully by linear programming.

2. The programming analysis seems to conform more closely to the way managers view production. The language and concepts of linear programming, though abstract and by no means the same as those of management, seem to be closer to those of managers and engineers than the ones used by conventional theory. This means that often it is easier to apply linear programming to many types of production problems in industry and government.

## The Linear-Programming View of the Firm

To economists who use linear programming, *the technology available to a firm consists of a finite number of* **processes,** *each of which uses inputs and produces one or more outputs.* IBM can choose among a number of different processes to manufacture a computer, and Bethlehem Steel can use a number of processes to manufacture steel. Typically, a firm can use various alternative processes to do a particular job. An important assump-

[3] To understand this Appendix, the reader should have covered Chapter 22 (and its Appendix).

tion in linear programming is that *each process uses inputs in fixed proportions.* Consider the case of an automobile manufacturer that, among other things, assembles truck engines. Suppose that one process it can employ is Process X, which uses 10 hours of labor and 1 hour of machine time to assemble 1 truck engine. If this process uses inputs in fixed proportions—as assumed in linear programming—this 10:1 ratio of labor time to machine time must be maintained. It cannot be altered.

Any process can be operated at various activity levels; the **activity level** *of a process is the number of units of output produced with the process.* If Process X is used to assemble 3 truck engines, its activity level is 3; if it is used to assemble 100 truck engines, its activity level is 100. If the output of any process is varied, it is assumed that the inputs used by the process vary proportionately with the output of the process. Consequently, the amount of any input used by a process equals the activity level of the process—i.e., the number of units of output produced with the process—times the number of units of input the process requires to produce a unit of output. In our example, the amount of labor used by Process X to assemble 5 truck engines is 50 hours, since the process is operated at an activity level of 5, and Process X requires 10 hours of labor to assemble each truck engine.[4]

Linear programming views the firm's production problem as follows. *The firm has certain fixed amounts of a number of inputs at its disposal. Thus a manufacturing firm has available a limited amount of land, managerial labor, raw materials, and equipment of various kinds.* (These limitations on the amounts of various inputs that the firm can use are called **constraints.**) *Each unit of output resulting from a particular process yields the firm a certain amount of profit. This amount of profit varies in general from process to process. Knowing the profit to be made from a unit of output from each process and bearing in mind the limited amounts of inputs at its disposal, the firm must determine the activity level at which each process should be operated to maximize profit.* This is the firm's problem in a nutshell—a linear-programming nutshell, that is.

## Removing Defects from Sheet Metal: An Example

No general description of linear programming can give more than a very incomplete idea of the nature of linear programming and its power to solve real-life problems. We can get a somewhat better idea from a simple case study which concerns a metalworking firm that removes defects from sheet metal. Suppose that there are three processes the firm can use— Processes A, B, and C. Process A requires 2 hours of labor and 1 hour of machine time to remove the defects from 1 square foot of sheet metal, Process B does the same job with 1.5 hours of labor and 1.5 hours of machine time, and Process C requires 1.1 hours of labor and 2.2 hours of machine time. The same kind of machine is used for each process.

Assume that the firm has contracted to remove the defects from 100 square feet of sheet metal per week, and that it will receive a price of $10 a square foot for this service. Also assume that the firm must pay $3 per hour for labor and that the cost of an hour of machine time is $2. (The firm is located in a low-wage country, which explains the low wage rate for labor.) Given these circumstances, the firm must decide which process

---

[4] It is also assumed that, when two or more processes are used simultaneously, they do not interfere with one another or make each other more productive.

or processes it should use to satisfy this contract. Should it use any single process to remove the defects from all 100 square feet of sheet metal per week? If so, which process should it use? Should it use some combination of processes, such as Process A for 50 square feet and Process B for the rest? Which of the myriad of possibilities will maximize the firm's profits?

Since the firm receives $1,000 a week for the work (100 square feet × $10 per square foot) regardless of which processes it uses, the firm will maximize its profits by minimizing its costs. Thus, in this simple case,[5] the problem boils down to determining which process or processes can do the job at least cost. We begin by assuming that the firm can hire all the labor that it wants and that it has plenty of the necessary machines. (This assumption is contrary to our earlier statement that linear programming views the firm as having limited amounts of certain inputs, but we relax this assumption in a later section.) Letting $Q_1$ be the number of square feet of sheet metal subjected to Process A, $Q_2$ be the number of square feet subjected to Process B, and $Q_3$ be the number of square feet subjected to Process C, *the firm's problem can be regarded as the following simple linear programming problem. Choose the lowest possible value for*

$$\text{total cost} = 8.0\,Q_1 + 7.5Q_2 + 7.7Q_3 \qquad (B.1)$$

*subject to the constraints —*

$$Q_1 + Q_2 + Q_3 = 100 \qquad (B.2)$$

$$Q_1 \geq 0;\ Q_2 \geq 0;\ Q_3 \geq 0. \qquad (B.3)$$

Why should the firm seek the lowest possible value for the expression in Equation (B.1)? Because this expression equals the firm's total weekly costs of doing the job. The cost of each square foot of sheet metal subjected to Process A is $8.00, since Process A requires 2 hours of labor (at $3 per hour) and 1 hour of machine time (at $2 per hour). Thus the total cost of the sheet metal subjected to Process A is $8.0Q_1$. Similarly, the total cost of the sheet metal subjected to Process B is $7.5Q_2$, since the cost of each square foot of sheet metal subjected to Process B is $7.50. And the total cost of the sheet metal subjected to process C is $7.7Q_3$, since the cost of each square foot subjected to Process C is $7.70. Clearly, the total cost of the job is the sum of whatever costs are incurred using each of the processes, which is the expression Equation (B.1).

Why must the firm conform to the constraints in Equation (B.2) and Inequality (B.3)? Equation (B.2) must hold if the firm is to meet its contract, since it states that the sum of the amounts of sheet metal subjected to each process must equal 100 square feet. That is, $Q_1 + Q_2 + Q_3$ must equal 100. Also, the inequalities in (B.3) must hold. All they say is that the number of square feet of sheet metal subjected to each process must be either zero or more than zero, which certainly must be true. (If you wonder why such an obvious constraint must be specified, remember that electronic computers won't recognize it as being true unless they are told.)

## Solving the Problem: No Constraints on Inputs

It is convenient to begin solving the problem by providing a graphic representation of each of the three processes. Since a process is defined to

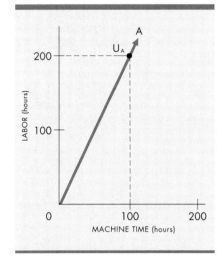

**Figure B.1**
**Graphical Representation of Process A**
The ray $OA$ includes all points where labor time is combined with machine time in the ratio of 2:1, since this is the ratio used by Process A. The point $U_A$ corresponds to an output of 100 square feet of sheet metal per week. (Why? Because Process A uses 2 hours of labor and 1 hour of machine time per square foot of sheet metal. Thus 200 hours of labor and 100 hours of machine time are required to produce an output of 100 square feet.)

[5] In general the problem of maximizing profit does not boil down to the minimization of cost because the firm's total revenue is not fixed as it is in this simple case.

have fixed input proportions and since all points where input proportions are unchanged lie along a straight line through the origin, we can represent each process by such a line or **ray**. In Figure B.1, the ray $OA$ represents Process A. Process A uses 2 hours of labor and 1 hour of machine time per square foot of sheet metal—in other words, 2 hours of labor for every hour of machine time. Consequently, the ray $OA$ includes all points where labor time is combined with machine time in the ratio of 2:1.

Two things should be noted about ray $OA$. First, *each point on this ray implies a certain output level.* For example, Point $U_A$, where 200 hours of labor and 100 hours of machine time are used, implies an output of 100 square feet of sheet metal per week. Second, *every possible output rate corresponds to some point on this ray.* This is true because all possible points at which labor time is combined with machine time in the ratio of 2:1 are included in the ray $OA$.

In Figure B.2, we show the rays corresponding to all three processes: $OA$ corresponds to Process A, $OB$ to Process B, and $OC$ to Process C. Each ray is constructed in the same way. Using these rays, we can draw the isoquant corresponding to the output of 100 square feet of sheet metal processed—the curve that includes all input combinations that can produce this amount of output. Focusing first on Processes A and B, point $U_A$ is the point corresponding to an output of 100 square feet of sheet metal with Process A, and Point $U_B$ corresponds to an output of 100 square feet with Process B. Thus $U_A$ and $U_B$ are points on the isoquant corresponding to an output of 100 square feet of sheet metal.

Moreover, *any point on the line segment joining $U_A$ and $U_B$ is also on this isoquant,* because the firm can simultaneously use both Process A and Process B to remove defects from a total of 100 square feet of sheet metal. For example, point $U_D$ corresponds to the case in which Processes A and B are each used to remove defects from 50 square feet of the metal;

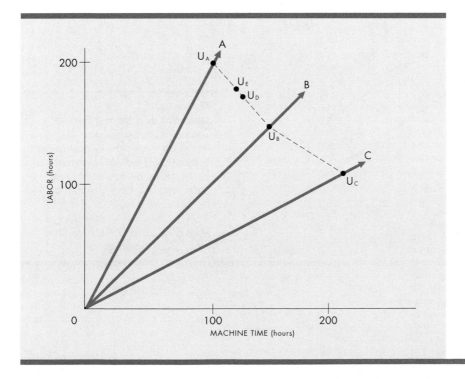

**Figure B.2**
**Graphical Representation of Processes A, B, and C**
Ray $OA$ pertains to Process A, ray $OB$ to Process B, and ray $OC$ to Process C. Based on these rays, we derive the isoquant corresponding to an output of 100 square feet per week, $U_A U_B U_C$. (Since Process B uses 1.5 hours of labor and 1.5 hours of machine time per square foot of sheet metal, point $U_B$ is at 150 hours of labor and 150 hours of machine time. Since Process C uses 1.1 hours of labor and 2.2 hours of machine time per square foot of sheet metal, point $U_C$ is at 110 hours of labor and 220 hours of machine time.)

and point $U_E$ corresponds to the case in which Process A is used for 60 square feet and Process B for 40 square feet. By varying the proportion of the total output subjected to each of these two processes, one can obtain all points on the line segment that joins $U_A$ to $U_B$.

To complete the isoquant, we must recognize the existence of Process C, too. In Figure B.2, $U_C$ is the point corresponding to the use of Process C to remove defects from 100 square feet of sheet metal. Thus U$_C$ *is also a point on this isoquant.* Moreover, *any point on the line segment joining* U$_B$ *and* U$_C$ *is also on this isoquant,* because the firm can simultaneously use both Process B and Process C to remove defects from a total of 100 square feet of sheet metal.[6] Consequently, *the entire isoquant is* U$_A$U$_B$U$_C$. Note that this isoquant, like all in linear programming, consists of connected line segments, and, while not smooth, has the same basic shape as the isoquants of conventional theory.

Given the isoquant $U_A U_B U_C$, it is simple to solve the firm's problem. All we have to do is construct Figure B.3, which contains this isoquant as well as some isocost curves, each of which shows all input combinations that cost the firm the same amount. The isocost curves corresponding to $600 and $750 are shown in Figure B.3. To find the input combination that minimizes the cost of removing defects from 100 square feet of sheet metal, we need only follow the procedure recommended in the Appendix to Chapter 22: *find the point on the isoquant that is on the lowest isocost*

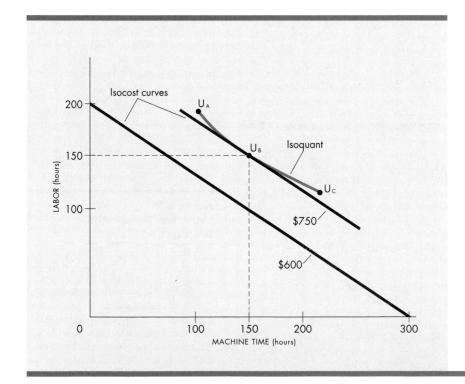

**Figure B.3**
**Isoquant and Isocost Curves**
The point on the isoquant $U_A U_B U_C$ that is on the lowest isocost curve is point $U_B$. (The $600 isocost curve shows all combinations of labor and machine time that can be obtained for $600. The $750 isocost curve shows all combinations of labor and machine time that can be obtained for $750.)

[6] At first glance, one might wonder why the line segment joining $U_A$ to $U_C$ is not part of the iso-quant. After all, it too represents various combinations of labor time and machine time that can remove the defects from 100 square feet of sheet metal. This line segment is excluded because the points on it are inefficient. They use as much of one input and more of the other input than some point on $U_A U_B U_C$. Recall from the Appendix to Chapter 22 that an isoquant contains only efficient combinations of inputs.

*curve.* This is $U_B$—the point corresponding to the use of Process B alone. Thus the firm should use only Process B, its total costs will be $750, and it will make a profit of $250 per week on the contract, which is the best it can do.

## Solving the Problem: Constraint on Machine Time

The foregoing problem is simple—so simple that it can easily be solved outside the framework of linear programming.[7] Let's complicate the problem a bit and make it somewhat more realistic. In the previous section, we assumed that the firm could use all the machine time it wanted—at $2 per hour. But in the short run, the firm is likely to have only a certain number of machines available. It therefore is constrained to use no more than a certain number of machine hours per week. Specifically, suppose that the firm can use no more than 120 hours of machine time per week; this is the maximum capacity of the machines it owns or to which it has access. Now which process or processes should be used to satisfy the contract?

This problem recognizes that the firm has limited amounts of certain inputs in the short run; thus it contains constraints of the sort visualized in the linear-programming view of the firm. The objective is still to minimize the expression in Equation (B.1), and the constraints in Equation (B.2) and Inequality (B.3) must still be met, but there is now a new constraint:

$$Q_1 + 1.5Q_2 + 2.2Q_3 \leq 120. \tag{B.4}$$

Why? Because the number of hours of machine time per week must be less than (or equal to) 120, and the total number of hours of machine time used per week equals $Q_1 + 1.5Q_2 + 2.2Q_3$.

To see that this is so, recall that the removal of defects from each square foot of sheet metal by Process A requires 1 hour of machine time; thus, since $Q_1$ is the number of square feet of sheet metal treated per week by Process A, the number of hours of machine time per week used on Process A must also equal $Q_1$. Similarly, the number of hours of machine time per week used on Process B must equal $1.5Q_2$ since the removal of defects from each square foot of sheet metal by Process B requires 1.5 hours of machine time. Moreover, the number of hours of machine time per week used on Process C must equal $2.2Q_3$ since Process C requires 2.2 hours of machine time per square foot of metal. Thus the *total* amount of machine time used per week on *all* processes must be $Q_1 + 1.5\ Q_2 + 2.2\ Q_3$.

How can this problem be solved? The constraint in Inequality (B.4) means that many of the points in Figure B.3 are no longer feasible, because they require more than 120 hours per week of machine time. These nonfeasible points are shown in the shaded area of Figure B.4. To solve the problem, we must find that *feasible* point on the isoquant $U_AU_BU_C$ that is on the lowest isocost curve. The feasible points on this isoquant are all on line $U_AU_E$ in Figure B.4. Isocost curves representing costs of $600 and $780 are also shown in Figure B.4. It is evident that the point on $U_AU_E$ that

---

[7] All this problem really entails is a choice among three methods of production, the cost of producing a unit of output being constant for each process and no constraint being placed on the amount that can be produced with a certain process. In such a case, the answer is obvious. Produce the required volume of output with the process with the lowest cost per unit of output. The simplicity of this case does not detract from its usefulness as a first step in the discussion of the nature of linear programming.

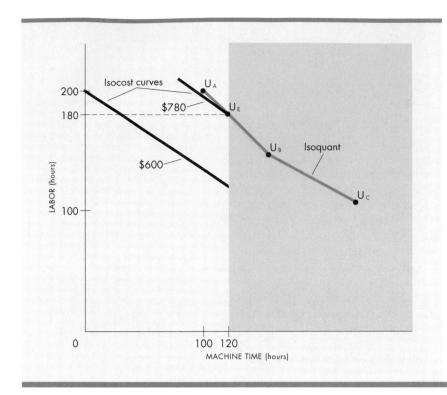

**Figure B.4**
**Isoquant (with Constraint on Machine Time) and Isocost Curves**
If the firm cannot use more than 120 hours of machine time per week, the shaded area is no longer feasible, so the feasible point on the isoquant that is on the lowest isocost curve is $U_E$. (The $780 isocost curve, which is the lowest isocost curve touching the line $U_A U_E$, shows all combinations of labor and machine time that can be obtained for $780.)

is on the lowest isocost curve is $U_E$. Thus the firm should use 180 hours of labor and 120 machine hours per week—which means that Process A should be used on 60 square feet of sheet metal per week and Process B on 40 square feet.[8] The firm's total cost is $780, and it makes $220 per week—which is the best it can do under these circumstances.

## Linear Programming and Management Science

Linear programming is only one of a number of analytical tools that have been developed in the past 40 years to aid decision making in the private and public sectors of the economy. These techniques form the core of ***management science*** or ***operations research,*** a very important field that draws on economics and other disciplines. Although management is still very much an art, the development and application of techniques like linear programming are making it more and more a science. Many problems that were "solved" 20 years ago by guesswork and seat-of-the-pants judgment are now being handled by linear programming and other such techniques, with the result that decisions are better, firms are more efficient, and society gets more out of its available resources.

---

[8] Since the total amount of hours of labor used equals 180 hours, $2Q_1 + 1.5Q_2 = 180$. And since the total amount of machine time used equals 120 hours, $Q_1 + 1.5Q_2 = 120$. Solving these two equations simultaneously, $Q_1 = 60$ and $Q_2 = 40$. Thus Process A should be used on 60 square feet and Process B on 40 square feet.

# APPENDIX C: GENERAL EQUILIBRIUM ANALYSIS AND INPUT-OUTPUT MODELS[9]

## Partial Equilibrium Versus General Equilibrium Analysis

In this book, we looked in detail at the behavior of individual decision-making units and the workings of individual markets. We looked at consumers, at firms, and at various types of product markets and input markets. We almost always viewed each single market in isolation. According to the models we have used, the price and quantity in each such market are determined by supply and demand curves, with these curves drawn on the assumption that other prices are given. Each market is regarded as independent and self-contained for all practical purposes. In particular, it is assumed that *changes in price in the market under consideration do not have serious repercussions on the prices in other markets.* This is ***partial equilibrium analysis.***

   ***General equilibrium analysis*** recognizes that *changes in price may affect other prices, and that the changes in other prices may have an impact on the market under consideration.* No market can adjust to a change in conditions without causing *some* change in other markets, and in some cases this change may be substantial. Suppose that an upward shift occurs in the demand for barley. In previous chapters, it was generally assumed that when the price and output of barley changed in response to this change in conditions, the prices of other products would remain fixed. However, the market for barley is not sealed off from the markets for rye, corn, wheat, and other foodstuffs. (For that matter, it is not completely sealed of from the markets for nonfood products like sewing machines and autos.) Thus the market for barley cannot adjust without disturbing the equilibrium of other markets *and having these disturbances feed back on itself.*

   Both partial and general equilibrium analyses are very useful, each in its own way. Partial equilibrium analysis is perfectly adequate when a change in conditions in one market has little repercussion on prices in other markets. Thus, in studying the effects of a proposed excise tax on the production of a certain commodity, we often can assume that prices of other commodities are fixed and remain close to the truth. However, if a change in conditions in one market has important repercussions on other prices, a general equilibrium analysis may be required.

## Input-Output Analysis

***Input-output analysis,*** due largely to Nobel laureate Wassily Leontief, puts general equilibrium analysis in a form that is operationally useful to governments and firms faced with a variety of important practical problems. An important feature of input-output analysis is its emphasis on the *interdependence* of the economy. Each industry uses the outputs of other industries as its inputs, and its own output may be used as an input by the same industries whose output it uses. Recognizing this interdependence, input-output analysis attempts to determine the amount each industry must produce so that a specified amount of various final goods will be turned out by the economy. This type of analysis has been used to help predict production requirements to meet estimated demands. Economic planners have applied it to military mobilization, to problems

---

[9] To understand this Appendix, the reader should have covered Chapter 24.

of economic development in less developed countries, and to many other areas.

To put general equilibrium analysis in a usable form, input-output analysis makes a number of simplifying assumptions. Thus it generally uses as variables the *total* quantity of a particular good demanded or supplied, rather than the quantity demanded by a particular consumer or supplied by a particular firm. This reduces enormously the number of variables and equations in the analysis. Also, in the simpler versions of input-output analysis, it is assumed that consumer demand for all commodities is known. Input-output analysis attempts to find out what can be produced, and the amount of each input and intermediate good that must be employed to produce a given output. It views these questions as largely a matter of technology.

Finally, input-output analysis assumes that inputs are used in *fixed proportions* to produce any product and that there are *constant returns to scale*. This is a key assumption of Leontief's input-output system. In the production of steel, Leontief would assume that, for every ton of steel produced, a certain amount of iron ore, a certain amount of coke, a certain amount of fuel, and so on would be required. The amount of each input required per unit of output is assumed to be the same, whatever the level of output. If a certain amount of iron ore is required to produce 1 million tons of steel, it is assumed that 10 times that amount is required to produce 10 million tons of steel.[10]

## A Numerical Example

With some basic algebra, the essentials of input-output analysis are quickly grasped. Suppose that the economy consists of only three industries—coal,chemicals, and electric power. Each industry uses the products of the other industries in the proportions shown in Table C.1. Thus the second column of Table C.1 states that every dollar's worth of coal requires \$.30 worth of electric power, \$.10 worth of coal, and \$.60 worth of labor. (One could just as well carry out the analysis with inputs and outputs measured in physical units—labor-hours or tons per year—as in money.)

This economy has set consumption targets of \$100 million of electric power, \$50 million of coal, and \$50 million of chemicals. Input-output analysis takes up the question: *How much will have to be produced by each industry in order to meet these targets?* Let's begin with coal. If electric power output is $E$, chemical output is $C$, and coal output is $X$ ($E, C$, and $X$ are measured in millions of dollars), it follows from Table C.1 that

$$X = .5E + .1X + 50 \qquad \text{(C.1)}$$

if the target is met. Why? Because the electric power industry needs an amount of coal equal in value to $.5E$, the coal industry needs an amount equal in value to $.1X$ and an amount equal in value to 50 must be produced for consumption. Thus the total output of coal must be equal to the sum of these three terms, as shown in Equation (C.1.)

If we construct similar equations for electric power output and chemi-

**Table C.1**
**Amount of Each Input Used per Dollar of Output (Dollars)**

| TYPE OF INPUT | TYPE OF OUTPUT | | |
| | ELECTRIC POWER | COAL | CHEMICALS |
| --- | --- | --- | --- |
| Electric power | .10 | .30 | .00 |
| Coal | .50 | .10 | .00 |
| Chemicals | .20 | .00 | .90 |
| Labor | .20 | .60 | .10 |
| Total | 1.00 | 1.00 | 1.00 |

---

[10] In previous chapters, we said that the proportion in which inputs are combined can generally be altered. This is a direct contradiction of the assumption of fixed proportions in input-output analysis. But it often takes a fair amount of time for changes to be made and they are often gradual, with the result that Leontief's assumption of fixed proportions may work reasonably well in the short run.

cal output, we find that

$$E = .1E + .3X + 100 \qquad \text{(C.2)}$$
$$C = .2E + .9C + 50 \qquad \text{(C.3)}$$

if the targets are to be met. For example, Equation (C.3) must hold because chemical output must equal the amount needed by the electric power industry ($.2E$) plus the amount needed by the chemical industry itself ($.9C$) plus 50 for consumption.

## What's the Answer?

Since Equations (C.1) to (C.3) are three equations in three unknowns, $X$, $E$, and $C$, we can solve for the unknowns, which turn out to be $X = 144$, $E = 159$, and $C = 818$. We have answered our question—*$144 million of coal, $159 million of electric power, and $818 million of chemicals must be produced to meet the consumption targets.* We can also find out how much labor will be required to meet these targets, since (according to Table C.1) the total value of labor required equals

$$.2E + .6X + .1C. \qquad \text{(C.4)}$$

Substituting the 144, 159, and 818 for $X$, $E$, and $C$, respectively, in Equation (C.4), we find that $200 million of labor is required. If this does not exceed the available labor supply, the solution is feasible; otherwise the targets must be scaled downward.

This simple example illustrates the fundamentals of input-output analysis. It also suggests why the assumption that inputs are used in fixed proportions is so convenient. Without this assumption, the input-output table in Table C.1 would not hold for each output level of the industries. Instead, the numbers in the table would vary depending on how much of each commodity was produced. The added complexity that would arise (without this assumption) is obvious. Even with this assumption, the computational and estimation problems involved in solving large input-output models can be substantial. Government agencies, such as the Departments of Commerce and Labor, have constructed a model of the U.S. economy involving several hundred industries. Usually, however, far fewer industries are included in such models.

## Applicability of Input-Output Analysis

Whether input-output analysis can be applied fruitfully in a particular situation depends in part on whether the ***production coefficients***—the numbers in Table C.1—remain constant. (See footnote 10.) There are at least two important factors that might cause changes over time in such coefficients. First, changes in technology may change the relative quantities of an input used. For this reason, among others, the amount of coal required to produce many goods decreased considerably in the years since World War II. Second, changes in the relative prices of inputs may result in changes in production coefficients as cheaper inputs are substituted for more expensive ones.

In recent decades, much has been done to implement and extend input-output analysis. Basic research has been conducted by academic economists interested in the quantitative significance of various types of economic interdependence. Applied research has been devoted to formulating techniques that would be useful in decision making in government and business. Other countries have used input-output analysis to determine the relationship of imports and exports to domestic production, as well as to analyze various problems of economic development. Also, business firms have used input-output analysis to forecast their sales.

# APPENDIX D: OPTIMAL RESOURCE ALLOCATION AND PERFECT COMPETITION[11]

One of the great goals of economics is to determine how best to allocate society's scarce resources. Questions concerning the optimal allocation of inputs among industries and the optimal distribution of commodities among consumers are general equilibrium problems, since the optimal usage of any input cannot be determined by looking at the market for this input alone, and the optimal output of any commodity cannot be determined by looking at the market for this commodity alone. On the contrary, the optimal allocation of resources between two products depends on the relative strength of the demands for the products and their relative production costs.

The term **welfare economics** covers the branch of economics that studies policy issues concerning the allocation of resources. (Do not confuse welfare economics with the various government "welfare" programs you read about in Chapter 30). It should be stressed from the start that welfare economics, although useful, is certainly no panacea. By itself, welfare economics can seldom provide a clear-cut solution to issues of public policy. But in combination with other disciplines, it can frequently show useful ways to structure and analyze these issues.

## Interpersonal Comparisons of Utility

Perhaps the most important limitation of welfare economics stems from the fact that *there is no scientific way to compare the utility level of different individuals.* There is no way to show scientifically that a bottle of Château Haut-Brion will bring you more satisfaction than it will me, or that your backache is worse than mine. This is because there is no scale on which we can measure pleasure or pain so that interpersonal comparisons can be made scientifically. For this reason, the judgment of whether one distribution of income is better than another must be made on ethical, not scientific, grounds. If you receive twice as much income as I do, economists cannot tell us whether this is a better distribution of income than if I receive twice as much income as you do. This is an ethical judgment.

However, most problems of public policy involve changes in the distribution of income. A decision to increase the production of jet aircraft and to reduce the production of railroad locomotives may mean that certain stockholders and workers will gain, while others will lose. Because it is so difficult to tell whether the resulting change in the distribution of income is good or bad, it is correspondingly difficult to conclude whether such a decision is good or bad.

[11] To understand this Appendix the reader should have covered Chapters 19 to 25 of this book.

Faced with this problem, economists have adopted a number of approaches, all of which have significant shortcomings. Some economists have simply paid no attention to the effects of proposed policies on the income distribution. Others have taken the existing income distribution as optimal, while still others have asserted that less unequal income distributions are preferable to more unequal ones. Purists have argued that we really cannot be sure a change is for the better unless it hurts no member of society, while others have suggested that we must accept the judgment of Congress (or the public as a whole) on what is an optimal distribution of income.

For now, the major thing to note is that the conditions for an optimal allocation of resources, described in the following sections, are incomplete, since they say nothing about the optimal income distribution. Whatever the income distribution you or I may consider best on ethical or some other (nonscientific) grounds, the conditions below must be met if resources are to be allocated optimally. Remember, however, that there may be many allocations of resources that meet these conditions, and the choice of which is best will depend on one's feelings about the optimal income distribution.

## Optimal Resource Allocation: Condition 1

Fundamentally, there are three necessary conditions for optimal resource allocation. The first pertains to the optimal allocation of commodities among consumers, and states that *the ratio of the marginal utilities of any two goods must be the same for any two consumers who consume both goods.* That is, if the marginal utility of good A is twice that of good B for one consumer, it must also be twice that of good B for any other consumer who consumes both goods. The proof that this condition is necessary to maximize consumer satisfaction is quite simple. We need only note that, if this ratio were unequal for two consumers, both consumers could benefit by trading.

Thus assume that the ratio of the marginal utility of good A to that of good B is 2 for one consumer, but 3 for another consumer. This means that the first consumer regards an additional unit of good A as having the same utility as 2 extra units of good B, whereas the second consumer regards an additional unit of good A as having the same utility as 3 extra units of good B. Then, if the first consumer trades 1 unit of good A for 2.5 units of good B from the second consumer, both are better off. (Why? Because the first consumer receives 2.5 units of good B, which he prefers to 1 unit of good A, and the second consumer receives 1 unit of good A, which she prefers to 2.5 units of good B.)

## Optimal Resource Allocation: Condition 2

The second condition, which pertains to the optimal allocation of inputs among producers, states that *the ratio of the marginal products of two inputs must be the same for any pair of producers that use both inputs.* That is, if the marginal product of input 1 is twice that of input 2 in one firm, it must also be twice that of input 2 in any other firm that uses both inputs. If this condition does not hold, total production can be increased merely by reallocating inputs among firms.

To illustrate this, suppose that for the first producer the marginal product of input 1 is twice that of input 2, whereas for the second producer the marginal product of input 1 is three times that of input 2. Then, if the first producer gives 1 unit of input 1 to the second producer in exchange for 2.5 units of input 2, both firms can expand their output. To see this, suppose that the marginal product of input 1 is $M_1$ for the first producer and $M_2$ for the second producer. Then the output of the first producer is reduced by $M_1$ units because of its loss of the unit of input 1, but it is increased by $2.5 \times M_1/2$ units because of its gain of the 2.5 units of input 2, so that on balance its output increases by $M_1/4$ units because of the trade. Similarly, the output of the second producer is increased by $M_2$ units because it gains the 1 unit of input 1, but it is decreased by $2.5 \times M_2/3$ units because it loses the 2.5 units of input 2, with the consequence that on balance its output increases by $M_2/6$ units because of the trade.

## Optimal Resource Allocation: Condition 3

The third condition pertains to the optimal output of a commodity. It states that *any commodity's output level, if it is optimal, must be such that the marginal social benefit from an extra unit of the commodity is equal to its marginal social cost.* If this condition is violated, social welfare can be increased by altering the output level of the commodity. Specifically, if the marginal social benefit from an extra unit of the commodity exceeds its marginal social cost, an increase in the output of the commodity will increase social welfare. (Why? Because the extra social benefit resulting from an extra unit of the commodity outweighs the extra social cost.) And if the marginal social benefit from an extra unit of the commodity is less than marginal social cost, a decrease in the output of the commodity will increase social welfare.

## Optimal Resource Allocation: A Case Study

Let's turn now to a case study of how these conditions can be applied to one of our most important commodities—water. If the first condition is to hold, the ratio of the marginal utility of water to that of any other good must be the same for all consumers. To be specific, suppose that the other good is money. Then the ratio of the marginal utility of water to the marginal utility of money must be the same for all consumers. That is, if resources are allocated optimally, *the amount of money a consumer will give up to obtain an extra unit of water must be the same for all consumers.* This follows because the ratio of the marginal utility of good A to the marginal utility of good B equals the number of units of good B that the consumer will give up to get an extra unit of good A.

The common sense underlying this condition has been described well in a study of water resources done at the RAND Corporation:

The RAND Corporation

> Suppose that my neighbor and I are both given rights (ration coupons, perhaps) to certain volumes of water, and we wish to consider whether it might be in our mutual interest to trade those water rights between us for other resources—we might as well say for dollars, which we can think of as a generalized claim on other resources like clam chowders, babysitting services, acres of land, or yachts. . . . Now suppose that the last acre-foot of my periodic entitlement is worth $10 at most to me, but my neighbor would be willing to pay anything up to $50 for the right. . . . Eventually, if I transfer the right to him for any compensation between $10 and $50, we will both be better off in terms of our own preferences. . . . But this is not yet the end. Having given up one acre-foot, I will not be inclined to give up another on such easy terms (and) my

neighbor is no longer quite so anxious to buy as he was before, since his most urgent need for one more acre-foot has been satisfied. . . . Suppose he is now willing to pay up to $45 (for another acre-foot), while I am willing to sell for anything over $15. Evidently, we should trade again. Obviously, the stopping point is where the last (or marginal) unit of water is valued equally (in terms of the greatest amount of dollars we would be willing to pay) by the two of us . . . . At this point no more mutually advantageous trades are available—and efficiency has been attained.[12]

If people can trade water rights freely—as in this hypothetical case—an efficient allocation of water rights will be achieved. But what if water rights cannot be traded freely, because certain kinds of water uses are given priority over other types of uses, and it is difficult, even impossible, for a low-priority user to purchase water rights from a high-priority user? The effect is to prevent water from being allocated so as to maximize consumer satisfaction. Unfortunately, this question is not merely an academic exercise. It focuses attention on a very practical problem. In fact, there is a wide variety of limitations on the free exchange of water rights in the United States. Thus some legal codes grant certain types of users priority over other types of users, and free exchange of water is limited. Experts believe that these limitations are a serious impediment to the optimal allocation of water resources. (For related material, see Example 28.1 on page 591.)

## Perfect Competition and Welfare Maximization

One of the most fundamental findings of economic theory is that a perfectly competitive economy satisfies the three sets of conditions for welfare maximization set forth in previous sections. An argument for competition can be made in various ways. Some people favor it simply because it prevents the undue concentration of power and the exploitation of consumers. But to the economic theorist, the basic argument for a perfectly competitive economy is that such an economy satisfies these three conditions. In this section we prove that this is indeed a fact.

*Condition 1—The Ratio of the Marginal Utilities of any Pair of Commodities Must Be the Same for All Consumers Buying Both Commodities.* Recall that under perfect competition consumers choose their purchases so that the marginal utility of a commodity is proportional to its price. Since prices, and thus price ratios, are the same for all buyers under perfect competition, it follows that the ratio of the marginal utilities between any pair of commodities must be the same for all consumers. If every consumer can buy bread at $.50 a loaf and butter at $1 a pound, each one will arrange his or her purchases so that the ratio of the marginal utility of butter to that of bread is 2. Thus the ratio will be the same for all consumers—2 for everyone.

To make sure you understand this point, let's consider any two goods, A and B. Based on our discussion in Chapter 20, we know that each consumer will buy amounts of these goods so that

$$\frac{MU_A}{P_A} = \frac{MU_B}{P_B},$$

where $MU_A$ is the marginal utility of good A, $MU_B$ is the marginal utility of good B, $P_A$ is the price of good A, and $P_B$ is the price of good B. Multiply-

[12] J. Hirshleifer, J. Milliman, and J. DeHaven, "The Allocation of Water Supplies," in E. Mansfield (ed.), *Microeconomics: Selected Readings,* 4th ed., New York: Norton, 1982.

ing both sides of this equation by $P_A \div MU_B$, it follows that

$$\frac{MU_A}{MU_B} = \frac{P_A}{P_B}.$$

Since $P_A \div P_B$ is the same for all consumers, $MU_A \div MU_B$ must also be the same for all of them, which means this condition is satisfied.

*Condition 2—The Ratio of the Marginal Products of any Pair of Inputs Must Be the Same for All Producers Using Both Inputs.* We have already seen in Chapter 22 that under perfect competition producers will choose the quantity of each input so that the ratio of the marginal products of any pair of inputs equals the ratio of the prices of the pair of inputs. Since input prices, and thus price ratios, are the same for all producers under perfect competition, it follows that the ratio of the marginal products must be the same for all producers. If every producer can buy labor services at $8 an hour and machine tool services at $16 an hour, each one will arrange the quantity of its inputs so that the ratio of the marginal product of machine tool service to that of labor is 2. Thus the ratio will be the same for all producers: 2 for each.

To make sure you understand this point, let's consider any two inputs, *X* and *Y*. Based on our discussion in Chapter 22, we know that each firm will buy amounts of these inputs so that

$$\frac{MP_X}{P_X} = \frac{MP_Y}{P_Y},$$

where $MP_X$ is the marginal product of input *X*, $MP_Y$ is the marginal product of input *Y*, $P_X$ is the price of input *X*, and $P_Y$ is the price of input *Y*. Multiplying both sides of this equation by $P_X \div MP_Y$, it follows that

$$\frac{MP_X}{MP_Y} = \frac{P_X}{P_Y}.$$

Since $P_X \div P_Y$ is the same for all firms, $MP_X \div MP_Y$ must also be the same for all of them, which means this condition is satisfied.

*Condition 3—The Marginal Social Benefit From an Extra Unit of any Commodity Must Be Equal to Its Marginal Social Cost.* Recall from Chapter 24 that under perfect competition firms will choose their outputs so that price equals marginal cost. If a commodity's price is an accurate measure of the marginal social benefit from producing an extra unit of it, and if its marginal cost is an accurate measure of the marginal social cost of producing an extra unit of it, the fact that price is set equal to marginal cost insures that this condition will be met.

Thus, in summary, *all three conditions for optimal resource allocation are satisfied under perfect competition.* This is one principal reason why many economists are so enamored of perfect competition and so wary of monopoly and other market imperfections. If a formerly competitive economy is restructured so that some industries become monopolies, these conditions for optimal resource allocation are no longer met. As we know from Chapter 25, each monopolist produces less than the perfectly competitive industry that it replaces would have produced. Thus too few resources are devoted to the industries that are monopolized, and too many resources are devoted to the industries that remain perfectly competitive. This is one of the economist's chief charges against monopoly. It wastes resources because it results in overallocation of resources to competitive industries and underallocation of resources to monopolistic industries. The result is that society is less well off. Similarly, oligopoly and monopolistic competition are charged with wasting resources, since the conditions for optimal resource allocation are not met there either.

However, in evaluating this result and judging its relevance, one must be careful to note that it stems from a very simple model that ignores such things as technological change and other dynamic considerations, risk and uncertainty, and external economies and diseconomies. Also, there is the so-called *theory of the second-best*, which states that unless *all* of the conditions for optimal resource allocation are met, it may be a mistake to increase the number of such conditions that are fulfilled. Thus piecemeal attempts to preserve or impose competition may do more harm than good.

# BRIEF ANSWERS TO ODD-NUMBERED TEST-YOURSELF QUESTIONS*

## CHAPTER 1 (P. 8)

1. (a) Iron ore that is still in the ground is included in land. (b) The 747 is capital. (c) These inventories are capital, as explained on p.6. (d) If the University owns the telephone, it is part of the university's capital.

3. Yes, use of the catalyst alters the relationship between inputs of crude oil and the refined oil output. By making the refining process more efficient, the catalyst allows a larger volume of refined oil to be gleaned from a barrel of crude oil. The services of engineers and scientists, as well as research laboratories, were used to obtain the invention.

## CHAPTER 1 (P. 16)

1. Preparing the meal costs the family $50.00, assuming that Ms. Harris could see patients during that hour.

3. The $1,000 figure is correct because the remaining cost of room and board must be met whether the student goes to college or works instead.

## CHAPTER 2 (P. 23)

1. 2 million bushels generate $2 million; 1 million bushels generates $2 million. No, I would produce 1 million bushels since I can sell it for as much as I can get for 2 million bushels.

3. The demand curve in Figure 2.2 shifts to the right when preferences change in favor of playing tennis.

## CHAPTER 2 (P. 36)

1. (a) No. (b) Yes. (c) The combination of 20 million tons of food and 6 million tractors is inside the curve. Possible contributory factors: unemployment, inefficiency, or bad weather.

3. Yes, it is on the new curve. The horizontal intersection is 24 million tons, and the vertical one is 60 million tractors.

---

* The answers provided here are meant only to be brief guides, not complete or exhaustive treatments. Many were contributed by Michael Claudon of Middlebury College, who is responsible for the *Instructor's Manual* accompanying this book.

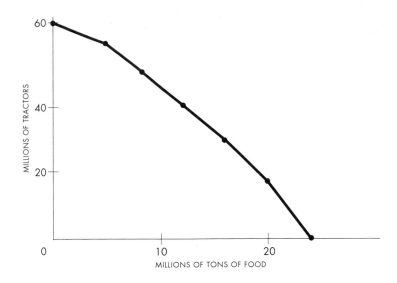

5. This statement is true. Of course, it is also important to note that not all individuals have the same number of votes, because of income inequality.

## CHAPTER 3 (P. 46)

1. This is a direct relationship. Supply curves are generally direct relationships.

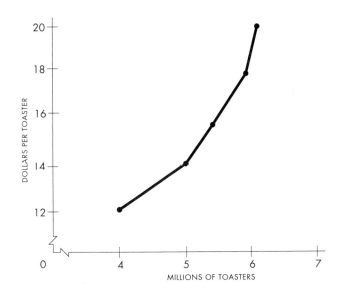

3. No, quantity demanded will exceed quantity supplied. Black markets and queues may arise. If black markets develop, the price may rise above the official price of $14. Such a ceiling might be introduced as part of an anti-inflationary program or to help the poor.

5. Equilibrium price = $3.33, and equilibrium quantity = 6.67 million pounds.

## CHAPTER 3 (P. 62)

1. The toaster demand curve shifts: (a) right; (b) right; (c) left; (d) right; (e) no shift.

3. The impact on price is ambiguous. Equilibrium quantity rises.

5. The demand for beets and beet growers' profits rise. The opposite happens for string beans. Bean growers spy beet growers' high profits and plant beets instead of beans. Beet supply rises and string bean supply falls.

## CHAPTER 4 (P. 73)

1. The figures are 1,000 for 1974, 1,200 for 1976, 1820 for 1978, 2,400 for 1980, and 1,600 for 1992.

3. No. If GNP is used to gauge the net social value of economic output, pollution's costs should be subtracted from the market value of the goods produced.

## CHAPTER 4 (P. 82)

1. GNP = $1,900 millions; NNP = $1,800 millions.

3. GNP = $93 millions, the sum of all items except for transfer payments.

5. Inventories represent goods that can be sold without drawing upon the economy's current productive capacity. Ignoring inventory increases excludes the value of these goods from the GNP calculation, even though they were produced during the year.

## CHAPTER 5 (P. 98)

1. (i) Unemployment benefits are temporary, and averaged less than $200 per week in 1990. (ii) Unemployed workers involve an opportunity cost to the country in the form of the goods and services that these workers could produce.

3. Frictionally unemployed people have left one job (often voluntarily) and have not as yet begun a new one. Structural unemployment occurs when jobs are available for qualified workers, but the unemployed do not have the necessary qualifications. Cyclical unemployment occurs when, because of an insufficiency of aggregate demand, there are more people looking for work than there are jobs. The government should not attempt to reduce all types of unemployment to zero because severe inflation would be likely to result.

# CHAPTER 5 (P. 106)

1. The point is that there may be tradeoffs between inflation and un-employment, and a full-employment policy should take inflation into consideration as well. Much more will be said on this score in subsequent chapters.

3. About 7 years.

5. Recessions tend to reduce inflation substantially. There are lots of excess capacity and unemployed resources, which put a damper on price increases.

# CHAPTER 6 (P. 116)

1. The marginal propensity to save = 0.1. The marginal propensity to consume = the average propensity to consume = 0.9 in this example. The consumption function has been assumed to pass through the origin. In this example, the marginal propensity to consume is unrelated to the income distribution, which is unrealistic since different socioeconomic groups have different spending and savings habits.

3. The marginal propensity to consume is not constant. The average propensity to consume falls as disposable income rises.

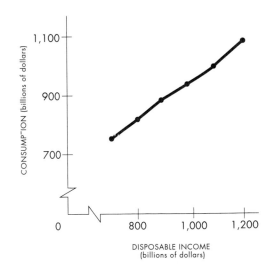 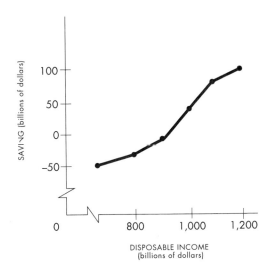

5. (a) Decrease; (b) increase; (c) increase; (d) decrease; (e) increase.

# CHAPTER 6 (P. 130)

1. GNP will increase by $2 billion, from $500 billion to $502 billion, as shown below.

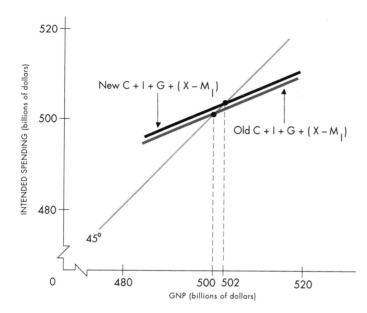

3. Multiplier = 1 ÷ .2 = 5.

5. The marginal propensity to save equals 0.25, and the multiplier is 4.

# CHAPTER 7 (P. 145)

1. Increases in the price level will tend to push up interest rates, which will lower investment. They will reduce the real value of currency and government debt held by the public, thus reducing consumption expenditures. Also, they tend to lower net exports because foreigners cut back their purchases from us (and we purchase more from them).

3. As production increases, it eventually pushes against capacity constraints, and it becomes increasingly difficult and costly for firms to increase their output further. Bigger and bigger increases in the price level are required to elicit an additional unit of output.

# CHAPTER 7 (P. 153)

1. A leftward shift in the short-run aggregate supply curve, combined with a rightward shift in the aggregate demand curve, that kept their intersection at the same output level, would result in a constant real output but a higher price level.

3. Q falls by $2 billion from $18 billion to $16 billion.

5. The principal effect will be on the short-run aggregate supply curve, which will shift upward and to the left. All other things equal, the result will be a higher price level and a lower real output level.

## CHAPTER 8 (P. 170)

1. After Iraq invaded Kuwait, the price of oil rose substantially because there was widespread concern that oil supplies would be reduced. Such an increase in the price of oil can shift the short-run aggregate supply curve to the left, thus reducing output. Also, the uncertainties associated with impending war affected the confidence and expectations of consumers. Reduced confidence can shift the aggregate demand curve to the left, also reducing output.

3. If consumers acted upon their optimism and actually began to buy more autos and appliances, the consumption function might shift to the right, thus increasing GNP (and having a multiplier effect).

## CHAPTER 8 (P. 177)

1. Economic cycles are not so regular that one can use them alone to forecast accurately.

3. An important input into any forecast is the nature of federal economic policy, since this policy has a big effect. The implications are that you must be sensitive to policy changes, and try to anticipate them as well as possible.

5. If the estimate of $G + I + (X - M_I) = \$700$ billion + \$10 billion, the \$2 trillion forecast will be in error by \$28.6 billion.

## CHAPTER 9 (P. 191)

1. Yes. No.

3. From top to bottom, the figures are: 500; 625; 750; 875; 1,000.

5. See the right-hand panel of Figure 9.2.

## CHAPTER 9 (P. 197)

1. The government might adopt certain rules governing the behavior of taxes and/or government spending. As we shall see in Chapters 14 and 15, there is considerable controversy among economists over the roles that discretion and rules should play in determining fiscal and monetary policy.

3. If the government spends money on a useless program, the result is waste. There is no sense in establishing wasteful and foolish spending programs merely to make jobs.

## CHAPTER 10 (P. 209)

1. The paper content of a dollar has little value. Money derives value from its ability to be exchanged for goods and services, because it is a unit of account, and because it acts as a store of value.

3. Time deposits can be transformed into a medium of exchange, currency, by savings withdrawal. They represent a store of value. But the traditional argument against including them in the money supply has been that, in most instances, you could not pay directly for anything with them.

## CHAPTER 10 (P. 220)

1. Yes, according to $MV = PQ$, $V$ must increase by 10 percent. If people and firms conserve on the use of cash because of higher interest rates or the use of new technologies and payment methods, velocity will increase.

3. (a) Simple Keynesian model: Changes in the money supply influence total spending through interest rates.
(b) Crude quantity theory: The quantity of money affects the price level, but not real output, thereby influencing nominal GNP.
(c) Model in Figure 10.5: Changes in the money supply affect the aggregate demand curve, thus influencing (usually) both real and nominal GNP.

## CHAPTER 11 (P. 238)

1. Reserves, demand deposits, total assets and total liabilities (including net worth) rise by $50,000. Loans and investments and net worth are unchanged.

3. Effect on balance sheet:

| Assets | | Liabilities and Net Worth | |
|---|---|---|---|
| Reserves | +$20,000 | Demand deposits | +$50,000 |
| Loans | +$30,000 | Net worth | 0 |
| Total | +$50,000 | Total | +$50,000 |

## CHAPTER 11 (P. 248)

1. The loans made by banks within the limits of reserve requirements do create money.

3. No, calling in loans and selling investments increase the bank's reserves. They do not increase demand deposits.

5. If the reserve ratio is 1/10, the system can support an additional $1,000 million with $100 million in excess reserves. If the reserve requirement is 1/6, $100 million in excess reserves can support a $600 million increase in the money supply.

# CHAPTER 12 (P. 258)

1. All entries should be +$5 million.

3. No, increasing reserve requirements reduces excess reserves, but does nothing to total member bank reserves.

5. You probably should wait to invest as a dramatic increase in the discount rate is likely to mean higher interest rates and lower bond prices.

# CHAPTER 12 (P. 269)

1. Keeping interest rates low in no way guarantees prosperity. In fact, such a policy could lead to serious inflation at times when the economy is becoming overheated.

3. The answer should focus on the material included in the section on "Should the Fed Pay More Attention to Interest Rates or the Money Supply?"

# CHAPTER 13 (P. 279)

1. No, they tend to be caused by massive shifts to the right of the aggregate demand curve.

3. The plot shows a downward-sloping Phillips curve. Friedman would reject it as a long-run Phillips cuve since it is not vertical.

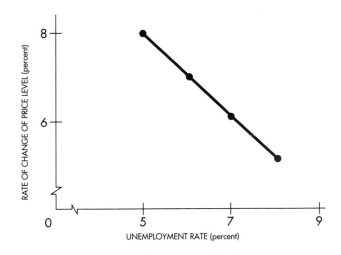

# CHAPTER 13 (P. 288)

1. The theory of rational expectations says that individuals and firms do not make systematic errors in forecasting the future. Whether or not people conform closely to this theory, it may produce predictions that are

useful. How good these predictions are is a matter to be settled by empirical studies.

3. Take the case of expectations of the inflation rate. Whereas the assumption of adaptive expectations means that people change their forecasts of the inflation rate to conform with whatever inflation rate currently exists, the theory of rational expectations says that, *on the average,* forecasts are correct.

## CHAPTER 14 (P. 301)

1. Critics of the new classical macroeconomics maintain that many unemployed workers would be willing to work if offered a job at a reasonable wage. They say that, if you ask the unemployed workers or actually offer them jobs, you'll see that this is true. The new classical macroeconomists deny this.

3. Market clearing means that the quantity supplied equals the quantity demanded in each market. Critics of the new classical macroeconomics deny that markets continually clear in this way.

## CHAPTER 14 (P. 312)

1. Critics of this view maintain that unemployed workers sometimes are unwilling to take jobs that would pay them in accord with their worth to potential employers and that, if they were willing to settle for a reasonable wage, they could get a job. The new Keynesians, on the other hand, believe that wages tend to be sticky, and that the quantity of labor supplied may exceed the quantity of labor demanded, particularly in recessions.

3. No. The rise of trade unions in the United States occurred largely in the 1930s and 1940s. Thus, it seems very unlikely that long-term labor contracts between unions and firms could explain the stickiness of wages and prices—or the existence of business fluctuations—before 1930.

## CHAPTER 15 (P. 321)

1. Large budget deficits financed by government borrowing can push up the interest rate, which in turn can cut private investment. Because of the cut in private investment, the nation's capital stock may grow less rapidly than otherwise would be the case.

3. Large deficits financed by borrowing can push up the interest rate, which will tend to increase the value of the dollar relative to other currencies. Thus, U.S. exports will tend to fall (because U.S. goods become more expensive relative to foreign goods) and U.S. imports tend to rise (because foreign goods become cheaper relative to U.S. goods). Consequently, net exports tend to fall.

## CHAPTER 15 (P. 330)

1. If the federal budget deficit rises, but the cyclically adjusted budget deficit is falling, most economists would feel that fiscal policy is not becoming more expansionary. If the federal budget deficit falls, but the cyclically adjusted budget deficit is rising, most economists would feel that fiscal policy is not becoming more contractionary.

3. Supporters of a balanced budget say that it would help curb government spending (which they regard as excessive). Opponents say that, if the government had to balance its budget, it could not use fiscal policy to help stabilize the economy.

## CHAPTER 16 (P. 339)

1. Yes, there was an increase in output per capita. The economy was operating inside its production possibilities curve in 1991, and on its production possibilities curve in 1992.

3. 2 bushels per hour; 2 bushels per hour; zero. The law of diminishing marginal returns sets in beyond 3 million hours of labor input.

5. The equilibrium labor force occurs where the annual average product of labor is 1,400 bushels. The factors responsible are described in Figure 16.3 of the text. The technological advance would increase the equilibrium labor force.

## CHAPTER 16 (P. 352)

1. The capital-output ratio is 2. No, this ratio can change; its value depends on technological change, among other things.

3. Ricardo did not assume that the capital-output ratio was fixed. He believed that it would increase.

## CHAPTER 17 (P. 364)

1. Yes, since the domestic opportunity cost of a computer is 1,000 cases of wine in the United States and 2,000 cases in France. The United States has a comparative advantage in computers, and France has one in producing wine. The United States is three times as efficient as France in computers, but only 50 percent more efficient in wine production.

3. No, forces of supply and demand will set the price of each good in world markets so that U.S. firms will find it profitable to make and export computers, while French firms will find it profitable to make and export wine.

## CHAPTER 17 (P. 376)

1. Yes, protection is likely to reduce, not increase, a country's standard of living. On the other hand, a country's standard of living tends to be directly related to its productivity.

3. The United States may have a comparative advantage in computers, but not in TV sets.

## CHAPTER 18 (P. 390)

1. Demanders of marks include buyers of German exports, foreign tourists in Germany, and foreign buyers of German financial assets. Both the demand curve and the supply curve (in question 2) are shown below.

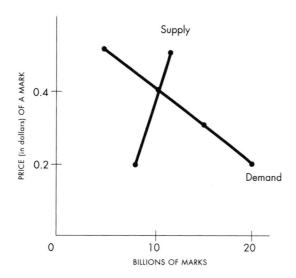

3. $.40 per mark, since at this exchange rate the quantity of marks demanded equals the quantity supplied. In recent years, there has been considerable flexibility in exchange rates, as described on p. 392.

## CHAPTER 18 (P. 401)

1. See the section on "Should the Value of the Dollar Be Stabilized?"

3. The market, through changing exchange rates, tends to erase payments imbalances within a flexible exchange rate system. Reserves are required to maintain fixed exchange rates in the face of payments imbalances.

## CHAPTER 19 (P. 412)

1. About 0.4. About 1.4. Teenagers have lower income than adults.

3. It is price elastic.

## CHAPTER 19 (P. 417)

1. (a) not true; (b) not true for some goods; (c) true.

3. Because of changes in tastes and incomes, and greater familiarity with cars, the demand curve may have shifted to the right between 1914 to 1916. Also, the price elasticity of demand may have been different then than in more recent years.

## CHAPTER 20 (P. 427)

1. 2 utils. 1 util. Yes.

3. Air is cheap because its marginal utility is quite low. In general, people are willing to pay relatively higher prices for commodities having higher marginal utilities.

## CHAPTER 20 (P. 432)

1. The quantity demanded is 26 at a price of $1, 23 at a price of $2, 19 at a price of $3, 14 at a price of $4, and 11 at a price of $5.

3. Bill's consumer's surplus = 6 cents. This number tells us how much more Bill would have been willing to spend on the two apples per day he consumes.

## CHAPTER 21 (P. 451)

1. The new olefins plant is not a firm; it is part of Exxon, which is a firm. A proprietorship is unlikely to build such a plant due to a lack of resources.

3. (a) and (b) are false because neither the University of Texas nor Massachusetts General Hospital are run to make profits. (c) is false because many firms are individual proprietorships with only one owner. (d) is false because many stockholders or partners do not participate in the management of the firms of which they are part owners.

5. Bondholders are not owners of the corporation, but stockholders are. Bondholders have lent money to the corporation at an agreed-upon interest rate, whereas stockholders' returns are based upon the profitability of the corporation they own.

## CHAPTER 21 (P. 460)

1. All but (h).

3. Column 1: $700,000; Column 2: $1,100,000 and $2,000,000. The owners owe $1,600,000. The owners have contributed $400,000. The difference between current assets and fixed assets is the length of time before they will be converted into cash.

## CHAPTER 22 (P. 468)

1.

OUTPUT PER HOUR

6

4

2

Average product

Marginal product

0    2    4    6
HOURS PER YEAR (thousands)

3. Labor is a variable input since the amount of labor is not fixed. Machines are a fixed input; their number cannot be changed during the period.

## CHAPTER 22 (P. 473)

1. The price of a unit of capital is $8.00.

3. This does not seem sensible. For one thing, it denies the existence of diminishing marginal returns in the short run.

## CHAPTER 23 (P. 487)

1. Total fixed costs = $20,000. The total variable cost of 4 units of output is $500.

3. The average costs are: $20,100, $10,100, $6,767, $5,125, and $4,160.

5. The marginal cost increases with output, since each extra unit of output increases total variable cost by more than the previous one does.

## CHAPTER 23 (P. 496)

1. (a) False, the statement describes increasing returns to scale. (b) False, the statement confuses the short run (decreasing marginal returns) with the long run (returns to scale). (c) False, what is important in determining the optimal number of firms in an industry is the shape of the long-run average cost function.

3. No. A linear total cost curve implies constant marginal cost. If the actual marginal costs rise quickly with output, the break-even chart is not likely to be very accurate.

## CHAPTER 24 (P. 510)

1. Between 3 and 4 is the optimal output.

3. Marginal cost is unchanged since the total variable cost function is unchanged.

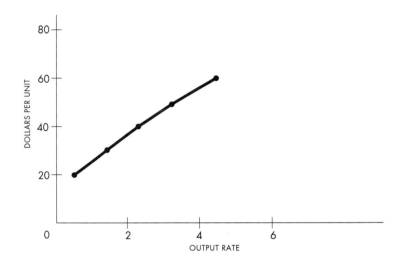

## CHAPTER 24 (P. 520)

1. Quantity supplied increases by about 0.1 percent.

3. Price = 1/2. The market period supply curve is vertical.

## CHAPTER 25 (P. 534)

1. No, because marginal revenue is negative when demand is price inelastic. Thus a reduction in output will raise total revenue. Since it is also likely to reduce total cost, it will increase profits.

3. Marginal cost equals average variable cost over this range of output. Output will be between 2 and 3 units per year, and price will be between $6,000 and $7,000.

5. Output falls to between 1 and 2 units of output, and price increases to between $7,000 and $8,000.

## CHAPTER 25 (P. 541)

1. See the sections in the text on "Perfect Competition and Monopoly: A Comparison" and "The Case Against Monopoly."

3. Perfectly competitive firms can earn high accounting profits if they are more efficient than are other firms. Also, in the short run, they may earn large profits.

## CHAPTER 26 (P. 553)

1. Cartel output will be 3,000 units per year.

3. If other members of the cartel hold their prices fixed (in accord with the agreement), each firm has a strong motive for lowering price, expanding sales, and increasing its profits.

## CHAPTER 26 (P. 566)

1. Lever Brothers still has a dominant strategy (concentrate on magazines), but Procter and Gamble no longer has a dominant strategy. If Lever Brothers concentrates on TV, Procter and Gamble should concentrate on TV, but if Lever Brothers concentrates on magazines, Procter and Gamble should concentrate on magazines.

3. As the demand curve becomes closer and closer to horizontal, it is tangent to the long-run average cost curve at a point that is closer and closer to the minimum point.

## CHAPTER 27 (P. 579)

1. The statement is incorrect. One cannot prove that perfect competition results in an optimal distribution of income. Also, the United States really hasn't opted for perfect competition, which is an abstract model.

3. The four-firm concentration ratio is 90 percent.

## CHAPTER 27 (P. 585)

1. The issue is whether firms can escape the discipline of the market. According to this quotation, they can: many (probably most) economists take a different view.

3. The answer should touch on the difficulties of establishing intent and, in some circumstances, its irrelevance.

## CHAPTER 28 (P. 599)

1. The maximum is $3,600, since if the wage exceeded this amount, the firm would hire 3, not 4, years of labor. The minimum is $3,000, since if

the wage were below this amount, the firm would hire 5, not 4, years of labor. These wage rates seem unrealistically low for the United States at present.

3. If a bonus payment system results in a worker's working harder, thus increasing the firm's sales or productivity, it may increase the firm's profits even though the worker may get paid more because of its existence.

## CHAPTER 28 (P. 606)

1. The focus of the answer should be upon whether the unions can be considered as monopolizers of a service.

3. This is not an easy task, as you would need data relating output responses to changes in various types of labor. No, the theory is not useless. Employers must form judgments of some sort on this score.

## CHAPTER 29 (P. 619)

1. Borrowers might include: consumers purchasing durable goods, businesses financing inventories, and local, state, and federal governments financing expenditures.

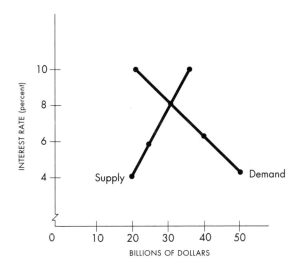

Eight percent is the equilibrium interest rate. If usury laws put a 6 percent ceiling on interest rates, there would be an excess demand for loanable funds.

3. The capitalized value of the asset is $1,000 \div .10 = $10,000.

## CHAPTER 29 (P. 627)

1. $1,000 \div (1.08)^2 = $857.34.

3. As indicated in the chapter, much of the apparent increase in labor's share may have little to do with the growth of labor's power. Moreover, in

recent years, it is not clear that labor's power has grown. The links to the alleged shortage of capital also are unclear.

## CHAPTER 30 (P. 640)

1. The proportion of total income received by families with incomes of $2000 equals $40 \times 2,000 \div (40 \times 2,000 + 30 \times 4,000 + 20 \times 6,000 + 10 \times 10,000) = 19.0$ percent. The proportions received by families with incomes of $4,000, $6,000, and $10,000 are 28.6 percent, 28.6 percent, and 23.8 percent, respectively. Thus the Lorenz curve is as follows:

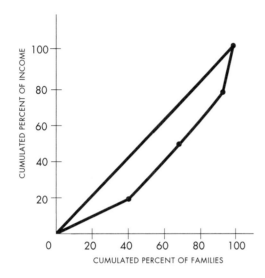

3. (a) Yes, since people can sell assets to maintain consumption. (b) No. (c) Yes.

## CHAPTER 30 (P. 648)

1. To be free of dependency, welfare recipients must be able to earn a living. Training and job placement seem to be worthwhile activities, but it may be difficult to train some welfare recipients effectively, since they lack basic education and skills.

3. See p. 642 on "Social Insurance."

## CHAPTER 31 (P. 663)

1. It is very difficult in many cases to know whether a certain activity can be performed better by government than private citizens can do for themselves. But the first half of this chapter indicates a number of areas where most economists believe the government has legitimate functions.

3. You can consume the services provided by national defense without depriving another person of also doing so simultaneously. Also, citizens cannot be prevented from benefiting from national expenditures on defense, whether they pay money toward defense or not. A rifle is not a

public good; the hallmark of a public good is that it is consumed collectively or jointly.

5. Such activities result in external economies.

## CHAPTER 31 (P. 670)

1. The socially optimal output of paper is less than *OQ*. The supply curve reflecting true social costs lies to the left of the one shown because the latter neglects part of the social cost of paper production.

3. Government programs supported prices of farm products. See pp. 663–69 of the text. Federal government programs have not solved the problem. See the section of the text on "Evaluation of Government Farm Programs."

5. The essential point here is one shared by many government programs, be they protective tariffs or farm subsidies. The benefits of the programs are concentrated on a relatively small and highly organized group of people, while the programs' costs are spread across the population at large.

## CHAPTER 32 (P. 681)

1. The government should build the road from A to B since its benefits exceed its costs. The numbers imply that the cost of the road between B and C exceeds its benefits. The cost equals $15 million – $10 million = $5 million, while the benefit equals $22 million – $20 million = $2 million.

3. No. It is impossible to tell in which sector the inefficiency exists. The nonattainment of potential production might result from inefficiency in either sector.

## CHAPTER 32 (P. 689)

1.

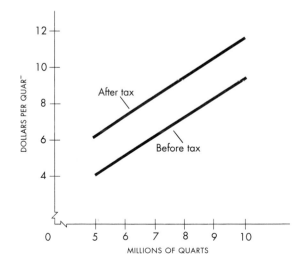

3. The equilibrium price of gin is $6 per quart both before and after the tax. None of the tax is passed on to the consumer.

# CHAPTER 33 (P. 704)

1. No, the private costs are less than the social costs because of the required downstream water treatment.

3. The output prevailing after the industry has to reimburse others is more desirable, because it reflects the social costs of paper manufacture.

5. The total cost equals $10 - 2P + 5P = 10 + 3P$. Thus it is minimized when $P = 0$. No.

# CHAPTER 34 (P. 718)

1. Hypotheses might include differential savings, investment, population growth, and literacy rates, a more poorly developed capital market in India, and sociological and cultural differences between the two countries.

3. No, not in the sense that population growth has been higher in India than Taiwan. In fact, the opposite was true.

# CHAPTER 34 (P. 729)

1. No. For example, consider the case of Chile, cited on p. 719.

3. The point here is that cultural differences among nations greatly influence the countries' abilities, and even their will, to generate rapid economic development. Obviously, they also set limits on what both the developed countries and the LDCs themselves can do effectively to promote development.

# CHAPTER 35 (P. 744)

1. Both have declined for reasons given on pp. 741–43.

3. The response should focus on the differences between the price mechanism and planning in solving the basic economic problems (what, how, for whom, and how much growth). See the section on "Prices in the USSR."

# CHAPTER 35 (P. 749)

1. Some people have stated this view, but so many factors are not held equal that it is hard to see that very much can be learned from this simple comparison. Nonetheless, comparative studies of this sort, if conducted carefully, can be valuable.

3. For the views of the radical economists on this score, see the section on "Radical Economics."

# BRIEF ANSWERS TO "PROBING DEEPER" AT THE END OF "CENTRAL ECONOMIC ISSUES"

## HOW TO MAKE THE TRANSITION FROM COMMUNISM TO CAPITALISM: THE CASE OF POLAND (PP. 54–56)

1. The central planners must have a great deal of information concerning the technology of each industry, in order to try to determine whether resources should be allocated to one industry or another. Also, the output set for one industry often depends on how much another industry will produce, so the planners must look at the economy as a whole, not just at specific industries in isolation.

2. Because individuals do not own the firms, they often do not receive any substantial reward if they increase the firms' efficiency. Thus, there often is little incentive for their improving resource allocation.

3. If managers receive little reward for innovation or for improved quality of product, they will have little incentive to carry out innovations or to improve quality.

4. Very few people in Poland have sufficient wealth to make a bid, and even if they did, it would be very difficult for them to determine how much to bid since Poland does not have a well-developed price system.

5. Because such subsidies tend to reduce the incentives for managers to reduce costs and to operate efficiently and effectively.

6. If a nation adopts a capitalist system, it must tolerate some bankruptcies and unemployment. Firms that are unsuccessful must be allowed to fail. People who want to leave a particular job must be able to do so. Firms must be able to fire people who cannot succeed at a particular occupation.

## WILL THE BANKS GO THE WAY OF THE SAVINGS AND LOAN INDUSTRY? (PP. 234–36)

1. Many real estate loans were "nonperforming;" borrowers were not paying interest and/or principal fully and on time. The market for real estate was much poorer than expected by the borrowers (and lenders).

2. The Bush administration argued that, if industrial companies could own banks, this would enable banks to attract additional capital and

allow them to diversify their risks. If they could sell insurance, they would be able to diversify into potentially profitable areas, according to the proponents of this proposal.

3. The Bush administration argued that this could save the banking industry a lot of the costs incurred in opening new bank branches in different states.

4. They invested their money in low-yielding mortgages that paid the same low rate of interest over the life of the mortgage, often 20 or 30 years; but to attract and keep deposits, they had to pay higher interest rates than their investments in these mortgages were earning.

5. To survive, a bank (like any firm) must be profitable. It is unwise for banks to get involved in risky businesses about which they know little. The banks should be encouraged to increase the amount of capital provided by their owners. Regulators and others should be sensitive and alert to problems arising from incompetence, fraud, and improper political influence. Also, changes may be required in the system of deposit insurance.

## "HAS THE UNITED STATES LOST ITS TECHNO-LOGICAL EDGE?" (PP. 348–49)

1. If American firms develop and introduce a relatively large proportion of the new products and processes in the industry, take out a relatively large proportion of the significant patents, do a relatively large share of the research and development, and have relatively high levels of productivity, these are signs that the U.S. has a technological lead.

2. It depends to a large extent on how much American industry and government spend (relative to other countries) to advance technology, on the quality of our educational system, the competitiveness of our markets, the alertness of our managers, and a host of other factors.

3. Such an industry may find it difficult to compete with foreign rivals. Jobs may be lost, and profits may decline. Communities where this industry is located may be depressed.

4. In some cases, firms may underinvest in particular types of research and development, because they cannot appropriate the benefits fully. More will be said on this score in Chapter 31.

5. No.

6. Yes. The United States has tried in many ways to promote the economic welfare and political stability of its European and Asian allies, as well as other countries. The fact that the technological gap has narrowed is, in many respects, from the point of view of the world as a whole, a healthy sign.

## "AMERICA'S CHRONIC TRADE DEFICIT" (PP. 398–400)

1. Many observers have been concerned about the trade deficit and about our becoming an international debtor country. As Paul Volcker has

put it, we "can't afford to become addicted to drawing on increasing amounts of foreign savings to help finance our internal economy. Part of our domestic industry—that part dependent on exports or competing with imports—would be sacrificed. The stability of the dollar and our domestic financial markets would become hostage to events abroad."

2. It can change exchange rates; that is, the value of the dollar can fall relative to that of other currencies. It can also reduce the federal budget deficit. Further, it can try to make American goods and services more competitive in international markets.

3. Because of the weak dollar, it was relatively easy for American firms to compete with imported goods in the 1970s. Thus there was less pressure on American firms to improve their technology, lower their costs, and make better products.

4. Because people became convinced that inflation really was going to be curbed in the United States. As indicated on p. 382, such a change in expectations would be expected to result in a stronger dollar.

5. No. See the answer to question 2 above.

6. See the answer to question 1.

## "CAN AMERICAN FIRMS COMPETE?" (PP. 492–94)

1. No. Advertising, styling, finance, and a variety of others.

2. Because it costs money to hold, store, and finance inventories.

3. Because if a worker makes a single item and passes it to the next worker immediately (rather than making a large batch of the items and then passing them on all at once), the first worker will be informed very soon if the next worker finds them defective. Thus the causes of defects tend to be nipped in the bud.

4. Absenteeism raises a firm's costs, because redundant labor must be hired to cover for unexpected absence of workers. Greater incentives can be established to induce workers to reduce absenteeism.

5. Yes. Using Japanese managerial techniques, plants that formerly were relatively inefficient have been transformed into efficient ones without substantial investments in advanced automation.

6. A firm can invest in spotting the causes of product defects, so the problems can be dealt with at the source rather than after the fact.

## MEDICAL CARE: CAN BENEFIT-COST ANALYSIS BE USED? (PP. 675–77)

1. A great many people have health insurance (for example, Blue Cross), much of it paid for by employers.

2. The advantage is that the hospitals have an incentive to reduce costs. One problem is that the hospitals may respond by lowering the quality of health care.

3. Economists feel that more competition would tend to bring down the costs of health care and promote efficiency, as well as reduce the price of health care.

4. It is very difficult to measure the benefits of saving a life or improving the quality of life. Are some lives more valuable than others? Are some extensions of life more beneficial than others?

5. It depends on the valuation one places on this person's life, and while economists can contribute to a discussion of this topic, economics alone cannot provide a full or completely satisfactory answer.

## WHAT SHOULD BE DONE ABOUT GLOBAL WARMING? (PP. 701–3)

1. See page 695 for a discussion of why a fee would result in a least-cost reduction in emissions of pollutants. The reasons are essentially the same for a system of transferable emissions permits.

2. Because the costs would outweigh the social benefits, thus reducing the rate of economic growth.

3. Because if some countries limited emissions, but other countries failed to do so, little might be achieved.

4. Because, if only some greenhouse gases are covered, but other greenhouse gases are not covered, little may be achieved.

5. See page 695 for a discussion of why an effluent fee is likely to be less costly than direct government regulation as a means of reducing pollution.

# GLOSSARY OF TERMS

**Absolute advantage** the ability of one country to produce a good or service more cheaply than another country.

**Adaptive expectations** situation where people change their forecasts of the variable in question to conform to its current level.

**Aggregate demand curve** a curve, sloping downward to the right, that shows the level of real national output that will be demanded at various economy-wide price levels.

**Aggregate production function** the relationship between the amount used of each of the inputs available in the economy and the resulting amount of potential output, i.e., the most output that existing technology permits the economy to produce from various quantities of all available inputs.

**Aid to Families with Dependent Children (AFDC)** an antipoverty program that provides cash payments to families with children.

**Alternative cost** the value of what certain resources could have produced had they been used in the best alternative way; also called **opportunity cost.**

**American Federation of Labor-Congress of Industrial Organizations (AFL-CIO)** a federation of national labor unions formed in 1955 by the merger between the American Federation of Labor (originally a federation of unions organized along craft lines) and the Congress of Industrial Organizations (originally a federation of unions organized along industrial lines).

**Antitrust laws** legislation (such as the Sherman Act, the Clayton Act, and the Federal Trade Commission Act) intended to promote competition and control monopoly.

**Appreciation of currency** an increase in the value of one currency relative to another.

**Asymmetric information** situation where all participants in a market do not have the same information (for example, sellers may know more about the quality of a product than do potential buyers).

**Automatic stabilizers** structural features of the economy that tend by themselves to stabilize national output, without the help of new legislation or government policy measures.

**Average fixed cost** the firm's total fixed cost divided by its output.

**Average product of an input** total output divided by the amount of input used to produce this amount of output.

**Average product of labor** total output per unit of labor.

**Average propensity to consume** the fraction of total disposable income that is spent on consumption; equal to personal consumption expenditure divided by disposable income.

**Average total cost** the firm's total cost divided by its output; equal to average fixed cost plus average variable cost.

**Average variable cost** the firm's total variable cost divided by its output.

**Backward-bending supply curve for labor** a supply curve for labor inputs showing that, beyond some point, increases in price may result in smaller amounts of labor being supplied.

**Balance-of-payments deficit** the difference between the quantity supplied and the quantity demanded of a currency when the currency is overvalued (i.e., priced above its equilibrium price).

**Balance-of-payments surplus** the difference between the quantity demanded and the quantity supplied of a currency when the currency is undervalued (i.e., priced below its equilibrium price).

**Balance sheet** an accounting statement showing the nature of a firm's assets, the claims by creditors on those assets, and the value of the firm's ownership at a certain point in time.

**Balanced budget** a budget in which

A 4 9

tax revenues cover government expenditures.

**Barometric firm** in an oligopolistic industry, any single firm that is the first to make changes in prices, which are then generally accepted by other firms.

**Base year** a year chosen as a reference point for comparison with some later or earlier year.

**Bond** a debt (generally long-term) of a firm or government.

**Break-even chart** a chart that plots a firm's total cost and total revenue, and that shows the output level that must be reached if the firm is to avoid losses.

**Budget** a statement of the government's anticipated expenditures and tax revenues for a fiscal year.

**Budget deficit** a budget in which tax revenues fall short of government expenditures.

**Budget line** a line showing the market baskets that the consumer can purchase, given his or her income and prevailing prices.

**Budget surplus** a budget in which tax revenues exceed government expenditures.

$C + I + G + (X - M_1)$ **line** a curve showing total intended spending (the sum of consumption expenditure, investment expenditure, government expenditure, and net exports) at various levels of gross national product.

$C + I + G$ **line** a curve showing total intended spending (the sum of intended consumption expenditure, investment expenditure, and government expenditure) at various levels of gross national product, in the simple case where net exports are zero.

**Capital** resources (such as factory buildings, equipment, raw materials, and inventories) that are created within the economic system for the purpose of producing other goods.

**Capital consumption allowance** the value of the capital (i.e., the plant, equipment, and structures) that is worn out in a year; also called **depreciation.**

**Capital formation** investment in plant and equipment.

**Capital goods** output consisting of plant and equipment that are used to make other goods.

**Capital-output ratio** the ratio of the total capital stock to annual national output.

**Capitalism** an economic system characterized by private ownership of the tools of production; freedom of choice and of enterprise whereby consumers and firms can pursue their own self-interest; competition for sales among producers and resource owners; and reliance on the free market.

**Capitalization of assets** a method of computing the value of an asset by calculating the present value of the expected future income this asset will produce.

**Cartel** an open, formal collusive arrangement among firms.

**Central bank** a government-established agency that controls the supply of money and supervises the country's commercial banks; the central bank of the United States is the Federal Reserve.

**Closed shop** a situation where firms can hire only workers who are already union members.

**Collective bargaining** process of negotiation between the union and management over wages and working conditions.

**Collusion** a covert arrangement whereby firms agree on price and output levels in order to decrease competition and increase profits.

**Commercial banks** financial institutions that hold demand and other checkable deposits and permit checks to be written on them, and lend money to firms and individuals.

**Common stock** certificate of ownership of a corporation. Holders of common stock are owners of the corporation.

**Comparative advantage** the law that states that a nation should produce and export goods where its efficiency *relative to other nations* is highest; specialization and trade depend on comparative, not absolute advantage.

**Compensation of employees** the wages and salaries paid by employers to the suppliers of labor, including supplementary payments for employee benefits (such as payments into public and private pension and welfare funds).

**Complements** commodities that tend to be consumed together, i.e., commodities with a negative cross elasticity of demand such that a decrease in the price of one will result in an increase in the quantity demanded of the other.

**Constant dollar amounts** amounts measured in base-year dollars (i.e., according to the purchasing power of the dollar in some earlier year), in order to express value in a way that corrects for changes in the price level.

**Constant returns to scale** a long-run situation where, if the firm increases the amount of all inputs by the same proportion, output increases by the same proportion as each of the inputs.

**Consumer** an individual or household that purchases the goods and services produced by the economic system.

**Consumer goods** output consisting of items that consumers purchase, such as clothing, food, and drink.

**Consumer Price Index** a measure of U.S. inflation, calculated by the Bureau of Labor Statistics, originally intended to measure changes in the prices of goods and services purchased by urban wage earners and clerical workers; in 1978, expanded to cover all urban consumers.

**Consumer's surplus** the difference between the maximum amount that a consumer would pay for a good or service and what he or she actually pays.

**Consumption function** the relationship between consumption spending and disposable income, i.e., the amount of consumption expenditure that will occur at various levels of disposable income.

**Corporate profits** the net income of corporations (i.e., corporate profits before income taxes), including dividends received by the stockholders, retained earnings, and the amount paid by corporations as income taxes.

**Corporation** a fictitious legal person separate and distinct from the stockholders who own it, governed by a board of directors elected by the stockholders.

**Cost function** the relationship between cost and a firm's level of output, i.e., how much cost a firm will incur at various levels of output.

**Council of Economic Advisers** a group established by the Employment Act of 1946, whose function is to help the president formulate and assess the economic policies of the government.

**Craft union** a labor union that includes workers in a particular craft (such as machinists or carpenters).

**Creeping inflation** an increase in the general price level of a few percent per year that gradually erodes the value of money.

**Cross elasticity of demand** the percentage change in the quantity demanded of one commodity resulting from a one percent change in the price of another commodity; may be either positive or negative.

**Crowding-out effect** the tendency for an increase in public sector expenditure to result in a cut in private sector expenditure.

**Crude quantity theory of money and prices** the theory that if the velocity of circulation of money remains constant and real gross national product remains fixed at its full-employment level, it follows from the equation of exchange that the price level will be proportional to the money supply.

**Cyclical unemployment** joblessness that occurs because of business fluctuations.

**Cyclically adjusted budget balance** the difference between tax revenues and government expenditures that would result if gross national product were at its potential, not its actual, level.

**Decreasing returns to scale** a long-run situation where, if the firm increases the amount of all inputs by the same proportion, output increases by a smaller proportion than each of the inputs.

**Deflating** the conversion of values expressed in current dollars into values expressed in constant dollars, in order to correct for changes in the price level.

**Demand curve for loanable funds** a curve showing the quantity of loanable funds that will be demanded at each interest rate.

**Demand curve for money** a curve representing the quantity of money that will be demanded at various interest rates (holding real gross national product and the price level constant).

**Demand deposits** checking accounts; bank deposits subject to payment on demand.

**Demand-side inflation** an increase in the general price level that is triggered by rightward shifts of the aggregate demand curve (too much aggregate spending, too much money chasing too few goods).

**Depreciation** the value of the capital (i.e., plant, equipment, and structures) that is worn out in a year; also called a **capital consumption allowance.**

**Depreciation of currency** a decrease in the value of one currency relative to another.

**Depression** a period when national output is well below its potential (i.e., full-employment) level; a severe recession.

**Derived demand** demand for labor and other inputs not as ends in themselves, but as means to produce other things.

**Devaluation of currency** under the gold standard, a decrease in the value of a currency as a consequence of an increase in the price of gold.

**Differentiated oligopoly** a market structure (such as those for automobiles and machinery) where there are only a few sellers of somewhat different products.

**Diffusion process** the process by which the use of an innovation spreads from firm to firm and from use to use.

**Direct regulation** government issue of enforceable rules concerning the conduct of firms.

**Discount rate** the interest rate the Federal Reserve charges for loans to commercial banks.

**Discretionary policy** policy that is formulated at the discretion of the policy makers (in contrast to rigid policy rules or feedback policy rules).

**Disposable income** the total amount of income people can keep after personal taxes.

**Diversifiable risk** risk that can be avoided by diversification.

**Dominant firm** in an oligopolistic industry, a single large firm that sets the price for the industry but lets the small firms sell all they want at that price.

**Dominant strategy** a strategy that is best for a player regardless of what the other player's strategy may be.

**Easy monetary policy** a monetary policy that increases the money supply substantially and reduces interest rates.

**Economic profits** the excess of a firm's profits over what it could make in other industries.

**Economic resources** resources that are scarce and thus command a nonzero price.

**Economics** the study of how resources are allocated among alternative uses to satisfy human wants.

**Economies of scale** efficiencies that result from carrying out a process (such as production or sales) on a large scale.

**Efficiency wage** a wage rate that is higher than the perfectly competitive wage. Firms may pay such a wage to reduce shirking and raise worker productivity.

**Effluent fee** a fee that a polluter must pay to the government for discharging waste.

**Equation of exchange** a way of restating the definition of the velocity of circulation of money, such that the amount received for the final goods and services during a period equals the amount spent on those final goods and services during the same period (that is, MV = PQ).

**Equilibrium** a situation in which there is no tendency for change.

**Equilibrium level of gross national product** the value of national output at which the flow of income generated by this level of output results in a level of spending precisely sufficient to buy this level of output.

**Equilibrium price** a price that shows no tendency for change, because it is the price at which the quantity demanded equals the quantity supplied; the price toward which the actual price of a good always tends to move.

**Exchange rate** the number of units of one currency that can purchase a unit of another currency.

**Excise tax** a tax imposed on each unit sold of a particular product, such as cigarettes or liquor.

**Expansion** the phase in the business cycle after the trough during which national output rises.

**Explicit cost** the cost of resources for which there is an explicit payment.

**Exports** the goods and services that a nation sells to other nations.

**External diseconomy** an uncompensated cost to one person or firm resulting from the consumption or output of another person or firm.

**External economy** an uncompensated benefit to one person or firm resulting from the consumption or output of another person or firm.

**Featherbedding** a practice whereby a union restricts output per worker in order to increase the amount of labor required to do a certain job.

**Federal Open Market Committee (FOMC)** a group, composed of the seven members of the Federal Reserve Board plus five presidents of Federal Reserve Banks, which makes decisions concerning the purchase and sale of government securities, in order to control bank reserves and the money supply.

**Federal Reserve Board** the Board of Governors of the Federal Reserve System, composed of seven members appointed by the president for 14-year terms, whose function is to promote the nation's economic welfare by supervising the operations of the U.S. money and banking system.

**Federal Reserve System** a system established by Congress in 1913 that includes the commercial banks, the twelve Federal Reserve Banks, and the seven-member Board of Governors of the Federal Reserve System.

**Feedback policy rule** a rule allowing the behavior of the variable governed by the policy rule to change, depending upon future circumstances.

**Final goods and services** goods and services that are destined for the ultimate user (such as flour purchased for family consumption).

**Firm** an organization that produces a good or service for sale in an attempt to make a profit.

**Firm's demand curve for labor** a curve showing the relationship between the price of labor and the amount of labor demanded by a firm, i.e., the amount of labor that will be demanded by a firm at various wage rates.

**Firm's supply curve** a curve, usually sloping upward to the right, showing the quantity of output a firm will produce at each price.

**Fiscal policy** the policy of the government regarding taxes and government expenditures, the object being to stabilize the economy.

**Fixed input** a resource used in the production process (such as plant and equipment) whose quantity cannot be changed during the particular period under consideration.

**Food programs** federal antipoverty programs that distribute food to the poor, either directly from surpluses produced by farm programs or indirectly via stamps that can be exchanged for food.

**45-degree line** a line that contains all points where the amount on the horizontal axis equals the amount on the vertical axis.

**Fractional-reserve banking** the practice whereby banks hold less cash than the amount they owe their depositors.

**Free resources** resources (such as air) that are so abundant that they can be obtained without charge.

**Frictional unemployment** temporary joblessness, such as that occurring among people who have quit jobs, people looking for their first job, and seasonal workers.

**Full employment** the minimum level of joblessness that the economy could achieve without undesirably high inflation, recognizing that there will always be some frictional and structural unemployment.

**Game** a competitive situation where two or more players pursue their own interests and no player can dictate the outcome.

**Gold exchange standard** an exchange rate system developed after World War II, under which the dollar was directly convertible into gold at a fixed price, and other currencies, since they could be converted into dollars at fixed exchange rates, were thus indirectly convertible into gold at a fixed price.

**Gold standard** a method of exchange rate determination prevailing until the 1930s, under which currencies were convertible into a certain amount of gold.

**Government purchases** federal, state, and local government spending on final goods and services, excluding transfer payments.

**Gross national product (GNP)** the value of the total amount of final goods and services produced by the economy during a period of time; this value can be measured either by the expenditure on the final goods and services, or by the income generated by the output.

**Gross private domestic investment** all additions to the nation's stock of private investment goods, i.e., all investment spending, including purchases of tools, equipment, and machinery, all construction expenditures, and the change in total inventories.

**Historical cost of assets** what a firm actually paid for its assets.

**Hysteresis** situation where the natural rate of unemployment depends on the actual rate of unemployment.

**Implicit contracts** agreements between workers and firms that are not found in any formal, written contracts.

**Implicit cost** the cost (for which there is no explicit payment) of the resources that are provided by the owner of a firm, measured by what these resources could bring if they were used in their best alternative employment.

**Imports** the goods and services that a nation buys from other nations.

**Income effect** the change in the quantity demanded by the consumer of a good due to the change in the consumer's level of utility resulting from a change in the price of the good.

**Income elasticity of demand** the percentage change in the quantity demanded of a commodity resulting from a one percent increase in total money income (all prices being held constant).

**Income statement** an accounting statement showing a firm's sales, costs, and profits during a particular period (often a quarter or a year).

**Income tax** a federal, state, or local tax imposed on personal income and corporate profits.

**Incomes policy** a policy to control inflation that sets some targets for wages and prices in the economy as a whole; gives particular firms and industries detailed guides for making wage and price decisions; and provides some inducements for firms and unions to follow these guidelines.

**Increasing returns to scale** a long-run situation where, if a firm increases the amount of all inputs by the same proportion, output increases by a larger proportion than each of the inputs.

**Indifference curve** a curve representing market baskets among which the consumer is indifferent.

**Indirect business taxes** taxes (such as general sales taxes, excise taxes, and customs duties) that are imposed not directly on the business itself but on its products or services, and hence are treated by firms as costs of production.

**Individual demand curve** a curve showing the relationship between individual consumer demand and prices, i.e., how much of a good an individual consumer will demand at various prices.

**Industrial union** a labor union that includes all the workers in a particular plant or industry (such as autos or steel).

**Inflation** an increase in the general level of prices economy-wide.

**Innovation** the first commercial application of a new technology.

**Innovator** a firm that is first to apply a new technology.

**Input** any resource used in the production process.

**Interest** the payment of money by borrowers to suppliers of money capital.

**Interest rate** the annual amount that a borrower must pay for the use of a dollar for a year.

**Intermediate good** a good that is not sold to the ultimate user, but is used as an input in producing final goods and services (such as flour to be used in manufacturing bread).

**IS curve** a curve showing, for each level of the interest rate, the level of GNP that will satisfy the equilibrium condition that intended spending on output must equal GNP.

**Isocost curve** a curve showing the input combinations the firm can obtain for a given expenditure.

**Isoquant** a curve showing all possible efficient combinations of inputs capable of producing a certain quantity of output.

**Keynesians** economists who share many of the beliefs of John Maynard Keynes. His principal tenet was that a capitalist system does not automatically tend toward a full-employment equilibrium (due in part to the rigidity of wages). Keynesians tend to believe that a free-enterprise economy has weak self-regulating mechanisms that should be supplemented by activist fiscal (and other) policies.

**Labor** human effort, both physical and mental, used to produce goods and services.

**Labor force** the number of people employed plus the number of those unemployed (i.e., actively looking for work and willing to take a job if one were offered).

**Labor productivity** the average

amount of output that can be obtained for every unit of labor.

**Laffer curve** a curve representing the relationship between the amount of income tax revenue collected by the government and the marginal tax rate, i.e., how much revenue will be collected at various marginal tax rates.

**Land** natural resources, including minerals as well as plots of ground, used to produce goods and services.

**Law of diminishing marginal returns** the principle that if equal increments of a given input are added (the quantities of other inputs being held constant), the resulting increments of product obtained from the extra unit of input (i.e., the marginal product) will begin to decrease beyond some point.

**Law of diminishing marginal utility** the principle that if a person consumes additional units of a given commodity (the consumption of other commodities being held constant), the resulting increments of utility derived from the extra unit of the commodity (i.e., the commodity's marginal utility) will begin to decrease beyond some point.

**Law of increasing cost** the principle that as more and more of a good is produced, the production of each additional unit of the good is likely to entail a larger and larger opportunity cost.

**Legal reserve requirements** regulations, imposed by the Federal Reserve System in order to control the money supply, requiring banks (and other institutions) to hold a certain fraction of deposits as reserves.

**Liabilities** the debts of a firm.

**LM curve** a curve showing, for each level of the interest rate, the level of GNP that will satisfy the equilibrium condition that the public be satisfied to hold the existing quantity of money.

**Loanable funds** funds (including those supplied by households and firms that find the rate of interest high enough to get them to save) that are available for borrowing by consumers, businesses, and government.

**Local unions** labor unions, organized around either craft or industrial lines, that are set up in particular geographical areas or plants, and which may or may not belong to a larger national union.

**Long run** the period of time during which all of a firm's inputs are variable,

i.e., during which the firm could completely change the resources used in the production process.

**Long-run aggregate supply curve** a vertical line showing the level of real national output at various economy-wide price levels when input prices are flexible.

**Long-run average cost function** a representation of the minimum average cost of producing various output levels when any desired type or scale of plant can be built.

**Lorenz curve** a curve that measures income inequality by showing what percentage of the people receive what percentage of total income.

**Lucas aggregate supply curve** according to Robert Lucas, only unexpected changes in the price level will result in changes in aggregate supply (holding the expected price level constant, the level of real GNP is directly related to the actual price level, according to the Lucas aggregate supply curve).

*M*-1 narrowly defined money supply, which includes coins, currency, demand deposits, and other checkable deposits.

*M*-2 broadly defined money supply, which includes savings deposits, small time deposits, money market mutual fund balances, and money market deposit accounts, as well as the components of the narrowly defined money supply, *M*-1 (coins, currency, demand deposits, and other checkable deposits).

**Marginal cost** the addition to total cost resulting from the addition of the last unit of output.

**Marginal cost pricing** a pricing rule whereby the price of a product is set equal to its marginal cost.

**Marginal product of an input** the addition to total output that results from the addition of an extra unit of input (the quantities of all other inputs being held constant).

**Marginal product of labor** the additional output resulting from the addition of an extra unit of labor.

**Marginal propensity to consume** the fraction of an extra dollar of disposable income that is spent on consumption

**Marginal propensity to save** the fraction of an extra dollar of disposable income that is saved.

**Marginal revenue** the change in total revenue that results from the addition of one unit to the quantity sold.

**Marginal tax rate** the proportion of an extra dollar of income that must be paid in taxes.

**Marginal utility** the additional satisfaction derived from consuming an additional unit of a commodity.

**Market** a group of firms and individuals that are in touch with each other in order to buy or sell some good or service.

**Market demand curve** a curve, usually sloping downward to the right, showing the relationship between a product's price and the quantity demanded of the product.

**Market demand curve for labor** a curve showing the relationship between the price of labor and the total amount of labor demanded in the market.

**Market period** the relatively short period of time during which the supply of a particular good is fixed and output is unaffected by price.

**Market structure** the type or organization of a market. Markets differ with regard to the number and size of buyers and sellers in the market, the ease with which new firms can enter, the extent of product differentiation, and other factors.

**Market supply curve** a curve, usually sloping upward to the right, showing the relationship between a product's price and the quantity supplied of the product.

**Market supply curve for labor** a curve showing the relationship between the price of labor and the total amount of labor supplied in the market.

**Medicaid** a federal program that pays for the health care of the poor.

**Medicare** a compulsory hospitalization program plus a voluntary insurance plan for doctors' fees for people over 65, included under the Social Security program.

**Model** a theory composed of assumptions that simplify and abstract from reality, from which conclusions or predictions about the real world are deduced.

**Monetarists** economists generally sharing the belief that business fluctuations are due largely to changes in the money supply. Many monetarists think that a free-enterprise economy has ef-fective self-regulating mechanisms that activist fiscal and monetary policies tend to disrupt. Some monetarists, like Milton Friedman, advocate a rule for stable growth in the money supply of 3 to 5 percent per year.

**Monetary base** the reserves of commercial banks plus currency outside banks.

**Monetary policy** the exercise of the central bank's control over the quantity of money and the level of interest rates in order to promote the objectives of national economic policy.

**Money** anything that serves as a medium of exchange and a standard and store of value; the unit in which the prices of goods and services are measured.

**Money income** income measured in current dollars (i.e., actual money amounts).

**Monopolistic competition** a market structure in which there are many sellers of somewhat differentiated products, where entry is easy, and where there is no collusion among sellers. Retailing seems to have many of the characteristics of monopolistic competition.

**Monopoly** a market structure (such as those for public utilities) in which there is only one seller of a product.

**Monopsony** a market structure (such as that for the single firm that employs all the labor in a company town) in which there is only a single buyer.

**Moral suasion** the Federal Reserve's practice of exhorting banks to go along with its wishes, in the absence of any actual power to force the banks' compliance.

**Multinational firm** a firm that makes direct investments in other countries, and produces and markets its products abroad.

**National debt** the amount owed by the government. To cover the difference between its expenditures and its tax revenues, the government sells bonds, notes, and other forms of IOUs.

**National income** the total amount of wages, interest, rents, and profits paid out (or owed) by employers, approximately equal to gross national product minus indirect business taxes and depreciation.

**Natural monopoly** an industry in which the average costs of producing the product reach a minimum at an output rate large enough to satisfy the entire market, so that competition among firms cannot be sustained and one firm becomes a monopolist.

**Natural rate of unemployment** the unemployment rate when the economy is at full employment.

**Near-money** assets (such as government bonds) that can be converted into cash, though not quite as easily as time and savings accounts.

**Negative income tax** a system whereby families with incomes below a certain break-even level would receive, rather than make, a government income tax payment.

**Net exports** the amount spent by foreigners on a nation's goods and services (exports) minus the amount a nation spends on foreign goods and services (imports).

**Net national product (NNP)** gross national product minus depreciation. (Depreciation equals the value of the plant, equipment, and structures that are worn out during the relevant period of time.)

**New classical macroeconomists** a group, led by Robert Lucas, that believes that the government cannot use monetary and fiscal policies to close recessionary and inflationary gaps because, if firms and individuals formulate their expectations rationally, they will tend to frustrate the government's attempts to use activist stabilization policies.

**New Keynesians** a group that believes, like the Keynesians, that prices and wages tend to be rigid in the short run, but in contrast to the Keynesians this group has developed theories to explain why such wage and price stickiness can be expected.

**Nominal** expressed in current dollars (i.e., actual money amounts).

**Nondiversifiable risk** risk that cannot be reduced by diversification.

**Normative economics** economic propositions about what ought to be, or about what a person, organization, or nation ought to do.

**Old-age insurance** benefits paid under the Social Security program to retired workers, from taxes imposed on both workers and employers.

**Oligopoly** a market structure (such as those for autos and steel) in which there are only a few sellers of products that can be either identical or differentiated.

**Open market operations** the purchase and sale of U.S. government securities on the open market by the Federal Reserve in order to control the quantity of bank reserves.

**Open shop** a situation where a firm can hire both union and nonunion workers, with no requirement that nonunion workers ever join a union.

**Opportunity cost** the value of what certain resources could have produced had they been used in the best alternative way; also called **alternative cost.**

**Overvaluation of currency** the setting of a currency's price above the equilibrium price.

**Parity** the principle that a farmer should be able to exchange a given quantity of farm output for the same quantity of nonfarm goods and services he would have been able to purchase at some point in the past; in effect, the principle that farm prices should increase at the same rate as the prices of the goods and services that farmers buy.

**Partnership** a form of business organization whereby two or more people agree to own and conduct a business, with each party contributing some proportion of the capital and/or labor and receiving some proportion of the profit or loss.

**Payoff matrix** a table showing each player's payoff (often profit) if various strategies are chosen by each player.

**Peak** the point in the business cycle where national output is highest relative to its potential (i.e., full-employment) level.

**Perfect competition** a market structure in which there are many sellers of identical products, where no one seller or buyer has control over the price, where entry is easy, and where resources can switch readily from one use to another. Many agricultural markets have many of the characteristics of perfect competition.

**Personal consumption expenditures** the spending by households on durable goods, nondurable goods, and services.

**Phillips curve** a curve representing the relationship between the rate of increase of the price level and the level of unemployment.

**Positive economics** descriptive statements, propositions, and predictions about the economic world that are generally testable by an appeal to the facts.

**Potential gross national product** the total amount of goods and services that could have been produced had the economy been operating at full capacity or full employment.

**Precautionary demand for money** the demand for money because of uncertainty about the timing and size of future disbursements and receipts.

**Price discrimination** the practice whereby one buyer is charged more than another buyer for the same product.

**Price elastic** the demand for a good if its price elasticity of demand is greater than one.

**Price elasticity of demand** the percentage change in quantity demanded resulting from a one percent change in price; by convention, always expressed as a positive number.

**Price elasticity of supply** the percentage change in quantity supplied resulting from a one percent change in price.

**Price index** the ratio of the value of a set of goods and services in current dollars to the value of the same set of goods and services in constant dollars.

**Price inelastic** the demand for a good if its price elasticity of demand is less than one.

**Price leader** in an oligopolistic industry, a firm that sets a price that other firms are willing to follow.

**Price supports** price floors imposed by the government on a certain good.

**Price system** a system under which every good and service has a price, and which in a purely capitalistic economy carries out the basic functions of an economic system (determining what goods and services will be produced, how the output will be produced, how much of it each person will receive, and what the nation's growth of per capita income will be).

**Primary inputs** resources (such as labor and land) that are produced outside of the economic system.

**Principal-agent problem** the problem that arises because managers or workers may pursue their own objectives, even though this reduces the profits of the owners of the firm.

**Prisoners' dilemma** a situation in which two persons (or firms) would both do better to cooperate than not to cooperate, but where each feels it is in his or her interests not to do so; thus each fares worse than if they cooperated.

**Private cost** the price paid by the individual user for the use of a resource.

**Product differentiation** the process by which producers create real or apparent differences between products that perform the same general function.

**Product group** a group of firms that produce similar products that are fairly close substitutes for one another.

**Product market** a market where products are bought and sold.

**Production function** the relationship between the quantities of various inputs used per period of time and the maximum quantity of output that can be produced per period of time, i.e., the most output that existing technology permits the firm to produce from various quantities of inputs.

**Production possibilities curve** a curve showing the combinations of amounts of various goods that a society can produce with given (fixed) amounts of resources.

**Profit** the difference between a firm's revenue and its costs.

**Progressive tax** a tax whereby the rich pay a larger proportion of their income for the tax than do the poor.

**Prohibitive tariff** a tariff so high that it prevents imports of a good.

**Property tax** a tax imposed on real estate and/or other property.

**Proprietors' income** the net income of unincorporated businesses (i.e., proprietorships and partnerships).

**Proprietorship** a firm owned by a single individual.

**Prosperity** a period when national output is close to its potential (i.e., full-employment) level.

**Public goods** goods and services that can be consumed by one person without diminishing the amount of them that others can consume. Also, there is no way to prevent citizens from consuming public goods whether they pay for them or not.

**Public sector** the governmental sector of the economy.

**Pure rate of interest** the interest rate on a riskless loan.

**P-star** an indicator of the price level

about five years hence used by the Federal Reserve.

**Quota** a limit imposed on the amount of a commodity that can be imported annually.

**Rate of return** the annual profit per dollar invested that business can obtain by building new structures, adding new equipment, or increasing their inventories; the interest rate earned on the investment in a particular asset.

**Rational expectations** expectations that are correct on the average (that is, forecasting errors are random); the forecaster makes the best possible use of whatever information is available.

**Real** expressed in constant dollars.

**Real business cycle models** theories asserting that business fluctuations are due largely to shifts in the aggregate supply curve resulting from new technology, good or bad weather, and so on.

**Real income** income measured in constant dollars (i.e., the amount of goods and services that can be bought with the income).

**Recession** the phase in the business cycle after the peak during which national output falls.

**Regressive tax** a tax whereby the rich pay a smaller proportion of their income for the tax than do the poor.

**Rent** in the context of Chapter 29, the return derived from an input that is fixed in supply.

**Reproduction cost of assets** what the firm would have to pay to replace its assets.

**Resource market** a market where resources are bought and sold.

**Resources** inputs used to produce goods and services

**Retained earnings** the total amount of profit that the stockholders of a corporation have reinvested in the business, rather than withdrawing as dividends.

**Ricardian equivalence** the idea, proposed by Robert Barro, that government budget deficits do not really matter because debt financing and taxes are basically equivalent. (This idea can be traced back to David Ricardo.)

**Rigid policy rule** a rule specifying completely the behavior of the variable governed by the policy rule (for example, Milton Friedman's suggestion that the money supply be set so that it grows at a fixed, agreed-on rate).

**Rule of reason** the idea that not all trusts, but only unreasonable combinations in restraint of trade, require conviction under the antitrust laws.

**Runaway inflation** a very rapid increase in the general price level that wipes out practically all of the value of money.

**Sales tax** a tax imposed on the goods consumers buy (with the exception, in some states, of food and medical care).

**Saving** the process by which people give up a claim on present consumption goods in order to receive consumption goods in the future.

**Saving function** the relationship between total saving and disposable income, i.e., the total amount of saving that will occur at various levels of disposable income.

**Say's Law** the principle that the production of a certain amount of goods and services results in the generation of an amount of income precisely sufficient to buy that output.

**Short run** the period of time during which at least one of a firm's inputs (generally its plant and equipment) is fixed.

**Short-run aggregate supply curve** a curve, sloping upward to the right, that shows the level of real national output that will be supplied at various economy-wide price levels when input prices are fixed.

**Social Security** a program that imposes taxes on wage earners and employers, and provides old-age, survivors, disability, and medical benefits to workers covered under the Social Security Act.

**Special drawing rights (SDRs)** a reserve asset established since 1968 by the International Monetary Fund, which member countries can use to exchange for other currencies, much as they have used gold.

**Stagflation** a simultaneous combination of high unemployment and high inflation.

**Structural unemployment** joblessness that occurs when new goods or new technologies call for new skills, and workers with older skills cannot find jobs.

**Substitutes** commodities with a positive cross elasticity of demand (that is, a decrease in the price of one commodity will result in a decrease in the quantity demanded of the other commodity).

**Substitution effect** the change in the quantity demanded (by a consumer) of a commodity resulting from a change in the commodity's price, if the consumer's level of utility is held constant.

**Supply curve for loanable funds** a curve showing the relationship between the quantity of loanable funds supplied and the pure interest rate.

**Supply-side economics** a set of propositions concerned with influencing the aggregate supply curve through the use of financial incentives such as tax cuts.

**Supply-side inflation** inflation resulting from leftward shifts of the aggregate supply curve.

**Tariff** a tax imposed by the government on imported goods (designed to cut down on imports and thus protect domestic industry and workers from foreign competition.)

**Tax avoidance** legal steps taken by taxpayers to reduce their tax bill.

**Tax evasion** misreporting of income or other illegal steps taken by taxpayers to reduce their tax bill.

**Technological change** new methods of producing existing products, new designs that make it possible to produce new products, and new techniques of organization, marketing, and management.

**Technology** society's pool of knowledge concerning how goods and services can be produced from a given amount of resources.

**Terms of trade** the ratio of an index of export prices to an index of import prices.

**Tight monetary policy** a monetary policy that restrains or reduces the money supply and raises interest rates.

**Tit-for-tat** a strategy in game theory where each player does on this round what the other player did on the previous round.

**Total cost** the sum of a firm's total fixed cost and total variable cost.

**Total fixed cost** a firm's total expenditure on fixed inputs per period of time.

**Total revenue** a firm's total dollar sales volume.

**Total variable cost** a firm's total expenditure on variable inputs per period of time.

**Trading possibilities curve** a curve showing the various combinations of products that a nation can get if it specializes in one product and trades that specialty for foreign goods.

**Transactions demand for money** the holding of money in cash or in checking accounts in order to pay for final goods and services; the higher the level of real GNP and the price level, the greater the quantity of money demanded for transactions purposes.

**Transfer payments** payments made by the government or private business to individuals who do not contribute to the production of goods and services in exchange for them.

**Trough** the point in the business cycle where national output is lowest relative to its potential (i.e., full-employment) level.

**Tying contract** the practice whereby buyers must purchase other items in order to get the product they want.

**Undervaluation of currency** the setting of a currency's price below the equilibrium price.

**Unemployment** according to the definition of the Bureau of Labor Statistics, joblessness among people who are actively looking for work and would take a job if one were offered.

**Unemployment rate** the number of people who are unemployed divided by the number of people in the labor force.

**Union shop** a situation where firms can hire nonunion workers who must then become union members within a certain length of time after being hired.

**Unitary elasticity** a price elasticity of demand equal to one.

**Utility** a number representing the level of satisfaction that a consumer derives from a particular market basket.

**Value-added** the amount of value added by a firm or industry to the total worth of a product.

**Value of the marginal product of labor** the marginal product of labor (i.e., the additional output resulting from the addition of an extra unit of labor) multiplied by the product's price.

**Variable input** a resource used in the production process (such as labor or raw material) whose quantity can be changed during the particular period under consideration.

**Velocity of circulation of money** the rate at which the money supply is used to make transactions for final goods and services, i.e., the average number of times per year that a dollar is used to buy the final goods and services produced by the economy. It equals GNP divided by the money supply.

**Wage and price controls** limits imposed by the government on the amount by which wages and prices can increase, in order to reduce the inflation rate at a given unemployment rate.

**Wage rate** the price of labor.

## Photograph Credits

# INDEX

Definitions of terms appear on pages set in **boldface** type.

junk bonds, **234**
Justice Department, U.S., 548
 Antitrust Division of, 574–75, 576, 578

Kahn, Alfred, 539
Kalt, J., 491*n*
Kanban system, 492–93
*Kapital, Das* (Marx), 731–34
Kaysen, Carl, 580*n*
Kennedy, John F., 322, 661
Kennedy–Johnson guidelines, 291
"Kennedy Round" negotiations, 372–73
Keohane, Nanneri, 450
Keynes, John Maynard, 98, 446, 450
 classical economics criticized by, 94–96
Keynesian model, simple, 250–51, 258–60,
  299, 302
 consumption function as viewed by,
  **108**–10
 federal budget in, 292–93, 329
 GNP level, 209–13
 Great Depression in, 94–96, 143–44
 liquidity preference theory in, **612**
 money supply in, 209–16, 250–51, 258–60
 short-run aggregate supply curve in,
  143–44, 285
 unemployment as viewed by, 94–96
Keynesian-monetarist debate, 214–15,
  292–313, 329
 business fluctuations and, 292–93,
  297–300
 GNP in, 474–76, A1–A8
 historical background of, 292–93
 inflation policy in, 286–87, 474–76, A5,
  A7–A8
 IS-LM model of, 474–76, A1–A8
 policy activism and, 307–11
 stability of economy and, 250–51, 286–87
Keynesians, new, 292–93, 312
 inflation policy and, 287
 new classical macroeconomists and,
  **96**–97, 292–**301**, 307–12
 old Keynesians vs., 302
 policy activism of, 307–11
 rational expectations theory and, 301
 unemployment as veiwed by, 97, 296–97
 wage and price policy of, 97, 287, 299,
  302, 303–7
Kinney, R.G., 576
Klein, L., 175
Kneese, Allen, 699
Knickerbocker Trust failure, 231
Knight, Frank, 623
Korean War, inflation and, 101, 167
Krugman, Paul, 369
Kuznets, Simon, 65, 67, 718
Kuznets cycles, 160*n*

labor, labor force, 6, 14, 86, 291, 587–606,
  717
 average product of, **335**, 465, 466
 economic growth and, **332**–36
 as economic resource, 6
 equilibrium price and, 592–94
 firm demand curve for, **589**–90
 government's role in, 604, 659–62
 implicit contracts and, **304**–6
 international trade and, 370–71, 375–76
 marginal product of, **334**–36, 338–39, 342,

465, 590-92
 market demand curves for, **590**, 604
 market supply curves for, 590–**92**, 603
 monopsony and, **599**–601
 perfect competition and, 589–96
 price of, 587–88. 592–94, 603–5
 as primary input, **614**–15
 principal-agent problem and, 597
 profit-maximizing quantity of, 589
 U.S. occupational composition of, 588
 *see also* income; unemployment; wages
laboratory experimentation in economics,
  514
Labor Department, U.S., A17
labor productivity, **3**, 31
 technological change and, 347–51
labor unions, 602–6
 concessions of, 605–6
 incomes policies and, 290–91
 insider-outsider hypothesis and, 307
 internal problems of, 602
 long-term contracts of, 303–4
 national vs. local, **601**
 recent membership trends in, 602–3
 technological change and, 347–51
 wages increased by, 603–6
 *see also specific unions*
Laffer, Arthur, 193
Laffer curve, **193**
La Follette, Robert, 67
lagging series, **172**
Lamb, Charles, 592, 608
land, **619**–21
 as economic resource, 6
 opportunity cost and, **9**
 as primary input, **614**–15
Latin America, trade with, 355, 356
Lave, Lester, 692*n*, 700
leading indicators, **172**–73
leading series, **172**
leisure, GNP and, **71**
Lenin, V. I., 734
Leontief, Wassily, A15–A16
less developed countries (LDCs), 5, 21, 332,
  668, **707**–29
 balanced growth in, 709, **719**–20
 barriers to development in, 710–11
 characteristics of, 707–10
 development planning in, 720–23
 entrepreneurship and social institutions in,
  716
 foreign aid to, **711**, 724–29
 government's role in, 718
 industrialization in, 711, 719–20, 721
 investment selection in, 710–711, 723–24
 labor in, 717
 mutinational firms in, 364
 natural resources in, 716–17
 population growth in 338, 711–13, **712**
 poverty in, 707–8
 technology in 713–14, 715, 725
Lever Brothers, 554–55
Levine, H., 743*n*
Lewis, W. Arthur, 717
liabilities:
 on balance sheets, 230, 240–43, 252,
  454–55
 current, **455**
 of Federal Reserve Banks, 252–53

long-term, **455**
 type of business organization and, 443–45
liberals, 726
 Federal Reserve criticized by, 263, 268
 government's role as viewed by, 649–51
 rational expectations theory challenged
  by, 286–87
life-cycle hypothesis, 112–**13**
Lincoln, Abraham, 371
Lindbeck, Assar, 307
Lindzen, Richard, 702
linear programming, 720, A8–A14
 case study of, A9–A14
 management science and, **A14**
line-item veto, **330**
Lintner, John, 625
liquidity preference theory, **612**
Little, S., 58*n*
Litton Industries, 576
LM curves, A1–A8
 definition and derivation of, A2–A3
 monetary policy and, A5–A6
loanable funds theory, **609**–**10**
local governments:
 bonds issued by, 225, 684
 expenditures of, 660
 tax revenues of, 662
local unions, **601**
long run, 464–65
 cost functions in, **487**–90, 494–95, 563–64
 equilibrium in, 151–52, 513–17, 520–23,
  530–33, 563–65
 GNP in, 215
 government expenditures in, 189
 monopolistic competition in, 564
 monopoly in, 531
 perfect competition in, 512–18, 521–23
 Phillips curve in, 275–79
 as planning horizon, 464–65
 price and output in, 513–16, 531
long-term liabilities, **455**
Lorenz curves, **631**–32, 634
Louvre Accord (1987), 395
Lucas, Robert, 286–87, 294
Lucas aggregate supply curve, **295**–96

M-2, **202**–3, 218*n*, 263, 267*n*
McDonald's, 562
NcNamara, Robert, 729
macroeconomics, **96**–97
 *see also* new classical macroeconomics
Maisel, Sherman, 269
Malkiel, Burton, 446
Malthus, Thomas, 336–40, 712
management, 462, 602, 604
 economic growth and, 347, 351–52
 in Soviet Union, 736–38
management science, linear programming
  and, **A14**
Manne, Alan, 701
Mansfield, E., 56*n*, 337*n*, 348*n*, 463*n*, 544*n*,
  571*n*, 580*n*, 590*n*, 637*n*, 651*n*, 715*n*
marginal cost, **482**–87, 526–28
 average costs in relation to, 484–85
 diminishing returns and, 483–85
 measurement of, 491–96
 in monopolistic competition, 563–65
 in monopoly, 529–31, 532–33, 534–35,
  543–44

Switzerland, international trade of, 365

Taft-Hartley Act (1947), 604
takeovers, corporate, 577–78
target zones, **393**–95
tariffs, **365**–77
  arguments for, 371
  prohibitive, 365
  social costs of, 366
  U.S. changes in, 373–76
tastes, *see* consumer tastes and preferences
tax avoidance, 684
tax-based income policies, 291
tax credits, 194, 196
  investment, 194, 196
  for pollution-control equipment, **696**–97
tax cuts:
  of 1964, 194–95, 195
  of 1975, 194
  of 1978, 196
  of 1981, 195, 196
  supply-side views on, 191–93, 196
taxes, 12, 662, 688–89
  burden of, by income level, 632–34
  death, 632–33
  estate, 632–33, 683
  excise, **634$n$,** 662–63, 685–88
  as fiscal policy tool, 189–91
  incidence of, 634, 685–88
  income, *see* income tax
  income inequality and, 632–33, 684
  in income redistribution, 325, 652–54
  indirect business, **77**
  legislative process and, 681–85
  personal property, **685**
  principles of, 682–83
  progressive vs. regressive, **632**–33
  property, 100, 633, 657, **662,** 682–83,
    **685**–88
  Proposition 13 and, 662
  public goods supported by, 654–57
  sales, 632–33, 654, 657, **662**–63, 683
  **685**–88
  sensitivity issue and, 686–88
  single, 621
  Social Security, 641–42, 662
  turnover, **738**
tax evasion, 684
tax schedule, 683
tax surcharge, 194, 293
Teamsters Union, 549, 601, 602
technological change:
  case study of, 346–47
  determinants of, 347–51
  diffusion process in, 345–**46**
  diminishing marginal returns and, 336
  economic growth and, 334, 336, 339,
    342–43, **345**–47
  first application of, *see* innovation
  investment and, 114–15
  labor productivity and, 347–51
  monopoly and, 536–37, 570–71
technology, **6**–7, 42, 345–49, 452–54
  agriculture and, 663–64
  changes in market supply curves and, 42
  choice and, 6–7
  efficiency of resource use and, 53
  in investment decision, 114–15
  in less-developed countries, 713–14, 715,

    725
technology gap, 362–63
technology transfer, 348–49, 725
teenagers, unemployment of, 86, 87–88
Tennessee Valley Authority (TVA), 30, 655
Texas Instruments, 650, 653
Thackeray, William M., 615$n$
thrift institutions, 224, 228$n$, 234–36
time, consumption decisions and, 433
time deposits, 223–24, 247$n$
  in money supply, 201–2
  reserves in relation to, 255–57
time inconsistency, discretionary policy and,
  **310**
tit-for-tat strategy, **558**
tobacco industry, 450
Tobin, James, 73
Tokyo Round, 373
total cost, **479**–80, 486–87
  average, 482, **486**
  measurement of, 491–95
  in monopoly, 528–29
  in perfect competition, 502–3, 506–7
total fixed cost, **478**–79
  in perfect competition, 502, 506–7
total revenue, 502–7, **526**–27
  in monopoly, 525–29, **526**
  in perfect competition, 502–4, 505–7
total utility, 422
total variable cost, **479**
  in perfect competition, 502–3, 505–7
trade, *see* international trade
Trade Acts (1988), 373
Trade Agreements Act (1934), 372
trading possibilities curve, **359**
training, wage differentials and, 594
transactions demand for money, 206–7
transferable emissions permits, **696**
transfer payments:
  business, **81**$n$
  GNP's exclusion of, 67
  government, **66, 658**
  private, **66**
  *see also* welfare
Treasury Department, U.S., 175, 315–17, 681
  Brannan plan and, **413**–14, 668
  Federal Reserve and, 221, 251–52, 253,
    267, 268–69
  national debt and, 326
troughs in business cycle, **159**–60, 161–63
  variables and, 172–73
Truman administration, 413, 668
Turner, Donald, 530$n$
turnover tax, **738**
two-person games, 554–55
tying contracts, **573**

uncertainty, profits and, 623–24
underemployment, 86–87
unemployment, 84–96, 159–60, 268
  automatic stabilizers of, **188**–89, 190
  business fluctuations and, 85, 136, 158–60,
    294
  in classical economics, 90–93, 94–96
  costs of, 87–92
  cyclical, **85**–86
  duration and reasons for, 88–89
  in Europe, 95

  expectations and, 271–80
  foreign trade and, 366, 370–71
  frictional, **84**–**85,** 87–88
  government and, 86, 94–96, 147, 162–64,
    189–95, 275–79, 654
  in Great Depression, 1, 85, 87, 161–62,
    652–54
  inadequate growth of money supply and,
    258
  inflation and, 1–3, 61, 84–107, 162, 195,
    271–91, 688–89
  Keynesian view of, 94–96
  measurement and incidence of, 86–92
  monetary policy and, 280
  natural rate of, 91–92, 275–79
  new Keynesian view of, 97, 296–97
  production possibilities curve and, 26–28
  profit sharing and, **305**
  quantity of money and, 205
  structural, **85,** 87–88, 275
  tariffs and, 366
  theories of, 90–93, 96–97, 181
  types of, 84–85
  U.S., 2–3, 86–88
  voluntary, 84–85, 97
  wage-increase rate in relation to, *see*
    Phillips curve
  *see also* employment
unemployment insurance, **642**
  as automatic stabilizer, 188–89, 190
Union Carbide Corporation, 364
unions, *see* labor unions; *specific unions*
union shops, **604**
unitary elasticity, **411**
United Auto Workers, 601
United Nations Relief and Rehabilitation Administration (UNRRA), 724
United States Steel Corporation (USS), 574
  price leadership and, 550
Upward Bound program, benefit-cost analysis of, 674–78
Uruguay Round, 373
utility, 421–**22**
  indifference curves and, 437
  marginal, **422**–27, **423,** 429–30, 439,
    **465**–66
  maximizing of, 422–27, 437–39
  total, 422
  welfare economics and, A18–A19

value:
  of currency, 200
  of marginal product of labor, **589**–90
  Marx's theory of, 624, **732**–33
  of money, 203–5
  money as standard of, 199–200
  of output, limitations of GNP and, 71–73
  surplus, 624, **732**
value-added, **70**–71
values:
  economic role of, 15
  income redistribution and, 652–54
variable inputs, **464**
variables:
  in business fluctuations, 172
  direct vs. inverse relationship between, 21
  graphs and, 19–21
velocity of circulation of money, **215**–18,
  219

vertical mergers, 576
veterans' benefits, 189
Vietnam War, 162
    inflation and, 101, 162, 167, 189
Vishny, R., 453*n*, 578*n*
Volcker, Paul A., 251, 262, 263, 266, 400
von Neumann, John, 346
*Von's Grocery* case, **575**–76

wage controls, 162, **289**–91
    disadvantages of, 344
wage differentials, 594–97
wage-price guidelines, *see* incomes policies
wages, 75–76, 181, 603–4
    determinants of, 587–607
    efficiency, **306**–7
    equal pay issue in, 635
    equilibrium and, 589–90, 599–601
    flexibility of, 94–96
    incentive systems and, 598–99
    income inequality and, 632
    labor unions and, 603–6
    Marx's theory of, 732–34
    minimum, 646–47, 660
    money vs. real, 102, 588–89
    monopsony and, **599**–601
    new Keynesians view of, 97, 287, 296,
        299, 302, 303–7
    perfect competition and, 594–97
    sticky, 303–4
    unemployment related to increases in,
        *see* Phillips curve

*see also* income; income distribution
Wagner, S., 571*n*
Wallace, Neil, 294, 317
*Wall Street Journal,* 550
Warner, Kenneth, 412
Warren, Earl, 575–76
water, value of, 591
watermelons, price elasticity of supply for,
    511–12
water pollution, 691–92
    control of, 693–97
    as external diseconomy, 650, 657
Water Quality Improvement Act (1970), 700
Watt, James, 703
wealth:
    as determinant of consumption, 124–25
    inflation's impact on, 101–3
*Wealth of Nations, The* (Smith), 11–12, 533
Webb-Pomerene Act (1918), 583
Weiss, Leonard, 562*n*
Weitzman, Martin, 305
welfare, 4–5, 36, **643**–48, **652**–54, 660
    as automatic stabilizer, **188**–89
    as fiscal policy tool, 189–91
    measured economic, 71–72
welfare economics, A18–A23
welfare reform act (1988), 644
Westinghouse, 575
Wharton model, 175–76
"what if" questions, 122
wheat:
    equilibrium price of, 43–45, 47–48

isoquants for, 474–75, A7–A8
marginal cost and, 482–84
market demand curves for, **39**–42,
    49–50, 407–9, 414
market supply curves for, **42**–43
optimal input decisions and, 468–69
perfect competition and, 500, 516–19
price and income supports for, 662
price elasticity of demand for, 407–9
Wicksteed, Philip, 4
Williamson, John, 393–95
women:
    equal pay and, 635
    in labor unions, 602
workfare, 644
World Bank, 723, **728**–29
World War I, 205, 595
    German inflation after, 99, 204–5, 217–18
    labor in, 161–62
World War II, 28, 85, 162, 658
    aggregate demand curves in, 162
    agriculture in, 664
    consumption function shift in, 127
    inflation and, 101, 162, 167, 202, 269
    national debt and, 611–12
    national output in, 160
    price system in, 53–54, 60
    production possibilities curve and, 27

zero economic profits, **513**–15
zero pollution, 698–99